READINGS IN LAW AND PSYCHIATRY

READINGS IN LAW AND PSYCHIATRY

edited by

RICHARD C. ALLEN, J.D.
*Professor of Law and Forensic Sciences, and
Director, Institute of Law, Psychiatry, and Criminology
The George Washington University*

ELYCE ZENOFF FERSTER, J.D.
Professor of Law, The George Washington University

JESSE G. RUBIN, M.D.
*The Psychiatric Institute, Washington, D.C.,
and Associate Clinical Professor of Psychiatry,
The George Washington University School of Medicine*

Revised and Expanded Edition

THE JOHNS HOPKINS UNIVERSITY PRESS
Baltimore and London

Manufactured in the United States of America

The Johns Hopkins University Press, Baltimore, Maryland 21218
The Johns Hopkins University Press Ltd., London

Library of Congress Catalog Card Number 74–24384
ISBN 0–8018–1692–0

Originally published, 1968
Revised and Expanded Edition, 1975

Library of Congress Cataloging in Publication Data

Allen, Richard C   1926–   comp.
    Readings in law and psychiatry.

    Includes bibliographies.
    1. Forensic psychiatry. 2. Mental health
laws—United States. 3. Insanity—Jurisprudence—
United States. I. Ferster, Elyce Zenoff.
II. Rubin, Jesse G. III. Title. [DNLM: 1. Forensic
psychiatry. W740 A428r]
KF3828.A7A53   1975   614'.19   74–24384
ISBN 0–8018–1692–0

More and more we lawyers are awaking to a perception of the truth that what divides and distracts us in the solution of a legal problem is not so much uncertainty about the law as uncertainty about the facts—the facts which generate the law. Let the facts be known as they are, and the law will sprout from the seed and turn its branches toward the light.

Benjamin Nathan Cardozo, "What Medicine Can Do for Law"
Address before the New York Academy of Medicine, November 1, 1928

Preface to the Revised and Expanded Edition

Much has taken place since the first edition of *Readings in Law and Psychiatry* was published in 1968. Psychiatric treatment has been undergoing dramatic changes: increased use of chemotherapy, group psychotherapy, the therapeutic community, community mental health, and preventive psychiatry. And the law has kept pace. There have been court decisions of landmark proportions: *Jackson v. Indiana, Powell v. Texas, U.S. v. Brawner*, to name but a few. And the "public interest" bar has at last discovered the most discriminated against minority groups of all —the mentally ill and the mentally retarded—and has brought (often successfully) right to treatment, "least restrictive alternative," anti-peonage, and right to education cases on their behalf. Electroshock, psychosurgery, behavior modification, and experimental use of drugs have aroused whirlwinds of controversy. Reform movements addressed to the laws regulating or proscribing abortion, sterilization, involuntary hospitalization, sexual psychopathy, homosexual acts, alcohol and drug abuse have had varying degrees of success.

It is for these reasons, and because of the growing interest of law schools and psychiatric residency programs in coursework in forensic psychiatry, that this revised and expanded edition has been prepared. We hope that you will find it a timely, useful, and informative book.

R. C. A.
E. Z. F.
J. G. R.

Washington, D.C.

vii

Preface to the First Edition

This book of readings is intended to provide sufficient material—including excerpts from the literatures of law, psychiatry, and psychology; trial transcripts; psychiatric evaluations and reports; appellate briefs; empirical research findings; and leading case decisions and statutes; together with commentaries, questions for discussion, and suggested additional readings—for a two- or three-hour basic course or seminar in law and psychiatry. It is primarily intended for use in teaching graduate and undergraduate law students, and for the practicing lawyer, but is also appropriate for use in schools of medicine, psychiatric residency, and continuing professional education programs. In addition, inclusion of extensive excerpts from the *Diagnostic and Statistical Manual: Mental Disorders*, the American Psychiatric Association's *Glossary* in its entirety, and previously unpublished monographs on the training and functions of medical and paramedical personnel, psychological testing and assessment, the current status of physician-patient privileged communication laws, the techniques of direct and cross-examination, and other materials, will, we believe, make it a valuable reference book for practitioners of both disciplines.

We are indebted to many more people than can be listed here. We would, however, like to thank especially the following:

Drs. Karl Menninger, Joseph Satten, and Herbert Modlin, and the late, and beloved, Dr. Will Menninger of the Menninger Foundation, with whom Professor Allen collaborated in developing the coursework in law and psychiatry at the Menninger School of Psychiatry.

Hon. John Biggs, Jr., Judge of the United States Court of Appeals for the Third Circuit, revered friend and mentor of Professor Ferster.

Dr. Leon Yochelson, Chairman of the Department of Psychiatry, The George Washington University School of Medicine, Co-Director of the Institute of Law, Psychiatry and Criminology, and professional colleague of Dr. Rubin.

Professor Charles B. Nutting, Professor and Vice President Louis Mayo, and Dean Robert Kramer of The George Washington University National Law Center, without whose encouragement and support this book could not have been written.

And our able secretarial staff, especially Betsy Heusinger and Bonnie Davis.

R. C. A.
E. Z. F.
J. G. R.

Washington, D.C.

Introduction

The lawyer owes entire devotion to the interest of his client, warm zeal in the maintenance and defense of his rights, and the exertion of his utmost learning and ability. . . .

Canons of Professional Ethics
American Bar Association

The principal objective of the medical profession is to render service to humanity with full respect for the dignity of man. Physicians should merit the confidence of patients entrusted to their care, rendering to each a full measure of service and devotion. . . .

Principles of Medical Ethics
American Medical Association

When one considers the enormous conceptual gulf that lies between proximate cause and multiple causality, jural responsibility and psychic determinism, advocacy and psychotherapy, *stare decisis* and the scientific method, one is almost driven to conclude that law and psychiatry share about the same degree of ideological kinship as does the Mafia with the Women's Christian Temperance Union (indeed, perhaps even less, since at least the latter two organizations have a common concern about sin, albeit they view it somewhat differently). There are, of course, significant differences in the orientation, responsibilities, and methods of lawyers and psychiatrists. Several of the conceptual dichotomies are considered in the article "The Dynamics of Interpersonal Communication and the Law" in Chapter 3, and appear in sharper focus in the psychiatric testimony in the Andrews and Volbrecht cases in Chapter 7. Yet there is a "lowest common denominator" which, as is illustrated by the quotations with which this introductory note was begun, is at the same time the highest professional responsibility of both disciplines: the duty of rendering full and competent professional service to the client or patient. It seems to us that this is a shared premise which provides a pretty firm foundation for bridge building.

Patients and clients have an annoying habit of having problems that do not fit precisely into neat little disciplinary cubbyholes. It is a rare patient who, presenting a clinical picture of severe emotional disturbance, does not have associated legal problems—of which he, and perhaps the psychiatrist as well, is quite unaware—relating to the management of his property, the validity of his marriage, his legal status if he is hospitalized, or his interest in safeguarding the privacy of his communications with the doctor. And it is a rare client who, under the stress of an impending divorce, or potential liability for an act of negligence, or a criminal charge, can be said to have a purely "legal" problem. Whether or not there is need for a psychiatric evaluation or for expert testimony, the client's emotional response to the situation is at least a factor of which the attorney must take account if he wishes to render effective professional service. It would seem, then, that in order to provide appropriate professional help, the practitioner of each discipline needs to know something about the other.

In perhaps no other aspect of the law has there been such dynamic growth as that which has occurred and is occurring in the areas of interrelationship of law and behavioral science. The use of expert psychiatric (and psychological) testimony in criminal law, tort, probate, family law, hospitalization, guardianship and incompetency, and juvenile court cases has resulted in changes in legal theory and psychiatric practice, posited new areas of multi-disciplinary collaboration, aroused old antagonisms, revealed barriers to meaningful communication between clinician and advocate, and given rise to disturbing and challenging questions about the basic assumptions which underlie traditional methods.

Unfortunately, it is still true that most students come to law school with little or no background in the behavioral sciences, and in at least half of the accredited law schools in the country there is no course or seminar exploring in depth the interrelationship of law and the study of human behavior. Similarly, few psychiatrists have had significant exposure in their premedical work to the history, purposes, and functioning of the legal system, and in most medical schools and psychiatric residency programs they are unlikely to find more than a few hours devoted to "forensic medicine" —and that, largely confined to a consideration of the legal aspects of medical partnerships and the omnipresent ogre, "malpractice," with perhaps passing reference to the "superiority" of Durham or the ALI Rule to M'Naghten. As a result, the psychiatrist may avoid involvement with cases that might lead to litigation, and if required to render an opinion or to testify in the course of a legal proceeding involving his patient, may, through his ignorance of the ways in which his special insights and knowledge could be of value in resolving the problems with which the court is confronted, prejudice substantial rights of his patient. And the lawyer unsophisticated in the principles of human behavior will be compelled to learn them—if indeed he does learn them—through painful experience to himself and his clients. When he is made a judge, he will probably adopt one of two extreme, and equally undesirable, attitudes toward the role of the behavioral sciences in law: arbitrary rejection of the insights which psychiatry and psychology may bring to bear upon the social problems to be resolved, or uncritical acceptance of anything and everything the expert may have to say—in effect an abdication of the law's adjudicative function.

It is the purpose of this book to provide an overview of the significant areas of interaction of law and its sister disciplines; to expose the lawyer to some of the constructs of dynamic psychiatry dealing with human personality and behavior and to relate them to problems encountered in legal practice; and to acquaint the psychiatrist with the social and legal dimensions of the kinds of controversies in which his insights and opinions may be sought. While the book is designed primarily for classroom use, it is believed that the nature of the readings included will make it a reference source of continuing usefulness.

The selection and arrangement of materials reflect the combined experiences of the authors in teaching law and psychiatry courses and seminars over the last decade or more to undergraduate law students, to practicing attorneys, judges, and lawyers in government and military service, to graduate students seeking masters and doctoral degrees in law or in the forensic sciences, to medical students, and to psychiatric residents; and these reflect, most recently, and significantly, their collaboration for the last several years at The George Washington University School of Law (The National Law Center).

To the extent that guiding principles can be identified in our eclecticism, they might well include the following:

1) We have not assumed an already sophisticated reader/student. For example, our experience has been that most law students have only the haziest notion of what a psychoanalyst is and how he differs from a psychologist, a neurologist, or a psychiatrist. We begin at that point.

2) We have sought balance. We have not avoided stridently polemical writings—on the contrary, when controversies over critical issues exist, we feel it important that the student be made aware of them (e.g., the sometimes conflicting schools of psychiatric thought; varying opinions about the "sociopath"—now "antisocial personality"—and "behavior mod"; Dr. Szasz's articulate, if extreme, criticisms of contemporary psychiatry)—but we have sought to compel the student to question, to accept no theory—no point of view—as divine revelation, but rather as hypothesis (e.g., see Dr. Diamond's articulate and persuasive article on "impartial" testimony and the questions following it).

3) We have emphasized intensivity of experience rather than exhaustiveness of coverage. That is to say, we have sought to identify basic issues—social, ideological, and cross-disciplinary—and to provide the reader with an armamentarium of skills—linguistic and conceptual—which will enable him to approach any legal-psychiatric problem with understanding and an enhanced critical facility. We have not, however, attempted to provide the psychiatrist with all the appellate decisions necessary to write a legal brief, or to equip the lawyer to engage in psychotherapy.

4) We have striven for viability, including in the selection of readings not only articles and opinions *about* psychiatric evaluations and testimony, but also *actual* evaluations and testimony; not merely laws, but empirical studies of their operation as well; not alone opposing "rules" (e.g., the competing definitions of criminal responsibility), but also questions about the basic assumptions underlying them. And throughout, we have given preference to the pre-trial and trial aspects of professional practice over appellate decision-making, since it is in these initial phases that it is most necessary that there be meaningful dialogue between the disciplines. Thus, unlike the traditional law school "casebook," appellate opinions play a secondary role to evaluation reports, empirical research findings, and trial transcripts.

The first major division of the book is entitled "Basic Concepts in Psychiatry." It begins with a brief introduction to the history of psychiatric treatment and an analysis of contemporary attitudes about mental illness and the mentally ill. In Chapter 2 we introduce the dramatis personae, the members of the mental health professions, and their training, learned societies, accreditation, and licensure; and we present to the student the different orientations of the schools of psychiatric practice. In Chapter 3 we consider "normality" and "psychiatric illness," beginning with an outline of basic psychiatric constructs and their relationship to problems encountered in legal practice, and continuing with an analysis of the social significance of assignment to a "normal" as opposed to a "sick" role, and consideration of the generally accepted criteria of diagnosis as set forth in the American Psychiatric Association's *Diagnostic and Statistical Manual of Mental Disorders*, together with recent materials on mental retardation and sexuality. Chapter 4 considers changes in treatment concepts and etiology, and the growing concern about electroshock, psychosurgery, and behavior modification.

Part II, "The Psychiatrist and Psychologist in a Legal Setting," begins with an analysis of the psychiatric evaluation and report, with illustrative clinical-legal materials. In Chapter 6, the psychological assessment is discussed, and the first trial transcript of expert testimony is presented. Chapter 7 includes intensive analyses of the processes and techniques of direct and cross-examination, problems in cross-disciplinary communication, and the pros and cons of impartial medical testimony. In Chapter 8, we present materials on privilege and confidentiality in the physician-patient relationship.

Part III, "The Psychiatrist and the Civil Law," includes chapters on psychiatric hospitalization; alternatives to civil commitment; the rights of the mentally impaired, including the right to treatment and the right to refuse treatment; guardianship and incompetency; traumatic neurosis, malpractice, and family law.

Part IV, "The Psychiatrist and the Criminal Law," covers mental impairment and the criminal law, competency to stand trial, and criminal responsibility (the insanity defense), with a concluding chapter on "special categories" of offenders: the drug addict, the alcoholic, the sex offender and the "sexual psychopath," and the "defective delinquent."

A professor who begins his class at page one of a textbook, or casebook, and works consecutively through it is a rarity in the groves of academe. Therefore, although the authors understandably feel that there is some merit in the arrangement of materials they have devised, they offer the following suggestions for alternative approaches.

The book begins with an introduction to some of the basic concepts in psychiatry, in part through excerpts from the psychiatric literature. If the professor feels that law students should be introduced to the subject on more familiar ground, he might well begin with the "rights" cases in Chapter 10, or with one of the substantive legal areas, such as confidentiality and privilege in Chapter 8, or guardianship in Chapter 11. If the course is to be addressed primarily to graduate students with some experience in the field, the professor may wish to adopt a topical approach. For example, the relationship of the legal concepts of "knowledge" and "awareness" to dynamic constructs of personality and behavior might be pursued through discussions of "normality" and "illness" in Chapter 3, the nature of the psychiatric evaluation in Chapter 5, and of psychological testing in Chapter 6; then through some specific legal areas in which variations on the theme appear: e.g., guardianship and incompetency in Chapter 11, "informed consent" in Chapter 10, competency to stand trial in Chapter 16 and criminal responsibility in Chapter 17, and finally discussion of the problems posed by the dichotomy in direct and cross-examination of the expert witness, through analysis of the trial transcripts in Chapter 7. The book also lends itself to presentation of the materials through a series of short courses, perhaps for continuing professional education students. Each of the four major parts, for example, could be offered as a short course consisting of four, six, or eight classroom hours.

It is urged that, if possible, the classroom presentation be conducted collaboratively by a lawyer and a psychiatrist, although the materials are amenable to use by a knowledgeable law professor or physician without such collaboration. In addition, it has been found most helpful in presenting the materials to law students to supplement them with patient interviews conducted by a psychiatrist, and with field trips to local clinical facilities. Following such sessions, law students have a tendency to want to exercise their assumed diagnostic ability rather than to concentrate on the ways in which psychiatric insights might be useful in resolving the legal problems of patients. This "diagnosis syndrome" can probably best be channeled into more productive discussion by direct confrontation. We sometimes introduce the subject by informing the class that we have categorized all students who came to class late that day as "hostile," those who came to class early as "insecure," and the ones who came on time as "compulsive."

It is still largely true, as was pointed out nearly two decades ago by Professor Lasswell: "As matters stand today, a bright graduate goes directly into practice or teaching; there is no 'ladder up' in the profession for the man who wants to establish himself as a serious expert in the relationship between the law and other special fields of knowledge, such as psychiatry." It is our earnest hope that *Readings in Law and Psychiatry* may provide a first step.

RICHARD C. ALLEN

Contents

Part I

Basic Concepts in Psychiatry

Part II

The Psychiatrist and Psychologist
in a Legal Setting

Part III

The Psychiatrist and the Civil Law

Part IV

The Psychiatrist and the Criminal Law

I

Basic Concepts In Psychiatry

The Development of Psychiatric Concepts

As the name suggests, the purpose of Chapter 1 is to provide the reader with an historical perspective of psychiatry. The first selection, tracing significant developments in the evolution and concepts of treatment, from the flogging out of demons to contemporary psychotherapy, was written by the late Dr. Winfred Overholser over two decades ago. An editorial note updates Dr. Overholser's sketch and will be amplified in Chapter 4. The chapter continues with a brief note on the magnitude of psychiatric illness in the United States and excerpts from a survey of public attitudes toward mental illness and the mentally ill. It concludes with a recent article by Dr. Robitscher outlining the expansion of interest in the field of forensic psychiatry. This article contains references to most of the important current literature in forensic psychiatry.

AN HISTORICAL SKETCH OF PSYCHIATRY

Winfred Overholser, M.D., Sc.D.

If we are to define psychiatry as the study and the treatment of mental disorder, then we are forced to say that the history of psychiatry goes back to the earliest written records of human activities, even though the views of causation and of therapy have fluctuated vastly in the period that has intervened between then and the present. The early Egyptians, as much as 1500 years before Christ, attributed mental disorder to the activities of evil spirits and describe senile and alcoholic mental disease as well as depression. In the early books of the Old Testament we find references to the Lord "smiting with madness," and the accounts of the alternating maniacal and depressed attacks from which King Saul suffered, ending with his suicide, are as well known as is the lycanthropy of King Nebuchadnezzar. In the Bible we read that "the spirit of the Lord descended" upon someone or that an "evil spirit entered into him." This has been the almost universal interpretation of primitive peoples in all periods. The Homeric poems, for example, refer to the "ancient wrath"; they attributed mental disorder to the special visitation of Hera, the wife of Zeus. By about the sixth century before Christ, however, Greek philosophers and physicians were paying considerable attention to the problem of mental illness and as a result of their observations and speculations enunciated some doctrines which are not unlike some of those which prevail at the present time. Pythagoras, for example, before 500 B.C. had said that the brain is the central organ of intellectual activity, and Hippocrates had described several types of mental disorder to which he applied the names of phrenitis, mania, and melancholia. These disorders he attributed to an unbalancing of the humors and the effect of this imbalance upon the brain. . . .

The medical torch of Greece seems to have passed to Rome after the destruction of Corinth in 146 B.C., and among the Roman writers we likewise find considerable attention to disturbances of personality. About the beginning of the Christian era Aretaeus, for example, foreshadowed the concept of manic-depressive psychosis by suggesting that melancholia is the commencement and a part of mania, while Celsus discussed in some detail the use of chains and flogging on the one hand and of sports and music on the other hand in the treatment of the mentally ill.

Reprinted from the *Journal of Clinical Psychopathology*, vol. 10, no. 2 (April 1949).

Galen (142–200) was one of the most influential writers on medicine of his time, and his influence prevailed in a most astonishing manner until the later part of the Renaissance. He was inclined to give a physiological interpretation to mental symptoms, and showed a truly scientific spirit in his investigations. His contributions to the knowledge of neuroanatomy were advanced indeed. He described the brain and the meninges, the ventricles and the cranial nerves, and he divided the nerves into the motor and sensory. The seat of the soul, he said, was in the substance of the brain, a portion of the anatomy which he considered highly dependent upon the humors. . . .

Very little was contributed to the topic of psychiatry by the Romans, at least, after the passing of Galen. The Christian church was developing, and maintained the tradition of demoniacal possession which it found in the New Testament as well as in the Old. The demonological interpretation was again in the ascendancy, together with a closely related belief in witchcraft, and with the growth and influence of the Church the professional attention given to mental deviation was administered by the priest rather than the physician. The treatment of mental disorder had passed from the physician, and now fell entirely within the priest's domain. The stagnation of the observation and rational treatment of mental disorder was unfortunately to last until well into modern times. . . .

During the Middle Ages much of the tradition and influence of the Greek and Roman medical writers was kept alive by the Arabs. They did not add materially to the sum total of knowledge but we, nevertheless, owe much to them for keeping extant the works of the earlier writers at a time when the religious zeal of the monks tended to result in destruction of the writings of the pagans. Avicenna, who lived in the early part of the eleventh century, deserves especial mention; he was a follower of Aristotle and listed a large number of types of mental disorder. He referred to changes in the pulse-rate caused by emotional stimuli and even spoke of curing epilepsy with quartan malaria! The Arabs in general had a sympathetic approach to mental disorder and, indeed, looked on the mentally ill as being under the special protection of Allah, so that on the whole this group was kindly treated. By contrast, during the same period in the Christian portions of Europe, the mentally ill were being persecuted and executed as witches in numbers which for size seem to us now fantastically incredible.

It is difficult at this distance to appreciate the depth of scientific blackness which descended upon Europe during the Middle Ages. Whitwell[1] summarizes the four principal factors in this scientific stagnation as the following: First, the dictatorial power of the Church; second, the inertia of the human mind; third, the tyranny of the Galenic teaching; and finally the persistent belief in demons and witches which acted as a "poison" to the human mind. . . .

The Inquisition was founded by Gregory IX in an effort to suppress heresy—an organization which was to exist in full force for about 400 years. Although physical illness was to a considerable extent recognized as natural in origin, almost everything of what we would today call mental disorder was considered supernatural and the victim of it was either subjected to exorcisms or to persecution as harboring a devil or having relations with an incubus or a succubus. This particular form of activity received great impetus when two Dominican monks, Sprenger and Kraemer, were given authority by Pope Innocent VIII in 1484 to detect and punish those persons who "had abandoned themselves to the devils, the incubi and succubi, who had slain infants, blasted trees and otherwise done great damage by means of their supernatural associations." These two monks wrote a book called *The Malleus Maleficarum* or *The Witch's Hammer*, which was for many years the guide to the "diagnosis" and punishment of witchcraft. The power and the persistence of the movement typified by *The Malleus Maleficarum* may be appreciated from the statement that as late as 1775 a witch was executed in Germany, and one in Switzerland seven years later!

It can readily be seen that the atmosphere was not conducive to psychiatric practice. . . .

The most brilliant protest against the *Malleus* was uttered by a physician, a former student of Henry Cornelius Agrippa, Johann Weyer was born in 1515 and died in 1588. Being physician to one of the local princes, he was in a protected position when he wrote his epoch-making work *De praestigiis Daemonum*, which appeared in Latin in 1562 and in German in 1567. In this book he even dared to speak of "incendiary bishops," and he attacked vigorously the thesis upon which the Inquisition was proceeding against witches. He said that the witches were the mentally ill and that the monks who punished them should themselves be punished. His was a scientific, as well as a humanitarian approach, and in many ways he may be looked upon as one of the early founders of modern psychiatry. He was a careful clinical observer, who reduced the clinical

[1] J. R. Whitwell, *Historical Notes on Psychiatry* (London: H. K. Lewis and Company, 1936), p. 141.

problems to the terms of everyday life and succeeded for the first time in many centuries in divorcing medical psychology from theology. He studied the mental effects of drugs and outlined a sort of psychotherapy. His views were cast aside very casually by the Saxon criminal code of 1572 with the statement that they were not very important "because Weyer is a physician and not a jurist"! In this respect we are reminded of the hesitancy of the law even today to accept well-demonstrated psychiatric principles.

The century following Weyer witnessed the turning of the tide and the ascendancy of scientific investigation as opposed to theological dogmatism. By the middle of the seventeenth century the power of the Church over scientific thought was ebbing rapidly. The change did not come all of a sudden, of course. Felix Plater, who lived in the latter part of the sixteenth century, was interested in mental diseases and wrote a classification but prescribed chains for the disturbed and exorcism for the quiet psychotics, believing the latter to be possessed of devils. Thomas Willis, indeed, the famous discoverer of the circle, and a great contributor to the knowledge of brain anatomy and pathology, still believed in devils as causative factors of mental disorder and recommended severe treatment for the mentally ill. Such psychiatry as he developed was, as Zilboorg[2] puts it, a psychiatry without psychology. John Locke, who happened to be a physician but is best remembered as a philosopher, wrote on the human understanding and speculated at considerable length upon problems of mental disorder, as did the lay philosophers Descartes, Hobbes, and Spinoza. It was the philosophers, then, who were studying at this time and speculating about mental disorder while the physicians were trying to develop a strictly organic psychiatry. Indeed, the struggle at this particular period of the eighteenth century was largely one between the organically-minded physicians and the humanitarian non-physicians. . . .

In the latter part of the eighteenth century Reil wrote his famous *Rhapsodies*, but his treatment consisted largely in ducking, in firing cannon, and in other forms of what he called "non-injurious torture"—another modification of the concept of shock therapy. The French writer, de Sauvages, wrote a three-volume nosology in 1771 in which he devoted 326 pages to mental diseases. Cullen, the eminent Scottish physician, at about the same time, had written extensively on neuropathology, inter alia, and established a classification of mental disease.

The name of Gall (1758–1818) has been so firmly associated with the rise of phrenology that some of his more substantial contributions to neurology have been forgotten. Phrenology was for a considerable period of time at the close of the eighteenth century and well into the earlier years of the nineteenth century a moving force in psychiatry and neurology. It was based on the theory that there were certain functions of certain portions of the brain, these functions being referred to in the phrenological literature as "organs," such as those of time, honesty, philo-progenitiveness, and so on, the development or lack of development of which could be detected by palpating the "corresponding" protuberances and depression of the skull. Phrenology had a tremendous vogue in this country as well. . . .

Contemporaneously with Gall, Haslam, at the Bedlam Hospital in London, was making close studies of the clinical course of his patients and describing in most lucid language the results of his post-mortem examinations. He is generally given the credit for the first description of general paresis in 1798. At the same time, too, Kant, the great German philosopher, was discussing the relation of the needs and demands of the patient in relation to the frustrations which he met in his environment.

Such, then, was the milieu, into which came the physician who . . . has not been given the credit which he deserves as a close observer and one who applied the scientific method in drawing deductions from his observations. This man was Philippe Pinel. The fame which has properly come to Pinel as a result of his epoch-making humanitarianism in striking the shackles from the mentally ill patients at the Bicêtre in 1793 has been so great and widespread that it has obscured, if anything, the very substantial contributions which he made to medical literature in general and psychiatric literature in particular. He may properly be looked upon as the father of modern psychiatry. In 1793 [he] was appointed Physician-in-Chief at the Bicêtre, the famous mental hospital in Paris. Shocked and horrified at the conditions which he found there, he sought and secured the grudging permission of the governmental authorities to strike the shackles from the patients. This, however, was not all. He started a régime of sound hospital administration, not only humanitarian, but according to the best lights of the medicine of his time. He frowned upon bloodletting, was skeptical of the "bath of surprise" and the other drastic treatments of his day, and depended very much upon what he termed moral treatment, that is, as we should say today, psychotherapy. He started a system of case records and was evidently a very close observer. Although he was interested

[2] G. Zilboorg, *A History of Medical Psychology* (New York: W. W. Norton & Co., 1941), p. 264.

in classification, and, indeed wrote a three volume work entitled *Nosographie Philosophique* and in 1801 his classical *Traité Médico-Philosophique sur l'Aliénation Mentale*, he was primarily a clinician and therapist, a reformer and reorganizer.

Pinel's approach to the problem of treatment and classification may be gathered from his introductory remarks to the first edition of his treatise: "Symptoms so different, and all comprehended under the general title of insanity, required on my part much study and discrimination; and to secure order in the establishment and success to the practice, I determined upon adopting such a variety of measures, both as to discipline and treatment, as my patients required, and my limited opportunity permitted. From symptoms of nosology, I had little assistance to expect; . . . I, therefore, resolved to adopt that method of investigation which has invariably succeeded in all the departments of natural history, viz. to notice successively every fact, without any other object than that of collecting materials for future use; and to endeavor, as far as possible, to divest myself of the influence, both of my own prepossessions and the authority of others. . . .*,[3]

By his application of clinical methods, by his emphasis upon psychotherapy as against the harsh treatments then prevalent, and by the introduction of a medical atmosphere into mental institutions which had not existed before, Pinel's influence must be considered a highly significant one; it gave a new turn to the stream of psychiatry.

The work of Pinel was well carried on by his able student Esquirol. He, too, emphasized the importance of the emotional factors in mental disorder. . . . The result of his studies and clinical observations was presented in his two volumes entitled *Maladies Mentales* published in 1838. Esquirol may well be considered the first writer to have applied the statistical method to the study of mental disorders. To him, likewise, we are indebted for the use of the word "hallucination" in its modern sense. . . . He also devoted some attention to mental disorder as a defense to charges of crime. The names of Pinel and Esquirol stand out brilliantly in the history of psychiatry. They were succeeded in France by such outstanding writers as Georget, Falret, and Baillarger.

While a young and sincere physician, Philippe Pinel, was on his way to Paris, another physician of quite a different type was also arriving, one Anton Mesmer. Mesmer had

found the atmosphere of Vienna somewhat uncomfortable, but was warmly received by the Parisians with his magnetizing seances. The "animal magnetism" which Mesmer preached and demonstrated, at least to the satisfaction of the Parisians, had an extraordinary spread and influence. The studies of hypnotism by Braid and by Charcot were direct outgrowths of the work of Mesmer. . . .

While these developments were taking place in France, England was likewise making progress. The founding of the York Retreat by William Tuke in 1792 was a progressive step of the first magnitude since it represented, as did the work of Pinel in France, the substitution of kindness and humanitarian treatment for the abuses to which the mentally ill had hitherto been subjected. Tuke, although a layman, was the founder of a line of distinguished psychiatrists, and his principles were ably supported by Conolly and Gardiner Hill, the great advocates of non-restraint. It is interesting in this connection to note that the doctrine of non-restraint was accepted much less readily in America than in England. In the earlier days of what is now the American Psychiatric Association resolutions were passed, indicating that this doctrine of non-restraint was looked upon as a dangerously novel one! . . .

While these developments were taking place in the Old World, America was not stationary, although progress was far more guarded and cautious—a psychological state of affairs which Oscar Wilde probably had in mind when he spoke of the youth of America as being one of its oldest traditions. Benjamin Rush in 1812 wrote the first treatise on mental disorders published in America, *Medical Inquiries and Observations upon Diseases of the Mind.* . . . Rush looked upon mental disorder as due to disturbance of the circulation of the brain; he was strictly an organicist. Since the circulation was disturbed, presumably through an excess of blood, the proper treatment consisted in bloodletting, purging, and other depleting procedures. A little was said about moral treatment, but far more was said about treatments which we should look upon as decidedly rough. He speaks of the use of the lash and of the chain and of the propriety of putting the patient in fear of death if the depleting methods already mentioned should not be effective. He invented two terrifying apparatuses, the "gyrator" and the "tranquilizer," which certainly had an effect upon the luckless patient.

The first institution of any sort to care for the mentally ill was the Pennsylvania Hospital in Philadelphia (1752), and gradually a few other institutions, some public and some voluntary (private) in nature, were founded. The first public mental institution had been opened

---

* [Ed. note: This remains good practice, especially for the forensic psychiatrist.]

[3] P. Pinel, *A Treatise on Insanity*, trans. D. D. Davis, M.D. (Sheffield, England, 1806), p. 2.

at Williamsburg, Virginia in 1773 under the control, not of a physician, but a "keeper." In 1846 John Minson Galt, then Superintendent at Williamsburg and one of the founders of the American Psychiatric Association, published a valuable book entitled *The Treatment of Insanity* in which he had compiled abstracts of practically all of the then extant European literature upon the treatment of mental disorder. . . .

In 1844 the American Psychiatric Association had been founded and the American Journal of Insanity (now the American Journal of Psychiatry) was established. . . . The most significant psychiatric document published in this period, however was *The Medical Jurisprudence of Insanity*, the first volume on the subject to appear in the English language. It was published in 1838 by Isaac Ray, then an obscure practitioner in the remote town of Eastport, Maine, but later to become a founder of the American Psychiatric Association and a leader in American psychiatry. The volume had a profound effect upon legal, as well as psychiatric, thought, and was for almost half a century quoted freely as authority in the decisions of courts in the United States. The scope of its thought and of its scholarship stamp it as one of the great books of psychiatry. . . .

During a large part of the nineteenth century the psychiatric trend was toward the somatic point of view. This was true, for example, with Maudsley in England, with Heinroth and Griesinger in Germany, with Meynert in Austria, and with Weir Mitchell and some of his colleagues in the United States. Particularly in Germany this trend was emphasized by the rise of neuropathology, which had been given a very considerable impetus in the eighties through the development of new staining processes as the aniline dyes were discovered. Delusions and hallucinations were explained by Meynert as due to subcortical irritation of the brain, and melancholia and mania to the changes in the cortical blood vessels or cortical cells. There was strong opposition to speculative psychology, but while much of this opposition delayed the development of the psychological study of mental disorder, it promoted the study of such organic diseases as general paresis, alcoholic mental disorders and the senile psychoses by Nissl, Alzheimer, and others. In the meantime, especially in Germany, a new school of psychology was developing in the universities under such men as Weber, Fechner, and Wundt, the latter establishing in 1878 the Institute for Experimental Psychology.

It was into this field of the conflicting approaches of psychologists and of organic psychiatrists that Emil Kraepelin was born in 1855. In 1878, the same year in which Charcot started his studies of hysteria at the Salpêtrière, Kraepelin became assistant at the clinic in Munich, and five years later brought out the first edition of his *Psychiatrie*. He was an acute observer, an excellent describer of symptoms, and a systematic classifier; his classification, indeed, is still the basis of that used today in mental hospitals. To him mental disease was a predetermined entity, arising from constitutional causes and running a fixed course. It is to Kraepelin that we owe the concept of dementia praecox, later expanded (in 1911) by Bleuler to our present one of schizophrenia. He also defined clearly the paranoias, and emphasized the unitary nature of mania and depression. His classification was largely an abstract one rather than one that dealt with the individual patient's problems, and his concepts of treatment and, indeed, of curability were essentially pessimistic. His great contribution was that at last he had brought psychiatry into medicine. . . .

Only one year after the birth of Kraepelin was born another man who was to revolutionize and to vitalize psychiatry, namely, Sigmund Freud. After some early investigations of local anesthesia, he became interested in clinical neurology, and left Vienna to study with Charcot in Paris. While there he developed an interest in the neuroses and in the possibilities of hypnotism in their treatment, and on returning to Vienna in 1886 he carried out his studies further. In 1895 he published his *Studien uber Hysterie*, followed in 1900 by his *Traumdeutung*. Freud's discoveries concerning the role of the unconscious and the instinctual life were revolutionary, and, as is to be expected with anything new, aroused great opposition. . . . Since then they have gained a wide acceptance and have been incorporated into the body of psychiatric thought. There were early offshoots from the parent stem, such as the developments under C. G. Jung of Zurich, W. Stekel and Alfred Adler of Vienna. Since Freud's death there have been still other developments and modifications of the so-called orthodox psychoanalytic doctrines, such as those formulated by Karen Horney, Harry Stack Sullivan, and Franz Alexander. Such developments are healthy signs, and further growth is to be expected as our knowledge of mental processes increases.

In this country a significant psychiatric development has taken place under the leadership of Dr. Adolf Meyer. . . . From the start he emphasized the general pathological evolution of the symptoms of the patient, physical and mental. He viewed the patient as a whole, studying his past and present, synthesizing the various points of view and developing what is now referred to generally as the psychobiological school. . . .

The dynamic approach of Freud and of Meyer gave tremendous impetus to attempts at psychotherapy. The early writers in this country, as on the continent, had spoken of "moral treatment" as meaning occupational therapy, environmental therapy, encouragement, recreation, and so on. This treatment was largely empirical and general, and on the whole very superficial. Freud and his interpreters, such as Brill, Jelliffe, and White, pointed out that mental symptoms are essentially symbolic, the true meanings being usually hidden, but that much can be learned from a study of them as to what is going on within the patient's unconscious, thus enabling an approach of a helpful nature. The orthodox psychoanalytic procedure, although helpful in the neuroses, was found to be largely inapplicable to the psychoses. Other approaches were, therefore, sought. Bleckwenn and Lorenz in 1930 demonstrated that the intravenous use of sodium amytal permits a more direct approach to the patient's unconscious and that it serves in large measure as a "short cut" to psychotherapy even in uncooperative patients. Moreno developed a dramatic method, the outgrowth of the Spontaneity Theatre of Vienna, which he terms psychodrama, and which has enabled even refractory patients to give vent to attitudes and feelings which they would hardly have been expected to verbalize in a formal interview. Other forms of group therapy have developed from World War II and have shown themselves to be applicable to groups of psychotics and non-psychotics alike.

In the field of treatment one significant and revolutionary advance should be mentioned, namely, the treatment of general paresis.[4] One of the most important events in clinical psychiatry occurred in 1913 when Joseph E. Moore of New York first demonstrated (as confirmed by Noguchi) the spirochete in the brains of general paretics, thus proving the truth of a suspicion that had existed for a long time. Hard on the heels of this revolutionary discovery, namely in 1918, came the demonstration by Wagner-Jauregg of Vienna that malaria could cure general paresis, a disease which up to that time had been considered entirely refractory to any sort of treatment. This method, first demonstrated in the Western Hemisphere at St. Elizabeths Hospital in Washington by White and Eldridge, has completely revolutionized the prognosis of general paresis.

World War I gave a very substantial impetus to the development of psychiatry in the United States. At the outset of the war the Army called upon the National Committee for Men-

tal Hygiene and through them secured the services of Dr. Thomas W. Salmon, one of the great psychiatric statesmen of this country. Psychiatry was put to work early in the Army and given a comparatively free hand. It was well demonstrated that psychiatry could make a valuable contribution to the efficiency of the Army and in addition much was learned concerning the early treatment of the neuroses of war. . . .

The National Committee for Mental Hygiene . . . was the direct outgrowth of the experience of Clifford W. Beers, who on his release from a mental hospital in which he had undergone a serious depression wrote *A Mind that Found Itself*, a volume which has had world-wide sale and has been translated into numerous foreign languages. Immediately thereafter, in 1909, he organized the National Committee for Mental Hygiene for the purpose of improving the hospital care of the mentally ill and making it more accessible to the public by easier admission, extending public knowledge concerning the true nature of mental illness, and stimulating the establishment of preventive activities. The contributions of the National Committee, not only to the development of psychiatry in World War I but to the amelioration of the lot of the mentally ill in hospitals and to a wider public understanding, have been highly significant.

Soon after World War I the child guidance movement which had started primarily in the Juvenile Court at Chicago with William Healy in 1909 developed rapidly under such men as Lowrey, Levy, Plant, and Thom. This movement has amply justified its aim of correcting in early life those trends of behavior in children which, if allowed to go unchecked, may easily develop later on into fully developed neuroses or psychoses. During the period since 1918 clinical psychology, occupational therapy, and social work, all valuable auxiliaries of psychiatry, have shown a sound and healthy growth. In the field of clinical psychology, the development of the Rorschach and the other projective techniques has vastly increased the value of the clinical psychologist to the psychiatrist. The social worker has proved herself invaluable in hospital work particularly and also in the child guidance field, not only in interpreting the home situation to the psychiatrist and the psychiatrist, clinic, or hospital to the home, but in readjusting the individual to community life and in some instances in administering psychotherapy to the family.

Researches of many sorts have been prosecuted, and recent impetus has been given in this field by the passage of the National Mental Health Act. Schizophrenia has been the principal topic of research, and especially since

---

[4] I.e., central nervous system syphilis.

1934, when the Scottish Rite Masons of the Northern Masonic Jurisdiction began a systematic support of research in this field, a vast amount of literature has developed. A recent survey of the literature on this disorder by Leopold Bellak,[5] indeed, lists over 3000 articles. Next to schizophrenia in numerical importance in the literature we find epilepsy; the work of Lennox, Gibbs, Davis, and Merritt has done much, not only to shed light upon the nature of this disorder but to make possible more effective treatment, at least of a palliative nature.

In recent years the work of Sherrington, Cannon, and others has done much to stimulate interest in the relationship between the emotions and the autonomic nervous system, a phase of medicine which has achieved considerable currency under the title of psychosomatic or comprehensive medicine. Over 100 years ago the term "psychosomatic medicine" was used by Nasse and Jacobi, so that neither the term nor the concept is a new one. Indeed, it may be doubted whether psychosomatic medicine is essentially a psychiatric specialty. Every physician should have the psychosomatic approach, namely, the realization that he is dealing not solely with an organ, nor with the mental reactions of the patient, but with a human being who is reacting to a given situation and who may manifest his reactions at any level, whether chemical, physiological, or social. . . .

At the outbreak of World War II there were about 4000 physicians over the entire country who indicated that they had at least an interest in psychiatry. Many of them, however, were not available for military service, so that the number who could be used by the armed forces was far from adequate. . . .

The sodium amytal method of Bleckwenn and Lorenz was developed in the Army with great success under the name of narcosynthesis, and gave excellent results in the early treatment of the acute neuroses. The various so-called shock therapies which have been developing since the late thirties and especially the electroconvulsive therapy of Bini and Cerletti were utilized to a considerable extent in the Army. A modification of the insulin treatment developed by Sargant and Slater in England as "sub-shock" therapy proved of value, as it has proved since in civilian institutions.* Out-patient clinics were maintained by

the Army, and social workers and clinical psychologists worked with the psychiatrists, in selection, in the maintenance of morale, and in the treatment of casualties. In addition the experience of many medical officers in World War II satisfied them that there was a need for psychiatrists and that it was a field in which they should have an interest. . . .

Another outgrowth of the World War has been a considerable breaking down on the part of the public of their previous fear of mental disorder. Through the returning soldiers the public has learned that emotional difficulties, major or minor, may occur in anybody, particularly under stress, and that there is nothing shameful or especially mysterious or incurable about them. The improvement of the public attitude should do much to promote the use of outpatient departments, psychiatric departments of general hospitals, and indeed all psychiatric facilities, as well as making easier the path of the patient returning to the community from the mental hospital.

The official stamping of psychiatry as a specialty may properly be dated from 1934, when the American Board of Psychiatry and Neurology was established. Up to the present time over 3100 physicians have been certified in one or the other specialty, or both. The standards are constantly becoming more stringent, and in a considerable number of positions already the possession of a diploma from the Board is a prerequisite. It is to be hoped that eventually the courts of the country will require a physician to show the possession of a diploma before he is permitted to testify as a psychiatric expert in court.* Such a step would do much to improve the status of psychiatric testimony.

So far almost nothing has been said about the care of the mentally ill in the United States and, indeed, if one were to deal properly with this topic a separate essay would be called for. The scholarly volume by Albert Deutsch entitled *The Mentally Ill in America*[6] can be strongly recommended to any who are interested in this topic. Certainly the history of the care of the mentally ill in this country casts no great glory upon the ability or the willingness of the various state governments to practice adequate mental medicine. With a few notable exceptions the state hospitals of the country have been inadequately provided with funds, inadequately manned, the patients inadequately and crowdedly housed, and in too many instances the state hospital systems have as well become the prey of political spoilsmen. . . .

We now have hopes for . . . increased appro-

[5] Leopold Bellak, *Dementia Praecox. The Past Decade's Work and Present Status: A Review and Evaluation* (New York: Grune & Stratton, 1948).

* [Ed. note: Although electroshock therapy continues as an important treatment modality, the use of insulin coma has, by and large, ceased since publication of Dr. Overholser's article.]

* [Ed. note: Sadly, this has not yet been done.]
[6] Garden City, N.Y.: Columbia University Press, 1949. P. 555 (2d ed.).

priations, higher professional standards, and freedom from political meddling. The methods of admission to these hospitals, too, should more nearly approach those in effect for general hospitals, and in those cases in which legally authorized detention is necessary the formalities should be reduced to the minimum, rather than demanding notices, hearings, counsel, subpoenas, and the rest of the legal armamentarium.*

In the field of medical education a substantial advance is being made in presenting psychiatry to medical students as a subject which is closely related to the other topics studied. Clinical contacts not only with the psychoses but with the neuroses and with the emotional aspects of general diseases are being provided as never before in the medical schools of the country, . . .

This trend in medical education has been accomplished and strengthened by the development of psychiatric wards in general hospitals. . . . In 1902 the Albany Hospital established a psychiatric pavilion, and a few hospitals, notably the Henry Ford Hospital in Detroit, followed suit. In the last few years it has become almost the usual practice to provide wards in general hospitals which are available to mental patients. In this manner transient and intercurrent psychotic episodes may be cared for without commitment; the neurotic symptoms of medical and surgical patients may be treated appropriately, and in addition the rest of the staff are exposed to psychiatric influences. The advantages to patient and staff alike are at last widely recognized.

As one looks back over the development of psychiatric therapy in modern times, certain swings of the pendulum seem evident. Rush, carrying on the earlier tradition, emphasized physical methods such as bloodletting and purging. Pinel, on the other hand, emphasized psychological factors in causation and treatment, and for a time "moral treatment" took the lead. With the rise of the neuropathologists the pendulum swung again to neural explanations and either no treatment at all or "general" therapy. Under the influence of Freud the psychogenic point of view came again into the ascendant, and with it much emphasis on psychotherapy—more than ever before, for far more was known of psychic mechanisms. It can safely be said that the past quarter century represents the brightest era of psychiatric therapy.

For the past decade, however, a regressive tendency has appeared, a suggestion of another swing of the pendulum. Reference is made, of course, to the so-called drastic therapies. When Sakel's "insulin shock" method was introduced about 1933 great claims were made for its effectiveness in schizophrenia, claims which have been considerably modified as time has passed. Meduna's metrazol shock therapy, originally recommended for schizophrenia, was found to yield better results in the depressions, but was soon abandoned for the electro-convulsive therapy of Bini and Cerletti. The dangerously deceptive ease of administration of the latter form of treatment has given more than a few inadequately trained psychiatrists and neurologists the mistaken notion that all they need for the practice of psychiatry is the little box which contains the shock apparatus! . . .

The free use of prefrontal leucotomy is even more doubtful. A multilating operation at best, it should be employed only when all other therapeutic methods have been tried thoroughly and have failed over a substantial period and even then only in the presence of certain symptoms such as extreme restlessness or aggressiveness.

It should be said in fairness that one reason alleged by the advocates of "shock therapy" is that it brings about results much more rapidly than psychotherapy, and they point to the orthodox psychoanalytic procedures with their expense and their course of a year or more. The answer to such criticisms lies not in abandonment of all that has been learned of psychoanalytic principles, but in the development of new and briefer technics of psychotherapy. . . .

So much progress has been made in psychotherapy that it is to be hoped that the present tendency of the pendulum of progress to reverse its direction will be short-lived. The physical can never be overlooked in psychiatry, but it must never be allowed to eclipse all use of psychologic approaches and methods.

The crying need today is for a synthesis of all the schools of thought and methods of approach; no one method has a monopoly of the truth. . . . We need urgently a selection and coordination of the best and most helpful in neurophysiology, neurology, psychoanalysis, psychobiology, "psychosomatic medicine," neurosurgery, physical methods of treatment (physical medicine in its broadest and newest sense), anthropology, and sociology. When that time comes, we shall have a truly American psychiatry, and psychiatry will truly have come of age.

---

* [Ed. note: More about this controversial suggestion in Chapters 9 and 10.]

ADDENDUM TO DR. OVERHOLSER'S ARTICLE

Although the quarter century since Dr. Overholser's article appeared has not entirely fulfilled the hopes stated in his last paragraph, significant movement toward the synthesis of a "truly American psychiatry" has been made, and enormous advances in research and treatment have revolutionized the theory and practice of psychiatry. To oversimplify somewhat the state of affairs in 1948 when Dr. Overholser wrote, psychiatric patients were stereotyped into either those with severe mental illness (the psychoses) and those with less serious illness (the neuroses and personality disorders). The former generally responded to no known treatment except electroshock. Those not responding to this treatment too often became chronic custodial patients requiring lifelong hospitalization in state or private institutions. The neuroses were treatable only by common-sense advice, sympathy, or "support," or by lengthy and expensive psychoanalysis.

Dr. Overholser emphasizes the dichotomy between the physical-medical-organic view of psychiatric illness on the one hand, and the psychological-psychoanalytic-psychosocial view on the other. This dichotomy is gradually being replaced by a single, more empiric and eclectic approach. The synthesis of psychosocial and biological psychiatry has been made possible by advances in psychological and biological science as well as by the development of multiple effective treatment modalities. The latter include the introduction in 1953 of the tranquilizers, followed by the antidepressants and most recently by lithium carbonate. In terms of "talking treatment," brief individual therapy, group therapy, family therapy, therapeutic community modalities, and behavior modification treatments have been introduced and refined.

In tandem with the development of new treatment approaches has come a major shift in the philosophy of treatment. Since the days of Wier Mitchell (in the nineteenth century), psychiatric patients have been thought best treated in the atmosphere of a "retreat" or "asylum," which optimally offered rest, peace, quiet, and separation from the noxious influences of family and community. However, since World War II, the pendulum has swung 180 degrees toward an approach that views as optimal the maintenance of the patient within a family and community structure, insofar as the illness permits. This trend has been most vigorously promulgated since the National Mental Health Act of 1963. This Act established a series of community mental health centers across the country, which emphasize preventive and treatment services within the patient's own community. Since then, both public and private sectors of psychiatry have seen community-based treatment as an essential component of psychiatric care.

Finally, since Dr. Overholser wrote, there has been a great surge of interest in the field of forensic psychiatry, which had unfortunately been a neglected stepchild of both psychiatry and the law. During the past decade, pioneering cases in the areas of patient's rights, the right to treatment, the requirement of least restrictive alternatives, the rights of the mentally retarded and children, and the complex issues of privilege and confidentiality have finally become concerns of organized psychiatry.

These recent developments will be more fully elaborated upon in Chapter 4 and in other sections of the book.

Editorial Note: *Prevalence of Psychiatric Disorders*

In terms of seriousness to the individual, the family, and the nation as a whole, psychiatric illnesses should rank as among the three or four major health problems confronting this country. However, precise data as to the magnitude of the problem are hard to come by. As Reed states, "Unfortunately, annual morbidity statistics on the incidence and prevalence of mental disorders do not exist for the U.S.—or for that matter, for any other country."[1] The statistics that do exist probably underestimate the incidence of psychiatric disorders, given the reluctance of many people to seek psychiatric care or to admit psychiatric disability. Some studies, however, have been carried out. In Baltimore, a survey concluded that approximately 10 percent of the population have conditions or symptoms that could be characterized as "mental illness." Selective service statistics from World War II indicate an incidence between 1.8 and 6.7 percent of the population examined. A New York City study estimated that 23.4 percent of a large sample of the population had some impairment in life functioning because of mental disorder. In this study psychiatric impairment was considerably higher in the lower socioeconomic group.[2]

Further evidence of the magnitude of the problem is that suicide is the second leading cause of death (after accidents) among 18 to 25 year old white males,[3] and among the twelve leading reported causes of death generally,[4] though it is grossly underreported. In addition, there are millions of aged people with depression and early signs of diminished brain functioning who could benefit from adequate and early psychiatric care; millions of mentally retarded, most of whom can be trained to be productive members of society, given adequate multidimensional treatment and rehabilitation; an estimated 9 million alcoholics; and an estimated 250,000 narcotic addicts.[5] A total of about 870,000 patients are admitted to public and private psychiatric hospitals each year,[6] and in 1970 there were an estimated 2.7 million psychiatric outpatient visits.[7] Valium, a tranquilizer and muscle relaxant, is the nation's leading prescription drug.[8]

Less definitive, but perhaps more revealing than any of these statistics, is the commonly accepted figure among medical practitioners that at least 50 percent of all visits to internists, pediatricians, and general practitioners result from psychological and emotional problems rather than primarily physical illness.

What is the public's attitude toward the mentally ill and emotionally suffering, who constitute such a large percentage of our population? The following excerpt reports a study of public attitudes toward mental illness and mental health services.

[1] L. S. Reed, E. S. Myers, P. L. Scheidemandel, *Health Insurance and Psychiatric Care: Utilization and Cost* (Washington, D.C.: The American Psychiatric Association, 1972), p. 11.

[2] "A Survey of Mental Disease in an Urban Population: Prevalence by Race and Income," in B. Pasamanick (ed.), *Epidemiology of Mental Disorder* (Washington, D.C.: American Association for the Advancement of Science, 1959), quoted by L. S. Reed, Ibid., p. 11.

[3] *Leading Components of Upturn in Mortality for Men, United States—1952–67* (Rockville, Maryland: DHEW Publication No. (HSM) 72–1008, 1971), p. 9.

[4] *Suicide in the United States, 1950–1964* (Washington, D.C.: DHEW Publication No. (HSM) 73–1259, 1967), p. 1.

[5] M. E. Chafetz, Foreword to *Alcohol and Alcoholism* (Rockville, Maryland: DHEW Publication No. (HSM) 72–9127, Revised 1972), p. iii.

[6] "The Menninger Clinic Is Changing Its Ways; Patients Help Run It," *Wall Street Journal*, 13 March 1974.

[7] *Building a National Health-Care System* (New York: Committee for Economic Development, 1973), p. 52.

[8] "Prescription Leaders," *Chain Store Age/Drug Editions* (February 1974), p. 94.

PUBLIC IMAGE OF MENTAL HEALTH SERVICES

Jack Elinson, Ph.D., Elena Padilla, Ph.D., and Marvin E. Perkins, M.D.

This is the first general report of the findings obtained from a household survey on the public image of mental health services in New York City, conducted by the Columbia University School of Public Health and Administrative Medicine and the New York City Community Mental Health Board during the fall and winter of 1963. New York City adults living in each of the five boroughs were selected for interviews by probability sampling techniques to represent the opinions and attitudes of the adult population of the city. More than a hundred interviewers and researchers participated in the survey operations.

The survey tapped public knowledge and opinion about mental health care, appraisals of mental health facilities and professionals, and attitudes toward the mentally ill. The survey also explored public perceptions and conceptions of mental illness, experience with professional mental health help, including hospitalization, and the sources and recognition of personal problems. How New Yorkers go about seeking help, their awareness of the help system available, and their appraisal of the need for community-based mental health services were among the major mental health areas covered.

The survey showed clearly that there are chinks in the traditional public armor of rejection of the mentally ill. There is widespread support for a variety of ideas for community-based services currently being suggested by mental health professionals for the care of mentally ill people, and especially for those services offering quick assistance, such as a telephone information service and walk-in clinics. The view is now equite prevalent that "mental illness is an illness like any other," and optimism prevails that mental illness is treatable.

Mental illness is not perceived as so strange a phenomenon as may once have been the case. One out of two adults in New York City personally has known someone who has had help for mental or emotional problems. And almost as many New Yorkers admit to having had personal problems themselves for which they could have used help.

Yet not all the old views about mental illness have been completely dispelled. The public shares the view expressed in the report of the Joint Commission on Mental Illness and Health that mental illness tends to repel people; but, interestingly, only a small minority admit to being repelled themselves by mental illness.

Nearly every other adult (45%) can think of times in his life when he has had personal problems that might have been helped by going somewhere or seeing someone. An additional one in seven (15%) has had personal problems but does not believe that going somewhere or seeing someone might have helped. The rest, two out of five (38%), deny having ever had any "great personal problems."

One out of eleven adults (9%) reports having ever gone for help for a mental or emotional problem or condition. Of those who have gone for help, half say they have seen a psychiatrist. Other professionals seen, in order of frequency of mention, are physicians (nonpsychiatric), psychologists, social workers, and counselors. Fewer report having seen clergymen or lawyers, among others.

The main reasons why persons with mental or emotional troubles do not go for help, as seen by the public, are: fear of what people will think or say; fear of finding out if it is serious, of losing their freedom, or of being hurt; the lack of recognition of the trouble or the inability to realize that they are sick; emotional blocks such as shyness, denial, temporizing, desire for privacy, pride, etc. Less frequently mentioned reasons are related to general ignorance and ignorance of help available; the cost involved; belief in self-reliance; and lack of faith in the efficacy of help.

In the public view, the professional identity of psychiatrists and psychologists appears to be blurred and ambiguous. Nearly half (47%)

Excerpted with permission from *Public Image of Mental Health Services* by Jack Elinson, Elena Padilla, and Marvin E. Perkins (1967). Published for the New York City Community Mental Health Board by the Mental Health Materials Center (104 East 25th Street, New York, N.Y.).

either do not know or deny that a psychiatrist is a doctor of medicine. The same proportion (47%) either do not know or deny that anyone but a psychiatrist can treat a person for emotional or mental conditions. One in four (24%) is not sure that a psychiatrist and a psychologist are different, and 8% more think they are the same.

Half (49%) believe that psychologists treat people for mental or emotional conditions, and three in ten (29%) believe that social workers also do.

Better than half of New York City adults (54%) share the view that "mental illness is not the most serious health problem in this country." An even larger proportion, nearly nine out of ten (86%), agree with the statement that "most people feel very helpless about mental illness"—as many as hold this opinion concerning helplessness regarding cancer (87%).

The influence of socio-environmental factors is more favored by adults as explanation for mental illness than hereditary, moralistic, or organic causes. Conflict between parents as a childhood influence is seen as a cause of mental illness by nearly two out of three (64%), who agree that "the mental illness of many people is caused by a lot of fighting and quarreling between their parents during childhood." A majority (57%) also agrees that "the mental illness of many people is caused by the separation or divorce of their parents during childhood." A majority (55%) sees parental love as a deterrent to mental illness, but more than a third (38%) deny this. In the opinion of three out of four (73%), "kindness and understanding from others can usually head off a mental illness."

Opinion is divided regarding a hereditary component of mental illness: two out of five (44%) believe that "a mental illness can happen just because it runs in the family"; but just as many (48%) do not concur.

Public opinion is also divided with regard to an organic etiology: nearly half (48%) agree to the statement that "mental illness is usually caused by some disease of the nervous system," although one out of three (33%) is in disagreement.

A similar dichotomy of opinion appears with regard to the "strength of character" explanation of mental illness: half (49%) believe that "one of the main causes of mental illness is lack of moral strength or will power," but nearly as many, two out of five (44%), do not accept this explanation.

Two out of three adults (69%) agree with the assertion that "mental illness is an illness like any other." Yet, at the same time, more than three out of four (77%) agree with the statement that "unlike physical illness, which makes most people sympathetic, mental illness tends to repel most people." Notwithstanding that most people believe that others are repelled by mental illness, few (16%) admit to being repelled by mental illness themselves.

Doubt about the reliability of persons who have been under mental health care is expressed by over half (56%), who disagree that "most women who were once patients in a mental hospital could be trusted as babysitters." Just as many (55%) believe the same about "most women who have gone to mental health clinics."

Two out of five (40%) agree that "anyone who is in a hospital for mental illness should not be allowed to vote," and one in five (21%) does not believe that patients discharged from mental hospitals should be allowed to marry although they "may seem all right."

Fear or protectiveness is expressed by more than two out of five (44%) who agree that "it is unfair to the women and the children of a community to mix mental patients among them." But just as many disagree with this view (49%).

A series of "symptom" questions about certain psychophysiologic reactions were asked. Positive responses to those questions—which in other studies have been considered as pathognomonic—are shown in summary form below.

Respondents are often bothered by: great restlessness (18%), sudden hot flashes (14%), nervousness (14%), sour stomach (12%), worries that get one down physically (12%), trouble sleeping (11%), weakness (10%), clogging of head or nose (10%), fainting spells (8%), headaches (7%), poor appetite (4%), unexplained shortness of breath (4%), heart beating hard (3%), trembling hands (2%), cold sweats (1%).

Questions about thoughts and feelings indicative of psychologic status were also asked. Respondents' replies are summarized thus: 40% say they are worrying types, 21% have periods of feeling depressed, 21% can't help wondering if anything is worthwhile any more, 20% have special thoughts that keep bothering them, 17% have special fears that keep bothering them, 15% have trouble with memory, 13% feel somewhat apart even among friends, 13% have periods when they cannot get going, 13% feel that nothing ever turns out the way one wants it, 13% have special habits that keep bothering them, 8% feel "very high" so that it is difficult to concentrate, 8% are in low spirits most of the time.

ADDENDUM TO ELINSON ARTICLE

Other recent surveys confirm growing acceptance of psychiatric illness in this country. For example, a study conducted by Lewis Harris and Associates for the Blue Cross Association[1] notes that 80 percent of those polled would favor "education in the schools on ways to recognize and care for mental illness," and that the majority of respondents indicated they would personally like to have more information about mental illness. Similarly, a study by Drs. W. Kenneth Bentz and W. Wilbert Edgerton, published in the journal, *Social Psychiatry*,[2] noted greater public accept-

[1] *Psychiatric News*, May 19, 1972.
[2] As reported in *Psychiatric News*, May 19, 1972.

ance of the mentally ill and willingness to work alongside ex-mental patients in rural areas of North Carolina and Virginia, in contrast to findings in a similar study done in 1957. They also found no evidence that identifying a person as mentally ill resulted in rejection or isolation. Public attitudes toward the former mental patient may indeed be moving in a positive direction. But that the chimeras still exist is illustrated by the furor—pro and con—over the removal of Senator Eagleton as a vice-presidential candidate in 1972 when it was learned that he had been hospitalized—and received electroshock—for depression several years prior ot his nomination.

THE NEW FACE OF LEGAL PSYCHIATRY

Jonas Robitscher, J.D., M.D.

The nineteenth-century psychiatrist occupied an important but circumscribed position in society; his influence did not extend far. He was primarily the custodian, the hospital superintendent. He dealt with the mentally ill and did not concern himself with social reform except as it applied to patients in his custody.

One of the few times he assumed a more prominent role was when he appeared as a forensic psychiatrist, taking the witness stand as an expert in order to testify that a defendant did or did not have criminal responsibility or that a deceased testator had or did not have testamentary capacity.

When Freud's medical psychology promulgated a theory of the cause and cure of neuroses, the psychiatrist expanded his role and became an office practitioner who now dealt with outpatients as well as inpatients. Although his views began to influence child raising, education, the structure of social and family life,

and arts and letters, the psychiatrist remained essentially a private individual, once-removed from the legislative and the administrative process. Psychiatrists continued to have a "low visibility profile."

One reason for the privatism of psychiatrists was the Freudian ideal of anonymity; another was the medical tradition that prohibited self-advertising and self-aggrandizement; and still another was the low level of public concern with many phases of the psychiatrist's activities, such as his work with state hospital patients, in a prison setting, and with juvenile delinquents.

Our modern changing and complicated society has thrust psychiatrists into a more public role at the same time that it has stimulated the profession to reexamine concepts of health and disease. The forensic psychiatrist is the main emissary of psychiatry to society; he is the psychiatrist who appears in court, works in

Excerpted and reprinted with permission from *Amer. J. Psychiat.*, 129 (1972): 315–21. Copyright 1972, the American Psychiatric Association.

This work was supported by Public Health Service grant MH-12555 from the National Institute of Mental Health.

corrections, advises on legislation, teaches lawyers.

The courtroom, and the criminal trial in particular, continues to be the place where forensic psychiatrists receive the most exposure; the testimony of Manfred Guttmacher in the Jack Ruby case, which emphasized Ruby's weak ego structure and its disruption under the impact of the Kennedy assassination, and the testimony of Bernard Diamond in the Sirhan Sirhan case, where Diamond proposed a theory of the reactivation of a self-hypnotic state as a cause of the second Kennedy assassination, led to great public exposure for the testifying psychiatrists. The Leopold and Loeb and Alger Hiss cases are other examples of the psychiatrist in the public eye. New legal rules of criminal responsibility and new psychiatric theories relating social factors to psychopathology lead to testimony that assumes increased importance in the trial process (1).

But the forensic psychiatrist has widened his role to include much more than the courtroom appearance. He uses his psychiatric background and his familiarity with law and the legislative process to deal with juvenile delinquency, aggression, violence, drugs, sexual standards, and a host of other problems that have psychiatric, legal, social, and even political and economic components.

In this atmosphere forensic psychiatry finds itself forced to become more truly interdisciplinary. In place of the old psychiatrist-law professor dialogue, which often bogged down in philosophical discussions of free will and determinism, the conversation has broadened into a colloquium in which law, psychiatry, sociology, psychology, social work, and other behavioral science disciplines all share. As one illustration of the merging of disciplines and the merging of legal and social psychiatry, let me cite the program I headed until recently at the University of Pennsylvania. After searching for a name to fit the National Institute of Mental Health sponsored program, which emphasized teaching at the medical school and residency levels and the preparation of teaching materials, the older titles such as "Legal Psychiatry" or "Forensic Psychiatry" seemed too narrow, so the title eventually emerged as "Social-Legal Uses of Forensic Psychiatry" (2). The term "social-legal psychiatry" seems to describe better than the older ones the multidisciplinary quality of the patient-society interaction (3).

Growing Interest in Forensic Psychiatry

Two developments indicate the growing interest in forensic psychiatry. First, a number of interdisciplinary courses and institutes have been developed to foster research and to sponsor advanced training. Boston University, Harvard, Yale, the Menninger Foundation, George Washington University, Emory University, Temple, Tulane, the University of Pittsburgh, the University of Maryland, the University of Southern California, and the University of California, Los Angeles, are some of the pioneers in these programs.

Second, in late 1969 the American Academy of Psychiatry and the Law (AAPL) was formed. This formal group was the outgrowth of an informal group of about 15, mainly directors of forensic psychiatry fellowship training programs, who had met in connection with the American Psychiatric Association meeting in Boston in 1968. This new group now has about 250 members, all interested in some phase of legal psychiatry; it has published eleven issues of a quarterly newsletter, which is more truly a small journal, and it has held two annual meetings (4). The by-laws of AAPL list six aims: to exchange ideas and experience among forensic psychiatrists in North America; to elevate the standards of study and practice in this field; to develop training programs for psychiatrists desirous of acquiring skills in forensic psychiatry; to take leadership in initiating and monitoring research in the field; to improve relationships between psychiatrists on the one hand and attorneys, legislators, jurists, and penologists on the other; and to take leadership in informing the public of the needs of those involved with the law and the contributions available from psychiatry (5).

An indication of the broadened application of forensic psychiatry is the definition found in the by-laws:

. . . The phrase "forensic psychiatry" will include all aspects of psychiatry which remain in close and significant contact with the law, legislation or jurisprudence, including, but not limited to, problems in the psychiatric aspects of testamentary capacity, criminal responsibility, guardianship, evidence, competency, marriage, divorce, annulment, custody of children, commitment procedures, personal injury evaluation, malpractice litigation, preservation of the civil rights of the mentally ill, addiction to alcohol and drugs, psychiatric testimony in courts and before other tribunals or legislative bodies, management and treatment of all offenders, and confidentiality of records (5).

Legal psychiatry can be defined simply enough as the area where law and psychiatry meet or as the body of law and customs that accords special treatment (sometimes specially favorable and sometimes specially unfavorable) to individuals whose mental or emotional status entitles them to be treated differently. But as the field extends, these simple definitions are seen to encompass a host of not-so-simple relationships to other disciplines.

The relationship of forensic psychiatry to law requires an understanding of the historical development of this specialized branch of law. Also, since law deals with analogies and precedents that originate in one field of law but are then applied to another, the forensic psychiatrist soon finds himself a victim of "cultural spread"; he has to become aware of other branches of law, other aspects of medicine, other aspects of society.

For example, the law dealing with psychiatric patients is very similar to the law dealing with minors or the law dealing with seamen—both groups need special protection because of their diminished capacity to deal effectively with authorities—and very similar to superseded law dealing with the inferior position of women (especially married women), blacks, and indentured servants. The protection of the rights of the mentally disabled requires a knowledge of the legal problems of other minorities. Legal psychiatry and race relations become intertwined in decisions like *Brown v. Board of Education* (6), in which the basis for overturning the concept of school segregation is the psychological harm caused by the segregation; they are related more generally in that both fields are concerned with the enforcement of the legal rights of those at a legal disadvantage.

The treatment of juveniles in juvenile courts, the treatment of mental or "moral" defectives under defective delinquency laws, and the treatment of sexual deviates under sexual psychopath laws are topics that carry the forensic psychiatrist away from the narrow definition of legal psychiatry and involve him in a broader world of criminology, sociology, and rehabilitation by nonpsychiatric means. The question of whether an involuntarily committed patient should be entitled to a lawyer at the time of his commitment cannot be studied without getting into such related areas as the question of whether a prisoner who has violated the conditions of his parole should be entitled to a lawyer when the parole board considers returning him to jail, or the question of whether an indigent who cannot afford a lawyer because of poverty is entitled to legal help.

Law deals with analogies and precedents, and the logic that develops in one area is applied to another. This forces the legal psychiatrist to consider not only the problems of the mentally disabled under the law but to delve into other legal areas: it forces him to understand the problems of those suffering from nonpsychiatric disability (nonadults, racial minorities, the indigent, the imprisoned) and to find out how the law has developed in those areas.

Besides being forced into other legal fields, the forensic psychiatrist is forced to extend himself into nonpsychiatric areas of medicine, the nonmedical therapies, and other helping professions. For example, confidentiality is a major concern of legal psychiatry—especially during this period of developing community mental health centers—but although there are special concerns that make confidentiality more important in psychiatric therapy than in other therapies, confidentiality is of concern to doctors generally (7, 8).

Informed consent is of special concern to psychiatrists. How can we be sure that a patient who is psychotic, mentally retarded, and (just to make the example as difficult as possible) is also a minor, has her rights protected in a decision for eugenic sterilization (9)? But informed consent is also of concern to doctors generally; the use of patients as subjects for scientific experiments and for testing the efficacy of drugs has medical implications that are of interest to internists as well as psychiatrists.

Psychiatric malpractice is a specialized topic because psychiatric practice is difficult to define and includes treatment methods unknown to medicine generally; nevertheless, psychiatric and medical malpractice are topics that are closely related.

The forensic psychiatrist can no longer define his field narrowly. Since many of the topics that have special meaning for forensic psychiatry have meaning for other branches of medicine as well, some forensic psychiatrists have suggested that the home for their specialty is not the department of psychiatry—although this is where it is usually found—but as an independent medical school department of medical jurisprudence.

THE PRESENT STATE OF LEGAL PSYCHIATRY

The present state of legal psychiatry represents a reaching out, although still somewhat amorphous and ill-defined, into other branches of medicine and other disciplines. These areas are of concern primarily to five disciplines—psychiatry, law, psychology, sociology, and social work—although other disciplines as varied as anthropology, education and special education, and hospital administration can also be involved (3). It would not be difficult to give a list of 50 or 100 topics, all of which involve other disciplines, that interest a forensic psychiatrist. They might range from abortion and addiction at one end of the alphabet to violence and victims at the other, in contrast to the three traditional aspects that previously attracted attention from forensic psychiatrists and lawyers—criminal responsibility, commitment processes, and testamentary capacity. Although criminal responsibility remains interesting and although it represents complicated moral and philosophical questions that underlie all phases of social-legal psychiatry, it has not deserved the 90 percent of the attention that it has received.

In descriptions of the history of forensic psychiatry in America, the names that appear are all identified with legal psychiatry mainly because of their contributions to the law of criminal responsibility—Isaac Ray; Bernard Glueck, who studied Sing Sing prisoners; Vernon Briggs, author of the Massachusetts "Briggs Law," which provides for the psychiatric examination of certain classes of defendants by impartial psychiatrists; Manfred Guttmacher, long connected with the Baltimore court system and author and co-author with Professor Henry Weihofen of books and articles on criminal responsibility; Winfred Overholser; Franz Alexander; Gregory Zilboorg; and Benjamin Karpman. Starting in 1952, APA has presented the Isaac Ray Award (annually if a suitable candidate is available) to a specialist particularly distinguished in the field of psychiatry and law; the award includes the obligation for a lecture series, which usually appears in book form. With only four exceptions the award winners have used their lectureships to make further contributions to the field of criminal responsibility and correctional psychiatry—Gregory Zilboorg (10); Judge John Biggs, Jr. (11); Professor Henry Weihofen (12); Philip Roche (13); Manfred Guttmacher (14); Alastair MacLeod (15); Judge David Bazelon (16); Sheldon Glueck (17); Karl Menninger (18); George Sturup (19); and Bernard Diamond (20).

The award has been presented only four additional times. The 1959 winner, Maxwell Jones, contributed a volume (21) that was undoubtedly important but, with the exception of a brief chapter on prison psychiatry, dealt with social psychiatry rather than legal or social-legal psychiatry. The 1963 award winner, Judge Morris Ploscowe, delivered a lecture series at Vanderbilt University on sex and law, the theme of a book he had published twelve years previously (22); the lecture series has never been published.

It thus appears that only two of fifteen winners produced books that dealt with the widened scope of legal psychiatry. In 1952 the first award winner, Winfred Overholser, in *The Psychiatrist and the Law* (23) sought a closer relationship between law and psychiatry, considered the lot of the committed mental patient, and discussed the role of the psychiatrist as witness. In 1964 Judge Justine Wise Polier dealt with such noncriminal aspects of legal psychiatry as adoption, custody, and the availability of psychiatric services for noncriminals; the series, published as *The Rule of Law and the Role of Psychiatry* (24), stimulated an important discussion by Tapp of the relationship of law and the behavioral sciences, especially social psychology (25).

But although the Isaac Ray Award Committee has stressed the criminal functions of forensic psychiatry, a flood of major texts and monographs in the last decade has emphasized the widened scope of social-legal psychiatry. An important event in 1960 was the appearance of the comprehensive, carefully researched study by the American Bar Foundation, *The Mentally Disabled and the Law* (26). This book brought together and tabulated the laws of all jurisdictions on a comprehensive range of legal psychiatric topics and has been the chief research source of many subsequent studies.

CURRENT LITERATURE

We have had a number of other meaningful books: the huge Katz, Goldstein, and Dershowitz text *Psychoanalysis, Psychiatry and Law* (27); the less comprehensive but still very helpful and much less overpowering text of Allen, Ferster, and Rubin, *Readings in Law and Psychiatry* (28); a new edition of Davidson's *Forensic Psychiatry* (29); and my own *Pursuit of Agreement: Psychiatry and the Law* (9). There have also been specialized works on criminal responsibility such as Yale Law School Dean Abraham Goldstein's (30) and in England, F. A. Whitlock's (31); on mental incompetency, including Allen, Ferster, and Weihofen's *Mental Impairment and Legal Incompetency* (32); on confidentiality in psychiatry, such as Slovenko and Usdin's *Psychotherapy, Confidentiality and Privileged Communication* (33); compilations such as *Psychopathic Disorders and Their Assessment* (34), *The Mentally Abnormal Offender* (35), and *Sexual Behavior and the Law* (36); specialized studies on commitment such as *Mental Illness and Due Process* (37) and *Hospitalization and Discharge of the Mentally Ill* (38). Within the past decade social-legal psychiatry has developed its own literature. Instead of the earlier subject matter, emphasizing psychic determinism and free will and the old debate about criminal responsibility, this is a varied literature emphasizing many practical problems of a host of people.

Much work is now going on. A. Louis McGarry, Director of the Division of Legal Medicine for the Massachusetts Department of Mental Health; Donald Hayes Russell, Director, Massachusetts Court Clinics Program; William Curran, Professor of Legal Medicine, Harvard Medical School; Alan A. Stone, Lecturer in Law, Harvard Law School, and Associate Professor of Psychiatry, Harvard Medical School; Jay Katz, Adjunct Professor of Law and Psychiatry, Yale Law School; the George Washington University Institute of Law, Psychiatry and Criminology, headed by Richard Allen (who has collaborated with Elyce Zenoff Ferster and Professor Henry Weihofen of the University of New Mexico School of Law); John Suarez, Director of the Psychiatry and Law Program at UCLA; Seymour Pollack, Director of the Institute of Psychiatry and Law at the University of Southern California School of Medicine; John Macdonald, Director of Forensic Psychiatry of the University of Colorado Medical Center; Jonas Rappeport, Clinical Professor of Psychiatry, the Psychiatric Institute, University of Maryland School of Medicine; Ames Robey, Director, State of Michigan Center for Forensic Psychiatry, Ann Arbor; Andrew Watson, Professor of Law and Professor of Psychiatry, University of Michigan; Seymour Halleck, Wisconsin Division of Correction and the University of Wisconsin Medical School; Melvin Heller, Co-Director, and Robert Sadoff, Training Supervisor in Forensic Psychiatry, Unit in Law and Psychiatry, Temple University Schools of Law and Medicine; Irwin Perr, Clinical Professor of Legal Medicine, Case Western Reserve Law School; Herbert Thomas, University of Pittsburgh's Schools of Law and Medicine—these are representative of a growing list of psychiatrists and lawyers, many of whom have published only in the last ten years, who are developing an imposing body of books and studies on varied aspects of legal psychiatry.

There is also a growing literature in antipsychiatric thought by such people as Michael Hakeem (39); Thomas Szasz (40, 41) and Ronald Leifer (42), respectively Professor of Psychiatry and Associate Professor of Psychiatry, State University of New York in Syracuse; and Alan Dershowitz (43), Professor, Harvard University Law School; as well as the legal and sociological works of Edwin Schur (44, 45). Professor and Chairman of the Department of Sociology, Tufts University, and Herbert Packer (46), Professor of Law, Stanford University, which if not overtly antipsychiatric would like us to redefine many of those we view as patients as merely socially different. These works make many psychiatrists uncomfortable, but they also force psychiatrists to redefine our fields and our roles.

In another category, not antipsychiatric but critical of our failure to define our role and to provide meaningful help, are papers by Saleem Shah, Chief of the Center for Studies of Crime and Delinquency, National Institute of Mental Health, who has written about our incapacity to precisely define what is social deviancy and the harm to the individual that may result (47), and by Bertram Brown, Director of the National Institute of Mental Health, and Thomas Courtless, Director of Criminological Studies, the George Washington University Institute of Law, Psychiatry, and Criminology. Brown and Courtless (48, 49) have called our attention to the plight of the mentally retarded offender caught up in the correctional process and of the mentally abnormal offender; these offenders are not provided with meaningful help by either mental health or correctional systems. "The Right To Be Different" by Nicholas Kittrie (50), Professor of Criminal and Comparative Law at American University, is an important recent addition to this category.

Besides the growing literature there is a growing list of important court decisions: the Robinson (51), Driver (52), and Easter (53) cases, and *Powell v. Texas* (54), all of which deal with addiction and alcoholism as medical problems; *Carter v. General Motors* (55), which upheld the finding of a Workmen's Compensation Board that schizophrenia had been caused by work stress; *Marable v. Alabama* (56), the case that did for the segregated state hospital system what *Brown v. Board of Education* did for the school system; and *Wyatt v. Stickney* (57), which said that state hospital patients have a constitutional right to treatment that meets standards approved by the court. A host of other recent cases attempt to define the law's position on abortion, commitment, confidentiality, psychiatric disability, and homosexuality. We also have an accumulating library of legal psychiatric teaching materials —compilations of cases and records on family law, marriage, divorce, custody, and adoption, which are not yet published but are available, for teaching purposes. So we can see that forensic psychiatry in the last decade has developed a body of literature to be taught.

CONCLUSIONS

Forensic psychiatry—or, more appropriately, social-legal psychiatry—has burst its boundaries. It has found itself a broadened subject matter, it has extended out to cooperate with other disciplines, it has established in the

AAPL its own "trade association," and it has developed its own literature and teaching materials.

Most important, it has involved itself in the body politic and the life of society. It has become the connection between psychiatry and a host of institutions—the courts, the prisons, administrative bodies, social agencies, and legislatures. It is now a focus for students who want to find ways to use psychiatric knowledge in the larger context of society.

REFERENCES

1. Robitscher, J. Medical limits of criminality. *Ann. Intern. Med.* 73:849–51, 1970.
2. Robitscher, J. Three forensic psychiatry programs in the greater Philadelphia area. *Newsletter of the AAPL* 2(1):1–9, 1970.
3. Robitscher, J. Social legal psychiatry. Read at the 12th International Conference on Legal Medicine, American College of Legal Medicine, Miami Beach, Fla., May 12–13, 1972.
4. Rappeport, J. The American Academy of Psychiatry and the Law: a history. *Newsletter of the AAPL* 2(3):23–32, 1971.
5. By-laws of the American Academy of Psychiatry and the Law. *Newsletter of the AAPL* 1(1), 1969.
6. *Brown* v. *Board of Education* 349 US 310 (1955).
7. Robitscher, J. Doctors' privileged communications, public life, and history's rights. *Cleveland-Marshall Law Review* 17:199–212, 1968.
8. Robitscher, J. Public life and private information. *JAMA* 202:398–400, 1967.
9. Robitscher, J. *Pursuit of Agreement: Psychiatry and the Law.* Philadelphia: J. B. Lippincott Co., 1966, pp. 68–92.
10. Zilboorg, G. *The Psychology of the Criminal Act and Punishment.* New York: Harcourt, Brace & Co., 1954.
11. Biggs, J. *The Guilty Mind: Psychiatry and the Law of Homicide.* New York: Harcourt, Brace & Co., 1955.
12. Weihofen, H. *The Urge to Punish.* New York: Farrar, Straus and Cudahy, 1956.
13. Roche, P. *The Criminal Mind.* New York: Farrar, Straus and Cudahy, 1958.
14. Guttmacher, M. S. *The Mind of the Murderer.* New York: Farrar, Straus and Cudahy, 1960.
15. MacLeod, A. W. *Recidivism—A Deficiency Disease.* Philadelphia: University of Pennsylvania Press, 1965.
16. Bazelon, D. L. Equal Justice for the Unequal. Washington, D.C., American Psychiatric Association, 1961 (processed).
17. Glueck, S. *Law and Psychiatry: Cold War or Entente Cordiale?* Baltimore: Johns Hopkins Press, 1962.
18. Menninger, K. *The Crime of Punishment.* New York: Viking Press, 1968.
19. Sturup, G. K. *Treating the "Untreatable": Chronic Criminals at Herstedvester.* Baltimore: Johns Hopkins Press, 1968.
20. Diamond, B. *Criminal Responsibility of the Mentally Ill.* Baltimore: Johns Hopkins Press (to be published).
21. Jones, M. *Social Psychiatry.* Springfield, Ill.: Charles C Thomas, 1963.
22. Ploscowe, M. *Sex and the Law.* Englewood Cliffs, N.J.: Prentice-Hall, 1951.
23. Overholser, W. *The Psychiatrist and the Law.* New York: Harcourt, Brace & Co., 1953.
24. Polier, J. W. *The Rule of Law and the Role of Psychiatry.* Baltimore: Johns Hopkins Press, 1968.
25. Tapp, J. What rule? What role? Reacting to Polier's *Rule of Law and Role of Psychiatry. UCLA Law Review* 17:1333–1344, 1970.
26. Brakel, S. J., Rock, R. S. (eds.), *The Mentally Disabled and the Law,* Report of the American Bar Foundation, rev. ed. Chicago: University of Chicago Press, 1971.
27. Katz, J., Goldstein, J., Dershowitz, A. M. *Psychoanalysis, Psychiatry, and Law.* New York: Free Press, 1962.
28. Allen, R. C., Ferster, E. Z., Rubin, J. G. *Readings in Law and Psychiatry.* Baltimore: Johns Hopkins Press, 1968.
29. Davidson, H. A. *Forensic Psychiatry,* 2nd ed. New York: Ronald Press Co., 1965.
30. Goldstein, A. S. *The Insanity Defense.* New Haven: Yale University Press, 1967.
31. Whitlock, F. A. *Criminal Responsibility and Mental Illness.* London: Butterworths, 1963.
32. Allen, R. C., Ferster, E. Z., Weihofen, H. *Mental Impairment and Legal Incompetency.* Englewood Cliffs, N.J.: Prentice-Hall, 1968.
33. Slovenko, R., Usdin, G. L. *Psychotherapy, Confidentiality and Privileged Communication.* Springfield, Ill.: Charles C Thomas, 1966.
34. Craft, M. (ed.), *Psychopathic Disorders and Their Assessment.* Oxford: Pergamon Press, 1966.
35. De Reuck, A. V. S., Porter, R. (eds.). *The Mentally Abnormal Offender.* Boston: Little, Brown and Co., 1968.
36. Slovenko, R. (ed.), *Sexual Behavior and the Law.* Springfield, Ill.: Charles C Thomas, 1965.
37. Special Committee to Study Commitment Procedures, Association of the Bar of the City of New York: *Report and Recommendations on Admission to Mental Hospitals Under New York Law: Mental Illness and Due Process.* Ithaca, N.Y.: Cornell University Press, 1962.
38. Rock, R. R. *Hospitalization and Discharge of the Mentally Ill.* Chicago: University of Chicago Press, 1968.
39. Hakeem, M. Critique of the psychiatric approach to crime and correction. *Law and Contemporary Problems* 23:650–682, 1958.
40. Szasz, T. S. *Psychiatric Justice.* New York: Macmillan Co., 1965.
41. Szasz, T. S. *The Myth of Mental Illness.* New York: Dell Publishing Co., 1967.
42. Leifer, R. *In the Name of Mental Health: The Social Functions of Psychiatry.* New York: Science House, 1969.
43. Dershowitz, A. M. The psychiatrist's power

in civil commitment: a knife that cuts both ways. *Psychology Today* 2(9):42–47, 1969.

44. Schur, E. M. *Law and Society.* New York: Random House, 1968.
45. Schur, E. M. *Our Criminal Society: The Social and Legal Sources of Crime in America.* Englewood Cliffs, N.J.: Prentice-Hall, 1969.
46. Packer, H. L. *The Limits of the Criminal Sanction.* Stanford, Calif.: Stanford University Press, 1968.
47. Shah, S. Crime and mental illness: some problems in defining and labeling deviant behavior. *Ment. Hyg.* 53:21–33, 1969.
48. Brown, B. S., Courtless, T. F. The mentally retarded in penal and correctional institutions. *Amer. J. Psychiat.* 124:1164–1169, 1968.
49. Brown, B. S., Courtless, T. F. The Mentally Retarded Offender, Department of Health, Education, and Welfare Publication no (HSM) 72-9039. Washington, D.C.: U.S. Government Printing Office, 1971.
50. Kittrie, N. N. *The Right To Be Different: Deviance and Enforced Therapy.* Baltimore: Johns Hopkins Press, 1972.
51. *Robinson* v. *California* 370 US 660 (1962).
52. *Driver* v. *Hinnant* 356 F 2d 761 (4th Cir. 1966).
53. *Easter* v. *District of Columbia* 361 F 2d 50 (DC Cir. 1966).
54. *Powell* v. *Texas* 392 US 514 (1968).
55. *Carter* v. *General Motors* 361 Mich 577, 106 NW 2d 105 (1960).
56. *Marable* v. *Alabama* 297 F Supp. 291 (MD Ala. 1969).
57. *Wyatt* v. *Stickney* 325 F Supp. 781 (MD Ala. 1971).

SUGGESTIONS FOR ADDITIONAL READING

Alexander, F., and Selesnick, S. *The History of Psychiatry.* New York: Harper and Row, 1966.

Arieti, S., ed. *American Handbook of Psychiatry.* New York: Basic Books, 1974. 1:3–58.

Bockover, I. "Moral Treatment in American Psychiatry." *Journal of Nervous and Mental Diseases* 124 (1956): 167–94, 292–321.

Deutsch, A. *The Mentally Ill in America.* 2d ed. New York: Columbia University Press, 1949 (4th printing, 1962). Esp. pp. 1–23, 88–113, 158–85, 483–519.

Joint Commission on Mental Illness and Health, Action for Mental Health. New York: Basic Books, 1961, Chapters 2 and 3.

Menninger, K. *The Human Mind.* 3d ed. New York: Alfred A. Knopf, 1953, pp. 1–15.

Reed, L. S., Myers, E. S., and Schneidmandel, P. L., *Health Insurance and Psychiatric Care: Utilization and Cost.* Washington, D.C.: The American Psychiatric Association, 1972.

Zilboorg, G. *A History of Medical Psychology.* New York: W. W. Norton and Company, 1941, pp. 27–36, 312–41, 450–64, 500–6, 558–89.

In addition to the above, there are a number of well-written novelized and first person accounts of mental illness, which the reader will find instructive as well as entertaining. The classic first person description of psychosis is Clifford Beers, *A Mind That Found Itself,* New York: Doubleday, 1921, by the man who subsequently founded the National Association for Mental Health. Among other, more recently published, such works, are:

Kessey, Ken. *One Flew Over the Cuckoo's Nest.* New York: Viking Press, 1962 (available in paperback, Signet Books).

Green, Hannah. *I Never Promised You a Rose Garden.* New York: Holt, Rinehart and Winston, 1964 (available in paperback, Signet Books).

Benziger, Barbara. *The Prison of My Mind.* New York: Walker and Company, 1969 (also available in paperback).

Smith, Nancy. *Journey Out of Nowhere.* Waco, Texas: World Books, 1973.

Aldren, Col. Edwin E. ("Buss"), with Wayne Warga. *Return to Earth.* New York: Random House, 1973.

2

Who Is Involved in the Treatment Process?

MEDICAL AND PARAMEDICAL PERSONNEL IN THE MENTAL HEALTH FIELD

Jesse G. Rubin, M.D.

As a prerequisite for understanding what is to follow, it is essential to know who the behavioral expert is and to know something about his educational background, professional qualifications, and point of view. It is suggested that the attorney acquaint himself with the position of his particular consultant, expert witness, or correspondent in the framework outlined herein.

The chief professional persons with whom the attorney will be dealing in the behavioral field are the following: the psychiatrist (and the subspecialists within the field, particularly the child psychiatrist and the psychoanalyst); the clinical psychologist; and the psychiatric social worker. (Other professional specialists may occasionally be encountered, such as the group worker, the psychiatric nurse, the adjunctive therapist—occupational, recreational, etc.) The credentials of these professional people should be clearly known to the attorney when he deals with them. (Essential data about each of these specialists will be found in the chart on p. 25.)

THE PSYCHIATRIST

The psychiatrist is, by training and professional identity, a physician. He will have obtained an M.D. degree prior to the beginning of his psychiatric training. Information about the quality of the psychiatrist's medical background may be found in the *Directory of*

Medical Specialists or the *American Psychiatric Association Biographical Directory (1973)*.

The psychiatrist will usually be a graduate of an accredited United States medical school or its Canadian equivalent. As in most educational fields, there are distinctions in prestige among these schools. However, any graduate of an accredited United States or Canadian medical school may be considered to have had a well-rounded and adequate medical education. When a psychiatrist is a graduate of a foreign school, the reputation of that school must be ascertained on an individual basis.

Until 1970, it was necessary to serve a one year internship in general medicine prior to beginning post-graduate training in a psychiatric residency. In 1970, the requirement for an internship was dropped, and one may now proceed directly from medical school to psychiatric residency.*

Postgraduate training in psychiatry proper usually begins immediately after internship, although some psychiatrists practice as general practitioners or in one of the medical specialties before beginning their psychiatric training. The standard period of training for psychiatry consists of a three-year residency program at an institution accredited by the American Board of Psychiatry and Neurology. Once again, it may be desirable to check into the

* Accrediting bodies are currently reconsidering this issue and the one-year internship requirement may be reinstated.

The author would like to acknowledge the help of Dr. Al Zients and Dr. Ruth Wanger in the preparation of this paper. This selection was written expressly for this volume and has not been previously published.

quality and specific orientation of the psychiatrist's residency training program; however, all approved residencies may be considered to provide an acceptable level of psychiatric education.

The psychiatrist is therefore a medical specialist working within the area of emotional or behavioral illness. As such, his function, analogous to that of other physicians, consists of evaluating patients, making recommendations about treatment, and providing therapy through a variety of psychological, pharmacological, and physical techniques.

Although it is most useful to view the psychiatrist as a medical specialist pure and simple, certain problems are peculiar to the practice of psychiatry. Among these problems are the fact that emotional or mental disease may be viewed differently from physical illness, and that its presence is often veiled in secrecy and shame; and that hospitalization for such illness may have to be on an involuntary basis. Also, because psychiatry is the specialty dealing most with interpersonal problems, the psychiatrist tends to be drawn more into the social arena than his medical colleagues.

Specialty certification in psychiatry is granted by the American Board of Psychiatry and Neurology. In order to obtain Board certification, the psychiatrist must have completed three years of psychiatric residency at an accredited institution, must have been in clinical psychiatric practice for two years after his residency, and must then pass a rigorous oral and written examination. The standards of the American Board of Psychiatry and Neurology are comparable to those of other specialty certifying boards in medicine. Like them, Board certification is not a prerequisite to psychiatric practice, but is a significant recognition of professional status in the field. Sometimes the phrase "Board eligible" is used, indicating that the psychiatrist has completed all the requirements for Board certification except examination.

There is no specific licensure for the practice of psychiatry. The practicing psychiatrist, as a medical specialist, obtains his license in the same way any other physician does. Each jurisdiction in the United States has its own constituted licensure procedures and examination standards. The examination for licensure is generally taken at the end of internship and therefore precedes specialty training in psychiatry. Although each jurisdiction has its own examination, many jurisdictions reciprocate with each other and with the National Board of Medical Examiners.

The American Psychiatric Association, with headquarters in Washington, D.C., is the recognized professional association of psychiatrists. Membership in this organization, which stands at approximately 22,000 persons, generally indicates, first, that the psychiatrist has completed an acceptable training program, and second, that he has not violated the ethical standards of the Association. There are a number of other societies which devote themselves to subspecialties within psychiatry, such as the American Psychosomatic Association, and the Group for the Advancement of Psychiatry.

The most widely circulated journals in the field of general psychiatry are the *Archives of General Psychiatry* and the *American Journal of Psychiatry*. As in all the fields to be discussed, there are a number of reputable journals other than these.

THE CHILD PSYCHIATRIST

Child psychiatry is a subspecialty of psychiatry concerned with the study of growth and development, the psychopathology of young children and adolescents, and other aspects unique in work with normal and disturbed children.

The child psychiatrist has the same educational background as the general psychiatrist, but with additional training and expertise in matters relating to emotional disturbances in children. He also will be a physician, with an M.D. degree. The postgraduate training of a child psychiatrist consists of two years' residency in general psychiatry and two years of fellowship in child psychiatry.

During his fellowship program, the child psychiatrist receives supervised training in the diagnosis and treatment of a large number of children. Typically, the training program emphasizes an understanding of all facets of mental retardation. Collaboration with other professionals responsible for the care of children is also emphasized. The child psychiatrist often has had direct experience with institutionalized children and in understanding the advantages and disadvantages of placement away from the home. He also receives special training in dealing with family dynamics.

Specialty certification is by the American Board of Child Psychiatry, which requires that the above-mentioned educational standards be met, that the applicant be a diplomate of the American Board of Psychiatry and Neurology, and that he pass a rigorous examination. Licensure is the same as for general physicians, as described above. The qualifications of a particular child psychiatrist may be found in the same reference books as those mentioned above for psychiatrists. The leading periodicals and learned society for this group may be found in the chart.

Child psychiatry is related to pediatrics in the same way that general psychiatry is related to the fields of medicine and surgery. The child psychiatrist is responsible for the evaluation and treatment of the psychiatrically disturbed child and adolescent and, increasingly, for the mentally retarded child as well. There are 760 board-certified child psychiatrists.

The background of the child psychiatrist provides him with certain skills that are often invaluable in assisting the law in questions regarding the best interests of children. His understanding of growth and development and the everchanging needs of the child are of assistance in appreciating the complexities of early life. For example, the child psychiatrist's understanding of cognitive development can assist the Court in its need to comprehend the child's ability to understand the nature of the legal proceedings. His expertise regarding psychopathology in childhood can be helpful in answering questions regarding etiology, prognosis, and optimal treatment.

THE PSYCHOANALYST

Much confusion exists among laymen as to the distinction between a psychoanalyst and a psychiatrist. A psychoanalyst is a psychiatrist who has additional training in psychoanalysis. This is both a specific theoretical view of the mental apparatus and a method of treatment, first developed by Sigmund Freud. As will be discussed more fully in the excerpt to follow, psychoanalysis is used in its complete, or in a modified, form by many, though certainly not all, psychiatrists practicing in the United States today. Although a few psychoanalysts are psychologists in background and training, the overwhelming majority of practicing analysts in the United States have a medical background. Therefore, all that has been said about the psychiatrist will apply also to the psychoanalyst. In addition, postgraduate training will consist of four to ten years of work in the theory and practice of psychoanalysis at a recognized psychoanalytic institute.

The psychoanalyst, then, is essentially a practicing psychiatrist who devotes all or part of his time to the method of treatment known as psychoanalysis. Though definitions of this treatment vary to some degree, it is generally agreed that psychoanalytic treatment involves exploration in depth of the total personality, the goal being a healthier integration of the whole personality. To accomplish this, treatment must be given on an intensive basis (e.g., four or more visits per week, of forty-five to sixty minutes each, for several years). Psychotherapy, on the other hand, which is prac-

ticed to varying degrees by almost all psychiatrists, has more circumscribed aims, involves less frequent visits, and is generally of shorter duration. Although there is no formal certification for psychoanalysts in the sense that there is for psychiatrists, there is certification of a sort in graduation from a recognized institute and in subsequent admission to membership in a local analytic society. After two years of such membership, the analyst may become a member of the American Psychoanalytic Association. Leading journals and the learned society may be found in the chart. The qualifications of psychoanalysts will be found in the same reference sources cited above. There are approximately 1,340 qualified psychoanalysts in the United States.

THE PSYCHOLOGIST

Those engaged in the practice of law will in all probability become associated in their work with only one of the many types of psychologists, the clinical psychologist. There are, in addition, other psychologists who are engaged only in experimental or scholarly work and who do not practice clinical psychology. What follows will apply to the clinical psychologist.

Unlike the psychiatrist, the psychologist is not a physician, and his graduate degrees consist of an M.A. and a Ph.D. in psychology. The Ph.D. in clinical psychology requires a minimum of four years of graduate work after college in a graduate school approved by the American Psychological Association, and a one-year internship, during which time the psychologist engages in supervised diagnostic and therapeutic work with psychiatric patients. It is useful here to distinguish between the full-fledged clinical psychologist and the psychometrician. The former is fully qualified in all areas to be discussed below, while the latter, usually holding a master's degree but not a doctorate, is qualified to give and interpret the simpler psychological tests, but not to make a full interpretation of all the psychological data gathered on a patient.

Specialty certification is granted by the American Board of Examiners in Professional Psychology, which grants diplomate status to qualified individuals who pass a written and oral examination. The examination may be taken only after five years of clinical practice and certifies specialty in one of four areas: clinical, counseling, industrial and organizational, and school. Licensure for practicing psychologists at present is required in forty-six states. Several other jurisdictions are currently considering legislation requiring licensure for

	Graduate degree	Postgraduate training	Certification	Licensure	Learned society	Journals
Psychiatrist	M.D.	Usually 1 year internship (medicine, surgery, or rotating); 3 years residency—general psychiatry	American Board of Psychiatry and Neurology	As M.D., by state law	American Psychiatric Association	*A.M.A. Archives of General Psychiatry; American Journal of Psychiatry*
Child psychiatrist	M.D.	Usually 1 year internship; 2 years residency—general psychiatry; 2 years fellowship—child psychiatry	American Board of Child Psychiatry	As above	Academy of Child Psychiatry	*American Journal of Child Psychiatry; American Journal of Orthopsychiatry*
Psychoanalyst	M.D.	Same as psychiatrist, plus 4 or more years training at an accredited psychoanalytic institute	Acceptance into American Psychoanalytic Association	As above	American Psychoanalytic Association	*Journal of the American Psychoanalytic Association; International Journal of Psychoanalysis*
Clinical psychologist	Ph.D. in psychology	None required, but internship included in Ph.D. work	American Board of Examiners in Professional Psychology	As a psychologist, by state law (currently applies in 46 states)	American Psychological Association	*Journal of Abnormal Psychology; American Psychologist*
Psychiatric social worker	M.S.W.	None required	Academy of Certified Social Workers	As a social worker, by state law (currently applies in 12 states)	National Association of Social Workers	*Social Work; Social Casework*

clinical psychologists. The learned society that approves the training program is the American Psychological Association, which has 35,254 members, listed in a *Directory* published periodically by the society. Leading journals in psychology are noted in the chart.

One universally accepted area of special competence for psychologists is the administration and interpretation of psychological tests. Many psychologists also practice individual, group, and family therapy; however, there is some question within the psychiatric community as to whether psychologists should provide independent and medically unsupervised diagnostic evaluation and psychotherapy.*

* The clinical psychologist and his work are described in greater detail in the Silber article in Chapter 6.

THE PSYCHIATRIC SOCIAL WORKER

The psychiatric social worker will have obtained a Master of Social Work (M.S.W.) degree from an accredited school of social work. This takes a minimum of two years of full-time graduate study. A portion of each of the two years of graduate study is spent in a field placement in the community. During this time, the psychiatric social worker attains a beginning competence in the areas of knowledge of individual development and behavior, dynamics of interpersonal interaction, skill in dealing with disturbed patients and their families, techniques of individual, group, and family therapy, and use of community resources for psychiatrically disturbed patients. Certification is by the Academy of Certified Social Workers (ACSW) and is obtained after two years of full-time practice beyond the Master's degree, during which the applicant must be supervised by a member of the Academy.

At this writing, twelve states regulate licensure for social workers. In eighteen other states such legislation is pending. Leading journals and learned societies are listed in the chart.†

The psychiatric social worker often engages in duties far removed from those traditionally associated with social work. Psychiatric social workers generally are not "welfare workers," but are concerned with the relationship of the emotionally disturbed individual to his community and with the best use of community and family resources in helping him. Work within this field is quite varied and may include social evaluation of patients, liaison with patients' families, work with hospitalized patients, work in child guidance clinics, private diagnostic and treatment work, and work in community mental health centers. Although some psychiatric social workers function independently in private practice, the vast majority work as a part of a mental health team.

† The National Association of Social Workers proposes a set of guidelines (NASW Policy Statement 4) which differentiate among various levels of education and competence within the field. These may eventually serve as prototypes for accreditation and/or future licensure legislation.

OTHER MENTAL HEALTH WORKERS AND COUNSELORS

Paraprofessionals are gaining increasing importance in the team approach to the treatment of mental illness, particularly in community mental health centers, day care centers, and inpatient units. Such workers are generally referred to as mental health technicians. They will rarely be encountered by the attorney in his work, involving liaison with psychiatry and allied fields. However, when they are, their experience and formal academic training must be ascertained on an individual basis.

In addition, there are a number of other individuals engaged in various forms of counseling, including pastoral counseling, marital counseling, sensitivity group training, transactional analysis, and the newer "consciousness raising" techniques, including meditation techniques. While psychiatrists and other mental health professionals may utilize any of these modalities, their expertise derives from their professional standing rather than the fact of their being leaders of sensitivity groups, etc. Nonprofessionals engaged in these activities may be well-trained and ethical within the limits of their activities, but their expertise in forensic matters is questionable and must be judged on a highly individualized basis.

EDITORIAL COMMENT

The selection to follow provides a further definition of the role and orientation of the psychiatrist. As pointed out in Chapter 1, the past twenty-five years has seen a great deal of progress toward the development of a scientifically based eclectic psychiatry. However, differences in approach and treatment modalities still exist among American psychiatrists. At the time of this writing, American psychiatry seems to be moving away from psychogenetic and psychotherapeutic approaches toward a well-grounded organic approach. Within this broad movement, however, there still exist many diversities among psychiatrists. This movement has resulted from increasing sophistication in the fields of neurophysiology, neurochemistry, and psychophysiology. For the lawyer, understanding where a particular expert witness stands with regard to the various psychiatric approaches will enable him better to evaluate the psychiatrist's testimony and report.

PSYCHIATRY AND PSEUDOPSYCHIATRY

Hagop S. Akiskal, M.D., and William T. McKinney, Jr., M.D.

Crucial philosophical-methodological issues confront psychiatrists of the 1970s. This paper will examine some of these issues within the context of recent developments in the behavioral and neurobiologic sciences. Obviously, this broad aim cannot be fully accomplished in a single article, but some attempt to sketch out the needs and possibilities of this kind of perspective seems needed. Data generated in the past two decades are beginning to provide a comprehensive framework in which many psychiatric disorders can be understood. Yet several trends, including the recent emergence of an anti-intellectual movement in psychiatry, seriously threaten further advances in our scientific understanding of human psychopathology. We believe it is important to consider the implications and consequences of some of these trends for the future development of psychiatry and for the public which is in need of psychiatric services. . . .

ORIGINS OF PSYCHIATRY

Psychiatry, as an independent discipline, is not much older than a hundred years.[1,2] It was created by physicians who utilized the medical-neurologic knowledge of the day to conceptualize a multitude of serious deviations in human behavior, which were thus given the status of "illnesses" of the mind. The major investigative tool was clinical observation. Neuropathology did not shed much light on the commoner psychiatric conditions with the exception of general paresis of the insane. Yet vague concepts like "degeneration" and "constitution" were postulated to be important in the genesis of the commoner syndromes, though lesser degrees of deviant behavior were occasionally subsumed under "moral causes" or ascribed to "poverty."[3] Psychology and sociology, which were just then emerging, were not respected scientific disciplines and, on the whole, had little impact on this early developmental phase of psychiatry. Sigmund Freud,

for instance, borrowed concepts from physics and evolution, as well as from literature and mythology.[4] These were supplemented by introspection, e.g., *The Interpretation of Dreams*,[5] considered by many—including Freud himself—as his masterpiece; and unsystematic clinical impressions often deriving from single cases or cases he had not even seen. The famous Schreber case,[6] where the latent homosexuality theory of paranoid psychoses was enunciated, is an example of the latter.

The pioneering work sketched above was mostly conducted in France and in German-speaking central European countries. Its value can only be appreciated when placed within the context of 19th-century science and society. A new field was created; clinical entities were defined, delineated and classified; hypotheses were proposed about their nature and causation. All these were essential first steps in establishing a new discipline. One can easily see how primitive were the methods available to the early pioneers compared to those developed by contemporary science. Yet the definitions, descriptions and formulations of psychiatric syndromes in many present-day clinical texts and official systems of classification are almost identical to those available at the turn of the century despite monumental advances, both in methodology and basic principles, in the psychological, sociological, and neurobiological sciences in the past two decades. . . .

PSEUDOPSYCHIATRY

Although there is much talk these days about eclecticism, general systems theory, multiple causation, and the rest; at a pragmatic level there appears to be little change. Monolithic separatist postures prevail. Psychiatry is divided into multiple factions of pseudopsychiatry that do not communicate—biological psychiatrists, Pavlovians, Skinnerians, rational-emotive-therapists, orthodox Freudians, Jungians, Adlerians, Sullivanians, transactionalists, Rogerians, existentialists, Gestalt therapists, so-called eclectics, etc. Abroms hails the publication of Redlich and Freedman's *Theory and Practice of Psychiatry*" and Freedman and Kaplan's *Comprehensive Textbook of Psychiatry*[53] as signs of a "new eclecticism."[54] This may say more about hopes and wishes than the actual state of psychiatric education and practice. In spite of these two excellent texts, signs of true eclecticism are rare indeed. In the same year in which this article on the new eclecticism appeared (1969), Grinker wrote[55]

Let us be absolutely clear when we talk about psychotherapy that we are not discussing psychiatry, within which the former is only a small technical part. Psychiatry as a branch of medicine is heavily dependent on the basic, the behavioral and social sciences. For this field, which encompasses all of life, a broad education is necessary. Efforts to provide it are often woefully inadequate in our universities, but also in our medical schools and psychiatric training centers.

We shall attempt to illustrate the present status of confusion by a systematic analysis of pseudological and semantic issues which consume much ink, paper, and rhetoric in present day psychiatry.

Heredity vs Environment Controversy— Though this belongs to the history of the science of genetics, it persists unabated in modern psychiatry. . . .

One cannot speak of pure genetic diseases, since genes do not operate in a vacuum; nor could one conceptualize purely environmental diseases, since all environment can do is to interact with genetic endowment. Hence the important questions to be raised in relation to a psychiatric disorder are the following: (1) What are the differential contributions of genes and environment? (2) What is the mode of inheritance? (3) What specific environment(s) are involved? (4) How do they interact? At what developmental periods? What prior environmental conditions make the individual more vulnerable to the effect of genes or new environments later in life?[57] (5) Since biochemistry is the most basic level at which genes interact with their environments, one should determine the mechanism of interaction at this level too.

Questions 3 and 4 have important implications for preventive psychiatry, sociotherapy, and to a lesser extent for psychotherapy. Questions 4 and 5, among the least-understood areas in behavior, are roughly equivalent to what is termed pathogenesis in general medicine. From a chemotherapeutic standpoint,

item 5 represents a particularly important challenge for modern psychiatry in terms of understanding the mechanism of action of the available empirical somatic therapies and, possibly, in terms of facilitating the development of more specific treatment modalities.

Ruling out significant genetic contribution from specific mutant genes does not constitute evidence for psychosocial causation. Environment is not synonymous with a field of psychosocial forces or events. It is a much wider concept and includes other genes, the physiochemical matrix of the cells and body fluids, the placenta and nutrition; as well as "overprotective parents," living in an alien culture, exposure to a civilian catastrophe, etc.

Organic vs Functional Dichotomy.—Apparently many physicians, including psychiatrists, have not yet given up this myth. At a metaphysical level it is represented by the "mind-body" dichotomy which goes back to the earliest days of Greek philosophy. In the early part of this century it largely disappeared from philosophical discourse. Bertrand Russell, for instance, states that the mind-body dilemma is nothing but a linguistic misconstruct, "mental" and "physical" being merely different words or languages in describing the same phenomenon.[58]

Graham[59,60] advocates a similar solution in clinical medicine:

. . . no state, disease, reaction, or anything else is psychological or physical. It *is* itself; we choose the way in which we wish to talk about it. . . In particular, an emotion is some collection of events in the organism; we can give it a name like "fear" or "anger" which are words in the psychological language, *or*, we can use the names of processes in the nervous system, glands, and muscles, names which are words in the physical language. . . .

The classification of psychiatric disorders into organic brain syndromes and the so-called functional disorders—though based on valid phenomenological criteria—has unfortunately contributed to the belief that psychosocial factors are not operative in the former and that physiochemical factors are absent in the latter.

Are Mental Disorders Illnesses?—This question has become an obsessive preoccupation of many mental health professionals.[61] Although the number of psychiatrists who have abandoned the medical model has increased during the past few years, such trends appear to have found their widest appeal among militant intellectuals outside the field of psychiatry. Szasz is generally credited for having initiated this movement.[62] The semantic aspects of this problem were exhaustively reviewed in a recent article.[63] At this juncture we will only be concerned with the implications of this question for methodological issues in psychiatry.

Those who reject the medical model argue that only changes that are manifestations of demonstrable physical abnormality qualify as medical illnesses.[62,64] By what criteria one is supposed to measure such changes is not clearly spelled out. Also, the definition of disease offered by these authors completely disregards the principles of clinical psychophysiology. All emotional states—whether described in psychological language or not—are organismic states and, therefore, have physiochemical correlates.[59] Nevertheless, they state that organic or biological defects are absent in the so-called functional mental disorders, and mental illness is labeled as the "great operating delusion of psychiatry."[64,65] One can respond to this argument by pointing out that the alternative psychosocial formulations of mental disorders are at least as speculative in nature as the biological ones. The plain fact is that the causation of most mental disorders is only beginning to be understood. Consequently, dogmatic assertions about their nature are unwarranted at the present time. Moreover, whatever the multiple factors that enter into the causation of the schizophrenias and affective disorders, the contribution of genetic vulnerability to these conditions can no more be brushed away as being merely a myth.[65,66]

Another assumption about disease considers it to be a discontinuous state that can be sharply demarcated from so-called normal or healthy states. Since there seems to exist a continuity between normal behavior and extremes of psychopathological states, it is argued that mental disorders should not be classified as diseases. Yet many of the commonest medical conditions imperceptibly merge with normal physiological states,[59,67] e.g., essential hypertension, atherosclerosis, cancer of the cervix.[68] It can be concluded then, if one so wishes, that these are not diseases but problems of living. Ultimately, the debate about the disease model seems unresolvable and dependent on one's definition of disease.

The crucial point is that, from a methodological standpoint, the antimedical orientation contravenes the biological investigation of mental disorders. Such a narrow perspective is no longer permissible in psychiatry.

SCIENCE, HUMANISM AND PSYCHIATRY

It would not be too farfetched to suggest that there exists a deep schism in present-day US psychiatry as outlined in the Table. Though most psychiatrists would probably refuse to identify with either camp exclusively, it is our contention that the majority of US psychiatrists (and clinical psychologists) can be classified either as "more or less soft-headed" or as "more or less tough-headed." The Table outlines, in an exaggerated format, the characteristics of each camp as viewed by the opposite camp. Only a small group would occupy a middle camp in belief, word, and action: the true eclectics, who might be designated as "more or less even-headed." At the present time, US psychiatry seems to be dominated by the more or less soft-headed camp.[69] . . .

The soft-headed category, in this case, is a heterogeneous group which, in addition to the (psychoanalytic) group, includes many new schools that are in open rivalry with it. The major representatives of soft-headed psychiatry can be classified into five groups: (1) more or less psychoanalytic-orthodox Freudians and neo-Freudians; (2) existential

The Schism in US Psychiatry

Soft-Headed	Tough-Headed
Psychosocial (adaptational) model	Medical (illness) model
'Functional' etiology	"Organic" etiology
Existential ("problems of living")	Biological (Neurophysiological, biochemical)
Environment	Heredity
Psychotherapy, sociotherapy, family therapy	Pharmacotherapy, ECT
Value Judgments	
"Contractual psychiatry"	"Institutional psychiatry"
Personality: "Warm, human"	Personality: "Rigid, cold"
"Politically liberal"	"Politically conservative"
Clinical "Humane"	Research "Scientific"
Representative Schools	
Psychoanalytic schools Existential schools Family psychiatry Political psychiatry Other schools of psychotherapy	Biological psychiatry

(and Rogerian) schools; (3) sociotherapists and family and systems therapists; (4) the political psychiatrists; and (5) others—followers of Haley, Moreno, Perls, Berne, etc—covering the endless list of schools of psychotherapy originating in the US. (Behavior schools do not figure in our scheme, because with few exceptions, most of the eminent theoreticians in this area are academic psychologists.) It would appear almost outrageous that we have included under the soft-headed rubric many schools of psychiatric thinking which are in open polemic. The major defining characteristic of this group is their antibiological bias, resulting in various degrees of alienation from their medical backgrounds; and, in extreme form, culminating in a total abandonment of the canons of scientific reasoning, with heavy reliance on a primitive and anecdotal type of evidence.

The more a psychiatrist falls on the extreme side of the soft-headed continuum, the more the likelihood for biologic-medical formulations to be rejected; hence, the limitation of therapy exclusively to the various psychotherapeutic and sociotherapeutic modalities (eg, Szasz[71,50] Laine[72,73]). The less extremists among the soft-headed would be more aware of and sympathetic to the biological formulations and, consequently, somatic therapies would be used as adjuncts to the psychosocial therapies. . . .

There may not be any living psychiatrist who would be on the extreme side of the tough-headed continuum, ie, categorically denying the contribution of psychosocial factors to psychopathology. This should not be surprising, since psychiatry by its very nature —dealing with the entire life of human beings —would negate an extreme organic stance. On the other hand tough-headed psychiatrists regard psychosocial formulations with extreme skepticism and, therefore, rely most often on somatic therapies.

Unfortunately, as would be evident from an examination of the table, there are value judgments attached to the activities and practice of both camps, which are not only mostly untrue, but maintain and widen the schism in US psychiatry.

Research is mistakenly identified with biological investigations and with psychiatrists, who are "rigid" and "cold"; while clinicians are regarded "warm" and "humane."[77] . . .

We shall finally focus on what we believe to represent the differential contributions of soft-headed and tough-headed psychiatrists to the field of psychiatry and the patient population they serve.

Major Positive Contributions of Soft-Headed Psychiatry.—(1) With their deemphasis on mental illness, they have contributed to lessening the fear which the concept engenders in the patient, his family, and the public; and therefore, they have contributed to a more liberal and humane handling of those afflicted with mental disorders.

(2) They have ventured into innovative "process techniques," e.g., family therapy, couples therapy, group psychotherapy. Although theoretically sound and fruitful from a pragmatic standpoint, their differential indications and effectiveness should be studied more rigorously.

(3) Several psychiatrists from the ranks of the soft-headed have done a remarkable service in cautioning the US public against too much psychologizing—and the abuses which could ensue from psychoauthoritarianism,[78-80] We believe this is to be the positive and important message of the Szaszian school.

What is Negative in Soft-Headed Psychiatry? —(1) Extremists from this camp have generated an anti-intellectual climate which has even permeated academic circles. To the extent its proponents have assumed antimethodological postures, they represent a serious hindrance to the scientific development of psychiatry. They rely mainly on ill-defined, nonstandardized, and somewhat mystical techniques which at times have led to serious casualities.[81] Finally, because of their antimedical orientation, they might deprive seriously disturbed schizophrenics, manics, and severe depressives of the effective somatic therapies available for such patients. Laing and his followers have seriously proposed that psychotic disorganization should be approached with other than somatic therapies in order to permit the individuals so afflicted to gain "self-actualization."[72,82] This is an example of unscientific extrapolation from the reasonable belief that some degree of anxiety could be useful for psychological growth in the process of psychotherapy.

What factors have led to the emergence of anti-intellectualism—which has already identified itself as anti-psychiatry?[82] (1) The rhetoric and charisma of its leaders has seduced bright young men into its ranks. Doctors who go into psychiatry usually do so because they value feeling as an important aspect of human life. The anti-intellectuals would obviously have great appeal for such residents because, in their romantic rejection of science, they endorse feeling, touch, intuition, encounter, and sensitivity. (2) The furor they have created appeals to the radical left among the student body. The general disillusionment with science—which characterizes such youth on US campuses—would naturally make them vulnerable to what on the surface appears more humanistic. (3) Their lierature is sensational (eg, *The Manufacture of Madness: A Comparative Study of the Inquisition and the Mental Health Movement*[71]) and makes easy, fascinating, and provocative reading, e.g., Haley,[81] Laing,[72] (4) With an increasing number of anti-intellectuals present among the faculty of psychiatry departments, they serve as models of identification for those residents who abhor the self-discipline implied in rigorous scientific methodology. This makes the novice the peer of the experienced; for instance, the resident who has not yet learned how to deal with a sociopath in a one-to-one relationship decides to institute therapy for his patient's neighborhood.

(2) Another unfortunate outcome of soft-headed thinking in psychiatry is the dilution of the concept of mental illness to such a degree that it is no longer meaningful. Even as early as the fifties Hollingshead and Redlich[70] had remarked that the "in our society psychiatrists treat individuals whose behavior would be ignored in a second society." Those psychodynamic schools which do not utilize rigorous diagnostic criteria—yet still cling to standard medical metaphors—are largely responsible for this state of affairs. We are told that "at the present point in the evolution of human culture a neurotic process is universal."[84] The last few years have seen a pseudoepidemic of mental illness because of fashionable diagnoses like borderline schizophrenia; as an example of such trends one can examine Chessick's *How Psychotherapy Heals*,[85] where this diagnosis appears on almost every other page.

In addition to overdiagnosis of mental illness by psychiatrists, the present era has witnessed a pathological pre-occupation with psychology and psychiatry, resulting in self-attribution[86] of mental illness among the educated. In our opinion, with a more rigorous application of diagnostic criteria, the "prevalence" of mental illness would be greatly diminished in the United States. Psychiatrists' differential diagnosis should include the label "318—No Mental Disorder." After all, it is in the diagnostic manual!

What About Tough-Headed Psychiatry?— Overindulgence in somatic therapies in cases where the latter are not indicated and failure to resort to the interpersonal modalities of therapy constitute the major shortcoming of this camp.

On the other hand, biological psychiatry has been instrumental in fostering a rigorous scientific methodology which has advanced our knowledge of the neurobiology of mental functioning and opened new horizons beyond imagination. Moreover it has provided psychiatry with some of the most effective therapeutic modalities (chemotherapy and ECT) in the treatment of the most serious mental disorders. To this extent it has been extremely effective in destroying therapeutic nihilism as regards the psychotic disorders. Actually it is difficult to see how community psychiatry—which soft-headed psychiatry appropriates as its own contribution—could have come about without psychopharmachotherapy.

THE FUTURE

To protect psychiatry from the trap of anti-intellectualism, from excessive soft-headed thinking, and from too much neurologizing, and to foster true eclecticism (even-headed thinking) we propose:

(1) Inclusion in psychiatric residency programs of training in the philosophy of science, with special emphasis on epistemology and linguistics.

(2) Increasing the number of true eclectics —those capable of real synthesis—on the faculties of psychiatry departments as models of identification for the psychiatrists of tomorrow. Psychiatric educators with extreme viewpoints should clearly indicate that their approaches merely represent different languages in describing the same phenomena—and do not negate or invalidate other approaches, but supplement them.

(3) The "development of research-minded psychiatrists who must introduce their clinical colleagues to developments outside the confines of the discipline" in forms that are "less corrupted and banal than they have often been."[87] The net result would be a modern psychiatry based on the foundations of social psychology, anthropology, sociology of deviant behavior, ethology, primatology, generics, neuroanatomy, neurophysiology, psychophysiology, neurochemistry, neuropharmacology, and psychology of perception, learning, attention, memory and motivation. (It should be obvious that scientific methodology is not synonymous with biological investigations.) Unfortunately, in most residency programs these subjects are covered in one or two lectures each, if at all.

We conclude with a quote from Bailey addressed to the American Psychiatric Association in 1956[88]: "The task for the psychiatrists it seems to me is to get back into the asylums and laboratories which they are so proud to have left behind them, and prove, by established criteria, that their concepts have scientific validity."

Humanism and science cannot be based on rhetoric and wishful thinking. They require hard work and dedication to *both* scientific methodology and humanistic concerns.

The writing of this paper was supported in part by Research Scientist Development Award MH47, 353 (Dr. McKinney) from the National Institute of Mental Health.

REFERENCES

1. Zilboorg, G., Henry, W. G. *A History of Medical Psychology*. New York: W. N. Norton & Co., 1941.
2. Alexander, F. G., Selesnick, S. T. *The History of Psychiatry*. London: George Allen & Unwin, 1967.
3. Tourney, G. History of biological psychiatry in America. *Am. J. Psychiatry* 126:29–42, 1969.
4. Jones, E. *The Life and Work of Sigmund Freud*. New York: Basic Books, 1961.
5. Freud, S. *The Interpretation of Dreams (1900)*, Standard Edition, J. Strachey (trans.). London: Hogarth Press, vol. 4-5.
6. Freud, S. *Psychoanalytic Notes on an Autobiographical Account of a Case of Paranoia (1911)*, Standard Edition. London: Hogarth Press, vol. 14.
7. American Psychiatric Association. *DSM-11: Diagnostic and Statistical Manual*, ed. 2, 1968.
8. Kraepelin, E. *Manic-Depressive Insanity and Paranoia*. Edinburgh: E. & S. Livingston, 1921.
9. Bleuler, E. *Dementia Praecox or the Group of Schizophrenias (1911)*. New York: International Universities Press, 1950.
10. A guide to the American Psychiatric Association's new diagnostic nomenclature. *Int. J. Psychiatry* 7:356–428, 1969.
11. Buss, A. H. *Psychopathology*. New York: John Wiley & Sons, 1966, p. 187.
12. Henderson, D., Batchelor, I. R. C. *Henderson and Gilespies' Textbook of Psychiatry*, ed. 9. London: Oxford University Press, 1962, pp. 262–67.
13. Klein, D. F., Davis, J. M. *Diagnosis and Drug Treatment of Psychiatric Disorders*. Baltimore: Williams and Wilkins, 1969, pp. 10, 41–48.
14. Schneider, K. *Clinical Psychopathology*. New York: Grune & Stratton, 1959, pp. 95–130.
15. Fish, F. *Schizophrenia*. Bristol, England: John Wright & Sons, 1962.
16. Taylor, M. Schneiderian first rank symptoms and clinical prognostic features in schizophrenia. *Arch. Gen. Psychiatry* 26:64–67, 1972.
17. Feighner, J. P., et al. Diagnostic criteria for use in psychiatric research. *Arch. Gen. Psychiatry* 26:57–63, 1972.
18. Langfeltd, G. Diagnosis and prognosis of schizophrenia. *Proc. R. Soc. Med.* 53:1047–52, 1960.
19. Shakow, D. Psychological deficit in schizophrenia. *Behav. Sci.* 8:275–305, 1963.
20. Cromwell, R. I., Dokecki, P. R. Schizophrenic language: A disattention interpretation, in Rosenberg, S., Koplis, J. H. (eds.), *Developments in Applied Psycholinguistics Research*. New York: Macmillan, 1968, pp. 209–61.
21. Buss, A. H., Lang, P. I. Psychological deficit in schizophrenia: I. Affect, reinforcement and concept attainment. *J. Abnorm. Psychol.* 70: 2–24, 1965.
22. Kristofferson, M. W. Shifting attention between modalities: A comparison of schizophrenics and normals. *J. Abnorm. Psychol.* 72:388–94, 1967.
23. Moon, A. F., et al. Perceptual dysfunction as a determinant of schizophrenic word associations. *J. Nerv. Ment. Dis.* 146:80–84, 1968.
24. Kornetsky, C., Mirsky, A. F. On certain psychopharmacological and physiological differences between schizophrenic and normal persons. *Psychopharmacologia* 8:309–18, 1965.
25. Callaway, E., Jones, R. T., Layne, R. S. Evoked responses and segmental set of schizophrenia. *Arch. Gen. Psychiatry* 12:83–89, 1965.
26. Orzack, M. H., Kornetsky, C., Freeman, H. The effects of daily administration of carphenazine on attention in the schizophrenic patient. *Psychopharmacologia* 11:31–38, 1967
27. Callaway, E. Schizophrenia and interference: An analogy with a malfunctioning computer. *Arch. Gen. Psychiatry* 22:193–208, 1970.
28. Storms, I. H., Broen, W. E., Jr. A theory of schizophrenic behavioral disorganization. *Arch. Gen. Psychiatry* 20:129–44, 1969.
29. Blumenthal, M. Heterogeneity and research on depressive disorders. *Arch. Gen. Psychiatry* 24:524–31, 1971.
30. Coppen, A., Walk, A. (eds.). *Recent Developments in Affective Disorders. Br. J. Psychiatry* (special pub. 2), Headly Brothers Ltd. Ashford, Kent, England: 1968.
31. Mendels, J. *Concepts of Depression*. New York: John Wiley & Sons, 1970.
32. Lundquist, G. Prognosis and course in manic-depressive psychoses. *Acta Psychiatr. Neurol.* (suppl. 35):1–96, 1945.
33. Perris, C. The course of depressive psychoses. *Acta Psychiatr. Scand.* 44:238–48, 1968.
34. Beigel, A., Murphy, D. I. Unipolar and bipolar affective illness: Differences in clinical characteristics accompanying depression. *Arch. Gen. Psychiatry* 24:215–20, 1971.
35. Perris, C. A study of bipolar (maniac-depressive) and unipolar depressive psychoses. *Acta Psychiatr. Scand.* (suppl. 194) 42:7–189, 1966.
36. Winokur, G., Clayton, P., Reich, T. *Manic-Depressive Illness*. St. Louis: C. V. Mosby, 1969.
37. Winokur, G., et al. Depressive disease: A genetic study. *Arch. Gen. Psychiatry* 24:135–44, 1971.
38. Gershon, E. S., Dunner, D. L., Goodwin, F. K. Toward a biology of affective disorders. Genetic contributions. *Arch. Gen. Psychiatry* 25:1–15, 1971.

39. Cadoret, R. J., Winokur, G. Genetic principles in the classification of affective illnesses. *Int. J. Ment. Health* 1:159–75, 1972.

40. Goodwin, F. K., Murphy, D. L., Bunney, W. E., Jr. Lithium carbonate treatment in depression and mania. *Arch. Gen. Psychiatry* 21:286–496, 1969.

41. Murphy, D. L., Brodie, H. K., Goodwin, F. K. Regular induction of hypomania by L-Dopa in 'bipolar" manic-depressive patients. *Nature* 229:135–36, 1971.

42. Buchsbaum, M., et al. AER in affective disorders. *Am. J. Psychiatry* 128:19–25, 1971.

43. Borge, F., et al. Neuropsychological correlates of affective disorders. *Arch. Gen. Psychiatry* 24:501-04, 1971.

44. Purtell, J. L., Robins, E., Cohen, M. E. Observations on clinical aspects of hysteria. *JAMA* 902–08, 1951.

45. Guze, S. The diagnosis of hysteria: What are we trying to do? *Am. J. Psychiatry* 124:491–98, 1967.

46. Slater, E. Diagnosis of "hysteria." *Br. Med. J.* 1:1395–99, 1965.

47. Walsh, F. Diagnosis of hysteria. *Br. Med. J.* 2:1451-54, 1965.

48. Lewis, W. C., Berman, M. Studies of conversion hysteria: I. Operational study of diagnosis. *Arch. Gen. Psychiatry* 13:275–82, 1965.

49. Broughton, R. J. Sleep disorders: Disorders of arousal? *Science* 159:1070–78, 1968.

50. Slater, E., Roth, M. *Mayer-Gross' Clinical Psychiatry*, ed. 3. Baltimore: Williams & Wilkins, 1969, Chap. 3.

51. Redlich, F. C., Freedman, D. X. *The Theory and Practice of Psychiatry*. New York: Basic Books, 1966, pp. 347–402.

52. Heston, L. The genetics of schizophrenia and schizoid disease. *Science* 167:249–56, 1970.

53. Freedman, A. M., Kaplan, H. I. *Comprehensive Textbook of Psychiatry*. Baltimore: Williams and Wilkins, 1967.

54. Abroms, G. M. The new eclecticism. *Arch. Gen. Psychiatry* 20:514–23, 1969.

55. Grinker, R., Jr. Emerging concepts of mental illness and models of treatment: The medical model. *Am. J. Psychiatry* 125:865–69, 1969.

56. Fox, M. W. Neurobehavioral development and the genotype-environment interaction. *Q. Rev. Biol.* 45:131–47, 1970.

57. Scott, J. P. Critical periods in behavioral development. *Science* 138:949–58, 1962.

58. Russell, B. *Human Knowledge: Its Scope and Meaning*. New York: Simon & Schuster, 1948.

59. Graham, D. T. Psychophysiology and medicine. *Psychophysiology* 8:121–31, 1971.

60. Graham, D. T. Health, disease and the mind-body problem: Linguistic parallelism. *Psychosom. Med.* 29:52–71, 1967.

61. Albee, G. W., et al. Emerging concepts of mental illness and models of treatment. *Profess. Psychol.* 2:129–45, 1971.

62. Szasz, T. *The Myth of Mental Illness.* New York: Harper & Row, 1961.

63. Reiss, S. A critique of Thomas S. Szasz's "Myth of Mental Illness." *Am. J. Psychiatry* 128:1081–85, 1972.

64. Albee, G. W. Emerging concepts of mental illness and models of treatment: The psychological point of view. *Am. J. Psychiatry* 125:870–76, 1969.

65. Werry, J. S. Psychotherapy: A medical procedure? *Can. Psychiatry Assoc. J.* 10:278–82, 1965.

66. Pollin, W. The pathogenesis of schizophrenia: Possible relationships between genetic, biochemical and experiential factors. *Arch. Gen. Psychiatry* 27:29–37, 1972.

67. Kashgarian, M. The concepts of prevalence and incidence as applied to the study of development and duration of disease. *Methods Inf. Med.* 7:111–17, 1968.

68. Kashgarian, M., Dunn, J. E., Jr. The duration of intraepithelial and preclinical squamous cell carcinma of the uterine cervix. *Am. J. Epidemiol.* 92:211–22, 1970.

69. Rugow, A. A. *The Psychiatrists.* New York: G. P. Putnam's Sons, 1970.

70. Hollingshead, A. B., Redlich, F. C. *Social Class and Mental Illness.* New York: John Wiley & Sons, 1958, pp. 155–67.

71. Szasz, T. *The Manufacture of Madness: A Comparative Study of The Inquisition and the Mental Health Movement.* New York: Harper & Row, 1970.

72. Laing, R. D. *The Politics of Experience.* New York: Ballantine Book, 1967.

73. Laing, R. D. *The Divided Self: An Existential Study in Sanity and Madness.* Harmondsworth, England: Penguin Books, 1965.

74. Lidz, cited by Boyers, R., Orill, R. (eds.): *R. D. Laing and Anti-Psychiatry.* New York: Harper & Row, 1971, pp. 152–53.

75. May, P. R. Psychotherapy and ataraxic drugs, in Bergin, A. E., Garfield, S. L. (eds.). *Handbook of Psychotherapy and Behavior Change.* New York: John Wiley & Sons, 1971, pp. 495–540.

76. Freyhan, F. A. Therapeutic implications of different effects of new phenothiazine compounds. *Am. J. Psychiatry* 115:577–85, 1959.

77. McKinney, W. T., Jr. Researchers-clinicians: Is a merger possible? Read before the annual meeting of the American Psychiatric Association, Dallas, May 1972.

78. Halleck, S. L. *The Politics of Therapy.* New York: Science House, 1971.

79. Halleck, S. L., Miller, M. H. The psychiatric consultation: Questionable social precedents of some current practices. *Am. J. Psychiatry* 120:164–69, 1963.

80. Szasz, T. S. *Law, Liberty and Psychiatry.* New York: Macmillan, 1963.

81. Yalom, I. D., Lieberman, M. A. A study of encounter group casualties. *Arch. Gen. Psychiatry* 25:16–30, 1971.

82. Cooper, D. *Psychiatry and Anti-Psychiatry.* London: Tavistock Publications, 1967.

83. Haley, J. *The Power Tactics of Jesus Christ and Other Essays.* New York: Grossman Publishers, 1969.

84. Charny, I. W. Marital love and hate. *Fam. Proc.* 8:1–24, 1969.

85. Chessick, R. *How Psychotherapy Heals.* New York: Science House, 1969.

86. Valins, S., Nisbett, R. E. *Attribution Processes in the Development and Treatment of Emotional Disorders.* New York: General Learning Press, 1971.

87. Offer, D., Freedman, D. X., Offer, J. L. The psychiatrist as researcher, in Offer, D., Freed-man, D. X. (eds.): *Modern Psychiatry and Clinical Research.* New York: Basic Books, 1972, p. 210.

88. Bailey, P. The new psychiatric revolution. *Am. J. Psychiatry* 113:387–406, 1956.

QUESTIONS FOR DISCUSSION

1. If you were handling a custody dispute, which one of the professionals described above would most appropriately make a home visit and best present the over-all family situation to a jury?

2. If you wanted to use a child psychiatrist in the custody case, what information should you know about:

   a. his professional training;
   b. professional recognition of him as a specialist?

How would you assure yourself of his ethical standing in the medical community?

3. Assume you are defending a client accused of rape and are using the defense of insanity. Would you want:

   a. a "soft-headed" psychiatrist?
   b. a "tough-headed" psychiatrist?
   c. either?

4. Also assume that psychological tests are indicated in the rape case:

   a. Who would you want to give the tests?
   b. Who would you want to testify about the test material and its significance?
   c. Who would you want to integrate the test findings with the other data?

SUGGESTIONS FOR ADDITIONAL READING

Davidson. *Forensic Psychiatry.* 2d ed. New York: Ronald Press, 1965, Chapter 18.

Stetler and Moritz. *Doctor and Patient and the Law.* 4th ed. St. Louis: C. V. Mosby, 1962, Chapters 1, 2, and 3.

Alexander and Selesnick. *The History of Psychiatry.* New York: Harper and Row, 1966, Chapters 14, 18, 19, and 20.

Sundberg and Tyler. *Clinical Psychology.* New York: Appleton-Century-Crofts, 1962, Chapters 20 and 21.

Guttmacher and Weihofen. *Psychiatry and the Law.* New York: W. W. Norton, 1952, Chapters 1 and 2.

Goldstein, ed. *Concepts of Community Psychiatry.* U.S. Dept. of Health, Education and Welfare, 1965. Esp. Caplan, "Community Psychiatry—Introduction and Overview," p. 3; Goldstein, "Community Psychiatry and the Legal Process—1," p. 117; Pulver, "Community Psychiatry and the Legal Process—2," p. 125; Kreisler, "Is This Psychiatry?", p. 147.

Rogow, A. A. *The Psychiatrists.* New York: G. P. Putnam's Sons, 1970.

3

"Normality" and Psychiatric Illness

It is our hope that after completing Chapters 1 and 2 the reader will know who the behavioral experts are, what their educational and professional background is, and what the standards are by which the latter may be measured. It is equally important for the lawyer to understand something about the field in which these experts operate—the field of the behavioral disorders. The purpose of this chapter is to give the attorney a working knowledge of what the psychiatrist considers to be emotional normality, and in what major ways people deviate from the norm. Professor Allen's article will serve as an introduction to general psychiatric theory as it usefully pertains to the problems of psychiatry and the law. The Halleck article provides a dimension of the dichotomy of the "sick" and "well" roles. Next, the selections from Redlich and Freedman and from Sabshin discuss concepts of emotional normality. They highlight some of the difficulties in differentiating "normality" and illness. Dr. Rubin presents an approach to the broad categories of psychiatric illness based on current generally accepted diagnostic criteria. The American Psychiatric Association's *Diagnostic and Statistical Manual*, 1968 revision, as we will see in later sections of the book, provides the generally accepted norms for psychiatric diagnosis. The chapter continues with discussions of two special and rapidly changing areas of psychiatric diagnosis: homosexuality and mental retardation.

THE DYNAMICS OF INTERPERSONAL COMMUNICATION AND THE LAW

Richard C. Allen, LL.M.

I. INTRODUCTION AND SCOPE

Save only the functioning of the autonomic nervous system, it would seem that the major activity of man in our "civilized" (or at least complex) society, is communicating with his fellows. The cynic might observe that the capacity to communicate effectively appears to vary inversely with age. An infant communicates his desire for the breast or a dry undergarment with unmistakable clarity, as his parents will readily attest; and that same infant perceives signals of love or rejection with unerring accuracy, however they may be disguised.[1]

interpersonal communication with understand- With increasing years, however, our facility for ing seems to diminish.

The problem is, of course, a universal one, pervading every activity of man, and has been studied by a variety of professional disciplines.

[1] Erik Erikson refers to resolution of the conflict of trust vs. mistrust as the "first task of the ego," which derives from earliest infantile ex-

perience and "does not seem to depend on absolute quantities of food or demonstrations of love, but rather on the quality of the maternal relationship." Erikson, *Childhood and Society* (New York: W. W. Norton & Co., 1950), p. 221. As to the disastrous effects of deprivation of maternal love in infancy even under conditions of excellent physical care, see Rene Spitz and K. M. Wolf, "Anaclitic Depression: An Inquiry into the Genesis of Psychiatric Conditions in Early Childhood," *The Psychoanalytic Study of the Child*, vol. 2 (New York: International Universities Press, 1946).

Excerpts reprinted with permission from 3 *Washburn L. J.* 135 (1964).

Semanticists are interested in the *content* of communication, as the use of terms in a verbal exchange to which quite different values may be assigned by the participants ("civil rights," "welfare state," "liberal," "peaceful co-existence," are obvious illustrations). Sociologists have conducted empirical research into the *patterns* of communication in group interaction—studying, for example, the effect of status variations between communicants (e.g., foreman and work crew, or professional co-ordinates) or of differential "goal orientations," "normative expectations," or "values" (e.g., the administration of a university and its teaching personnel; lawyers and behavioral scientists; the guard and inmate "sub-cultures" in a prison). While sociologists are thus concerned with variables existing on a "social system" level, psychiatrists emphasize "individual level" variables. Psychiatry looks behind the communication to find its often *unconscious determinants;* for example, the assertion "My neighbors falsely accuse me of being a homosexual" may be found to mask the communicant's own unconscious doubts as to his masculine identity.

Communication is the stock-in-trade of lawyers, who pride themselves on being architects of language. Classically, their approach has been non-empirical, and at the level of "common sense." Many of the more successful practitioners have developed considerable proficiency in the "art" of communication. Concern, however, is often expressed, as in a recent article in the *Missouri Bar Journal*, entitled "Do Your Clients Ignore Your Advice?"[2]

Such lawyers have learned, for example, that a client's statement, "I want a divorce," can be taken at face value only at the client's and the attorney's peril. They have discovered that there are a number of signals which, if correctly perceived, may indicate that other needs and expectations lurk behind the verbal facade —perhaps realizable within the framework of the lawyer's expertise, perhaps not.[3]

Communication is, of course, of paramount concern for the lawyer in the courtroom setting. As law students discover, usually in their second year of law school (except that they already knew it from watching "Perry Mason" on television), the law has evolved a complex set of rules dealing with the admission and exclusion of evidence and the process of cross-examination. Some of them seem to run starkly contrary to "common sense,"[4] but unhappily the student hasn't the equipment nor the teacher the time to question their soundness (when one has to add some thirty-odd exceptions to the hearsay rule to his trial armamentarium in the course of a couple of weeks of class time, he has precious little opportunity— or desire—to debate the propriety of the rule itself).

A somewhat more educated common sense might perceive that much of the present law of evidence rests—rather precariously—on two basic assumptions: that witnesses either give a reasonably accurate picture of objective facts or that they deliberately lie, and that the best way to get to the "Truth" is through cross-examination and the exclusionary rules. Some witnesses lie, and some (though blessed few)[5] perhaps observe, remember, and recount with a high degree of fidelity to what "really happened," but by far the greater number do neither. Witnesses (like plumbers, lawyers, psychiatrists, and even judges) filter what they perceive through a complex maze of ego-preserving defense mechanisms (to be considered in some detail at a later point in this article) which have the effect of deluding themselves most of all into believing that they are telling the truth, the whole truth, and a great deal of it.

---

[2] 1962 *Mo. B. J.*, reprinted in 67 *Case and Comment* 26 (Nov.–Dec., 1962), where it is followed by a cartoon depicting a happily smiling jury, whose foreman is saying to a sober-faced judge and an ecstatic litigant: "Before we announce the verdict, we would like to thank the defendant for the delicious drinks and sandwiches which he sent us during our long hours of deliberation." Even lawyers realize that the most effective communications are often non-verbal.

[3] For example, when the "divorce-minded" client comes into the office with his or her spouse, the attorney would be wise to look a little deeper into the situation. The fact that enough solidarity exists to permit co-operation in soliciting the legal tools to dissolve the union may indicate that what

the parties are unconsciously seeking is the involvement of a disinterested third person to resolve their own ambivalence. Making the divorce decision for them by preparing legal documents and starting the (for them) magical and irreversible process of legal action may work incalculable harm. Again, the client who describes her spouse's shortcomings in vehement and emotion-laden terms may be communicating, to the attuned ear, by the very heat of her verbal castigation, that considerable emotional investment remains in the relationship, and that the marriage may require something other than legal amputation.

[4] As the practice of striking a witness's comment from the record and instructing the jury to "disregard" it in order to cure its prejudicial effect, which even the most untutored common sense ought to perceive enormously enhances the importance of the stricken evidence, as dozing jurors nudge their fellows, asking "What did he say?"

[5] See Houts, *From Evidence to Proof* (Springfield, Ill.: C. C Thomas & Co., 1956), especially his chapter on the "Eyeball Witness."

This article, then, will seek to present in broad outline some of the insight of three of our sister disciplines, an awareness of which can become an important resource of the lawyer in surmounting barriers to effective communication. It will be in no wise a scientific exposition of the theories of semantics, psychiatry, sociology, or law; the very breadth of the subject here considered and the complexity of multi-disciplinary interest in it will permit little more than a sampling of relevant information. However, perhaps some light can be cast on a problem of increasing importance to the law in this era of court clinics, marriage counseling, and individualized treatment of offenders, which will indicate the need for employment of empirical research techniques in resolving legal problems,[6] and for increased exposure of law students to the knowledge of other disciplines, to the end that their own professional services can be rendered more effectively.

II. "A ROSE IS A ROSE IS A ROSE"—OR IS IT? THE SEMANTICIST'S VIEW OF COMMUNICATION

One of the author's law school professors delighted in provoking his freshman classes with the epigram "Words are a device to conceal thought"—a disconcerting paradox for law students just beginning to savor the comforting certainty of the magical phrases which transform "negotiation" into offer and acceptance, and thus create a "contract," and which result in conveyances of land in "fee simple absolute." Professor Henry Weihofen, in a recent address given at the Menninger Foundation in Topeka, Kansas, provided some "case authority" for the principle. A lawyer with whom he is acquainted was defending a very serious personal injury suit against his corporate client, in which liability seemed clear, and the plaintiff was claiming nearly total disability. Happily, however, his opponent's case on damages seemed speculative and unconvincing, and the principal witness for the defense—a medi-

cal specialist of high repute—left little room for doubt. Therefore, the defense lawyer, after taking his witness through a meticulous description of his examination of the claimant, confidently resumed his chair at counsel table when the expert electrifyingly declared: "In my opinion, the plaintiff is a complete and total malingerer." There was no cross-examination. After the jury had returned with a whopping verdict for the plaintiff, defense counsel interrogated the foreman, who informed him that it was only fair to demand full compensation from a defendant whose negligence had caused so dread a condition as "malingery"— and especially where its effect was "total and complete."

F. J. Roethlisberger, Donham Professor of Human Relations in the Harvard Graduate School of Business Administration, wrote: "In thinking about the many barriers to personal communication, particularly those that are due to differences of background, experience, and motivation, it seems to me extraordinary that any two persons can ever understand each other. Such reflections provoke the question of how communication is possible when people do not see and assume the same things and share the same values."[7] What then of the famous phrase of Gertrude Stein quoted in the title above? To my three-year-old son all flowers are "roses," and a "rose" is hardly the same thing to a poet that it is to a botanist.

Alfred Korzybski, founder of the "Institute of General Semantics," based his "non-Aristotelian system" in part on the concepts of "non-all-ness" and "non-identity," affirming that while people behave as if they identified words with things, no matter how much is said *about* something, *what* is said can only be true in part, and the words used can never fully describe or, of course, *be* the thing itself.[8]

This construct is very close to that of the "propositional function" of Lord Bertrand Russell, viz., that, although, in application of the principles of classical logic, one can devise simple statements and arrange them in syllogistic style as though they were propositions— and hence either true or false, and capable of being dealt with as such—in fact, most such statements are "propositional functions," neither true nor false in themselves, but *either* true or false depending on the values attributed

---

[6] Empirical research is still a relatively unused tool in the law. Our researches have largely been carried on within the paneled walls of law libraries, prompting some of our critics to accuse us of inbreeding of doctrine almost to the point of incest. It is the view of the author that in order to make the law more responsive to the needs of a dynamic society, we can no longer afford the academic indulgence which Professor Lon Fuller once attributed to the "Vienna School" of legal positivists, who "never let the green fields of life lure them away from the gray path of logic." Fuller, *The Law in Quest of Itself* (Evanston: Northwestern University Press, 1940).

[7] Roethlisberg, "Barriers to Communication Between Men," in *The Use and Misuse of Language*, ed., S. I. Hayakawa (New York: Premier Books, 1962).

[8] Korzybski's classic work in his *Science and Sanity: An Introduction to Non-Aristotelian Systems and General Semantics*, 3d ed. (Connecticut: Institute of General Semantics, 1948).

to the terms employed.[9] A psychiatric evaluation which recently came to the author's attention illustrates the point. The psychiatrist first diagnostically characterized the subject as a "sociopathic personality," and then proceeded in the rest of his report to draw conclusions and make predictions based on what "sociopaths" are like—that is, on the label and not the individual.[10] But the label is *not* the person, and statements like "A is a Negro," "B is

a delinquent," "C is a sociopathic personality," are not propositions, but propositional functions; and to the extent that we "label" people and then react to the label rather than to the person, we permit ourselves to be tyrannized by language.

The late Irving J. Lee, author of several books on public speaking and group discussion, observed: ". . . values and meanings are assigned to terms by a human nervous system. But so pervasive is the unexamined notion that words can have exact meanings compounded in and of themselves in the way a tree has branches, that it is often difficult to persuade a listener that in discussion the other fellow may be assigning a value to his variables which is not at all the one the listener would assign if he were speaking." He cites as an example the differing values assigned to the term "democracy" by an American and a Soviet official.[11]

One would think that lawyers, accustomed to the vagaries of statutory construction, would be well aware of the hidden traps concealed beneath the apparent clarity of verbal expression; yet such is not the case. However, it is a blight from which our colleagues in other disciplines are not immune. Thus, lawyers and judges continue to ask of the psychiatrist, "Doctor, is this man insane?", and the expert

---

[9] Rappoport, 'What is Semantics," in *The Use and Misuse of Language.*

[10] Psychiatrists as well as semanticists are, of course, aware of such pitfalls. Jurgen Ruesch has observed that, due to the peculiarities of language and the resulting difficulties in the description of behavior, certain verbal classifications are employed. These classifications are not applied because they are descriptive of all or even most of the essential aspects of human functioning or pathology of the patient, but to serve the linguistic convenience of the human reporter. "Analytic dissections . . . are frequently assigned substance and body as if they existed independently of the organism and had a life of their own. . . . [However], terms such as schizophrenia and Oedipus complex do not refer to something the patient experiences or the onlooker can observe . . . gradually the psychiatrist forgets this inherent distortion and becomes a victim of verbal unreality." Ruesch, *Disturbed Communication* (New York: W. W. Norton & Co., 1957), p. 22.
'Giving something a name seems to have a deadening influence upon all our relations to it. It brings matters to a finality. Nothing further seems to need to be done. The disease has been identified. The necessity for further understanding of it has ceased to exist." William Alanson White, *The Autobiography of a Purpose* (New York: Doubleday & Co., 1938), p. 53.
"I do not use the word 'schizophrenia' because I do not think any such disease exists. . . . I know it means widely different things to different people. With a number of other psychiatrists, I hold that the words 'neurosis,' 'psychoneurosis,' 'psychopathic personality,' and the like, are similarly valueless. I do not use them, and I try to prevent my students from using them, although the latter effort is almost futile once the psychiatrist discovers how conveniently ambiguous these terms really are. . . . In general, we hold that mental illness should be thought and spoken of less in terms of disease entities than in terms of personality disorganization. We can precisely define organization and disorganization; we cannot precisely define disease. . . . Of course, one can describe a 'manic' or a "depressed" or a 'schizophrenic' constellation of symptoms, but what is most important about this constellation in each case? Not, we think, its curious external form, but rather what it indicates in regard to the process of disorganization and reorganization of a personality which is in a fluctuant state of attempted adjustment to environmental reality. Is the imbalance increasing or decreasing? To what is the stress related? What psychological factors are

accessible to external modification? What latent capacities for satisfaction in work, play, love, creativity, are discoverable for therapeutic planning? And this is language that can be understood. It is practical language and not language of incantation and exorcism." Karl Menninger, "Communication and Mental Health," *The Menninger Quarterly* (1962), p. 1.
The law—and particularly the criminal law—has, of course, its language of "incantation and exorcism." It is so much simpler to deal with "criminals" or "sex offenders" or "incompetents" than with individual human beings who get into trouble, or who need special care or protection. Often movements to effect penal reform have become stalled at the level of semantics, little affecting the realities of incarceration. For example, guards are now called "treatment officers" in many prisons, but their function is still custodial rather than rehabilitative. As Hon. George Edwards, former Justice of the Michigan Supreme Court, and now Detroit Police Commissioner, recently observed at a seminar in Juvenile Court Practice and Procedure, held at the University of Michigan: "We do strange things with language. We find the idea of putting children in jail offensive, so we build jails for children and call them detention 'homes' and somehow assuage our consciences. But they are jails all the same. What is 'homelike' about enforced silence, marching in lock-step, and bars on the window?"
[11] Irving J. Lee, "Why Discussions Go Astray," the *The Use and Misuse of Language.*

witness continues to answer "yes" or "no," and we all blithely assume that an intelligible communication has taken place. Yet the lawyer or judge assumes that "insane" (though perhaps a disfavored term in the art) refers to some medically recognized entity which either exists or doesn't: psychiatrist A, who has read about the M'Naghten Rule, believes that "insanity" invariably refers to the concept of "knowledge of the difference between right and wrong," whatever the legal matter under inquiry, and answers accordingly, whether the question be one of criminal responsibility, competency to make a will, involuntary hospitalization, or the legal sufficiency of a ground of divorce (quite unaware that the legal standard of competency varies depending on the legal question to be resolved); psychiatrist B, seeking to avoid giving either a legalistic or a moralistic answer, infers that by "insane" the questioner means "psychotic"; to psychiatrist C "insanity" is synonymous with "mental illness"; while to psychiatrist D, who is in charge of a ward housing judicially committed patients, the term denotes "dangerousness." Lest it be thought that the examples given are fanciful, it should be noted that each comes from the author's personal experience in serving as a legal consultant in state hospitals.[12]

But even if the judge is aware of the ambiguity of the term "insane," and uses instead the specific *ad hoc* legal standard—for example, the actor's "knowledge that he was doing what was wrong"—has he avoided the propositional function? Indeed not, for again the words used have no inherent or essential meaning. Nouns like "knowledge," "awareness," and "appreciation" are simply undefined points on a continuum running from superficial intellectual comprehension (e.g., that the law prohibits homicide, or that a gun can shoot) to an engagement of the entire personality, including adequate feeling, significant and appropriate experiencing—knowledge "fused with affect."[13] In successive terms of court, the Supreme Court of Kansas ran the gamut in applying the concept of "knowledge": from mere intellectuality in a murder case ("knowledge" that the acts committed were "proscribed and prohibited by the laws of the state")[14] to the concept

of "full appreciation" as opposed to mere "comprehension" in construing the law of assumption of risk in a tort suit.[15] In the former case the defendant, who "knew," was hanged; and in the latter the plaintiff, who didn't, recovered money damages.[16]

Again, one might assume that in the sixty years or so of interdisciplinary communications in the operation of our juvenile courts the participants would have become alert to the pitfalls of professional jargon; but again the assumption is a dangerous one. Recently a psychiatrist in a report to the court employed the term "homosexual" to denote, in the context of his discipline, merely a point in the psychosexual development of the child, but the judge construed the term colloquially, and the child was committed, because "you can't have 'homosexuals' running around loose."

Sometimes, these linguistic communication barriers are a more or less artful device to conceal inadequate understanding on the part of the communicator—a sort of sheepskin curtain behind which it is hoped that omission of essential detail can safely be hidden. Thus, a juvenile court case worker who has not dug up the facts supporting a recommendation to remove a child from the parental home may seek to conceal the deficiency by resorting to "expertise," e.g., the parents' inability to "relate to the child," or their failure to provide "structure"; the judge, not understanding the lingo and not knowing what to ask for, in turn "explains" his failure to follow the recommendation in his own technical jargon—the absence of "legal grounds" and "due process of law."[17] There has indeed been communication, but little understanding.[18]

---

[12] " 'The question is,' said Alice, 'whether you can make words mean so many different things.' 'The question is,' said Humpty Dumpty, 'which is to be master—that's all.' "—Lewis Carroll.

[13] Weihofen, *Mental Disorder as a Criminal Defense* (New York: Dennis & Co., Inc., 1954), p. 77; see also Hall, *General Principles of Criminal Law*, 2d ed. (New York: Bobbs-Merrill, 1960), p. 550.

[14] State v. Andrews, 187 Kan. 458, 469, 357 P.2d 739 (1960).

[15] Shufelberger, v. Worden, 189 Kan. 379 (1961).

[16] Recent cases upholding a broader concept of "knowledge" are Hardy v. Barbour, 304 S.W.2d 21 (1957) (testamentary capacity), and Dusky v. U.S., 362 U.S. 402 (1960) (competency to stand trial).

[17] Lawyers have occasionally complained—not entirely without justification of the overuse by social scientists of professional "gobbledygook" (see Fahr, "Why Lawyers are Dissatisfied with the Social Sciences," 1 *Washburn L. J.* 161 [1961]); yet our own legal jargon is infested with phrases like "clear and present danger," which "tend to convey a delusion of certitude when what is most certain is the complexity of the strands in the web of freedoms which the judge must disentangle." Freund, *The Supreme Court of the United States* (Cleveland, Ohio: World Publishing Co., 1961), p. 44.

[18] In addition to those already described, among the highly readable works on general semantics are: Hayakawa, *Language in Thought and Action* (New York: Harcourt, Brace & Co., 1949)—

[Section III. Sociological Approaches to Communication, has been omitted.]

IV. Psychiatry and Communication

Communication is that human function which enables people to relate to each other. By means of signals and signs, human beings exchange views, express inner thoughts and feelings, make agreements, and state disagreements. . . . Among the behavioral disciplines, psychiatry is that field of human endeavor which is devoted to the study and treatment of conditions which prevent the successful interrelation of people.[19]

Thus defined, psychiatry's involvement with the problems of interpersonal communication is as broad as the discipline itself, and any adequate treatment of the subject would necessitate consideration of the whole spectrum of thinking, emotion, and behavior viewed in light of the theoretical constructs of dynamic psychiatry. It is not the author's purpose, nor is he qualified, to enter into so extensive a review.[20] Neither is it the author's purpose to relate psychiatric principles to the structuring of specific legal relationships (such as the "legal interview"[21]). Rather, it is hoped that through a brief discussion of some of the factors which influence behavior, together with illustrative material, another dimension of understanding of communication problems facing the lawyer may be brought into focus.

Hon. Arthur H. Schwartz, President of the New York County Lawyers' Association and a former Justice of the New York State Supreme Court, recently declared: "I have been persuaded that our profession needs an understanding of psychiatric principles. . . . I think . . . a knowledge of people's behavior and their reactions to various stimuli or arguments are vital to our basic equipment." Quoting a statement made in 1955 by Dean Griswold of the Harvard Law School, viz., ". . . Lawyers constantly deal with people. They deal with people far more than they do with appellate courts. They deal with clients; they deal with witnesses; they deal with persons against whom demands are made; they carry on negotiations; they are constantly endeavoring to come to agreements of one sort or another with people, to persuade people, sometimes when they are very reluctant to be persuaded. Lawyers are constantly dealing with people who are under stress or strain of one sort or another . . . ," Mr. Schwartz concluded: "The use of psychiatric principles should aid the clients, improve the value of our services, and . . . widen our important social function."[22] We will now discuss some of these principles.

A. The Concept of the Unconscious

During the course of man's brief tenure in this best of possible worlds, scientific research has confronted him with three great humbling discoveries. Each was first greeted with extreme scepticism; each at first seemed to conflict with essential religious tenets, and its proponents were labeled "heretics," or worse; and each has at last won general acceptance among civilized and literate men. The first was the discovery that the earth is not the center of the universe, but only a relatively insignificant planet revolving about a relatively insignificant star. The second was the discovery that man did not come into being whole and entire in a moment of divine creation, but rather represents but the most advanced stage in a continuous evolutionary development from the

perhaps the most widely read book in the field; Lee, *How to Talk with People* (New York: Harper & Bros., 1952)—cataloging communication breakdowns in some 150 group deliberations in universities, military organizations, community agencies, and private business; and Chase, *Power of Words* (New York: Harcourt, Brace & Co., 1954)—where twelve "kinds of communication failure" are noted (including such logical non-sequiturs as [e.g., "The train is going 20 miles an hour"—fact; confusing facts, inferences, and value judgements "At this rate we will arrive late"—inference; "Trains never run on time any more"—value judgment]; the use of abstractions without apparent referents; spurious identification [e.g., "Communists are against Chiang. The State Department disapproves of Chiang. Therefore the State Department must be run by Communists"]; and wholesale application of "two-valued logic" [i.e., all things are either black or white, with no allowance for shades of gray]).

The reader's special attention is invited to the Western Reserve University School of Law Symposium on "The Language of Law," published in 9 *Western Res. L. R.* 115, *et seq.*

[19] Ruesch, *Disturbed Communication.*

[20] A most excellent introduction to the concepts of psychoanalytic psychiatry has been published in paperback form: Brenner, *An Elementary Textbook of Psychoanalysis* (New York: Doubleday Anchor Books, 1957).

[21] The Unit in Law and Psychiatry of Temple University School of Law has recently produced a pamphlet on the subject, which should be in the library of every practicing lawyer: M. Heller, E. Polen, and S. Polsky, *An Introduction to Legal Interviewing,* National Legal Aid and Defender Association (1960). We will, however, have some comments to make about interviewing.

[22] A. Schwarz, "Introductory Remarks at the Seminar on Psychiatry and Psychology as a Tool for Lawyers," 16 *N.Y. County Lawyers Assn. Bar Bulletin* 131 (Jan.–Feb., 1959).

most primitive forms of life. The third was, of course, the contribution of Sigmund Freud: that despite the ringing phrase of *Invictus*—"I am the master of my fate; I am the captain of my soul"—man's behavior is to a very great extent determined by drives, repressed wishes, and proscriptions of which he is not consciously aware.[23]

Employing the technique of listening to patients' "free associations,"[24] Freud and his successors found clinical proof of the enormous influence of unconscious processes on mental functioning. Additional evidence was provided by the phenomenon of post-hypnotic suggestions;[25] through the interpretation of dreams,[26] and in those "slips" of the tongue, pen, and memory which we may term "accidental," but which have often—even before Freud's day—been regarded as something more than chance occurrences.

"Forgetting" a name or event, false recollections, mistakes in speech, misplaced word order, creation of unintended neologisms, and the like are "often the consequence of a *failure* to repress completely some unconscious thought or wish. In such cases the speaker or writer expresses what he would unconsciously have liked to say or write, despite his attempt to keep it hidden."[27] In other words, through such *parapraxes* the unconscious is in some way revealing itself. Sometimes the "meaning" is apparent,[28] while at other times it can be dis-

covered only through intensive analysis. As additional evidence of the unconscious determinants of such "slips," Freud noted the frequency with which intelligent and honest people are offended if told that they have made a verbal bobble, or become angry at their inability to recall a name, observing that "the emotional trace which clings to the demonstration of the mistake, which manifestly belongs to the nature of shame, has its significance."[29]

Such "slips," including the "forgetting" by a client of an appointment, or his failure to bring in important papers requested by the lawyer in order to proceed with a case, should be clues to the attorney that an unconscious problem may be present. Indeed, the latter two examples given may be indications of such ambivalence on the part of the client about the services which he has requested the lawyer to perform for him that if the clue is ignored the attorney's efforts will in the end be frustrated by the client's withdrawal or "lack or cooperation."[30]

Judge Jerome Frank has noted that opinions and legal textbooks are full of observations about the fallibility of human testimony, such as "men are prone to see what they want to see" and ". . . a witness may have a strong bias

---

[23] "To accept such a concept was, at least at that time, a painful blow to the self-esteem of the average person. For essentially the same reason it is not always easy to impress the student of modern psychiatry with the tremendous importance of the unconscious. There are additional reasons why an understanding of the unconscious is so difficult. There are forces operating within the psyche which maintain a constant vigilance to prevent unconscious material from entering into the conscious." English and Finch, *Introduction to Psychiatry*, 2d ed. (New York: W. W. Norton & Co., 1957), p. 34.

[24] "Free" only in the sense that they are not subject to *conscious* control.

[25] Brenner, *Elementary Textbook of Psychoanalysis*, p. 10.

[26] Which Freud termed the "royal road to the unconscious." His classic work, *The Interpretation of Dreams*, ranks as one of the most revolutionary and significant scientific books of all time. It may be found in *The Basic Writings of Sigmund Freud* (New York: Modern Library, 1938).

[27] Brenner, *Elementary Textbook of Psychoanalysis*, p. 145.

[28] As in an example cited by Freud, whose patient, while he was writing a prescription for her, said to him, "Please do not give me big *bills*, because I cannot swallow them," then immediately corrected herself saying that she had meant to say "*pills*." The real source of her concern, how-

ever, was obvious. Freud, "Psychopathology of Everyday Life," in *The Basic Writings of Sigmund Freud*, p. 82. Brenner offers another example—that of an attorney, who, while boasting of the confidences he received from his clients, wished to say that they told him "their most *intimate* troubles." Instead, however, what be actually said was "their most *interminable* troubles," thus revealing what he was desirous of hiding: "that sometimes what his clients told him of their troubles bored him and made him wish that they would talk less about themselves and not take up so much of his time." *Elementary Textbook of Psychoanalysis*, p. 145.

[29] Freud, *Psychopathology of Everyday Life*, p. 80.

[30] The unconscious may be revealed in more dramatic form in "accidental" injuries which may mask an unconscious desire for punishment or self-destruction. Although behavioral science literature is replete with illustrations of such phenomena, the law has not yet sought to deal with the problem. "Legal" recognition of the Freudian concept, from an unexpected source, is noted by A. A. Brill, who recounts that in 1936 the Berlin press wired to the *New York Times* the text of a speech by Rudolf Hess lauding the "Hitler Youth" for taking part in a great *Freiheitsbewegung* ("movement of liberty"), but using instead the word *Freheitsberaubung* ("robbery of liberty"). Retaliatory measures were taken against the authors of the "mistake," Brill observing that "It seems that the Nazis who burned Freud's works, nevertheless recognize the truth of Freud's teachings." (*Ibid.*, p. 91.)

from what he conceives to be the justice of the case, so that with entire innocence he may recall things which have never occurred, or forget important instances which have occurred, through the operation of sympathy for a good man threatened with a loss";[31] yet while "judges and lawyers are astute enough in their observation of the effect of non-rational factors in the thought-processes of *witnesses* . . . as to the effect of these factors on the thought-processes of *judges*, they are singularly blind."[32] That the donning of judicial robes confers upon one no immunity from the influence of his unconscious should, however, be apparent. To the extent that judges can become more alert to their non-rationally-determined hostilities and partialities; to the extent that judges gain awareness of, and can become responsive to, the emotional factors which are a part of every legal controversy, the processes of law will become a part of the "science of human nature"; but "that development cannot come to fruition until the judges come to grips with the human nature operative in themselves."[33]

As has been indicated, some understanding of the operation of unconscious processes can be a great asset to the lawyer in making appropriate evaluations of information, which his work continually demands of him. As Heller *et al.* have observed, ". . . by the agency of unconscious psychic processes, is brought to bear an unconscious *screen* or *censorship* which often serves to protect the client from embarrassing or anxiety-laden material that may be consciously or unconsciously associated with the manifest content of the interview."[34] Dr. Herbert Modlin of the Menninger Foundation has noted:

Your client . . . may present what he thinks you want to hear or ought to hear. . . . The motivation which brings the client to you may be clearly apparent in his problem; then again it may not. Impelled by unconscious as well as conscious motives, one type of client may try to use the lawyer as a diversion channel for hidden hostile and aggressive impulses. If the lawyer agrees to take his case, even provisionally, he feels abetted and justified in his stand and invigorated to pursue his litigious course. Another client may be unconsciously seeking, behind the conscious façade of his legitimate claim, relief from guilt. If he can get you to agree that his deeds or intentions were wholly or partially justified or could be exonerated through a legal

technicality then he has achieved his goal. You have, in effect, temporarily taken over the functions of his own conscience. . . . Lawyers are frustrated by clients who seek legal aid, participate fully in their investigative efforts, express appreciation for the legal counsel they receive, and yet take no steps to implement it. . . . It is a sober fact of psychic reality that people soliciting help frequently resist, avoid, and sabotage that very help once it is forthcoming.[35]

We have noted a few—but only a few—of the clues which may indicate the existence of unconscious determinants and motivations. Among others which should at least be noted are: indications of anxiety, inappropriate affect (that is, evidences of feeling or emotion inappropriate to the circumstance apparently eliciting it; or, of course, the absence of emotional response to a situation which would seem to call for some expression of feeling), evasion (leaving out an essential piece of the story and persisting in the evasion—or showing anxiety—under further questioning concerning the omission), perseveration ("protesting" too much), and evidences of ambivalence or hostility on the part of the communicant.[36]

Dr. Modlin urges that the lawyer "try to see the whole person, not just the legal problem," and to "see the whole situation, not just the client." "Narrow focusing on the presenting issues may blind you to peripheral factors in the client's personality or job or marriage that bear on the problem. Attention to the client only may limit your awareness of his susceptibility to important people and circumstances. . . . His wife or father-in-law . . . may be effectively counteracting your efforts." He poses the following questions for the lawyer to ask himself: "What is he saying? . . . (then) What is he *really* saying? . . . measure the emotional charge in his remarks; look for the irrational. 'I want a divorce,' may really mean 'sympathize with me; tell me I've been mistreated, but talk me out of it.' . . . (finally)

[31] Frank, *Law and the Modern Mind* (New York: Coward-McCann, Inc., 1949), p. 107.

[32] *Ibid.*, p. 143.

[33] *Ibid.*, p. 147.

[34] Heller *et al.*, *Introduction to Legal Interviewing*, p. 17.

[35] H. Modlin, 'The Client and You," 16 *N.Y. County Lawyers Assn. Bar Bulletin* 151, 153 (Jan.–Feb., 1949).

[36] The anxious, suspicious, or hostile client or witness is frequently encountered. Often "reassurance" is not the best way to handle such reactions, since they represent emotional responses to danger or frustration. What is needed is to convey a feeling that it is "all right" for the other to be concerned or angry, or to "test" the lawyer; that such feelings will be dealt with in a non-threatening way. Heller *et al.* suggest such responses on the part of the lawyer as "I can see that you are frightened. Why don't you tell me something about your fears?" or "You are obviously very angry. Tell me about it." *Introduction to Legal Interviewing*, p. 24.

What is the client *not* saying? The omission, the gaps, the silences are always significant and are usually motivated by unconscious determinants."[37]

Dr. Andrew Watson, a psychiatrist on the faculty of the University of Michigan School of Law, has summed it up with the phrase, "hear the music as well as the words." Psychiatry has learned to make use of intuition—the "feel" for the situation—"listening with the third ear." The law has largely placed its chips on "logic" and "rationality"; but people do not always act "rationally" or "logically," as it is hoped this brief discussion has demonstrated. Thurman Arnold once asked ". . . how does it happen that rational societies achieve more irrational results in trying to follow their reason than when they act on impulse?"[38] Perhaps the law can begin to cultivate that intuitive "third ear," based on an understanding of and sensitivity to unconscious emotional processes.

B. *The Content of the Unconscious: The Instinctual Drives, the Superego, and the Mechanisms of Defense*

Freud's hypotheses about instinctual forces within the human psyche, pressing for immediate gratification, and carrying or generating psychic energy, or *cathexis*, changed and developed over the course of some three decades. Ultimately, he postulated two basic *drives*, the *sexual* and the *aggressive*. By the former, he referred to the erotic, or creative component of mental activities, and by the latter to their destructive component. Under his duel theory of drives, however, he emphasized that, in both normal and pathological manifestations, *both* the sexual and the aggressive drives participate.[39]

Structurally, the personality is divided into three parts: the *id*, which is unconscious, being the repository of the psychic equivalent of the drives; the *ego*, the "seat of consciousness and tester of reality," partly conscious and partly unconscious, having to do with the individual's relation to his environment, and having mediative functions with regard to the demands of id and the prohibitions of superego; and the *superego*, which contains what we often call "conscience" (its conscious portion) and a primitive, guilt producing, punitive unconscious portion.[40]

As Anna Freud has pointed out, although psychoanalytic psychiatry is frequently described in terms of explorations into unconscious motivations, repressed wishes, infantile fantasies, and the like (the area of the id), in practice, it is concerned primarily with the ego and its aberrations, investigation of the id being only a means to the end of restoration of the ego to its integrity.[41] The ego, defending against anxieties caused by the demands of reality, pressures from the instinctual drives, and from the "moral code" of the superego, may resort to one or more of a group of *defense mechanisms*. These defense mechanisms, which are themselves for the most part unconscious, represent an order, or level, of personality organization designed to ward off anxiety. Most of them are regarded as to some degree pathological, since they operate relatively inefficiently and entail certain "costs" to the ego. If they fail, and anxiety becomes overwhelming, or instinctual drives assume command, or if they are employed to an inordinate degree, the personality has reached a sufficient state of disorganization that the person may be deemed "mentally ill." Such defense mechanisms are widely employed by persons under stress, and hence are factors with which the lawyer as well as the psychiatrist is directly concerned.

The picture is complicated by the fact that distinctions between the mechanisms are not easy to make, and by the further fact that "one usually sees a combination of perhaps three or four mechanisms utilized by an individual to deal with his conflicts."[42] Only one defense is regarded as well within the limits of normality —that of *sublimation*, in which the instinctual drive is diverted into a new, socially useful and acceptable channel and is then gratified.[43]

We have already seen the operation of *repression* in our discussion of the forgetting of names and events. Most lawyers have at one time or another observed its effects in causing a client to omit, in recounting the details of an automobile collision, for example, certain facts which tend to establish his own negligence. When, at the trial, such facts are ultimately revealed, the lawyer may blame his client for "lying" or "not trusting him," but, from the client's standpoint, he did indeed "forget" or obliterate a memory destructive of his own self-

---

[37] Modlin, "The Client and You," p. 156.

[38] Thurman Arnold, *The Symbols of Government* (New York: Harcourt, 1962).

[39] See Brenner, *Elementary Textbook of Psychoanalysis*, p. 28.

[40] See English and Finch, *Introduction to Psychiatry*, p. 36.

[41] A. Freud, *The Ego and the Mechanisms of Defense* (New York: International Universities Press, 1946).

[42] English and Finch, *Introduction to Psychiatry*, p. 53.

[43] As transformation of destructive impulses into a socially useful career as a surgeon; or sublimation of the desire to exhibit into the hobby of amateur theatrics.

concept, and it may be that the fault lies with the lawyer who failed to take into account this possibility.

Rationalization is a commonly employed defense, in which the ego supplies us with an acceptable reason for a given action or attitude instead of an unacceptable one, thereby avoiding the shame or guilt which is associated with the latter. The law student, for example, who has not adequately prepared for his examination, may "tell" himself on the night before the test that "cramming" is bad, and that he might strain his eyes by late studying, and will "do better" if he attends a movie. This enables him to avoid study and enjoy a picture which he wants to see, without guilt; whereas to admit that he would really prefer the movies to law, or, at an even deeper level, that he is preparing himself with a rational "excuse" for failure ("I didn't really try"), would engender considerable guilt.

Projection is "the dynamism by which an individual, in order to protect himself against ideas or wishes that he cannot admit he has, projects them onto another person or object in a more or less disguised form."[44] Thus the client seeking a divorce may ascribe to her spouse the very inadequacies which she unconsciously feels she has, and may behave as if she considers herself to possess all of the virtues of a good wife and mother. At the extreme, of course, are the paranoiac delusions, which may be represented by a simple formula which wards off conscious recognition of homosexual impulses: "I love him. No, that is shameful. I don't love him—I hate him. No, that is sinful. It is *he* who hates *me*. And thus my distrust of him and hatred for him are justified."[45] The paranoiac is especially likely to come into contact with the law, either as a direct actionist (e.g., committing a homicide) or as a frequent litigant. He often displays an impressive façade of reasonableness, earnestness, and "normality."

Conversion translates the threatening impulse from the id into a symbolic expression of pain, distress, or functional disorder. To some degree, this is present in all of us (as in bodily reactions to anticipated situational problems), and in more pathological form may be of concern to the lawyer in cases which have come to bear the label "traumatic neurosis."

Introjection is the incorporation into the self of some external characteristic, trait, or force, either for the purpose of using it or of destroying it. Thus, children "ingest" the standards and mores of parents to form the nucleus of their superego. Parents in many households lay down rules of conduct (washing hands before dinner, not getting intoxicated, not shouting angrily at one's peers, etc.), but regularly violate them in their own conduct. The communication to the child is to proclaim one thing and do another. "Stating the rule thus becomes the sanction for doing the opposite." Similarly, two sets of "rules" may be communicated: a set for "insiders" and another for "outsiders." Such inconsistent directives, or rules based on arbitrary distinctions, lead to misunderstanding, confusion, and the undermining of communicative interchange.[46] In more pathological terms, one may "incorporate" a person toward whom he has strong feelings of both love and hate. Thus when one is rejected by or loses through death one toward whom he has strong ambivalent feelings, he may literally introject the person—hate, love, and all—becoming himself the recipient of all the hate which he formerly directed against the other, resulting in extreme guilt and depression.[47] In a recent case in juvenile court, in which the social history disclosed that the child's father had died soon after he had committed an act of juvenile van-

---

[46] Ruesch, *Disturbed Communication*, p. 155. In research extending over a period of more than ten years, it was discovered that a major cause of, and the specific stimulus for, such juvenile antisocial behavior as fire-setting, stealing, truancy, and unacceptable sexuality in apparently "normal" families of good reputation was the usually unconscious parental sanction of such behavior, representing "a specific defect in the parents' own conscience or integration in this area of behavior." Selection of a child as the family "scapegoat"; parental vacillation between "conscience-dictated prohibition and the permissive loophole of 'if he insisted' "; parental suspiciousness, acute anxiety, or inordinate curiosity about the dating child's sexual experiences; and indeed overt seductive behavior from the parent of the opposite sex, are difficult to detect. "Direct questioning is fruitless. Unearthing of parental sanction for antisocial behavior in children is one of the most formidable challenges that confront psychiatrists." A. Johnson and S. Szurek, *"Etiology of Antisocial Behavior in Delinquents and Sociopaths,"* 154 *J.A.M.A.* 814 (1960), reprinted in Harper and Skolnick, *Problems of the Family*, rev. ed. (New York: Bobbs-Merrill, 1962), p. 335. So also "the law" may communicate confusion and misunderstanding through inconsistent rules, harsh police measures, arbitrary conditions of probation, and the like.

[47] English and Finch, *Introduction to Psychiatry*, p. 61.

---

[44] Will Menninger, *Psychiatry—Its Evolution and Present Status* (Ithaca: Cornell University Press, 1948).
[45] Article on paranoia by Dr. Karl Menninger, from 1957 edition of the *Encylopaedia Brittanica*.

dalism, the precipitating event which brought him before the court was his unsuccessful attempt to kill himself after declaring to his mother: "I killed my father—I don't deserve to live."

This mechanism, which in group psychology is more often referred to as *identification*, is, of course, a highly important factor in dealing with the juvenile offender. "Certain groups . . . are held together by virtue of the fact that each of the members of the group has introjected or identified with the same person, who is the leader of the group. The consequence of this identification is that the image of the leader becomes a part of the superego of each of the members of the group."[48] We have a tendency to look on the "herd" activity of adolescents as abnormal and undesirable, but "such a judgment disregards the universal need for group activity as a setting in which to work out new and potentially more mature social relationships. . . . [A]dolescence is a time when the normal tendency is to move away from the patterns, activities, and values of the family and to test and experiment with new techniques for living. The normal child does not undertake this frightening experiment alone. He turns to his age-mates and others who can satisfy his powerful psychological needs. If this happens to be in a neighborhood where the only group activities available are of an anti-social character, he has little choice but to ally himself with these groups. It would almost be a sign of abnormality if he were to do otherwise."[49]

Redl and Wineman have noted that "submergence into a delinquent group code" seems almost an "antidote against the remainders of individual superego demands," recounting the juvenile "strategies of tax evasion": "He did it first," "Everybody else does such things anyway," "We were all in on it," "But somebody else did that same thing to me before," "He had it coming to him," "I had to do it, or I would have lost face," etc. They point out that it is important to differentiate between the mechanisms of defense and use of "arguments" to fool authority figures or evade punishment once one has been caught. "Whenever the latter is being done, the same arguments quoted here may be used, but we then have to deal with an entirely different layer of 'defenses of the delinquent ego.' . . . What we have in mind . . . is an actual attempt of the ego to ward off *inner* conflict . . . not to ward off outside consequences. . . . The defenses employed here

prove both the existence of pathology and the functioning of the ego defending it."[50]

In *reaction formation*, the ego sets up a more or less rigid attitude or character trait which serves to prevent emergence of a painful or undesirable attitude or trait, usually of the opposite type.[51] Common examples include the overly prudish person who may be unconsciously battling unacceptable sexual thoughts, or the too agreeable, anxious-to-please attitude which masks hostility. Gross disparities in sentencing—particularly in cases involving sex or extreme violence—indicate the existence of reaction formations on the part of judges as well as offenders. A corollary mechanism is that of *isolation*, in which *affect* or emotion is repressed. Persons employing this defense may show very little emotion of any sort.[52]

Regression is the "readoption, partially or symbolically, of more infantile ways of gratification," and is most often seen in severe psychoses.[53] The most extreme example of regression is the catatonic schizophrenic, who may be so disorganized that he cannot care for his bodily needs. At a more "normal" level is such oral behavior as excessive use of alcohol, or increasing dependency upon a father figure.[54]

Displacement is the mechanism by which an affect which was originally attached to one object is displaced to another, as in the common example of the husband, berated during the day by his boss for some mistake he has made, who represses his anger, then arrives home to find dinner five minutes late and becomes unreasonably angry with his wife.[55] In more pathological terms, phobias—fears of animals, places, objects, or situations—represent displacement of negative affect.

Turning against the self—directing feelings of anger toward some outside object inward against the self, which "despite its seeming

[48] Brenner, *Elementary Textbook of Psychoanalysis*, p. 139.

[49] A. Watson, "Psychiatry for Lawyers" (unpublished MS, cited with permission of the author).

[50] Redl and Wineman, *Children Who Hate* (New York: Collier Books, 1962), p. 172. (First publication by The Free Press, 1951.)

[51] English and Finch, *Introduction to Psychiatry*, p. 61.

[52] Brenner, *Elementary Textbook of Psychoanalysis*, p. 98.

[53] *Psychiatric Glossary*, published by the Committee on Public Information of the American Psychiatric Association (1957).

[54] Working on the manuscript for this article, the author's typist contributed at this point a charming illustration of parapraxis (discussed earlier). Some seven months pregnant, she engagingly mistyped the phrase to which this note is appended: "increasing dependency upon a *fatter* figure."

[55] English and Finch, *Introduction to Psychiatry*, p. 67.

strangeness, plays more of a role in normal mental life than is ordinarily recognized."[56] It may well be a part of the punishment compulsion which is often a factor in anti-social behavior.

Other descriptive terms have been employed to describe ego reactions to anxiety: *idealization*—lack of critical judgment about self or loved ones; *undoing*—chiefly characterized by compulsive acts or obsessive thoughts; *denial*—closely related to repression; *compensation*—"making up" for perceived physical, mental, or social deficiencies by exaggerating opposite characteristics (the "tough guy" whose "toughness" is a façade for his own perception of weakness or fear); however, perhaps enough has been said to indicate their importance in understanding communicative behavior.

C. The Phenomena of Transference and Counter-Transference

Transference has been defined as "the unconscious attachment to others of feelings and attitudes which were originally associated with important figures (parents, siblings, etc.) in one's early life."[57] Thus, patients in psychoanalysis experience impulses and attitudes toward the analyst, not newly created by the objective analytic situation, but having their source in the earliest object-relations, revived by the *repetition-compulsion*. Anna Freud described interpretation of the transference as the most powerful of the analytical techniques.[58]

Similarly, in legal and other relationships, attitudes and responses by one communicant to the other may represent less a reaction to the reality of the situation than the revival of similar attitudes and responses originally directed toward a person of significance in the communicant's childhood. Such responses may be triggered by some superficial similarity (facial characteristic, manner of speech, and the like), or by the perceived similarity of relationship (the lawyer or judge, for example, representing an "authority figure"—or perhaps a "father figure"—to the client or litigant). The point is that the communication may involve elements of irrationality which can be understood only in terms of the transference.

English and Finch offer the following example: ". . . the man who comes from a home where his father was a brutal, sadistic, demanding person is stirred from early childhood to

rebellion against this type of treatment. He has never been able to get along with his bosses, with officers while in the service, or with any other figure of authority. Soon in the analytic situation he becomes rebellious toward the analyst, finding all sorts of faults with the treatment situation, feeling the analyst is unkind to him and even resentful of him. Thus he transfers hostile feelings of the type that he originally had toward his father to the analyst. . . . Meantime, of course, the analyst's attitude remains friendly and understanding so that eventually the patient can be helped to see the unreality in his feelings and behavior."[59]

Psychoanalysts later "discovered" another phenomenon—that of *counter-transference*. At one time, the analyst thought of himself as merely a "mirror," reflecting but not contributing to the psychoanalytic situation. In the colorful language of Erikson: "In analogy to a certain bird, he has tried to pretend that his values remained hidden because his classical position at the head of the 'analytic couch' removed him from the patient's visual field."[60] However, there are at least two participants to every communication, and the psychiatrist is not a "mirror," but a human being, with emotional reactions—conscious and unconscious—toward his patient.

It is safe to say that the less the physician knows and understands his own personality, the more his own counter-transference will interfere with the efficiency of the procedure. As an example, the insecure therapist may almost overwhelm the patient with friendliness and positive overtures purely as a result of his own inner insecurity. . . . On the other hand [he] may react with unrealistic hostility to any insinuation on the part of the patient that the treatment is inadequate. . . . Anxiety on the part of the therapist about certain areas in his own life may well lead to his mishandling of discussions by the patient of similar areas.[61]

Watson describes transference and countertransference as the "two halves of a circle of dynamic interaction between the personalities of the two individuals in the relationship. . . .

---

[56] Brenner, *Elementary Textbook of Psychoanalysis*, p. 103.

[57] *Psychiatric Glossary*, cited above, note 53.

[58] A. Freud, *The Ego and the Mechanisms of Defense.*

[59] English and Finch, *Introduction to Psychiatry*, p. 532.

[60] *Childhood and Society* (New York: W. W. Norton & Co., 1960), p. 379.

[61] English and Finch, *Introduction to Psychiatry*, p. 537. It has been stated that the function of the psychotherapist is not to impose his values on the patient, but rather to make him ". . . aware of his character, able to accept the limitations which belong to his nature, to recognize life's value in spite of them, and to see a possibility for self-realization." K. Goldstein, "Organismic Approach," *American Handbook of Psychiatry* (1959), ed. S. Arieti.

The mere acknowledgment of the possibility of such unconscious reactions permits the participants to look more objectively at relationships and to question causes. The capacity to accept the possibility that one's feelings about another may be due to unconscious and unrealistic coloring rather than to the other's reality traits is a great step forward toward understanding."[62] In the words of Dr. Heller and his collaborators: "If the attorney detects his own anxiety rising during the interview, he must ask himself why, and what it is about the client that might be threatening or discomforting. He should then spend a moment or two resolving this, rather than ignoring it and rushing on in a state of nervousness or uneasiness."[63]

Involved, of course, in the phenomenon of counter-transference are the conflicts and motivations which led to the lawyer's choice of law as a career, and his perception of himself in that role. As Dr. Modlin has observed:

Why law as a life work? Conscious motives, societal influences, and chance play their part, but the ubiquitous unconscious, uninfluenced by reason or will, has been a powerful determinant. . . . One well-known factor is a youth's conscious and unconscious identification of himself with a lawyer father. This may be positive—a wish to follow, imitate or join the father; or it may be negative—a wish to compete, surpass or destroy. . . . The lawyer's unconscious compulsion in his life work may be to find *the* rule, *the* authority, *the* completely unshakeable precedent. Or, his unguessed motive may be to test the rule, overthrow the precedent, challenge the authority.[64]

The author recently observed a juvenile hearing involving a young girl of fifteen. At a prior hearing it had been decided that the girl, whose parents had "lost control" of her to the extent that she was freely engaging in drinking and sexual adventures of a character likely to cause injury to herself, should go to a private institution for a time. She had not gone, and the "explanations" made to the referee were conflicting. Essentially, she had "talked her father out" of sending her, despite the court's order that she go. Her father appeared to be an insecure, rather weak person, whose threats and commands were verbally decisive, but lacked inner conviction. The child was communicating rather freely to the court; her need was quite obviously for strength and decisiveness from the referee. She wanted to be told that she "must" go, or that the order was rescinded but any further promiscuity would

be severely dealt with by the court. She transferred to the referee her child's image of the strong, decisive male, and began to relate to him as such. She was an attractive and physically mature young lady, and her behavior —while not overtly seductive—obviously conveyed a sensuality which was disturbing to the referee. He reacted by becoming "flustered" and uneasy, and began to observe at several points that he felt that an adjournment and a period of "seeing how things will work out" was indicated. Almost immediately, her candor and positive response toward him stopped; she "clammed up," and the session ended with an exchange of stereotyped, monosyllabic responses to the referee's injunctions to "see if she couldn't behave herself."

In the words of Dr. Watson:

Whenever we react with emotion, more strongly than the situation would seem to warrant, we may be sure there is some underlying unconscious attitude toward the problem. . . . For these reasons it behooves the lawyer to understand himself and his attitudes just as thoroughly as he can. . . . Although his professional role calls for objectivity, this is not achieved by blocking emotions. True objectivity requires direct dealing with one's emotional responses. . . . Hidden emotions powerfully direct decisions, and only the person himself is deceived.[65]

D. Non-Verbal Communication

We know today that communication is by no means primarily a verbal matter: words are only the tools of meaning.[66]

We communicate unintentionally by our actions as well as through our more or less calculated verbal and non-verbal expressions. Ruesch and Kess in their fascinating volume *Nonverbal Communication*[67] provide photographs of many strikingly revealing expressive moments (an arm about the shoulder, a child touching a favored toy, etc.): "Such ordinary actions as taking off a coat, diving into a pool, or merely walking are as understandable as words to those who see them. Sometimes they enable the onlooker to predict future events more accurately than if he relied upon words alone. And, if he is familiar with the individuals or situations he observes, the possibility of accurate prediction of subsequent behavior becomes even more likely. . . . These statements are not pinpointed for another person's

[62] Watson, "Psychiatry for Lawyers."

[63] Heller *et al.*, *Introduction to Legal Interviewing*, p. 10.

[64] Modlin, "The Client and You."

[65] Watson, "Psychiatry for Lawyers."

[66] Erikson, *Childhood and Society*, p. 379.

[67] Berkeley: University of California Press, 1956.

consumption, but they are nonetheless statements."[68]

As Karl Menninger has observed:

There are so many forms of communication —gesturing, grimacing, smiling, pouting, stealing, exhibiting, shouting, whispering, weeping, all of which both express and signal. Psychiatrists must learn to translate these into their simple meanings of "I like you." "Do you like me?" "See how beautiful or clever I am!" "I'm not getting enough attention." "I am angry!"[69]

So also in the practice of law:

. . . much of what is passed from client to attorney and in turn from attorney to client is communicated by glances, silences (what is omitted may be of greater significance than what is spoken), and the general tone and manner of both participants. . . . Even the novice might be aware of a withdrawn client who refuses to communicate. An equal amount of withdrawal . . . may hide behind the lighting of a cigarette, an evasive straightening of a cuff or the crossing of one leg over the other.[70]

Ruesch and Kess refer to the "international emergency language" of emotional expression when people are overwhelmed by anger, anxiety, fear, or shame; for example, the cues of intensity, periodicity, and crescendo which enable a mother to distinguish between the feeling states expressed by her child's cries. Other less intense "emotional modifiers"—especially contractions of various muscle groups associated with facial expression and posture, which may or may not have communicative intent, are nevertheless interpreted by the observer as revealing of the personality and temperament of the observed.[71] Indeed, in cases of gross disorganization, psychiatrists have found that communication through nonverbal means may be the only way to reach the patient.[72]

Again, we must call attention to the other party to the exchange. The attorney or judge may be communicating—much more effec-tively than he wishes—through non-verbal gestures which reveal, or are interpreted as revealing, his reactions, value judgments, and evaluations of the material being transmitted to him. Through judicious use of neutral responses, "open" questions, pauses, non-judgmental attitudes, offering an opportunity for "feedback," refraining from rendering premature opinions or speculations, he may insure the receipt of fuller, more helpful information. As pointed out by Heller et al.:

If the lawyer is busy writing (i.e., taking notes), the client assumes, not without some reason, that the lawyer must think that this material is important. Hence, the client may tend to pursue this train of thought. The end result is that the lawyer unwittingly encourages the client to talk about certain material, and conversely, by not taking notes, may discourage the same client from talking about other material. In much the same way the attorney may neglect the subtle effect of a stifled yawn, a glance at a clock, or even the shifting of his position during the course of the interview. All of these manifestations of "body language" might be interpreted by the client as a subtle suggestion to "Move on to another area that is more important to your case. I, the attorney, the authority, the expert, advise and suggest that you do this"—or so it might seem to the client.[73]

E. Communication between Psychiatrists and Lawyers—Mental Illness

A man also or woman that hath a familiar spirit, or that is a wizard, shall surely be put to death; they shall stone them with stones, their blood shall be upon them. (*Leviticus* 20:27)

The law has come a long way in dealing with mental illness. Yet this area which, perhaps more than any other in the law, demands unfettered exchange of information between persons of varying disciplinary backgrounds, seems plagued with communication breakdowns.

There is now a vast amount of material in the literature of both psychiatry and law bearing upon the areas of our mutual concern. Yet, with all that has been spoken and written about our pooling of intellectual resources, when the "chips are down" psychiatrists and lawyers often seem unable to communicate effectively. Why? Why do so many judges and lawyers dismiss psychiatry as something less than a science, because "psychiatrists can never agree on anything," or distrust a psychiatric evalua-

---

[68] *Ibid.*, p. 45.

[69] "Communication and Mental Health," *The Menninger Quarterly* (1962).

[70] Heller *et al.*, *Introduction to Legal Interviewing.*

[71] Ruesch and Kess, *Nonverbal Communication*, p. 64.

[72] See Marguerite Sechehaye's classic account of her nonverbal communication with a psychotic child (*Autobiography of a Schizophrenic Girl* [New York: Grune and Stratton, 1951]; and *Symbolic Realization* [New York: International Universities Press, 1952]). For a more recent study see Khan, "Silence as Communication," *Bulletin of the Menninger Clinic* (Nov., 1963), p. 300.

[73] Heller *et al.*, *Introduction to Legal Interviewing.*

tion of the defendant in a criminal case, because "psychiatrists don't believe in free will and want to excuse everybody"? Why are so many psychiatrists reluctant to testify, or indeed to become involved in a case which may bring them into contact with the law, because "lawyers are venal—they are not interested in truth, but only in winning their case," or because they "never ask the right questions"?

The interrelationship of law and psychiatry covers virtually the length and breadth of both disciplines. The "law" governs the contractual relationship between the psychiatrist and his patient, and measures the scope of the legally enforceable duties which such relationships entail: professional responsibility (and its correlative, that anxiety-producing word "malpractice"), confidentiality, and privileged communications. The psychiatrist provides the information which lawyers and courts must have to determine legal status in a variety of situations: competency to perform jural acts, enforceability of a contract, the "fitness" of a parent or prospective parent, involuntary hospitalization, whether a will should be probated, whether certain acts should be recognized as a ground for divorce, whether recovery should be granted for psychic disability following trauma, and, of course, the area of sharpest conflict—criminal responsibility.

Despite our "model mental health acts" and "model penal codes"; increased use of court clinics and pre-sentence investigations of offenders; improvement of state hospitals; creation of diagnostic centers within state penal systems and the addition of psychiatrists and clinical psychologists to the staffs of custodial institutions; and the offering of courses in law to psychiatric residents and courses in the behavioral sciences to law students, we have not found ultimate "answers" to the fantastically complex problems with which both our disciplines are confronted. Perhaps there are none; but we are beginning to deal with the problems which exist rather than continuing to indulge our fantasies of problem-solving by rubric and fiat; we are beginning to communicate with each other in terms of reality, rather than of value judgment and invective.[74] Yet it is only a beginning.

Let us return for a moment to some of the "value judgments" referred to earlier. First, however, a general observation: the objectives and responsibilities of psychiatrists and lawyers are not the same, and we are deluding ourselves if we pretend that they are. In psychiatry —as in all of medicine—the focus of concern is the patient; the world in which the patient lives and functions is of interest primarily in terms of the stresses and conflicts with which he must learn to deal. The law, on the other hand, exists primarily to preserve social values through the orderly resolution of controversies; thus the individual litigant is less of concern as an individual than as an instrumentality whose activities and relationships with others create rights, duties, privileges, and immunities which must be given legal effect in the interest of the community. That is not to say that psychiatry has no interest in the world at large except as it forms the milieu for an individual patient— the rapidly growing field of community psychiatry belies so parochial a concern. Nor is it fair to say that the law cares nothing for people as people, but seeks only to regulate their conduct—the lawyer's highest duty is to the client whom he represents, and he conceives of himself as counselor as well as advocate. Yet to say that all that needs to be done is to join hands and advance to our common goals is to ignore what should be most obvious—that psychiatrists are not lawyers and lawyers are not psychiatrists, and our objectives and responsibilities, while not necessarily antithetical to each another, are not identical.

Of course there is disagreement among psychiatrists, as might be expected in any discipline dealing with so complex an organism as the human mind (and for a profession in which it is quite possible for a tribunal to split 4 to 3 in deciding that an issue is one on which "reasonable minds could not differ," it would seem that the law should be rather charitable about disagreements). Lawyers should know that there is a school of thought among psychiatrists which views man essentially in organic terms. Such psychiatrists tend to discount maladaptations and emotional disturbances as *illness* without some demonstrable organic involvement; or, if willing to consider functional impairments as within the context of illness, see them as a less significant factor in producing deviant behavior than do their psychoanalytically oriented colleagues.[75] However, many of the apparent disagreements are at the level of nosology rather than substance. That is to say, the psychiatrists on both sides of the case see essentially the same symptomatology, but give it different "labels" (see our earlier discussion

---

[74] ". . . when two people respond to each other by using value judgments, communication becomes strained. Under such circumstances, denotative statements are omitted, information ceases to be exchanged, and correction cannot occur; and unless one person yields and submits to the values of the other, the relationship breaks down." Ruesch, *Disturbed Communication.*

[75] Such psychiatrists are in a distinct minority today (though rather popular with some prosecuting attorneys).

in Section II);[76] or, as happens even more frequently, are in agreement on what they have observed and on the significance which they attribute to it, differing only in their response to the "legal question" posed to them: does he "know," can he "appreciate," is he "competent"?

To psychiatrists it should be made clear that the institutions of law do not function as a scientific inquiry to determine "truth." The law exists to resolve controversies. The world can wait, if it must, for a score of centuries for the discovery of a Salk vaccine; but the case of *Doe* v. *Roe* must be decided seasonably, or justice fails. Thus all that can be hoped for is an approximation of truth, and, in the resolution of essentially moral issues, the adversary process is the best tool which society has been able to come up with to make such resolutions and yet afford the individual protection against arbitrary excesses of the state. This is an idealized picture of the law, and heaven knows it doesn't always work out so neatly in specific cases; yet perhaps with an increased understanding of how hard won (and how easily subverted) are the concepts of "due process of law" (representation by counsel; the right to be confronted by one's accusers; the right of judgment by one's peers; protection against self-incrimination and prolonged confinement without charge or hearing; etc.), the psychiatrist would be less resentful of the lawyer's zeal in defending his client's interests, and of having his own diagnosis called into public question through cross-examination.

It should further be observed—to both disciplines—that the issues which the law has to decide are not psychiatric but moral. It may be incontrovertible, from a psychiatric standpoint, that John Jones would be a happier, better adjusted person if he were to receive treatment in a hospital; but society has, and should have, no right to compel him to submit to hospitalization on such a basis. The question of "how sick" John must be (or rather, what risks to himself and to others must be present) before the agencies of government may be permitted to deprive him of his freedom, is not a matter for "expert" determination, although the observations and predictions on which the "trier of fact" must base its judgment are necessarily expert in character. So also, although it is clear that Bill Smith is suffering from gross mental illness, the question of how this factor should be taken into account in determining whether he, or some other person with whom he has come into contact (as an innocent party with whom he has made a contract, fair in its inception, who has acted in reasonable reliance that the relationship imposed mutual obligations; or someone whom he has injured through some tortious act), should bear a necessary economic loss, is a question for determination by the tribunals of moral judgment, and not by the expert witness. When, however, a judge or lawyer poses the question to a psychiatric witness: "Doctor, is this man competent," or "responsible," or "insane," and the witness answers the question in the same terms, the law has abdicated its proper area of decision-making, and the psychiatrist has assumed a function outside his area of expertise. From the standpoint of the psychiatrist, this leaves him in a position which he cannot defend, either on the basis of his training or of his examination of the patient—thus he is "fair game" for the astute cross-examiner. From the standpoint of the law, the onus of decision—and responsibility—has been assumed by the psychiatrist; communication failure has reached its zenith.

What questions then should be asked? Those which the psychiatrist is peculiarly qualified to answer. It is not—or should not be—for his opinion on legal or moral issues that he is called to testify, but rather for the light which his examination and expert knowledge can shed on the emotional strengths and weaknesses, capacity to test reality, motivations, and quality of integration of personality of his patient; for his appraisal of the probable effect of alternative modes of treatment; and for his predictions of future behavior.

Unhappily—particularly in the field of criminal law—the law continues, in most jurisdictions, to elicit moral judgments from the psychiatrist. It is not the purpose of this article to weigh the relative merits of the various "tests" of criminal responsibility,[77] but perhaps the point should be noted, that in a majority of jurisdictions where the M'Naghten rubric is still applied in as strict and literal a form as was recently enunciated by the Supreme Court

---

[76] The point, for example, at which a line is drawn between "schizophrenic reaction"—a psychosis—and "schizoid personality"—a "mere" personality disturbance—is essentially an arbitrary one (*Diagnostic and Statistical Manual of Mental Disorders*, American Psychiatric Association, 13th printing [1960], pp. 26 and 34), and perhaps of little consequence (see Karl Menninger *et al.*, "The Unitary Concept of Mental Illness," *Bulletin of the Menninger Clinic* [Jan., 1958], p. 4), although the law seems to accord greater significance to the name given than to the degree and quality of disorganization and its probable trend of development.

[77] A most comprehensive analysis of the various "rules" may be found in Judge Biggs's landmark opinion in U.S. v. Currens, 290 F.2d 751 (C.A. 3d 1961); see also Comments to Sec. 4.01, Model Penal Code.

of Kansas,[78] a road block of massive proportions has been placed in the way of effective communication. As the Group for the Advancement of Psychiatry has observed: "The law does not allow the psychiatrist to communicate his unique understanding of psychic realities to the Court and Jury. More often, the mutual quest for the 'whole truth' cannot get past a barrier of communication which leaves the psychiatrist talking about 'mental illness' and the lawyer talking about 'right and wrong.' "[79]

V. CONCLUDING REMARKS

In the course of this discussion of the importance to the law, and to lawyers, of an understanding of the dynamics of interpersonal communication, we have examined a number of subjects, including: the use and abuse of words; empirical studies of social interaction; the court viewed as an organization; obstacles to effective interdisciplinary coordination; the unconscious, and the ego's defense mechanisms; the transference and counter-transference phenomena; lawyer-client relationships; non-verbal communications; and the psychiatrist as expert witness.

Similarities and overlappings will have been noted among the constructs of the several disciplines herein considered. Other disciplines might also have been explored: anthropology, social psychology, linguistics, mathematics, cybernetics, and neuro-physiology, for example, have made important contributions to the understanding of the process of communication.

No consideration of communication could be complete without at least one reference to the greatest of all earthly communicators. Shakespeare's *Comedy of Errors* closes with these lines, not inappropriate to an interdisciplinary study of communications: "We came into the world like brother and brother; / And now let's go hand in hand, not one before another."

[78] "The law recognizes no form of insanity, although the mental faculties may be disordered or deranged, which will furnish immunity from punishment for an act declared by the law to be criminal, so long as the person committing the act had the capacity to know what he was doing and the power to know that his act was wrong." State v. Andrews, see above, note 14.

[79] *Criminal Responsibility and Psychiatric Expert Testimony*, G.A.P. Report No. 26 (1954).

THE CRIMINAL'S PROBLEM WITH PSYCHIATRY

Seymour L. Halleck, M.D.

Increasingly, humanistic and scientific principles of dynamic psychiatry are being applied to the field of criminology, and behavior once regarded as merely "bad" is seen as a product of mental illness. Resistances to this trend have in the past been blamed on the punitiveness of society and the reluctance of lawyers and psychiatrists to completely abandon older moralistic codes.[1] Perhaps it is time to examine more carefully another resistance—namely, that which comes from the offender himself.

It is my impression that a large segment of the criminal population vigorously struggles against the type of role implicit in the more deterministic, less retaliative philosophy of the Durham decision or in the application of psychiatric principles to penology. To state this

[1] Henry Weihofen, *The Urge to Punish* (New York: Farrar, Straus & Cudahy, 1956), p. 189. M. H. Miller, P. L. Eichman, and E. M. Burns, "The Sanity Hearing," *Bulletin of the Meninger Clinic*, 23 (1959): 97–105. Arthur Koestler, *Reflections on Hanging* (New York: Macmillan, 1957), p. 22.

Reprinted with permission from *Psychiatry: Journal for the Study of Interpersonal Processes* 23, no. 4 (November 1960): 409–12. Reprinted by special permission of the William Alanson White Psychiatric Foundation, Inc., which holds the copyright to this article.

simply, some offenders find advantages to living the role of a criminally deviant person, rather than a sick person. While it would be difficult to separate the conscious and unconscious motivations for the adoption of a particular role, there seem to be certain economic, social, and psychological advantages to the "bad" role, as opposed to the sick role. Careful examination of some of these advantages may throw some light on the problem of criminal responsibility as well as the more urgent question of effective treatment of offenders.

While working as a staff psychiatrist in a hospital for federal offenders, I became aware of the vigorous attempts prisoners often made to avoid being seen as sick. Inmates who, during the course of their imprisonment, became mentally ill were transferred to the hospital, where the environment was permissive, more privileges were given, and some opportunity for psychiatric treatment was provided. Despite the apparent advantages of hospital life, most prisoners transferred there made strenuous efforts to return to the prison, long before they had fully reconstituted their defenses. Often they would devise elaborate rationalizations, such as claiming that they had feigned insanity. They seemed to be saying: *It is permissible to get medical attention only when you are desperately sick. When you feel the least bit better, you should immediately get out of a situation in which people regard you as sick instead of bad.* It sometimes seemed that the psychiatrist was feared more than the custodial officer.

Psychiatrists who have had experience in examining offenders awaiting trial have frequently encountered a similar phenomenon. While the usual assumption of legal workers and of society in general is that most offenders would welcome a chance to plead insanity, if not actually malinger, the fact is that many criminals will go to great lengths to avoid cooperating with examining psychiatrists, even though it is almost obvious that they are ill and that a plea of mental illness might avert a lengthy sentence. Since lawyers are loath to make a plea of mental illness if the client is resistant to it, in these cases there is frequently a superficial and inadequate application of psychiatric testimony. The following case is illustrative:

A 26-year-old Negro man was accused of having criminally assaulted two women in a large city. Although he had been having severe anxiety symptoms and had demonstrated peculiar behavior for several years, he resisted psychiatric examination when this was suggested by his attorney, insisting that he was not mentally ill and was fully capable of standing trial. At the insistence of the court, however,

he was eventually examined by a psychiatrist, who found him uncooperative, angry, and surly, and made a diagnosis of sociopathic personality disturbance, anti-social type.

The offender was given a long prison sentence. As soon as he began to mingle with other prisoners, it became apparent that he was psychotically disturbed, and a further psychiatric examination showed him to be extremely anxious and subject to delusions of persecution and auditory and visual hallucinations. He had begun hearing voices approximately seven years before his arrest, and it seemed quite likely that the crimes had been committed at least partly in response to delusional thinking. On the basis of this new psychiatric information, another trial was scheduled. In the courtroom, the prisoner denied the information he had given to four different prison psychiatrists, explaining that he had fabricated it to avoid difficult prison situations. He insisted that he was not mentally ill and did not want to be considered so. He was again judged to be without psychosis and was returned to prison.

Thus, although the prisoner was seriously disturbed, he was still able to determine a considerable part of his future. He chose to remain in a prison environment, clearly preferring the role of offender to the role of patient.

THE ADVANTAGES OF BEING BAD

The economic advantages of criminally deviant behavior are reflected in the fact that activity associated with crime accounts for a sizable percentage of the national income. While there are certainly many unsuccessful criminals, the old adage that crime does not pay is not always true. Nevertheless, economic gain is probably the least of the advantages of being "bad."

There are definite social advantages to the person who chooses the criminally deviant role. The attractions of the criminal culture can be enormous. It is a seductive culture in which guilt feelings are easily rationalized away and in which the rewards for effective performance are great. It rewards those who conform with acceptance, a definite role in life, and status. While some offenders are probably unable to form close interpersonal relationships, others can do so, and associations between offenders may be close and sometimes meaningful.

In the prison situation, psychiatry can offer few attractions to compete with the gratifications of the criminal culture. The rigid, clear, and concise standards for conduct and behavior of the criminal culture are an inviting prospect in comparison with the ambiguities and hazinesses of psychiatry. It is far easier for the criminal to consider his behavior in terms of the ready explanations his own culture gives him than to begin to delve into the meaning of his behavior. Even in prison he finds a definite social structure and close alliances with others as a definite gratifying possibility. If he accepts psychiatry, he may be expelled from this culture.

Moreover, in spite of the great volume of literature and publicity designed to point out the evils of crime, the offender remains a romantic figure in the eyes of the general public. Even if he is apprehended and punished, he is not, on his emergence from prison, fully rejected by the wider culture. On occasion communities have been militantly proud of their reformed criminals, who live in their midst as respected citizens.

The person who is mentally ill reaps none of these advantages. There is no "sick culture" that compares in any way with the deviant culture; there is no quasi-respectable society which will accept him, as there is for the offender. In most cases, he is unable to form close, gratifying interpersonal relationships with others. The society in general accords him no glamour, but persecutes him in most of the ways in which a society can persecute an individual. Recovery does not accomplish for him what reform does for the criminal; long after he has fully recovered, he may be looked upon suspiciously by his fellow citizens and regarded as not entirely capable of being trusted.

The idea that certain types of behavior represent attempts to deal with unconscious psychological difficulties has been discussed by Freud, Reich, and others.[2] The offender is frequently described as a person unwilling to change because his behavior in effect is responsible for maintaining a state of psychological homeostasis. His degree of discomfort is less than that of a person with a painful neurosis or a psychosis.

A less discussed advantage of being bad is that it offers a clear and easy channel for aggression. Whether the offender is in or out of prison, there is always a definite enemy, whom it is permissible to hate. The offender need not feel guilty because of his aggressive feelings

toward law enforcement officers, prison guards, or society in general, for his peer group supports him. Many criminals can tolerate serious deprivations and punishments which the normal person might find devastating; for instance, I have seen prisoners spend many days in solitary confinement and yet retain their ego integrity, developing none of the psychotic-like symptoms which seem to be characteristic in other cases of isolation. But these men were angry and bitterly resentful; they had objects on which to focus their aggressive impulses, and they knew that their peer group supported them.

The person with a mental illness also struggles with aggressive impulses, but he finds little in the way of socially acceptable channel for expressing them. Often these impulses are internalized and lead to feelings of depression. While he may, like the offender, project them onto others, he lacks the peer support for these projections which would make him more comfortable about them. Thus, while for the "bad" person his aggressive feelings are a means of sustenance, for the sick person they are a source of torture.

The delinquent's acceptance by his own culture, together with his relative psychological comfort, makes it possible for him to hold to a self-concept that is close to his ego ideal. He has a definite identity which may not always be completely satisfying but which can provide him with comfort. He is spared the trials of ambiguity and the continual necessity of choice, since the criminal code provides him with ready answers. Like the member of the democratic society described by Erich Fromm, whose freedom leaves him with painful feelings of aloneness, of overpowering responsibility, and of vagueness,[3] the delinquent finds an escape from freedom in a way of life which partially solves these problems.

If the suppositions thus far advanced are valid, it would follow that cases would be seen in which acting-out or "bad" behavior solved the problems of people who were struggling with emotional conflicts, and left them more comfortable. It would also follow that offenders who through correctional religious or psychotherapeutic experiences abandon the "bad" role might experience serious psychological stress. A psychiatrist who works with delinquents sees many examples of the first situation—of offenders whose delinquent behavior seems to have warded off depression, alleviated anxiety, or solved sexual or dependency problems. I have seen the second situation in three different institutions for treatment of offenders

---

[2] Sigmund Freud, "Three Contributions to the Theory of Sex," in *The Basic Writings of Sigmund Freud* (New York: Modern Library, 1938), pp. 553–629. Freud, "Some Character-Types Met with in Psycho-Analytic Work," in *Collected Papers* (London: Hogarth Press, 1934), 4:313–44, especially pp. 342–44. Wilhelm Reich, *Character-Analysis*, 3d ed. (New York: Orgone Institute Press, 1940). Kate Friedlander, *Psychoanalytical Approach to Juvenile Delinquency* (London: Routledge and Kegan Paul, 1951). Benjamin Karpman, "Criminal Psychodynamics: A Platform," *Archives of Abnormal Psychodynamics* (1955), 1:3–100.

[3] Erich Fromm, *Escape from Freedom* (New York: Rinehart, 1941).

at which I have worked. It happened that each of these institutions was in the process of improving its rehabilitation program, and, in each case, as the program improved, the neurotic and psychotic symptoms among the institution population increased. Apparently the average delinquent remains fairly comfortable as long as he is allowed to associate with other delinquents and is not forced to delve too intensively into his own motivations. When a solid rehabilitation program develops, he is in a sense correct when he looks upon it as a threat. Apparently an increasing emphasis on rehabilitation makes it difficult for him to continue his identification with the "bad" role. Older staff members at these institutions have made such comments as, "We just don't get the same type of tough offender any more; they're just a bunch of sick, helpless people." Such statements are usually indicators that the program is moving forward.

Implications for Treatment of Offenders

If delinquency can be thought of as a symptom, it can be considered to have the primary gain of the solution of unconscious conflict, and a secondary gain in terms of some of the social and psychological advantages of the "bad" role which I have described. Since punitive methods only assuage what guilt the criminal might have and afford him a still clearer identification with the "bad" role, treatment must begin with efforts to reduce this secondary gain. But the successful therapist must have some appreciation of what he is asking the offender to give up in order to change, and must be able to communicate this appreciation in some way.[4] He must provide a climate in which there are inducements toward acceptable behavior that are almost as alluring as those of delinquency.

Thus a major prerequisite for treatment of delinquency, whether as out-patient psycho-

[4] For instance, Aichhorn, in his presentation of himself to his patients, was able to show that he could understand the delinquent's gratifications from acting-out behavior; and Noshpitz empathized with the advantages of the delinquent role by actually entering into delinquent fantasies with the patient. See August Aichhorn, *Wayward Youth* (New York: Viking Press, 1935); and Joseph D. Noshpitz, "Opening Phase in the Psychotherapy of Adolescents," *Bulletin of the Menninger Clinic*, 21 (1957): 153–64.

therapy or in a residential treatment program, is an attitude of acceptance and identification with the person and his milieu—an attitude that recognizes that "there are advantages to being bad," at the same time that it states that "there are gratifications in not being bad." The aim must be to encourage identification with persons or goals that may be gratifying enough to encourage the delinquent to examine himself more closely. When neurotic symptoms appear, as they inevitably will, there must be adequate skills and facilities to deal with them. Aggressive outlets can be provided either in the form of the patient's freedom to express his feelings directly to the therapist, or through the more conventional channels of an occupational or recreational program. The sense of pride and self-esteem that goes with the ability to control oneself and to sublimate in a productive manner must be supported in an enormous degree. The latter is perhaps more easily accomplished in an institution, where controls and "ego-building" activities can be more easily provided, than in out-patient treatment. When all the above prerequisites are met, it is possible for some offenders to give up their delinquent symptoms. Inevitably, however, this is an extremely painful task for the offender and requires considerable skill on the part of the therapist. The recidivism rate for offenders remains depressingly high, and the number of psychiatrists interested in treating the delinquent remains shamefully low.

Society, and the psychiatrist in particular, may be imposing an almost intolerable burden on the delinquent in asking him to exchange the "bad" role for the sick role. Thus the offender who comes to trial may go to extremes to prove his normality, and the unsophisticated examiner or the defense attorney may overlook serious pathology. A prison psychiatrist sees frequent examples of prisoners who supposedly have become mentally ill during incarceration but who, as becomes apparent, would have been shown by careful examination at the time of trial to be psychotically ill.

Thus it is not surprising, too, that the criminal looks upon the usual rehabilitation program with cynicism and distrust. Only when those in charge of treatment searchingly ask themselves what they are doing to the delinquent when they try to make him into a comforting citizen, and are able to appreciate what he is giving up in accepting the sick role, can therapy be successful.

THE PROBLEM OF NORMALITY

Frederick C. Redlich, M.D., and Daniel X. Freedman, M.D.

NORMAL AND ABNORMAL BEHAVIOR

The concepts of normality and abnormality are more complex in psychiatry than in general medicine, and some people have suggested abandoning the concepts of normal and abnormal behavior entirely because simple concepts of health and disease do not apply. Marie Jahoda and other social psychologists are using the concept of positive mental health, which is supposed to designate more than an absence of mental illness. Three traditional approaches to the concept of health in psychiatry can be distinguished: (1) the statistical approach, (2) the clinical approach, and (3) the normative approach. The statistical approach focuses on average behavior and determines what deviates from the statistical average. Few exact data, however, are available on the frequency and distribution of behavior traits. Such an approach presupposes that behavior is quantifiable and measurable, but obviously many forms of behavior are not. Good examples of this approach are the data supplied by Alfred C. Kinsey *et al.* on sexual behavior, socioeconomic data—income, consumption, and production of goods—as well as the broad investigations of intelligence. Few data, however, exist on the prevalence and the incidence of psychiatric symptoms, such as anxiety, hallucinations, phobias, and so forth. Statistical data are, of course, not helpful in determining whether a given individual is sick or well, which may have something to do with the fact that clinicians have, without justification, a deprecating attitude toward morbidity statistics.

The clinical approach defines as abnormal anything that does not function according to its design. This approach is useful in somatic illness, including brain disease, but it is less helpful in behavior disorders, because all too often we do not know what design or function a certain behavior pattern serves. Heinz Hartmann and also George L. Engel view adaptation as a crucial criterion for normality. We find this concept, which is supposed to explain just about everything, only of very limited use in differentiating normal and abnormal behavior. Hartmann's concept of the "average expectable environment," however, is useful for an assessment of normality because it stresses that normality of behavior is judged not under extreme conditions of stress but under average conditions. In general terms, clinical normality is not ideal performance but minimal performance for a given individual.

Another practical attempt to define normality in terms of maturity has been suggested by John G. Whitehorn: adult and mature behavior are normal; infantile and immature behavior are abnormal. Much of what clinicians consider abnormal is immature behavior. Carl Binger pointed out that a two-year-old with temper tantrums, endowed with the physical and intellectual abilities of the adult, would be a veritable monster.

An important clinical and theoretical approach is Kubie's assumption that predominance of conscious and preconscious motivations over unconscious motivation of behavioral acts determines normality. Normal behavior is flexible and characterized by the capacity to learn. Unconscious behavior is rigid, repetitive, and insatiable. In criticism of Kubie's proposals, one may point to the fact that in many types of normal and socially desirable behavior, unconscious and preconscious motivations occur: in passionate love or in ecstatic religious experience, or in projections and identifications that are instrumental for the appreciation of art or empathy with our fellow human beings. In an effort to meet these objections, Kubie differentiated more rigorously between preconscious and unconscious motivations; the unconscious acts, according to him, are tantamount to bad, irrational, non-adaptive behavior, a psychosocial orientation that he wanted to avoid. Kubie's theory also fails to apply to phenomena like mental deficiency and many forms of abnormal behavior determined by brain disease.

In the authors' opinion, most propositions on

Chapter 4 from *The Theory and Practice of Psychiatry* by Frederick C. Redlich and Daniel X. Freedman, © 1966 by Frederick C. Redlich and Daniel X. Freedman (New York: Basic Books, 1966); reprinted with permission.

normality and abnormality depend on value judgments. Take Karl Menninger's statement: "Let us define mental health as the adjustment of human beings to the world and to each other with a maximum of effectiveness and happiness. Not just efficiency, or just contentment, or the grace of obeying the rules of the game cheerfully. It is all of these together. It is the ability to maintain an even temper, an alert intelligence, socially considerate behavior, and a happy disposition. This, I think is a healthy mind." There is nothing wrong with such a statement, as long as it is recognized as a value proposition; abnormality depends on the cultural values of defining persons. What is normal drinking? In many Irish, French, Italian, German, and Scandinavian families, moderate drinking is normal; to Protestant fundamentalists and Moslem believers, any imbibing of alcohol is abnormal. Prostitution is accepted in some cultures but not in others. There are remarkable differences in aggression, sexuality, and dependency needs in the different social classes of a single culture, and there are notable differences in the acceptance of mental illness in different cultures. The Indian sage, Ramakrishna, was considered a prophet and a saintly man by many of his companions, but he would have been judged as mentally disturbed by Western psychiatrists (and in all likelihood he also would have behaved differently had he lived in a Western cultural setting). Although some social scientists do not accept a relativistic point of view, it would seem that only extreme forms of behavior, such as indiscriminate murder, cannibalism, or absolute disregard for property are almost universally rejected. The more severe a behavior disorder, the more likely is it to be considered abnormal, regardless of the cultural context. In actual practice, psychiatrists use a composite approach; they diagnose behavior as clearly abnormal when it is seriously disabling, frustrating, deviates from established cultural norms, hence occurs relatively rarely; however, in borderline cases such an approach does not work well.

One of the revealing pieces of empirical research on normality is by Roy R. Grinker, Sr., et al., who studied monoclites, or persons who follow the common rule. Their subjects were male students of a college that specializes in teaching group work, recreation, and physical education. Grinker found these students amazingly free of disabling symptoms. The subjects were of average intelligence, worked well, but were not ambitious or creative; they had adequate stable adjustment to reality. They were middle-of-the-roaders and had warm human relationships with parents, teachers, friends, and girls; they had a firm sense of

identity, with relatively few areas of conflict. Grinker noted the following contributing factors: good health, parental cooperation in child-rearing, strong identification with parents, sound early religious training, reasonable and consistent punishment and also definite limitations set on behavior, early work history and eagerness to tackle problems in a commonsense fashion, a disinclination to introspection, and an emphasis on good fellowship. For these people money was only a means and not a goal.

In summary, the concept of health and normality is still quite muddled, with empirical research mostly lacking. Only gross deviations are clearly recognized and agreed upon in all civilized societies; borderlines of normal and abnormal behavior are fuzzy and overlapping. Cultural relativism with respect to milder disorders is the rule. The judgments of psychiatrists cannot in reality be far removed from those of the common man of the societies and cultures in which psychiatrists and patients live. At present, we cannot make precise statements about normal and abnormal; we can, however, define to a certain extent the psychiatric sick role.

THE PSYCHIATRIC SICK ROLE

Diseases and injuries put the patient into the sick role, legitimately excusing him from work and social obligations and granting him the rights of special attention, while requiring him to do his best to recover. Psychosocial losses are balanced by certain advantages that are quite similar to those offered by neuroses (the secondary gains). Patients may exploit their somatic illnesses to evoke support and avoid obligations. Illness may become a style through which comfort can be achieved. Symptoms of somatic illness may become a part of one's identity, inducing the patient to stay entrenched in incapacity rather than to adapt more creatively to his limitations. Such factors are contributory but remarkably potent in sustaining behavior disorders related to physical illness.

The "psychiatric sick role"—a term that may be questioned by purists—is considerably more complex than the medical sick role. The bulk of psychiatric patients are not sick in the ordinary sense; if the term were less awkward we might speak of a "disordered behavior role." We suggest two basic types: (1) the sick role of the patient with severe behavior disorders; (2) the sick role of the patient with mild to moderate disorders. The first group corresponds to the psychotic and severely neurotic groups. In all technologically advanced societies, such patients require attention, and psychiatrists and other mental health workers are charged with this task. Patients need not be cooperative; if necessary, society enforces treatment and confinement to psychiatric institutions. Such patients, like medical patients, are excused from work and other social obligations; they are not considered accountable for antisocial acts. If the patients with obvious and unequivocally severe behavior disorders commit crimes they are treated—or at least restrained—in psychiatric rather than in penal institutions, although Western society is far from certain what it should do with the less obvious behavior disorders associated with criminal acts. In patients with severe disorders, the goal of therapy is to free the patient from his most severe, undesirable, and crippling symptoms. In treating these patients, therapists employ a wide variety of therapeutic means, ranging from the biological to the psychosocial; moreover, generally speaking, they maintain a medical therapeutic role. In the light of new empirical knowledge the sick role of patients in mental hospitals is quite complex. Daniel L. Levinson and Eugene B. Gallagher examined patienthood or the human conditions in a mental hospital. They view the mental hospital as a quasi-bureaucratic institution —somewhere between a prison, a boarding school, and a general hospital—with a therapeutic-educative-corrective task. In such a system, patients assume complex patient-student-inmate roles. The patient role in the second group is quite different. Patients in this category, roughly corresponding to the moderate to moderate-mild group (which cannot be readily differentiated from the "normal" general population), request therapy or are advised to seek therapy, not because they are helpless or severely troubled in most spheres of living; rather, they hope for the realization of their capabilities. These patients are accountable for their acts; they do not receive, generally speaking, the benefits of the medical sick role, such as being relieved from work and other social obligations. Their relationship with the therapist is, at least in adult patients, a voluntary one, and the goal of therapy is the patient's self-actualization. The therapy of this group is entirely psychosocial. The extent to which the sick role is granted to neurotics and sociopaths is far from settled, both in the minds of experts and the general public.

These two types surely do not encompass all possible variants of the psychiatric sick role. Indeed, many people come to psychiatrists neither in total despair nor for self-actualization; they come for temporary relief of a troublesome state. Yet the distinction between the two basic roles can be helpful in answering: "Who becomes a psychiatric patient?" Psychological status and behavioral signs alone do not establish what a case is; the process of becoming not only disturbed but a case depends on those social and cultural factors that determine the sick role. Beyond any doubt, the psychiatric sick role depends on socioeconomic status and ethnic factors, as well as on the availability and general orientation of therapeutic facilities.

PSYCHIATRIC PERSPECTIVES ON NORMALITY

Melvin Sabshin, M.D.

. . . I should like to discuss the four perspectives of normality as conceived and formulated by Offer and Sabshin.[3] My purpose is to call attention to and identify the divergent approaches, but also to indicate some areas of commonality. I am distinctly hopeful that new research will lead to syntheses of the apparently discrepant positions. My presentation involves an attempt at identification and classification of those who are groping in relative darkness.

[The author presents] four perspectives, labeled (1) normality as health; (2) normality as utopia; (3) normality as average; and (4) normality as process. None of these positions is original with us, although the over-all classifi-

Excerpted and reprinted with permission from *Archives of General Psychiatry* 17 (Sept. 1967): 258. Copyright 1967, American Medical Association.

cation is new. It is certainly not the final word in conceptualizing the perspectives, since newer typologies will of necessity evolve out of empirical research.

NORMALITY AS HEALTH

The first functional perspective, normality as health, includes the traditional medical-psychiatric approach which equates normality with health and views health as an almost universal phenomenon. Many investigators have assumed and continue to assume behavior to be within normal limits when no manifest pathology is present. Concentration is then focused on definitions of pathology, leaving the large residue normal, or "healthy." Transposed on a scale, normality would be the major portion of a continuum, and abnormality the small remainder. This definition of normality relates quite clearly to the classical role function of the doctor who attempts to free his patients from grossly observable symptoms: the lack of unfavorable symptoms indicates health. Health in this context refers to a reasonable rather than an optimal or ideal state of functioning.

This perspective is illustrated in its simplest form by Romano,[4] who states that a healthy person is one who is reasonably free of undue pain, discomfort, and disability. Others have commented about this point of view. Barton,[5] for example, has stated: "Medicine has developed this useful way of looking at health and the normal to the extent that health, as the antonym of disease, has become a part of the philosophy, or tradition of physicians." . . .

NORMALITY AS UTOPIA

The second functional perspective, normality as utopia, which is best typified by but certainly not limited to psychoanalysts, conceives normality as that optimal structuralization of the diverse elements of the psychic apparatus and its mental characteristics that culminates in optimal functioning, or, in Maslow's terms, "self-actualization."[9] Such definitions emerge clearly, although most often implicitly, when psychoanalysts grapple with the complex problem of discussing their criteria of successful treatment.

Dating from Freud's conception of normality as an "ideal fiction,"[10] the normality as utopia view has almost become the trademark of the psychoanalyst. Here is an area where Freudian and neo-Freudian analysts speak in similar terms in their tendency to equate the normal person with the ideal or idealized one. . . . [They] relate normality to an individual's self-knowledge, concluding that there can be no completely normal person, since self-knowledge is always incomplete. Thus, normality is a utopia not to be attained, but only approximated. . . .

The general psychiatrist sets his goals of therapy as alleviation of suffering and removal of symptoms. The psychoanalyst, however, seeks to facilitate the patient's development of the healthiest character structure. He hopes to help the patient effectively to utilize all the resources with which he is endowed. He hopes that the patient will have freer access to his unconscious and also become freer of infantile conflicts in order to function more optimally. These goals of therapy correspond to the analyst's own conception of the healthy state he wishes his patient to attain. Most psychoanalysts realize that these are ideal goals that rarely, if ever, can be attained, but they nevertheless continue to measure their own treatment results in terms of their distance from, or proximity to, ideal results.

Comparison between cardiac functioning and ego structure may be helpful in elucidating the normality as utopia position. A heart, free of any congenital or acquired disease, never functions at its maximum capacity. Inevitable exposures to environmental stresses hamper its functioning, even if the decrement in function is subtle. The heart at best can operate only close to what it could if everything had been "perfect"; clearly, the ideal heart remains a fiction. Similarly, according to the structural and economic psychoanalytic theory, the ego of a person, under the average expectable environment[13] is only slightly injured. . . .

The normality as utopia position is being adopted increasingly by theorists in preventive medicine who have enlarged the horizons of illness to its earliest origins and most subtle manifestations. To these theorists at the vanguard, physical health is an ideal fiction. Indubitably, this utopian perspective will become more and more important in the medicine of the future, as grosser pathology is steadily decreased and prevention becomes a more dominant mode of practice. . . .

NORMALITY AS AVERAGE

The third functional perspective, normality as average, is commonly employed in normative studies of behavior. This approach is based on the mathematical principle of the bell-shaped curve and its applicability to physical, psychological, and sociological data. London[15] states it thus:

Technically, normal is a term that describes a particular kind of mathematical graph and statistical phenomenon. If certain measurements are made of a very large number of individuals, for example, and half of them fall above and half below a certain point, with most falling very close to it and diminishing numbers falling further and further from that point in precisely equal proportions on both sides of it, then the entire array of measurements is called a normal distribution.

The application of the "normal" bell-shaped curve to human data contrasts sharply with the other two perspectives described above. Those perspectives visualize normality and abnormality primarily as a straight-line continuum; they differ sharply as to where the line should be drawn. The normality as average perspective conceives the middle range as normal and both extremes as deviant. The normative statistical approach is used to find a way of describing each individual in terms of general assessment and total scores; interindividual variability is explained only within the context of the total group. . . .

Normality as Process

The fourth functional perspective, normality as process, stresses that normal behavior is the end result of interacting systems that change over time. In contrast to proponents of the other three perspectives, those who advocate this position insist that normality must be consistently viewed from a standpoint of temporal progression. . . .

Central to Erikson's[23] concept of the epigenesis of personality development is successful mastery of the stages of development essential to the attainment of normal adult functioning and maturity. Here Erikson defines normality in terms of the end product in a continuously unfolding process over time. He has emphasized this frame of reference. . . . For Erikson, the temporal or process approach is clearly and consistently central to his thesis. . . .

References

1. Grinker, R. R. Psychiatry Rides Madly in All Directions, *Arch. Gen. Psychiat.* 10:228–237, 1964.
2. Grinker, R. R. "A Dynamic Story of the 'Homoclite,' " in Masserman, J. H. (ed.), *Science and Psychoanalysis*, New York: Grune & Stratton, 1963, p. 128.
3. Offer, D., and Sabshin, M. *Normality: Theoretical and Clinical Concepts of Mental Health*, New York: Basic Books, 1966.
4. Romano, J. Basic Orientation and Education of the Medical Student, *JAMA* 409:143, 1950.
5. Barton, W. E. "Viewpoint of a Clinician," in Jahoda, M. (ed.), *Current Concepts of Positive Mental Health*, New York: Basic Books, 1959.
6. Alexander, F. *Fundamentals of Psychoanalysis*, New York: W. W. Norton & Co., 1948, p. 194.
7. Hsu, F. L. K. (ed.). *Psychological Anthropology: Approaches to Culture and Personality*. Homewood, Ill.: Dorsey Press, 1961.
8. Kallmann, F. J. "The Genetics of Mental Illness," in Arieti, S. (ed.). *American Handbook of Psychiatry*, New York: Basic Books, 1959.
9. Maslow, A. H. *Motivation and Personality*. New York: Harper & Bros., 1954.
10. Freud, S. "Analysis Terminable and Interminable," in Strachey, J. (trans.), *Collected Papers of Sigmund Freud*, New York: Basic Books, 1959.
11. Money-Kyrle, R. E. "Psychoanalysis and Ethics," in Klein, M.; Heimann, P.; and Money-Kyrle, R. E. (eds.), *New Directions in Psychoanalysis*, New York: Basic Books Inc., 1957.
12. Wallerstein, R. S. The Current State of Psychotherapy: Theory, Practice, Research, *J. Amer. Psychoanal. Assoc.* 14:183–225, 1966.
13. Hartmann, H. *Ego Psychology and the Problem of Adaptation*, New York: International Universities Press, 1958.
14. Rogers, C. R. "A Theory of Therapy, Personality, and Interpersonal Relationships as Developed in a Client-Centered Framework," in Koch, S. (ed.), *Psychology: A Study of a Science*, New York: McGraw-Hill, 1959, vol. 3.
15. London, P. The Sources of Therapeutic Morality, *Columbia University Forum 5*, No. 3, 1962.
16. Kardiner, A. *The Individual and His Society*, New York: Columbia University Press, 1939.
17. Kardiner, A. *The Psychological Frontiers of Society*. New York: Columbia University Press, 1945.
18. DuBois, C. *The People of Alor*, Minneapolis: University of Minnesota Press, 1944.
19. Child, C. M. *Physiological Foundations of Behavior*. New York: Henry Holt & Co., 1924, p. 222.
20. Freud, S. *Civilization and Its Discontents*, Strachey, J. (trans.), London Hogarth Press, 1961.
21. Freedman, L., and Roe, A. "Evolution and Human Behavior," in Roe, A., and Simpson, G. G. (eds.), *Behavior and Evolution*, New Haven, Conn.: Yale University Press, 1958, p. 461.
22. Feibleman, J. K. Ecological Factors in Human Maladaptation, *Amer. J. Psychiat.* 118: 118–124, 1961.
23. Erikson, E. H. *Childhood and Society*, New York: W. W. Norton & Co., 1950.
24. Parsons, T. "Definitions of Health and Illness in the Light of American Values and Social Structure," in Jaco, E. G. (ed.), *Patients, Physicians, and Illness*, New York: The Free Press of Glencoe, 1958, p. 176.
25. Offer, D. Normal Adolescents, *Arch. Gen. Psychiat.* 17:30–36, 1967.

PSYCHIATRIC ILLNESS

Jesse G. Rubin, M.D.

The definitions of health and illness in the emotional sphere are more difficult than in the other fields of medicine. Although certain categories of behavioral deviation are generally accepted as "diseases"[1] in the medical sense, often the question whether someone is actually ill cannot be answered as clearly as when he has pneumonia or a fractured leg. It should be emphasized that, as generally defined by mental health professionals, psychiatric illness causes only a small part of the total pool of socially deviant or maladaptive behavior. All sorts of unusual, culturally unacceptable, extreme or extraordinary behavior patterns exist which are unrelated to classical psychiatric diagnoses. To the psychiatrist who defines his profession in a relatively narrow way, therefore, the study of these latter behaviors and life styles are not the province of psychiatry. On the whole, the author is rather inclined toward this more conservative view of the profession and of the population that properly can come under its scrutiny and care. Quite clearly, neither the criminal justice system nor the psychiatric profession as a whole recognizes the distinction between deviant behavior and psychiatric illness. Thus, psychiatrists sometimes speak as experts in court and in public forums on many human problems about which they have little or no special knowledge. Such diverse aspects of human behavior as common criminal assault, prostitution, "normal" grieving, and even "streaking" have become the subjects of psychiatric "explanations." If all atypical human behavior is not a manifestation of psychiatric illness, what does constitute such illness?

In general, we may approach the problem of defining the major categories of psychiatric illnesses by dividing them into two groups.[2] The first includes conditions that are generally agreed to constitute illness in the same way that pneumonia or a fractured leg is an illness. These emotional problems cause the patient to suffer "dis-ease" (in the sense of psychic discomfort or pain) or to function in a way which is "dis-ordered." Thus, questions of competency and criminal responsibility aside, the first group is composed of people in the "sick" role.[3] In the second category include people who do not function or behave in a normal manner, but who may or may not be defined as diseased, depending on the role that their society and the criminal justice system gives them, and on who defines the term "illness." It may make a considerable difference in the outcome of a specific case, for example, as to whether the decision to call somebody "mad or bad" is left up to a psychiatrist, a judge, or a jury.

Although certain criteria set this latter group of patients apart from those in the first group, it should be noted that the degree of their deviation from normal ("disability," "dangerous," etc.) is not one of them. For example, contrast the chronic alcoholic who compulsively forges checks with someone suffering moderate fits of depression. Clearly, both the medical and legal professions would consider someone subject to severe depression to be ill and in need of medical help. However, there is no general agreement on whether the alcoholic check forger is medically ill ("mad") or is a social deviant to be dealt with legally ("bad"), even though he may be more severely deviant than the depressive.

The first major group (those definitely ill) may be subdivided into two classifications: the functional and the organic. The functional subgroup is composed of those people who suffer from an emotional disorder for which no *definite* medical, biochemical, or neurological

---

[1] They are not universally accepted. Thomas Szasz, for example, would dispute the concept that many of the conditions to be described below are illness. However, the statement stands that among the psychiatric profession there exists a general consensus that certain categories of deviant behavior are symptomatic of illness in the classic medical sense.

[2] See the chart below.

[3] See Redlich and Freedman, above, page 56.

This selection was written expressly for the 1st edition of this volume and has not been previously published. It has been revised for the current edition.

	Definitely ill (Group I)	Questionably ill (Group II)
Functional	1. Mild—the neuroses 2. Severe—the psychoses	Character disorders (or personality disorders), sexual deviation.
Organic	1. Acute and chronic brain syndromes 2. Mental retardation	Ill-defined "constitutional inadequacy," some cases of inadequate personality, "episodic dyscontrol."

basis has as yet been found. As we will see in the selections to follow, there is evidence that constitutional or organic factors may operate in these illnesses.[4] However, at present, the precise nature of these organic factors and their degree of importance in the illnesses is unknown. This functional group may again be divided into a milder and more serious group of illnesses.[5]

In the category of milder functional illnesses are the neuroses, defined in the American Psychiatric Association *Diagnostic and Statistical Manual* as follows:

"Anxiety is the chief characteristic of the neuroses. It may be felt and expressed directly, or it may be controlled unconsciously and automatically by conversion, displacement, and various other psychological mechanisms. Generally, these mechanisms produce symptoms experienced as subjective distress from which the patient desires relief.

"The neuroses, as contrasted to the psychoses, manifest neither gross distortion nor misinterpretation of external reality, nor gross personality disorganization."

The neuroses (or psychoneuroses) are classified as "mild" because they do not generally interfere in a global way with the functioning of the individual, nor do they interfere with his capacity to know what reality is. They may, however, hamper his style of living in a variety of ways. Neurotic symptoms are, to some degree, experienced by everyone. We all suffer at times from anxiety and depression. In a similar fashion, under conditions of sleep deprivation, long-distance driving, or severe fatigue, anyone may experience a type of dissociative state. It is the severity and persistence of these symptoms, as well as the inability of the person to deal with them by the conventional means (going on vacation, getting a little more rest or sleep, or one or another of our usual home cures), that defines when one of these normal "stress and strain" reactions becomes a neurosis.

The more severe subgroup among the functional disorders includes the psychoses. They are defined by the APA *Manual* as follows: "Patients are described as psychotic when their mental functioning is sufficiently impaired to interfere grossly with their capacity to meet the ordinary demands of life. The impairment may result from a serious distortion in their capacity to recognize reality. Hallucinations and delusions, for example, may distort their perceptions. Alterations of mood may be so profound that the patient's capacity to respond appropriately is grossly impaired. Deficits in perception, language, and memory may be so severe that the patient's capacity for mental grasp of his situation is effectively lost."

There are essentially two criteria in this definition for the diagnosis of a psychotic state: First, the person suffers from global dysfunction. That is, he is not able to work, or is able to work only minimally, and is unable ot function in his home life or to take on the responsibilities appropriate to his age and station. Second, the psychotic is no longer able to test reality. That is, he can no longer tell the difference between his fantasies, hallucinations, and delusional ideas and the real world around him. Psychosis is the medical term *roughly* equivalent to the lay terms "insanity," "mental illness," and "craziness."

Failure to test reality and a global breakdown in functioning of an individual may well raise questions of his legal competency. Therefore, although psychosis in and of itself does not define legal incompetency or irresponsibility, it is largely with the group of psychotics that these issues are raised. Because of the degree of disability caused by psychosis, compensation cases often involve psychotic reactions. Psychosis may be a factor in family law practice, particularly in divorce, annulment, or in custody cases.

The psychoses are not psychic states that are close to the experience of most people. Although nonpsychotic people may have transient moments when they feel the world is unreal, or that their own fantasies are quite vivid, or suffer brief periods of relatively severe malfunctioning, the true psychotic state of mind is not generally known to the nonpsychotic person (except possibly, in dreams). Thus, the psychotic individual strikes the layman as a strange and alien creature; hence, the old term "alienist" for those doctors who treat mental illness.

Included in the category of organically determined diseases definitely considered as illness are the behavioral disorders associated with

---

[4] See Chapter 4, selections by Durell and Zubin.

[5] It is suggested that the remainder of this section be read in close conjunction with the excerpts from the *Diagnostic and Statistical Manual*, below, which describes more fully the specific types of reactions in each category dealt with here.

central nervous system damage (the organic brain syndromes). They are defined by the *Manual* as follows:

"These disorders are manifested by the following symptoms: (a) Impairment of orientation; (b) Impairment of memory; (c) Impairment of all intellectual functions, such as comprehension, calculation, knowledge, learning, etc.; (d) Impairment of judgment; (e) Lability and shallowness of affect.

"The organic brain syndrome is a basic mental condition characteristically resulting from impairment of brain tissue function from whatever cause. Most of the basic symptoms are generally present to some degree, regardless of whether the syndrome is mild, moderate, or severe. . . .

"(Brain syndromes may be caused by) . . . senility . . . alcohol . . . infection . . . trauma . . . (etc.)"

With relatively few variations, all brain syndromes will have about the same symptomatology The acute or chronic brain syndrome, whether from epilepsy, drug toxicity, encephalitis, meningitis, brain tumor, stroke, diabetic acidosis, or any one of a number of other causes, will present a clinical picture different from that of the functional psychoses. A careful diagnostic evaluation, sometimes including psychological tests, an electroencephalogram, and a neurological examination, will usually enable the psychiatrist to differentiate between brain disorder and functional psychosis. Even in cases where there is a mixed picture, this should be susceptible to sorting out by careful study and repeated examinations.

For the layman, a behavioral disorder caused by impairment of brain tissue function is easier to understand, and perhaps to excuse, than a functional disorder. The memory loss, confusion, clouded sensorium, and impaired intellectual facility of the organic brain syndrome may be appreciated by normal people who have experienced a febrile illness, prolonged physical stress, severe alcohol intoxication, or recovery from surgical anesthesia.

The second major category of organic impairment is mental retardation.[6] This is defined by the *Manual* as follows: "Mental retardation refers to subnormal general intellectual functioning which originates during the developmental period and is associated with impairment of either learning and social adjustment or maturation, or both. The diagnostic classification of mental retardation relates to IQ as follows: *Borderline mental retardation* —IQ 68–85; *Mild mental retardation*—IQ 52–67; *Moderate mental retardation*—IQ

[6] See also section H, article by Begad and the AMA handbook.

36–51; *Severe mental retardation*—IQ 20–35; *Profound mental retardation*—IQ under 20.

"It is recognized that the intelligence quotient should not be the only criterion used in making a diagnosis of mental retardation or in evaluating its severity. It should serve only to help in making a clinical judgment of the patient's adaptive behavioral capacity. This judgment should also be based on an evaluation of the patient's developmental history and present functioning, including academic and vocational achievement, motor skills, and social and emotional maturity.

[Mental retardation may be caused by] . . . infection . . . physical trauma . . . chromosomal abnormalities . . . psychosocial deprivation . . . [etc.]."

The effect of mental retardation on the individual's actions, his capacity to be responsible, and society's expectation that he should control his impulses is directly related to the degree of intellectual deficit. However, environmental factors also play a critical role.

Our second major group consists of deviations from the norm that may or may not be defined as illness, and as a result of which the deviant person may or may not be granted "the sick role"—depending on who does the defining.

One major functional subgroup in this category is the personality or character disorders. These are defined by the APA *Manual* as follows:

"This group of disorders is characterized by deeply ingrained maladaptive patterns of behavior that are distinctly different in quality from psychotic and neurotic symptoms. Generally, these are lifelong patterns, often recognizable by the time of adolescence or earlier. Sometimes the pattern is determined primarily by malfunctioning of the brain, but such cases should be classified under one of the non-psychotic organic brain syndromes rather than here."

Because these deviations are not clearly defined as "illness," because they may seem to be under more conscious control than are those of the first group, because their presence usually involves little or no psychic pain or "disease," and because their symptom patterns are often mixed with those of the more commonly accepted diseases, the personality disorders present particularly difficult problems for psychiatry and the law. Among those that present the most difficult problems are the *schizoid personality*, *anti-social personality*, *addiction*, *alcoholism*, and *sexual deviation*.

The diagnosis of schizoid personality is important because the issue of whether an individual is to be held "responsible" for a crime

may hinge largely on the differential diagnosis between schizoid personality and schizophrenic psychosis.[7]

The most perplexing personality disorder to confront the field of psychiatry and the law is the antisocial personality (formerly known as the psychopathic personality and later as the sociopathic personality disorder). Antisocial personality includes the "con artist," the "manipulator," the smooth embezzler. His criminal behavior is compulsive, often self-destructive, and "makes no sense," and his attempts to avoid apprehension may be negligible. The antisocial personality is not universally defined as medically and psychiatrically diseased in the sense that the schizophrenic is.[8] Since 1835, when Pritchard coined the term "moral insanity" to describe this syndrome, a battle has been raging in forensic psychiatric circles as to whether antisocial personalities are to be considered ill, and 139 years later no end to the controversy is in sight. Before deciding where such a person stands with regard to the law, one must know who is classifying the individual as well as who is interpreting the law.

The psychiatric status of individuals whose usual patterns of sexual behavior deviate from that of genitally oriented heterosexual relationships is currently a matter of much debate within psychiatric circles.[9]

Finally, there are organic conditions that fall into the questionably ill category. There are a number of ill-defined syndromes, probably with organic bases, which lead people into the courts; some criminals, particularly of the impulsive type, have marginally abnormal electroencephalograms, chromosomal abnormalities,[10] a history of either birth trauma or severe physical insult to the central nervous system in childhood, repeated head injuries, tics or other evidence of neuromuscular malfunction, borderline low intelligence, and mild physical deformity. (Jack Ruby; and Perry Smith, one of the "Clutter killers," described in *In Cold Blood*, are examples of this type.) It is difficult to decide on the significance of the physical and neurological findings in these cases, and the decision as to whether they should be held responsible for their acts can be a most difficult one. Recently, the diagnosis of "episodic behavioral disorder" or "episodic dyscontrol" has appeared in the psychiatric literature.[11] As described by a number of workers, people who suffer from this disorder complain of "seizure-like" outbursts with an alleged loss of contact with the environment during the outbursts, with occasional warnings of the outburst to come, as well as post-"seizure" symptoms which include depression, fatigue, and sleep. These outbursts may involve physical and sexual assaultive behavior as well as many traffic violations and serious automobile accidents. Workers who have described this syndrome feel there is the high probability of brain dysfunction as at least a partial basis for it. However, other investigators disagree with this conclusion and the concept is not universally accepted at this time. The diagnosis, it should be noted, is not included in the *Diagnostic and Statistical Manual* of the APA.

---

[7] See the Andrews and Volbrecht cases below.

[8] See the "Caveat paragraph" in the A.L.I. insanity rule and Judge Biggss' discussion of it in the *Currens* case, *infra*.

[9] For further discussion, see selection below.

[10] See Chapter 4, below.

[11] Department of Health, Education, and Welfare, National Institutes of Health, National Institute of Neurological Diseases and Stroke, *Report on the Biomedical Research Aspects of Brain and Aggressive Violent Behavior*, October 23, 1973.

DIAGNOSTIC AND STATISTICAL MANUAL OF MENTAL DISORDERS

American Psychiatric Association

I. MENTAL RETARDATION

Mental retardation refers to subnormal general intellectual functioning which originates during the developmental period and is associated with impairment of either learning and social adjustment or maturation, or both. The diagnostic classification of mental retardation relates to IQ as follows: *Borderline mental retardation*—IQ 68–85; *Mild mental retardation*—IQ 52–67; *Moderate mental retardation*—IQ 36–51; *Severe mental retardation*—IQ 20–35; *Profound mental retardation*—IQ under 20.

It is recognized that the intelligence quotient should not be the only criterion used in making a diagnosis of mental retardation or in evaluating its severity. It should serve only to help in making a clinical judgment of the patient's adaptive behavioral capacity. This judgment should also be based on an evaluation of the patient's developmental history and present functioning, including academic and vocational achievement, motor skills, and social and emotional maturity.

[Mental retardation may be caused by] . . . infection . . . physical trauma . . . chromosomal abnormalities . . . psychosocial deprivaiton . . . [etc.].

II. ORGANIC BRAIN SYNDROMES (DISORDERS CAUSED BY OR ASSOCIATED WITH IMPAIRMENT OF BRAIN TISSUE FUNCTION)

These disorders are manifested by the following symptoms: (*a*) Impairment of orientation; (*b*) Impairment of memory; (*c*) Impairment of all intellectual functions such as comprehension, calculation, knowledge, learning, etc.; (*d*) Impairment of judgment; (*e*) Lability and shallowness of affect.

The organic brain syndrome is a basic mental condition characteristically resulting from diffuse impairment of brain tissue function from whatever cause. Most of the basic symptoms are generally present to some degree regardless of whether the syndrome is mild, moderate, or severe.

The syndrome may be the only disturbance present. It may also be associated with psychotic symptoms and behavioral disturbances. The severity of the associated symptoms is affected by and related to not only the precipitating organic disorder but also the patient's inherent personality patterns, present emotional conflicts, his environmental situation, and interpersonal relations.

These brain syndromes are grouped into psychotic and non-psychotic disorders according to the severity of functional impairment.

It is important to distinguish "acute" from "chronic" brain disorders because of marked differences in the course of illness, prognosis, and treatment. The terms indicate primarily whether the brain pathology and its accompanying organic brain syndrome is reversible. Since the same etiology may produce either temporary or permanent brain damage, a brain disorder which appears reversible (acute) at the beginning may prove later to have left permanent damage and a persistent organic brain syndrome which will then be diagnosed "chronic."

[Brain syndromes may be caused by] . . . senility . . . alcohol . . . infection . . . trauma . . . [etc.].

The Psychoses

Patients are described as psychotic when their mental functioning is sufficiently impaired to interfere grossly with their capacity to meet the ordinary demands of life. The impairment may result from a serious distortion in their capacity to recognize reality. Hallucinations and delusions, for example, may distort their perceptions. Alterations of mood may be so profound that the patient's capacity to respond

---

Excerpts reprinted with permission from the *Diagnostic and Statistical Manual of Mental Disorders*, American Psychiatric Association, Washington, D.C., 2d ed., 1968.

appropriately is grossly impaired. Deficits in perception, language, and memory may be so severe that the patient's capacity for mental grasp of his situation is effectively lost.

Some confusion results from the different meanings which have become attached to the word "psychosis." Some non-organic disorders, in the well-developed form in which they were first recognized, typically rendered patients psychotic. For historical reasons these disorders are still classified as psychoses, even though it now is generally recognized that many patients for whom these diagnoses are clinically justified are not in fact psychotic. This is true particularly in the incipient or convalescent stages of the illness. To reduce confusion, when one of these disorders listed as a "psychosis" is diagnosed in a patient who is not psychotic, a qualifying phrase *not psychotic* or *not presently psychotic* should be noted even though there is no code number assigned to these phrases.

Example: *Schizophrenia, simple type, not psychotic.*

It should be noted that this Manual permits an organic condition to be classified as a psychosis only if the patient is psychotic during the episode being diagnosed.

If the specific physical condition underlying one of these disorders is known, indicate it with a separate, additional diagnosis.

III. Psychoses Not Attributed to Physical Conditions Listed Previously

Schizophrenia

This large category includes a group of disorders manifested by characteristic disturbances of thinking, mood, and behavior. Disturbances in thinking are marked by alterations of concept formation which may lead to misinterpretation of reality and sometimes to delusions and hallucinations, which frequently appear psychologically self-protective. Corollary mood changes include ambivalent, constricted, and inappropriate emotional responsiveness and loss of empathy with others. Behavior may be withdrawn, regressive, and bizarre. The schizophrenias, in which the mental status is attributable primarily to a *thought* disorder, are to be distinguished from the *Affective psychoses* (q.v.), which are dominated by a mood disorder. The *Paranoid states* (q.v.) are distinguished from schizophrenia by the narrowness of their distortions of reality and by the absence of other psychotic symptoms.

Schizophrenia, simple type. This psychosis is characterized chiefly by a slow and insidious

reduction of external attachments and interests, and by apathy and indifference leading to impoverishment of interpersonal relations, mental deterioration, and adjustment on a lower level of functioning. In general, the condition is less dramatically psychotic than are the hebephrenic, catatonic, and paranoid types of schizophrenia. Also, it contrasts with schizoid personality, in which there is little or no progression of the disorder.

Schizophrenia, hebephrenic type. This psychosis is characterized by disorganized thinking, shallow and inappropriate affect, unpredictable giggling, silly and regressive behavior and mannerisms, and frequent hypochondriacal complaints. Delusions and hallucinations, if present, are transient and not well organized.

Schizophrenia, catatonic type (Schizophrenia, catatonic type, excited; Schizophrenia, catatonic type, withdrawn). It is frequently possible and useful to distinguish two subtypes of catatonic schizophrenia. One is marked by excessive and sometimes violent motor activity and excitement, and the other by generalized inhibition manifested by stupor, mutism, negativism, or waxy flexibility. In time, some cases deteriorate to a vegetative state.

Schizophrenia, paranoid type. This type of schizophrenia is characterized primarily by the presence of persecutory or grandiose delusions, often associated with haullucinations. Excessive religiosity is sometimes seen. The patient's attitude is frequently hostile and aggressive, and his behavior tends to be consistent with his delusions. In general the disorder does not manifest the gross personality disorganization of the hebephrenic and catatonic types, perhaps because the patient uses the mechanism of projection, which ascribes to others characteristics he cannot accept in himself. Three subtypes of the disorder may sometimes be differentiated, depending on the predominant symptoms: hostile, grandiose, and hallucinatory.

Acute schizophrenic episode. This diagnosis does not apply to acute episodes of schizophrenic disorders described elsewhere. This condition is distinguished by the acute onset of schizophrenic symptoms, often associated with confusion, perplexity, ideas of reference, emotional turmoil, dream-like dissociation, and excitement, depression, or fear. The acute onset distinguishes this condition from simple schizophrenia. In time these patients may take on the characteristics of catatonic, hebephrenic, or paranoid schizophrenia, in which case their diagnosis should be changed accordingly. In many cases the patient recovers within weeks, but sometimes his disorganization becomes progressive. More frequently remission is followed by recurrence.

Schizophrenia, latent type. This category is for patients having clear symptoms of schizophrenia but no history of a psychotic schizophrenic episode. Disorders sometimes designated as incipient, pre-psychotic, pseudoneurotic, pseudopsychopathic, or borderline schizophrenia are categorized here.

Schizophrenia, residual type. This category is for patients showing signs of schizophrenia but who, following a psychotic schizophrenic episode, are no longer psychotic.

Schizophrenia, schizo-affective type. This category is for patients showing a mixture of schizophrenic symptoms and pronounced elation or depression. Within this category it may be useful to distinguish excited from depressed types.

Schizophrenia, childhood type. This category is for cases in which schizophrenic symptoms appear before puberty. The condition may be manifested by autistic, atypical, and withdrawn behavior; failure to develop identity separate from the mother's; and general unevenness, gross immaturity, and inadequacy in development.

Schizophrenia, chronic undifferentiated type. This category is for patients who show mixed schizophrenic symptoms and who present definite schizophrenic thought, affect, and behavior not classifiable under the other types of schizophrenia. It is distinguished from *Schizoid personality* (q.v.).

Major Affective Disorders (Affective Psychoses)

This group of psychoses is characterized by a single disorder of mood, either extreme depression or elation, that dominates the mental life of the patient and is responsible for whatever loss of contact he has with his environment. The onset of the mood does not seem to be related directly to a precipitating life experience and therefore is distinguishable from *Psychotic depressive reaction* and *Depressive neurosis.*

Involutional Melancholia. This is a disorder occurring in the involutional period and characterized by worry, anxiety, agitation, and severe insomnia. Feelings of guilt and somatic preoccupations are frequently present and may be of delusional proportions. This disorder is distinguishable from *Manic-depressive illness* (q.v.) by the absence of previous episodes; it is distinguished from *Schizophrenia* (q.v.) in that impaired reality testing is due to a disorder of mood; and it is distinguished from *Psychotic depressive reaction* (q.v.) in that the disorder of mood is not due to some experience. Opinion is divided as to whether this psychosis can be distinguished from the other affective disorders. It is, therefore, recommended that involutional patients not be given this diagnosis unless all other affective disorders have been ruled out.

Manic-depressive Illnesses (Manic-depressive Psychoses). These disorders are marked by severe mood swings and a tendency to remission and recurrence. Patients may be given this diagnosis in the absence of a previous history of affective psychosis if there is no obvious precipitating event. This disorder is divided into three major subtypes: manic type, depressed type, and circular type.

Manic-depressive illness, manic type (Manic-depressive psychosis, manic type). This disorder consists exclusively of manic episodes. These episodes are characterized by excessive elation, irritability, talkativeness, flight of ideas, and accelerated speech and motor activity. Brief periods of depression sometimes occur, but they are never true depressive episodes.

Manic-depressive illness, depressed type (Manic-depressive psychosis, depressed type). This disorder consists exclusively of depressive episodes. These episodes are characterized by severely depressed mood and by mental and motor retardation progressing occasionally to stupor. Uneasiness, apprehension, perplexity, and agitation may also be present. When illusions, hallucinations, and delusions (usually of guilt or of hypochondriacal or paranoid ideas) occur, they are attributable to the dominant mood disorder. Because it is a primary mood disorder, this psychosis differs from the *Psychotic depressive reaction*, which is more easily attributable to precipitating stress.

Manic-depressive illness, circular type (Manic-depressive psychosis, circular type). This disorder is distinguished by at least one attack of both a depressive episode *and* a manic episode. this phenomenon makes clear why manic and depressed types are combined into a single category.

Paranoid States

These are psychotic disorders in which a delusion, generally persecutory or grandiose, is the essential abnormality. Disturbances in mood, behavior, and thinking (including hallucinations) are derived from this delusion. This distinguishes paranoid states from the affective psychoses and schizophrenias, in which mood and thought disorders, respectively, are the central abnormalities. Most authorities, however, question whether this group of disorders are distinct clinical entities and not merely variants of schizophrenia or paranoid personality.

Paranoia. This extremely rare condition is characterized by gradual development of an intricate, complex, and elaborate paranoid system based on and often proceeding logically from misinterpretation of an actual event. Frequently the patient considers himself endowed with unique and superior ability. In spite of a chronic course the condition does not seem to interfere with the rest of the patient's thinking and personality.

Involutional paraphrenia. This paranoid psychosis is characterized by delusion formation with onset in the involutional period. Formerly it was classified as a paranoid variety of involutional psychotic reaction. The absence of conspicuous thought disorders typical of schizophrenia distinguishes it from that group.

Psychotic depressive reaction (Reactive Depressive Psychosis). This psychosis is distinguished by a depressive mood attributable to some experience. Ordinarily the individual has no history of repeated depressions of cyclothymic mood swings. The differentiation between this condition and *Depressive neurosis* (q.v.) depends on whether the reaction impairs reality testing or functional adequacy enough to be considered a psychosis.

IV. NEUROSES

Anxiety is the chief characteristic of the neuroses. It may be felt and expressed directly, or it may be controlled unconsciously and automatically by conversion, displacement, and various other psychological mechanisms. Generally, these mechanisms produce symptoms experienced as subjective distress from which the patient desires relief.

The neuroses, as contrasted to the psychoses, manifest neither gross distortion nor misinterpretation of external reality, nor gross personality disorganization. A possible exception to this is hysterical neurosis, which some believe may occasionally be accompanied by hallucinations and other symptoms encountered in psychoses.

Traditionally, neurotic patients, however severely handicapped by their symptoms, are not classified as psychotic because they are aware that their mental functioning is disturbed.

Anxiety neurosis. This neurosis is characterized by anxious over-concern extending to panic and frequently associated with somatic symptoms. Unlike *Phobic neurosis* (q.v.), anxiety may occur under any circumstances and is not restricted to specific situations or objects. This disorder must be distinguished from normal apprehension or fear which occur in realistically dangerous situations.

Hypochondriacal neurosis. This condition is dominated by preoccupation with the body, and with fear of presumed diseases of various organs. Though the fears are not of delusional quality as in psychotic depressions, they persist despite reassurance. The condition differs from hysterical neurosis in that there are no actual losses or distortions of function.

Hysterical neurosis. This neurosis is characterized by an involuntary psychogenic loss or disorder of function. Symptoms characteristically begin and end suddenly in emotionally charged situations and are symbolic of the underlying conflicts. Often they can be modified by suggestion alone.

Hysterical neurosis, conversion type. In the conversion type, the special senses or voluntary nervous system are affected, causing such symptoms as blindness, deafness, anosmia, anaesthesias, paraesthesias, paralyses, ataxias, akinesias, and dyskinesias. Often the patient shows an inappropriate lack of concern or "belle indifference" about these symptoms, which may actually provide secondary gains by winning him sympathy or relieving him of unpleasant responsibilities. This type of hysterical neurosis must be distinguished from psychophysiologic disorders, which are mediated by the autonomic nervous system; from malingering, which is done consciously; and from neurological lesions, which cause anatomically circumscribed symptoms.

Hysterical neurosis, dissociative type. In the dissociative type, alterations may occur in the patient's state of consciousness, or in his identity, to produce such symptoms as amnesia, somnambulism, fugue, and multiple personality.

Phobic neurosis. This condition is characterized by intense fear of an object or situation which the patient consciously recognizes as no real danger to him. His apprehension may be experienced as faintness, fatigue, palpitations, perspiration, nausea, tremor, and even panic. Phobias are generally attributed to fears displaced to the phobic object or situation from some other object of which the patient is unaware. A wide range of phobias has been described.

Obsessive compulsive neurosis. This disorder is characterized by the persistent intrusion of unwanted thoughts, urges, or actions that the patient is unable to stop. The thoughts may consist of single words or ideas, ruminations or trains of thought often perceived by the patient as nonsensical. The actions vary from simple movements to complex rituals such as repeated handwashing. Anxiety and distress are often present if the patient is either prevented from completing his compulsive ritual or if he is concerned about being unable to control it himself.

Depressive neurosis. This disorder is manifested by an excessive reaction of depression due to an internal conflict or to an identifiable event such as the loss of a love object or cherished possession.

Neurasthenic neurosis. This condition is characterized by complaints of chronic weakness, easy fatigability, and sometimes exhaustion. Unlike hysterical neurosis the patient's complaints are genuinely distressing to him and there is no evidence of secondary gain. It differs from *Anxiety neurosis* (q.v.) and from the *Psychophysiological disorders* (q.v.) in the nature of the predominant complaint. It differs from *Depressive neurosis* (q.v.) in the moderateness of the depression and in the chronicity of its course.

Depersonalization neurosis (Depersonalization syndrome). This syndrome is dominated by a feeling of unreality and of estrangement from the self, body, or surroundings. This diagnosis should not be used if the condition is part of some other mental disorder, such as acute situational reactions. A brief experience of depersonalization is not necessarily a symptom of illness.

V. Personality Disorders and Certain Other Non-Psychotic Mental Disorders Not Mentioned Previously

Personality Disorders

This group of disorders is characterized by deeply ingrained maladaptive patterns of behavior that are distinctly different in quality from psychotic and neurotic symptoms. Generally, these are lifelong patterns, often recognizable by the time of adolescence or earlier. Sometimes the pattern is determined primarily by malfunctioning of the brain, but such cases should be classified under one of the non-psychotic organic brain syndromes rather than here.

Paranoid personality. This behavioral pattern is characterized by hypersensitivity, rigidity, unwarranted suspicion, jealousy, envy, excessive self-importance, and a tendency to blame others and ascribe evil motives to them. These characteristics often interfere with the patient's ability to maintain satisfactory interpersonal relations. Of course, the presence of suspicion of itself does not justify this diagnosis, since it may be warranted in some instances.

Cyclothymic personality (Affective personality) This behavior pattern is manifested by recurring and alternating periods of depression and elation. Periods of elation may be marked by ambition, warmth, enthuisasm, optimism, and high energy. Periods of depression may be marked by worry, pessimism, low energy, and a sense of futility. These mood variations are not readily attributable to external circumstances. If possible, the diagnosis should specify whether the mood is characteristically depressed, hypomanic, or alternating.

Schizoid personality. This behavior pattern manifests shyness, over-sensitivity, seclusiveness, avoidance of close or competitive relationships, and often eccentricity. Autistic thinking without loss of capacity to recognize reality is common, as is daydreaming, and the inability to express hostility and ordinary aggressive feelings. These patients react to disturbing experiences and conflicts with apparent detachment.

Explosive personality (Epileptoid personality disorder). This behavior pattern is characterized by gross outbursts of rage or of verbal or physical aggressiveness. These outbursts are strikingly different from the patient's usual behavior, and he may be regretful and repentant of them. These patients are generally considered excitable, aggressive, and overresponsive to environmental pressures. It is the intensity of the outbursts and the individual's inability to control them which distinguishes this group. Cases diagnosed as "aggressive personality" are classified here. If the patient is amnesic for the outbursts, the diagnosis of *Hysterical neurosis, Non-psychotic OBS with epilepsy,* or *Psychosis with epilepsy* should be considered.

Obsessive compulsive personality (Anankastic personality). This behavior pattern is characterized by excessive concern with conformity and adherence to standards of conscience. Consequently, individuals in this group may be rigid, over-inhibited, over-conscientious, over-dutiful, and unable to relax easily. This disorder may lead to an *Obsessive compulsive neurosis* (q.v.), from which it must be distinguished.

Hysterical personality (Histrionic personality disorder). These behavior patterns are characterized by excitability, emotional instability, over-reactivity, and self-dramatization. This self-dramatization is always attention seeking and often seductive, whether or not the patient is aware of its purpose. These personalities are also immature, self-centered, often vain, and unusually dependent on others. This disorder must be differentiated from *Hysterical neurosis* (q.v.).

Asthenic personality. This behavior pattern is characterized by easy fatigability, low energy level, lack of enthusiasm, marked incapacity for enjoyment, and oversensitivity to physical and emotional stress. This disorder must be differentiated from *Neurasthenic neurosis* (q.v.).

Antisocial personality. This term is reserved for individuals who are basically unsocialized and whose behavior pattern brings them repeatedly into conflict with society. They often are incapable of loyalty to any individuals, groups, or social values. They are grossly selfish, callous, irresponsible, impulsive, and unable to feel guilt or to learn from experience and punishment. Frustration tolerance is low. They tend to blame others or offer plausible rationalizations for their behavior. A mere history of repeated legal or social offenses is not sufficient to justify this diagnosis. [N.B. This classification includes those individuals formerly classified as *Psychopaths* or *Sociopaths*].

Passive-aggressive personality. This behavior pattern is characterized by both passivity and aggressiveness. The aggressiveness may be expressed passively, for example by obstructionism, pouting, procrastination, intentional inefficiency, or stubbornness. This behavior commonly reflects hostility which the individual feels he dare not express openly. Often the behavior is one expression of the patient's resentment at failing to find gratification in â relationship with an individual or institution upon which he is over-dependent.

Inadequate personality. This behavior pattern is characterized by ineffectual responses to emotional, social, intellectual, and physical demands. While the patient seems neither physically nor mentally deficient, he does manifest inadaptability, ineptness, poor judgment, social instability, and lack of physical and emotional stamina.

Sexual Deviation

This category is for individuals whose sexual interests are directed primarily toward objects other than people of the opposite sex, toward sexual acts not usually associated with coitus, or toward coitus performed under bizarre circumstances as in necrophilia, pedophilia, sexual sadism, and fetishism. Even though many find their practices distasteful, they remain unable to substitute normal sexual behavior for them. This diagnosis is not appropriate for individuals who perform deviant sexual acts because normal sexual objects are not available to them. [These include]—Homosexuality; Fetishism; Pedophilia; Transvestitism; Exhibitionism; Voyeurism; Sadism; Masochism.

Alcoholism

This category is for patients whose alcohol intake is great enough to damage their physical health, or their personal or social functioning, or when it has become a prerequisite ot normal functioning. If the alcoholism is due to another mental disorder, both diagnoses should be made. The following types of alcoholism are recognized:

Episodic excessive drinking. If alcoholism is present and the individual becomes intoxicated as frequently as four times a year, the condition should be classified here. Intoxication is defined as a state in which the individual's coordination or speech is definitely impaired or his behavior is clearly altered.

Habitual excessive drinking. This diagnosis is given to persons who are alcoholic and who either become intoxicated more than twelve times a year or are recognizably under the influence of alcohol more than once a week, even though not intoxicated.

Alcohol addiction. This condition should be diagnosed when there is direct or strong presumptive evidence that the patient is dependent on alcohol. If available, the best direct evidence of such dependence is the appearance of withdrawal symptoms. The inability of the patient to go one day without drinking is presumptive evidence. When heavy drinking continues for three months or more it is reasonable to presume addiction to alcohol has been established.

Drug Dependence

This category is for patients who are addicted to, or dependent on, drugs other than alcohol, tobacco, and ordinary caffeine-containing beverages. Dependence on medically prescribed drugs is also excluded so long as the drug is medically indicated and the intake is proportionate to the medical need. The diagnosis requires evidence of habitual use or a clear sense of need for the drug. Withdrawal symptoms are not reliable evidence of dependence. While always present with the use of opium derivatives, they may be entirely absent with the use of cocaine or marihuana. The diagnosis may stand alone or be coupled with any other psychiatric diagnosis.

VI. Psychophysiologic Disorders

This group of disorders is characterized by physical symptoms that are caused by emotional factors and involve a single organ system, usually under autonomic nervous system innervation. The physiological changes involved are those that normally accompany certain emotional states, but in these disorders the changes are more intense and sustained. The individual may not be consciously aware of his emotional state. If an accompanying psychiatric disorder is present, it should be diagnosed separately whether or not it is presumed to contribute to the physical disorder. The specific physical disorder should be named and classified in one of the following categories: [skin, musculoskeletal, etc.].

VII. Special Symptoms

This category is for the occasional patient whose psychopathology is manifested by a single specific symptom. An example might be anorexia nervosa under "Feeding disturbance" as listed below. It does not apply, however, if the symptom is the result of an organic illness or defect or other mental disorder. For example, anorexia nervosa due to schizophrenia would not be included here.]Examples are]— Speech disturbances; Specific learning disturbance; Tic; Other psychomotor disorder; Disorders of sleep; Feeding disturbance.

VIII. Transient Situational Disturbances

This major category is reserved for more or less transient disorders of any severity that occur in individuals without any apparent underlying mental disorders and that represent an acute reaction to overwhelming environmental stress. A diagnosis in this category should specify the cause and manifestations of the disturbance so far as possible. If the patient has good adaptive capacity his symptoms usually recede as the stress diminishes. If, however, the symptoms persist after the stress is removed, the diagnosis of another mental disorder is indicated. Disorders in this category are classified according to the patient's developmental stage.

IX. Behavior Disorders of Childhood and Adolescence

This major category is reserved for disorders occurring in childhood and adolescence that are more stable, internalized, and resistant to treatment than *Transient situational disturbances* (q.v.) but less so than *psychoses, neuroses,* and *personality disorders* (q.v.). This intermediate stability is attributed to the greater fluidity of all behavior at this age. Characteristic manfestations include such symptoms as overactivity, inattentiveness, shyness, feelings of rejection, over-aggressiveness, timidity, and delinquency.

X. Conditions Without Manifest Psychiatric Disorder and Non-Specific Conditions

Social Maladjustment Without Manifest Psychiatric Disorders. This category is for recording the conditions of individuals who are psychiatrically normal but who nevertheless have severe enough problems to warrant examination by a psychiatrist. Following examination, these conditions may either become or precipitate a diagnosable mental disorder. [Examples are]—marital, social, and occupational maladjustment.

Dyssocial behavior. This category is for individuals who are not classifiable as anti-social personalities, but who are predatory and follow more or less criminal pursuits, such as racketeers, dishonest gamblers, prostitutes, and dope peddlers.

Editorial Note: *Change in Nomenclature with Regard to Homosexuality*

Special attention is given here to the classification of homosexuality for two reasons. First, the issue is most timely, and attitudes toward homosexuality within the mental health profession are in flux. Second, it is likely that if homosexuality is officially removed from the APA *Diagnostic and Statistical Manual* (referred to below as DSM-II), there will follow changes in civil rights and equal employment opportunities for homosexuals. Such a change may also have an impact on sodomy laws. (With regard to the latter, however, it must be remembered that the Wolfenden Report in Great Britain, intended to have similar aims, did not have legal consequences for a full decade.)

The proposal to remove homosexuality from DSM-2 came largely as the result of pressure from homosexual groups from 1964 through 1969. The first official statement within the American Psychiatric Association was made by Dr. Judd Marmor, then vice-president, in 1971. After the Nomenclature Task Force of the APA worked on the question, the APA Board of Trustees, on December 15, 1973, approved the deletion of unconflicted homosexuality from the *Diagnostic and Statistical Manual.** It reserved as a diagnosis "sexual orientation disturbance" for those who are "either disturbed by, in conflict with, or wish to change their sexual orientation." The Board of Trustees amplified their stand by issuing the statement quoted in full below. Subsequently, a group of members of the American Psychiatric Association issued a statement disagreeing with the Board of Trustees and asked that the matter go before the APA membership in a referendum vote. The membership voted to support the trustees and to delete unconflicted homosexuality from DSM-2. The notion of declaring homosexuality (or indeed any other culturally deviant lifestyle) either normal or an illness by virtue of an APA referendum has its unscientific and even absurd side. Nevertheless, this matter constitutes a clear example of the serious and sober issues involved in defining the limits of psychiatric illness, particularly those questionable illnesses that fall within Rubin's second major category (see above).†

* By unanimous vote, with two absentions.

† This brief historical summary of the events culminating in the current debate is taken from the article "Deleting Homosexuality as Illness: A Psychiatric Challenge to Values," *Frontiers of Psychiatry* 4, no. 3 (February 1, 1974).

AN ACTION OF THE BOARD OF TRUSTEES OF THE AMERICAN PSYCHIATRIC ASSOCIATION

Change in DSM–II, 6th Printing, page 44—Approved by APA Board of Trustees, December 15, 1973 (unanimously with two abstentions)

Sexual orientation disturbance [Homosexuality]

This category is for individuals whose sexual interests are directed primarily toward people of the same sex and who are either disturbed by, in conflict with, or wish to change their sexual orientation. This diagnostic category is distinguished from homosexuality, which by itself does not necessarily constitute a psychiatric disorder. Homosexuality per se is one form of sexual behavior and, like other forms of sexual behavior which are not by themselves psychiatric disorders, is not listed in this nomenclature of mental disorders.

STATEMENT FOR THE BOARD OF TRUSTEES
ACTION

For a condition to be considered a *mental disorder*, it must either regularly cause subjective distress or regularly be associated with some generalized impairment in social effectiveness or functioning. With the exception of homosexuality (and perhaps some of the other "sexual deviations"), virtually all of the mental disorders in DSM-II fulfill either of these two criteria.

A significant proportion of homosexuals are apparently satisfied with their sexual orientation, show no significant signs of manifest psychopathology, and are able to function as effectively as heterosexuals. Homosexuality per se, therefore, cannot be considered a mental disorder. It is significant that DSM-II does not list many heterosexual forms of sexual behavior that, like homosexuality, also do not meet these criteria for a mental disorder, such as frigidity, premature ejaculation, asexuality, and Don Juanism. Clearly, there is no scientific reason for their omission from the nomenclature of mental disorders and the inclusion of homosexuality (not only exclusive homosexuality).

The purpose of DSM-II is to list and describe *mental disorders*, not all of the forms of human psychological functioning which some believe are invariably the result of childhood conflicts and intra-psychic anxieties. The revision in the nomenclature has not been presented as largely a question of civil rights, nor does it sacrifice scientific principles in order to further the struggle for the civil rights of homosexuals. Quite the contrary: it has been the unscientific inclusion of homosexuality per se in a list of mental disorders which has been the main ideological justification for the denial of the civil rights to individuals whose only crime is their sexual orientation. To restore the original diagnostic classification of homosexuality as a mental disorder, because of unfounded assertion about "anatomy and biological reality" of questionable and certainly unproved applicability to *human* sexuality, would not only be scientifically unsound, it would be socially irresponsible.

The revision was approved unanimously by the Council on Research and Development, The Reference Committee and the Board of Trustees, and approved by the Assembly precisely because it is scientifically sound and a reasonable compromise between two extreme viewpoints about homosexuality held by many members of our profession. It avoids commitment to either the notion that homosexuality is invariably a mental disorder or that it is merely a normal variance of heterosexuality.

Alfred M. Freedman, M.D., President
John P. Spiegel, M.D., President-Elect; Chairman of the Reference Committee
Warren S. Williams, M.D., Speaker of the Assembly
Russell R. Monroe, M.D., Chairman, Council on Research and Development
Robert L. Spitzer, M.D., Member, Task Force on Nomenclature and Statistics

STATEMENT BY THE PETITIONERS

Those who support the deletion of homosexuality from the DSM-II define this condition as simply "one form of sexual behavior like other forms of sexual behavior which are not by themselves psychiatric disorders." They do not specify what "other forms" are meant or, in fact, give any clinical information by which to assess their comparison. Further, they seek to present the entire issue as if it were largely a matter of civil rights.

It is the assumption of those of us who oppose this deletion that every member of the American Psychiatric Association already agrees that all social injustices inflicted on the homosexual should be ended immediately. Our profession need not be influenced via its nomenclature to concur in the necessity for abolishing civil wrongs against anyone. However, the sacrifice of scientific standards of excellence in diagnosis serves neither the goal of individual liberties nor the best interests of our society. In summary, we object to the deletion because we believe:

1) That exclusive homosexuality (repetitive sexual behavior with same sex partners in adult life) develops experientially and is a disorder of psycho-sexual development.
2) That homosexuality is an outcome of conflicts beginning in early childhood.
3) That it is scientifically fallacious to assert, as is done in the Nomenclature Committee's definition of "Sexual Orientation Disturbance" that individuals are disturbed *only* if they cannot adjust to homosexuality. The term "Sexual Orientation Disturbance" does not include that large group of homosexuals who are disturbed by the very pathology which creates homosexuality.

To claim that homosexuality does not belong in our diagnostic manual is not to advance psychiatry but, rather, to regress to an earlier time when our knowledge of human behavior had not yet developed to its current status. It countervails the gains of painstaking scientific progress and renders chaotic fundamental truths about the inter-relationship of anatomy and psychosexual identity. It is put forth by those advocating this change that homosexuality does not meet the criteria for a psychiatric disorder i.e., it does not cause subjective distress and it is not associated with impairment in functioning. We assert on the basis of *clinical* findings that the homosexual suffers from multiple intra-psychic anxieties which are causative of his disorder and force him to flee from opposite sex partners. Furthermore, the homosexual's impairment in functioning is an extreme one: he is unable to function in his appropriate sexual role in accordance with anatomy and biological reality.

Charles W. Socarides, M.D., New York
Robert J. McDevitt, M.D., Cincinnati
Armand M. Nicholi, M.D., Boston
  et al.

Editorial Note: *Action Paper on Sexuality*

The American Psychiatric Association has also been struggling with the issue of the civil rights of homosexuals. The following resolution on homosexuality and civil rights was approved by the APA assembly and presented for consideration to the Committee on Psychiatry and the Law of the APA (as reported in the Washington Psychiatric Society *Newsletter*, November 1973).

WHEREAS, Homosexuality per se implies no impairment in judgment, stability, reliability or general social or vocational capabilities,

THEREFORE, BE IT RESOLVED, That the American Psychiatric Association deplores all public and private discrimination against homosexuals in such areas as employment, housing, public accommodations, and licensing, and declares that no burden of proof of such judgment, capacity or reliability shall be placed upon homosexuals greater than that imposed on any other persons.

FURTHER, The American Psychiatric Association supports and urges the enactment of civil rights legislation at the local, state and federal level that would offer homosexual citizens the same protections now guaranteed to others on the basis of race, creed, color, etc.

FURTHER, The American Psychiatric Association supports and urges the repeal of all legislation making criminal offenses of sexual acts performed by consenting adults in private.

(The American Psychiatric Association is, of course, aware that many other persons in addition to homosexuals are irrationally denied their civil rights on the basis of pejorative connotations derived from diagnostic or descriptive terminology used in psychiatry, such as schizophrenia, and deplores all such discrimination. This resolution singles out dicrimination against homosexuals only because of the pervasive discriminatory acts directed against this group and the existence of specific laws directed against homosexual behavior.)

EDITORIAL COMMENT

All too often, persons afflicted with mental retardation are seen only in terms of a number—their IQ. It is not appreciated that within the limits of their mental capacity they represent a varied population in terms of their capacity for habilitation, medical and psychiatric treatment, vocational usefulness within the community, and utilization of various civil rights, such as the right to make a will, the right to marry, the right to hold a driver's license, etc. The following selections will provide some indication of current scientific thinking about these issues, as well as indicate some of the problems to be faced in research, in diagnosis, and in finding a common language (nomenclature).

DIAGNOSIS OF MENTAL RETARDATION

The identification and diagnosis of mental retardation can prove one of the most challenging problems confronting the primary physician. Over 200 causes of retardation have been identified, yet in most cases the physician can make no specific etiological diagnosis. He can define retardation only in terms of functional characteristics, of significant impairments in intellectual functioning, and in the social adaptation of the individual.

A recent definition of mental retardation—a modification of that proposed by the American Association on Mental Deficiency—is as follows: "Mental retardation refers to significantly sub-average intellectual functioning which manifests itself during the developmental period and is characterized by inadequacy in adaptive behavior (Kidd, J. W.: *Ment. Retard.* 2:209 [Aug.] 1964)."

The nature of impairment varies with the age of the individual. Below school age it is a lag in self-help, locomotion, eating, and communications skills; in school, disability in learning; and at the adult level, inability to remain independent or to meet employment requirements. Hence the process of evaluation and provision of services is a dynamic one, and the physician's role changes with the advancing age and individual needs of each retardate.

Considered in this way, as individuals the retarded do not fall neatly into any classification. They vary widely in degree of intellectual deficit and social adaptability. Some have associated physical handicaps and emotional problems; some do not. Some require protective care; others achieve a striking degree of independence. Some remain identified as retarded; others slip back into the general population without occasioning any further special concern.

Granted this difficulty in tidy classification, the physician may wish to become familiar with the definition of commonly used terms. Seen in terms of intellectual potential, the "mildly" retarded child is generally defined within the intelligence-quotient range of 50 to 70; the "moderately" retarded, 35 to 50; the "severely" retarded, 20 to 35; and the "profoundly" retarded, below 20.

In terms of educational potential, retarded children are described as "educable," "trainable," or "totally dependent." The educable individual may achieve an academic competence of fourth- or fifth-grade level, a moderate amount of social adjustment, and a satisfactory degree of self-support via occupations not requiring abstract thought. The trainable child may attain an acceptable level of self-care, social adjustment to home and neighborhood, and a degree of economic usefulness via the home, residential facility, or sheltered workshop. The totally dependent child requires assistance in personal care, makes little response to the environment, and usually requires permanent institutionalization.

The magnitude of the problem of retardation is probably best expressed by the fact that 3% of newborn infants will be diagnosed at some time during their lives as suffering from this syndrome. This figure on incidence may not be translated into an equivalent figure on prevalence, however. We do not know how many mentally retarded individuals there are in a community of 100,000 at any given moment. Diagnostic difficulties hamper such studies. While it is relatively easy to measure intelligence, diagnosis also requires consideration of impairment in adaptation, a characteristic much harder to quantify.

Present evidence indicates that prevalence varies with age. Only during the school years do general adaptation and measured intelligence correlate to a high degree. Therefore, most retarded children, particularly the mildly impaired, become clinically visible only upon school entrance and become asymptomatic again in adulthood. In the more severely affected groups, increased mortality takes many. In all probability, the diagnosed mentally retarded are closer to 1% than to 3% of the population.

Excerpted with permission from *Mental Retardation, A Handbook for the Primary Physician*, Report of the American Medical Association Conference on Mental Retardation, April 9 to 11, 1964.

MENTAL RETARDATION: DEVELOPMENT OF AN INTERNATIONAL CLASSIFICATION SCHEME

Michael J. Begab, Ph.D., and Gerald D. LaVeck, M.D.

Mental retardation is a universal phenomenon. It occurs, with varying degrees of frequency, in families from all walks of life in both developed and underdeveloped countries. In its most severe forms it is a source of great trauma, hardship, and despair to parents and is an economic and social burden to communities. Even the milder forms of intellectual handicap pose serious threats to individual self-fulfillment, family security, and national productivity. The most affluent of nations can ill afford such losses in their human resources.

The prevention and treatment of mental retardation on both the individual and societal levels rest fundamentally on a fuller understanding of its causes and pathogenesis, on concerned and skilled professional practitioners, and on the commitment of appropriate resources at all levels of government. Efforts to reach the first of these goals have been greatly enhanced in recent decades through basic and applied research. During this period we have identified additional clinical syndromes, developed a technology for prenatal diagnosis and prevention, improved nutritional and medical intervention techniques, and made progress toward solving the mysteries surrounding the transmission of genetic materials at the cellular level.

In the behavioral sciences much has been learned about the impact of environmental deprivation on mental growth and the compensating effects of early stimulation, about methods for promoting language development and reading skills, and about the untapped capacities of many retarded individuals for socially useful living. Perhaps most important of all is the growing recognition that in most forms of retardation, even where a single etiological factor can be isolated, the individual's functional performance is the product of the interaction of his biological makeup and environmental events and can be modified. The potential for behavioral change, sometimes to the point of reversibility, represents one of the most significant concepts in the field to emerge in recent years.

The changing attitudes of psychiatrists, pediatricians, and obstetricians toward the mentally retarded stem in part from this new conceptualization of the problem and the growing conviction that even where "cures" are not possible, informed treatment of the individual and his family can significantly aid life adjustment. To capitalize more fully on this burgeoning interest, these disciplines need more precise information on hazards to fetal development, symptomatology and treatment potentials for specific diagnostic conditions, and the values and limitations of psychological test measurements. Furthermore, to keep abreast of new discoveries and program developments, these disciplines must share a terminology and language that permit communication. Our failure in this latter area has seriously handicapped efforts of professionals from different countries to learn from one another.

The World Health Organization, mindful of these deficiencies and of our increasing fund of knowledge, has embarked upon a series of seminars to develop an international scheme for the diagnosis, classification, and reporting of statistics in psychiatric disorders, including mental retardation. This effort comes at a most opportune time. Comparative data among countries on the incidence and prevalence of mental retardation and the factors with which specific conditions are associated are not highly reliable. Although there are significant variations in prenatal care, population homogeneity, disease control, degree of environmental deprivation, and other factors causative or contributory to mental retardation, reported statistical differences may be more artifactual than real. Differences in the definition and conceptualization of mental retardation, inadequacies and variations in classification schemes used, confusion of terminology, and cultural variability in demands and expectations for human performance are only a few of the artifacts that preclude valid comparisons. Within and among countries, meaningful planning for the retarded cannot be accomplished until these issues are resolved.

Excerpted and reprinted with permission from *American Journal of Psychiatry* 128. (May Supplement, 1972): 1. Copyright 1972, The American Psychiatric Association.

QUESTIONS FOR DISCUSSION

1. Be prepared to present an illustration from your own experience, or from a case you have read about in law school, of the operation of one or more of the "ego defenses": of the transference–counter-transfenence phenomena.
2. Why might as much as thirty percent of the text of a psychiatrist's report on a forty-year-old man be devoted to a description of the first ten years of his life?
3. How might different concepts of psychic normality account for conflicting testimony by psychiatrists as to the *degree* of psychopathology in a defendant?
4. With which psychiatric observations is there most apt to be disagreement:
   a. Whether the patient is "mentally ill"?
   b. What type of mental illness he has?
   c. Whether the diagnosed condition affected his behavior?
5. What significance does such disagreement have for the lawyer?
6. What might constitute "secondary gains" from the "psychiatrically sick role" for a fifty-year-old employee whose work entails hard manual labor? What, if any, significance do such "gains" have in the field of workmen's compensation?
7. How might the criminal law more adequately take account of the "advantages" of the "bad" role as opposed to the "sick" role?
8. How might defense counsel in a capital case approach the problem of conflicting diagnoses, where the defense psychiatrist testifies that the defendant is a "schizophrenic" and the prosecution witness that he is "merely" a "schizoid personality"?
9. How might differential concepts of "functional" and "organic" disorders be of concern to the lawyer?

SUGGESTIONS FOR ADDITIONAL READING

Brenner, C. *An Elementary Textbook of Psychoanalysis.* New York: International Universities Press, 1955. (Also available in paperback edition), pp. 1–32.

Brill, A. *Freud's Contribution to Psychiatry.* New York: W. W. Norton & Co., 1944, pp. 13–46.

Cleckley, H. *The Mask of Sanity.* 2d ed. St. Louis: C. V. Mosby, 1950, pp. 395–484.

Erikson, E. *Childhood and Society.* New York: W. W. Norton & Co., 1950, pp. 44–67, 219–33.

Freeman, T., Cameron, J. L., and McGhie, A. *Chronic Schizophrenia.* New York: International Universities Press, 1958, Chapters 2, 11, and 15.

Freud, A. *The Ego and the Mechanisms of Defense.* London: Hogarth Press, 1937, pp. 3–113.

Freud, S. "History of the Psychoanalytic Movement," *The Basic Writings of Sigmund Freud.* New York: Random House, 1938, pp. 931–77.

Freud, S. *New Introductory Lectures on Psychoanalysis.* New York: W. W. Norton & Co., 1933, pp. 82–112.

Menninger, K. *The Vital Balance.* New York: Viking Press, 1963.

Menninger, W. *Psychiatry—Its Evolution and Present Status.* Ithaca: Cornell University Press, 1948.

Peters, F. *The World Next Door.* New York: Farrar, Straus, and Cudahy, 1949.

Hollingshead, A., and Redlich, F. *Social Class and Mental Illness.* New York: John Wiley and Sons, 1958.

4

Current Methods of Psychiatric Treatment and Their Legal and Ethical Implications

INTRODUCTION

As noted in the addendum to Dr. Overholzer's article (See above, Chapter 1), the changes in psychiatry over the past twenty-five years are basically of two types. First, there have been changes in treatment toward the concept that psychiatric care is optimally delivered within the family and community. Second, there have been the introduction and refinement of a number of specific new treatment techniques, both organic and psychotherapeutic.

Changes in treatment philosophy. The major conceptual change in psychiatry during the last generation has been from treating major psychiatric illness in an isolated "asylum" (either a public state hospital or a private mental institution) to an attempt to keep the patient in his own home and community setting. Most important in this change was the passage of the National Mental Health Act in 1963, directing that a number of Community Mental Health Centers be established throughout the country. There are now 391 such centers operating in the United States, with another 150 funded and in the planning stage.[1] Each center is mandated to provide comprehensive psychiatric services (including inpatient and outpatient care, an emergency 24-hour walk-in clinic, day hospital services, and consultation and educational services to the community) in a setting close to the patient's home. Due to uncertainty of state and federal funding, the future of the community mental health centers is unknown. This writer's guess is that they will continue performing valuable functions, but will need increasing supplementation from the private sector and possibly from existing state hospital systems. These will be necessitated by funding reductions, increased reliance on contractual relationships with private facilities, and the as yet uncertain parameter of national health insurance legislation.

Both public and private providers of psychiatric inpatient care have moved toward more liberal use of day care (partial hospitalization) facilities and the provision of open-door inpatient units (as contrasted with the locked units of prior decades).

Along with the community psychiatry approach there has been an increase in the number of psychiatric units in general hospitals. It is estimated that such units have increased about 60 percent in the past decade, from about 485 units in 1963 to about 785 units in 1973.[2] These units refute the notion that psychiatric illnesses are uniquely different from other medical illnesses. They promote the ideal of treatment within the community, and of rapid return to work, school, and home. The average length of stay in such units is about eighteen days.

Private psychiatric hospitals are also now being built within the community rather than in the countryside. Recognition of the specialized needs of many patients has spurred development of a number of private hospitals devoted to quality, multimodality treatment.

Newer psychiatric treatment methods. The community-oriented approach outlined above would have yielded little result had it not been for the simultaneous proliferation of useful treatment modalities. As indicated in Chapter 1, prior to World War II, psychiatry could offer only custodial

---

[1] Personal communication, Mr. Giraldi, Department of Health, Education, and Welfare, Public Health Services, Alcohol, Drug Abuse, and Mental Health Administration. March 26, 1974.

[2] Personal communication, Joint Information Service of The American Psychiatric Association and National Association for Mental Health, March 26, 1974.

care to the severely ill, electroshock treatment to the depressed, sedatives to calm the insomniac, and intensive and lengthy individual psychotherapy and psychoanalysis to the neurotic. In the past twenty years, however, a number of new treatment modalities have been introduced and refined.

Organic therapies. Psychiatry witnessed a major breakthrough in 1953 with the introduction of chlorpromazine (Thorazine[tm]), the first effective tranquilizer for severely disturbed patients. Within a few years a variety of antianxiety agents, such as chlordiazepoxide (Librium)[tm] and related compounds, were developed. They have done much to hasten recovery from neurotic (less severe) illness. In the late 1950s the first antidepressant compounds were shown to be clinically effective and safe. Use of antidepressants, such as impramine (Tofranil[tm]), has obviated the need for hospitalization in many cases of depression. In the late 1960s lithium carbonate passed from a research tool to a clinically useful drug in the treatment of manic depressive illnesses.

Along with these specific biological modes of therapy, a body of experimental data has accumulated, indicating that biological factors operate as contributory agents in many, if not most, serious psychiatric diseases. The fruits of this research are just now being applied to clinical treatment. The time is near when the diagnosis of specific chemical and constitutional factors will guide the selection of specific types and doses of medication.

Experimental modalities in organic therapy that offer promise for the future include electrosedation, the use of heroin substitutes in the treatment of addiction, and the refinement of psychosurgical and electroconvulsive techniques. The legal and ethical implications of electroshock therapy and psychosurgery will be dealt with in more detail later in this chapter.

The psychotherapies. A number of advances have also been made in psychotherapeutic technique. Under the pressures of World War II, military psychiatry began to recognize the value of short-term individual psychotherapy and of group therapy. Short-term individual psychotherapy, often in combination with drug therapy, is today a common form of effective outpatient treatment.[3]

Until recently, group therapy had been thought of chiefly as a second-best treatment choice for those who could not afford individual psychoanalysis. However, group therapy is now seen as a primary treatment modality, with results equal to or better than individual therapy in properly selected cases.[4] In Washington, D.C., a psychiatrically sophisticated city, group therapy is the most widely used form of treatment in terms of number of patients served.[5]

Family therapy is an effective way of dealing with multiple neurotic problems occurring within a family. Ineffective, nonproductive family interaction can be treated efficiently by seeing the family together as a unit or together with similarly troubled families in a multiple family group.

Therapeutic community approaches to day care and hospital treatment have tended both to increase treatability of many psychiatric difficulties and to make more efficient use of the physician's time. The therapeutic community approach involves a change from the traditional one-to-one doctor-patient relationship (with the healing or cure transmitted from the physician to the patient) to a team approach in which the physician, nurse, paramedical technicians, patients, and families work together to effect a total, 24-hour-a-day therapeutic experience.

Two new types of "talking treatment" exist apart from the investigation of "psychodynamics" or family dynamics: (1) The first is behavioral therapy, in which specific psychiatric symptoms (such as fear of flying or social shyness) are subjected to relatively brief courses of outpatient treatment. Basically, behavior therapy endeavors by a variety of means to treat psychiatric problems by reinforcing healthy, adaptive behavior and "extinguishing" neurotic behavior, without reference to underlying "causes." Because some types of behavior therapy dealing with token economies and negative reinforcement techniques raise special legal and ethical questions, the behavior therapies will be dealt with in greater detail in a later section. (2) The second is sexual therapy. A number of sexual dysfunctions can be treated rapidly and effectively by methods first developed by Drs. Masters and Johnson.[6]

---

[3] Reed (*Health Insurance and Psychiatric Care: Utilization and Cost*, by Lewis S. Reed, Evelyn Myers, and Patricia Scheidmandel, American Psychiatric Association, 1972, Washington, D.C.) reports data from ten group practice plans showing that the average number of visits per patient per year ranged from 4.2 to 18.8. Data presented by one typical group plan showed that 91 percent of all patients had 20 or fewer visits.

[4] James T. Quattlebaum, "Medically Speaking . . . Group Psychotherapy, New Respect For an Old Technique," *Maryland State Medical Journal* (February 1969).

[5] Results of questionnaire sent to all members of the Washington Psychiatric Society, as reported in the Washington Psychiatric Society *Newsletter*, January 1973.

[6] William H. Masters and Virginia E. Johnson, *Human Sexual Response* (Boston, Massachusetts: Little, Brown, 1966). William H. Masters and Virginia E. Johnson, *Human Sexual Inadequacy* (Boston, Massachusetts: Little, Brown, 1970).

In addition to these newer methods, psychoanalysis and psychoanalytic psychotherapy have remained essential treatment techniques for appropriately selected patients. Psychoanalysis has also provided the basic personality theory from which many of the newer treatment modalities derive.

Still in the experimental stage, but showing promise for the future, are biofeedback techniques, which combine elements of both organic and psychological methods in the treatment of psychosomatic disorders, tension states, and anxiety neuroses.

It is the purpose of this chapter to give the reader a general idea of the state of psychiatric theory today. The articles by Dr. Durell and Dr. Zubin present clear expositions of the growing eclectism in psychiatry. Basically, Drs. Durell and Zubin point out that concepts of multicausality seem more appropriate to the state of the art today than the futile "nature versus nurture" controversy that has plagued psychiatry for so long. The selection from Jarvik indicates the difficulties inherent in trying to determine a single cause for behavioral aberration: in this case the XYY chromosomal pattern. Professor Ferster's article confronts some of the perplexing issues that the criminal justice system must face in the light of such new findings as the XYY chromosome. The chapter concludes with a section devoted to three special forms of treatment that have come to the public's attention or have generated considerable controversy recently. Dr. Lebensohn discusses the facts about electroshock therapy and sorts them out from the myths. The articles from the American Medical Association, the excerpts from the TV program, "Firing Line," and the excerpt from Dr. Brown's testimony before the Senate Committee highlight the current controversy about the use and abuse of psychosurgery. Finally, the articles by Ferster and Halleck deal with some questions raised by behavior therapy. In this latter connection, the reader's attention is also directed to the Editorial note in Chapter 15, on "behavior mod" in corrections.

INTRODUCTION TO *BIOLOGICAL PSYCHIATRY*

Jack Durell, M.D.

. . . Psychiatry is a branch of medicine. . . .

Its primary goal is the prevention or alteration of psychological states that are considered disordered or undesirable. As in other branches of medicine its practitioners apply techniques for producing change that have been empirically derived prior to the development of a comprehensive understanding of the processes that are disordered. Its investigations are most properly concerned with characterizing and classifying the disordered states that come within its domain and discovering and validating techniques for altering them.

Traditionally, medical scientists have also concerned themselves with investigating the etiology and pathogenesis of disordered states and the mechanism of action of the agents altering them. From an intellectual point of view, the value of such studies is self-evident.

The justification often given, however, is that only through a knowledge of the etiology can there be effective treatment of the "basic causes" of disordered states. Although the elucidation of etiology is important, an overemphasis of the need to identify single "basic causes" is undesirable. Rarely in medicine is it possible to define a single necessary and sufficient cause for a disordered state and even when such is possible, many other factors may be causative in the sense that they increase the probability of occurrence of the necessary and sufficient event.

To illustrate the complexity of the problem, let us consider two infectious diseases, chronic pulmonary tuberculosis and general paresis. In both these diseases, the statement is generally made that the etiological agent is known, that is, the tubercle bacillus and spirochete, *Trepo-*

Excerpted and reprinted with permission from *Biological Psychiatry* by Jack Durell (New York: John Wiley and Sons, 1973).

*nema pallidum,** respectively. Is that not, however, simplistic? By definition, these agents are necessary conditions for the disease. It should not be forgotten, however, that this is brought about by a process of circular logic. If these diseases were defined by any clinical criteria other than the presence of the infectious organisms, certain patients would probably be included in whom the organisms were not present! This is not to argue against the value of arbitrarily defining the presence of a certain condition as necessary for the diagnosis of a disordered state. It cannot be said, however, that the exposure to a given dose of the agents involved is sufficient for the development of the disease. Whether tuberculosis will be acquired with a given exposure depends on factors of resistance which in turn are dependent on genetic, nutritional, and other environmental factors (Vaillant 1962). Furthermore, the likelihood of exposure depends on socioenvironmental factors. In addition, the progress of the disease once contracted is strongly dependent on genetic and environmental factors.

Similar considerations apply to general paresis.† It is strikingly apparent that social factors play a strong role in determining the probability of both the acquisition of primary syphilis and its progress untreated into general paresis. Is the "basic cause" of general paresis *Treponema pallidum* or social factors that lead to the transmission of syphilis and the failure to treat certain individuals early in the progress of the disease? The answer probably depends on whether the responder is a bacteriologist or a sociologist. The practitioner interested in the prevention and cure of general paresis had better not become overconcerned with "basic causes"; he must learn from both the bacteriologist and the sociologist.

Perhaps the point above has been labored, but there are elements in it that have been only slowly learned by many psychiatrists. Too often psychiatry has seemed to polarize itself into psychological and biological camps.‡ Each have argued the essential validity of their approaches, and within the two major camps minor warring tribes have emerged. Some psychoanalysts have discouraged the application of techniques derived from learning theory to symptom removal because such techniques do not get at "basic causes," for example, unresolved oedipal conflicts. On the other hand,

some biologically oriented psychiatrists viewing schizophrenia as a genetically determined defect state have discouraged the active social rehabilitation of schizophrenic patients because that could not alter the basic disease process assumed to be operative. In our view, because no school of thought has developed a comprehensive scientific psychology based on full knowledge of the human organism, there are no sufficient logical grounds to exclude any of the multiple approaches to treatment and research. . . . [*The ultimate intellectual task is the integration of all the bits of knowledge obtained through each of the multiple approaches*]. . . .

Though mention was made above of factionalism in psychiatry, there is increasing evidence of the opposite tendency. An intellectual atmosphere appears to be developing that allows for the importance of multiple physical and psychological factors in the etiology and pathogenesis of the psychological disorders (eclecticism). Similarly, it is acknowledged that treatment ideally often consists of the skillful utilization of somatic and psychological agents of change. Even though this eclectic attitude appeals intellectually, it should be remembered that with each disorder a well-controlled empirical demonstration that clinically significant change can be produced by either psychological, somatic intervention, or both is necessary. Similarly, certainty as to whether multiple factors are involved in etiology also requires empirical validation. . . .

Little is known of the nature of the somatic etiological factors in the disorders of major concern to psychiatrists. In part, this is due to the tendency of psychiatry to focus on the functional disorders (those without known organic etiologies) and to virtually exclude from its attention those psychological disorders with known somatic etiologies: for example, the mental deficiencies secondary to inborn errors of metabolism; the psychoses associated with endocrinopathies or other metabolic diseases, general paresis, and many others. On the other hand, the extensive studies of the familial incidence of certain psychological disorders are strong evidence for the importance of genetic factors, thus somatic factors in etiology. Most recent have been the studies of familial incidence of psychological disorders in the biological and adoptive families of schizophrenic patients who had been adopted early in life. These provide strong evidence for the importance of genetic factors in the etiology of schizophrenia and are perhaps the most conclusive evidence for the role of somatic factors in the etiology of any "functional disorders" (Kety et al. 1968; Heston & Denney 1968). . . .

---

* [Ed. note: The infectious agents in tuberculosis and syphilis, respectively.]

† [Ed. note: i.e., syphilis of the central nervous system.]

‡ See Akiskal article, Chapter 2, above.

REFERENCES

Bourne, H. R., Bunney, W. E., Jr., Colburn, R. W., Davis, M. J., Davis, J. N., Shaw, D. M., and Coppen, A. J. Noradrenaline, 5-hydroxytryptamine, and 5-hydroxyindoleacetic acid in hindbrains of suicidal patients. *Lancet*, 2, 805–8 (1968).

Bunney, W. E., Jr., and Davis, J. M. Norepinephrine in depressive reactions: A review. *Arch. Gen. Psychiat.*, 13, 483–94 (1965).

Bunney, W. E., Jr., Goodwin, F., and Murphy, D. Theoretical implications of the switch process. *Arch. Gen. Psychiat.*, in press.

Caspari, E. W. Gene action as applied to behavior. Chap. 6 in *Behavior-genetic analysis*, J. Hirsch (ed.). McGraw-Hill, New York, 1967, pp. 112–34.

Dole, V. D., Nyswander, M. E., and Warner, A. Successful treatment of 750 criminal addicts. *J.A.M.A.*, 206, 2708–11 (1968).

Durell, J., Baer, L., and Green, R. Electrolytes and psychoses. Chap. 10 in *Biochemistry, schizophrenias and affective illnesses*, H. Himwich (ed.). Williams and Wilkins, Baltimore, Maryland, 1970, pp. 283–307.

Evarts, E. V. A discussion of research methods as applied to physiological studies of psychiatric patients. *Psychiatric Research Reports*, No. 9, American Psychiatric Association, 1958.

Ginsburg, B. E. Genetic parameters in behavioral research. Chap. 7 in *Behavior-genetic analysis*, J. Hirsch (ed.). McGraw-Hill, New York, 1967, pp. 135–53.

Gottesman, I. I., and Shields, J. In pursuit of the schizophrenic genotype. Chap. 6 in *Progress in human behavior genetics*, S. G. Vanderberg (ed.). Johns Hopkins Press, Baltimore, Md., 1968, pp. 67–103.

Grinker, R. R., Sr. Reception of communication by patients in depressive states. *Arch. Gen. Psychiat.*, 10, 576–80 (1964).

Hamburg, D. A. Genetics of adrenocortical hormone metabolism in relation to psychological stress. Chap. 8 in *Behavior-genetic analysis*, J. Hirsch (ed.). McGraw-Hill, New York, 1967, pp. 154–75.

Heston, L. L., and Denney, D. Interactions between early life experience and biological factors in schizophrenia. *J. Psychiat. Res.*, 6, Suppl. 1, 363 (1968).

Horwitt, M. K. Fact and artifact in the biology of schizophrenia. *Science*, 124, 429 (1958).

Hsia, D. Y-Y. The hereditary metabolic diseases. Chap. 9 in *Behavior-genetic analysis*, J. Hirsch (ed.). McGraw-Hill, New York, 1967, pp. 176–210.

Hyde, R. W. Psychological and social determinants of drug action. In *The dynamics of psychiatric drug therapy*, G. J. Sarwer-Foner (ed.). Springfield, Illinois, 1960, pp. 297–315.

Jones, E. In *The life and work of Sigmund Freud*, Vol. 1. Basic Books, New York, 1953, p. 395.

Kety, S. S. Biochemical theories of schizophrenia. *Science*, 129, 1528–1532; 1590–1596 (1959).

Kety, S. S., Rosenthal, D., Wender, P. H., and Shulsinger, F. The types and prevalence of mental illness in the biological and adoptive families of adopted schizophrenics. *J. Psychiat. Res.*, 6, Suppl. 1, 345 (1968).

Klein, D. F., and Davis, J. M. In *Diagnosis and drug treatment of psychiatric disorders*. The Williams and Wilkins Co., Baltimore, Md., 1969.

Kringlen, E. Clinical variability in schizophrenic twin partners. Chap. 8 in *Progress in human behavior genetics*. S. G. Vandenberg (ed.). Johns Hopkins Press, Baltimore, Md., 1968, pp. 127–35.

Lapin, I. P., and Oxenkrug, G. F. Intensification of the central serotoninergic processes as a possible determinant of the thymoleptic effect. *Lancet*, 1, 132–36 (1969).

Pare, C. M., and Yeung, D. P. H. 5-Hydroxytryptamine noradrenaline, and dopamine in brainstem hypothalmus, and caudate nucleus of controls and of patients committing suicide by coal-gas poisoning. *Lancet*, 2, 133–35 (1969).

Pollin, W., Stabenau, J. R., Hoffer, A., Mosher, L. R., and Spillman, B. The NIMH study of a series of monozygotic twins discordant for schizophrenia. In *Progress in human behavior*, S. G. Vandenberg (ed.). Johns Hopkins Press, Baltimore, Md., 1968, pp. 137–49.

Rosenthal, D., and Kety, S. S. (eds.). The transmission of schizophrenia: Proceedings of the second research conference of the foundation's fund for research in psychiatry, Dorado, Puerto Rico, June 26–July 1, 1967. *J. Psychiat. Res.*, 6 (1968).

Schildkraut, J. J. The catecholamine hypothesis of affective disorders: A review of supporting evidence. *Am. J. Psychiat.*, 122, 509–22 (1965).

Schildkraut, J. J., Gordon, E. K., and Durell, J. Catecholamine metabolism in affective disorders: I. Normetanephrine and VMA excretion in depressed patients treated with imipramine. *J. Psychiat. Res.*, 3, 213 (1965).

Schildkraut, J. J., and Kety, S. S. Biogenic amines and emotions. *Science*, 156, 21–37 (1967).

Schou, M. Lithium in psychiatric therapy and prophylaxis. *J. Psychiat. Res.*, 6, 67 (1968).

Shaw, D. M., Camps, F. E., and Eccleston, E. G. 5-Hydroxytryptamine in the hind brain of depressive suicides. *Brit. J. Psychiat.*, 113, 1407–11 (1967).

Unger, S. M. Mescaline, LSD, psilocybin and personality change: A review. *Psychiatry*, 26, 111–25 (1963).

Vaillant, G. E. Tuberculosis: An historical analogy to schizophrenia. *Psychosom. Med.*, 24, 225 (1962).

SCIENTIFIC MODELS FOR PSYCHOPATHOLOGY IN THE 1970's

Joseph Zubin, Ph.D.

. . . It is too late in the age to try to reduce etiology to a unidimensional framework such as that provided by genetics or ecology, since the evidence is so clear that multiple etiology will be found to be the rule rather than the exception. Nevertheless, it is important to push each unidimensional model as far as we can, before inquiring into its interaction with other models. We are somewhat in the same position as a statistician faced with a problem in the analysis of variance. He knows full well that none of his main effects operate independently and is fully aware that he must look at their interactions, but before he can do so, he must first separate the main primary effects. This is how we will proceed. We will formulate each one of our models independently and then look for their interactions.

There are six such models now in the field:

1) The *ecological model* simply stated assumes that the sources of man's mental disorders are to be sought in the characteristics of the ecological niche which he occupies and that all of us are vulnerable to noxious niches. According to this model, the ecological forces impinging on the niche determine the particular nodal point occupied by the individual and thus determine his behavior. Among the contributions of this model have been the establishment of the importance of such factors as population density and crowding, socioeconomic level, educational level, occupation, degree of neighborhood disorganization, minority or majority status in the community, degree of isolation, and similar ecological factors in the productions of not only mental disorders but also of physical disorders. . . .

2) The *developmental model* stipulates that the origin of mental disorders is to be sought in the transitional stages which man passes through as he develops from fertilized ovum to fetus, neonate, child, adolescent, adult, presenium, and senium stages. Should there be lacking any of the needed nutrients or supplies that are required in passing from one level to the next, or should noxious events intervene, e.g., toxemia of pregnancy, perinatal difficulties, fetal or neonatal anoxia, isolation and deprivation in childhood, the probability of mental disorder is increased. Thus, if there is insufficient protein available while the brain is developing, if there are no suitable peers to help the shift from family dependence to peer acceptance, if in passing from later adulthood to the senium he fails to make the proper gradual disengagement, he may be at high risk of mental disorder. Some of the studies based on this model have indicated that in animals, the absence of peer play is far more important than the absence of mothering in later psychosexual and personality development, and in humans, absence of intimacy with friends during adolescence characterizes those who later become schizophrenic. . . .

3) The *learning and conditioning model* stipulates that one learns to become mentally ill even as he learns to become mentally well. According to the strict behavioral view, there is no need for assuming an underlying disorder which produces deviant behavior; instead the deviant behavior itself *is* the disorder and it is learned through experience, and not produced by an underlying disease. Since the abnormal behavior is learned, the usual methods of acquisition of normal behavior will describe the paths to abnormality.

Indeed, according to this model, many behaviors generally accepted as normal might well be labeled psychopathologic—by the community or even by the individual himself—if they occurred with markedly different frequency or intensity or on other than the typical or "acceptable" occasions. . . .

We have covered the three scientific models which may be regarded as *exogenous* since ecology, development, and learning depend so much on the influence of external forces impinging on the behavior of the individual.

Excerpted and reprinted with permission from *Seminars in Psychiatry* 4, no. 3 (August 1972): 283–96.

Some difficulty may arise in distinguishing among these three exogenous models. The ecological model is primarily concerned with the forces that produce a complex balanced system of interlocking subsystems in the niche an individual occupies and which may lead to maladaptive behavior. A learning theorist regards the world as does an engineer, subject to his manipulative ingenuity, and psychopathology is the result of manipulations of the environment by a person or his family and others leading to maladaptive behavior. Development is separated from learning in the same way as ethology differs from experimental learning theory. The former approaches the problems of psychopathology naturalistically and intervenes experimentally only to determine the underpinning of development, while the latter regards schedules of reinforcement, reward, and punishment as the basic underpinnings of maladaptive behavior. . . .

4) The *hereditary model* for the etiology of psychopathology is so well established that I am not going to spend any time discussing its importance, except to point out as a challenge, rather than as a conviction that strictly speaking *there are probably no genetic disorders nor any environmental disorders in our field. We designate a disorder as genetic when we are still ignorant of its environmental parameters and vice versa.** In most so-called genetic disorders, the hereditary component is necessary but not sufficient for producing a disorder. Similarly, for most so-called environmental disorders, the noxious environmental parameters are necessary but not sufficient. It is the interaction of both hereditary and environment factors that is both necessary and sufficient for producing a disorder. I can conceive of a genotype that could survive and maintain its health and prosper in the most inhospitable niche which our planet or any other planet can offer. By the same token I can conceive, at least in theory, of an ecological niche which could maintain the health and well-being of even the most deficient genotype who could hardly survive in the usual niches on our planet. . . .

5) So far as *the model for the internal environment* is concerned it stipulates that the sources of mental disorder are to be sought in the interior milieu—in the metabolic and biochemical characteristics of the organism, its body fluids, enzymes, and metabolic products. However, we must remember that the biochemical agents, like the genetic, may be necessary but not sufficient.

6) We now come to the last model, *the*

* See Rubin article, "Psychiatric Illness," Chapter 3, above.

neurophysiologic model which, simply stated, stipulates that the sources of psychopathology are to be sought in deviations in brain function, especially the electrophysiologic aspects of its functioning. . . .

To discover the full import of each of the six etiological models for mental disorder, we have to resort to a strategy which will permit the assessment of each of them separately. This presents us with a dilemma, since none of these models are sufficient in themselves. They are often necessary, but not sufficient alone in eliciting a given disorder. . . .

The most fruitful studies now in process are those which involve the intersection between two or more models. In fact, the very name neuropsychopharmacology is a testimony to the fact that it is in the intersection between neurophysiology, psychology, and pharmacology that the pay dirt lies. Perhaps the best known interaction is that between the ecological and genetic models or, as it used to be known, the interaction between nature and nurture. Another well-known interaction is that between the learning, the internal environment, and the neurophysiologic models which is best represented by the concept of psychosomatics and somatopsychics.

The interaction between the internal environment and neurophysiologic models is exemplified in the assumption that the modulation of neural transmitters by foreign substances (drugs) or by excess of endogeneous substances within the internal milieu is what lies at the bottom of the disturbances in processing information in schizophrenia or development of mood disturbance in affective disorders. . . .

We have omitted perhaps the most important determinant of man's stage behavior—his ability to be a self-starter, to alter developmental trends, to modify the internal environment as well as his neurophysiologic equipment. Unlike other organisms which are shaped by their environment through eons of gradual evolutionary developments, man can shape his own environment if he chooses to do so and has developed the know-how to apply changes not only to the exogenous but also to the endogenous environment. It is in these directions that the future of man's normal development, as well the containment and improvement of abnormal development, lies. . . .

REFERENCES

1. Barker, R. G. *Ecological Psychology*. Stanford, Calif.: Stanford University Press, 1968.
2. Blackburn, T. R. Sensuous-intellectual complementarity in science. *Science* 172:1003, 1971.

3. Brady, J. V., and Hunt, H. F. An experimental approach to the analysis of emotional behavior. *J. Psychol.* 40:313, 1955.

4. Dohrenwend, B. P., and Dohrenwend, B. S. *Social Status and Psychological Disorder.* New York: Wiley, 1969.

5. Dubos, R. *Am. Scholar* 41:16, 1971.

6. Estes, W. K., and Skinner, B. F. Some quantitative properties of anxiety. *J. Exp. Psychol.* 29:390, 1941.

7. Hammer, M., Polgar, S., and Salzinger, K. Speech predictability and social contact patterns in an informal group. *Hum. Organization.* 28:235, 1969.

8. Haughton, E., and Ayllon, T. Production and elimination of symptomatic behavior. *In* Ullmann, L. P., and Krasner, L. (eds.), *Case Studies in Behavior Modification.* New York: Holt, Rinehart & Winston, 1965.

9. Hefferline, R. F., and Perera, T. B. Proprioceptive discrimination of a covert operant without its observation by the subject. *Science* 139:834, 1963.

10. Jarvik, L. F., and Erlenmeyer-Kimling, L. Survey of familial correlations in measured intellectual functions. *In* Jervis, G. A., and Zubin, J. (eds.), *Psychopathology of Mental Development.* New York: Grune and Stratton, 1967, pp. 447–59.

11. Kaplan, A. *The Conduct of Inquiry.* San Francisco: Chandler, 1964.

12. Landis, C., and Zubin, J. The effect of thonzylamine hydrochloride and phenobarbital sodium on certain psychological functions. *J. Psychol.* 31:181, 1951.

13. Levit, R. A. Averaged evoked potential correlates of information processing in schizophrenics, psychotic depressives and normals. Ph.D. thesis, Columbia University, 1972.

14. Moore, D. J., and Shiek, D. A. Toward a theory of early infantile autism. *Psychol. Rev.* 78:451, 1971.

15. Murphy, H. B. M. Cultural factors in the genesis of schizophrenia. *In* Rosenthal, D., and Kety, S. S. (eds.), *The Transmission of Schizophrenia.* New York: Pergamon, 1968, pp. 137–54.

16. Murphy, H. B. M. Sociocultural factors in schizophrenia: a compromise theory. *In* Zubin, J. and Freyhan, F. (eds.), *Social Psychiatry.* New York: Grune & Stratton, 1968, pp. 74–92.

16a. Pasamanick, B. Epidemiologic investigations of some prenatal factors in the production of neuropsychiatric disorder. *In* Hoch, P. H., and Zubin, J. (eds.), *Comparative Epidemiology of the Mental Disorders.* New York: Grune & Stratton, 1961.

17. Reynolds, G. S., Catania, A. C., and Skinner, B. F. Conditioned and unconditioned aggression in pigeons. *J. Exp. Anal. Behav.* 6:73–74, 1963.

18. Rosenthal, D., and Kety, S. S. (eds.), *The Transmission of Schizophrenia.* New York: Pergamon, 1968.

19. Salzinger, K.: Behavior theory models of abnormal behavior. *In* Kietzman, M., Sutton, S., and Zubin, J. (eds.), *Experimental Approaches to Psychopathology.* New York: Academic, in press.

20. Sidman, M., Herrnstein, R. J., and Conrad, D. G. Maintenance of avoidance behavior by unavoidable shocks. *J. Comp. Physiol. Psychol.* 50:533, 1957.

21. Sutton, S. Fact and artifact in the psychology of schizophrenia. *In* Hammer, M., Salzinger, K., and Sutton, S. (eds.), *Psychopathology: Contributions from the Biological, Behavioral, and Social Sciences.* New York: Wiley, 1972, in press.

22. Ulrich, R. E., and Azrin, N. H. Reflexive fighting in response to aversive stimulation. *J. Exp. Anal. Behav.* 5:511, 1962.

23. Vernon, W., and Ulrich, R. Classical conditioning of pain-elicited aggression. *Science* 152:668, 1966.

24. Wenar, C. *Personality Development from Infancy to Adulthood.* Boston: Houghton Mifflin, 1971, p. 419.

25. Zubin, J. The biometric approach to psychopathology—revisited. (The Paul H. Hoch Lecture, 1968, of the American Psychopathological Association.) *In* Zubin, J., and Shagass, C. (eds.), *Neurobiological Aspects of Psychopathology.* New York: Grune & Stratton, 1969, pp. 281–309.

EDITORIAL COMMENT

As pointed out by Dr. Durell and Dr. Zubin, concepts of multicausality are gaining ascendency in modern psychiatric thought. This complicates the issue of whether a particular piece of behavior was determined by specific genetic, constitutional, or indeed even early environmental factors. In criminal proceedings it reduces the issue of free will to a matter of probabilities and degrees of freedom. It does the same in areas in which psychiatry and the law struggle together to predict human behavior; for example, in such issues as treatability, dangerousness, fitness for custody of a child, readiness for parole.

The discovery of the XYY chromosomal aberration highlights these issues and has already been a matter of concern in particular court cases. The article by Drs. Jarvik et al. summarizes the literature to date on the effects of the extra Y chromosome. The statistical review of the literature is too detailed for our present purposes, hence this excerpt. Those interested may refer to the original article or the references. The author's conclusions have been left intact. The implications of the scientific findings that Dr. Jarvik reviews for the criminal justice system are elucidated in Professor Ferster's article.

HUMAN AGGRESSION AND THE EXTRA Y CHROMOSOME: FACT OR FANTASY?

Lissy F. Jarvik, Victor Klodin, and Steven S. Matsuyama

. . . The scientific community has been divided for many years by a major question: Is human aggression an inborn biological urge which must become manifest in some form of violent or antisocial behavior, or is aggression learned as a response to particular environmental conditions or experiences which, under properly controlled circumstances, need not break through into overt acts of hostility?

Despite a great deal of attention, this serious question has never been answered satisfactorily. Such a determination is critical, however, because applied research aimed at curbing unnecessary and excessive violence proceeds either from the assumption that as a biologically based urge, aggression can be treated biologically or else channeled into some socially acceptable areas, or from the hypothesis that as a learned response, aggressive modes of behavior are not acquired if neither the need nor the opportunity exists for such learning to occur.

Recently uncovered clues may herald the revival of a biological approach and may have a profound effect on all future studies of aggressiveness in man. These clues emanate from the discovery that a chromosomal aberration in some mentally retarded male criminals of exceptionally tall stature and unusually aggressive temperament may be responsible for their violent behavior characteristics.

Chromosomes are thin threads of genetic material (DNA) and contain hereditary instructions for the growth and reproduction of every living cell in an organism. Physical traits, such as eye color, hair color, and height, are controlled by these hereditary messages. New and improved methods for studying human cells have permitted an accurate description of the chromosome complement (karyotype) and have led to the discovery of many chromosomal aberrations. The cells of the human body normally contain 46 chromosomes, 2 of them ("X" and "Y") being sex chromosomes responsible for sex determination. Cells in a normal woman's body have 2 X chromosomes, whereas each cell in a normal man has 1 X and 1 Y chromosome.

Instead of the normal complement of 46 chromosomes, the cells of some mentally retarded, tall criminals were found to contain 47, the extra one being a Y chromosome. This abnormality is known as the XYY genotype. When the association of an extra Y chromosome with tall stature, mental retardation, and aggressive behavior was first made (Jacobs, Brunton, Melville, Brittain, & McClemont 1965), it had a profound impact on the scientific community, the legal and medical professions, and the public at large. The reason for the excitement can be readily understood in the perspective of the knowledge available at the time, which consisted of only 11 cases in the entire world literature of what was then considered a rare syndrome. Suddenly, there was the study by Jacobs et al. reporting 7 additional cases among 197 mentally retarded criminals. An outstanding feature of these 7 cases was that they had no physical stigmata that would differentiate them from other males,

Excerpted and reprinted with permission from the *American Psychologist* 28 (August 1973): 674.

patients or not, except for their great height. Such had not been true of the earlier cases, many of whom had shown one or more physical abnormalities. Moreover, this was the first time that a specific behavioral abnormality, other than mental deficiency, had been linked to a chromosomal aberration. Soon, other investigators began to look for persons with the extra Y chromosome among tall retarded inmates of institutions for criminal offenders and discovered more than 100 of them in a scant four years.

Although there are exceptions, and they will be discussed later, the dominant features associated with the presence of an extra Y chromosome include unusual height, excessive episodic aggressiveness, and borderline intelligence. Not surprisingly, an extra Y chromosome has been detected in some of the most renowned murderers of our time. One of the first such cases was that of Robert Peter Tait, an Australian who was convicted in 1962 of bludgeoning to death an 81-year-old woman in a vicarage where he had gone seeking a handout. In 1965, Daniel Hugon, a 31-year-old French stablehand brutally strangled a Paris prostitute, with no apparent motivation. During the course of his trial in 1968, he was found to have an extra Y chromosome. In April 1969, six-foot, eight-inch, 240-pound John Farley, nicknamed "Jolly Green Giant" because he was usually good-natured and "Big Bad John" because he was subject to fits of violent temper, confessed to having beaten, strangled, raped, and mutilated a Queens, New York, woman. He was defended on the grounds that due to the presence in his cells of an extra Y chromosome, he had no control over his actions or his judgment, and should therefore be found not guilty "by reason of insanity resulting from a chromosome imbalance [Evansasbury 1969, p. 54]."

These and other similarly grisly cases were brought to public attention by attorneys who pleaded that their clients, charged with committing crimes of particular violence, could not be judged responsible for their actions. In some instances, the defense was successful; in others, it was not. . . .

Is There an XYY Syndrome?

Even though the triad of tall physique, short temper, and limited intelligence, as exemplified by the patient described above, is characteristic of the XYY syndrome, not one of the attributes is either necessary or sufficient for its diagnosis. Thus, great height is typical, and yet, several cases of record did not even grow to be six feet tall. Of course, the possibility exists that without the second Y chromosome these partic-

ular persons might have been even shorter than they were. Similarly, with regard to intelligence, although there is a preponderance of cases on the borderline of the dull normal range, there is a fair representation of persons with average intelligence and even a few with superior intelligence. Finally, not even aggressive, antisocial, or criminal behavior is a *sine qua non* of the XYY karyotype, as first demonstrated by the accidental discovery in Australia of an extra Y chromosome in a solid citizen and family man whose only outstanding characteristic was that he volunteered as a blood donor and thus happened to have his chromosomes scrutinized.

Indeed, the mounting number of exceptions to the characteristic features of the extra Y syndrome led to a series of headlines at the time of the 1969 annual meeting of the American Psychiatric Association questioning the relationship between the extra Y chromosome and aggressive behavior. "It appears that the XYY males in general have been falsely stigmatized" proclaimed the headlines; and the consensus was that "most XYY men are solid citizens." This opinion was not restricted to newspaper reporters, but appeared in a learned journal under the title "XYY Chromosomes: Premature Conclusions." Kessler and Moos (1969) concluded from their survey of the literature: "That XYY males are uncontrollably aggressive psychopaths appears to be nothing more than a myth promoted by the mass media [p. 442]." Others have refused to accept this conclusion (Gardner & Neu 1972).

Where are the data to resolve this controversy? Unfortunately, the tedious, time-consuming nature of human chromosome analysis and the requirement for highly skilled personnel make large-scale population surveys practically impossible.[2] Nonetheless, a thorough survey of the literature leads to the conclusion that a sufficient amount of information has been accumulated throughout the world to warrant an attempt at comparing the frequency of the XYY karyotype among various population groups. . . .

[The authors survey the literature extensively and conclude:]

It would seem that patients in mental hospitals are more prone to have an extra sex chromosome than men in the general population, but that the tendency is nonspecific, the probability of an extra X chromosome being as great as that of an extra Y chromosome. . . .

Criminals are the *only* group in which an extra Y chromosome occurs significantly more often than an extra X chromosome. *The data available so far, therefore, provide strong presumptive evidence for an association between criminal behavior and the extra Y chromo-*

some. Within a short time, the question should be settled definitively, since a new technique (fluorescent staining), which has become available during the past two years (Caspersson, Zech, Johansson, Lindsten, & Hulten 1970; Pearson, Bobrow, & Vosa 1970; Zech 1969), makes mass screening for extra Y chromosomes feasible.

XYY AND VIOLENCE

Whatever incidence may eventually be determined, it is safe to predict that persons with an extra Y chromosome will constitute but an insignificant proportion of the perpetrators of violent crimes. Yet, quite apart from questions of law and ethics, the XYY genotype may have importance exceeding by far its numerical impact in contributing to our understanding of aggressive behavior. As previously noted, the Y chromosome is the male-determining chromosome; therefore, it should come as no surprise that an extra Y chromosome can produce an individual with heightened masculinity, evinced by characteristics such as unusual tallness, increased fertility (although most XYYs do not have children, some have produced as many as 10), and powerful aggressive tendencies.

The XYY genotype may be seen as highlighting the association between maleness and violence. Being genetic, such a relationship cannot depend exclusively on external factors, although undoubtedly home environment, early upbringing, and a host of sociocultural factors have either reinforcing or inhibiting effects. In this respect, the extraordinarily large size of many XYY males dating back to early infancy (Hook & Kim 1971; Nielsen, Friedrich, & Zeuthen 1971) may lead to their being taunted by their peers and encouraged to physically aggressive behavior as a means of retaliation. However, this explanation is not sufficient to account for the hostile behavior, since children afflicted with other forms of gigantism have not shown noticeably aggressive behavior (Stephenson, Mellinger, & Manson 1968). . . .

Although the majority of violent crimes are committed by chromosomally normal persons, the increased frequency of XYY individuals among perpetrators of such crimes suggests that an extra Y chromosome predisposes to aggressive behavior. . . .

As discussed in the beginning of this article, many individuals have been recorded who, despite the presence of an extra Y chromosome, displayed no unusual aggressive behavior. How much the lack of aggression in certain persons with an extra Y chromosome can be ascribed to the particular genic content of their

Y chromosome and how much can be attributed to a fortuitous combination of environmental circumstances remain to be established. . . .

The novelty of the XYY approach to aggression is most important, for this approach takes as its basis an inherent or internal predisposition, yet seeks its solution in an understanding of external or environmental variables. It is this synthesis of positions which gives such research its enormous potential. . . .

REFERENCES

Abdullah, S., Jarvik, L. F., Kato, T., Johnston, W. C., & Lanzkron, J. The extra Y chromosome and its psychiatric implications. *Archives of General Psychiatry*, 1969, 21, 497–501.

Akesson, H. O., Forssman, H., & Wallin, L. Chromosomes of tall men in mental hospitals. *Lancet*, 1968, 2, 1040.

Baker, D., Telfer, M. A., Richardson, C. E., & Clark, G. R. Chromosome errors in men with antisocial behavior. *Journal of the American Medical Association*, 1970, 214, 869–78.

Bartlett, D. J., Hurley, W. P., Brand, C. R., & Poole, E. W. Chromosomes of male patients in a security prison. *Nature*, 1968, 219, 351–54.

Casey, M. D., Blank, C. E., Street, D. R. K., Segall, L. J., McDougall, J. H., McGrath, P. J., & Skinner, J. L. YY chromosomes and antisocial behavior. *Lancet*, 1966, 2, 859–60.

Caspersson, T., Zech, L., Johansson, C., Lindsten, J., & Hulten, M. Fluorescent staining of heteropycnotic chromosome regions in human interphase nuclei. *Experimental Cell Research*, 1970, 61, 472–74.

Close, H. G., Goonetilleke, A. S. R., Jacobs, P. A., & Price, W. H. The incidence of sex chromosomal abnormalities in mentally subnormal males. *Cytogenetics*, 1968, 7, 277–85.

Court-Brown, W. M., & Smith, P. G. Human population cytogenetics. *British Medical Bulletin*, 1969, 25, 74–80.

Daly, R. F. Neurological abnormalities in XYY males. *Nature*, 1969, 221, 472–73.

Davis, R. J., McGee, B. J., Empson, J., & Engel, E. XYY and crime. *Lancet*, 1970, 2, 1086.

Evansasbury, E. Chromosome slaying trial begins in Queens. *New York Times*, 1969, April 16, 54.

Falek, A., Craddick, R., & Collum, J. An attempt to identify prisoners with an XYY chromosome complement by psychiatric and psychological means. *Journal of Nervous and Mental Disease*, 1970, 150, 165–70.

Fattig, W. D. An XYY survey in a Negro prison population. *Journal of Heredity*, 1970, 61, 10.

Gardner, L. I., & Neu, R. L. Evidence linking an extra Y chromosome to sociopathic behavior. *Archives of General Psychiatry*, 1972, 26, 220–22.

Goodman, R. M., Miller, J. F., & North, C. Chromosomes of tall men. *Lancet*, 1968, 1, 1318.

Goodman, R. M., Smith, W. S., & Migeon, C. J. Sex chromosome abnormalities. *Nature*, 1967, 216, 942–43.

Graham, H. D., & Gurr, T. R. *Violence in America: Historical and comparative perspectives.* Washington, D.C.: U.S. Government Printing Office, 1969.

Griffiths, A. W., Richards, B. W., Zaremba, J., Abramowics, T., & Stewart, A. Psychological and sociological investigation of XYY prisoners. *Nature*, 1970, 227, 290–92.

Griffiths, A. W., & Zaremba, J. Crime and sex chromosome anomalies. *British Medical Journal*, 1967, 4, 622.

Hobbes, T. *Leviathan.* Oxford: Basil Blackwell, 1960.

Hook, E. B., & Kim, D. S. Height and antisocial behavior in XY and XYY boys. *Science*, 1971, 172, 284–86.

Howell, F. C. *Early man.* New York: Time, Inc., 1965.

Jacobs, P. A., Brunton, M., Melville, M. M., Brittain, R. P., & McClemont, W. F. Aggressive behavior, mental subnormality and the XYY male. *Nature*, 1965, 208, 1351–52.

Jacobs, P. A., Price, W. H., Court-Brown, W. M., Brittain, R. P., & Whatmore, P. B. Chromosome studies on men in a maximum security hospital. *Annals of Human Genetics*, 1968, 31, 339–47.

Jarvik, L. F. Cytogenetic aspects of psychopathology. In J. Zubin & C. Shagass (eds.), *Neurobiological aspects of psychopathology.* New York: Grune & Stratton, 1969.

Kessler, S., & Moos, R. H. XYY chromosome: Premature conclusions. *Science*, 1969, 165, 442.

Kjessler, B. Karyotype, meiosis and spermatogenesis in a sample of men attending an infertility clinic. *Monographs in Human Genetics*, 1966, 2.

Knox, S. J., & Nevin, N. C. XYY chromosomal constitution in prison populations. *Nature*, 1969, 222, 596.

Maccoby, E. E., & Jacklin, C. N. Sex differences and their implications for sex roles. Paper presented at the annual meeting of the American Psychological Association, Washington, D.C., September 1971.

Maclean, N., Harnden, D. G., Court-Brown, W. M., Bond, J., & Mantle, D. J. Sex chromosome abnormalities in newborn babies. *Lancet*, 1964, 1, 286.

Marcus, A. M., & Richmond, G. The XYY syndrome: A short review, a case study and investigatory model. *Journal of Forensic Sciences*, 1970, 15, 154–72.

Marinello, M. J., Berkson, R. A., Edwards, J. A., & Bannerman, R. M. A study of the XYY syndrome in tall men and juvenile delinquents. *Journal of the American Medical Association*, 1969, 208, 321–25.

Masterson, J., Power, M., & O'Brien, E. Cytogenetic studies in a maximum security hospital. *Journal of the Irish Medical Association*, 1970, 63, 362–64.

McDanal, C. E., Jr. A survey among tall male prisoners for the XYY karyotype. *Alabama Journal of Medical Science*, 1969, 6, 295–96.

Melnyk, J., Derencsenyi, A., Vanacek, F., Rucci, A. J., & Thompson, H. XYY survey in an institution for sex offenders and the mentally ill. *Nature*, 1969, 224, 369–70.

Money, J. Behavior genetics: Principles, methods and examples from XO, XXY and XYY syndromes. *Seminars in Psychiatry*, 1970, 2, 11–29.

Nielsen, J., Friedrich, U., & Zeuthen, E. Stature and weight in boys with the XYY syndrome. *Humangenetik*, 1971, 14, 66–68.

Nielsen, J., Stürup, G., Tsuboi, T., & Romano, D. Prevalence of the XYY syndrome in an institution for psychologically abnormal criminals. *Acta Psychiatrica Scandinavica*, 1969, 45, 383–401.

Nielsen, J., Tsuboi, T., Tuver, B., Jensen, J. T., & Sachs, J. Prevalence and incidence of the XYY syndrome and Klinefelter's syndrome in an institution for criminal psychopaths. *Acta Psychiatrica Scandinavica*, 1969, 45, 402–23.

Noel, B., Quack, B., Durand, Y., & Rethoré, M. O. Les hommes 47, XYY. *Annales de Genetique*, 1969, 12, 223–36.

Pearson, P. L., Bobrow, M., & Vosa, C. G. Technique for identifying Y chromosomes in human interphase nuclei. *Nature*, 1970, 226, 78–80.

Penrose, L. S. *The biology of mental defect.* New York: Grune & Stratton, 1963.

Rainer, J., Abdullah, S., & Jarvik, L. F. XYY karyotype in a pair of monozygotic twins: A 17-year life history study. *British Journal of Psychiatry*, 1972, 120, 543–48.

Ratcliffe, S. G., Stewart, A. L., Melville, M. M., Jacobs, P. A., & Keay, A. Chromosome studies on 3,500 newborn male infants. *Lancet*, 1970, 1, 121.

Recherche Coopérative sur Programme No. 85. Fréquence de la constitution XYY dans la population générale. *Annales de Genetique*, 1968, 11, 245–46.

Sergovich, F., Valentine, G. H., Chen, A. J. C., Kinch, R. A. H., & Smout, M. S. Chromosome aberrations in 2159 consecutive newborn babies. *New England Journal of Medicine*, 1969, 280, 851–55.

Stenchever, M. A., Chlebowski, R., & Jarvis, J. XYY syndrome. *Journal of the American Medical Association*, 1971, 215, 798.

Stephenson, J. N., Mellinger, R. C., & Manson, G. Cerebral gigantism. *Pediatrics*, 1968, 41, 130–38.

Walzer, S., Breau, G., & Gerald, P. S. A chromosome survey of 2,400 normal newborn infants. *Journal of Pediatrics*, 1969, 74, 438–48.

Welch, J. P., Borgaonkar, D. S., & Herr, H. M. Psychopathy, mental deficiency, aggressiveness and the XYY syndrome. *Nature*, 1967, 214, 500–1.

Wiener, S., Sutherland, G., Bartholomew, A. A., & Hudson, B. XYY males in a Melbourne prison. *Lancet*, 1968, 1, 150.

Wilton, E., & Lever, A. XYY male. *South African Medical Journal*, 1967, 41, 284–86.

Zech, L. Investigation of metaphase chromosomes with DNA binding fluorochromes. *Experimental Cell Research*, 1969, 58, 463.

THE XYY CHROMOSOME—HOW SHOULD THE LAW RESPOND?

Elyce Zenoff Ferster

Scientists frequently charge that the law is much too slow in responding to scientific advances. Lawmakers and legal scholars too often plead guilty to this charge, forgetting the various occasions on which the law has responded swiftly but inappropriately. For example, when knowledge about genetics was still in its infancy, laws authorizing compulsory sterilization of the mentally ill and mentally retarded were drafted and upheld on the assumption that science had proved these conditions were hereditary. Years later, after thousands of persons had been sterilized, many scientists reported that the inheritability of these conditions was still and always had been in doubt.

A more recent example is the legislative response to the battered child syndrome. In less than five years after the initial articles describing the syndrome, almost every state enacted a child abuse law. However, most of them failed to specify what was to happen after the report was made and, also, failed to supply any funds to carry out the law's reporting provisions, much less to provide anything for treatment or prevention. Yet, for a number of years many communities were under the impression that they had solved the problem because they had passed a battered child law.

Unfortunately, when the question of a new law to implement advances in science is being considered, the assumption is that the law will solve the problem, and the proponents concentrate their efforts on getting a law passed. Frequently, many important issues relevent to the law's desirability and efficiency are overlooked. For example:

1) How certain is the scientific knowledge on which the proposed law is based?
2) What action is the law supposed to take because of it?
3) Who will be affected by the proposed action?
4) How will the action affect the rights of involved persons?
5) What will be the benefits or detriments of the action to society?
6) What will happen if the interests of the affected person and society conflict?

I would like to briefly explore some of these questions and their relationship to the XYY chromosome, because it has had such widespread attention during the last few years, not only in medical and legal literature but also in the press. Although only a few years have elapsed since the XYY syndrome was identified, it has been an issue in at least five trials, three of them in the United States,[1] and the question whether the defendant had an XYY chromosome was raised in two other cases.[2] In each case, the XYY syndrome was used as a defense to a criminal charge, and in most of these cases the defense was supported by the testimony of an expert witness. In other words, the defendant admitted that he had committed the alleged crime, but said he should not be held responsible for it because of his chromosomal abnormality.

The first question that occurs to me is: "What was the attorney's purpose in raising

[1] *People* v. *Farley*, No. 1827, Sup. Ct., Queens Cty., April 30, 1969; *People* v. *Tanner*, No. 102, 072, Los Angeles County, Cal. Super. Ct., March 5, 1969, affd. 13 Cal. App. 3d 596, 1970; *State* v. *Millard*, Criminal No. 8334–37, Pr. George's County Cir. Ct., Feb. 5, 1969, affd. *Millard* v. *State* 8 Md. App. 419, 1970; for the two foreign cases, see the Report on the XYY Chromosome Abnormality National Institute of Mental Health, Center for Studies of Crime and Delinquency, October 1970, p. 3.

[2] Chromosome tests were performed on Richard F. Speck, who was convicted of murdering eight nurses in Chicago; Richard D. Lyons, *New York Times*, April 22, 1968, p. 143; and on Joseph W. Perkins who was convicted of shooting two men to death in a bar in Maryland, *Washington Post*, October 23, 1968, p. B6.

Excerpted and reprinted with permission from a talk before the American Association for the Advancement of Science, December 1971.

this defense?" Several of these cases involved charges of murder, where the consequences of a guilty verdict, of course, would be severe. Presumably, the defense attorney thought any disposition on a successful XYY defense would be preferable to the death penalty or life imprisonment on conviction for murder. In one case, however, the charge was robbery and, presumably, the sentence if the defendant was convicted would have been less severe than in a murder case.[3] Many attorneys would question whether the client's best interests were served by raising the XYY defense in such cases. Whether or not the defense should be used depends to some extent on what happens to the defendant if he is not found guilty by reason of his chromosomal abnormality. Usually, a person who is found not guilty by reason of insanity is institutionalized until he is cured. Is there a cure for the XYY syndrome? If there is no cure, hospitalization would be tantamount to a life sentence. If the crime resulted in death or severe bodily injury, although loss of liberty is tragic it can be justified, as it is in the use of insanity defense, on the ground that the public is entitled to protection against repetition of the offense. The question what to do with the person with an XYY chromosome becomes much more difficult if his act, although a dangerous one, such as robbery, did not result in serious harm. Should he be deprived of his freedom forever because there is no cure for his condition, while the "normal" robber is returned to the community after a few years of imprisonment?

No one has been acquitted on the basis of the XYY chromosomal abnormality, but the judge in one case made it clear that he was not ruling it out as a defense,[4] and in another case the issue was sent to the jury,[5] so it is possible that there may be a successful defense in the near future. If this happens, the law would face some difficult questions quickly. For example, a prosecutor may raise the issue in a case where the defense would prefer to litigate the issue of guilt or may prefer a verdict of guilty to not guilty because of an XYY chromosome abnormality. Should the prosecutor or the court be allowed to raise the issue of the XYY syndrome over the objections of the defense? Should the ability vary with the seriousness of the offense? Could institutionalization for life be justified if conviction on the criminal charge would merit a punishment of only five years imprisonment?

A successful XYY defense in a rape or murder case would probably be followed by a good deal of publicity, with the result that many people might be afraid of anyone having this condition. It is likely that legislation would be proposed requiring testing of certain population groups. Would such legislation be desirable? Would it be constitutional? Does it make any difference whether the testing is done on new-born infants or on persons who have been accused or convicted of a violent crime?

Should it make any difference what use is made of the information? The choices could vary from an offer of services through compulsory treatment, sterilization, to removal from the community. Is enough known about the XYY chromosome to justify any legislation that affects the rights of persons having this condition?

The parade of horribles I have raised are not just the figment of a law professor's active imagination. We took drastic action about eugenic sterilization in the early twenties with very little information about eugenics. We have come perilously close to doing so again in the case of the XYY chromosome. A good deal of thought should be given to how rapidly the law should follow scientific advances, how certain the scientific proof should be, and the effect the comtemplated action will have upon the persons involved, before responses are made to the next cry for "action."

REFERENCES

1. Chandler, J. A., and Rose, S. F. "The Constitctional Dilemma of a Person Predisposed to Criminal Behavior," 26 *Vanderbilt L.R.* 69, 1973.
2. Report on the XYY Chromosomal Abnormality, National Institute of Mental Health, Center for Studies of Crime and Delinquency, October 1970.
3. "Note, XYY Syndrome, The XYY Syndrome: A Challenge to Our System of Criminal Responsibility," 16 *N.Y.U. Law Rev.* 232, 1970.
4. Amer and Berman. "Chromosomal Derivation & Crime," 34 *Fed. Prob.* 55, 1970.
5. Epstein. "Genetics and the Law," 21 *Hastings L. J.* 35, 1969–70.
6. Clark, Telfer, Baker, & Rosen. "Sex Chromosomes, Crime and Psychosis," *American Journal of Psychiatry*, 126:1659 (1970).
7. Farrell. "XYY In Criminal Law: an Introduction," 44 *St. John's L. Rev.* 217, 1969.
8. Burke. "The XYY Syndrome: Genetics, Behavior and the Law," 46 *Denver L. J.* 261, 1969.
9. "Note, the XYY Chromosome Defense," 57 *Geo. L. J.* 892, 1969.
10. "Note, XYY Chromosomal Complement: Brief Application to Criminal Insanity Tests," 14 *St. Louis W. L. J.* 297, 1969.
11. Sergovitch, "Chromosome Aberrations and Criminal Behavior: A Brief Review," 11 *Crim. L. Quart.* 303, 1968–69.

[3] *State* v. *Millard*, supra n.1.
[4] *Millard* v. *State*, supra n.1.
[5] *People* v. *Farley*, supra. n.1.

EDITORIAL COMMENT

Of all the changes in psychiatric knowledge and treatment reviewed in the introduction to this chapter, three have been singled out for particular attention, partly because they all currently share the public limelight, and partly because they raise many more baffling issues for forensic psychiatry than the other forms of treatment. These are electroconvulsive therapy, psychosurgery, and some of the behavioral therapies.

Electroconvulsive therapy came prominently to the public view during the 1972 presidential election. To many laymen this very valuable treatment technique seems a relic of the middle ages. Its application is the most common reason for malpractice suits in psychiatry. In addition, the issue of informed consent is a difficult one between doctor and patient when electroconvulsive therapy is contemplated.

Psychosurgery has been so much in the news that an introduction to the controversy hardly seems necessary. Unfortunately, the media are not the best vehicle for gaining understanding of the real issues involved in the psychosurgery debate. The excerpts from a series of articles which appeared in the Journal of the American Medical Association touches on all sides of this psychosurgery debate. The excerpts from the Firing Line program were chosen because the participants, Dr. Bloomer and Mr. Valenstein, are neither proponents nor propagandists on either side of the controversy, but are basic scientists who present a well-balanced view of the subject. Similarly, the excerpts from Dr. Bertram Brown's testimony, included in the *Congressional Record*, indicate that there are more questions than answers in the field at the present time, and Dr. Brown speaks from a position of considerable governmental responsibility.

While behavioral therapy takes many forms that are neither controversial nor of much interest to forensic psychiatry (for example, the desensitization treatment of phobias), certain procedures and treatments that fall within the broad category of behavior therapy have raised issues concerning patient's rights, coercion, informed consent, and the proper limits of behavioral control techniques. Some of these issues will be dealt with in a later chapter. The purpose of the Ferster and Halleck articles is to give the student (reader) enough understanding of the field of behavior therapy to be able to read intelligently the later selections.

THE PLACE OF ELECTROSHOCK THERAPY (EST) IN PRESENT-DAY PSYCHIATRY

Zigmond M. Lebensohn, M.D.

In the hot, humid days of July 1972, electroshock therapy (EST) suddenly became a household word when it was revealed that a candidate for the vice-presidency of the United States had been successfully treated for a psychiatric disorder with EST. Eventually his name was withdrawn from the ballot. Whether his withdrawal was prompted primarily by the nature of his past illness or by the nature of the treatment he received is still not clear. However, during the ensuing weeks and months, the American public was bombarded by a barrage of information and misinformation about EST. Psychiatrists were sharply

Based in part on an editorial "In Defense of Electroshock Therapy," *Medical Annals of the District of Columbia* 42, no. 6 (June 1973).

divided, and the general medical profession itself was confused. Was EST harmful? Was it on the way out? Had it been supplanted by the newer chemical antidepressants and tranquilizers? What was the truth of the matter?

Electroshock therapy, also known as electroconvulsive therapy (ECT), has been an accepted form of treatment for certain types of psychiatric disorders ever since its discovery by the Italian psychiatrists Cerletti and Bini in 1938. For many years, psychiatrists had been searching for a more effective treatment method for schizophrenia because results with psychotherapy and drugs had been largely disappointing. Attention was first directed to the physical methods of treatment by Manfred Sakel of Vienna, who noted that convulsive seizures that occasionally occurred during the course of insulin treatment, rather than harming the patient, seemed to have a beneficial effect. Working on this hypothesis, Dr. von Meduno of Budapest began injecting metrazon intravenously for the express purpose of inducing a controlled convulsive seizure that would have a therapeutic effect on the mental disorder. By 1938, when Cerletti and Bini administered the first electroshock treatment to a human being, it was clear that the convulsive seizures did produce improvement, and that the treatment was more effective in depressive disorders than it was in the schizophrenias. Therefore, it was inevitable that a simpler and safer method of producing a convulsive seizure by electrical means was devised.

When properly used, no somatic treatment in psychiatry has been as consistently or as dramatically effective over such a long period. During the intervening years the procedure has been greatly refined and is now a well accepted treatment modality. But in some psychiatric centers it has fallen into disuse, or worse, has been treated with disdain, often by psychiatrists who have had little personal experience with the procedure and seem to be guided more by emotion than by reason.

There seem to be many reasons for this state of affairs. There is no doubt that over the years individuals and groups have misused or abused EST for a variety of reasons. However, such practices are not confined to psychiatry. Any procedure in medicine that gains popularity and that is relatively easy to administer is subject to the same abuse. Although this is no excuse, the so-called "shock mills" have contributed to the negative professional and public attitudes regarding EST.

Another factor contributing to the negative attitudes has been the dominance of psychoanalytic teaching in medical schools and in psychiatric residency training programs. Little time is given to teaching the indications for and techniques of EST. The new generation of psychiatric residents includes many who have never witnessed, much less administered, an electroshock treatment. The attitude toward EST is often one of smug condescension. The psychiatrist who still administers EST is often regarded with the kind of disdain that gynecologists used to reserve for colleagues who performed "therapeutic" abortions, in the old days before legalization. In many medical schools a double standard seems to exist. I have known psychiatrists who preach publicly against the use of EST, but who have privately recommended it for members of their own family or for individual patients.

Still another reason for the negative attitude toward EST may be found in the scores of articles, horror stories in Sunday supplements, sensational books and plays (e.g., "One Flew Over the Cuckoo's Nest") that portray EST as a form of punitive therapy controlled by sadistic doctors and nurses. Anyone familiar with the workings of a modern psychiatric hospital, with its insistence on clear criteria and informed consent, can dismiss this as sensational hogwash, which can only create needless anxieties in the minds of the suggestible lay public.

TECHNIQUE

The psychiatrist himself gives the treatment, using a specially designed electronic instrument. In some instances he may be assisted by an anesthetist, but in many areas the psychiatrist himself is trained and experienced in the techniques that are required for the successful administration of this treatment method. The treatment consists of passing a carefully controlled electric current between two electrodes applied to the patient's temples. Before this happens, the patient is given an intravenous anesthetic that induces sleep in a matter of seconds. This is followed by a second injection that produces as much musuclar relaxation as the physician deems necessary to diminish the strength of the muscular contractions. The patient experiences no discomfort or pain during the treatment. He does not feel the electric current and has no memory of the treatment after it is over.

Once the patient is asleep and his muscles relaxed, the electrodes are applied to the temples and the predetermined electrical stimulus is given. This results in a softened but generalized convulsive seizure that lasts approximately sixty seconds. Complete relaxation follows, and several minutes later the patient slowly awakens. As he gradually regains consciousness, he may show transitory confusion similar to that seen in any patient emerging from brief anesthesia. In less than an hour the confusion clears and the patient is able to recognize his surroundings. Headache and nausea sometimes occur, but these are infrequent and usually respond rapidly to simple treatment.

The number and frequency of individual treatments for each patient varies with the condition being treated, with the individual's response to treatment, and with the medical judgment of the treating psychiatrist. The usual course of electroshock therapy may consist of four to ten individual treatments spaced approximately two days apart. However, in some instances, less may be sufficient or more treatments may be required. As the treatment progresses, usually after the third or fourth treatment, a certain amount of confusion and haziness of memory develops. This is an expected side effect of the treatment and usually clears up within several weeks following the last treatment.

RISKS

Electroshock therapy, like any other medical or surgical procedure, involves a certain amount of calculated risk. In spite of this, literally hundreds of thousands of individual treatments have been administered without incident. The fractures and/or dislocations that used to occur during the early days, rarely occur, due to the use of muscle relaxants. Adverse reactions to the intravenous medications may sometimes occur, but these are very infrequent. Fatalities have been reported but these usually occur in cases where there is a known added risk due to the presence of other hazardous organic diseases, the risk of which had been carefully considered and accepted by the patient being treated. Such complications, although infrequent, may occur in spite of all precautions and must be looked upon as recognized hazards of electroshock therapy.

CONVALESCENCE

Following the last treatment the patient begins a convalescent period the duration of which varies with each case. During this period (usually one to two weeks) the patient should either remain in the hospital or be discharged under the supervision of a family member or some responsible person selected by the family.

INDICATIONS FOR EST

As previously indicated, the somatic or "shock" treatments were originally designed for schizophrenia. Later it was discovered that electroshock therapy was much more effective in the depressive disorders. It is still true that cases of severe depression with suicidal preoccupation and an overwhelming sense of hopelessness respond remarkably well to a brief course of electroshock therapy. Modern antidepressants are only 40 to 60 percent effective and require weeks and sometimes months to effect a cure. During this time the patient may experience intolerable distress or may be so suicidal as to require hospitalization. With electroshock therapy the immediate results are from 90 to 95 percent effective in carefully selected cases, and improvement takes place within a matter of seven to ten days in a protected hospital setting.

Although severe depressions of varying types (the depressed phase of manic depressive illness, psychotic depression, involutional depression, agitated depression, etc.) are primary indications for electroshock therapy, there are other conditions for which it is also effective. These include severe catatonic schizophrenia, schizophrenia with depressive features, the manic phase of manic depressive illness, acute toxic psychoses, and senile depressions. In certain acute illnesses, the proper use of electroshock therapy can be a life-saving measure.

THEORETICAL CONSIDERATIONS

No one yet knows precisely how electroshock therapy works. For that matter, no one yet knows why aspirin relieves a headache; we simply know that it does. Such treatments in medicine are called "empirical," a fact that in no way lessens their usefulness. There is no doubt that producing a series of convulsive seizures causes profound changes in brain chemistry. This is particularly true of certain of the neurohormones and the catecholamines. Research has indicated changes in the level of the stress hormones, norepinephrine, serotonin, and dopamine, to mention but a few. The final chapter has yet to be written in this regard.

Although there are a number of theories as to how electroshock works, no single one has as yet been completely accepted by those who work in the field. One useful way of explaining the treatment to patients is that the electroshock treatments break up *recently* acquired abnormal patterns of thinking, feeling, and behaving and permit the *older*, more established, and presumably more healthy, patterns of thinking, feeling, and behaving, to regain command. This rather simplistic theory fits in well with the clinical observation that the treatment produces an amnesia for recent events (including many of the symptoms of the presenting illness) and does not affect older and more established memory traces. This finding can sometimes be turned to unexpected advantage. I remember once treating a highly skilled technician in the Census Bureau for a suicidal depression, in the early 40's. Prior to his illness he was trying to remember a technique that he had used with great effectiveness in the 1930 census but was unable to recapture. During the amnesia that followed his successful electroshock therapy, he was able to recapture perfectly the details of what happened some fourteen years earlier.

CONCLUSIONS

Electroshock therapy remains, to this day, one of the most effective treatment methods for the rapid relief of severe depressive reactions and for various other severe psychiatric disorders. It should not be allowed to fall into disuse because of popular and professional prejudices based on erroneous information. Psychiatry covers a vast range of disorders, some of which respond to physical methods, some to psychodynamic approaches, and some to a combination of both. Success in psychiatric treatment consists largely of selecting the right treatment or combination of treatments for the individual case and not in espousing one form of treatment for all psychiatric disorders.

The position of electroshock therapy today was well summarized in a recent Task Force Report on Electroconvulsive Therapy in Massachusetts. It is so broad and fair in its statement that it deserves to be quoted at this point: "The history of ECT and its relationship to psychodynamic psychiatry captures the essence of the struggle for identity within the psychiatric profession. As the mainstay (until the era of psychotropic drugs) of those who sought a biological approach to the treatment of psychiatric illness, ECT became an emblem maligned by some and hallowed by others. . . . What emerges clearly is that ECT is neither the villain of the piece nor its all-conquering hero. Although definite answers to some questions are still not available and the pressing need for extensive long term comparative studies of the current treatment modes is clear, enough information is already at hand in the collective experience of psychiatrists and in the reports of a few top caliber investigators for ECT to be recognized as a necessary part of psychiatric treatment."*

* "Electro-convulsive Therapy in Massachusetts, A Task Force Report," Fred H. Frankel, M.B. Ch.B., D.P.M., *Massachusetts Journal of Mental Health* 3, no. 2 (Winter 1973).

DEBATE OVER BENEFITS AND ETHICS OF PSYCHOSURGERY

Virginia Snodgrass

PART I

A treatment of the future or a horror from the past? What is psychosurgery and where is it going?

When prefrontal lobotomy was introduced in the thirties, only to be rejected almost totally (though not until an estimated 50,000 operations had been performed), many physicians thought that ended the matter. But now it appears that the dispute about lobotomies was only the prelude to a more bitter controversy.

Psychosurgery—surgery to alter behavior—the highly refined cousin of prefrontal lobotomy, has become a subject of discussion in scientific literature, lay publications, in Congress, and in the courts.

People are asking if psychosurgery has a place in the treatment of behavioral aberrations, or whether it constitutes an unjustified attack on a defenseless patient. Does psychosurgery enable a troubled person to rewind the tangled threads of his life, or does it turn an imperfect human into a perfect vegetable?

Excerpted and reprinted with permission from the *Journal of the American Medical Association* 225, no. 8 (1973): 913, [Part I], and 225, no. 9 (1973): 1035 [Part II].

These are important questions, but the answers often are based on feelings rather than facts. Physicians cannot claim to be much better informed on the subject then the general public. And yet, no matter how this issue is resolved, the decision will have far-reaching implications for all of society. . . .

Some hope that the permissibility of psychosurgery will be made a matter of law. Others ask if that—in effect letting courts and legislators prescribe for patients—would constitute good medicine. But if psychosurgery is not regulated, will there not continue to be excesses, possible abuses in the name of progress? And, of course, if the lawmakers step in —why shouldn't they also regulate other areas of medicine that might be considered sensitive? . . .

Rising public interest can be traced to some extent to newspaper and magazine articles, some of which assert that the real purpose of psychosurgery is social control. Depending upon the publication, the targets are identified as blacks, women, Jews, prisoners, recalcitrant children . . . the list is practically endless.

Logistically, psychosurgery for social control is highly unlikely, simply because there are not enough neurosurgeons. Yet, there can be no doubt that there are serious ethical and moral questions connected with psychosurgery.

Two of the thorniest specific ethical points are (A) who can give informed consent and when, and (B) who should be eligible for treatment. For instance, is a prisoner's consent truly voluntary (often mistakenly referred to as "informed") when he knows his decision may influence whether he will be free again? For that matter, can inmates of a mental hospital give informed consent?

If a person cannot cope with, or live in, his environment, and yet lacks the inner resource to change either, is it wrong for him to seek out a treatment that may enable him to adapt? Finally, psychosurgery is often referred to as a treatment of last resort—but who determines that everything else has been tried and has proved unsuccessful?

One group that has given much thought to the social aspects of psychosurgery is at the Institute of Society, Ethics, and the Life Sciences, Hastings-on-Hudson, N.Y.

Dan Callahan, Ph.D., director of the institute, appeared at the American Association of Neurological Surgeons (AANS) meeting in Los Angeles to discuss the social and ethical implications of psychosurgery. He said the subject has received both more and less attention than it deserves—too much from the media and too little from physicians.

"It is clear," he said, "that further development must proceed in a scientific way. I believe that all present procedures should be classified as experimental until there is enough evidence to justify further use or abandonment of psychosurgery." . . .

The term psychosurgery covers a variety of surgical procedures, of which those most often done are cingulotomy, amygdalatomy, thalamotomy, and lobectomy.

The actual operating time varies with the procedure and ranges from about two hours for cingulotomies to more than five hours for an amygdalatomy. This does not include the preoperative workup which runs into hours of tests, over a period of weeks and months, in order to locate the various centers in the brain. . . . Given the amount of time needed for such a procedure, one can see that the logistics of using psychosurgery for social control are formidable. There are approximately 3,000 neurosurgeons in the United States. Taking things to the ultimate absurdity, if each did nothing but psychosurgery and each did two procedures a day, six days a week, the total would be 1.9 million a year. Actually, however, neurosurgeons usually operate in teams and 95% of their work is totally unrelated to anything psychosurgical. Complete concentration on psychosurgery would mean there would be no one available to operate for head injuries, brain tumors, slipped discs, and many other conditions.

The actual number of psychosurgical operations performed in this country in any given year appear to be between 300 and 500, the latter figure being considered generous by several neurosurgeons. (The 50,000 figure, quoted by some critics of psychosurgery refers to lobotomies that were performed in the 1940s and 1950s, often by psychiatrists rather than neurosurgeons.) . . .

Undoubtedly the one person most responsible for politicizing psychosurgery is Peter Roger Breggin, M.D., a man violently opposed to a procedure that he says "partially destroys a human being."

He has been very active in Washington where he practices psychiatry and has testified before Congressional committees and in court, as well as appearing at scientific meetings, evaluating patients, and writing, all in service of putting a stop to any practice of psychosurgery.

"It's an unscientific operation," he said, "and there is no way to make it scientific." . . .

Dr. Breggin claims that the prime candidates for psychosurgery are young people, women, blacks, and prisoners. He also indicates that Jews may be among targets, although he is less specific on this point.

There are many who dispute Dr. Breggin's contention that certain groups are "targets" for psychosurgery. A recent article in *Ebony* magazine, which called psychosurgery another tool for controlling the black population, was widely disputed by physicians who say relatively few black patients are considered candidates for psychosurgery. The logistics would also seem to rule out psychosurgery as a method of social control, or at least as one that could be applied on wide scale.

As far as women are concerned, Dr. Breggin contends that a housewife whose brain has been damaged by psychosurgery can fit into society; that so long as she no longer gives her husband any trouble, he (and the surgeon) will consider the operation successful, even if most of her basic personality has been destroyed. This line of thought has some appeal for many women who are at odds with their psychiatrists over role identification, but it leaves the surgeons aghast. They deny that to them a "good" female patient is a docile one. . . .

Vernon Mark, M.D., has performed thirteen "psychosurgical" procedures in the last ten years. All these patients were diagnosed as epileptics with a history of violent behavior.

Of his book, *Violence and the Brain*, he says: "The sole purpose of the book was to expound the idea that the abnormal (or diseased) brain may respond to environmental stimuli."

Writing in the February issue of the *Hastings Center Report*, Dr. Mark noted the public response to the book has underscored the fact that the medical issues of neurosurgery are no more interesting than the issues of its social role. The book stresses what he calls "an unfortunate dichotomy" in basic approaches to behavior, noting that certain kinds of behavior (such as paralysis and blindness) were put into the province of organic neurology while, on the other hand, many workers in the field tend to regard other behavioral abnormalities, such as intractable depression and aggressive assaultive behavior, as pure reflections of unusual or abnormal environmental stress.

The way he sees it, there are two factions in psychiatry that are against diagnosis of mental illness—one group that claims everyone has mental illness (the "sick society" theory) and the other that subscribes to the view that everyone is well (the "individual variations" theory).

"How can it be said we have a 'sick society,' " Dr. Mark said, "if they don't have norms established or controlled outcome studies? Then, on the other hand, we have the political psychiatrists saying there is no such thing as mental illness. Doesn't that make them somewhat hypocritical?"

He continued: "In my view, anyone who tries to stop treatment of these sick individuals is himself unethical."

Dr. Mark stresses the importance of assessing the effects of any given treatment. "Drug therapy," he said, "has been extremely effective in calming disturbed schizophrenics, but at what price? Studies have shown that long-term treatment with psychotrophic drugs causes basal ganglia disruption, tardive dyskinesia in from 0.2% to 40% of patients. It seems quite possible to have emotional blunting in patients on long-term drug therapy."

He expressed surprise that the public knows so little about possible hazards of drug therapy, affecting hundreds of thousands of people (although visible symptoms usually do not appear until some years after the beginning of treatment), while raising such an outcry about fewer than 500 cases of psychosurgery.

Dr. Mark is not alone in his concern about the use of antipsychotic drugs. Both the July 13 issue of *Science* and the April 1973 *Archives of General Psychiatry* carry warning articles. . . .

He is keenly aware of the psychosurgery controversy and is strongly opposed to surgical intervention when there is no organic brain disease. But he does not agree with those who think it is too early to use the procedures on patients:

"There is a group of scientists who want a moratorium on psychosurgery—they say more animal experiments are needed, even though there already is a tremendous volume of studies and experiments in the literature. When can we treat these patients if a moratorium is imposed, and what happens to them in the meantime? The political psychiatrists would say let them commit suicide, but I disagree."

Some critics of Dr. Mark have said that his patients suffer severe emotional blunting after surgery and that he suppresses this fact in his writings. Dr. Mark says this is not true, that he believes in full disclosure of pertinent medical information. He adds that he does not believe public disclosure of all details of a patient's history is always in keeping with that patient's best interests. . . .

He is on record against psychosurgery for prisoners. Again, writing in the *Hastings Report*, he said, "Prison inmates suffering from epilepsy should receive only medical treatment; surgical therapy should not be carried out, because of the difficulty in obtaining truly informed consent."

With regard to informed consent, he said that when the surgery is for violence, the patient should have the assistance of "an impartial, noninvolved professional group to determine whether surgery or other forms of treatment should be undertaken. In practical terms, this means a committee of some sort, composed of physicians, or in some cases, physicians and informed laymen." . . .

Some physicians who are deeply concerned about the ethics of psychosurgery do not agree with either Dr. Vernon Mark or Dr. Peter Breggin.

One of these is Karl H. Pribram, M.D., who holds appointments in the departments of psychiatry and psychology at Stanford University.

Dr. Pribram has tried to bring the moral issue into focus for many years now.

"As a former neurosurgeon," he said, "I feel that intervention into the functions of the human brain can indeed be therapeutic. Further, I feel that sometimes we must work in partial ignorance . . . simply to relieve suffering."

However, he rejects suggestions that psychosurgery should be considered as a means to control violent behavior of unknown etiology.

"I suggest," he said, "that we limit direct therapeutic brain manipulation to those patients whose brain has been shown to be abnormal in function, and that we resort to behavioral means to treat those people for whom we have been able to demonstrate only behavioral abnormalities."

Dr. Pribram believes drugs could be considered an intermediate form of therapy, one over which the patient has more control. However, he pointed out that pharmacology has its pitfalls and noted the ethical problems that arise when therapy leads to addiction.

Dr. Pribram does animal studies primarily, although his main interest is the functioning of the human brain. He has written extensively on the moral issues raised by psychosurgery, including a proposed "biological bill of rights" in one publication for the Hastings Center. In that, he suggests that "the right to integrity" supplements the right to life. Acceptance of this proposal, he says, would mean that a scientist should examine the consequences of psychosurgery, psychopharmacology, genetic manipulation, and even cloning before going ahead with the procedure because the right to integrity would demand identity and individuality.

PART II

The controversy over psychosurgery began among scientists, but the public is also becoming involved.

Quite a few newspaper and magazine articles have been written on the subject, often with "scare" headlines, and frequently combining the discussion of psychosurgery with that of two other topics—human experimentation and the use of prisoners in clinical testing.

Government is beginning to get involved, too, and as of now, the critics of psychosurgery have been far more effective in presenting their views, both before legislative committees and in the courts. The California legislature has held up funds for a proposed Center for the Study of Reduction of Violence, and the measures submitted to this term of Congress include both a House bill that would forbid psychosurgery and a Senate resolution calling for a moratorium on such operations (see stories on pages 1042 and 1044).

The chief sponsor of the Senate resolution, J. Glenn Beall, Jr. (R-Md), in asking for his colleagues' support, cited the outcome of six days of hearings by the Subcommittee on Health of the Senate Committee on Labor and Public Welfare last February and March.

During that hearing, Bertram S. Brown, MD, director of the National Institute of Mental Health, testified that he does not believe enough is known about the human brain to justify most of the current behavior-altering attempts.

"The goal of responsible researchers in psychosurgery is to pinpoint the exact locus of the undesirable behavior in the brain and destroy only those tissues and nerve cells, leaving other functions and behaviors of the patient unaffected," Dr. Brown testified. "Frankly, current practice of psychosurgery falls short of this goal, and even the best research in this field is not able to achieve such precision."

Sen Edward M. Kennedy (D-Mass) asked Dr. Brown if he considered psychosurgery a valid technique for treating behavioral disorders. Dr. Brown responded with "Maybe."

Other witnesses at the hearing included Orlando J. Andy, M.D., chairman of the Department of Neurosurgery at the University of Mississippi, Robert G. Heath, M.D., chairman of the Department of Psychiatry/Neurology at Tulane University, and Peter R. Breggin, M.D., a Washington psychiatrist and a leading critic of psychosurgery.

Dr. Andy described psychosurgery as "one of the most effective methods of treating structural pathology of the brain. Psychosurgical procedures are not experimental as implied by some critics." Both he and Dr. Heath described the outcome in a number of cases treated by psychosurgery, and Dr. Heath also noted that direct stimulation of the pleasure sites caused two chronic marihuana users to stop craving the drug. He added that the chances of mass use of such technique are extremely small because of the cost and complexity of the necessary equipment.

Dr. Breggin charged that many psychosurgeons are guilty of unethical practices, especially in the area of securing consent for the operations. He also disputed Dr. Andy's statements on the outcome of some cases, and accused Dr. Brown of misleading the committee on several points. "The reliance on professional ethics and medical control over these issues [involving psychosurgery] leaves the physicians in charge of the situation," Dr. Breggin said. "It creates for themselves an elitist power over human mind and spirit. If America ever falls to totalitarianism, the dictator will be a behavioral scientist and the secret police will be armed with lobotomy and psychosurgery. And by the way, lobotomy is still with us. . . .

"Lobotomy and psychosurgery is an ethical, political and spiritual crime. It should be made illegal.". . .

Another psychiatrist who has spoken up on the issue recently is Leo Alexander, M.D., of Boston. Dr. Alexander was a psychiatrist at the Nürnberg war crimes trials after World War II, and he disagrees—strongly—that psychosurgery is comparable to the crimes of which some German physicians and scientists were convicted after the war.

Dr. Alexander's main concern is that politicization of medical matters may come between the physician and his patient. For instance, a recent Massachusetts law limits the number of electroconvulsive treatments administered to a single patient to thirty-five in one calendar year. While that number is rarely exceeded, Dr. Alexander pointed out that sometimes this could be necessary for the patient's welfare.

As an example of what he calls the capriciousness of temporal law as compared to medical ethics, he says:

"Two years ago, if a physician performed an abortion, he was a criminal; but if subsequently, after his patient developed a severe depression, he brought about her recovery by 40 electroconvulsive treatments, he was a good doctor. Now the situation is reversed. When he performs the abortion, he a good doctor, but if he later finds it necessary to relieve the severe depression by 40 electroconvulsive treatments, he is a criminal."

At the recent APA meeting, Drs. Alexander and Breggin clashed in an open session in which Dr. Alexander expressed doubt that his colleague was primarily concerned with patient welfare.

He also complains that the opposition to psychosurgery is based almost solely on an emotional stand which may "condemn people to remain victims of disease, because it abridges their right to be judged ill."

Asked about the personality-altering aspect of psychosurgery, he replied: "The personality needs to be altered in that the patient is sick.

However, results show that what usually happens is that the patient's personality is restored to what it was before he became ill. It certainly is not as if an entirely new personality emerged."

Other psychiatrists have made similar statements. Many say they believe an official position statement by the American Psychiatric Association would be a useful tool for physicians thinking of recommending a patient for psychosurgery. . . .

The word "psychosurgery" is also being heard more and more often in court. One widely publicized case occurred in Detroit, where a prisoner scheduled for psychosurgery was freed by the judge. The prisoner, who had been an inmate of the Ionia (Mich.) State Hospital for eighteen years, had a history of uncontrollable rages. During one of these rages, he allegedly raped and killed a nurse. He had little hope of release until he volunteered to participate in a research program set up at the Lafayette Clinic of Wayne State University to compare the effects of psychosurgery and drug therapy. (The program had been set up with a $228,400 grant from the Michigan legislature.)

A Michigan Legal Services attorney, who is also a member of the Medical Committee for Human Rights, found out about the proposed operation. He charged that the patient had not given informed consent (and that he was in fact incapable of giving informed consent) and that public funds should not be used for such operations. The prisoner-patient himself changed his mind and said he had not been fully informed about the possible effects of psychosurgery. The court ordered the patient's release, though he may now go to prison for murder and rape.

Another case, in Virginia, involved a self-mutilating mental patient who had been intermittently hospitalized since 1968. The patient blinded himself in one eye and injured his other eye, either by burning himself with a cigarette or by banging his head against a wall. Drug therapy and other modalities of treatment had no effect, and so his parents and physicians agreed to try psychosurgery. But someone alerted the Virginia attorney general's office, the hospital, and the *Washington Post,* which raised questions about the need for psychosurgery and, again, the patient's ability to give informed consent. Surgery has been postponed until the questions can be resolved.

In Kentucky, a woman blinded as a result of a psychosurgical procedure received a substantial out-of-court settlement. The record is unclear on whether the surgery was recommended for long-standing intractable back and leg pain, or for the psychiatric problems resulting from the pain. In any event, the woman's attorney says there is reason to believe that she was not fully informed about the risks and possible benefits, so that neither she nor her husband had given informed consent.

None of the court cases so far has led to a head-on clash of proponents and foes of psychosurgery in the full glare of publicity. But the Congressional hearings and court cases—and the prospect of becoming involved in such a public battle—have had the effect of making anybody think twice before considering a psychosurgical procedure. One medical administrator says that residents interested in brain and/or behavioral research now stop to weigh the potential personal problems this research could lead to—an attitude that the administrator feels will have a detrimental effect on investigative medicine in the future. . . .

Until recently, psychiatrists have said very little about psychosurgery. Many of them obviously thought (and hoped) that the issue would quietly resolve itself, but it has not, and the American Psychiatric Association's Council on Emerging Issues has appointed a task force to study the situation and make recommendations. This group had not yet begun work in late July.

This does not mean, of course, that individual psychiatrists have no opinions about psychosurgery. It probably is a fair statement that most psychiatrists have reservations about surgical intervention to alter behavior. Some have no hesitation about referring patients with certain types of mental illness; others may refuse to consider psychosurgery even if they feel there may be merit in the procedure.

The point is that the APA has no official spokesmen on the subject—all the opinions expressed by psychiatrists reflect their own views.

For instance, there is Milton Greenblatt, M.D., professor of psychiatry at UCLA and chief of service at the Sepulveda VA Hospital. For many years, Dr. Greenblatt was commissioner of mental health for Massachusetts.

"Years ago when psychosurgery first started," he said, "the question of ethics came up almost immediately. In addition to physicians thought, the Roman Catholic Church decided that it was a licit operation if done for the benefit of the patient. They [the Church] established a policy of judging each case on empirical grounds. So the question of ethics is not new at all.

"I would say," he continued, "that the whole thing weighs on the issue of indications:

- How sick is the patient?
- What is the prognosis without surgery?
- What is the risk in relation to the benefit?"

Dr. Greenblatt thinks there has been enough study, that it can be determined when psychosurgery is indicated as a form of treatment—"drastic, but indicated."

Dr. Greenblatt has known Peter R. Breggin, M.D., well for years, and suggested one thing that may upset his colleague is that there may not necessarily be any gross lesions present when surgery is indicated or performed.

"However," he continued, "I have known of a patient with a frontal lobe tumor that was hidden; the only overt symptoms were unusual behavior and depression, both of which lifted when the tumor was removed. Therefore, I can't see why neurophysiological changes couldn't be as much an indication for surgery as gross pathology." (The patient's symptoms personality included obsession, anxiety, and phobia, all of which interfere with the functioning of the individual.)

"The basic, or so-called core personality," Dr. Greenblatt said, "is not so much altered by psychosurgery that you can't recognize the patient, and this has been fully documented."

With regard to the problem of prisoner-patients, Dr. Greenblatt commented:

"Prisoners should not be experimented on, but they should not necessarily be denied treatment. It depends on whether you can set up a situation where the surgery is not used as coercion."

In that opinion, his thinking is similar to many of his colleagues who also recognize that it is hard to take a "coercive element" out of prison situations.

"I deeply regret that psychosurgery has become a political issue," Dr. Greenblatt concluded. "Zealotry has hurt us. This doesn't mean that I am not in favor of 'politicizing medicine,' if by that you mean increasing public knowledge on medical needs. What I oppose is having a small group of people grab an issue and run with it, without facts, but based only on emotion. Certainly there has been excessive political interest in this issue." . . .

FIRING LINE: DISCUSSION OF PSYCHOSURGERY AND BRAIN CONTROL

I should like to begin by asking Mr. Valenstein if he would tell us what are the procedures at this moment that lead to neurosurgery when the intention is to affect behavior. . . .

MR. ELLIOT VALENSTEIN: It depends upon the hospital. In many hospitals these days there are lawyers, ministers, and even something that we've come to call an ombudsman who is supposed to represent the patient. How effectively the patient is represented in these review processes varies from place to place and is certainly in transition. My own feeling is that up until very recently, when the heat has certainly started to be generated, much of this review has simply been hand-washing on the part of physicians, where physicians within a hospital would approve the procedures—sometimes experimental procedures—of another physician and the patient was not really represented very well. Peer review meant not the patient's peers but the physician's peers.

MR. WILLIAM F. BUCKLEY JR.: And the purpose was to avoid, for instance, malpractice suits or that kind of thing?

MR. VALENSTEIN: Very often, yes.

MR. BUCKLEY: It was just sort of formalistic. Now, when you say "up until recent times," are you alluding to any spectacular failures that have caused public clamor?

MR. VALENSTEIN: Well, I think there has been a tremendous amount of concern because of the popularization of an idea that these techniques may have much greater application than to a few patients who are at the end of their rope, patients whom all psychiatric treatment, all physical therapies, all drugs have failed. But now there have been some claims that these techniques may be applicable to a much greater range of people and that there may be a significant amount of violence that we're all concerned with, violence that seems to be increasing, that may be related to brain pathology. At least there have been *some* claims that some of these techniques may be applicable. They certainly have not been used in this way up to this point but these claims have created such an undercurrent of anxiety and fear and passion that there has been an examination of the review process and the conditions that exist before psychosurgery would be considered, and that has caused a lot of heat. . . .

My own work has emphasized that there's a tremendous amount of lack of predictability in the effects of any of these procedures, not only in terms of psychosurgery where a particular part of the brain is destroyed but also in terms of electrical stimulation of the brain, where we have been told in the popular media—it's a very current topic—that we can get tremendous control over people by stimulating specific areas in the brain, that we can turn sex on, we can turn aggression on, or we can turn it off. We can tame bulls. My own work has emphasized that these reports are clearly unrepresentative and do not really state the true situation scientifically. My own work has emphasized the lack of predictability in many of these procedures and, therefore, the hesitation and danger in using them, the hesitation that we should exercise. . . .

DR. DIETRICH BLUMER: I think we run primarily into a lack of understanding of the complexity of this topic. Of course, the brain is highly complex, the most complex organ. So is human behavior. And there are very few people who have any understanding how both these parts work together. We have just made a beginning of understanding how certain lesions of the brain effect changes of behavior.

Excerpted and reprinted with permission, from transcript of the Firing Line television program taped on October 18, 1973.

Dietrich Blumer, professor of psychiatry, Harvard Medical School.
Elliot Valenstein, neuroscientist, professor of psychology, University of Michigan Neuroscience Laboratory.

Now, of course, generally the psychiatrist works with the notion that disturbed behavior has to do with stress and strain in the past. Perhaps genetics plays a part. But how the brain comes in there is sort of still a mystery. There just isn't a training for this particular area which falls right between neurology and psychiatry. That is sort of an unfortunate state of affairs. I think among those psychiatrists who have been seriously interested with the type of patient who is intractable and may be a candidate for certain psychosurgical procedures, there are relatively little disagreements.

Now, of course, one problem in particular is that if we talk about psychosurgery we talk really about two very different things. In the very strict sense of the word this is an operation on the totally intact brain, and perhaps in a wider sense—

MR. BUCKLEY: You mean assuming there's no malformation?

DR. BLUMER: There's no malformation, there has been no brain damage, and if you have the opportunity to examine such a brain, the only lesion you will find is the one produced by the neurosurgeon.

MR. BUCKLEY: Yes.

DR. BLUMER: The other case in point is the patient who does have a lesion, usually, and these are only certain forms of epilepsy, which are called temporal lobe epilepsies. These types of seizures are very intractable, they don't respond well to medication. These patients, although there is some difference of opinion—but for those who have looked at this very carefully, there is an agreement that these patients are particularly prone to behavior disturbances. And then if one eliminates this area of the brain which has caused the seizures and, we believe, the behavior disturbance at the same time, then one *can* bring about considerable improvement. If epilepsy is eliminated, you will usually also find an improved behavior, sometimes very dramatic. . . .

MR. BUCKLEY: The work that you referred to Mr. Valenstein, on sexual disorders, is it now simply accepted that there is a cure, let's say, for satyriasis or for homosexuality?

MR. VALENSTEIN: Oh, absolutely not. There are actually some people who are doing psychosurgery for types of homosexuality, one type called pedophilic homosexuality, generally middle-aged men who have a propensity for young boys. There is a team in Germany who is doing some surgery on a particular part of the brain and my own view is that this is not at all acceptable work, that they are, in effect, doing a functional castration on these people and lowering sexual desire of any type and, in general, these people then don't become a problem in terms of committing crimes. But, simply, what they have done is do something that is illegal, that is, castration in Germany, by a brain operation. . . .

MR. VALENSTEIN: I think a point that has to be emphasized is that clinicians as a group, and there are certainly some exceptions, but as a group are not trained to evaluate a lot of experimental animal data and the relationship between the experimental animal data and clinical applications is, for those of us who work with animals, almost embarrassingly close.

The whole history of psychosurgery—if one studies it, it is abundantly clear that techniques that were first developed with animals were borrowed by clinicians who looked at just one aspect of the behavior change of an animal, an aspect that looked like it might have some use for some seriously disturbed patients, and simply neglected to pay attention to the somewhat more subtle but still devastating changes that occurred in other areas.

I think a very good example, and one that's known by quite a few people but perhaps not enough, is the story of how lobotomy effectively began. The man who started prefrontal lobotomy, at least in this modern age, was Egas Moniz, a Portugese neurologist who eventually won the Nobel prize for this work. He did do—and it's not much less known—he did actually do some very interesting and important work on the blood vessels of the brain, but he won the Nobel prize for developing the lobotomy procedure, and it developed as a result—

MR. BUCKLEY: Why is that a joke? Is that a professional joke that he got it?

MR. VALENSTEIN: Well, there are many people who feel that the whole era of lobotomy, in which some 40,000 to 50,000 people were lobotomized in 1945 to 1955, where rather crude techniques were used at that time, was just rampant with abuses, where people were not studied sufficiently, that alternative methods were never really explored—

MR. BUCKLEY: Oh, oh.

MR. VALENSTEIN:—that overly optimistic reports led many neurosurgeons to rush into these procedures.

MR. BUCKLEY: But one doesn't blame that on Dr. Moniz?

MR. VALENSTEIN: No, no. Actually, Dr. Moniz was rather cautious and preferred to wait for the results on his first few patients. But the point I wanted to make is that at an international congress of neurology in 1935 in London, an experimental physiologist and psychologist, Carlyle Jacobsen, reported on the effect of destroying a part of the frontal lobes of monkeys and chimpanzees. And there was one interesting anecdote in that report. There was a chimpanzee named Becky, and I mention the name because the animal has become famous, who had a habit of throwing temper tantrums prior to any operation. The animal was tested in a procedure in which a reward was hidden under one of three cups and the animal had to retain that information. It was shielded from the cups for some period of time and then when the shield was lifted up the animal had to show that it retained the information and make the correct response.

Well, this one particular chimpanzee, Becky, prior to the operation, had a habit of throwing temper tantrums, would defecate and throw the product all over the room, scream whenever it made an error and didn't get the reward. After this prefrontal operation, the animal was very accepting of its fate and accepted rewards and non-rewards with equal equanimity.

Dr. Moniz got up at that meeting and asked if this technique would not be applicable to very agitated patients, and many people were horrified at that suggestion. But he actually went back and convinced a neurosurgical colleague of his . . . to do some operations in a hospital in Lisbon and, within two months, the first operations were done. But the important part of that report of those animals was that after the operation, after this prefrontal operation, none of these chimpanzees or monkeys could solve these tasks any more. They were unable to solve the simple task of retaining information for a period of time. That was completely neglected, and that is sort of characteristic, I think, of the kind of tunnel vision that many clinicians show toward experimental data. I think this work that we were talking about in Germany for hypersexuality, that actually that procedure is well developed as a result of some animal experimentation and a very limited view of the changes in behavior that resulted in performing a brain operation on animals.

MR. BUCKLEY: Well, now, what are some of the less obvious social implications of that kind of problem? Is it your opinion that the laws or that the procedure, as it now exists, puts people too quickly on an operating table under the care of a neurosurgeon expecting miracles that it has no grounds for accepting? Or do you find, on the contrary, a reluctance to move in the direction that you think has to be restored to to help certain kinds of people?

DR. BLUMER: No, I think currently any psychosurgical procedure is done with great reluctance.

MR. BUCKLEY: In every state or are you just talking about Massachusetts?

DR. BLUMER: I would think in most states of the Union. There has been tremendous publicity. There has been a lot of distortion of facts. These patients who come for help have been described as victims. It has been said these were the blacks, women, children who were being attacked.

MR. BUCKLEY: Yes.

DR. BLUMER: Almost murderous motives have been imputed to the neurosurgeons and it has frightened people a little bit. And this, of course, is a lot of nonsense. This is presented by people who are not involved with actual neurosurgical procedures in patients who have problems with their behavior. . . .

DR. BLUMER: One is excessively cautious. The question is really: Do the current psychosurgical procedures have any effect because these are such discrete lesions? . . .

DR. BLUMER: These very drastic lobotomies of the past are something very different from the modern psychosurgical procedures because of their extent. These are now very discrete lesions, usually bilateral either in the cingulum or in the orbital frontal area. And, as I said, it is really a question of how effective they are. The side effects are probably almost minimal. We don't have to fear it anymore, like with the old procedures.

Again what is really very necessary are very careful psychiatric studies of how these patients improve. And these patients should be evaluated by an independent team of psychiatrists; not even the same one who recommended the operation should reevaluate the patient, because he may be inclined to see these things a little bit too favorably. Plus we have to consider that a patient who is reexamined by the same person who has performed surgery—

MR. BUCKLEY: Doesn't have the perspective.

DR. BLUMER: Yes, and he tends to give a rather good picture. He likes to please the one he felt close to, the one—after all, both were involved in this. So this should be outside service before and after these very refined psychosurgical procedures, and my real question at this point is: Are they indeed so effective? That is what I would like to know better by better follow-up studies. I am not concerned that we have this great deal of side effects like apathy or this inhibited behavior, like we had with the old, very gross procedure. . . .

MR. BUCKLEY: Do you develop a sense of familiarity with the brain that has you saying things like, "Gosh, if I just had that guy on the operating table, I know just what I'd push and pull in order to make him more this way or more that way"? Do you think of the brain as sort of a console which you've mastered? . . .

MR. VALENSTEIN: It would be a delusion, because I think if there is anything we should emphasize in our discussion, it is the ignorance we have about the brain. I think the popular press, and that's the reason I mentioned it before, has given the impression that we are able to control a lot more than we are able to control. . . .

MR. BUCKLEY: As a matter of numbers, what are we talking about? For instance, in the last year in America how many brain operations of this kind would you say there were? Dozens, hundreds, thousands?

MR. VALENSTEIN: Hundreds. The most accurate report that I have been able to get in the United States is somewhere on the order of 500 to 600 such operations as should be called psychosurgery, that is, where there is not clear indication of a tumor or some kind of disease process in the brain that has led to psychiatric disturbance.

MR. BUCKLEY: And of those, what percentage would you say, if any, were ordered by a court, by a political authority?

MR. VALENSTEIN: I hesitate to give you a figure, but I would say very few, *very*, very few.

MR. BUCKLEY: Most of them were completely voluntary?

MR. VALENSTEIN: They were voluntary. Of course, the problem of voluntary and con-

sent, when you're dealing with a psychiatric patient, becomes very complex. But most of them were certainly not referred by courts. I think that those were very, very few. . . .

MR. JEFF GREENFIELD: Let me give you this example. You're called in by the head of the Federal Bureau of Prisons, or a state prison bureau, and he says, "Look, we have a rehabilitation rate failure of 75 percent. We simply do not know how to do what we want to do. We don't know how to change behavior. That's what we're supposed to do, but they go back on the streets, commit violent crimes, go back into prison. Can you develop through psychosurgery an operation which will lessen aggressiveness such that no one that we now have in our prison will commit a violent crime?"

MR. BUCKLEY: Or fewer. How about fewer?

MR. GREENFIELD: All right. You can develop a success rate, say, of 80 percent and there will be the other consequences, generally more emotionally flat, less intelligent, but they will not be criminals. Do you think that is an appropriate future or present use of psychosurgery?

DR. BLUMER: No, n-o.

MR. GREENFIELD: Okay, why not, n-o-t? (laughter) I mean what's the difference between changing a person's personality by psychosurgery and changing it by incarceration for fifteen years?

DR. BLUMER: The difference is in the individual. I mean, no. We deal with patients who ask for help. They themselves come for help. . . .

MR. GREENFIELD: What I'm asking—I guess I'm raising a philosophical question, which is: Does a person who commits a violent crime or a series—I mean, set your own example— three straight violent crimes, convicted by a jury beyond a reasonable doubt, sacrifice a certain right to free will? We're willing to lock him up for twenty years; why shouldn't we be willing to change his mode of behavior?

DR. BLUMER: No, not at all. Experience shows that this type of behavior gets much milder over the years. And there is absolutely no indication to treat somebody who doesn't want to be treated, certainly not for a physician. . . .

MR. BUCKLEY: Let me just ask—Suppose the state of the science was sufficiently developed to make it possible for you to perform such an operation without totally dehumanizing the person or changing his personality. Would you then have philosophical objections to doing it over his protest?

DR. BLUMER: Oh, yes.

MR. BUCKLEY: You would.

DR. BLUMER: I think any good neurosurgeon, physician, would just not get involved with that. . . .

MR. FRED KRUPP: Dr. Valenstein, early on you said that the technology of brain control lacked a certain predictability and that, therefore, what you were trying to publicize was the fact that the state of the art was not such that it could be applicable to a widespread scale. I wonder if our fears are to be allayed given the fact that the Office of Naval Research and the United States Air Force have supported your colleague Jose Delgado's work, and given the fact that Delgado claims that you could, through electrical stimulation technology, give a patient an orgasmic response or a tremendously painful response. Combining that with Skinnerian technology, aren't those techniques available and isn't there a legitimate cause for fear?

MR. VALENSTEIN: Not to the extent that you are implying. I think the fact that Dr. Delgado has grants from the Federal Government is not really germane to the issue because the Federal Government may be wrong in assuming that he can do things that he really can't do. . . .

We have an illusion that if we put an electrode in a specific part of the brain that that part of the brain is responsible for one function and only one function. The brain is just simply not organized that way. It does not conform to our social needs by having nice little compartments that deal with aggression, sexuality and eating. I can give you many examples of people who study the same part of the brain, but from their own perspective. So one man is studying temperature regulation, another thirst, another sexual behavior. They are all studying the same part of the brain. The truth of the matter is that the very same single units, the very same nerve cells, are probably contributing to many different circuits. So we will never really have the kind of predictability with these techniques. The personality of the

animal or of the human is constantly exerting its influence over the effects of stimulating any one part of the brain.

MR. KRUPP: Not even enough predictability to isolate pleasure centers and pain centers, so that you can implant a little listening device and say, you know, "Shoot," and if he doesn't it's pain and if he does, later on give him an orgasm or something. You don't have that control?

MR. VALENSTEIN: It is true that you can stimulate parts of the brain that can be very painful and that there are enough reports, certainly from animal work as well as human work, to lead us to believe that animals and humans can experience a certain amount of pleasure by having their brains stimulated. But the amount of pleasure is not that exquisitely supreme that you can bend their will and force them to do what you want. There's absolutely no evidence that that is true at all; in fact the evidence is quite to the contrary. You can give people pain by a thumbscrew. You don't have to put an electrode in their brain. You don't have any more control by doing that, and the notion that because somehow you have penetrated the brain, penetrated this inner barrier, you have now grabbed control of the person is just not true.

MR. KRUPP: Except you could do it by remote control, through a computer or through a remote system.

MR. VALENSTEIN: That's true. You could, but you are simply delivering pain to a person by remote control. I suppose if you wanted to develop some science fiction notion, you might very well elaborate on this, but there are other ways of doing the same thing and mankind has been pretty ingenious about thinking of tortures. One doesn't have to have a host of neurosurgeons implanting electrodes in order to gain control of our populace. Certainly if we lose our freedom it won't come by this means. . . .

DR. BLUMER: I perhaps would disagree just to some amount about this. I believe, for instance, as far as sexual pleasure, sexual arousal, is concerned, there are a number of relatively discrete cerebral areas which are potent—. . .

I have definitely to share your opinion that there has been so much science fiction spread. I've been sort of abhorred about some of the vitriolic responses to psychosurgical procedures, which, after all, are only done on very sound grounds, in very few patients, tormented, totally intractable to anything else. But then if I've read what some proponents of psychosurgery have said, and these are actually not the clinicians but some neurophysiologists, and so on, this smacks so much of, you know, *1984* and is so far away from what we actually are capable of achieving at this state of our knowledge in man. . . .

MR. BUCKLEY: Of these 500 operations last year, roughly speaking, how would you divide them up? How many of those 500, say, concerned an attempt to cure epilepsy or alleviate epilepsy? Half, a third?

MR. VALENSTEIN: I think none of the figures that I gave.

MR. BUCKLEY: None?

MR. VALENSTEIN: Yes.

MR. BUCKLEY: Well, what do they mostly concern themselves with, or in part?

MR. VALENSTEIN: Well, the patient population who are considered candidates for psychosurgery have varied quite a bit over the years. Originally the backward deteriorated schizophrenic was considered the person that one would do such an operation on. Gradually, over the years, it turned out that they were the poorest candidates, that nothing ever happened that looked like it was worth undertaking the surgery with such people.

Now the kinds of people that are considered candidates by those who do these procedures are people who are ridden with obsessions or anxieties in which no psychiatric treatment or drugs seem to be able to alleviate this. And these are not minor psychiatric disorders. These are people who are completely unable to cope with life, many times trying to commit suicide and completely intractable to other types of treatment. . . .

MR. GREENFIELD: I'm curious. There seems to be a—I, too, find it reassuring—hostility to involuntary operations like this and I am playing devil's advocate to ask what is worse about that than letting a person go to set fires which cause damage to life and limb? In a social cost—social benefit area, wouldn't it be better just to plant an electrode?

MR. VALENSTEIN: I think not. I think my own view is similar to Dr. Blumer's. I think that no surgical procedure should ever be done for the good of society. I think that we should use confinement or other kinds of social interventions. I think that even though one might be able to justify it on an individual, a narrow case, taking the narrow point of view, I think the dangers of establishing a precedent where surgery or any kind of therapeutic procedure is undertaken for social purposes, rather than for individual therapy, is just too great. . . .

MR. GREENFIELD: Why is it more totalitarian to operate on an individual than to lock that individual up for twenty years? Locking up someone abused is what totalitarianism is all about.

MR. BUCKLEY: Because it's irreversible, presumably. . . .

MR. VALENSTEIN: Well, it's not irreversible in the sense of psychosurgery. There's probably only a few cells that are destroyed while the electrode is entering the brain and penetrating it. But since those of us who are over 18 are losing cells at a rapid rate anyway, it probably doesn't matter that much. There is a small element of risk. But the point is there are other means that can be used. There are other kinds of therapies that can be tried. The use of electrodes for this purpose has really very little scientific foundation. . . .

MR. KRUPP: If we do reach the state of technology that Mr. Blumer says we're already at and you claim that we are not quite at, what is going to prevent perhaps some other country from utilizing these techniques for control of their populations? Let's assume the United States is too free, and I would like to believe that, to let some doctor go around doing this, but let's assume another country, like Spain, would. How can we stop that?

MR. BUCKLEY: Oh, can't you do better than Spain?

MR. KRUPP: Oh, the People's Republic of China would be better. (laughter)

MR. BUCKLEY: Yes.

MR. VALENSTEIN: Yes. Well, my point would be that we aren't on that track, that is, I think that we haven't found the right code. So it isn't a matter of getting more accurate stereotaxic devices to place our electrodes more precisely. I don't think that's the question. We aren't even proceeding along that path where I can see that down the road, to have that kind of predictability.

And if the purpose of this is simply to control people, I maintain there are much simpler ways of controlling people than putting electrodes in everyone's head. There was actually a science fiction story that appeared in *Esquire* a few years back in which a society, called an "electroligarchy" was described in which the classes were divided on the basis of free will that they had left depending on the number of electrodes implanted in their brains.

I think the whole notion is sheer fantasy and if you want to worry about such notions, it's okay, but I think it is not based on any techniques that I can see developing in the near future, nor do I think it very likely. If a population were willing to submit to having electrodes placed in their brain, they would already have lost their freedom. . . .

MR. BUCKLEY: Do you see the technique being developed, or do you simply start on the assumption we will never reach that point.

DR. BLUMER: I think we are very far from that. I think another limitation not pointed out is the very limited number of neurosurgeons. If you just figure out how many years it takes to train a neurosurgeon so he can go into the brain without raising havoc, you know, how many patients can be operated on with such few neurosurgeons around, if this ever should become some kind of mass treatment, you know, in a tyranny? . . .

TESTIMONY OF DR. BERTRAM BROWN BEFORE THE SENATE

We need to know the answers to such questions as: What chemicals are responsible for transmission of nerve impulses within the brain and how do these chemicals control different forms of behavior? What chemical or physical changes occur when learning takes place or when a memory is recovered from the brain? What anatomical systems and what chemicals are responsible for aggressive behavior, sexual behavior, eating behavior, drinking behavior, and the common state of sleep and dreaming? How is the brain and central nervous system related to the autonomic nervous system which controls many life processes such as heart rate, blood pressure, and a wide variety of visceral functions? What happens to the behavior and cognitive processes of men when portions of the brain are damaged through accident, birth injury, malnutrition or disease? Can functions that have been lost through such disruption of the brain be recovered or taken over by other portions of the brain?

In response to a question, Dr. Brown stated that we know much more about the functioning of the human brain today than we did 30 years ago—"but we know very little of what we need to know." I believe that this observation succintly sums up the reasons for suspending Federal support to psychosurgical projects until such time as we have, at our disposal, the type of comprehensive information needed to make a valid policy decision. Dr. Brown reinforced this point when he stated:

We have no reliable data on the extent of the practice or psychosurgery in this country, the types of patients subjected to this technique, or the after effects on patient behavior. The most systematic attempt (in this country) to assess the effects of psychosurgery on patient behavior and intellectual capacities was the Columbia-Greystone project which was conducted in 1954. Since then, many changes in psychiatric and medical practice have taken place: chemotherapy has dramatically changed the nature of the patient population in mental hospitals, and new surgical procedures have been introduced which are quite different from those studied by the Columbia-Greystone project. In order to make any specific recommendations for overseeing or controlling the clinical practice of psychosurgery a systematic survey of the field must be conducted—perhaps by one of the many professional societies and private foundations that have recently begun to focus on ethical issues in life sciences. We need to gather existing data available from patient histories and other sources which

---

Excerpt from the *Congressional Record*, 3/29/73; excerpt from speech by Senator Bealle, summarizing and quoting testimony by Dr. Bertram Brown, director of the National Institute of Mental Health.

never come to our attention because they are not federally funded. In order to answer the "hard" questions, we must first find out what's going on.

Later on in his testimony, Dr. Brown sought to explain some of the problems confronting the Department of Health, Education, and Welfare with regard to human experimentation for medical purposes. He outlined the HEW regulations related to "informed consent" which cover only those cases involving Federal funds. It became clear during the course of these hearings that these guidelines are most often observed in the breach.

EDITORIAL COMMENT

The selections that close this chapter will introduce the reader to some of the fundamental theoretical issues underlying psychological modalities of behavior control. The Ferster article demonstrates that learning theory supplies basic knowledge through which human behavior can be controlled more precisely than previously known noncoercive techniques. This may be applied to such relatively noncontroversial matters as the outpatient "desensitization" therapy of a phobia. On the other hand, when the behavior to be altered is not necessarily considered by the patient part of an illness, or when the initiative for altering the behavior does not lie with the patient, grave implications for forensic psychiatry exist. The brief selection from Halleck further points out these questions and dangers.

BEHAVIORISM, BEHAVIOR MODIFICATION, AND BEHAVIOR THERAPY

C. B. Ferster, Ph.D.

Behaviorism has a tradition that goes back much further in the history of psychology than the current modes of behavior therapy and behavior modification. It has its origins in the work of I. Pavlov and other biologists who were interested in the study of the behavior of organisms. They studied the interaction between the animal and its environment to gain an understanding of how the brain worked. Pavlov, for example, described his studies on conditioned reflexes as "the psychological activities of the cerebral cortex"; yet, his studies were primarily behavioral because they mostly involved the way in which the external environment influences reflex behavior (like salivation). Although the language was couched as "higher nervous activity," the actual measurements and experiments involved reflexes and stimuli in the external environment, and these were basically behavioral.

J. B. Watson (1934), who is usually described as the founder of modern behaviorism, brought the work of Pavlov on the conditioned reflex to the attention of American psychology. Watson founded a school of psychology, which asserted that all human behavior should be accounted for objectively, that thinking was the product of muscle activity,

This selection was written expressly for this volume and has not been previously published.

and that all human behavior would eventually be catalogued as a collection of predictable and known reflexes. The harbinger of behavior therapy (Wolpe 1969; Franks 1969) was an early experiment reported by Watson and a colleague (Watson & Rayner 1920) in which a very young infant was made fearful by a loud noise in the presence of a furry animal. The fearful reaction was established and then generalized to include not only the furry animal but also cotton and other furry objects. Then the process was reversed by exposing the child first to a ball of cotton, then to a piece of fur, and so on, in the absence of the fearfully loud noise. As the child tolerated each object without fear, he was exposed to new stimuli more closely resembling the furry animal, until he could tolerate the original conditioned stimulus, the white rat. After a gap of many years, much behavior therapy was to follow this paradigm.

After Watson founded the behavioral school of psychology, academic psychology became increasingly behavioral, particularly in university departments, while clinical psychology, for the most part, followed the directions laid down by Freud. Two characteristics of Watson and the Watsonian behaviorists set the style for later behaviorists. First, there was the use of data from animal experiments and the conviction that these were processes of phylogenetic generality; that is, they could be discovered in animals, but could then be generalized to help understand human behavior. Second, and closely related, was a bent for practical application. Laboratory experimenters and academic theoreticians were concerned about the solution of day-to-day problems of human existence.

Skinner's entry into psychology to extend the tradition of behaviorism was marked in 1938 with the publication of *The Behavior of Organisms*, a report of his research with rats. Skinner made three outstanding contributions that were to reverberate in psychology during the next forty-five years. First, was the distinction between reflexes, as described by Pavlov, and operant behavior, the ongoing activity that moves the animal in, and acts on, the environment. This distinction increased the relevance of behavior theory for the bulk of human conduct and allowed experimental psychology to look at human conduct as a primary datum rather than as an extrapolation from Pavlov's theory and findings. Second, was the discovery that the major dimension of operant behavior is its frequency, in marked contrast to reflexes that occurred only when they were elicited by a particular stimulus. The discovery of these important characteristics of operant behavior was accomplished by studying the

behavior of a rat pressing a bar reinforced by the delivery of a food pellet after occasional bar presses. Pressing the bar took a short time to execute and thus left the rat in a position to press again quickly. Therefore, frequency of bar pressing provided a measure of performance equivalent to "inclination, habit, disposition, or motivation." Third, the processes studied were orderly and demonstrable in an individual animal, eliminating the need for statistical averages and other artificial devices. This facet of Skinner's approach encouraged thinking about practical applications to the problems affecting individual humans.

Behavior modification, as it is applied to human problems today, owes its origins to B. F. Skinner. His study of the learning process in animal behavior led him to the same convictions as the behaviorists who preceded him: (1) that the study of human behavior was a part of natural science, and (2) that important behavioral processes were phylogenetically general and, hence, were applicable to both animals and people. Skinner and those who followed had confidence in the usefulness of animal behavior principles, because their relevance to human problems seemed obviously valid from common everyday observation of human behavior. Skinner set forth evidence for wide applicability of behavior principles to human behavior first in *Walden Two* (1948), a novel that speculated about the kinds of social structures that a community would adopt if it utilized knowledge of behavior principles maximally; and in *Science and Human Behavior* (1957), a systematic extension of behavior principles to self-control, law and government, religion, education, culture, and private events. The principles, originally validated intuitively and anecdotally, were later confirmed by a wide range of experiments.

Probably the most important experience shared by Skinnerian psychologists was the experience of shaping behavior in animals (such as a pigeon or rat) using food reinforcement. A food-deprived pigeon eats grain from a hopper, which can be raised to within the bird's reach by the experimenter's pressing a button. (This activates an electrically operated solenoid.) The experimenter selects some performance, such as hopping, that he wishes to occur more frequently and reinforces it with food by presenting the food, signaled by a correlated light and sound, immediately following the performance. The experience, shared alike by beginners and advanced professionals, is a dramatic one in which the experimenter, contacting the animal only through the button which operates the food dispensing mechanism, increases the frequency of the desired performance in a matter of minutes. Extinction provides an equally dramatic experience by either eliminating totally or drastically reducing the frequency of the performance by discontinuing the reinforcement (food).

The experience is significant because of the sense of complete control over a single animal's behavior. The experimenter creates or removes the behavior in a single organism rather than the average of a group. The situation has a clinical flavor because there is an adjustment and interaction between the person operating the feeder and the pigeon. Also significant is that each action depends on what happened previously (i.e., the sequence of performance and reinforcement or lack of reinforcement). The novice who carries out such a demonstration feels, like the early behaviorists, that the range behavior of organisms is plastic and virtually unlimited if a properly reactive environment can be arranged.

Behavior is altered so precisely and self-consciously in this experimental environment that it seemed natural to think that the same approach in more complex situations would resolve pressing social problems. The ability to change behavior for the betterment of mankind became as powerful a challenge for the experimental behavioral psychologist as it had been to other mental health professionals and educators, such as Freudian psychologists, group theorists, and nursery school teachers. This conviction about the plasticity of human behavior is reminiscent of the early Watsonian behaviorists and Carl Rogers's faith that every person in life has the "capacity to deal constructively with all aspects of his life which can potentially come into conscious awareness" (Rogers 1951). Skinner's (1948) *Walden Two* is an early statement of the conviction that man can design a social structure to make him the kind of human being he wants to be. Ferster (1957) expressed the same hope when he wrote of the potential in the everyday environment for avoiding the distress of mental illness. "A potential reinforcing environment exists for every individual, however, if he will only emit the required performances on the proper occasions. One has merely to paint the picture, write the symphony, produce the machine, tell the funny story, give affection artfully, and the world will respond in kind with prestige, money, social response, and love. Conversely, a repertoire which will make contact with the reinforcements of the world will be subsequently maintained because of the effect of the reinforcement on the performance."

Large numbers of experiments with human subjects, patterned after animal laboratory paradigms, continued to reinforce the belief in the importance of reinforcement principles for modifying human behavior (Ayllon & Azrin 1968; Bijou 1965; Bijou et al. 1966; Wolf et al. 1964; Lindsley 1956). Experiments with psychotic children, mostly autistic and very psychiatrically disturbed, considered untreatable at that time (Ferster 1961), were among the early extensions from the animal laboratory to clinical practice. At the start of the experiment the children behaved in only the simplest and most primitive ways, both in the experimental room and out. Toward the end of the experiment, they were earning pennies to use in a device that would deliver a towel with which they could go swimming later; they were matching simple with complex stimuli; they were saving money for later use; and they were engaging in other tasks that required paying attention to a host of stimuli and conforming to complicated procedures, most of these reinforced by food or tokens. Furthermore, the children sustained these complex activities for two and three hours at a time, even though they were not able to do so for as long as five minutes elsewhere. Obviously, the main achievement in these experiments was not the literal repertoires that emerged. The experiments did demonstrate, however, that an environment arranged to interact with the child's repertoire delicately and in small steps could develop complex activities. The patient, cumulative construction of a reactive environment, and the skill of the experimenter seemed to be the critical factors rather than any inherent limitations of the child.

Later experiments by Lovaas and others confirmed both the technical power of reinforcement and the child's sensitivity to carefully designed environments. Using food as a reinforcer, Lovaas (1966) patiently, through thousands of trials, taught several mute autistic children, first to mimic words and phrases and describe objects around them and later to request food and other needs verbally. Hundreds of reports in the literature corroborated the technical efficiency of the experiments and the susceptibility of the behavior of the most disturbed child to behavior modification. Interest in such behavioral modification heightened because there is such a shortage of trained clinical workers, and because the target behaviors were day-to-day items of conduct that would ease the burden of the children's custodial care, such as using the toilet, dressing, or eating with spoons or forks.

Food tokens, or other tangible motivational devices, however, have obvious drawbacks, despite their usefulness to make contact with a child who does not appear sensitive to ordinary social influence and for whom there would otherwise be no adequate care. A child who speaks or otherwise acts to get food is not likely to continue later when he is not hungry. Food procedures also raise moral problems because they give the therapists arbitrary power to deprive the child in order to make the reinforcer effective. The explicitness of behavioral procedures make them more overt and obvious than in other situations where the coerciveness may not be so obvious because it is unspoken. The emphasis on behavioral objectives may also emphasize goals relevant to the therapist rather than the child.

Fortunately, the extension of behavioral concepts to clinical problems does not depend upon the use of food, tokens, or any particular procedure for modifying behavior. The answer to the discrepancy between these obvious drawbacks in the use of food and token procedures on the one hand and their frequent effectiveness on the other lies in collateral and indirect efforts, apart from the specific behaviors that are intended to be reinforced. For example, one collateral result of reinforcement procedures is that the person who reinforces observes the child or patient most carefully because he has to identify specific detailed acts in order to deliver the tokens or other reinforcers accurately. The teacher delivering tokens in a classroom has to observe very small, otherwise unnoticed, increments in the child's performance in order to deliver the tokens and react to *individual* children, whereas, before she had lectured to them as a *group*. Indeed, any teacher or clinician who can observe small details of conduct becomes much more personally reactive. Thus the attention or personal reactivity of the therapist, particularly as it occurs uniquely to the individual child or patient, may serve as a powerful reinforcer, perhaps more effective or relevant than the food or token. Although there is no guarantee that a person who observes small details of an individual's conduct will as a result interact more humanely and closely with that individual, it is a step in the right direction. The ability to observe small changes in the patient's behavior also serves as a motivational device for the therapist. The therapy is often seen as a continuous development of the patient's conduct over a week, three months, or even a year. Neophyte clinicians frequently become discouraged because global changes in behavior happen slowly. Reinforcement procedures visualize tiny changes that in turn sustain (reinforce) the therapist, while larger changes accumulate gradually.

Fortunately, the usefulness of behavioral psychology for the solution of clinical problems is not limited to specific techniques of behavior modification. Behaviorists are able to enter into clinical work as objective observers who can describe the therapy of gifted and effective therapists, who act intuitively and cannot themselves describe what they do.

The following account of a gifted therapist working with a mute, profoundly psychotic 4-year-old child illustrates the power of an objective behavioral description.

"Jeanne Simons placed Karen on a rocking horse where she stayed without crying as long as Miss Simons rocked the horse and sang to her. After a few minutes Miss Simons stopped rocking the horse for brief periods but kept on singing. She carefully sensed how long she could stop rocking the horse without losing control of Karen. The return to rocking always followed some behavior other than crying. In general Miss Simons stopped rocking the horse whenever she judged that Karen's behavior was strongly maintained by some current factor, such as playing with the handles of the rocking horse. Next, Miss Simons took the plastic doll from Karen's hands, set it on a nearby table, and quickly moved the table next to Karen who promptly picked up the doll. One would guess that under other circumstances taking the doll away from Karen would lead to screaming. Although Karen was without the doll only for a few seconds, this situation provided the basis for the reinforcement of a specific constructive piece of behavior—reaching for the doll. This was the first time that Miss Simons required some behavior of Karen."

"Now Karen moved the rocking horse slightly, and Miss Simons' singing usually occurred contingent on the rocking. When Karen sat quietly, Miss Simons simply watched, smiled, and hummed gently. When Karen rocked, Miss Simons sang in rhythm to the movements of the horse. Then the episode with the doll repeated, but this time the movements were a little slower and Karen was without her doll for a few seconds longer. When Karen returned to rocking, Miss Simons sang in rhythm. Soon Karen placed the doll on the table herself. This probably occurred because the behavior controlled by the rocking horse was becoming prepotent over that controlled by the doll. Also, it was difficult for Karen both to clutch the doll and to hold the handles of the rocking horse. Karen continued rocking without the doll for over a minute as Miss Simons sang along. The magnitude and rhythm of the rocking were quite vigorous."

"Next Miss Simons kept silent for brief periods while Karen rocked. Technically this was intermittent reinforcement of the rocking. At this point Karen turned to the doll, possibly because she was less inclined to rock the horse when Miss Simons did not sing. But in picking up the doll Karen dropped it to the floor, perhaps accidentally, and for the first time during the episode, she began to cry. Miss Simons asked, 'Do you want to pick up your doll? I'll help you,' and extended her hands to Karen. When Karen touched Miss Simons' hand, Miss Simons clasped Karen's hands and helped her from the rocking horse. When Karen did not lift her foot over the saddle, Miss Simons simply held her there until she made some movement. When Karen did not move, Miss Simons prompted the behavior by moving the foot partially over the saddle and allowed Karen to complete the final part of the action. Miss Simons then held Karen in the vicinity of the doll until Karen picked it up, and once more she offered her hands as she said, 'Do you want to get up?' Karen lifted her hands in the gesture which many children characteristically use as a demand for being picked up, but Miss Simons simply continued to hold her hands out until Karen touched them. Back on the horse, Karen now rocked without Miss Simons' singing. Once again, she dropped her doll and the same episode was repeated. This time Miss Simons supported the behavior slightly less than she had on the previous occasion."

The whole interchange lasted about twenty minutes, during which several hundred reinforcements altered the child's repertoire substantially. In contrast to food reinforcement, in the usual animal experiment, very simple features of the child's environment were manipulated skillfully and rapidly in a symphony of action. Although every principle of behavior known from the animal laboratory could be illustrated by events from this episode, there was a content here that could not come from laboratory experience. A functional analysis of what happened is not equivalent to actually carrying out the interaction.

Miss Simons weakened the doll's compulsive control of Karen by waiting until Karen's behavior was strongly controlled by other reinforcers, so that she could remove the doll for brief periods. She very slowly lengthened the intervals during which Karen was without the doll by pacing them with the development of these other behaviors. At no point during the intervention was the frequency of crying decreased in the way that we carry out extinction in an animal experiment. With my limited experience with children I might have kept Karen on the horse until her crying stopped before I handed her the doll or lifted her off. When Karen dropped her doll and began to cry, Miss Simons reacted immediately and used the doll itself as the reinforcer for generating a small increment in the child's repertoire. Instead of simply carrying out extinction, Miss Simons identified the operant reinforcer, maintaining crying, and began to apply this reinforcer differentially in favor of behaviors, other than crying, which she judged to be more useful for the child. The weakened control by the doll and the extinction of the crying were by-products of the reinforcement of other behaviors. In the meantime, the amount of crying and emotional states were kept small enough so they did not disrupt the new emerging repertoire.

Not only did the observations fit the therapist's view of what had actually occurred, but it served also to communicate more clearly what happened in therapy. Despite her consumate skill as a therapist, she had not been able previously to teach her skills to other staff members, either by demonstration or by verbal instruction.

Although much of modern behavior therapy focuses on new techniques of psychotherapy, a powerful contribution of behaviorism may be the objective description of therapy, such as was presented above, as a language in a theoretical framework that can convey what happens (Ferster 1972). Not all therapists have the consumate skill of the one previously described, and clinical training programs frequently involved years of training. Even when the programs were successful there was no real conviction about what part of the training was responsible for what part of the therapist's clinical skill. If experimental psychology could provide tools to identify the effective elements of the therapist's interaction with the patient, and if therapy could be described objectively, then clinicians could become sure, quick, and more frequent in their effectiveness with the child.

Clinically skilled people who work with children are in short supply. Part of the problem is economic, because pay levels and, correspondingly, educational levels of those who work with children are so low. More distressing, however, is the possibility that persons with clinical skill who are in daily contact with the children would not be available even if pay scales were higher. This shortage of clinically trained people is a vacuum into which operant conditioning has stepped, in the form of behavior modification. Many procedures have been developed to conform a child's conduct to daily routines administered by the custodial staff. These are simple procedures usually requiring very little training. They frequently involve tokens that the child can cash in later for privileges, food, or an opportunity for an outing. Often the target behaviors of the reinforcement procedures were the day-to-day items of conduct required to manage the children in custodial care, such as using the toilet, eating with utensils, or dressing. When the children were capable of self-care, procedures were designed to sustain them at a high enough frequency.

Token systems also have been used in the classroom, as exemplified by the work of Bijou (1966), a pioneer in the development of programmed classrooms.* Reinforcement procedures in the classroom also involved an analysis of the educational repertoire, so that reinforcement could be delivered in a step-by-step program that developed complex repertoires in small, rationally designed increments. The work of Bijou and others who experimented in the classroom, like the experiments with emotionally disturbed children, showed that the limits of educability seemed to lie in the limits of our skills and knowledge about arrangement of an effective classroom environment, rather than the limits inherent in the child. When tokens and the teacher's reactivity met the student's existing repertoire, when each task set for the child was a small increment from what he already knew, there was always a corresponding increase in the child's competence.

Tokens, of course, are only a step removed from food, and they share some of the same problems. There is the danger of coercing the child into performing a rote act, meaningless to the important parts of his life. Like food, however, they have the advantage that they can be applied objectively as a visible procedure to all who observe, including the person who applied them. They direct the teacher's attention to small increments in the child's behavior, if for no other reason than that the increments have to be seen before a token can be delivered. The increase in the child's behavior reinforces the teacher's behavior, increasing the frequency of teaching. The clinician's task is usually a continuous one, lasting over a week, a month, three months, or even a year. The ability to sustain such continuous procedures would, as a matter of course, depend on being able to observe the relevant constituent details of the interactivity. Neophyte clinicians frequently become discouraged because global changes in behavior happen slowly. Reinforcement procedures visualize tiny changes in the child's behavior, which in turn sustain the therapy along the way to larger changes. Theoretically, at least, we can expect behavioral training to develop the trainee's ability to see the small step-by-step changes in behavior that the

experienced, sensitive clinician reacts to so intuitively.

Even though many token procedures and programmed environments appear to be unusually successful practically (Ayllon & Azrin 1968); Atthowe & Krasner 1968;), they raise puzzling questions because there are theoretical reasons why they should not work. There is something unreasonable, for example, about a child's learning to read in order to get food or candy. Later in the real world reading will have to occur because of its natural consequences—the other repertoires in the child's life it makes possible—rather than from the arbitrary intervention of a "feeder." Or to put the matter in the reverse direction, the inclination to interact with the social environment by reading appears to be more crucial than the components or content of the reading behavior. A child who learns to read because of food may stop reading as soon as it is withdrawn. A child who is inclined to read because it makes possible experiences that are important to his life will sustain and enlarge his repertoire. Perhaps the solution to the paradox is the indirect effects of the token procedures discussed above, rather than the specific behaviors that are reinforced.

Such objective definition of small units of the child's repertoire is essential for programming and for successive approximation of a large repertoire in small increments. The token may also have the same purpose for the child as for the teacher. It is not only backed up with food, but it also amplifies the child's conduct, making his progress and competence visible. When the child can visualize his own competence and accomplishment in directions relevant to his own needs, then natural reinforcers will take precedence over the tokens.

The close identification of behaviorism with behavior therapy, behavior modification, or operant conditioning is necessarily valid. The natural consequence of a child's behavior in a normal environment may be as effective and durable a reinforcer as food or other concrete things. In order to teach a child to dress himself, for example, an obvious procedure would be to use food to build the performances in successive approximations, beginning, perhaps, with just touching or picking up the coat. At each step, reinforcement shifts to a performance that is a small variation in the desired direction. The procedure is little different from that used to shape complex behavior with an animal, and the result would be equally predictable. The same performance could also be developed with natural reinforcers. If we begin with a child who is inclined to go outside and play on a cold day, we have two natural events—the outside play activity and the out-

* Editor's note: Dr. Ferster's article chiefly uses the teacher-child-classroom paradigm to explain behavior modification. To understand much of the current controversy over behavior modification programs, it should be clear to the reader that all of the author's examples apply equally well to therapy of adult outpatients and to behavior modification of prisoners, psychiatric inpatients, and human experimental subjects.

side temperature—as the ultimate reinforcers to sustain the performance. To start with, reinforcement occurs when the child is intercepted at a time when he is inclined to go outside to play. His arm is put into one sleeve of the coat and his other arm put half way in the other sleeve. All the while the child is kept loosely and good naturedly in the vicinity of the therapist by the crook of the arm and the position of the body. With enough sensitivity to the situation, the child will push his hand the remaining distance, perhaps 3 inches, into the coat sleeve. As the coat goes on, the therapist says, "Fine, Timmy, let's go outside," and he is out in a flash. The reinforcer is immediate, natural, and effective. On the next occasion for going outside the child's hand is only started into the sleeve, so that this time he has to extend it farther in order to get the coat on. Step by step, less of the activity is supplied by the therapist and more is controlled by its contribution to getting the coat on, until the child eventually takes full responsibility for dressing, reinforced by getting the coat on, which is in turn reinforcing because it is an occasion when he can go to the playground.

The objectivity and specific application of reinforcement principles is the same with the natural consequences of putting on a coat and going out as with food and tokens as reinforcers. The main difference is that the natural reinforcer has to be discovered by observing the individual child, while food and tokens can usually be applied arbitrarily. The control of the behavior by the outside temperature is a little more complicated because the consequences are not so immediate as with going through a door, but the principles are similar. The picture that emerges, when we combine the view of the behaviorist who emphasizes the frequency of identifiable performances occuring because they are reinforced and the clinician who deals with natural events basic to the child's immediate life, is that of a classroom or clinic in which ordinary events are molded and energized into a highly reactive environment. All of the advantages of reinforcement procedures are preserved because each performance makes possible another one that has an important place in the child's life. Seemingly innocent events may be substantial reinforcers if used effectively. A change in location, the child's clear view of his own activity, an increase in repertoire, or one event enabling the next can contribute to maintaining and expanding a repertoire. Instead of "making the child learn," the teacher reacts to performances that achieve the child's goals rather than those that annoy the teacher.

An important contribution that a functional analysis of behavior brings to clinical subject matters is communicability and the possibility of teaching others. Traditionally, the master teacher and the intuitive clinician just "grew like topsy." Training programs for clinicians are uncertain and the supply is short. The structure and design of a classroom in which the main events are visible can provide support for a teacher to operate at a higher level of technical skill than would be otherwise possible. Furthermore, training of teachers and clinicians in the functional analysis of behavior could provide a tool that would give them access to the knowledge of the skilled clinician and the skill to function adequately in a properly structured environment while they are gaining the long experience required for effective intuitive clinicians. Behaviorism is a way to describe human nature objectively in the manner of natural science. It is not necessarily different in its content or form from clinical views. Behavior modification describes specific techniques for modifying behavior by applying explicit reinforcement.

REFERENCES

Atthowe, J. M., Jr., & Krasner, L. "A preliminary report on the application of contingent reinforcement procedures," *Journal of Abnormal Psychology* 73 (1968): 37–43.

Ayllon, R., & Azrin, N. *Token economy: a motivational system for therapy and rehabilitation.* New York: Appleton-Century-Crofts, 1968.

Bijou, S. W. Application of operant principles to the teaching of reading, writing and arithmetic to retarded children. *New Frontiers in Special Education,* 1965. Washington: National Education Association, pp. 1–6.

Bijou, S. W., Birnbrauer, J. S., Kidder, J. D., & Tague, C. "Programmed instruction as an approach to teaching of reading, writing and arithmetic to retarded children," *Psych. Rec.* 16 (1966): 505–22.

Ferster, C. B. "Reinforcement and punishment in the control of human behavior by social agencies," *Psych. Res. Repts.* (Dec. 1958): 101–18.

Ferster, C. B., & DeMyer, M. K. "The development of performances in autistic children in an automatically controlled environment," *J. of Chron. Dis.* 13 (1961): 312–45.

Ferster, C. B. "An experimental analysis of clinical phenomena," *Psych. Rec.* 22 (1972): 1–16.

Franks, C. M. *Behavior therapy: Appraisal and status.* New York: McGraw-Hill, 1969.

Lindsley, O. R. "Operant conditioning methods applied to research in chronic schizophrenia," *Psych. Res. Repts.* 1956 (American Psychiatric Association): 118–39.

Lovaas, O. I., Berberich, J. P., Perloff, B. F., & Schaeffer, B. "Acquisition of imitative speech of schizophrenic children," *Science* 151 (1966): 705–7.

Rogers, C. *Client centered therapy.* Boston: Houghton Mifflin Co., 1951.

Skinner, B. F. *Walden Two.* New York: Macmillan, 1948.

Skinner, B. F. *Science and human behavior.* New York: Macmillan, 1953.

Watson, J. B. *Behaviorism* (2nd ed.). New York: Norton, 1930.

Watson, J. B., & Rayner, R. "Conditioned Emotional Reactions," *J. expl. Psychol.* 3 (1920): 1–14.

Wolf, M., Risley, T., & Mees, H. "Application of operant conditioning procedures to the behavior problems of an autistic child," *Behavior Research and Therapy* 1 (1964): 305–12.

Wolpe, J. *The practice of behavior therapy.* New York: Pergamon Press, 1969.

EDITORIAL COMMENT

Dr. Ferster's article describes behaviorism and behavior modification at its most ideal and ethical level. It also points out (for example, on p. 112) the pitfalls of applying behavior principles in a mechanistic and oversimplified way.

At this time, there is a great deal of ferment and controversy over the use of behavior modification programs, especially in mental institutions and prisons.* It is important to understand that behavioral modification is not good or bad per se, but that each proposed program must be judged in terms of the ethical and moral standards implied in Dr. Ferster's article. Each must also be judged in the light of its scientific validity, respect for the subjects rights, and due regard for informed consent.

* See Editorial note by Professor Allen, Chapter 5, for details.

LEGAL AND ETHICAL ASPECTS OF BEHAVIOR CONTROL

Seymour L. Halleck, M.D.

THE POTENTIALITIES OF BEHAVIOR CONTROL

The new fear of psychiatric treatment is best understood in terms of the concept of behavior control. Perry London has defined behavior control quite simply as getting people to do someone else's bidding. I would like to expand slightly on this definition. Most psychiatric treatments are designed to change the patient's behavior. In its broadest sense behavior control can be viewed as a special form of behavioral change. It is treatment imposed on or offered to the patient that to a large extent is designed to satisfy the wishes of others. Such treatment may lead to the patient's behaving in a manner which satisfies his community or his society. Of course, behavioral change that satisfies the wishes of others may also satisfy many of the wishes of the patient. It is sometimes necessary to include even this category of behavior change under the heading of behavior control.

The question of behavior control has been made more critical by the growing effectiveness

Excerpted and reprinted with permission from the *American Journal of Psychiatry* 131 (April 1974): 4.

of psychiatric treatment. The newer drugs and new behavior therapy techniques make it possible to change behavior in a relatively efficient and rapid manner. Long-term psychotherapeutic techniques can, of course, also modify behavior. However, traditional psychotherapy works slowly. It gives the patient time to contemplate the meaning of behavioral change and to resist such change. It also offers the patient the opportunity to learn to behave in ways which do not meet the needs of others. Some traditional psychotherapists even welcome changes that leave the patient more aggressive, more rebellious, and perhaps more abrasive to those around him. (This may, of course, just be a variant of behavior control in which the patient does the bidding of his therapist rather than the bidding of members of his community.)

Biological and behavior therapies, on the other hand, seem to be peculiarly adaptable to serving the needs of society. Lobotomy, electric shock, and tranquilization are likely to increase conformity and to decrease assertiveness. Behavior therapies are used somewhat more flexibly. Some forms of behavior therapy may help the patient develop greater assertiveness. In practice, however, there is little evidence that they have been used to promote assertiveness. Biological and behavior therapies also work quickly. They can be used without giving the patient a chance to contemplate the meaning of his behavior. Once the patient agrees to or is coerced into treatment, he is unlikely to consider the interpersonal or social causes of his behavior or the social consequences of his treatment. . . .

SUGGESTIONS FOR ADDITIONAL READING

Freedman, Alfred M., and Kaplan, Harold I., eds. *Comprehensive Textbook of Psychiatry.* Baltimore: The Williams & Wilkins Company, 1967.

Freedman, Alfred M., Kaplan, Harold I., and Sadock, Benjamin J. *Modern Synopsis of Comprehensive Textbook of Psychiatry.* Baltimore: The Williams & Wilkins Company, 1972.

Ferster, C. B., and Perrot, Mary C. *Behavior Principles.* New York: Appleton-Century-Crofts, Division of Meredith Corporation, 1968.

Redlich, Fredrick C., and Freedman, Daniel X. *The Theory and Practice of Psychiatry.* New York, London: Basic Books, 1966.

Reed, Louis S., Myers, Evelyn S., and Scheide-

mandel, Patricia L. *Health Insurance and Psychiatric Care: Utilization and Cost.* Washington, D.C.: The American Psychiatric Association, 1972.

Arieti, Silvano, ed. *American Handbook of Psychiatry.* New York: Basic Books, 1959 (reprint 1974) 3 vol.

Noyes, A., and Kolb, L. *Modern Clinical Psychiatry.* Philadelphia: W. B. Saunders, 8th ed., 1973.

Weihofen, H. *Legal Services and Community Mental Health Centers.* Washington, D.C.: The American Psychiatric Association, 1969.

"The Fires of Irrelevance," The Nader Report on Community Mental Health with Response by Bertram Brown, Director, NIMH, *M.H.,* vol. 56, no. 4 (Fall 1972): 6.

II

The Psychiatrist and Psychologist in a Legal Setting

5

The Psychiatric Evaluation

We begin our consideration of the psychiatrist and the psychologist in a legal setting with a discussion of the psychiatric evaluation (in this chapter) followed by consideration of the psychological assessment (in Chapter 6). These reports are the cornerstones on which legal behavioral science collaboration in adversary proceedings must be built. It is essential, therefore, that the lawyer be able to understand them and to appraise their validity and significance. After reading the articles by Dr. Whitehorn, Dr. Rubin, and Dr. Danto, the reader should be reasonably well equipped to "evaluate the evaluation"; the psychiatric reports in the Strong and Smith cases will provide an opportunity for testing that skill.* Psychiatric evaluations and testimony will be found in many of the chapters to follow. They have been selected because they are illustrative of some facets of the topic under discussion in each chapter; but it is important also for the reader to approach them critically in light of the criteria for all such professional reporting discussed in this chapter.

* Readers should assess these pretrial reports in light of the guidelines suggested by Dr. Rubin in "The Psychiatric Report." Lawyers and law students are invited to consider what questions they would have—as judge, prosecutor, or defense counsel in the case—for the psychiatrist who prepared the report.

Editorial Note: *Introduction to Whitehorn Article*

Dr. Whitehorn's article, written thirty years ago, is a clear, nontechnical description of the professional skills and interpersonal sensitivity required to conduct successfully a psychiatric interview. Though he writes about the psychiatric interview generally, his points are particularly appropriate for the forensic interview. Dr. Whitehorn's article demonstrates that the gathering of psychiatric data about a patient or client involves a great deal more than simply, "talking to the patient." ("You mean, doctor, all you did was talk with the accused?") Dr. Whitehorn points out that the objective data gathered is only half of the psychiatric material obtained through an evaluation. The patient's attitudes, feelings, capacity to verbalize his problems, and his nonverbal behavior are just as important as the specific information elicited.

GUIDE TO INTERVIEWING AND CLINICAL PERSONALITY STUDY

John C. Whitehorn, M.D.

LEARNING ABOUT THE PATIENT'S ATTITUDES

Human psychobiology, which is concerned with the integrated adaptive behavior of the human being, is of major importance in all fields of medicine. It is a fundamental purpose of psychiatric instruction and training to help the physician learn how to deal with the psychobiologic unit—the person—in action. The primary technical psychiatric procedure is the interview between the physician and the patient.

The aims and methods of psychiatric interviewing can be learned thoroughly only by experience, reflection, and discussion with teachers, but a somewhat detailed discussion of the matter is offered here for preliminary guidance.

The universal aim of the physician at the beginning of the first interview with the patient in any case is to learn about the presenting problem, or chief complaint. Thereafter, aims diverge somewhat. One line of inquiry tries to answer the questions, "What noxious agent causes this patient to be ill; how does it do so, and how can it be eliminated?" Another line of inquiry concerns the patient himself, "What is his reaction to the noxious influence, or influences, and how can a knowledge of his personality be utilized in his care?" This study of the patient as a person acquires an enormous importance in certain instances from a surprising fact: The patient is often his own worst enemy. His attitudes are sometimes the most noxious agencies with which the physician has to contend. . . .

The clinical study of personality depends fundamentally on the physician's first-hand study of the patient's attitudes. Sometimes the matter is left at the level of his getting a few opinions about the patient from relatives or other sources, but this information is inadequate, and often misleading. To learn about the patient's attitudes is somewhat more difficult than to make a physical examination, largely because of two factors: first, the factual information sought is somewhat more subtle than that which the examiner seeks through inspection, palpation, percussion, or auscultation; and, second, the technic involves the "personal equation" to a much more important degree. Indeed, one may truly say that the personal interaction between examiner and examinee constitutes the most vital part of this examination. The examiner must be doing two things—he participates in the interview and he observes at the same time. For purposes of logical discussion, these two roles may be separated, but in actual work they have to be combined.

ELEMENTARY STEPS

Getting the Interview Started

In learning to interview patients, one is inclined to depend on a prepared series of questions or topics, to "cover the ground" for one's superior; and it remains always a valuable aid to thoroughness to have in the back of one's mind, or in the back of one's desk, some scheme of systematic survey. . . . Yet mere questioning, in an impersonal and completely unresponsive manner, tends to defeat the examiner's purpose of learning about the patient's attitudes, for patients do not talk revealingly to an interviewer who does not show signs of interest and of increasing understanding, that is, unless what the patient says seems to mean something to the interviewer. The patient's attitudes are not likely to appear at first, in answer to prepared questions, but later, in reaction to what he feels is the interviewer's response to his statements. Some response is needed to draw the patient out. The responses most helpful in eliciting significant statements are, in general, facial expressions and gestures—the ordinary

Excerpts from "Guide to Interviewing and Clinical Personality Study," *Archives of Neurology and Psychiatry* 2, no. 3 (September 1944): 197–202; reprinted with permission.

human signs of interest and appreciation. The interviewer need not talk a great deal, and he surely does not need to begin framing and stating opinions. If he does have to talk a bit to get the patient started, he needs to be alert to what may be suggested thereby. Letting the patient tell his own story is the best way to avoid the troubles that arise from suggestibility. An attitude of alert interest and appreciation is the best means of avoiding the opposite extreme of having the patient "freeze up."

Furthermore, every interview has its psychotherapeutic or psychonoxious implications. It is incorrect to think that the examiner can first gather the information and then start the psychotherapy. The psychotherapy begins at the very first contact, in the sense of a mutual understanding and rapport. This does not mean that the interviewer has to start at once to offer advice and opinion—far from it.

THE PRESENTING PROBLEM AND THE PRESENT ILLNESS

With relatively few exceptions, interviews begin with the "presenting problem," corresponding to the classic medical term "chief complaint." The presenting problem is likely to be the topic which provides the soundest basis for a conversation of mutual serious interest. Why did the patient come to the hospital, clinic, or physician? What circumstances led to his coming at just this time? Had everything been going well up to this time?

The examiner should be sure to record verbatim the sentence in which the patient expresses his chief complaint. The manner in which this is stated generally indicates not only the chief complaint but the patient's attitude toward it, the record of which is lost if the complaint is translated into medical terms. Furthermore, all subsequent discussion is likely to revolve around this chief complaint; so it is a great help to be able to refer to it just as the patient stated it.

The story of the development of this chief complaint from the time the trouble began (the "present illness," as it is designated in the record) is usually the next topic to arise; here, again, the form of the patient's statement is important, although it is usually necessary to condense it for the record.

Some patients may say, "Well, doctor, you saw my record," or "You saw my sister," or "Do I have to go over all that again?" It may help, then, to say, "Yes, but we want most of all to know your story of the matter," or "We need to understand how the situation has been affecting you—your life, your feelings, your activities, or your welfare." It is of chief importance to get the patient's own formulation of the presenting problem. This will tell the physician a good deal about the patient himself, as well as about his sickness. The patient should also be encouraged to tell what he expects that the physician or the hospital can do about this presenting problem and what kind of help he is prepared to receive. Patients are seldom aware of all the resources of the medical profession. A patient who feels only moderately ill may say, "Well, doctor, maybe I need only a pill." Another, feeling gravely ill, may say, "Maybe I need an operation." Some patients find it difficult to accept the kind of help that can, and should, be given. So it is necessary to get an idea of what the patient expects and is ready for and the attitudes which must be met in gaining acceptance for the proper therapeutic measures. . . .

DEPRESSED STATES AND THEIR INFLUENCE ON THE INTERVIEW

When the patient is found to be in a sad mood or is gloomily irritable, consideration should be shown to his thinking difficulty. An apparently simple conversation may be overwhelmingly difficult for the retarded patient. It is the moderately or mildly depressed patient who is most likely to have this feature of his condition overlooked, and who therefore runs the greatest risk of being exhausted by an unduly complex or prolonged interview. An exhausted depressed patient may be a source of much misinformation, either because he misunderstands the context of a discussion or because, in order to be spared further effort, he may answer "yes" to any question or, in an indiscriminating way, disagree with everything.

ROUTINE QUESTIONS AND EXAMINATIONS

The discussion of the chief complaint and the present illness will often bring spontaneous statements on many of the points of information needed for the medical record, but some points will usually be left untouched. When a measure of rapport and mutual understanding has been reached through some minutes of rather informal and spontaneous interviewing, the examiner will usually find it acceptable to change the pace and style of the interview, in order to complete the routine information. He may say, "Now I have some specific questions to ask you about your past life. When and where were you born? What illnesses or operations have you had? Where and when?" and so on, through the usual simple questions about school, jobs, marriage and children, and social and economic circumstances, including, in a matter-of-fact way, questions about habits (use of alcohol and tobacco and sex experience). The patient may be asked for a simple self-evaluation of his personality traits (whether he is reserved, moody, tense, excitable, or steady). With regard to the family history, the examiner may at first quickly review the ages and general health of the parents and siblings and the occurrence of any illnesses among them comparable in the patient's eyes to his own condition, and later expand the inquiry as needed for the biographic understanding of family relationships. Information from other persons may be required to complete, supplement, or check the patient's account.

For an adequate personality study, the biography of the patient is, next to actual interview and observation, the most important source of information. . . .

SPECIAL ASPECTS OF INTERVIEWING

Common Difficulties in Psychiatric Interviewing

The examiner should avoid getting into unprofitable arguments with a patient. Some patients, especially those with a chronic, obscure disease or a neurosis, may put an uncomplimentary interpretation on any evidence of interest in their personal reactions, saying, "So you think I'm normal, do you?" or "Do you think I am only imagining these things?" Such remarks may at times be turned to advantage by asking in turn, "What suggested that to you?" Whereupon the patient may tell of relatives, friends, or physicians who have "accused" him of being neurotic. The physician's quizzical eyebrow or his repetition in a questioning tone of the word "accused" may then elicit a revealing rush of self-defensive remarks about "misunderstandings" over what someone may have called "imaginary" illness or over a lack of appreciation of the patient's trouble.

Sometimes a patient may sink or retire into a bog of tearful self-pity or self-defensiveness and need a bit of assistance in climbing out or a bit of stimulation. Restraint and discretion should be exercised in order not to overdo it.

If the examiner has already picked up some facts of encouraging or appreciative potentialities, he can bring this knowledge into play at this point. He may say, for example, "But, in spite of these difficulties and misunderstandings, I understood you had kept active in the care of your home (or in church duties, or looked after your sister's child, or were secretary of your club)."

It is well to be specific in such remarks, as in any questions concerning successes and achievement. A generalized question about such matters can be disheartening to one who cannot at the moment recall any achievements.

Sometimes a patient may stick on the issue that the physician thinks him abnormal. If it is not possible to get around this point unobtrusively, the examiner may say something like this: "I had not thought particularly that you were 'abnormal' (or 'imagining things' or 'neurotic' or whatever point the patient has raised), but just that you are human, and as a doctor I am of course concerned about how your human interests and activities affect your illness and your health. It is a necessary part of my business to learn about such matters."

The experienced interviewer will sometimes find it an advantage to acknowledge promptly, if it is true, that the patient's behavior or remarks have raised in his mind the possibility that the patient has become seriously handicapped by depression or has been confused or is jumping to conclusions too quickly, and will remark, "Well, you do seem depressed," or "What you have just said sounds very strange to me," or "Well, maybe so, but tell me more, so I can better understand your difficulty."

"IRRELEVANT TALK" AND ITS RELEVANCE FOR PERSONALITY PROBLEMS

Some patients do not need such careful maneuvering to get them talking about their sickness and themselves. Indeed, some physicians who are untrained in using the interview for personality study complain at times of the patient who talks too much, who "hands out just a lot of circumstantial and irrelevant talk." If one is studying the personality of a patient, there is no such thing as "irrelevant talk." The irrelevance is merely a condition of the interviewer's mind—he doesn't know what to make of it. The observer may listen, out of politeness, or because he has been told there is psychotherapeutic value in letting the patient talk, but he may not know what to listen for; in that case, the psychotherapeutic value may not be very great, for the patient may sense that no progress is being made.

The inexperienced interviewer may wonder how he can get the facts required for a respectable case record while letting the patient ramble. It is sometimes necessary to sacrifice the value of an unobstructed statement in order to hasten along to some other task. Actually, however, much of the information needed will come out spontaneously, and opportunities will also arise spontaneously for the necessary factual questions, such as those concerned with ages and names and the relationships of parents, siblings, and others. The interviewer will often find it distinctly helpful to pick up promptly the familiar names of persons as they are spontaneously mentioned. A relatively few seconds of intense effort, applied successfully at the first opportunity, in learning names and chronologic sequences may gain him a rapport with the patient which is worth hours of subsequent effort.

Without getting into deeper meanings at this stage, I may say that the patient's "irrelevant talk" usually means that he feels the need of self-justification, for some reason or other. To discover the "some reason or other" may be sometimes of much greater medical importance than anything else the physician can do. He should get down at least a few sentences for careful study. The interviewer does well, in general, to keep his mouth shut and his mind alert to all evidences from which he can infer the nature of the implied accusation or guilt against which the "irrelevant talk" or behavior constitutes a defense. He has the opportunity to learn in this way what "it is all about," by a process somewhat analogous to the surveyor's triangulation, thus: He may take two statements of the patient and imaginatively construct a statement to which they could be logical replies. If a considerable number of these construction lines converge toward the same point, the interviewer thus acquires a tentative idea as to what the talk is all "about." He may even throw out tentative questions or remarks to check his inferences. It is not recommended to seize the patient, so to speak, and make him face this central issue. In whatever the interviewer says he should keep to the same tangential lines which the patient has already laid down, and use as far as possible words which the patient has used. Skill in such "triangulation" is gained by close attention to detail and careful review of recorded interviews.

The Interview as a Constructive Experience for the Patient

The aim of this guide is primarily to aid the student of medicine as clinical clerk or intern in the task which to him is paramount. That task is, primarily, the diagnostic responsibility of arriving at a sound knowledge of the patient and an insight into his condition and reactions. Nevertheless, it should be clearly recognized that the interview between patient and physician may have meanings for the patient which are quite different. Why should any patient wish to carry on an interview?

The student's common sense tells him that the patient should wish to cooperate in order to establish a correct diagnosis, and the patient may, of course, acknowledge the logic of this proposition and yet be impatient, and a bit emotionally resistant, about what may seem unnecessary personal exposures.

The most general and reliable incentive for the patient's participation in interviews is the desire for understanding and an appreciative response. Frequently this desire is a stronger motive than is the desire to cooperate with complete truthfulness for the purpose of getting relief from pain or other symptoms of illness. The physician comes to expect a certain amount of falsification and deceit, as automatic human reactions, not to be viewed with too much indignation. The "rate of discount" varies with the patient and, also, with the rapport. When the interviewer senses keenly the patient's need for understanding, it is a common error to say hastily and reassuringly, "Yes, I understand," when, it fact, he does not understand. Such empty reassurance defeats its own purpose and blocks further progress. Real understanding, useful to the patient, is best shown in appreciative listening, with brief comments and questions geared closely and simply to the theme of the patient's preoccupations. Courtesy and respect shown in this way need not excessively prolong the interview; in fact, the session is often thereby speeded up and brought around to certain objectives of the interviewer much more promptly and effectively than by his keeping the patient crowded to the wall by a barrage of questions.

In any interview which invites spontaneity, the person interviewed may make constructive use of the opportunity to gain a better perspective and orientation. In therapeutic interviews this opportunity is systematically developed and used. Through the respectful, but candid, interaction between the attitudes of the two participants, knotty problems may be untangled with much greater effectiveness than in any purely logical analysis. In this sort of work the interviewer needs to have a fairly sound understanding of his own attitudes as they bear on the patient's problem, lest he impose on the patient new difficulties.

The Immediate Situation and the Patient's Attitude toward It

The foregoing suggestions have been formulated primarily as aids to the physician in the outpatient department. If the patient comes to the interview from a psychiatric ward, or is interviewed right in the ward, there will, of course, be a somewhat different set of expectations to deal with. The patient may be guardedly self-defensive, or he may be openly self-assertive, with delusional material prominently thrust into the foreground; and the interviewer may be blinded to the real opportunity for understanding because of prejudiced or inadequate conceptions of what such behavior means. On the other hand, if the patient is in a surgical or an obstetric service, both he and the interviewer are likely to have quite another sort of expectations, and may perhaps be temporarily blind to the importance of emotional factors. . . .

The patient usually finds himself, by reason of his illness—whatever it may be—in a state of unaccustomed helplessness. How does he take this? He may be chagrined or embarrassed about it and strive to minimize his helplessness, or he may welcome the invalid state. The manner in which a patient, in the situation of dependency imposed by illness, accepts or solicits sympathetic consideration may provide ready clues to this aptitude for the invalid role. In some persons this aptitude for invalidism is great indeed at all times, and it may be the main difficulty with which the physician has to contend. Or it may be that a tendency to welcome invalidism may represent only the need to escape from a temporary, but unusually harassing, set of anxieties. The physician's awareness of the need to evaluate such a factor will ordinarily lead to inquiries as to the patient's responsibilities. At the same time, he will feel the need to frame the discussion in terms acceptable to the patient, and so will find himself discussing occupational fatigue or point rationing or the children's school difficulties, not as irrelevant intrusions in the history-taking, or as separate and unrelated items, but as integrally related and medically significant affairs, pertinent to the evaluation of the patient's capacity to tolerate responsibility and anxiety. . . .

SUMMARY

In a brief summary of all the preceding elementary discussions, it may be said that, in whatever conditions the personality of the patient is considered to constitute an important factor in the causation or management of his illness, the examiner should seek, preferably through interviews with the patient himself, to establish the following points: (1) the patient's own spontaneous statement of his presenting problem (or "chief complaint"); (2) the special pressures in the patient's situation—personal, economic, and social (including legal, political, and military factors)—and the patient's attitudes thereto; (3) the way in which the patient's responsibilities or anxieties are increased or decreased by the illness; (4) the patient's general predisposition or resistance to the invalid state; and (5) the attitude of the patient to the physician, the hospital, etc.

EDITORIAL COMMENT

It is hoped that Dr. Whitehorn's article has given the reader a feeling for the manner in which psychiatric data ought to be gathered. The interview and interviewing techniques described by Dr. Whitehorn should result in a *product* useful to the attorney and to the court. This product is the psychiatric report. The article by Dr. Rubin discusses the report and what it should and should not contain.

THE PSYCHIATRIC REPORT

Jesse G. Rubin, M.D.

In order to use the psychiatric report as the foundation for further useful collaboration, the attorney must be in a position fully to understand each section of the report and to follow the psychiatrist's reasoning in coming to his conclusions and recommendations on the case. In addition, the attorney should know something about the criteria by which the adequacy of the report is to be measured. He must recognize whether parts of the report are weak, particularly if he is involved in an adversary proceeding. It is our purpose here to help the attorney orient himself to the psychiatric report in terms of the types of data it contains, its components and how to approach an evaluation of its strengths and weaknesses.

I. CLASSIFICATION OF DATA

In reading a psychiatric report, the attorney should keep in mind that certain of the data it contains may be thought of as "hard," other data as "soft," and still other data as of intermediate type. As he reads the report, the attorney should bear in mind the question of the position (along the "hard-soft" spectrum) of the report as a whole, and of its various components.

Hard data in this context refers to *direct objective observation* of the patient, which sometimes includes direct quotations from him. All hard data could presumably be verified and duplicated by someone observing the interview through a one-way mirror or a closed circuit television. An example of such observation would be, "During most of the interview the patient displayed a marked tremor of the hands, which was particularly notable when he lit his cigarettes. He sweated profusely when discussing the events of the day of the alleged crime. During his discussion of these events, there was also a marked quaver in his voice, in contrast to his tone during the rest of the interview." It is important to keep in mind that such hard data are the essence of good medical and scientific observation, and that the

doctor's final diagnosis and opinion can be substantiated or invalidated on the basis of the hard data presented.

Soft data consists of *inferences* and *abstractions* concerning the patient. Inferences may appear in the form of opinion, diagnoses, judgmental statements, and hypotheses about psychodynamics. The interview above might instead have been described as follows: "This patient was obviously guilty and was trying to cover up a lot of things about his life in general, and particularly about the day of the alleged crime." Note that the statement about the patient's inner feelings of "guilt" is not based on a quotation from the patient, and his supposed intent to "cover up" is an inferential conclusion of the examiner. *All soft data in a psychiatric report should be verifiable by hard data contained elsewhere in the report or available upon later elaboration.*

In reporting a psychiatric examination, it is best to stay as close as possible to hard data. However, since an evaluation may take several hours, precise and objective reporting of it would take an inordinate amount of time and would produce a cumbersome jumble of detail. Therefore, summarization is an acceptable and common practice in psychiatric reporting. Such summarization may be held to constitute *intermediate data.*

In the example given above, an intermediate data summary might read as follows: "Such common evidences of anxiety as tremor and perspiration were present during the interview and were heightened when discussing the day of the alleged crime." It may be seen that there is some inferential or soft data quality to this sentence. It is *inferred* that the patient under observation was suffering anxiety: there was no statement of the patient to that effect. Also, the specifics of the increase in anxiety at one part of the interview are not spelled out. On the other hand, the statement is brief and conveys enough of the flavor of the interview to substantiate the inferences contained.

The chart gives some further examples of hard and soft data.

This selection was written expressly for this volume and has not been previously published.

II. COMPONENTS OF A COMPLETE PSYCHIATRIC REPORT

There are seven basic parts to a psychiatric report. Given the needs of a specific case, it may not be necessary to include all of them. However, when one of these parts is omitted, it should be clear to both the psychiatrist and the attorney why this was done. Psychiatrists may record these components in varying orders. Some feel that the past history should come first as a background to the present situation. Others feel that the mental status should be recorded first so that the person reading the report can have a picture of the patient before getting into the current situation and history. The important thing to remember is that all of the components should be there or the reason for any omissions should be clearly explained.

1. Introduction

This is a brief statement with essential identifying data, concise reasons for the evaluation, and dates and length of examination procedures. For example, "At the request of Mr. A.,

Attorney at Law, I saw Mr. X., a forty-two-year-old married male, for purposes of evaluating his capacity to make a will. Patient was interviewed in my office for one hour on June 1, 1967, and for one hour on June 15, 1967. Psychological tests were performed on June 9, 1967, by Dr. Z."

2. Present Illness or Current Situation

Here the reasons for the examination are given more fully and the current legal situation or present psychiatric illness *as described by the patient* are recorded. If the patient is in legal trouble, *his views* of how he got there are essential here. This part of the report should consist essentially of hard data, with quotations from the patient when needed, and, in other instances, an accurate summary of the patient's position. The reliability of the "hardness" of the data in this context does not refer to the truthfulness of the patient's statements, but to the accuracy with which they are reported or summarized. The doctor's job here is not to pass judgment on the patient's reliability or truthfulness, but faithfully to observe

Hard Data	Soft Data	Intermediate Data
Patient reported many instances in her childhood during which her father would come home drunk and physically assault her and her mother. She stated that from the time she was twelve until the time she was seventeen she was the sole support of both parents. Although patient never saw any evidence of real physical sickness in her mother, the latter was always complaining about being too ill to work or help support the family. In addition, mother constantly complained to the patient about father's inadequacy. Patient's delinquency began at age sixteen.	This patient had a very traumatic childhood which is the cause of her current delinquent behavior.	Patient told in some detail about her early life. Her father was characterized as drunk and violent, and her mother as hypochondriacal and complaining. Such backgrounds are common in delinquent girls.
Patient spoke in a rapid, high-pitched tone about his purpose in planning the crime. His eyes were intense and his facial expression earnest as he said, "God told me I should do this. He told me I should do it because I can save the world that way. I will be the resurrection and the life. These are the necessary sacrifices on God's altar."	Patient's description of his crime was senseless and his manner appeared totally grandiose.	Patient spoke in a grandiose manner. He described his crime as a way of saving the world, and seemed to have no capacity to see himself in a realistic way.

and record what the patient tells him. If there are omissions or inconsistencies or areas of evasion in the patient's story, these may be noted, but not filled in by inferential processes.

3. Past History

This is a summary of the total life history of the patient up to the present time. It should include a picture of his childhood and adolescence, focusing particularly on his family life, peer relationships, and any evidence of early emotional disturbance. Any history of psychiatric disturbances in his family should be noted. In most cases, a summary of his capacity to socialize as a child and of his school performance should be noted, if it is obtainable. Pertinent family history of serious medical problems should be recorded.

Next, a more or less chronological history of the major areas of the patient's adult life should be recorded. If the patient has been in the armed services, something about his service career and the type of discharge he obtained is useful. Marital history, level of function as a spouse and parent, and work performance should be noted. Any previous emotional symptoms, such as depression, sleeplessness, etc., and prior psychiatric treatment should also be included here. General health problems may also be important, as are any legal difficulties. The total life history of a patient consists of a number of broad areas. It is a matter of clinical judgment to decide which of these areas requires detailed investigation.

4. Mental Status

Mental status is here used in the broad sense of a description of the psychological processes of the patient as related to his observable behavior and verbalization. The patient's appearance, motor activity (fidgeting, stance, gait, characteristic facial movement and hand gestures, etc.), his apparent mood, the flow and patterning of his speech, his capacity to think logically, his degree of insight into his current circumstances or illness, his emotional responsiveness during the interview, his degree of openness or evasiveness, are all part of the mental status examination. In this part of the psychiatric report there is a mixture of hard and soft data. Such inferences as, "The patient is depressed" or, "The patient displays a great deal of illogical thinking," or "The patient is evasive and dishonest with the interviewer," should all be verifiable by concrete examples and observation.

In addition, a formal mental status examination may be required. This consists of a fairly well standardized set of mental tasks designed to demonstrate certain qualitative and quanti-tative aspects of the patient's thinking. These tasks include his capacity to repeat a given number of digits, to interpret common proverbs, to do mental arithmetic, to understand similarities and differences between objects (a horse and a dog, for example), as well as tests of his recent and distant memory. This more formal mental status examination is useful in a variety of circumstances, most commonly when evaluating possibly brain-damaged, mentally deficient, and/or psychotic patients.[1]

5. Ancillary Data

Information gathered from sources other than direct examination of the patient should be reported if it contributes to the task at hand. Such data may consist of summaries of or quotations from previous psychiatric reports or hospitalizations; a brief summary and comparison of current and prior psychological tests; electroencephalographic reports; neurologic or medical examinations and laboratory tests; and interviews with family members, parole officers, or others whose observations may be of value in arriving at appropriate psychiatric conclusions.

6. Diagnosis

A psychiatric diagnosis is necessarily "soft data." It is an inferential or abstract statement, like any medical diagnosis. It is made after the psychiatrist, using his clinical experience, skills, and judgment, has collected many bits of hard data and ancillary data and has put them together. The diagnosis should conform to the American Psychiatric Association *Manual*,[2] unless there is some good reason not to do so. It will often be helpful to supplement the diagnosis with the qualifying adjectives, "mild," "moderate," or "severe." It may also be useful (following the custom of the armed services and the Veterans Administration) to note the pre-morbid personality of the patient, his predisposition to psychiatric illness, and the severity and type of stress which precipitated the current problem.

7. Recommendations, Conclusions, and Opinions

At this point, the psychiatrist has processed in his own mind all the information at his disposal and has come to a diagnostic impression. He then reprocesses the data with specific reference to the problem at hand and to the reason for the referral. He arrives at recommendations and opinions regarding the disposition and mental status of the patient. These

---

[1] See "Smith" evaluation, below.
[2] Chapter 3, above.

recommendations should flow naturally and in a logical fashion from the preceding parts of his report. In this last part of the report will come such issues as the psychiatrist's opinion as to the patient's competence to stand trial; whether the patient's act was causally related to a diagnosed mental condition; whether he has a disability that may be compensable under Workmen's Compensation or other laws; the fitness of the person to be a parent; the advisability of divorce, or separation, or therapeutic abortion; or any one of the varied problems for which the attorney refers a client for psychiatric opinion.

III. USING AND EVALUATING THE PSYCHIATRIC REPORT

A psychiatric report, properly understood, provides the framework for productive collaboration between psychiatrist and attorney. Before such collaboration can take place, however, the attorney must understand and adequately evaluate the report. To do so, he should ask himself the following questions:

1. How much time and effort have been spent in doing the evaluation? This will usually be apparent from part 1 of the report.

2. Are the data in parts 1 to 5 of the report chiefly "hard"? When these parts of the report contain soft or intermediate data the attorney should ascertain whether they will stand up to subsequent explanation, expansion, and cross-examination.

3. Does he understand all the language in the report? Is the language used in the first three parts of the report consistent with lay language? If not, is the technical language used in a way which can be clarified by reference to a standard psychiatric glossary or dictionary? Are the diagnostic labels consistent with those in the A. P. A. *Manual* (selections from which are included in Chapter 3 of this book)? The attorney should keep in mind that the psychiatrist may use technical terms which are meaningful for other psychiatrists but not for a lay person. For example, the psychiatrist may report in the mental status section that the patient's behavior was "schizoid." Most psychiatrists would know what was being referred to. However, a lawyer, judge, or jury will not approach the report with the same degree of medical sophistication. A request should be made to clarify and amplify such usages.

4. Do the diagnosis, recommendations, and opinions in parts 6 and 7 logically flow from the hard data in parts 1 to 5? If in the attorney's view they do not, he should discuss this with the psychiatrist. Perhaps, for example, certain theoretical positions of the psychiatrist may lead to conclusions which are surprising to the attorney even after he has read the first parts of the report.

5. Is the report complete in the sense outlined above? If it is not, why has the psychiatrist omitted parts of the report?

Optimally, work between attorney and psychiatrist demands a collaborative effort to achieve maximum consensus about what the psychiatrist is saying, why he is saying it, and how this relates to the attorney's specific objectives. This goal is easily stated, but its realization in any given case may require much time and effort.

WRITING PSYCHIATRIC REPORTS FOR THE COURT

Bruce L. Danto

. . . The psychiatrist is in a position to influence judicial process in various ways. Much of his success will depend upon his ability to write clearly and impressively or to offer effective verbal testimony. It has been my experience, that it is in this area in which the psychiatrist frequently fails his legal counsel, his client-defendant, and the court. In the following I am going to offer examples of both effective and ineffective reports.

Excerpted and reprinted with permission from the *International Journal of Offender Therapy and Comparative Criminology* 17, no. 2 (1973): 123–28.

All too often the psychiatrist uses words and concepts that not only the layman is at a loss to understand, but which are unclear to other psychiatrists. Another mistake is to cite numerous psychiatric experts whose work the court may rule "not admissible" and dismiss as "hearsay." The psychiatrist is open to criticism if his quotations are inexact, if he quotes a poor source or one out of date with contemporary thinking. In the adversary setting the opposing side will be quick to take advantage of such errors.

An example of ineffective writing:

"The mental status examination on admission showed him to be acutely psychotic. He appeared quite evasive, excited and generally over-active. He appeared very voluble and incoherent when first interviewed. His affect denoted exultation and a state of euphoria. This pseudo-manic overactivity appeared totally inappropriate to the boy's present life and to his thought content. He expressed paranoidal ideas and alluded in many ways to feelings of unreality, to a strange loss of identity and to feelings of depersonalization. The patient claims that he changed himself. His sense of identity appeared quite indistinct for he often assumed someone else's name or someone else's personality for a short period of time in association with others. He further claimed to be religiously inspired. Behind this perceptive disorder there appeared to be a great deal of rage."

As a psychiatrist I have trouble in understanding how the above material would assist its writer or the court in understanding either the defendant or anyone else. Psychological terms are used, but no concrete illustrations are offered. The report fails to give a conceptual framework that enables one to see the person about whom the report is being written. Each report should represent a picture of sorts, enabling to visualize the personality and background of the defendant, and how his usual behavior pattern related to the crime with which he is charged. Further, it should offer and substantiate an opinion both in legal as well as psychiatric terms as to whether he was temporarily insane at the time of the offense. The psychiatrist may hopefully assume that the many mystical sounding words which only a qualified expert could have written will impress the court or the attorneys. But possibly the involved parties may react instead on the lines of "this report is a bunch of garbage. The doctor doesn't know what we want to know or maybe he doesn't know anything at all and is only writing to impress someone." The more academically oriented forensic psychiatrist may resent his expertise not being appreciated, but he should realize that his written reports should serve effective communication.

A report should quote from the defendant so that the court can learn what was actually said. Statements should be followed by interpretations and these lead to conclusions, so that the reader can see how the forensic psychiatrist arrived at his expert opinions regarding criminal responsibility.

"Charles said: 'That day, it was automatic, like driving a car. I didn't plan the shooting. I was going through the motions. I had had an accident before and I never could remember the motorcycle accident. Vaguely, I can remember the shooting.' Here we see an absence of intent, or rather an uncontrollable unconscious impulse, one which I will tie up later with his suicidal behavior. Continuing, he said, 'I can remember people silhouetted in my sights and see them falling down. I was numb. I kind of wish there were voices telling me what to do but there weren't any. I would have had an excuse then. Can X-rays tell if you've had a concussion?' Here again, his thoughts switch to another subject, one which he hopes unconsciously will help him account for the killing of two people, so that he would not be diagnosed as *sociopath* as he was by other doctors prior to this examination.

Throughout the interview he expressed little concern for the victims. He said, 'Right now I am remorseful, but then (at the time of the shooting) I didn't have any feelings. At the time I was shooting I felt that I was getting even with someone. It's hard to point it down. I guess you could say, society, the world, or government. If I knew it was wrong, I wouldn't have done it. Did I use more than one gun? Hm, I think it was a rifle?' Again, here we see his level of confusion, his struggle to keep his thoughts straight and connected. Also it would appear that he did not know the difference between right and wrong when he did the shooting. In reply to my question about whether he would have shot anyone if the police had been present in the room or across the street, he said, 'I would have aimed more likely at him (policeman) instead of them (actual victims). I had a grudge against them (the police) for what I was comitted to a mental hospital for in 1970. I felt they had gone too far. I would have rather been put in jail instead. To me, I've never been in a mental hospital and consider that as low as you can go. I was ashamed and embarrassed of being put into one.' He had been committed because he had pulled a knife on the police who had been called when he threatened his parents during a family argument. In regard to his current commitment to a mental hospital for forensic study he said, 'I deserve what I have coming. I don't feel bitter about this.' Clearly, from his answer to the question about the policeman being in his room or near the actual victims, he failed the 'policeman-at-the-elbow test.' In the light of this, plus his apparent lack of conscious intent and the suddenness of his act which occurred on impulse that morning, I feel that his killing the two people was the product of an irresistible impulse and that he did not know the difference between right and wrong at the time of the shooting and that he would have killed even if policemen had been present. This man used the killing to bring in the police so that he could manipulate them into killing him. He had attempted to provoke such action on their part some months previously when he entered a federal court with his hands in his pockets, purposely giving the impression that he was ready to pull out a gun and start shooting. He confessed that he looked mean and angry in order to stimulate anxiety so that the US Marshal would shoot him. However, this did not happen. Had he been killed he hoped that public indignation over police brutality and unnecessary shooting would have been aroused when it would be brought out that he was unarmed. In this vein, he said, 'When I did away with them (shooting the two neighbors) I wanted the police in trouble. I surrendered and thought they would shoot me as they were under stress. I thought they would be put in jail for shooting me. When I was in jail I thought I would commit suicide by gassing myself.' Here we see more evidence of his psychotic process since it would be unrealistic to commit suicide in that manner in a jail setting."

The above portion of the report, illustrates some of the points previously discussed. Aside from the use of *unconscious* and *psychotic*, psychiatric terminology was reduced to a minimum. A more traditional psychiatric approach would have involved terms like *dissociative thinking, impaired concentration* and *reality testing*. Instead, those very concepts were described and concretely illustrated, so that readers could sense the degree of his personality fragmentation, his tenuous hold on reality, his disturbed view of himself and others, and his inability to lock-in and follow the subject of conversation. An attempt was made to recreate his state of mind at the time of the shooting so that the reader could, as it were, crawl inside the defendant and fathom what he was thinking and feeling both at the time of the offense and for some time afterwards.

The psychiatrist may also be called upon to determine whether a psychiatric condition is present which may affect a defendant's competence to stand trial. The following is a section of a report for mental competency examination.

"It is striking that she shows a childish denial of responsibility for having written the bad check. This action is so typical of her diagnostic condition, namely, sociopathic personality, antisocial type. It would appear also that she suffers from some consequences of alcoholism and that there may be an underlying schizophrenic condition. A severe mental disease like schizophrenia is suggested by the way she makes up words (neologism). She gives peculiar inappropriate answers and frequently strays away from one question and winds up by talking about something unrelated, suggesting a psychotic style of thinking. However, her mental illness is not of such intensity as to make her incompetent to stand trial. She appears childish and helpless and cannot assume full care of her child. Rather, she is herself a child in search of a parent and that is why she wrote a bad check. She does know the nature of the charge against her. She was able to basically follow my questions and answer them sufficiently. It is likely that she is able to assist her counsel in her defence. There is no indication at this time that her underlying mental illness will become so uncontrolled as to interfere with the judicial process. I do feel that she should receive treatment for her alcoholism and be given some tranquilizers and supportive psychotherapy. She is not motivated for intensive psychotherapy and her over-all prognosis is poor."

This report attempts to describe the fact that despite the presence of a mental illness, the defendant is competent to stand trial. In the past, such persons might well have been declared incompetent to stand trial. Many mentally ill defendants may be actively hallucinating and be mildly delusional. However, with tranquilizers and supportive care they can obtain justice and due process of law, even in spite of a fairly intense psychiatric condition. By making every effort to assist the defendant in becoming competent to stand trial, the latter benefits in the long run and is able to proceed with his future with greater certainty. Handled otherwise, a mentally ill defendant could deteriorate like so many others who have inhabited hospitals for the criminally insane for twenty years or more—still awaiting trial!

EDITORIAL COMMENT

The following reports are included so that the reader may evaluate them in terms of the articles by Drs. Whitehorn and Rubin. Two of the reports (on Mr. Strong) involve the same patient, but were done independently by two different psychiatrists. The report on Mr. Smith raises several complex issues involving questions of responsibility and "normality."

PSYCHIATRIC EVALUATION OF MR. STEVEN STRONG

This 51 year old, widowed, white male was referred for pretrial psychiatric evaluation. He is charged with the murder of his wife. Mr. Strong was seen by me for psychiatric evaluation on December 2, 5, and 14, 1969, and had psychological testing performed on January 18, 1970. Mr. Strong acknowledged without much emotion that he did shoot his wife, but he appears not really to have accepted his wife's death. "It's just like she's gone out of my life right now." In the context of marital discord of long standing, he shot his wife in the back while she was seated in their apartment. Later he "took a whole bottle of aspirin—but all it did was make me sick." He has had little emotional reaction to the whole past sequence of events.

He stated he had had problems with his wife for a long time and that there was a long-standing tension between them. He stated that his wife had had a number of affairs and had "rebelled against me over the years." He was particularly irritated that she apparently wanted the freedom to have affairs and to be married at the same time.

Mental Status: The evaluation showed an apparently guarded, underweight man who showed little emotion and volunteered a minimum of information about himself. It was not possible to judge to what extent he was withholding emotion and other data about himself or to what extent he simply was not aware of psychological and interpersonal factors.

Past History: The patient grew up in Kansas City, Kansas, the oldest of four boys. He said he had a normal childhood and that his mother and father were also normal. But, "my mother didn't show any emotions. My father was more emotional." They were in average economic circumstances; his father was a postman. The patient graduated from high school and subsequently got a Bachelor of Arts degree in Business Management at the University of Kansas. At the time of the alleged murder he was working as personnel manager for a large firm in this city. I understand that there is no record of previous criminal or antisocial conduct. Psychological testing showed at least bright average intelligence and no evidence of organicity or psychosis. The psychological testing was not able to elicit much information as to the referral questions.

Summary: This patient remains somewhat enigmatic despite several psychiatric interviews and complete psychological testing. Apparently he committed the one offense of his life in the setting of extreme, long-standing, but suppressed, marital discord. He was dangerous only to one person and only in the context of a long intimate and strained relationship. There is no indication that he has posed or would pose a danger to society under any other circumstances. Consequently, in spite of the serious nature of the alleged offense, this patient may be considered by the court to prove suitable for a disposition which does not require incarceration. If such proves to be the case, probation or parole supervision, combined with periodic psychiatric reevaluation, is recommended.

BARTON CRANWELL, M.D.

ANOTHER PSYCHIATRIC EVALUATION OF MR. STEVEN STRONG

745 Connecticut Avenue, N.W.
Washington, D.C. 20006

John Rhodes, Esq.
Rhodes and Dickenson
2185 K Street, N.W.
Washington, D.C. 20037

Dear Mr. Rhodes:

I am writing you concerning Mr. Steven Strong, a 51 year old man who was referred for psychiatric and psychological evaluation pending sentencing on a charge of murder. Data and conclusions in this evaluation are based on the following sources: (1) Mr. Strong was seen for individual 50 minute interviews on February 20, March 10 and March 26, 1970; (2) Review of your letter of February 12, 1970, which included the previous psychiatric and psychological evaluation and letters from his relatives; (3) Discussions with Dr. Susan Wagner and review of Dr. Wagner's psychological test report.*

History: (The following is the history as obtained from the patient. Additional historical information obtained from other sources will be dealt with separately, below.) Because Mr. Strong's behavior of last August can best be understood in the context of his total life story, his past history will be given first, and the events leading up to the alleged offense will follow.

The patient was born and raised in Kansas City, Kansas, the oldest of four brothers. Family history is negative for psychiatric illness except that one of the siblings has been in a state hospital several times. Patient's mother died a year and a half ago and his father is still alive and living in Kansas City.

Patient described his early family life as relatively normal though financially things were difficult. He felt that the parent's marriage was reasonably good, but marred by the fact that his father was an alcoholic. He could get quite nasty when drunk and this was directed almost exclusively at the patient's mother. Patient further criticized father's character in saying, "He always thought he was right and that the world was picking on him."

His aggressiveness was confined to yelling and there were no physical assaults or violence in the house. Patient's father worked as a postman and made a marginal living.

Patient described his mother as a quiet woman who didn't show her feelings and who was rather wishy-washy. Because of the financial situation, mother had to go to work when the patient was 10. With both parents working patient assumed the role of the surrogate father for his brothers.

As a child, the patient had few close friends, but did very well in school, graduating 10th in a class of 400 in high school. There was no history of childhood neurosis, such as bedwetting, frequent nightmares, feeding problems, etc.

After high school, the patient continued living at home and worked as a salesman for 10 years. During this time he met and married his wife. She was 10 years his junior. He knew they would marry from the first date because she was different from the other girls he knew. "She always seemed so bright and vivacious."

They moved to Washington in 1948, where he took a job in the personnel department of a large local company. He continued with this career up to the present time.

Patient states that marital problems began within a month of the wedding, when his wife informed him that she did not want children but strongly desired a career of her own in the advertising field. Prior to getting married she had spoken of becoming a wife and mother. He felt bitter and disappointed about this.

Another difficulty in the marriage was their sexual relationship. She always used sex as a weapon. That is, at times when he would not do what she demanded she would withhold intercourse.

Despite all this, when asked if there were good things in the marriage, he replied that his wife could often be a nice companion and a woman with whom he had much in common. However, year by year these good things became more and more outweighed by the disappointments and bad things listed above.

The marriage took a turn for the worse in 1960 when he began to advance to positions of significant responsibility and better pay. At the same time, she felt competitive because her own career had reached a dead end.

* See Chapter 6, post.

By the mid-1960's the difficulties in the marriage had become severe. When asked why he had not thought of divorce during this time, he replied that he had hoped she would become more mature and that the marriage would become a happy one.

The marriage took still another turn for the worse a year or two later. Mr. Strong said he felt increasing anger from his wife, which she now expressed in the form of interpersonal and sexual withdrawal. He felt he could no longer express his own anger because she would simply become extremely distant. Therefore, whatever ability he had to express his anger and communicate with her was blocked. His wife was increasingly depressed because her job had gone sour and she was not advancing at all. She began drinking excessively and he felt that their marriage was in profound trouble.

Beginning early in 1967 she began openly having affairs with other men. After an evening out with another man, she would come home intoxicated and boast to him about her sexual encounters.

By 1968 she demanded that he allow her to live two lives. That is, she wanted complete freedom to see other men, but she also wanted the comfort and security of married life with him. They had a series of increasingly bitter arguments about this. To this day, the patient believes that his wife's running around was not so much because she liked other men but because, "She wanted to get back at me because I was succeeding and she wasn't."

Despite several arguments, Mrs. Strong continued going out with another man about once a week.

Things seemed about to reach a head one week prior to Mrs. Strong's death. They were having almost continual arguments and she was taunting him overtly about her relations with other men, always casting aspersions on his virility. Finally, on the day prior to his death, she came home, "in a foul mood, looking for a fight." They started fighting verbally and fought continuously for the next 24 hours, except for brief periods of sleep. The next day, August 15, 1970, she finally said to him, "You complain a lot, but you don't have the guts to do anything. You're not enough of a man to take any action. If you were, you'd probably shoot me." When she said this, he felt a calm come over him. He went to the drawer where they kept the gun. Though he had never used it, he knew it was loaded and read the instructions. He pointed the gun at his wife and told her to turn around. She refused. He then shot her in the back. He thinks she died instantly.

Following the shooting, he says he does not know how he felt, but several thoughts occurred to him. First, he thought he would just continue living there with his wife, denying the fact that she was dead. However, he began realizing that eventually people would begin to ask questions. He also thought of running away but rejected that. Finally, he thought that the best thing to do would be to commit suicide. He then took a whole bottle of aspirin in a deliberate way but without any feelings. He maintains that he is quite ignorant of pharmacology and thought that this would be lethal. However, it resulted only in his becoming nauseated and vomiting. He says he really had wanted to die and was sorry that he didn't. Finally, not knowing what else to do, he called his brother, who came right over and then called the police and you.

Mr. Strong said that throughout these events he was aware of what was going on, but felt in a "state of shock." He was let out on bond and was able to go to work the next day. I questioned him about this and he said that that was better than sitting at his brother's house or his own apartment just thinking things over and over again.

The patient was tried and pled guilty to second degree murder. The judge ordered a psychiatric evaluation prior to sentencing, for which you referred the patient to me.

For the past few months, there have been no recurrence of suicidal ideas, though the patient says he has been quite depressed most of the time.

Mental Status: Mr. Strong is a tall thin man who looks about 10 years older than his stated age. He was not anxious during the interview, but at times he was overtly depressed. He was tearful while talking about the events immediately before and after his wife's death and about his suicidal thoughts. He exhibited some questionable borderline signs of a thought disorder: his affect was somewhat bland throughout much of the history-taking and he apparently denied that his wife had really died for as long as 24 hours after the murder. His description of this time had a rather inappropriate somewhat bizarre quality. There was no other overt evidence of psychotic thought disorder. There was no evidence of any organic brain dysfunction.

Collateral Background Information: This was contained in letters from two of the patients brothers. One confirmed the history as given by Mr. Strong, particularly reemphasizing the fact that the patient functioned as a surrogate parent for the younger brothers. It also confirmed the long-standing marital tensions between the patient and his wife.

A second brother confirmed the family history of psychiatric disorder and said he believed the diagnosis was paranoid schizophrenic reaction. He also noted that Mr. Strong had always had a great deal of trouble expressing anger, particularly at his wife, even though she "treated him poorly."

Psychological Tests: The psychological test report done by Dr. Wagner is attached to this letter. Therefore, my comments here will be confined to three important aspects of the psychological testing: First, testing confirms my clinical impression that Mr. Strong is not basically psychotic. Second, testing confirmed that he utilizes predominantly obsessional defenses and has difficulty dealing with angry feelings. Third, testing neither confirms nor refutes my clinical impression that he is strongly masochistic in his orientation to life.

Impression: Obsessive-compulsive personality with strong masochistic tendencies. I believe that at the time he shot his wife, the long-standing defenses against rage (a combination of obsessional, intellectual defenses and turning against the self through masochistic processes) broke down under the extreme prodding and goading of his wife, and the rage poured out at her. This rage was directed not only at her, but was also displaced rage originally directed at his parents (who imposed a premature burden of responsibility on him); and at his brothers who have always been overly dependent on him. With the evidence of his wife's increasing sense of failure, the episode may also be viewed as Mr. Strong's passively serving as the instrument of his wife's suicidal impulses. She literally asked him to shoot her.

Based on the above material, the following is my best judgment with regard to specific questions which have been posed by yourself and the court social worker.

1. Is Mr. Strong dangerous to himself or others?
I do not believe that he is dangerous to others. His obsessional and masochistic defenses certainly lasted throughout almost all of his years and broke down under extraordinary stress. Unless he got into another situation in which he was goaded into turning his rage outward, he would not be dangerous to others. I think there is a small suicidal risk in this man. The amount of his masochism, as well as the fact that he was quite seriously suicidal after the murder, indicates that should he get into another situation in which he feels life is hopeless he could conceivably make another suicide attempt. He certainly does not seem to be in that sort of state now.

2. Does he have a mental illness as defined legally and psychiatrically?
I do not believe he has a mental illness as defined either legally or psychiatrically in the sense of having a psychotic diagnosis. I believe that his basic diagnosis is of a character disorder with an intercurrent depression around the event of the murder. Clearly the very high degree of situational stress under which he was living with his wife, combined with his personality disorder, diminished his control somewhat so that his life-long defenses broke down.

3. What is the likelihood of recurrence of murderous behavior?
Quite unlikely. Entering with him into a detailed reconstruction of the last several years of his married life, and a very detailed reconstruction of the last day of his wife's life, make it seem that such a sequence of events will not recur and lead to future murderous behavior.

4. Will Mr. Strong benefit from therapy?
This must be answered at two levels. At a deep level, his way of handling his feelings is relatively habitual, ingrained, and rigid. I do not believe basic change is likely. More superficially, I think he relates and talks easily and could use a non-intensive, supportive counseling relationship to help him face whatever may lie ahead with a maximum of reality-planning and a minimum of depression and pain. If I can be of further assistance in this case, please do not hesitate to phone or write.

Sincerely,
JERRY ROBINSON, M.D.

PSYCHIATRIC EVALUATION OF THEODORE SMITH

745 Connecticut Avenue, N.W.
Washington, D.C. 20006

John Allman, Attorney at Law
409 13th Street, N.W.
Washington, D.C.

Dear Mr. Allman:

I am writing you concerning my evaluation of Theodore Smith. Evaluation consisted of a review of the file of material which you sent me; a 1¾ hour psychiatric interview conducted on December 11, 1968, and a review of the available hospital and youth center homes records on Mr. Smith. Mr. Smith is a 23 year old single male who was examined in the context of pending disposition of a murder charge. Evaluation was requested to see whether Mr. Smith's mental condition warranted an insanity defense and also whether anything useful regarding sentencing could be learned.

Past History: Patient was born and raised in North Carolina. Records indicate that he was hospitalized at age 2 months with head injuries, possibly caused by his father. He is the oldest of three children. His parents split up about 15 years ago and his father's whereabouts are unknown. Mother and children moved to Baltimore for several years and then came to Washington. His earliest memory is of his father physically assaulting him and he is quite angry about this. He says that when he was about 7 or 8, there was a fire in the house, which he believed was started by his father intentionally. A sister died in the fire and as a result of his reaction to this he states he was in a mental hospital for two years, though he does not remember where. He states he is amnesic for this period and that his mother has told him that when she visited him he did not know her. After a couple of years, he says, his memory returned. However, he feels that as a result of the trauma of the fire and the fact that his father hit him on the head a great deal when he was a child, he has had recurrent loss of memory since then. These lapses have included all the times when he has been charged with criminal offenses, starting when he was 10 or 11 years old and was caught stealing.

He says that after they left North Carolina, his mother tried to raise the children alone. She was unable to do so and had to put him and his sisters in various orphanages and foster homes, all of which provided unstable environments. Since age 15, a great deal of his life has been spent in institutions. In 1960, he says, he was sent to Baltimore City Hospital, though he is not sure why. He says he remembers having a positive brain wave test there. Records indicate that he was in a youth center facility in 1962 charged with housebreaking, a charge he denied, according to the records. The impression was that of an immature, impulsive adolescent, with poor judgment. It was noted that he made a good adjustment and worked hard. It should also be noted that at the facility, Dr. John Sherman, a trained child psychiatrist, diagnosed psychomotor epilepsy. The basis on which this diagnosis is entered is not clear, however. It may be that this refers to the electroencephalogram which the patient says had been done at Baltimore City Hospital.

Records indicate that the patient was in another state mental hospital in 1964 after being charged with assault. He was diagnosed as a passive aggressive personality and judged to be competent to stand trial. Psychological testing at that time revealed a full scale IQ of 91 with no evidence of organicity.

Between hospitalization and the youth center, he was free only 11 months during the past several years. During that time he worked on construction jobs. As a result of blackouts on the job sites, he had to stop working. Blackouts are characterized as a loss of consciousness, balling up in a knot, but with no tongue biting or incontinence. In February 1967 he was charged with possession of narcotics. He was in the local reformatory until December 1967, when he went into a treatment program for narcotic offenders.

When asked about his history of narcotics use, he says that he has used approximately ½ spoon of heroin every other day for two years. He denies that this has varied much either on the up side or down side. He says he has always used narcotics for two reasons: (1) They help relieve the "spells" of amnesia; (2) They help relieve worry. He denies use of alcohol because it has the reverse effect.

He remained in the halfway house, without incident, from December 1967 through June 1968. While he was still in an outpatient role there, the alleged homicide took place. Since that time, he has either been incarcerated or in a state hospital for reevaluation.

With regard to the current episode, he denies

memory of the incident. He says, "They say I stabbed a man. I don't remember." He says the last thing he remembers before the alleged offense is heading down the street with some friends to a club and the next thing was waking up the next morning. He went to a friend's house and was informed by his mother that the police were looking for him. He said he could not remember what happened the night before. He stayed with a neighbor on his mother's advice. He stayed with a friend for three weeks, when, as a result of having been "jumped" on the street, he was hospitalized and then picked up by the police. He went through "cold turkey" withdrawal in jail, then tried Methadone but found he could neither take fluids or eat, and stopped Methadone.

Records indicate that during the amnesic time the patient is alledged to have participated with two other men in the robbery and fatal stabbing of a man.

Mental Status: Mr. Smith is a young white male who looks about his stated age. He appeared somewhat distant, withdrawn, and moderately depressed during the interview, but not anxious. He also appears rather stiff and constricted in his muscular movements. He appeared to be cooperative and tried to answer questions as best he could, but it seemed that it was difficult for him to keep things in a chronologic order. There was no evidence of overt thought disorder, however. Speech was slow and deliberate. Memory varied from being fairly clear about such distant episodes as the fire, to being hazy about things involving his criminal record. At one point toward the end of the interview he had what he later described as one of his "spells." This consisted of his stopping all muscular movement, staring into space, not answering questions, and appearing quite distant. It lasted about a minute and ended by the patient shaking himself and asking me what the last question had been. There was no overt seizure activity during this time.

Formal mental status exam revealed patient's digit span on repeated testing was 6 forward and 3 backward. Serial 7's were repeatedly failed on the second digit. On similarities he responded as follows: dog-horse: "both animals." Table-chair; "both made of wood." Tree-grass; "both plants." He failed to find any meaning in the proverbs, "Don't count your chickens before they hatch," and, "A rolling stone gathers no moss." He did adequately abstract on, "Don't cross your bridges until you come to them."

In view of the above history, it was recommended that neurological evaluation, to include an electroencephalogram, be performed. This seemed essential because if the patient truly suffered from psychomotor or another type of epilepsy, his behavior controls could have been essentially nonexistent at the time of the alleged offense. These examinations were accomplished. The report submitted was extremely brief but indicated that the findings had been negative and the electroencephalogram had been normal. Thus, evidence of the recent examination was against the diagnosis of active epilepsy. However, the report was extremely brief and extensive observations of the patient which might have included positive or negative observations with regard to the question of seizures were not recorded.

Impression: (1) Explosive personality disorder, severe. This diagnosis fits with the history of very poor impulse control and the impulsive nature of Mr. Smith's aggressive and antisocial behavior in the past. In addition, I had the impression during the interview of a young man who was sitting on explosive rage which he was continuously trying to control. This was most evident when he talked about his father and said that if he ever saw him he would kill him. When Mr. Smith said this, I believed him, because he appeared overwhelmed with rage. Regardless of the source of the rage (father or other relationships) it is never far from the surface and is always threatening to erupt into a violence with which Mr. Smith cannot cope.

(2) Borderline mental retardation. This diagnosis includes people who test with IQ's in the 68 to 85 range. Though this tested IQ, as revealed by past records, is slightly above this, I believe that his total intellectual functioning as reflected in total judgment and ability to think ahead, and his poor capacity to abstract and verbalize, would place him in the borderline category. This, combined with the rage mentioned above, would serve markedly to impair his impulse control. In summary, this man does not have much capacity to think ahead or to govern his actions by long-range goals. He is very apt to act on impulse and is driven mostly by very angry impulses.

(3) The diagnosis of psychomotor epilepsy must be considered here, though I believe that the weight of evidence is against it. In favor of the diagnosis are the history of a positive electroencephalogram in 1966 and the fact that at times psychomotor epilepsy does display itself in antisocial and violent acts. Against the diagnosis are the recent neurological conclusions and normal EEG; the overly dramatic nature of the "spell" he had during our interview; and the lack of any observed seizure in any of the records.

In summary, Mr. Smith presents a history of

lack of interpersonal stability for the past twelve years of his life; enormous murderous rage directed at his father; a poorly organized psychological defense structure which leaves him vulnerable to outbursts of impulsive unpremeditated aggressive behavior; inadequate intellectual equipment to deal with his impulses or to adequately plan his behavior in a long-range way. He has taken to using drugs in the last few years, which seems clearly related to a build-up of anxiety about stressful life events and to an attempt to dull the hostility within him. He is therefore driven to continued use of drugs as a sort of self-medication and tranquilizer. Drug use in turn contributes to his antisocial behavior, since he may engage in unlawful acts in an attempt to get the very medications which he hopes will calm him down.

Given that the weight of evidence is against the diagnosis of psychomotor epilepsy, the question arises as to whether diagnoses 1 and 2 (explosive personality disorder and borderline mental retardation) constitute mental disease sufficient to produce a lack of substantial capacity to conform to the law or rob Mr. Smith of the capacity to modify a wrongful act. It is my belief that his controls were somewhat impaired but that basically he did not lack substantial capacity to conform to the right or knowledge that he was indeed acting wrongfully. Even should the diagnosis of psychomotor epilepsy be established, one would then have to substantiate that the alleged murder was accomplished during one of the epileptic seizures.

As to sentencing, while I am not in general optimistic about the outcome of psychiatric intervention with this patient, I feel that three things would be worth trying. First, further investigation of the times in his life when he functioned well (for example, the brief time he was working on a construction job) might bring to light more of his assets. Once these are assessed, he could then be taught to recognize these and also to use them in dealing with his anger. Second, legitimately prescribed tranquilizers might be a useful alternative to self-administered narcotics. Third, counseling groups may be of help in providing him contact with others who are learning to deal with their impulses in a more productive way.

Sincerely,
SUZAN MOYER, M.D.

EDITORIAL COMMENT

The following article is included because it demonstrates many of the difficulties inherent in the utilization of psychiatric reports. Though the article concerns itself with judges and the sentencing of sex offenders, the points it makes are well taken with regard to all uses of psychiatric reports in the judicial process. Difficulties similar to those described in the article in cross-professional communication exist not only between psychiatrists and judges, but also between psychiatrists and attorneys working together.

JUDICIAL USE OF PSYCHIATRIC REPORTS IN THE SENTENCING OF SEX OFFENDERS

Carol Bohmer, Esq.

There has been, over the past number of years, an increased use and acceptance by the courts of psychiatrists' opinions about the disposition of offenders. One area in which psychiatrists have been called on with greater frequency regarding disposition is that of the sexual offender.

This type of offender has been viewed by the judiciary as a "sick" or "abnormal" individual whose behavior needs to be understood in order to aid in rendering an appropriate type of sentence which may often be medical treatment rather than punitive incarceration.[1] The focus of the present study is on the role of the psychiatrist in the judicial sentencing of these offenders.

This study arose from an interest in assessing the extent of the impact of psychiatry and psychiatric methods on the U.S. sentencing process. It was hoped that some insight could be obtained into the importance judges currently place on psychiatric evidence as an aid to their task of sentencing, Interviews were conducted with 42 judges in the Philadelphia Common Pleas Division whose work involved them in the sentencing of sex offenders. . . .

The material about which the judges were questioned was provided by the Philadelphia Court Clinic which prepares reports both in pre-trial and pre-sentence situations.

[1] Evidence of this tendency to see the sex offender as one amenable to psychiatric description and care may be found in the existence of sexual psychopath statutes in many states. For a discussion and critique of these statutes, see E. Sutherland, "The Diffusion of Sexual Psychopath Laws," *American Journal of Sociology*, LVI (1950): 142 and P. W. Tappan, "Sentencing for Sex Criminals," *Journal of Criminal Law and Criminology and Police Science*, XLII (1951): 332. For a discussion of the area of sexual deviation, see B. Karpman, *The Sexual Offender and His Offenses* (New York: The Julian Press, 1954) and J. W. Mohr, R. E. Turner, and M. B. Jerry, *Pedophilia and Exhibitionism* (Toronto: University of Toronto Press, 1964).

TECHNIQUE

Judges present difficult subjects for interviewing. It is not that they are unwilling to be interviewed.[2] Rather, they seem unwilling to disclose information about how they go about their job of sentencing. They may be reluctant to reveal information that could lead to criticism by the public. In view of these difficulties, I tried to be as emphatic as possible in the interviews and to reassure the judges that the information obtained would be used solely for the purpose of academic inquiry. However, despite my best efforts, there were large informational gaps in some of the interviews. . . .

As the interview progressed, they felt more comfortable and made remarks to indicate that, unconsciously at least, they felt powerless to use the psychiatrists' reports properly, even if they could understand the language used, and that they felt threatened by what they saw as a corrosion of their power to make sentencing decisions.

The results of this study indicate an increasing trend to see offenders, especially sexual offenders, in a psychiatric frame of reference. Despite this trend . . . there remains a lack of . . . understanding and communication between the psychiatrist and the judge, which can be seen in the more general responses of the judges. . . .

Thus, while the judges are ostensibly interested in and assisted by the entire report, it is apparent from further probing that their interest revolves around certain specific areas. They are interested in concrete facts that they are able to understand, such as IQ and background. They are interested in evidence of gross mental disturbance, such as the judge who said: "The question I want answered is how serious a psychotic a man is; is he so

[2] John Hogarth, "Sentencing as a Human Process," *Canadian Studies in Criminology* (Toronto: University of Toronto Press, 1971), I, esp. pp. 16 and 25.

seriously psychotic that I can send him to a mental institution?" Sometimes the interest has little to do with psychiatry. For example, one judge said he would get a report to find out if there was any justification for the evidence in a rape case, where the defense was that the defendant was impotent.

The other major area of concern among the judges in which they hope for help from the psychiatrist is in the making of a prognosis. Some judges appear to believe that minor sex offenders will progress to become "violent sex maniacs," as one of them put it. Another judge told me of a course he took with someone in the FBI which taught him that "no matter how insevere [sic] the crime is in a sex case, that person would be capable of murder." Another said that indecent exposure cases were the one situation in which he would immediately order a report, "because the person has an obvious mental problem and we should find out if they are dangerous because very often they are homicidal."

Thus what the judges really want to know from the psychiatrist is how dangerous the man is. This wish is constantly frustrated by the psychiatrists' understandable reluctance to make such specific predictions. However, because the judges are aware that the report is supposed to serve a greater function than that of prediction, they say that they find the reports helpful, and at the same time address their complaints to specific parts of the reports. Some of these complaints . . . come from their comments and use of words such as "jargon," "gobblegook," and phrases such as "you've read one, you've read them all," "after a while, I feel as if I could write them myself," "the reports have pat phrases in them," and "why can't they write them in laymen's terms?"

Another problem which the judges clearly had was in understanding the reports. . . . Thus, one judge who said that overall he had very few complaints with the reports, answered in response to a question about the value of the diagnosis "well, you sort of get bogged down with the terms of trade that you are not completely familiar with . . . it's nice to have it there." This judge also told me that he uses a book given out to judges called *A Glossary Of Psychiatric Language*, and admitted that generally one did not have time to do much more than gloss.

None of the judges have had any official training in psychiatric concepts; a few took psychology courses at college. Nevertheless, some judges indicated an understanding and familiarity with psychiatric concepts which they said had been picked up during prior experience in private practice or from a personal interest in the field. The judge, in his role as judge, is unlikely to have much time or opportunity to learn about psychiatric concepts but he does have experts available to whom he could turn if necessary, although shortage of time is a problem here. At the same time, he is required to understand and interpret the psychiatric reports presented to him. . . .

In opening the interview, I asked what made them decide to call for a psychiatric presentence report in sex offense cases. All gave some instances in which they thought a report was needed on an offender, even those who told me flatly that the reports were of no assistance to them whatsoever. It may be that calling for a report was used as a backup in case any questions were asked in the future about the correctness of the judge's handling of a case that might reflect badly. . . . It is interesting that the large proportion of these reasons do not deal directly with areas related to psychiatric concepts but rather to matters related to criminal justice concepts. . . .

After completing the interviews of a number of judges it became apparent that there were two relatively distinct approaches being used by the judges in their use of psychiatric reports. First, there was the group of judges who ordered a report in cases they determined were serious and in which they were therefore contemplating imposing a severe sentence. The second group were those who would impose a serious sentence without reference to a report but who used the reports in borderline cases when they were deciding between probation and imprisonment.

It seems that the reports are here being used for a different purpose in each case. In the first situation the judge is using the report more as support for imposing a serious sentence, and is likely to be looking only for information sufficiently unexpected to make him change his mind, such as information suggesting that the offender should instead be sent to a mental hospital.[3]

The second group of judges is likely to be comprised of those who are more influenced by the report since for them the decision to imprison or not is left in abeyance until after the report is submitted. Twenty-seven of the judges said they are more likely to get a report

---

[3] It is not likely in this situation that the reports will greatly influence the decision except perhaps to change slightly the length of the sentence. It is not possible at this stage of the research to state whether this happens, but further research presently being undertaken will correlate the ordering of reports with actual decisions made and will hopefully suggest whether and in which direction sentencing is influenced by the presence of a psychiatric report.

in cases where they are not sure what the best decision will be. . . .

It must also be pointed out that it is very difficult for an individual to adequately answer a question about a complex process which is also likely to be partly unconscious. To quote a prominent jurist, "Every important principle which is developed by litigation . . . is the unconscious result of instinctive prejudices and inarticulate convictions."[4]

Some judges were more aware of this unconscious element and indicated that they felt that they had the ability to coordinate all relevant facts and come up with the right decision. The spectrum here ranged from one judge who said he was not at all interested in the recommendation of the psychiatrist because he was the coordinator of information, not the follower of the suggestions of the psychiatrists, to several judges who humbly said that they could only hope they were doing the best thing in a sentencing decision but had no way of testing the rightness of this decision. . . .

It is clear that most judges feel sentencing is a difficult problem and they need all the help they can get. As Smith and Blumberg say in their recent article on decision-making: "The harsh fact about being a criminal court judge is, that some men may glory in it, still others are entirely ambivalent about the responsibilities imposed in sentencing their fellow men to prison or death."[5] The latter for the most part fits the central session judges (the subject of Smith and Blumberg's study), who have arranged for eleaborate probation and psychiatric services in the form of reports which they can lean on in deciding the otherwise dubious case. . . .

Unlike the recommendations of the psychiatrists about the sentence (which according to the judges interviewed they do not always follow), recommendations about treatment are much more often followed by the judges and incorporated in the sentence. This is because they feel that treatment is the province of the psychiatrist while sentencing is their province.

The high nonresponse rate to the questions . . . (about psychiatric recommendations for therapy) seems to be partly explained by the fact that some judges could not verbalize what they intended when they added a recommendation of psychotherapy to a sentence and therefore did not answer the question at all. It seems evident that they are relying on the fact that, as one of them said, "If the psychiatrist says he needs therapy, then I'll add it to my sentence." They feel that this decision is in the psychiatrist's field of expertise much more than is the recommendation as to sentencing and they simply do what the psychiatrist suggests without much idea of the purpose or outcome of such a recommendation. In fact, they make such a recommendation even if they do not think it will do any good, but with the idea that it cannot do any harm. An interesting aspect of the treatment part of the sentence is its frequently punitive nature, which is antithetical to the psychiatric model of treatment as basically a voluntary measure (although there are psychiatrists who work with apparent success in a compulsory setting). In many cases the order of the judge will read "two years strict psychiatric probation" or "one year strict medical probation," which seems to have not only a compulsory component, but also a punitive ring.

The judges use aids such as the psychiatric reports which were the subject of this study to lighten their burden of responsibility in making sentencing decisions. How useful the reports are other than for sentencing is, however, another question. Judges cannot really understand the reports written for them by psychiatrists, simply because they are psychiatric reports and are the result of a very different educational process and area of specialization. Examples can be seen in the feeling of judges that the language of the report is too "psychiatric," and in their concentration on those parts of the reports they can most easily understand. . . .

It is doubtful that even if the judges could understand the reports, it would help them much, since their freedom of choice of disposition is so limited within the present system. Basically, all the judge can do in a specific situation is to sentence the offender to incarceration or probation. Any variation to the sentence is not of great significance, except in the one specific situation where the offender is sufficiently psychiatrically sick that he should be committed to a mental institution rather than to prison. The conflict inherent in the judges' decision-making is very evident here. On the one hand, the reports are not helping them enough because of vagueness and psychiatric terms[6]. . . . while on the other hand the judge feels that a psychiatrist is somehow usurping his role as sentencer when he makes

[4] Oliver W. Holmes, *The Common Law* (Boston: Little Brown and Company, 1881), pp. 35–36.

[5] Alexander B. Smith and Abraham S. Blumberg, "The Problem of Objectivity in Judicial Decision-Making," *Social Forces*, XLVI (1967): 102.

[6] One judge said, "I'd rather have them say that it's a dark area, it stumps us; if they were honest they'd say it was in an area they were not able to diagnose."

specific recommendations.[7] Therefore, any vague generalizations by the psychiatrist, while not threatening to the judges' fear of encroachment into *their* role do not particularly help the decision-making process. The judge is a pragmatist both by training and by necessity; he is the one who had to decide to do something in this specific situation. The judge may also feel a little uncomfortable with specific suggestions (though data show he is interested in them) because of his perception of the role as one who makes decisions rather than one who rubberstamps the recommendations~ of others. If the recommendation is not in accord with the ideas of the judge or if it is unrealistic in view of available options to the judge (a common complaint[8]), then the judge is likely to view the recommendation as well as its maker with some scepticism. I was told by a psychiatrist in the Philadelphia Court Clinic that unrealistic recommendations were made to publicize the need for increased options, but some of the judges apparently did not know or appreciate this.

Another element in this problem of understanding between the judge and the psychiatrist is the absence in the psychiatric model of a diagnosis called "normal." The psychiatrist has problems defining what is meant by normal[9] and therefore does not use it as a diagnosis. In this context this means that some other diagnosis will be used which will fall within the psychiatric model. In looking through reports for cases of sex offenders over a 2-year period, I found three (out of approximately 150 reports) in which the psychiatrist said that there was nothing psychiatrically wrong with the offender....

A common diagnosis, which is actually teleological[10] is one in which the offender is diag-

nosed as having a psychopathic personality disturbance and the evidence used is the fact that he has committed this offense. The extreme of this kind of diagnosis was found in one of the reports in which a 21-year-old statutory rapist was diagnosed as "sociopathic personality disturbance, sexual deviance as manifested by repeated instances of sexual relations with fifteen year old girls."[11] . . .

The judge does not necessarily want to receive a "sick" psychiatric diagnosis on every offender he sends for a report. One judge wondered, rather cynically, if the fact that he always received some psychiatric diagnosis was due to the extraordinary skill he had in choosing which offenders to send for a report. He also does not want a recommendation that he thinks is unrealistically mild. The judge sees himself as the buffer between the community and the offender, with a three fold duty:

1. to punish the offender for his crime,
2. to do what in his opinion is best for the offender in terms of rehabilitation.
3. to do what is best for the community and also to some extent, to carry out the community's wishes, as he sees them, from current public opinion.

The separate aspects of this duty are of course interrelated. The judges on a number of occasions expressed this duty and spoke of the conflicts it engendered in them. Some judges were more aware of the protection of the community responsibility than of the others (12 mentioned it specifically). For example, since they feel they are representatives of the community that elected them, they do not feel they can grant probation as suggested by the psychiatrist for someone they see as a bad risk[12] and potential danger to the community.

---

[7] A judge said, "I find the reports helpful, but it is still my responsibility to decide how much reliance to put on it. One can only be guided by the recommendations"; and another said, "What I should do with a defendant is my job, not the psychiatrist's. I am not interested in any recommendation the psychiatrist may have."

[8] A judge told me, "I do not want to belittle the psychiatrist but I do not think he is qualified to help, even if he has unlimited time. He knows there is no facility for therapy, so why recommend it? In case after case I have sent men for attention and they don't get it"; another said, "The tragedy is the lack of adequate facilities for the treatment of persons convicted of crime."

[9] See the paper presented at the conference on New Directions in Research on Normal Behavior, by Melvin S. Sabshin published under the title "Psychiatric Perspectives on Normality," *Archives of General Psychiatry*, XVII (Sept. 1967): 258–64.

[10] See, Seymour Halleck, "The Psychiatrist in the Legal Process," *Psychology Today* (Feb.

1969): 26 where he says, "Whenever a psychiatrist bases his diagnosis of mental illness upon the peculiarity of unreasonableness of the criminal act, he is defining illness in terms of the crime and in effect arguing that the cause and effect are similar or identical." "The Psychopath is . . . par excellence and without shame or qualification, the model of the circular process by which mental abnormality is inferred from anti-social behavior while anti-social behavior is explained by mental abnormality." Barbara Wooten, *Social Science and Social Pathology* (New York: Macmillan, 1959), p. 250.

[11] Given the nature of the recommendation and the punitive tone of the report, I can only assume that it was the fact that the boy had actually impregnated two of the girls which provoked this reaction.

[12] One judge gave as an example the case of a man with a record of two previous burglaries, one with a gun. The psychiatrist said that the man was upset, gave a diagnosis, and said that the man was an "average risk on probation." "If the physi-

In contrast, when the psychiatrist's suggested sentence does not strike the judge as molly-coddling (when the psychiatrist recommends commitment or long term incarceration), accord appears likely to be high between them. When the psychiatrist sees someone as having a sufficiently bad record to require a punitive disposition, he does not need to hide (as he may do otherwise, to the great annoyance of the judges) behind vague generalizations about rehabilitation and intensive psychotherapy, which he sees as unavailable within the present system.[13] He is able to say specifically that the offender needs "a long period of external controls," i.e., prison. If, as is likely, that suggestion agrees with the judge's ideas on the subject he can feel justified in ordering a long sentence, and the psychiatrist can feel that he was psychiatrically justified in recommending that sentence.

Some judges consciously recognize communication problems between themselves and psychiatrists and do try to alleviate them by speaking directly to the psychiatrists in certain situations. . . . However, such contact is restricted to limited situations, or when the judge has a specific question to ask. Communications are most likely to be over the telephone. The pressures of their work mandate that judges and psychiatrists have little time to sit down together and share their disciplines in such a way as to make communication and understanding possible between them.[14] More

important, these two professional groups are very different in their ways of thinking, their training in problem-solving, and their positions in relation to the legal system.

It would seem that beyond a certain point no amount of training in psychiatric concepts on the part of the judges or understanding of what the judges want on the part of the psychiatrists can significantly improve the situation, for not only does the psychiatrist not help the judge fundamentally, he *cannot* in our present system. No matter how well informed the judge is on the background and psychological make-up of an individual offender, he can still choose only between incarceration and freedom (whether restricted or not)—a decision which despite increased psychiatric intervention in the sentencing process, continues to be tied in with numerous other factors.

The psychiatric report can, as Smith and Blumberg state in the passage cited above, make the judge feel less alone and helpless in his role of making decisions about other men's lives.[15] As Halleck says, in speaking of the psychiatrist's role in court generally: "The most important reason for psychiatric participation in the criminal trial is humanitarian zeal to temper the harshness of punishment."[16]

discussions. See, for example, Nathan Blackman, M.D. *et al.*, "The Social Maladjustment Unit: A Community Wide Approach to the Problem of Delinquent Behavior," *American Journal of Psychiatry*, XI, no. 6 (Dec. 1957): 536.

[15] Another possible influence of the psychiatrist in court is to reduce the length of sentences, though whether this in fact actually happens to any great extent will not be known until all the research presently being undertaken by the writer is completed.

[16] Seymour L. Halleck, "Current Psychiatric Roles in the Legal Process," *Wisconsin Law Review* (Spring 1966): 395.

cian thinks I am going to let that man out on the street . . ."

[13] Thomas S. Szasz, *Law, Liberty and Psychiatry: An Inquiry into the Social Uses of Mental Health Practices* (New York: Macmillan, 1963).

[14] This kind of approach has been tried, but only to a very limited extent does the interdisciplinary approach include judges in the group

---

SUGGESTIONS FOR ADDITIONAL READING

Butler, "Psychiatric Evaluation of the Aged," 18 *Geriatrics* 220 (March 1963).

Comment: "Psychiatric Examination of the Mentally Abnormal Witness," 59 *Yale L. J.* 1324 (1950).

Curran. *Law and Medicine.* Boston: Little, Brown & Co., 1960, Chapter 8.

Marshall. "Evidence, Psychology, and the Trial: Some Challenges to Law," 63 *Colum. L. Rev.* 197 (1963).

Meyers. "The Psychiatric Examination," 54 *J. of Crim. L., Criminol. and Police Science* (1963).

Goulett, H. M. *The Insanity Defense in Criminal Trials.* St. Paul, Minn.: Est Publishing Co., 1965.

See also the readings noted in Chapters 3 and 6.

6

Psychological Evaluation

Dr. Silber's article describes the training and professional role of the clinical psychologist and the most frequently encountered types of psychological testing. The two assessments of Mr. Strong should be read in conjunction with the psychiatric evaluation in the same case given in the previous chapter. They should be evaluated in the light of Dr. Silber's article and their strengths and weaknesses carefully considered. In the Kent case, psychological test results and diagnoses are subjected to vigorous cross-examination. The techniques used will be considered more fully in a subsequent chapter. A careful reading of all these selections should provide the reader with a basis for appraising psychological diagnosis and testimony.

The reader is invited to consider, in reading the excerpts from the trial transcript in Kent, which, if any of the tests, diagnoses, and perhaps witnesses, were substantially discredited by the cross-examination, and which, if any, stood up well. The same criteria could be applied to potential cross-examination in the Strong case. Lawyers and law students should consider how, as counsel for Kent or Strong, or as prosecutor in either case, they might have handled things (in preparing witnesses for trial, in direct or cross-examination, motions and objections, redirect, etc.) in order to thwart, or at least ameliorate, the impact of the opposing counsel's attack.

The somewhat inconsistent reception given to psychological testimony is pointed out in the excerpt from Professor Allen's article, in which contrasting views, including those of organized psychiatry, are discussed. The article concludes with Judge Bazelon's thoughts on the matter.

CLINICAL PSYCHOLOGY—ITS ROLE AND METHODS

David E. Silber, Ph.D.

Many people (including some lawyers) have a confused or unclear picture of what psychology is, and what a psychologist, and especially a clinical psychologist, does. The purpose of this monograph is to discuss and clarify some of the salient aspects of clinical psychology, and some of its tools and methods. The first section will describe the training of the psychologist; the next, what he does and where he generally works; and the final section will cover the techniques and tools used in clinical work. Since this is intended as a brief, rather general, overview, certain aspects of clinical psychology must be dealt with briefly.

THE CLINICAL PSYCHOLOGIST AND HIS TRAINING

There is no way to define clinical psychology concisely, for the field has been rapidly expanding during the past twenty-five years. However, there is general agreement that clinical psychology is first and foremost the study of the individual, his personality and behavior in his total life situation. "Total life situation" encompasses not only one's social environment, but also the effects of one's past experiences, one's physical circumstances, and one's interrelationships with others.

This selection was written expressly for this volume and has not been previously published.

Although such a definition may suggest that clinical psychology is primarily an academic or research-oriented field, the opposite is true for the majority of clinical psychologists. Such psychologists are usually clinicians operating within an institutional framework. It is important to note, however, that they provide such services in the context of certain theoretical assumptions about personality and behavior. The basis of modern psychology is the empirical study of behavior and psychological processes. Therefore, although the clinical psychologist must be knowledgeable about biological and physiological functions, his interest focuses on the ways in which they may affect behavior. He is interested also in sociological and cultural influences on the patterns of individual behavior. And, because psychology is an empirical science, the clinical psychologist should strive to express his explanations of behavior and his theoretical assumptions in terms accessible to investigation, and he should strive to buttress his conclusions with methodologically adequate research.

Thus, the clinician must learn the clinical techniques unique to clinical psychology; but their application must rest on a broad foundation of knowledge that includes other areas of psychology, physiology, sociology, anthropology, statistics, and research methodology. The generally accepted academic qualification is the Ph.D. degree, and many students pursue a postdoctoral training program for one or two additional years.

Requirements for the undergraduate degree in psychology (A.B.) vary, but thirty hours of psychology courses are usually included, plus courses in related areas. Basic courses in the principles of learning, theories of personality, abnormal psychology, experimental psychology, and systems of psychology are usually required. In addition, the student is encouraged to take courses in basic sociology, anthropology, statistics, physiology and anatomy, and chemistry. The Bachelor of Arts degree in psychology does not adequately prepare the student for professional work.

Most post-graduate programs accept only highly qualified students who show potential for continuing at the doctoral level. Doctoral training is generally contained in a five-year program, although surveys have found that the median time for fulfilment of the requirements for the Ph.D. is over six years. During the first two years the student receives training in the basic substantive areas of psychology, including social psychology, psychopathology (the psychology of abnormal behavior), physiological psychology, research methodology, and psychological measurement. He is introduced to clinical subjects that include psycho-

diagnosis (personality assessment of normal and abnormal individuals), theories of psychotherapy, individual testing, and professional ethics. The second phase of the doctoral program is usually begun when the student has fulfilled the requirements of the M.A. degree, which usually requires completion of original research of thesis proportions, and a series of qualifying examinations. He then begins practicum clinical training under close supervision. Most Ph.D. programs require a year's internship at an approved clinic or mental hospital, and a majority of students have had more than this minimum by the time they complete their doctorates.

The internship experience of a clinical psychologist can be as varied as the settings within which he functions as a professional. For example, in a large mental hospital the intern may receive supervised training in the administration and interpretation of personality tests, report-writing, and case presentation. He will usually participate in case conferences where decisions about treatment and disposition are made. He usually attends seminars on various types of treatment, theories of mental illness, etc., often along with the psychiatric residents at the hospital. The intern puts into practice the theories of diagnosis and test interpretation learned in classroom settings, and begins to use various treatment techniques. Most important, he goes over his work with his supervisors in (occasionally painful) detail, constantly striving to increase his clinical skills.

Finally, he must complete his doctoral dissertation, which must be based upon significant original research. This latter requirement may entail a period of years beyond completion of the academic and residency programs.

The Work of the Clinical Psychologist

The field that the psychologist enters is vast and constantly expanding. He works in mental hospitals of all kinds, in guidance clinics, children's clinics, university counseling centers, and various specialized agencies (e.g., agencies for crippled or handicapped children, schools for retarded children, and homes for the aged). As the need for personal rehabilitation has been recognized, psychologists have become involved in penitentiaries and training schools. Government and business have long employed psychologists in evaluating prospective employees.

Increasingly in recent years, clinical psychologists have engaged in private practice, providing a variety of clinical services, including psychotherapeutic treatment. Questions have been raised by psychiatrists and others as to the propriety of such private clinical practice, in part on the basis of the inadequacy of contemporary licensing and certification laws and regulations, and in part on the basis of the belief of many physicians that diagnosis and treatment should be under medical supervision. It should be noted that professionally qualified psychologists have been in the forefront of efforts to obtain protective licensing and certification laws.

In a clinical or hospital setting, the psychologist has primary responsibility for the psychological assessment of clients and patients. The assessment procedure will be described in greater detail in a later section; however, to anticipate, the procedure usually involves ascertaining the nature of the individual's problem, and assessing the personality of the individual through psychological interviews and tests. The assessment is reported and discussed at case conferences, at which decisions regarding treatment or case disposition may be made. Such conferences usually include psychiatrists, social workers, psychiatric nurses, and rehabilitation therapists, as well as the psychologist.

A second major activity, in the clinic or hospital setting, is providing psychotherapeutic treatment. There are many different types of psychotherapy, but all are aimed at modifying the behavior and feelings of the client to a point where he can interact successfully in his life setting. Individual psychotherapy involves the individual patient and the therapist; here the focus may be on the current behavior of the patient, on his feelings, on his relationships with others, or on the antecedents of his disordered behavior. There is no single "approved" personality theory or technique that is used by psychologists. Many prefer to work in a Freudian psychoanalytic framework, while others prefer to focus on specific abnormal habit patterns. Some use very recent developments, such as learning theory principles to "decondition" maladaptive behavior, while others ignore the behavior in favor of examining the feelings and attitudes of the patient. A therapist may be quite directive in explaining to the client how he can achieve better functioning, or he may be consciously nondirective, attempting only to understand (and communicate this understanding to) the client. Occasionally hypnosis or special relaxing techniques are used, but the psychologist never employs "medical" treatment, such as tranquilizers or shock therapy.

Group therapy may also be employed, with a family unit, a married couple, several unrelated clients, etc. It has been found that many of the barriers to meaningful communication can be overcome in such settings. Clients are often amazed to find that someone else shares their fears or impulses; and often a client can analyze another client's problems in a manner which, though not technically sophisticated, goes directly to the heart of the matter in a way that can be understood and accepted by him. It need hardly be added that group therapy allows for wider utilization of professional personnel, a factor that is extremely important in most, generally understaffed, hospitals.

Psychologists may also counsel clients, plan vocational programs, assess applicants for industrial and governmental jobs and programs, and carry out research on diagnostic and therapeutic processes. The Peace Corps is an example of how psychological assessment procedures can be effectively utilized. Because each candidate is thoroughly assessed throughout the training period, nearly ninety-five per cent of the corpsmen have been able to complete their assignments satisfactorily, often in stressful and demanding foreign settings. Recent congressional inquiries have shown, however, that some businesses and government agencies have employed testing techniques inappropriately, or in ways in which basic human rights, such as the right to privacy, may be infringed.

PSYCHOLOGICAL TECHNIQUES

A major portion of psychological work concerns psychological assessment. This section will describe the assessment process and then discuss the principal tools employed. Psychological assessments are made, most often, as an aid to psychiatric diagnoses, but may also be used as a basis for making decisions about vocational training, admittance to special programs, or for planning psychotherapy strategy. It is important to note that the clinician looks not only for weaknesses and difficulties, but also for potential assets and strengths.

The assessment process includes (1) the preliminary stage; (2) data-gathering; (3) data-processing, or interpretation of the data; and (4) reporting and communicating results. In the preliminary stage the psychologist receives a referral request giving the purpose of the assessment to be made. This information is vital in making decisions as to the areas of personality or behavior to concentrate on, whether testing should be used, and if so, what type. For example, if the request is for information to aid in making vocational plans for a patient who is recovering from a psychological illness, the psychologist would need not only a measure of the client's intelligence, his vocational interests and aptitudes, but also a basis for determining his emotional readiness for vocational training. On the other hand, if the person is referred by the court for testing incident to a determination of commitability or competency to stand trial, the tests, procedures, and reports would be quite different.

During the data-gathering stage, the psychologist interacts with the client (and occasionally with others who know the client, or who work with him, etc.), interviews him, may administer psychological tests, and, not infrequently, revises his assessment strategy on the basis of the client's reactions and responses. The clinician often obtains a history from the person, interviews him about present activities, observes the client's dress, behavior, and facial expressions, and in general begins to formulate hypotheses about his personality. Psychological interviewing and testing will be discussed later in the paper.

Interpretation of data is the most difficult phase of assessment. During the process of data-gathering, empirical, observable data are collected. Two reasonably observant individuals might well agree about what was said, what the client did, how he reacted, etc., when tested or interviewed. However, once these data are collected, the clinician must draw hypotheses about the personality of the person on the basis of data, and as soon as he does that, he leaves the world of the verifiable, and enters the region of inference. Contemporary science in general notes the difference between empirically derived data ("hard" data) and hypothetical deductions drawn from the data ("soft" data).

The basic assumption underlying the interpretation of data is that there is no such thing as random or chance behavior: all behavior is meaningful, and all behavior has antecedent causes, however accidental or random it may appear.

Interpretation of empirical data is a complex process; however, there are several criteria that can be applied, and these have been well summarized by Schafer as follows:

1. There should be sufficient evidence (data) for the interpretation.

2. The depth of the interpretation should be appropriate to the material available. That is, if one is going to speculate about unconscious wishes, or the residue of childhood experiences, one ought to have a wide variety of data and not, for example, answers to a handful of questions.

3. The manifest form of the interpreted tendency should be specified. If, for example, "homosexual impulses" are inferred, one should specify their nature, whether they will become overt, or whether the person will be able to resist them.

4. The intensity of the interpreted trend should be specified.

5. The positive and negative aspects of an inferred characteristic should be specified.[1]

The above is a way of cautioning the would-be interpreter against interpretations not adequately supported by the data. Of course, clinical experience and skill play a vital role, and what might appear to the layman as inadequate evidence may amply support the conclusions drawn by the clinician.

Let us consider the following: a man is asked to define the word "radio." His response, after some thought, is "an electromagnetic apparatus which transmits communist emanations, and is used to erode men's minds." Applying the criteria specified above, one inference that could be drawn would be that the person has a rather extensive vocabulary which he uses well (if somewhat pedantically). In addition, a much more tenuous inference could be made that the person is suffering from a disturbance of thought. The reason that this is tenuous is because there is only one piece of evidence available: his verbal connection of radio and communism. This in and of itself isn't sufficient basis for the diagnosis suggested (e.g., the person might be expressing a political point of view as a loyal "John Bircher"; if, however, he later states that his electric razor is broadcasting communist propaganda, or that the Kremlin is aiming radar beams at him, then the inference about disturbed thought functioning would be strengthened).

One other point about data processing should be mentioned. The clinician's inferences will reflect psychological knowledge—and theories—of human personality. If the person in the example above went on to tell the clinician that his radio set was calling him vile names and accusing him of "unnatural acts with his fellow man," the clinician would make inferences concerning feelings of inadequacy, and fears about homosexual impulses. The danger here is that occasionally theory rather than empirical data dictates the interpretation.

After making all relevant inferences, the clinician formulates recommendations based on his interpretations and the reasons for the referral. For example, if the client is a patient in a mental hospital, the clinician would suggest a diagnosis (usually based on the American Psychiatric Association's *Diagnostic and Statistical Manual*), formulate a suggested treatment plan, and make a prognosis.

The final phase of the assessment procedure is the report of his findings, usually in written form. Sometimes this document is beclouded with so many technical terms and with so much

[1] R. Schafer, *Psychoanalytic Interpretation in Rorschach Testing* (New York: Grune & Stratton, 1954).

jargon that the individual being assessed virtually disappears from view. This kind of report may result from the psychologist's assumption that the only readers of his report will also be clinicians, but in some cases it may be deliberately employed to mask a basic lack of knowledge concerning the person being assessed.

The first section of the report usually includes demographic data—the client's name, age, marital status, and information about the dates he was seen, the procedures which were used, and the reason for referral. The second portion contains information about the client's behavior in the assessment situation, including his clothing, his gestures, any signs of anxiety or discomfort, his verbal behavior, and his response to the tests. In general, these data are empirical, with occasional low-level inferences such as "in general, he gave little evidence of being uncomfortable and remained calm throughout the rather long testing session."

The third, and longest, portion of the psychological report contains the "Results of Testing." A global portrait of the person is constructed, drawing on the data from the test responses, the behavior of the person in the test situation, and interview responses. Major conflicts are identified, an assessment of internal controls made, and hypotheses concerning the genesis of difficulties are often suggested. Styles vary, so that one report may contain no reference to the primary test data, while another will be replete with test examples drawn to illustrate a particular point. It is suggested that when an important and far-reaching conclusion is made, that inference be buttressed with the evidence leading to it.

A fourth section may include the background and history of the client, usually as given by the client. The section is included even when other, more reliable, sources are available, because it tells something about the way the person sees himself. In cases where the person's actual background appears to be different from his retelling of it, both are stated. The final section is usually a "Summary and Conclusion," in which the salient points are briefly reiterated, the diagnosis and prognosis made, and recommendations formulated.

THE TOOLS OF PSYCHOLOGICAL ASSESSMENT

Assessment tools include interviews, observation, and tests. Ordinarily the clinical assessment begins with a brief interview. Pertinent data are obtained, and the person is invited to tell something about himself and his problems as he sees them. In general, the interview is "open-ended." That is, the person is asked general questions designed to allow him to express himself freely and to reveal his anxieties, fears, and coping strategies. During the interview the psychologist must be alert to revelations of conflicts or problems; for example, if the client persistently avoids a particular subject, the psychologist may bring it up in a relatively non-stressful way, viz., "I noticed that you didn't mention whether your problems were related to sexual activities; could you tell me something about that area?"

During the interview and the subsequent testing session, the clinician is constantly observing the behavior of the person being assessed. Note is taken of his dress, his grooming, and his deportment. More important, the clinician is alert to the person's behavior patterns, including facial expressions and gestures, particularly behavior indicating emotionality. All persons being assessed and tested are usually nervous at the beginning; however, most relax shortly. If the person doesn't, this may indicate a chronic level of anxiety. After rapport has been established, and the interview concluded, the person is given the test battery previously selected by the clinician for this particular client and the particular purposes of testing.

PSYCHOLOGICAL TESTING

There is a wide variety of psychological tests, and their use is extensive. For example, Buros[2] lists 1,200 different psychological tests, and Sundberg[3] estimated that at least 700,000 individuals are tested in public clinic facilities each year.

A psychological assessment procedure usually involves a battery of tests designed to yield information concerning all facets of the person's capabilities and personality. Although the specific tests used vary from one psychologist to another, a typical test battery generally includes an intelligence test and several (from two to five) personality tests. It is a curious footnote to the history of psychological testing that the most widely used test of personality, the Rorschach Test, was designed and developed by a psychiatrist.

[2] Oscar Buros (ed.), *The Sixth Mental Measurement Yearbook* (New Jersey: Gryphon Press, 1965).

[3] N. D. Sundberg, "The Practice of Psychological Testing in Clinical Services in the United States," *American Psychologist* 16 (1961): 79–83.

INTELLIGENCE TESTING

Intelligence is one of those concepts which is constantly used, yet is elusive and difficult to define. Usually it is thought of as a capacity for problem solving or abstract thinking. Wechsler has given a definition that many find acceptable: "The aggregate or global capacity of the individual to act purposefully, to think rationally, and to deal effectively with one's environment."[4] It is important to point out that intelligence is a concept, or inference, about a person's capacity. This is extremely important to remember, for intelligence test scores have become so important in modern society that sometimes the scores are confused with intelligence itself.

An intelligence test can only measure, in an indirect way, the person's performance relative to some standard. Obviously, performance is influenced by a wide variety of factors, such as drive, motivation, psychological state, interest, and even fatigue, so that a given intelligence test score may not be representative of a person's *potential* score. In particular, two factors that may adversely affect a person's score are the presence of emotional disability, and a background of cultural deprivation.

The second of these points may be looked at from a different angle. Note that intelligence test scores are measures of functioning in relation to a standard. If the standard is poor, or inadequate, the scores will not convey as much meaning as they might otherwise. A concrete example of this is the Wechsler-Bellevue Test (1939), which was the first individually-administered test designed expressly for adults. The standards were based on a Caucasian sample only, and hence were not adequate for non-Caucasians. When the Wechsler-Bellevue was revised into the WAIS,[5] the standards were based on samples of both Caucasians and non-Caucasians in approximately the same proportion as in the nation as a whole.

The Stanford-Binet, the Wechsler Adult Intelligence Scale (WAIS), and the other individually administered intelligence tests require skilful administration and scoring to yield reliable scores. These tests sample from a wide variety of the different aspects of intelligence: use of words and numbers; symbol manipulation; puzzle-solving; finding logical similarities; general information; and other areas.

Group tests are much more restricted in subject matter than individually administered tests, but they can be administered and scored by less highly qualified persons. The scores are much less reliable and can only be used as crude indices of the person's functional intelligence. It is extremely important, when evaluating an intelligence test score, to know what test was used and under what circumstances the test was given. Group tests are inappropriate for the educationally or culturally deprived, because they lean heavily on verbal material likely to be acquired through schooling or experiental richness.

It has been found that the distribution of IQ scores in the general population is "normal." That is, the scores approximate a bell-shaped curve, with the majority clustering around the middle, and only a few at either the low or high end. For example, on the WAIS, 67 percent of the population have scores between 85 and 115, while 95.4 percent of the population fall within the range of 70 to 130.

Intelligence test scores have been correlated with every imaginable variable, and have been found to be related to every imaginable variable. Intelligence is a key factor in functioning successfully (or unsuccessfully) in the world; IQ scores are useful in assessing a person's competency for schooling, his ability to profit from experience, his capabilities for certain vocations, and a wide variety of other situations. Intelligence scores are not as stable over time as once thought, and they can be modified by experience and education.

Personality Tests

There are two main types of personality assessment tests: projective tests and paper-and-pencil questionnaires. Most tests used in job selection or vocational advancement are of the paper-and-pencil type, which yield "profiles" of personality traits. However, in clinical assessment, projective tests are usually used (with one notable exception, to be discussed later). Although different clinicians have different preferences, the most widely used projective devices are the Rorschach Test, the Thematic Apperception Test (TAT), and the Draw-A-Person Test. Other newer tests are also used, but less frequently.

Projective devices are most often used because they allow the clinician to gain data about personality that he couldn't otherwise obtain. The reasons for this are these: a client is likely to *suppress consciously* aspects of his personality that he considers bad or undesirable; and a client *represses unconsciously* those aspects of his personality that are too painful or unacceptable to bear consciously. Projective devices aim to circumvent such defenses by presenting situations where there are no guide-

---

[4] D. Wechsler, *The Measurement and Appraisal of Adult Intelligence* (Baltimore: Williams and Wilkins, 1958).

[5] D. Wechsler, *Wechsler Adult Intelligence Scale* (New York: Psychological Corporation, 1955).

lines to the "correct" or "acceptable" responses, and where, therefore, such defenses are unusable. That is, the projective device is constructed in such a way that the person's responses to the tests will be governed primarily by his own personality configuration. Without being aware of it, he will "project" his wishes, wants, hopes, fears, conflicts, and impulses, and his manner of dealing with them, into the content of his responses. To illustrate, suppose that a given test consists of ten carefully selected inkblots that vary in configuration, shading, and coloring. These are given to the client and he is asked to tell what they remind him of—what they "look like." Since the inkblots do not actually picture anything it is assumed that the images which the person gives will be determined by his own personality. Further, it is assumed that his manner of approach to the task will mirror his typical manner of approach to the uncertain exigencies of everyday living.

What has just been described is the Rorschach series of inkblots. This, the most widely used of the projective tests, is based on the premise that perception is a product of personality; when the stimulus is equivocal, the individual will project his own inner self into it. The person who only uses minute areas of the blot, or who can give only a single response to a blot, or none, or who takes a great deal of time, is unconsciously telling something about himself to the clinician. In practice, one inkblot at a time is exposed, and the person is asked to tell what it looks like to him. Little or no additional instructions are given, to allow maximum freedom in approaching the task. When the person indicates that he has completed his responses to the blot, he is asked to tell what it was about it that suggested that response to him (sometimes this is done after all the blots have been shown). Some persons find it easy to give many responses, and some find it difficult to "see" anything in the blots. The average number of responses for all ten blots is twenty-five to thirty-five, but as few as one or as many as one hundred are occasionally recorded. Five of the blots are completely black; of the remainder, two are black and red, and three are in pastel colors. It has been found that certain blots, and certain areas on each blot, give rise to "usual" responses. Thus, on Card I about sixty per cent of those tested say it looks like a bat. This does not mean that the response has no value for understanding the particular person. One person may say "a fearsome bat," while another may say "a flying bat." The clinical psychologist immediately wonders why one sees it as "fearsome" and another is able to project movement into the static blot.

In addition to noting what the person says, and how he approaches the task, the examiner is alert to any other clues to the person's personality, and he may make notes such as the following: "client becomes tense when he sees the red and black card"; "all cards are immediately turned upside down"; "client hesitates abnormally long before responding," etc.

Following the administration of the cards, the clinician scores the responses. There are three categories usually tabulated: the area of the blot used in the response (was it the whole blot, a frequently used area, or a minute, infrequently used area?—enough experience has been accumulated that atlases are available to help the clinician); the determinants (did the person use the shape, the shading, or a combination; was there movement projected into the response? etc.); and the content (animal, human, inanimate object, abstract idea, etc.). Various ratios of these scores aid the clinician in interpretation. To take just one, suppose that a person has perceived a number of humans in motion, say six, over the entire series. This empirical data (six human movement responses) suggests several inferences about the testee: the testee has relatively good imaginative abilities, for the imposition of movement on a static blot requires imaginative resources; the testee has empathetic feelings toward other people in his environment, for the number of humans he perceived was higher than the average; the testee has a fairly high intelligence level, for it has been shown that it is more difficult to integrate the blots into perceptions of humans than it is to integrate them into perceptions of animals or objects. Given these inferences, based on the scores assigned to the responses, the clinician returns to actual responses themselves and to other ratios for further confirmation. He will probably go beyond these inferences in his interpretation, however. He will check to see whether the humans were described as males or females; whether they were threatening or benign; whether the description pictured them as grotesque or comely, etc. Each card is viewed independently of the others, and hypotheses developed for each one. After all the cards have been inspected, the inferences are reviewed for commonality, and the ones that survive are integrated with inferences derived from the scores and ratios.

The overriding assumption, as stated earlier, is that all behavior has meaning. A seemingly insignificant comment is not without some meaning in relation to the testee's personality. A client who sees "broken bats," "tiny autos," and who asks, "am I doing okay?" may, in all three of these responses, be communicating indirectly a sense of inadequacy or insecurity in his self-concept. Interpretation is, of course, much more complicated than the above hypothetical illustrations.

In addition to the Rorschach, most test batteries would include the Thematic Apperception Test. The TAT is, in stimuli and task, quite different from the Rorschach. It consists of a group of twenty pictures of varying degrees of clarity and of different content. The client is asked to make up a story about each picture, to include what happened in the past, what is happening in the present, what will happen in the future, and what the people are thinking, saying, or feeling. Again, as in the Rorschach, there is no clearly apparent "correct" answer, so the story made up by the person will reflect the internal dimensions of his personality, particularly his social perceptions, and—through his identification with the principal character of the story—his feelings about himself. The following story (given by a client of the writer) illustrates how powerfully the storyteller may project himself in his stories: "Here are some people operating on me. Using one knife, but so greatly painful. You just don't know how it feels. And if they was laying here on this table, as I am, they would feel these pains rushing, rushing through their body. Their hands would be numb, their chest sore. For just one bullet to be taken from my body, with a dull knife." This intense identification is admittedly somewhat unusual, but it points up clearly how involved with the stimuli and task a person may become (this, of course, holds true for any projective task; on the Rorschach a client may spontaneously comment, "a hairy monster—I don't like it").

The TAT stories are recorded verbatim and then examined for dominant themes concerning the person's needs and the environmental pressures he feels surrounding him. In addition, his perception of relationships between himself and significant others are highlighted by his stories for various cards. The first ten cards are less ambiguous than the last ten, and occasionally are given alone. In fact, the TAT —unlike the Rorschach—is often tailored to the person. That is, the clinical psychologist will select only those cards which he feels will result in the most relevant themes and stories.

As with other projective techniques, adequate interpretation of the TAT stories demands a wealth of clinical training and experience. Perhaps even more than other techniques, the TAT lacks standards and norms that can be turned to for aid. This is in part because the stories do not lend themselves easily to scoring, and in part because a good deal of the clinical inference is "global." A number of scoring systems have been proposed,

but the effort involved is too great to make them practical, considering the light that scores shed on personality dynamics. (These scoring systems have, however, been used extensively in research.)

A third projective technique, quite unlike the previous two, is the Draw-A-Person Test.[6] The task is simple: a number of sheets of paper and a pencil are given to the person, and he is asked to "draw a person. Spend as much time as you like, and make it as good as you can." The theory is that a figure drawing is as much—or more—a projection of the person's personality as it is a reflection of artistic talent. After the first figure is drawn, the person is asked to draw a figure of the opposite sex, and then asked to tell about the figures he has just drawn. As with other projective techniques, interpretation is based on a wealth of clinical hypotheses gained after wide experience with the test. The inferences drawn from the DAP are the least well validated, although the test is second in popularity only to the Rorschach. First, the clinician notes the placement and size of the figures. If the figures are small, and at the edge of the page, insecurity may be shown. Excessive emphasis on hair is thought to be related to sexual feelings, while erasures of awkwardness in the region of the crotch is hypothesized to indicate conflicts over sex. Hands may be utilized in expressing aggression; and hands that are jammed in pockets, clasped behind the body, or left off entirely may be indicative of conflicts over aggressive impulses. The above are only a few of the numerous hypotheses related to the DAP and personality.

The Rorschach, TAT, and DAP are but three of a number of projective techniques in use. Every day sees the addition of more— and often ingenious—techniques, designed to provide more precise methods for assessment of personality. One of the more interesting ones is the Hand Test. This test consists of a series of cards showing hands in various positions (clenched, open, pointing, etc.). The person is asked to tell what the hand is doing, and in this way provides data as to his own needs and urges, for the behavior attributed to the hands is assumed to reflect the personality of the testee.

Reliability and Validity
Problems with Projectives

At one time, during the thirties and forties, it was felt that projective techniques unfailingly elicited the "inner dynamics" of personality

[6] Karen Machover, *Projection in the Drawing of the Human Figure* (Springfield, Ill.: Charles C Thomas, 1949).

and were not influenced by transient or extraneous factors. However, a number of well-controled experiments carried out in the late forties and fifties showed that projectives were just as much influenced by transient and situational factors as any other test. Thus, a Rorschach protocol obtained by a hostile examiner was likely to contain a good deal of aggressive imagery. A person suspicious of the test situation gives few responses, and the ones he does give are apt to be stark, simple, and unrevealing. Sundberg and Tyler[7] point out that in interpreting test data several major factors must be considered, including stimulus characteristics (of the projective device), situational characteristics (lighting, transient fatigue, examiner influence), and characteristics of the person. Characteristics of the person include not only enduring aspects of his personality, but also his test-taking attitude, psychological conditions (such as emotional strain, ability to maintain attention, etc.), and sociocultural interpretations of the stimuli.

All of this is one way of saying that test responses fluctuate, depending on the conditions noted, and to the degree that they fluctuate they are unreliable. This is one reason why the Rorschach, with ten cards, and the TAT, with twenty, are superior to the DAP, which depends on one trial only. Further, the use of a test battery is itself an attempt to increase reliability. If such disparate techniques as the DAP, TAT, and Rorschach *all* contain evidence of, say, overwhelming anxiety, then the psychologist can place more confidence in his conclusion than if just one test has been used.

Reliability, then, is the degree to which a response tends to recur on two different occasions, or the degree to which responses on part A of a test are similar to those on part B. The various investigations of the Rorschach, TAT, and other tests have provided estimates of reliability that range from fair to quite good; when tests are used in combination, the reliability is higher.

Validity is, simply, the degree to which a test does what it is designed to do. A test may have great reliability, but no validity. For instance, a test of honesty may yield the same score time after time, but the score may have no relation at all to how honest a person actually is. (The reverse cannot be true: a test cannot have validity if it is not reliable.) When the question is: how well do projective techniques measure personality? no answer can be given. The question must be amended, to begin with, to: how well do projective techniques in the hands of skilled interpreters measure personality? Even at that the question is difficult to answer because of the problem of establishing evaluative criteria.

Some inroads on the problem have been made, but at present it must be noted that a majority of the experimental attempts to establish validity have not been adequate. One method is to take groups with known personality differences and see if they respond differently on a given test. For example, Purcell[8] gave cards of the TAT to two groups of inductees. One group had a history of aggressive antisocial behavior, and the other had a history of social compliance. The two groups, it was hypothesized, ought to manifest different amounts of fantasy aggression, which they did. Another method of validating a test is to see if its users can, given test responses, predict or diagnose accurately on the basis of their inferences concerning the testees. It is here that the results have so far been discouraging, with little predictive validity emerging. In fairness to the projective techniques, however, it should be noted that the tasks of prediction of behavior involve consideration not only of personality by also a host of unknowable environmental variables.

There are a great many other personality tests which are not projective, or are perhaps only semi-projective. The questionnaire-type personality inventories make basically different assumptions about personality than do the projective technique theories. For example, projective techniques assume that a person is governed by unconscious and conscious forces, wishes, urges, and conflicts, and that his personality is a product of the dynamic interaction between wish and taboo, urge and control, impulse and defense. The questionnaires are constructed on the principle that personality is an aggregate of traits (honesty-dishonesty, introversion-sociability, masculinity-femininity, etc.) which can be measured quantitatively. The profile of trait-scores then provides a measure of the individual's personality. The most successful such scale, by any standard, is the empirically derived Minnesota Multiphasic Personality Inventory (MMPI). The MMPI consists of five hundred and fifty self-referral questions (e.g., "I sleep about as well as I ever did") that can be answered yes or no. Nine clinical scales representing extreme pathological states (e.g., hysteria, depression, hypochondriasis, psychopathic deviation, mania, paranoia, schizophrenia, psychaesthenia, and masculinity-femininity) were derived

[7] N. D. Sundberg and Leona Tyler, *Clinical Psychology* (New York: Appleton-Century-Crofts, 1962).

[8] K. Purcell, "The Thematic Apperception Test and Antisocial Behavior," *Journal of Consulting Psychology* 20 (1956): 449–56.

from the answers of patients in these categories. A person's score on each scale is based on the number of questions for each scale that he answers in the "pathological" direction. The fact that the questions making up each scale were derived empirically means that the content of the question does not necessarily indicate which scale it is on. For example, "I know I would do better if people didn't have it in for me" might be on the paranoid scale, but it would not be if most people tended to answer it affirmatively.

The MMPI, along with the Rorschach, Thematic Apperception Test, and Draw-A-Person, frequently make up the personality testing portion of the assessment test battery. On the basis of results, the clinician makes an inferential statement about the main aspects of the client's personality. Research and experience together have shown that certain conclusions are apt to be more reliable and valid than others. The following classifications of statements are listed in decreasing order of validity:

1. Statements concerning the present personality functioning of the individual:
   (a) thought processes and abilities, including intelligence level and potential, clarity of thought, and degree of thought disturbance present:
   (b) emotional level and breadth of the person, including degree of felt anxiety, comfort with his impulses, and general tension level;
   (c) conscious and unconscious attempts to protect the self against the experience of anxiety, or the awareness of conflicts;

   (d) conflicts, impulses, urges, and motives that are unconscious;
   (e) degree of psychological disturbance present;

2. Statements and inferences concerning past experiences and antecedents of present personality;

3. Statements and inferences about future personality trends, including:
   (a) possible prognosis, or outcome;
   (b) ability to profit from various types of psychotherapy or counseling;
   (c) predictions concerning overt behavior, such as the likelihood of suicide, or the chance of becoming psychotic.

Conclusion

To reiterate, then, the basic study of clinical psychology is the unique experiencing organism in his total environment. The psychologist is not only involved in assessment of the individual, but also in the modification of psychologically maladaptive behavior. Assessment is a combination of evidence-gathering and inference-generating activity, designed to answer questions about a particular person in a particular situation; it depends on the adroit combination of a wealth of minute data into an integrated description of personality. Although still in the formative stages, it has been used successfully in a wide range of circumstances ranging from the courtroom to the Peace Corps. Thoughtfully used, it can be of invaluable aid in enhancing the human condition through providing a valid picture of the measurement of man.

PSYCHOLOGICAL ASSESSMENT OF STEVEN STRONG*

NAME: Steven Strong
TEST DATE: January 8, 1970
REFERRED BY: Barton Cranwell, M.D.
TESTED BY: Patrick Payton, Ph.D.
AGE: 51 Years
BIRTH DATE: 9/26/19

Referral and Observation: Mr. Strong is currently being evaluated by Dr. Cranwell

* See also psychiatric evaluation of Mr. Strong, Chapter 5.

relative to his upcoming trial for murder of his wife. His attorney is raising an insanity defense, and also hopes to obtain a more lenient sentence if it can be shown that Mr. Strong is no longer dangerous. Psychological testing was requested to help ascertain whether Mr. Strong is still dangerous and what are the underlying psychodynamics.

Mr. Strong is a very thin, unattractive, middle-aged man who appears older than his 51 years. He is left-handed. Mr. Strong was overtly cooperative, but rather guarded for the testing. In doing the tests, he tended to assume a bit of the martyr role. For example, when he complained that his elbow hurt when he wrote, it was suggested that he could tape record his responses rather than writing them. He insisted, however, that never mind the pain, he would write anyway. He performed all the tests without complaint (despite a facial expression of distaste on some of them), but tended to be constricted in response and obviously was attempting consciously to monitor what he revealed. An example of such monitoring was on one TAT card commonly interpreted as a man who either raped or murdered a woman. After interpreting the woman sick or dead from an illness (also a common interpretation), the patient mused over the card and said, "but his expression . . . the way he's looking at the . . . No! never mind!" Throughout the session, Mr. Strong was not very communicative and was obviously avoiding any talk of his wife. When I asked even a peripheral question pertaining to her, he stiffened so that I avoided direct questioning about her for fear of losing his cooperation for the testing. At times he just sat there in silence getting more uncomfortable and angry. He could offer no particular explanation why he did this.

Tests Administered: Partial WAIS (Comprehension, Similarities, Block Design, Picture Arrangement); Bender-Gestalt; Goodenough Draw-a-Person; Rorschach; TAT; Sentence Completion; and MMPI.

Evaluation: Mr. Strong's guardedness in responding, particularly to the projective tests, make it impossible adequately to answer the referral questions. Throughout the testing, Mr. Strong rather successfully maintained a bland, conventional façade. His MMPI was within normal limits but quite defensive. His sentence completions were bland and conventional, except for quite appropriate concern about what his future holds and expressions of regret for causing so much trouble to his loved ones. His Rorschach was rather constricted and consisted primarily of popular or other innocuous responses. Thematic stories were also generally bland and unrevealing. There were, however, a few flaws in the façade which allow a few tentative hypotheses about underlying dynamics and character structure.

Mr. Strong is an intelligent man, with at least bright average and probably superior intelligence who shows no signs of either organicity or psychosis. He presents himself as a man who holds high standards for himself and others, who values efficiency and is somewhat impatient of others who are inefficient, who do not do their share, or otherwise do not meet his standards. Although these characteristics may sometimes cause interpersonal difficulties, he does have adequate capacity for forming close interpersonal relationships. He also appears capable of experiencing appropriate feelings of guilt about his actions. His knowledge and understanding of social expectations and prohibitions are excellent. However, his judgment in an actual interpersonal situation may be faulty at times because of his tendency to ignore the subtleties of a situation or misinterpret them in terms of his own emotional needs. He is quite capable of denying, "not seeing," realities which are unpleasant or incongruous with his view of himself or his world. It is quite likely that at this time he is trying to deny to himself the emotional and realistic implications and ramifications of the behavior responsible for his current difficulties.

The one clear area of psychological conflict for Mr. Strong which emerged on the testing was some confusion around sexual identification. Mr. Strong could not specify the sex of any of his human percepts on the Rorschach, avoided depicting any sexual characteristics in his male drawing, gave his lowest level Rorschach response to card VII, which is generally associated with one's feelings about femininity, and consistently interpreted ambiguous TAT figures as females. It is possible that difficulty in accepting his masculinity may have made adjustment to marriage more difficult for Mr. Strong and have contributed to the conflicts between him and his wife.

Evaluating Mr. Strong's current level of hostility and degree of impulse controls is impossible at this time. He was obviously making an effort to conceal any hostility or impulsiveness throughout the testing and was pretty much successful in this. There was some mild evidence that he had some underlying concerns about impulse controls, certainly understandable in view of his current situation. There are also hints that he, possibly in accordance with lower middle class origins, sees physical violence as one way of enforcing compliance or obedience from others, particularly children. This, however, is a commonly held view, and the question remains as to his level of generalized hostility, readiness to use violence as a solution to interpersonal difficulties, and ability to control violent impulses should they occur.

Overall, the psychological testing was not very helpful in throwing much light on the referral questions. Mr. Strong appears to be an intelligent man, neither psychotic nor organic, with a capacity for the normal range of human emotions and relationships. Standards for himself and others may be unrealistically high and possibly rigid; he tends to handle psychological difficulties through denial, which may at times cloud his judgment, and he clearly has some conflicts in the area of sex identification. The primary question, however, of whether Mr. Strong is currently dangerous is not answerable at this time.

PATRICK PAYTON, PH.D.

ANOTHER PSYCHOLOGICAL ASSESSMENT OF STEVEN STRONG

NAME: Steven Strong
AGE: 51
DATE TESTED: March 4, 1970
REFERRED BY: Jerry Robinson, M.D.
EXAMINER: Susan Wagner, Ph.D.

TESTS ADMINISTERED. Bender Gestalt, Minnesota Multiphasic Personality Inventory, Draw A Person, Rorschach, Rotter Incomplete Sentence Test, Thematic Apperception Test.

REASON FOR REFERRAL. Psychological assessment was requested as part of a pre-sentencing psychiatric evaluation to rule out psychosis and capacity for destructive behavior. A description of the underlying psychodynamics of his personality was also requested.

OBSERVATION. Mr. Strong's appearance was that of a plain-looking, neatly dressed, thin man who displays a forthright, sincere approach to his present circumstances. While he was at first quite guarded about the details, he watched the examiner very closely for clues and seemed to open up as the session progressed. He was cooperative and involved in the tasks, working quickly and efficiently. His facial expression was very bland, and there was little if any display of or expression of feelings during the session. He conveyed the overall impression of an overly controlled, logical person who is very task-oriented in his approach to problems.

TEST RESULTS. Mr. Strong is a man whose basic approach to life is extremely logical and intellectual. He utilizes a systematic, analytical, computer-like style in dealing with his problems and functions quite effectively as long as situations lend themselves to this rational approach.

However, when faced with problems requiring an emotional solution, Mr. Strong does not have the capacity to deal with them effectively and continues to resort to intellectual solutions. He shields himself from emotions by utilizing basically obsessional defenses—denial, intellectualization, and repression—with which he successfully maintains rigid control over his behavior. His attempts to busy himself with routine, structured activities are another means by which he achieves control.

It is quite clear that Mr. Strong has set very high standards for himself and strives hard to achieve them. He does not believe in complaining or giving in to adversity and finds it necessary to "keep up a good front" at all times. This may explain his seemingly bland emotional tone and resigned attitude throughout the testing session. The expression of emotion is exceedingly difficult for him and seems to be viewed as a sign of weakness. This is true even in intimate relationships and is well exemplified by his reaction to a TAT card that pictures a woman obviously crying and in despair:

> She looks like she's been given sad news.
> She's leaving the room because she doesn't want them to see that she's crying. She'll stay there, get hold of herself and then go back into the room. I would say someone probably died. Otherwise she'd have gotten further away before she cried.

It is quite possible that Mr. Strong's reluctance to deal with his feelings and his great difficulty in expressing them contributed to escalating an already difficult marital situation. Not feeling able to discuss his difficulties with even close family members or friends must have created feelings of frustration and the desire for some resolution, no matter how extreme, of what had become an intolerable situation.

Both the test results and Mr. Strong's own account of his history and the circumstances preceding his wife's death also suggest that he has very stereotyped notions about appropriate behavioral roles for men and women, and some uncertainty about his own sexual identity. In addition, his wife's resentment about her career and financial failure and her open admission of relationships with other men all added to his negative feelings of self-worth. His very traditional views of male superiority and the binding obligations of marriage apparently placed him in a position where he felt he had no options open to him. Viewed in this context, the murder was his attempt to find a logical, rational solution to what had become an intolerable situation.

Mr. Strong is feeling appropriately guilty and uneasy about the future. His lack of overt display of anxiety may be related in part to his need to conceal emotional concerns and his use of rigid intellectual controls that work quite effectively for him. Because of his rigid defenses, it is difficult to predict how well he would respond in any therapeutic involvement. He does demonstrate capacity to relate to others and is certainly intelligent. Supportive therapy focusing on expression of emotions, instilling awareness of his attributes, and broadening his outlook on future options could be very useful to him.

SUMMARY. Mr. Strong is an intelligent, responsible man who approaches problems in a logical, rational way. He finds the handling of emotional situations extremely difficult and resorts to intellectual solutions even when inappropriate. He maintains rigid control over his behavior by using an obsessional defensive style of intellectualization, denial, and repression. There is no indication of any psychotic process. Mr. Strong's difficulty in expressing feelings and his need to maintain a stoic front may explain his bland expression and matter of fact attitude about his present circumstances. The test results and the details surrounding his wife's death point to his very stereotyped and traditional views of appropriate sexual roles and binding marital obligations. There was evidence of some confusion and uncertainty about his own identity, probably intensified by his wife's relationships with other men. The murder was apparently his attempt to solve an intolerable situation logically. There was no evidence of poor impulse control or any indication that he would be a danger to others or to himself.

His ability to profit from therapy is questionable due to his use of excessively rigid controls, especially in areas dealing with the display of or expression of emotion.

SUSAN WAGNER, PH.D.

JENKINS v. UNITED STATES: TESTIMONY BY THE PSYCHOLOGIST

Brief for American Psychological Association

I. STATEMENT OF THE CASE

In the Court below, defendant was convicted of the crimes of housebreaking with intent to commit an assault, assault with intent to rape, and assault with a dangerous weapon. At the trial, defendant relied solely upon the defense of insanity. In support of this defense, defendant presented the testimony, *inter alia,* of three clinical psychologists with from three to twenty-five years' clinical experience, who had received Ph.D. degrees in institutions approved for clinical training by the American Psychological Association.

One of these three was the Chief Psychologist of St. Elizabeths Hospital; one was the Chief Psychologist of the District of Columbia General Hospital; and the third was a psychologist on the Staff of St. Elizabeths Hospital at the time he examined the defendant.

Upon the basis of personal contact with the defendant, review of his case history, and upon

---

Excerpts from Brief for American Psychological Association, *Amicus Curiae,* in the United States Court of Appeals for the Disrtict of Columbia Circuit, No. 16, 306.

the basis of the results of standard psychological tests administered by these psychologists or under their direction, they all testified that on the date the alleged crimes were committed, defendant had been suffering from schizophrenia. One of the three testified that he could give no opinion concerning the relationship between the illness and the crimes but the other two gave it as their opinions, respectively, that the disease and the crimes were "related," and that the crimes were the product of the illness.

At the conclusion of the trial, the judge instructed the jury to disregard the opinions of the psychologists.

On appeal to this Court from the conviction, the panel of the Court which heard the case held, *inter alia,* one judge dissenting, that the Trial Court had committed reversible error in excluding the psychologists' expert opinions.

Upon motion of the Government, the Court ordered a rehearing *en banc* limited to the issue of the correctness of ". . . the ruling of the District Court which excluded from consideration by the jury the testimony of the psychologist concerning the existence and effects of the 'mental disease or defect.' "

By motion filed January 15, 1962, the American Psychological Association sought leave to file this brief *amicus curiae* with respect to the issue stated above. Neither appellant nor appellee opposed the motion, and the Court granted it by order dated January 29, 1962.

[Sections II and III omitted.]

IV. ARGUMENT

A. *Psychology Is an Established Science*

In any inquiry as to the testimonial competence of a psychologist to express an expert professional opinion, it is important to understand that psychology is an established science which makes use of the same fundamental methods of investigation and inquiry and the same criteria of objectivity and thoroughness as are used in all recognized scientific disciplines.

Psychology, the science of human behavior, has its origins in many areas of inquiry. It grew in part from the great philosophical concerns with human behavior and conduct. Its immediate origins as a science, however, can be placed in the period of scientific development in the mid-nineteenth century. It was at the University of Leipzig in 1879 that Professor Wilhelm Wundt established the first laboratory in scientific psychology. Since that time the major emphasis in the development of psychology has been along scientific lines, with increased application of the results of research to a wide variety of problems of human behavior.

It is interesting to note that the first intelligence test, the derivatives of which are so widely used today in education, industry, government, and institutions, was developed in 1905 by Alfred Binet, a French psychologist who was Director of the Psychological Laboratory at the Sorbonne. The first American adaptation of this test was published the same year, but the 1916 Stanford Revision set the pattern for the measurement of mental ability throughout the United States. Further modified in 1937 as the Revised Stanford-Binet Scale, and again modified in 1960, this test continues to be extensively used today.

From a scholarly discipline and science developed mainly in university centers, the result of psychological effort has become recognized as capable of application in many fields of human activity. In the interval between the two World Wars, applications were taking place in business and industry and in education. During World War II, the methods and techniques developed by psychologists found extensive application in the wide range of events covered by the war years, and played a vital role in the recruitment, selection, classification, assignment, and training of individuals accepted for military service. Newer applications of psychology were possible in such areas as psychological warfare, aviation and submarine operations, treatment of casualties and offenders, design of equipment, such as radar, with a view toward the best utilization of the skills of the human operator, food and nutrition research, the effect of drugs on behavior, morale and productivity of groups, and a host of other problems. Since World War II, new and vitally important practical uses of the skills of psychologists have taken place at a remarkable rate. . . .

B. *The Practice of Psychology Is a Learned Profession*

As in the case of all sciences, a distinction may be drawn between psychologists whose total or primary endeavors are devoted to basic research and those whose total or primary endeavors are devoted to using their scientific skills and knowledge for the solution of practical problems and the achievement of practical results. Since the founding of the American Psychological Association, the number of psychologists engaged in work of the latter sort has greatly increased. From a primarily academic discipline pursued almost exclusively in the colleges and universities, psychology has developed a full-fledged professional segment. For example, it is estimated that of the more than 20,000 members of the American Psychological Association, approximately half find their primary employment in academic work, and the remainder find their primary employment in Federal, state, and municipal government, in private practice, and in business and industry. . . .

The Association has been seriously concerned with the problems of education and training in psychology. Among the permanent Boards and Committees of the Association is the Education and Training Board. By Article X, paragraph 9 of the Association's Bylaws, this Board is charged with "general concern for all educational and training affairs which involve psychology. . . ." Among other duties, this Board has the continuing responsibility for reviewing and reporting upon the adequacy of graduate training programs in clinical and counseling psychology offered by the different colleges and universities. A list of approved universities is maintained and published. Additionally, the Board also evaluates and approves a list of predoctoral internships in clinical and counseling psychology which meet minimal qualifications.

The Association's evaluation of educational institutions has been going on since 1947. This practice is analogous to the practice of the American Bar Association in conferring or withholding approval of Law Schools. . . .

All recognized educational institutions with departments of psychology that offer advanced training utilize a variety of selection techniques for admitting students to such advanced training. Some of these are: analysis of collegiate records and previous training, evaluations and recommendations from professors, special qualifying examinations such as the Graduate Record Examination and the Miller Analogies Test, and personal interview.

Over and above these evaluations, there was established in 1947, the American Board of Examiners in Professional Psychology. This organization confers Diplomate status upon those individuals who are judged to be qualified. The basis for evaluation is experience and the successful completion of rigorous oral and written examinations. Those individuals who have demonstrated their competency are awarded Diplomate status in one of three areas: Industrial Psychology, Counseling Psychology, and Clinical Psychology. The last of these specialties is of particular relevance to the case at bar. Through August, 1961, 1,520 Diplomas have been issued by the American Board, of which 1,100 were in clinical psychology, 243 were in counseling psychology, and 177 were in industrial psychology.

In addition to the intraprofessional standards and criteria of status discussed above, the profession of psychology is now given legal recognition in the statutes of seventeen states, four of which have licensing requirements and thirteen of which have certification requirements for psychologists. It is interesting to note that in eleven of these seventeen states, clients of psychologists are granted a testimonial privilege similar to the attorney-client privilege.

In view of all the foregoing, it is submitted that psychology in its present state of development is clearly an established science and that psychologists are clearly engaged in the practice of an established profession. It would obviously be foolish to assert that any psychologist is testimonially competent to express an expert professional opinion upon all questions relating to the science of psychology. In fact, the Association would oppose any such rule as being contrary to the professional standards to which it and its membership adhere. It is submitted, however, that a psychologist is clearly competent under well-established rules of evidence to testify as an expert upon matters within the scope of his professional experience.

C. *A Clinical Psychologist Is Competent to Express Professional Opinions upon the Existence or Non-Existence of Mental Disease or Defect and upon Their Causal Relationships to Overt Behavior*

. . . the principal functions of the clinical psychologist are threefold, namely: (1) diagnosis, (2) therapy, and (3) research. These three functions are closely interrelated. From the standpoint of the profession of psychology, no one of them is of greater importance than the others. However, the diagnostic function is obviously the most relevant to the issue to be decided in the case at bar. For this reason, the diagnostic function will be discussed in this brief, to the exclusion of the therapy and research functions.

In the diagnosis of mental disease and mental defect, including the formulation of professional opinions as to causal relationships between mental disease or defect and overt behavior, a principal tool of the clinical psychologist is found in psychological tests. These tests fall into two major categories.

The first category consists of tests designed to measure a broad band of abilities or capacities by requiring a person to answer specific questions which can be unequivocally scored as correct or incorrect. The Stanford-Binet test . . . is one of the best-known tests of this sort. Another is the Wechsler-Bellevue Intelligence

Scale, which, as the Court will recall, was one of the tests administered to the defendant in this case. The Wechsler-Bellevue Scale was specifically designed for testing adults and ranks first in frequency of use among all psychological tests designed to measure individual intelligence.

The second major category of psychological tests is designed to reveal information about the personality structure and emotional make-up of a person. In tests of this kind, there is obviously no such thing as a right answer or a perfect score. Rather, the person's responses are classified by comparison with those of defined groups of people exhibiting differential personality or emotional characteristics.

Personality tests, themselves, are of two basic types. The first type is represented by the personality inventory which seeks to obtain information about an individual's personality by having him select statements which most nearly describe his feelings or behavior. One of the most widely known of these tests is the Minnesota Multiphasic Personality Inventory, often used in education, business, and industry.

The second type of personality test is represented by the projective instrument which seeks to stimulate a person to project or reveal his personality or emotions through his interpretation of or reaction to materials that are not in question-and-answer form. The person may be asked to tell what he sees in patterns derived from ink blots, as in the Rorschach Test; to select pictures of people he particularly likes and dislikes, as in the Szondi Test; or to tell a story about what is going on in a series of action pictures, as in the Thematic Apperception Test; or to copy groups of dots, lines, and geometrical figures as in the Bender-Gestalt Test; or to draw a picture of a man or woman as in the projective drawing tests.

In general, both ability and personality tests are based on extensive normative samples of human behavior, developed according to established principles of psychological measurement, and standardized in administration to eliminate, insofar as possible, extraneous factors which might affect the interpretation of their results.

Infallibility is not claimed for any psychological test, and no professional psychologist would assert that he could reach a valid diagnosis upon the basis of test results alone. However, the use of test results, in conjunction with a review of a person's history and evaluative interviews, can be extremely useful to the clinical psychologist in reaching informed opinions as to the nature and existence or non-existence of mental disease or defect in a given subject and as to the causal relationship or lack thereof between such mental disease or defect and the subject's overt behavior. . . .

D. Experience Is the Essential Legal Ingredient of Competence to Give an Expert Opinion

Although the question presented upon this rehearing is one of first impression in this jurisdiction, it does not involve any new or novel legal principles, but rather involves the application of well-established and simple legal principles to a factual situation which this Court has not heretofore been asked to consider.

The fundamental legal principle governing the competence of a witness to express a professional expert opinion is in essence no different from that which governs the competence of any witness to testify in a judicial proceeding. As has been aptly observed by Wigmore, the essential qualifications of any witness, lay or expert, is that he have sufficient *experience* with the subject of his testimony to enable him to testify reliably. In the case of the lay witness, this essential experience is usually nothing more than suitable ability and opportunity to observe and remember the event or occurrence as to which he testifies. Except in the case of children of tender years and perhaps a few other special cases, it is assumed that the lay witness possesses these essential requisites and he is not required to demonstrate them before giving the substance of his testimony.

In the case of the expert witness there must be a showing that he possesses some special and peculiar experience before he is permitted to proceed to the substance of his testimony. However, there is nothing arcane about this requirement of a showing of special and peculiar experience. As stated by Wigmore:

This special and peculiar experience may have been attained, so far as legal rules go, in any way whatever; all the law requires is that it should have been attained. Yet it is possible here to group roughly two classes of experience which are usually, though not necessarily, found separately:

(a) There is, first an *occupational* experience—. . .

(b) There is, secondly, a *systematic training*. . . .

Now, the line, if any can be drawn, between these two has no general legal significance. In truth, no accurate line can be drawn. Each shades into the other imperceptibly. In some instances, the witness will need both; in some instances he may have both, though he does not need both. Neither is generally favored above the other by the Courts. The question in each instance is whether the particular witness is fitted as to the matter in hand.

Applying the foregoing basic principle to the issue presented upon this rehearing, we submit that the clinical psychologist is fully qualified both by occupational experience and by systematic training to express a professional expert opinion in a criminal case upon the existence or non-existence of mental disease or defect and the causal relationship or lack of causal relationship between such mental disease or defect and the criminal conduct with which the defendant is charged.

It is submitted that the case of *People* v. *Hawthorne* (1940) 293 Mich. 15, 291 N.W. 205, cited and discussed in the briefs of both appellant and appellee herein, illustrates the correct application of established legal principles to the question of the clinical psychologist's competence to testify in criminal cases as an expert witness of professional standing. In that case, a defendant charged with murder proffered a psychologist as an expert witness in support of his defense of insanity. The trial court refused to permit the psychologist to give his professional opinion upon the defendant's mental condition in response to a hypothetical question. On appeal from conviction, a majority of the Supreme Court of Michigan, although affirming the conviction upon other grounds, joined in an opinion declaring that the trial court had erred in rejecting the professional opinion of the psychologist. In reaching this conclusion, and in rejecting the argument that only a doctor of medicine

should be permitted to give such testimony, the opinion states: "There is no magic in particular titles and degrees, and in our age of intense scientific specialization we might deny outselves the use of the best knowledge available by a rule that would immutably fix the educational qualifications to a particular degree."

V. CONCLUSION

In light of the foregoing it is clear that psychology is an established science and profession. It is also clear that psychologists are highly trained experts in their profession. As an adjunct to these conclusions it is also clear that the clinical psychologist, through systematic professional training and through professional experience, is qualified to formulate and express expert professional opinions in the field of mental disease and mental defect.

By reason of this professional competence, it is submitted that the clinical psychologist is fully qualified under the established legal principles governing competence of expert witnesses, to express a professional expert opinion in criminal cases upon the issues governing criminal responsibility under the *Durham* rule.

For these reasons it is respectfully urged that the issue presented upon this rehearing was correctly decided by the panel of this Court that first heard this appeal.

Statement of Interest and Position of the American Psychiatric Association

---

The American Psychiatric Association, founded in 1844, is the national membership organization of Doctors of Medicine who specialize in the diagnosis, treatment, and care of mental illnesses. Doctors of Medicine who qualify and specialize in the field of mental illness are psychiatrists and alienists. The Association is comprised of those twelve thousand qualified Doctors of Medicine who specialize and practice as psychiatrists.

Psychiatrists have traditionally been called upon by our Courts to give expert medical

testimony concerning mental illnesses, the productivity thereof and their effects.

The question of whether a person *not* trained in medicine, *not* a Doctor of Medicine, and *not* a doctor trained as a specialist in the diagnosis, treatment, and care of the mentally ill, can qualify as a *medical* expert and give expert *medical* opinions concerning the diagnosis of specific mental diseases and the *medical* effects thereof is of grave concern to psychiatrists and their Association.

Psychiatrists, or alienists as they have also

Excerpts from Brief for American Psychiatric Association, *Amicus Curiae*.

been termed in times past, are qualified Doctors of Medicine who specialize in the diagnosis, care, and treatment of mental illnesses (Webster's International and Concise Dictionaries). Briefly, the psychiatrist now receives a minimum of thirteen years of medical training and special experience, needed to qualify a Doctor of Medicine as a Psychiatrist. This special training in medicine is discussed later in this brief. . . .

A psychologist is not so trained. . . . Psychology basically deals with philosophy. Psychologists study philosophy, not medicine, and their objectives as stated in the "purposes" of their Association, "shall be to advance psychology (not medicine) . . . as a means of promoting human welfare. . . ."

In the Divisions created by the American Psychological Association, some twenty in number, none deal with medical diagnosis, treatment, and care of mental illnesses. The nearest approach to mental illness and its effects is a category called "Division of Clinical Psychology." As the psychologists who testified at the trial had some experience as clinical psychologists, let us comment on the part the clinical psychologist plays in the diagnosis and treatment of the mentally ill. These psychologists studied philosophy, not medicine, and have Ph.D. degrees, i.e., Doctors of Philosophy. The clinical psychologists, like "teachers, ministers, lawyers, social workers, and vocational counselors," all utilize their skills as aids only to the psychiatrist in his medical diagnosis, care, and treatment of the mentally ill. That the clinical psychologist only passes on his contribution as a part of the medical picture to be evaluated only by a qualified psychiatrist, was resolved by a Resolution on the Relationship of Psychotherapy to Medicine, approved by the Board of Trustees of the American Medical Association, the Council of the American Psychiatric Association, and the Executive Council of the American Psychoanalytical Association in 1954. This joint Resolution reads as follows:

For centuries the Western world has placed on the medical profession responsibility for the diagnosis and treatment of illness. Medical practice acts have been designed to protect the public from unqualified practitioners and to define the special responsibilities assumed by those who practice the healing art, for much harm may be done by unqualified persons, however good their intentions may be. To do justice to the patient requires the capacity to make a diagnosis and to prescribe appropriate treatment. Diagnosis often requires the ability to compare and contrast various diseases and disorders that have similar symptoms but different causes. Diagnosis is a continuing process, for the character of the illness changes with its treatment or with the passage of time, and that treatment which is appropriate may change accordingly.

Recognized medical training today involves, as a minimum, graduation from an approved medical school and internship in a hospital. Most physicians today receive additional medical training, and specialization requires still further training.

Psychiatry is the medical specialty concerned with illness that has chiefly mental symptoms. The psychiatrist is also concerned with mental causes of physical illness, for we have come to recognize that physical symptoms may have mental causes just as mental symptoms may have physical causes. The psychiatrist, with or without consultation with other physicians, must select from the many different methods of treatment at his disposal those methods that he considers appropriate to the particular patient. His treatment may be medicinal or surgical, physical as (electroshock) or psychological. The systematic application of the methods of psychological medicine to the treatment of illness, particularly as these methods involve gaining an understanding of the emotional state of the patient and aiding him to understand himself, is called psychotherapy. This special form of medical treatment may be highly developed, but it remains simply one of the possible methods of treatment to be selected for use according to medical criteria for use when it is indicated. Psychotherapy is a form of medical treatment and does not form the basis for a separate profession.

Other professional groups such as psychologists, teachers, ministers, lawyers, social workers, and vocational counselors, of course, use psychological understanding in carrying out their professional functions. Members of these professional groups are not thereby practicing medicine. The application of psychological methods to the treatment of illness is a medical function. Any physician may utilize the skills of others in his professional work, but he remains responsible, legally and morally, for the diagnosis and for the treatment of his patient.

The medical profession fully endorses the appropriate utilization of the skills of psychologists, social workers, and other professional personnel in contributing roles in settings directly supervised by physicians. It further recognizes that these professions are entirely independent and autonomous when medical questions are not involved; but when members of these professions contribute to the diagnosis and treatment of illness, their professional contributions must be coordinated under medical responsibility.

Reduced to simple terms, clinical psychology . . . "remains simply one of the possible methods" to be selected by the psychiatrist in evaluating and treating a specific mental illness. Its use in any specific case is for the psychiatrist to determine, because this is a medical function reserved by joint agreement of the American Medical Association, the American Psychiatric Association, and the American Psychoanalytical Association to the qualified psychiatrist. As their joint Resolution expresses this principle, "For centuries the Western world has placed on the *medical* profession responsibility for the diagnosis and treatment of illness" and "Psychiatry is the *medical* specialty concerned with illness that has chiefly mental symptoms." [Italics supplied.]

SUMMARY OF ARGUMENT

I. Psychiatrists undergo a minimum of thirteen years of special training and experience to quality as medical experts in the mental health field. The psychologists who testified below lack such medical training and experience, hence they are not medical experts in the mental health field. While they are skilled in psychology, this does not qualify them to diagnose or to prescribe treatment and care for a specific mental illness. Traditionally, ultimate medical diagnosis, care, and treatment for the mentally ill are reserved to the psychiatrist.

The diagnosis of mental illness should be based on the *synthesis* of data from several sources. One source could be observations of and tests given by a clinical psychologist under direct medical supervision, but this is but a part of the history. Diagnosis to be ultimate must be made by a medical specialist, the psychiatrist, and psychological data play only a part in this diagnosis. A clinical psychologist lacking medical training and experience is not qualified as a medical expert in this field and cannot diagnose, prescribe care and treatment

of a specific case of mental illness, or give expert medical opinions on these end results. Traditionally, medical men have been relied upon by our Courts for expert testimony in medical fields.

II. The clinical psychologists who testified below admittedly are not educated, trained, and experienced in medicine. They are not graduates of medical schools. They are not Doctors of Medicine. They are not psychiatrists or alienists. Traditionally, it is the primary function of the trial judge to pass upon the qualifications of any purported expert witness and to decide if expert testimony can be given in a particular instance. Here the instance was the giving of expert testimony concerning the existence of specific mental illness in Appellant, its diagnosis, its productivity, and the relationship of the particular mental illness to the criminal acts of Appellant. While the Trial Judge permitted the psychologists to testify to their observations and the various tests given to the Appellant, in exercising his sound discretion he excluded expert medical opinions of these psychologists "as to a mental disease or defect," obviously, as the majority pointed out in the decision of October 26, 1961, "because psychologists lack medical training." The Trial Judge's decision was correct and certainly was not an abuse of his discretion.

III. The positions urged by the American Psychological Association's brief *amicus curiae* that "psychology is a learned profession," hence, a "clinical psychologist is competent to express professional opinions upon the existence or non-existence of mental disease or defect and upon their causal relationships to overt behavior" are unsound.

Decision of Court of Appeals

BAZELON, Circuit Judge.

Appellant relied solely upon the defense of insanity in a jury trial which culminated in his conviction for housebreaking with intent to commit an assault, assault with intent to rape, and assault with a dangerous weapon. He

alleges that the District Court erred in (1) determining his competency to stand trial, (2) excluding diagnostic opinions of two defense psychiatrists on the ground that their opinions were without "proper basis," (3) instructing the jury to disregard the testimony of three defense psychologists that appellant had a men-

---

Jenkins v. United States, United States Court of Appeals, District of Columbia Circuit, 307 F.2d 637 (1962); footnotes deleted.

tal disease or defect on the ground that "a psychologist is not competent to give a medical opinion as to a mental disease or defect," and (4) depriving him of a fair trial by conducting a lengthy and disaparaging examination of some expert witnesses.

I. THE FACTS

The record discloses the following pertinent information. After indictment, appellant was committed to the District General Hospital for a mental examination on September 4, 1959, to determine his competency to stand trial and his condition at the time of the alleged offense. Appellant was given a series of psychological tests on October 20 and 22, 1959, by staff psychologists under the supervision of the Chief Psychologist Dr. Bernard I. Levy. Appellant scored 63, high moron, on the I.Q. section of the tests. He was also interviewed three or four times by Dr. Richard Schaengold, Assistant Chief Psychiatrist. Appellant's test performance and his "dullness and inability to relate correctly" led Dr. Schaengold to consider and reject the possibility of undifferentiated psychosis in favor of a diagnosis of mental defect: a basic, unchanging deficiency in brain function. His findings were confirmed by Dr. Mary V. McIndoo, District General's Chief Psychiatrist, on the basis of interviews on November 23, 24, and 25, and a review of appellant's history and test results. By letter of November 25, 1959, signed by Dr. Schaengold and countersigned by Dr. McIndoo, the District Court was advised that appellant was "suffering from an organic brain defect resulting in mental deficiency and impaired judgment. He is, therefore, psychotic, incompetent, and incapable of participating in his own defense." Appellant was adjudicated incompetent to stand trial on the basis of this report and was committed to "Saint Elizabeths Hospital until he is mentally competent to stand trial pursuant to Title 24, Section 301, District of Columbia Code, 1951 Edition, as amended August 9, 1955."

At St. Elizabeths, Dr. Lawrence Tirnauer, a staff psychologist, administered another battery of psychological tests on February 25 and March 2, 1960, in which appellant scored 74 an the I.Q. section. Dr. Tirnauer concluded that appellant was suffering from schizophrenia. Thereafter Dr. David J. Owens of St. Elizabeths interviewed appellant several times, "probably [for] fifteen or twenty minutes," and saw him at a staff conference on October 3, 1960. Dr. Owens found no evidence of mental disease or defect. He classified appellant as "a borderline intelligence." Dr. William G.

Cushard, another psychiatrist at St. Elizabeths, who saw appellant at the staff conference, reviewed the test reports and agreed with Dr. Owens' findings. Dr. Margaret Ives, Chief Psychologist at St. Elizabeths, was also present at the staff conference. Subsequently, she reviewed Dr. Tirnauer's test results and appellant's past history and administered one part of a six-part Szondi profile test. She agreed with Dr. Tirnauer that appellant "had a mental illness by name of schizophrenia."

Ten days later, the Acting Superintendent of the hospital notified the District Court that "it has been determined that he [appellant] is, at this time, mentally competent to stand trial and to consult with counsel and assist properly in his own defense. He is not suffering from mental disease. . . . Although he is not suffering from mental deficiency, he has only borderline intelligence." Upon appellant's objection to this report, the court conducted a hearing on November 4, 1960, wherein appellant was found competent and ordered to stand trial.

In preparation for their testimony at trial, Drs. McIndoo and Schaengold noted the later and different diagnosis and the apparent change in appellant's I.Q. reported by the St. Elizabeths psychologists. They requested Dr. Levy of their staff to retest appellant in order to reconsider their diagnoses that he was mentally defective on June 10, 1959, the date of the alleged offenses. This time appellant scored 90 on the I.Q. test, an improvement inconsistent with mental defect. In reporting this result, Dr. Levy, who had previously been unable to make a diagnosis, concluded that upon review of all test data appellant "is psychotic and schizophrenic." Considering this report in the light of the hospital record and "reports" from St. Elizabeths, Drs. McIndoo and Schaengold revised their previous diagnoses without seeing appellant again. Dr. McIndoo concluded that appellant was schizophrenic, and Dr. Schaengold diagnosed his condition as undifferentiated psychosis. . . .

[Section II omitted.]

III. ADMISSIBILITY OF THE PSYCHOLOGISTS' OPINIONS

The next assignment of error we discuss concerns the court's instruction to the jury to disregard testimony of three defense psychologists that appellant had a mental disease when he committed the crimes charged. Although appellant failed to object to this instruction, we consider it because it presents a question which is likely to arise upon a new trial.

The first psychologist, Dr. Tirnauer, administered a battery of tests to appellant, studied his case history, and concluded he had been suffering from schizophrenia when he committed the crimes. In his opinion, the disease and the crimes were "related." The second psychologist, Dr. Margaret Ives, had reviewed Dr. Tirnauer's test results, had seen appellant at a staff conference, and had administered part of a Szondi profile test. She stated that appellant was suffering from schizophrenia and that his crimes were the product of the disease. The third psychologist, Dr. Levy, interpreted test results obtained by members of the District General staff in October, 1959, and administered two additional tests shortly before trial. He testified that defendant had been suffering from schizophrenia on June 10, 1959, but could give no opinion concerning the relationship between the illness and the crimes. At the conclusion of the trial the court instructed the jury: "A psychologist is not competent to give a medical opinion as to a mental disease or defect. Therefore, you will not consider any evidence to the effect that the defendant was suffering from a mental disease or a mental defect on June 10, 1959, according to the testimony given by the psychologists."

The trial court apparently excluded these opinions because psychologists lack medical training. We agree with the weight of authority, however, that some psychologists are qualified to render expert testimony in the field of mental disorder.

We begin by placing this problem in the context of the considerations governing the reception of expert testimony.

An observer is qualified to testify because he has firsthand knowledge which the jury does not have of the situation or transaction at issue. The expert has something different to contribute. This is a power to draw inferences from the facts which a jury would not be competent to draw. To warrant the use of expert testimony, then, two elements are required. First, the subject of the inference must be so distinctively related to some science, profession, business or occupation as to be beyond the ken of the average layman, and second, the witness must have such skill, knowledge or experience in that field or calling as to make it appear that his opinion or inference will probably aid the trier in his search for truth. The knowledge may in some fields be derived from reading alone, in some from practice alone, or as is more commonly the case, from both. [McCormick, Evidence § 13 (1954), citing authorities.]

The test, then, is whether the opinion offered will be likely to aid the trier in the search for truth. In light of that purpose, it is hardly surprising that courts do not exclude all but the very best kind of witness. (See 2 Wigmore, Evidence § 569 [3d ed. 1940]. Accord: Fightmaster v. Mode, 31 Ohio App. 273, 167 N.E. 407 [1928].) Thus a general practitioner may testify concerning matters within a medical specialty if his education or experience, or both, involves demonstrable knowledge of the subject. (Sher v. DeHaven, 91 U.S. App. D.C. 257, 199 F.2d 777, 36 A.L.R. 2d 937 [1952], cert. denied, 345 U.S. 936, 73 S.Ct. 797, 97 L.Ed. 1363 [1953]; 2 Wigmore, Evidence § 569 [3d ed. 1940].) Nor need a skilled witness on a medical subject be duly licensed to practice medicine. (*Ibid.*) The general rule is that "anyone who is shown to have special knowledge and skill in diagnosing and treating human ailments is qualified to testify as an expert, if his learning and training show that he is qualified to give an opinion on the particular question at issue." "It is not essential that the witness be a medical practitioner." (32 C.J.S. Evidence § 537 [1942].) Thus, non-medical witnesses who have had experience in electrical work may testify to the effects of electrical shock upon the human body (Vessels v. Kansas City Light & Power Co., 219 S.W. 80 [Mo. Sup. Ct. 1920]; Blakeney v. Alabama Power Co., 222 Ala. 394, 133 So. 16 [1931]). Optometrists, whose training includes instruction in the symptoms of certain eye diseases, may testify to the presence of cataract discovered in the course of fitting glasses (Jackson v. Waller, 126 Conn. 294, 10 A. 2d 763 [1940]), and to the effect of a scar upon vision (Black Star Coal Corp. v. Reeder, 278 Ky. 532, 128 S.W. 2d 905 [1939]). A toxicologist has been permitted to testify to the effect of oxalic acid, a poison, upon the human eye (Reynolds v. Davis, 55 R.I. 206, 179 A. 613 [1935]). The kinds of witnesses whose opinions courts have received, *even though they lacked medical training and would not be permitted by law to treat the conditions they describe*, are legion. The principle to be distilled from the cases is plain: if experience or training enables a proffered expert witness to form an opinion which would aid the jury, in the absence of some countervailing consideration, his testimony will be received.

Suggesting the diagnostic category into which an accused's condition fits, and relating it to his past behavior, require skill far in excess of that possessed by laymen. Lest the jury be misled into relying on opinions which are not based upon relevant learning and experience, we must examine the reality behind the title "psychologist." Many psychologists may not qualify to testify concerning mental disease or defect. Their training and experience may not provide an adequate basis for their testimony. Some psychologists, for example, teach and engage in theoretical research in fields unrelated to the diagnosis and treatment of mental disease. Others are employed in personnel administration; still others advise industry on problems of employee morale. (See Western Personnel Institute, *Opportunities for Psychologists, Psychiatrists, Psychiatric Social Workers* [1958], pp. 8–10; Daniel and Louttit, *Professional Problems in Psychology* [1953], pp. 250–52, 297.) Such experience does not ordinarily provide the skill essential to offer expert testimony concerning mental disorders (cf. Albee, *Mental Health Manpower Trends* [1959], p. 116). Some psychologists, moreover, have had no post-graduate instruction (*ibid.*, pp. 121–22).

On the other hand, the Ph.D. in Clinical Psychology involves some—and often much—training and experience in the diagnosis and treatment of mental disorders. Typically, candidates are trained in, among other things, general psychology, theory of personality and psychodynamics, psychopathology, diagnostic methods, therapeutic techniques, selected aspects of physiology and anatomy, and clinical methods. A one-year internship in a mental hospital is required for this degree. After graduation, many clinical psychologists administer and interpret diagnostic tests which elicit the patient's intellectual level, defenses, personality structure, attitudes, feelings, thought, and perceptual processes (see Rapaport, *Diagnostic Testing*, 1 [1945]: 7–9). In many institutions and clinics their reports, which regularly include opinions concerning the presence or absence of mental disease or defect, are important aids to psychiatrists who customarily have the final responsibility for diagnosis. Some psychologists, moreover, regularly administer psychotherapy and related non-organic therapies in the treatment of certain types of mental disorders.

The determination of a psychologist's competence to render an expert opinion based on his findings as to the presence or absence of mental disease or defect must depend upon the nature and extent of his knowledge. It does not depend upon his claim to the title "psychologist." And that determination, after hearing, must be left in each case to the traditional discretion of the trial court subject to appellate review. Although there are no statutory criteria for licensing psychologists in the District of Columbia to assist trial courts, the American Psychological Association's list of approved graduate training programs provides some guidance. When completion of such training is followed by actual experience in the treatment and diagnosis of disease in association with psychiatrists or neurologists, the opinion of the psychologist may properly be received in evidence.

Some graduate clinical psychologists, moreover, are certified by the American Board of Examiners in Professional Psychology. Certification, which indicates exceptional professional competence, is awarded upon completion of written and oral examinations in, among other things, diagnosis and treatment. Applicants must have four years acceptable professional experience and must present credentials, including a sample of their work and letters of recommendation, showing sufficient professional achievement to warrant further examination. The purpose of Board certification is to identify and evaluate psychologists at an advanced professional level. If the post-doctoral experience required for certification has included substantial experience in a hospital or clinical setting in association with psychiatrists or neurologists, clinical psychologists who are Diplomates of the American Board of Examiners in Professional Psychology should ordinarily qualify as expert witnesses.

We need not decide whether the three psychologists who testified for the defense at the trial under review were qualified to offer expert opinions since they may not be called to testify at the retrial. We hold only that the lack of a medical degree, and the lesser degree of responsibility for patient care which mental hospitals usually assign to psychologists, are not automatic disqualifications. Where relevant, these matters may be shown to affect the weight of their testimony, even though it be admitted in evidence. The critical factor in respect to admissibility is the actual experience of the witness and the probable probative value of his opinion. The trial judge should make a finding in respect to the individual qualifications of each challenged expert. Qualifications to express an opinion on a given topic are to be decided by the judge alone. The weight to be given any expert opinion admitted in evidence by the judge is exclusively for the jury. They should be so instructed.

[Editor's note: The *Jenkins* case holding allowing a qualified psychologist to testify as an expert as to a party's mental condition has been approved and followed in the Fourth Circuit in *U.S.* v. *Riggleman*, 411 F.2d 1190 (4th Cir. 1969), and in several states: *People* v. *Davis*, 402 P.2d 142 (Cal. 1965); *Rollins* v. *Commonwealth*, 151 S.E. 2d 622 (Va. 1966); and *Buckler* v. *Sinclair Refining Company*, 216 N.E.2d 14 (Ill. 1966). For further discussion see the annotation 78 A.L.R.2d 919, plus 78 A.L.R.2d 919 Supplemental Service.]

UNITED STATES v. KENT

Editor's Note

Chronology of the Kent Case

September 5, 1961—Morris A. Kent, Jr., aged 16, was arrested by the Metropolitan Police of the District of Columbia on charges of having committed 14 serious offenses, all of which would be felonies if committed by an adult. At the time of arrest he had been under probation in the Juvenile Court for two years.

September 12, 1961—The Juvenile Court signed a waiver of its jurisdiction, and Kent was held for trial under the regular procedures of the United States District Court.

September 13, 1961—(1) Habeas corpus petition filed in the District Court challenging the District Court's jurisdiction to try the case.

(2) Order of waiver appealed to the Municipal Court of Appeals. (The habeas corpus petition was dismissed and the Juvenile Court's order was affirmed. See *In re Kent*, 179 A2d 727 [1962] and *Kent* v. *Reid*, 316 F.2d 331 [1963].)

September 25, 1961—Indictments by the grand jury, 3 counts housebreaking, 3 of robbery, and 2 of rape.

October 6, 1961—Defendant's motion for mental examination at D.C. General Hospital instead of at St. Elizabeths Hospital filed alleging:

(1) "his retention in the company of adults charged with crime is likely to inflict serious mental harm upon the defendant and to jeopardize the adequacy of the Mental Examination in his case."

(2) D.C. General Hospital, Psychiatric Division, maintains separate quarters for children and for adolescents and specializes in their care.

October 13, 1961—Defendant committed to D.C. General Hospital for 60 days. Leave granted the Government to have defendant examined by psychiatrists of its choice.

December 22, 1961—Letter from D.C. General Hospital advising that defendant is incompetent to stand trial filed.

January 4, 1962—Objection of Government to report of D.C. General Hospital and Government's requires for a judicial determination of the competency of the defendant to stand trial filed.

January 8, 1962—Defendant committed to St. Elizabeths Hospital for mental examination for a period not to exceed 90 days.

April 6, 1962—Letter from W. Overholser, Superintendent, St. Elizabeths Hospital, advising that defendant is mentally competent to understand the nature of the proceedings against him.

April 10, 1962—Defendant's motion for a hearing to determine his competency to stand trial filed.

November 23, 1962—Objection of defendant to treatment of defendant by District Jail authorities and to interference with effective assistance of counsel by refusing access to defendant by psychiatrists selected for him by counsel and affidavit in support thereof filed.

February 6, 1963—Motion for hearing to determine competency of defendant denied.

March 5, 1963—Memorandum vacating the denial of a motion for a hearing to determine the mental competency of the defendant and directing that the motion be set down for a hearing in due course filed.

March 7, 1963—Motion of defendant to determine mental competency heard. Finding: Mentally competent to stand trial.

March 14, 1963—Trial begun.

March 27, 1963—Found guilty on three counts of housebreaking and 3 counts of robbery and not guilty by reason of insanity on 2 counts of rape.

March 28, 1963—Order committing defendant to St. Elizabeths Hospital subject to being produced in court for sentencing upon counts of housebreaking and robbery.

May 17, 1963—Sentenced to 5 to 15 years on each count of robbery and 5 to 15 years on each count of housebreaking—said sentences to run consecutively. The defendant is to be credited with all time served as a mental patient in an institution against the sentence imposed in this case.

Criminal No. 798–61 (March, 1963); U.S. D.C. (D.C.). Excerpts from the Trial Transcript: Direct and Cross-examination of Psychologists.

August 22, 1963—Appeal filed.

October 16, 1964—Judgment of the District Court affirmed. *Kent v. U.S.* (U.S. Court of Appeals, D.C. Circuit) 343 F.2d 247, 1964.

March 21, 1966—The Supreme Court reversed and remanded the case to the District Court for a full-dress de novo hearing to determine the validity of the juvenile court's waiver of jurisdiction. *Kent* v. *U.S.*, 383 U.S. 541 (1966).

District Court, on remand, sitting as a juvenile court, found the waiver appropriate and proper. (Opinion not reported).

July 30, 1968—The U.S. Court of Appeals, District of Columbia Circuit, reversed the findings of the District Court sitting as juvenile court and held the waiver invalid. As the waiver was invalid, the court found that the subsequent criminal proceedings were also invalid and must be vacated. The court directed the government to release Kent or apply for civil commitment to St. Elizabeths Hospital.

Kent v. *U.S.*, 401 F.2d 408 (D.C. Cir. 1968).

October 10, 1968—Kent was committed to St. Elizabeths Hospital at his own request. If Kent had not made this request it is doubtful that he could have been committed. The issue at this hearing was his mental state at the present time, not at the time of the offenses which had taken place several years earlier. In fact, since the St. Elizabeths psychiatrist who testified at the hearing said Kent had completely lost the psychotic tendencies which had made him dangerous to himself and others, involuntary commitment would have been unjustified. However, Kent did not oppose the commitment. In fact, he felt it would be in his best interests saying, "I feel if I were thrown out on the street now it would cause a lot of problems for me."

October 20, 1969—Morris Kent was released from St. Elizabeth's Hospital.

The following are excerpts from the testimony of psychologists presented as expert witnesses on behalf of the defendant. Four psychologists testified for the defense; none for the prosecution. The defense also utilized the testimony of five psychiatrists and a psychiatric social worker. Two psychiatrists testified for the government.

Excerpts from the Trial Transcript:
Direct and Cross-Examination of
Psychologists, March 1963

[The first psychologist to testify was Dr. Katherine Beardsley, a clinical psychologist and Director of Training of the Psychology Branch at St. Elizabeths Hospital. She testified that she saw the defendant Kent for four sessions in March 1962, at St. Elizabeths Hospital.]

Direct Examination

Q. At those sessions did you give him certain standard psychological tests?

A. Yes.

Q. What tests were these, Doctor?

A. I administered the Wechsler Memory Scale, the Bender-Gestalt, the Behn–Rorschach, the Thematic Apperception test, the House-Tree-Person test, and the Szondi.

Q. Doctor, what is the purpose for giving these psychological tests?

A. The purpose for giving these particular tests was a referral from the psychiatrist with a question of differential diagnosis and a question of organicity. This is in accordance with the practice at St. Elizabeths Hospital, where the psychology branch receives referrals from psychiatrists or other staff people with certain specific questions. This was a routine referral.

Q. Doctor, would you tell what in your professional opinion is your diagnostic impression of the mental condition of the defendant.

A. In my opinion, on the basis of my tests, the test results were consistent with a diagnosis of chronic undifferentiated schizophrenia.

Cross-Examination

Q. Now then, on this Szondi test that you administered, that test is comprised of a series of six sets of eight cards apiece. Isn't that right?

A. That is correct.

Q. And those eight cards in a series of six were exhibited by you to this defendant, Kent, here. Isn't that correct?

A. Yes.

Q. And the question that you asked this defendant, Kent, when you exhibited the first set of Szondi profiles, the first eight cards, was to pick out, was it, the person or the two persons you would most like to be with, or the one person? The two that you'd like the best and the two you don't like?

A. The two you dislike the most.

Q. Alright, now then, what is the purpose of this Szondi test?

A. To give a picture of a personality based upon a very complex theory put forth by Dr. Szondi himself.

Q. I am still trying to find out what is the purpose of it.

A. The purpose of it is to give a picture of a person's personality.

Q. Well now, when you administered the Szondi test to Kent here, the pictures of the individuals that you showed him and asked him to pick out the two from the set he would most like to be with, and the two that he would least like to be with, the pictures of those individuals were photographs taken of persons who lived either in the late part of the last century or the early part of this century, isn't that right?

A. Some may have been as late as the 1930's.

Q. That is a little early for me, Doctor. That is about the latest though, isn't it?

A. Yes.

Q. Now the photographs also, Doctor, include persons way back, I mean along around 1800 and even before that, do they not?

A. I have not reviewed this recently, so I don't know precisely.

Q. How many times have you administered that profile?

A. Many times.

Q. Well now, they are all persons who, with no disrespect to them, are not native-born Americans, isn't that right?

A. As far as I know.

Q. Furthermore, all the persons whose photographs appear in the six sets of eight cards apiece of profiles of Dr. Szondi were at the time those photographs then were taken, were actually insane persons, weren't they?

A. Not only that, they were extreme types.

Q. Yes, they were extreme psychotics, weren't they?

A. Not all psychotics, no.

Q. But extreme types of insanity, isn't that correct?

A. That is right. That is part of the theory.

Q. Yes, now then, and you are supposed to be able, according to the Szondi theory, from the responses of persons looking at six sets of eight cards of pictures of persons who at the time they were taken were insane, and from the two that he liked the most to be with and the two he wouldn't like to be with, you are supposed to be able to figure out his personality.

A. We were able to get some picture of his personality, yes.

Q. Well now, did this defendant answer on all the profiles? Did he pick out two, or by any chance, did he say he didn't like the looks of any of them?

A. He may have. I don't know. He may have said that. If so, I would have recorded it in my notes, but the important point is he responded to all.

Q. I take it you also administered the ink-blot test, did you not?

A. The Behn-Rorschach, yes.

[At this point, the results of this test were received in evidence as the government's exhibits. The witness was next questioned as to the House-Tree-Person test.]

Q. Now then, in administering the House-Tree-Person test, you first gave him this paper which at the time was blank and now contains a drawing and bears the notation "Government's exhibit 22A" on the reverse side of it. This paper was blank at the time you handed it to the defendant, wasn't it?

A. That is correct.

Q. And you requested him, at that time, to draw a house. Is that right?

A. Yes, I asked him to draw a house.

Q. And he drew what appears on this paper.

A. That is right.

Q. Now what, if anything, psychological-wise did you see from this drawing of the house that this defendant, Kent, made?

A. I had a feeling, particularly from the windows there and from the absence of a door on the front of the house, that he saw, psychologically, saw a home as a jail rather than as a warm dwelling-place.

Q. Well now, Doctor, didn't you realize from looking at this picture that this defendant wasn't trying to give you the view of the front of the house? He was trying to show you the side, because he has some steps coming down with a little portiere or something over it.

A. That is a very good observation, particularly when we find this with people who are not very accessible to the outside world. They would like to hide from accessibility.

Q. You mean that people, when they draw this house, don't put the door so that you can see it, but put it on the side, to hide from accessibility to the world?

A. Statistically this has been shown in the literature to be very often true.

Q. Well now, these bars that you see in the window, did he tell you, Kent, that these were bars?

A. No, this is my interpretation . . . as a clinician.

Q. Well then, you didn't know whether Kent, when he drew these lines in the windows, had in mind bars or had in mind the things that you pull up and down, the Venetian blinds?

A. No.

Q. And you didn't bother asking him, did you?

A. I didn't ask him.

Q. Alright. Now, if you had asked him and he, Kent, had said to you, Dr. Beardsley, that oh, no, he didn't intend for you as a clinician to view these cross lines on the windows as bars, but rather that he was trying to put Venetian blinds in his drawing, would that have made any difference diagnostically to you?

A. No.

Q. None? Now, what, if any, significance is there to the line that appears on this drawing, kind of a, I suppose, a line coming up from the right to the left across the house? Does that have any significance?

A. That is sometimes interpreted as indicating a feeling of need for security because one feels insecure.

Q. Well, couldn't it also be interpreted that he is trying to put the contour of the landscape, the lawn on which the house is sitting, at a little rise here?

A. That still could have the same psychological implication.

Q. The chimney with the smoke coming out of it, what is the matter with that?

A. You notice the chimney is particularly dark. You notice it is almost the darkest part of the drawing. Very often we find this in drawings, particularly of adolescents who are very disturbed about sexual feelings. The smoke coming out very often is found in drawings of people who have a great deal of inner daydreaming life and sometimes this indicates that.

Q. Well now, I want to find out, for His Honor and the jury, about this sex business and the chimney. What is that? Unless I misunderstood you, didn't you just get through with saying something about chimneys being dark and so forth?

A. Yes, very often, as I say, we have found this in the drawings of both adolescents and older people who are very disturbed about sexual feelings.

Q. Chimneys drawn dark?

A. Yes, dark would indicate anxiety.

Q. What pencil was this defendant using, one, two, three or four?

A. Ordinarily, we use number two.

Q. Well, what was he using?

A. I assume a number two. That is what I usually use.

Q. Well now, in drawing, doesn't the drawer try to sometimes accentuate certain parts of the drawing by making them lighter and other parts heavier in order to lend reality to his drawing?

A. The question is why does he choose those particular parts psychologically.

Q. Well now, what about this article over here to the left as you face it, Doctor? What did you clinically, as a clinician, interpret this to be?

A. It is a tree, I believe.

Q. Well now, what, if anything, does the fact that Kent put a tree on this landscape scene here have to do?

A. Again, this is sometimes interpreted as related to feelings of the number of siblings or number of children in the family. I, myself, do not always go along with this particular interpretation and in this case, I did not make an interpretation.

Q. You just let the tree go?

A. This one, yes. I used the tree which I asked him to draw.

Q. Now, this test that we are on now was devised and redevised by two psychologists, Buck and Goodenough, isn't that right?

A. Well, at different times.

Q. Yes, now in regard to these little, I shouldn't say little, it is fine writing here, Doctor. I take it, it is yours. It says, "Country suburban one-family, four." I take it, this is your writing, is it not, down at the bottom of this picture here?

A. That is right.

Q. Now then, when this defendant got through with drawing this house, you then asked him, did you not, what that house represented, how many people in it, ... etc.?

A. I said, "Where is it and who lives in it?"

Q. And he said it was in the country?

A. Yes.

Q. And he said it was a one-family dwelling, didn't he?

A. Yes.

Q. Did he say there were four people in it or four children in the house?

A. Four people.

Q. Now, assuming that this defendant, for purposes of this question, has no formal education in sketching a drawing in art, would you say that it would be unreasonable clinically to say that this was a rough drawing of a house in the country in the suburbs and that it was a one-family house?

A. Oh no, it is not unreasonable.

Q. Now then, after Kent got through drawing the one-family suburban house with the smoke in the chimney and a tree, you then gave him this piece of paper which at the time was blank and I am referring to government exhibit 22B . . . and you asked him to draw a tree?

A. That is correct. . . . We have found in the literature that a person very often expresses feelings about himself that are on a subconscious level when we ask him to draw a tree.

Q. Alright. Well now, did you just say draw a tree.

A. That is right.

Q. This tree here that the defendant drew, what clinically did you deduce from that about his personality?

A. When I asked him, as you see recorded in my handwriting, he said the tree was a sequoia and it was fifteen hundred years old and it was diseased. From this, I would say this reflected feelings of a very great deal of self-depreciation for a young boy of seventeen to feel fifteen hundred years old and to feel diseased. I felt it indicated a very strong feeling of depression and self-depreciation. You will notice, also, that it has no leaves and it leans in a left direction. Again, we have found in drawings of people who tend to withdraw a tendency toward drawing towards the left side of the paper. The absence of leaves is an absence of effective contact with the outside. Now all of these things are based on a great deal of theory and of practice.

Q. Doctor, did you request this defendant to draw a tree with leaves on it?

A. Oh no.

Q. Well, you can look outside the courthouse this morning and you won't find any leaves on any trees out there yet, will you?

A. That isn't the point.

Q. Well, isn't that true?

A. That is true.

Q. Isn't it true that this individual, when he drew this tree, may have had in his mind a season of the year in which there were no leaves on the tree? Now, is there anything else here that you found significant, clinical-wise, from this sequoia that is fifteen hundred years old according to Kent?

A. I think the only other thing which I notice in my notes here is something which I have said, but which I think bears repeating. I think a feeling of being stripped of emotions, that is stripped of leaves, was one of my interpretations.

Q. Now, in regard to this drawing, which is the third which I want to show you, government exhibit 22C, for identification, that is a drawing by Kent and that is your handwritten note at the bottom. Is that right?

A. That is right.

Q. At the time you handed this third paper to him, it was blank, . . . and you told this defendant to draw a person. Is that right?

A. That is correct.

Q. You didn't tell him to draw a person of one sex or the other. You just said, "Draw a person."

A. That is right.

Q. Alright, and he drew what appears on the paper which I am holding before you, His Honor and the jury of a what?

A. Of a man.

Q. You had no difficulty recognizing that this drawing was the drawing of a man.

A. That is right.

Q. Alright. What significance clinically did you

as a psychologist attach to this drawing . . . of a man?

A. You notice that he appears to be running and Mr. Kent also says that he is running. Notice again, he is running towards the left. There are two things here: a feeling of very strong anxiety and agitation, and of an attempt to run away from reality. . . .

Q. What if he was running to the right?

A. That would be interpreted as trying to run into the environment.

Q. What else did you derive from this drawing?

A. That was the only comment I made on the drawing.

Q. You mean you deduced as a clinical psychologist that this figure running toward the left of the page shows that the person who drew it tends to withdraw from reality.

A. Not in and of itself, but in connection with all the other tests.

Q. Well now, didn't you attach any significance to the sharp appearing fingers on the hands and the neck and the hair and the profile instead of a full-face view and so forth?

A. Oh yes, I did. I could have elaborated much more. The very sharp fingers, you notice they are going in both directions, are often interpreted as a person's need to express hostility towards the environment.

Q. The neck was fairly long, was it not, and had a very dark collar on it?

A. Yes, the neck is fairly long, the head is small, and this is very often found in people who have difficulty in controlling emotions. We speak of it as a sort of split between intellect, that is the head, and emotions, that is the body. The very dark hair, the very dark tie, the very dark shoes and the very dark buckle on the belt, again, Karen Machover . . . has done an intensive study of the drawings of adolescents and has found this to be related to feelings of anxiety about sexual problems which the adolescent often has.

Q. Dr. Beardsley, after the defendant got through making this drawing, you determined in your own mind that this was the drawing of a male, did you not?

A. Yes.

Q. And then you asked this defendant to tell you who this male was and what he was doing and his age. Isn't that correct?

A. I said, "What is the name of this person?"

Q. Alright, and he told you that his name was George and that he was twenty-five years old and that he was running and that he was an attendant. Isn't that correct?

A. That is right.

Q. And did you question him as to whether or not, when he said an attendant that was running, it might have been a gas station attendant running to service someone's car?

A. No.

Q. Now Doctor, does this drawing appear to you . . . , assuming for the purposes of my question, a person who does not have formal training in art, that it reasonably depicts a person, a male, around twenty-five, running, who is an attendant?

A. Except for the very small head, yes.

Q. Well now, you say except for the very small head. You mean the head is out of proportion to the rest of the drawing?

A. Yes.

Q. I ask you to assume for purposes of my question that the person who drew this was not skilled in drawing. Did you take that into consideration when you asked the person to draw it?

A. Yes.

Q. Did you ask this defendant whether he, Kent, had had any formal education in drawing?

A. No.

Q. And you say then that other than for the small head, to you this does reasonably represent a male, twenty-five years old, running.

A. Yes.

[The witness then testified that she had asked the defendant, Kent, to draw a person of the opposite sex.]

Q. Alright, now, when Kent got through drawing this drawing here on government's exhibit 22D, did you have any difficulty in arriving at a conclusion yourself that this was a drawing of a female?

A. No.

Q. Now what, if any, conclusion did you arrive at, as a psychologist, from this drawing of a female about the personality of this defendant, Kent?

A. Note the absence of hands. Note the extremely dark piercing eyes. Again, based on experience, we have found that often people who feel they have been strongly rejected by parents, in this case by women or by mother, do not draw the hands. The dark piercing eyes suggest a tremendous amount of feeling of being looked at and viewed by women with hostility. A very strong feeling of hostility is shown. Notice how dark they are.

Q. Well, Doctor, with no offense intended to the ladies around the courthouse, don't some ladies use, I think they call it mascara . . . do you know whether or not when this defendant, Kent, was drawing these dark piercing eyes here that he may have

had in mind some young lady who used mascara to enhance her beauty?

A. The question is why did he use that particular one psychologically.

Q. Well now, when this defendant got through with drawing this drawing here, incidentally, I notice that the feet, what appeared to be the feet down here, are also dark. Is there anything clinically significant to that?

A. Again this might be interpreted as feelings of anxiety about women.

Q. What about black shoes?

A. Yes, again.

Q. Don't many ladies walk around wearing black shoes?

A. Yes. The critical point is why in connection with all the other things he did in the test, did he choose to make them black shoes. That is the important thing.

Q. Well now, you asked this defendant after he got through with drawing this figure here, the lady's name, age, and what she was doing; isn't that right?

A. That is correct.

Q. And he told you the lady's name was Doris and she was any age, about twenty-five, and that she was walking; isn't that right?

A. That is correct.

Q. Well now, assuming for purposes of my question again that the person who drew this drawing here had no formal art education, doesn't this, to you as a clinician, reasonably represent a person by the name of Doris about twenty-five years of age walking?

A. Not without the hands.

Redirect Examination

Q. Now Doctor, when you consider giving psychological tests and results and you reach a diagnostic impression, what is more important to you, the total view of tests or something else?

A. I am not sure what you mean by "something else."

Q. When you reach your diagnostic impression as you have testified in direct examination, did you only take one test in view or did you take them all?

A. No, I took all the tests.

Q. Certain tests only go to certain various areas of personality, is that correct?

A. They accentuate certain areas of personality.

[The next psychologist to testify was Dr. John Lawrence Endacott, the Assistant Chief Clinical Psychologist in the Mental Hygiene Clinic at the Veterans' Administration. He testified that he had been a practicing psychologist for roughly twenty-five years and that he had seen the defendant Kent on four different occasions: three times in D.C. General Hospital and once at St. Elizabeths Hospital.]

Direct Examination

Q. Doctor, did you give a standard battery of psychological tests?

A. Yes. I gave him the Wechsler-Bellevue Adult Intelligence Scale, the Graham-Kendall test for organic brain damage, the Rorschach test, and the Symonds Picture Story test.

Q. Now Doctor, based upon these tests and your experience, do you have a diagnostic impression as to the mental condition of Morris Kent from June of 1961 to the end of September, 1961?

A. Yes, I do.

Q. Would you tell us what your diagnostic impression is?

A. The results of this battery of tests would indicate first of all that he has average intellectual ability. The Rorschach test clearly indicated that he was suffering from schizophrenia, undifferentiated type. The Graham-Kendall test results were in what we call the doubtful range which would suggest that there is about a fifty-fifty chance that the causing basis for this disturbance might have been some sort of organic basis. The patient does have a history of several blows on the head, I might say.

Cross-Examination

Q. Dr. Endacott, I think one of the tests that you said you administered to defendant, sir, was the W.A.I.S., the Wechsler Adult Intelligence Scale.

A. That's right.

Q. What was his overall intelligence quotient?

A. Ninety-six.

Q. Now that put this defendant in what range from your viewpoint as a psychologist?

A. The range of average intellectual ability.

Q. In other words, no mental deficiency.

A. That's right.

Q. Well now, did you administer the Szondi profiles?

A. No.

Q. Don't you usually in your capacity as a psychologist administer the Szondi profile?

A. No I don't. I don't use the Szondi test very often.

Q. Why not?

A. Oh, I don't happen to think very much of it.

Q. I want you, Doctor, to capsule if you will, but with full impression, too, why, in your capacity as a psychologist of twenty, twenty-five years experience, you do not hold in your esteem the Szondi test and do not administer it.

A. Well, the Szondi test is a series of pictures of people who were mental patients in European mental hospitals . . . and the subject sorts these particular pictures in terms of ones that he likes and ones that he dislikes; and it is based on the premise that these particular individuals represent different mental disease categories and because people like or dislike a picture of a schizophrenic or the picture of an epileptic that this means something in terms of their own particular disturbance. That is, it works on the assumption that an epileptic looks a certain way or a schizophrenic looks a certain way, and we have a good deal of evidence in American psychology to support the notion that this just isn't so.

Q. Alright, in other words, as I understand you, Doctor, in your professional opinion as a psychologist, the Szondi test profiles are not worth too much.

A. I don't happen to think so. Others do.

Q. Now, Doctor, did you administer the House-Tree-Person test?

A. No.

Q. You know of the test?

A. Yes, I know of the test.

Q. And you didn't administer that because you personally don't think much of that either?

A. No, the House-Tree-Person test is a perfectly good test. It's just that I happen to feel that the particular tests that I gave him were more valid and more reliable. I think that you get more from them. I think they are more useful, in other words. Other people that are more skilled with the House-Tree-Person or some other perspective [*sic*] tests that we could mention prefer them.

Q. Now in this Symonds Picture Story test, what is the purpose of that?

A. Well, that is a personality test from which one can get, you might say, corroborative diagnostic information about the individual depending on what kind of results that you get.

[When questioned about the Graham-Kendall test, the witness testified that this was a test of the possibility of organic brain damage. He further testified that he was aware of the fact that an extensive physical examination had shown no evidence of organic disease of the nervous system. "I'm also aware, however, that one could have those findings and still have organic brain damage."]

Q. Dr. Endacott, looking at government's exhibits 23A through J inclusive, those are, if you will look at them please, a standard set of the Rorschach ink blots, is that right?

A. That is right, sir.

Q. Now, this test is the one that you said yesterday was the test that clearly showed to you as a psychologist that this defendant was suffering from undifferentiated schizophrenia, is that right?

A. That is right, sir.

Q. Alright, now in administering this test, did you sit in front of, to the side of, or behind Kent when he took this test?

A. Let's see, I am trying to think. I think I sat in front of him, sir. I don't quite remember the physical arrangements.

Q. Is it not usual in administering this test for the psychologist to sit to the rear so that he can see what, if anything, the person taking the test points out on these different cards?

A. No, some people do this. It is not absolutely essential.

Q. Alright, . . . there are ten cards here, are there not?

A. That is right.

Q. Before you showed Kent the first card in point of sequence, did you tell him what you were going to do?

A. I told him I was going to show him some ink blots and I wanted him to tell me what they looked like to him.

Q. In regard to card number one, which I now hold before you, what did Kent say he saw in this one?

A. Well, first of all, he said that the whole thing looked like a canine or a wolf. He meant the head of a wolf. This is a fairly common response.

Q. What else did he say?

A. Those things on the side sections, he said they looked like two angels and then those two little claw things, he said those looked like a sort of a crab. He explained later that he meant the claws of a crab. Lastly, those two little middle bumps at the top there looked like two breasts of a woman.

Q. Now, what did those responses to card number one of the Rorschach test indicate to you as a psychologist?

A. Well, by itself, they don't indicate anything in particular.

Q. Now, in regard to card number two, what did Kent say that he saw in this one?

A. First of all, he thought the whole thing was like a butterfly.

Q. Isn't that the common response?

A. No, that is a very poor response. Then those two red things at the top there he thought looked like two kinds of birds. Then, he said down in lower middle red section there, he said a vagina. Then he said all the red on the blot looked like blood. Then, just the dark areas there, he said looked like a pelvis.

Q. In regard to card number three, what did Kent say this looked like to him?

A. First of all, the middle red area looked like a butterfly, then the two side red areas looked like two stomachs and the dark area looked like two women and then to the same area, he said it looked like, his word was "hermaphrogas," he meant a hermaphrodite, but he used the wrong word. Then the lower middle black area there looked like a tub of water and that was all on that one.

Q. In regard to card number four, what did Kent say this looked like?

A. He said the whole thing looked like some kind of a monster. He said the whole thing looked like a bat and then the top middle area, clear up at the top, he said that looked like a vagina.

Q. Card number five?

A. He gave two responses on that one. First of all, he said a bat, and secondly, he said the whole area looked like a butterfly.

Q. Card number six?

A. First of all, he said the whole thing looked like a floor mat made out of an animal skin. Secondly, it turned out because of the whiskers on the top there that the whole thing looked like a cat or feline. Then down there through the middle, he said looked like a highway and then there are some tiny little white things in there, in the middle, he said those looked like two cars on a highway. Then all down through the middle there, he said that looked like a vaginal tract.

Q. Card number seven?

A. To the whole thing, he said two Indian girls having sexual relations. Then he gave one more response. In the lower middle black area, there is a real tiny black area, he said this was blood dripping.

Q. Card number eight?

A. To the side pink areas there, he said two pink lizards and then in the middle of the blue area, he said a backbone and then he said the whole thing looked like different kinds of flowers. Then he said the whole thing looked like maybe a butterfly also.

Q. Number nine card? What responses?

A. First of all, he said it looked like a butterfly, the whole thing. Then he said the whole thing looked like flowers. Then he said all through the center area there, that looked like a vaginal tract and then he said that the whole thing looked like a woman because the middle part of the lower pink area looked like the buttocks of a woman.

Q. The tenth and last card, which I now hold before you?

A. The side blue areas there were spiders. Then

that top gray area there, two animals holding up and supporting a monument. Then the whole thing, all kinds of flowers and last of all, that top gray area again, it could be a penis going into a vagina and that was all on that one.

Q. Now, from those responses that you have testified to now on the ten cards you've reached a clinical diagnostic impression that this defendant was suffering from undifferentiated schizophrenia.

A. That is right, sir.

[The witness was next questioned as to the Wechsler Adult Intelligence Scale test which he administered to the defendant.]

Q. In the part of this test which is called information, there are twenty-nine words, one through twenty-nine and isn't it true that those words progress not only arithmetically but in order of difficulty as they get to higher numbers?

A. That is right, sir.

Q. Alright, now in regard to the sixteenth word, the word "Vatican," what did you ask this defendant in regard to the "Vatican"?

A. The standard question is, "What is the Vatican?"

Q. And he said, "The Pope's home." You recall that? Do you recall how you scored him on that?

A. Yes, that is an acceptable answer.

Q. That would be a one answer, is that right?

A. Yes.

Q. Now in regard to the next word "Paris," which is the seventeenth word in the list, what did you ask him? How far is it from New York to Paris?

A. That is right, sir.

Q. And you scored him zero and according to your writing here, Doctor, this defendant said 1,200 miles. What is the right answer on that?

A. Around 3,000 miles. We have standard norms by which we score this. I believe the acceptable answer is between 2,500 and 3,500. It has to be in that area. Obviously his was wrong.

[The witness was then questioned as to the various words which he asked as part of this test and why the defendant's answers were unsatisfactory.]

Q. Did you know at the time you administered this test what grade of education this defendant had completed?

A. Yeah, I think I have it marked on the front there. I asked him.

Q. Ninth grade?

A. Yes.

Q. Now, the next two words, the twenty-fifth phrase here, the two words "blood vessels." What did you ask him, Doctor?

A. The question is "What are blood vessels?"

Q. Well, he has got down there, in your handwriting, sir, "CAP" and then a comma and then "veins," are those blood vessels? Capillaries and veins, I assume that is what he said.

A. They are not blood vessels. The blood is carried by capillaries, veins, and arteries. I don't know, I don't quite understand what I have there. I am sorry, sir.

Q. According to your writing, doesn't that say that he told you, this defendant, when you asked him "What are blood vessels?" that he told you capillaries and veins? Why did you mark him zero on that answer?

A. Because the norms don't accept that as an acceptable answer.

Q. What norms?

A. The norms in the book.

[At this point the defense counsel objected saying that the government counsel was trying to put the test on trial. The court, however, overruled his objection, finding his cross-examination proper since it was on the basis of the tests that the witness reached his diagnostic impression. The Court asked, "To what book are you referring, Doctor?"]

A. Dr. Wechsler has written a book entitled *The Measurement of Adult Intelligence.* That is the handbook that goes along with this particular test on which the norms and so forth are all based.

[The witness was then questioned on the B section of the test entitled "Comprehension." The answers to these questions may be scored two, one, or zero.]

Q. Alright, now the third word on this Comprehension Section of the test is the word "envelope." Is it not true that you asked this defendant, Kent, "What would you do with an envelope if you found it lying on the sidewalk?"

A. No, the question is "What should you do if you found in the middle of the street an envelope that was sealed, addressed, and had a stamp on it?"

Q. Alright, and he said according to your handwriting, "Turn it in." Do you recall how you scored him?

A. I think I might have scored him one, I might.

Q. You scored him one, Doctor. Why didn't you score him two?

A. Well, first of all, partly because of the

norms. You see there is some area for the tester to make some discretion in judgment. An acceptable answer for that is, "mail it or take it to the Post Office." An answer like "I would turn it in" is too vague. It has some merit so it gets the score of one, but it isn't specific enough to get a score of two.

[The witness was questioned as to most of the words in this comprehension series and questioned as to the scoring norms. In response to each question, he testified that he went through every answer in considerable detail in terms of the norms and then made a judgment about the answer which the defendant had given him. According to the norms, most of the defendant's answers had some merit, but "just isn't an answer that is specific enough in terms of the norms that are given in the book." The third section of the test about which the witness was questioned was the Vocabulary Section. Again this section is scored 2, 1, and 0. The words progress in difficulty as they go from 1 to 40.]

Q. Alright, the fourth word is the word "winter" and he said, "It's a season of the year," and you scored him 1. Why?
A. Well, we are back to the same old thing again. It's a matter of the norms. Season is a general answer. To get a 2, he has to be able to say, "It is the cold season of the year."
Q. The eighth word, Doctor, is the word "slice" and he said "to cut," and you gave him a 1. Doesn't the word "slice" mean to cut?
A. Yes, that it does. I don't precisely remember what the norms say for a two answer here, but I think it includes some notion that you cut off something into thin pieces.

[The attorney continued to question the witness as to each of the words in the section. In answering these questions, the witness again referred to the necessity of looking at Kent's answers in comparison with the norms. "You remember all of these have been pretested and these norms have been set up in a very standard sort of way using hundreds, maybe even thousands, of people, and there is very little latitude for judgment here, some but not much." The witness was next questioned as to the Graham-Kendall Memory for Designs test in which there are fifteen cards.]

Q. Now, Doctor, how many times do you show the series of fifteen cards to the defendant.
A. You show them once.
Q. At the time you showed them, had you provided this defendant with the paper which is now government's exhibit 25 for identification and which at the time you gave it to him contained no forms on it, no drawings?

A. That is right. I told him, "I am going to show you a series of designs, one at a time, for five seconds, and after I show you the design I will take it away and I want you to draw for me what you have just seen." That, centrally, was the substance of the instructions and what the defendant did.

[The witness testified that the defendant would look at the card for the period of time specified and then be asked to draw the design which he had seen. In response to the question how these drawings are scored, he testified that if there is no distortion, the figure is scored 0, and then if there is some distortion, the scores run 1, 2, and 3. The greatest distortion is 3 and defendant had two drawings which according to the standard norms received a score of 2.]

Q. Now then, out of all the cards shown to him on the Graham-Kendall test, he missed on two cards.
A. That is right.
Q. And from that, you say there is a fifty-fifty chance of organic brain damage. Is that right?
A. That is right. This test is very sensitive.

Redirect Examination

Q. Dr. Endacott, with reference to the Rorschach cards, can you tell us whether each individual card is as significant as the total picture from the test?
A. Neither each individual card nor each individual response is important, it has some importance, but you have to consider the test in its entirety.
Q. Why?
A. Well, you have to consider all the responses. Actually, this particular test has a regular complex way of scoring responses and one has to consider how this particular instrument is scored and evaluated from that.
Q. Does the skill of the examiner play any part in the interpretation of the Rorschach test?
A. The skill of the examiner is very important. People have to have years of experience to be skilled for this.

[The third psychologist to testify for the defense was Dr. Malcolm Meltzer, who testified that he was a clinical psychologist with the Psychological Department of the Veterans Hospital in Durham, North Carolina, and also associated with Duke University. He testified that while on the staff of D.C. General Hospital he administered the following tests to the defendant: the Wechsler Adult Intelligence Scale, the Rorschach, the Human Figure Drawing Test, the Porteus Maze Test, the Kohn, and the Thematic Apperception Test. He further testified that on the basis of these tests his opinion was that the defendant was mentally ill—a chronic undifferentiated schizophrenic.]

Direct Examination

Q. But for the existence of this mental disease which you saw from the tests, what is your opinion as to whether the defendant would have committed these acts?

A. I saw a struggle to control his impulses, to see things realistically, being a struggle he wasn't really able to win. From this I would say if he were better in a sense, then he might not have seen some of these things [in the tests]. I felt very definitely the struggle, the feeling to try to control these impulses.

Cross-Examination

A. This is a test [Thematic Apperception Test] that is comprised of 30 or 20 or 10, depending on how many you want to give, pictures of people and scenes and the test that the person is asked to do is to tell a story as to each picture. It is not primarily a test to diagnose mental disorder. Instead it is a test designed to give some idea of what the person's problems, feelings, and attitudes are. It is not used primarily for diagnosis—it is used rather for the describing of a personality. For example, the first picture is a little boy sitting in front of a violin and the task the person has is to make up a story to this, saying what happened, what is happening, what might have led up to this, what the characters were feeling and thinking and how it might turn out. There are a series of pictures like this. I think I gave about 10.

Q. These pictures, are they photographs, sketches, or what?

A. Both, some of them are photographs and some are taken from magazines and some art work—a variety.

[The witness was next asked to identify the Porteus Maze test. He testified that there were seven cards which run from the age level of seven years to adult level. You administer as many as are indicated. When a person fails two age levels, then you stop. You continue through adult.]

Q. Now what is this supposed to show, the Porteus Maze?

A. This is a known verbal test of intelligence. It has been used as such. It also has been used to discriminate between delinquents and non-delinquents. It is very effective. There is a great deal of research showing that delinquents show certain qualities of response on this test. I was interested in

whether this boy would conform to the usual delinquent pattern. He did not.

Q. When you say he did not conform to the usual delinquent pattern, when you use that phrase "usual delinquent pattern," what do you mean by that?

A. There is a particular kind of behavior on this test that has been well [documented] that one finds in juvenile delinquents, that is they may solve the items correctly, but in doing so they disregard the instructions. It is a particular style that reflects the disorientation, disregard of the rules completely.

Q. Well, isn't it a fact, Doctor, that you handed this defendant one card at a time in this Porteus Maze?

A. That's correct. The test, you see, is to go from the beginning to the end.

Q. In other words, you put your pen down where the arrow goes in and then you go all the way through without bumping any lines and come out where the arrow goes up.

A. Right, without bumping any blind alleys.

Q. So you get out of the maze.

A. That's right.

[The witness was next questioned as to the Human Figure Drawing Test. He testified that he had handed the defendant a blank piece of paper and asked him to draw a whole person. After he had drawn this person, he was asked to draw a picture of a person of the opposite sex.]

Q. You asked him to draw a house and a tree?

A. No, I did not.

Q. Does this test differ from the House-Tree-Person?

A. It is very often interpreted—the person is the house-tree-person—yes.

[When shown a third drawing which the witness had asked defendant to make, he answered:]

A. In this picture we have a very rare occurrence. A person is asked to draw a human figure and he usually draws a profile or a front view [in this case, the defendant had drawn a rear view]. Statistically it is very uncommon to have someone draw a rear view of a person. I cannot quote you the exact statistics. I have seen a couple thousand patients and this is the second time I have gotten this. The usual interpretation is something like this: the person is hiding guilt feelings; there are guilt feelings and he is turning away from reality; this might be a paranoid indication. It is so unusual to get this.

Q. Do you mean from the fact that this is supposed to be a drawing from the rear of a male?

A. That is correct.

[When questioned about the picture of a woman which Kent had drawn, he testified that the drawing presented him with the idea that the defendant saw women as hostile, unapproachable, and denying.]

Q. Well now, Doctor, what in this drawing leads you to your hunch that women to this defendant were hostile and so on?

A. The pose, the facial expression, it suggested to me rather hostile rejecting women.

Q. What in the pose suggested to you a hostile woman?

A. Just the way she is standing there with her hands on her hips, the look on the face, they all suggested to me that there might be something in here that I should look into.

Q. What in the look on the face of this picture gave you that hunch?

A. The way the facial features are arranged, the closed mouth, it seemed to be a hard-looking face from the drawing. I think it is the features all taken in conjunction with one another, sir, that suggests this facial expression. I might just say I use this test to get hunches and not to make definite statements. I wanted to have him draw a forward figure. The most important thing I got out of this [forward figure] was the size of the ears. There is research in the literature that suggests that as the ears become more prominent on a drawing so that they are completely out of proportion, the possibility of a paranoid kind of outlook is possible, even perhaps in the sense of hallucinations. This was the most important thing that came out of this drawing, so once again I was alerted to the possibility about these things and I wanted to investigate them further.

[The witness further testified as to the lack of feet in the drawing, "some might interpret that as lack of security and insecurity feeling. Also interesting was that he attempted to comply with instructions in this, and he attempted to do what was asked of him. He indicated a kind of approach. This is important, also." The witness was then asked questions concerning the reasons why he gave the Rorschach test and the Wechsler Adult Intelligence test.]

Q. Now which of these batteries of tests did you use, if any, or did you use them all together to arrive at this diagnostic impression of schizophrenia reaction?

A. I used them all to some extent. I relied most heavily on the Wechsler and the Rorschach for the diagnosis of schizophrenia.

Q. Is it customary to give the Wechsler Adult Intelligence test to a person and give him the same test within oh, say, four months later?

A. Yes sir, one must take into account that it has been given before.

Q. Now what in the Wechsler Adult Intelligence Scale test indicated to you that this defendant was suffering from a schizophrenia reaction [sic]?

A. The first thing that was important to me was that he did better on the verbal test than on the performance test. Now then, there are some tests where there are verbal questions asked and there are others where there is manipulation material. The first thing that struck me about this was this boy is probably some poor psychotic delinquent, since the pattern—once again a psychotic delinquent will do much better on the performance report than on the verbal report. He had the exact opposite pattern. He does better at verbal patterns. Some of his reasoning through the hearing tended to be a little unreasonable. For example, when you asked him how many days in the year, he said 365 days in the year. Then he was asked how many weeks are in a year. He said, "Let's see, there are 365 days in a year and 20 times into 365. I don't know. I never took any interest. There are 10 billion people in the United States." This is a little unusual. All of these things are minor sorts of things, but they do add up. On the question, "What should you do if you found an envelope in the street that is sealed and addressed and has a new stamp?" 93 percent of the population of this country will respond, "Put it in the mail box" or "Take it to the Post Office." His response is, "I would open it up and find out who it belongs to, I guess. I will show you I know right from wrong," so that he gave a very inaccurate answer. Some of the other important aspects of this is [sic] the spottiness of his performance, where he does very poorly at times on some easy items and then when you get the much more difficult ones later. There is a striking amount of this in subtests, and this is something that one expects to find in cases of emotional disturbances. It reaches a point where a person where on a block design, this is one of the more difficult of these subtests, where a person is to arrange some blocks to conform to a pattern. He couldn't go on with the second one which I demonstrated at first. He had two trials at this but he never did get it. He was never able to get them in order or to get the ninth one. This is something roughly 98 per cent of the people can do. There were some comments that suggested . . . overevaluation of his ability. For example, he said, "Oh, I will be able to do all of those," then he would run into difficulty. At other times, when he ran into difficulty, he would suddenly accuse me of tricking him in some fashion and then he would say, "Well, all of these blocks aren't exactly alike," and all of them are alike. When faced with some kind of stress or failure or not doing what he thought he could do, he would very often distort the situation. He blames it on the other person, on the materials. There is another element that I want to mention here and that is the low score on what we call the comprehension subtest. This is lower than any of his other scores. What this is, in a sense, is a measurement of common sense, practical judgment. His score on this is below his score on some of the other tests; this suggests there is difficulty in showing good judgment. So these are sufficient things, that once again by themselves don't prove anything, but the overwhelming set of all these things put together and combined with the other tests leads me to feel very strongly he is schizophrenic.

[The final psychologist to testify was Dr. Bernard Levy, the Director of Psychological Services for the D.C. General Hospital. Dr. Levy testified that he had seen the defendant once and had administered the Rorschach test and attempted to administer the Human Figure Drawing test but was unsuccessful because defendant's father was announced by a member of the staff at the Receiving Home and defendant became disturbed and agitated.]

Direct Examination

Q. Now Doctor, when you have the Rorschach test you show certain cards, is that correct?
A. Yes.
Q. What role does the psychologist . . . play in this testing procedure?
A. The cards provide a very standard set of materials which the patient uses to describe images he constructs out of the ink blots. It is the psychologist's job to prepare this information as a set of symbols and to evaluate the symbols as well as the material that the patients say and then to arrive at an interpretation of these materials in accordance with the principles of psychopathological diagnosis.

Cross-Examination

Q. Do you usually arrive at a diagnosis on the administration two times of the Rorschach tests, consuming about an hour, without administering other psychological tests?
A. Frequently.
Q. And does the examiner's skill have any part in reaching this diagnosis?
A. The examiner's skill is primary.

[In response to one of the ink blots the defendant had informed Dr. Levy that it looked like a "jet airplane."]

Q. Now a jet airplane at the time that this test was devised by Dr. Rorschach wasn't in existence, was it?
A. I don't think so, no.
Q. Well have the—for the lack of a better term, Doctor, the answer books, the psychological explanation books that you studied to evaluate answers given to these Rorschach cards, have they been revised through the years as science and our mode of living have progressed to take into consideration jet airplanes and so forth? . . .
A. The answer books are only guides for students primarily. In the minds of the people who use the test, yes, one takes into consideration the developments. . . .

Redirect Examination

Q. You testified as to certain tests which you are familiar with and which you give and certain tests that other psychologists give with which you were not familiar. Do certain psychologists choose certain tests as a matter of preference over others?
A. Yes.
Q. Does that indicate anything about the validity of the individual psychologist's choice of test materials?
A. It indicates nothing about them; it is a matter of personal preference.

ON PSYCHOLOGICAL TESTIMONY

Richard C. Allen, J.D.

Another issue on appeal [in the *Brawner** case], closely related to that of the insanity defense, was the propriety of the prosecutor's efforts to discredit the testimony of a St. Elizabeths psychologist who had testified concerning the results of projective tests he had administered to the defendant, in part by doing a little testifying himself in cross-examination in his closing argument. For example, he told the jury in summation:

Ladies and gentlemen, then we come to that ink blot. . . . Fourteen responses and four of them turn out to be anatomical things—hearts or whatever it happened to be. Is there something unusual about that? Is a man crazy when he sees a heart or something else four times . . . ? After all, they are just blots of ink. Is a man crazy when he sees them? And how about that last one, that rocket one. He says he sees a rocket going off. I asked him, doctor, was there any rocket fired during that period of time that might stick in a man's brain and might suggest it to him. The doctor doesn't know. But there is something explosive about a personality if he sees a rocket on a little ink blot.
Well, ladies and gentlemen, there is not much I can say about that; I am not an expert. . . . But I can say one thing; that it is a jury decision. It is your province. It is your function to take that evidence and weigh that evidence and decide whether what that doctor said as far as you are concerned made any sense at all.[1]

The American Psychological Association [*amicus curiae*], as might have been expected, was most vehement in its denunciation of the prosecutor's tactics; William H. Dempsey, Jr., in his amicus brief, also criticized the prosecution:

In the case at bar . . . the gravest damage to the defense was worked through the prosecutor's cross-examination of the clinical psychologist and his closing argument. The thrust of the questions and

argument was that either the psychological tests were unreliable or that the expert did not know how to administer them, or both. But there is nothing in the record to support either point. Indeed, the government evidently employs such tests itself when the results are favorable.[2]

Among the other amici, only the American Psychiatric Association commented at length about the question of the psychologist's treatment at the hands of the prosecutor, but its remarks suggest that it was more interested in attacking the psychologist than in reproving the prosecutor:

[P]sychologists are not trained in medicine, are not doctors of medicine, and on the basis of psychological testing alone should not be permitted to testify as to a specific diagnosis of a mental disease or defect and to relate the alleged criminal act to that disease or defect. The final diagnosis and the relation of the disease to productive acts is a complicated scientific medical and psychiatric problem. Laymen should not be permitted to testify as the final expert in diagnosing medical mental illnesses or defects, and certainly are not qualified to relate specific acts on a productivity basis to these medical problems.[3]

While some of the phrases in the paragraph quoted above are far from clear,[4] the Association's ultimate objective is quite clear: reversal of Judge Bazelon's decision in *Jenkins*

---

* For text of the Brawner opinion, see Chapter 17.

[1] Record at 36, *United States* v. *Brawner*, 471 F.2d 969 (D.C. Cir. 1972).

[2] Brief of William H. Dempsey, Jr., as *Amicus Curiae* at 8.

[3] Brief for American Psychiatric Association as *Amicus Curiae* at 20.

[4] E.g., what does "final expert" mean—would the American Psychiatric Association require that psychological evidence be admitted only as ancillary to psychiatric testimony, or would it bar psychological testimony as to diagnosis and "productivity" altogether? Also, what are "medical mental illnesses or defects," since both psychiatrists and psychologists—and, indeed, other mental health professionals and para-professionals—purport to treat functional mental illness?

Excerpted and reprinted with permission from "The Brawner Rule: New Lyrics for an Old Tune," *Washington University Law Quarterly* (Winter 1973): 73.

v. *United States*,[5] in which it was held that, assuming proper qualifications,[6] a psychologist may state his clinical findings and opinions. In that case, too, the American Psychiatric Association had filed a brief *amicus curiae*, to very much the same effect as the quotation above, if in somewhat less sophisticated terms; viz., "Psychology basically deals with philosophy. Psychologists study philosophy, not medicine . . . and have Ph.D. degrees, i.e., Doctors of Philosophy."[7]

Observing that "there was neither testimony adduced on cross-examination, nor testimony of a prosecutor's witness, to support a disparagement of the very concept of projective tests, as based on mere ink blots," the Court of Appeals in *Brawner* criticized the prosecutor's questioning and summation as a "know-nothing appeal to ignorance," adding the veiled threat that it is "an approach we do not expect to recur." However, it did not find it so persistent and aggravated as to result in reversible error (perhaps because of the judge's "clarifying questions," or the fact that defense counsel failed to object).[8] Interestingly, just two months prior to the decision in *Brawner*, the court had to deal with a somewhat similar *judicial* disparagement of psychological testing. In *United States* v. *Alexander & Murdock*,[9] the trial judge took over the questioning of the clinical psychologist testifying for the defense:

WITNESS: On the Minnesota Multiphasic Personality Inventory, it is a series of 500 or so true and false statements which have been standardized against people with known mental symptoms and complaints. There are various patterns, profiles we call them, based on the way an individual responds. Mr. Murdock's pattern of responses is very similar to standardized groups of people who are known to have—known to be sullen, known to be alienated, known to be a kind of loner, not being identified with any of the establishment's kinds of views.

THE COURT: That is an opinion.

WITNESS: No, I am telling you a fact.

THE COURT: I beg your pardon, Doctor. That is an opinion. Give them the facts on which you reached that opinion. What answers did he give you that led you to that opinion? Give us some examples of sullen answers to questions. . . .

WITNESS: I don't have the raw—the actual MMPI which I want to talk about. I have the summary sheet. I don't have the actual 568 questions. I have his responses, but I don't know what the actual questions were. . . . I do have the results of other tests which I perhaps. . . .

THE COURT: Mr. Witness, you are entitled to those opinions, but you are not the judge. The jury is the judge of the facts and, therefore, you are required to explain to the jury in factual terms . . . what the underlying material is from which you reach your opinion, because the jury is not required to accept the opinion of any expert and they have to weigh the testimony of experts and to do that they need to know what it is that the expert relied on to reach his conclusion.[10]

Concluding that the witness's answers were unsatisfactory, the court ruled that his testimony was entitled to no weight, and instructed the jury to disregard it, and Murdock's counsel moved for a mistrial. The Court of Appeals did not rule squarely on the propriety of the judge's questioning or on his instruction to the jury to disregard the psychologist's testimony, but affirmed the conviction and described the situation as a "failure of communication ending in evident mutual exasperation."[11] Judge Bazelon in his dissent observed:

It would have been perfectly appropriate to question Dr. Blum further about the precision of his tests, the margin of error in their results, and the significance of his findings in this particular case. He might well have been asked how closely Murdock's responses matched the standard profile on which Dr. Blum based his evaluation—whether Murdock fit squarely in a standard category or whether the psychological evaluation was more tentative. By asking exclusively for specific test responses, which would add little to the jury's understanding of the expert's opinion, the trial judge may have inadvertently cut off the flow of information about the statistical nature of the tests, information without which the jury could not evaluate Dr. Blum's opinion testimony.[12]

This is, of course, a more charitable characterization than the "know-nothing appeal to igno-

---

[5] 307 F.2d 637 (D.C. Cir. 1962).

[6] Id., p. 645. "The determination of a psychologist's competence to render an expert opinion based on his findings as to the presence or absence of mental disease or defect must depend upon the nature and extent of his knowledge. It does not depend upon his claim to the title "psychologist."

[7] The briefs of both the American Psychiatric Association and the American Psychological Association are excerpted above, pp. 155–60.

[8] *United States* v. *Brawner*, 471 F.2d 969, 1003–04 (D.C. Cir. 1972). Cf. *King* v. *United States*, 372 F.2d 390 (D.C. Cir. 1967).

[9] 471 F.2d 923 (D.C. Cir. 1972).

[10] Id., pp. 953–54.

[11] Id., p. 967.

[12] Id., p. 955.

rance" charge leveled against the prosecutor in *Brawner*, but it may amount to very much the same thing.[13]

The problem of dealing effectively with testimony based on psychological tests is not a new one for this court. We have frequently seen attorneys and judges elicit from a psychologist a series of test

[13] See the instructive monograph by David Silber, Ph.D., *Clinical Psychology—Its Role and Methods*, pp. 143–52, above.

questions and answers, thereby setting up an easy target for ridicule. It would be inappropriate to shield these tests from scrutiny by prohibiting such questions. . . . Indeed, it may be that the validity of the tests is so doubtful that they should be excluded from evidence as a matter of law. But if courts are willing to accept the tests as legitimate diagnostic tools, it is troublesome to see counsel or the court attempting to discredit them in a particular case by ridicule, rather than exploring their acknowledged strengths and weaknesses.[14]

[14] *United States* v. *Alexander and Murdock*, 471 F.2d 923 (D.C. Cir. 1972).

SUGGESTIONS FOR ADDITIONAL READING

Anastasi, Anne. *Psychological Testing*, 3d ed. New York: Macmillan, 1968.

Cronbach, Lee J. *Essentials of Psychological Testing* (Murphy Holtzman Series) New York: Harper & Rowe, 3d ed., 1970.

Pope, Benjamin, and Scot, Winfield. *Psychological Diagnosis in Clinical Practice*. New York: Oxford University Press, 1967.

Goldman, Leo. *Using Tests in Counseling*. New York: Appleton-Century-Crofts, 1971.

Schafer, Roy. *The Clinical Application of Psychological Tests*. New York: International Universities Press, 1970.

Sundberg, Norman D., et al. *Clinical Psychology: Expanding Horizons*, 2d ed. New York: Appleton-Century-Crofts, 1973.

7

The Psychiatrist and Psychologist
as Expert Witnesses

Chapter 7 is concerned with the psychiatrist and the psychologist in court. We begin with a comment about the role of the expert witness, followed by illustrations of direct examination and cross-examination of psychiatric witnesses in two Kansas criminal cases. Both cases deserve careful reading: the Andrews case for the insights it provides about the differential meanings ascribed to "knowledge" and "awareness" by law and the behavioral sciences, a dichotomy which will appear again in subsequent chapters; and the Volbrecht case because it is an excellent vehicle for a discussion of the cross-examination techniques frequently employed with the psychiatric witness. It is suggested that the reader first go through the cross-examination in Volbrecht and try to identify for himself the techniques used; then, that he go back over the testimony in light of the Questions for Discussion which follow it.

The Roberts article summarizes a number of the problems involved in the interaction of lawyer and forensic psychiatrist in the courtroom setting. The article by Dr. Diamond has become something of a classic on "impartial" expert testimony. It is followed by a series of questions re-examining the Diamond thesis, and an article by Dr. Kubie about the Ruby case, taking a position quite different from that of Dr. Diamond. Finally, there is an editorial from the *American Journal of Psychiatry* by the late Dr. Henry Davidson: "The Coach, Yes; The Umpire, No."

EDITORIAL COMMENT

Of course the psychiatrist, like anyone else, may be called as an ordinary (i.e., nonexpert) witness, or indeed may be a party to litigation. However, when the psychiatrist testifies as an expert, he generally appears in one of three roles:

1. as the attending physician (that is, he is called to testify about his diagnosis, prognosis, and treatment of his own patient);
2. as examining physician where the examination was made for the purpose of providing a basis for expert testimony, rather than as incident to rendering treatment (the psychiatrist may have conducted the examination at the instance of the patient or his attorney, or pursuant to court order); or
3. as a nontreating, nonexamining expert: (a) with respect to standards of medical care and practice (e.g., in malpractice cases); or (b) who is asked to render an

opinion in response to a hypothetical question; or (c) to render an opinion based on collateral evidence (testimony at trial, correspondence, documents, observation of the demeanor of a witness, etc.).

The applicable substantive and procedural rules (e.g., as to whether the person about whom the witness is to testify may assert the rule of privilege, whether the expert witness may be subpoenaed, whether pretrial discovery can be employed, etc.) may vary depending on the category in which the proposed testimony falls. It is not the purpose of these pages to describe the rules and their variations (these matters are considered in any good textbook on evidence or trial practice), but rather to discuss some of the basic considerations in presenting expert psychiatric testimony.

First, the matter of payment. In most states counsel is permitted to pay the expert witness in excess of the statutory witness fee. In some states there is a specific statutory regulation; but in most, not. In half a dozen or so states, contingent fee contracts with expert witnesses have expressly been declared against public policy; but in some states the practice is regularly followed.

Any expert witness is entitled to be compensated for his time: in preparation for trial (conducting examinations, examining documents, conferring with counsel, etc.) and at the trial itself (including time spent actually giving testimony, serving as a trial consultant to counsel during the testimony of others, and, indeed, simply waiting in court until he is called). There is nothing dishonorable, or even faintly disreputable, in offering such compensation. There should be a clear understanding between counsel and the expert as to what the expert is expected to do (simply testify? conduct an examination? if so, for what purpose? examine records, documents? have conferences to assist counsel in preparing his case? sit with counsel at trial during opposing medical testimony and advise him regarding possible cross-examination approaches?) and what his compensation shall be. That compensation, it seems to us, should *never* be contingent on a favorable result in the case. Such an agreement *may* be unlawful, but more significantly, the witness may be questioned about it on cross-examination and the results may be catastrophic.

In some jurisdictions it is fashionable on cross-examination to ask the witness: "Doctor, you are getting paid for your testimony (or, less charitably, "your opinion") are you not?" The witness should be prepared for the possibility that such a question will be asked. If it is, he should of course answer it honestly. Either in his answer, or later on redirect examination, it should be made clear that the witness is being compensated for his *time*, not for his opinion; and, if possible, the point should be made that the witness is receiving his normal fee for the time expended—in other words, no more than he would have received through devoting an equivalent period of time to his own practice.

As to the use of the subpoena, it has been indicated that the subpoena may not be available (where the psychiatrist has no prior knowledge of the case and is called merely to give an opinion based on matters stated to him, or observed by him, at the trial). Where the subpoena is available, there is no inflexible rule as to its appropriate use. Some attorneys subpoena every witness as a matter of routine. If the attorney tries to accommodate the physician (in arranging a time for him to appear that is least inconvenient to him, minimizing as

much as possible the time he must spend in court waiting for his name to be called, etc.), and if he explains to him the purpose of the subpoena, the psychiatrist will probably not resent it. In fact, it may serve as a reminder to him of the time of the case; and, if he has never testified before, he will probably be a little proud of it, and show it to his friends. The subpoena may even be helpful to the witness. For example, if he is a low-ranking member of a hospital staff, it may obviate possible objections by his administrative superior, who may feel that the work of the institution will suffer by reason of the diversion of the time and efforts of one of its key personnel; and who may be apprehensive about possible embarrassment to the institution as a result of the testimony.

In rare cases, use of the subpoena may be essential, if the witness is unwilling to appear and his testimony is crucial to the case. However, it should be self-evident that where a subpoena is used to compel testimony from an unwilling physician the risks are great. A resentful medical witness can be devastating to one's case; and if his testimony is damaging, the party calling him *may* not be permitted to impeach his own witness.

In presenting psychiatric evidence, no investment of time will pay off more handsomely than the hours spent with the witness in preparation for the trial. An exchange of letters and a hurried conference a few minutes before the witness is called to testify is as good a way to lose a case as any we know.

It is counsel's responsibility to make sure that the witness understands what the case is about and to consider with him the probable nature of the opposing medical evidence and the kind of cross-examination he can expect. It is probably also a good idea to discuss with the doctor the "why" of the adversary process. Many physicians (even those who frequently testify) do not understand why their testimony is presented in partisan fashion, and resent having their opinions challenged by the other side.

Counsel should be sure that *he* understands what the doctor is going to say. If your witness is unable to make his testimony clear, understandable, persuasive to *you*, he will never be able to convince the jury.

In his conferences with the psychiatrist, the attorney should encourage him to discuss the case fully—and from his own point of view. The doctor should not be restricted to responding to counsel's legal phrasing of questions. Through such an unfettered discussion counsel may gain a new perspective of the issues in the case; or, indeed, may discover a cherished bias of the doctor's that, if revealed at trial, might partially discredit his testimony (e.g., he may feel that *everyone* who commits a criminal offense is mentally ill—which is not very helpful when you are hoping to prove that the physician's diagnosis of mental illness in *this* case was based on the most carefully and rigorously applied diagnostic techniques).

Although the matter should be approached delicately, it is a good idea for counsel to discuss with the psychiatric witness his demeanor on the stand. Many physicians are intimidated by the position of the witness vis-à-vis counsel (who is permitted to ask the questions, may press, look for contradictions, even be hostile, etc.). Few doctors—even psychiatrists (!)—realize that it is the *witness* who has the advantage. Even if he is an expert in a field with which the jurors are totally unfamiliar, they find it much easier to identify with him than with the attorney or judge—a fact the expert witness should bear in mind when the cross-examination becomes vigorous.

Of course, counsel should go over all of the expert's testimony with him prior to trial, beginning with his qualifications. It is a truism in law—but worth repeating—that counsel should not consent to a stipulation at trial that his witness is qualified to testify. If such a stipulation is offered, counsel should thank his colleague for recognizing his witness's expertness, but state that he feels the jury is entitled to know about the witness's background in order properly to evaluate his testimony.

In addition, it would be well to remind the witness of the importance of his maintaining his composure on the stand—especially when opposing counsel is hostile. Displays of petulance on the part of the expert antagonize the jury: they seem unprofessional, and make the witness appear to be excessively partisan. Nor should the witness offer a "smart" or "flip" answer; nor should the attorney impose "stock" or "cute" rejoinders on him. If the witness's responses are not natural to *him*, they will sound "pat" or "rehearsed."

The witness should be instructed never to answer a question he doesn't understand (some doctors are afraid to ask for a clarification or repetition of a question), or one which incorporates unacceptable premises (some witnesses answer the last part of a question and ignore the fact that they are conceding the truth of an earlier statement to which they would strongly have dissented had it been asked alone). Indeed, the response, "I don't know" can be a devastatingly effective answer on occasion. Such problems will be less likely to arise if counsel does his job of protecting the witness by objecting to questions calling for speculation, or misstating facts, or assuming facts not in evidence. Further, the witness should answer

the question asked and not offer gratuitous comments; and this applies to direct as well as to cross-examination.

The witness should avoid attempting to support a sound medical judgment with an unsound generalization (the "Doctor, isn't it possible that . . ." to which he responds that "it couldn't happen" or "it has never happened," when all he can truthfully say is that because of factors *a*, *b*, and *c* it is highly unlikely in this case). Some witnesses who have done so have been "cured" by the cross-examiner's next question: "Doctor, have you *ever* made a mistake?"

The content of the testimony, as has been indicated, should be in the words of the witness; but the attorney should be aware of the problem of semantics: no obscure or technical terms should be used without definition—or be used at all if the meaning can be conveyed without them. To this point should be added the *caveat* that the testimony should not sound "folksy" or patronizing to the jury.

There are some terms which are clearly terms of art in the lexicon of psychiatry (terms such as abreaction, etiology, hebephrenic, neologism, oedipus complex, psychometric, schizophrenia, etc.). There are other terms, however, which have both a colloquial and a technical meaning, and the attorney should be especially alert to them, for they are likely to be interpreted by the jury in their colloquial sense unless they are appropriately defined (terms such as acute, anxiety, complex, conversion, delusion, depression, deterioration, erotic, euphoria, fabrication, homosexual, hysteria, transference, etc.).

Finally, the attorney should discuss with the doctor some of the "sneakier" kind of cross-examination questions which might be asked (see the Volbrecht cross-examination to follow), and how they can most effectively be answered (questions like: "Doctor, you mean all you did was *talk* with him; how did you know he was telling you the truth?" or "You mean you didn't conduct *any* neurological tests?"—or, if he did, but no organic brain damage was shown—"And all of the neurological tests were negative—that is, *normal*—weren't they?" or "Now, doctor, isn't it true that thousands of people are a little shy and introverted—they aren't *all* psychotics, are they?" or "Are you saying that *anyone* who has daydreams is insane?" or "Doctor, if Mr. Jones is so sick and has all these symptoms, how could he have carried on a business?" or "If he were all that sick, why didn't he display any symptoms during his stay at the county jail, or right now in this courtroom?" etc.).

Most important of all—but this is true, of course, in any case, and with any witness—the attorney must know his case. If that case involves complex nosological differentiations, he must know what they are. But he should be aware also that what should be made significant for the jury is what the doctors *saw*, not what they chose to call it. It is, after all, not a label on trial, but a human being.

It might be well at this point for the reader to note the "Court's Instruction to Expert Witness in Case Involving the 'Insanity Defense,'" contained in *Washington* v. *U.S.* (Chapter 17, post).

R.C.A.

STATE OF KANSAS v. LOWELL LEE ANDREWS

Excerpt from *In Cold Blood* by Truman Capote

The following excerpt, describing the case which led to the habeas corpus proceeding from which the transcript to follow was taken, is from Truman Capote's *In Cold Blood* (New York: Random House, Inc., 1965), and is reprinted with the permission of the author and copyright holder, Mr. Capote, and the publisher. *In Cold Blood*, which has already become a literary classic, is primarily concerned with another Kansas case of note—the wholesale murder of four members of the Clutter family, and the subsequent trial, conviction, and execution of two young men, Dick Hickock and Perry Smith, for that crime. For several months, Hickock, Smith, and Lowell Lee Andrews shared the rather somber facilities of death row at Kansas State Prison, and Mr. Capote includes considerable detail about Lee Andrews and his brief relationship with the "Clutter killers":

. . . Lowell Lee Andrews, an enormous, weakeyed boy of eighteen who wore horn-rimmed glasses and weighed almost three hundred pounds, had been a sophomore at the University of Kansas, an honor student majoring in biology Though he was a solitary creature, withdrawn and seldom communicative, his acquaintances, both at the University and in his home town of Wolcott, Kansas, regarded him as exceptionally gentle and "sweet-natured" (later one Kansas paper printed an article about him entitled: The Nicest Boy in Wolcott"). But inside the quiet young scholar there existed a second, unsuspected personality, one with stunted emotions and a distorted mind through which cold thoughts flowed in cruel directions. His family—his parents and a slightly older

sister, Jennie Marie—would have been astounded had they known the daydreams Lowell Lee dreamed throughout the summer and autumn of 1958; the brilliant son, the adored brother, was planning to poison them all.

The elder Andrews was a prosperous farmer; he had not much money in the bank, but he owned land valued at approximately two hundred thousand dollars. A desire to inherit this estate was ostensibly the motivation behind Lowell Lee's plot to destroy his family. For the secret Lowell Lee, the one concealed inside the shy churchgoing biology student, fancied himself an ice-hearted master criminal: he wanted to wear gangsterish silk shirts and drive scarlet sports cars; he wanted to be recognized as no mere bespectacled, bookish, overweight, virginal schoolboy; and while he did not dislike any member of his family, at least not consciously, murdering them seemed the swiftest, most sensible way of implementing the fantasies that possessed him. Arsenic was the weapon he decided upon; after poisoning the victims, he meant to tuck them in their beds and burn down the house, in the hope that investigators would believe the deaths accidental. However, one detail perturbed him: suppose autopsies revealed the presence of arsenic? And suppose the purchase of the poison could be traced to him? Toward the end of summer he evolved another plan. He spent three months polishing it. Finally, there came a near-zero November night when he was ready to start.

It was Thanksgiving week, and Lowell Lee was home for the holidays, as was Jennie Marie, an intelligent but rather plain girl who attended a college in Oklahoma. On the evening of November 28, somewhere around seven, Jennie Marie was sitting with her parents in the parlor watching television; Lowell Lee was locked in his bedroom reading the last chapter of *The Brothers Karamazov*. That task completed, he shaved, changed into his best suit, and pro-

---

Andrews v. Hand, No. 1361 H.C.

ceeded to load both a semi-automatic .22-caliber rifle and a Ruger .22-caliber revolver. He fitted the revolver into a hip holster, shouldered the rifle, and ambled down a hall to the parlor, which was dark except for the flickering television screen. He switched on a light, aimed the rifle, pulled the trigger, and hit his sister between the eyes, killing her instantly. He shot his mother three times, and his father twice. The mother, eyes gaping, arms outstretched, staggered toward him; she tried to speak, her mouth opened, closed, but Lowell Lee said: "Shut up." To be certain she obeyed him, he shot her three times more. Mr. Andrews, however, was still alive; sobbing, whimpering, he thrashed along the floor toward the kitchen, but at the kitchen's threshold the son unholstered his revolver and discharged every chamber, then reloaded the weapon and emptied it again; altogether, his father absorbed seventeen bullets.

Andrews, acording to statements credited to him, "didn't feel anything about it. The time came, and I was doing what I had to do. That's all there was to it." After the shootings he raised a window in his bedroom and removed the screen, then roamed the house rifling dresser drawers and scattering the contents: it was his intention to blame the crime on thieves. Later, driving his father's car, he traveled forty miles over snow-slippery roads to Lawrence, the town where the University of Kansas is located; en route, he parked on a bridge, dismantled his lethal artillery, and disposed of it by dropping the parts into the Kansas River. But of course the journey's true purpose was to arrange an alibi. First he stopped at the campus house where he roomed; he talked with the landlady, told her that he had come to pick up his typewriter, and that because of the bad weather, the trip from Wolcott to Lawrence had taken two hours. Departing, he visited a movie theater, where, uncharacteristically, he chatted with an usher and a candy vendor. At eleven, when the movie let out, he returned to Wolcott. The family's mongrel dog was waiting on the front porch; it was whining with hunger, so Lowell Lee, entering the house and stepping across his father's corpse, prepared a bowl of warm milk and mush; then, while the dog was lapping it up, he telephoned the sheriff's office and said, "My name is Lowell Lee Andrews. I live at 6040 Wolcott Drive, and I want to report a robbery—"

Four officers of the Wyandotte County Sheriff's Patrol responded. One of the group, Patrolman Meyers, described the scene as follows: "Well, it was one in the morning when we got there. All the lights in the house was on. And this big dark-haired boy, Lowell Lee, he was sitting on the porch petting his dog. Patting it on the head. Lieutenant Athey asked the boy what happened, and he pointed to the door, real casual, and said, 'Look in there.' " Having looked, the astonished officers summoned the county coroner, a gentleman who was also impressed by young Andrews' callous nonchalance, for when the coroner asked him what funeral arrangements he wished to have made, Andrews replied with a shrug, "*I* don't care what you do with them."

Shortly, two senior detectives appeared and began to question the family's lone survivor. Though convinced he was lying, the detectives listened respectfully to the tale of how he had driven to Lawrence to fetch a typewriter, gone to a movie, and arrived home after midnight to find the bedrooms ransacked and his family slain. He stayed with the story, and might never have altered it if, subsequent to his arrest and removal to the county jail, the authorities had not obtained the aid of the Reverend Mr. Virto C. Dameron.

The Reverend Dameron, a Dickensian personage, an unctuous and jolly brimstone-and-damnation orator, was minister of the Grandview Baptist Church in Kansas City, Kansas, the church the Andrews family attended regularly. Awakened by an urgent call from the county coroner, Dameron presented himself at the jail around 3:00 a.m., whereupon detectives, who had been strenuously but abortively interrogating the suspect, withdrew to another room, leaving the minister to consult privately with his parishioner. It proved a fatal interview for the latter, who many months afterward gave this account of it to a friend: "Mr. Dameron said, 'Now, Lee, I've known you all your life. Since you were just a little tadpole. And I knew your daddy all his life, we grew up together, we were childhood friends. And that's why I'm here—not just because I'm your minister, but because I feel like you're a member of my own family. And because you need a friend that you can talk to and trust. And I feel terrible about this terrible event, and I'm every bit as anxious as you are to see the guilty party caught and punished.'

"He wanted to know was I thirsty, and I was, so he got me a Coke, and after that he's going on about the Thanksgiving vacation and how do I like school, when all of a sudden he says, 'Now, Lee, there seems to be some doubt among the people here regarding your innocence. I'm sure you'd be willing to take a lie detector and convince these men of your innocence so they can get busy and catch the guilty party.' Then he said, 'Lee, you didn't do this terrible thing, did you? If you did, now is the time to purge your soul.' The next thing was, I thought what difference does it make, and I told him the truth, most everything about it. He kept wagging his head and rolling his eyes and rubbing his hands together, and he said it was a terrible thing, and I would have to answer to the Almighty, have to purge my soul by telling the officers what I'd told him, and would I?" Receiving an affirmative nod, the prisoner's spiritual advisor stepped into an adjacent room, which was crowded with expectant policemen, and elatedly issued an invitation: "Come on in. The boy's ready to make a statement."

The Andrews case became the basis for a

legal and medical crusade. Prior to the trial, at which Andrews pleaded innocent by reason of insanity, the psychiatric staff of the Menninger Clinic conducted an exhaustive examination of the accused; this produced a diagnosis of "schizophrenia, simple type." By "simple," the diagnosticians meant that Andrews suffered no delusions, no false perceptions, no hallucinations, but the primary illness of separation of thinking from feeling. He understood the nature of his acts, and that they were prohibited, and that he was subject to punishment. "But," to quote Dr. Joseph Satten, one of the examiners, "Lowell Lee Andrews felt no emotions whatsoever. He considered himself the only important, only significant person in the world. And in his own seclusive world it seemed to him just as right to kill his mother as to kill an animal or a fly."

In the opinion of Dr. Satten and his colleagues, Andrews' crime amounted to such an undebatable example of diminished responsibility that the case offered an ideal chance to challenge the M'Naghten Rule in Kansas courts. The M'Naghten Rule, as has been previously stated, recognizes no form of insanity provided the defendant has the capacity to discriminate between right and wrong—legally, not morally. Much to the distress of psychiatrists and liberal jurists, the Rule prevails in the courts of the British Commonwealth and, in the United States, in the courts of all but half a dozen or so of the states and the District of Columbia, which abide by the more lenient, though to some minds impractical, Durham Rule, which is simply that an accused is not criminally responsible if his unlawful act is the product of mental disease or mental defect.

In short, what Andrews' defenders, a team composed of Menninger Clinic psychiatrists and two first-class attorneys, hoped to achieve was a victory of legal-landmark stature. The great essential was to persuade the court to substitute the Durham Rule for the M'Naghten Rule. If that happened, then Andrews, because of the abundant evidence concerning his schizophrenic condition, would certainly be sentenced not to the gallows, or even to prison, but to confinement in the State Hospital for the Criminally Insane.

However, the defense reckoned without the defendant's religious counselor, the tireless Reverend Mr. Dameron, who appeared at the trial as the chief witness for the prosecution, and who, in the overwrought, rococo style of a tent-show revivalist, told the court he had often warned his former Sunday School pupil of God's impending wrath: "I says, there isn't anything in this world that is worth more than your soul, and you have acknowledged to me a number of times in our conversations that your faith is weak, that you have no faith in God. You know that all sin is against God and God is your final judge, and you have got to answer to Him. That is what I said to make him feel the terribleness of the thing he'd done, and that

he had to answer to the Almighty for this crime."

Apparently the Reverend Dameron was determined young Andrews should answer not only to the Almighty, but also to more temporal powers, for it was his testimony, added to the defendant's confession, that settled matters. The presiding judge upheld the M'Naghten Rule, and the jury gave the state the death penalty it demanded.

. . .

Andrews' conviction was affirmed on appeal by the Kansas Supreme Court, and, following two unsuccessful petitions for a writ of certiorari to the United States Supreme Court, sentence was executed upon him by hanging.

The following excerpt illustrates some of the problems of relating psychiatric testimony to legal concepts. The principal issues in this habeas corpus proceeding were, of course, the constitutional propriety of the M'Naghten rule, strictly and literally applied, and of admission of the confession as a "free and voluntary" statement.

Excerpts from Transcript of Proceedings on Petition for a Writ of Habeas Corpus

The . . . matter came on for hearing before The Honorable Kenneth Harmon, Judge of the District Court for The First Judicial District of Kansas, at 2 P.M., Tuesday, November 21, 1961.

Direct Examination

By Mr. Allen:

Q. Doctor, would you state your name, address, and professional affiliation for the record?

A. My name is Joseph Satten; I live at 1500 Stratford Road in Topeka, Kansas; I work at The Menninger Foundation where I am the Director of the Division of Law and Psychiatry.

Q. You are a medical doctor and a psychiatrist; is that correct?

A. I am a physician specializing in the practice of psychiatry.

Q. Are you the same Doctor Satten who examined Lowell Lee Andrews pursuant to order of the district court of Wyandotte County, Kansas, some time subsequent to June 14, 1959, and who testified in the trial of the case of State vs. Andrews?

A. Yes, I am.

Q. Will you describe the nature of that examination briefly for us, Doctor?

A. The examination consisted of a series of interviews by me over a period of weeks, lasting about 12 hours in all; a series of tests by the clinical psychologist, psychological tests lasting about six hours; interviews by our psychiatric social worker of an aunt and uncle of the patient, as well as contacts by the psychiatric social worker with some of his teachers, particularly his band leader at the University of Kansas. In addition, I had access to some information by various people who had known the patient, including the reactions, including the observations of police officers who brought him to and from the clinic.

Q. Would you describe briefly the nature of any physical or psychological tests which were performed on Lee Andrews?

A. There was a complete physical and neurological examination by the neurologist and by the internist; there were blood tests, x-rays, and electroencephalographic brainwave tests, you might call it, in addition to the psychiatric and psychological examinations.

Q. Based upon your examination of Andrews, Doctor, do you have an opinion, based on reasonable medical certainty, as to whether Lee Andrews was then suffering from a mental disease?

A. I do.

Q. What is that opinion, Doctor?

MR. FOTH: I object to that, Your Honor. The mental condition of Lowell Lee Andrews at the time Dr. Satten examined him is not an issue in this case.

MR. ALLEN: I don't see how it could help but be, Your Honor. We will certainly relate this to the time of the taking of the confession and the time of the offense as well. This examination could hardly do other than reveal his condition at the time of the examination.

THE COURT: We will overrule the objection and take his answer.

Q. Would you state that opinion, Doctor?

A. I found that he was suffering from a severe mental illness at the time of my examination, a mental illness which, in my opinion, had lasted some period of time prior to the time of my examination.

Q. Can this illness be described in terms of a diagnostic category and, if so, what is that category?

A. The illness I found him to be suffering from can be called, in kind of medical shorthand, schizophrenic reaction, simple type.

Q. Can you describe that illness, Doctor, and tell us what factors were significant in making your diagnosis?

. . .

A. This illness is primarily considered to be a psychological illness, an illness of the mental functioning, traditionally unassociated with any physical damage to the brain. The major findings that I observed had to do with defects in Andrews' emotional functioning in which I observed a blunting or a diminution of his emotional reactions, a disharmony between his emotional reactions and the thoughts that were going on at the time. In addition, I found him to be somewhat awkward, stilted in his speech, often preferring elaborate, complicated ways of saying things in a way that covered up confusion in his thinking.

The next most important finding was his attempt to try to convince himself and me that he was a rational human being; that he was not sick; that he was not insane, in an attempt to continually try to convince himself that his actions were rational and made sense to him.

These were the major findings, although there were some minor findings as well that I would like to refresh my memory about by looking at my notes if I may. There were two other important aspects of this man's functioning. One was the fact that he was able to entertain in consciousness contradictory ideas like, for example, loving or hating someone—loving and hating someone—and not really being aware of the fact that this was a contradiction and that the contradiction had to be logically resolved.

The other important point—I am sorry that I said I had covered the major points—the other important point was really a distortion of the way he visualized the world. It relates, in part, to his disintegrated emotional functioning, but he perceives the world as a place in which people, as people, don't exist, much less human feeling and closeness existing as important things, and in this image of the world he sees himself as a kind of almost all-powerful figure above everybody else, having rights to do things that others don't have, without being aware that right under the surface are extreme and intense feelings of inadequacy, failure, and inability to function as an ordinary human being. These are the major findings.

Q. Doctor, I believe you testified that it was your opinion that Lee Andrews was trying to convince you that he was not insane?

A. Yes.

Q. Does this fit consistently with the pattern that you have described, that one will deny in himself the presence of mental illness at the risk of his life? Can you expand on this point?

A. That is extreme but it is not at all unusual

for many kinds of patients with the existence of mental disorders to try to diminish or deny the seriousness of the mental disorder, and it is not uncommon with seriously disorganized people to attempt to deny the presence of that disorder, even at the cost of their life.

Q. Doctor, what is your opinion with respect to whether or not Lee Andrews was suffering from this condition on November 28, 1958, the date of the alleged offense?

A. My opinion is that he was suffering from this condition at that time.

Q. On what do you base this opinion that the condition had existed for some months prior to your examination and that it existed at the time of the death of Lee's parents and sister?

A. I base this opinion on two factors: (1) The clinical examination in which the constellation of all the symptoms I have noted traditionally come, or traditionally develop, over a long period of time. This constellation of symptoms I have described rarely appears suddenly, but gradually builds up over years and years. So, on the basis of the clinical aspect of the case, this was one important criterion.

The second, and perhaps less important criterion had to do with the reports of other people who had described his withdrawn, somewhat isolated, functioning over a period of years preceding the offense in a way that was entirely consistent with the clinical picture that I found.

A third factor which plays some part, but which I deliberately tried to play down in my thinking, is the nature of the offense itself and the light that this kind of offense throws on the kind of mental functioning that was going on at the time, but since this offense and the disposition of Andrews in regard to this offense was a point at issue, I deliberately, in my own thinking, tried to play down that aspect. But it is from the point of view of psychiatrists, the scientists, that one of the criteria enters into consideration.

Q. Doctor, you mentioned observations of others and occurrences prior to the time of the offense. Could you specify more particularly some of these observations of which you became aware prior to the date of the offense?

A. I didn't understand the question.

Q. Let me rephrase it. You mentioned as confirmatory of your opinion that this condition was one of long standing and specifically that it had existed at the time of the offense; you mentioned observations of others who had come in contact with Lee,

and events that had occurred prior to the commission of the offense. I wonder if you would care to specify any particular or special observations or special incidents occurring prior to the alleged offense which you took into account.

A. I can specify a few. I think I mentioned the observations of his band leader as reported to the psychiatric social worker; the observation of an aunt and uncle. A third had to do with the observations of a fellow student who saw him brandishing a gun, and in a sense, almost threatening the life of this student. A fourth had to do with a report that some disturbance in him had been noticed on some personality tests at the university, a report conveyed to me by the psychiatrist at the university. These were the main ones, I think. There were others along the same line confirming the idea that this was a somewhat withdrawn, peculiar kid, as they called him. Subsequent to the trial I have had additional reports from other sources confirming this man's isolatedness, withdrawal, and detachment; for example, from the warden of the penitentiary, from a neighbor of the family, people like that. These are the specific ones that come to my mind.

Q. These latter points you have mentioned have occurred subsequent to your testimony at the trial?

A. Yes.

Q. In your opinion, Doctor, was the killing of Lee Andrews' parents and sister brought on by the mental disease you have described?

A. I would say so, without much question. But for this peculiar kind of thing—but for the illness that he had—I doubt very much that this tragedy would have occurred. To put it another way, the tragedy was an outgrowth of his peculiar and perverted thinking and feeling.

Q. Doctor, in your experience is such a gross and violent act as this was a rare occurrence among persons who are mentally ill, and how does it relate to this specific mental illness which you have described?

A. Fortunately, such tragic acts are relatively rare in people who are mentally ill, but when they do occur, when an act occurs without reported anger or feeling, such as is reported in this case, they are almost always a murder of someone very close, like a mother, a father, a husband or child. When they occur in such a context, they are almost always associated with the kinds of emotional and mental disturbances that exist in this case. But, fortunately, they are relatively rare among mental patients, and also they are even rarer among the community as a whole.

Q. In your opinion, did Lee Andrews at the time of the act, by reason of his mental disease, lack substantial capacity to appreciate the criminality of his conduct?

A. I would think so; yes.

Q. In your opinion, did he lack substantial capacity to conform his conduct to the requirements of the law?

A. Very definitely.

Q. Doctor, as you know, the test of criminal responsibility, or insanity as the law calls it, in Kansas is a two-fold test. The defendant may be acquitted by reason of insanity if the jury finds that at the time of the offense, by reason of mental illness, he could not appreciate the nature and quality of the act he was doing, or, if he could do so, that he did not know that what he was doing was wrong. Testimony is usually elicited from psychiatrists, and sometimes from laymen, with respect to these two questions, as was done in the Andrews case. I should like for you, if you will, to comment briefly with respect to the findings which you made concerning Lee Andrews and the condition from which he was, and is, suffering in light of these questions, and specifically whether he could appreciate the nature and quality of his conduct, and whether he knew what he was doing was wrong.

. . .

A. Well, I can answer the question as follows: The question, the test—the rule as it were —possesses a special difficulty for me as a psychiatrist, and I think for other psychiatrists, because it does two things that make it difficult to convey to the Court and to the jury the clinical findings: (1) It requires an absolute answer on one side or the other side of a scale, when, in reality, as we examine people, we find not absolutes, but relatives. It requires us to talk in terms of black and white when, by the nature of the people we examine, we see mostly shades of gray.

The second point is that it places a tremendous, almost 100 per cent, emphasis on one element of mental functioning and mental malfunctioning; namely, the capacity to know, and on a relatively narrow conception of the word "know." As scientists, as psychiatrists we are very well aware that there are different levels of knowing. There is knowing which is simply awareness of something. And there is knowing which represents a full rational comprehension of the situation and I testified in this case that to the casual observer Andrews did have

the capacity to know but to the scientist looking at this carefully the kind of knowing that he was capable of is a knowing that is completely divorced from emotional functioning so that this is in another sense of the word and a deeper sense of the word, really not a full rational comprehension of the situation. The rule makes it difficult to get these points across and makes it necessary to try to bring into the definition of "knowing" other aspects of personality functioning, like emotional functioning.

One last point about this: It places an emphasis on the superficial aspects. At the risk that analogies create, it is like looking at a counterfeit bill and the casual observer saying, "The color is right; the paper is right; the printing is right"—and the expert looking at it, pointing out that while all of this may be right, there are little defects in the engraving which are not right, and then an argument ensues as to whether the superficial aspects are more important than the few technical details. This is an analogy, and it runs the risk of all analogies.

Q. Doctor, I will ask you, if you will, to define schizoid personality and to describe the differences between this condition and schizophrenic reaction.

A. Schizoid personality is a term used to describe one type of mental disorder in which the disorder is characterized primarily by the behavior of the individual, such behavior being mainly withdrawal from people, difficulty in interpersonal relationships, and inability to respond spontaneously and actively. It is also associated in the traditional definition with extensive fantasies, usually fantasies of omnipotence and power. The distinction—or, let me correct myself— many, many patients, who at a later point in their lives develop overt schizophrenic reaction with gross distortions in thinking, feeling, and behavior, have had as their primary way of reacting to the world a personality which can be described as a schizoid personality. Schizophrenic reactions don't occur out of the blue, but they usually develop in individuals who are predisposed to such reactions as a result of their personality structure and are somewhat more vulnerable to certain kinds of stresses that are placed upon them.

The distinction between that and schizophrenic reaction of various sorts is, in part, a question of degree, and in part, a question of new things appearing. The different schizophrenic reactions that can appear in individuals are classified usually on the basis of the predominant disturbance that is seen. If that predominant disturbance is in thinking with certain kinds of delusions and feelings of persecution, it is called a paranoid reaction, but the disturbances in emotion are still present. If the primary disturbance happens to be in behavior, it is apt to be called catatonic reaction. It is apt to be called a catatonic reaction, but the disturbance in feeling and thinking is also present. If the disturbance is primarily in feeling, with a disintegration of feeling, the traditional giggling kind of insane patient, it is called hebephrenic reaction.

But where the reaction doesn't take one of those three main forms, disturbances in thinking, feeling, or behavior predominantly, but represents mainly a disintegration of personality functioning, with the thinking relatively intact, and the emotions relatively intact, but a disharmony between them, that's called a schizophrenic reaction, simple type, and the distinction between that and a schizoid personality is: (1) A question of degree, the schizophrenic reaction being more disabling than the schizoid personality; and also a question of historical development. Over the years the individual with a schizoid personality tends to remain more or less stable except that under conditions of stress he may develop briefly overt insane periods or overt psychotic episodes.

On the other hand, the individual with a schizophrenic reaction, simple type, is apt, without treatment, over the years to progressively get worse and worse and worse, so that his thinking, which at one point was apparently intact, gets completely deteriorated.

Q. Now, Dr. Roth, in his deposition, spoke about decompensation, although the reporter heard it as "decomposition." If "decompensation" is a word in your psychiatric terminology, I wonder if you would, Doctor, tell us what this is. What is decompensation?

A. Decompensation is a word used in psychiatry to describe a worsening of a way of functioning in which the individual relapses or becomes sicker by having disturbances in thinking or disturbances in behavior. It assumes that all individuals function in a kind of balance between themselves and their environment and that this balance is one in which they are able to evaluate the stresses placed upon them by their environment, the stresses that come from their own existence, and are able to work out solutions for themselves in a relatively mature and grownup and satisfactory way. Decompensation means that in any kind of pattern, a reaction under the impact of certain stress, either coming from inside the individual or from the outside, the pattern gives way and in its place one sees patterns of greater distortion, greater illness.

Q. Now, Doctor, in your opinion, was Lee Andrews in a condition of stress on and prior to November 28, 1958?

A. Yes, he was. The stress that I feel that he was under is a relatively common stress that most individuals face; namely, the stress that's involved in growing from adolescence to manhood, a kind of biological stress period; and, secondly, the stress that is involved in going away from home, attempting to, in a sense, grow up and grow away from his parents in a setting that places certain demands for maturity and for independent functioning on him, and the period of going away to school is a period of great stress to most people, and here again, fortunately, most people respond well to this period of stress, which is both psychological and biological, and grow out of it more stable and more mature.

Q. What can you tell us about the dynamics of the acts which he committed on that date?

A. If by "dynamics" you mean what was going on inside of him that might have led to those acts, I have a hypothesis or inference based on the findings that I have made and the observations of others about him, as follows: Here was a young man . . . . who, a large part of his life, has been isolated and withdrawn, mocked because of his awkwardness and overweight by other students, having ambivalent attachments to his family, attachments that involved mixed feeling of love and hate, going away to the university where he sees himself—in his fantasies—as accomplishing great things. His actual performance, though not failing, is far from his fantasy of what he perceived himself able to do, and instead of being able to look at his own failings, his own inadequacies, he begins, in his mind, to place the blame on his relatively blameless family and then begins to entertain a very sick, crazy idea that if they were out of the picture, somehow his problem would be solved, and in the course of this kind of sick brooding and rumination, straps on a pistol, picks up a rifle, in a way that's almost like the behavior of a child, and then shoots in a way that overkills the members of his family, without any point, either then or afterwards, with[out] really realizing that this has solved nothing for him.

Q. Now, Doctor, did you at my request read the transcript of Lee Andrews' trial, and are you familiar with the testimony in that case regarding the circumstances under which Lee made a confession or statement to Reverend Dameron and later to the county attorney and the police?

A. Yes.

Q. Now, first, I should like for you to describe Lee's mental condition as it might relate to the giving of a statement involving his own personal criminal liability for a serious offense.

A. Well, here was a young man, or a boy, who, as I have described before, is able to entertain contradictory ideas of all sorts, including love and hate, who needs to think of himself as powerful and controlling, cannot bear the idea that he might have lost control of himself or that he might be sick, who has difficulty in interpersonal relations and getting along with people, so that at times he may be abnormally suspicious or either extremely gullible, an individual who has gotten rid of some of the most important people in his life and yet has a wish somewhere to have attachments with people. I think these were the main points of the examination.

Q. Doctor, in the making of a statement pursuant to the investigation of a crime, what comments, if any, do you have with respect to Lee's capacity to evaluate the importance of such questions from the standpoint of his own self-interest and to make decisions based on his self-interest in response to such questions?

A. His awareness of his own self-interest would be, as a result of his illness, severely disturbed. He would be dominated in part by a delusion that he is all-powerful and that he can't be hurt, and at the same time, if he were to feel that someone had hurt him or tricked him, he would feel that he would have to deny that he had been tricked, but rather that he had wished to do it of his own accord.

Q. Doctor, did you also, at my request, read the text of the confession taken by the county attorney?

A. Yes, I did.

Q. Do you have any comments with respect to the confession, as you recall it, as it might relate to Lee Andrews' mental condition?

A. Yes. In other words, the confession that I read reflected some of his symptomatology in the sense that his apathy or pathological lack of concern for himself reflects itself when he is asked a question, in a kind of perplexed answer or "I don't know" or "Maybe" or "Uh-huh," and then his subsequent willingness to accept someone else's interpretation of what might have been going on in his mind, even though he may have known it was wrong in terms of his own recollection, rather than going to the trouble of correcting the issue. In other words, a kind of passive suggestibility—"They said it was that way. Okay. Let it be that way."—without any awareness that his own self-interest is at stake, or without any substantial awareness. Again, this is a question, not of black and white, but in this case of substantial graying.

Q. Doctor, you have described a boy whose mental illness is characterized, among other things, as I recall your testimony, by blunted emotions, a distorted perception of the world and of customary social and moral values, suffering from dissociation between his thinking and emotions and a pathologically diminished capacity to interrelate with people. Now, the minister Dameron's appeal, if I may call it that, to the boy—I think it was described by Dr. Roth in response to a hypothetical question as an appeal to what he called the more "normal" aspects of Lee's personality, as an attempt to break down his resistance in an insinuating, emotionally appealing way, as opposed to coercion.

Now, Dr. Roth qualified his answers by describing the brevity of his examination, and he was not as familiar as you are with the circumstances under which the questioning of Lee took place by the minister. I would like for you to tell us, Doctor, based upon your knowledge of Lee and your examinations of him and your knowledge of the circumstances under which the confession was taken, of the meaning to Lee Andrews of his minister's presence in the county jail and what effect, if any, the role of the minister, had with regard to Lee's subsequent confession to him and to the county attorney.

A. I think the minister represented to Lee, in spite of—let me rephrase that, Lee had just lost by his own action the three most important people in his life, and although he had to deny that these were important to him, they were, and so, in a way, was the minister who was one of the close friends of the family and had been for many years, and in one sense I think the minister represented some kind of—represented a person, at least, with whom Lee, however distorted his capacity to relate to people was, represented a person with whom he was apt to have some kind of relationship and who, indeed, may have represented to him some tie with the deceased family, so that I would agree in one sense with Dr. Roth that the appeal of the minister was certainly to whatever islands of personality functioning that remained intact, or relatively intact, but the disabilities that were present, in terms of his inability to care about himself, his pathological gullibility, these disabilities prevented him from exercising the normal kind of care and concern about what he would say and much later prevented him from admitting that in any way he felt disappointed or tricked by the action of the minister.

Q. Now, you mentioned, among other things, Doctor, a proneness to accept suggestion, and balanced with that an inability to respond in a self-protective, in a normally self-protective way. Can you conclude from this anything with respect to the possible reliability of statements which might have been made in such a context?

A. I would have to make an educated guess about that, that on the basis of what I have found about Andrews' personality functioning, I don't think that we can place great weight on the reliability of what he said, in this sense: That what is apt to come out would be his distorted image of what he conceived himself to be and to have done, rather than any picture that might represent a more balanced understanding, as, for example, a scientific observer on the scene might have or someone being present at that time. He would need then, as he did throughout the examination with me, to try to maintain that he was powerful and clever, could outwit the police, could outwit me, could outwit anybody, in spite of being confronted with many instances, sometimes small and sometimes big, in which this was not, of course, true.

Q. Doctor, one final question, if I may. In your opinion was Lee Andrews, under the conditions and with the mental illness which you have described, capable of making a voluntary statement?

A. I think that I would have serious doubt about even a normal boy of 18 being able to make a voluntary statement under those conditions of the minister and so forth, but with the added weight of the mental illness that I found in Lowell Lee Andrews there is no doubt in my mind that he was not capable of making a voluntary statement at that time.

Cross-Examination

By Mr. Wells:

Q. Dr. Satten, you have gone over your testimony that you would give here today with Mr. Allen, have you not, sir?

A. I had a conference with him, yes.

Q. If I remember correctly, Doctor, when you testified at the Wyandotte County District Court trial you testified that the petitioner, Lowell Andrews, knew that if he fired bullets into the heart and brain of his mother and his father and his sister that death would ensue, did you, sir?

A. Yes, I testified as to that.

Q. And that when Andrews fired these shots that he knew that it was a gun that he held in his hand, did he not?

A. May I—

Q. Now, will you answer the question, please?

A. I don't know what you mean by the word "know." What definition of "know" are you using?

Q. "Know" is not a psychiatric term, is it, Doctor?

A. "Know" is a word in the English language that has certain technical meanings both in psychiatry and different meanings in the English language.

. . .

Q. Will you state whether or not the petitioner knew that it was a gun in his hand and that he was shooting bullets into the bodies of his mother and father and sister at the time of the slayings?

A. At the risk of repeating what I said at the trial, there are two kinds of knowledge. One is a superficial knowledge that this represents a gun, and the second is the full emotional and rational knowledge of the implications of what one act has in relationship to another act. From the point of view of the superficial meaning of the word "know," limited to simply intellectual awareness, yes, of course, he knew. From the point of view of this second meaning of the word "know" that I have raised, the meaning that some psychiatrists—perhaps not all—use, there is a much deeper meaning to the word "know," and some Courts have recognized this variation in meaning, I understand.

Q. Now, in your opinion, did the petitioner "know" that what he was doing was against the law in that his act could possibly result in the death penalty being imposed on him if he were apprehended for this crime?

A. Did he know at which point? At the time he pulled the trigger?

Q. Yes.

A. At the time he fired the bullet?

Q. Yes.

A. I honestly don't know.

Q. Do you think he knew it back at the time in these preceding months when he was planning the crime? Do you think he knew it then?

A. I think he had some intellectual awareness in that sense of the word, yes. I think he knew that, in the sense of some superficial knowledge, somewhere, some place there was a death penalty, but at the same time he had the delusional idea: (1) That he was above all this; and (2) that somehow he would never be caught, and if he were caught, nothing would happen, and if it did happen, it wouldn't make any difference.

Q. You have examined the x-rays and the blood tests and encephalogram and so forth that were taken there at your clinic in Topeka, have you not?

A. Yes.

Q. And were the findings on these tests normal?

A. Yes, they were. I tried to say that the kind of illness that he is suffering from is predominantly a mental one with no associated organic findings. This is one of the cardinal points in making a diagnosis of schizophrenic reaction, that there is no organic brain damage.

Q. Dr. Satten, did Andrews tell you about these other plans that he had gone over in his mind some months before he actually committed these murders as to the possibility of him using poison to kill his mother and father and his sister?

A. Well, I wouldn't call them plans. He described to me peculiar brooding ruminations, but I don't know that I would honor them by giving them that quality of thinking that is necessary to call something a plan. But, yes, he did tell me of thoughts that he had had about differing kinds of ways of solving his problem, quote unquote.

Q. One of them was by using poison?

A. That's one of the thoughts that had crossed his mind.

Q. And he discarded that because of the fact if all the rest of his family was poisoned and he was not, that the finger of suspicion would point to him?

A. I am not sure that's why he discarded it. That's ascribing to his thinking a kind of rational quality that I don't think he is capable of, because the same finger of suspicion would point to him with death by another source.

Q. Is that what he told you, though, Doctor?

A. No, it is not what he told me. I can't create the precise words, but I can give the image of the kind of examination it was. Basically, what he said was, "I had thoughts like these: poison occurred to me." Something else, "Fire occurred to me." And then he tried to, in retrospect, figure out why he had done what he did.

Q. Did he also tell you, Doctor, that he had planned to kill his family and then burn the house down, and he had discarded that plan, too?

A. No. Again, I must say you are trying to ascribe to him a kind of logical thinking. All these thoughts from time to time existed in his mind in a kind of melange, sometimes logically related and sometimes illogically related to each other. These thoughts from time to time were present, yes, but I can't say on the basis of examination that they were in the nature of logical connections, or that one was discarded or one was not discarded on the basis of logical considerations. I failed to find much logic in what he did with reference to his mother, father, and sister.

Q. He did discard these other plans because they were impractical, though?

A. Well, I didn't think the one that he picked was any more practical.

Q. Did he tell you, Doctor, that he had finally decided to shoot his parents and sister and then make it appear that a burglary had occurred there so that he could mask this crime?

A. No; he didn't put it that way. That, again, is giving it a quality of logical thinking.

Q. Did he tell you, Doctor, about having pulled the things out of drawers in the house and thrown them around on the bed and the floor and taking the screen off a window and opening the window to make it appear like an outsider had come in the house and been caught in the perpetration of a burglary and these murders had ensued?

A. I can answer yes to the first half of your question. He told me about doing these things.

Q. Did he tell you why he did them?

A. No. This was the interesting thing about the examination. Constantly I tried to get from him some answers as to why he did what he did or why he thought what he did, and his response was usually a kind of perplexity or "I am not sure," or "I don't know," and it was very easy for me to suggest some kind of logical connection because he would immediately grasp it and say, "That's it." Then I would ask him, "Now, was this really in your mind?" And he would say, "No."

Q. Did he ever tell you that he wanted you to testify that he was insane?

A. No.

Q. He never did say that or indicate to you that he wanted you to testify that he was insane at the time of the murders?

A. He did not. Now, I discussed the question of my testifying with him, and his answer was in the nature of "If you do it, it isn't really because I want you to but because somebody else thinks it may be helpful to me."

Q. Didn't he tell you that his great mistake was in underestimating the ability of the police department to solve this crime?

A. I don't remember his making that statement. The closest he came to telling me what his great mistake was, was in thinking that he could—his great mistake, he felt (to the extent that he could allow himself to consider that he made a mistake)—his great mistake, he felt, was feeling that he couldn't leave home and get away from the domination, from what he felt was the domination of his parents, without having to kill them. That was the closest that he would admit to making a mistake of any sort.

Q. Did he tell you about disassembling these guns and throwing them over the bridge at Lawrence at the swiftest point in the river in order to get rid of the evidence of the crime?

A. He told me about that, yes, sir.

Q. Wouldn't that indicate to you that was good planning and good thinking?

A. It was good planning for getting rid of the guns. The point about mental illness is not that it is an all-or-none phenomenon. Certain isolated parts of functioning can be present, and there are many, many mental patients, for example, in the criminally insane ward at Larned that can do a lot of scheming and planning that holds together up to a certain point.

Q. Didn't the petitioner tell you that he made it a point to get out of the car there in the filling station on his way back to Lawrence in his shirt sleeves and talk to the attendant there in the gas station in this freezing weather so that he would make an impression on that attendant and he would remember he was in Lawrence at that particular time on the evening of the murders?

A. I don't remember his telling me exactly that, but he was trying to make a big point of showing me how clever he was; he was really doing all he could to show me that.

Q. Didn't he tell you that he had made a particular point to talk to his landlady in the rooming house so that she would remember that he was there at the particular time on that evening?

A. I think he did, yes.

MR. ALLEN: Your Honor, if I may again interpose an objection. Counsel was so gracious to me I don't like to interrupt, but this series of questions, "Didn't he tell you?" in which counsel is now reciting all

of the evidence at the trial seems a little bit remote from the point under inquiry here. If counsel is going to go through the transcript, page by page, with "Didn't he tell you?". . .

MR. WELLS: We have been doing this, Your Honor, for two days—the day we were up here before and today—and actually I think if we examine the record and the testimony of the doctor today, that there are some conflicts, either in his testimony—I don't know whether he has changed his mind about some of these things, but I think an examination of the record will disclose some discrepancies in the testimony.

THE COURT: You may proceed.

Q. Doctor, you were talking about some incident in response to one of Mr. Allen's questions where the petitioner had a conversation in a rooming house with his roommate concerning a gun; is that correct?

A. Yes.

Q. And, as a matter of fact, he didn't threaten the life of this roommate; he told him to be careful of the gun, that the gun was loaded, and might go off and injure him; isn't that right, as you remember that?

A. No. Here is an instance where, in terms of examining an individual who is mentally ill, one has to be extremely precise. I think, as I testified today, I made the qualification when I spoke of threats; the exact words of the defendant, as I recall, and as reported to me, were, "I could kill you with this gun," that, "I have got nothing against you, or nothing special against you," or something like that. Now, this, in one sense, of course, could be construed as a threat and in another sense it could be construed as saying, "Watch out," but in neither of those two instances does it accurately describe the kind of thinking or kind of interchange that was going on in the defendant's mind at the time.

. . .

Q. Well, now, Dr. Satten, you have seen the confession, have you not, that the petitioner gave to Mr. Foster, the county attorney, after the commission of the crime?

A. I read it in the transcript of the trial.

Q. There is nothing that is not true in the statement so far as you know and so far as the investigation revealed, is there, sir?

A. It depends on what you mean by "true." It creates a certain—the confession, as given, creates a certain picture about the capacity to plan that I don't think Andrews had at that time, and it also is worded in such a way that doesn't represent the state of mind that he was in at the time, but rather represents a kind of feeding to him of a certain picture of what happened, which he then parroted back as patients like this are frequently able to do.

Q. He repeated back the events that transpired in the preceding few hours, did he not, Doctor, so far as you know, and he repeated them back correctly, did he not, sir?

A. It depends on how you define "correctly."

Q. Now, if he wasn't capable of giving you these, or giving the police officers or the county attorney these voluntary statements and telling the truth, was he any more capable of giving you the truth when he made these statements and had these conversations with you in Topeka?

A. Absolutely not. That's the whole point of the psychiatric examination. It doesn't depend on the truth or falsity of the individual statements, but rather on an attempt to evaluate what he is trying to do and the nature of his thinking processes. It is more difficult to do, but a psychiatric examination can be done on somebody who is telling all lies.

Q. You mean that you think you can get at the truth when other persons can't?

A. I didn't say that. I said I think I can get at a description of a person's mental functioning independent of the truth or falsity of the statements that he gives.

Q. Well, do you think that when he made this confession that he knew who Robert Foster was and whether or not he was the county attorney when he was making the confession to him?

A. Before I could answer that I would have to ask you what you mean by the word "know."

Q. Well, do you think that he was aware that Robert Foster was the county attorney when he was asking him these questions concerning the murders?

A. Yes, I do.

. . .

Q. Now, Dr. Satten, are you opposed to the so-called M'Naghten Rule?

A. It presents a certain difficulty in conveying medical findings. I would prefer a rule that would allow the physician to present more of the medical findings for the consideration of the Court and jury. If the M'Naghten Rule were broadened so that the word "know" at least had more of the psychiatric meaning to it, I think one could convey to the jury a good bit of the facts about a defendant. My objection to it is to the way it excludes, I feel, what is perti-

nent information about the defendant from the consideration of the Court and jury.

Q. All right. I have a couple more questions and I'll stop, Doctor. Now, you stated that the petitioner in this case was always a clumsy and awkward boy and he wasn't accepted in high school and he led a rather secluded and withdrawn life; is that right?

A. Relatively speaking. There were attempts that he made to try to mix with people; there were certain areas in which he had some degree of confidence and felt he could be accepted by others. For example, with the band. Things like that. He was struggling, and the balance was not resolved in the direction of illness until sometime, I think, after he was in college.

Q. Now, he was in the band and he was in plays and he was in the Pep Club and he was on the school paper and attended the functions there in the school. That doesn't indicate that he was withdrawn.

A. I think each of the people who saw him in those places noticed a certain peculiarity and withdrawal about him, and it was true he did these things, and they were healthy attempts to break out of the difficulty he was having, but at the same time they failed, in my opinion.

Q. Well, were you aware, sir, that he made some of the highest grades that have ever been made at Washington High School in Wyandotte County?

A. Indeed I was.

Q. Were you arare also, that he was in the upper 25 percent of the class that entered K.U. the year that he started there?

A. Yes. That is a point that I wanted to make, that he did very well in high school while he was able to be home, and he had a high opinion of himself, but under the pressure that was demanded of him in college, his performance began to slip, and while the performance itself was not bad by ordinary or average standards, it was not the previous high level that he had before, and this began, I think, to prey on his mind.

Q. It is not too unusual for a person to make excellent grades in high school and find that when they get to college that a little bit more is expected of them and for their grades to be a little bit lower than they were in high school?

A. You are absolutely right. His reaction to that was a sick reaction. The point is: this is a normal experience for many of the so-called bright kids, geniuses in high school, and part of the normal stress and strain in college which that group of bright kids meet and they have to come to grips with. Some of them will be at the top and some of them would have to fall a little bit below. He couldn't come to grips with this.

Q. He did all right in his first year there, didn't he?

A. I don't know what you mean by "he did all right." He doesn't think he did.

Q. Well, the grades reflect that he did, don't they, Doctor?

A. The grades reflect something that you or I or the average person would consider all right or satisfactory during the first year, and the first part of the second year the grades began to slip even more than they had in the first year, and this represented—this, in a sense, was both a result of the difficulty he was having and then creating a kind of vicious circle which then added to more difficulty.

Q. Didn't he tell you the reason he killed his mother and father and sister was so that he could inherit the farm out there at Wolcott and would be comparatively wealthy, sir?

A. No, this he didn't say. We talked about this, and we talked about the farm and the possibility of his inheriting it, and to the best of my recollection, as I reconstruct the examination, his feelings, in his words, were: "I was aware that there was a farm there, and I was aware that ultimately this might come to me"; but this is as far as the discussion went, as far as he was able to carry it out, and when specifically asked about whether this was a factor in his thinking, his response was, "I don't know." Just "I don't know. I couldn't ignore it." And my opinion, on the basis of the total picture, was that this man has an awareness of things arounds him, but the kind of

impact they have on him is different from the kind of impact these things have on other, normal persons, and he would like for people to think that he is okay, that he is not crazy.

Q. Well, he did tell you, didn't he, Doctor, that he had heard his parents talking about this farm possibly having a potential value of a quarter of a million dollars.

A. No.

Q. Dr. Satten, I will ask you: Are you completely and unequivocally and categorically opposed to capital punishment?

A. I don't know what you mean by "completely"—

Q. Are you opposed to capital punishment?

A. I think capital punishment is the wrong treatment for mental patients.

Q. Are you opposed to capital punishment?

A. Well, I would say that, by and large, I am opposed to capital punishment, yes. I can conceive of certain instances whereby I might not be opposed to it, but by and large—in thinking back in response to your original question—my objection and hesitation was in terms of the complete and unmitigated, etc. I would not take that position about something like capital punishment or anything about which there was a serious disagreement.

MR. WELLS: I have no further questions, Your Honor.

MR. ALLEN: No questions, Your Honor.

THE COURT: You may step down, Doctor. (Witness excused.)

STATE OF KANSAS v. VOLBRECHT

COMMENT

There is no published report of the Volbrecht case. The case was tried without a jury; the court found the defendant legally sane and guilty of robbery and first-degree murder on October 25, 1960, and sentenced him to life imprisonment. The defendant's family, fearing that a retrial might result in a sentence of death, directed defense counsel not to enter an appeal.

The following feature story by reporter Ron Kull of the *Topeka Daily Capital*, dated No-

vember 6, 1960, describes the crime—and the defendent, Pvt. Donald W. Volbrecht, United States Army.

JUNCTION CITY—Toward the end of last July, a pulp magazine called "True Police Cases" appeared on newstands here. In a short time, more than 500 copies were sold. The reason for the popularity of the magazine was obvious: It contained a supposedly factual account of the murder of Anthony Troncone, a Junction City service station attendant, the previous Feb. 6.

In an article entitled "A Sad End for a Gay

G.I.," the magazine told how the murderer, who was ending a love tryst with a "petite brunette companion" who had "shapely nylon-clad legs" . . . "calmly . . . told of having robbed the filling station attendant . . . in order to get money with which to carry on his gay fling with the lovely brunette" and of the subsequent murder. The article generously admits in an agate-print note at the end that some of the names in the story were changed "to protect the actual persons and places involved." But although the article mentions nothing about changing the facts in the case, about the only truth in the article is that Anthony Troncone was robbed and murdered. The rest is bunk. Indeed, Pvt. Donald W. Volbrecht of Cleveland was sentenced to life imprisonment last week for the murder and robbery, but there the similarity ends.

Volbrecht, far from being the "tall, powerfully built young man" mentioned in the magazine article, is somewhat tall—5 feet, 11 inches —but is scarcely powerfully built. He is skinny, pale. He slumps. In Volbrecht's short career in the Army, he said, he could do 15 pushups "with the help of the instructor." "That was when he picked me up by my shirt and lifted me." Volbrecht, according to his statement and statements by his parents, never had a date in his life.

Volbrecht, at 22, has no particular desires. No strong likes or dislikes. Emotionally, he's a near-perfect zero. Two psychiatrists have classified him as a "chronic undifferentiated schizophrenic." Volbrecht admits to being "really mad" only once in his life. That was when he picked up a piece of steel—probably a tire iron—and struck Anthony Troncone on the head 17 times with blows any one of which could have been fatal, a physician later testified.

Why did he do this? "I was just getting homesick, I guess," Volbrecht said.

Volbrecht, who arrived at Ft. Riley in January, was there about three weeks. A week of this was spent in the hospital, undergoing treatment for a strep throat. "When I came out of the hospital I had a whole bunch of stuff piled up and I knew I was going to have inspection the next day." "Besides," he added, "I'd got chewed out by one of the cadre (instructors) because I didn't know the answers to an oral test. He told me I should have known them. I walked into Junction City late at night —or early in the morning—I wasn't paying too much attention. I remember going in the filling station, getting a candy bar, and going in the men's room. But after that, everything happened so fast—I just don't know."

Volbrecht, however, admitted under questioning that he remembered hitting Troncone with what he now says was a tire iron. "I'm not sure I hit him five or six times—or what. I didn't know whether he was dead or not." Was he angry at the time? "Not at him," Volbrecht said. "I was angry about all the things that had been happening to me—going to the hospital, having all that extra work and those tests sprung on me."

After the killing, Volbrecht took a bus to Cleveland and checked into a hotel. He eventually went to his parents' home there. After spending about a month in Cleveland, Volbrecht's parents realized something was wrong, tried to make an appointment with a psychiatrist for him, but later turned him over to military authorities.

Volbrecht expresses neither approval nor disapproval of his imprisonment:

"Do you like it here?" he was asked.

"Not too much."

"Do you dislike it here?"

"No."

"Are you happy?"

"I feel all right."

"Are you sad?"

"No."

"Do you miss your parents?"

"Not too much."

But Volbrecht is more definite on one thing —his sanity. During his trial, one of the principal contentions of the defense was that he didn't know right from wrong at the time the crime was committed, and was therefore legally insane. But Volbrecht, asked whether in his opinion he is insane answered with a firm "No. I act normal, don't I?" Asked whether he'd rather be sent to the Kansas State Penitentiary at Lansing or to the Larned State Hospital, Volbrecht first answered, "I don't know." Then he said, "I'd rather go to Lansing. When I was at Larned I talked to a couple of fellows there. One had been there 25 years, but they wouldn't release him."

EXCERPTS FROM TRIAL TRANSCRIPT

Cross-Examination of Defense Psychiatric Witness by the Prosecutor

Q. Doctor, are you qualified to be a member of the American Psychiatric Association?

A. Yes.

Q. Have you passed the Psychiatric Boards?

A. No.

Q. You say you are in the process of studying at the present time?

A. Yes, residency in psychiatry is sort of a training program, although of course, what I do is see patients all day. . . . I have to spend an hour a week with another psychiatrist, sort of review of the work and go over the problems that I have had and so on, and I see patients all week long. This is what I do.

Q. The other psychiatrist is helping you with your work?

A. What do you mean?

Q. Is he helping you?

DEFENSE COUNSEL: To which we object for the reason it is immaterial whether it helps him or not.

THE COURT: Overruled.

A. Yes, he is of help. That is what he is there for. He is actually in consultant capacity for the work that I do.

Q. Now, I believe you based your opinion on matters other than the examination and your talks with the defendant, is that correct?

A. No, I don't think so.

Q. That is, all you based your decision on in this case is talks with the defendant?

A. And you said "and other examinations."

Q. Did you base your—

A. I based my opinion on talks with the defendant, other laboratory and x-ray tests, as much social history as we could gather, as much record from the court as we could gather, as much material as we could gather.

. . .

Q. Now, was any of this information obtained from his parents?

A. We had some information from his parents.

Q. Did you check that information to determine its validity?

A. Well, no, we got a social history, somebody in Cleveland talked to his parents and we got this material, although I might say that this material only reached Larned after we had had the conference and sent the report back here to the court. You know, they are kinda slow about getting information taken. The examinational findings that I have reported came from the patient, of course.

Q. Then all of this information that you have in the report that you sent back came from the patient himself?

DEFENSE COUNSEL: We object to that as argumentative. He just stated twice that the opposite was the case. He said he based his opinion on the examination of the defendant and then the County Attorney says, "Well, you got a social report," and he says, "Yes, but it didn't arrive until after we had our consultation and had written our report." I think it is argumentative.

PROSECUTOR: I think my question is simple enough.

THE COURT: Objection overruled.

Q. Was all of your report based on your conversation, then, with the defendant?

. . .

A. No, we had ancillary . . . , I mean we knew as much as possible from the court here for example, you know that you sent us as much information as you had.

Q. What was the nature of that information?

A. Well, pretty sparse as I remember it, that he had been charged with murder on a certain date, and that he was coming to trial pretty soon, and his home address, and things of that kind.

. . .

Q. Have you studied any of his confessions before you came here?

A. I read two of the confessions, the one that was made on the tape recorder today, and the one that you read.

Q. It is true, isn't it, Doctor, that you found some of the defendant's statements to be inaccurate?

A. Yes, uh-huh.

. . .

Q. Generally, did you have the opinion that he was telling you the truth?

A. Generally, I think so, yes.

. . .

Q. Have you made any tests of his intelligence?

A. We—I made a clinical estimate of his intelligence.

Q. Is it true, Doctor, that his intelligence is fairly high?

A. Yes, I would say that his intelligence is around the level that would permit him to go to college.

Q. You would say, then, that he had normal intelligence?

A. Yes.

Q. What did you find regarding his vocabulary?

A. Pretty good considering his background and education.

Q. Isn't it true that occasionally normal people have lapses of normal logic and occasionally lose trains of thought?

A. It can happen, yeah.

Q. What did you find regarding his knowledge of current events?

A. It is pretty good. He knew in a general way what was going on.

Q. Isn't it true, Doctor, that you found that he had a fear of being executed in this case?

A. One or two occasions when I talked with the defendant and he became anxious, almost panicky, when we mentioned the possibility—or, he said "execution," this is his word, somebody had told him this.

Q. Did you not notice the defendant bowing his head at times when the confession was read and twitching at certain times in court?

A. I didn't notice it specifically, I wasn't watching it.

DEFENSE COUNSEL: In any case, we object, that is not in evidence.

PROSECUTOR: If it please the Court, he said he observed the defendant in court.

THE COURT: Overruled. The objection is overruled.

A. I wasn't watching the defendant. I was watching during the time they were showing the pictures. I didn't see any reaction to this.

Q. Were you watching at all times?

A. No, I glanced occasionally.

Q. Of course, the normal thing for him to do if he wanted to show that he was in this particular category would be for him to act like he was unconcerned, wouldn't it?

A. Not necessarily. This guy doesn't have any idea about what the normal thing to do to pretend like he is insane.

Q. But he does have a good knowledge of current events?

A. He knows who is running for president. I would assume that he knows what happened in the news yesterday.

Q. And he can separate, can he not, reality from fantasy?

A. As far as his daydreams are concerned, at the time we examined him we felt that he knew where his daydreams left off and where reality took up.

Q. Isn't it actually true that daydreams are rather common in people?

A. I don't know anybody that doesn't daydream.

Q. Isn't it true, Doctor, that the dividing line between people would be the ordinary individual who imagines himself, as, say, catching a big fish or hitting a long baseball and the individual in a mental institution who prances around and calls himself God or Napoleon?

A. What?

Q. Isn't that the difference between the normal person and the person who is psychotic?

A. Not necessarily. On the basis of whether he knows the daydream is a daydream? . . . —a daydream, even the most psychotic people have daydreams and realize that they are daydreams. . . .

Q. But he tends more toward the normal type of daydream, does he not?

A. Well, there is—no, a daydream is a daydream, and the quantity and the use to which the daydream is put is more important than the content of the daydream. In other words, anybody in this courtroom might daydream, but when you begin to prefer to daydream to living out experiences, when you begin to retreat into this world for the gratification that you get rather than going out and mixing it up in the world, this is the point when they become pathological.

Q. Did he tell you about these daydreams?

A. Yes.

Q. Were these some of his statements that you found to be inaccurate?

A. Well, I don't know if they were. There is no way to check that. Maybe they were.

. . .

Q. Isn't it true that everyone to a certain extent relies on their daydreams?

A. People don't rely on them much. Two- or three-year-old kids will rely on them perhaps, but most people don't.

Q. I said to a certain degree.

A. Everbody has daydreams to a certain extent, that is true.

Q. And rely on them to a certain degree?

A. Rely on them for what?

Q. Well, they serve some purpose, don't they?

A. Yeah, a daydream serves the purpose of partial outlet. Now, everybody is probably familiar with sexual daydreams, and maybe more people, more normal people have these than any other because instead of having what you want in the daydream you can drift off and achieve some of these things. Everybody has these but everyone doesn't rely on them.

Q. Now, you would say even in normal people they furnish somewhat of a partial outlet?

A. They can. Not in every person. I know some normal people who are so actually [sic] oriented that they don't actually daydream, and I know other people, so-called normal people, they usually do.

Q. You feel in this individual he does more than normal people?

A. Tremendous amount more. He doesn't exist in a world of reality.

Q. Wouldn't you categorize his daydreaming as a neurosis?

A. No, a neurosis is something else. A neurosis is another sort of configuration of symptom. This guy doesn't—this is not a neurosis.

Q. Why would you say that it is not a neurosis?

A. That daydreams aren't neurosis?

Q. Why would you say that it was not a neurosis?

A. That what was not neurosis?

Q. His daydreams.

A. Well, daydreams is just one of our symptoms. I have already explained it can be a symptom of neurosis. Now a guy has daydreams and this and this and this, then you can say he has a neurosis, but dreams by themselves, even used to a pathological extent, even used to a pathological extent are not a neurosis, don't constitute neurosis in themselves.

Q. Then would you say if he just had—disregarding everything else and he just had this problem with daydreaming, you would say then that it did not constitute a neurosis?

A. No.

Q. Would you say if it was just for the daydreaming and nothing else that that would constitute a psychosis?

A. No.

. . .

Q. Now, the defendant's father testified that the defendant was depressed because he could not find a job. Would you say that was a reaction of a normal individual?

A. I would say that any individual might feel a little depressed if he were looking for a job and wasn't able to find it.

Q. Now, the reactions of a schizophrenic are flattened, are they not?

A. The reactions, what do you mean?

Q. Well, reactions to ordinary daily things that would cause ordinary people to be depressed or have fear, the real things in life.

A. You mean emotional reaction, is that what you are talking about?

Q. Yes are they flattened or dulled?

A. They tend to be, uh-huh.

Q. And you found that the defendant's reactions in such situations were flattened and dulled?

A. In what situations?

Q. In a situation such as the reality of daily living.

A. Yes.

Q. Then would not the fact that the defendant was depressed over his not being able to find a job be contrary to the normal pattern of a schizophrenic?

A. No, no, schizophrenics are subject to depression, to fear, to extreme anger. This is not inconsistent with the emotional blandness we are talking about.

Q. Would it not be inconsistent with the finding that his emotions were flattened or dulled?

A. Not necessarily. The dulling or the blandness in relation to objects, or other people, object relationships, and so on, doesn't—isn't inconsistent with variation or expression of other emotions, and in schizophrenia the emotions are inappropriate frequently although this doesn't mean that there can't be feelings of depression, feelings of fear, feelings of extreme anger.

Q. Well, would the depression over not being able to get a job be inappropriate?

A. Not necessarily, no.

Q. But it would be normal?

A. It might be normal, yes.

. . .

Q. Well, then, Doctor, if it is normal, how can you say it isn't inconsistent with schizophrenia?

. . .

A. Well, because there are times that the reaction of a schizophrenic may appear pretty near to what the normal person—well, I think of one example of a person who wrote about schizophrenics. He described it as an apple that had been chopped in pieces. A normal person is the whole apple. And he described the schizophrenic as an apple chopped up in pieces so that you didn't see a continuity of the personality process, that here and there you see a piece of apple sticking up with the skin over it. This person was writing about psychopathic personalities, and his point in making the analogy is that the skin of the apple is analogous to the normal reactions to people and in this analogy you occasionally see a piece of apple sticking up with a piece of skin still over it but it is not an integrated whole, that here and there are areas of inappropriateness.

Q. I think I understand a little better, Doctor.

A. In fact, there is one sub-classification of schizophrenia which is called schizo-affective schizophrenia, and in this, the picture is like that of a manic-depressive.

Q. Did you find any evidence of the manic-depressive reaction in the defendant?

A. No, huh-uh.

Q. As a matter of fact, you found that his condition was one that was rather unchangeable or static?

A. His condition is relatively chronic.

Q. Remained about the same from day to day, did it not?

A. Pretty much, uh-huh, although as you have pointed out, there were variations in the way that he felt.

Q. As a matter of fact, then, you say that it is possible that he would have a normal reaction to such a matter as not finding a job?

A. Yeah. He might have more than a normal reaction. This is a guy who has always been inadequate in a number of areas and so that finding a job might make him more depressed than a person who has more confidence in himself.

Q. As a matter of fact, he does have a capacity to have normal reactions to daily matters of reality?

A. Reactions that he might have could be those that a normal person might have.

Q. Now, Doctor, did you find any—first of all, will you define a hallucination for us.

A. Well, a hallucination is a false sensory perception.

Q. Did you find that there was any evidence of hallucination in the personality of the defendant?

A. We didn't find any evidence that he has had a hallucinatory experience.

Q. Are not hallucinations common in schizophrenics?

A. Relatively common. They occur in about fifty per cent of people with schizophrenia.

Q. Will you please explain what is meant by the term delusional ideation?

A. A delusion is a false belief. It is really more than a false belief, it is a false—it is a belief in some fact which is not normally held to be truthful by the majority of people in the culture in which the person happens to be living. Many people have a false belief, but if they have a false belief together, we don't call it a false belief.

Q. Did the defendant have any evidence of such a condition?

A. We didn't see anything of this sort, no.

Q. Would not this condition be common in schizophrenics?

A. It is fairly common, yes, uh-huh.

Q. Did you make a determination as to whether or not the defendant was orientated as far as time, place, and person?

A. Yes.

Q. What did you find?

A. I found that he was.

Q. Did you make a determination of whether or not the defendant was aware of what was happening about him?

A. Yes.

Q. Tell the Court what you found.

A. He was pretty well aware of the things that were going on about him at the time that I examined him.

Q. Doctor, did this individual show a radical alteration of speech?

A. Of what?

. . .

Q. Tell the Court what is meant by radical alteration of speech.

A. I never heard of it. It doesn't make any sense to me.

Q. Doctor, are you familiar with this textbook of *Principles of Abnormal Psychology* by Maslow and Mittleman?

A. Huh-uh. I never read it.

Q. Now, there is a reference here to radical alteration of speech. (Handing book to witness.)

A. I will see. (Looking at book handed to him by counsel.)

. . .

A. This is a term I don't use and I don't think is common.

. . .

Q. Would you agree with this interpretation in this book which states "Radical alteration of speech, including the coining of new words, rambling, monosyllables, nonsensical utterances," would you agree with that as radical alteration of speech?

A. I don't use the term and it is not commonly used in psychiatry. This is the first time I have ever heard of it. This is a psychological textbook and I am not familiar with the term. I don't use it now and I don't intend to use it in the future, and I wouldn't—

. . .

Q. Would you agree with this textbook in the statement that this is one of the symptoms that is usually found in schizophrenic reaction?

A. I wouldn't use this term.

Q. Well, you understand what they meant?

A. You are not telling me what you mean, see?

Q. Well, you understand what would be meant by the coining of new words and rambling?

A. Yeah. Okay, the coining of new words, rambling.

Q. Would you agree that this is one of the symptoms usually found in schizophrenics?

A. Not usually the coining of new words. These words that are formed by schizophrenics are called neologisms. They are not commonly found but they are a symptom of schizophrenics. Also the rambling sort of speech, the rambling sort of thought. Speech is just a reflection of thought, and some rambling and disorganization of thought is frequently a symptom of schizophrenia.

Q. This textbook states these symptoms are usually found in schizophrenia. Would you disagree with that?

A. I disagree that they are usually found in schizophrenia. I would say that, oh, maybe 20 per cent of the schizophrenics I have dealt with show this sort of thing.

Q. Did you find any evidence of such a condition in the personality of the defendant?

. . .

A. . . . The defendant's thinking doesn't show any gross disorganization. You can listen to him and the things that he says flow along and are understood; however, there are hints of difficulty such as of blocking, shows at times that he will lose a train of thought, be talking along and if he stops for a moment, he may lose a train of thought or may drift off into another subject. Now, these are sort of precursors of the sort of gross disorganization that many schizophrenics show. This answer your question?

Q. Now, Doctor, you heard his taped confession or admission in court?

A. Yes.

Q. Did you find any evidence in that that he lost his train of thought?

A. No. The tape recordings were interesting. The answers that he made were coherent and organized, but, of course, the type of interview which the Sheriff conducted is what we in psychiatric terms call a highly structured interview. He asked a question that could be answered in one or a number of words. I did notice that the Sheriff, and also in this other confession, they said, "Now tell me in your own words what occurred," and he gave his short choppy sentences, and then the examiner said, "Well, maybe you prefer questions," and he says, "Yes." Now this is the sort of thing we saw at Larned, too. He is not capable of sustained explanations, that his initiative tends to die down. His power of organizing thoughts is not too good but there is no gross disorganization. The answers that he gave are quite coherent. I thought, incidentally, the Sheriff did an excellent job of interviewing as far as the structured interview goes.

. . .

Q. Doctor, in other words, you are talking about rapid-fire questions one after another?

A. Not rapid-fire, but questions which are not open-ended. None of the questions that were asked were open-ended, questions that can be answered on a concrete basis.

Q. Can you tell us what is meant by the term "bizarre thinking"?

A. Well, this is thinking which contains elements which are foreign to most normal thought content, elements which are strange.

Q. They are elements, are they not, that are extremely strange, they are bizarre, isn't that correct?

A. Well, you are using the term to define the term.

Q. All right, did you find any evidence of such a condition in the personality of the defendant?

A. No.

Q. Is not this a common condition of a schizophrenic, or commonly found?

A. It frequently occurs in schizophrenics.

. . .

Q. Would you not say, Doctor, on your determination, that the individual is close to the line between neurosis and psychosis?

A. Not between neurosis and psychosis.

. . .

Q. How many classifications are there of schizophrenics?

A. There is paranoid, catatonic, simple, acute undifferentiated, chronic undifferentiated, schizo-affective. Six.

Q. What about catatonic?

A. I mentioned that, didn't I?

DEFENSE COUNSEL: He did mention it.

Q. Now, a person suffering from a schizophrenic reaction would be classified as a schizophrenic, isn't that right?

A. Yes, uh-huh.

Q. And tell the Court what is meant by a hebephrenic schizophrenic.

A. This is a silly sort of laughing type of schizophrenic, really sort of schizophrenic that to the lay person is considered as one really off, a crazy person . . . may wear bizarre clothing or put on strange makeup or go through strange gestures, frequently hallucinated laugh, giggle sort of silly.

Q. Can you tell the Court what a paranoid schizophrenic is?

A. A paranoid schizophrenic is a person who has sort of the basic elements of schizoprenia plus having a tendency to project feelings of his own out onto other people, a person more likely to feel that others are persecuting him. The "Mad Bomber" in New York was such a person. He might have a high intelligence, considerable ability to organize his thoughts, considerable ability to plan and execute actions, and may have only incapsulated illusional [sic] situations. It varies of course, in paranoid schizophrenia.

Q. Can you tell the court what condition that the defendant has that a simple schizophrenic would not have, if any?

A. Actually, he is fairly close to simple schizophrenia.

Q. Then you can't tell the court anything that he has that a simple schizophrenic wouldn't have?

A. Well, I would stay that the level of intelligent function is higher in the defendant. Simple schizophrenics we think of as a person who has been inadequate most of their lives. Many of the bums you see riding the rails and people like dishwashers who drift from place to place never form relationships with other people, who never have any ambition to plan things of this sort. These are the types that we think of as simple schizophrenics. There was a good simple schizophrenic in John Steinbeck's

"Grapes of Wrath," remember the oldest brother, Joad?

Q. Now, will you tell the court, or will you define a schizoid personality?

A. A schizoid personality is a person who has —who tends to withdraw from contacts with other people, has much the same emotional blandness that we have talked about, who spends much of his time drawn back in a little world of his own, who may—is reluctant to deal with people and may prefer to deal with things than involve himself with any personal relationships.

Q. In other words, it is the type of personality exactly as you have described the defendant, isn't it?

A. The defendant carries many of these, fits quite well into the description of the schizoid personality, but he goes beyond this. In our psychiatric evaluation he goes over the line into the classification we call chronic undifferentiated schizophrenia.

Q. Now, tell the Court how he goes over this particular line.

A. The schizoid personality is frequently able to function much better than the patient in social situations. The schizoid personality doesn't have as severe an emotional disturbance, as great a degree [of] blandness, inappropriateness as the defendant has. The schizoid personality tends to be able to make a better adjustment, and the schizoid personality, last of all would never be capable of breaking out into a ferocious, violent reaction such as this patient.

Q. You say a schizoid would never be capable of breaking out into a violent reaction?

. . .

A. I shouldn't have said that.

Q. I didn't think you should, Doctor. You wish to retract that statement?

A. I will retract it and change it a little bit. You can't say that anyone will never do anything and certainly aggressive outbursts of the uncontrolled type might be seen in a schizoid personality, but something—

Q. And it might be—

DEFENSE COUNSEL: Just a minute, would you let the witness answer your question?

PROSECUTOR: I think he answered.

DEFENSE COUNSEL: I object to counsel in-interrupting the witness.

THE COURT: Sustained.

DEFENSE COUNSEL: Go ahead, Doctor, you were interrupted again. Go ahead and give us your answer.

A. Getting back to the act, this boy has never been able to even talk back to anyone, and for him suddenly to beat someone else to a pulp indicates to me a violent rupture.

Q. Will you explain to the Court how you are able to determine that he has never been able to talk back?

A. Well, in the ward at Larned State Hospital, any matters that were told to him by the patients, by the aides, by myself, he did it submissively. It was at this point that we formed the opinion that he could not adequately express aggressive feeling, and this was corroborated by views from the family. They say the same thing. I can't say that he never did, from my own knowledge, but I say that he didn't at Larned, and I say that the family said that he never had.

Q. Would you like to retract your arbitrary statement that he has never been able to talk back?

DEFENSE COUNSEL: Object to that question, the word "arbitrary."

THE COURT: Sustained. I think he said he wished to modify it a while ago, and I think he did. The objection is sustained.

Q. Would you say that a person suffering from a schizoid personality is psychotic?

A. No.

. . .

Q. Well, Doctor, I will go to another subject. You stated that the defendant had a hatred of his father, is this true?

A. Yes.

Q. Now, is it your opinion that he was basically attacking his father when he committed this offense?

A. I think that unconsciously this certainly played a part in the commission of the offense. I don't think he was aware of this.

Q. Do you think this would have any connection with the fact he talked back to his father in the plumbing incident?

A. The fact that he talked back to his father in the plumbing incident indicated, I think, the strong aggressive feelings in the man were coming closer the surface at that time, which was just prior to his going in the army.

Q. Then he would have the ability to talk back if he did?

A. Yeah, I would say that.

. . .

Q. Do you think that the defendant was acting under the realm of reality when he decided to go AWOL?

A. I think that the decision to go AWOL was a

rational one determined by his strong emotional attachment to the family, and the feelings had been aroused in that by his training.

Q. Do you think that he had an awareness that he was actually going AWOL?

A. Yes, I think so.

Q. Now, you listened to the defendant's statement in court, did you not?

A. Yes.

Q. Do you think that he knew the nature of his thoughts when he decided to take the money while in the service station?

A. I think that he had some awareness of what he was doing.

Q. Now then, Doctor, would the fact that the defendant, if it is a fact, took the keys from the deceased, would that indicate that he had an awareness at that time of his act?

A. Indicates a certain awareness of what is going on. Of course, he carried the keys home with him to Cleveland which sort of goes the other way.

Q. Would you think that act would be odd?

A. No, but it would be inconsistent with good criminality. There is some degree of awareness, but there is some degree of confusion.

Q. Doctor, probably you think if he was thinking well, he would probably have thrown it in the river with the weapon?

A. Well, I don't know.

Q. Well, what do you think he should have done with it, if he was acting as a good criminal should?

A. Well, I think he would have gotten rid of them some way.

Q. Well, actually it would be rather a normal act to the individual to stick the keys in his pocket and walk off with them. Would that not be normal?

A. Well, he was borrowing them or something.

Q. Especially as he was holding a weapon in his hand and tossing it in the river.

A. Doesn't seem normal to me.

Q. Well, to stick keys in your pocket?

A. These keys had grown enormously in importance by the time we are talking about. This isn't a matter of carrying off somebody's cigarette lighter or something like that.

Q. Doctor, in one of the defendant's statements, and in answer to a question, "You said you had no intention of what?" the defendant said, "To kill him or anything like that. I just wanted to take the money and that was all." Now, would this indicate that the defendant had the act of taking the money in his mind at the time that he struck the deceased?

A. It might or might not. I think there was some awareness of this, but I am extremely doubtful as to whether this was—provided the main motivation, the main driving power, for the commission of the crime.

. . .

Q. Well, Doctor, would the fact that the defendant threw the weapon in the river, if he did, would this fact indicate a guilty knowledge?

A. Not necessarily a guilty knowledge.

Q. Would it not indicate an awareness?

. . .

THE WITNESS: . . . I would say the question can't be answered clearly unless you sort of clear up the word "guilty."

Q. You mean you would like to have me define the word "guilty"?

A. I don't understand what you mean by it.

THE COURT: The legal meaning, Doctor, we define guilty as evil intent, if that will help any.

DEFENSE COUNSEL: And an intent which is punishable under the law, I believe, is that correct, Your Honor?

THE COURT: Well, that might be added to it.
PROSECUTOR: I don't think that would fit with guilty knowledge.

DEFENSE COUNSEL: That just shows you why that isn't a fair question. Now, if that isn't an example of an unfair question—

THE COURT: You may proceed with the next question, Mr. Prosecutor.

THE WITNESS: Guilty has a different psychiatric connotation.

Q. Well, would not the fact that he had thrown a weapon in the river tend to indicate that he had an awareness that he had committed a wrong act?

A. There is some degree of awareness in this.

Q. Doctor, in the defendant's statement in answer to this question, which I quote, "Donald, when you struck this man, what was your intention? Actually why did you hit him?" and the answer to this was, and I quote, "I guess he surprised me, I mean I had no intention of killing him or anything like that, I just wanted to get away, and I just needed the money." Now, would this answer indicate that he had an awareness of the act?

. . .

A. This statement begins with "I guess" which indicates to me that the patient may be applying some rational idea or be trying to explain why it was that he did this at the time he did it, and I don't necessarily feel that he means—

Q. I am sorry, I didn't read that too clearly. He doesn't exactly start off that way, "I guess, comma, he surprised me. . . ." That is the end of the question [*sic*], "I guess he surprised me."

. . .

A. Well, why doesn't he know whether the guy surprised him or not? This is the most important event in this man's life, why would —(interrupts self)

. . .

Q. Doctor, did you not, in a telephone conversation on October 22, 1960, state that the defendant had some awareness of what he was doing when he threw the weapon in the river?

A. Yes.

Q. During that same conversation, did you not tell me . . . in answer to a question, and I quote the question, "Based on what you now know as an expert, are you in a position to state whether or not the defendant knew right from wrong at the time of the offense?" and did you not reply at that time that "I would not make a categorical statement that he did not know right from wrong." Is that not correct, Doctor?

A. I don't remember my replies verbatim, but I would say that that is consistent with the spirit of what I told you.

PROSECUTOR: No further questions.

. . .

Recross Examination

Q. Doctor, in this brutal beating, do you feel that this defendant was taking his anger out on this individual, I believe you said that he was acting in anger?

A. It wasn't so much conscious taking out of anger as an explosion of a lot of feelings that had been building up.

Q. He was taking them out on this individual?

A. Taking out implies that he consciously did this and I don't think that he was, but I saw it was an explosion rather than a taking out.

Q. Do you feel that he had an awareness of the situation but did not have the will power to resist the act, is that correct?

A. I feel that he had some awareness of the situation but that no rational processes were operating in his mind.

Q. Now, then, Doctor, you said that you placed a great deal of significance on the killing itself. Now, would it not be true that you would not have classified this individual as a schizophrenic had you not known of the killing?

A. It certainly would not. I would call this man a chronic undifferentiated schizophrenic if he had been admitted to Larned for any other reason. I would like for this to be clear if nothing else is.

Q. Then how did you place such great significance on the killing?

DEFENSE COUNSEL: Object to that as argumentative. I don't think he said that. He said it is considered.

THE COURT: Well, it is argumentative and the objection is sustained.

PROSECUTOR: No further questions.

QUESTIONS FOR DISCUSSION

1. In the first series of questions (down to defense counsel's interjection), the prosecutor is clearly attacking the witness' qualifications: not directly, but by subtly suggesting that the doctor is really "only a student," who cannot even be trusted to treat patients on his own. How might defense counsel have guarded against this attack on his witness's credentials?

The transcript excerpt is not presented as a model of effective cross-examination technique. Indeed, it is somewhat atypical, since the case was not tried to a jury. Rather, it is presented because it illustrates in fairly concise fashion many of the more frequently encountered lines of attack employed against a psychiatrist testifying for the defense in a capital case. R.C.A.

2. The doctor notes in one of his answers that laboratory and x-ray tests were made. The prosecutor is aware that there were no demonstrable organic signs of the defendant's illness. How might he have pursued the witness' reference to such tests had the case been tried to a jury? How should the matter of negative test findings be handled on direct examination by defense counsel; or should they be referred to at all?

3. Note the recurrence in the prosecutor's questioning of the theme: "Then all you did was talk with him." Assuming that defense counsel had his witness prepare a brief lecture on the nature and significance of clinical interviewing which would be given as a part of his direct testimony, the jury would not be left with the impression that the witness' opinion is based merely on a "chat" he had with the defendant. But note the subtlety of the question, "Generally, did you have the opinion that he was telling you the truth?" which is of the genre of "Have you stopped beating your wife?" Had the case been tried to a jury, the prosecutor might have followed up the witness' affirmative answer with: "Then you believe just about everything he told you?" (leaving the jury with impression that the psychiatrist's answer betrays an astonishing naïveté); or "You didn't try to verify the things he told you, did you?" (which entails a certain amount of risk for the prosecutor, since the psychiatrist may well have obtained factual information from other sources; but the prosecutor holds in reserve the question, "Wouldn't you say a man on trial for his life has some motivation to lie?"). If the psychiatrist answers "No" to the first question, the prosecutor hopes to reap the benefit of its "tails you lose" aspect; viz., that the jury must conclude: first, that the defendant is so confirmed a liar and a fraud that he would seek to mislead the doctor hired to help him "avoid punishment"; and, more importantly, that a tissue of lies is not a very firm basis for a psychiatric judgment. What, if anything, can defense counsel do in preparing his witness for trial to guard against the damaging effect of the "Did you think he was telling you the truth?" technique in cross-examination?

4. The defense has never contended that the defendant was mentally retarded. Why then the series of questions about intelligence testing? Do you see any relationship to the questions much later in the examination about defendant's "knowledge" and "awareness" of what he was doing at each point in his commission of the alleged offense? Can anything be done in a M'Naghten state to convey to the jury that "knowledge" and "awareness" mean more than mere intellectual comprehension?

Compare this witness' testimony with that of the psychiatrist in the Andrews case vis-à-vis "knowledge" and "awareness."

5. An affirmative answer to the question "Isn't it true, Doctor, that you found that he had a fear of being executed?" makes at least three significant points for the prosecution: (1) it seems to show that the defendant was in good contact with reality; (2) fear is certainly an appropriate emotional response to being on trial for one's life—hence, it seems to militate against the psychiatrist's finding of "blandness" and "inappropriate affect"; and (3) it makes again the point that the defendant had good reason for feigning insanity. Note how quickly the prosecutor injects another question when the psychiatrist's response seems to be tending toward an affirmative answer (and incidentally, the prosecutor gets in a bit of testimony himself). Should defense counsel go back over this point in redirect?

6. Note the frequent repetition of the word "normal" in the prosecutor's questions. This semantical characterization is followed at a number of points in the remainder of the examination by more pointed efforts to equate defendant's symptoms with "normal" behavior. Note also the artfulness of the following question: "Of course, the normal thing for him to do if he wanted to show that he was in this particular category [i.e., insane] would be for him to act like he was unconcerned, wouldn't it?" Here again the cross-examiner feels that he cannot lose: if the psychiatrist agrees, then a symptom of schizophrenia is conceded to be at the same time "normal" behavior under the circumstances; if the psychiatrist disagrees, his answer is contrary to the widely held assumption that feigning mental illness is a fairly common ploy in criminal cases. What do you think of the psychiatrist's answer to the question? How else might he have answered it?

7. Again, the question "Isn't it actually true that daydreams are rather common in people?" is a variation on the theme that the defendant was really pretty "normal" after all. How should the psychiatrist respond to a question that isolates a symptom, omits any reference to its persistence or severity, or to the fact that it was but a part of a total observed pattern of response, and then asks whether it is not true that "normal" people exhibit similar behavior (e.g., "Are all people who are a little introverted or shy mentally ill?" "We all get a little depressed at times, don't we, Doctor?" etc.)?

8. The question "Wouldn't you categorize his daydreaming as a neurosis?" is a rather clumsy attempt to confuse the witness and the jury with nosological labels, and perhaps to convince the jury that the dividing line between

neurosis and psychosis is hazy and that the diagnosis could have gone either way. More often, especially where there is conflicting psychiatric testimony, the questioner will attempt to obscure the distinction between schizophrenia and schizoid personality (see question 14). How can the lawyer avoid being led into a semantical cul-de-sac in which the dispute over labels obscures for the jury the significance of the substance of the illness seen? Suppose the defense counsel in the Volbrecht case were confronted with a prosecution psychiatrist who insisted that the defendant had a "personality disorder" and not a psychosis? How should he construct his cross-examination?

9. The question "Would you say if it was just for the daydreaming and nothing else that that would constitute a psychosis?" is another illustration of the isolation of a single symptom. How should the psychiatrist be prepared to answer such a question?

10. The question about daydreaming is followed by the first concerted attack on the psychiatrist's finding of blandness in the defendant. The prosecutor's reasoning goes something like this: (1) Isn't the defendant's unhappiness (note here the questioner's colloquial use of the term "depressed" and the doctor's assent to such use in his answer) over not finding a job a "normal" reaction? (2) If it would be "normal" to experience such an emotional reaction, then a schizophrenic could not experience it. Indeed, the prosecutor asks the witness: "Would it [being "depressed" about not finding a job] not be inconsistent with the finding that his emotions were flattened or dulled?" He reasons that if the witness answers "No" he thereby obscures the relevancy of flattened affect, and if he answers "Yes" he casts doubt on his diagnosis of schizophrenia. What do you think of the witness' response?

11. The cross-examiner continues to pursue the witness on the thesis that if the defendant experienced a reaction that "normal" people can experience, then the defendant must himself be "normal" (how can you be "crazy" and "normal" at the same time?), and the psychiatrist feels impelled to draw an analogy. The analogy, of the schizophrenic to a piece of an apple that yet has a portion of its skin intact, was rather obviously one which occurred to the good doctor on the spur of the moment and had not been carefully thought out beforehand. Tone of voice, unfortunately, cannot be recreated; but it seems probable that the prosecutor's "I think I understand a little better, Doctor," was perceived by everyone in the courtroom—except the witness—as irony. The witness, however, accepts it as approval, and

goes on further to educate the lawyer: "In fact, there is one sub-classification of schizophrenia which is called schizo-affective schizophrenia, and in this picture is like that of a manic-depressive"; and the cross-examiner promptly makes him regret it. What does this interlude suggest about preparing one's witness to meet the rigors of cross-examination?

12. What is the purpose of the series of questions about textbook symptoms which the defendant did *not* have (hallucinations, delusions, disorientation as to time, place, and person, "radical alteration of speech," "bizarre thinking")? How might defense counsel proceed on redirect to correct any false impressions these questions may have left with the jury?

13. The prosecutor succeeds in ruffling the witness' composure with a series of questions based on a psychology textbook definition of "radical alteration of speech." What, if anything, would you have done at this point if you had been defense counsel?

14. In the next series of questions, the cross-examiner returns to his confusion-of-labels ploy (simple, hebephrenic, and paranoid schizophrenia; schizoid personality vs. schizophrenia [see question 8]). Probably because the nosological categories are imprecise and overlapping, the psychiatrist succumbs to the temptation on two occasions to overstate the case: viz., "the schizoid personality . . . would never be capable of breaking out in a ferocious violent action such as this patient"; and "this boy has never been able to even talk back to anyone." As to the latter statement, although it does not appear in the portion of the transcript here excerpted, there was evidence—unknown to the psychiatrist—that the defendant had had a vigorous argument with another soldier several weeks prior to the incident at the filling station. Why does not the prosecutor confront the witness with this piece of evidence in his cross-examination?

15. In the next series of questions, the prosecutor isolates minute steps in the behavioral sequence, asking the witness repeatedly: "Did he know what he was doing at that point?" This is a frequently employed technique in cross-examining the psychiatric expert: it provides an opportunity for the questioner to re-emphasize for the jury each of the factual events of the crime; by compelling the psychiatrist to evaluate each physical act in isolation and not as a total pattern of behavior, it often elicits responses indicating "knowledge" or "awareness," which responses it is hoped the jury will have in mind when they are instructed under the M'Naghten rule; and finally, it

drives the point home that the act was planned (premeditation) and that the defendant sought to avoid arrest ("knowledge that he was doing what was wrong"). How might defense counsel counter this line of attack?

16. A fundamental rule of cross-examination is to know when to quit. How many instances can you find in which the prosecutor asked the proverbial "one question too many" and got an answer he didn't want?

17. Another rule of cross-examination is to end on a high point. Note the last question posed to the witness in the cross-examination in chief (which the prosecutor saved for this purpose). How might the witness have been rehabilitated on redirect?

SOME OBSERVATIONS ON THE PROBLEMS OF THE FORENSIC PSYCHIATRIST

Leigh M. Roberts, M.D.

The professions of law and psychiatry currently interact with greater intensity and frequency than at any prior point in time. The opinion of the psychiatrist may be sought in widely ranging legal areas. He may become concerned with civil cases involving personal injuries, wills, contracts, deeds, annulments, divorce, guardianship, and commitment to mental institutions. The psychiatrist's opinion is also crucial in criminal cases involving the alleged offender's mental state at the time of trial and at the time of the commission of the alleged offense. His recommendations are sought regarding the possible rehabilitation of a criminal offender. Furthermore, juvenile delinquents and sex offenders are often referred for diagnosis or treatment.

Yet the professions of psychiatry and law frequently engage in vitriolic exchanges involving matters of mutual concern. The issues which have developed involve differences in theory, values, and practices. It is evident that although some significant issues remain unresolved between the two professions, many relatively minor differences are magnified in the heated debates. There is no doubt that basic methods of cooperation must be evolved if the needs of society are to be served.

It is my belief that points of misunderstanding between the two professions may be more easily eliminated once these problems are comprehended. First, the areas of conflict will be examined. Then a functional approach to the solution of some existing problems will be offered. Finally, some of the areas of current debate will be presented, in an attempt to clarify the issues or to propose solutions to these more specific problems.

Numerous problems are present for the psychiatrist as he deals with the legal profession. Some of these are caused primarily by the psychiatrist. For example, frequently minimal psychiatric evaluation is presented as a full evaluation, or less than optimally competent psychiatric practitioners are selected to work with attorneys. There may be a failure in active cooperation by the psychiatrist or he may expect remarkably high remuneration for his forensic psychiatric services. Many psychiatrists try to avoid dealing with legal problems, and others participate as partisan advocates to the point they become poor witnesses. A general emotional flavor of hostility toward lawyers is held by some psychiatrists. These concerns create difficulties for the legal profession, but there are many other areas that create difficulties for the psychiatrist.

THE ADVERSARY SYSTEM

There are occasions when the attorney seeks to make the psychiatrist a partisan witness for his client. While such an approach is part of the adversary system, it is a type of approach that psychiatrists may not understand. The adversary approach may well lead to a "battle of psychiatric experts." This may lead to expression of lack of respect by fellow physicians and even public abuse. A good example

Wisconsin Law Review (Spring 1965): 240–67; reprinted with permission.

of such abuse is seen when a psychiatrist testifies in a proceeding involving a brutal crime. The public usually demands punishment for such offenders, and a verdict of not guilty by reason of insanity is subject to extreme public criticism.

More importantly, the psychiatrist may not understand the adversary system of justice itself. To him the courtroom battle may appear only to obstruct justice. A source of this confusion is the various rules of procedure and evidence, such as, for example, the hearsay exclusionary rule. These rules seem only to obstruct the search for truth in the psychiatrist's eyes. Furthermore, many psychiatrists object to substantive rules of law which they feel do not accurately reflect advances made in the field of psychiatry. An example of this is the current debate involving the *correct* definition of "legal insanity."

THE UNFAVORABLE APPEAL OF FORENSIC PSYCHIATRY

One of the most significant limitations of current psychiatric practice is that relatively few psychiatrists are willing to participate in medical-legal problems.[1] This is demonstrated when many of the most highly respected psychiatrists refuse to testify in court. Forensic psychiatry is therefore left to less qualified psychiatrists by default. This is particularly unfortunate at a time when psychiatric testimony is more in demand than ever before.[2]

Part of the problem stems from the psychiatrist's current position in society. The possible areas of involvement for the psychiatrist are vast, with great public and private demands for mental health information and care. This places the psychiatrist in the privileged position of being in a "seller's market." Thus he is able to select those aspects of psychiatric practice in which he wishes to engage. He selects those patients with whom he chooses to work and avoids those who are less rewarding, often in terms of emotional and monetary satisfaction. He is able to work in conjunction with large public mental hospitals or to establish a private practice. He participates in those professional activities which he enjoys and which reward him, while abstaining from pursuits which he feels make less suitable use of his skills or which are substantially unpleasant in their conduct.

These are some of the aspects of the professional seller's market in which the psychiatrist finds himself. All of this does not mean that the psychiatrist does not donate substantial skills, energy, and time to the betterment of society, with minimal or no economic compensation. It has meant, however, that up to this point a majority of psychiatrists have had relatively minimal contact with legal-psychiatric problems.

Some of the reasons for this lack of involvement, such as personal abuse and public criticism, have previously been noted. Yet there are additional reasons. It is difficult for the psychiatrist to schedule his time for courtroom testimony. Such testimony is a time-consuming process and, additionally, must be fitted into the total proceedings of the trial rather than being primarily for the convenience of the physician. The relatively low compensation for his time in legal proceedings also takes a psychiatrist away from legal-medical work. Equally important is his rather poor relationship with the legal profession. The association of some members of the legal profession with unfounded malpractice claims has caused, in part, this poor relationship.

Yet, the major threat posed by the legal system to the psychiatrist is his imagined loss of dignity and status if he testifies in court. This stereotyped picture finds him in the midst of a dramatic criminal trial.[3] He visualizes himself as the victim of sharp-tongued lawyers who distort his testimony. He envisions the rapture of a hostile gathering of judge, attorneys, jurors, press, spectators, and the community at large. The distortion in such a view is, of course, obvious. Yet the psychiatrist is driven away from legal involvement to the extent that he believes in the truth of this stereotype.

The courtroom or the attorney's office is therefore viewed as a place of uneasiness and unfamiliarity by the psychiatrist. The legal proceedings do not prove accommodating to the psychiatrist, quite in contrast to his position of status and prominence. He greatly prefers the customary work setting of the office, hospital, or agency in which he determines events in his own way. He finds it particularly difficult to accustom himself to being dealt with as an adversary in cross-examination and to being cut off in presentation of testimony he believes essential to presenting a relatively complete picture of an individual. It is hard

---

[1] Watson, "Communication between Psychiatrists and Lawyers," *International Psychiatry Clinics*, 1 (1964): 186.

[2] Cf. Oleck, "A Cure for Doctor-Lawyer Frictions," *Clev.-Mar. L. Rev.*, 7 (1958): 473, 474.

[3] Dr. Watson verbalizes this view in a dramatic manner: "When most psychiatrists contemplate communicating with lawyers, they visualize the witness stand—which in their fantasies appears to have been wired for execution, or, at least, torture." Watson, "Communication between Psychiatrists and Lawyers," p. 193.

for him to repress data he is never asked to reveal and to have questions phrased for him in ways which are poorly translatable into his own technical jargon.

There is no easy solution to this problem. But it is safe to say that as long as a psychiatrist feels abuses he will continue to avoid legal-medical involvements. Yet is is certain that a clearer understanding of his function may eliminate this and many of the other problems outlined above.

An Approach to Solving the Problems of Conflict

Psychiatrists misunderstand how the legal system works, and their role in it. And this is compounded because lawyers fail to realize that psychiatrists so misunderstand, and thus do nothing to eliminate this lack of understanding. Conflicts are increased in proportion to the degree of this mutual misunderstanding. What I offer here is a practical and realistic approach to the solution of many of these problems.

The Training of the Psychiatrist

It is essential for lawyers to recognize how much they may rely upon a psychiatrist's advice and conclusions. Correlatively, it is important for psychiatrists to understand how far they may go in giving such advice and stating such conclusions. I believe that this understanding may be furthered by a discussion of the kind of training a psychiatrist receives, for this training shapes to a great extent the psychiatrist's views.

The psychiatrist emerges in his professional role as the product of two differing types of professional education. He first enters medical school with a background of pre-medical college preparation. At this point his primary assets are a high level of intelligence and a motivation to be of service to fellow human beings.[4] He also brings with him a background of personal life experiences and values. Then for four years he is molded by a concentrated curriculum of basic science and clinical experience with medical disease entities.

Following completion of medical school, the physician enters a period of internship in a hospital. It is only after completion of this training that he enters the three-or-more-year period of training to become a psychiatrist.

[4] American Psychiatric Association, *Psychiatry and Medical Education*, Vol. II (1952).

Further training may be taken in an institute for psychoanalysis or in specialized areas such as community psychiatry, child psychiatry, psychiatric research, or crime and delinquency. It should be noted that a major transition occurs from the scientific orientation of the physician in medical school to the more humanistic orientation in specialized psychiatric training.

The training patterns are of relatively recent origin. Medical schools have shifted markedly within the past half century, and the present model of psychiatric residency training programs dates back only three decades. Major current trends in psychiatric orientation are dynamic psychiatry and community psychiatry.[5] Dynamic psychiatry has emerged as a synthesis of psychoanalysis and psychobiology. Community psychiatry has provided an extension of psychiatric services into smaller urban and rural areas. It has resulted in availability of psychiatrists to a greater extent for legal problems in such areas than has ever been true in the past.

The core of clinical psychiatry is the doctor-patient interaction. In that relationship the psychiatrist comes to intimately know, understand, accept, and treat the individual who has come to him. This one-to-one treatment relationship is the central area of psychiatric practice and is the place in which the psychiatrist is most uniquely expert. A psychiatrist has a degree of expertness which is substantial in the clinical evaluation of individuals and their treatment, in the treatment of groups of emotionally disturbed persons, in the understanding of individual human behavior and its motivations, and, further, in the conscious and unconscious processes and related human problems.

It is important for the lawyer to remember

[5] Dynamic psychiatry is concerned with the multiple interacting mental forces which result in human behavior, thought, and emotion. Treatment is based on modifying these factors to reduce symptoms of a mentally disordered individual (Hinsie and Campbell, *Psychiatric Dictionary* [3d ed., 1960]).

Community psychiatry is a newly emerging type of psychiatric theory and practice. It is defined in several ways by different psychiatrists. A common definition states that it provides for prevention, recognition, treatment, and rehabilitation of the mentally ill and emotionally troubled in a given population. The development of positive mental health, as defined by Jahoda, within that given population, is another aspect of community psychiatry. Jahoda, *Current Concepts of Positive Mental Health* (1958). See also Roberts, Halleck, and Loeb, eds., *Community Psychiatry: What It Is and What It Isn't* (1965).

Psychobiology is the study of the functioning of the mind and the behavior of a person in relation to his environment.

that the psychiatrist is on less firm ground when he moves farther afield from the clinical setting, such as when he is asked to diagnose society's problems or when he is asked to apply his knowledge to more hypothetical questions. In these areas his knowledge and competence should be demonstrated before they are given automatic recognition.

The Selection of the Psychiatrist and the Pre-Examination Conference

Some of the lawyer's problems may be solved by trying to retain a psychiatrist who already understands the problems of the legal system. The lawyer should make a preliminary investigation of available psychiatrists. After he has several, tentatively, he should arrange a conference with each of them. This conference serves two purposes. First, the attorney can explain many of the problem areas of the law to the psychiatrist. This, as I have stated before, should go a long way toward solving problems. Secondly, the way that the psychiatrist responds to the attorney's explanation will help the attorney decide if he should employ the psychiatrist. One point should be emphasized here. The attorney's needs for a psychiatrist are, in many cases, two-fold: he must select a psychiatrist who is competent to evaluate his client, and one who is qualified to offer supporting testimony in court.

Certain criteria are helpful in the selection of an expert:[6]

1. Membership in local and national professional organizations—American Psychiatric Association, American Medical Association.

2. Certification by the professional specialty organization—American Board of Psychiatry and Neurology.

3. Academic sources of information regarding the specialty, such as the nearest university medical school department of psychiatry. Assistance may be obtained from such faculty members; at least information may be obtained from them regarding competent professionals in the area of forensic psychiatry.

The forensic psychiatrist who may be best suited for the attorney's purpose is one who rates well in the opinion of his professional colleagues, is a member of the national professional organization,[7] and has a number of publications in his field.

Once the psychiatrist is selected, the attorney should arrange a conference with him before he examines the client. It should begin with an explanation of the legal procedures which will be followed in the case. The role of the judge and the jury should be clearly explained to the psychiatrist. Relevant substantive law ought to be explained. For example, the distinction between mental illness and legal insanity should be clarified.[8] It must be made clear that the psychiatrist's testimony will be considered in relation to legal, and not medical, standards.

I have said before that the adversary system is perhaps the most confusing aspect of the legal process for the psychiatrist. It would be well for the lawyer to explain in great detail the aspects of the adversary system. The attorney should point out that the power of the state can only be exerted within clearly defined legal limits and procedures. This includes the right of each of the parties to challenge the evidence and the witnesses testifying against him and to introduce counter-evidence and witnesses. The attorney should try to clarify the reasons for this procedure. While many psychiatrists may not agree, at least they will understand, and through understanding they may be able to cooperate more effectively.

Relevant rules of evidence must also be explained to the psychiatrist at the pre-examination conference. In particular, the requirements of the hearsay rule should be carefully explained. Legal problems involving the hearsay rule require close cooperation between the two professions, and it is absolutely necessary that the psychiatrist be aware of the problems before the examination of the client is undertaken.

The attorney should also tell the psychiatrist exactly what is required from the evaluation— the psychiatric process is multi-faceted and can accomplish a number of different things. The nature of the particular legal problem, the

[7] The type of membership in the American Psychiatric Association, the major national professional organization for psychiatrists, is one useful criterion for the attorney in selecting a psychiatrist. Particular qualification standards must be met to achieve membership in this organization. Full membership is given only to psychiatrists who have three years of training or experience. Fellowship is bestowed upon members with outstanding contributions in particular areas of psychiatric practice. The bibliographic directory of the APA provides further useful preliminary data on which to base a decision to engage a particular psychiatrist.

[8] See generally, Stein, "Mental Competency and the Law," *Med. Trial Tech. Q.*, 10 (1964): 155.

[6] See generally, Davies, "Finding an Expert in the Sciences," *Clev.-Mar. L. Rev.*, 13 (1964): 309.

legal standards involved, and the specific questions for which answers are required help to determine the information the psychiatrist will try to obtain.

The following situations are illustrative of the type of legal problems which the psychiatrist may be asked to help solve. In each instance the types of questions to be answered by the psychiatrist should be presented to him in advance of the examination and related to the prevailing legal standards pertinent in the particular situation.

In a criminal case the opinion of the psychiatrist may be sought with respect to issues of the defendant's ability to stand trial; the presence of a mental disorder and its nature, both currently and at the time of the alleged offense; the degree of danger of the individual to himself or others; the relationship of a mental disorder to the alleged offense; the possible benefit from available psychiatric therapy; and the predicted effect of incarceration on the alleged offender. With respect to alleged sex offenders the presence of a mental disorder and its nature, the relationship of the disorder to the alleged offense, the danger to others posed by the alleged offender, the degree of benefit anticipated from available outpatient or institutional psychiatric therapy and the likelihood of the repetition of the alleged offense may be questions asked of the psychiatrist.

In an annulment or divorce case the opinion of the psychiatrist may be sought to determine the presence and nature of a mental disorder in one or both of the parties. His opinion may be used to assess the possible benefit of available psychiatric therapy, the impact of divorce upon the parties' mental health, and the retrospective determination of mental health prior to marriage. In contested custody hearings the psychiatrist may be asked to assess the mental health of one or both parents with respect to their fitness for the custody of the children, the presence of mental disorder and its nature, and the degree of danger, physical or mental, posed by a parent toward the children.

In a will contest the psychiatrist may be asked to evaluate retrospectively the mental health of the testator, the presence of a mental disorder and its nature at the time of the making of the will, and relationship of the mental disorder to the making of specific provisions of the will. In a civil suit for damages based on psychiatric disability the attorney may seek psychiatric expert opinion on the nature of the mental disorder and its relationship to an alleged event, as well as the degree of benefit anticipated from available psychiatric therapy, and the permanence of the disability.

Through the use of the conference technique it is hoped the attorney will be able to select a psychiatrist with whom he can work. At the same time some of the problems the psychiatrist notes as inherent in the legal system will be clarified. One warning should be made at this point: it is important to reexplain and reemphasize all aspects of the legal process continually throughout the interprofessional relationship to a point that they are clearly understood by the participating psychiatrist. I shall return to this topic later.

THE EXAMINATION OF THE CLIENT

During the evaluation of a client referred by a lawyer the psychiatrist is confronted by legal, psychological, and ethical considerations beyond the usual scope of his psychiatric practice. The preceding clarification of the type of examination desired and the legal questions to be answered facilitates the examination. Standards of the examination will now be discussed; both the attorney and the psychiatrist must agree on what is desired if optimal results are to be obtained from the psychiatric evaluation.

It is important that both professionals be fully cognizant of the need for an adequate evaluation of the client. It is undesirable to impose significant time limitations, either through pressure of events or because of inadequate funds. Sufficient time must be devoted by the psychiatrist if his evaluation is to be meaningful. In certain matters a single interview may be sufficient, though for most cases a more intensive evaluation is desirable. Frequently two separate interviews, constituting a minimum of approximately two hours, produce more adequate data upon which to base the evaluation. In fact, it can develop that in cases involving highly complex psychiatric problems the required evaluation time may extend to several days or even weeks in an in-patient institutional setting.

The clinical psychaitric evaluation should lead to both a clinical diagnosis and a psychodynamic diagnosis.[9] Psychological testing also

---

[9] A psychodynamic diagnosis includes a description of individual personality factors which are operative in daily living, including thoughts and behavior, and their attached emotions. This type of diagnosis, in non-technical language, provides the best means of describing human behavior and its causation.

A clinical diagnosis is a descriptive "shortcut" which (1) provides a brief means of characterizing a specific person in relation to the symptoms of a particular mental disorder and (2) gives a rough basis of predicting future behavioral patterns for members of the group of persons so labeled. A clinical diagnosis is frequently more succinct but less useful in portraying a specific individual than is a psychodynamic diagnosis.

provides useful data to corroborate the findings of the psychiatrist. It also assists him in extending the scope of his inquiry with the client. However, psychological testing without a clinical psychiatric evaluation is usually less meaningful in providing answers to the types of questions the attorney wants answered.[10]

The evaluation in most cases should include a complete psychiatric evaluation with a full past and present history of the client. It should also include a mental status examination. This includes assessment of intelligence, competence of organic brain functioning, symptoms of mental disorder, patterns of coping with stressful situations, and levels of anxiety and depression. The determination of ability to respond to treatment requires detailed knowledge of the specific person, his mental disorder, motivation for therapy, responsivity of the particular disorder to known treatment techniques and available treatment resources. With alleged sex offenders, the detailed history of prior sexual activity, relationship of sexual problems to the alleged offense, and assessment of danger to past victims are all important. In each instance the psychiatric evaluation is highly individualized, but within a broad framework which is similar each time.

The performance of a physical examination may or may not be required in a particular psychiatric evaluation. In many instances the physical examination may be performed by another physician. Whenever organic brain functioning is a question, it is necessary that the physical examination, including a complete neurological examination, be performed. Indicated laboratory procedure should also be used to supplement the examination. Such laboratory procedure includes serological testing, skull x-rays, electroencephalogram, spinal fluid examination, and other specialized tests on clinical indication. Hospitalization for these detailed neurological tests may be necessary in order to study adequately the functioning of the central nervous system.

A detailed history is essential as part of a psychiatric evaluation. Such a complete history may be difficult to obtain from a client because of his concern about revealing certain information which might be relayed to either his attorney or to the court. It is therefore very helpful for the psychiatrist to obtain information from outside sources in order to broaden the scope of his inquiry during the interview. The opinions of significant persons in the individual's life such as spouse, parents, teachers, and religious leaders may be helpful. In the area of criminal law, confessions, police statements, and various statements made to other persons may be very useful. The psychiatrist should be cautioned that such material frequently constitutes hearsay evidence. He should be aware that he cannot, therefore, use such data as the specific basis for forming his opinion. This evidence is still important, however, in helping the psychiatrist focus on areas which otherwise might be overlooked and which can serve as corroborative data in forming an opinion, if the opinion is based on statements made by the client which confirm information obtained from other sources.

The method of conducting the examination is also an important consideration. It is always preferable to conduct the examination in privacy. An alleged criminal offender should not be restrained by handcuffs or the like during any portion of the interview, if at all possible. The likelihood of obtaining more meaningful interview material is significantly enhanced by these measures.

Introductory comments by the psychiatrist to the client should state the reason for the examination and the relationship of the psychiatrist to the client.[11] The absence of confidentiality in this relationship should be revealed at the outset. It is common in psychiatric evaluations that a great deal of private and highly personalized material is revealed. Since any information revealed by the client to the psychiatrist becomes possible content for subsequent public revelation in a document or in a court proceeding, he should be fully informed about this prior to making any such statements. In a criminal proceeding, for example, further revelation regarding the alleged offense may be forthcoming in the context of the psychiatric evaluation. Rapport for the relationship between the psychiatrist and the client is also enhanced by a straightforward, honest approach on the part of the psychiatrist.

During the course of his examination the psychiatrist arrives at a clinical diagnosis in accordance with the standard psychiatric nomenclature. In addition to his clinical diag-

[10] Psychological testing provides a useful tool for evaluating an individual. Such tests may assess such things as intelligence, intellectual functioning of the central nervous system, and possible impairment in organic brain functioning, personality components, and disordered thinking and emotions. Administration of a number of different tests by the clinical psychologist provides additional data useful to the psychiatrist who clinically evaluates the individual. The psychological test results, in the absence of clinical evaluation, do not usually conclusively answer the attorney's questions. This is true even in the case of the determination of a level of intelligence, the area in which psychological testing affords the greatest precision.

[11] See generally, McDonald, *Psychiatry and the Criminal* (1958), p. 39.

nosis, he also formulates a psychodynamic diagnosis. The latter includes a description of the personality factors in the individual which are operative in daily living, including his thoughts and impulses and their attached emotions. At times it is difficult to complete this type of evaluation due to limitations in the examination situation. On the other hand, the stress of the examination may assist in providing much information which is useful in making such a dynamic diagnosis.

A concluding statement is rendered by the psychiatrist which represents his medical-legal opinion. This is based upon his total examination in relation to the specific problems presented by the client in his legal situation. Questions posed by the attorney prior to the examination are answered as fully as possible in this opinion. The report must be lucid, concise, and contain minimal technical language. Such technical terms as may be used should be fully defined.[12]

PRE-TRIAL CONFERENCES BETWEEN ATTORNEY AND PSYCHIATRIST

Upon completion of the examination it is advisable for the psychiatrist to meet again with the attorney. This is useful because it helps to redefine the basic issues in terms of what the evaluation has shown. The specific legal issues should be outlined for the psychiatrist, and he should present the specific psychiatric findings to the attorney. The chief benefit of the conference is the clarification of the basic issues in addition to reaffirming for the psychiatrist his exact role in any anticipated courtroom proceedings. If this is adequately done, the psychiatrist feels more free to testify and will likely present more effective testimony.

Adequate cross-examination requires significant knowledge on the attorney's part in relation to the specialized field in question. The expert witness testifying for a party in the adversary proceeding can be of significant assistance in acquainting the attorney with information about the client's specific illness. He can also provide the attorney with material to further enhance his understanding of the issues involved. We will see that this same cooperation can be used when the attorney prepares his hypothetical questions for the adverse expert witness. With the psychiatrist's help the questions can be intelligible and focused on the specific psychiatric issues involved in the case.

One other important factor should be discussed at this meeting. This involves the fee which the psychiatrist is to receive for his courtroom appearance. It should be on a fixed and not on a contingent basis. A contingent fee tends to deprive the witness of his objectivity and raises questions about the validity of his testimony. However, at the same time the fee should be adequate. As noted before, the psychiatrist is, for the most part, in a seller's market. While it is nice to argue that the psychiatrist should recognize his duty, all too often he will not participate unless paid sufficiently. In the case of the poor client, it is recognized that unpaid psychiatric evaluation and testimony may have to be sought. Even here, contingent fees should not be resorted to. In a criminal case where the defendant is indigent, however, some states provide for the appointment of an impartial expert witness.[13]

PSYCHIATRIC EXPERT TESTIMONY

The general area of psychiatric expert testimony probably creates more problems for the psychiatrist than any other aspect of his involvement with the legal system. Many psychiatrists have firm notions on how the legal system operates and some feel that it operates poorly, particularly insofar as it deals with psychiatric matters in the criminal area. They are perturbed by what they feel are unnecessary legal restrictions. But a basic point is that they do not adequately understand why these restrictions exist. And the psychiatrist may not understand what role he is to play in the total process of the trial. Needless to say the expert testimony will be found lacking to the extent that any of these problems exist.

The psychiatrist's objections to various rules of procedure and evidence may be alleviated if he can be made to understand either the purpose of the rules, or why they exist, even if outmoded. Thus the purpose of each relevant rule should be explained. And if a rule is outmoded, the attorney should explain why it has not been changed. For example, the fact that the legal system moves slowly in initiating change and that present-day thought generally recognizes that a certain rule is poor will create a feeling of understanding upon the psychiatrist's part. To the extent he understands the reasons, his whole attitude may change, and thus his testimony will be far more effective.

As pointed out before, many psychiatrists are disturbed by substantive rules of law which they believe are not in harmony with current

---

[12] See generally, Watson, "Communication between Psychiatrists and Lawyers," pp. 191–92.

[13] See, e.g., Cal. Civ. Proc. Code & 1871; Wis. Stat. & 957.27 (1963).

psychiatric knowledge.[14] A prime example of this atttiude may be seen in the current debate over the proper definition of "legal insanity." However, the attorney must impress the psychiatrist with the fact that testimony is given within a legal framework. The psychiatrist's basic role is to provide information which only he can give. He is not to try the case, and his interests are not legal interests.

There is an additional point that lawyers should consider when briefing their expert witnesses on trial procedure. I should state, however, that this consideration has been gained through practical experience with some trial courts and is by no means an absolute proposition. The consideration is that some courts tend to be more flexible than the laws under which they function. For example, courts may tend to give the psychiatrist great leeway in his testimony; I find this to be especially true with a psychiatrist who presents testimony that demonstrates an adequate psychiatric examination and an understanding of the necessary legal procedures involved in the case. Thus, the lawyer should, if possible, try to brief the psychiatric witness as to the attitudes of the trial judge who will try the case.

Testimony that can be Expected from the Psychiatrist

Attorneys frequently have little idea of the standard they should require a psychiatrist to fulfill when he testifies. Before discussing standards, however, it is necessary to raise a preliminary point. Psychiatrists may feel, either consciously or unconsciously, that their testimony must be guarded. This is because they fail to distinguish the two situations concerning the confidences of the client. There is, first the very important consideration of confidentiality when a person *voluntarily* consults a psychiatrist for treatment. On the other hand, there is no confidentiality barrier when a psychiatrist examines a person as part of a procedure to determine legal rights and liabilities. This distinction must be clarified before the attorney can get optimum testimony from the psychiatrist. And a failure to do so will, in many cases, color the testimony of the expert witness.

The attorney should advise the psychiatrist on the most meaningful method of presenting testimony. For example, the demeanor of the witness is usually not stressed by the attorney as a factor that the jury seriously considers in evaluating testimony. He should explain that

bombastic comments are far less well received than an earnest "soft sell" approach. The testimony should be concise and lucid. And it is of the utmost importance that the psychiatrist be constantly advised not to use technical terms in his testimony, since a very meaningful point may not be comprehended by the jury if couched in the psychiatrist's jargon.

Both professions should recognize that psychiatric testimony will be most effective if it is presented in an impartial and unbiased manner. Findings which tend to support an opposite point of view should be readily conceded, rather than grudgingly admitted. Yet it should be understood that psychiatrists cannot be impartial in the sense of having no allegiance to a school of thought or point of view. The personal biases and prejudices of the psychiatrist which are evident in his daily activities are also difficult to exclude from his testimony. For example, one expert may be more optimistic than another. These biases are components of the human personality and must be accepted as such. Yet the expert should not be partial in the sense of an allegiance to either party in a law suit. As one observer has stated:

In legal proceedings he should be jealous of the prerogatives of the profession and appear always as an advisor rather than as an advocate, telling the truth as he sees it to the best of his ability, unmoved by the prospect of gain or fame. He should, in the legal field particularly, avoid so far as possible any controversies with his colleagues and seek opportunity for joint examination and report in contested cases.[15]

Lawyers and psychiatrists are frequently confused on the exact content of the expert's testimony. Basically, it is the function of the psychiatrist to present the mental state of the examined party at the relevant times in issue. The psychodynamic basis of any relevant behavior, including both conscious and unconscious processes, should be described. This will include presentation of the mental processes, forces, and motivations which result in specific behavior. Although different situations will call for different kinds of testimony, the following quotations will be illustrative. It should be noted that they are confined to the criminal law context.

When a psychiatrist who has examined the defendant testifies concerning his mental condition, he shall be permitted to make a statement as to the nature of his examination, his diagnosis of the mental condition of the defendant at the time of commission of the

---

[14] State v. Esser, 16 Wis. 2d 567, 115 N.W. 2d 505 (1962), is a nice illustration of this point.

[15] Overholser, "Presidential Address," *American J. of Psychiatry*, 105 (1948): 5.

offense charged. . . . He shall be permitted to make any explanation reasonably serving to clarify his diagnosis and opinion. . . .[16]

Guttmacher, discussing the psychiatrist's role in testifying on the responsibility issue in a criminal case, becomes even more specific as to what questions the psychiatrist should address himself to:

1. Whether the defendant was suffering from a definite and generally recognized mental disorder and why and how this conclusion was reached; 2. The name, the chief characteristics and symptoms of the disorder, with particular emphasis on its effect on judgment, social behavior, and self-control of the affected individual; 3. The way and the degree to which the malady has affected the particular defendant's behavior, especially in regard to his judgment, social behavior and self-control; 4. Whether the alleged act could be considered symptomatic of the disorder.[17]

Preparing the Psychiatrist for the Hypothetical Questions

The psychiatrist must understand that in his role as expert he usually serves as advisor to one of the advocates in the court proceedings. In this role he may be asked a hypothetical question which is framed to permit consideration of all pertinent "facts" in the case useful to the advocate's position. This commonly presents difficulty for the psychiatrist since he may be confronted with "facts" which are contrary to his own experience with the client whom he has examined.[18] If often appears to the psychiatrist that the hypothetical question fails to present a fair summary of the facts in the case. The question may assume some facts which appear wholly inconsistent with those actually known to the psychiatrist through his evaluation of the client. He may be confused when a differing set of facts about another hypothetical individual is introduced by the opposing lawyer to establish an opposite point of view.

The psychiatrist needs to understand that responses to hypothetical questions must be based solely on the "facts" of the hypothetical question itself, and must not reflect any other

information about the client possessed by the psychiatrist. The point is usually not made clear to the psychiatric expert by either the lawyer or the court. He should know that his position as an expert in responding to a hypothetical question is not to determine the existence or non-existence of the facts posed in the question but to assume those facts to be true and respond accordingly.

He is similarly troubled by the great length of the hypothetical question. It may become somewhat clearer to him, if it is explained as being analogous to the medical model of a case presentation at a clinical-pathological conference.

The framing of the hypothetical question may be best done cooperatively by the lawyer and the psychiatrist. It becomes much easier for the psychiatrist to testify if the facts contained in the hypothetical question are essentially in agreement with his own findings. Since the hypothetical question may play a significant role in some legal proceedings, the psychiatrist's familiarity with it prior to his court appearance is very beneficial to his total testimony.

Preparing the Psychiatrist for Cross-Examination

The cross-examination phase of a trial presents many problems for the psychiatrist. Frequently he anticipates cross-examination as an ordeal to which he feels he should not be subjected. The possibility of personal abuse at the hands of the cross-examining attorney frequently results in his refusal to participate in courtroom activities. On the other hand, the attorney should explain that with adequate preparation, frank objectivity, and familiarity with legal procedures, cross-examination can be a stimulating experience. The pontifications of positions and reification of theoretical concepts will be challenged in court. Undocumented or speculative views will be exposed as being of little merit.

The attorney must explain the actual function of the cross-examination to the psychiatrist. While some trial attorneys feel that "ordinarily the best cross-examination of medical experts is no cross-examination," it is clear that the cross-examination will not always be eliminated.[19] For example, everyone should realize that a person, even though an expert witness, may inadvertently testify outside the

[16] Model Penal Code § 4.07 (Tent. Draft No. 5, 1955).

[17] Guttmacher, "What Can the Psychiatrist Contribute to the Issue of Criminal Responsibility?," *J. of Nervous Mental Disorders*, 136 (1963): 103, 107.

[18] See generally, "The Physicians' Testimony, Including the Hypothetical Question," *N.Y.S.J. of Medicine*, 63 (1963): 2056.

[19] Goldstein, "Cross-examination of Expert Medical Witnesses," in *American Medical Association, Medical Legal Symposium Proceedings* (1959), p. 241.

realm of his particular training or experience. Such consequences can be avoided by the use of a vigorous cross-examination.

Specific techniques used by a cross-examining attorney should be explained to the psychiatrist. Testimony may be discredited by trying to impeach the expert's testimony. One method is to attempt to show that the psychiatrist is biased because he has a relationship with the hiring attorney under which he will receive substantial fees for the testimony that he gives. Another method is to challenge the psychiatrist's educational background to show that he is unqualified to give testimony on the particular issue in question. While the psychiatrist may view this as a personal attack, it is probable that the psychiatrist will be a more meaningful participant if the legal validity and purpose of this technique are made clear to him.

Specific detailed information may be sought during cross-examination to test the witness's knowledge. The attorney should brief his expert on the types of questions that are likely to be asked and advise him on the proper way to answer these questions. Some of the more important aspects of this phase of the preparation for cross-examination should be outlined.

If the detailed information requested is beyond the immediate recall of the witness, and outside the scope of material which he ordinarily uses for recall, he should be advised to state that medical reference sources are used for such information, and not to rely upon his memory. Particular reference sources may be used by the cross-examining attorney in an effort to cite conflicting points of view in the literature. An appropriate response by the expert to this line of questioning is a statement that his knowledge is based upon many sources, including his training and experience;

the psychiatrist should state that he is not relying upon any particular single source book in forming his opinion. In the event specific books are recognized as authorities in the field, it is important to review statements in their proper context and to be sure that the most recent publication of the particular volume is being cited.

The psychiatrist should be advised to acknowledge rationally and unemotionally differences with other experts. Errors in previous testimony, if these are noted during later testimony or on cross-examination, should be recognized. The meaning of earlier statements may be distorted, misquoted, or taken out of context during the course of cross-examination. If such is the case, this should be brought to the attention of the court by the expert. This may be effectively done by asking the court reporter to quote from the earlier testimony.

The expert witness should not attempt to engage in legal debate with the cross-examining attorney while on the witness stand, since his skilled adversary is likely to be far more expert in this arena. Questions should not be answered with a categorical "yes" or "no" if qualification is necessary for a complete answer. Efforts by the attorney to limit the answer to "yes" or "no" may be resisted by the witness who needs to clarify his response to make it complete, and this will ordinarily be sustained by the court.

Thorough examination of the alleged offender, careful preparation for testimony, knowledge of the legal procedure, and a helpful impartial demeanor in the courtroom will ordinarily lead to good testimony on both direct and cross-examination, and with this pattern as a base the psychiatric expert can be assured that he need not fear cross-examination.

THE FALLACY OF THE IMPARTIAL EXPERT

Bernard L. Diamond, M.D.

It is quite generally assumed that the battle of the experts, that always disconcerting and often sensational disagreement of psychiatrists in testifying on issues of legal insanity and criminal responsibility, could be eliminated through the device of the neutral or impartial expert.

Such a neutral expert witness is supposedly

Archives of Criminal Psychodynamics 3 (Spring 1959): 221–36; excerpts reprinted with permission.

entirely outside the traditional adversary system of the courts. Not in the employment of either the defense or the prosecution, but acting in the name of the court, such a witness presumedly can remain detached and objective. Disagreement between expert witnesses is supposed to be greatly reduced; thereby aiding the court in reaching a higher level of fair, just, and impartial decisions.

As a by-product of the elimination of the battle of the experts, it is claimed, the public relations of the psychiatric specialist would be much improved. For a considerable segment of the population the only direct contact with psychiatry and the psychiatrist is that obtained through the media of sensational trial reports in the newspapers, radio, and television. It is entirely understandable that this segment of the population regards psychiatry as a most uncertain affair, with violent disagreements, contradictory opinions, and dubious ethics the hallmarks of its practitioners.

I would guess that, today, nine-tenths of the psychiatrists in this country would unhesitatingly agree to the desirability of removing the psychiatric expert from the legal adversary system. It is the purpose of this editorial to challenge this widespread agreement. It is proper that this discussion take the form of an editorial, rather than that of a scientific paper. For opinions pro and con this matter can hardly be considered as objective facts to be solemnly presented as a scientific advance. Quite properly they are to be considered as personal opinions of the author and nothing more.

It is a fiction of the law that only the immediate parties to a legal action—the defendant and the plaintiff or prosecutor and their counsel—are adversaries. All else: the judge, the jury, and the witnesses, are not to be partisans. All witnesses, both expert and lay witnesses of fact, are sworn to tell the truth, the whole truth, and nothing but the truth. This truth, as revealed in the testimony of the witness, may favor one or the other side, but the witness may not. That is a fiction, not a reality, as evidenced by the customary manner of labeling witnesses as *for* the defendant or *for* the prosecution.

I will thus concede at the outset that the expert witness called by either adversary is likely to be biased to some degree, that his opinions are not truly impartial, and that he, himself, is an advocate. I concede this with full awareness that both legal and medical codes of ethics demand the impartiality of the expert witness, irrespective of the side that calls him. The desirability of such an ethical ideal must not blind us to the reality that the ideal is seldom, if ever, achieved.

The crude charge is sometimes asserted that under the adversary system the expert witness sells his opinion. Because he is paid by one or the other side, he is accused of prostituting his medical knowledge in providing untruthful testimony in return for the money he is paid. This charge is too base to defend by more than just a simple statement: I do not believe that this happens.

Undoubtedly, what does happen is that the expert witness, through his close operational identification with one side of the conflict, does become an advocate. Because his testimony does in fact support one side of the legal battle, he, if he is at all human, must necessarily identify himself with his own opinion, and subjectively desire that "his side" win. This can vary all the way from a deliberate, conscious participation in the planning of the legal strategy with the lawyers who call upon him for expert advice and opinion, to a more aloof, detached facsimile of impartiality that masks his secret hope for victory of his own opinion. Such a detached witness may be totally unconscious of the innumerable subtle distortions and biases in his testimony that spring from this wish to triumph.

This is well recognized by our courts of law. It is the duty of the counsel for the opposing side to cross-examine the witness, revealing these distortions and biases, attempting to impeach his testimony. It is wholly legitimate to impeach the testimony through an attack upon the witness himself. That is, by eliciting evidence to show that the witness is not the expert he proclaims himself to be, that the clinical facts upon which the expert bases his opinions are not complete or may not even be true, that the skill and knowledge of the expert in his professional field are deficient, and that his expert opinions are faulty and unwarranted. Under such cross-examination or through redirect examination by the counsel who engaged him, the expert is expected to defend his expert status, his clinical facts, his professional knowledge, and to justify his opinions. It is absurd to pretend that the psychiatric expert remains neutral under such a legal procedure. For the sake of his own ego integrity, he must identify himself with his own opinions and become the advocate of those opinions. But in proportion as those opinions favor one side or the other, the witness loses his hypothetical impartiality.

Because both the impartial, court-appointed, independent witness as well as the adversary witness are required to submit to cross-examination and defend their opinions, it is here asserted that there is no such thing as a truly impartial expert; that all witnesses, regardless of who engaged them, identify closely with their own opinions and unintentionally introduce as a result a certain degree of bias and deviation from their oath to tell the truth, the whole truth, and nothing but the truth.

Certain other factors also contribute to the lack of impartiality of the court-appointed expert. However, let us first place these issues within the framework of a specific case. I deliberately chose a trial in which all elements are greatly exaggerated. I do not mean that the description of the trial to be given below is exaggerated, for the description is entirely itself, and the circumstances of the expert examinations and testimony are far more extreme than is usual.

A certain California multi-millionaire was charged with perverse sexual acts on two adolescent boys. It was a matter of common public knowledge that the defendant had overtly and unashamedly practiced homosexuality for many years, but he had never been accused of seducing children. He pleaded not guilty by reason of insanity. The defendant had no insight into his mental illness, nor did he consider himself insane in any sense of the word. However, he consented to the plea on the insistence of his attorneys and his family. Practically unlimited sums of money were available for purposes of his defense. An exceptionally high-powered battery of attorneys, headed by the most outstanding criminal lawyer in the area, represented him. He was quickly convicted of the acts charged in the indictment, for the evidence was conclusive. Then he was tried on the question of his insanity, as is required by the peculiar split-trial system used in California. A jury trial had been waived.

Two court-appointed psychiatrists had examined him and submitted reports to the court stating that he was sane under the M'Naghten rules; that he was a sociopath, manifesting a sexual deviation which made him a menace to society; hence he came under the California sexual psychopathy law permitting indefinite confinement.

Two other psychiatrists, who had been engaged by the defense, testified that they had examined the defendant, and found him to be suffering from a major psychosis; that he was insane under the M'Naghten rules; that his long-standing homosexuality as well as the specific perverse sexual acts with children were symptoms of his psychosis; and that he was not a sociopath or a sexual psychopath.

The court-appointed psychiatrists received the usual fee for their examinations and time spent in court, probably not over fifty or one hundred dollars each. The two defense psychiatrists were each paid several thousand dollars for their examinations and time in court.

Here we have an extreme instance of the battle of the experts. How to explain the disparate testimony of the experts? Would the verdict of the judge have been more just if all four psychiatrists had been neutral? What role did the sharp discrepancy in fees paid to the witnesses play?

The differences in the diagnoses reached by the court-appointed witnesses and the defense witnesses hinged largely upon the question as to whether certain statements asserted by the defendant were actually delusions or whether they were true, or possible exaggerations, or perhaps even deliberate lies. The neutral experts had only the usual hour or so of examination time, and no sources of information outside the defendant's statements, to formulate their opinion on this very difficult question. The defendant had no intention of admitting even the possibility that he might be suffering from a psychotic thinking disorder. He went to great lengths to rationalize his peculiar thoughts and to justify his conduct, both past and present, as the actions of a sane person who chose voluntarily to lead an eccentric life. He concealed from the court-appointed psychiatrists the details of his past history, which included hospitalization in private sanitariums in England and in France on nine previous occasions.

It was certainly no reflection upon the clinical abilities of the two neutral experts that they reached the conclusions they did. Under the limited circumstances of their examination and with the restricted information that they had access to, it is difficult to imagine how they could have reached any other conclusions.

On the other hand, the defense psychiatrists were paid to spend practically unlimited time and to use all possible clinical facilities in their study of the defendant. Batteries of psychological tests were administered. An exhaustive neurological investigation was done, including spinal puncture and an EEG (certain symptoms suggested general paresis). An attorney was dispatched to Europe to obtain copies of the previous hospital records and to take depositions from all of the European physicians who had previously treated him over a period of thirty years. The aged mother of the defendant was brought to California from her home in Europe and made available for a social history. When the clinical evidence was all in, the conclusion was inescapable that this man was psychotic and not responsible for his actions. The judge agreed and found him not guilty by reason of insanity, and he was committed to a state hospital.

Beyond doubt the verdict was just. The great wealth of the defendant was not used to purchase biased and untruthful testimony from dubious experts. Rather it was used to make certain that every scrap of evidence, every clinical possibility was exhaustively investigated, and that nothing was overlooked. The injustice inherent in this extreme example, is, of course, the fact that if this defendant had been a poor man he would probably have been found to be sane, and would have been imprisoned.

The assumption is often made that the elimination of the adversary expert witness will lead to testimony of greater objectivity, thoroughness, and accuracy. Corollary to this assumption is the implication that examinations performed by adversary witnesses are neither objective, thorough, nor accurate. In our case of the millionaire sex offender, just the opposite was true. But how about in ordinary cases? It is very difficult to give a definite answer to this question without having some basis of statistical information. However, I believe there are logical reasons to infer that quite generally psychiatric investigations done for the defense are likely to be more thorough than those done by the ordinary court-appointed psychiatrist. The latter is apt to approach the examination situation in a routine manner, a job to be done, so to speak, and to restrict his time, energy, and thought on the case to a level determined by the habitual fees paid for this work. The public funds available to the court-appointed psychiatrist are very limited, the courts taking it for granted that he should be able to perform an adequate examination and reach a conclusion in one or two hours. Rarely is money available for auxiliary examinations, such as projective techniques. The fact that there are a few notable exceptions to this situation does not alter the general inference. I refer to the City of Baltimore, where, under the dedicated direction of Dr. Manfred Guttmacher, a court clinic has evolved by which any defendant has available to him a type of psychiatric investigation approaching that which was utilized for the millionaire defendant described above. Also, in Washington, D.C., where Dr. Winfred Overholser has followed the great Dr. William Alanson White in developing St. Elizabeths Hospital into an outstanding center for medico-legal psychiatric training and research.

Leaving aside these special instances, it is clear that the psychiatrist engaged by defense counsel is in quite a different position than the usual court-appointed expert. Whatever money can conceivably be scraped together by the defendant or his family is used freely to reimburse the psychiatrist for whatever time he feels necessary to perform an adequate investigation and examination. Occasionally, a defense counsel, particularly a public defender, may call upon a psychiatrist with the express

understanding that only a very limited amount is available for examination time. The psychiatrist is under no obligation to accept the case, and may decline, or, as very often happens (especially when the case is unusual or challenging), the psychiatrist may accept the case, agreeing in advance to spend whatever time is necessary without adequate remuneration.

In short, I think it is possible to make the generalization that court appointments tend to be handled by psychiatrists as a kind of routine job, in which, despite totally unreasonable time restriction, there nevertheless results a fairly medium level of clinical competence. The psychiatrist called by the defense, on the other hand, is much more apt to regard the examination situation as a highly challenging task, to which he devotes considerable time and effort, with or without adequate remuneration. If for his own personal reasons he cannot enter into the case on this superior level, he is likely to turn it down, altogether, rather than handle it as just routine.

Does the fact that a psychiatrist is called as a witness for the court, that he is neither directly involved with the prosecution nor the defense make it more likely that his opinion is less biased and more truthful and objective than that of the adversary witness? . . . The selection of court-appointed psychiatrists is seldom made from the random universe of the psychiatric population. Certain psychiatrists tend to be appointed over and over again. These are generally men who have an active interest in forensic psychiatry. More often than not they tend to be Kraepelinian and less dynamic in their approach to their cases. They are often drawn from the ranks of administrative psychiatry, an area deficient in psycho-analytically oriented therapists. They are less inclined to probe deeply, more inclined to accept uncritically surface manifestations, and prone to interpret the legal criteria for insanity in a narrowly restricted way. (Many of my forensic psychiatrist friends will take me to task for making these assertions—I will merely tell them that they are the exceptions who prove the rule.)

A second reason for this biased selection of court-appointed experts is the unfortunate fact that dynamically oriented psychotherapists with liberal, enlightened, and non-moralistic attitudes toward mental illness and criminal behavior, shamefully avoid their social responsibility to participate in the administration of justice. They make it clearly known that they would not accept appointment as expert witness, and they ensure that they will not even be asked by having an abysmal ignorance of even the basic principles of forensic psychiatry.

Thirdly, in many communities, the District

Attorney has an undue influence over the courts in the selection of the panels from which the court-appointed expert is drawn. Psychiatrists who have more liberal views which have been revealed through their testimony in previous cases may be systematically excluded from appointment by the court. It is only natural for the District Attorney to recommend a panel of psychiatrists who are known to be reliable in expressing extremely conservative opinions, and who follow the strictest possible interpretation of the M'Naghten rules. Granted that the defense psychiatrist is chosen by counsel just because he is more liberal and more advanced in his views. And probably those psychiatrists who do a great deal of defense work are apt to be unconsciously identified with the defendant, to be overly sympathetic and motivated to be an advocate for the underdog. But I assert that those psychiatrists who seek out and tend to receive appointment by the court as a so-called impartial witness have an equal probability of being overly identified with authority, of being a sort of watch-dog of the public morals, and motivated toward seeing that no criminal "gets away with anything."

The defense of insanity is nearly always raised in crimes of violence, especially homicide. Such acts of violence arouse strong emotions within everyone, and psychiatrists are no exception. Premature and prejudicial judgements must inevitably occur. Such emotions demand that one identify himself with either the defendant or with the authority of society, usually the latter. The determining factors which will decide the direction of the identification frequently have less to do with the facts and circumstances of the crime and criminal than with the predisposition and temperament of the observing individual. It is far-fetched to suppose that even an experienced psychiatrist remains neutral in his evaluation of acts of violence and murder.

So I claim that there is no such thing as a neutral, impartial witness. No matter whether a psychiatrist is engaged by the defense or the prosecution or is allowed to remain completely outside of the system of adversary conflict, he is bound to be biased and partial and strongly motivated toward advocacy of his particular prejudiced point of view.

This lack of impartiality of the expert witness need not be a serious obstacle to the administration of justice. It is inherent in our traditional system of adversary procedure that both sides be presented to the jury and the jury is to choose within the conflict of evidence that side which is most credible. However, serious injustice may occur when an adversary witness is disguised as a neutral witness. When actual partiality is masked as impartiality, the judge and jury are deceived, and misled. The response is less to the credibility of the witness and the logic of his testimony and more to his status as a so-called neutral. In Massachusetts, where the Briggs law has been in operation for a good many years, it is still permissible for the defense to call its own expert witnesses. But advocates of the neutral system of expert testimony use as one of their chief arguments the fact that the jury almost invariably accepts the opinion of the neutral experts. They consider it progress that under such circumstances it is hardly worth while for the defense to call in its own experts. Thus the battle of the experts is eliminated. But does this provide a better brand of justice than does the adversary method? I doubt it. In a legal situation where impartiality is impossible, let us frankly label the witness for what he is, and let the jury choose. To be sure, there will be instances of bad choice, of incorrect, illogical, and injust verdicts. But to disguise the partisan character of the expert through status labels of neutrality and court appointment will not contribute to more rational jury decision.

Sending a defendant to a state hospital, supposedly an independent agency, for medical-legal evaluation, does not remedy this situation. In fact, it may only further distort the issues. For example, a defendant is committed to a public hospital for observation and is detained in that hospital for, let us say, a period of three months. He is assigned to a staff physician who takes a history and performs a mental examination. In better hospitals they will also obtain a social history from the family and write for records of previous medical care. The patient is presented to the staff at least once and usually several times; the case is discussed; a decision is reached, and a report is sent to the court. The staff physician or an administrative official of the hospital will appear in court as a witness. He will testify that the defendant has been under continual observation for three months, that he has been thoroughly examined, and that the hospital staff has agreed as to the diagnosis and legal responsibility of the defendant.

On the surface this would seem like a very superior solution. Months of observation time are certainly better than a few hours of clinical examination; and the opinion of an entire hospital staff is more reliable than that of a single examiner. It is understandable why a judge or juror would give much greater weight to the testimony of such an institutional report than they would to that of an adversary expert.

However, a closer scrutiny of the institutional examination procedure casts considerable doubt on whether this greater weight is justified. In the first place it is not true that defendant has been under observation for the period of time claimed. It is more likely that the ward physician has spent only from one to a few hours in direct contact with the patient. All public hospitals are extremely busy places, with a heavy over-load of patients. Ward physicians invariably have many more patients than they can adequately examine and care for. Time is very precious and must be strictly rationed among the patients. Medical-legal cases in the average mental hospital or psychopathic ward of the large city hospital are not welcomed with enthusiasm. Because there is no treatment contemplated, but merely diagnosis and medical-legal evaluation, there is apt to be much less time and interest devoted to the case. Most physicians are treatment oriented. Justifiably, the hospital physician regards the need of those patients who are hospitalized for treatment purposes as taking priority over those who are there merely for diagnostic or custodial purposes. Over and over again I have examined hospital records of forensic cases and found the clinical investigation to be second-rate compared to the quality of professional care provided for the active treatment case. I see little to choose between a one- or two-hour examination done in the hospital followed by three months of non-observational custodial care, and the same amount of time spent by an ordinary court-appointed examiner in the county jail setting. Yet the court and jury are misled into believing that the defendant has been subjected to a more exhaustive scrutiny for a prolonged period of time by the full hospital staff.

It is customary in most public mental hospitals to present the case at a staff conference. Each staff member, having listened to an abstract of the history and examination findings, then expresses his opinion. There may be varying amounts of discussion and then a sort of vote is taken. In some hospitals, the majority vote decides the issue. In others, the superintendent or the physician who is in charge of the conference has the final say. There are many different systems used. But whatever method is utilized in reaching a decision, the report that goes to the court just about invariably implies that the decision was unanimous.

A case some time ago, which I had occasion to look into, involved a most difficult diagnostic problem. He was a seventeen-year-old boy, who, while confined as a patient in a state hospital, strangled another patient. He was regarded as too mentally ill to be subject to trial and was sent by the court to another state hospital for medical-legal observation.

The diagnostic choices lay between schizophrenia and schizoid personality disorder. Which diagnosis was made would naturally have great bearing on his criminal responsibility. When the case was presented to the staff conference there was great division of opinion among the staff physicians. He was recommended back to his ward for further observation. In a few months, he was staffed again. And again there was no agreement. After repeated staffing over a period of a year, it was agreed that further observation was futile, and that a diagnosis would have to be agreed upon. The vote was five to four in favor of psychopathy. A report was then sent to the court stating that this diagnosis had been made, following a year's observation, and that he was now sane and could stand trial. The wording of the report clearly implied that the diagnosis was definitely established and that there was full agreement. There was no reference to the uncertainty of the actual diagnostic formulation, nor any knowledge conveyed to the court that the hospital staff was strongly divided, sometimes voting one way, and sometimes the other. With such a report the court erroneously assumed that the matter was settled beyond dispute.

What we have here, of course, is nothing else than the familiar star chamber proceeding. The hospital staff usurped the function of the jury, settled the whole matter within the hospital star chamber, and the court was then deprived of the full evidence, the conflict of medical opinion, and the grave doubt of the correctness of the diagnosis and the boy's legal responsibility.

Such hospital reports are false and misleading, and certainly do not contribute to the proper administration of justice. The only thing they seem to accomplish is to create the illusion that psychiatrists are more consistent, more omniscient, and more unanimous than they actually are.

Furthermore, the public mental hospital is not the independent agency it claims to be. In a criminal case the adversary to the defendant is the People of the State. The institutional psychiatrist is a full-time employee of the People of the State. It is only logical to suppose that persons who are permanently employed by the State tend to identify themselves with that State, and to be prejudiced in its favor. Because of the hierarchal system within the hospital, the attitude of the hospital superintendent tends to influence unduly the decisions of the entire staff. The hospital superintendent, as a permanent State employee, with ambitions within the State bureaucratic system, may be totally identified with the authority of the State. He may be an excellent hospital administrator, yet be completely out of touch with modern psychiatric attitudes toward criminal behavior. Such an administrator may not actually have practiced clinical psychiatry for many years. He may give his staff a free hand in ordinary clinical decisions; but he considers medico-legal evaluation as basically administrative and within his province. He may utilize only outmoded, moralistic, or even theological criteria for his evaluation of questions of legal responsibility. As a consequence, what purports to be the impartial decision of a group of doctors, may in fact be only the expression of a particular doctor's prejudice or limited clinical knowledge.

Again, I reiterate my concession that there are exceptions. There are hospitals where none, whatsoever, of the above criticisms would apply. But the advocates of the impartial witness system seem to take it for granted that hospital observation would lead to a superior type of justice.

Everyone would concede, I think, that the ideal solution would be to provide each and every defendant with the extensive type of clinical investigation which was afforded to the millionaire defendant of our example above. Unlimited funds would be available for investigational purposes and only the most competent and experienced witnesses well skilled in the presentation of technical clinical data to lay audiences, would be utilized in the courtroom. Obviously this is not going to be the case in the foreseeable future. The average defendant is going to be examined and evaluated in a highly abbreviated procedure by experts with varying degrees of skill, experience, bias, and partiality.

The traditional adversary system of calling witnesses for each side and then examining the witnesses by direct and cross-examination has been evolved for just the purpose of exposing these shortcomings and biases. The court and jury are then free to take them into consideration in alloting the weight which it will attach to the testimony of each witness. To utilize a system in which the expert witness is labeled as "impartial" in no way eliminates the shortcomings; it merely conceals them from the jury and creates the illusion of psychiatric omniscience. Such illusions may be good for the public relations of psychiatry, but they are not good for the administration of justice.

If and when the time comes when the following conditions are approached, I would freely abandon the adversary system insofar as it applies to problems of mental illness:

1. When each defendant, rich or poor, rural and urban, in enlightened communities and in backward communities, can be reasonably guaranteed the type of exhaustive clinical investigation that is now available to only a few fortunate defendants.

2. When all expert witnesses are highly trained and experienced and adept in transmitting their findings to the court.

3. When observation hospitals are staffed with dynamically oriented psychiatrists who fully appreciate the important role they play in the administration of justice.

4. When such psychiatrists, through their own enlightenment and self-understanding, can be relied upon to detach themselves from their own prejudices and refrain from homogenizing their moral judgments with their medical opinions.[1]

5. When our whole profession of psychiatry is less preoccupied with its own omniscience and is sufficiently secure in its public status that it is unafraid to expose its deficiencies of knowledge about some of the most fundamental problems of human nature.

6. When the forensic psychiatrist is permitted to operate within a legal framework which allows him to apply his professional judgment to appropriate questions of psychological reality and not to philosophical and theological rules and syllogisms—when he can apply his knowledge to human reality instead of legal fiction.

7. When society is able to leave behind its archaic need for vengeance and retribution and learn that its own best protection is inextricably woven in with the rehabilitation of the individual deviant; that to degrade any member of that society with either the formal vengeance of punishment or the stigmata of legal insanity is to degrade only itself.

Then and only then would I admit the superiority of the impartial expert over the adversary witness. But then, if such a utopia were to be achieved, perhaps there would be no need for experts.

[1] Paraphrased from a book review by Andrew S. Watson, M.D. *University of Pennsylvania Law Review*, 107 (1959): 899. Compare with comment by Reginald S. Rood, M.D., *American Journal of Psychiatry*, 115 (May, 1959): 1038.

QUESTIONS FOR DISCUSSION

(RE-EXAMINING THE DIAMOND THESIS)

1. Dr. Diamond's first major point is that: "It is a fiction of the law that only the immediate parties to a legal action . . . are adversaries." He goes on: "That this is a fiction, not a reality, is evidenced by the customary manner of labeling witnesses as *for* the defendant or *for* the prosecution." Is his argument persuasive?

Is not Dr. Diamond's "proof" that witnesses are inevitably partisan an irrelevancy? Physical evidence is also labeled "for the defendant" or "for the prosecution," but is a document or a set of fingerprints partisan? Does not the phrase to which Dr. Diamond attributes so much significance simply identify the party who *introduced* the evidence or testimony?

2. Of course many witnesses *are* partisan (the arresting officer who testifies probably consciously or unconsciously hopes that his arrest of the defendant will be validated by a conviction; defendant's brother-in-law who testifies for the defense as a character witness may earnestly hope that the defendant will be acquitted so that he, rather than the witness, will have to support the defendant's wife). But what do the biases, ties of blood, friendship, or finances of the non-expert witness have to do with the role of the expert? Ordinary witnesses are not permitted to state opinions. The expert is, and his opinion is deemed worth listening to because it is presumed that it will be an objective and scientific one.

3. Next, Dr. Diamond asserts that: "Undoubtedly, what does happen is that the expert witness, through his *close operational identification* with one side of the conflict, does become an advocate," and that the expert "may be totally unconscious of the innumerable subtle distortions and biases in his testimony that spring from this *wish to triumph*" (italics added). But is not the very purpose of the court's calling its own expert to testify to avoid such an "operational identification with one side of the conflict," and the concomitant wish for it to triumph?

4. Is not the following statement a logical non sequitur: "Because both the impartial, court-appointed, independent witness as well as the adversary witness are required to submit to cross-examination and defend their opinions . . . there is no such thing as a truly impartial expert"? Compare the following statements:

Because I lock my door at night there is no such thing as an honest man.

Because graduates of both Harvard and Podunk medical schools are required to take licensure examinations, one school must be as good (or as bad) as the other.

5. Now let us look at the case of the "California Multi-Millionaire." Dr. Diamond takes great pains to detail the medical procedures that were made available to this defendant under our glorious free enterprise system, under which one can get excellent medical testimony—if he can afford to pay for it. He concludes the vignette by observing that "if this defendant had been a poor man he would probably have been found to be sane, and would have been imprisoned." One is moved to ask: "Might not an indigent defendent have been helped by a court-appointed expert?" At least it might have been better than having no expert at all.

6. Dr. Diamond makes the telling point that often the court-appointed psychiatrist performs his role in a routine, perfunctory manner—principally because of limitations of time and money. But do not these same limitations apply in the case of most criminal defendents, relatively few of whom happen to be "California multi-millionaires"? Why not improve the breed of court-appointed experts: pressing for legislation that will improve the system of selection; require that an adequate examination be made, and provide the funds to pay for it? In other words, cannot all of the shortcomings alluded to be corrected within the framework of the non-partisan plan?

7. Dr. Diamond asserts that the psychiatrists selected by courts as non-partisan experts tend to be "men who have an acitve interest in forensic psychiatry . . . Kraepelinian [i.e.,

---

Dr. Diamond's paper is, as he describes it, an "editorial" rather than a scientific paper—and a most articulate one. For that reason, we have employed a similar form for our questions, in order to sharpen the issues surrounding use of the "impartial" expert.   R.C.A.

excessively preoccupied with labels] and less dynamic in their approach to their cases . . . and are prone to interpret the legal criteria for insanity in a narrowly restricted way."

But are not these observations almost invariably true of prosecution witnesses under the adversary system? The non-partisan approach permits the positing of minimum qualifications, establishment of a system of selection and rotation, and, hopefully, it prevents "shopping" for an opinion. For example, the Peck plan in New York requires board certification; and admission to the panel from which non-partisan experts are selected requires approval by the medical society.

8. It is probably true, as the article points out, that "dynamically oriented psychotherapists with liberal, enlightened, and non-moralistic attitudes towards mental illness and criminal behavior, shamefully avoid their social responsibility to participate in the administration of justice." But isn't it *adversary* appointment that they primarily shun?

9. "Thirdly," says Dr. Diamond, "in many communities, the District Attorney has an undue influence over the courts in the selection of the panels from which the court-appointed expert is drawn." Again, does this not seem to be a quarrel with method and application rather than with the theory and objectives of non-partisan testimony?

10. Is not the following an interesting observation: "The defense of insanity is nearly always raised in crimes of violence, especially homicide. Such acts of violence arouse strong emotions within everyone, and psychiatrists are no exception . . . *such emotions demand that one identify himself with either the defendent or the authority of society, usually the latter* . . . it is far-fetched to suppose that even an experienced psychiatrist remains neutral in his evaluation of acts of violence and murder. So I claim that there is no such thing as a neutral, impartial witness. . . . [H]e is bound to be biased and partial and strongly motivated toward advocacy *of his particular prejudiced point of view.*" [Italics added.] If the statements just quoted were indeed true— that no psychiatrist is capable of making a diagnosis and prognosis of a patient who hap-

pens to be a defendent in a criminal case that is not a reflection of his own emotions and moral judgments—then would it not seem that the inquiry may be misdirected? Rather than questioning whether there is any merit in having a psychiatrist called as an expert by the court, perhaps the question should be whether a psychiatrist should be called as an expert at all.

11. Dr. Diamond makes a strong point when he asserts that there is danger in the aura of authority which cloaks any witness who is called by the court. Under most non-partisan expert testimony plans the parties are free to present their own expert witnesses and to cross-examine the court-appointed expert in the same fashion as they would cross-examine a witness presented by the other party. But is this enough to insure a fair trial of disputed medical issues? Could a carefully drafted instruction help to dissipate the assumption of infallibility that seems to attach to the non-partisan expert?

12. Closely related to this point is the inescapable fact that some psychiatrists are dynamically and some organically oriented, and an adherent of either school may have impeccable credentials. If it is unavoidable that the non-partisan witness will appear in a more favorable light to the jury than a witness called by either of the parties, then the outcome of a criminal case might well depend on the basic orientation of the person whose name next appears in rotation on the psychiatric panel. Professor Goldstein of Yale University Law School has observed that "perhaps the only way to eliminate the undesirable aspects of the impartial-expert proposal would be to have the court call more than one psychiatrist, each representing a different viewpoint and training, as 'its' witness," but he does not regard this as a very satisfactory solution (Goldstein, "The Psychiatrist and the Legal Process: The Proposals for an Impartial Expert and for Preventive Detention," *Amer. J. of Orthopsychiatry,* 33 [January, 1963]: 123).

13. What do *you* think of the arguments for and against "impartial" expert testimony?

THE RUBY CASE: WHO OR WHAT WAS ON TRIAL?

Lawrence S. Kubie, M.D., D.Sc.

The adversary system and the role of the psychiatrist in court is examined and the conclusion is drawn that a psychiatrist should not be a witness for either side. An alternative is suggested; that he should be hired by both parties in order to counteract the bias inherent in becoming an advocate for either side. Another alternative suggested is that the court appoint psychiatrists to testify as impartial witnesses. Finally, the use of psychiatric testimony in the Jack Ruby case is examined to show how the adversary system can destroy the value of psychiatrists' testimony.

In no meaningful sense was Jack Ruby ever tried for anything. Nor was the knowledge or integrity of the "experts" on trial; although some sharply critical reporters wrote as though they had been. It was a system which was on trial: a system of courtroom procedure which is called the "adversary system."[1] More specifically what we will consider is the effect of the adversary system on "expert" testimony. The term "expert" is a loaded and misleading one. It is misleading because it carries an unjustified assumption of unquestionable "expert" judgment and knowledge. An alternative term, such as "specialized" would not be perfect, but would have the advantage of making no assumptions beyond the fact that the witness in question has had an opportunity for long and special experience and study of the problems under consideration. It would carry no implication of comparative expertise.

[1] My thesis is that the adversary system, whatever its value in other respects, as used at present, destroys whatever potential values the testimony of the specialist, expert might have. In a personal letter to the author, the Honorable Emory Niles, for many years before his retirement, Chief Justice of the Baltimore Supreme Bench made the following comments on this article. I am quoting him verbatim with his permission: "I agree with the main thrust of your article against the paid 'expert' for one side. I agree that they should be selected by the court or by both sides together. In fact I instituted such a system in Baltimore when I was on the Bench. It exists in other places but it has not been used as widely as it should be."

Here I will interject a comment the purpose of which is to try to avoid any misunderstanding or misinterpretation of my position. On purely psychological grounds I have frequently questioned the present value of the adversary system not for the resolution of disagreements as to facts but for the resolution of disagreements among "experts." I have tried to make clear this distinction only to find that judges and lawyers would usually persist in their assumption that I was implying that it had *never* had any value, and even that I was also questioning at the same time the value of the jury system itself as a whole, as though the two were inseparable. I want to make it explicitly clear that my doubts about the value of the adversary system as a method of evaluating specialized opinions do not mean that I fail to recognize that its introduction into courtroom procedure in the past meant a great advance; and that I do not question the value of the jury system.

Therefore, when I challenge the adversary system with respect to its influences on "specialist" testimony, I do not question what it has contributed in the past. I question whether it is the *only* method or necessarily the best method by which the testimony of specialists can be ensured impartial expression and an impartial hearing. I also challenge my legal friends for not facing up to some of its deficiencies, especially the fact that it can be misused to becloud the truth, to make it less accessible, to distort evidence, and in the end to make proof impossible. Finally, I challenge it especially vigorously for debasing men of specialized experience, for attacking the value of their testimony, and for confusing the jury by doing so. No matter how great an advance it once represented, it must still be challenged if lawyers fail at the same time to acknowledge or to study its deficiencies and the distortions and limitations which it may have acquired with the passage of time.

Because the adversary system once constituted such an enormous advance, it holds a justifiably honored position in the minds of

---

Excerpted and reprinted with permission from the *Journal of Psychiatry and Law* 1, no. 4 (Winter 1973): 475. Copyright 1973 by Federal Legal Publications, Inc., 95 Morton Street, New York, New York 10014.

legal scholars and historians. This makes it difficult for them even to consider the possibility that some other system might be devised which could be better. Yet the unhappy fact is that the adversary system often makes a mockery even of competent and honest specialists and their testimony. . . .

Moreover when nonlegal specialists are introduced into the courtroom battle, the contending lawyers turn on them, aiming not to reconcile honest differences of opinion, but to attack and belittle them. They question their training, their veracity and their opinions and often end up by setting conscientious error (or even venal error) on a par with truth. In this way they make a mockery of any degree of specialized wisdom, skill, and special knowledge which the specialist may actually have brought to the proceedings.

One palliative suggestion worth considering might be that all questioning of specialists might be the exclusive privilege of the judge alone, perhaps prodded by the opposing lawyers, but also guided, if the judge so desires, by his own impartial specialists in the same field, and introduced into the proceeding as friends of the court. This would constitute at least a modest step toward the elimination of some of the more serious distortions which the adversary system imposes on specialist testimony. Of course, each of the contending parties could be allowed to have his own specialists in addition; but this would raise closely related and difficult problems, on which I will not venture an opinion here.[2]

Most practicing lawyers are opposed to any changes in this framework. So are many physicians, but not all. The opposition to change

[2] In order to clarify this let me quote from Dressler a brief word about the obvious psychology of the courtrooms. "In a trial, a lawyer plays a game. His goal and his duty to his client as he conceives it is less to find the 'truth' or what is 'right' than to defeat the opponent as resoundingly as possible. Therefore the lawyer's strategy aims to make the most of his own strong arguments and to minimize the weak ones, at the same time playing up the weaknesses of his opponent's arguments and minimizing its strengths. The adversary process may arise out of the sound principles that a man is innocent until proven guilty, that he must be defended in court, and that he is entitled to the best defense that can be devised for him. In practice, however, the objective of each lawyer is to win his client's case at any cost. Therefore the courtroom is a battleground where, once the battle is joined, the principles which underlie what is being fought about become relatively unimportant. What is of supreme importance is to win." Condensed from: David Dressler, *Trial by Combat in American Courts* (New Haven, Conn.: Yale University Press, 1964), pp. 423–32.

grows, in part, out of habituation; partly out of a fear of losing the social and judicial gains which current practices first achieved many years ago.

As actually practiced in the courtroom the adversary system has deteriorated into a battle between opposing lawyers who attempt not to establish the truth but to make an effective record of everything that can be said on one side of a question, and to rule out as far as possible, and often on the basis of technicalities, that which might be said for the other side. The resulting battle of wits is often masterly. It requires skill, ingenuity, scholarship and fast foot-work. It is not strange that lawyers enjoy it, take pride in it, and defend it. Furthermore the "experts" (both legal and nonlegal) profit by it financially. Yet, it is by no means clear that it does not impede and distort the search for evidence and its validation.

Compare this with the situation which confronts the scientist in his search for truth in the laboratory, in the field, or in the clinic. Here the scientist has three adversaries: (1) his own unconscious biases, which can warp both his perceptions of data and the concepts with which he generalizes from these percepts; (2) the complex maze of multiple concurrent variables from which the relevant variables must be extricated. As a result of these alone, the scientist in his laboratory may have to follow many misleading clues before he can eliminate them; and (3) his methods that may conceal errors for a long time, before he detects them. But in nature itself no other man lies to the scientist. Nor as he talks about his work does anyone leap to his feet to object to his evidence on the basis of precedent alone. Other scientists may challenge his evidence by pointing to flaws in the techniques by which it has been gathered, or because it is insufficient, inconclusive or inaccurate, or because some particular explanatory hypothesis is not adequate, necessary or unique. This, however, is basically different from the role of opposing lawyers under the adversary system, as each attempts to tear down the data and the opinions which the other presents.

Is it impossible for human integrity to devise better ways of using both legal talents and specialist testimony and better methods by which to compare the relative values of different procedures?

As an example let us review at this point the complex medical and psychiatric issues which the court in the trial of Jack Ruby was supposed to examine, expose and clarify, and not to obscure. There were several points which the court did *not* have to prove: *i.e.*, that Lee Oswald had been shot to death and that Jack Ruby had done the shooting. Millions witnessed this via TV. Sceptics might say that it was necessary nonetheless to prove that no other gun had been fired by someone else, that the whole thing had not been an affair staged by actors and that Oswald did not suffer from some concurrent fatal disease. I have no quarrel with precision in such matters; but to enable me to proceed with my essential argument allow me to by-pass these questions, which incidentally were never even raised in the courtroom battle. Instead I will assume that the fact of the killing and the identities of the killer and of the victim were self-evident and did not have to be proved in court. If this is so, then the one point that remained for the court to establish was the mental and physical condition of the killer *as he planned* the killing, *during the moment of the killing* and not merely while he was being held for trial, nor during the trial, nor after it. Was Ruby sick or well when he was planning to shoot Oswald and while he was shooting? These questions alone raise difficult questions. Does medical science today have at its command psychological or psychophysiological methods by which such questions can be decided retrospectively? If so, what are they? And how can such data be adduced in any courtroom procedure? And especially during a courtroom procedure which is conducted under the adversary system?

The technical difficulties of the relevant medico-psychological investigations are formidable but not insurmountable. Let us assume for the sake of argument that from time to time Ruby lapsed into that state of psychological disorganization which for want of a better label we call "insanity" or "psychosis." Even then we would confront questions which may not be answerable in the present state of our knowledge. Few if any patients are psychotic continuously for 24 hours a day and without fluctuating interruptions over days, weeks, and months. Therefore, even if it had not been proved that for years Ruby had suffered from psychotic episodes of variable duration, we still could not claim to know on the basis of statistical probabilities alone whether Mr. Ruby was sane or insane as he planned and executed the killing.

The same thing is true for disordered brain waves. It was generally known and acknowledged that Ruby's brain waves showed periodic disturbances. Yet such disturbances are not constant. Therefore, only continuous round-the-clock studies of his brain waves over days and nights, awake and asleep and for weeks could have determined what percentage of the time out of every week or month his brain wave tracings were disordered and what percentage of the time they were more normally

organized. Such round-the-clock studies could ascertain whether there was any consistent tendency for these abnormalities to show up in certain parts of the diurnal cycle and not in others. Students might then go further and compare his general behavior and his performance on psychiatric examinations and on appropriate psychological tests in relation to the varied phases in the electrical activity of his brain. They could check to see if the records of his brain waves during sleep showed correlations with any special types of dreams. Such data could then be correlated with studies of eye movements during sleep. All of these studies, although possible, are attended by formidable but not insurmountable difficulties. Unhappily no such round-the-clock studies have ever been made on any accused person; and certainly not on Jack Ruby.

Even if they had been, we would still not have been medically justified in drawing any conclusions from them as to the mental state of Ruby as he was planning the shooting or at the time when he shot Lee Oswald. Therefore, it is preposterous to claim that it is ever possible to make a statistically accurate extrapolation out of the present into the past.

Furthermore, we should not forget that, with exquisite accuracy and detail, paranoid patients can plan and execute a criminal killing based on their delusional system. Therefore, the capacity to plan and to execute is clearly no proof that anyone is insane or well. The proof lies in the delusional system that pervades the thinking and underlies and produces the act.

We could not say that if Ruby showed disordered brain waves associated with disordered psychological productions and behavior 50 percent of the time during any period of observation before and/or during the trial, there would be a 50-50 chance that his brain waves had been in a disordered state when he planned and carried out the shooting. Nor could we make any such a claim if the figures were 10 percent or 90 percent. This is because the frequency of such outbursts of disordered electrical activity can vary in any patient from once an hour, day, week or month to other phases in which they are almost continuous. . . . Therefore, unless there had been electrodes on the head of Ruby almost continuously both before and after the shooting, as well as during it, and unless someone had drawn blood samples for chemical analysis before, during and after the act, no diagnosis of his psychophysiological state during the act would be possible based on statistical probabilities alone, not for a neurologist, neurobiochemist, neurophysiologist, psychiatrist, psychologist, judge or jury.

We must add one other complication: namely, that most epileptics never commit crimes. Some do so only when they are wholly free from the epileptiform disturbance. The same thing is true for psychomotor epilepsy. Into which group Ruby belonged no one knows. How then was the judge, jury, lawyer or specialist furthering the cause of justice in that courtroom in Dallas?

To all of this we must add one further complication: that even if we had such data as I have outlined, we would not be able to interpret it with confidence unless similar comparative studies had been made on a random and representative sample of many thousands of other human beings of all ages, men with and without recordings of disordered brain waves, with and without records of disturbed or antisocial behavior, sane and insane, criminal and noncriminal, and with and without records of neurotic or psychotic disturbances, and from different cultural, educational, economic, and racial backgrounds. Not the Department of Justice of the federal government or of any state, nor any penologists, nor any foundation, nor the NIMH, nor any law school has conducted such vast studies. Yet without any such data the questions before the judge and jury were unanswerable by *any* specialists. This is why I say that the procedure itself was on trial; not the man. It was on trial for its lack of scientific sophistication and integrity, for not publicly acknowledging its own limitations.

Note that this is not an attack upon nor a criticism of my colleagues. But this does not mean that I cannot question the wisdom of their having consented to testify on these issues under the circumstances which were prescribed for them.

The late Dr. Manfred Guttmacher, who testified at Ruby's trial, was for many years the chief medical officer of the Supreme Bench of Baltimore and as such was always the impartial expert *for the court*, never for any side. My deep conviction is that he and the other experts would have been wise to refuse to testify in the Ruby case unless they had been retained by both sides or by the court. Had such a challenge been refused, they could have repeated the offer publicly, and in this way might have forced the whole procedure into sounder channels, thus setting up a sound precedent and protecting their own testimony and that of their colleagues from the distortions to which they are regularly subjected under the battering of the adversary system.

I do not acept as valid the objection that it is useless to point out the defects of an existing system, unless you can immediately propose a better one. It is not useless to prove that gold salts do not cure cancer unless one can come up at once with a cure; because the elimination of erroneous leads is often an essential preliminary to launching a search for better ways. As a contrast to the adversary system I will mention tentatively only one alternative method as a possible improvement; and I mention this only as an example. In the first place lawyers themselves could serve as expert legal advisors to the court itself, and not for the prosecution or for the defense. It would then be their duty to assemble data, to sift evidence, to examine and summarize the history of all relevant law and its precedents and to present this material, perhaps not in open court where it might merely serve to befuddle the jury, but in briefs submitted to the judge for his later exposition to the jury.

Now let us consider comparable ways in which the adversary system misuses not only lawyers, but also nonlegal specialists. It is a paradoxical anomaly for any "expert" to appear as an "expert for a side." Furthermore, honest testimony when used in the framework of the adversary system may actually damage the side for which the specialist offers testimony. For myself I will say that, with only three exceptions in nearly 40 years of practice, I have refused to participate as an expert witness in any medico-legal procedure unless I was retained by both sides. The three exceptions were situations which involved the protection of a child from destructively sick, alcoholic, dishonest, promiscuous and sometimes overtly incestuous parent. Under these circumstances I put aside my scruples and consented to appear as an "expert"; but in my mind this was done not for the sake of the battling adults of one side or the other, but for the protection of the child.

Apart from such special situations it is my conviction that all specialists (not only medical and psychiatric but also specialists from other fields) should refuse to appear as specialists for a side. The specialist himself may be wholly incorruptible whether by a fee or by anything else; but when he comes into court as the special pleader for a side his opinions and even his data encounter a powerful tide of sceptical distrust. Against this his personal honesty is no protection. He faces the suspicion, whether spoken or unspoken that his testimony has been colored by his loyalty to the side which pays him or to which he has close personal ties. This can be true even when he is unpaid and appears out of personal friendship for one of the contestants, or out of a sense of civic duty. No matter what the reason, the mere fact that the specialist is *for* one side or *for* the other will inevitably color the attitudes of both the judge and the jury toward everything he says.

Furthermore, if the expert is a psychiatrist or clinical psychologist he must acknowledge that his personal loyalties and his general social and political convictions inevitably, if unconsciously, will bias both his observations and his judgment. In spite of every effort to correct for such biases, the psychologist or psychiatrist is no more immune to such self-deception than is the layman. No one is invulnerable to the subtle effects of loyalties, especially where quantifiable and objective data are scarce, and where the specialist has to depend largely on intuitive judgments and feelings.

Subtle influences of this kind can never be wholly eliminated from human judgment. What we can do is to create situations in which their biasing influences will be minimized. Therefore, if we come into court as special pleaders retained either by the court, or alternatively retained by both sides jointly, our testimony will have a better chance of being based upon objectively perceived and summarized data, and also of being heard without suspicions of bias.

How else can the specialist be a friend of the court and a friend of justice? That there will still be disagreements among them is as it should be. One would never want to eliminate honest disagreement. But the presentation of that disagreement would then be in the hands of men who were biased neither by mercenary considerations nor by subtle emotional affiliations of any kind. The lawyers too would then be friends of the court and friends of the experts, cooperating with them for the clarification of their testimony, instead of attacking their testimony to destroy its clarity. No consideration of the jury system is complete if it omits consideration of the distortions which are injected into its procedures by the adversary system.

If all experts of any kind were to boycott procedures such as the Ruby trial, we might influence the legal profession to abandon or alter a procedure which distorts the entire jury process and the potential values of all specialist testimony.

Most impartial and disinterested specialists long for such a change and would welcome it. They do not really enjoy being put into an arena with their hands tied so that the opposing lawyer can slug away at them, at their competence and integrity, and at their testimony.

In the Ruby case the issue which confronted the experts was not whether Ruby had shot and killed Oswald, but whether Ruby was mentally sick while planning and executing the act, and whether his electroencephalogram showed disordered brain waves *at that moment*. No "expert" could answer such questions. As I have said above, it is doubtful whether anyone is psychotic 24 hours a day. Patients go into and out of states of psychotic disorganization sometimes in the course of a few minutes or in the midst of a sentence. Brain waves change similarly from moment to moment. Therefore, the relevant question was whether as he planned the act and at the moment that he shot Oswald Ruby was sick or well, mentally responsible or irresponsible. Under any circumstances these are difficult questions on which to present objective and conclusive testimony. Does the adversary system contribute to a clarification of such questions or to their obfuscation?

The court's attempt to reconstruct retroactively the mental condition of the perpetrator of a criminal act is at best extremely difficult. When the attempt is made in the face of conflicting testimony of paid "experts" for a side it becomes impossible. The least we can do is to modify the system so as to eliminate these grosser sources of bias. The *Ruby* case was a demonstration of how the adversary system can be misused to destroy the value of the testimony of witnesses with specialized knowledge. These so-called "experts" can better assist the processes of justice when they are retained by the court or by both sides jointly; but not when retained by one side.

THE COACH, YES; THE UMPIRE, NO

Henry A. Davidson, M.D.

It sometimes looks as if psychiatry promises more than it can deliver, that the gap between promise and performance is too wide. This is especially true at the interface between psychiatry and law. The defense attorney pleads to have the sexual deviate or the aggressively antisocial personality turned over to the psychiatrist, not the jailer. He has been told that these defendants are patients to be treated, not criminals to be scorned. So he turns to us and says: treat him! Now and then we present statistics showing that such and such a percentage of alcoholics or compulsive thieves or severe gamblers have been cured by deep psychotherapy, reconditioning, or by the prescription of behavior-modifying drugs. But we don't assert that our batting average, at best, is very high.

There is a current cry for changes in legal policy and legal procedure, most of which depend on the theory that there *is* a psychiatric technique of reform. Thus, we hail legislation which outlaws the repetitive arrest of alcoholics or narcotic addicts. If a defendant is arrested for rape, rioting, or robbery, we suggest—or at any rate we welcome—hospitalization for "therapy." When such a patient demands his release on the basis that he is not getting treatment, we resist by arguing that the entire hospital milieu provides treatment—or at least a therapeutic atmosphere. If the court were to suggest (as some of them have) that proper treatment would require electroshock therapy or tranquilizing drugs or psychotherapy, we retort that no judge can write such a prescription. We are the only ones who can do that.

The use of the mental hospital for law violators may seem like a progressive step. But it is impaled on the horns of a dilemma. If we treat the disturbed offender the way we treat the psychotic nonoffender, then, with an open ward and an extended privileges philosophy, he may walk out through the policy-fixed open door. If we take steps to keep him from walking out, we are, instead of converting the prison into a hospital, doing just the opposite and converting our hospitals into prisons.

A similar dichotomy has developed around commitment laws. We don't like the "legalistic" flavor of commitment procedures, so we suggest reforming the laws so that they will have more of a medical and less of a legal tincture. For instance, giving a patient notice that he is to be committed is an article of faith among lawyers and civil libertarians. But we know of patients who were made more depressed, more excited, or more paranoid when confronted by witnesses testifying to their mental illness. If we rewrite the commitment laws so that no such confrontation is required we may spare the patient this kind of embarrassment; but then we deprive him of a legal right. If we preserve his constitutional rights, we may injure medical and psychiatric care. A patient locked into a ward against his will has every right to look to the law to protect his freedom. If we tell the judge to go away because this is a medical question, we set up a possible tyranny by doctors who make decisions about keeping a patient locked up. If we let the court make the final decision (and this is, in the last analysis, how it always has to be), then the commitment procedure, no matter how "medical" at top, becomes legal at bottom.

If we abandon the Magna Carta-based privilege of habeas corpus, we threaten the very foundations of the Law with a capital "L." If we retain the privilege, we entrust the disposition of the mental patient to the courts.

Suppose we insist on a psychiatric justification for abortion. If we allowed a curettage because the woman is depressed or anxious, we put psychiatrists at the doorway to life—since any woman worried about her pregnancy can develop anxiety or depression about it.

The problem is not just giving a psychiatrist a role in law reform but rather how to keep the bench, the bar, and the public from becoming disenchanted if we fail to reform juvenile delinquents, cure alcoholics, straighten out deviates, and rehabilitate addicts. One phase of the problem is this: The psychiatrist may say "Maybe yes; maybe no" or that there is something to be said on both sides, or that the chances are thus and so. This is a commendable

Reprinted with permission from the *American Journal of Psychiatry* 125 (1968): 825–26. Copyright 1968, the American Psychiatric Association.

caution in any phase of medical science. But the courts must make a decision. The judge cannot say: "Maybe the plaintiff is right, but then there is much to be said for the defense, too." The court may certainly be wrong. But one thing the judge may not be is indecisive.

By all means, let us play a vigorous role in suggesting reforms in the law. We may have some very sage advice to give. But legal procedures and constitutional rights are fashioned in the lawyer's ball park. We may be useful coaches, but we cannot be the umpires.

SUGGESTIONS FOR ADDITIONAL READING

Diamond, B. "The Psychiatrist as Advocate," *Journal of Psychiatry and Law* (Spring 1973): 5.

English, O. S., and Finch, S. *Introduction to Psychiatry*, 3rd ed. New York: W. W. Norton Co., 1964, pp. 70–100.

Goldstein, A. S. "The Psychiatrist and the Legal Process: The Proposals for an Impartial Expert and for Preventive Detention," *Amer. J. of Orthopsychiatry* 33 (1963): 123.

Guttmacher, M. S. *The Mind of the Murderer*. New York: Farrar, Straus and Cudahy, 1960, pp. 109–26. (Also available in paperback.)

Haward, L. R. C. "Psychological Evidence," *Forensic Sciences Soc. J.* 2 (September 1961): 8.

Lapain, "The Psychologist as an Expert Witness in Assessing Mental Diseases or Defect," *A.B.A.J.* 50 (March 1964): 239.

Marshall, J. *Law and Psychology in Conflict*. New York: Bobbs-Merrill, 1966; Anchor Books, 1969.

Polier, J. *The Rule of Law and the Role of Psychiatry*. Baltimore, Md.: The Johns Hopkins Press, 1968.

"Psychologist as Witness on Mental Incompetency," *JAMA* 198 (October 10, 1966): 313.

Symposium. *Psychiatry and the Courts, American Journal of Psychiatry* 126, no. 4 (October 1969).

Symposium. *Psychiatry and Law, American Journal of Psychiatry* 129, no. 3 (September 1972).

"The Principles of Medical Ethics, American Medical Association, with Annotations Especially Applicable to Psychiatry," *American Journal of Psychiatry* 130, no. 9 (September 1973).

"Admissibility of Physiological or Psychological Truth and Deception Test or its Results to Support Physician's Testimony," 41 ALR FED 1369 (1971).

"Construction and Application of Provision in Subsection (e) of Criminal Justice Act of 1964 (18 USC Sec. 3006A [e]) Concerning Right of Indigent Defendant to Aid in Obtaining Services of Investigator or Expert," 6 ALR FED 1007 (1971).

"Necessity and Admissibility of Expert Testimony as to Credibility of Witness," 20 ALR 3d 684 (1968).

"Qualification of Nonmedical Psychologist to Testify as to Mental Condition or Competency," 78 ALR 2d 919 (1961).

8

Privileged and Confidential Communications

Chapter 8 examines the problems that occur when a patient's wish to keep communications to a therapist from being disclosed, conflicts with the needs of the state, an employer, or other person, to information about his mental condition. Dr. Shah's article focuses on the patient's right to prohibit disclosure of communications made to a psychologist during legal proceedings. However, issues discussed in the article are equally applicable to communications between patients and other therapists, e.g., psychiatrists and lay analysts, because the premise underlying protection of communications is based on the function performed or service rendered, not the profession of the confidant. The Shah article is followed by a summary of contemporary privilege statutes. Next, some of the practical problems encountered by therapists trying to maintain patients' privacy are described in excerpts from two panel discussions. The last selection on the question of privilege deals with a new issue: Does the therapist have a right to refuse to disclose such communications, regardless of the wishes of a patient, in a particular case? Until this argument was advanced in the *Lifschutz* case, it was generally agreed that privilege belongs solely to the patient.

The problems encountered by patients and therapists when the information requested will not be used in a legal proceeding, but to determine such matters as whether the patient will be employed, admitted to a school, given a driver's license, etc., are the subject of the last two selections in the chapter.

PRIVILEGED COMMUNICATIONS, CONFIDENTIALITY, AND PRIVACY

Saleem A. Shah, Ph.D.

GENERAL CONSIDERATIONS

Privileged communication protects a client from having his confidential and private discussions revealed to the public during legal proceedings without his permission. It is a legal right which exist by statute. Except for the attorney-client privilege which existed in common law, other confidential communications are privileged only if the right has been created by statute. Although there have been one or two exceptions to the above rule, for example, Binder v. Ruvell (1952),[1] the decision in which case was not appealed, appellate courts nevertheless have uniformly held that privilege cannot be created by judicial decision.

It is important to remember that the privilege belongs to the client and he alone has the right to exercise it. The privilege does not

[1] Civil Docket 52 C 25 35, Circuit Court of Cook County, Ill., June 24, 1952.

In addition to the valuable contributions of the Committee members in preparation of the aforementioned report, the author would also like to acknowledge the helpful comments and suggestions made by the following persons during various stages of preparation of this material: Elyce Z. Ferster, Jane D. Hildreth, Paul D. Lipsitt, Marcia MacNaughton, Stephen Rosenberg, Ralph K. Schwitzgebel, and Jay Ziskin.

Excerpted and reprinted with permission from Privileged Communications, Professional Psychology vol. 1. no. 1 (Nov. 1969).

belong to the professional and neither is it meant for his protection nor for the enhancement of his professional status. Once the client has waived his privilege or, as described later, has compromised it through his actions, the professional has no grounds for withholding disclosure of the relevant information.

The privilege actually refers to the admissibility of testimony under procedural rules of evidence. In this regard, the rules are analogous to those imposed upon other nonadmissible evidence. Thus, other testimony would be excluded when based, for example, upon constitutional and due process considerations such as "search and seizure" and "self-incrimination."

A brief historical perspective on privilege should facilitate understanding of these exceptions to the general rule that the proper administration of justice requires disclosure of all pertinent information. Originally, under English law, a person who qualified as a witness could not be compelled to testify in judicial proceedings. However, for about the past 400 years the rule has been that a witness must testify. This rule was based on the important principle that the administration of justice is of benefit to all and, therefore, all competent persons had a public duty to contribute to its proper functioning. However, shortly after the policy of testimonial compulsion was adopted, the courts began to be confronted with witnesses who refused to answer particular questions on the grounds that the information was confidential. Eventually, it was decided that the state considered some relationships to be of sufficient importance that communications pertinent to them would be privileged. It should be evident that exemptions from the obligation to testify impede in some degree the achievement of the fair administration of justice. This interference with the administration of justice has been justified on the basis that the injury to the relationship resulting from disclosure would be greater than the loss to justice if the information was considered privileged.[2]

This, then, is the critical basis for the consideration of new privileges: whether, from a social policy standpoint, the injury to the relationship resulting from disclosure would be greater than the loss to justice if the information were considered privileged.

Since the privilege interferes with the administration of justice, quite understandably this protection is rarely conferred and then only to protect relationships with specially situated persons who, in a sense, become instruments of some larger social policy.

The privileged relationships that the law protects in this category may be viewed as those in which the communicant becomes in a sense an extension of the communicator. For example, confidential statements by a husband to a wife are protected from disclosure in court because it is considered important that married couples be free to communicate with each other in an intimate fashion and without fear of revelation; husband and wife, it is said, are one. Likewise, the client talking to his lawyer is talking to his own representative, his advocate, and in colloquial expression, to his "mouthpiece." The latter term, while common and somewhat indecorous, does express the concept of the extension of self. In addition, the attorney's function in being advocate for his client is one which can be performed effectively only if the client is cloaked in a privilege that assures him full protection from harm when he seeks the legal services to which he is entitled by law. The client disclosing his deepest thoughts, his most private feelings, his fears, anxieties, and problems to his therapist, in an even more obvious sense is in an especially close, private, and personal relationship.

In essence, then, the issue of privileged communication involves the drawing of a balance between two important social values: (1) society's right to have access to information of safeguarding the individual's right to privacy in certain relationships which serve the larger interests of a society. It should be clear that these privileges are not a matter of constitutional right, but rather are a matter of public policy.

Wigmore's four criteria. There has been much dispute concerning the factors which should exist before a particular relationship is judged to merit protection by the privilege. Four criteria suggested by Dean Wigmore, one of the country's leading legal authorities on the rules of evidence, have generally been accepted as essential (Wigmore 1961).[3]

1. The communications must originate in a confidence that they will not be disclosed.

2. This element of confidentiality must be essential to the full and satisfactory maintenance of the relation between the parties.

3. The relation must be one which in the opinion of the community ought to be sedulously fostered.

[2] E. Ferster, Confidential and Privilege Communications. *Readings in Law and Psychiatry* (Baltimore: The Johns Hopkins Press, 1968), p. 153.

[3] J. H. Wigmore, *Evidence in Trials at Common Law*, vol. 8. (McNaughton rev.) (Boston: Little Brown, 1961).

4. The injury that would inure to the relation by the disclosure of the communications must be greater than the benefit thereby gained for the correct disposal of litigation.

Emphasis on the key words and phrases in Wigmore's criteria can readily be perceived as indicating the rather obvious qualification of psychotherapeutic and related consultations for the protection offered by the privilege. Thus, even though the appropriateness of some privileges, namely, the physician-patient privilege, has been seriously questioned (e.g., Baldwin 1962,[4] Chafee 1943[5]), the psychotherapeutic relationship would appear clearly to merit such protection.

Goldstein and Katz (1962)[6] point out that society could not tolerate such interference with its processes for resolving disputes unless it were reasonably clear that other and more important objectives were served by nondisclosure. In regard to extensions of the privilege to psychotherapeutic and related situations Goldstein and Katz have stated: "Treatment of the mentally ill is too important and the assurance of confidentiality too central to it, to risk jeopardizing the whole because of the relevance of some patients' statements to some legal proceedings [p. 735]."

Privileged Communications and Clients of Psychologists

In many states the statutes providing privilege to clients of psychologists simply cite the attorney-client law as the model. A typical statement, for example, reads as follows: "The confidential relations and communications between a certified psychologist and his client are placed on the same basis as provided by law for those between an attorney and his client. Nothing in this act shall be construed to require such privileged communications to be disclosed."

There are a few statutes which attempt to delineate specific guidelines applicable to the relationship between psychologists and their clients. The following are two examples of such laws:

Connecticut (amendments approved June 24, 1969. Section 13):

As used in this section, "person" means an individual who, for the purpose of securing psychological services, consults a licensed psychologist practising in the area of clinical psychology. Except as hereinafter provided, in civil and criminal cases, in proceedings preliminary thereto, and in legislative and administrative proceedings, a licensed psychologisy shall not disclose any communication made to him by a person while he is engaged in the practice of clinical psychology, unless the person or his authorized representative waives such privilege. There shall be no privilege for any relevant communications under this section: (a) If a judge finds that any person after having been informed that the communications would not be privileged, has made communications to a clinical psychologist in the course of a psychological examination ordered by the court provided that such communications shall be admissible only on issues involving such person's psychological conditions; or (b) in a civil proceeding in which any person introduces his psychological condition as an element of his claim or defense or, after such person's death, when such condition is introduced by any party claiming or defending through or as a beneficiary of such person and the judge finds that it is more important to the interests of justice that the communication be disclosed than that the relationship between such person and psychologist be protected.

Illinois:

No psychologist shall disclose any information he may have acquired from persons consulting him in his professional capacity, necessary to enable him to render services in his professional capacity, to such persons except only (a) in trials for homicide when the disclosure related directly to the fact or immediate circumstances of the homicide, (b) in all proceedings the purpose of which is to determine mental competency, or in which a defense of mental incapacity is raised, (c) in action, civil or criminal, against the psychologist for malpractice, (d) with the expressed consent of the client, or in the case of his death or disability, of his personal representative or other person authorized to sue or of the beneficiary of an insurance policy on his life, health, or physical condition, or (e) upon an issue as to the validity of a document as a will of his client.

It is important to note that, while statutes modeled after the well-established attorney-client laws have the virtue of relative simplicity of definition and may also be somewhat easier to get enacted, such statutes do not consider the many specific situations unique to the psychologist-client relationship.

[4] R. Baldwin, "Confidentiality between Physician and Patient," *Maryland Law Review* 22 (1962): 181–89.

[5] Z. Chafee, "Privilege Communication: Is Justice Served or Obstructed by Closing the Doctor's Mouth on the Witness Stand?" *Yale Law Journal* 52 (1943): 607–9.

[6] A. S. Goldstein, and J. Katz, "Psychiatrist—Patient Privilege: The Gap Proposal and the Connecticut Statute," *American Journal of Psychiatry* 118 (1962): 733–39.

Fisher (1964)[7] has also referred to the above problem of a privilege modeled after that of attorney-client and has remarked: "It is unreasonable to unthinkingly impose, for the sake of 'simplicity,' such a rule on the newly privileged relationship if there is good reason to do otherwise. The unqualified use of the attorney-client parameters in these new statutes is irrational" [p. 641].

SOME SPECIFIC ISSUES REGARDING PRIVILEGE

It needs to be emphasized that it is very difficult to make definite and precise statements about interpretations of the law relating to the psychologist-client privilege, since specific particulars are still relatively unexplored and untested. In addition, not only are there variations in the phrasing of the statutes in different states, but there are also differences in the rules governing federal and state courts. Besides, when disputes arise for adjudication, the specific facts involved can and do vary widely, hence we can anticipate differences in court rulings among different judges. In view of this, the discussion in this report should be viewed only as offering rather general guidelines. When faced with specific problems or questions on such legal issues, psychologists would be well advised to seek proper legal counsel and to be guided by such information.

Before discussing a number of specific issues pertaining to the topic of privilege it should be made clear that, to the extent that most psychologist-client laws are modeled after that of the attorney-client relationship, the discussion very largely will draw upon the rules and interpretations developed within the latter context. To the extent that these two professional relationships differ in many regards, and also because of the relative absence of case law regarding the psychologist-client privilege, the statements that will be made should be considered tentative.

Circumstances in which the privilege prevails. Even though the statute may not so specify, it is generally understood that only those communications are protected which are intended to be private and confidential. Thus, communications in the presence of "casual third persons," or which have also been made to other persons in the absence of any privacy or confidentiality, or discussions in a social context, would not be protected. Where the privilege has been compromised by the client by

virtue of his communications in other situations, such information may be properly divulged by the professional on the stand. However, the privilege remains intact for portions of the communications which have not been compromised in the above manner. The privilege hinges upon the client's belief that he is consulting a qualified professional. It may, therefore, be sufficient that the client believes the person qualified. It has been argued by some (e.g., Geiser & Rheingold 1964)[8] that even a client's communications with a quack passing himself off as a qualified professional would very likely be protected, since the privilege belongs to the client and is meant for his protection.

It has also been held that communications, in the course of preliminary discussions, with a view to obtaining further professional services are privileged, even though the services may not be obtained later. Likewise, payment or agreement to pay a fee is not essential to the establishment of privileged communications in the professional-client relationship. However, the consultation has to be in the context of a professional confidential relationship—not discussions with a professional simply as a friend or acquaintance.

Who may assert or waive the privilege? The privilege belongs to the client and is designed to protect him, since he would be the one hurt by disclosures of his confidences. Therefore, it is the client who decides whether he wishes to assert or to waive his privilege. For the privilege to be exercised it must be asserted by the client, or at times by his counsel or the professional, by an explicit affirmative declaration. Failure to claim such protection can be ruled to constitute a waiver. In the client's absence, the judge has the discretion to enforce the protection which the statute provides, either on his own initiative or on suggestion of counsel or the other professional involved in the confidential relationship.

If the client on direct examination testifies in regard to his confidential communications with the professional, this would constitute waiver of the privilege in respect to such consultation. There is a general rule that the client cannot tell some and then seek to withhold the rest of such communications. If he decides to open the door by discussing certain aspects of the private communication from the stand, then there is no privilege for any other portion of such communication. In somewhat similar fashion, when several professionals have par-

[7] R. M. Fisher, "The Psychotherapeutic Professions and the Law of Privileged Communications," *Wayne Law Review* 10 (1964): 609–54.

[8] R. L. Geiser and P. D. Rheingold, "Psychology and the Legal Process: Testimonial Privileged Communications," *American Psychologist* 19 (1964): 831–38.

ticipated jointly in a consultation and the client calls one of them to disclose part of the shared information, he cannot then object to the testimony of the other participating professionals who may be called by the adversary.

When the client is judged to be mentally incompetent, or if he is a minor (i.e., under the age of 18), assertion or waiver of the privilege should come from the parents or legal guardians.

Whenever a psychologist examines a client privately for an attorney, the information thus obtained is covered by the attorney-client privilege, since the psychologist is functioning as an agent of the attorney. Likewise, when the psychologist serves as the agent of a physician or psychiatrist in certain situations, the information disclosed by the client will be covered by the physician-patient or psychiatrist-patient privilege, even though there may be no statutory protection for the client's communications with a psychologist in that particular jurisdiction.

Exceptions to the privilege. All statutes pertaining to privileged communication provide certain exceptions to the general rule against disclosure. In the sphere of public health law, physicians are required by law in many states to report certain facts. For example, they are required to report certain communicable and occupational diseases to the local health officer. In addition, they must report gunshot and knife wounds, suicide attempts, abortions, and, in some instances, addiction to narcotics. Disclosure of such information is seemed a safeguard for the community. (In a strict sense, however, the aforementioned reporting laws are not exceptions to the privileged communication laws, since the privilege relates only to the disclosure of confidential communications in legal proceedings.)

There also are situations in which the rule against disclosure of privileged communications does not apply. Many of the physician-patient and attorney-client privilege statutes and also some of the psychologist-client laws, for example,l the Illinois statute, have several explicitly stated exceptions. Among the most common exceptions are criminal prosecutions for homicide and in workmen's compensation cases; disputes between persons involved in the special relationship, namely, malpractice suits; civil commitment proceedings and contests regarding the validity of a document as a will of the client; legal actions in which the condition of the person's mental functioning has been introduced as an element in the claim or defense. (Although this situation may also be viewed as an operational or implicit waiver of the privilege, rather than as an exception to the rule.)

Since many of the psychologist-client statutes follow the attorney-client model, it is very important to remember that in the latter relationships the privilege does not extend to situations in which the legal advice or service sought is in reference to either the client's plans or intentions to commit a crime or fraud. This is sometimes referred to as the "future crime or fraud" exception.

Finally, we may note that certain privilege statutes have explicit qualifying clauses. For example, the psychologist-client privilege law in North Carolina states:

No person, duly authorized as a practicing psychologist or psychological examiner, nor any of his employees or associates, shall be required to disclose any information which he may have acquired in rendering professional psychological services, and which information was necessary to enable him to render professional psychological services: Provided, that the presiding judge of a superior court may compel such disclosure, if in his opinion the same is necessary to a proper administration of justice [General Statute of North Carolina, Section 8-53.2, emphasis added].

The above provision restricting the privilege rule also occurs in the physician-patient privilege in North Carolina (McCormick 1954).[9] In states having the above restrictions, the privilege is, therefore, only a qualified right because its use depends on the judges' discretion. The above qualification in some of these laws tends to defeat the purpose of the privilege, since the client cannot be entirely sure it is safe to reveal himself.

Circumstances in which the privilege does not exist. As noted earlier, in the case of the attorney-client, privileged communications occurring in the presence of a "casual third party" are not deemed to be confidential and hence are not protected. The reasoning for this particular rule is that if the communications were confidential or private they would not have taken place in the presence of such "casual" third persons. However, this rule does not apply to situations where the other persons present are the professionals' associates who are necessary and customary participants during consultations.

The question is raised as to what implications the above rules would have for joint marital counseling and therapy, family therapy, and group therapy. One might well be able to argue that in these situations the presence of spouse, other members of the family, and the

[9] C. T. McCormick, *Handbook of Law of Evidence* (St. Paul, Minnesota: West, 1954).

other group members, respectively, are necessary and customary participants in such forms of therapy.

MacCormick (1959)[10] has discussed the importance of confidentiality of communications in a therapy group within a correctional setting and favors such therapeutic relationships being included in the privilege. Certainly, the importance and significance of legal protection for confidential communications with a therapist loom even larger when the treatment is carried on is such institutional settings.

It should be remembered, however, that the above viewpoints are not reflected in the more conservative judicial interpretations of the privilege. Furthermore, since the privilege is an exception to the general requirement of full disclosure of all pertinent information to assist in the proper administration of justice, it typically is subject to strict judicial interpretation.

It is interesting to note that a recent amendment to the Colorado statute specifically refers to the group therapy situation:

A certified psychologist shall not be examined without the consent of his client, as to any communication made by the client to him or his advice given thereon in the course of professional employment; nor shall a certified psychologist's secretary, stenographer, or clerk be examined without the consent of his employer concerning any fact, the knowledge of which he has acquired in such capacity; nor shall any person who has participated in any psychological therapy sessions, be examined concerning any knowledge gained during the course of such therapy without the consent of the person or persons to whom the testimony sought relates [Colorado Statute (amendment of July 1, 1967), Section 16]

Confidentiality in court-ordered mental examinations. As discussed earlier under Exceptions to the privilege, once the issue of the client's mental condition has been introduced as an element in the trial, no privilege attaches to information obtained as a result of court-ordered mental examinations on that issue, for example, pretrial incompetency examinations. It is, therefore, very important that whenever conducting court-ordered examinations, the psychologist should explicitly and even repetitiously inform the defendant about the nature and purpose of the examination and the possible use of the findings. He should clearly advise the client that no privilege is involved in that particular examination situation, and that the client may decline to answer questions if he so chooses. This cautionary instruction to the defendant is also very much related to Principle 7(d) of the "ethical Standards of Psychologists" relating to client welfare (APA, 1968): "The psychologist who asks that an individual reveal personal information in the course of interviewing, testing, or evaluation, or who allows such information to be divulged to him, does so only after making certain that the responsible person is fully aware of the purposes of the interview, testing or evaluation, and of the ways in which the information may be used" [p. 358].

In this connection, a procedural rule followed in federal courts holds that any information pertaining to the defendant's guilt or innocence which has been adduced during the course of the aforementioned examinations is either restricted or nonadmissible. Thus, whether the examination is in reference to the issue of competence to stand trial or when insanity has been interposed as a defense against criminal responsibility, only that information can be reported or be testified to which relates to legal questions concerning the defendant's mental condition. Even though information pertaining to the defendant's guilt or innocence may have been obtained during the examination, it cannot be reported. However, in the above as also in other matters, there are important differences between federal and state courts. Nevertheless, psychologists and other mental health professionals involved in such examinations have an obligation and professional responsibility to become aware of all such issues pertaining to legal and ethical questions.

(Parenthetically, it may be noted that the defendant is in a sense asked to waive some of his rights when he agrees to a court-ordered examination in a criminal action. If the person were to be examined by a private professional acting as an agent of the defendant's attorney, the information obtained would first be placed in the hands of the counsel, and not—as in the case of court-ordered examinations—given directly to the court. Recent amendments to the Federal Rules of Criminal Procedure broaden the possibilities for reciprocal discovery and inspection, for example, when motions are to be filed regarding medical, mental, or other such examinations. Thus, at least in federal courts, the aforementioned problems are not so serious. However, such problems as are indeed involved could be avoided were the services of private professionals obtained to act as agents of the defendant.)

[10] A. MacCormick, "A Criminologist Looks at Privilege," *American Journal of Psychiatry* 115 (1959): 1068–70.

STATUTORY SUMMARY OF PHYSICIAN–PATIENT PRIVILEGED COMMUNICATION LAWS

Elyce Zenoff Ferster

In forty states communications between psychiatrists and their patients are privileged (six of these by specific psychiatrist-patient statutes and the remainder by physician-patient statutes). Twenty-two of these states also recognize, by statute, a psychologist-client privilege. It is noteworthy that an additional five states do not confer a privilege upon psychiatrist-patient communications, yet give this privilege to psychologists.

The following are the states providing these privileges:

Psychiatrist: Connecticut, Florida, Georgia, Illinois, Kentucky, Maine.

Physician, Surgeon: Arizona, Arkansas,[4] California, Colorado, Hawaii, Idaho, Illinois, Indiana, Iowa, Kansas, Kentucky,[2] Louisiana, Maine, Massachusetts, Michigan, Minnesota, Mississippi, Missouri, Montana, Nebraska, Nevada, New Hampshire,[2] New Jersey, New Mexico, North Carolina, North Dakota, Ohio, Oklahoma, Oregon, Pennsylvania, South Dakota, Utah, Washington, West Virginia, Wisconsin, Wyoming, District of Columbia.

Psychologist: Alaska,[1] Alabama,[2] Arizona,[3] Arkansas,[4] California,[5] Colorado, Connecticut, Delaware, Idaho,[2,6] Illinois, Indiana, Kansas, Michigan, Mississippi, Nevada, New Hampshire,[2] New York,[2] North Carolina,[4] Ohio,[7] Oklahoma,[2] Oregon, Pennsylvania,[2] Tennessee,[2] Utah, Washington,[2] Wyoming, District of Columbia.

[1] Includes counselor and psychometrist.
[2] Placed on same basis as attorney-client privileged communications.
[3] Clinical or counseling psychologists.
[4] Licensed psychologist or psychological examiner.
[5] Includes clinical social workers, marriage, family, and child counselors, as well as psychologists.
[6] Includes certified counselor, psychologists or psychological examiner employed by any public or private school.
[7] Licensed psychologist or licensed school psychologist.

STATUTORY SUMMARY OF PSYCHIATRIST, PSYCHOLOGIST LAWS CONCERNING PATIENT PRIVILEGED COMMUNICATION

State	Action		Coverage	Privileged Testimony	Exceptions
	Civil	*Criminal*			
Alaska §08.86.200			Psychologist or psychological associate (includes a counselor and psychometrist)	Any matter concerning which the client has employed the psychologist or psychologist associate	Written consent of patient

State	Action		Coverage	Privileged Testimony	Exceptions
	Civil	Criminal			
Alabama 46 §297(36)			Psychologist	Confidential relations and communications between licensed psychologist and client are placed on same basis as those provided by law between attorney and client	
Arizona §32–2085			Clinical or counseling psychologist	Same as Alabama	
§13–1802		X	Physician or surgeon	Any information acquired in attending the patient which was necessary to enable him to prescribe or act for the patient	No privilege where, prior to court-ordered mental examination, patient was told that a report would be made to the court
§12–2235	X		Physician or surgeon	Any communication made by patient with reference to any physical or supposed physical disease or any knowledge obtained by personal examination of patient	A person who offers himself as a witness and voluntarily testifies with reference to the communications referred to in §2235, thereby consents to the examination of such physician or surgeon
Rules of Crim. Proc. 11.7		X		The state may not make use of evidence obtained by compulsory mental examination of defendant unless defendant offers, either directly or through cross-examination, evidence in support of the affirmative defense of insanity	
Arkansas 72–1518	X	X	Licensed psychologist or psychological examiner	Same as Alabama	
28–607	X	X	Physicians and nurses	Same as Arizona 13–1802	If two or more physicians or nurses have treated patient for same ailment waiver of privilege for one physician or nurse will waiver privilege for other
California Evidence Code §§990 et seq.	X		Physician	Information, including information obtained by examination of patient, transmitted between patient and physician in the course of that relationship and in confidence party claiming through	No privilege: as to a communication relevant to an issue concerning the condition of patient, if such issue has been tendered by the patient, any and includes diagnosis

State	Action Civil	Action Criminal	Coverage	Privileged Testimony	Exceptions
(California, cont.)				or under the patient, any party claiming as a beneficiary of a contract to which patient is or was a party, or the plaintiff in action for damages for injury or death of the patient; in a proceeding to commit the patient or otherwise place him or his property under the control of another because of his alleged mental or physical condition; in will contests or contested documents transferring title to property	and advice given by physician in the course of that relationship
Evidence Code 1014	X	X	Psychotherapist (including clinical social workers, marriage, family, and child counselors, as well as psychologists)	Confidential communications between client and psychotherapist	Same as under physician plus: when court appoints psychotherapist (except when at request of defendant in criminal proceedings in order to furnish defendant with information to plead); in action initiated by defendant in criminal action to determine defendant's sanity; if psychotherapist has reasonable cause to believe patient dangerous to himself or others and that disclosure is necessary to prevent the danger; in action brought by patient to establish his competency; if patient is a child under 16 and psychotherapist has reason to believe patient has been victim of crime and disclosure is in the best interests of the child
Colorado 154–1–7	X	X	Physician or surgeon	Same as Arizona 13–1802	Where patient or legal representative (heir) brings suit against doctor on any cause of action arising from doctor's cure or treatment. No privilege regarding evidence of child's injuries or cause thereof
			Certified psychologist	Same as Alaska	
Connecticut 52–146	X	X	Licensed clinical psychologist	Any communication made to him by any person while he is engaged in the practice of clinical psychology	Patient or authorized representative may waive privilege

State	Action Civil	Action Criminal	Coverage	Privileged Testimony	Exceptions
(Connecticut, cont.)					Court ordered examination if patient informed in advance that no privilege would attach
					Where patient in civil action introduces his psychological condition as a claim or defense, if judge finds it in the interests of justice (or if raised by heirs or beneficiaries)
			Psychiatrist	Same as above but includes communication with patient's family	Patient's waiver must be in writing
					Consent may be withdrawn at any time
					When psychiatrist determines substantial risk of imminent physical injury by patient to himself or others
					Court ordered examination
					In civil action when patient claims or defends on mental condition
Delaware 24–3534	X	X	Psychologist	Same as Alabama	
Florida 90–242	X	X	Psychiatrist and patient and patient's family and psychiatrist	Same as Connecticut	Court ordered examination. Proceeding where patient introduces his condition as a claim or defense
					After death, if issue introduced by his beneficiary
Georgia 28–418	X	X	Psychiatrist	Admissions and communications	Court appointed psychiatrist. When patient calls psychiatrist to testify as to his mental condition
Hawaii 621–20	X		Physician	Same as Arizona 13–1802	
Idaho 54–2314	X	X	Psychologist	Any information acquired in the course of his professional services. Same basis as attorney-client privilege	
9–203	X		Physician or surgeon	Same as Arizona 13–1802	No privilege when physical abuse of child by par-

State	Action		Coverage	Privileged Testimony	Exceptions
	Civil	*Criminal*			
(Idaho, cont.)					ent, guardian, or legal custodian. After death of patient in any action regarding validity of will or other instrument transfering property, physician *may* testify regarding patient's mental or physical condition and disclose information acquired in the course of treatment. In a wrongful death or personal injury action the privilege is waived
9–203(6)	X	X	Certified counselor, psychologist, or psychological examiner employed by any public or private school	Any communication made by any student so counseled or examined	Student must be party to action to claim privilege
Illinois 51 §5.1	X	X	Physician	Any information acquired in attending a patient in a professional capacity which was necessary to enable him to serve such patient	Will contests; malpractice suits; actions by or against patient when his physical or mental condition is in issue; proceedings for hospitalizing the mentally ill; any criminal action where the charge is murder by abortion, attempted abortion, or abortion; and homicide trials when disclosure relates directly to fact or immediate circumstances of homicide
51 §5.2	X	X	Psychiatrist	Same as Connecticut	Same as Conn. plus exception for action by patient against psychiatrist for malpractice
91 1/2 §406			Psychologist	Same as Physician	Same as Physician, without the abortion exceptions
Indiana 2–1714 9–1602	X	X	Physician	Communications by patients or advice from physician in the course of their professional business	
63–3617			Psychologists	Same as Illinois 91 1/2 §406	
Iowa 622.10	X	X	Physician	Any confidential communication given physician in his professional ca-	In action against physician for wrongful death or personal injury, infor-

State	Action Civil	Action Criminal	Coverage	Privileged Testimony	Exceptions
(Iowa, cont.)				pacity and necessary and proper to enable him to discharge the functions of his office according to usual course of practice	mation and communication relating to condition alleged are not privileged
Kansas 60–427	X	X	Physician	Any communication with reference to any physical or supposed physical disease, defect, or injury, or time, manner, or circumstance under which it was incurred, or any knowledge obtained by examination	When patient voluntarily testifies concerning such examination
74–5323	X	X	Psychologist	Same as Alabama	
Kentucky 213.200 421.215				Confidential communications between physician and patient are placed on same basis as attorney-client	
			Psychiatrist		When psychiatrist determines need for commitment to mental hospital. When court-ordered examination and patient is informed that there will be no privilege. Civil proceedings where patient introduces his mental condition as a claim or defense
Maine 32 § 3295	X	X	Physician	Any information acquired from patient while attending, examining, or treating in professional capacity, if such information was necessary to enable him to furnish care to patient	When physical or mental condition of patient is at issue, or when the court in the exercise of sound discretion deems such disclosure necessary to the proper administration of justice
16 §60	X	X	Psychiatrist	Any communication between client and psychiatrist	
Massachusetts 233 §20B			Psychotherapists (defined as persons licensed to practice medicine who devote substantial time to psychiatry)	Any communication relative to diagnosis or treatment of patient's mental or emotional problem	If psychotherapist determines patient needs hospitalization, or that patient is dangerous to himself or others and on the basis of such determination discloses communications either for purpose of placing patient in hospital or retaining him in hospital. Court-ordered psychiatric

State	Action		Coverage	Privileged Testimony	Exceptions
	Civil	Criminal			
(Massachusetts, cont.)					examination, if patient is informed in advance that there would be no privilege. Any proceeding, except child custody, where the patient introduces his mental or emotional condition as a claim or defense and judge finds interests of justice require disclosure. In child custody cases, where psychotherapist believes disclosure necessary because condition of patient would impair ability to care for child, disclosure to judge who determines interests of justice. In action by patient against psychotherapist for malpractice, crime or license revocation hearings in which disclosure necessary or relevant to the claim or defense of psychotherapist
Michigan 27A.2157 28.1045	X	X	Physician	Same as Arizona 13–1802	Personal injury or malpractice case, when patient offers testimony of a physician who has treated him for condition on which suit is based
14.677	X	X	Psychologist	Any information acquired from consultations in professional capacity, which was necessary to enable him to render services to patient	Disclosure with consent of patient if over 18, with consent of parent or guardian if under 18. In will contest, may be waived by any heir or personal representative of deceased
Minnesota 595.02	X	X	Physician	Any information or opinion based thereon acquired in attending patient in a professional capacity and which was necessary to enable him to act in such capacity	
Mississippi §13–1–21	X	X	Physician	All communications made by patient under treatment or seeking professional advice. Any communication made by client or advice given him in course of professional employment	Will contests
§73–31–29	X	X	Psychologist		

State	Action Civil	Action Criminal	Coverage	Privileged Testimony	Exceptions
Missouri 491.060	X	X	Physician	Same as Arizona 13–1802	
Montana 93–701–4 66–3212	X		Physician	Information acquired in attending the patient, which was necessary to enable him to prescribe or act for the plaintiff	
Nebraska 25–1206–07	X	X	Same as Iow	Same as Iowa	When patient voluntarily offers testimony of his physical or mental condition
Nevada 49.215 et seq.	X	X	Doctor (person licensed to practice medicine or psychology in any state)	Confidential communications among patient, his doctor or persons who are participating in the diagnosis or treatment, including members of patient's family	Proceedings to hospitalize patient for mental illness, if doctor has determined hospitalization necessary. Court-ordered examination. Where condition of patient is an element of a claim or defense in any proceeding
New Hampshire 330–A:19 329:26	X	X	Psychologist Physician	Same basis as attorney-client relationship	
New Jersey 2A:84A–22.2	X	X	Physician	Confidential communications between physician and patient necessary or helpful to enable physician to make diagnosis of condition of patient or render treatment therefor	Commitment proceedings, or competency hearing; action to recover damages on account of conduct of patient, which constitutes a criminal offense other than a misdemeanor; will contests; upon an issue between parties claiming by testate or intestate succession from a decreased patient
New Mexico 20–4–504	X	X	Psychotherapist (defined as a person authorized to practice medicine in any state or nation, or reasonably believed by the patient so to be, while engaged in the diagnosis or treatment of a mental or emotional condition, including drug addiction,	Same as Nevada	Proceedings for hospitalization for mental illness. Examination by court order. When condition is an element of a claim or defense in any proceeding

State	Action		Coverage	Privileged Testimony	Exceptions
	Civil	*Criminal*			
(New Mexico, cont.)			or, a licensed or certified psychologist while similarly engaged		
New York CPLR 4507	X	X	Psychologist	Same as attorney-client privilege	
North Carolina §8–53	X	X	Physician	Same as Arizona 13–1802	
§8–53.3	X	X	Psychologist or psychological examiner	Any information received in rendering professional services and which information was necessary to enable him to render psychological services	Judge of Superior Court may compel disclosure if necessary for proper administration of justice
North Dakota 31–01–06 31–01–07	X	X	Physician	Same as Arizona 13–1802, but does not require necessity of information for doctor to prescribe or act for patient	When patient voluntarily testifies concerning communications
Ohio 2317.02 2945.41 4732.19	X	X	Physician	Communications made by or advice given patient in a professional relationship	When patient voluntarily testifies concerning communications. When patient is deceased, by express consent of surviving spouse or executor or administrator of deceased patient's estate
			Licensed psychologist or licensed school psychologist	Same as physician-patient above	
Oklahoma 12 §385 22 §702 59 §1372	X	X	Physician	Same as Arizona 12–2235	When patient voluntarily testifies concerning communication
	X	X	Psychologist	Same as attorney-client privilege.	
Oregon 44.040	X		Physician	Same as Arizona 13–1802	When patient voluntarily testifies concerning communications
			Psychologist	Communication by client or advice to client given in the course of professional employment	
Pennsylvania 28 §328 63 §1213	X		Physician	Any information acquired in a professional capacity which was necessary to enable him to	Personal injury actions

State	Action		Coverage	Privileged Testimony	Exceptions
	Civil	Criminal			
(Pennsylvania, cont.)				act in that capacity and which would tend to blacken character of patient	
	X	X	Licensed psychologist	Any information acquired in course of professional services. Such information is placed on the same basis as the attorney-client privilege	
South Dakota 19–1–1 19–2–3	X		Physician	Same as Arizona 13–1802	When patient voluntarily testifies concerning communications
Tennessee 63–1117	X	X	Psychologist	Same basis as attorney-client	
Utah 78–24–8	X		Physician	Same as Arizona 13–1802	
58–25–9	X	X	Certified psychologist	Any information acquired in course of professional services on behalf of client	
Virginia 8–289.1	X			Information received in attending, examining, or treating patient in a professional capacity, if such information was necessary to furnish professional care to the patient	When physical or mental condition of patient is at issue, or when necessary for proper administration of justice (judge's discretion)
Washington 5.60.060	X		Physician	Same as Arizona 13–1802	Child's injuries, neglect, or sexual abuse
18.83.110	X	X	Certified psychologist	Same basis as attorney-client	
West Virginia 50–6–10(e)	X	X	Physician	Same as Arizona 13–1802	
Wisconsin 971.16		X			Criminal defendant pleading N. G. B. R. I. given court-ordered examination—no privilege
885.21	X	X	Physician	Same as Arizona 13–1802	Malpractice actions, homicide trials, when disclosure relates directly to fact or immediate circumstances of homicide and lunacy inquiries; in case of death or disability, personal representative may consent to

State	Action Civil	Action Criminal	Coverage	Privileged Testimony	Exceptions
(Wisconsin, cont.)					waiver of privilege; in situations where a hospitalized person is adjudicated mentally ill, infirm, or deficient or is a voluntary mental patient and the release of medical information is necessary so that the person can qualify for insurance benefits or some type of government benefit or pension either for himself or his dependants; where abused or invalid child is involved
Wyoming 33–343.4	X	X	Licensed psychologist	Communications or advice given in course of professional employment	
1–139	X	X	Physician	Communications or advice given in physician-patient relationship	When patient voluntarily testifies concerning communications
District of Columbia §14–307	X	X	Physician	Any information, confidential in nature, acquired in attending patient in a professional capacity and that was necessary to enable him to act in that capacity, whether the information was obtained from patient or from his family or the person or persons in charge of him	In criminal case where causing death or injury patient is charged with to a human, and disclosure is required in the interests of public justice. Mental competency or sanity in criminal trial, where patient raises defense of N.G.B.R.I.; or where a question arises concerning the mental condition of an accused or convicted person. Mental competency or sanity of a child alleged to be delinquent, neglected, or in need of supervision, in any proceeding before Family Division of the Superior Court
§2–496	X	X	Psychologists	Above §14–307 applies	

A DISCUSSION OF CONFIDENTIAL AND PRIVILEGED COMMUNICATION PROBLEMS IN PRIVATE PSYCHIATRIC PRACTICE

DR. THEODORE ROBIE (East Orange, New Jersey):

In our state, psychiatrists do not have "privilege," but we are particularly fortunate that we do have liberal judges, and on the stand, the judge carefully informs us of our rights, though we know that we don't have any! We do not have "privilege," and I believe that every psychiatrist should bend his effort in every state to bring about law that will allow "privilege" to professional persons.

DR. CARL BREITNER (Phoenix, Arizona):

There is a problem of keeping records of what happens in psychotherapeutic situations. Are we in any way protected against such records being subpoenaed? This has happened to me and it has been very embarrassing.

DR. JONAS RAPPEPORT (Baltimore, Maryland):

We have just gotten through trying to get a Privileged Communication Law for psychiatrists, designed after the Connecticut Law, through the Legislature of the State of Maryland, and were not successful. It passed the House of Delegates but not our Senate. It has been most disturbing to me that many psychiatrists in our community are willing to accept the kindness of the courts on some occasions by the court allowing the psychiatrists to forget, to not keep records, and to do other things.

In this way, of course, we play into this, and we also have situations in Maryland in which psychiatrists have been forced to testify and reveal to the court damaging information about patients, and have done this with impunity, not wishing to martyr themselves.

I have a plea today. We will be back with our Bill before the Legislature in 1965, and I would appreciate anyone here in those states that do have privilege, being kind enough to have their attorney or attorneys that they work

with, send me information which I might present to our main opposition, the Bar Association, to the effect that the privilege has not caused them difficulty and how they have been able to work with the privilege in insurance cases and other cases. My address is Dr. Jonas Rappeport, 2 East Read Street, Baltimore, Maryland, 21202.

DR. IRWIN N. PERR (Cleveland, Ohio):

I would like to mention an incident which involved a psychologist, not a psychiatrist, although in this situation a difference not of great significance. This was a domestic relations case involving custody of children. The psychologist, who had seen the mother, was asked to assist her in showing that she was capable of maintaining custody of the children. He brought his records with him, although not subpoenaed. He had recorded in one interview that she had fleeting delusional thoughts that the children were not her children at all. The attorney for the other side snatched these records and readily picked this out and made much to-do about it. The result was that the woman lost custody of the children, at least in part, some thought, because of the statements in the records.

If records are subpoenaed, the psychiatrist should be conversant with their content and be prepared to use them in the most helpful and pertinent manner possible. There are other ways in which people try to manipulate this situation. I know of certain training centers where the records, official hospital records, say: Date Patient Interviewed, and Initials; and in the valut somewhere are another set of records, not official, so that when the hospital records are subpoenaed, the ones in the valut are not considered official hospital records and remain hidden.

Sometimes the psychiatrist must help a patient, not for psychiatric reasons, but

The following discussion took place at the 1963 meeting of the American Psychiatric Association during a program on "The Medico-Legal Aspects of Private Psychiatric Practice," presented by the Section on Private Practice. Reprinted, with permission, from *Diseases of the Nervous System*, 26 (March 1965): 169–75.

because he is the patient's doctor and friend in the eyes of society. To give you an example—somebody apparently wants to obtain custody of the children. The fact of psychiatric treatment is known and will be brought out. That psychiatrist is on the spot. If he refuses to come, if he had that option, will he be helping his own patient?

I do not think that it is easy to separate psychotherapy of any kind from the rest of the patient's functions. The psychotherapeutic process does not exist in a vacuum. There are many other problems facing the patient, and the psychiatrist is often called upon to help patients in other than psychiatric areas.

JUDGE MORRIS PLOSCOWE:

Frankly, I must confess that I am shocked at the suggestion that there be two sets of records—one for the public and one for your office. Once you start keeping two sets of records, where is it going to stop? I do not recommend that at all. If the psychiatric profession or the medical profession wants to be allowed a privilege, that privilege is a legal proposition and should cover all records. There should be privilege unquestionably. To me it seems ridiculous that you have to stand here in this day and age and plead for that kind of a law, for a privilege to cover that area of confidentiality; but once that is formulated into law, don't get the notion that you must keep two sets of records.

DR. GENE L. USDIN (New Orleans, Louisiana):

Psychiatry and psychiatrists need to take a position, but I do not think we should flagrantly and possibly abusively twist legal positions. Many of us are familiar with the position taken by Dr. Grinker in Chicago when, although Illinois does not recognize privileged communication, Dr. Grinker refused to testify about a patient in therapy. There is a distinct possibility that Dr. Grinker might have been found in contempt and fined. It has been pointed out that the law is lenient, and I would not subscribe to an action such as destruction or concealment of records. To make our point in jurisdictions where privileged communication does not exist, some psychiatrists may have to be martyrs—but if so, we should do this in a direct manner as did Dr. Grinker.

Another point we might keep in mind when we deal with courts is that there sometimes are valuable practical techniques. For example, in marital disputes, we may have a patient in therapy and be subpoenaed to relate details of the patient's condition and personal life. A procedure that I have used in two instances and have recommended to other psychiatrists is to telephone the attorney who has subpoenaed me and advise him that if I am compelled to testify under subpoena, I want to warn him that the information to which I would testify as coming from my patient could be very embarrassing and harmful to his client. That I would not hesitate on the stand to mention that while it was difficult for me to bring out this information, I had warned the attorney of the opposing side. I was not subpoenaed.

DR. ABRAHAM HALPERN (Syracuse, New York):

I would like to take this question out of court and ask Dr. Hollender if a patient communicates an intent to commit suicide, whether he would risk the patient-oriented psychotherapeutic encounter and reveal his information to anyone?

DR. WILLIAM BELLAMY (San Francisco, California):

The matter of records is an extremely complicated one and in the past five years as Chairman of the Ethics Committee of Northern California Psychiatric Society, I have had the opportunity of putting an item in our newsletter to our membership, and the one thing that I haven't been able to write on was records. It defeats me.

I would like to offer, however, my informal thoughts on the subject. I disagree with those who would keep dual records. I consider it dishonest and you might end up in jail.

The alternative which I would suggest may sound like a bit of sophistry, but I don't think so—I think judges do it too, namely, we keep two sets of thoughts. After all, why did God give us two cerebral hemispheres? You don't have to write down in your record with your right hand what you are thinking with your left hand. And if the examining attorney happens to suspect you, what you know, and is pressing you under cross-examination, which is his right under the philosophy of advocacy, in the interest of shaking out hte truth, you can say: "Your Honor, could I please talk to you in chambers?" Dr. Melvin Somers did just this and his request was granted. He explained to the judge why he could not answer these questions in good conscience, that if he did it would bring irreparable harm to his patient, it would sever the therapeutic relationship which he needed desperately—a very sick woman—and it had nothing to do with the case at bar. It was a divorce situation, and the information which the lawyer was trying to drag out was just a smear tactic. The judge backed up Mel

Somers one hundred per cent. He didn't have to answer the questions once the Judge knew what this "cat and mouse game" was all about.

A further step is the bold one that Roy Grinker took in the case in Cook County, Illinois, reported in 47 Northwestern Law Review, page 384, and it tells how Roy Grinker said on the stand, "I cannot answer in good conscience." Although there was no law protecting confidentiality in the State of Illinois, which surprised the judge and all the attorneys and made a big flurry—and that is why it is in the Law Review—he, nevertheless, was not cited for contempt, however, he took the risk of going to jail or a fine or both, and, mind you, it was Roy Grinker's stature as a psychiatrist that kept him out of contempt, and 99 per cent of us had better be a little more careful.

DR. IRWIN PERR:

I am not for two sets of records. I think it is a bad practice. I mention it because I know that it does exist, and I feel that it is morally reprehensible as well as legally questionable.

No. 2, I thought you would be interested in knowing that there has been another Roy Grinker-type case in Canada, where in one of the provinces where there was no medical-patient-doctor privilege, another psychiatrist refused to reveal information and was upheld by the court. There are now two such cases and, perhaps, this represents a trend toward a common law doctor-patient privilege in areas, states, and provinces where it does not exist.

I just would like to bring up another problem—that of hsopital records involving all kinds of para-medical (to use that expression) information, reports of social workers, letters from agencies, nurses' notes—all kinds of material that lie around in medical records which are then subpoenaed. Where these records stand today is questionable; this is a separate problem but a very important one because all kinds of extremely damaging information coming from a variety of unchecked sources lies in hospital records. This is an area which might be explored.

DR. HOLLENDER:

The points that have been brought up, by a number of you, are of considerable interest to me.

I would certainly agree with the point made by Dr. Robie, that although it is very nice to have lawyers who are reasonably kind and judges who are reasonably considerate, there is really no substitute for a statute to protect us.

In regard to Dr. Halpern's question about a suicidal threat: many patients make such threats but you do not always run to their relatives. You evaluate the threat. If you feel that it is so serious that it is imperative to take action, then obviously you would have to dissolve the patient-oriented type of relationship and you would not return to it. From then on the relationship would be different than it had been. Relatives and others would now be involved in the process. The patient himself would no longer be engaged in therapy in which he would make the decisions about changes in his life, etc.

Finally, I would like to say a few words about the keeping of records. What I am about to say will probably shock the Judge more than the keeping of double records, and that is, that I do not keep any records at all. Very candidly, I do not want any records that could ever be subpoenaed into court, and records cannot be subpoenaed if they do not exist. I do not keep records other than the form cards that my secretary makes out, listing the dates of appointments and my charges and collections, and that's it.

I did keep records some years with the idea that I was collecting pure gold, that some day I would refine into journal articles. Then one day I woke up and came to the conclusion that this was nonsense. I did not have a precious metal. At best I had a few alloys and what I really wanted to write was probably in my head anyway. So at that point I have not written anything other than brief notes about things that I especially wanted for some purpose quite detached from the patient.

SILENCE IS GOLDEN, OR IS IT?

INFO: Mr. Allen, what do you see as the future of privileged information relative to the medical practice? Should it be expanded or restricted?

ALLEN: Well, both really. . . . I see no immediate revolutionary trends. But I think over the long haul, privilege will be extended to cover the psychotherapeutic relationship of physician and patient, or clinical psychologist and patient, perhaps to some of the adjunctive therapists who provide psychotherapeutic help. I think it will tend to be restricted over the long haul in the general physician-patient relationship, where there's less need to safeguard confidentiality than perhaps was seen 50 or 75 years ago.

INFO: To the extent of its elimination?

ALLEN: I would think so, yes.

INFO: Isn't it a fact that the right of privilege is the patient's, and that the doctor has an obligation to protect the patient?

RAPPAPORT: That's correct.

INFO: How can you have both of these things that you suggest?

RAPPAPORT: Well, no. I'm saying that . . . the patient should, have privilege with reference to any physician, and not just the psychiatrist or psychotherapist. The privilege is the patient's, and the patient can waive the privilege. But the patient should have this opportunity for all concerned, that is, for the psychiatrist or the general physician, or the surgeon. Can you not imagine the serious problems that can arise in terms of public exposure for the patient who discusses with his urologist, say, some very personal sexual problems that he has, and then to feel that later on in a divorce case this might be brought out in the courtroom.

RUBEN: I think I would tend to agree with Dr. Rappaport. Looking at the general picture of privilege-communication statutes in the country today, there were 32 states in 1966 that had physician-patient privilege, and in 1971 there were 45 states that have it. So I think that although there are numerous legal scholars who would agree with you on the need perhaps for some type of decreasing privi-

lege for physicians in general, I think state legislatures are coming out in favor of the privilege for physicians.

ALLEN: Now I don't entirely disagree with the points that you and Dr. Rappaport have made. I was asked to forecast trends, and I think the trends are in the direction of restricting rather than enlarging general physician-patient privilege. Though I do recognize that there are some areas in which disclosures are made that could be embarrassing, could jeopardize the relationship. But let me emphasize that in addition to the fact that privilege belongs to the fact that privilege belongs to the patient—to the communicant —it is not an absolute. We're talking about a balancing of two important social principles. One is safeguarding a relationship, which may depend upon confidentiality for its preservation; that is, people may be deterred from seeking professional help if they feel that their disclosures might be sought out by subpoena. So the safeguarding of the relationship is an important social principle. But there's another important social principle—the principle that in a civil or criminal case, the jury is entitled to hear all relevant evidence bearing on the issues in the case. To withhold evidence from the jury means that it's going to be making decisions—perhaps involving the liberty or lives of litigants —on less than all the facts, when the doctor asserts privilege on behalf of the patient in response to a subpoena. It means that if the assertion is successful, the jury is not going to hear evidence which is relevant, pertinent, and maybe determinative of the issue before it.

INFO: Dr. Szasz, by now you must have an opinion on what has been said so far.

SZASZ: Yes, I do. I tend to agree, so far, most with Mr. Allen. But if I may, I'd like to enlarge the scope of our inquiry by not just talking about privilege—not just talking of this in the traditional way—but by really asking what the communication is about, and why; who is paying for it, and with whom is it going to be shared; and last, but

The panel discussion participants are: Richard C. Allen, Dr. Harvey Ruben, Dr. Jonas Rappaport, and Dr. Thomas Szasz. Excerpted and reprinted with permission from *M.H.* (Journal of the National Association for Mental Health) 57, 1 (Winter 1973): 21.

not least, what is the expectation at the beginning of the relationship on the part of both patient and physician. Now the two classic situations are in psychoanalytic training and with the very seriously disturbed or depressed patient. In both situations the therapist, without the consent of the patient, communicates information that he obtained from the patient to other persons.

RAPPAPORT: Well, I think there's no question, Dr. Szasz, that in both of those situations the patient's complete privacy is invaded by the physician without the patient knowing it. On the other hand, the communications in a certain sense are officially acceptable to other people. If you would feel that it would be improper for a doctor to communicate with another physician anything about a patient without his permission, it would certainly make usual medical communications very difficult, whereby a doctor speaks with another physician for just advice about dealing with a patient. If you had to ask your patient, "May I speak to Dr. X about you, because I'm worried about whether I'm making the right diagnosis here, or about this little difference that I see," it would certainly undermine the patient's confidence, to say the least. One could take such an absolute position—this is certainly very possible.

SZASZ: Well, the point really I'm trying to make is that one can take all sorts of positions, but what is important—and here I am relying on the tradition really of the law—is for the patient, for the client, for the buyer, as it were, of the service to be fully informed of what it is he's buying. Clients nowadays think they are buying unqualified privacy, analogous to what happens with a confessor in a confessional.

RUBEN: . . . Physicians . . . become confused when they start talking about privacy versus confidentiality versus privilege. Perhaps it would be best to differentiate those entities at this time. I feel the patient has the right to privacy and, I guess, Mr. Allen, you could support this—that there are legal scholars who say that there is no constitutionally guaranteed right to privacy; whereas, others say that some of the amendments do give us a right to privacy. But I think privacy belongs to the patient himself, and that is his own thoughts about his own life, his own feelings, his own actions. But when he communicates his private thoughts to another person, in this case his physician, then we get into the realm of confidentiality, which is a moral and ethical tenet mandated by the oath of Hippocrates, and also by the principles of medical ethics of the American Medical Association. But then when we get

into privileged communication, we're talking about statutory degree within various jurisdictions. And I think that we get confused when we start using these terms interchangeably. . . .

ALLEN: . . . As Dr. Ruben says, we're really talking about two different, though related, concepts in the law. The first, the concept of confidentiality, can be sustained on common law privacy grounds or on grounds of violation of contract, or breach of statutory regulations of the practice of medicine, or perhaps other bases as well. It is a right that a patient has that his confidences, information learned as a result of his examination and diagnosis, will not be revealed. Now some states require that that revelation be made other than in the course of treatment and in a professional relationship. If damage results to the patient as a result of his photograph being published, or the nature of his illness revealed, or facts about his background learned in taking a medical history, published—he has a right to sue at law to recover, I think that right is also a constitutional one —right of privacy is probably subsumed in the 9th Amendment. But whether it's a constitutionally based right or one based on the common law, it is a right to recover. The other doctrine is that of privileged communication, under which a communicant in certain protected relationships—including that of priest and penitent, lawyer and client, physician and patient and, in some jurisdictions, others—has a right that confidences communicated by him in the course of professional treatment will not be revealed. And that right extends even to court cases in which a subpoena is issued to the doctor. I think all of these concepts have a firm foundation in medical practice, in the Hippocratic oath, in the principles of ethics of the American Medical Association. And there are counterpart traditions in the practice of law. I think it would be a mistake, however, to regard the concept of privilege as one in any way belonging to the physician. It protects a relationship, and not the professional person. And that is true as much of the lawyer-client relationship as it is of that of physician and patient. . . .

INFO: Well, how much can a doctor resist, faced with a subpoena?

RAPPAPORT: Doctors do all sorts of things that are basically dishonest and certainly can't be condoned. They forget, they lose their records, they can't—you know—can't remember, or they really don't think the patient said that, etc. This is basically dishonest and is certainly a poor premise on which to establish any kind of relationship.

ALLEN: There have been physicians—Dr. Grinker, Dr. Lifschutz and, doubtless, others —who have stood firm and said: "I will not reveal it, even under threat of contempt citation and imprisonment." That I can admire. But a physician who lies about the existence of a record or claims that he's lost recollection of an event in order to evade subpoena, I think is taking a dishonorable course.

RUBEN: I think this is a problem that exists in the military, because with the lack of statutory privilege within the military, many times military physicians will not record information in records, and keep things within their heads that perhaps should be on paper for the good of the patient. . . .

SZASZ: Gentlemen, I'm a little perturbed that some of this discussion is on a rather exalted level and does not hit everyday occurrences that I think are more to the point. . . . I think a great deal of psychotherapy is self-incrimination. And then, the next thing that happens is that the psychiatrist talks to this patient's husband or wife, or daughter, and informs these people that the patient is very depressed and ought to be hospitalized, and then they take steps to hospitalize the person against his will. This kind of thing is far more common and constitutes a situation in which a psychiatrist, in effect, abridges the patient's confidences. Now, of course, the whole thing is done for the patient; therefore, there is nothing actionable. This could never be litigated successfully, because everything is done for the patient. . . .

INFO: Where do you see the problem, Dr. Szasz?

SZASZ: I see the problem in the paternalism of the medical relationship, in one sentence. I see it in neither doctor nor patient being entirely clear in their relationship at the beginning and as they go along, as to who is entitled to information and who is there to get information. I'm basing my argument entirely on the fundamental principle of informed consent—what is the patient consenting to?

RAPPAPORT: I think that all patients—perhaps this is a naive statement—but I would believe that most patients understand that when they are saying anything to a doctor that the doctor will have what he considers and what you consider this paternalistic approach, that he will have this approach and that he will take this approach, and that the doctor feels that the patient needs such protection, that he will carry it out.

SZASZ: Well, now, wait one second. You see, this is the complete contrast with the relationship between a penitent and the priest, or even between a client and the lawyer. If a client hires a lawyer for divorce, and in the middle of the proceeding the lawyer decides that what this client needs is not a divorce but a reconciliation, and if he then acts on that, in opposition to his client's wishes— every lawyer would be subject to a malpractice suit, which I think he would use.

ALLEN: I find it hard to disagree with anything you're saying, Dr. Szasz. It seems to me that if a relationship is sufficiently important to warrant application of a rule of privilege, then there is even greater importance in there being a full disclosure to the patient or client at the beginning of the relationship of what that relationship is.

SZASZ: This is all—for the moment—what I am urging, more than a legalistic distinction between privilege, confidentiality, and privacy, which really does not come into play, usually.

ALLEN: I think it should be emphasized also that there is a possibility not only of less than full disclosure of the nature of the relationship, but also of the posibility that the doctor or the lawyer may have a conflict of interest.

SZASZ: Correct.

ALLEN: If the patient consults his company's doctor, and the physician feels himself bound to report any adverse findings to the employer, it seems to me that ought to be very clearly stated, that something other than the normal physician-patient relationship exists here: "I may take actions which are against your interest because of my greater duty of allegiance to your employer." That has to be, it seems to me, stated at the very outset. And if it is not, I think the physician has misrepresented his position.

SZASZ: Let me tell you a very simple illustration that occurs to me. If a patient goes to a psychotherapist and in the course of his therapy reports that he's cheating on his income tax, the therapist wouldn't dream of calling the FBI or the Bureau of Internal Revenue and reporting it. But if the same patient would report that he's going to go home and kill himself, that therapist is going to be inclined to commit the patient. I submit that there is no moral difference.

ALLEN: Supposing he says, "I'm going to go home and kill my wife." What would you say in that event?

SZASZ: Same thing. If the expectation is that everything that the patient tells the doctor is private—or let me put it more clearly—if the contract is for the doctor to help the patient, and not do anything to the patient doesn't want done to him.

RAPPAPORT: I don't, well, disagree with you

entirely, Dr. Szasz, and I don't think any physician would accept that level of confidentiality. It's been my experience that patients accept, I think, the paternalism of the medical profession. And I believe that when a patient suspects he's going to tell you something—such as: "I'm going to go kill my wife," or even that: "I've cheated like heck on my income tax"—he will, in fact, ask you beforehand: "If I give you certain information, what are you going to do about it?" And I've had this happen repeatedly, and then I tell him what I'm going to do about it: "If this is information that endangers you or anyone else, I will have to take action on it."

ALLEN: If you'll forgive me, I think I'm in disagreement with both of you on this point. I think there is a difference between reporting to a physician: "I have cheated on my income tax," and reporting to him: "I am going home tonight and kill my wife." One is information about a past crime, the other is information about a proposed crime. The law has always recognized that a physician or an attorney has a duty to report and to take steps to prevent the commission of a crime of violence. Now, I take it that would include an attempted suicide, which is still recognized as a crime in most jurisdictions. I think that this one of those areas of exception to the rule of privilege, recognized both in law and, I think, in the traditions of the medical profession. . . .

INFO: How big a problem is the release of privileged information from medical record libraries and hospitals, perhaps without even the knowledge of the doctor or patient involved?

RUBEN: As I understand it—speaking about the military in my case—one of the problems we're confronted with is that there are a lot of instances where investigating agents will go through the registrar of a hospital and say, "I have authorization," under some unspecified regulation, "to have access to Mr. X's record." And usually somebody of junior position within records libraries will give them the information merely on the fact that they present their credentials as investigators. . . .

RAPPAPORT: . . . Medical records, unfortunately I think, get invaded in various ways. They become invaded by the secretary in the record room who types up a report and recognizes somebody that she knows, then tells it to a friend. . . .

INFO: Don't you see this record problem as a growing one?

RAPPAPORT: Worse and worse with our computers. The whole idea of a national health file, which I think Professor Allen has some ideas about, causes us great concern.

ALLEN: Well, I'm not sure that I have any ideas other than those you've very ably expressed. That if we go to a compulsory national health scheme, records are going to be collected, computerized, made generally available throughout the country. And it seems to me we are going to have to build in some protection about what information may be collected, how it is to be safeguarded, what software restrictions are to be applied, and under what circumstances and to whom is it to be disseminated. Potentially, there is a grave area of invasion of privacy, an area of potential damage to employment and marital relationships, to criminal liability, and to the totality of one's life.

INFO: How do you feel, any of you gentlemen, about a patient signing a waiver of privilege? Do you feel he really knows what he's doing when he does that?

SZASZ: I think the situation of a patient who goes into a hospital with acute appendicitis is just so totally different from the patient who is in the psychiatric situation as to make it impossible to discuss them together. Now, I think some of our problems come from amalgamation and mixing of such very, very different situations, where on the one end of the spectrum there is really no conflict between the patient's needs and societal needs, and at the other end the two are actually at complete opposites, almost like in the criminal situation. . . .

ALLEN: I think it's also important, again, to emphasize something that maybe is self-evident but perhaps deserves repetition. That the purpose of the rule of privilege, in large part, is to facilitate a relationship under which people feel free to consult without fear of revelation. To avoid, in other words, deterring people from making use of the professional skills of the physician. To the extent that we require physicians to report matters—child-beating or drug addiction or depression that might be a basis for compulsory hospitalization—to that extent we are impairing or deterring people from seeking out a professional consultation which, perhaps, they very much need.

SZASZ: Let me add to that. I feel about this very strongly. We are now, I think, going in a very immoral direction, if I may put it that way. . . .

RUBEN: I agree totally with what you're saying, Dr. Szasz, but the problem that concerns me is, when the man, perhaps through a minor defect in judgment, then decides that, no, it's just not best for my wife to know.

SZASZ: See, here we go—no defect of judgment. You can't bring in the issue of incompetence in this way.

RUBEN: I think this is the bind that the doctor gets into, because of the Hippocratic oath and the principles of ethics of the AMA. We're dealing in the patient's best interests and we're supposed to protect the patient's privacy, but we're also given the responsibility of doing what we feel is best, and that becomes judgmental. If I, as the physician, feel, knowing the man—he's been my patient for 10 years, I've treated him and his family—that under any other circumstance I would never want to violate his confidences, but I see here that he's leading his family into destruction by not telling them something, then I've got to try to make some sort of decision that I can live with morally, within my own conscience, about what to do about that.

SZASZ: Well, I respect that. I don't agree with it, but I respect it.

ALLEN: I'm not sure to what extent we may be in disagreement, Dr. Ruben. But I think it should be emphasized that the law does not require or permit the physician to be guided only by what is best for the patient. We've been talking about a cancer patient. Supposing the cancer is operable, and an operation, we might generally agree, would be in the best interest of the patient. If the patient doesn't want to be operated, he doggone well has a right not to be operated—whatever someone else may think is in his best interest. Do you disagree with that?

RAPPAPORT: I certainly wholeheartedly agree if a patient is competent to make this decision—in fact, I'm not even sure I would pass judgment as to his not being competent—I would think that's a matter for a court to decide, but certainly no operation should be forced on him. . . . A priest told me, not long ago, about an 80-year-old man in a hospital who had cardiac irregularities and was going to be given a pacemaker, and refused it. Thereupon, the family and the psychiatrist were called in, and he was declared incompetent. And a pacemaker was put on him. Same thing is not unusual, from what I am told; around the country this kind of thing is quite routine. This probably happens in thousands of cases per year; probably more often than that.

RAPPAPORT: I agree with Dr. Szasz. I think one has to be very careful about using this thing of incompetency to make people have pacemakers, operations, or anything else that they have a perfect right to refuse.

ALLEN: I think we're talking about questions that are enormously difficult for the physician to resolve. There is a delicate line between respect for the right of a patient to decide for himself, and respect for the right of privacy on the one hand, and the physician's duty to his profession and to society on the other. If the law compels disclosure as it does, I take it, in the case of suicide or prospective criminal acts, as it sometimes does with respect to reporting gunshot wounds, reporting drug addiction, reporting child battering, or whatever—then it seems to me society has decided for the physician that the higher duty is to make the disclosure: to follow the rule of a statute. Some physicians who feel a higher call of conscience have stood firm. Whether I would subscribe to their tenet or not really makes little difference. I think such a stand as a matter of principle may be heroic. . . .

INFO: Dr. Ruben, are there any problems in the Army as far as confidentiality and privacy that are distinct from the civilian world?

RUBEN: I think what actually happens is that —what you're speaking about is the dual responsibility that the military physician has, both for the good of the Army and for the good of the patient. And the physician frequently feels that the Army is saying, "Put the good of the Army before the good of the patient." And the Surgeon General takes marked exception to that and says, "No, we have to protect both interests." And I think in this sense—this is why I say it's analogous to the civilian situation, because in the civilian world—although Dr. Szasz may take issue with this—I feel that the physician has a responsibility to a civilian community equal to that which he has to the patient, and depending on the situation, he is going to have to—at least as I see it—in certain instances, violate the patient's confidentiality, for the good of the community.

RAPPAPORT: We're making this a one-way street. We're forgetting that the patient has responsibility as a soldier to see that he doesn't have a gun in his hand when perhaps he shouldn't. . . .

ALLEN: Well, I think we're kind of blurring the fact that a variety of relationships are being discussed here. One might involve a private physician and a private patient. That's one kind of relationship. Another that you are now suggesting is a physician who is retained by a company, and one of the employees of the company is referred to him for a report. And that's quite a different situation. I think the physician owes a duty to the patient, to disclose to him on what basis the consultation is being held. If the patient is to be examined for purposes of reporting to some third person, then the physician ought to make that clear. Having done so, then I see no problem in his making such a report.

SZASZ: I very much appreciate Mr. Allen's remarks. This is a kind of point I was trying to make earlier. Mr. Allen made it more sharply. If I may make it even more sharply, at the risk of exaggerating just a bit. In the traditional sense, most people think of a doctor in the private relationship—a private patient, a private doctor. Now, in that sense—and again I'm saying this only to clarify it—in that sense the military physician is not a physician at all, because his contract is not to make the patient healthy. He has a contract, as it were, with the government. . . .

ALLEN: . . . We have touched on most of the sensitive points in both confidentiality and privilege. My feeling is that it is vitally important that a professional person—whether he's a physician, a lawyer, a priest, or anyone else occupying a special role of confidence—should respect that confidence. Disclosures—frivolous disclosures or disclosures operating against the interest of the patient—it seems to me, are to be discouraged. If the physician has a special relationship to this patient—as where he is representing an insurance company, or is being referred by a court, or in some other way represents a potentially adverse interest—it is vital that he disclose that to the patient at the outset, so that it is clear to him that the confidences that he might otherwise repose are subject to revelation. . . .

In Re Lifschutz
85 Cal. Rptr. 829
467 P.2d 557 (1970)

TOBRINER, Justice.

The instant proceeding arose out of a suit instituted by Joseph F. Housek against John Arabian on June 3, 1968, for damages resulting from an alleged assault. Housek's complaint alleged that the assault caused him "physical injuries, pain, suffering and severe mental and emotional distress." Defendant Abrabian deposed the plaintiff and during the course of that deposition Housek stated that he had received psychiatric treatment from Dr. Lifschutz over a six-month period approximately 10 years earlier. Nothing in the record indicates that the plaintiff revealed the nature or contents of any conversation with or treatment by Dr. Lifschutz.

Arabian then subpenaed for deposition Dr. Lifschutz and all of his medical records relating to the treatment of Housek. (Code Civ.-Proc. §§ 2016, 2019, subd. (a).) Although Dr. Lifschutz appeared for the deposition, he refused to produce any of his medical records and refused to answer any questions relating to his treatment of patients; the psychiatrist declined even to disclose whether or not Housek had consulted him or had been his patient. Although notified, neither plaintiff Housek nor his attorney were present at this deposition. Housek has neither expressly claimed a psychotherapist-patient privilege, statutory or constitutional, nor expressly waived such a privilege.

In response to the psychiatrist's refusal to cooperate, defendant Arabian moved for an order of the superior court compelling the production of the subpenaed records and the answers to questions on deposition (Code Civ.-Proc. § 2034, subd. (a)). Relying on the patient-litigant exception of section 1016 of the Evidence Code, the superior court determined that because the plaintiff, in instituting the pending litigation, had tendered as an issue his mental and emotional condition, the statutory psychotherapist-patient (Evid. Code, § 1014) privilege did not apply. On December 20, 1968, the court therefore ordered Dr. Lifschutz to comply with the subpena and to answer questions posed during deposition. On January 15, 1969, defendant attempted to continue with the deposition of Dr. Lifschutz as ordered by the superior court, but petitioner remained resolute in his refusal to respond or produce records.

The superior court held another hearing on December 5, 1969; when Dr. Lifschutz again refused to comply with the order, the court adjudged him in contempt and ordered him to be confined in the custody of the Sheriff of San Mateo County. After the Court of Appeals denied without opinion a petition for habeas corpus, this court agreed to hear the case. . . .

Dr. Lifschutz presents a novel challenge, attempting to raise far-reaching questions of constitutional law. From the affidavits and correspondence included in the record we note that a large segment of the psychiatric profession concurs in Dr. Lifschutz's strongly held belief that an absolute privilege of confidentiality is essential to the effective practice of psychotherapy.

We recognize the growing importance of the psychiatric profession in our modern, ultra-complex society. The swiftness of change—economic, cultural, and moral—produces accelerated tensions in our society, and the potential for relief of such emotional disturbances offered by psychotherapy undoubtedly establishes it as a profession essential to the preservation of societal health and well-being. Furthermore, a growing consensus throughout the country, reflected in a trend of legislative enactments,[1] acknowledges that an environment of confidentiality of treatment is vitally important to the successful operation of psychotherapy. California has embraced this view

[1] Until 20 years ago, no statutes dealt specifically with the question of the privilege for psychotherapeutic communications; protection was available only under the terms of existing physician-patient privileges. Such privilege only applied to medical practitioners who fell within the terms of various state statutes; often psychiatrists were covered, but clinical psychologists, though using many of the same techniques of psychotherapy, were not. In the nineteen-fifties and sixties several states, responding to the demands of organized spokesmen of psychology, enacted new privilege statutes, often granting psychologist-patient communications much broader protection than was provided by existing physician-patient privileges. (See Ferster, "Statutory Summary of Physician-Patient Privileged Communication Laws" in Allen, Ferster & Ruben, Readings in *Law & Psychiatry* (1968), pp. 161–65.) In 1960 California enacted such a statute, providing: "[T]he confidential relations and communications between psychologist and client shall be placed upon the same basis as those provided by law between attorney and client. . . ." (Bus. & Prof.Code, § 2904 (since repealed).)

Although commentators who analyzed the need for a privilege in this specific area unanimously supported the position that greater protection be extended to communications of psychotherapeutic treatment (see, e.g., Louisell, The Psychologist in Today's Legal World: Part II (1957) 41 Minn.L. Rev. 731; Slovenko, Psychiatry and a Second Look at the Medical Privilege (1960) 6 Wayne L.Rev. 175), they pointed out the anomaly of affording more protection to patients of psychologists than to patients of psychiatrists, as most of the existing statutory schemes did. To eliminate this irrational distinction, California enacted the current psychotherapist-patient privilege (Evid.Code, § 1014) in 1965.

through the enactment of a broad, protective psychotherapist-patient privilege.

The primary contention of Dr. Lifschutz's attack on the judgment of contempt consists of the assertion of a constitutional right of a psychotherapist to absolute confidentiality in his communications with, and treatment of, patients. Although, as we understand it, the alleged right draws its substance primarily from the psychological needs and expectations of patients, Dr. Lifschutz claims that the Constitution grants him an absolute right to refuse to disclose such confidential communications, regardless of the wishes of a patient in a particular case. In separating the interest of the psychotherapist from that of the patient for the purposes of analyzing this contention, we conclude that the compelled disclosure of relevant information obtained in a confidential communication does not violate any constitutional privacy rights of the psychotherapist.

Petitioner founds his far-reaching constitutional claim on the United States Supreme Court decision of Griswold v. Connecticut, supra, 381 U.S. 479, 85 S.Ct. 1678. In *Griswold* the court struck down a state criminal statute prohibiting the use of contraceptives as an unconstitutional infringement of a marital right of privacy.

I

The *Griswold* court quite explicitly explained, however, that the constitutional privacy interests and rights underlying its decision were those of the "patients" of the birth control clinic, rather than of physicians. "We think that appellants have standing to raise *the constitutional rights of the married people* with whom they had a professional relationship. . . . *The rights of husband and wife*, pressed here, are likely to be diluted or adversely affected unless those rights are considered in a suit involving those who have this kind of confidential relation to them." (Italics added.) (381 U.S. at p. 481, 85 S.Ct. at p. 1679.) It is the depth and intimacy of the *patients'* revelations that give rise to the concern over compelled disclosure; the psychotherapist, though undoubtedly deeply involved in the communicative treatment, does not exert a significant privacy interest separate from his patient. We cannot accept petitioner's reliance on the *Griswold* decision as establishing broad constitutional privacy rights of psychotherapists.

In addition to his claim as to a "right of privacy," petitioner urges that the provisions of the Evidence Code requiring a psychotherapist to reveal confidential matters under some circumstances unconstitutionally impair the practice of his profession. This position rests on two distinct legal contentions: first, that the impairment is so severe as to constitute an unconstitutional "taking" of a valuable property right, the doctor's right to practice psychotherapy; and second, that compelled disclosure of any psychotherapeutic communication renders the continued practice of psychotherapy impossible and thus unconstitutionally constricts the realm of available medical treatment. Although psychotherapists should, of course, be entitled to the constitutional protections requisite to the right to practice their profession we doubt that the disclosure involved here goes so far as to constitute the claimed unconstitutional deprivation of that right.

Insofar as petitioner's argument rests on the economic loss that psychotherapists may suffer as a result of the disclosure requirement, his position runs contra to the current trend of constitutional adjudication involving the regulation of economic interests. Legal requirements prescribing mandatory disclosure of confidential business records are of course regular occurrences, and although all compelled disclosures may interfere to some extent with an individual's performance of his work, such requirements have been universally upheld so long as the compelled disclosure is reasonable in light of a related and important governmental purpose.

In order to facilitate the ascertainment of truth and the just resolution of legal claims, the state clearly exerts a justifiable interest in requiring a businessman to disclose communications, confidential or otherwise, relevant to pending litigation. Although we appreciate, as petitioner suggests, that because of the peculiar nature of psychotherapy, the debilitating effect of disclosure is particularly acute, the incidental infringement of the psychotherapist's economic interest in such practice does not succumb to constitutional challenge so long as the circumstances of disclosure are properly confined to serve a legitimate governmental interest. Moreover, because, as we explain below, the patient-litigant exception at issue involves only that special instance in which a patient has chosen to forego the confidentiality of the privilege, we question whether the deterrence of patients and the impairment to the practice of psychotherapy will be as great as petitioner anticipates.

The second basis of petitioner's contention raises a more serious problem. Petitioner claims that if the state is authorized to compel disclosure of some psychotherapeutic communications, psychotherapy can no longer be practiced successfully. He asserts that the unique nature of psychotherapeutic treatment, involving a probing of the patient's subconscious thoughts and emotions, requires an environment of total confidentiality and absolute trust. Petitioner claims that unless a psychotherapist can truthfully assure his patient that all revelations will be held in strictest confidence and never disclosed, patients will be inhibited from participating fully in the psychotherapeutic process and proper treatment will be impossible. Petitioner concludes that the patient-litigant exception involved here conflicts with the preservation of an environment of absolute confidentiality and unconstitutionally constricts the field of medical practice.

Petitioner's argument, resting as it does on assertions of medical necessity, exemplifies the type of question to which the judiciary brings little expertise. Although petitioner has submitted affidavits of psychotherapists who concur in his assertion that total confidentiality is essential to the practice of their profession, we cannot blind ourselves to the fact that the practice of psychotherapy has grown, indeed flourished, in an environment of a non-absolute privilege. No state in the country recognizes as broad a privilege as petitioner claims is constitutionally compelled.

Petitioner's broad assertion, moreover, overlooks the limited nature of the intrusion into psychotherapeutic privacy actually at issue in this case. The patient-litigant exception of section 1016 of the Evidence Code compels disclosure of only those matters which the patient himself has chosen to reveal by tendering them in litigation. We do not know, of course, to what extent patients are deterred from seeking psychotherapeutic treatment by the knowledge that if, at some future date, they choose to place some aspect of their mental condition in issue in litigation, communications relevant to that issue may be revealed. We can only surmise that an understanding of the limits of section 1016, and the realization that the patient retains control over subsequent disclosure, may provide a measure of reassurance to the prospective patient.

II

Section 1034 of the Evidence Code provides that: "a clergyman . . . has a privilege to refuse to disclose a penitential communication if he claims the privilege"; the code provides no exceptions to the clergyman-penitent privilege comparable to the numerous exceptions to the psychotherapist-patient privilege. Petitioner contends that the Legislature, in so distinguishing between clergymen and psychotherapists, has denied psychotherapists the equal protection of the laws in violation of the Fourteenth Amendment. . . . The differing degrees of non-disclosure essential to the relationship and the value of preserving the particular confidential aspect involved, has led states to adopt a variety of different kinds of privileges. The distinction drawn in the California Evidence Code between clergymen and participants in other privileged communications parallels the distinction recognized in the 44 states that have established a distinct clergyman-penitent or "priest-penitent" privilege.

Petitioner maintains, however, that, given the purpose of the clergyman-penitent privilege, the distinction between clergymen and psychotherapists cannot stand. Dr. Lifschutz characterizes the "modern" purpose of the clergyman-penitent privilege as fostering a "sanctuary for the disclosure of emotional distress": as so characterized, relevant distinctions between clergymen and psychotherapists do diminish. Petitioner's portrayal of the clergy-man-penitent privilege, however, while perhaps identifying one of the supporting threads of the statutory provision, does not reflect a complete analysis of the foundation of the privilege.

Realistically, the statutory privilege must be recognized as basically an explicit accommodation by the secular state to strongly held religious tenets of a large segment of its citizenry. . . .

Recognizing that the toleration of religious beliefs and practices forms the basis for this privilege, we cannot say that the Legislature acted irrationally in granting the privilege to clergymen and not to psychotherapists. Although in some circumstances clergymen and psychotherapists perform similar functions and serve similar needs, fundamental and significant differences remain. While many psychotherapists are no doubt strongly committed to the "tenets" of their profession, as indeed Dr. Lifschutz has exhibited by his determined action in the instant proceeding, the source of this commitment can be reasonably distinguished from the distinctive religious conviction out of which the penitential privilege flows.

III

Although, as we have discussed above, Dr. Lifschutz on his own behalf can claim no constitutional privilege to avoid disclosure, he may in some circumstances assert the statutory privilege of his patient.

The psychotherapist . . . cannot assert his patient's privilege if that privilege has been waived or if the communication in question falls within the statutory exceptions to the privilege. Evidence Code, section 912, subdivision (a), provides that: ". . . the right of any person to claim a privilege provided by Section . . . 1014 (psychotherapist-patient privilege) . . . is waived with respect to a communication protected by such privilege if any holder of the privilege, without coercion, has disclosed a significant part of the communication or has consented to such disclosure made by anyone. Consent to disclosure is manifested by any statement or other conduct of the holder of the privilege indicating his consent to the disclosure, including his failure to claim the privilege in any proceeding in which he has the legal standing and opportunity to claim the privilege."

Since Housek, the holder of the privilege, disclosed at a prior deposition that he had consulted Dr. Lifschutz for psychiatric treatment, he has waived whatever privilege he might have had to keep such information confidential.

The questions posed to Dr. Litschutz, however, have inquired only into whether he treated Mr. Housek, and whether he possessed records regarding this patient. Defendant has not yet asked Dr. Lifschutz about the nature of his treatment of the plaintiff, his diagnosis, or the content of any communication. Certainly, in admitting the existence of a psycho-therapist-patient relationship, plaintiff has not disclosed "a significant part of the communication" between himself and Dr. Lifschutz so as to waive his right subsequently to claim the privilege as to other elements of the communication.

Defendant contended in the superior court, however, that *any* communication between the plaintiff and Dr. Lifschutz has lost its privileged status because the plaintiff has filed a personal injury action in which the claims recovery for "mental and emotional distress." Defendant relies on section 1016 of the Evidence Code, the patient-litigant exception to the psycho-therapist-patient privilege, which provides that: "[t]here is no privilege under this article as to a communication relevant to an issue concerning the mental or emotional condition of the patient if such issue has been tendered by: (a) the patient. . . ."

As we explain more fully below, the patient-litigant exception allows only a limited inquiry into the confidences of the psychotherapist-patient relationship, compelling disclosure of only those matters directly relevant to the nature of the specific "emotional or mental" condition which the patient has voluntarily disclosed and tendered in his pleadings or in answer to discovery inquiries. Furthermore, even when confidential information falls within this exception, trial courts, because of the intimate and potentially embarrassing nature of such communications, may utilize the protective measures at their disposal to avoid unwarranted intrusions into the confidences of the relationship.

In interpreting this exception we are necessarily mindful of the justifiable expectations of confidentiality that most individuals seeking psychotherapeutic treatment harbor.

We believe that a patient's interest in keeping such confidential revelations from public purview, in retaining this substantial privacy, has deeper roots than the California statute and draws sustenance from our constitutional heritage. In Griswold v. Connecticut, supra, 381 U.S. 479, 484, 85 S.Ct. 1678, 1681, 14 L.Ed.2d 510, the United States Supreme Court declared that "Various guarantees [of the Bill of Rights] create zones of privacy," and we believe that the confidentiality of the psychotherapeutic session falls within one such zone. Although *Griswold* itself involved only the marital relationship, the open-ended quality of that decision's rationale evidences its far-reaching dimension.

Even though a patient's interest in the confidentiality of the psychotherapist-patient relationship rests, in part, on constitutional underpinnings, all state "interference" with such confidentiality is not prohibited. In section 1016 we do not deal with a provision which seeks to proscribe the association of psychotherapist and patient entirely, but instead we encounter a provision carefully tailored to serve the historically important state interest of facilitating the ascertainment of truth in connection with legal proceedings. In the past this state interest has been viewed as substantial enough to compel the disclosure of a great variety of confidential material.

Moreover, since the exception compels disclosure only in cases in which the patient's own action initiates the exposure, "intrusion" into a patient's privacy remains essentially under the patient's control. As such, we find no constitutional infirmity in it.

Although no previous cases have arisen under the patient-litigant exception to the psychotherapist-patient privilege, decisions applying an analogous exception to the physician-patient privilege have identified two distinct grounds for the exception. First, the courts have noted that the patient, in raising the issue of a specific ailment or condition in litigation, in effect dispenses with the confidentiality of that ailment and may no longer justifiably seek protection from the humiliation of its exposure. Second, the exception represents a judgment that, in all fairness, a patient should not be permitted to establish a claim while simultaneously forclosing inquiry into relevant matters. As we explained in City and County of San Francisco v. Superior Court, supra, 37

Cal.2d 227, 232, 231 P.2d 26, 28 (the *Catton* case), "The whole purpose of the [physician-patient] privilege is to preclude the humiliation of the patient that might follow disclosure of his ailments. When the patient himself discloses those ailments by bringing an action in which they are in issue, there is no longer any reason for the privilege. The patient-litigant exception precludes one who has placed in issue his physical condition from invoking the privilege on the ground that disclosure of his condition would cause him humiliation. He cannot have his cake and eat it too."

Although defendant reads the above quoted language of the *Catton* case as implying that the patient-litigant exception contemplates an automatic, complete waiver of privilege whenever a patient institutes a claim for any physical or mental injury, we find nothing in either the rationale of the exception as explained in the *Catton* case, or in the cases applying the exception, to justify the breadth of this description. In previous physician-patient privilege cases the exception has been generally applied only to compel disclosure of medical treatment and communication concerning the very injury of impairment that was the subject matter of the litigation. There is certainly nothing to suggest that in the context of the more liberal psychotherapist-patient privilege this exception should be given a broader reading.

If the provision had as broad an effect as is suggested by petitioner, it might effectively deter many psychotherapeutic patients from instituting any general claim for mental suffering and damage out of fear of opening up all past communications to discovery. This result would clearly be an intolerable and overbroad intrusion into the patient's privacy, not sufficiently limited to the legitimate state interest embodied in the provision and would create opportunities for harassment and blackmail.

In light of these considerations the "automatic" waiver of privilege contemplated by section 1016 must be construed not as a complete waiver of the privilege but only as a limited waiver concomitant with the purposes of the exception. Under section 1016 disclosure can be compelled only with respect to *those mental conditions* the patient-litigant has "disclose[d] . . . by bringing an action in which *they* are in issue" communications which are not directly relevant to those specific conditions do not fall within the terms of section 1160's exception and therefore remain privileged. Disclosure cannot be compelled with respect to other aspects of the patient-litigant's personality even though they may, in some sense, be "relevant" to the substantive issues of litigation. The patient thus is not obligated to sacrifice all privacy to seek redress for a specific mental or emotional injury; the scope of the inquiry permitted depends upon the nature of the injuries which the patient-litigant himself has brought before the court.

Because only the patient, and not the party seeking disclosure, knows both the nature of the ailments for which recovery is sought and the general content of the psychotherapeutic communications, the burden rests upon the patient initially to submit some showing that a given confidential communication is not directly related to the issue he has tendered to the court. (Cf.Evid.Code, § 404 (person claiming privilege against incrimination bears burden of showing proffered evidence might tend to incriminate him).) A patient may have to delimit his claimed "mental or emotional distress" or explain, in general terms, the object of the psychotherapy[2] in order to illustrate that it is not reasonably probable that the psychotherapeutic communications sought are directly relevant to the mental condition that he has placed in issue. In determining whether communications sufficiently relate to the mental condition at issue to require disclosure, the court should heed the basic privacy interests involved in the privilege in general, the statutory psychotherapist-patient privilege "[is to] be liberally construed in favor of the patient."

Even when the confidential communication is directly relevant to a mental condition tendered by the patient, and is therefore not privileged, the codes provide a variety of protections that remain available to aid in safeguarding the privacy of the patient. When inquiry into the confidential relationship takes place before trial during discovery, as in the instant case, the patient or psychotherapist may apply to the trial court for a protective order to limit the scope of the inquiry or to regulate the procedure of the inquiry so as to best preserve the rights of the patient.

Such a protective order may be sought at any time during the deposition, and, in appropriate cases, the trial court may issue such an order on its own motion.

[2] Although ordinarily a patient cannot be required to disclose privileged information in order to claim the privilege (Evid. Code, § 915, subd. (a)), because the privileged status of psychotherapeutic communications under the patient-litigant exception depends upon the *content* of the communication, a patient may have to reveal some information about a communication to enable the trial judge to pass on his claim of irrelevancy. Upon such revelation, the trial judge should take necessary precautions to protect the confidentiality of these communications; for example, he might routinely permit such disclosure to be made *ex parte* in his chambers. (Compare the procedure suggested in Evid.Code, § 915, subd. (b).)

When the questioning of the psychotherapist or patient as to confidential communications occurs at the trial itself, the danger of publicity and embarrassment is increased. Of course, unless the information sought is directly relevant to the issue as revealed by the evidence at trial, the communication is privileged and no disclosure can be compelled. Moreover, as with any evidence, the court court retains discretion to "exclude evidence if its probative value is substantially outweighted by the probability that its admission will . . . (b) create substantial danger of undue prejudice, ..." (Evid.Code, § 352.)

In sum, we conclude that no constitutional right enables the psychotherapist to assert an absolute privilege concerning all psychotherapeutic communications. We do not believe the patient-psychotherapist privilege should be frozen into the rigidity of absolutism. So extreme a conclusion neither harmonizes with the expressed legislative intent nor finds a clear source in constitutional law. Such an application would lock the patient into a vice which would prevent him from waiving the privilege without the psychotherapist's consent. The question whether such a ruling would have the medical merit claimed by petitioner must be addressed to the Legislature; we can find no basis for such a ruling in legal precedent or principle.

Furthermore, the existence of a broad statutory privilege in clergymen does not deny psychotherapists the equal protection of the laws. Finally, although we recognize the legitimacy and importance of the concern over governmentally sanctioned intrusions into a patient's psychotherapeutic history, the patient-litigant exception, as properly limited, does not necessarily entail an overbroad intrusion into the patient's privacy.

Inasmuch as plaintiff had already disclosed that he had consulted Dr. Lifschutz for psychotherapeutic treatment, petitioner could not properly have refused to answer at least that question concerning the communications; since neither plaintiff nor the psychotherapist has as yet made any claim that the subpenaed records are not directly relevant to the specific "mental and emotional" injuries for which plaintiff is claiming relief, Dr. Lifschutz had no right to refuse to produce the records. Thus the trial court's order requiring the production of records and the answering of questions was valid; the trial court properly adjudged Dr. Lifschutz in contempt of court for intentionally violating that valid court order.

The order to show cause is discharged and the petition for writ of habeas corpus is denied.

CONFIDENTIAL COMMUNICATIONS

Elyce Zenoff Ferster

The first problem that confronts a person who wants to understand the subject of communications between patients and therapists is the frequently confused and mistaken use of the terms "confidential" and "privileged." Unfortunately, these terms are often employed as synonyms to describe communications between a therapist and his patients.

Confidential communications refer to the therapist's ethical duty to keep secret the information obtained about a patient while acting in a professional capacity. These communications are privileged only if a statute provides that such information may not be disclosed in a legal proceeding without the patient's consent.

The ethical duty of confidentiality probably was first expressed by Hippocrates. He vowed: "Whatever, in connection with my professional practice, or not in connection with it, I may see or hear in the lives of men which ought not to be spoken abroad I will not divulge as reckoning that all should be kept secret." The substance of this position is incorporated into principles of ethics of both the Americal Medical Association and the American Psychological Association.[1] The APA's confidentiality principle, although much more detailed, is substantially similar. It also includes a subsection directing that provisions be made "for the maintenance of confidentiality in the preservation and ultimate disposition of confidential records."[2] The ethical duty of confidentiality is reinforced in many states by the fact that a breach is grounds for revocation of a license to practice.[3]

Consequently, most therapists who receive requests for confidential information about a patient should have little trouble deciding what action to take when the patient has not requested the disclosure. Except for the very few situations in which there is a clear danger to the patient or society, the information should not be released.[4] In fact, for the protection of both the patient and the therapist, disclosure should not be made without the patient's written consent.

Many people assume that there should also be little difficulty in making a decision about releasing confidential materials when the patient has consented. Since the communication is the patient's and he has consented to its being divulged, it is assumed that the therapist should release it. One problem that is not answered by this assumption is whether a patient in therapy can give an informed consent, since he cannot know what the therapist's records may reveal about him.[5] For that matter, even if the therapist does not keep written records, the patient or ex-patient does not know what the therapist will say about him. Also, at least one therapist states that such disclosures raise a therapeutic problem. He states that the patient may regard the therapist as a potential informer, even if the patient believes that information will be furnished only with written consent.[6]

Even if it is assumed that the consent is informed and that disclosure raises no therapeutic problems, there is still the problem of the voluntariness of the patient's consent. Little attention has been paid to the issue of whether a consent is truly voluntary, when the consequence of denying consent is likely to be failure to obtain employment, a driver's license, etc.

---

[1] A.M.A. Principles of Ethics §9.

[2] A.P.A. Principles of Ethics §6.

[3] E. Zenoff Ferster, "Confidentiality and Privileged Communications," *Journal of American Medical Association* 182 (1962): 656.

[4] But see A. A. Davidson, "Legal and Ethical Aspects of Psychiatric Research," *American Journal of Psychiatry* 126 (Aug. 1969), who points out that some psychiatrists believe to breach a doctor-patient confidence is justifiable in a wide variety of circumstances.

[5] West, "Ethical Psychiatry and Biosocial Humanism," *American Journal of Psych.* 126 (1969): 226, 228.

[6] M. H. Hollender, "Psychiatrist and Release of Patient Information," *American Journal of Psychiatry* 116 (March 1960): 828.

This selection was written expressly for this volume and has not been previously published.

Even less attention has been paid to such questions as:

1. Does the party requesting the information need to know that the patient has seen a therapist?
2. Assuming that some information from the therapist is necessary, is his opinion of the patient's fitness for the task in question sufficient or should records and the substance of the communications be made available?
3. Should information be required only if the patient:
   a. is currently seeing a therapist;
   b. has seen a therapist within the last two years;
   c. has never seen a therapist;
   d. has been hospitalized for mental illness?
4. Should information be sent directly to the employer, school, etc., or only to a therapist selected by the person or institution inquiring about the patient?

It is difficult to discuss these various questions without some description of the different situations in which the issue of voluntary release of confidential information may come up. First, and perhaps the simplest, is the request of an insurance company for information before it will reimburse the patient for medical and/or hospital bills. Certainly, the company is entitled to know that the patient was seen by a therapist, the number of times, and some data that would indicate that the visits were for a professional purpose. However, at times companies ask for all the therapist's records on the patient. Their need for this amount of information in order to determine whether the claim is valid is questionable. Nor should the policy be justified by saying the patient does not object, since his only option may be to pay the therapist's fee, which he probably cannot afford, himself.

Another situation in which confidential information may be requested is when a patient applies for a driver's license. For example, the patient may have lost the license as a consequence of hospitalization for mental illness. In some states the license is suspended or revoked when a person is hospitalized for an indeterminate period. In others, the hospital is required to forward the patient's license to the motor vehicle bureau.[7] In either situation, the patient must either apply for a new license or ask for his old one back, and he may be required to undergo a psychiatric examination or furnish psychiatric records in order to be considered for a new license.

Restrictions on driving and requests for confidential information are not necessarily confined to cases in which the patient was hospitalized. Most states ask for information concerning mental illness on the motor vehicle license form, and in California, for example, applicants are asked whether they have ever been afflicted with a "nervous breakdown," "mental illness" or "insanity." Refusal of applicants who answer "yes," to furnish psychiatric records, or to undergo an examination constitutes an independent basis for refusing or revoking a license.[8] Similarly, in the District of Columbia any applicant admitting that he is being, or has recently been, treated for a mental disorder is required to sign a release authorizing his therapist to respond to an inquiry by the Department of Motor Vehicles concerning his condition.[9]

To criticize existing laws and procedures is, of course, simpler than to come up with sound solutions. It is easy to say that motor vehicle department administrators should refuse to revoke licenses only when it is likely that a person is dangerous. Suggesting criteria for determining dangerous drivers is much more difficult. However, it should be remembered that there is virtually no reliable information indicating that persons suffering from any disease (including mental disease) except alcoholism have higher accident rates than do persons free from disease.

Even if motor vehicle administrators believe it necessary to screen all persons who have been hospitalized for mental illness to insure against licensing dangerous drivers, a statement of "fitness" from a treating physician should be sufficient. There seems to be no justification for requiring a release of confidential records.

Nor does there seem to be any reason to assume that people who are seeing or have seen therapists regularly are more dangerous drivers than the general public. Insistence upon requiring the release of confidential information in order for such people to obtain driver's licenses is more likely to lead to lying, or refusal to seek treatment than it is to lower accident rates.

Although the areas of insurance and motor vehicle licensure illustrate some of the problems patients and ex-patients face when asked to consent to disclosure of confidential communications they have made to therapists, the

[7] R. C. Allen, E. Z. Ferster, H. Weihofen. *Mental Impairment and Legal Incompetency.* Prentice-Hall, 1968, pp. 66–63, 344–50.

[8] Idem. at 348–49.
[9] Ibid.

employment area seems to be the first one in which some of the issues involved will be litigated.

The first problem for an applicant who is or has been in therapy is how to answer a question worded like question 29 on the standard application form for federal employment: "Have you ever had a nervous breakdown?" The initial question the applicant probably will ask himself is "What does that mean?" The phrase is at best ambiguous. It has neither a scientific nor a legal meaning. In fact, the American Psychiatric Association's Psychiatric Glossary describes it as "A nonmedical, nonspecific term for emotional illness; primarily, a euphemism for psychiatric illness or psychosis."

Therefore, it is not surprising that countless patients and therapists have assumed that the question is directed at finding out whether the applicant has been hospitalized for severe mental illness or has been so incapacitated by illness that he has been unable to carry out routine activities, such as attending school, carrying out his job, etc. Thus, thousands of persons who have been in individual or group therapy or in analysis on an out-patient basis while pursuing their routine activities and interests have assumed the question is not applicable to them and have answered "No."

However, the federal government currently seems to be taking the position that anyone who has ever seen a therapist has had a "breakdown" or a mental disease. At least this seems to be the only logical deduction that can be drawn from the government's assertion in the case of *Anonymous* v. *Rogers* that an employee who had attended a few group therapy sessions and had twice seen a psychiatrist "falsely answered" the question "Have you ever had a nervous breakdown or had treatment for a mental condition?"

The problem of the question's ambiguity will probably be resolved by the *Rogers* case. The Court will probably decide that the employee did not give a "false answer," either on the grounds that the question is so vague that the applicant can only guess at an answer or on the grounds that the answer was correct since the question is normally interpreted as requesting information only about severe mental illness.

Such a decision would not decide, however, the more important question of "What information, if any, is an employer entitled to about an applicant's present or past therapeutic experiences?" For example, let us assume that *Anonymous* v. *Rogers* is decided in favor of the employee and the government revises its form by substituting such questions as: "Have you ever been in individual or group psycho-

therapy?" "How long and with what frequency did you see a therapist?" Is the government entitled to such information or would such questions constitute an invasion of privacy? The answer to this question may depend on how the information is used. For example, if an admission of seeing a therapist automatically disqualifies an applicant it may not be allowable, while it may be a proper question if the government merely wants assurance that the applicant is capable of performing the required work.

Questions about the frequency and duration of therapeutic consultation probably would not be very productive. For example, psychiatrists may decide that seeing a patient once a week for six months constitutes a "prolonged evaluation" and is not therapy. More important, however, is the fact that the information about the number of sessions is not useful. In psychiatry, unlike other branches of medicine, intensity and duration of treatment is *not* correlated (in fact, it may be inversely correlated) with the severity of the condition. For example, analytic patients who see therapists three or four times a week may well be healthier than the severe neurotic who goes to the therapist once a week for support and medication.

Even if it is decided that an employer is entitled to know that a prospective employee has had any or some therapy in order to determine fitness, there are still difficult questions to answer about the extent to which the patient's privacy may be invaded in making this determination. Should a statement of fitness from the patient's therapist be sufficient to answer questions about the applicant's mental health? Or may the employer require an examination by a therapist of its own choosing? Is the employer entitled to demand that the applicant sign a waiver of confidentiality, so that the therapist will release records about the patient? Presently, waivers of confidential communications are routinely requested, and this requirement is another of the issues in the *Rogers* case.

A Court's decision in *Anonymous* v. *Rogers* and in possible future cases would have ramifications beyond the employment situation. Schools, too, ask applicants about their mental condition, and they, too, sometimes require clearances. For example, one university asks: "Are you receiving, or have you received, care for an emotional condition or disorder of any kind within the past five years? If yes give dates and state briefly the nature of the condition." Schools seem less entitled to this information than employers. An employer might at least argue that it has a right to be concerned about whether a potential employee's condition is such that he is more likely to miss work, have trouble with fellow employees, be indiscreet, etc., than the average employee. A school, however, would seem to have no other reason for the information than to assure itself that a prospective student will not be dangerous to himself or others. It may be reasonable to ask for clearance when the applicant is or has recently been hospitalized for mental illness, but safety does not require students to be screened or to give up the confidentiality of their communications because they have seen a therapist.

To date, the principal problem with requests for confidential information about people who have seen therapists is that they are too broad. The point of view of the insurance company, the motor vehicle department, the employer, the school, etc., has been to obtain as much information as possible, on the assumption that

it may be useful. Thus far, their view has prevailed and has resulted in unnecessary invasions of privacy.

Hopefully, this situation is about to change and the point of view of the patient will also be considered. The result should be a balance between the needs of the inquirer and those of the patient with attention being focused on

1. Why does the questioner need to know the information?
2. Is the information sought relevant to the question asked?
3. Can the question be answered without releasing confidential communication?
4. If confidential information is to be released, who will have access to it?
5. What safeguards are provided to insure that only authorized persons will have access to the information?

ANONYMOUS v. ROGERS

*Brief of the American
Psychiatric Association*

STATEMENT OF THE NATURE OF THE INTEREST OF THE AMICUS

The Association and its member doctors are deeply concerned over any invasion into the privilege and extent of the confidentiality existing between psychiatrists and their patients. Inviolate confidentiality is an integral part controlling the degree and quality of the specialized care afforded by psychiatrists to their patients. This privilege and confidentiality differs considerably from the confidentiality involved in the ordinary practice of medicine. The practice of psychiatry transcends State Lines and the privilege and confidentiality regarding psychiatrists' records, findings and diagnoses should be covered and protected by a quality of confidentiality as high as that afforded lawyers and clergymen. Underlying the treatment given by a psychiatrist is the express or inferred binding, understanding and

agreement that the highly personal disclosures freely made by the patient and necessary to appropriate psychiatric diagnosis and treatment are to be held in the utmost confidence and are not to be divulged.

Amicus and psychiatry as a whole view with alarm any intrusion into the needed personal confidence privilege underlying psychiatric treatment and contend that such intrusion disregards the interests of society. Society will be better served if psychiatrists are able to assure their patients that their confidences are inviolate.

ISSUES PRESENTED FOR REVIEW WHICH ARE OF CONCERN TO THE AMERICAN PSYCHIATRIC ASSOCIATION

1. When an applicant for Government employment answers "No" to the question:

Excerpts from Brief of the American Psychiatric Association, *Amicus Curiae*, in the United States Court of Appeals for the District of Columbia Circuit, No. 73–1141.

"Have you ever had a nervous breakdown or have you ever had treatment for a mental condition" on a security questionnaire, does the fact that he had previously consulted a psychiatrist more than a year earlier for anxiety compel the conclusion that he had "falsely answered" the question?

2. Should a Government employee release to lay personnel officials and others the records of the psychiatrist who saw the employee when the Government employee has offered to disclose highly personal information to a Government psychiatrist through his psychiatrist for evaluation, rather than release the records of the psychiatrist to the mentioned lay personnel officials and others, is his discharge for "refusal to cooperate" arbitrary and capricious and, therefore, unlawful?

STATEMENT OF THE CASE

On November 14, 1968 Appellant began working at the Peace Corps as a Correspondence Analyst in Foreign Service Reserve Grade 8. In September, 1968 Appellant was required to fill out Standard Form 86, "Security Investigation Date for Sensitive Position."

On Form 86, Question No. 19 reads as follows: "Have you ever had a nervous breakdown or have you ever had medical treatment for a mental condition?"

Appellant answered "No" to Question No. 19, stating that this answer was "true, complete and correct to the best of (his) knowledge and belief" and was "made in good faith." Appellant did not report an incident which occurred while he was a minor (aged 20), following his parents' divorce, when he had become upset and anxious. Appellant had consulted his physician who referred him to a psychiatrist who had him participate in a few group therapy sessions. Group therapy involves several patients meeting at the same time with one or more psychologists or psychiatrists, where all work together toward alleviating emotional concerns. Many normal and stable persons participate in group therapy.

Appellant performed his position superbly as a Correspondence Analyst after receiving temporary security clearance. On February 5, 1969, without any warning or notice of any charges, Appellant was summoned and subjected to interrogation lasting some two hours by two Government investigators relating to his sex and his attitude towards sex and other personal matters. The General Counsel of the Peace Corps acknowledged that this interrogation was extraordinary. During this interrogation Appellant disclosed he had twice con-

sulted psychiatrists. One was in the early spring of 1967, a year before he applied for the position, and the other was in the fall of 1968, after he had applied for the position. At the latter time he had become tense and upset over personal matters. In consulting these physicians, no medication was prescribed for or used by Appellant. Appellant at no time has been hospitalized and never received any treatment, and has not had any mental illness.

During the February interrogation, the Government investigators questioned Appellant about his two previous visits to two psychiatrists and Appellant signed releases giving the Government access to his medical records in the psychiatrists' possession at a time when he was without legal counsel. Up to that time the Government never approached the psychiatrists to ask for Appellant's records. Appellant consulted counsel, and on his counsel's advice did not keep an appointment to see a Government psychiatrists who was a consultant under contract to the Peace Corps, and rescinded the releases he signed in February.

In March Appellant was informed by the Government that he would be dismissed from the Peace Corps if he did not release his medical records and submit to questioning by the Government psychiatrist. On the advice of counsel Appellant declined to release his medical records or to submit to a psychiatric examination by the Government psychiatrist.

Appellant offered to have the psychiatrist he had consulted furnish detailed reports for review by the Government psychiatrist. The Government refused this offer.

Counsel for Appellant then made a further offer of having Appellant meet with the Government psychiatrist, accompanied by his counsel and by the psychiatrist Appellant had seen in 1968. This offer was also refused by the Government, and [the Government insisted Appellant again release his medical records and submit to an examination by the Government psychiatrist, not accompanied by anyone else.]

On April 15, 1969 the Government dismissed him from the Peace Corps "to promote the sufficiency of the Service."

On October 31, 1969 Appellant filed an Amended and Supplemental Complaint. . . . This Complaint sought (a) a declaration that his dismissal was unlawful, (b) an Order directing defendants to correct his record, (c) back pay pursuant to 5 U.S.C., Sec. 5596(b) and (d) a declaration that Appellant be deemed to have rendered satisfactory service.

On October 26, 1972 the court below . . . granted defendants' Motion for a Summary Judgment.

This appeal followed.

ARGUMENT

1. *The negative answer of Appellant to question No. 19 is not a false answer.*

2. Question No. 19 on Standard Form 86 is ambiguous, is dual and poorly phrased. To characterize Appellant's negative answer to this involved and difficult question as "false" in Amicus' view is incorrect. This involved question would be difficult for a trained psychiatrist or psychologist, much less a layman, to answer. The terms "nervous breakdown" and "medical treatment" and "mental condition" are difficult to define and in medicine certainly have meanings which are not known to the layman. On the facts in this case, the reasons why Appellant went to his family physician a year before he applied for the Government job, when he was only 20 years of age, because of difficult personal and family problems which upset him emotionally, in no sense would be construed in medicine to be a "nervous breakdown." Nor is the Amicus prepared to state that the referral of Appellant by his family physician to a psychiatrist who had this young man sit in on several group therapy sessions, constitute "medical treatment" for a "nervous breakdown" or a "mental condition." Appellant was given no medical treatment by way of medication or otherwise. His attending several sessions of group therapy cannot be construed medically as medical treatment for a mental condition or for a nervous breakdown.

Appellant has insisted that he never considered his visit to his family physician and a psychiatrist, and the attending of these group therapy sessions as constituting medical treatment for a mental illness or for a nervous breakdown. Appellant honestly believes, and the facts support him, that he never has had a mental illness and has never had a nervous breakdown. On this premise, Appellant contends, and properly so, that he did not falsely answer this question and that he did not engage in deception in answering this question in the negative.

3. *Appellant's offer to disclose highly personal information to a Government psychiatrist through his psychiatrist and to attend and be examined by the Government psychiatrist in the presence of his counsel and his psychiatrist does not constitute refusal to cooperate under the facts involved in this brief.*

Appellant offered reasonable alternatives to the demands of the Government. Appellant's first offer was that the psychiatrist he had consulted furnish detailed reports for review by the Government psychiatrist, notwithstanding that his counsel advised him that the Government had no such rights to such reports.

This offer was rejected by the Government. Appellant made a second offer in which Appellant offered to meet with the Government psychiatrist, accompanied by his counsel and the private psychiatrist Appellant had seen in the previous year, in order to furnish the Government with detailed reports concerning Appellant and to have the Government psychiatrist examine Appellant. This offer also was rejected by the Government. This offer involved the furnishing of the Government psychiatrist with the opportunity to evaluate the confidential and medical problems involved without participation in these confidential areas of Government lay personnel in order to evaluate Appellant's stability. Obviously, if the Government psychiatrist after reviewing the material furnished through Appellant's psychiatrist, and after his interviewing and examining Appellant, would give Appellant a clean bill of health, there would be no reason for the Government to pursue the matter further. The Government psychiatrist has confirmed that Appellant's first offer was a sensible one.

As we have pointed out in the Statement of the Amicus' interest in this case, the practice of psychiatry involves unqualified privilege and confidentiality, and in this respect psychiatry differs considerably from the ordinary practice of medicine which also involves confidential relationships. The right of privacy, including the right of a physician in this area of privacy, has been constitutionally recognized. *Griswold* v. *Connecticut*, 381 U.S. 479 (1965), *Roe* v. *Wade*, 41 U.S.L.W. 4213 (S.C.U.S. Jan. 22, 1973), *Scott* v. *Macey* (II), supra.

Underlying the treatment given by a psychiatrist to a patient is the express or inferred binding understanding and agreement that the highly personal disclosures made by the patient and necessary to appropriate diagnosis and treatment are to be held in the utmost confidence and are not to be divulged. To permit this confidence to be breached on the demand of lay personnel in Government involving Federal employment would decrease the capabilities of psychiatrists to make accurate diagnoses and to provide for adequate and proper medical psychiatric treatments. Involved also in this confidential situation is the problem inherent in psychiatry which arises when the patient makes such disclosures to a psychiatrist in good faith, with the belief, understanding or agreement that these disclosures will be kept confidential, but are later compelled to be divulged by force of a demand by laymen in Government. The results are unreasonable and in effect compel the citizens to testify against themselves without prior knowledge of the problems and dangers involved in free discosures made to a psychiatrist in inviolate confidence. Treatment of the mentally ill is too important (the assurance of inviolate confidentiality is central to this treatment) to risk jeopardizing the theory and success of treatment because of possible and questionable relevance of some of the patient's personal statements when demanded by a layman in the Government. Also involved are the deep rooted ethics of the profession as they apply to the psychiatrist. He should not be forced or required, even with the consent of the patient, to breach the basic and inviolate confidentiality existing between the psychiatrist and his patient. *Disclosure and the turning over of patients' records to laymen in Government is contrary to his ethics and his Hippocratic Oath.*[1] Such could subject the psychiatrist to

[1] The Hippocratic Oath, which is still administered to medical graduates, states: "Whatever, in connection with my professional practice or not in connection with it, I see or hear, in the life of men, which ought not to be spoken abroad, I will not divulge, as reckoning that all such should be kept secret."

severe criticism by his peers or by the community. Disclosures of personal confidences and the turning over of psychiatric records at the demand of laymen in Government could cause many persons who would otherwise seek needed psychiatric help for even slight emotional problems to be reluctant to seek this needed, learned, professional, medical assistance and thus interfere with the proper rendering of psychiatric care to our citizens.

The demand of a psychiatric examination by a Government employed psychiatrist and the demand for the turning over by Appellant and his psychiatrist of his confidential medical records to laymen in the Peace Corps [are arbitrary and unreasonable, and an unwarranted invasion into the privacy of Appellant and his psychiatrist.]

Amicus submits that the confidentiality existing between the psychiatrist and his patient should be inviolate, and should be protected by the same quality of confidentiality as is afforded lawyers and clergymen in the practice of their learned professions.

SUGGESTIONS FOR ADDITIONAL READING

American Psychiatric Association, "Position Statement on Guidelines for Psychiatrists: Problems in Confidentiality," *American Journal of Psychiatry* 126, no. 10 (April 1970): 1543.

"Communications to Social Worker as Privileged," 50 ALR 3d 563, 1973.

Group for the Advancement of Psychiatry, Report No. 45 ("Confidentiality and Privileged Communication in the Practice of Psychiatry"), 1960.

Guttmacher, M. S. *The Mind of the Murderer.* New York: Farrar, Straus, 1960, pp. 157–226.

Modlin, H. "How Private is Privacy," *Psychiatry Digest* (Feb. 1969): 13.

"Physician's Tort Liability, Apart from Defamation, for Unauthorized Disclosure of Confidential Information about Patient," 20 ALR 3d 1109, 1968.

"Privilege, in Judicial or Quasi-Judicial Proceedings, Arising from Relationship between Psychiatrist or Psychologist and Patient," 44 ALR 3d 24, 1972.

Slovenko, R. (ed.) *Psychotherapy, Confidentiality and Privileged Communication.* Springfield, Ill.: C. C Thomas, 1966.

Watson, A. "Levels of Confidentiality in the Psychoanalytic Situation," *Journal of the American Psychoanalytic Assoc.* 20, no. 1 (January 1972).

III

The Psychiatrist and the Civil Law

9

Psychiatric Hospitalization

This chapter, which begins our consideration of specific substantive areas of civil law, is concerned with psychiatric hospitalization. It begins with the testimony of Albert Deutsch, the author of the classic work in the area, *The Mentally Ill in America,* before the Subcommittee on Constitutional Rights of the Senate Judiciary Committee. It is both an articulate and an accurate description of the problems of the state mental hospital and its patients. The Ervin Act, drafted by the Subcommittee, indicates the defects of the hospitalization laws of the past and identifies areas of legislative reform for the present and the future. The five cases which follow illustrate the various problems the courts have been grappling with in recent years: the extent to which allegedly mentally ill persons are entitled to rights not granted by the legislatures; the special problems of hospitalizing the young and the old; and the emergence of the concept of "the least restrictive alternative."

The next group of selections deals with the other side of the coin: Has there been too much "reform"? Has the emphasis on the rights of the mentally ill resulted in a decrease in protection of both the mentally ill and the public?

Problems surrounding the standards and procedures for release of the involuntarily hospitalized patient are the focus of the next group of selections. The final reading, Professor Chambers' *Alternatives to Civil Commitment of the Mentally Ill,* is a thoughtful exploration of the question whether we can or should eliminate involuntary psychiatric hospitalization.

TESTIMONY OF ALBERT DEUTSCH

*Before the Subcommittee on Constitutional Rights
of the Senate Judiciary Committee,
87th Congress, First Session*

I share with many of my fellow citizens a deep sense of gratification that this splendid subcommittee is now turning a powerful searchlight on one of the darkest and most shameful areas of public neglect. As historian, journalist, and citizen, I have been actively interested in the right of the institutionalized mentally sick for a quarter century. With many others, I have been picking at the public conscience in their behalf, relying mainly on medical, economic, moral and humanitarian persuasion. Now, by a paradox of progress that I'll define later, a new and, I trust, more effective instrument of reform comes to hand—the demand for constitutional protection, for basic justice guaranteed to every American citizen not as a matter of mere charity or sympathy but of inalienable right.

I wish to make it clear at the outset that throughout this statement I shall concern myself only with the so-called "civil insane," as distinguished from the "criminal insane"— that is, with those who are neither suspected nor convicted of antisocial acts or crimes.

Hearings on the Constitutional Rights of the Mentally Ill before the Subcommittee on Constitutional Rights, Senate Committee on the Judiciary, 87th Congress, 1st Session, Part I, at 40 (1961).

There are about 650,000 of them in American mental hospitals today. More than 97 per cent of this number are in public institutions. For the most part, they represent an oppressed minority in our midst. In a period when civil rights for minority groups constitute a major national issue, theirs remains the most ignored and neglected of all.

None can doubt the impressive progress made during the past decade or so in the institutional care and treatment of the mentally ill. But neither can the sober student doubt that the rate of progress has been grossly exaggerated in many reports that reach the public eye and ear or that overoptimistic appraisals have tended to lull the interested public into a false complacency about present conditions.

The melancholy fact is that, in spite of recent progress, these conditions remain for the most part a disgrace to any civilized society, more so to a society that boasts a special concern for the civil liberties of the individual citizen.

About a dozen years ago I conducted a nationwide survey of mental hospital conditions in the United States; I reported my findings in a book *The Shame of the States*. Some physicians I interviewed frankly admitted that the animals of nearby piggeries were better housed, fed, and treated than many of the patients on their wards. I saw hundreds of sick people shackled, strapped, straitjacketed, and bound to their beds. I saw mental patients forced to eat meals with their hands because they couldn't be trusted to eat like humans. I saw them crawl into beds jammed together, in dormitories filled to twice or three times their normal capacity. I saw them incarcerated in "seclusion rooms"—solitary isolation cells, really—for weeks and months at a time. I saw signs of medical neglect, with curable patients sinking into hopeless chronicity. I found evidence of physical brutality, but these paled into insignificance when compared with the excruciating suffering stemming from prolonged, enforced idleness, herdlike crowding, lack of privacy, depersonalization, and the overall atmosphere of neglect. The fault lay not with individual physicians, nurses or attendants—underpaid, undervalued, and overworked as they were—but with the general community that not only tolerated but enforced these subhuman conditions through financial penury, ignorance, fear, and indifference.

Conditions, as I noted earlier, have improved considerably since them. The advent of the tranquilizing drugs a few years ago reduced tremendously the resort to straitjackets and other mechanical restraints which our British cousins proved unnecessary in the first place more than a century ago. The "disturbed wards" are not the bedlams they were a decade ago. The application of the "therapeutic community" concept in a few hospitals—where patients, instead of being herded like animals and reduced to subhuman status, are given greater measures of freedom, participation, and responsibility—has tended to transform asylums to hospitals where it is adopted. So have other therapeutic devices. But these improvements, heartening though they be, must be measured soberly against the primitive level they proceeded from, the great distance we remain from achievable goals, and the continuing injustices and deprivations still inflicted on hundreds of thousands of our fellow citizens.

Let us trace, briefly, the *via dolorosa* of the typical mental patient from the time of admission to the time of discharge, keeping in mind that there are notable exceptions in some communities and some States:

Firstly, there are the consequences of our outmoded, often outrageously unjust, commitment laws in most States. The mental patient is "suspected" of being insane. He or she is "apprehended" or "arrested" by a sheriff or other law-enforcement official. In many instances, he is thrown into jail and lodged there like a criminal, awaiting determination of his mental status.

A recent survey in Indiana revealed that hundreds of harmless mental patients were thus confined in jail, many for long periods, while awaiting commitment.

If adjudged insane, he is committed by court order much as a criminal is committed to prison. Although modern psychiatry has demonstrated that individual mentalpatients differ vastly in their capacities for responsibility, mental hospital commitment in most States automatically strips them *en masse* of specific civil rights—sometimes of all such rights, regardless of their individual capacity.

In most cases, the committed patient is transported to the hospital by a police officer, often in handcuffs or a straitjacket, although he or she may be perfectly harmless.

In spite of recent reforms here and there, commitment procedures in most States remain unsound, archaic, and even vicious in their operation. The combination of police, jail, and court can do incalculable harm to the patient, gravely impeding his chances of recovery. It often reinforces the delusions of persecution in some and the morbid feelings of guilt in others. Psychiatrists generally are appalled by the cumbersome, callous, and sometimes brutal legal machinery that "processes" sick people as though they were criminals.

Current commitment procedures, as with the institutional process itself, reflect in great measure the outworn popular misconceptions of the mentally sick or insane as either raving maniacs, dangerous lunatics, or gibbering idiots. The fact is that the great majority of hospitalized mental patients are too passive, too silent, too fearful, too withdrawn. Yet, for every real or potentially dangerous mental patient, we penalize [a] thousand or more sick people, perfectly harmless to the public peace or safety. This is in direct violation of our democratic concept of fair play—indeed, of the basic law itself.

Now, let us follow the mental patient into the institution. It is estimated that about 90 per cent of all State hospital patients in this ountry are there on commitment, rather than on voluntary admission.

I should say, gentlemen, that this is a rather educated guess that I got from a member of the staff of the NIMH only yesterday. Now, New York, which is one of the most advanced in the movement toward voluntary admission, in 1959 admitted 20 per cent of its hospitalized patients; 25,000 admitted, I believe it was, and about 5,000 on voluntary admission. That is 20 per cent.

And that is a very creditable percentage in our time. We will see later how it compares with what the British and the Europeans have been doing in this same field. If we said 8 to 9 percent on commitment, we would probably be roughly right. . . .

That is, we send them to these institutions without their approval or against their will. We do so on the implicit or explicit premise or promise that they will be treated with a view toward aiding their recovery. But what happens?

Recent studies—notably those of Drs. Erving Goffman, William Caudill, and Ivan Belknap, based on prolonged ward observation—attest to the continuance of the stripping of the patient, loss of his individuality and dignity, depersonalization, and demoralization. The chronically acute shortage of physicians in most wards makes the term "psychotherapy" a hideous mockery for most patients. In most public mental hospitals, the average ward patient comes into person-to-person contact with a physician about 15 minutes every month—not a day or a week, but a month. The wonder is that so many patients achieve social recovery, under these dismal circumstances. The grim tragedy of it all is that reliable psychiatrists tell us that the recovery rate could be doubled in many mental hospitals if modern therapeutic procedures were put to optimum use.

In return for depriving the institutionalized mental patient of his civil rights, we promise him treatment for his illness. In failing to redeem this pledge, we not only do not aid his recovery; in many cases, we make him worse.

Dr. Robert C. Hunt, superintendent of the Hudson River State Hospital in Poughkeepsie, N.Y., is one of our foremost institutional administrators. He is a conservative psychiatrist. In 1955 he made a study of several leading British mental hospitals, where patients were given maximum freedom and vigorous modern therapy. In 1957, he delivered a remarkable paper summing up the situation in most of our mental hospitals, as follows:

The enormous disability associated with mental illness is, to a large extent, superimposed, preventable, and treatable.

Disability is superimposed by rejection mechanisms stemming from cultural attitudes.

Hospitalization as such is an important cause of disability.

The best of treatment-minded State hospitals perform a disabling function.

The custodial culture within a State hospital is largely created by public pressure for security.

In short, under prevailing conditions, we superimpose new disabilities upon existing disabilities—at least in many cases—when we forcibly commit sick people to places called mental hospitals which in reality remain custodial asylums.

Hollingshead and Redlich, in their epochal book, *Social Class and Mental Illness*, published in 1958, add another dimension to this tragic situation by demonstrating, to a degree undreamed of in the treatment of physical ills, that treatment, nontreatment, and maltreatment of mental patients is significantly affected by socioeconomic status.

Highly significant associations, they write,

exist between class status . . . and the kinds of treatment psychiatrists administer to their patients . . . Higher classes get what they want, lower classes do not.

Low man on the psychiatric totem pole is the State hospital patient, and even there class status usually determines treatment, with the lowest class swiftly relegated to the back wards.

In 1948 I visited several English mental hospitals, including Warlingham Park, one of the first open hospitals. An open hospital is one where all patients are in wards with doors unlocked during the day, with patients free to move in and out. I was astounded by the peace and order of the institution, and by the noticeable therapeutic atmosphere, and I came back and wrote it up. It is significant that several British hospitals unlocked their doors years before the advent of the tranquilizing drugs.

In 1958 I visited the first completely open State hospital in this country, at Embreeville, Pa. As I walked through its open wards and noted the free movement and relaxed postures of the patients, there flashed through my mind many scenes of tragedy and despair that I had witnessed in my journalistic rounds, over the years, of nearly 100 mental hospitals.

You approach a ward. The doctor, nurse, or attendant escorting you turns a key in the lock and opens the door. You enter. The door is locked behind you. Within that ward may be anywhere from 30 to 300 sick humans, guilty of no crime, yet locked up as securely as prison inmates.

For many of them, the ward is their total living space. Here they are shut in day and night, save for brief periods when they are marched out, under close guard, to the dining room for meals or outdoors in good weather. That is, when there is enough personnel on hand to take them out. Many mental patients, perfectly able to move about without risk to themselves or others, are confined in crowded wards for days and weeks on end, sometimes for months and even years.

Today, of the more than 200 State mental hospitals in this country, five or six are completely open, or nearly so—notably St. Lawrence and Hudson River in New York and Embreeville in Pennsylvania.

In New York State, under the leadership of Dr. Paul Hoch, wards have been opened with fair speed, so that today about 60 per cent of New York's nearly 100,000 hospitalized mental patients are in open wards. Other States have been opening their wards here and there, but the process is much too slow, and there are still civil mental hospitals with all their wards locked tight.

This is in spite of the overwhelming evidence, not only abroad but now in this country, that loss of liberty harms the mental patient and is unnecessary for the public safety. Indeed, it has been amply demonstrated that freedom is a therapeutic tool, that it speeds recovery, and that it therefore is conducive to economy.

Here is what I found in Embreeville after two years of operation as a completely open hospital:

The discharge rate of patients had doubled. Thanks to the zooming discharge rate, the hospital population had been reduced in the face of a doubled monthly admission rate.

The relapse rate was cut almost in half.

There was a sharp drop in violence. Patients got along better with themselves and the staff. Staff morale was raised tremendously. Property damage by patients was reduced 75 per cent.

There had not been a single serious incident in the surrounding community involving a patient. There were no more escapes than before the doors were opened. Patients were expected to act like human beings, and acted like human beings.

In 1958 a group of Massachusetts State hospital superintendents made an inspection tour of British and European mental hospitals. Here is what they reported:

The most significant difference apparent to one familiar with American mental hospitals is the greater respect for the patient as an individual noted in nearly all psychiatric institutions in Europe. It might have been expected that in the United States, where individual freedom is a revered tradition, this attitude would be reflected in mental hospital care. In some places this is evident, but not to the extent generally observed in Europe.

For some time, American mental hospitals have stressed control of deviant behavior and emphasized security as necessary for the protection of the patient and the public.

In nearly every place visited, the patient was given as much freedom as he could manage. All patients were placed on privileged status, which was withheld only for the period during which a patient might show himself unable to assume so much responsibility.

"Self-esteem," in this view, "cannot be achieved when one person is the prisoner of another."

There it is, for the record. In olden times we burned, hanged, and tortured mentally sick persons because we believed they were witches or possessed of demons. Then we imprisoned them because we regarded them as sinful or as criminals.

Later still we confined them because we didn't know what else to do.

The plea of ignorance is no longer open to us as an excuse of needlessly depriving mentally sick people of sacred rights. We know what can be done, what is being done. I am not advocating that all the so-called insane be loosed on the community. But I am convinced that all but a very small proportion of the civil insane need not be subjected to degrading commitment proceedings and then locked up in custodial institutions. We can no longer tolerate the paradox of depriving mental patients of their civil rights in the name of hospital treatment when we know that it is not only unnecessary for security but harmful to potential recovery.

I feel strongly that very day we tolerate the needless confinement of a mental patient in a locked ward is a day of ignominy for all of us, a day in which we passively participate in a social crime against individual liberty.

I subscribe to Dr. Morton Birnbaum's thesis that deprivation of the hospitalized mental patient of his civil rights is a violation of the "due process" clause in our Constitution. I advocate the initiation of test cases that would challenge existing deprivations in the courts on constitutional grounds. I agree with Dr. Birnbaum that the courts may have to allow a reasonable interim period between the recognition of the right to treatment and the enforcement of that right. But court action could accelerate that process, using the desegregation of public schools decision as a precedent.

I recommend, in addition, the following steps, some of them spelled out in the final report of the Joint Commission on Mental Illness and Health, released last week under the title *Action for Mental Health:*

1. Federal financial and technical aid to States for mental hospital treatment, thus helping to speed up progress toward the restoration of civil rights. Federal aid in the treatment area could be just as effective as aid for research and training has already proved.

2. Speeded action by States and communities toward alternatives to hospitalization—through day and night hospitals, psychiatric wards in general community hospitals, mental health clinics, psychiatric treatment in the home, et cetera.

3. Abandonment of monstrously huge State mental hospitals—some with patient populations of 10,000 and more—as speedily as possible. I would prefer a limit of 500 beds on all future State hospitals, but would accept the Joint Commission's recommendation of a 1,000 bed limit.

4. The rapid recruitment and training of nonpsychiatrist professional personnel—such as psychologists, social workers, and public health nurses—to participate in the therapeutic process, recognizing that it would take two generations or more to develop enough psychiatrists to provide adequately for the needs of the mentally ill.

5. Rapid relinquishment of quasi-criminal commitment procedures in favor of voluntary admission. In England, upward of 70 percent of hospitalized mental patients are there on voluntary status; in some public mental hospitals the percentage runs to 90. Here it is the other way around. There is much talk about the advantages of voluntary admission, but too little active support and encouragement. Indeed, in a number of States providing for voluntary admission as an alternative, hospitals are so crowded that the authorities accept only committed patients. In several States, the patients who wish to enter voluntarily are forced to go through humiliating commitment procedures to become eligible for admission.

All along the line, the pace of progress is far too slow. Acceleration is possible. Simple justice demands it.

THE ERVIN ACT

Public Law 88–597, 88th Congress, S.935
To Protect the Constitutional Rights of Certain Individuals Who Are
Mentally Ill, to Provide for Their Care, Treatment, Hospitalization,
and for Other Purposes

DEFINITIONS

Sec. 2. As used in this Act—

1. the term *mental illness* means any psychosis or other disease which substantially impairs the mental health of an individual;

2. the term *mentally ill person* means any person who has a mental illness, but shall not include a person committed to a private or public hospital in the District of Columbia by order of the court in a criminal proceeding;

3. the term *physician* means an individual licensed under the laws of the District of Columbia to practice medicine, or an individual who practices medicine in the employment of the Government of the United States or of the District of Columbia;

4. the term *private hospital* means any non-

---

78 Stat. 944 (1964) (Now D.C. Code §§ 21–501 to 591 [Supp. V. 1966]).

governmental hospital or institution, or part thereof, in the District of Columbia, equipped and qualified to provide inpatient care and treatment for any individual suffering from a physical or mental illness;

5. the term *public hospital* means any hospital or institution, or part thereof, in the District of Columbia, owned and operated by the Government of the United States or of the District of Columbia, equipped and qualified to provide inpatient care and treatment for any individual suffering from a physical or mental illness;

6. the term *administrator* means an individual in charge of a public or private hospital or his delegate; and

7. the term *chief of service* means the physician charged with overall responsibility for the professional program of care and treatment in the particular administrative unit of the hospital to which the patient has been admitted or such other member of the medical staff as shall be designated by the chief of service.

Commission on Mental Health

Sec. 3. The United States District Court for the District of Columbia (hereinafter referred to as the "court") is authorized to appoint a Commission on Mental Health, composed of nine members. One member shall be a member of the bar of such court, who has engaged in active practice of law in the District of Columbia for a period of at least five years prior to his appointment. He shall be the Chairman of the Commission and act as the administrative head of the Commission and its staff. He shall preside at all hearings and direct all of the proceedings before the Commission. He shall devote his entire time to the work of the Commission. Eight members of the Commission shall be physicians who have been practicing medicine in the District of Columbia and who have had not less than five years' experience in the diagnosis and treatment of mental illnesses. Each member of the Commission shall hold office for four years, the appointments of physician members to be staggered. The physician members shall serve on a part-time basis and shall be rotated by assignment of the chief judge of the court, so that at any one time the Commission shall consist of the Chairman and two physician members. Physician members of the Commission may practice their profession during their tenure of office, but may not participate in the disposition of the case of any person in which they have rendered professional service or advice. The court shall also appoint an alternate lawyer member who shall have the same qualifications as the lawyer

member of the Commission and who shall serve on a part-time basis and act as Chairman in the absence of the permanent Chairman. The salaries of the members of the Commission and its employees shall be fixed in accordance with the provisions of the Classification Act of 1949, as amended. The alternate Chairman shall be paid on a per diem basis at the same rate of compensation as fixed for the permanent Chairman. It shall be the duty of the Commission on Mental Health to examine alleged mentally ill persons, inquire into their affairs and the affairs of persons who may be legally liable for their support, and to make reports and recommendations to the court. Except as otherwise provided in this Act, the Commission may conduct its examinations and hearings either at the courthouse or elsewhere at its discretion. The court may issue subpoenas at the request of the Commission returnable before the Commission, for the appearance of the alleged mentally ill person, witnesses, and persons who may be liable for the support of the mentally ill person. The Commission, or any of the members thereof, shall be competent and compellable witnesses at any trial, hearing, or other proceeding conducted pursuant to this Act and the physician-patient privilege shall not be applicable.

Voluntary Hospitalization

Sec. 4. (a) Any individual may apply to any public or private hospital in the District of Columbia for admission to such hospital as a voluntary patient for the purposes of observation, diagnosis, and care and treatment of a mental illness. Upon the request of any such individual eighteen years of age or over (or in the case of any individual under eighteen years of age, upon a request made by his spouse, parent, or legal guardian), the administrator of a public hospital shall, if an examination by an admitting psychiatrist at such public hospital reveals the need for such hospitalization, and the administrator of a private hospital may, admit any such individual as a voluntary patient to such hospital for observation, diagnosis, and care and treatment of a mental illness in accordance with the provisions of this Act.

(b) Any voluntary patient admitted to any hospital pursuant to this section shall, if he is eighteen years of age or over, be entitled at any time to obtain his release from such hospital by filing a written request with the chief of service. The chief of service shall, within a period of forty-eight hours after the receipt of any such request (unless such period shall expire on a Saturday, Sunday, or legal holiday, then not later than noon of the next succeeding day which is not a Saturday, Sunday, or legal holiday), release the voluntary patient making such request. In the case of any voluntary patient under the age of eighteen years, the chief of service shall release such patient, according to the provisions of this section, upon the written request of his spouse, parent, or legal guardian. The chief of service may release any voluntary patient hospitalized pursuant to this section whenever he determines that such patient has recovered or that his conoinued hospitalization is no longer beneficial to him or advisable.

Hospitalization of Nonprotesting Persons

Sec. 5. (a) A friend or relative of an individual believed to be suffering from a mental illness may make application on behalf of that individual to the admitting psychiatrist of any hospital by presenting the individual, together with a referral from a practicing physician. Such individual may be accepted for examination and treatment by any private hospital and shall be accepted for examination and treatment by any public hospital if, in the judgment of the admitting psychiatrist, the need for such is indicated on the basis of the individual's mental condition and such individual signs a statement at the time of such admission stating that he does not object to hospitalization. Such statement shall contain in simple, nontechnical language the fact that the individual is to be hospitalized and a description of the right to release set out in subsection (b) of the section. The admitting psychiatrist may admit such an individual without referral from a practicing physician if the need for an immediate admission is apparent to the admitting psychiatrist upon preliminary examination.

(b) Any person hospitalized under the provisions of Subsection (a) of this section shall be immediately released upon his written request unless proceedings for hospitalization under court order pursuant to Section 7 have been initiated.

Emergency Hospitalization

Sec. 6. (a) Any duly accredited officer or agent of the Department of Public Health of the District of Columbia, or any officer authorized to make arrests in the District of Columbia, or the family physician of the individual in question, who has reason to believe that an individual is mentally ill and, because of such illness, is likely to injure himself or others if he is not immediately detained may, without a warrant, take such individual into custody, transport him to a public or private hospital, and make application for his admission thereto for purposes of emergency observation and diagnosis. Such application shall reveal the circumstances under which the individual was taken into custody and the reasons therefor.

(b) Subject to the provisions of Subsection (c) of this section, the administrator of any private hospital may, and the administrator of any public hospital shall, admit and detain for purposes of emergency observation and diagnosis any individual with respect to whom such application is made, if such application is accompanied by a certificate of a psychiatrist on duty at such hospital stating that he has examined the individual and is of the opinion that he has symptoms of a mental illness and, as a result thereof, is likely to injure himself or others unless he is immediately hospitalized; not later than twenty-four hours after the admission pursuant to this section of any individual to a hospital, the administrator of such hospital shall serve notice of such admission, by registered mail, to the spouse, parent, or legal guardian of such individual and to the Commission on Mental Health.

(c) No individual admitted to any hospital under Subsection (b) of this section shall be detained in such hospital for a period in excess of forty-eight hours from the time of his admission (unless such period shall expire on a Saturday, Sunday, or legal holiday, then not later than noon of the next succeeding day which is not a Saturday, Sunday, or legal holiday), unless the administrator of such hospital has, within such period, filed a written petition with the court for an order authorizing the continued hospitalization of such individual for emergency observation and diagnosis for a period not to exceed seven days from the time such order is entered.

(d) The court shall, within a period of twenty-four hours after the receipt by it of such petition (unless such period shall expire on a Saturday, Sunday, or legal holiday, then not later than noon of the next succeeding day which is not a Saturday, Sunday, or legal holiday), either order the hospitalization of such individual for emergency observation and a diagnosis for a period of not to exceed seven days from the time such order is entered, or order his immediate release. In making its determination, the court shall consider the written reports of the agent, officer, or physician who made the application under Subsection (b) of this section, the certificate of the examining psychiatrist which accompanied it, and any other relevant information.

(e) Any individual whose continued hospitalization is ordered under Subsection (d) of this section shall be entitled upon his request to a hearing before the court entering such order. Any such hearing so requested shall be held within a period of twenty-four hours after receipt of such request (unless such period shall expire on a Saturday, Sunday, or legal holiday, then not later than noon of the next succeeding day which is not a Saturday, Sunday, or legal holiday).

(f) The chief of service of any hospital in which an individual is hospitalized under a court order entered pursuant to Subsection (d) of this section shall, within forty-eight hours after such order is entered, have such individual examined by a physician. If the physician, after his examination, certifies that in his opinion the individual is not mentally ill to the extent that he is likely to injure himself or others if not presently detained, the individual shall be immediately released. The chief of service shall, within forty-eight hours after such examination has been completed, send a copy of the results thereof by registered mail to the spouse, parents, attorney, legal guardian, or nearest known adult relative of the individual examined.

(g) Any physician or psychiatrist making application or conducting an examination under this Act shall be a competent and compellable witness at any trial hearing or other proceeding conducted pursuant to this Act and the physician-patient privilege shall not be applicable.

(h) Notwithstanding any other provision of this section, the administrator of any hospital in which an individual is hospitalized under this section may, if judicial proceedings for his hospitalization have been commenced under Section 7 of this Act, detain such individual therein during the course of such proceedings.

Hospitalization Under Court Order

Sec. 7. (a) Proceedings for the judicial hospitalization of any individual in the District of Columbia may be commenced by the filing of a petition with the Mental Health Commission by his spouse, parent, or legal guardian, by any physician, duly accredited officer or agent of the Department of Public Health, or by any officer authorized to make arrest in the District of Columbia. Such petition shall be accompanied (1) by a certificate of a physician stating that he has examined the individual and is of the opinion that such individual is mentally ill, and because of such illness is likely to injure himself or others if allowed to remain at liberty, or (2) by a sworn written statement by the petitioner that (A) the petitioner has good reason to believe that such individual is men-

tally ill and, because of such illness, is likely to injure himself or others if allowed to remain at liberty, and (B) that such individual has refused to submit to examination by a physician.

(b) Within three days after the receipt by it of any petition filed under Subsection (a) of this section, the Commission shall send a copy of such petition by registered mail to the individual with respect to whom it was filed.

(c) The Commission shall promptly examine any individual alleged to be mentally ill after the filing of a petition provided by Subsection (a) of this section and shall thereafter promptly hold a hearing on the issue of his mental illness. Such hearing shall be conducted in as informal a manner as may be consistent with orderly procedure and in a physical setting not likely to have a harmful effect on the mental health of the individual named in such petition. In conducting such hearing, the Commission shall hear testimony of any person whose testimony may be relevant and shall receive all relevant evidence which may be offered. Any individual with respect to whom a hearing is held under this section shall be entitled, in his discretion, to be present at such hearing, to testify, and to present and cross-examine witnesses. The Commission shall also hold a hearing in order to determine liability under the provisions of Subsection (g) of this section for the expenses of hospitalization of the alleged mentally ill person, if it is determined that he is mentally ill and should be hospitalized as provided under this Act. Such hearing may be conducted separately from the hearing on the issue of mental illness. If conducted separately, it may be conducted by the Chairman of the Commission alone.

(d) The alleged mentally ill person shall be represented by counsel in any proceeding before the Commission or the court, and if he fails or refuses to obtain counsel, the court shall appoint counsel to represent him. Any counsel so appointed shall be awarded compensation by the court for his services in an amount determined by it to be fair and reasonable. Such compensation shall be charged against the estate of the individual for whom such counsel was appointed, or against any unobligated funds of the Commission, as the court in its discretion may direct. The Commission or the court, as the case may be, shall at the request of any counsel so appointed, grant a recess in such proceeding (but not for more than five days) to give such counsel an opportunity to prepare his case.

(e) If the Commission finds, after such hearing, that the individual with respect to whom such hearing was held is not mentally ill or, if mentally ill, is not mentally ill to the extent that he is likely to injure himself or others if allowed to remain at liberty, the Commission shall immediately order his release and notify the court of that fact in writing. If the Commission finds, after such hearing, that the individual with respect to whom such hearing was held is mentally ill, and because of such illness is likely to injure himself or others if allowed to remain at liberty, the Commission shall promptly report such fact, in writing, to the United States District Court for the District of Columbia. Such report shall contain the Commission's findings of fact, conclusions of law, and recommendations. Any alleged mentally ill person with respect to whom such report is made shall have the right to demand a jury trial and shall be advised of that right by the Commission orally and in writing. A copy of the report of the Commission shall be served personally on the alleged mentally ill person and his attorney.

(f) Upon the receipt by the court of any such report referred to in Subsection (e), the court shall promptly set the matter for hearing and shall cause a written notice of the time and place of the final hearing to be served personally upon the individual with respect to whom such report was made and his attorney, together with notice that he has five days following the date on which he is so served within which to demand a jury trial. Any such demand may be made by such individual or by anyone in his behalf. If a jury trial is demanded within such five-day period, it shall be accorded by the court with all reasonable speed. If no timely demand is made for such trial, the court shall determine such individual's mental condition on the basis of the report of the Commission, or on such further evidence in addition to such report as the court may require. If the court or jury (as the case may be) finds that such individual is not mentally ill, the court shall dismiss the petition and order his release. If the court or jury (as the case may be) finds that such individual is mentally ill and, because of that illness, is likely to injure himself or others if allowed to remain at liberty, the court may order his hospitalization for an indeterminante period, or order any other alternative course of treatment which the court believes will be in the best interests of such individual or of the public. The Commission, or any member thereof, shall be competent and compellable witnesses at any hearing or jury trial held pursuant to this Act. The jury to be used in any case where a jury trial is demanded under this Act shall be impaneled, upon order of the court, from the jurors in attendance upon other branches of the court, who shall perform such services in addition to and as part of their duties in such court.

(g) The father, mother, husband, wife, and adult children of a mentally ill person, if of sufficient ability, and the estate of such mentally ill person, if such estate is sufficient for the purpose, shall pay the cost to the District of Columbia of such mentally ill person's maintenance, including treatment, in any hospital in which such person is hospitalized under this Act. It shall be the duty of the Commission to examine, under oath, the father, mother, husband, wife, and adult children of any alleged mentally ill person whenever such relatives live within the District of Columbia, and to ascertain the ability of such relatives or estate to maintain or contribute toward the maintenance of such mentally ill person; except that in no case shall such relatives or estate be required tp ay more than the actual cost to the District of Columbia of maintenance of such alleged mentally ill person. If any individual hereinabove made liable for the maintenance of a mentally ill person shall fail so to provide or pay for such maintenance, the court shall issue to such individual a citation to show cause why he should not be adjudged to pay a portion or all of the expenses of maintenance of such patient. The citation shall be served at least ten days before the hearing thereon. If, upon such hearing, it shall appear to the court that the mentally ill person has not sufficient estate out of which his maintenance may properly be fully met and that he has relatives of the degree hereinabove referred to who are parties to the proceedings, and who are able to contribute thereto, the court may make an order requiring payment by such relative of such sum or sums as it may find they are reasonably able to pay and as may be necessary to provide for the maintenance and treatment of such mentally ill person. Such order shall require the payment of such sums to the District of Columbia treasurer annually, semiannually, quarterly, or monthly as the court may direct. It shall be the duty of the treasurer to collect such sums due under this section, and to turn the same into the Treasury of the United States to the credit of the District of Columbia. Any such order may be enforced against any property of the mentally ill person or of the individual liable or undertaking to maintain him in the same way as if it were an order for temporary alimony in a divorce case.

(h) No petition, application, or certificate authorized under Sections 6(a) and 7(a) of this Act may be considered if made by a physician who is related by blood or marriage to the alleged mentally ill person, or who is financially interested in the hospital in which the alleged mentally ill person is to be detained, or, except in the case of physicians employed by the United States or the District of Columbia, who are professionally or officially connected with such hospital. No such petition, application, or certificate of any physician shall be considered unless it is based on personal observation and examination of the alleged mentally ill person made by such physician not more than seventy-two hours prior to the making of the petition, application, or certificate. Such certificate shall set forth in detail the facts and reasons on which such physician based his opinions and conclusions.

PERIODIC EXAMINATION AND RELEASE

Sec. 8. (a) Any patient hospitalized pursuant to a court order obtained under section 7 of this Act, or his attorney, legal guardian, spouse, parent, or other nearest adult relative, shall be entitled, upon the expiration of ninety days following such order and not more frequently than every six months thereafter, to request, in writing, the chief of service of the hospital in which the patient is hospitalized, to have a current examination of his mental condition made by one or more physicians. If the request is timely it shall be granted. The patient shall be entitled, at his own expense, to have any duly qualified physician participate in such examination. In the case of any such patient who is indigent, the Department of Public Health shall, upon the written request of such patient, assist him in obtaining a duly qualified physician to participate in such examination in the patient's behalf. Any such physician so obtained by such indigent patient shall be compensated for his services out of any unobligated funds of such Department in an amount determined by it to be fair and reasonable. If the chief of service, after considering the reports of the physicians conducting such examination, determines that the patient is no longer mentally ill to the extentt hat he is likely to injure himself or others if not hospitalized, the chief of service shall order the immediate release of the patient. However, if the chief of service, after considering such reports, determines that such patient continues to be mentally ill to the extent that he is likely to injure himself or others if not hospitalized, but one or more of the physicians participating in such examination reports that the patient is not mentally ill to such extent, the patient may petition the court for an order directing his release. Such petition shall be accompanied by the reports of the physicians who conducted the examination of the patient.

(b) In considering such petition, the court shall consider the testimony of the physicians who participated in the examination of such patient, and the reports of such physicians accompanying the petition. After considering such testimony and reports, the court shall either (1) reject the petition and order the continued hospitalization of the patient, or (2) order the chief of service to immediately release such patient. Any physician participating in such examination shall be a competent and compellable witness at any trial or hearing held pursuant to this Act.

(c) The chief of service of a public or private hospital shall as often as practicable, but not less often than every six months, examine or cause to be examined each patient admitted to any such hospital pursuant to section 7 of this Act and if he determines on the basis of such examination that the conditions which justified the involuntary hospitalization of such patient no longer exist, the chief of service shall immediately release such patient.

(d) Nothing in this section shall be construed to prohibit any person from exercising any right presently available to him for obtaining release from confinement, including the right to petition for a writ of habeas corpus.

RIGHT TO COMMUNICATION—EXERCISE OF CERTAIN RIGHTS

Sec. 9. (a) Any person hospitalized in a public or private hospital pursuant to this Act shall be entitled (1) to communicate by sealed mail or otherwise with any individual or official agency inside or outside the hospital, and (2) to receive uncensored mail from his attorney or personal physician. All other incoming mail or communications may be read before being delivered to the patient, if the chief of service believes such action is necessary for the medical welfare of the patient who is the intended recipient. However, any mail or other communication which is not delivered to the patient for whom it is intended shall be immediately returned to the sender. But nothing in this section shall prevent the administrator from making reasonable rules regarding visitation hours and the use of telephone and telegraph facilities.

(b) Any person hospitalized in a public hospital for a mental illness shall, during his hospitalization, be entitled to medical and psychiatric care and treatment. The administrator of each public hospital shall keep records detailing all such care and treatment received by any such person and such records shall be made available, upon that person's written authorization, to his attorney or personal physician. Such records shall be preserved by the administrator until such person has been discharged from the hospital.

(c) No mechanical restraint shall be applied to any patient hospitalized in any public or private hospital for a mental illness unless the use of restraint is prescribed by a physician and, if so prescribed, such restraint shall be removed whenever the condition justifying its use no longer exists. Any use of a mechanical restraint, together with the reasons therefor, shall be made a part of the medical record of the patient.

(d) No patient hospitalized pursuant to this Act shall, by reason of such hospitalization, be denied the right to dispose of property, execute instruments, make purchases, enter into contractual relationships, vote, and hold a driver's license, unless such patient has been adjudicated incompetent by a court of competent jurisdiction and has not been restored to legal capacity. If the chief of service of the public or private hospital in which any such patient is hospitalized is of the opinion that such patient is unable to exercise any of the aforementioned rights, the chief of service shall immediately notify the patient and the patient's attorney, legal guardian, spouse, parents, or other nearest known adult relative, and the United States District Court for the District of Columbia, the Commission on Mental Health, and the Board of Commissioners of the District of Columbia of that fact.

(e) Any individual in the District of Columbia who, by reason of a judicial decree ordering his hospitalization entered prior to the date of the enactment of this Act, is considered to be mentally incompetent and is denied the right to dispose of property, execute instruments, make purchases, enter into contractual relationships, vote, or hold a driver's license solely by reason of such decree, shall, upon the expiration of the one-year period immediately following such date of enactment, be deemed to have been restored to legal capacity unless, within such one-year period, affirmative action is commenced to have such individual adjudicated mentally incompetent by a court of competent jurisdiction. . . .

(f) Any patient, and the patient's spouse, parents, or other nearest known adult relative, shall receive, upon admission of the patient to the hospital, a written statement outlining in simple, nontechnical language all release procedures provided by this Act, setting out all rights accorded to patients by this Act, and describing procedures provided by law for adjudication of incompetency and appointment of trustees or committees for the hospitalized individual.

VETERANS' ADMINISTRATION FACILITIES [omitted]

PENALTIES

Sec. 11. (a) Any individual who (1) without probable cause for believing a person to be mentally ill, causes or conspires with or assists another to cause the hospitalization of any such person under this Act or (2) causes or conspires with or assists another to cause the denial to any person of any right accorded to him under this Act, shall be punished by a fine not exceeding $5,000 or imprisonment not exceeding three years, or both.

(b) Any individual who, without probable cause for believing a person to be mentally ill, executes a petition, application, or certificate pursuant to this Act, by which such individual secures or attempts to secure the apprehension, hospitalization, detention, or restraint of any such person, or any physician or psychiatrist who knowingly makes any false certificate or application pursuant to this Act as to the mental condition of any person, shall be punished by a fine not exceeding $5,000 or imprisonment not exceeding three years, or both.

NON-RESIDENT

Sec. 12. If an individual ordered committed to a public hospital by the court pursuant to Subsection (f) of Section 7 is found by the Commission, subject to a review by the court, not to be a resident of the District of Columbia, and to be a resident of another place, he shall be transferred to the State of his residence of an appropriate institution of that State is willing to accept him. If the person be an indigent, the expense of transferring him, including the traveling expenses of necessary attendants, shall be borne by the District of Columbia. For the purposes of this section, a "resident of the District of Columbia" means an individual who has maintained his principal place of abode in the District of Columbia for more than one year immediately prior to the filing of the petition referred to in Subsection (a) of Section 7 of this Act.

WITNESS FEES [omitted]

NOT TO BE CONFINED IN JAIL

Sec. 14. No person apprehended, detained, or hospitalized under any provision of this Act, shall be confined in jail or in any penal or correctional institution.

FORMS [*omitted*]

SURETY

Sec. 16. The court in its discretion may require any petitioner under Section 7 of this Act to file an undertaking with surety to be approved by the court in such amount as the court may deem proper, conditioned to save harmless the respondent by reason of costs incurred, including attorney's fees, if any, and damages suffered by the respondent, as a result of any such action.

INDIVIDUALS PREVIOUSLY HOSPITALIZED

Sec. 17. The provisions of Sections 8, 9, 12, 14, 15, and 16 of this Act shall be applicable to any person who, on or after the date of the enactment of this Act, is a patient in a hospital in the District of Columbia by reason of having been declared insane or of unsound mind pursuant to a court order entered in a noncriminal proceeding prior to such date of enactment; except that any request for an examination authorized under Section 8 may be made by such person, or his attorney, legal guardian, spouse, parent, or other nearest adult relative, after the expiration of the thirty-day period

following the date of the enactment and not more frequently than every six months thereafter.

APPOINTMENT OF CONSERVATORS

Sec. 18. The first section of the Act of October 24, 1951 (65 Stat. 608), is amended by adding after "mental weakness (not amounting to unsoundness of mind)" the following: "mental illness (as such term is defined in the District of Columbia Hospitalization of the Mentally Ill Act)."

ACTS REPEALED [*omitted*]

CONTINUANCE OF COMMISSION ON MENTAL HEALTH

Sec. 20. The Commission on Mental Health to which reference is made in Section 3 of this Act is the Commission established by the Act of June 8, 1938 (52 Stat. 625), as amended. Nothing contained in any amendment made by this Act shall be construed to affect or impair the existence of the Commission serving as such on the day preceding the date of enactment of this Act.

HOSPITALIZATION OF THE MENTALLY ILL: A DECADE AFTER THE ERVIN ACT

Elyce Zenoff Ferster

The Ervin Act, at least on paper, was a significant step forward in society's treatment of the mentally ill. At last a legislature, and one whose lead the states were likely to follow, the United States Congress, asserted that mentally ill and allegedly mentally ill persons had a variety of rights. The most important of these were:

1. the right to hospitalization on a voluntary basis;
2. the right of a voluntary patient to leave the hospital;
3. the right to due process in hospitalization proceedings including notice, counsel, and a hearing;
4. the right of a hospitalized patient to re-

This article was written specifically for this book and has not been previously published. The author was Counsel for the 1961 Senate Subcommittee on Constitutional Rights Hearings on the Constitutional Rights of the Mentally Ill, helped to develop the Ervin Act, and was the Consultant to the Committee's 1969 hearings on the same subject.

tain his civil rights unless adjudicated incompetent in an independent proceeding;

5. the right to periodic review of commitment, including an examination by an independent psychiatrist;
6. the right to treatment.

However, it is unrealistic to regard the passage of legislation as the sole criterion of success in achieving a specific goal, such as protecting the rights of the mentally ill. Although a new law is often a necessary step in this process, it frequently is not sufficient. Therefore, a look at the law in action also is necessary.

Unfortunately, it is not unusual for reformers to discover that despite their success in getting their views embodied in a statute, the problem that was supposed to be solved, remains. This disappointing result may be due to one or more of the following reasons:

1. the problem is not susceptible to a legislative solution;
2. the law was not implemented, e.g., necessary funds to carry it out were not provided;
3. the law solved some problems while creating others which were as bad or worse than those that led to its adoption;
4. opponents of the law gained enough support to have it amended or repealed.

The Senate Subcommittee on Constitutional Rights, in order to evaluate the impact of the Ervin Act, held new hearings on the "Constitutional Rights of the Mentally Ill" in 1969, five years after its enactment. Although the Subcommittee always had planned to hold such hearings, the immediate impetus for their being held in the fall of 1969 was to consider some proposed amendments to the bill which were contained in S.2869, the Administration's bill to revise the criminal laws in the District of Columbia.

One of these amendments, which was suggested by the Department of Justice, would have changed the Act's voluntary hospitalization procedure. One of the principal purposes of the Act was to encourage voluntary hospitalization.[1] The merits of voluntary admission have been recognized for many years and an excellent summary of them appears in the Commentary accompanying the National Institute of Mental Health's Draft Act Governing Hospitalization for the Mentally Ill:

A fully operating program of voluntary admissions will reduce materially the harmful experiences often associated with compulsory hospitalization and at the same time encourage the mentally ill and their families to obtain care at an early stage, when the promise of recovery is greatest. Another important consideration is the need . . . for the patient's cooperation with his physician. This is most likely to be obtained if the patient is in a hospital environment because he recognizes his need for it and affirmatively seeks it. Making hospitalization, and when, recovery having become ill . . . should reduce the financial and human cost of mental illness which is greatest when the patient's condition has been aggravated by delay in treatment or by the experience of forcible hospitalization, and when, recovery having become impossible, lifelong custody is the only prospect.

Despite the desirability of voluntary hospitalization, at the time of the Subcommittee's hearings in 1961, 90 percent of the patients at St. Elizabeth's Hospital were there by judicial commitment.[2] In an effort to enlarge the number of voluntary patients, the Ervin Act required that public hospitals *accept* voluntary patients instead of merely *allowing* them to, and gave these patients the absolute right to release after notice to the hospital. Voluntary admissions to St. Elizabeths did increase. They comprised almost 38 percent of admissions during the first nine months after the Act's adoption, and by fiscal 1970 accounted for 53 percent of the admissions. The Justice Department's amendment would have deprived the voluntary patient of the right to leave after giving the hospital notice.[3] Instead, it allowed hospitals to detain such patients and initiate emergency commitment proceedings whenever the patient's physician had reason to believe that he might injure himself or others. Witnesses representing medical organizations, psychiatric organizations, lawyers, etc., overwhelmingly favored retention of the Ervin Act provisions. They believed that changing the law would significantly decrease the number of people who would enter the hospital voluntarily.[4]

Another of the Justice Department's proposed amendments would have seriously restricted the benefits established by the Act —the right to a periodic examination. Section 21–546 provides that a patient is entitled to current examination of his mental condition at least every six months, and the right to have a

---

[1] U.S. Senate, Subcommittee on Constitutional Rights, Hearings On Constitutional Rights, of the Mentally Ill (1969–70).

[2] Id. at 2.

[3] Id. at 961.

[4] For example, see Id. at 18, American Psychiatric Association; 112 D.C. Medical Society; 147 D.C. Mental Health Association; 151 Neighborhood Legal Services; 174, 193 D.C. Legal Aid Agency; 211–12—American Civil Liberties Union.

physician from outside of the hospital participate in the examination. If at least one physician, as a result of the examination, believes
that hospitalization is no longer necessary, the
patient is entitled to judicial review. The Justice Department proposal would have eliminated the right to judicial review. Again, the
witnesses did not support this amendment.
Instead, their concern was that the periodic
examination provision needed further implementation. The Act provided that examinations by outside physicians would be paid for
by the patient if he had funds and by unobligated funds of the Department of Public
Health if the patient was indigent. Unfortunately, the Department usually did not have
such funds and was therefore unable to meet
the obligation.[5] In addition to the problem of
the lack of funds to pay physicians for the
periodic examination, there was also the problem of paying attorneys who served as counsel
for indigent patients.

The need for implementation was the main
theme at the hearings. By and large, there
was almost a continuous chorus of praise for
the substantive provisions of the Act. There
were no substantial complaints about the language of the statute or its procedures. Instead,
the problems brought to the Subcommittee's
attention invariably involved the lack of facilities, personnel, and funds available for carrying out the Act's provisions.

Lack of funds also curtailed the implementation of another innovative provision of the
act. Too often the right to be placed somewhere other than a mental hospital was not
meaningful, because there was no alternative
facility available in which the judge could
place a patient. The most important deficiency,
however, was that despite the statute's acknowledgment of a right to treatment, unfortunately,
there was often not sufficient staff to provide
it. Yet, no one suggested that any of these provisions be abandoned as an "impossible
dream." In fact, it was hoped that their presence would stimulate administrative agencies.
Congress, the Courts, and/or the public to turn
these rights into realities.

It is now five years since the Subcommittee's
1969 hearings and, as the witnesses hoped,

reality has begun to conform to the Ervin Act,
instead of the goals being modified to meet the
status quo. Independent physicians to conduct
the periodic examinations are being supplied
by the Mental Health Service Administration's
Department of Forensic Psychiatry. Patients
are now represented at all hearings, from
emergency commitment through appeals by a
special division of the District of Columbia
Public Defender Service, by staff attorneys and
law students from all of the local law schools.
More, though not enough, patients are being
treated in community facilities. Of course,
further implementation of the right to treatment is needed. But it has already become a
concept recognized not only in the literature
about the mentally impaired but also in the
case law. This recognition is illustrated by the
fact that a whole section of the next chapter
is devoted to this topic. The most significant
indication of the importance however, is that
the United States Supreme Court has agreed
to review a right-to-treatment case.

The effects of the Ervin Act are being felt
beyond the District of Columbia. By the time
of the 1969 hearings some progress had been
made in protecting the rights of the mentally
ill, not only in the District of Columbia (which
was the only jurisdiction in which the Act applied) but also in other states, such as Georgia,
Hawaii, Illinois, Kentucky, Nevada, and Tennessee. Many of these states drew on the Ervin
Act for revising their own laws.[6]

In the last five years more states have revised their laws in order to strengthen the
rights of the mentally ill. Massachusetts, for
example, has abolished, at least on paper, indefinite commitment, and has introduced the
concept of "likelihood of serious harm" as a
prerequisite to commitment.[7] California is trying to treat most mentally ill people in their
own communities.[8]

The reader will be better able to make an
evaluation of the extent to which progress has
been made, the problems that remain, and the
likelihood that they will be resolved in another
decade, after reading the rest of this chapter
and the chapter on Patient's Rights which
follows.

---

[5] Id. at 136.

[6] Id. at 94–98.
[7] Gen. Laws of Mass., Chapter 123, Supp. 1973.
[8] Cal. W. & I. Code §§ 5000–5401, Supp. 1973.

LESSARD v. SCHMIDT

SPRECHER, Circuit Judge.

Alberta Lessard was picked up by two police officers in front of her residence in West Allis, Wisconsin, and taken to the Mental Health Center North Division, Milwaukee, on October 29, 1971. At the Center, the police officers, defendants James D. Mejchar and Jack Schneider, filled out a form entitled "Emergency Detention for Mental Observation," following which Miss Lessard was detained on an emergency basis. On November 11, 1971, the same police officers appeared before defendant Judge Christ T. Seraphim, Milwaukee County Court, and restated the allegations contained in the petition for emergency detention. On the basis of this ex parte proceeding, Judge Seraphim issued an order permitting the confinement of Miss Lessard for an additional ten days. Thereafter, on November 4, 1971, defendant Dr. George Currier filed an "Application for Judicial Inquiry" with Judge Seraphim, stating that Miss Lessard was suffering from schizophrenia and recommending permanent commitment. At this time Judge Seraphim ordered two physicians to examine Miss Lessard, and signed a second temporary detention document, permitting Miss Lessard's detention for ten more days from the date of the order. This period was again extended on November 12, 1971. Neither Miss Lessard nor anyone who might act on her behalf was informed of any of these proceedings.

On November 5, 1971, Judge Seraphim held an interview with Miss Lessard at the Mental Health Center. At this interview, Judge Seraphim informed Miss Lessard that two doctors had been appointed to examine her and that a guardian ad litem would be appointed to represent her. He asked her if she wished to have her own doctor examine her. Miss Lessard replied that she had no physician. Miss Lessard was not told of this interview in advance and was given no opportunity to prepare for it. Following the interview, Judge Seraphim signed an order appointing Daniel A. Noonan, an attorney, as guardian ad litem for Miss Lessard.

Miss Lessard, on her own initiative, retained counsel through the Milwaukee Legal Services.

. . . At the November 24 hearing before Judge Seraphim, testimony was given by one of the police officers and three physicians and Miss Lessard was ordered committed for thirty additional days. Judge Seraphim gave no reasons for his order except to state that he found Miss Lessard to be "mentally ill." Although the hospital authorities permitted Miss Lessard to go home on an out-patient "parole" basis three days later, the thirty day commitment order has been extended for one month each month since November 24, 1971. . . .

Miss Lessard alleges that the Wisconsin procedure for involuntary civil commitment denied her due process of law in the following respects: in permitting involuntary detention for a possible maximum period of 145 days without benefit of hearing on the necessity of detention; in failing to make notice of all hearings mandatory; in failing to give adequate and timely notice where notice is given; in failing to provide for mandatory notice of right to trial by jury; in failing to give a right to permit counsel to be present at psychiatric interviews; in failing to provide for exclusion of hearsay evidence and for the privilege against self-incrimination; in failing to provide access to an independent psychiatric examination by a physician of the allegedly mentally ill person's choice; in permitting commitment of a person without a determination that the person is in need of commitment beyond a reasonable doubt; and in failing to describe the standard for commitment so that persons may be able to ascertain the standard of conduct under which they may be detained with reasonable certainty. . . .

Even a brief examination of the effects of civil commitment upon those adjudged mentally ill shows the importance of strict adherence to stringent procedural requirements and the necessity for narrow, precise standards.

An individual committed to a mental institution loses numerous civil rights. In Wisconsin, hospitalization for mental illness, whether by voluntary admission or involuntary commitment, raises a rebuttable presumption of incompetency. The presumption continues as long as the patient is under the jurisdiction of hospital authorities. Wis.Stat.Ann.

349 F. Supp. 1078 (E. D. Wisc. 1972).

§ 51.005(2). An individual adjudged mentally ill in Wisconsin also faces restrictions on making contracts and limitations on the right to sue and be sued. . . . Restrictions on licenses required to engage in certain professions also accompany an adjudication of mental illness in Wisconsin. Persons found mentally ill in Wisconsin are, like felons, unable to vote. . . . The mentally ill are also prohibited from driving a car and serving on juries. . . . No person found to be "insane, imbecile, or feeble-minded" may participate in a marriage contract. . . .

It is obvious that the commitment adjudication carries with it an enormous and devastating effect on an individual's civil rights. In some respects, such as the limitation on holding a driver's license, the civil deprivations which follow civil commitment are more serious than the deprivations which accompany a criminal conviction.

In addition to the statutory disabilities associated with an adjudication of mental illness, and just as serious, are the difficulties that the committed individual will face in attempting to adjust to life outside the institution following release. The stigma which accompanies any hospitalization for mental illness has been brought to public attention in the news stories surrounding the recent resignation of a vice-presidential aspirant from further candidacy. Evidence is plentiful that a former mental patient will encounter serious obstacles in attempting to find a job, sign a lease or buy a house. One commentator, noting that "former mental patients do not get jobs," has insisted that, "[i]n the job market, it is better to be an ex-felon than ex-patient." Testimony of Bruce J. Ennis, ACLU, New York City, 1970 Hearings at 284.

Perhaps the most serious possible effect of a decision to commit an individual lies in the statistics which indicate that an individual committed to a mental institution has a much greater chance of dying than if he were left at large. Data compiled in 1966 indicate that while the death rate per 1000 persons in the general population in the United States each year is only 9.5 the rate among resident mental patients is 91.8. Furman & Conners, Jr., "The Pennsylvania Experiment in Due Process," 8 *Duquesne L. Rev.* 32, 65-66 (1970). Figures for Wisconsin are similar. The study showed a death rate for the Wisconsin populace in general of 9.7 per 100 population per year (or less than one percent) and a death rate in Wisconsin mental institutions of 85.1 per thousand (or 8.51 percent). Id. at 66.

Although part of this difference may be accounted for by a larger number of older persons in mental institutions, studies indicate

that other factors also are involved. One factor is the smaller number of physicians per patient in public mental institutions in comparison to the ratio of doctors to individuals in the general population. . . .

In summary, an adjudication of mental illness in Wisconsin carries with it loss of basic civil rights and loss of future opportunities. The damage done is not confined to a small number among the population. In 1963, 679,000 persons were confined in mental institutions in the United States, only 250,000 persons were incarcerated in all prisons administered by the states and federal government. . . . It would thus appear that the interests in avoiding civil commitment are at least as high as those of persons accused of criminal offenses. The resulting burden on the state to justify civil commitment must be correspondingly high. We turn to the specific practices challenged by the plaintiffs in this case.

NOTICE AND AN OPPORTUNITY TO BE HEARD

Plaintiffs challenge the constitutionality of the sections of the Wisconsin civil commitment statute which permit involuntary detention for a possible total of 145 days without a hearing which fail to provide for meaningful notice and which allow the court to dispense with notice at all in cases in which notice is deemed "injurious or without advantage" to the patient. We believe sections 51.02(1), 51.03, and 51.04(1), (2) and (3) are uncon-

---

[1] Section 51.04(1) permits a five-day involuntary detention of "any person who is violent or who threatens violence and who appears irresponsible and dangerous." Under § 51.04(2) the court may require an additional ten-day detention of any person "if it appears from the application for his mental examination or otherwise that safety requires it." Section 51.04(3) permits a further 30-day detention, which may be extended to 90 days. A person may therefor be detained a total of 105 days without any hearing at all. If the patient requires a jury trial under § 51.03 the period may be extended another 40 days, for a total of 145 days.

[2] Wis.Stat.Ann. § 51.02(1)(a) provides: "on receipt of the application or of the report of the examining physicians, the court shall appoint a time and place for hearing the application and shall cause notice thereof to be served upon the patient . . . , which notice shall state that application has been made for the examination into his mental condition (withholding the names of the applicants) and that such application will be heard at the time and place named in the notice; but if it appears to the satisfaction of the court that the notice would be injurious or without advantage to

stitutional on their face and as applied to the named plaintiff in this action, Alberta Lessard. . . .

It can be argued that no deprivation of liberty is permissible under the due process clause without a prior hearing. We think, however, that the state may sometimes have a compelling interest in emergency detention of persons who threaten violence to themselves or others for the purpose of protecting society and the individual. Cf., Boddie v. Connecticut, supra, 401 U.S. at 377-378, 91 S.Ct. 780. Such an emergency measure can be justified only for the length of time necessary to arrange for a hearing before a neutral judge at which probable cause for the detention must be established. The individual detained and members of his family must be given notice of this hearing and attendance by the detained party cannot be waived.

We do not decide the precise time when this hearing must take place. The Wisconsin legislature may decide that a preliminary hearing should be held within a much shorter shorter time than that required by this decision. We set down only the minimum standards which we believe are required by the due process clause. In this connection, we believe that the maximum period which a person may be detained without a preliminary hearing is 48 hours. It must be remembered that at this time the necessity for commitment of an individual has not yet been established. Those who argue that notice and a hearing at this time may be harmful to the patient ignore the fact that there has been no finding that the person is in need of hospitalization. The argument also ignores the fact that even a short detention in a mental facility may have long lasting effects on the individual's ability to function in the outside world due to the stigma attached to mental illness.

There is no necessity for us to determine at the present time the precise nature of the hearing that is required. . . . The exigency of the situation, encompassing an emergency situation and lack of time to marshal all facts necessary to an ultimate determination, however, precludes a requirement that a hearing

at this time encompass all requirements which may be deemed essential at a subsequent hearing. Furthermore, 'subsequent proceedings" should rectify any shortcomings in this preliminary procedure. We note, though, that due process is not accorded by an ex parte hearing in which the individual has no meaningful opportunity to be heard either because of incapacity caused by medication or lack of counsel. . . .

. . . [A] full hearing on the necessity of continued confinement . . . must be held as soon after detention as possible within the limits made necessary in order for psychiatrists to make their examination and reports and for the patient to be able to prepare any defense. There does not seem to be any reason why psychiatrists cannot be scheduled to make their examinations within two or three days of the patient's entering the hospital, particularly when the examinations consist, as in Miss Lessard's case, of ten or fifteen minute interviews. Even if more thorough examinations were to begin to be made there is surely no need for the twenty-six day lapse between detention and hearing which occurred in the instant case. We believe that from ten to fourteen days should be the maximum period which an individual can be detained without a full hearing. If the facilities of the state hospitals do not permit full examination within this period because of inadequate personnel, it is difficult to see how continued detention can be said to be beneficial to the patient.

Notice of the scheduled hearing, "to comply with due process requirements, must be given sufficiently in advance of scheduled court proceedings so that reasonable opportunity to prepare will be afforded," and it must set forth the basis for detention with particularity. In re Gault, 387 U.S. 1, 33. (1967). Notice of date, time and place is not satisfactory. The patient should be informed of the basis for his detention, his right to jury trial, the standard upon which he may be detained, the names of examining physicia and all other persons who may testify in favor of his continued detention, and the substance of their proposed testimony.

Judged by these standards, the Wisconsin statutory scheme for involuntary civil commitment fails to afford persons alleged to be mentally ill with adequate procedural safeguards. . . .

---

the patient by reason of his mental condition, the service of notice may be omitted. The court may, in its discretion, cause notice to be given to such other persons as it deems advisable. If the notice is served the court may proceed to hold the hearing at the time and place specified therein; or, if it is dispensed with, at any time."

The validity of the provision permitting the withholding of names of the applicants is not contested here. See, however, Willner v. Committee on Character & Fitness, 373 U.S. 96, 103–104, 83 S.Ct. 1175, 10 L.Ed.2d 224 (1963).

STANDARDS FOR COMMITMENT

Under Wis.Stat.Ann § 51.02(5), the court may order a patient involuntarily committed if it is "satisfied that he is mentally ill or infirm or deficient and that he is a proper subject for custody and treatment . . ." . . .

Wisconsin defines "mental illness" as "mental disease to such extent that a person so afflicted requires care and treatment for his own welfare, or the welfare of others, or of the community." Wis.Stat.Ann. § 51.75, Art. II(f) (1971 Supp.). Interpreting § 51.02(5) in the light of this provision in Humphrey v. Cady, 405 U.S. 504, 509, 92 S.Ct. 1048, 1052, 31 L.Ed.2d 394 (1972), the Supreme Court noted (in dicta) that implicit in this definition is the requirement that a person's "potential for doing harm, to himself or to others, is great enough to justify such a massive curtailment of liberty." In other words, the statute itself requires a finding of "dangerousness" to self or others in order to deprive an individual of his or her freedom. The Court did not directly address itself to the degree of dangerousness that is constitutionally required before a person may be involuntarily deprived of liberty. However, its approval of a requirement that the potential for doing harm be "great enough to justify such a massive curtailment of liberty" implies a balancing test in which the state must bear the burden of proving that there is an extreme likelihood that if the person is not confined he will do immediate harm to himself or others. Although attempts to predict future conduct are always difficult, and confinement based upon such a prediction must always be viewed with suspicion, we believe confinement can be justified in some cases if the proper burden of proof is satisfied and dangerousness is based upon a finding of a recent overt act, attempt or threat to do substantial harm to oneself or another. See Cross v. Harris, 135 U.S.App.D.C. 259, 418 F.2d 1095, 1102 (1969).

. . . Persons in need of hospitalization for physical ailments are allowed the choice of whether to undergo hospitalization and treatment or not. The same should be true of persons in need of treatment for mental illness unless the state can prove that the person is unable to make a decision about hospitalization because of the nature of his illness. It is certainly true that many people, maybe most, could benefit from some sort of treatment at different periods in their lives. However, it is not difficult to see that the rational choice in many instances would be to forego treatment, particularly if it carries with it the stigma of incarceration in a mental institution, with the difficulties of obtaining release, the curtailments of many rights, the interruption of job and family life, and the difficulties of attempting to obtain a job, drivers license, etc., upon release from the hospital. . . .

This leaves the question of what standard of proof is required to prove that an individual is "mentally ill" and a "proper subject for custody and treatment," i.e., treatable and "dangerous.". . .

The Supreme Court has stated in regard to the deprivation of liberty involved in deportation that it is impermissible for an individual to be "banished from this country upon no higher degree of proof than applies in a negligence case." Woodby, supra, at 285, 87 S.Ct., at 487. The deprivation of freedom involved in civil commitment is greater than that involved in deportation. The deported person may still have his family with him, may take up new citizenship and vote in elections, travel unfettered where he wishes for the most part, make contracts and marry and hold a job. The person confined in a Wisconsin mental institution is deprived of all of these rights. Civil commitment cannot, therefore, be justified upon a mere preponderance of the evidence.

There remains the formulation of a permissible standard. . . .

At least one court would require proof beyond a reasonable doubt on all questions relating to civil commitment. Denton v. Commonwealth, 383 S.W.2d 681 (Ky. 1964). In In re Winship, 397 U.S. 358, (1970), the Supreme Court held that proof beyond a reasonable doubt was required to prove every fact necessary in juvenile delinquency proceedings. . . . The Court reiterated its previous holding in In re Gault, that "civil labels and good intentions do not themselves obviate the need for criminal due process safeguards in juvenile courts, for '[a] proceeding where the issue is whether the child will be found to be "delinquent" and subjected to the loss of his liberty for years is comparable in seriousness to a felony prosecution.'" In re Winship, supra, 397 U.S. at 365-366, 90 S.Ct. at 1073. The Winship Court reached its conclusion despite its findings that an adjudication of delinquency "does not deprive the child of his civil rights, and that juvenile proceedings are confidential." Id. at 366, 90 S.Ct. at 1074.

The argument for a stringent standard of proof is more compelling in the case of a civil commitment in which an individual will be deprived of basic civil rights and be certainly stigmatized by the lack of confidentiality of the adjudication. We therefore hold that the state must prove beyond a reasonable doubt all facts necessary to show that an individual is mentally ill and dangerous.

Even if the standards for an adjudication of mental illness and potential dangerousness are satisfied, a court should order full-time involuntary hospitalization only as a last resort. A basic concept in American justice is the principle that "even though the governmental purpose be legitimate and substantial, that purpose cannot be pursued by means that broadly stifle fundamental personal liberties when the end can be more narrowly achieved. . . .

Perhaps the most basic and fundamental right is the right to be free from unwanted restraint. It seems clear, then, that persons suffering from the condition of being mentally ill, but who are not alleged to have committed any crime, cannot be totally deprived of their liberty if there are less drastic means for achieving the same basic goal. In Lake v. Cameron, 124 U.S.App.D.C. 264, 364 F.2d 657, 660 (1966), the court ruled that the state should "bear the burden of exploration of possible alternatives" to commitment. We believe that the person recommending full time involuntary hospitalization must bear the burden of proving (1) what alternatives are available; (2) what alternatives were investigated; and (3) why the investigated alternatives were not deemed suitable. These alternatives include voluntary or court-ordered out-patient treatment, day treatment in a hospital, night treatment in a hospital, placement in the custody of a friend or relative, placement in a nursing home, referral to a community mental health clinic, and home health aide services. . . .

We now turn to the procedure followed in the commitment hearing of the named plaintiff in this action, Alberta Lessard. At the close of the hearing held 26 days after Miss Lessard was initially detained, Judge Seraphim ordered her committed for an additional 30 days to the Milwaukee County Mental Health Center. Although the hospital authorities released her conditionally three days later, Judge Seraphim's order has been extended for 30-day periods each month subsequent to this hearing. In the course of the November 24 hearing, Miss Lessard requested that the judge permit her to go home and agreed that if this were allowed she would seek treatment voluntarily on an out-patient basis. Judge Seraphim denied her request without giving a basis for his decision. Neither did the judge give a basis for his decision to commit except to state that he was "finding that she is mentally ill." He made no finding on dangerousness despite the fact that all of the evidence that she had attempted "suicide" 26 days earlier was of a hearsay character and the fact that Dr. Kennedy, staff psychiatrist at the mental hospital, testified that in his opinion she had no present suicidal tendencies. There is no indication in the record that the judge considered alternative methods of treatment which would have a less drastic effect on the curtailment of Miss Lessard's freedom and civil liberties; in fact, the little evidence in the record indicates that he

refused to consider less restrictive alternatives. Finally, the record gives no indication whether the judge found the existence of a need for confinement beyond a reasonable doubt or by a preponderance of the evidence or by any standard whatsoever. . . .

RIGHT TO COUNSEL

The Wisconsin civil commitment statute has no provision providing for a right to counsel. The statute does provide for the appointment of a guardian ad litem in the discretion of the court. Wis.Stat.Ann § 51.02(4). Elsewhere, it is required that the guardian be an attorney. Wis.Stat.Ann. § 256.48. Nowhere is there any indication of the role which the guardian is to play in the proceedings. The record in this case makes clear, however, that the guardian does not view his role as that of an adversary counsel, and thus cannot take the place of counsel unless his role is restructured.

There seems to be little doubt that a person detained on grounds of mental illness has a right to counsel, and to appointed counsel if the individual is indigent. . . .

The state argues, however, that Wisconsin does provide for counsel in the person of the guardian and litem. . . . The attorney appointed as guardian [for Miss Lessard] did not see his role as that of defense counsel. . . .

A recent study of the Wisconsin civil commitment procedures supports our belief that the guardian and representative attorney occupy separate roles. The study concluded: "In present practice, it seems clear that in almost all cases where a guardian is appointed he sees his role not as an advocate for the prospective patient but as a traditional guardian whose function is to evaluate for himself what is in the best interests of his client-ward and then proceed, almost independent of the will of the client-ward, to accomplish this." Dix, "Hospitalization of the Mentally Ill in Wisconsin: A Need For a Reexamination," 51 Marquette L.Rev. 1, 33 (1967). . . .

We think it apparent, therefore, that appointment of a guardian ad litem cannot satisfy the constitutional requirement of representative counsel.

The more important question in this action relates to the role of counsel in the proceedings inasmuch as Miss Lessard retained counsel prior to the commencement of the judicial hearing on commitment. The plaintiffs insist that one charged with mental illness has a right to counsel at every step of the procedure, including interviews with psychiatrists. . . . Certainly the detained individual must have counsel at the preliminary hearing on detention, with time enough before that hearing to prepare any initial defenses which may be available. Otherwise the right to representation by counsel may be a "formality [and a] grudging gesture to a ritualistic requirement." Kent v. United States, 383 U.S. 541, (1966). Counsel must also have access to all reports, psychiatric and otherwise, which will be introduced at the hearing on commitment. See Kent v. United States, supra. The need for counsel at an early stage is also apparent from the provision for a jury trial on demand. Clearly, the subject of the civil commitment proceeding cannot competently decide whether to exercise that right without the aid of counsel. . . . The right to a jury trial has been shown to be critical, numerous studies indicating that the exercise of that right may well mean the difference between release and commitment. . . .

We are unable at this point, however, to be so certain that assistance of counsel will prove materially beneficial at the psychiatric interview as to be able to determine that the right to effective aid of counsel outweighs the interests of the state in meaningful consultation. . . . It may be that a person charged with mental illness will be unable to properly exercise his rights of cross-examination without the presence of counsel at this critical stage in the proceeding. However, we think it appropriate to permit the state to demonstrate that other means, such as recording the interviews and making available to defense counsel the written results of the interview, will prove as effective in maintaining the individual's rights with less disruption to the traditional psychiatrist-patient relationship.

The Privilege against Self-Incrimination

Plaintiffs assert that the privilege against self-incrimination is applicable to civil commitment proceedings. As may readily be seen, application of the privilege involves conflicting considerations. On the one hand, statements made by a prospective mental patient may well be the basis for total involuntary loss of freedom, and thus it will not do to simply label these proceedings civil. In this respect at least the Supreme Court's opinion in In re Gault, 387 U.S. 1, (1967), is directly applicable:

. . . [C]ommitment is a deprivation of liberty. It is incarceration against one's will, whether it is called 'criminal' or 'civil.' And our Constitution guarantees that no person shall be 'compelled' to be a witness against himself when he is threatened with deprivation of his liberty—a command which this Court has broadly applied and generously implemented in accordance

with the teaching of the history of the privilege and its great office in mankind's battle for freedom.

On the other hand, the prospect of a seriously ill individual being prevented from obtaining needed treatment, in a situation in which treatment is possible and will actually be given, on the basis of counsel's advice to refuse to make any statements to a psychiatrist appears ludicrous. As the majority stated in Tippett v. Maryland, 436 F.2d 1153, 1158 (4th Cir. 1971), cert. dismissed sub nom., Murel v. Baltimore City Criminal Court, 407 U.S. 355, 92 S.Ct. 2091, 32 L.Ed.2d 791 (1972), "[i]t is difficult to imagine anything more stultifying to a psychiatrist, as dependent as he is upon the cooperation of his patient, than the presence of a lawyer objecting to the psychiatrist's questions and advising his client not to answer this question and that."

The conflicting interests are thus difficult to reconcile. The Supreme Court found it unnecessary to reach this question in McNeil v. Director, Patuxent Institution, 407 U.S. 245, 250, 92 S.Ct. 2083, 32 L.Ed.2d 719 (1972), but Justice Douglas in a concurring opinion found that the privilege was indeed applicable:

Whatever the Patuxent procedures may be called—whether civil or criminal—the result under the Self-Incrimination Clause of the Fifth Amendment is the same. As we said in In re Gault, 387 U.S. 1, 49–50, 87 S.Ct. 1428, 18 L.Ed.2d 527, there is harm and self-incrimination whenever there is "a deprivation of liberty"; and there is such a deprivation whatever the name of the institution, if a person is held against his will. Id. at 257, 92 S.Ct. at 2091.

We find Justice Douglas' opinion and the underlying decision in Gault persuasive. Wisconsin may not, consistent with basic concepts of due process, commit individuals on the basis of their statements to psychiatrists in the absence of a showing that the statements were made with "knowledge" that the individual was not obliged to speak. We do think, however, that the safeguards of the privilege may be obtained without the presence of counsel in the psychiatric interview. The patient should be told by counsel and the psychiatrist that he is going to be examined with regard to his mental condition, that the statements he may make may be the basis for commitment, and that he does not have to speak to the psychiatrist. Having been informed of this danger the patient may be examined if he willingly assents. . . .

To conclude, statements made to a psychiatrist by the subject of a commitment proceeding, unless voluntarily given after notice of the possible consequences, cannot be the basis for an order of commitment.

EXCLUSION OF HEARSAY EVIDENCE

Plaintiffs final challenge to the constitutionality of the Wisconsin civil commitment statute lies in the use of hearsay evidence at the commitment hearing. Defendants do not seriously dispute the validity of plaintiffs' contentions, stating that they "recognize fully well that hearsay wherever possible should be prevented in any type of legal proceeding." We agree. . . .

Where standard exclusionary rules forbid the admission of evidence, no sound policy reasons exist for admitting such evidence in an involuntary mental commitment hearing. Indeed, as noted throughout this opinion, the seriousness of the deprivation of liberty and the consequences which follow an adjudication of mental illness make imperative strict adherence to the rules of evidence generally applicable to other proceedings in which an individual's liberty is in jeopardy. . . .

We conclude that the Wisconsin civil commitment procedure is constitutionally defective insofar as it fails to require effective and timely notice of the "charges" under which a person is sought to be detained; fails to require adequate notice of all rights, including the right to jury trial; permits detention longer than 48 hours without a hearing on probable cause; permits detention longer than two weeks without a full hearing on the necessity for commitment; permits commitment based upon a

hearing in which the person charged with mental illness is not represented by adversary counsel, at which hearsay evidence is admitted, and in which psychiatric evidence is presented without the patient having been given the benefit of the privilege against self-incrimination; permits commitment without proof beyond a reasonable doubt that the patient is both "mentally ill" and dangerous; and fails to require those seeking commitment to consider less restrictive alternatives to commitment.

Alberta Lessard and the other members of her class are entitled to declaratory and injunctive relief against further enforcement of the present Wisconsin scheme against them. . . .

The unnamed plaintiffs in this case, all persons 18 years of age or older who are being held involuntarily pursuant to any emergency, temporary or permanent commitment provision of the Wisconsin involuntary mental commitment statute, are also entitled to relief against further detention pursuant to the defective Wisconsin procedure. . . .

POSTSCRIPT

On appeal to the U.S. Supreme Court, Schmidt v. Lessard, 94 S.Ct. 713, 715 (1974), the District Court's order was vacated and remanded for a more specific injunctive relief order. The Supreme Court held: "Neither the . . . order nor the accompanying opinion is 'specific' in outlining the 'terms' of the injunctive relief granted; nor can it be said that the order describes 'in reasonable detail . . . the act or acts sought to be restrained'. . . ."

IN RE THE MATTER OF THE INCOMPETENCY OF LOMAX SEALY

WIGGINTON, Chief Judge.

Lomax Sealy has appealed a judgment rendered by the County Judge's Court of Duval County finding him to be mentally incompetent, and from an order entered pursuant thereto committing him to the Superintendent of the State Hospital as Director of Mental

Health, for detention, treatment, and care. The sole point presented by his appeal challenges the sufficiency of the evidence to support the adjudication of incompetency and order committing appellant to the state hospital.

Appellant is a white male 26 years of age and professes to be what is commonly referred to as a "hippie." During the past eight years he

218 So. 2d 765 (1969).

has been in and out of several universities, and at the time of the incompetency hearing was enrolled as a student in a beauty college in Jacksonville. While at one state university, he sought emotional guidance from an out-patient clinic. Between attending sessions of college he worked sporadically but was unable to hold a position of employment for any appreciable length of time. In addition to his beliefs in love and nonviolence, appellant professed to be an atheist. His beliefs and personal conduct brought him into disagreeable conflict with his natural father who lived in Alabama, as well as his mother and her husband who lived in Jacksonville. Appellant returned from New York and took up residence in his mother's home at Jacksonville in order to be near a girl friend who had borne him an illegitimate child. He resented the attitude adopted by his mother and stepfather toward this child whose relationship they refused to recognize. At one time he either threatened or considered suicide, and on one or more occasions threatened bodily harm to his mother. One night when his mother and stepfather were out for the evening, he brought to their home as his date a Negro girl whom he had known for some time. When his parents returned home, his stepfather became incensed and ordered both him and the girl out of the house. A rather unpleasant altercation ensued in which appellant either shoved, pushed, or struck his stepfather, causing the latter to fall against a table and injure his head. Appellant was arrested on a criminal warrant charging him with trespass and assault, following which his mother filed in the County Judge's Court a petition alleging appellant to be incompetent and praying that an examination be made as to his mental condition as provided by law.

A committee of two medical doctors and one lawman were appointed by the County Judge who made an examination of appellant and filed their written report in which they found that appellant was incompetent, the apparent cause being chronic schizophrenia. The committee found that appellant was suffering from hallucinations which were delusional, inappropriate affect, and dictatorial confusion. They found that he possessed propensities for using LSD and marijuana and that he had poor insight. The committee concluded that appellant required mechanical restraint to prevent him from self-injury or doing violence to others.

At the hearing held before the court for the purpose of determining appellant's competency, the latter was represented by counsel furnished by the Legal Aid Association of Duval County. No members of the examining committee appeared to testify in person, but their written report was filed in evidence before the court. Appellant's mother and stepfather testified to the facts hereinabove set forth and expressed their opinion that appellant was insane or mentally ill and in need of psychiatric treatment. Other than the scuffle between appellant and his stepfather on the night he was ordered out of the home, there was no evidence that appellant ever actually injured himself or committed acts of violence toward any other person.

Appellant called as a witness in his behalf a qualified psychologist who gave his expert testimony concerning his examination and observation of appellant, and his professional opinion as to appellant's mental condition. This witness testified that he found appellant to be sane and rational in all respects; that he was mentally competent; and there were no indications that appellant would do violence either to himself or others. He defined a mentally competent person as one who is in contact with reality, knows where and who he is, what he is doing, and is able to relate to the world around him in a rational fashion. He expressed the opinion that appellant's condition should be more accurately categorized as a character disorder rather than schizophrenia, manic or any of the psychotic sources. This witness, in response to questions propounded on cross-examination, testified that from his examination it was his opinion that although some of the beliefs espoused by appellant represented philosophies with which many would disagree, and that his conduct and manner of speech would be considered by some to be socially inappropriate, that nevertheless these tendencies are not indicative of psychological incompetencies.

Appellant testified at length in which he admitted an inability to conform his beliefs and standard of values to those shared by his father, his mother and stepfather, which inability resulted in considerable friction between them and himself. He denied any suicidal tendencies or propensity to do violence to anyone. He frankly admitted that his behavior from time to time was adolescent in character and palpably unwise, but attributed it primarily to the fact that he had been encouraged to depend too greatly upon his parents for financial responsibility of caring for his own needs. He steadfastly denied that he needed psychiatric care but expressed a willingness to accept psychiatric help only as an out-patient and on his own terms.

Following the hearing the County Judge entered his final judgment which found appellant to be mentally incompetent by reason of chronic schizophrenia, his particular hallucinations being delusional, inappropriate affect, dictatorial, and his propensities being confusion, poor insight, and use of marijuana. An order was entered upon the judgment directing the sheriff to deliver appellant to the superintendent of such state hospital as the Director of Mental Health might designate. In pursuance of this order appellant was taken into custody and placed in the Northeast Florida State Hospital for observation, treatment, and care. After a period of 59 days a competency discharge signed by three members of the medical staff of the hospital and approved by the superintendent was issued, finding appellant to be mentally competent and discharging him from the hospital. After receipt of such discharge by the County Judge, and no objections being made thereto, a mandatory order of restoration of competency was entered by the court on June 12, 1968. It is from the judgment of incompetency and the order of commitment that this appeal is taken.

As noted above, the only medical proof of appellant's incompetence is the statement contained in the written report filed by the examining committee consisting of two medical doctors in which they diagnosed appellant's condition as chronic schizophrenia. The report did not attempt in any manner to classify the type of schizophrenia of which they found appellant to be suffering. These medical experts did not testify at the hearing and were not subject to cross-examination by appellant's counsel on this vital question. Such general diagnosis is in direct conflict with the opinion expressed by the expert produced by appellant who did appear and testify in person at the hearing, and was subjected to intensive cross-examination by the court and petitioner's counsel.

In the case of In re Pickles' Petition[1] this court had for consideration an appeal from a judgment of incompetency in which the sufficiency of the evidence to support the judgment was questioned. The diagnosis of appellant's condition by the examining committee was that of chronic schizophrenia. Neither in their written report, nor in their testimony at the incompetency hearing, did the medical members of the committee attempt to classify the type of schizophrenia of which the alleged incompetent was suffering. In reversing the judgment appealed, this court said: "Maloy in his treatise entitled *Nervous and Mental Diseases* quotes Obernoff as stating":

[1] In re Pickles' Petition, (Fla.App.1965) 170 So.2d 603, 613, 614.

"As time went on everyone recognized that the borderline . . . between schizophrenia and the neuroses (nervous diseases) is a fine one, that probably everyone is a bit schizoid as well as neurotic, and that it is the degree of constancy that determines whether the patient becomes schizophrenic in the pathologic (pertaining to disease) sense. The normal person has transitory schizoid episodes. The deduction from the above is, first, that in borderline cases—in cases in which there is not yet a preponderance of universally accepted symptoms of dementia praecox, there is often present a possibility of error in diagnosis; second, that much is yet to be learned about the disease; and third, that many persons apparently normal sitting in judgment in a case of insanity may not be entirely sound in mind themselves." Thus, it is apparent that a diagnosis of schizophrenia standing by itself (which is not classified as to type) is insufficient to support an adjudication of incompetency within the purview of Florida Statutes 394.22, F.S.A. Weighing the evidence presented to the trial judge in light of the foregoing principles of law, we are compelled to conclude that he applied erroneous legal concepts in deciding that Muriel Pickles was incompetent as contemplated by Florida Statutes 394.22, F.S.A.

In the Pickles case, supra, this court held that in incompetency proceedings ". . . the determinative question is not whether the person is suffering from a mental illness, is in need of psychiatric treatment, is in need of counseling, is staying out of trouble, or is leading a normal life. The pertinent question presented to the judge in cases such as this is whether the alleged incompetent is suffering from a mental illness to such an extent that he is incapable of caring for himself, or managing his property or is likely to dissipate or lose his property or become the victim of designing persons. . . ."

The evidence in the record before us reveals that appellant engaged in profitable employment from time to time during which periods he was capable of providing for his own financial needs. It is true that he frequently called on his parents for financial help, primarily when he was attending college, and each call was met with an affirmative response from the indulgent parent. There is no evidence that appellant mismanaged, dissipated or lost any property of which he was possessed, or ever became the victim of designing persons.

As we view the record in this case it seems apparent that partially because of a broken home appellant adopted a way of life which caused him to entertain philosophies and beliefs foreign to those of his parents. He lived the life of a typical "hippie," at times scrounging for a living, indulging in the use of hallucinogenic drugs and engaging in free love with members of the opposite sex in the sincere belief that his way of life was preferable to that of his parents and the great majority of those comprising our society. He took advantage of his parents' love by making monetary demands on them to which he was not necessarily entitled, and accepting their largess instead of providing for his own needs by pursuing gainful employment. His demands upon his parents became burdensome, and his personal appearance, conduct and beliefs offensive, embarrassing and objectionable. The fact that he elected to lead the kind of life, entertain beliefs and engage in conduct which was offensive, repulsive, and objectionable to others does not necessarily indicate mental incompetence, nor does it justify confining him in a mental institution primarily in order to alleviate the financial drain upon his parents and the embarrassment he was causing them.

The record before us leaves little doubt but that appellant's mother, in petitioning the court for an adjudication of incompetency, was motivated by a sincere desire to save appellant from a life of waste and degradation, and by medical treatment to have him restored as a useful and respected member of society. Appellant's judicial sanity having been heretofore restored by court order, the only apparent purpose of this appeal is to remove the stigma of incompetency from his record, and although the evidence of appellant's personal conduct and beliefs is sufficient to raise a substantial question as to his mental stability, we think the weight of the evidence militates against the conclusion that he is legally insane.

We therefore conclude that the evidence is insufficient to support the judgment of incompetency under which appellant was committed to the state hospital. The judgment appealed is accordingly reversed and the cause remanded with directions that an order be entered vacating, setting aside, and holding for naught the judgment appealed.

HOHNSON and SPECTOR, JJ., concur.

Hospitalization of Minors

MELVILLE v. GARDNER

BERDON, J.

Cameron Melville, hereinafter referred to as the plaintiff, brought this application for a writ of habeas corpus against Dr. Charles W. Gardner,[1] Director of the Yale Psychiatric Institute, hereinafter referred to as the defendant. The plaintiff's parents, Frank Melville and Alan W. Melville, were added as defendants in this matter upon the granting of their motion to intervene as such.

Yale Psychiatric Institute is a private hospital located in New Haven, which provides long term psychiatric care and specializes in the treatment of adolescents.

The plaintiff is seventeen years of age and has been a patient confined at the Yale Psychi-

atric Institute since he was fifteen years old. He was admitted upon the written request of his parents under a "voluntary admission." The written request was entitled "Application for Admission To The Yale Psychiatric Institute." This application was dated January 18, 1972, signed by the father of the plaintiff and read as follows: "I the undersigned, do hereby apply for admission (for my son/daughter) to the Yale Psychiatric Institute for observation and treatment in accordance with Section 17–187 of the General Statutes of the State of Connecticut, Revision of 1960."

The plaintiff acknowledges that he is in need of psychiatric therapy, but he desires to obtain the same on an out-patient basis. On August 18, 1973, the plaintiff gave to the defendant notice in writing of his desire to leave Yale Psychiatric Institute in ten days. The parents of the plaintiff objected to his release because

[1] Upon agreement of all parties, Dr. Charles W. Gardner was substituted for the original named defendant, Dr. Joseph Sabbatino.

Superior Court, New Haven County, Connecticut, October 5, 1973, No. 135894.

they and the physicians at Yale Psychiatric Institute felt he needed additional treatment in a structured environment. The defendant refused to release the plaintiff at the expiration of the ten day period. This application for a writ of habeas corpus was brought by the plaintiff to obtain his release.

Counsel for the parties agreed that the court should follow the orderly procedure of first determining whether the plaintiff was entitled to release from confinement at Yale Psychiatric Institute upon his own demand under proceedings outlined in sub-section a of Section 17–187. If not, the court would then hear evidence, including medical testimony to determine whether the confinement is necessary and legal.

First, it must be noted and all parties agree that the constitutional safeguard of due process as guaranteed by the Fourteenth Amendment of the Constitution of the United States must be afforded the plaintiff, even if he is an unemancipated minor. *In re Gault*, 387 U.S. 1.

But, like *Gault*, and of utmost importance, we have a situation in which the liberty of an individual is at stake, and we think the reasoning in *Gault* emphatically applies. It matters not whether the proceedings be labeled "civil" or "criminal" or whether the subject matter be mental instability or juvenile delinquency. It is the likelihood of involuntary incarceration—whether for punishment as an adult for a crime, rehabilitation as a juvenile for delinquency, or treatment and training as a feebleminded or mental incompetent—which commands observance of the constitutional safeguards of due process. *Heryford* v. *Parker*, 396 F. 2d 393, 396

The defendants and the parents claim that because the plaintiff is a minor, the parents' decision as to the child's welfare is controlling. Since the child was admitted at the request of the parents, it is their position that in order for the plaintiff to be released, the parents must request his release or he must have reached his majority. The defendant and the parents suggest that the reasonableness and legality of the parents' decision can be constitutionally tested under the procedure set forth in Sections 17–200 and 17–201 of the General Statutes.

Although it is not controlling in this decision, the court feels compelled to comment on Sections 17–200 and 17–201 of the General Statutes. The appointment of a commission to inquire whether a person is "unjustly deprived of his liberty by being detained or confined in any hospital for mental illness" under Section 17–200 apparently had its origin from the Lunacy Commissions of early ages. The statute does not require notice and an opportunity for the patient to be heard. It provides in part that "(s)uch commission need not summon the

party claimed to be unjustly confined before it, but shall have one or more private interviews with him." The procedures suggested and dictated by the statute are so violative of the basic constitutional guarantees of due process that it shocks the conscience of modern jurisprudence. *In re Gault*, supra. See also *Lessard* v. *Schmidt*, 349 F. Supp. 1078.

Section 17–201 makes it clear that writs of habeas corpus are available to persons confined in a hospital for mental illness. Its main thrust is to furnish a procedure to test the legality of a commitment made by a court of probate.

There is no question that as a general proposition when a dispute arises between parents and an unemancipated minor, the parents' decision as to the child's welfare is controlling. *Draus* v. *International Silver Co.*, 105 Conn. 415, 419, 135 A. 437. "Parental power probably cannot be defined except as a residue of all power not lodged elsewhere by law. . . . Much authority of this sort supports the general proposition that except where there is some authoritatively expressed public policy to the contrary, parental power extends to all areas of a child's life." Kleinfeld, *The Balance of Power Among Infants, Their Parents and the State*, 4 Family L. Q. 413.

Although the authority of the parent is generally controlling, this does not mean as indicated above that such authority is unlimited. For example, parents could not compel a minor to have an abortion, *In re Smith*, 16 Md. App. 209, 295 A. 2d. 238, or the parents could not compel their child to accept their attorney in proceedings initiated by them for the commitment of the child to a mental hospital, *In re Sippy*, 97 A. 2d. 455, or parents could not place a child in a psychiatric school when such a structured environment was not necessary. *Application for the Certification of Anonymous*, 248 N.Y.S. 2d 608.

Turning to Connecticut law on the subject matter, all parties agree that the plaintiff can be confined at Yale Psychiatric Institute only if his admission and continued confinement are authorized by Section 17–187 of the General Statutes which provides the following:

Sec. 17–187. Voluntary Admissions. (a) Any hospital for mental illness may receive for observation and treatment any person who in writing requests to be received; but no such person shall be confined in any such hospital for more than ten days after he has given notice in writing of his desire to leave, without commitment by some court of competent jurisdiction. (b) Any person desiring admission to a hospital for mental illness for care and treatment of a mental illness may be admitted as a patient without making formal or written application therefor if the superintendent deems such person clinically suitable for such admission, care and treatment, and any such person may be free to leave the hospital at any time after admission.

Certainly the statute by its express terms does not authorize "voluntary admission" of a minor by his parent. Apparently, it has been the practice that psychiatric hospitals will accept as a voluntary admission a minor child acting through his parent under the statute, as was the case with the plaintiff.

The legislature in 1971 enacted Public Act 834 which is commonly known as "Patient's Bill of Rights," Section 17–206a through 17–206k of the General Statutes. The act not only codifies certain constitutional guarantees which must be afforded to all patients in a hospital for the mentally disordered, but it also provides that any minor of the ages of sixteen or over can apply in writing for and be admitted to such a hospital as a voluntary patient. It also formally gave to parents and legal guardians the right to apply in writing for the voluntary admission of their minor child or ward if under the age of sixteen. Section 17–206a (d) of the General Statutes.[2] It is clearly apparent by the very terms of the Patient's Bill of Rights Act that it applies to all admissions and confinements under Chapter 306 of the General Statutes, including Section 17–187. This act must be read with all the statutory sections pertaining to commitment of mentally ill persons in order "to constitute a uniform body of law."

It therefore logically follows that if one between the ages of sixteen and eighteen can admit himself into an institution as a voluntary patient, he has the same right to sign himself out under Section 17–187 whether or not his parents originally initiated the admission.[3] For purposes of voluntary admission and release under Section 17–187, the plaintiff in this case being of the age of seventeen has become emancipated. The Patient's Bill of Rights clearly lodges in a minor between the ages of sixteen and eighteen the power to demand on

[2] Section 17–206(a) "(d) 'voluntary patient' means any patient over sixteen years of age who applies in writing for and is admitted to a hospital for observation, diagnosis or treatment of a mental disorder or any patient under sixteen years of age whose parent or legal guardian applies in writing for such observation, diagnosis or treatment;"

[3] Quaere—Whether since the enactment of the Patient's Bill of Rights, a parent can apply in writing for a voluntary commitment under Section 17–187 of a minor child of the age of sixteen or over, or whether such admission would require the application to be signed by such minor? This court is not called upon to determine the matter.

his own authority his release under such a voluntary admission.

In re Smith, supra, presents an issue identical in nature to the present case. The Maryland Court in holding that a parent could not compel her daughter to have an abortion, reasoned at page 246 as follows:

Under the conditions as set out, the minor having the same capacity to consent as an adult, is emancipated from the control of the parents with respect to medical treatment within the contemplation of the statute. We think it follows that if a minor may consent to medical treatment as an adult upon seeking treatment or advice concerning pregnancy, the minor, particularly a minor over 16 years of age, may not be forced, more than an adult, to accept treatment or advice concerning pregnancy. Consent cannot be the subject of compulsion; its existence depends upon the exercise of voluntary will of those from whom it is obtained; the one consenting has the right to forbid. *In re Smith*, at 246.

At this point it should be noted that no one has questioned the sincerity of the parents or that their sole purpose in demanding the continued confinement of the plaintiff is their concern for his welfare. But the parents' good intentions cannot set the standard for voluntary admission to and continued confinement at a psychiatric hospital, especially for a minor of the age of sixteen or over. Confinement at the Yale Psychiatric Institute, although for purposes of medical treatment, does deprive the plaintiff of his liberty. It appears that the enactment of the Patient's Bill of Rights legislation has clearly dictated that minors of the ages of sixteen and over are to exercise for themselves the rights of a "voluntary patient," which includes the right under subsection (a) of Section 17–287 to leave the institution after giving appropriate notice.

If the plaintiff is in need of medical treatment in a structured environment such as the Yale Psychiatric Institute, the parents have a remedy. The legislature clearly granted to the courts of probate the jurisdiction to commit mentally ill persons. Section 17–177 of the General Statutes. Under such commitment proceedings before the court of probate, a person alleged ot be mentally ill is given reasonable notice of the time and place of hearing, he is guaranteed representation by counsel, he is guaranteed the rights of cross-examination of witnesses, section 17–178 of the General Statutes, and the statutes further provide for the right of appeal to any person aggrieved by an order of the probate court, "including any relative or friend." Section 17–202 of the General Statutes. After providing for these procedural safeguards consistent with due process of law the statute provides that such courts of probate shall enter an order of commitment, if the "court finds that the person complained of is mentally ill and a fit subject for treatment in a hospital for mental illness or that he ought to be confined." Section 17–178, Connecticut General Statutes.

The parents of the plaintiff and the defendant director of the Yale Psychiatric Institute should be given an opportunity to commence commitment proceedings before the probate court, if they deem it necessary. Therefore, judgement is entered in favor of the plaintiff, execution of which shall be suspended for a period of fourteen days from the date of this memorandum of decision.

IN THE INTEREST OF MARY LEE, PAMELA WESLEY

SCHNEIDER, Circuit Judge.

This is a Class Action that was initiated on behalf of the plaintiffs Mary Lee and Pamela Wesley by their attorneys and of other persons similarly situated.

The stipulated facts are as follows: Both Mary Lee and Pamela Wesley were adjudicated neglected children by the Juvenile Division of the Court of Cook County and made wards of the Department of Children and Family Services. Both were placed in the Audy Home for protracted periods of time and in an institution (Lee) and foster homes (Wesley) as well. Their adjustments in the institutional and foster home placements were not satisfactory and subsequently voluntary applications for the hospitalization of both girls were signed by agents of the Department of Children and Family Services and they were hospitalized at Elgin State Hospital.

Pamela Wesley had been at Elgin State Hospital for one and a half years when she was charged with assaulting a matron at the hospital. A Delinquency Petition was filed in the Kane County Juvenile Court and after an adjudication that she was a delinquent, she was transferred from Elgin State Hospital to the Illinois State Training School for Girls at Geneva, Illinois, an institution conducted by the Department of Corrections.

Subsequent to the filing of the petition in this cause, Mary Lee made a written request to be released from Elgin State Hospital. A petition for hospitalization was then filed in the Circuit Court of Kane County and after a hearing, Mary Lee was found not to be a person in need of mental treatment and discharged from Elgin State Hospital by the Court.

The legal issue raised by the plaintiffs is whether persons under eighteen years of age are denied due process and equal protection of the laws when they are hospitalized as voluntary patients in a mental hospital upon the application for voluntary admission by their parents or guardians under Article V of the 1967 Mental Health Code, as amended, (*Ill. Rev. Stat.*, Ch. 91½,§5–1, et seq.) 1969. Article V of the Mental Health Code states the manner for the voluntary admission to a mental hospital.

Article V provides as follows:

Section 5–1. Any person may be admitted to a hospital as a voluntary admittee for care and treatment of mental illness or mental retardation upon the filing of an application with the superintendent of the hospital, if the superintendent deems such person suitable for admission as a voluntary patient.

Section 5–2. The application for admission as a voluntary patient may be executed by, and the superintendent shall accept application from:

1. The person seeking admission, if 18 years of age or over,
2. Any relative, or attorney for him, with his consent, or
3. If he is below the age of 18 years, by a parent, guardian, person in loco parentis, the Illinois Youth Commission or Department of Children and Family Services.

Circuit Court of Cook County Juvenile Division, State of Illinois, Nos. 68 J(D) 1362, 68 J(D) 6383, 68 J 15805, Feb. 29, 1972.

The written application form shall contain in large, bold-face type a statement in simple non-technical terms that the person becoming a voluntary patient by execution of such form may leave the hospital within 5 days, excluding Saturdays, Sundays and holidays, after giving a written notice of his desire to leave. This right to leave must be communicated orally to the admittee at the time of his admission, in a language he understands, and a copy of the application form given to the admittee and to any parent, guardian, relative, attorney or friend who accompanied the patient to the hospital.

Section 5–3. Each voluntary admittee shall be allowed to leave the hospital within 5 days, excluding Saturdays, Sundays and holidays after he gives any professional staff person written notice of his desire to leave, unless prior to leaving the patient withdraws such notice by written withdrawal, or unless within said five days a petition and the certificates of two examining physicians, at least one of whom shall be a psychiatrist, are filed with the Court and the Court shall order a hearing pursuant to Section 8–8. The patient may continue to be hospitalized pending a final order of the Court in the court proceedings.

The Court cannot agree with counsel for the plaintiffs that it is unconstitutional to treat minors in a manner different than adults. The State in the exercise of its concern for minors under the doctrine of parens patriae has rightfully interceded in their protection. The law is filled with many limitations upon the acts of minors. Even though there may be a difference of opinion as to the age at which a person should be allowed to file an application for his admission to a hospital, it is appropriate and consistent for the General Assembly to establish an age when a person may file a voluntary application, just as it establishes minimum ages at which persons may perform other acts. Section 5–2 clearly provides who may make the application. If a person is over 18 years of age, he may seek the application or it may be on his behalf by any relative or attorney for him with his consent. The General Assembly has stated that if the person is under the age of 18, the application must be made on his behalf by a parent, guardian, person in loco parentis, the Illinois Youth Commission or the Department of Children and Family Servises.

Who is defined as a "voluntary admittee?" Section 5–1 provides that *any person* may be admitted to a hospital as a voluntary admittee. . ." Section 5–2 provides among other things that the person becoming a voluntary patient may leave after giving a written notice of his desire to leave. Section 5–2 further provides "this right to leave must be communi-

cated orally *to the admittee* at the time of his admission, in a language he understands and a copy of the application form given to the admittee . . ." Section 5–3 provides "each *voluntary admittee* shall be allowed to leave the hospital . . ." Nowhere in Article V is any distinction made between a voluntary admittee under the ages of 18 or over that age. The language of the statute clearly gives the person under the age of 18 the same right to request to leave the hospital as any other person. (Underlining added.)

Counsel for the Department of Mental Health has stipulated that it had not been the policy of the Department to consider that the person under the age of 18 had a right to demand his release from the hospital. By taking this position, the Department of Mental Health, therefore, did not give persons under the age of 18 a copy of the written application nor was there any oral communication in a language understood by the person of his right to leave. Such a procedure is not consistent with the language of the statute and is a practice which does deny the person under the age of 18 due process and equal protection of the laws. The Court understands that the policy and practices of the Department of Mental Health in treating minors differently than adults was based upon a formal opinion of the Illinois Attorney General who is the legal advisor to the Department.

Counsel for the Department of Mental Health has represented to the Court that, the Department of Mental Health is prepared to promulgate a rule that in substance will provide as follows:

Proposed Rule on Hearings for Certain Minors
If any person 13 years of age or over admitted as a voluntary patient under Section 5–2(3) or any person authorized by him or on his behalf expresses a desire to leave the hospital, he shall be notified of his right to an examination and a hearing on his need for involuntary hospitalization. If after being informed of his rights the patient or any person on his behalf notifies in writing the superintendent or any professional staff person of his desire to leave the hospital, upon receiving the notification the superintendent shall proceed in accordance with section 5–3 of the Mental Health Code. Unwillingness or inability of the parent, guardian, or person or agency in loco parentis to manage, care for, or to obtain a place to live or care for the patient shall not be grounds for retaining him in the hospital or for finding a need for involuntary hospitalization.

There was no disagreement expressed by any of the parties to this proceeding to the proposed rule.

The treatment afforded the wards of this Court are a continuing concern of this Court.

On one hand, Pamela Wesley who was presumed to be at Elgin State Hospital because she was in need of mental treatment was adjudicated a delinquent because of an altercation at the hospital and transferred from that treatment facility to a training school for girls under the Department of Corrections. Mary Lee on the other hand was afforded a hearing after this pending suit was filed on her behalf and she was found to be not in need of mental treatment. In August, 1971 the Illinois Department of Mental Health issued a policy statement on services to children and adolescents. On page 5 of this policy statement we find the following:

"D. *Advocacy*
An interagency public and private body should be convened to determine the most effective mechanisms for assuming permanent administrative responsibility for the child or adolescent requiring services. The body shall also address the question of *child advocacy and the monitoring and evaluating of the systems of delivery of mental health services for children and adolescents.*" (Italics added.)

The right to adequate treatment is a present right of all persons and the protection of our children must be an immediate concern. Mary Lee and Pamela Wesley are no longer in a hospital of the Department of Mental Health but this Court is concerned about all of the other wards of this Court that are currently hospitalized in mental health facilities.

IT IS THEREFORE ORDERED:

1. This order applies to any and all minors between the ages of 13 through 17.

2. Any such minor under the age of 18 admitted to an Illinois Mental Health facility, pursuant to the provisions of Illinois Revised Statutes, Chapter 91½, Section 5–1 to 5–3 (1969) (Voluntary admission) must be informed as are adults, upon his admission to said facility, in simple, nontechnical language which the minor understands, that he may leave the hospital within five days, excluding Saturdays, Sundays and holidays, after giving a written notice of this desire to leave.

3. At the time of his admission any such minor must be informed in a language he understands, of his right to leave both orally and in writing, a copy of which must be given to the minor himself and any parent, guardian, relative, attorney or friend who either accompanied the minor to the hospital or who has demonstrated a substantial interest in the minor's admission or release. This shall be construed to include court-appointed guardians.

4. Any such minor under the age of 18 admitted pursuant to the foregoing statutory provisions must be informed both orally and in writing in a language he understands, that if his desire to leave the hospital within five days pursuant to the foregoing numbered paragraphs of this order is opposed by the mental health institution, that the institution must within the five-day period, file with the court a petition with the certificates of two examining physicians, at least one of whom shall be a psychiatrist, for a hearing to determine whether the minor is a person in need of mental treatment and whether the person is in need of hospitalization.

5. In the event of the filing of a petition as referred to in Paragraph 3 above, the minor must be informed in a language he understands both orally and in writing that he will be entitled to representation by counsel, and if he is unable to afford counsel, the Court will appoint one for him; that at said hearing he has the right to a jury or court determination of the question of his need for mental treatment; that he cannot be found to be in need of mental treatment without the testimony of at least one psychiatrist, physician or psychologist who has personally examined him with a view to determining his need for mental treatment.

6. In addition to the above required oral and written notices the Department of Mental Health shall take apropriate steps in every child and adolescent unit maintained by it to advise its employees of the provisions of this order and their duties and responsibilities in complying with and enforcing such provisions, including, if deemed appropriate, by the Director of the Department of Mental Health, posting in several convenient locations in such child and adolescent units written notice in large, bold-face print of the aforesaid rights of minors as they relate to their admission to a mental health facility.

7. Any and all such minors as defined herein, including all wards of the Circuit Court of Cook County currently hospitalized in Illinois mental facilities for whom the Department of Children and Family Services has been designated as guardian shall be immediately advised of their rights in a

manner consistent with the provisions of this order.

8. Moreover, on behalf of wards of the Juvenile Court who constitute the above-named class and for whom the Department of Children and Family Services is guardian, the Court hereby appoints Arthur Young, Director of the Legal Aid Bureau of the United Charities of Chicago, as attorney for the above named class of minors. Mr. Arthur Young or any person designated by him are authorized and directed to examine the social, medical and psychiatric histories of these minors and to interview in person said minors, if necessary, to determine in good faith whether or not a written request for release from the hospital shall be made by or in behalf of the minor.

9. The Department of Children and Family Services is directed to make available to Mr. Arthur Young or his designates, the names of the wards who are hospitalized in Illinois hospitals other than in facilities of the Department of Mental Health.

10. The Departments of Mental Health and Children and Family Services are authorized and directed to make available to Mr. Arthur Young or his designates, the names of the wards and the Department of Mental Health facility in which said ward is hospitalized, and to cooperate as fully as possible with the attorney for the minors in implementing this order, and in particular, the foregoing Paragraph 7 above.

11. This Court shall retain jurisdiction in this cause to enter whatever further orders may be necessary for the enforcement of this order.

RIGHTS OF MINORS

This rule applies to minors between the ages of 13 and 18 admitted to any facility of the Department under Article V of the Mental Health Code whether signed in by parents, guardian, the Department of Children and Family Services, the Department of Corrections–Juvenile Division, or any other person or agency having custody, control or guardianship of the minor.

1. If any person 13 years of age or over admitted as a voluntary patient under Section 5-2(3) of the Mental Health Code, or any person authorized by him or on his behalf, expresses a desire to leave the hospital, he shall be notified of his right to an examination and a hearing on his need for involuntary hospitalization. If, after being informed of his rights, the patient or any person on his behalf notifies in writing the Superintendent or any professional staff person of his desire to leave the hospital, upon receiving the notification, the Superintendent shall proceed in accordance with Section 5-3 of the Mental Health Code. Unwillingness or inability of the parent, guardian, or person in loco parentis to manage, care for, or to obtain a place to live or care for the patient shall not be grounds for retaining him in the hospital or for finding a need for involuntary hospitalization.

2. Any minor between 13 and 18 years of age admitted to an Illinois Mental Health facility, pursuant to the provisions of Section 5-3 of the Mental Health Code, must be informed as are adults, upon his admission to said facility, in simple, non-technical language which the minor understands, that he may leave the hospital within five days, excluding Saturdays, Sundays and holidays, after giving a written notice of his desire to leave.

Illinois Department of Mental Health Rules, Rule 8.04, added March 15, 1972.

3. At the time of his admission, any minor between 13 and 18 years of age must be informed in a language he understands of his right to leave, both orally and in writing. A copy of the written notice must be given to the minor, himself; the person tion, and any parent, guardian, relative, signing the voluntary admission applica- attorney or friend who has demonstrated a substantial interest in the minor's admission or release. This includes court-appointed guardians.

4. Any minor between 13 and 18 years of age admitted pursuant to the foregoing statutory provisions must be informed both orally and in writing in language he understands, that if his desire to leave the hospital within five days, pursuant to the foregoing numbered paragraphs of this rule, is opposed by the mental health institution, that the institution must within the five-day period, file with the court a petition with the certificates of two examining physicians, at least one of whom shall be a psychiatrist, for a hearing to determine whether the minor is a person in need of mental treatment and whether the person is in need of hospitalization.

5. In the event of the filing of a petition as referred to in Paragraph 4 above, the minor must be informed in a language he understands, both orally and in writing, that he will be entitled to representation

by counsel, and if he is unable to afford counsel, the Court will appoint one for him; that at said hearing he has the right to a jury or court determination of the question of his need for mental treatment; that he cannot be found to be in need of mental treatment without the testimony of at least one psychiatrist or physician who has personally examined him with a view to determining his need for mental treatment.

6. In addition to the required oral and written notices, the Director of each Children & Adolescent Unit shall be responsible for advising all employees on the Unit of the provisions of this rule and their duties under it. If the Director of the Children & Adolescent Unit deems it appropriate, he may post, in several convenient locations in the Unit, written notice in large, boldface print, the rights of adolescents under this rule.

7. Any and all minors between 13 and 18, including all wards of the Circuit Court of Cook County currently hospitalized in Department facilities for whom the Department of Children and Family Services has been designated as guardian, and all minors transferred from the Department of Corrections-Juvenile Division, shall be immediately advised of their rights in a manner consistent with the provisions of this rule.

LAKE v. CAMERON

Excerpts from Brief for Appellant

STATEMENT OF THE CASE

I. Chronology of Events

Appellant filed a self-style pleading in October 11, 1962, entitled "Petition for Writ of Habeas Corpus And Also A Writ of Prohibition," designating several parties as respondents. On the same day, appellant was transferred from the District of Columbia General Hospital to Saint Elizabeths Hospital, pursuant to an order of the District Court, for

---

United States Court of Appeals for the District of Columbia Circuit, No. 18,809; Catherine Lake, Appellant, v. Dale C. Cameron, Superintendent, Saint Elizabeths Hospital, Appellee. Appeal from the United States District Court for the District of Columbia. Brief for Appellant on Rehearing *en banc.* Brief by Hyman Smollar, Lawrence S. Shaffner, Armin V. Kuder (appointed by the Court).

mental observation pending her formal commitment in Mental Health No. 2012-62.[1]

Thereafter, the respondents who had been named by petitioner replied by return and answer to the effect that she was no longer in their custody. On November 2, 1962, appellant moved to amend her petition by adding Dale C. Cameron, Superintendent, Saint Elizabeths Hospital, as a party to the proceeding and alleged that she was being unlawfully detained. The District Court granted leave to amend and simultaneously therewith dismissed the petition. An appeal to this Court in forma pauperis followed.

On appeal, this Court reversed and remanded the case for further proceedings predicated on the ground that appellant had failed to be afforded an appropriate hearing on her allegation that she was being unlawfully detained by appellee (*Lake* v. *Cameron*, 118 U.S. App. D.C. 25, 331 F.2d 771 [1964)).

Pursuant to the remand, the District Court ordered a new writ to issue, returnable on April 24, 1964, and appointed counsel to represent appellant (Finding of Fact No. 10). A hearing was conducted on May 8, 1964, at the conclusion of which the District Court dismissed the petition and remanded appellant to the custody of appellee. On July 15, 1964, the District Court granted appellant's application to proceed on appeal without prepayment of costs. In due course, the case was briefed and argued before a division of this Court. On April 1, 1965, this Court entered its judgment and opinion sustaining the disposition of the Court below. A petition for rehearing *en banc* was then filed. This Court granted appellant's petition for a rehearing and ordered that the judgment and opinion entered herein on April 1, 1965, be vacated and that additional briefs be filed. . . .

II. *Evidence Adduced at the Habeas Corpus Hearing*

At the hearing, appellant testified initially to the circumstances attendant upon her admission to the District of Columbia General Hospital following her apprehension by a police officer (Tr. 6, 7, 11–14). Appellant also

[1] Appellant had been found by a member of the Metropolitan Police Department wandering in the vicinity of 5th and E. Streets, N.W., on September 29, 1962, and was thereafter taken to the District of Columbia General Hospital. On October 2, 1962, civil commitment procedures were initiated in the District Court. On November 21, 1962, appellant was adjudicated to be of unsound mind following a jury trial and was accordingly committed by the District Court to Saint Elizabeths Hospital.

alluded to the fact that she had been the recipient of a Navy allotment check which had been terminated by the Government following her son's death, and that at this juncture she had no current means of support (Tr. 9). She also stated that she thought she was completely capable of handling her own affairs and that upon her release she could manage herself (Tr. 11, 12). Furthermore, she added that she had never been previously hospitalized for mental illness, and that she would be able to live with her husband who had recently returned to Washington, D.C. (Tr. 14, 15).

Harry L. Berger, appellant's husband, also testified at the hearing (Tr. 23). He indicated that he had married appellant in May, 1950, and had thereafter left the city; that he was employed by the Volunteers of America and that if given the opportunity he was prepared to care for appellant if the Court were to release her (Tr. 24, 25, 26).

Also called as a witness in support of the petition was Mary Louise Ruth, a sister of the appellant. Mrs. Ruth testified that she had not been employed since 1956 (Tr. 28); that she receives public assistance and would endeavor to contribute whatever she possibly could to the support of her older sister (Tr. 31, 33). She was of the opinion that appellant was not mentally ill or likely to injure herself or others and that, accordingly, she was being detained unlawfully (Tr. 36, 37, 40–47).

In opposition to the petition, appellee introduced the testimony of a single witness—Dr. Ethel H. Friedman—a psychiatrist on the staff at Saint Elizabeths Hospital. No other expert testimony was introduced at the hearing. Dr. Friedman's testimony reflected that appellant had been a patient under her supervision for approximately eleven months (Tr. 47, 48). Based upon her observations of appellant and her familiarity with the pertinent hospital records, she concluded that appellant suffered from chronic brain syndrome, with cerebral arteriosclerosis (Tr. 49 and Finding of Fact No. 16). The witness stated that the symptoms of this mental disorder were manifested by appellant's inability to recall remote or recent events, and that in general she had a paranoid trend in that appellant felt she was being persecuted by the Police Department and Veterans Administration (Tr. 49, 50). She also testified that appellant was cooperative in the hospital and had been progressing favorably since her admission (Tr. 51). The psychiatrist felt that appellant could not adequately care for herself if she were released from the hospital because she was in need of supervision. Other than the custodial attention which appellant has received at the hospital, the record is devoid of any reference as to the treatment appellant is receiving or whether, if such were forthcoming, she would benefit from psychiatric therapy.

On cross-examination, it was revealed that Dr. Friedman did not believe appellant to be a source of potential physical danger either to herself or society if she were released, but that her only problem would be her exposure to difficulty if left unattended without the benefit of supervision (Tr. 54, 55). The doctor remarked that appellant did not need constant medical supervision but required attention because of her forgetfulness (Tr. 55). Moreover, the witness was of the opinion that appellant had become very well adjusted while at Saint Elizabeths Hospital (Tr. 55).

Upon inquiry of the Court, Dr. Friedman stated that she would have no objection to plaintiff's release if she could receive adequate attention under appropriate supervision. If appellant were in a nursing home or any place where there would be supervision, the witness would have no objection to her discharge (Tr. 56). Counsel for appellee likewise conceded that appellant's release would not be controverted if there were proper facilities available outside of the hospital to attend to appellant's physical and financial requirements (Tr. 57).

Upon the basis of this evidence, the District Court entered its order, accompanied by its Findings of Fact and Conclusions of Law, dismissing the petition but without prejudice to the filing by appellant of a new petition at such time that appellant's family was able to provide financially for her care and custody. . . .

ARGUMENT

I. Petitioner Is Not Likely to Injure Herself Within the Meaning of the Statute

A. *The Statute Requires a Likelihood of Serious Personal Harm to Petitioner.* The Standards of the District of Columbia Hospitalization of the Mentally Ill Act[2] authorizing indefinite, involuntary hospitalization of the mentally ill were not intended by their draftsmen to be interpreted so broadly as to encompass petitioner. If her enforced hospitalization is upheld, it can mean that any person with a mental disease who refused to undergo a recommended treatment or otherwise acts in any manner inimical to his own health, may be placed against his will in a mental hospital because he is thus "likely to injure himself" (Sec. 7[f]; D.C. Code § 21-545[b]).

Section 7(f) D.C. Code § 21-545(b) provides only one standard for hospitalization of an individual for an indeterminate period without his consent if he has a mental illness; that is, if because of his illness he is "likely to injure himself or other persons if allowed to remain at liberty." There has been no charge that petitioner is likely to injure others. The evidence is to the contrary (Tr. 54-55). Accordingly, the sole inquiry as to whether her continued hospitalization is authorized by the statute is whether she is likely to injure herself, and what this phrase means in the statute.

A starting point for the formulation of the 1964 Act for the District of Columbia was the "Draft Act Governing Hospitalization of the Mentally Ill" prepared and revised in 1952 by the National Institute of Mental Health and the Office of the General Counsel of the Federal Security Agency.[3] This Draft Act, which was the subject of extensive comment and analysis on the question of involuntary hospitalization,[4] furnishes an important comparison with the 1964 Act's standard for commitment. The Draft Act provided for the hospitalization of those likely to injure themselves or others and it contained an additional standard for judicial commitment in the case of an individual who "is in need of care or treatment in a mental hospital, and because of his illness, lacks sufficient insight or capacity to make responsible application therefor" (Draft Act, *supra*, § 6[a] [2] [C]).

During hearings on the pending hospitalization act for the District of Columbia, it was urged upon Congress that this alternative provision of the Draft Act be included in the bill.[5] This suggestion was never accepted.

However, the legislative history does reflect that one concession was made to the advocates for the addition of this provision for hospitalizing those without the capacity to choose for themselves. The Department of Health, Education and Welfare, in extensive comments on the bill (1963 Hearings 137), state that the phrase "injure himself or others" implied injury by violent action. In reporting its bill to the Congress, the Senate Judiciary Committee

---

[2] 78 Stat. 944 (1964), now codified at 21 D.C. Code, §§ 501–591 as a result of Public Law 89–183, 79 Stat. 685 (1965) (hereinafter referred to as the 1964 Act).

[3] See "Constitutional Rights of the Mentally Ill," Hearings Before the Subcommittee on Constitutional Rights of the Committee on the Judiciary, U.S. Senate. Part 1, 87th Cong. 1st Sess. 89, 501 (1961) (hereinafter cited as 1961 Hearings).

[4] See Lindman and McIntyre, *The Mentally Disabled and the Law* (1961), p. 20.

[5] Hearings on S. 935 before the Subcommittee on Constitutional Rights of the Senate Committee on the Judiciary, 88th Cong., 1st Sess. 29, 138, 177–178 (1963) (hereinafter cited as 1963 Hearings).

acknowledged this, but made no amendment; it only stated that the persons feared by the Department of Health, Education and Welfare to be outside the ambit of the statutory language, were customarily considered to be within it in the District of Columbia (S. Rep. No. 925, 88th Cong., 2d Sess. 28 (1964). The persons thus brought within the intent of the Congressional Committee are described as follows in the Departmental staff memorandum to which the Senate Committee report referred:

We do believe it important, however, not to exclude those "harmless" persons who are mentally ill, can be treated effectively only in a hospital, and, while not likely to do violence to themselves, are because of that illness so far incapable of attending to their immediate needs or safety as to be *in danger of serious personal harm* unless hospitalized. S. Rep. No. 925, supra, 28, 36. [Emphasis added].

The significance of the statement by the Senate Committee that those likely to suffer "serious personal harm" will be within the statute, and the Committee's refusal to accede to the requests that it insert the additional Draft Act provision is manifest. Even if violence is not required, more than neglect and refusing care is required.[6]. . .

A determination of capacity to choose between the risks of freedom and the benefits of hospitalization seems to be one which the Congressional Committee concerned wished to avoid in favor of an objective standard for commitment. This objective was accomplished by eliminating the second standard of the Draft Act from the 1964 Act.[7] All references in the legislative record are to "serious personal injury." This is consistent with the view that at the point the choice of the individual is irrational on its face, such as suicide or other serious personal harm, it cannot be accepted. But all other choices of the individual must be respected, even if they are not wise and would be harmful to him to a lesser degree. . . .

B. *There was Insufficient Evidence to Find Petitioner Likely to Suffer Serious Personal Harm.* The evidence presented to the court below can be summarized as demonstrating that petitioner was not dangerous to herself or others except for the tendency to wander peri-

odically and to neglect her person. The psychiatrist testifying from Saint Elizabeths Hospital said the petitioner needed custodial attention or supervision which could be found in a nursing home if it were available (Tr. 47–57).

Petitioner's diagnosis is chronic brain syndrome with cerebral arteriosclerosis (Tr. 49 and Finding of Fact No. 16). "The distinction between senility, which is not considered a mental illness, and senile brain disease, which is considered a mental illness, is almost imperceptible" (Note, 63 *Mich. L. Rev.* 562 [1965] and authorities cited therein). Chronic brain syndrome is little different from these senile diagnoses.[8]

In other words, petitioner may become confused, forgetful or vague (Tr. 49–51) and suffer the problems of the aged, but there is no evidence that she is psychotic, may inflict injury on herself, or take uncontrolled actions which have a substantial probability of resulting in serious harm. The incident cited by the psychiatrist for the hospital as indicating some danger to petitioner was one in which she had absented herself from the hospital for over 24 hours and returned evidencing a forgetfulness and vagueness as serious as at any other time described (Tr. 54). Still, there is no evidence that she was seriously harmed. In sum, there is inadequate support in the record for finding that petitioner is likely to harm herself other than the mere harm which can flow from neglect. The District Court's conclusion that she might be released at such time as custodial care could be obtained indicates that the likelihood of harm it acted upon was merely the harm of neglect. In this regard, the Court erred. As demonstrated in the previous section, such harm cannot be construed as warranting hospitalization under the 1964 Act.[9]

---

[6] Dr. Dale Cameron, appellee, characterized the standard used in the 1964 Act as being a "clear and evident danger of harm" (1963 Hearings 129).

[7] See Note, District of Columbia Hospitalization of the Mentally Ill Act, 65 *Colum. L. Rev.* 1062, 1066 (1965).

[8] Application for Certification, etc., 195 N.Y.S.2d 131 (Sup. Ct. 1959); see also, American Psychiatric Association, *Diagnostic and Statistical Manual: Mental Disorders* (1952), p. 21.

"Any definition of mental disease will involve value choices on questions of social philosophy." Swartz, "Mental Disease: The Groundwork for Legal Analysis and Legislative Action," 111 *U. Pa. L. Rev.* 389, 392 (1963).

[9] Highly significant are the provisions for emergency hospitalization of one who is likely to injure himself if not "immediately detained." Section 6(a), D.C. Code § 21–521. Should it ever appear to anyone such as an agent of the Department of Health, or anyone authorized to make arrests, or petitioner's family that she has become more than merely neglectful of her person and in her forgetfulness and vagueness is putting herself in a position where more serious harm is imminent, she can be easily hospitalized at that time. This possibility mitigates the necessity for prophylactic hospitalization on the likelihood of its arising in

II. Commitment to a Mental Hospital Is Not Authorized if No Psychiatric Care and Treatment Are Required

The District Court found that petitioner required "care and supervision" (Finding of Fact No. 17). This supervision is custodial in nature and the only psychiatrist offering evidence at the hearing stated that she would have no objection to petitioner's release to family or to a nursing home or other place provided she would receive the necessary attention (Tr. 56). In the preceding section of this brief, the similarity of petitioner's diagnosis to "senility" was noted. Guttmacher and Weihofen see "no point" in making the "fine differentiation."[10] In sum, petitioner is not a psychiatric but a geriatric patient.[11]

The whole basis for imposing hospitalization on an unconsenting person who is not dangerous to others is a need for treatment, and the assumption that they will receive it. In the absence of appropriate care, there seems to be little justification for hospitalization of the non-dangerous.[12]

The principal sponsor of the 1964 Act, Senator Ervin, reported his chief concern to his Senate colleagues:

Our concern has been to assure that when an individual is deprived of liberty because he is mentally ill, he will receive appropriate attention and treatment necessary to restore him to his place in society (110 Cong. Rec. 21346 [1964]).

Senator Ervin found the "fact that institutionalized patients often receive only custodial care" to be "shocking" (1963 Hearings 12).

A mental hospital is, in its own fashion, a jail to the person being held against his will.[13] Commitment to a mental institution carries a recognized "stigma."[14]

The 1964 Act seeks to insure that this stigma is justified only by the existence of a psychiatric problem requiring commitment to a mental institution. . . . Satisfying the physical requirements of a patient is not a justifiable basis for commitment to a mental hospital. The statutory test is that the mental condition of the patient must be of the type which lends itself to psychiatric care or treatment or the guarantee of the legislation is meaningless.

At least one jurisdiction has refused to order the commitment of geriatric patients with the same diagnoses as petitioner, and who like petitioner were not actively psychotic or overtly mentally disturbed. In *Application for Certification, etc.*, 195 N.Y.S.2d 131, 132 (Sup. Ct. 1959), the Court noted as follows:

They are all arteriosclerotic patients whose psychotic reactions are either mild or nonexistent. As I have often indicated, aged patients in this category do not deserve to be sent to mental institutions and that to do so is unconscionable and immoral . . . they deserve to go to a general hospital where they can receive treatment by specialists equipped with geriatric techniques and where their custodial care may be assured if their relations cannot provide it.

This same court refused to transfer to a mental hospital an elderly woman described as follows: "confused, disoriented and has a 'very poor mental grasp,'" with a diagnosis of chronic brain syndrome with senile brain disease, arteriosclerotic type.[15]

The D.C. Hospitalization of the Mentally Ill Act, and Saint Elizabeths Hospital, cannot be used as catch-alls because other facilities may not have been provided under other legislative programs or are not sufficiently attractive for the voluntary admission of aged patients requiring care and supervision.[16] . . . Outside

---

the future. This is especially true, as is seen in Argument IV, when other ways of providing assistance for petitioner are available in the community.

[10] Guttmacher and Weihofen, *Psychiatry and the Law* (1952), p. 138.

[11] The superintendent of Saint Elizabeths has testified in a similar fashion: "Approximately 50 per cent of the patients then hospitalized really required hospitalization in a mental institution. Many could quite appropriately be cared for in suitable nursing or foster homes, or in chronic disease hospitals were they available. To be sure, those who could have been cared for elsewhere had mental disturbances, but their mental difficulties were not so severe as to require hospitalization, granted the availability of suitable alternative facilities. *For many older patients, the primary need was found to be for physical rather than psychiatric care.*" Hearings on H.R. 9072 Before the Ad Hoc Subcommittee on St. Elizabeths Hospital of the House Committee on Education & Labor, 88th Cong., 1st Sess. 23–24 (1963). (Emphasis added.)

[12] Lindman and McIntyre, *Mentally Disabled and the Law*, pp. 19–20.

[13] Szasz, *Law, Liberty and Psychiatry* (1963), pp. 179–81.

[14] *State Ex rel. Bles* v. *Merrick*, 2 Ohio 2d 13, 205 N.E.2d 924, 926 (1965); see also Certification of Anonymous No. 1 to Anon. No. 12, 206 Misc. 909, 138 N.Y.S.2d 30 (1954).

[15] Application for Anonymous No. 13, 6 Misc. 2d 596, 159 N.Y.S.2d 842 (1956).

[16] As an example of other legislative steps being taken, see the Community Mental Health Centers Act, 77 Stat. 290 (1963), 42 U.S.C. § 2681–2687.

care or facilities not requiring compulsion are the answer to petitioner in her present condition.[17]

III. The District Court's Order Unconstitutionally Discriminates against Petitioner because of Her Indigency

The D.C. Hospitalization of the Mentally Ill Act contains no indigency test and does not purport to be on its face, or through any of the Committee reports accompanying it, an act based upon a finding of special reasons for providing compulsory hospitalization of the poor. Nevertheless, the conclusions of the District Court are that petitioner must remain involuntarily and for an indefinite period of time in a mental institution unless her family has "sufficient funds to employ a competent person" to supervise her. (Finding of Fact No. 17; Conclusion of Law No. 3). This result is offensive to the due process requirement of the Fifth Amendment to the Constitution.

States may not discriminate between the rich and the poor when a right, such as to appeal a criminal conviction, is granted their citizens (*Griffin* v. *Illinois*, 351 U.S. 12, rehearing denied, 351 U.S. 958 [1956]). This "equal protection of the laws" is required of the United States in governing the District of Columbia under the due process clause of the Fifth Amendment.[18]

Justice Jackson, concurring in *Edwards* v. *California*, 314 U.S. 160, 184–185 (1941), stated the impropriety of indigency as a constitutional factor:

We should say now, and in no uncertain terms, that a man's mere property status, without more, cannot be used by a state to test, qualify, or limit his rights as a citizen of the United States. *"Indigence" in itself is neither a source of rights nor a basis for denying them.* The mere state of being without funds is a neutral fact—constitutionally an irrelevance, like race, creed, or color. [Emphasis added.]

Contrary to this constitutional command, the court below dismissed the petition for

release at the same time saying that it was "without prejudice to file a new petition at a time when the family of the petitioner is able to provide for her care and custody" (Conclusion of Law No. 3.). Because petitioner cannot afford someone to attend to her, the District Court holds she must be involuntarily hospitalized in a mental institution. An individual with the same diagnosis, but with funds, would not lose her freedom. Or at the very least she would not go to a mental hospital. . . .

The California Supreme Court has held that care of the aged is not an individual problem but a community problem, the burden of which must be borne by the entire citizenry and not just particular individuals who happen to be related by birth to hospitalized aged persons.[19]

The Government can and does provide assistance and care for the aged population.[20] The point is that the method chosen by the District Court for petitioner is an involuntary and far-reaching loss of freedom. The statute specifically avoids the necessity of this result by authorizing the District Court to use alternatives to hospitalization, such as out-patient treatment (see *H.R. Rep. No. 1833, supra* at 14). There is no legitimate basis to make compulsory hospitalization turn on the fact of petitioner's indigency when the legislation provides such alternatives. . . .

IV. The District Court Erred in Failing to Consider Alternative Means of Care and Supervision for Petitioner

A. *Even If the Act Authorizes Hospitalization of Petitioner, The Court Must Consider Alternative Community Facilities.* Assuming that Congress authorized hospitalization of petitioner, under the previous law, as well as the new D.C. Hospitalization of the Mentally Ill Act, involuntary hospitalization in a mental institution does not automatically follow from a finding that the standards for commitment are met. Both statutes leave the disposition of the individual to the discretion of the court (D.C. Code, § 21–315 [1961 ed.]; D.C. Code,

---

[17] Dr. Sigmond M. Lebensohn, a leading District of Columbia psychiatrist, representing the American Psychiatric Association, the Washington Psychiatric Society, and the Medical Society of the District of Columbia, advised the Senate Committee: 'I would say that 80 or 90 per cent of the patients under the proper circumstances, that is, the proper psychiatric climate, the proper cultural climate, the proper socio-economic climate, and the proper legal climate could be persuaded to enter a hospital without any difficulty." 1963 Hearings 65.

[18] *Coppedge* v. *United States*, 369 U.S. 438 (1962); *Bolling* v. *Sharpe*, 347 U.S. 497 (1954).

[19] *Department of Mental Hygiene of California* v. *Kirchner*, 60 Cal. App. 2d 716, 388 P.2d 720 (1964). For the later history of this case as to whether the California court relied on federal or state grounds, see 280, U.S. 194 (1965) and—— ——Cal. App. 2d——, 400 P.2d 321 (1965).

[20] See President's Council on Aging, *Federal Payments to Older Persons in Need of Protection* (1965). O'Neill, *Protecting Older People*, Public Welfare 119 (April, 1965). Lehmann and Mathiasen, *Guardianship and Protective Services for Older People* (1963), contains an appendix detailing community services for the aged in several jurisdictions.

§ 21–545, 79 Stat. 685 [1965)]. Upon the finding that a person may be committed, "the Court may order his hospitalization for an indeterminate period, or order any other alternative course of treatment which the Court believes will be in the best interests of the person or of the public" (See. 7[f]; D.C. Code, § 21–545).

This provision was added to the original bill to insure that the Court would be free to order an individual to be placed in "half-way houses" or receive "outpatient care" or any other "alternative course of treatment" (*S. Rep. No. 925, supra* at 18; *H.R. Rep. No. 1833, supra* at 14). In commenting on this provision in its final report on *Comprehensive Mental Health Services in the District of Columbia* (1965), the Department of Public Health cited a number of alternative courses to be available to the Court:

This certainly provides the necessary flexibility to [commit] a patient to less than 24 hour care; for example, to an outpatient program, a Halfway House, etc. It also makes it possible for the court to send a senile patient to a non-psychiatric disease facility at St. Elizabeths or elsewhere. In short, the machinery of the Court can be used to obtain compulsory attendance at any variant of treatment, providing the person is found to be mentally ill and likely, because of that illness, to injure himself or others if allowed to remain at liberty. [P. 235.]

The policy of the Act is clear, the Court should exercise such discretion so as not to automatically commit a patient to a mental institution, but rather should inquire and assure itself that the welfare of the patient and the public are advanced to the maximum degree possible.[21] This is particularly true in the case of the aged patient, such as petitioner.

The following analysis of the problem of the older person facing possible commitment is particularly appropriate to the facts of this case, as taken from a project report supported by the National Council on the Aging:

For many older people the need for more care and supervision than their usual environment affords may be the result of gradual changes in physical or psychic energy or in capacity to function. These persons gradually withdraw from social contacts; do not eat regularly or adequately, cease to take proper care of themselves, their clothing or their house; grow increasingly irritable, are difficult and demanding; grow restless and wander indoors or out, at irregular hours or improperly clothed; take off on impractical expeditions; or seek inappropriate satisfactions, often at exorbitant costs.

The questions which need to be asked here are: What kind of help does the individual need? How can a community provide care and supervision so that he may care for himself and find meaningful satisfactions for his remaining years?

There are no very simple answers to these questions. They emphasize the necessity for careful screening for all applications for commitment, whether voluntary or involuntary, to a mental hospital or other facility.[22]

B. *There Is No Evidence That Alternative Care and Supervision Were Considered for Petitioner.* In its findings of fact, the District Court went no further than to find that petitioner was in need of "continuous attention and supervision." In its conclusions of law, the court states that this care and treatment are needed "in a mental institution," but there are no subsidiary findings which would substantiate this conclusion. A review of the record reveals that there is no such evidence. Quite the contrary, the sole psychiatrist testifying stated that she would have no objection to petitioner being released to an outside facility such as a responsible family or a nursing home (Tr. 56)....

There was no testimony that nursing home care or outpatient care were not available. The numerous public and private mental health facilities and services in the District of Columbia are not mentioned.[23] The Court requested no additional assistance of expert witnesses.[24] In sum, the District Court could not have exercised an informed discretion.

C. *The District Court Failed to Make Necessary Findings Supporting Its Conclusion That a Mental Hospital Was Needed.* The District Court was required to make findings of fact and conclusions of law adequate for approval by this Court and sufficient to support its order

---

[21] The obvious example of the public interest is the expense to the Government. "If the cost of day-care services cannot be financed through old-age assistance or if home-care is not available, an elderly person may need to be hospitalized. The total cost to the taxpayer in this instance may be many times the cost of the patient's care in his own home or at a day-care center." Lehmann and Mathiasen, *Guardianship and Protective Services*, p. 77.

[22] *Ibid.*, pp. 105–6.

[23] Existing facilities and programs are cited in Department of Public Health, *Comprehensive Mental Health Services in the District of Columbia* (1965), pp. 10–21.

[24] Cf. *DeMarcos* v. *Overholser*, 78 U.S.App. D.C. 131, 137 R. 2d 698, *cert. denied*, 320 U.S. 785 (1943).

(Rule 52 [a] F.R. Civ. P., 28 U.S.C., Appendix).[25]

Of course, findings of the District Court must be accepted unless they are "clearly erroneous" (Rule 52[a] F.R. Civ. P., *Von Moltke* v. *Gillies*, 332 U.S. 708 [1948]). But the court below did not make any findings of fact with respect to the necessity of treating petitioner in a mental hospital. It found only that she needed care and supervision.

The court characterizes as a "conclusion of law" its belief that this needed attention was to be found in a mental institution. This Court is not bound by conclusions of law (*Great A. & P. Tea Co.* v. *Super Market Equip. Co.*, 340 U.S. 147 [1950]). Accordingly, this Court is free to determine whether the findings of fact, even if supported by the evidence, justified the conclusion that a senile patient requiring only care and supervision must, as a matter of law, be restrained in a mental institution. The answer to this proposition seems clear. The discretion given the District Court by statute dictates that this is not a valid proposition of law.

If the District Court's finding concerning the need to put petitioner in a mental hospital is considered to be one of fact, regardless of its characterization in the order, it does not satisfy requirements for appellate review. The appellate court is "entitled to the benefit of clear and *explicit* findings in any factual issue tried without a jury." *United States* v. *Marchese*, 341 F.2d 782, 794 (9th Cir. 1965), remanded on other grounds, 374 U.S. 101 (1965) (habeas corpus):

[E]xplicit reference is likewise required between such findings and any conclusions resting thereon in order to enable this court to compare the conclusions and findings, and the facts found, with the evidence appearing in the record in our search for 'proper findings' to support the ruling. [*Ibid.*, 794, 795.]

Applicable law clearly puts in issue the question of what facility is best suited for petitioner and the public welfare. This is the type of issue that is traditionally left to the discretion of the trial court. Nevertheless, the court must explicitly set forth its reasons for choosing as it did, if in fact such a choice was made, in order to provide a proper basis for review. It is apparent that the court below believed that petitioner could be cared for by someone other than staff members of a mental institution (see Conclusion of Law No. 3). But there is no delineation of the reasons for arriving at the conclusion that in the absence of a family capable of supporting and caring for her, there was no other facility available for petitioner. The finding that petitioner must remain in a mental institution, therefore, is supported by neither evidence of the adequacy or inadequacy of other alternatives, nor a statement by the court how it reached this conclusion. Even if there were sufficient evidence, this Court cannot accept the absence of any indication that the court understood its discretion or if it did, how it exercised it.

V. The District Court Erred in Its Failure to Utilize an Independent Psychiatric Examination and an Evaluation of Appellant's Continued Commitment Under the Circumstances of This Case

Although not requested to at the hearing, appellant contends that under the compelling circumstances of this case the court should have invoked its discretionary powers and ordered an independent psychiatric examination by either the Mental Health Commission, Legal Psychiatric Services or some other appropriate expert to determine appellant's mental condition and evaluate the necessity for her continued confinement at St. Elizabeths. This is particularly appropriate where, in a "doubtful case" such as this, the District Court should have had all the information available in order to render an informed judgment (see *DeMarcos* v. *Overholser* at 133, 137 F.2d at 700).

This case can properly be called "doubtful" because the evidence at hand demonstrates that appellant's mental condition is not susceptible to conventional psychiatric treatment and at the same time she is unlikely to injure herself or be inimical to the safety of the community. In fact, but for her indigency as well as that of her family the only psychiatrist testifying would have her released without observation or restraint by the governmental authorities. Thus, it would appear that this is the "doubtful case" referred to in *DeMarcos*, above, where the rights of the indigent must be protected by courts acting sua sponte.

While there is no questioning the competence or dedication of those in whose custody petitioner has been placed, there are limitations inherent in this situation.

[25] Rule 81(a) (2), F.R. Civ. P. states that the Federal Rules apply to habeas corpus appeals. The same result follows from Local Rule 9 of this Court. There has been some question whether Rule 52(a) should apply to the trial judge's findings, but the general rule now seems to hold the rule to be applicable, see 5 Moore, *Federal Practice* 2621 (1955), and cases cited therein. In any case where, as here, findings have been made, there is no question that the Rules will be applied.

In the great majority of cases, the impecunious patient will have to rely on State medical authorities and hospital doctors who, as respondents in habeas corpus proceedings, may not always possess the desired impartiality.[26]

Whenever the physician is employed by someone other than the patient, his loyalty and responsibility to his employer must frankly be recognized.[27]

Considering the nature and degree of appellant's illness as well as the reasons advanced by the hospital for her continued confinement, at the very least, the court should have insured further examination. The failure of the District court to afford the patient such an examination was error.[28]

It has been recognized that following the commitment of a patient to a mental hospital he or she becomes a ward of the state (*Anonymous* v. *State, supra*). Therefore, the court acts as *parents patriae* of the civilly committed patient (*Overholser* v. *Treibly, supra* at 392, 147 F.2d at 708).

In *Boone* v. *Boone*, 80 U.S. App. D.C. 152, 150 F.2d 153 (1945), this Court found that the trial court had erred in its failure to "call to its aid experienced and disinterested persons . . . to make an unbiased examination of the qualifications" of the parties and the circumstances underlying a custody action. There this Court held that it was not satisfied that the decision of the trial court should be made upon the adversary evidence which had been introduced. No less should be required when a court sits in the case of an indigent, involuntary, and for the moment helpless, patient. The court should utilize the expertise of administrative and social officers to assist it in analyzing petitioner's specific needs and capabilities.[29]

Moreover, Section 8(*a*) of the 1964 Act (D.C. Code § 21–546) expressly requires that indigent patients be granted periodic mental examinations to determine their status for release. This statutory mandate supports the importance of periodic independent examinations for those committed due to mental illness.

In sum, appellant is an indigent who has been involuntarily committed for purposes of custodial attention rather than treatment; her mental disorder is not of such severity that she will constitute a serious danger to herself or others; and the hospital authorities would release her but for her indigency and that of her family. At the very minimum, the District Court should have sought independent expertise since "where an indigent confined in a mental hospital seeks habeas corpus it is more important to provide [her] with an independent psychiatric examination than to give [her] independent counsel" (*DeMarcos* v. *Overholser, supra* at 132, 137 F.2d at 699).

Therefore, for this additional reason the judgment of the District Court should be reversed and remanded to afford appellant an independent psychiatric examination and for such other expert assistance as may be required for the District Court properly to discharge its duties.

CONCLUSION

Wherefore, it is respectfully submitted that the judgment of the District Court should be reversed and remanded with directions to either release appellant from custody or to conduct such further proceedings as the Court may deem just and proper.

---

[26] 1961 Hearings 334. See Weihofen & Overholser, "Commitment of the Mentally Ill," 24 *Texas L. Rev.* 307, 335 (1946).

[27] Szasz, *Psychiatric Justice* (1965), p. 56.

[28] *Cf. Watson* v. *Cameron*, 114 U.S. App. D.C. 151, 312 F.2d 878 (1962); *Curry* v. *Overholser*, 109 U.S. App. D.C. 283, 287 F.2d 137 (1960). In *Curry*, this Court stated that "an inmate of St. Elizabeths petitioning for habeas corpus might demand the expert testimony of the members of the Commission on Mental Health, or that the Court *on its own motion might require it.* This gives any inmate of St. Elizabeths the protection of a diagnosis by independent experts. . . . We think this relief is available to all indigent inmates of the hospital. . . ." *Ibid.* at 286, 287 F.2d at 140 (Emphasis added.)

[29] See *In Re Anonymous*, 42 Misc.2d 575, 248 N.Y.S.2d 608 (1964), where the court conducted an independent investigation of the matter and arrived at a disposition contrary to the recommendations of the committing psychiatrists.

U.S. Court of Appeals Decision

BAZELON, Chief Judge.

Appellant is confined in Saint Elizabeths Hospital as an insane person and appeals from denial of release in habeas corpus. On September 29, 1962, when she was sixty years old, a policeman found her wandering about and took her to the D.C. General Hospital. On October 11, 1962, she filed in the District Court a petition for a writ of habeas corpus. The court transferred her to St. Elizabeths Hospital for observation in connection with pending commitment proceedings, allowed her to amend her petition by naming the Superintendent of St. Elizabeths as defendant, and on November 2, 1962, dismissed her petition without holding a hearing or requiring a return.

After she filed her appeal from denial of habeas corpus, she was adjudged "of unsound mind" and committed to Saint Elizabeths. At the commitment hearing two psychiatrists testified that she was mentally ill and one of them that she was suffering from a "chronic brain syndrome" associated with aging and "demonstrated very frequently difficulty with her memory. . . . Occasionally, she was unable to tell me where she was or what the date was." Both psychiatrists testified to the effect that she could not care for herself adequately. She did not take a timely appeal from the commitment order. We heard her appeal from the summary dismissal of her petition for habeas corpus and remanded the case to the District Court with directions to require a return and hold a hearing.

At the hearing on remand, the sole psychiatric witness testified that appellant was suffering from a senile brain disease, "chronic brain syndrome, with arteriosclerosis with reaction." The psychiatrist said she was not dangerous to others and would not intentionally harm herself, but was prone to "wandering away and being out exposed at night or any time that she is out." This witness also related that on one occasion she wandered away from the Hospital, was missing for about thirty-two hours, and was brought back after midnight by a police officer who found her wandering in the streets. She had suffered a minor injury which she attributed to being chased by boys.

She thought she had been away only a few hours and could not tell where she had been. The psychiatrist also testified that she was "confused and agitated" when first admitted to the Hospital but became "comfortable" after "treatment and medication."

At both the commitment hearing and the habeas corpus hearing on remand, appellant testified that she felt able to be at liberty. At the habeas corpus hearing her husband who had recently reappeared after a long absence and her sister said they were eager for her release and would try to provide a home for her. The District Court found that she "is suffering from a mental illness with the diagnosis of chronic syndrome associated with cerebral arteriosclerosis"; that she "is in need of care and supervision, and that there is no member of the family able to give the petitioner the necessary care and supervision; and that the family is without sufficient funds to employ a competent person to do so"; that she "is a danger to herself in that she has a tendency to wander about the streets, and is not competent to care for herself." The District Court again denied relief in habeas corpus, but noted appellant's right "to make further application in the event that the patient is in a position to show that there would be some facilities available for her provision." The court thus recognized that she might be entitled to release from Saint Elizabeths if other facilities were available, but required her to carry the burden of showing their availability.

Appellant contends in written and oral argument that remand to the District Court is required for a consideration of suitable alternatives to confinement in Saint Elizabeths Hospital in light of the new District of Columbia Hospitalization of the Mentally Ill Act [the Ervin Act, *supra*], which came into effect after the hearing in the District Court. Indeed, her counsel appointed by this court, who had interviewed appellant, made clear in answer to a question from the bench on oral argument that although appellant's formal pro se pleading requests outright release, her real complaint is total confinement in a mental institution; that she would rather be in another

U.S. Court of Appeals, District of Columbia Circuit, 364 F.2d 657 (1966).

institution or hospital, if available, or at home, even though under some form of restraint.

Habeas corpus challenges not only the fact of confinement but also the place of confinement. And the court is required to "dispose of the matter . . . as law and justice require." 28 U.S.C. § 2243. The court is not restricted to the alternative of returning appellant to Saint Elizabeths or unconditionally releasing her.

We are not called upon to consider what action we would have taken in the absence of the new Act, because we think the interest of justice and furtherance of the congressional objective require the application to the pending proceeding of the principles adopted in that Act. It provides that if the court or jury finds that a "person is mentally ill and, because of that illness, is likely to injure himself or other persons if allowed to remain at liberty, the court may order his hospitalization for an indeterminate period, or order any other alternative course of treatment which the court believes will be in the best interests of the person or of the public." D.C. Code § 21–545(b) (Supp. V, 1966). This confirms the view of the Department of Health, Education and Welfare that "the entire spectrum of services should be made available, including outpatient treatment, foster care, halfway houses, day hospitals, nursing homes, etc." The alternative course of treatment or care should be fashioned as the interests of the person and of the public require in the particular case. Deprivations of liberty solely because of dangers to the ill persons themselves should not go beyond what is necessary for their protection.

The court's duty to explore alternatives in such a case as this is related also to the obligation of the state to bear the burden of exploration of possible alternatives an indigent cannot bear. This appellant, as appears from the record, would not be confined in Saint Elizabeths if her family were able to care for her or pay for the care she needs. Though she cannot be given such care as only the wealthy can afford, an earnest effort should be made to review and exhaust the available resources of the community in order to provide care reasonably suited to her needs.

At the habeas corpus hearing, the psychiatrist testified that appellant did not need "constant medical supervision," but only "attention"; that the psychiatrist would have no objection if appellant "were in a nursing home, or a place where there would be supervision." At the commitment hearing one psychiatrist testified that "Mrs. Lake needs care, whether it be in the hospital or out of the hospital," and did not specify what, if any,

psychiatric care she needs. The second psychiatrist testified that she "needs close watching. She could wander off. She could get hurt and she certainly needs someone to see that her body is adequately cared for. . . . [She] needs care and kindness. . . ." It does not appear from this testimony that appellant's illness required the complete deprivation of liberty that results from commitment to Saint Elizabeths as a person of "unsound mind."

Appellant may not be required to carry the burden of showing the availability of alternatives. Proceedings involving the care and treatment of the mentally ill are not strictly adversary proceedings. Moreover, appellant plainly does not know and lacks the means to ascertain what alternatives, if any, are available, but the government knows or has the means of knowing and should therefore assist the court in acquiring such information.

We remand the case to the District Court for an inquiry into "other alternative courses of treatment." The court may consider, e.g., whether the appellant and the public would be sufficiently protected if she were required to carry an identification card on her person so that the police or others could take her home if she should wander, or whether she should be required to accept public health nursing care, community mental health and day care services, foster care, home health aide services, or whether available welfare payments might finance adequate private care. Every effort should be made to find a course of treatment which appellant might be willing to accept.

In making this inquiry, the District Court may seek aid from various sources, for example the D.C. Department of Public Health, the D.C. Department of Public Welfare, the Metropolitan Police Department, the D.C. Department of Vocational Rehabilitation, the D.C. Association for Mental Health, the various family service agencies, social workers from the patient's neighborhood, and neighbors who might be able to provide supervision. The court can also require the aid of the Commission on Mental Health, which was established "in recognition of the fact that the assistance of unbiased experts was essential to assist courts in dealing with insanity cases." The Commission's aid is available in habeas corpus proceedings as well as commitment proceedings. The Commission, like the court, may obtain the aid of appropriate groups and individuals.

We express no opinion on questions that would arise if on remand the court should find no available alternative to confinement in Saint Elizabeths.

We respectfully reject the suggestion that

our opinion may be read as amounting to a revival of all commitments that had already become final. This case has its special features within which the opinion is confined. This appears from the factual setting of the opinion. The District Court recognized the problem in suggesting that if this patient could show that there were other facilities available for her provision she could apply again to the court. Our decision does no more than require the exploration respecting other facilities to be made by the government for the indigent appellant in the circumstances of this case.

Habeas corpus proceedings always have been available to test the validity of a deprivation of liberty—see, e.g., *Stewart* v. *Overholser*, 87 U.S. App. D.C. 402, 186 F.2d 339 (1950); and where there has occurred, as here, a change in the applicable statutory law pending the appeal, remand for consideration by the trial court under the intervening statute is appropriate if not required. To require in a habeas corpus proceeding that the court consider an intervening statute applicable to the situation is not to require a new commitment proceeding, nor does it open one already concluded.

Remanded for further proceedings in accordance with this opinion.

WRIGHT, Circuit Judge, concurring:

I concur in the court's opinion, but wish to make clear my position that, while the District of Columbia may be able to make some provision for Mrs. Lake's safety under our statute, the permissible alternatives, on the record before us, do not include full-time involuntary confinement. The record shows only that Mrs. Lake is somewhat senile, that she has a poor memory, has wandered on a few occasions, and is unable to care for herself at all times. This evidence makes out a need for custodial care of some sort, but I cannot accept the proposition that this showing automatically entitles the Government to compel Mrs. Lake to accept its help at the price of her freedom.

BURGER, Circuit Judge, with whom DANAHER and TAMM, Circuit Judges, join, dissenting:

We disagree with remanding the case to require the District Court to carry out an investigation of alternatives for which Appellant has never indicated any desire. The only issue before us is the legality of Mrs. Lake's confinement in Saint Elizabeths Hospital and the only relief she herself has requested is immediate unconditional release. The majority does not intimate that Appellant's present confinement as a patient at Saint Elizabeths Hospital is illegal, or that there is anything wrong with it except that she does not like it and

wishes to get out of any confinement. Nevertheless, this Court now orders the District Court to perform functions normally reserved to social agencies by commanding search for a judicially approved course of treatment or custodial care for this mentally ill person who is plainly unable to care for herself. Neither this Court nor the District Court is equipped to carry out the broad geriatric inquiry proposed or to resolve the social and economic issues involved. This is particularly illustrated in the first alternative the majority commands the District Court to explore: ". . . whether the appellant and the public would be sufficiently protected if she were required to carry an identification card on her person so that the police or others could take her home if she should wander. . . ." The list of subjects to explore concludes with an admonition that "every effort should be made to find a course of treatment which appellant might be willing to accept."

Although proceedings for commitment of mentally ill persons are not strictly adversary, a United States court in our legal system is not set up to initiate inquiries and direct studies of social welfare facilities or other social problems. This Court exists to decide questions put before it by parties to litigation on the basis of issues raised by them in pleadings and facts adduced by those parties. D.C. Code § 21–545 (Supp. 1966) does not transmute the United States District Court for the District of Columbia into an administrative agency for proceedings involving the mentally ill. This statute provides only that "the court may order [a mentally ill person's] . . . hospitalization for an indeterminate period, or order any other alternative course of treatment which *the court believes* will be in the best interests of the person or of the public." (Emphasis added.) All this section does, or was intended to do, is authorize the court to order alternative courses of treatment, provided the evidence presented to it leads it to believe that some alternative is preferable to confinement in Saint Elizabeths Hospital. This appellant seeks only her release, not a transfer. We cannot find anything in this statute which even vaguely hints at a requirement that the court conduct broad inquiries into possible treatment facilities. In the absence of such language, we must interpret the statute as not enlarging the role of the court beyond its normal judicial function of deciding issues presented by the parties on the basis of such facts as the parties present.

Even if the statute were read to require the District Court or the Mental Health Commission to investigate alternatives during the commitment proceedings, clearly a petitioner in a habeas corpus proceeding bears the initial burden of establishing the illegality of the present confinement. If, in order to accomplish this end, it is relevant to show that there are preferable alternatives to confinement in Saint Elizabeths, then the burden is on the petitioner to show the existence of these alternatives. Yet, from the filing of Mrs. Lake's petition to the present moment, no one including the majority of this Court has demonstrated any alternative "course of treatment."

What the majority has done here is first rewrite Mrs. Lake's petition for her, to demand something which she has never requested, then it has proceeded to remand, ordering the District Court to consider this new "petition" written by this court. Mrs. Lake and her successive lawyers have never asked for exploration of alternatives; she requested total release. The majority orders the District Court to make "every effort . . . to find a course of treatment which appellant might be willing to accept" yet at the same time the majority flouts the petitioner's wishes. What she wants this Court to do is to decide the legality of her commitment; however, the majority explicitly reserves that question pending the results of the study of District of Columbia social welfare facilities which it has ordered the Trial Court to undertake. We believe that this court should decide the issues raised by Appellant, not the issues it feels the Appellant should have raised. The Court's failure to decide the issues raised leaves her confined in St. Elizabeths Hospital while the District Court conducts a study largely unrelated to the question of the legality of that confinement, and for which a court is not equipped.

To show that Appellant really does object to the *place* of her confinement, the majority is forced to rely on the response of her appointed counsel to a question from the bench at oral argument. Counsel said that Appellant's major objection was that she was confined in a mental institution, and he intimated that possibly she might not be so unhappy with confinement in some other institution. This indicates that a large part of what troubles both Appellant and the majority is the fact that she is being confined in a *mental* institution and not some type of home for the aged which would provide essentially the same care but would not have attached to it the "onus" of being associated with a mental institution.

If Appellant were to receive precisely the same care she is presently receiving in the geriatrics ward of St. Elizabeths at an institution elsewhere with a name like Columbia Rest Haven, it does not appear that there would be much disagreement over the propriety of her confinement. However, a person's freedom is no less arrested, nor is the effect on him significantly different, if he is confined in a rest home with a euphemistic name rather than at St. Elizabeths Hospital. The cases the majority cites to support the proposition that habeas corpus is available to challenge the place of custody all involved the quite different situation of challenges based on the nature rather than simply the name of the place of custody. Any conceivable relevance of those cases to the contentions made in the present case is eliminated by the fact that no one denies that Appellant is mentally ill.

We can all agree in principle that a series of graded institutions with various kinds of homes for the aged and infirm would be a happier solution to the problem that confining harmless senile ladies in St. Elizabeths Hospital with approximately 8,000 patients, maintained at a great public expense. But it would be a piece of unmitigated folly to turn this appellant loose on the streets with or without an identity tag; and I am sure for my part that no District Judge will order such a solution. This city is hardly a safe place for able-bodied men, to say nothing of an infirm, senile, and disoriented woman to wander about with no protection except an identity tag advising police where to take her. The record shows that in her past wanderings she has been molested, and should she be allowed to wander again all of her problems might well be rendered moot either by natural causes or violence.

MCGOWAN, Circuit Judge, dissenting:

I dissent for the reason that, with all respect, I am unable to understand just what the majority's concept of finality is in civil commitment proceedings for the mentally ill.

As for the instant case, appellant sought only her outright release on habeas corpus. Represented by counsel, she endeavored to show by evidence that her condition did not require further custody of any kind, and that, in any event, her husband and other relatives could furnish such care and supervision as might be required. The District Court found the facts to be otherwise on both of these approaches, and no one suggests that those finding are erroneous. That ordinarily would end the matter, subject always to the right of appellant to seek hereafter a different disposition of her person, either on habeas corpus or under the specific provisions of the new law referred to hereinafter.

Appellant's original commitment in mental health proceedings was under a statute which, effective September 15, 1964, was replaced by a new one, which is now codified as 21 D.C.

Code § § 501–91 (Supp. V, 1966). The majority opinion may perhaps mean that all those originally committed under the old law may, by means of habeas corpus, have a new original commitment hearing under the terms of the new statute. This would presumably be for the purpose of giving everyone a chance to have the committing tribunal consider "any other alternative course of treatment which the court believes will be in the best interests of the person or of the public" (21 D.C. Code § 545). Under this approach, all commitment proceedings which became final before the new statute are now open for a de novo inquiry, with the party seeking the commitment cast in the usual role of moving party. But, if the majority opinion be regarded as accomplishing this much, it is by no means clear that the replay on habeas corpus is limited only to those finally committed before the new law became effective.

I am by no means persuaded that Congress, by the enactment of the new statute, intended either of these consequences. The new law, indeed, contains its own provisions for periodic review of commitments made either under it or the old law, 21 D.C. Code § § 546, 589; and those provisions are hardly to be identified with what is prescribed on the remand which the court orders. And it may well come as a surprise to Congress to know that the new mental hospitalization act is fully retrospective in operation to the point of reopening all commitments which had become final earlier. It may have thought, contrarily, that such complete retroactivity was not necessary in view of the traditional availability of habeas corpus under which any person under commitment, aided by counsel either retained or provided, may come into court and show that the particular relief sought is justified. In any event, it seems likely that it was this kind of habeas corpus which Congress expressly preserved in the new law, 21 D.C. Code § 549, for the benefit of all persons originally committed under either the new or the old law.

Judges Danaher, Burger, and Tamm have authorized me to say that they concur in this opinion.

U.S. District Court Decision on Remand

Late in September 1962, Catherine Lake, patient-petitioner herein, was found by a member of the Metropolitan Police Department while she was wandering in the vicinity of Fifth and E Streets, N.W., and was taken to the Women's Bureau of the Police Department.

On October 3, 1962, civil commitment proceedings were instituted by the filing of a petition by the Police Department. This petition, signed by Detective Maude B. Knight, stated as grounds for the petition that Mrs. Lake ". . . was looking for a place to stay, without funds. She cannot remember last address. . . . This woman is incapable of making plans for herself or handling her own affairs, and it is felt that hospitalization is the only solution to her problem," [Mental Health Case No. 2012–62]. This Court, sitting as Motions Judge, signed an Order on October 3, 1962 granting the petition and ordering that Mrs.

Lake be referred to the Mental Health Commission, and that she be detained at D.C. General Hospital for thirty days or until discharged or transferred by order of the Court. A guardian ad litem was appointed.

On October 11, 1962, the medical staff of the hospital filed a certificate asserting that Catherine Lake was of unsound mind and should be committed for treatment of her mental condition, diagnosed as chronic brain syndrome associated with arteriosclerosis. She was transferred to St. Elizabeths Hospital on October 11.

On October 12 the Commission on Mental Health reported its findings that Mrs. Lake was of unsound mind, suffering from chronic brain syndrome and was incapable of managing her own affairs and recommending her committment for treatment; that she was without funds, and should be committed to St. Elizabeths Hospital. On October 15, the guardian

---

District Court, D.C., H.C. No. 439–62, April 17, 1967 (95 *Daily Washington Law Reporter* 829).

ad litem, reported that he concurred in the recommendation of the Commission.

Mrs. Lake appeared in open court before the undersigned on October 26, 1962, and requested a jury trial, and the case was set for trial before a jury on November 21.

In the meantime, on October 11th, Mrs. Lake filed the instant proceeding (Habeas Corpus No. 439–62) against the Superintendent and others of the D.C. General Hospital staff. Answers were filed by the respective respondents, all to the effect that the petitioner had been transferred to the custody of St. Elizabeths Hospital. Leave to file an amended complaint was granted; the amended complaint was filed, and was dismissed the same day. Thereafter leave to appeal without prepayment of costs was granted.

The trial by jury in Mental Health Case No. 2012–62 was held before Judge McGuire, and Mrs. Lake was found of unsound mind, and she was thereafter committed to St. Elizabeths "until she may be safely discharged therefrom."

The Circuit Court, in *Catherine Lake* v. *Dale Cameron, et al.*, No. 17,531, January 9, 1964 (331 F.2d 771, 118 U.S. App. D.C. 25), reversed and remanded the Habeas Corpus proceeding (H. C. 439–62) for further proceedings, on the grounds that the dismissal was a summary disposition in that the respondent had made no return, no hearing was held, and no findings made.

. . .

Hearing was held on May 8, 1964, at which petitioner testified on her own behalf. The Court also heard testimony from the sister and the husband of petitioner, as well as from the medical staff of St. Elizabeth's Hospital. On May 22, 1964, this Court entered its findings to the effect that the evidence showed petitioner was suffering from a mental illness and was in need of care and supervision: [that] there was no member of her family able to give her necessary care and supervision and the family was without sufficient funds to employ a competent person to do so; and further, that she was a danger to herself in that she had a tendency to wander about the streets and was not competent to care for herself. The Court dismissed the petition without prejudice to the filing of a new petition at a time when the family is able to provide for petitioner's care and custody. Petitioner was again granted leave to appeal without prepayment of costs.

In a Per Curiam opinion, *Lake* v. *Cameron*, No. 18,809, April 1, 1965, F.2d, U.S. App. D.C., the Circuit Court affirmed the lower Court's findings and dismissal of the petition.

The District of Columbia Hospitalization of the Mentally Ill Act, 78 Stat. 944 (1964), D.C. Code, Sup IV 1965, Sections 21–351 to 21–366, was amended by the Act of Congress of September 14, 1965, 79 Stat. 752, P.L. 89–183, Section 1, D.C. Code Title 21, Sections 501–591 (Supp. V. 1966), which became effective January 1, 1966.

The Circuit Court granted a rehearing *en banc*, and in a five to four opinion, *Catherine Lake* v. *Dale C. Cameron*, No. 18,809, decided May 19, 1966, amended September 19, 1966, 364 F.2d 657, U.S. App. D.C., remanded the matter of the Habeas Corpus proceeding to this Court for further proceedings in the light of the new Mentally Ill Act.

The pertinent section of that Act, D.C. Code 21–545(b), provides in part that if the court or jury finds a "person is mentally ill and, because of that illness, is likely to injure himself or others if allowed to remain at liberty, the court may order his hospitalization for an indeterminate period, or order any other alternative course of treatment which the court believes will be in the best interests of the person or of the public." The provision for "other alternative course of treatment" was not in the 1964 Act, and the Circuit Court remanded the case to this Court "for an inquiry into 'other alternative courses of treatment.' " . . .

The Circuit Court's opinion suggested that this Court seek aid from (1) The District of Columbia Department of Public Health, (2) the District of Columbia Department of Public Welfare, (3) the Metropolitan Police Department, (4) the District of Columbia Department of Vocational Rehabilitation, (5) the District of Columbia Association for Mental Health, and (6) the Commission on Mental Health. It was also suggested that this Court consider (1) having the petitioner carry on her person an identification card; (2) the acceptance of Public Health Nursing care; (3) the acceptance of day care services; (4) foster home care; (5) home health aid services; and (6) welfare payments for adequate private care.

The perplexing problems created by this case result from the above quoted portion of D.C. Code Section 21–545(b) (Supp. V 1966), which provides that the court may order hospitalization or order any other alternative course of treatment.

The statute places upon the District Court the burden of exploring alternatives that are in the best interest of the "person or the public." Such an exploration must necessarily be limited to alternatives designed to implement and satisfy the requisite course of prescribed treatment for the particular patient.

The medical testimony throughout the chronology of this case has remained constant. Mrs. Lake is suffering from chronic brain syndrome associated with arteriosclerosis, with psychotic reaction, and there has been no essential change in her condition or that diagnosis. As a result of this condition, the petitioner receives medication so as to reduce her generally confused state, and she has been placed in a closed ward.

The purpose of her confinement in a closed ward is to prevent her from wandering. Her medical background indicated that she has a strong propensity, when in a confused and disoriented state, to wander aimlessly through the streets until eventually picked up. The records of the Metropolitan Police Department Women's Bureau and the records of St. Elizabeths Hospital indicate that during these periods she has been accosted but has no specific recollection of the events which took place. She had wandered away from the Hospital on two separate occasions before her doctor became aware of "her pronounced tendency to wander." In order to prevent Mrs. Lake from wandering she must be maintained in a closed ward and under "constant supervision."

This Court finds from the testimony that it is quite clear that constant supervision is not only proper but required for the safety of this patient.

The requirement of constant supervision necessarily restricts the availability of other alternative courses of treatment. It means that if the patient is placed in a facility other than St. Elizabeths, the new facility must provide supervision commensurate with what Mrs. Lake is presently receiving. This reality precludes this Court from ordering the petitioner to wear an identification, from ordering her to accept community mental health and day care services, from ordering her to accept various family service agency services, or neighborhood supervision, or part-time supervision from social workers in petitioner's neighborhood.

The requirement of constant supervision dictates similar treatment and consequently channeled the major portion of this investigation into the location of other appropriate facilities. . . .

Since the Court finds that the actual medical and psychiatric treatment extended to Catherine Lake is fully warranted, there is no facility within the District of Columbia, other than St. Elizabeths, presently capable of treating the petitioner.

As Dr. Cameron pointed out in his reply to a question propounded by Mr. Browning, even if there were not the financial barrier, Mrs. Lake would have to be restrained of her liberty as she is at St. Elizabeths.

The majority opinion of the Court of Appeals indicates that economic dependency or indigency, as is present here, should be no reason for sending patients to mental hospitals. The note points out that inquiries such as this "will not only reveal the facilities available but will uncover the need for those that are not available." While this inquiry has shown the need, it has not shown the availability. The pathos of economic deprivation cannot detour well reasoned obligations of the Court.

Title 21, Section 545(b) D.C. Code, (Supp. V 1966) and the Court of Appeals majority opinion leave unanswered the two most difficult questions before this trial Court. As this Court remarked in its preliminary statement to this investigation, it has always, prior to the enactment of the new statute, considered alternative facilities for mental health patients. That inquiry was and is made with the aid of the Mental Health Commission and the social service agency at St. Elizabeths. While the opinion of the majority speaks mainly in terms of facilities, the statute speaks in terms of treatment. To be sure, the facility may be an element of treatment, but the facility as an entity itself, does not appear approachable under the statute.

A second problem is the Court's actual commitment power. The statute says the Court may "order any other alternative course of treatment." This raises the question of whether or not the Court may legally commit a patient to a facility or institution, other than St. Elizabeths. If the statute does clothe the District Court with authority to order the patient into a private nursing home or to a foster home, the question arises as to whom may the Court look as a responsible party.

At present, when a patient is committed to St. Elizabeths, and transferred by the Hospital to a foster home, the hospital is the responsible party. Their officials check on both the conditions in the foster home and the patient's adaptability to that environment. If the patient is unable to get along satisfactorily, he is not returned to the hospital.

If the Court were to order a patient directly to a foster home or a private nursing home, who would replace St. Elizabeths as the responsible party? It may be that the Court has the authority to order the patient into another facility and still place the responsibility on St. Elizabeths, but this point is not clear.

These unanswered questions need resolution before effective commitments for "alternative course of treatment" can become practical.

The Court would like to make it clear that the problems of (1) distinguishing between facility and treatment, (2) the scope of the Court's "order" authority under the new Act, and (3) the burden of responsibility to the patient and to the Court, had no bearing on this particular case. There is no question that Mrs. Lake reqires 24-hour supervision for her own safety, and that the only facility within the District of Columbia available to her which affords that type of treatment is St. Elizabeths Hospital.

EDITORIAL COMMENT

Two recent cases have followed the least restrictive alternative theory of *Lake* v. *Cameron* and *Lessard* v. *Schmidt*. A New York court in *In re Kesselbrenner*, No. 112 (N.Y. Ct. App., Nov. 23, 1973), held a section of the New York Mental Hygiene Law unconstitutional as violating due process. This section permitted the transfer of dangerously mentally ill patients from state civil hospitals to a penal institution for mentally ill convicted criminals. The court held that such transfer could not be permitted, since it failed to provide the least restrictive alternative and since confinement in a penal institution bore no reasonable relation to the patient's treatment. The other case, although not using the words "least restrictive alternative" established procedures governing placement in a maximum security unit of a state mental hospital. In *Barnes* v. *Hill*, No. 1821 (W.D. Mo., Dec. 3, 1973) the court held that all placements of patients in maximum security facilities of state mental hospitals by administrative decision must be reviewed within a specified period of time. If it is determined that the patient is to be kept in maximum security, he may challenge that decision through hearing procedures. The court also held the patient must receive written notice, giving the reasons for placement in maximum security and notice of a staffing conference (to be held within 90 days), on the necessity for continued hospitalization in maximum security, with the right to attend and submit comments. After this conference, the patient is entitled to a written statement of reasons for continued hospitalization in maximum security, his medical report must state what alternatives were considered and why they were rejected, and he must be informed of the right to appeal.

A DISTURBED LIFE AND A VIOLENT DEATH

She was standing in the near-freezing rain outside Union Station on Thursday, two shabby, open sacks of clothing and books at her feet, as dozens of sun-tanned vacationers from Florida transferred from strike-bound trains to buses.

"Have you been stranded by the train strike?" I ask. "Or are you just stranded?" (I was at the station to cover the railroad strike.)

Shabby in what once had been good clothing—a camel's hair coat and kid gloves and sneakers with holes in them—she admitted she had been living at Union Station for several days, had no money and no place to go, but insisted she was fine.

Less than 24 hours later her body, sexually molested and stabbed more than 20 times in the face, neck and chest, was found in a deserted garage in Southeast Washington.

Sheila Broughel, 26, daughter of a West Hartford, Conn., insurance executive, graduate of Chaffee School and Vassar College, who worked briefly at the *New Yorker* magazine and later was admitted to mental institutions on seven different occasions, talked freely about the past.

But she became withdrawn when asked about the future.

I talked to her and to four policemen who questioned her because they said she had been

---

Washington Post, February 14, 1973, p. A–1.

standing in the intermittent rain outside Union Station for "almost a week." Then I took her in to the snack bar, bought her lunch, gave her $5 when she said she had no money, and later persuaded her to see a psychiatrist at St. Elizabeths Hospital.

He suggested she sign herself in voluntarily, but she refused, said she had no problems of any kind and asked to be taken "home" to Union Station.

I left her in the rain outside the station, offered her my hand and wished her luck.

"I don't shake hands with anyone," she apologized, then smiled hesitantly, hugged her two bags to her and walked into the station.

Her body was found at 8:30 A.M. Friday by two construction workers in a garage in the 200 block of 13th Street SE.

Police said yesterday that she was wearing the camel's hair coat, three sweaters, three pairs of socks and a pair of slacks. A plaid scarf was found nearby. She was identified through a motel key found in her pocket. Police said the motel was in Virginia and that she hadn't been there for four days.

Her body was identified by an older sister who lives in Middleburg, Va., and whom she had come to visit in late January, police said.

Her father, James Broughel, a Hartford Insurance Group official, said last night that his daughter had problems "but I had no legal standing in court to do anything for her in any way."

He said she had been drifting for some time and that "perhaps 1,000 people have helped her . . . befriending her, giving her money, but she didn't understand the character of the beast in the jungle she found herself in" outside Union Station.

Standing outside Union Station on Thursday, her hands began shaking noticeably when two District and two railroad policemen came up to her. She picked up her sacks and began backing away.

"Do you have some place to stay? Some friends here? . . . Some identification? . . . Money?" the officers asked.

"Yes, I have friends . . . around." The officers spoke softly and were friendly but one took me aside.

"She's crazy . . . I saw her down on Pennsylvania Avenue waving her arms . . . but there's nothing we can do because of the Ervin law"—a 2-year-old District law that permits placement of persons in mental institutions only if they are a danger to themselves or others.

"I'm going to get a cup of coffee," she said

and looked at me. I'll buy her one," I said to the officers.

While we sat at the counter she ate a cheese sandwich, but didn't touch the soup she had ordered, and talked earnestly but disjointedly about her life.

"I was born to be famous . . . to be a writer . . . went to Vassar [she graduated in 1968] . . . and worked at the New Yorker for awhile, writing a letter occasionally, but mostly talking to people. . . . They advised me to leave and write on my own, in order to become famous. I have always insisted on intellectual excellence. This was drummed into me. My parents weren't intellectually excellent but they insisted we be." She was one of six children.

Whenever I asked what she planned to do and where she planned to go she just stared vacantly into the distance. "You can't stay here. The police told you that. And you just can't stand outside in the rain all night. Washington's a dangerous place, you could be raped or murdered." She never responded to any question about the present that the police, I, or the psychiatrist later asked her.

I asked her if she would see a psychiatrist at St. Elizabeths Hospital, and said that a personal friend of mine was a doctor there, working for the National Institutes of Mental Health. I said I'd pay her taxi fare there or take her over and that she would be free to leave if she wished. After a long silence she began shaking her head and said yes, if I would drive her.

Dr. Llewellyn Bigelow, a research psychiatrist studying schizophrenia with the mental health research division of NIMH at St. Elizabeths, said yes, he could see her, and to come right over.

But all she would discuss was the past, that she was born to be famous, believed in excellence, mentioning where she went to school and worked.

Dr. Bigelow could not, under law, arbitrarily order her committed to the hospital unless he determined that she was a threat to herself or others. He did not make this determination. He agreed to see Miss Broughel later on her stipulation that she would not be kept at St. Elizabeths against her will.

When Dr. Bigelow asked if she would consider voluntarily signing in to St. Elizabeths she said no and quickly began picking up her two threadbare sacks of dirty clothes and dog-eared books, the top one her Vassar edition of Rilke's poems. "Would you drive me home . . . to Union Station?" she asked me. I left her there.

Editorial Note

The article which follows describes a study of an admittedly small number (n=70) of psychiatrists with regard to the adequacy of their knowledge about commitment procedures and their attitudes regarding civil commitment. The study tends to show that psychiatrists' knowledge of the commitment laws under which they work is generally less than expert.

It should be noted that many of the psychiatrists participating in the study thought about commitment in terms of psychiatric symptoms and diagnoses rather than in terms of reasonably predictable behavior; yet, it is with the latter that most commitment laws deal. That is, for some psychiatrists, a diagnosis of severe acute schizophrenia could be considered grounds for commitment on the basis of the doctor's concern about the need of the patient for treatment, whether the patient wants it or not. The law, however, is concerned with behavior; for example, whether or not a patient will behave in a way that is dangerous to himself and/or the community in the immediate future. It is well to keep this distinction in mind.

EMERGENCY COMMITMENT— A TRANSCULTURAL STUDY

Michael A. Peszke, M.D., and Ronald M. Wintrob, M.D.

THE NATURE OF THE SURVEY

This paper reports the results of a questionnaire survey that sought information on psychiatrists' knowledge of and attitudes toward emergency involuntary hospitalization laws in their area of practice and the degree of their concern about possible litigation. Respondents were asked to discuss the statutes and to offer suggestions for improvements.

In addition, this brief clinical vignette was given: "If a patient (adult, single, without family, good physical health) examined by you or treated by you as an out-patient was preoccupied by suicidal thoughts, refused your advice for voluntary psychiatric admission, and shortly after that committed suicide, would you feel medically responsible?" Three response categories were provided for this vignette: (1) yes (i.e., responsible), (2) no (i.e., not responsible), and (3) can't say.

The questionnaire was sent to a selected sample of 200 members of the American Psychiatric Association in the United States, in all U.S. territories, and in three Canadian provinces, and also a sample of APA members in Asia, Africa, South America, Europe, and Australia.

FINDINGS

Seventy replies were received, representing a 35 percent return rate. For purposes of analysis the questions were divided into three categories: knowledge, attitude, and interest and involvement in the problem.

Knowledge of Commitment Procedures

Questions about knowledge concerned the respondents' subjective judgment as to their understanding of the statutes pertaining to involuntary medical (emergency) commitment in their area. In all cases for American states and English-speaking countries, respondents' statements were compared with the statutes, which were analyzed for us by an attorney.

Excerpted and reprinted with permission from *American Journal of Psychiatry* 131 (1974): 36–40. Copyright 1974 the American Psychiatric Association.

Only four psychiatrists judged their knowledge of commitment laws to be inadequate. All other respondents replied with an unqualified affirmative, which was not always justified, as to their knowledge of laws and criteria regarding commitment. Overall, the data indicate that many practicing psychiatrists do not have a true understanding of the laws governing emergency involuntary medical treatment in their states, provinces, and countries. Furthermore, most are confused by the two different concepts of statutory criteria and of appropriate medical practices. Some examples of responses that lead us to this conclusion follow.

Three respondents from one of the continental states replied in the affirmative as to their knowledge of the statutes for commitment in their state. However, their answers regarding the guidelines for such commitment were as follows:

First respondent: "A statement by two physicians regarding need for same."

Second respondent: "Contact coroner's office or notify sheriff's department with goal incarceration while evaluation is done."

Third respondent: "In theory requires action by parish coroner. However, in practice there is wide variability—some hospitals will admit voluntarily, some will not. Our biggest problem in this state is lack of adequate facilities, not legal civil rights, etc."

In fact, the statutes for that jurisdiction specify that there are three forms of involuntary commitment: by order of the coroner, by judicial order, and by emergency commitment. The description in the statutes of the emergency commitment for that state reads: "A relative, friend or curator may apply to the superintendent of a hospital for emergency commitment of an individual who is mentally ill and in need of immediate care. Application must be in writing and must be accompanied by the certificate of one qualified physician stating that the patient requires immediate care. Such certificate must be acted upon within 24 hours."

Two psychiatrists from another continental state also replied in the affirmative as to their knowledge of commitment. They described the statutory rule as follows:

First respondent: "Acutely homicidal or suicidal."

Second respondent: "Examination by a certified physician, licensed in the state and declaration by the physician that the patient is dangerous to himself or others. The clerk of courts can also issue holding order on basis of the petition of a relative."

These statements indicate a marked discrepancy in the respondents' understanding of the law, with the second respondent being basically correct.

We conclude this section with the example of two psychiatrists in the practice of general psychiatry who affirmatively answered the question regarding familiarity with the statutes and their implementation. The second respondent's statement is correct.

One wrote: "We have no provisions for emergency commitment."

The other stated: "The opinion of one physician. Psychiatrist not necessary. Sworn affidavit of insanity to the probate judge of the resident county or higher court judge. History of illness and circumstances signed by two relations or two persons knowing the circumstances."

Attitudes Regarding Commitment

On the issue of attitudes toward involuntary commitment there was a distinct difference in the extent to which certain questions were answered. In some instances psychiatrists in the same state or country gave quite different responses. In their reactions to the case vignette cited, eighteen respondents indicated a strong fear of possible malpractice litigation, should commitment procedures not be initiated. One psychiatrist wrote: "Would be liable for actions of persons not committed." Fourteen expressed fear of being sued by "an irate patient." One psychiatrist explained that, "I tried to rationalize my acting for or against [commitment] in a way that would be acceptable to a court of law."

The most striking finding, however, was the confirmation of our hypothesis that attitudes are subjective and that there is a lack of adequate criteria that are ethical, legal, and medically therapeutic for initiating emergency involuntary commitment. Compared with respondents in other states, those from California showed a greater degree of uniformity in stating the indications for involuntary commitment in their state, and they were "within the ballpark" as far as the statutory guidelines are concerned. The respondents otherwise listed the following indications for commitment (some listed more than one): potential harm to self or others (34, or 50 percent of the respondents), psychosis (14, or 20 percent), or inability of the patient to "take care of self" (11, or 16 percent).

Beyond these criteria agreed to by ten or more respondents, there was great variability in the commitment criteria that were cited. One psychiatrist proposed simply "mental alienation." Another indicated that he would commit a patient only on the basis of "solid criteria of psychiatric diagnosis." A third stated, "If the patient has symptoms of behavior which requires treatment and he refuses this voluntarily." A fourth psychiatrist proposed: "When patient is dangerous to himself and others and cannot be controlled in the home or community." One psychiatrist from a European country with a strikingly low homicide rate replied: "Mainly suicidal preoccupation; occasionally homicidal preoccupation or very bizarre behavior." Another psychiatrist from overseas stated that one criterion for commitment would be "to prevent patients ruining themselves socially and financially." Another replied, "If I can provide no other solution to a problem which in my opinion requires some action." At the other end of the spectrum was the statement: "A good psychiatrist will seldom need to commit."

A psychiatrist from one of the U.S. territories gave an answer that in effect is similar to the practice in Liberia. This psychiatrist wrote:

We very rarely have to commit patients. The poor people, without relatives, are taken directly to the state hospital and held there until they get better, even if they claim that they did not enter as a voluntary patient. Even better-off patients are held in private hospitals until they recover enough, or threaten a legal action if they are not released. Rarely do we have to go to court to commit a patient. I think that we don't have much problem in this respect since the poor are not usually if at all committed to mental hospitals. Pressure of the closest relatives usually makes the patient accept hospitalization. I would leave it the way it is now —otherwise, private hospitals may be very much afraid of hospitalizing a patient without his signature or that of the closest relative.

Interest and Involvement in the Problem of Commitment

These findings tend to confirm our hypothesis that psychiatrists do not have commonly accepted criteria for initiating commitment. It is interesting to note that a number of psychoanalysts who responded to the questionnaire stated that they did not think about the issues of commitment because their practice did not put them in touch with patients who might be committed. One distinguished academic psychoanalyst wrote that since he had "no ward responsibility" he had no way of answering the questionnaire.

In response to the clinical vignette, few respondents availed themselves of the third option ("can't say") and of thus avoiding a definitive position on medical responsibility for suicide. The majority of the respondents (37) expressed a feeling of responsibility for patients' suicide. This group included psychiatrists from all over the world, and there were no significant differences between respondents from this country and elsewhere. Nine respondents, all from the continental United States, gave an unqualified "no responsibility." Eight failed to answer this question, and the rest gave qualified answers including, "Can't say."

Some of the more illuminating answers and comments were as follows:

"I am responsible in every case in my practice."

"I think any psychiatrist must be able to predict suicide."

"When in doubt, hospitalize."

"Would want to indicate to that individual human being enough concern to intervene."

"Our custom is to accept actively the responsibility to prevent depressed people from committing suicide and I am unable to decide which ones should be allowed to die."

"This patient should have been committed." [This, incidentally, was from the same psychiatrist who wrote, "A good psychiatrist will seldom need to commit."]

"There is a risk of protecting civil liberties to the point that the patient may trade his liberty for his life."

"When a patient kills himself it is proper for his medical advisor to bear some responsibility and not merely to excuse himself."

"I would not feel medically responsible if I had in good faith reviewed all aspects of the patient's illness and had reached a judgment in an objective way that the actual risk of suicide was minimal."

"The fully trained psychiatrist has no need to resort to a commitment process which immediately brings in its turn personal and social consequences for patients that are antitherapeutic."

"The current thinking by radical social workers has not yet had a great deal of influence in this part of the world and I would regard such criticisms of our acting in the interests of our patients by commiting as being misinformed and biased by prejudice."

"If you never have a suicide you are hospitalizing a lot of people who really don't need it, along with a few who do."

"Society expects too much from psychiatry. Anyone likely to be unpredictable in behavior is susceptible to hospitalization. Dangerous people are released from prison every day after serving sentences. The sick can be incarcerated indefinitely. Something is wrong."

"If in responding to my best judgment, and taking into account my emotional reaction to the patient's sucidal threats, I did not commit him, I would feel guilty. If I did not feel he was a great risk, I would not feel guilty. I realize that no one will be right all the time, but feeling guilt would depend on whether I feel I acted with good judgment." [The question was specifically addressed to the issue of feeling medically responsible and did not address itself to the issue of personal guilt.]

"Many patients talk about doing away with their life, and don't do it. If I were to get scared, I would not be able to help patients at all. Of course, I would not take risks with certain patients." [This respondent, however, did not comment on the characteristics of these certain patients.]

DISCUSSION

There is a basic and probably irreconcilable difference of opinion and of philosophy between physicians, who wish to relieve suffering and preserve life, and lawyers, who are concerned about personal liability and justice. In problems of commitment the two professions have different views regarding the charge of protecting the rights of the individual. The medical profession views the best interests of the individual as being synonymous with possible benefit from treatment even if under duress, while the legal profession perceives liberty in terms of the individual exercising his freedom to behave as he wishes even if under duress of illness.

We argue that both professions are guilty of loose thinking. Psychiatry has never solved the problem of defining mental illness, while the statutory language is usually tautological. For example, a 1953 Delaware statute states, "Mentally ill person includes every idiot, lunatic, person or persons 'non compos mentis.'"

With such guidelines from the legal profession it is little wonder that psychiatrists use their own clinical judgment and their own conception and interpretation of statutes to guide their behavior as physician-healers.

The confusion in psychiatric thinking regarding a definition of mental illness is well illustrated by the difficulty that we have in accepting different cultural definitions of disturbed behavior and by the readiness with which we, as psychiatrists, diagnose psychopathology where it is minimal or nonexistent (1, 2). We do not identify with the segment of the profession that would deny the concept of mental illness, as well as ignore the fact that freedom under the duress of an illness whether its etiology is well documented, as in the case of a brain tumor, or is still to be elicited, as in schizophrenia, is spurious freedom at best. But it is because of our conviction that we have outgrown the unicausal germ theory in the medical model and because of our conviction that the treatment of mental illness is a medical responsibility that our concern is directed to a tightening of criteria for commitment and peer review and control. We should no more allow the ill to be neglected and untreated in the name of freedom than we should let the poor starve in the name of character development. Nonetheless, we should make sure that we do not incarcerate the deviant or the eccentric merely because a period of time in a hospital will do them no harm.

CONCLUSIONS

Two conclusions arise from this study. First it appears to us that the only viable practice is to have two forms of commitment:

1. Emergency medical holding actions for persons with clear-cut psychiatric problems who pose impending danger to themselves or others.

2. Judicial mental health tribunals that act as arbitrators and overseers for prolonged involuntary treatment, either inpatient or outpatient (3). The criterion for this should be evidence of psychosis with concomitant physical danger to self or others. The judge would have the option of ordering inpatient or outpatient enforced treatment, but no one who could manage his own affairs would be commited unless his disability was harmful to himslf or his family and only when treatment had a chance of success.

Second, given the confused and variable picture with respect to criteria for involuntary commitment, as demonstrated by this survey, we contend that psychiatrists need reasonably uniform commitment standards and that they will continue to exercise their well-intentioned but inchoate thinking until such guidelines are adopted.

We advocate two approaches to the problem of emergency commitments. With the current drive for peer review of all our actions, it would seem appropriate for psychiatric societies at the state or county level to give serious thought and consideration to instituting a peer review of all commitments. Since it appears reasonable for the medical profession to accept peer review for screening the length of hospital stay and the need for operative procedures, surely emergency involuntary commitment of an individual is at least as serious and requires as much thought and judgment as a cholecystectomy or hysterectomy.

Peer review has arisen primarily as a concern on the part of the physician at the thought that "outsiders" may become involved in the control of medical practices or standard. A study in New York has already well documented that when outsiders (in this case lawyers) oversee the disposition of psychiatric cases prior to probate court appearance, the discharge rate goes up 50 percent (4).

It is crucial that appropriate criteria be developed and the role of the physician in involuntary treatment be determined. We are facing the imminent danger of naively becoming the agents for thought control and political indoctrination, as appears to be happening in the Soviet Union (5). We have to fact the fact that in this age of anxiety and doubt, the mental health profession may become just such a fifth column for the control of the masses and that the profession's own political naivete could make this a serious danger.

REFERENCES

1. Rosenhan, D. L. "On being sane in insane places," *Science* 258 (1973): 179–250.
2. Kittrie, N. N. *The Right To Be Different: Deviance and Enforced Therapy.* Baltimore: The Johns Hopkins Press, 1972.
3. Peszke, M. "Involuntary treatment of the mentally ill: Law's all or nothing approach," *Connecticut Bar Journal* 46 (1972): 620–42.
4. Kumasaka, Y., Stokes, J., Gupta, R. K. "Criteria for involuntary hospitalization," *Arch. Gen. Psychiatry* 26 (1972): 399–404.
5. Medvedev, R. A., Medvedev, Z. *A Question of Madness.* New York: Random House, 1972.

EDITORIAL COMMENT

In *Logan* v. *Arafeh*, 346 Supp. 1265 (D.C. Conn. 1972) nine patients challenged the constitutionality of Connecticut's emergency commitment procedures. Under this law, an allegedly mentally ill person may be detained in a hospital for fifteen days if a physician certifies that he is dangerous to himself or others as a result of his mental illness. At the end of this period, the patient must either be released or the hospital must start involuntary commitment proceedings. Therefore, a person suspected of being mentally ill can be detained as long as forty-five days without a judicial determination of his mental condition.

The plaintiffs in *Logan* alleged that loss of liberty under these circumstances violated due process. However, the U.S. District Court for Connecticut said that confinement for forty-five days before a judicial determination is not so baseless as to be unconstitutional, because there is a reasonable connection between the time allowed and the objective sought.

The Court also was of the opinion that there was a compensating advantage to the patient, because in many cases during this period the hospital may alleviate his mental illness or determine by the use of diagnostic procedures that he does not need long-term commitment.

Also, the Court pointed out that the patient's right to liberty is protected by the right to bring habeas corpus proceedings. It rejected the plaintiffs contention that as a practical matter this remedy is unavailable, because there is no statute or administrative regulation which provides that patients be informed of this right, saying that though a notice provision would be both desirable and feasible, it is not constitutionally required.

The United States Supreme Court affirmed, without stating its reasons, in *Briggs* v. *Arafeh*, 93 S.Ct. 1556 (1973), Justices Douglas and Powell dissenting.

COMMITMENT

Lawrence S. Kubie, M.D., D.Sc.

Anyone who presumes to be a leader in his profession should himself give an example of thoughtful judgments carefully reached about subjects on which he is fully informed. It is saddening when instead such a leader, while posing as an authority on matters about which he subsequently betrays complete ignorance, misuses his position to distort a complex and painful topic by publishing inaccurate, misleading, and irresponsible statements. This is especially distressing when his misleading statements can do incalculable harm to patients, to their families, and to society.

I have never read a more distorted discussion of the hospital care of psychiatric patients than is expressed in the recent article by Dean Thomas L. Shaffer of the Law School of Notre Dame University, published in the *National Observer* of December 9, 1972. Not every word he says is inaccurate. Indeed almost every sentence contains some partial truths; but these are combined with vicious and destructive errors. This interweaving of truth and error makes them even more damaging, because the layman cannot distinguish one from the other.

Let me at once state my own point of view (or bias, if you will). I was first trained for four years under the late Dr. Adolf Meyer in the practice of hospital psychiatry. After four years in neurophysiology and experimental neuropathology this was followed by some twenty-five years of private practice and outpatient clinic practice, during which patients were free to come or not as they chose. Occasionally, the need arose to hospitalize such a patient temporarily, but this was usually welcomed by the patient, and the majority of such hospitalizations were voluntary. At the same time, I had extensive experience in teaching hospital psychiatry. Thus, I have seen the problems of hospital psychiatry from both outside and inside.

Of course it is true, as Dean Shaffer writes, that many public hospitals are so understaffed and so overcrowded that it becomes almost impossible even for a skilled and conscientious staff to do as high a calibre of work as they themselves struggle to achieve, but this does not justify his implications that even those hospitals which are adequately staffed and which are run as well as present knowledge and techniques permit are always destructive and never constructive. Nor does it mean that hospital care is never an essential ingredient in successful treatment. There are patients who for various reasons cannot possibly be treated at all outside of a hospital. Only rarely is hospitalization solely or predominantly for protective purposes. These are only a few samples of the inaccurate implications of Dean Shaffer's intemperate outburst.

Consider such sentences as, "If a kookie (sic) citizen wants to be kookie he has a right to be." Consider the nasty and untrue implication of this; that a man who is psychologically ill *wants* to be psychologically ill. Only shallowness can bring such prejudice to a discussion of the problems of how, why, and when to provide hospital care for mental patients. Again Dean Shaffer speaks of a commitment to a mental hospital as a "life sentence." Is he not aware that commitments are always reversible, and that there are a wide variety of well-known procedures by which to secure such reversals?

He writes that people are locked up only because their behavior "annoys" somebody who "has the power to commit." This statement embodies not one falsehood but three.

Again he writes of the right of patients to proper judicial procedures to protect their rights, as though he is unaware that every state (and I have worked in many) has specific laws to provide that the patient who wants to protest his hospitalization has a right to do so with legal defense and before a judge or jury as he prefers. The details of the methods vary from state to state; but the methods are always there.

Let me lean over backward to grant Dean Shaffer everything that we can. Let us grant that mental hospitals have faults. Certainly this is true; but they can never be improved if we shut them down and empty them; just as we could never learn either to prevent or to cure, if we were to kill off all patients who today are incurable.

Reprinted with permission from *Psychiatric News*, March 23, 1973, p. 2, col. 1.

Again he sounds as though he means that there are to be no limits to the patient's right to injure himself, his family, and the community, no matter what the nature of his disturbed conduct. Does he really mean this? Has society no right to protect children from the molester of children? I grant that among all psychotic patients not many commit murder and not many commit suicide or rape or seduce children, but the point is that some do. It is the duty of the psychiatrist to study these disturbances, until he learns to recognize these menaces ahead of time in order to have at least a chance to prevent them. Such studies usually require round-the-clock observations not by one observer alone but by many observers, observations of the patient's conduct alone and also when he is among others, and in different phases of the day's cycle. This can be done only in hospitals.

A tragic case in point was the young man in Chicago who murdered repeatedly in the grip of what the lawyers themselves call "an irresistible impulse," until in despair he scrawled on the wall over his bed, "Please somebody stop me before I commit another murder." Has society such a plea? Has a patient suffering from active pulmonary tuberculosis a right to spit in crowded public places? Has a patient suffering from active venereal disease a right to spread venereal disease until it becomes pandemic in proportions? Has the patient with a sick mind a right to spread filth and violence?

It is true, of course, that our techniques of prevention with or without hospitalization (or other forms of restraint) are not perfect, and that they do not always work perfectly, and they sometimes restrict the liberties of some who are less threatening; but even when protective hospitalization makes mistakes it still serves an indispensable function, often protecting the patient himself most of all. This is a vital need. We cannot withhold this from fellow humans who need this help.

DANGEROUSNESS: ARREST RATE COMPARISONS OF DISCHARGED PATIENTS AND THE GENERAL POPULATION

Jonas R. Rappeport, M.D., and George Lassen, Ph.D.

Although most psychiatrists will quickly say that the average mentally ill patient is not dangerous, we seem to be very cautious when it comes to releasing patients with "threatening" delusions or histories of previous antisocial behavior. . . .

We obtained the traditional hospital "face sheet" data for all male patients over 16 years of age discharged during fiscal 1947 and fiscal 1957 from all Maryland psychiatric hospitals (state, federal, and private—except one private institution). There were 708 patients in fiscal 1947, 2152 patients in fiscal 1957.

Unfortunately, no police agency in Maryland maintains a complete record of all felonies committed within the state, and therefore, the arrest records of all the police jurisdictions in Maryland were checked for these names for the five years preceding and five years subsequent to hospitalization.

Efforts were made to categorize our population into Urban and Rural and Negro and White as is done in the Uniform Crime Reports. However, the limited size of our samples did not lend itself to this type of analysis and consequently the crime rate for the entire

Excerpted with permission from the *American Journal of Psychiatry* 121 (1965): 776–83. Copyright 1965, the American Psychiatric Association.

state was used. This rate was obtained from the Uniform Crime Reports of the F.B.I. In order to equate our psychiatric populations to the F.B.I. rates it was necessary to recalculate their published data by eliminating all females and the general population under 16.

RESULTS

The data presented here represent only a preliminary report of our findings. A more detailed report, including information on females, will be published in the future. The arrests referred to are only for the five serious offenses of murder, negligent manslaughter, rape, robbery, and aggravated assault. We selected these offenses because they are felonies and represent danger to persons. . . .

DISCUSSION

We were most surprised to find our results not consistent with those reported in previous studies. We certainly do not find any clear-cut indications that the mentally ill are to any great extent less involved in criminal behavior than those in the general community. Instead, we find that for some offenses such as robbery and also probably rape, our patients were more frequently arrested than the general population. This suggests that we as psychiatrists may be biased when we malign others for suggesting that some of our patients represent a threat to the community.

That the hospital experience had a definite effect on reducing the total arrest rate as reported in the other studies . . . is not borne out by our findings. Some diagnostic groups, however, show changes after the hospital experience. The alcoholics showed a drop in arrests while the antisocial reactions showed a marked increase, but the schizophrenics showed no change. These results are a matter of some interest and we hope to further investigate this in the future. The arrests were spread out in all years. As best we can interpret our data, there was a tendency towards recidivism not unlike that seen in the general community.

There was no significant difference in the arrest rate experiences of our two populations. We would have expected that the newer treatment techniques would have been reflected in this variable. There are many factors which would seem to affect this type of research, such as the size of our populations, the accuracy of arrest information, the criteria of dangerousness, i.e., arrest versus conviction, the actual requirements for hospitalization, and the definitions of mental illness. Because of these various factors, it is difficult to come to any strong conclusions. However, we do feel that this project involved a more serious and accurate estimation of this problem than had the previous studies. One very difficult problem, and one which would appear to have affected the announced results of other studies if we understand them correctly, would be the need to adjust published arrest rates to fit the specific population being studied and that this be applied on a year to year basis.

SUMMARY

The incidence of arrest for two Maryland psychiatric populations, 1947 and 1957, were obtained for the five years preceding and following their discharge from psychiatric hospitals. Comparison of their arrest rates with that of the general population indicates that for some serious offenses the psychiatric population has a higher arrest rate than the general population. Comparison of pre- and post-hospitalization arrest rates were made and revealed no differences, nor did a comparison of the arrest rates of the two populations reveal any changes that might reflect the use of the newer treatment techniques. . . .

PSYCHIATRIC DISORDERS AND CRIMINALITY

Samuel B. Guze, M.D., Robert A. Woodruff, Jr., M.D.,
Paula J. Clayton, M.D.

A study of 500 psychiatric clinic patients indicated that serious crime (felony conviction) was chiefly associated with sociopathy, alcoholism, and drug dependence. Except for sexually deviant behavior leading to arrest and conviction, other psychiatric disorders are infrequently associated with felonies.

Serious crime, generally equated with felonies, is one of the country's major problems. Psychiatry's role in understanding, preventing, or treating criminal behavior is certainly not settled.[1] To help clarify this issue a series of investigations in this department, begun in 1959, have been addressed to the question, "What kinds of psychiatric disorders are associated with criminality?"

Systematic studies of convicted male and female felons indicated that sociopathy (antisocial personality), alcoholism, and drug dependence are the principal psychiatric disorders associated with adult criminality.[4-6] Among women felons, hysteria (Briquet Syndrome) is also frequent, but this is usually associated with sociopathy.[6] Schizophrenia or other psychotic states are not substantially increased in the criminal populations.

Having approached the question first by studying convicted criminals, it seemed appropriate to study psychiatric patients by asking the same question.

METHOD

A sample of 500 patients selected to constitute a cross section of our psychiatric clinic population have been examined systematically for ongoing, long-term, clinical, follow-up, and family studies.[7-15] The data for the present report were obtained from these patients at the time of the original interview. The research interview and diagnostic criteria have been presented elsewhere.[5, 16]

The interview included a section dealing with police trouble or imprisonment. The records were restudied to determine which patients had ever been convicted of a felony.

RESULTS

Twenty-two patients had a history of at least one felony conviction (26 convictions in all). They represented 4% of the entire sample, 10% of the men, and 1% of the women. The sex difference is statistically significant ($P<.01$), but there were no accompanying significant differences between the races controlled for sex.

The crimes, in order of frequency, for which the patient had been convicted included burglary (six cases), robbery (five cases), exhibitionism (four cases), larceny (three cases), forgery and shoplifting (two cases each), and attempted rape, auto theft, illegal possession of a weapon, and child molestation (one case each).

Five of the crimes were direct manifestations of sexual deviation: four cases of exhibitionism and one case of child molestation. In addition, one case of larceny involved stealing womens' clothes as an indirect manifestation of sexual deviation. Thus, six of the 22 patients, all men, were convicted because of behavior resulting from sexual deviation. Five of these men had no other psychiatric diagnosis; one was an alcoholic.

Fourteen of the remaining 16 patients were either sociopathic, alcoholic, or drug-dependent. The diagnosis of sociopathy was made in 13 of these cases, that of alcoholism in eight, and drug dependence in three.

One patient received the diagnosis of anxiety neurosis. She was a 34-year-old black woman who had been convicted of shoplifting six years earlier. The remaining patient was a 17-year-old black teen-ager with a history of delinquent and criminal behavior, including burglary, robbery, and attempted rape, who barely failed to meet the criteria for a diagnosis of his condition, sociopathy; thus, he was considered undiagnosed.

A felony conviction was reported by 37% of the 35 sociopaths, 13% of the 70 alcoholics, 23% of the 13 drug-dependents, 2% of the 62 anxiety neurotics, and 1% of the more than 100 undiagnosed patients in the entire sample. One of the 16 patients with mental retardation was also a sociopath, an alcoholic, and had been convicted of a felony. None of the other 15 with mental retardation had such a history.

Notably, none of the more than 200 patients with either schizophrenia, schizophreniform illness, or primary affective disorder reported a felony conviction.

COMMENT

The results are consistent with those previously obtained from studies of convicted felons. Sociopathy, alcoholism, and drug-dependence are the principal psychiatric disorders associated with serious crime. In fact, except for sexually deviant behavior leading to arrest and conviction, other psychiatric disorders are infrequently associated with felonies. While hysteria is frequent among women felons, felony conviction is infrequent among those suffering from hysteria; further, the comparative infrequency of serious crime among women makes the association of hysteria and crime of little general importance.

The implications of these results are important. To the degree that psychiatrists may be involved in the prevention or treatment of criminality, they must deal chiefly with sociopathy, alcoholism, and drug-dependence. These disorders are generally resistant to currently available treatment. At the same time,

because populations at high risk for these conditions may be easily identified,[17,18] hope for prevention must depend on further research with children and adolescents so recognized. Until more is known about prevention of these conditions, or until more effective treatments are developed, psychiatrists should be modest in their claims.

This investigation was supported in part by Public Health Service research grants AA–00209 and MH–19972.

REFERENCES

1. Menninger, K. *The Crime of Punishment.* New York: The Viking Press, 1968.

2. Szasz, T. Mental illness as an excuse for civil wrongs. *J. Nerv. Ment. Dis.* 147:113–123, 1968.

3. LeVine, W. R., Bornstein, P. E. Is the sociopath treatable? The contribution of psychiatry to a legal dilemma, *Wash. U. Law Quarterly* (1972):693–711.

4. Guze, S. B., et al. Psychiatric illness and crime with particular reference to alcoholism: A study of 223 criminals, *J. Nerv. Ment. Dis.* 134:512–521, 1962.

5. Guze, S. B., Goodwin, D. W., Crane, J. B. Criminality and psychiatric disorders, *Arch. Gen. Psychiatry* 20:583–591, 1969.

6. Cloninger, C. R., Guze, S. B. Psychiatric illness and female criminality: The role of sociopathy and hysteria in the antisocial woman, *Am. J. Phychiatry* 127:303–311, 1970.

7. Guze, S. B., Woodruff, R. A., Jr., Clayton, P. J. Hysteria and antisocial behavior. Further evidence of an association, *Am. J. Psychiatry* 127:957–960, 1971.

8. Woodruff, R. A., Guze, S. B., Clayton, P. J. Unipolar and bipolar primary affective disorders, *Br. J. Psychiatry* 119:33–38, 1971.

9. Woodruff, R. A., Guze, S. B., Clayton, P. J. The medical and psychiatric implications of antisocial personality (sociopathy), *Dis. Nerv. Syst.* 32:712–714, 1971.

10. Guze, S. B., Woodruff, R. A., Clayton, P. J. A study of conversion symptoms in psychiatric out-patients, *Am. J. Psychiatry* 128:643–646, 1971.

11. Guze, S. B., Woodruff, R. A., Clayton, P. J. Secondary affective disorders: A study of 95 cases, *Psychol. Med.* 1:426–428, 1971.

12. Woodruff, R. A., Guze, S. B., Clayton, P. J. Anxiety neurosis among psychiatric outpatients, *Compr. Psychiatry* 13:165–170, 1972.

13. Woodruff, R. A., Guze, S. B., Clayton, P. J. Divorce among psychiatric outpatients, *Br. J. Psychiatry* 121:289–292, 1972.

14. Woodruff, R. A., Clayton, P. J., Guze, S. B. Suicide attempts and psychiatric diagnosis, *Dis. Nerv. Syst.* 33:617–621, 1972.

15. Guze, S. B., Woodruff, R. A., Clayton, P. J. Sex, age, and the diagnosis of hysteria (Briquet Syndrome), *Am. J. Psychiatry* 129: 745–748, 1972.

16. Feighner, J. P., et al. Diagnostic criteria for use in psychiatric research, *Arch. Gen. Psychiatry* 26:57–63, 1972.

17. Robins, L. *Deviant Children Grown Up.* Baltimore: Williams & Wilkins Co., 1966.

18. Glueck, S., Glueck, E. *Predicting Delinquency and Crime.* Cambridge, Mass.: Harvard University Press, 1959.

REPORT ON THE BIOMEDICAL RESEARCH ASPECTS OF BRAIN AND AGGRESSIVE VIOLENT BEHAVIOR

1. Though there is extensive literature on murder, it appears that its prediction is difficult and the role played by such "organic" factors as brain tumors, dementia, epilepsy, etc., is slight, but deserving of further investigation.

2. The dimensions or the validity of the Episodic Dyscontrol Syndrome as a problem of cerebral dysfunction has not been established because of the newness of the proposal and the few reports on the subject.

3. There appears to be an association between the XYY genotype and presence in a mental-penal setting, but the nature and extent of this association are yet to be determined.

4. A surprisingly small number of case reports appear in the literature in regard to focal neuropathological lesions relating to aggressive or violent behavior in man. Rage attacks are more characteristic of hypothalamic lesions. The results of neuropathological lesions in the limbic system in man in regard to violence are poorly documented.

5. Epilepsy appears to be a rare "cause" for violent and aggressive behavior. Though there is some difference in the reported association between temporal lobe epilepsy and violent behavior, most neurologists believe that the relationship is equal to or only slightly higher than in the nonepileptic population.

6. Individuals diagnosed as sociopathic* have a higher incidence of EEG abnormalities (not necessarily epileptiform) than the normal population or than patients with psychoneurosis or schizophrenia. The explanation for this higher incidence of abnormality, such as a possible greater exposure to head trauma, has not been adequately studied.

7. Most reports agree that psychotherapy is ineffective for the symptoms of violence and aggression.

8. Pharmacological treatments have been used in relatively small numbers of patients and without the rigor necessary to appraise the effects accurately. Diphenylhydantoin and lithium may be potentially promising.

9. Operative treatments for patients suffering from severe psychiatric and/or neurological illnesses with intractable violence and aggression have been performed by many

* That is, antisocial personality.

Reprinted with permission from the National Institute of Neurological Diseases and Stroke, National Institute of Health, Department of Health, Education and Welfare.

neurosurgeons. Many responsible neuro-surgeons believe that withholding such therapy from individuals with otherwise uncontrollable violence and aggression may be depriving them of their only chance for assistance and relief. Though, most of these surgical procedures are reported as successful, the evaluation of the outcome is made difficult for the following reasons:

a) The diversity of symptoms in patient selection.

b) The paucity of information regarding the preoperative evaluation.

c) A lack of detail concerning the degree, character, and thoroughness of the follow-up.

d) Ambiguities in regard to additional therapeutic factors, i.e., drugs, psychotherapy, institutionalization, and change in the environmental situation.

SURGICAL TREATMENT FOR AGGRESSION AND VIOLENCE

The discussants are aware of some of the unique features surrounding the use of this modality. Though seemingly beyond the direct assignment to the participants in this review, the matter of informed consent and possible legal restriction is a current issue. Aside from this consideration, the suggestion can be made that surgical procedures should be undertaken only after an adequate trial of other types of treatment. This would be in keeping with the traditional medical model of the treatment of peptic ulcer by diet and antacids before gastric resection, or the use of every major anticonvulsant in epilepsy before surgery is considered. As developed in the body of this report, there are alternatives to surgery; however, they need to be examined for effectiveness with as much rigor as the surgical treatments themselves.

A PSYCHIATRIST VIEWS MENTAL HEALTH LEGISLATION

Thomas S. Szasz, M.D.

I. INTRODUCTION

In our day, when psychiatric mythology and rhetoric reign supreme as the "scientific" assessment of the "mental health" and "mental illness" of individuals, it is of the utmost importance that all thoughtful persons critically examine the principles and practices of modern psychiatry. Moreover, inasmuch as the social power of psychiatry rests squarely on the legal authentication of psychiatric coercion as medical treatment, a critical legal stance toward psychiatric ideas and interventions is especially important.

As will be apparent from a reading of my views, I consider the usual efforts at mental health reform useless, if not positively harmful. The reason for this is simple: Mental

hygiene laws constitute legislation for the control of a special category of persons—namely, the so-called mentally ill. Like legislation for the control of other "deviant" minorities, like Jews or Negroes, legislation for the control of the "mentally ill" may be more or less harsh. In either case, however, those who value individual freedom and dignity—in short, civil libertarians—must condemn and oppose such legislation; hence, they must advocate not its reform but its repeal.

Let me take this opportunity, then, to restate the reasons, as I see them, that compel the civil libertarian to reject all mental health legislation.

1. The term "mental illness" is a metaphor; more particularly, as this term is used in

Excerpted and reprinted with permission from *Washburn Law Review* 9 (1970): 224.

mental health legislation, it is not the name of a medical disease, but is a quasi-medical label concealing conflict as illness, and justifying coercion as treatment.

2. If not for the existence of mental hygiene laws—which create a category of individuals considered "mentally ill" by others, but who either do not consider themselves "mentally ill" or prefer not to be subjected to psychiatric interventions—there would be no need, and indeed no *raison d'être*, for agencies, laws, or organizations for the protection of the rights of so-called mental patients.

3. Inasmuch as it is the task of state Mental Hygiene Departments (and of similar federal agencies and organizations) to administer and enforce the appropriate mental hygiene laws, these agencies should be recognized as the adversaries, and not the allies, of the individual accused of mental illness or treated as an involuntary mental patient.

If the foregoing premises are valid, it follows that, as a matter of principle, no group or organization devoted to the protection of civil liberties should assist or collaborate in the drafting of "better mental hygiene" laws or of laws for the protection of the "rights of mental patients"; but that, instead, such groups should advocate the repeal, at the earliest moment, of all mental hygiene legislation.

I might note, in conclusion, that this position follows logically not only from my view (according to which "mental illness" is a metaphor and a myth), but also from the official view of the major mental health organizations, such as the American Psychiatric Association and the National Association for Mental Health (according to which "mental illness is like any other illness"). For if depression and schizophrenia are like pneumonia and myocardial infarction, then why have special laws for patients suffering from the former diseases but not for those suffering from the latter? And if depression and schizophrenia are not diseases at all, then what justifies mental health laws authorizing the use of the police power of the state for the involuntary "treatment" (by incarceration) of "patients" alleged to be suffering from such fictitious diseases?

Q. This distinction between voluntary and involuntary patients is evidently crucial to your whole thinking about psychiatric problems. Is it because of your view that the psychiatrist deals with human conflicts rather than medical diseases?

A. Yes. But, actually, my analysis of psychiatric problems rests not only on a distinc-

tion between the practice of psychiatry on voluntary and involuntary patients, but also on two related distinctions. The first is that between what constitutes a "psychiatric problem" for the self (the client or patient), and what constitutes such a problem for others (the "patient's" relatives, institutional psychiatrists, etc.); and the second is the distinction between the assumption of the role of "mental patient" by the self and its ascription to others.

Q. Do the people who work in state mental hospitals make this distinction between voluntary and involuntary patients, and the two corresponding kinds of psychiatric interventions?

A. Of course, they realize this distinction privately and I think they often suffer from the conflicts and turmoil of their work. But, officially, they do not make such a distinction. How could they? It would render their work, first, nonmedical—and the institutional psychiatrists, perhaps because what they do is so obviously nonmedical, always insist that their work is medical and can be done only by doctors; and second, it would render it non-therapeutic, indeed, antitherapeutic or noxious. This explains, I think, why institutional psychiatrists—even more than psychoanalysts (though they do it, too)—cast their activities into the idiom and imagery of medicine and therapy. After all, when you control bleeding in an accident victim, you are "treating" the person whether or not he has consented to your intervention. Wouldn't it be just lovely if the same imagery would apply to the maniacal "patient" whose "illness" consists of drinking too much and assaulting his wife, and perhaps also assaulting the policemen who come to take him to the mental hospital? When he is given Thorazine—if necessary, by injection while being held down by burly attendants—is that similar to or different from the accident victim's treatment? And when such a person's imprisonment—for weeks, months, years, often for life—can also be defined as "treatment," as commitment is, obviously we have a professional imagery and rhetoric that's immensely useful for those who deal with involuntary mental patients.

Q. Dr. Szasz, you seem to be opposed to involuntary mental hospitalization under any circumstances. Are there no situations when commitment, involuntary medication, or shock treatment, and similar psychiatric procedures, are good things, useful interventions?

A. There are none. I am unqualifiedly opposed to involuntary mental hospitalization and treatment. To me, it's like slavery: the problem is not how to improve it, but how to abolish it.

From a purely practical point of view, whenever commitment occurs, it *is* indicated or useful. Otherwise it would not occur. Someone has to *want* to commit a person, otherwise that person would not be committed. Now, for the person who wants the commitment, it's useful. It's as simple as that. In other words, commitment is *always* useful for the committers, for the patient's "loved ones," and others who are annoyed or disturbed by him. My analogy between commitment and slavery is not just a dramatic figure of speech. It should be taken quite seriously. When you ask, "When is commitment useful or when it is indicated?" you might as well ask, "When is Negro slavery useful or indicated?" The answer is obvious. Negro slavery is always a good idea for white men, assuming that they prefer not to work and have Negro slaves do the work for them. Similarly, commitment is always a good idea. It's always indicated, for those on the outside, for the "mentally healthy." That's why it's so popular.

Q. But how about the suicidal person? We prevent his suicide, and the chances are that when he recovers from his depression he will thank us for saving his life.

A. You are talking medicalese and psychiatrese. Let's speak English. What depression? What recovery? You have raised a complex moral question but are dealing with it as if it were a medical question. I just won't go along with that.

First, you must ask the question, "Who owns a person's life?" If the person does, then perhaps he has the "right" to destroy it; if he doesn't, then other implications follow. Second, you imply that good ends, namely, the prolongation of life, justify questionable means, namely, locking someone up in an insane asylum and probably stigmatizing him for life. I, for one, don't believe that. Third, you imply that physicians, especially psychiatrists, know when a person is going to kill himself, when he is a "suicidal risk." Well, of course, sometimes they do, and sometimes they don't. But there is obviously nothing easier than to *ascribe* suicidal intent to someone in order to justify controlling him, committing him. You don't say anything about what kinds of safeguards might be necessary to prevent such false ascription, even if one were to grant (as I don't for a minute) that the prevention of suicide by means of force and fraud (that is, involuntary hospitalization and deceptive diag-

nostic rhetoric) is a legitimate psychiatric activity.

Q. Still, what about a person who, having taken an overdose of pills, comes to an emergency room voluntarily thereby putting himself in a position where he can be committed to a mental hospital?

A. Well, of course, that's the way things are now. But by not succeeding with the suicidal act—that is, by not being dead, but instead by being a chemically poisoned, and hence sick, person—such an individual has, in effect, made himself into a medical patient. The proper place to treat him therefore is a medical hospital. Moreover, since he comes to the hospital voluntarily, there is obviously no need to commit him. It is precisely because such a person runs the risk of commitment that he may not go to a doctor or a hospital. Commitment is antitherapeutic. There are people who want medical and other care for their depression or dissatisfaction with life, and their suicidal ideas, and their case is jeopardized by the present concepts and legal status of psychiatry.

Q. How should this be changed?

A. Involuntary mental hospitalization should be abolished just as Negro slavery was abolished. It is an unqualified moral evil. There should be no such thing. There should be no place called a hospital from which a person cannot walk out without any further ado or by signing a piece of paper—that is, leaving against medical advice.

Q. But would it be possible to do away with involuntary mental hospitalization? There are hundreds of thousands of people in mental hospitals, most of them on a committed status. What would happen to them if you just opened the doors and said, "O.K., you can leave"?

Q. Many would stay.

A. Correct. Many would stay because they are poor, disabled, have no other place to go. In this sense, the mental hospital is an asylum. That's a nice, old term for insane asylum—but without the "insane." Civilized people ought to provide such places. The Salvation Army does, for example. Homes for the homeless. Orphanages for adults. But this has nothing to do with medicine. You don't need doctors to run such places. You don't even need psychologists or social workers. Just decent people.

Q. That way there would be no need for medicine or psychiatry to feel guilty that there are so few doctors in state mental hospitals.

A. Right. But it goes further than that. Millions of dollars could be saved that now go to prop up the stage-settings, so to speak, of a fraudulent and wasteful pseudomedical enterprise. This could be spent simply on food and lodging and the kind of help that people who would stay in such places would want and could use, like rehabilitation, job training. Also such a place could be just a haven where people could be left alone, away from annoying relatives.

Q. What about those people who, if there were no commitment, would want to leave, but who are considered dangerous or who are criminals?

A. I should like to refer you to *Law, Liberty, and Psychiatry*, where I answer this question in detail. Briefly, my position is that no one should be deprived of liberty with-out due process of law and, to me, due process includes the concept that the only justification for loss of liberty is the commission of an illegal act. In other words, if someone is suspected of lawbreaking, he should be accused, tried, and, if convicted, sentenced. If the sentence calls for loss of liberty, he should be confined in an institution that's penal, not medical, in character. I don't think doctors should be jailers. That's what hospital psychiatrists are now. I say, a man who locks up someone is a jailer, even if he has an MD and wears a white coat. If jails are bad, and of course many are, they should be improved. Placing lawbreakers, or suspected law-breakers, in mental hospitals against their will is not a proper substitute for prison reform.

ALTERNATIVES TO CIVIL COMMITMENT OF THE MENTALLY ILL: PRACTICAL GUIDES AND CONSTITUTIONAL IMPERATIVES

David L. Chambers

THE PRINCIPLE OF THE LEAST RESTRICTIVE ALTERNATIVE IN CONSTITUTIONAL ADJUDICATION

Stated succinctly, the principle of the least restrictive alternative would require courts to hold that, under state constitutions and the Constitution of the United States, committing courts and agencies must refrain from ordering hospitalization whenever a less restrictive alternative will serve the state's purposes as well or better. The appropriateness of insisting on the exploration of alternatives to hospitalization can be best understood by a brief exposition of the range of occasions when courts have insisted on the use of alternatives in other settings.

The United States Supreme Court has confronted hundreds of cases in which a party complains that the government has reached farther than it needed to achieve its purposes. The Court has responded variously—sometimes overturning legislation when convinced a less restrictive alternative existed and should have been used, sometimes refusing to listen at all to arguments about alternatives, and sometimes mentioning less restrictive alternatives without making clear their relation to the decision rendered.

At least in this century, the Justices have not regarded the principle that government should intrude as little as necessary into the lives of citizens as a principle independently worthy of veneration. In recent decades, when the Court has insisted on the use of a less restrictive alternative, it has done so because of its concern for a constitutionally protected interest at stake (for example, free expression), not because of loyalty to a view (sanctified in the Constitution, if at all, only in the little-used ninth and tenth amendments) that that government governs best which governs least. With their eyes focused on a particular social concern—public safety, free expression, free exercise of religion—the Justices have used the principle as simply one of several

Reprinted with permission from *Michigan Law Review* 70 (1972): 1108, 1145.

useful tools available to them to accommodate important constitutional and legislative interests when they conflict. When a consistent pattern of reliance on the principle appears, it reflects more a period of consistency in the Court's attitude toward a particular constitutional guarantee than an adherence to the principle itself.

In first amendment cases, particularly first amendment cases in which expression is commingled with conduct, the Court has on a few occasions upheld state and federal legislation curtailing free expression when it found no reasonable alternative available for serving the legislature's goal. It thus recently upheld criminal sanctions for the burning of draft cards, finding "the incidental restriction on free speech . . . no greater than essential" for serving the federal government's needs in raising armies.[1] More frequently, however, particularly when the expression at issue involved words rather than conduct, it has done just the reverse, striking down laws, even though the alternatives available to the state were plainly less adequate than the regulation chosen. The constitutional interest in preserving a greater level of free expression simply outweighed the legislative interest in having any regulation stronger than the weaker alternative available to it. In *Butler* v. *Michigan*,[2] for example, the Court held unconstitutional a statute forbidding the sale of books "tending to the corruption of the morals of minors," since it prevented adults from access to the same reading matter. The law was stricken even though a narrower statute—one forbidding the sale of such materials to minors—was almost certain to be less effective in keeping pornography and gore from coming before the eyes of youths.

In commerce clause cases, the Court has been more solicitous of the state's interests, but has still insisted in most, but not all, cases that the state protect its local interests by the means that interfere to the least extent necessary with the flow of interstate commerce.

As new concerns have caught the attention of the Court, the principle continues to serve as an aid in the resolution of conflict. In *Aptheker* v. *Secretary of State*,[3] the Court relied on the federal right to travel to strike down an act of Congress that denied passports for travel outside the Western Hemisphere to members of organizations identified as subversive by the Subversive Activities Control Board. The Court found that the act swept unnecessarily broadly in that the passport denial did not turn on a finding of the degree of the members' participation in the subversive organization or on the purposes or place of the proposed travel. Similarly, in *Shelton* v. *Tucker*,[4] the Court relied on the federal right of free association to invalidate an Arkansas law requiring school teachers to list all organizations to which they belonged. The Court, striving ardently to find a ground to invalidate legislation enacted as part of an effort to cripple the NAACP, again claimed that there were "less drastic means" for protecting the state's "legitimate and substantial" interests.

The principle of the least restrictive alternative offers an obvious possible application to civil commitment. Through commitment, the state seeks to serve its traditional functions of protecting its citizens from injury and providing care and treatment for the ill. However compelling these concerns may be, commitment also intrudes on equally compelling constitutionally based interests of the individual: freedom of movement, freedom of association, and, as I will demonstrate at some length, freedom from physical confinement. The search for alternatives to hospitalization may reveal in individual cases ways that the state's interests can be fully served with little or no constraint on the individual's freedom—that is, in ways that protect almost fully both sets of interests.

Despite the obvious place for the principle in the context of civil commitment and despite the numerous cases above that might support its application, the United States Supreme Court, in a recent decision, may conceivably have foreclosed its application as a requirement of federal constitutional law. In *Sanchez* v. *State*,[5] the New Mexico supreme court abruptly rejected a constitutional argument for application of the principle, distinguishing without comprehensible explanation the Supreme Court decisions cited by Sanchez's lawyer. Sanchez appealed to the United States Supreme Court, relying on *Shelton* and numerous first amendment cases. The Supreme Court dismissed the appeal in a single sentence "for want of a substantial federal question." The dismissal constituted a disposition on the merits and thus may have obliterated any chance of

---

[1] *O'Brien* v. *United States*, 391 U.S. 367, 377 (1968).

[2] 352 U.S. 380, 383–84 (1957).

[3] 387 U.S. 500, 512–14 (1964).

[4] 364 U.S. 479 (1960).

[5] 80 N.M. 438, 457 P.2d 370 (1968), appeal dismissed, 396 U.S. 276 (1969). Much about the New Mexico decision is disheartening. The case involved inordinately compelling circumstances for seizing an alternative. No one claimed that Sanchez posed threats to others, but simply that he was unable to care for himself, and his niece indicated to the court her willingness to provide the necessary care.

establishing a federal constitutional obligation to search for alternatives.

That the federal constitutional questions loom much larger than the Supreme Court implied is indicated by the fact that, since *Sanchez*, two federal courts (probably unaware of *Sanchez*) have indicated that the Constitution requires that alternatives to civil commitment be employed whenever effective for the state's needs. In 1969 in *Covington* v. *Harris*,[6] Judge Bazelon, writing for the Court of Appeals for the District of Columbia Circuit, reaffirmed the court's holding in the *Lake* case and went on to imply strongly that the *Lake* holding had roots in the Constitution: "The principle of the least restrictive alternative consistent with the legitimate purposes of a commitment inheres in the very nature of civil commitment, which entails an extraordinary deprivation of liberty. . . . A statute sanctioning such a drastic curtailment of the rights of citizens must be narrowly, even grudgingly, construed in order to avoid deprivations of liberty without due process of law.[7]

A three-judge federal district court in Pennsylvania also appears to have concluded that the search for alternatives is constitutionally required. In *Dixon* v. *Attorney General*,[8] Circuit Judge Biggs found unconstitutional Pennsylvania's procedure for committing persons to mental hospitals after they had served prison sentences. After a brief discussion of the constitutional infirmities, the court entered an order, with the consent of the parties, that not merely provided for elaborate procedural protections for those facing commitment but also required the hospital involved to explore alternatives before commitment. It further enjoined courts from committing an ill person except upon "a specific finding based on a preponderance of the evidence that placement at [the] Hospital is necessary." Whether this part of the consent order is supported by the court's finding that the Pennsylvania statute was unconstitutional is unclear. Unlike many cases involving consent decress, the court here did make its own findings of unconstitutionality. On the other hand, though the failure of the state courts to determine the need for inpatient hospitalization was one of the inadequacies alleged in the complaint, the issue is not one of those dealt with by the court in its brief discussion of the merits.

So far as I can find, no state court has been asked to decide whether a search for less restrictive alternatives to civil commitment is mandated under its own constitution. More-

over, the only state other than New Mexico asked to address the issue as a federal constitutional question has reached the same result as *Sanchez* even more abruptly. Counsel for an ill person in New York brought many Supreme Court decisions, as well as *Covington*, to a trial court's attention. The trial court dismissed the argument in a single sentence: "Plaintiff's contention as to alternative courses of treatment . . . does not state a constitutional claim (cf. *Lake* v. *Cameron* . . .)"[9]

In 1960, in *Shelton* the Supreme Court stated that whenever "fundamental personal liberties may be stifled" by a state regulation, states must use "less drastic means for achieving the same basic purposes." As we have seen, the Court's actions in other cases before and since have been largely consistent with this general precept. Thus its action in the *Sanchez* case, dismissing out of hand an appeal contending that state courts must explore less restrictive alternatives to commitment, may rest on a judgment, however hastily formed, that civil commitment endangers no "fundamental personal liberties."

Nearly forty state constitutions contain provisions establishing the right of their citizens to life, liberty, and the pursuit of happiness. Some state courts have read this language expansively and viewed it as a substantive limit on the legislature's powers. Many state appellate courts have indeed acknowledged the massive constriction of freedom that civil commitment entails.[10]

The place of freedom from confinement is more uncertain under the United States Constitution than under such state constitutions. Does civil commitment involve intrusions on fundamental personal liberties protected under the federal constitution? Or does it merely impinge on interests that, however important they may tower for the individual, are, like hunger, not a matter of federal constitutional concern? Judge Bazelon in the *Covington* case felt justified in requiring exploration of less restrictive alternatives to commitment by pointing to the "extraordinary deprivation of liberty" it involved. It is indeed hard to accept that there can be any "fundamental personal liberty," to use *Shelton's* term, more fundamental that personal liberty itself, and personal liberty of course, what is at risk in its most literal sense for the mentally ill. Yet, except

[9] *Fhagen* v. *Miller*, 65 Misc. 2d 163, 173, 317 N.Y.S.2d 128, 139 (Sup.Ct.1970), affd., as modified per curiam, 36 App.Div.2d 926, 321 N.Y.S.2d 61 (1971), affd., 29 N.Y.2d 348, 278 N.E.2d 615, 328 N.Y.S.2d 393 (1972).

[10] See, e.g., *State ex rel. Bles* v. *Merrick*, 2 Ohio St. 2d 13, 16, 205 N.E.2d 924, 926 (1965); In re Allison, 336 Mich. 316, 58 N.E.2d 90 (1953).

[6] 419 F.2d 617 (D.C. Cir. 1969).

[7] 419 F.2d at 623.

[8] 325 F.Supp. 966 (M.D. Pa. 1971).

for the cruel and unusual punishment clause and the excessive bail clause, the federal constitution places no explicit substantive limits on "extraordinary deprivations of liberty," providing by its terms only procedural protections. Judge Bazelon, however swift his reasoning, was nevertheless correct.

In short, the curtailment of the rights of travel and association, given the broadened view of those rights, is not a mere incidental side effect of commitment; curtailment of movement and social intercourse is often in fact one of the central purposes of commitment. And that is not the end of the commitment's curtailment of an ill person's liberties. His rights peaceably to assemble, to communicate and receive communications from others, to exercise his religious belief through ceremonies of his choice, and to enjoy his privacy in the company of his spouse, or even someone not his spouse, are all but totally ended.

The frequent insensitivity of American courts to the consequences of imprisonment is no less tragic than their insensitivity to commitment of the mentally ill, but there is at least analytically a significant difference between criminal and civil confinement—not a difference in the degree of the loss of freedom, but rather in the purposes for confinement and their susceptibility to review for alternatives. A principal historical function of the criminal sanction, apparently accepted by the Supreme Court, is retribution. Not so for civil commitment. Civil commitment may in many individual cases be motivated by a desire to punish the ill person for causing the rest of us discomfort, but I have never seen a judicial opinion or commitment statute recognizing punishment as a function of commitment. Thus, in criminal cases, if a state legislature has imposed a mandatory minimum jail term, state courts can do little but defer to the legislature's essentially political judgment about the length of punishment needed to satisfy society's need for revenge. When legislatures have imposed no minimum, state judges could be required to explore whether the community's need for retribution can be satisfied without incarceration—I would be glad to see them compelled to do so—but a judge's conclusions would at least be most difficult for another court to review.

Even if courts distinguished criminal from civil confinement, a holding that commitment of the ill requires scrutiny of lesser alternatives might still carry broad implications. Recognizing the fundamental rights impaired by commitment should all but answer the question of the right to counsel and other procedural protections in commitment proceedings —questions that, somewhat surprisingly, have

not been addressed by the Supreme Court. Moreover, several forms of noncriminal incarceration other than that of the mentally ill might be swept within the reasoning of any case requiring consideration of alternatives of civil commitment. Confinement of the tubercular, the epileptic, the defective delinquent, the retarded, and the juvenile delinquent involve the same curtailments of liberty. As to all of these, I can offer no sensible distinctions to the Court. They require no less attention than commitment of the mentally ill.

If other jurisdictions join the District of Columbia in requiring a search for less restrictive alternatives to commitment, the experience in the District warns that such decisions alone will not ensure that a meaningful search occurs. At least three further steps must be taken: (1) an adequate professional staff must be available to perform the inquiry into alternatives; (2) the court must have the power to compel the cooperation of community facilities the staff locates; and (3) the search must occur before, rather than after, commitment.

If the Constitution does require some sort of institutionalized system to ensure the examination of alternatives, it surely does not compel the adoption of any specific system—so long as the system adopted assures a reasonable likelihood that alternatives can be identified and evaluated. At least three models exist that states might be likely to consider. None is free of problems. Like the problem of choosing alternatives to commitment, each is less satisfactory than one of the others in at least one aspect. Under the first model, to me the most attractive, the responsibility for the search would rest in the hands of trained personnel employed by the court itself. Such a staff, probably best composed primarily of social workers, would be comparable in purpose to the probation officers employed by most juvenile and criminal courts and would be attuned to the functions that the particular judge serves through commitment. A court-based staff might also be able to clothe itself with some of the awesomeness of the judge's office and bedazzle those administering local programs and agencies into cooperation. And, perhaps most important, with the staff under the direction of the judge, the likelihood seems great, given the experience in the area of probation in criminal cases, that he will rely upon and trust their recommendations and, equally important, that he will become personally involved in the development of new community-based programs.

One difference between criminal and civil commitment, however, does complicate the matter: the central role in civil commitment of the diagnosing psychiatrists. Psychiatrists dominate the commitment process in almost all states. Their suggestions regarding commitment have been followed in the vast bulk of cases. It would therefore be highly desirable for the diagnosing psychiatrists to be in a position to work closely with the staff within the court engaged in exploring alternatives. On the other hand, since few well-qualified psychiatrists are likely to be interested in performing diagnostic work only, placing full-time psychiatrists on the court staff may be ill advised. One possible approach would be for the state to assign the entire task of diagnosing and exploring alternatives to a community mental health center. Such a center might be less firmly in touch with the judge's wishes, but would have the advantage of combining in one setting the range of mental health professionals who should contribute to the decision on placement. Operating in a closely analogous manner, at least one community mental health center has saved large numbers of persons from hospitalization by placing two of its social workers in the reception center of the state hospital and diverting to the center "a considerable majority" of those who live in the area it serves.

A second alternative open to the states would be to place the burden of exploring alternatives on the staff of the state hospital to which the patient is to be committed. Most hospitals already employ social workers whose functions include the exploration of community resources. States could thus, without the cost of adding an entirely new staff within the courthouse, expand their existing hospital staffs to ensure the exploration of alternatives for all patients. Because of the appearance of efficiency here, many states, if forced to adopt some system, would probably select this approach. And much can be said for it. Hospital social workers may well be able to work more closely with staff psychiatrists in arranging for the return of the patient to the community and thus avoid altogether the need for a final commitment hearing. On the other hand, there are several great drawbacks to placing sole responsibility in the hospitals. Unless the hospital is equipped to examine patients on an outpatient basis—which many hospitals far from cities are not—it either will be unable to perform the exploration for patients well enough to remain at home pending a hearing or will have to seek the temporary commitment of everyone for diagnosis. How sadly ironic to lock someone in a hospital, even on a short-term basis, simply to permit the staff to decide whether hospitalization is necessary.

Even if the hospital staff can examine the allegedly ill person as an outpatient, the hospital is still objectionable as the search instrument because it is caught in a disquieting conflict of interest in providing advice, a conflict that may raise doubts of constitutional dimensions about the fairness of a hearing in which the judge relies on the hospital's recommendation. Asked to advise about community care for a particular person, hospital staff may well feel consciously or unconsciously the need to justify inpatient care and overstate its probable values. They are certainly likely to appear to do so. Hospitals may also, in general, attract as staff those with the greatest confidence in the efficacy of inpatient care.

A third possible approach is to make available to the ill person himself the resources to examine alternatives. In New York City, for example, the Mental Health Information Service, a governmentally funded agency, provides counsel to persons facing commitment and hires psychiatric social workers to aid the attorneys in search for alternatives. Although New York courts neither acknowledge an obligation to employ the least restrictive alternative nor possess broad enough powers over the other agencies to compel their cooperation, if the courts were so equipped, the model of the Information Service might provide a constitutionally acceptable structure for exploring alternatives. The experience in New York indicates that the Information Service has brought about a decrease in hospitalizations and an increase in out-of-court agreements between counsel and hospital staff for community placement and treatment of the patient. In the District of Columbia the new Public Defender Agency is developing its staff along essentially the same lines and seems to be experiencing similar success. Many states, however, do not now provide counsel to persons facing civil commitment. Those that do generally use a system of court appointments from the regular bar. The abysmal records of such court-appointment systems (under which lawyers are almost uniformly reported to spend little, if any, time preparing for hearings) makes abundantly clear that such systems should be held constitutionally inadequate to ensure that alternatives are explored.

Even with a promising model such as the Mental Health Information Service a danger exists, somewhat like the danger of leaving the task to the hospital, that the agency cannot serve adequately as both advocate for the patient and adviser to the court. If its recommendations are regarded as simply an advocate's posturing, judges might understandably discount them. Perhaps the best system—more elaborate than the Constitution may require—would combine the three models: employing court and hospital personnel for those hospitalized prior to a hearing; employing court and mental health clinic personnel for those remaining in the community prior to the hearing; and providing to all persons counsel who are aided by psychiatric social workers.

The dilemma in civil commitment cases is that both summary commitment and the failure to commit summarily can in the same case produce substantial and irreparable harm—it is a human life that the government is temporarily impounding, not allegedly maggot-infested hams. In any event, state courts seem to have resolved the dilemma consistently in favor of state power to commit prior to a hearing. The New York court of appeals, for example, recently upheld a provision of its code permitting persons to be held for fifteen days without a hearing if simply "alleged to be in need of immediate observation, care or treatment for mental illness."[11]

The New York decision was unsound. Courts might indeed wisely invalidate even a commitment code that limits emergency commitments to those believed necessary to protect the public safety. They could do so either on the basis of the woefully inadequate capacities of psychiatrists and others in the mental health system to predict dangerousness to self or others, or, in a manner comparable to the Supreme Court's actions in some prior-hearing cases, because the risk of grave, even irreparable, harm to the public does not outweigh the interest of the allegedly ill person in his freedom. This belief that the individual's interest in freedom outweighs the community's interest in security does, after all, underlie the constitutionally-based right to bail in criminal cases, and the considerations in civil commitment, though not identical (because, in theory, hospitalization offers treatment), are at least in substantial part the same. Of course, the same argument resting on the individual's interest in his freedom taken to its logical extreme could yield a holding that civil commitment is never permissible whether or not there has been a full hearing.

If courts do insist on permitting temporary commitments before a hearing in some cases—and I can easily conceive of cases in which a total ban on summary commitment would be deeply troubling—the Supreme Court's decision in other areas should probably lead to the following resolution of the issue: In those cases, in which immediate and substantial harm is thought probable for the individual or others, a court may conduct its inquiry into alternatives—and even into illness—while the individual is held on a temporary basis. Nonetheless, the committing court and the hospital should

be required to perform an initial inquiry into alternatives as expeditiously as reasonably possible. Such a rule would permit the summary commitment not only of the suicidal and the assaultive but also of those apparently ill persons who, though not in danger of death, seem likely to deteriorate irretrievably without immediate inpatient care. On the other hand, what the rule would forbid is the common practice today of involuntarily committing in advance of an inquiry into alternatives those who behave peculiarly or are simply unable to care well for themselves but will irreparably harm neither themselves nor others if their commitment is postponed until after a review of alternatives. If hospital doctors would honor this standard—and it will be difficult to enforce otherwise—most patients should be spared inpatient hospitalization until after an inquiry into alternatives.

In setting the timetable for exploring alternatives, courts should insist on explorations not merely before commitment but also after commitment—not merely at the outset of governmental intervention but even after commitment and an initial thorough inquiry. A later inquiry may be especially desirable after a hospitalized person has passed through an acute episode of illness and has entered a more stable period, because finding an alternative then may intercept his transfer within the hospital from a moderately well-staffed intensive treatment ward to the sort of "extended treatment" or "rehabilitation" ward from which too few travelers ever return. Such a continuing inquiry may be seen as required by the principle of the least restrictive alternative itself or may be analyzed as part of the hospital's statutory or constitutional obligation to provide treatment.

In those states that provide for periodic judicial review of commitments by the hospital or by the court, the reviewer should be required to include a reexamination of alternatives as part of its decision on the need for continued confinement. Moreover, the availability of less restrictive alternatives should also be justiciable at habeas corpus hearings of the sort traditionally available to the mentally ill to test whether they remain within the statutory criteria for commitment. In fact, each of the principal District of Columbia decisions dealing with the use of alternatives arose in the context of habeas corpus proceedings, not in the context of appeals from initial commitments.[12]

Catherine Lake, the senile petitioner in the District of Columbia case establishing the obli-

---

[11] *Fhagen* v. *Miller*, 29 N.Y.2d 348, 278 N.E.2d 615, 328 N.Y.S.2d 393 (1972).

[12] *Covington* v. *Harris*, 419 F.2d 617 (D.C. Cir. 1969); *Lake* v. *Cameron*, 364 F.2d 657 (D.C. Cir. 1966).

gation of courts there to examine less restrictive alternatives, spent the remaining five years of her life in a public mental hospital. She died in April 1971, having received no visitors in the last year of her life. She did not need to be in a hospital. In the committing judge's view, a nursing home or similar residential facility providing some substantial measure of supervision, but not totally preventing access to the outside world, would have been sufficient. Such facilities—even ones of the sort the Nader study exposed—were simply unavailable in the District of Columbia for most aged people as poor as Ms. Lake.

For her, the principle of the least restrictive alternative proved a mirage, beckoning with hope and dissolving in disappointment. In many states, the principle would breed similar disappointment for many kinds of patients. In a commitment proceeding in Detroit, a judge told me that there was little point in requiring a search for community alternatives in most mental health cases, because alternatives simply do not exist. Across the country, the development in the last decade of community-based residential and outpatient programs for the mentally ill has been rapid, but has simply not kept pace with the demand. Nor has it kept pace with the research indicating their potential.

The failure to develop more extensive community-based programs poses a simple but perplexing question: For how much longer shall government be permitted to deny people their freedom, when it might easily develop programs and facilities that would permit both freedom and the service of the government's legitimate goals? Recall the simplicity of the alternative to incarceration found so successful in Pasamanick's experimental program in Louisville: seriously psychotic patients lived at home on medication, with periodic visits from nurses. If such a home-based program really would serve the state's interests, should the state nevertheless be permitted to continue indefinitely to hospitalize such people against their will by simply refusing to develop such programs? I am certain that the tone of my questions conveys my belief that the state should not be permitted to do so. But I do have a less rhetorical question more difficult to answer: By what process can citizens compel their states to reshape their mental health programs?

The obvious and traditional route for change has been the political process—through the ballot and pleas to the legislature. In the past few years, however, many legislatures, facing costs rising faster than revenues, have either pared the budgets of mental health programs or cut back on their rate of expansion. The

mental health lobby, though ardent, is neither rich nor widely feared. In some states, courts may be able to prompt legislatures to act. Two theories for judicial intervention can be offered: the developing right to treatment and the principle of the least restrictive alternative. Each may be instrumental in forcing change, yet at the same time responsive to the appropriate interests of the states.

Courts that have shaped a justiciable right to treatment for patients in hospitals have reasoned that, under the due process clause, states cannot be permitted to lock people up for their care and treatment and then fail to provide—or make a bona fide effort to provide —a decent level of care. Applied until recently only in suits brought by individual patients to secure their own treatment or release, the right has excited considerable interest within the legal profession and alarm among many psychiatrists, but has spurred little, if any, improvement in the quality of care provided in institutions.

In the past year, however, a right-to-treatment suit with spurs and considerable promise has been flourishing in a federal district court in Alabama. In this case, *Wyatt* v. *Stickney*,[13] patients involuntarily committed to two large state hospitals, brought a class action against the hospital administrators, alleging a violation of their constitutionally protected right to treatment. Two prestigious national mental organizations and the Department of Health, Education, and Welfare joined them as amici curiae. After an extensive trial, Chief Judge Frank M. Johnson found that many patients received no treatment whatever and others only treatment that fell well below any standard of minimal adequacy. He then ordered the state to move rapidly to provide "such individual treatment as will give each [patient] a realistic opportunity to be cured or to improve his or her mental condition"; subsequently he entered a further order fixing detailed standards by which the adequacy of the care at these hospitals will be judged. He expressly warned that he will not consider lack of staff or facilities a justification for providing less than adequate care. Indeed, in a phase of the suit attacking the particularly inhuman condi-

[13] One of the many orders in the case can be found at 325 F. Supp. 781 (M.D. Ala. 1971). A recent article is Drake, *Enforcing the Right to Treatment: Wyatt v. Stickney*, 10 *Am. Crim. L. Rev.* 587 (1972). The papers in the case can be obtained through the counsel for the amici curiae, American Psychological Association, American Orthopsychiatric Association, and American Civil Liberties Union: The Center for Law and Social Policy, 1600 20th St., N.W., Washington, D.C. 20009.

tions at an institution for the retarded, he has ordered the state either to close the institution or to hire 300 new personnel within four months.

The Wyatt litigants and Judge Johnson have, quite understandably, concerned themselves almost solely with the quality of care within Alabama's deplorable institutions. And courts in general might hold that, if a state provides "adequate" care within its institutions, the right to treatment does not require the creation of community-based facilities. The implications of the right-to-treatment cases, however, extend much further. Courts could appropriately hold that, given the known shortcomings of inpatient hospitalization, a state can be considered to provide "adequate treatment" for those whom it seeks to control against their will only by creating community-based programs as a supplement to institutional care.

The principle of the least restrictive alternative can reach as far as the right to treatment. Far less brittle in its logic, the principle, even in its most simply stated form, can justify a holding that states must not restrain a person in a mental hospital if fully as effective programs that are less restrictive of liberty might be employed—whether or not such programs are currently in existence in the state.

The hardest problem for lawyers interest in bringing suits of this sort will be to develop acceptable standards for determining just how high a price governments should be compelled to pay. Few, if any, of the Supreme Court cases that have insisted on the use of alternatives that were not yet created have compelled the creation of programs nearly so costly as vast new community-based alternatives to commitment. *Wyatt* in its present form may well cost Alabama annually millions of dollars in scarce revenues; if the suit's scope were expanded to demand an adequate system of outpatient care, many more millions might be entailed each year. Even if the state could offset much of the cost by closing down parts of its hospitals and rechanneling the savings into the required new programs, a court order might still have the impact of taking jobs away from many current hospital personnel or, at the least, of forcing a massive relocation and retraining of personnel.

Under either theory, further difficulties exist, wholly apart from dollar or resource cost, in determining the criteria for judging what sorts of community-based programs should be required. The right to treatment, typically held to require "adequate" care, might be found to demand an "adequate" system of community care tailored to aid the ill in avoiding hospitalization or rehospitalization. Unfortunately, even less agreement exists today about the components of an adequate system of community care than about the components of adequate hospital care. Complicating matters even more, the principle of the least restrictive alternative might seem, at least at first blush, to demand not merely "adequate" community-based programs, but rather the optimum—those programs, regardless of cost, that will permit the maximum number of ill persons to avoid hospitalization while serving the goals the states seek through commitment. Citing the principle, courts might conceivably demand dozens of new outpatient clinics, scores of well-staffed, humane nursing homes, and troops of trained visiting nurses.

In the end, perhaps only Congress and the legislatures can assure the development of alternatives to hospitalization. Many states have made encouraging beginnings. But Congress and the President have failed to uphold their side of a bargain the federal government initiated. Substantially greater development of alternatives may come into being only if community mental health proves irresistibly cheap, which is possible but unlikely, or if legislators accept the mentally ill as human beings whose self-worth and dignity deserve as much protection as their own. If that realization ever dawns, of course, legislators might put an end to involuntary commitment altogether. The issue of court-compelled use of alternatives would then vanish and with it the need for exhausting articles like this one.

SUGGESTIONS FOR ADDITIONAL READING

Allen, Ferster, and Weihofen. *Mental Impairment and Legal Incompetency*. Englewood Cliffs, N.J.: Prentice-Hall, 1968.

Andalman, E., and Chambers, D. "Effective Counsel for Persons Facing Civil Commitment," *Mississippi Law J.* 45 (Jan. 1974): 43.

Baynes, T. "Continuing Conjectual Concepts

Concerning Civil Commitment Criteria." *American Psychologist* 489 (1972).

Brakel, S., and Rock, R. *The Mentally Disabled and the Law* (revised ed.). Univ. of Chicago Press, 1971.

Chesler, P. *Women and Madness*. N.Y.: Doubleday & Co., 1972; Avon Books, 1973.

Committee on Laws Pertaining to Mental Disorders. Report: Study of the Commission on Mental Health of the District of Columbia. Judicial Conference of the District of Columbia, pub. November 1, 1969.

Ennis, B. *Prisoners of Psychiatry: Mental Patients, Psychiatrists, and the Law*. N.Y.: Harcourt, Brace & Jovanovich, 1973.

Golten, R. "On Casting the First Stone," *MH*, vol. 57, no. 3 (Summer 1973): 12.

Harris, A. "Mental Illness, Due Process and Lawyers," 55 *A.B.A.J.* (Jan. 1966): 65.

Hearings before the Subcommittee on Constitutional Rights of the Senate Judiciary Committee, 87th Congress (1961) and 88th Congress (1963).

Hearings before the Subcommittee on Constitutional Rights of the Senate Judiciary Committee, 91st Congress (1969 and 1970) on Constitutional Rights of the Mentally Ill.

Holzman, P., and Schlesinger, H. "On Becoming a Hospitalized Psychiatric Patient," *Bulletin of the Menninger Clinic*, vol. 36, no. 4 (July 1972): 383.

Lehmann and Mathiasen. *Guardianship and Protective Services for Older People*. National Council on the Aging, 1963.

Lindman and McIntyre (eds.). *The Mentally Disabled and the Law*. Chicago: University of Chicago Press, 1961.

Mental Illness and Due Process. Report of the Special Committee of the Association of the Bar of the City of New York, in Cooperation with Cornell Law School. Ithaca: Cornell University Press, 1962, chapters 2–6.

Note, *Harv. L. Rev.* 79 (1966): 1288.

Note, "The Language of Involuntary Mental Hospitalization: A Study in Sound and Fury," *Journal of Law Reform* 4 (Winter 1970): 195.

Practising Law Institute, The Mental Health Law Project. *Legal Rights of the Mentally Handicapped* (3 vols.), 1974.

Rappeport, J. (ed.). *The Clinical Evaluation of the Dangerousness of the Mentally Ill*. Springfield, Ill.: C. C Thomas, 1967.

Rock, R., et al. *Hospitalization and Discharge of the Mentally Ill*. Univ. of Chicago Press, 1971.

Ross, "Commitment of the Mentally Ill: Problems of Law and Policy," *Mich. L. Rev.* 57 (1959): 945.

Stetler and Moritz, *Doctor and Patient and the Law*, 4th ed. St. Louis: C. V. Mosby, 1962, pp. 179–93.

Symposium: "Mental Illness, The Law and Civil Liberties," 13 *Santa Clara Lawyer*, No. 3, 1973.

Weihofen, H. *Legal Services and Community Mental Health Centers*. American Psychiatric Association, 1969.

Annotation: "Right to Relief Under Federal Civil Rights Act of 1871 (42 USCS Sec. 1983) for Alleged Wrongful Commitment to or Confinement in Mental Hospital," 16 ALR FED 440, 1973.

Annotation: "Liability for Malicious Prosecution Predicated Upon Institution of, or Conduct in Connection with Insanity Proceedings," 30 ALR 3d 455, 1970.

10

The Rights of the Mentally Impaired

INTRODUCTION

Legal recognition of "patient's rights" is so new that five years ago, when the first edition of this book was published, it did not include a chapter on this topic.

At that time any author who referred to the "right to treatment" provision in the Ervin Act, the *Rouse* decision, and a few statutory provisions dealing with mechanical restraint, electroshock, and correspondence rights had covered the law on the subject. Today, it is difficult to send a book to press, as each day seems to bring a new precedent-breaking case.

This chapter does not purport to be an exhaustive compilation of the statutes, cases, and literature bearing on patients' rights. Instead, it focuses attention on the main developments and the problems involved in implementation. It also shows that once right to treatment was recognized, related rights, such as the right to refuse treatment and the right to receive the same benefits and services as the general public, also began to receive attention.

The organization of the chapter reflects this development. The McGarry and Kaplan article gives the historical background of the recognition of patients' rights and an overview of the subject. Section A, "Right to Treatment," starts with the two classic cases on the subject: *Rouse* v. *Cameron* and *Wyatt* v. *Stickney*. "Unanswered," the Robitscher and the Morris articles all deal with implementation problems.

The next section, which concerns the right to refuse treatment, is introduced by Kittrie's questions about the extent to which treatment should be forced. The other selections deal with such drastic treatment measures as behavior modification, electroshock, psychosurgery, and sterilization. The arguments for and against the use of such treatments are discussed, as well as the problems in requiring informed consent for them.

The last section deals, oddly enough, with the question whether the mentally impaired are entitled to the same rights as other citizens. Until fairly recently, they were deprived of most rights on the assumption that they were incapable of exercising them. Another reason, less often articulated, was that giving the impaired rights to an education (as in *Mills* v. *Board of Education*) or paying them for their labor (as in *Souder* v. *Brennan*) is very expensive.

OVERVIEW: CURRENT TRENDS IN MENTAL HEALTH LAW

A. Louis McGarry, M.D., and Honora A. Kaplan, M.P.A., J.D.

HISTORICAL BACKGROUND

In earlier times the primary concern of legislation relating to mental illness was the protection and security of society. In colonial America there were laws relating only to the violent and indigent insane. The violent insane were generally treated as common criminals

Excerpted and reprinted with permission from *American Journal of Psychiatry* 130, 6 (June 1973): 621.

and incarcerated in jails so "that they do not damify others" (2, p. 80). The indigent or dependent insane were dealt with no differently than paupers. Going as far back as 1639, communities enacted repressive stettlement laws that penalized paupers and vagabonds, and the dependent insane often roamed the countryside, literally without a home.

During the second half of the 18th century and during the early 19th century, when local communities began to deal with mental illness in a more organized fashion, jails and poorhouses were again used as solutions for the violent and indigent insane. There were, however, no statutes during this period that related to commitment of the mentally ill. Since only the violent or indigent were involved, commitment was easily accomplished. "A few words hastily scribbled on a chance scrap of paper . . . and the deed was done" (3, p. 62).

The early 19th century and the Age of Reason brought significant reform, albeit short-lived, to the treatment of the mentally ill. Due in large part to the ideas of Rush, Pinel, and Tuke, treatment and cure (rather than incarceration and punishment) seemed possible. The philosophy of "moral treatment" advocated the resocialization of the mentally ill individual within an institutional setting where his social and physical environment could be completely and therapeutically structured.

To carry out the precepts of moral treatment a few asylums or special institutions exclusively for the insane were developed in a number of states.[1] In response to the warm and open therapeutic milieu in these facilities, as well as to selective admission policies, the asylums providing moral treatment achieved impressive success. This "cult of curability," coupled with the effective humanitarian crusades for better care and treatment for the insane led by Dorothea Dix, resulted in the establishment of a network of public facilities for the insane in addition to those under private auspices. However, procedures for commitment remained undefined by statute.

The assumption by the government of broad responsibility for the mentally ill, who were viewed as a distinctly separate group, represented a significant change in public policy. However, public institutions for the mentally disabled could no longer be selective in their admission policies. Within a short period of time public hospitals exceeded their bed capacities, while patient turnover was almost non-existent. State facilities thus evolved into custodial, rather than therapeutic, entities, differing little from other kinds of custodial institutions, such as jails and poorhouses.

During this period of rapid growth of public asylums, a concern for the rights of the individual who had been committed to such a facility began to develop. This interest resulted more from public anxiety over the wrongful commitment of the sane than from a desire to protect the rights and liberty of the mentally ill. A vigorous campaign for strict commitment laws to prevent wrongful detention was led by Mrs. E.P.W. Packard, who herself had been confined in a mental hospital in Illinois for three years. Consequently, during the 1870s a number of states enacted fairly rigorous commitment laws, some of which included a jury determination of insanity. (Ironically, the jury trial resulted in more commitments of sane individuals than had ever been the case under any other procedure [4].) Legally, this period has been characterized as the "romance with the criminal law" (5). The overly legalistic approach to mental illness and civil commitment "contributed in no small degree to the stigma attached to mental disease" (3, p. 438). Because these statutes utilized the criminal-judicial model, they promoted the public's identification of civilly committed persons with criminals and thus created anxiety and isolation in the management of these patients.

Despite the advances in psychiatric knowledge and treatment that ensued in the 20th century, there was no major impetus for changing commitment laws until the middle of the century. After World War II, there was a growing conviction in the psychiatric community that the criminal law features of commitment statutes, including such concepts as notice and judicial hearings, were detrimental to the treatment of mental illness. During this period of "the romance with psychiatry" (5), model legislation was drafted that dispensed with criminalistic terminology, jury trials, and judicial procedures to decide the issue of commitment (6, pp. 454–475). New statutory provisions permitting commitment for varying periods of time based wholly on psychiatric certifications (rather than on judicial determinations) reflected this approach.

More recently there has been another shift, involving a "significant disenchantment . . . with both restrictive and punitive legal barriers and excessive reliance on psychiatric judgment" (5). There has been a growing attack on what is regarded as paternalism, particularly on the part of institutional administrators and

---

[1] The first private facilities were Friends Hospital, Philadelphia (1817); Bloomingdale Asylum, N.Y. (1817); and McLean Asylum, Mass. (1818). Among the early public institutions were the hospital at Williamsburg, Va. (1773), Eastern Kentucky State Hospital and South Carolina State Hospital (1824), and Worcester State Hospital, Mass. (1833).

clinicians. In contrast to the law of the past hundred years, which focused primarily on commitment procedures, increasing attention is now being paid to the rights, treatment, and living conditions of the mentally ill and retarded *after* they have been admitted to mental health facilities.

With the widespread growth of the open-door policy in mental health facilities and with the increase in voluntary admissions during the past two decades, we have entered an era in mental health law that might be called a "romance with the community."

JUDICIAL DECISIONS

Only in recent years have the courts been used to any significant degree as a forum for the mentally ill and mentally retarded.

While a comprehensive compilation of judicial decisions relating to the mentally disabled is beyond the scope of this paper, we will attempt to categorize and evaluate the impact of some of these decisions.

Right-to-Treatment Decisions

Of major significance is the recent line of cases recognizing the right to treatment of institutionalized mentally ill and mentally retarded persons. Beginning with the landmark decision in *Rouse v. Cameron* (7) in 1966, the District of Columbia Circuit Court of Appeals held that mental patients committed by criminal courts had the right to adequate treatment. The mental condition of such persons had resulted in their being found not guilty by reason of insanity; in the absence of criminal responsibility, punishment and incarceration were precluded. Although criminal commitment to a high-security mental hospital for therapeutic care and treatment would be both appropriate and constitutional, such confinement *without adequate treatment* was held tantamount to incarceration, thus transforming the hospital into a penitentiary. The *Rouse* decision stated that "the purpose of involuntary hospitalization is treatment, not punishment"; adequate treatment was in effect held to be the sine qua non of such criminal commitments. Two years later, again in the context of criminal commitments to mental hospitals, Massachusetts extended the right to treatment to persons found incompetent to stand trial (8).

In 1971, in response to a class action, an Alabama Federal District Court further extended the right to adequate treatment to *all* mentally ill and mentally retarded persons who were in institutions involuntarily, whether their commitments were under civil or criminal procedures (1). Moreover, the court based its decision on a constitutional guarantee of the right to treatment: "To deprive any citizen of his or her liberty upon the altruistic theory that the confinement is for humane therapeutic reasons and fail to provide adequate treatment violates the very fundamentals of due process" (1, p. 785).

Dissatisfied with the state plan for improvement of facilities required by the court in its first order (1, p. 785) and utilizing contributions and suggestions of a panel of national mental health experts, the court issued an order in April 1972 (9) that detailed the criteria for adequate treatment in three areas: 1) a humane psychological and physical environment, 2) a qualified staff with a sufficient number of members to administer adequate treatment, and 3) individualized treatment plans. However, the focus in the 1972 *Wyatt v. Stickney* order is exclusively on the allocation and expenditure of state funds for mental health institutions. Given limited resources for mental health services, the widespread application of the explicit and comprehensive *Wyatt* standards and requirements could be antithetical to the general movement toward community alternatives to institutional care. In October 1972, Judge Johnson, who wrote the *Wyatt* opinion, further applied its holding to require adequate medical treatment, including psychiatric services for prison inmates (10). In sharp contrast to these holdings a federal district court in the same Circuit (Georgia) held that determinations regarding the quality of mental health services and the adequacy of treatment rest with the "elected representatives of the people" and not with the courts (11).

These cases involved patients involuntarily committed under civil or criminal law. The increasing utilization of voluntary admissions to mental hospitals substantially mitigates the "incarceration" component of involuntary hospitalization. However, while the issue of adequacy of treatment for voluntarily admitted patients has not yet been addressed by the courts, there is no medical, legal, or ethical justification for compromising the quality of care and treatment at a mental health facility because of the legal status of the recipient. Minimum standards for adequate treatment should be no different, and certainly no lower, for voluntary patients than for involuntary patients. The constitutional guarantee of equal protection under the laws, particularly when one is dealing with state facilities, should mandate such a result.

Mental Retardation Law Suits

While *Wyatt v. Stickney* encompassed the rights of both the mentally ill and mentally retarded, there have been a number of recent cases that have specifically focused on the legal interests of the mentally retarded. Class actions on behalf of mentally retarded residents in state facilities have been brought in New York (12, 13), in Massachusetts (14), in Illinois (15, 16), and unsuccessfully (pending appeal) in Georgia (11). As in the *Wyatt* model, the plaintiffs seek the establishment and implementation of standards for adequate treatment and the improvement of the physical plant and treatment services. In the area of patient labor, class suits are under way in Tennessee (17) and in Florida (18) alleging the unconstitutional servitude of mentally retarded residents required to perform services in state facilities.

In an important decision in Pennsylvania in 1971, a federal court ordered that all mentally retarded children there be accorded access to a free public education program appropriate to their learning capacities (19). The potential impact of this decision on the custodial mental retardation facility could be enormous. In the District of Columbia plaintiffs in a class action had been suspended from school because of mental, behavioral, physical, or emotional handicaps or deficiencies. The court initially ordered the reenrollment of the named plaintiffs and the identification and readmission of other members of the class. In March 1972, judgment was made in favor of the plaintiffs, although the detailed order has not yet been handed down (20). In California a suit is currently being brought on the grounds of denial of education to a mentally retarded child in response to the state's attempt to terminate her placement in a state facility because of her "noneducability" (21). To date, the court has enjoined the state from interfering with the child's education until a final judicial determination is made.

Inaccurate and arbitrary classification and placement of mentally retarded children and the denial of their right to education is the basis for pending law suits in California (22), Louisiana (23), and New York (24). Other pending right-to-education suits are being brought in Michigan (25) and in North Carolina (26), others deal with autistic children (California) (27), special education in general (Delaware) (28), and emotionally disturbed children (Massachusetts) (29).

In addition to the broad categories of the right-to-treatment and mental retardation cases discussed here there have been several decisions delineating other rights of the mentally disabled. In *Commonwealth v. Wiseman* (30) the Massachusetts Supreme Judicial Court established the right to privacy of institutionalized mental patients and prohibited their

commercial exploitation. This was particularly significant since there had been no legal recognition of the right to privacy for anyone in Massachusetts until this decision (31, 32). In New York a federal court held that an involuntarily committed mental patient whom the court had not found incompetent was constitutionally guaranteed the right of refuse certain kinds of treatment because of religious beliefs (33). Still another court held that it would not permit the sterilization of a mental retardate who had given birth to two illegitimate children because the patient was unable to give consent (34).

While there are decisions and statutes in other jurisdictions that conflict with and contradict these cases, the examples cited here do represent some of the current judicial thinking in the area of mental health and retardation. Moreover, it is suggested that these decisions will have an impact beyond their jurisdictions. While the *Rouse* decision was narrowly grounded in a statutory right to treatment, subsequent decisions have not been legislatively derived.[2] Partially in response to the right-to-treatment decisions, legislative proposals have begun to reflect this legal concept (35) [Fla Stats ss 394.459 (1), (2), (3)].

The initial *Wyatt v. Stickney* order (1) required the State of Alabama to devise and submit a plan to the court for upgrading state institutions for the mentally disabled. This mechanism of administrative response and solution under judicial supervision has been emulated elsewhere (14, 36). In New York State the public furor resulting from the Willowbrook exposé and lawsuit (20) apparently resulted in the restoration of $5 million to the state budget. While such measures cannot be exclusively attributed to recent decisions protecting the legal rights of the mentally disabled, the impact of these landmark cases has most likely been significant.

As noted before, case law is essentially a response to past injustices and wrongs; appropriate redress is traditionally made to particular persons in particular situations. Thus judicial solutions, while occasionally broadly and innovatively applicable, are ordinarily limited in scope and tied to the past.

Statutory Change

Comprehensive and prospective legal change in protecting the rights of and providing services to the mentally disabled can be found primarily in legislative measures. In the past

---

[2] *Wyatt* v. *Stickney* (1) was based on constitutional grounds.

few years a number of states have enacted new legislation or have recodified and amended their existing statutes relating to mental health and mental retardation. An examination of some of these new laws has suggested several trends, or at least common problem areas for which legislative solutions have been undertaken. There is clearly no single or uniform method of dealing with these areas; what these new statutes have in common is a comprehensive attempt to correct the deficiencies of the past.

Areas of Change

The trends and changes in the new mental health statutes are generally in response to two broad problem areas: 1) the debilitative and dysfunctional effects of long-term custodial institutionalization, and 2) the neglect and, indeed, the abrogation of the rights and personal dignity of individuals committed to hospitals for indeterminate periods of time. The thrust of new mental health legislation has thus been toward shorter hospital stays, community alternatives to institutionalization, legal protection of the patient's rights, and substantial guarantees of the quality of treatment while under the care of the facility.

New Statutory Trends Related to Institutionalization

Variety of admission statuses. Less than 25 years ago "the World Health Organization reported that only 13,848 of 138,253 admissions to state mental hospitals in the United States, slightly more than 10%, were voluntary" (6, p. 17). Stated conversely, almost 90 percent of these patients had been involuntarily committed to mental institutions. In contrast to this almost monolithic system of hospitalization, more recent statutes provide a number of alternative routes to hospitalization and a variety of admission statuses. In addition to involuntary admissions there are the informal voluntary admissions based on the general hospital model [e.g., Pa Stats Title 50 s 4402; Ill Stats ch 91½ s 4-1; NY Mental Hyg Law s 31.15]. Another (and more common) voluntary admission status is a limited or conditional one in which release requires written notice and a lapse of generally three to ten days [e.g., Pa Stats Title 50 s 4403; Fla Stats s 394.465; Ga Code s 88-503; NY Mental Hyg Law s 31.13]. There are also pretreatment statuses such as emergency [e.g., Fla Stats s 394.463 (1); Ga Code s 88-504; Ill Stats ch 91½ s 7-1; Minn Stats s 253A.04], diagnostic [Pa Stats Title 50 s 4406], and evaluative [Fla Stats s 394.463 (2); Ga Code s 88-505.2; Calif Welf & Instits Code ss

5200, et seq] admissions that are usually of short duration and often precede admission for planned care and treatment.

Several legislative provisions explicitly state a presumption or a preference for voluntary admissions. "It shall be the duty of all state and local officers . . . to encourage any person suitable therefor and in need of care and treatment for mental illness to apply for admission as a voluntary or informal patient" [NY Mental Hyg Law ss 31.21(a), 31.23; see also Fla Stats s 394.465; Ga Code s 88-503]. In Massachusetts the right to conditional voluntary status and notice of that right on admission are absolute [Mass Gen Laws ch 123 s 12(c)].

The diversity in admission statuses, as well as the documented increase in the numbers of voluntary admissions to mental hospitals (6, pp. 17, 48), indicates substantial legislative effort to put an end to hospital stays of unlimited duration in which the patient could not initiate his discharge or his release. It also represents an increasing sophistication and an accommodation of the hospitalization episode to the particular needs of the particular patient. Finally, it represents enhanced emphasis on the rights of mentally disabled persons to freedom of movement and to self-determination.

Classification of mentally ill and mentally retarded persons. One of the disparate elements of the new mental health statutes is their inconsistent manner of classifying or categorizing mentally ill and mentally retarded persons. Nowhere is the terminology uniform from one state to another. This is partly the product of the differential variety of admission statuses available under the new laws. There are other distinctions as well. For example, eligibility for consenting admission to facilities often depends on age, ranging from 14 years in Georgia (Ga Code s 88-503] and Florida [Fla Stats s 394.465] to 18 years in most states [e.g., Pa Stats Title 50 s 4402, et seq; Ill Stats ch 91½ s 5-2; Minn Stats s 253A.03]. This disparity reflects the ambiguity in classifying adolescents as either children or adults.

In the past the law has generally not differentiated among disabilities; mental illness, epilepsy, mental retardation, and senility have often been jumbled together into a single statutory provision. Of special significance in recent legislative reform has been the degree of awareness and sophistication in particularizing these disabilities. For example, mental retardation has been clearly differentiated from mental illness: "A mentally retarded person may be considered mentally ill provided that no mentally retarded person shall be considered mentally ill solely by virtue of his mental retardation" [Mass Gen Law ch 123 s 1]. Moreover, the new laws specifically require the development of services that are adapted and appropriate to the needs of the mentally retarded (rather than acquiescing to watered-down mental health programs). Finally, there is awareness of variations within mental retardation: levels or degrees of retardation have now been recognized in statute and regulation [Mass Gen Laws ch 123 s 2; Mass Dept of Mental Health Regulation MR 116].

Few of the recent mental health statutes have reformed procedures relating to the category of the psychiatric offender, i.e., the mentally ill person who is within the criminal law system. Generally, provisions relating to this area will be found in the criminal statutes. With few exceptions [e.g., Pa Stats Title 50 ss 4407, et seq; Mass Gen Laws ch 123 ss 13-19] procedures governing the mentally ill criminal offender have tended to be neglected even in those states which have undergone substantial revision of their mental health statutes. There is a risk here that when civil statutes governing the mentally ill become procedurally complex or when standards for civil commitment become more restrictive, recourse to simpler criminal procedures may increase. Thus in California, with its new, restrictive civil procedures, an increase in the use of criminal procedures has been reported (37). It is a relatively simpler matter to allege "disorderly conduct" or "disturbing the peace" against a mentally ill person and bring about commitment in a mental hospital based on the question of his competency to stand trial.

However, attention is being focused on this area in case law (38, 39). Indeed, a recent decision by the United States Supreme Court stated: "Considering the number of persons affected, it is perhaps remarkable that the substantive constitutional limitations on this power [to commit mentally ill persons] have not been more frequently litigated" (39, p. 737). It is likely that statutory reform will eventuate in the area of the mentally ill offender.

Limitations on involuntary commitment. Closely linked to the greater variety of admission statuses and to the increasing use of voluntary admission have been significant limitations on the wholesale use of involuntary commitment. Indeed, a primary purpose of the new California mental health law is "to end the inappropriate, indefinite and involuntary commitment of mentally disordered persons . . ." [Calif Welf & Instits Code s 5001(a)]. The statutory standard for involuntary commitment has become somewhat more stringent in a number of states, contributing to a decreasing number of involuntary commitments. In 1959, only five states restricted involuntary hospitalization to those who were "dangerous." Ten years later nine states utilized dangerousness as the sole criterion for involuntary commitment, while 18 others permitted the need for care and treatment (or the welfare or best interests of the patient or society) to serve as alternative bases to dangerousness for involuntary hospitalization (6, p. 36). In 1971, Massachusetts adopted the concept of "likelihood of serious harm" (i.e., dangerousness) as its standard for commitment [Mass Gen Laws ch 123 ss 7, 8, 12]. It should be noted that in 1971, Massachusetts specifically rejected the concept of "social harm" (other than physical harm) as a basis for commitment; prior to this time, Massachusetts had been alone in its use of this standard (6, p. 36). New York, in a statute that became effective January 1, 1973, utilizes the standard of "likelihood of serious harm" for some commitments (NY Mental Hyg Law s 31.37], while Missouri in a 1969 law introduced "dangerousness" as one of its standards for commitment [Mo Stats s 202.800].

New statutory restrictions on involuntary commitment have had an effect on the institutionalization of the mentally retarded. In Massachusetts, for example, there can be no involuntary commitment of mentally retarded persons who are not also mentally ill [Mass Gen Laws ch 123 ss 1, 7(a)]. In some of the newer statutes providing for the involuntary commitment of the mentally retarded, the standard for commitment is distinct from that for commitment of the mentally ill; in New York it is limited to a person ". . . in need of inpatient care and treatment as a resident in a school, [where] such care and treatment is essential to his welfare and [where] his judgment is so impaired that he is unable to understand the need for such care and treatment" [NY Mental Hyg Law s 33.01].

Procedurally, involuntary commitment may be accomplished through the courts or through the medical certification of mental disability by a psychiatrist. In some of the new statutes a variety of commitment mechanisms have evolved, each appropriate to the particular involuntary status involved. For example, medical certification is often utilized for brief periods of involuntary hospitalization, such as emergency care [e.g., Pa Stats Title 50 s 4405 (ten days); Mo Stats s 202.795 (five days); Minn Stats s 253.04 (three days)]. (One court has held that involuntary commitment by medical certification for an indeterminate period of time is unconstitutional [39]. Judicial commitment usually relates to longer commitments and is accompanied by the full panoply of legal protections such as notice, hearing, representation by counsel, and so forth [Mass Gen Laws ch 123 s 5; Minn Stats s 253A.07; Ill Stats ch 91½ ss 8, 9; Ga Code s 88-507, et seq; Fla Stats s 394.67]. Falling somewhere between these procedures is a quasi-judicial or administrative commitment carried out by hearing officers [Fla Stats s 394.457 (6); Ga Code s 88-506]. It should be noted that administrative commitment is subject to judicial review [Fla Stats s 394.547 (6)(e)] (6, p. 57).

These statutory measures serve to restrict the availability and unnecessary utilization of involuntary commitment for long periods of time. In so doing they force closer scrutiny of the clinical status and particular needs of the mentally disabled individual and militate against the neglect of institutionalized patients.

Orientation of facilities toward the community. A number of the new mental health laws reflect the general shift in mental hospital treatment toward "open-door" policies and the effort to abolish locked and neglected back wards. New statutory provisions set forth explicit internal procedures for patient management and for administration of the institutions. For example, some provisions were designed to result in shorter patient stays, as we discussed previously Others mandate periodic clinical review (Ill Stats ch 91½ 10-2; Minn Stats s 253A.17-(7); NY Mental Hyg Law s 15.03; Mass Gen Laws ch 123 s 4]. This involves a close, individualized evaluation of a patient's progress, with a view toward discharge and continued treatment in the community rather than in the institution. The Massachusetts statute specifically requires the consideration of alternatives to hospitalization in its periodic review provision [Mass Gen Laws ch 123 s 4], while the Illinois law sets forth a similar requirement in its commitment hearings [Ill Stats ch 91½ s 9-6). It is likely that these provisions will contribute to an increasing patient turnover and a decreasing hospital census. This should make possible a reallocation of resources, perhaps directed toward community alternatives.

As a result of the impetus of the federal Community Mental Health Centers Act of 1963 (53, 54), more than 300 community mental health centers have been established throughout the country. Some recent statutes have recognized the halfway house and community residence as viable and homelike alternatives to the traditional hospital as well [Minn Stats s 245.691; Calif Welf & Instits Code ss 5115, 5705.5; NY Mental Hyg Law s 11.29; Mass Gen Laws ch 19 s 29; Mass Dept of Mental Health Regulation 5.2; Mo Stats s

202.645; Fla Stats s 393.015; Minn Stats s 252.021]. Advocates of the community residence model argue that rigorous state regulation and licensure of these programs risk their conversion into a "mine-institutions." On the other hand, legislative recognition and approbation of their intermediary function further encourage a change in the role of the state hospital and state school. Rather than providing custodial care for chronic patients, the large mental institutions may well be transformed into crisis-oriented facilities for more acutely ill patients.

The orientation of mental health programs toward the community, as well as the increasing use of voluntary hospitalization, represents acceptance into and by society of its mentally ill citizens and narrows the differences in legal and social status between the mentally healthy and the mentally ill.

Trends Related to Patients' Rights

Explicit statutory recognition in recent legislation of the civil and personal rights of the mentally ill and mentally retarded not only constitutes significant and needed reform, but also indicates the kinds of discrimination and illegal restrictions that had been placed on the mentally disabled in the past. Enumerated in recent legislation are such rights as that to communicate with persons outside the facility (via correspondence, telephone, and visits) [e.g., Pa Stats Title 50 s 4423; Mo Stats s 202.847; Fla Stats s 394.459 (4); Ga Code s 88-502.5; Ill Stats ch 91½ s 12-2; Minn Stats ss 253A.05, 253A.17; Calif Welf & Instits Code s 5235; NY Mental Hyg Law 15.05; Mass Gen Laws ch 123 s 23]; to keep clothing and personal effects [e.g., Fla Stats s 394.459 (5); Ga Code s 88-502.6; Calif Welf & Instits Code s 5325; NY Mental Hyg Law s 15.071]; to religious freedom [e.g., Pa Stats Title 50 s 4423; Minn Stats s 253A.17]; to vote [Fla Stats s 394.459 (6); Mo Stats s 202.847; Ga Code s 88-502.7; Ill Stats ch 91½ s 9-11; NY Mental Hyg Law s 15.01; Mass Gen Laws ch 123 s 25]; to be employed if possible [e.g., Pa Stats Title 50 s 4423; Ga Code s 88-502.8; NY Mental Hyg Law s 15.09]; to manage or dispose of property [Mo Stats s 202.847; Ill Stats ch 91½ s 9-11; Minn Stats s 253A.18]; to execute instruments such as wills [Mo Stats s 202.847; Minn Stats s 253A.18; Mass Gen Laws ch 123 s 25]; to enter contractual relationships [Mo Stats s 202.847; Ill Stats ch 91½ s 9-11; Minn Stats s 253A.18; Mass Gen Laws ch 123 s 25]; to make purchases [Mo Stats s 202.847; Minn Stats s 253A.18]; to education [Fla Stats s 394.459 (7); Ga Code s 88-502.9; NY Mental Hyg Law s 15.11]; to habeas corpus [e.g., Pa

Stats Title 50 s 4426; Ill Stats ch 91½ 10-6; Calif Welf & Instits Code s 7250[; to independent psychiatric examination [Pa Stats Title 50 s 4423; Fla Stats s 394.459 (3) (b)]; to civil service status [Ill Stats ch 91½ s 9-11; NY Mental Hyg Law s 15.01]; to retain licenses, privileges, or permits established by law such as a driver's or professional license [Minn Stats s 253A.18; Ill Stats ch 91½ s 9-11; NY Mental Hyg Law s 15.01]; to sue and be sued [Minn Stats s 253A.18]; to marry [Minn Op AG 1008 Sept 22, 1968; Mass Dept of Mental Health Regulation MH 16]; and not to be subject to unnecessary mechanical restraints [Mo Stats s 202.843; Ga Code s 88-502.4; Minn Stats s 253.17].

Mental illness does not necessarily impute incompetency in exercising one or more of these rights, and incompetency requires specific judicial determination. A number of statutes clearly differentiate between mental illness and mental incompetency [e.g., Mo Stats s 202.847; Mass Gen Laws ch 123 s 25; Fla Stats s 394.459 (1)] and make reference to this distinction in their catalog of patients' rights [e.g., Ill Stats ch 91½ s 9-11; NY Mental Hyg Law s 29.03].

The right to legal representation. The constitutional guarantee of the right to counsel or legal representation, which originated in the area of criminal law (40), has been incorporated into a number of new mental health statutes to protect the rights of patients in commitment hearings, including the appointment of counsel for indigent persons [e.g., Fla Stats ss 394.467 (2) (d), 394.467 (3), 394.473; Ga Stats ss 88-502.12, 88.503.3, 88.506.6; Ill Stats ch 91½ s 9-4]. The participation of an attorney representing the interests of the patient precludes the reality or the appearance of railroading commitment and establishes a true "adversary" setting, ensuring close adherence to statutory commitment standards.

Mechanisms for review, apprisal, and explanation of patients' rights are being introduced in several states. New York, for example, has established the Mental Health Information System, a court-affiliated service to review the admission and retention of all patients and to inform and advise patients of their rights (NY Mental Hyg Law s 29.09). A California court has instituted the use of a nonprofit legal services group to apprise involuntarily certified patients of their legal rights (41). In Minnesota, review boards examine the admission and detention of patients [Minn Stats s 253A.16], while Massachusetts requires the designation of a "civil rights officer" in each mental health facility to assist the patient in exercising his rights [Mass Dept of Mental Health Regulation MH 16]. In addition, apart from traditional guardianship and conservatorship provisions, new and more flexible forms of patient representation or patient advocacy have been statutorily established [Calif Welf & Instits Code s 5350; Fla Stats s 394.459; Ga Code s 88-502.19; Ill Stats ch 91½ ss 9-6, 9-7].

Legal representation of patients' rights and interests indicates a fundamental change in attitudes toward the mentally disabled; no longer is the mental patient passively subject to the legal, economic, and personal consequences of his illness, but may, with legal assistance if necessary, affirmatively and actively continue to control his own life.

Privacy and confidentiality. Protecting the privacy of mental patients, as well as the confidentiality of their communications and medical records, has become a significant legal concern. The "right of privacy" implies the right of the individual to keep some information about himself or access to his personality (as by a photograph or personality test) completely secret from others. "Confidentiality," on the other hand, presupposes disclosure of certain information to another person; however, the communication of such information is limited to specifically authorized parties. "Privileged testimonial communication" is an evidentiary concept, permitting the patient or client to prevent his physician, psychologist, etc., from disclosing confidential communications in court or in other legal proceedings.

All but three states (Rhode Island, Texas, and Wisconsin) recognize the right of privacy in some form (42, footnote 3), while approximately two-thirds of the states have enacted physician-patient testimonial privilege statutes (43). Interestingly enough, physician-patient testimonial privilege statutes in Connecticut [Gen Stats of Conn Title 52-146 (d), (e), (f)] (44, footnote 8) and in Massachusetts [Mass Gen Laws ch 322 s 203] protect only communications between psychotherapists and patients—one of the few areas where the legal interests of the mentally disabled have been given priority. In addition, most of the new mental health statutes specifically protect the confidentiality of patient records [Pa Stats Title 50 s 4602; Fla Stats s 394.459 (8); Ga Code s 88-502.10; Ill Stats ch 91½ s 12-3; Minn Stats s 246.13; Mass Gen Laws ch 123 s 36; Calif Welf & Instits Code s 5328 (cf. s 5328.2); NY Mental Hyg Law s 15.13]. The Massachusetts statute goes on to protect patients "from commercial exploitation of any kind. No patient shall be photographed, interviewed or exposed to public view without either his express written consent or that of his legal guardian" [Mass Gen Laws ch 19 s 29(f)].

Informed consent. Another issue relating to patient rights is the ability or capacity of the mentally disabled individual to give informed consent to his "voluntary" admission, to particular kinds of treatment or therapy, to surgical procedures, or to scientific research (including interviews, behavioral observation and testing, administration of drugs, and so forth). The case law regarding a mental patient's capacity to consent is ambiguous, and decisions support almost any position.[4] There are a few statutory provisions requiring patient consent to surgery and to specific modalities of treatment such as electroconvulsive therapy [Minn Stats s 253A.17; Calif Welf & Instits Code ss 5325, 5325.5; NY Mental Hyg Law s 15.03; Mass Gen Laws ch 123 s 23].

With regard to capacity to give informed consent to voluntary admission, some states have avoided the issue and created admission statuses such as "nonobjecting" [Ga Code s 88-506; NY Mental Hyg Law s 33.25] or "voluntary commitment" [Pa Stats Title 50 s 4403]. Finally, there is almost no statutory or case law relating to consent to scientific research (45). Federal (46) and state (47) guidelines requiring patient consent to participation in research are essentially hortatory but may indicate the direction of future statutory or regulatory amendment.

Statutory right to treatment. Corresponding to the growing body of case law relating to the right to treatment, recent legislation has begun to articulate substantive guarantees of adequate and humane treatment:

Each patient in a facility shall receive treatment suited to his needs which shall be administered skillfully, safely, and humanely with full respect for his dignity and personal integrity. Each patient shall receive such medical, vocational, social, educational, and rehabilitative services as his condition requires to bring about an early return to his community [Fla. Stats. s. 394.459 (3); also see Mo. Stats. s. 202.840; Ga. Codes ss. 88–502.2, 88–502.3; Ill. Stats. ch. 91½ s. 12–1; N.Y. Mental Hyg. Law s. 15.03].

Such guarantees would appear to be enforceable in court, if necessary. However, criteria for judicial assessment of the adequacy of treatment received remains a problematic area (48).

[4] Compare *Wilson* v. *Lehman* (60) and *Lester* v. *Aetna Casualty & Surety Co.* (61).

CONCLUSIONS

In one sense we have now come full circle in mental health law since the days of the "moral treatment" of the mentally ill. In those days admission to mental hospitals was selective and the unresponsive patient was turned away. Treatment was adequate, but only for the few. Now we are required to provide adequate treatment, but for the many. Fortunately, with the significant advances in the treatment of the mentally ill in the past 20 years, we should be able to make accelerated progress toward such a desideratum. This will require increased allotment of public resources for the mentally ill and the mentally retarded. However, much can be accomplished by the reallocation and more productive utilization of the resources we now have.

The role of the law that has emerged in recent years may be regarded as catalytic toward improving care and treatment for the mentally disabled. If some of the new statutes and case law appear to be excessively rigid or burdensome in their implementation, or if these reforms appear at times to be advanced by overly aggressive and overzealous lawyers, it is well to remember that there is no conflict regarding the ultimate ends to which all this energy is directed. Change is painful, but we know that it is both necessary and inevitable if we are to have progress.

It matters greatly, however, what the impact of change really is. It is of fundamental importance that the effects of these changes on the quality of people's lives and health be monitored carefully. Empirical follow-up of changes in mental health law is badly needed, and little has appeared in either the psychiatric or the legal literature. It is of great significance that the United States Supreme Court itself, beginning with the landmark school desegregation decision of 1954 (9) and most recently in *Jackson v. Indiana* (51) found such empirical studies to be persuasive in its decision making.

In closing we again underscore the dynamic, evolving nature of mental health law and the complex series of "experiments" that are now going on in this area. What we have written in this paper will therefore become dated rapidly. One can only wonder what new legal "romance" awaits us.

REFERENCES

1. Wyatt v. Stickney, 325 F. Supp. 781 (M.D. Ala. 1971).
2. Records of the Governor and Company of the Massachusetts Bay in New England, vol. 5, 1854.

3. Deutsch, A. *The Mentally Ill in America: A History of Their Care and Treatment from Colonial Times*, 2nd revised ed. New York: Columbia University Press, 1949.

4. Dewey, R. The jury law for commitment of the insane in Illinois (1867–1893), and Mrs. E. P. W. Packard, its author, also later developments in lunacy legislation in Illinois. *Am. J. Insanity* 69:571–584, 1913.

5. Curran, W. J. Community mental health and the commitment laws: a radical new approach is needed, *Am. J. Public Health* 57:1565–1570, 1967.

6. Brakel, S. J., Rock, R. S. The Mentally Disabled and the Law, revised ed. Chicago: University of Chicago Press, 1971.

7. Rouse v. Cameron, 373 F. 2d 451 (D.C. Cir. 1966).

8. Nason v. Superintendent of Bridgewater State Hospital, 233 N.E. 2d. 908 (Mass. 1968).

9. Wyatt v. Stickney, 344 F. Supp. 373 (M.D. Ala. 1972).

10. Newman v. State of Alabama, Civil Action No. 3501–N (M.D. Ala. 1972).

11. Burnham v. Department of Public Health of the State of Georgia, Civil Action No. 16385 (N.D. Ga. 1972).

12. New York State Association for Retarded Children et al. v. Rockefeller, 72 Civil Action No. 356 (E.D. N.Y. 1972).

13. Paresi et al. v. Rockefeller, 72 Civil Action No. 357 (Ed. N.Y. 1972).

14. Ricci et al. v. Greenblatt et al., Civil Action No. 72–469F (D. Mass. 1972).

15. Wheeler et al. v. Glass et al., Civil Action No. 71–1677 (7th Cir. 1971).

16. Rivera et al. v. Weaver et al., Civil Action No. 72 C. 135 (Ill. 1972).

17. Townsend v. Treadway, Civil Action No. 6500 (Tenn. 1972).

18. Roebuck et al. v. Florida Department of Health and Rehabilitative Services et al., Civil No. TCA 1041 (N.D. Fla., Tallahassee Division 1972).

19. Pennsylvania Association for Retarded Children v. Commonwealth of Pennsylvania, 334 F. Supp. 1257 (E.D. Pa. 1971).

20. Mills v. District of Columbia Board of Education, Civil Action No. 1939–71 (D.D.C. 1972).

21. Lori Case et al. v. State of California Department of Education et al., Civil Action No. 101679 (Cal. Superior Ct., Riverside Cy. 1972).

22. Larry, P., MS, MJ et al. v. Riles et al., Civil Action No. c–71–2270 (N.D. Calif. 1972).

23. LeBanks et al. v. Spears et al., Civil Action No. 71–2897 (E.D. La., New Orleans Division 1972).

24. Reid v. New York Board of Education, Civil Action No. 71–1380 (S.D. N.Y. 1971).

25. Harrison et al. v. Michigan, Civil Action No. 38557 (E.D. Mich. 1972).

26. North Carolina Association for Retarded Children, Inc. et al. v. State of North Carolina et al. (E.D. N.C. 1972).

27. Michael Burnstein, Fred Polk et al. and Alan Miller, Jonathan Booth et al. v. Board of Education and Superintendent of Contra Costa County School District (Cal. Superior Ct., Contra Costa Cy. 1972).

28. Catholic Social Services, Inc. et al. v. Delaware Board of Education et al. (Del. 1972).

29. Association for Mentally Ill Children, Lori Barnett et al. v. Greenblatt, Lee et al., Civil Action No. 71–3047–J (D. Mass. 1971).

30. Commonwealth v. Wiseman, 249 N.E. 2d. 610 (Mass. 1969).

31. Themo v. N. E. Newspaper Publishing Co., 27 N.E. 2d. 753 (Mass. 1940).

32. Kelly v. Post Publishing Co. 98 N.E. 2d. 286 (Mass. 1951).

33. Winters v. Miller, 446 F. 2d. 65 (2d. Cir. 1971).

34. Frazier v. Levi, 440 S.W. 2d. 393 (Texas 1969).

35. Senate Bill 1274, House Bill 2118, General Assembly of Pennsylvania, 1968.

36. Williams v. Lesiak, Civil Action No. 72–571W (D. Mass. 1972).

37. Abramson, M. F. The criminalization of mentally disordered behavior: possible side-effect of a new mental health law, *Hosp. Community Psychiatry* 23:101–105, 1972.

38. Baxstrom v. Herold, 383 U.S. 107 (1966).

39. Jackson v. Indiana, 406 U.S. 715 (1972).

40. Gideon v. Wainright, 372 U.S. 335 (1963).

41. Thorn v. Superior Court of San Diego County, 464 P. 2d. 56 (1970).

42. Medical practice and the right to privacy, *Minnesota Law Review* 43:943–963, 1959.

43. Curran, W. J., Stearns, B., Kaplan, H. Legal considerations in the establishment of a health information system in greater Boston and the State of Massachusetts (unpublished). Available upon request from Prof. William J. Curran, Harvard School of Public Health, 55 Shattuck St., Boston, Mass. 02115.

44. Felber v. Foote, 321 F. Supp. 85 (D.C. Conn. 1970).

45. State ex rel Carroll v. Junker, 482 P. 2d. 775 (Wash. 1971).

46. Department of Health, Education, and Welfare: The Institutional Guide to DHEW Policy on Protection of Human Subjects. DHEW Publication No. (NIH) 72–102. Washington, D.C., U.S. Government Printing Office, Dec. 1, 1971.

47. Massachusetts Department of Mental Health: Policies and Procedures Concerning Access to Subjects and Data Within the Massachusetts Department of Mental Health. Boston, MDMH, Sept. 1, 1972.

48. Robitscher, J. Courts, state hospitals, and the right to treatment. *Am. J. Psychiatry* 129:298–304, 1972.

A. *Right to Treatment*

ROUSE v. CAMERON

BAZELON, Chief Judge.

In this habeas corpus case appellant attacks has confinement in Saint Elizabeths Hospital. He was involuntarily committed in November 1962 by the Municipal Court, now the Court of General Sessions, upon finding him not guilty by reason of insanity of carrying a dangerous weapon, a misdemeanor for which the maximum imprisonment is one year. The District Court has held a hearing and denied relief in habeas corpus. It refused to consider appellant's contention that he has received no psychiatric treatment. The judge said: "My jurisdiction is limited to determining whether he has recovered his sanity. I don't think I have a right to consider whether he is getting enough treatment."

I

The principal issues raised by this appeal are whether a person involuntarily committed to a mental hospital on being acquitted of an offense by reason of insanity has a right to treatment that is cognizable in habeas corpus, and if so, how violation of this right may be established.

The purpose of involuntary hospitalization is treatment, not punishment. The provision for commitment rests upon the supposed "necessity for treatment of the mental condition which led to the acquittal by reason of insanity." [*Ragsdale v. Overholser*, 281 F.2d 943, 1960.] Absent treatment, the hospital is "transform[ed] . . . into a penitentiary where one could be held indefinitely for no convicted offense, and this even though the offense of which he was previously acquitted because of doubt as to his sanity might not have been one of the more serious felonies" [*ibid.*] or might have been, as it was here, a misdemeanor.

Absence of treatment "might draw into question 'the constitutionality of [this] mandatory commitment section' as applied." [*Darnell v. Cameron*, 348 F.2d 64, 1965.] (1) Lack of improvement raises a question of procedural due process where the commitment is under D.C. Code § 24–301 rather than under the civil commitment statute, for under § 24–301 commitment is summary, in contrast with civil commitment safeguards. It does not rest on any finding of present insanity and dangerousness but, on the contrary, on a jury's reasonable doubt that the defendant was sane when he committed the act charged. Commitment on this basis is permissible because of its humane therapeutic goals. (2) Had appellant been found criminally responsible, he could have been confined a year, at most, however dangerous he might have been. He has been confined four years and the end is not in sight. Since this difference rests only on need for treatment, a failure to supply treatment may raise a question of due process of law. It has also been suggested that a failure to supply treatment may violate the equal protection clause. (3) Indefinite confinement without treatment of one who has been found not criminally responsible may be so inhumane as to be "cruel and unusual punishment" [citing *Robinson v. California* and *Easter v. D.C.;* see Chapter 15].

Impressed by the considerable constitutional problems that arise because "institutionalized patients often receive only custodial care," Congress established a *statutory* "right to treatment" in the 1964 Hospitalization of the Mentally Ill Act. The Act provides:

A person hospitalized in a public hospital for a mental illness shall, during his hospitalization, be entitled to medical and psychiatric care and treatment. The administrator of each public hospital shall keep records detailing all medical and psychiatric care and treatment received by a person hospitalized for a mental illness and the records shall be made available, upon that person's written authorization, to his attorney or personal physician.

It appears that this provision, like the one limiting the use of mechanical restraints, was intended to cover persons hospitalized under any statutory authorization. Other sections of the Act apply only to patients "hospitalized

---

U.S. Court of Appeals, District of Columbia Circuit, 373 F.2d 451 (1966).

pursuant to [the 1964 Act]," or to "mentally ill persons," which term is defined by the Act to exclude persons committed by court order in a criminal proceeding. Since there are no such limitations in the "right to treatment" provision set forth above, that right necessarily extends to involuntary commitment under D.C. Code § 24–301.

Moreover, the considerations underlying the right to treatment provision in the 1964 Act apply with equal force to commitment under D.C. Code § 24–301. These considerations are reflected in the statement of Senator Ervin, sponsor of the bill in the Senate. He called mere custodial care of hospitalized persons "shocking" and stated that of all the areas in which reform is badly needed, the "right to treatment" was "perhaps the most critical." He further said:

Several experts advanced the opinion that to deprive a person of liberty on the basis that he is in need of treatment, without supplying the needed treatment, is tantamount to a denial of due process. [The Senate bill] . . . embodies provisions which will ameliorate this problem whereas existing law makes no provisions for safeguarding this right.

Regardless of the statutory authority, involuntary confinement without treatment is "shocking." Indeed, there may be greater need for the protection of the right to treatment for persons committed without the safeguards of civil commitment procedures. Because we hold that the right to treatment provision applies to appellant, we need not resolve the serious constitutional questions that Congress avoided by prescribing this right.

The Group for the Advancement of Psychiatry has urged that "provisions that safeguard the patient's right to good treatment as opposed to simple custody" are an essential element of commitment laws. [G.A.P. Report No. 61, see *supra.*] A right to treatment in some form is recognized by law in many states. The requirement in the 1964 Act that the hospital keep records detailing psychiatric care and treatment and make them available to the patient's attorney reinforces our view that Congress intended to implement the right treatment by affording a judicial remedy for its violation.

The patient's right to treatment is clear. We now consider how violation of the right may be established.

II

According to leading experts "psychiatric care and treatment" includes not only the contacts with psychiatrists but also activities and contacts with the hospital staff designed to cure or improve the patient. The hospital need not show that the treatment will cure or improve him but only that there is a bona fide effort to do so. This requires the hospital to show that initial and periodic inquiries are made into the needs and conditions of the patient with a view to providing suitable treatment for him, and that the program provided is suited to his particular needs. Treatment that has therapeutic value for some may not have such value for others. For example, it may not be assumed that confinement in a hospital is beneficial "environmental therapy" for all.

The effort should be to provide treatment which is adequate in light of present knowledge. Some measures which have therapeutic value for the particular patient may be too insubstantial in comparison with what is available. On the other hand, the possibility of better treatment does not necessarily prove that the one provided is unsuitable or inadequate.

It has been said that "the only certain thing that can be said about the present state of knowledge and therapy regarding mental disease is that science has not reached finality of judgment." [Frankfurter, J., in *Greenwood* v. *U.S.*, 350 U.S. 366, 1956.] But lack of finality cannot relieve the court of its duty to render an informed decision. Counsel for the patient and the government can be helpful in presenting pertinent data concerning standards for mental care, and, particularly when the patient is indigent and cannot present experts of his own, the court may appoint independent experts. Assistance might be obtained from such sources as the American Psychiatric Association, which has published standards and is continually engaged in studying the problems of mental care. The court could also consider inviting the psychiatric and legal communities to establish procedures by which expert assistance can be best provided.

Continuing failure to provide suitable and adequate treatment cannot be justified by lack of staff or facilities. Congress considered a Draft Act Governing Hospitalization of the Mentally Ill prepared by the National Institute of Mental Health and the General Counsel of the Federal Security Agency, which contained the following provision:

Every patient shall be entitled to humane care and treatment and, *to the extent that facilities, equipment, and personnel are available,* to medical care and treatment in accordance with the highest standards accepted in medical practice. [Emphasis supplied.]

The italicized language was omitted in the present Act. This omission plainly evidences the intent to establish a broader right to treatment. As the Fourth Circuit Court of Appeals said of the right to treatment under Maryland's "defective delinquent" statute, "[d]eficiencies in staff, facilities, and finances would undermine . . . the justification for the law, and ultimately the constitutionality of its application." *Sas* v. *State of Maryland,* 334 F.2d 506, 517 (4th Circuit 1964).

We are aware that shortage of psychiatric personnel is a most serious problem today in the care of the mentally ill. In the opinion of the American Psychiatric Association no tax-supported hospital in the United States can be considered adequately staffed. We also recognize that shortage cannot be remedied immediately. But indefinite delay cannot be approved. "The rights here asserted are . . . *present* rights . . . and, unless there is an overwhelmingly compelling reason, they are to be promptly fulfilled." *Watson* v. *City of Memphis,* 373 U.S. 526, 533, 83 S.Ct. 1314, 1318, 10 L.Ed.2d 529 (1963).

One who is "in custody in violation of the Constitution and laws" of the United States is entitled to relief in habeas corpus, and the court is required to "dispose of the matter as law and justice require." [28 U.S.C. §§ 2241(c) (3), 2243, 1964.] If the court finds that a mandatorily committed patient, such as appellant, is in custody in violation of the Constitution and laws, it may allow the hospital a reasonable opportunity to initiate treatment. In determining the extent to which the hospital will be given an opportunity to develop an adequate program, important considerations may be the length of time the patient has lacked adequate treatment, the length of time he has been in custody, the nature of the mental condition that caused his acquittal, and the degree of danger, resulting from the condition, that the patient would present if released. Unconditional or conditional release may be in order if it appears that the opportunity for treatment has been exhausted or treatment is otherwise inappropriate. It is unnecessary to detail the possible range of circumstances in which release would be the appropriate remedy.

The government says the record shows that appellant is receiving adequate treatment. Since the District judge found no right to treatment, he did not inquire into the question of adequacy. There was evidence that appellant voluntarily left group therapy several months before the hearing below. But there was no inquiry into such questions as the suitability of group therapy for his particular illness, whether his rejection of this therapy was a manifestation and symptom of his mental illness, and whether reasonable efforts were made either to deal with such rejection or to provide some other suitable treatment. Also, the government psychiatrist said that appellant was receiving "environmental therapy." But the suitability and adequacy of the "milieu" as therapy for *this* petitioner were not explored.

We think "law and justice require" that we remand for a hearing and findings on whether appellant is receiving adequate treatment, and, if not, the details and circumstances underlying the reason why he is not. The latter information is essential to determine whether there is "an overwhelmingly compelling reason" for the failure to provide adequate treatment.

III

The appellant challenges also the District Court's finding that he has not recovered his mental health. A person involuntarily committed and confined under D.C. Code § 24–301 is entitled to release if he has "recovered his sanity and will not in the reasonable future be dangerous to himself or others." That the "person so confined has some dangerous propensities does not, standing alone, warrant his continued confinement in a government mental institution under § 24–301 D.C. Code. The dangerous propensities . . . must be related to or arise out of an abnormal mental condition." The District Court's findings concerning mental illness and dangerous propensities are not to be disturbed unless they lack support in the record or rest on an erroneous legal principle.

Three psychiatrists gave conflicting testimony. Dr. Economon of Saint Elizabeths testified that appellant was suffering from "anti-social reaction" and described its symptoms. Dr. Marland, in private practice, and Dr. Bunge, of the Commission on Mental Health, testified that appellant was not suffering from mental illness. But we do not reach the question whether the record would have supported a finding of present mental illness and dangerous propensities. For the record shows that in assessing danger the District judge may have relied primarily on the nature of the offense with which the appellant had been charged in 1962 rather than his present condition. For example, the judge said to government counsel, after questioning him and Dr. Marland about the offense:

I venture to suggest, Mr. Silbert, that in these cases that arise out of a criminal proceeding it would be useful to know the facts of the crime in every case, even if you have to dig them up from the files of the Municipal Court, because I have to protect the public. That is the principal thing that I have to consider. I would consider myself derelict in my duty if I released him and then a few weeks later he shot somebody with a .45 Colt automatic. That is why I want to know how he came to be arrested for carrying a gun. He must have done something to call the attention of the police to the fact that he had a gun. The police don't just stop anybody on the street and say, have you got a gun.

. . .

You could talk to the arresting officer if he is still on the force. He would probably remember how he came to arrest this man. I think those facts are important.

There is a big difference between releasing a man, say, who overdrew his bank account and one who had a gun. If you release a man who overdrew his bank account, the worst that can happen, he might do it again; but when you release a man who has been carrying a .45 automatic, that is a pretty serious matter.

The judge concluded:

In view of the fact that the original arrest involved a dangerous weapon, an extremely dangerous weapon, with a great deal of ammunition, the Court is not going to undertake to release him unconditionally and would have great hesitancy in releasing him even conditionally.

The judge then continued the hearing pending a report from the Commission on Mental Health.

The Commission reported that appellant had "recovered" and that "further confinement would stifle his future development." The hearing resumed with the following colloquy:

COURT: The court has before it the report of the Commission on Mental Health. Is this the case in which the petitioner was arrested in possession of a .45 caliber revolver?

MR. SILBERT: With 600 rounds of ammunition, too. This was at 1:45 in the morning at 14th & Harvard Sts. N.W.

The judge then pursued at length with Dr. Bunge, as he had with Dr. Marland, appellant's purpose in possessing a gun and ammunition. At the conclusion of the doctor's testimony the judge said:

I do want to ask you one question, Doctor. I am going to ask you that question in view of the fact that [petitioner] . . . was caught in the possession of a .45 pistol and 600 rounds of ammunition. My principal interest must be to protect the public. Would he be dangerous to himself or others, in your opinion, if he is released?

Dr. Bunge replied: "I don't believe he would be at this time."

The judge made plain not only his reliance on the offense charged, but also his doubt whether the appellant was mentally ill. He said to Dr. Economon, the only psychiatrist who thought him so:

Do you mean to say, Doctor, that to carry —of course I strongly disapprove of anybody carrying a .45 automatic unless he is in uniform and on duty, and . . . of anybody carrying 500 rounds of ammunition, . . . but, certainly, that is not a symptom of insanity, Doctor, because many sane people do those things.

. . .

You know, we just couldn't accept any psychiatric testimony or theory to the effect that the commission of a crime is a sign of mental disease because if we accepted that our whole system of criminal law would have to break down.

. . .

You practically ask us to take your opinion for the sum total of the tendencies and all the data, instead of enumerating the data so that we could test the conclusion that you reach.

Appellant may not be held in custody for an offense of which he was found not guilty. Since, as we have pointed out above, he may not be held unless his dangerous propensities "are related to or arise out of an abnormal mental condition" and since the case is being remanded for a hearing and findings concerning treatment, the District Court may reconsider and clarify its findings concerning illness and dangerous propensities.

Reversed and remanded for further proceedings in accordance with this opinion.

[Relief was denied on remand and Rouse appealed. He also filed another habeas corpus alleging that his commitment was barred by *Lynch* v. *Overholser*, 369 U.S. 705 (1962), because he did not voluntarily introduce the insanity defense or authorize his counsel to do so. Relief was denied. Rouse's appeals on the "right to treatment" decision and introduction of the insanity defense were heard together. The Court of Appeals held that Rouse did not seek the insanity defense and ordered his release. It also held that its decision on that appeal rendered moot the issues in the "right to treatment" appeal. *Rouse* v. *Cameron*, 387 F.2d 741 (1967).]

WYATT v. STICKNEY

ORDER AND DECREE

This class action originally was filed on October 23, 1970, in behalf of patients involuntarily confined for mental treatment purposes at Bryce Hospital, Tuscaloosa, Alabama. On March 12, 1971, in a formal opinion and decree, this Court held that these involuntarily committed patients "unquestionably have a constitutional right to receive such individual treatment as will give each of them a realistic opportunity to be cured or to improve his or her mental condition." The Court further held that patients at Bryce were being denied their right to treatment and that defendants, per their request, would be allowed six months in which to raise the level of care at Bryce to the constitutionally required minimum. *Wyatt* v. *Stickney*, 325 F.Supp. 781 (M.D. Ala. 1971). In this decree, the Court ordered defendants to file reports defining the mission and functions of Bryce Hospital, specifying the objective and subjective standards required to furnish adequate care to the treatable mentally ill and detailing the hospital's progress toward the implementation of minimum constitutional standards. Subsequent to this order, plaintiffs, by motion to amend granted August 12, 1971, enlarged their class to include patients involuntarily confined for mental treatment at Searcy Hospital and at Partlow State School and Hospital for the mentally retarded.

On September 23, 1971, defendants filed their final report, from which this Court concluded on December 10, 1971, that defendants had failed to promulgate and implement a treatment program satisfying minimum medical and constitutional requisites. Generally, the Court found that defendants' treatment program was deficient in three fundamental areas. It failed to provide: (1) a humane psychological and physical environment, (2) qualified staff in numbers sufficient to administer adequate treatment and (3) individualized treatment plans. More specifically, the Court found that many conditions, such as nontherapeutic, uncompensated work assignments, and the absence of any semblance of privacy, constituted dehumanizing factors contributing to the degeneration of the patients' self-esteem.

The physical facilities at Bryce were overcrowded and plagued by fire and other emergency hazards. The Court found also that most staff members were poorly trained and that staffing ratios were so inadequate as to render the administration of effective treatment impossible. The Court concluded, therefore, that whatever treatment was provided at Bryce was grossly deficient and failed to satisfy minimum medical and constitutional standards. Based upon this conclusion, the Court ordered that a formal hearing be held at which the parties and amici would have the opportunity to submit proposed standards for constitutionally adequate treatment and to present expert testimony in support of their proposals.

Pursuant to this order, a hearing was held at which the foremost authorities on mental health in the United States appeared and testified as to the minimum medical and constitutional requisites for public institutions, such as Bryce and Searcy, designed to treat the mentally ill. At this hearing, the parties and amici submitted their proposed standards, and now have filed briefs in support of them. Moreover, the parties and amici have stipulated to a broad spectrum of conditions they feel are mandatory for a constitutionally acceptable minimum treatment program. This Court, having considered the evidence in the case, as well as the briefs, proposed standards and stipulations of the parties, has concluded that the standards set out in Appendix A to this decree are medical and constitutional minimums. Consequently, the Court will order their implementation. In so ordering, however, the Court emphasizes that these standards are, indeed, both medical and constitutional minimums and should be viewed as such. The Court urges that once this order is effectuated, defendants not become complacent and self-satisfied. Rather, they should dedicate themselves to providing physical conditions and treatment programs at Alabama's mental institutions that substantially exceed medical and constitutional minimums.

Federal courts are reluctant to assume control of any organization, but especially one operated by a state. Nevertheless, defendants, as well as the other parties and amici in this

U.S. Dist. Court, Middle District of Alabama, 334 F. Supp. 373 (1972).

case, are placed on notice that unless defendants do comply satisfactorily iwth this order, the Court will be obligated to appoint a master.

Because the availability of financing may bear upon the implementation of this order, the Court is constrained to emphasize at this juncture that a failure by defendants to comply with this decree cannot be justified by a lack of operating funds. As previously established by this Court:

There can be no legal (or moral) justification for the State of Alabama's failing to afford treatment—and adequate treatment from a medical standpoint—to the several thousand patients who have been civilly committed to Bryce's for treatment purposes. To deprive any citizen of his or her liberty upon the altruistic theory that the confinement is for humane therapeutic reasons and then fail to provide adequate treatment violates the very fundamentals of due process. *Wyatt* v. *Stickney*, 325 F. Supp. at 785.

From the above, it follows consistently, of course, that the unavailability of neither funds, nor staff and facilities, will justify a default by defendants in the provision of suitable treatment for the mentally ill.

* * * *

In the event . . . that the Legislature fails to satisfy its well-defined constitutional obligation, and the Mental Health Board, because of lack of funding or any other legally insufficient reason, fails to implement fully the standards herein ordered, it will be necessary for the Court to take affirmative steps, including appointing a master, to ensure that proper funding is realized and that adequate treatment is available for the mentally ill of Alabama.

This Court now must consider that aspect of plaintiffs' motion of March 15, 1972, seeking an injunction against further commitments to Bryce and Searcy until such time as adequate treatment is supplied in those hospitals. Indisputably, the evidence in this case reflects that no treatment program at the Bryce–Searcy facilities approaches constitutional standards. Nevertheless, because of the alternatives to commitment commonly utilized in Alabama, as well as in other states, the Court is fearful that granting plaintiffs' request at the present time would serve only to punish and further deprive Alabama's mentally ill.

Finally, the Court has determined that this case requires the awarding of a reasonable attorneys' fee to plaintiffs' counsel. The basis for the award and the amount thereof will be considered and treated in a separate order. The fee will be charged against the defendants as a part of the court costs in this case.

* * * *

APPENDIX A

MINIMUM CONSTITUTIONAL STANDARDS FOR ADEQUATE TREATMENT OF THE MENTALLY ILL

* * * *

II. *Humane Psychological and Physical Environment*

1. Patients have a right to privacy and dignity.

2. Patients have a right to the least restrictive conditions necessary to achieve the purposes of commitment.

3. No person shall be deemed incompetent to manage his affairs, to contract, to hold professional or occupational or vehicle operator's licenses, to marry and obtain a divorce, to register and vote, or to make a will *solely* by reason of his admission or commitment to the hospital.

4. Patients shall have the same rights to visitation and telephone communications as patients at other public hospitals, except that the Qualified Mental Health Professional responsible for formulation of a particular patient's treatment plan writes an order imposing special restrictions. The written order must be renewed after each periodic review of the treatment plan if any restrictions are to be continued. Patients shall have an unrestricted right to visitation with attorneys and with private physicians and other health professionals.

5. Patients shall have an unrestricted right to send sealed mail. Patients shall have an unrestricted right to receive sealed mail from their attorneys, private physicians, and other mental health professionals, from courts, and government officials. Patients shall have a right to receive sealed mail from others, except to the extent that the Qualified Mental Health Professional responsible for formulation of a particular patient's treatment plan writes an order imposing special restrictions on receipt of sealed mail. The written order must be renewed after each periodic review of the treatment plan if any restrictions are to be continued.

6. Patients have a right to be free from unnecessary or excessive medication. No medication shall be administered unless at the written order of a physician. The superintendent of the hospital and the attending physician shall be responsible for

all medication given or administered to a patient. The use of medication shall not exceed standards of use that are advocated by the United States Food and Drug Administration. Notation of each individual's medication shall be kept in his medical records. At least weekly the attending physician shall review the drug regimen of each patient under his care. All prescriptions shall be written with a termination date, which shall not exceed 30 days. Medication shall not be used as punishment, for the convenience of staff, as a substitute for program, or in quantities that interfere with the patient's treatment program.

7. Patients have a right to be free from physical restraint and isolation. Except for emergency situations, in which it is likely that patients could harm themselves or others and in which less restrictive means of restraint are not feasible, patients may be physically restrained or placed in isolation only on a Qualified Mental Health Professional's written order which explains the rationale for such action. The written order may be entered only after the Qualified Mental Health Professional has personally seen the patient concerned and evaluated whatever episode or situation is said to call for restraint or isolation. Emergency use of restraints or isolation shall be for no more than one hour, by which time a Qualified Mental Health Professional shall have been consulted and shall have entered an appropriate order in writing. Such written order shall be effective for no more than 24 hours and must be renewed if restraint and isolation are to be continued. While in restraint or isolation the patient must be seen by qualified ward personnel who will chart the patient's physical condition (if it is compromised) and psychiatric condition every hour. The patient must have bathroom privileges every hour and must be bathed every 12 hours.

8. Patients shall have a right not to be subjected to experimental research without the express and informed consent of the patient, if the patient is able to give such consent, and of his guardian or next of kin, after opportunities for consultation with independent specialists and with legal counsel. Such proposed research shall first have been reviewed and approved by the institution's Human Rights Committee before such consent shall be sought. Prior to such approval the Committee shall determine that such research complies with the principles of the Statement on the Use of Human Subjects for Research of the American Association on Mental Deficiency and with the principles for research involving human subjects required by the United States Department of Health, Education and Welfare for projects supported by that agency.

9. Patients have a right not to be subjected to treatment procedures such as lobotomy, electro-convulsive treatment, adversive reinforcement conditioning or other unusual or hazardous treatment procedures without their express and informed consent after consultation with counsel or interested party of the patient's choice.

10. Patients have a right to receive prompt and adequate medical treatment for any physical ailments.

11. Patients have a right to wear their own clothes and to keep and use their own personal possessions except insofar as such clothes or personal possessions may be determined by a Qualified Mental Health Professional to be dangerous or otherwise inappropriate to the treatment regimen.

12. The hospital has an obligation to supply an adequate allowance of clothing to any patients who do not have suitable clothing of their own. Patients shall have the opportunity to select from various types of neat, clean, and seasonable clothing. Such clothing shall be considered the patient's throughout his stay in the hospital.

13. The hospital shall make provision for the laundering of patient clothing.

14. Patients have a right to regular physical exercise several times a week. Moreover, it shall be the duty of the hospital to provide facilities and equipment for such exercise.

15. Patients have a right to be outdoors at regular and frequent intervals, in the absence of medical considerations.

16. The right to religious worship shall be accorded to each patient who desires such opportunities. Provisions for such worship shall be made available to all patients on a nondiscriminatory basis. No individual shall be coerced into engaging in any religious activities.

17. The institution shall provide, with adequate supervision, suitable opportunities for the patient's interaction with members of the opposite sex.

18. The following rules shall govern patient labor:

A. *Hospital Maintenance.* No patient shall be required to perform labor which involves the operation and maintenance of the hospital or for which the hospital is under contract with an outside organization. Privileges or release from the hospital shall not be conditioned upon the performance of labor covered by this provision. Patients may voluntarily engage in such labor if the labor is compensated in accordance with the minimum wage laws of the Fair Labor Standards Act, 29 U.S.C. § 206 as amended, 1966.

B. *Therapeutic Tasks and Therapeutic Labor*

(1) Patients may be required to perform therapeutic tasks which do not involve the operation and maintenance of the hospital, provided the specific task or any change in assignment is:

a. An integrated part of the patient's treatment plan and approved as a therapeutic activity by a Qualified Mental Health Professional responsible for supervising the patient's treatment; and

b. Supervised by a staff member to oversee the therapeutic aspects of the activity.

(2) Patients may voluntarily engage in therapeutic labor for which the hospital would otherwise have to pay an employee, provided the specific labor or any change in labor assignment is:

a. an integrated part of the patient's treatment plan and approved as a therapeutic activity by a Qualified Mental Health Professional responsible for supervising the patient's treatment; and

b. supervised by a staff member to oversee the therapeutic aspects of the activity; and

c. compensated in accordance with the minimum wage laws of the Fair Labor Standards Act, 29 U.S.C. § 206 as amended, 1966.

C. *Personal Housekeeping.* Patients may may required to perform tasks of a personal housekeeping nature such as the making of one's own bed.

D. Payment to patients pursuant to these paragraphs shall not be applied to the costs of hospitalization.

19. *Physical Facilities*

A patient has a right to a humane psychological and physical environment within the hospital facilities. These facilities shall be designed to afford patients with comfort and safety, promote dignity, and ensure privacy. The facilities shall be designed to make a positive contribution to the efficient attainment of the treatment goals of the hospital. . . . [Specific regulations governing residence units, toilets, nutrition, etc. omitted.]

* * * *

III. *Qualified Staff in Numbers Sufficient to Administer Adequate Treatment*

21. Each Qualified Mental Health Professional shall meet all licensing and certification requirements promulgated by the State of Alabama for persons engaged in private practice of the same profession elsewhere in Alabama. Other staff members shall meet the same licensing and certification requirements as persons who engage in private practice of their specialty elsewhere in Alabama.

22. a. All Non-Professional Staff Members who have not had prior clinical experience in a mental institution shall have a substantial orientation training.

b. Staff members on all levels shall have regularly scheduled in-service training.

23. Each Non-Professional Staff Member shall be under the direct supervision of a Qualified Mental Health Professional.

24. *Staffing Ratios.* The hospital shall have . . . minimum numbers of treatment personnel per 250 patients. Qualified Mental Health Professionals trained in particular disciplines may in appropriate situations perform services or functions traditionally performed by members of other disciplines. Changes in staff deployment may be made with prior approval of this Court upon a clear and convincing demonstration that the proposed deviation from this staffing structure will enhance the treatment of the patients. . . .

IV. *Individualized Treatment Plans*

25. Each patient shall have a comprehensive physical and mental examination and review of behavioral status within 48 hours after admission to the hospital.

26. Each patient shall have an individualized treatment plan. This plan shall be developed by appropriate Qualified Mental Health Professionals, including a psychiatrist, and implemented as soon as possible—in any event no later than five days

after the patient's admission. Each individualized treatment plan shall contain:

a. a statement of the nature of the specific problems and specific needs of the patient;

b. a statement of the least restrictive treatment conditions necessary to achieve the purposes of commitment;

c. a description of intermediate and long-range treatment goals, with a projected timetable for their attainment;

d. a statement and rationale for the plan of treatment for achieving these intermediate and long-range goals;

e. a specification of staff responsibility and a description of proposed staff involvement with the patient in order to attain these treatment goals;

f. criteria for release to less restrictive treatment conditions, and criteria for discharge;

g. a notation of any therapeutic tasks and labor to be performed by the patient in accordance with Standard 18.

27. As part of his treatment plan, each patient shall have an individualized post-hospitalization plan. This plan shall be developed by a Qualified Mental Health Professional as soon as practicable after the patient's admission to the hospital.

28. In the interests of continuity of care, whenever possible, one Qualified Mental Health Professional (who need not have been involved with the development of the treatment plan) shall be responsible for supervising the implementation of the treatment plan, integrating the various aspects of the treatment program and recording the patient's progress. This Qualified Mental Health Professional shall also be responsible for ensuring that the patient is released, where appropriate, into a less restrictive form of treatment.

29. The treatment plan shall be continuously reviewed by the Qualified Mental Health Professional responsible for supervising the implementation of the plan and shall be modified if necessary. Moreover, at least every 90 days, each patient shall receive a mental examination from, and his treatment plan shall be reviewed by, a Qualified Mental Health Professional other than the professional responsible for supervising the implementation of the plan.

30. In addition to treatment for mental disorders, patients confined at mental health institutions also are entitled to and shall receive appropriate treatment for physical illnesses such as tuberculosis.[1] In providing medical care, the State Board of Mental Health shall take advantage of whatever community-based facilities are appropriate and available and shall coordinate the patient's treatment for mental illness with his medical treatment.

31. Complete patient records shall be kept on the ward in which the patient is placed and shall be available to anyone properly authorized in writing by the patient. These records shall include:

a. identification data, including the patient's legal status;

b. a patient history, including but not limited to:

1) family data, educational background, and employment record;

2) prior medical history, both physical and mental, including prior hospitalization;

c. the chief complaints of the patient and the chief complaints of others regarding the patient;

d. an evaluation which notes the onset of illness, the circumstances leading to admission, attitudes, behavior, estimate of intellectual functioning, memory functioning, orientation, and an inventory of the patient's assets in descriptive, not interpretative, fashion;

e. a summary of each physical examination which describes the results of the examination;

f. a copy of the individual treatment plan and any modifications thereto;

g. a detailed summary of the findings made by the reviewing Qualified Mental Health Professional after each periodic review of the treatment plan which analyzes the successes and failures of the treatment program and directs whatever modifications are necessary;

h. a copy of the individualized post-hospitalization plan and any modifications thereto, and a summary of the steps that have been taken to implement that plan;

i. a medication history and status, which includes the signed orders of the prescribing physician (nurses shall indicate by signature that orders have been carried out);

---

[1] Approximately fifty patients at Bryce-Searcy are tubercular, as also are approximately four residents at Partlow.

j. a detailed summary of each significant contact by a Qualified Mental Health Professional with the patient;

k. a detailed summary on at least a weekly basis by a Qualified Mental Health Professional involved in the patient's treatment of the patient's progress along the treatment plan;

l. a weekly summary of the extent and nature of the patient's work activities de- effect of such activity upon the patient's scribed in Standard 18, *supra*, and the progress along the treatment plan;

m. a signed order by a Qualified Mental Health Professional for any restrictions on visitations and communication, as provided in Standards 4 and 5, *supra*;

n. a signed order by a Qualified Mental Health Professional for any physical restraints and isolation, as provided in Standard 7, supra;

o. a detailed summary of any extraordinary incident in the hospital involving the patient to be entered by a staff member noting that he has personal knowledge of the incident or specifying his other source of information, and initialed within 24 hours by a Qualified Mental Health Professional;

p. a summary by the superintendent of the hospital or his appointed agent of his findings after the 15-day review provided for in Standard 33 *infra*.

32. In addition to complying with all the other standards herein, a hospital shall make special provisions for the treatment of patients who are children and young adults. These provisions shall include but are not limited to:

a. Opportunities for publicly supported education suitable to the educational needs of the patient. This program of education must, in the opinion of the attending Qualified Mental Health Professional, be compatible with the patient's mental condition and his treatment program, and otherwise be in the patient's best interest.

b. A treatment plan which considers the chronological, maturational, and developmental level of the patient;

c. sufficient Qualified Mental Health Professionals, teachers, and staff members with specialized skills in the care and treatment of children and young adults;

d. recreation and play opportunities in the open air where possible and appropriate residential facilities;

e. arrangements for contact between the hospital and the family of the patient.

33. No later than 15 days after a patient is committed to the hospital, the superintendent of the hospital or his appointed, professionally qualified agent shall examine the committed patient and shall determine whether the patient continues to require hospitalization and whether a treatment plan complying with Standard 26 has been implemented. If the patient no longer requires hospitalization in accordance with the standards for commitment, or if a treatment plan has not been implemented, he must be released immediately unless he agrees to continue with treatment on a voluntary basis.

34. The Mental Health Board and its agents have an affirmative duty to provide adequate transitional treatment and care for all patients released after a period of involuntary confinement. Transitional care and treatment possibilities include, but are not limited to, psychiatric day care, treatment in the home by a visiting therapist, nursing home or extended care, outpatient treatment, and treatment in the psychiatric ward of a general hospital.

V. Miscellaneous

35. Each patient and his family, guardian, or next friend shall promptly upon the patient's admission receive written notice, in language he understands, of all the above standards for adequate treatment. In addition a copy of all the above standards shall be posted in each ward.

UNANSWERED

TUSCALOOSA—Board Eligible or Board Certified Psychiatrists: 5 opngs., immed. Will serve on team planning & implementing indvd. trtmt. of pts. Must be able to work well with all levels & disciplines of staff. Persons needed with solid skills in grp. & indvd. trtmt. techniques & in short-term psychotherapy. Will have freedom to dvlp. innov. trtmt. & transitional pgms. for all types of patients. Organization of hosp. being restructured—possibility of prominent clin. posns. becoming avlb. Sal. for bd. elig. psychiatrist nego. upward from $33,371; bd. cert., nego, upward from $36,792. Send letter, vita, & refs. to Roland Skelton, Director, Manpower Planning & Development, Bryce Hospital, Tuscaloosa, Ala. 35401 or call collect to Roland Skelton, (205) 752-7411.

We have never before reproduced on this page a classified advertisement as we do above, but this is a special classified advertisement. It has appeared at the back of this newspaper in its proper place for many months, but unlike most of our classified ads, it has gone unanswered.

As we have said, the ad is a special one. The hospital, named Bryce Hospital, will probably evoke in the minds of most readers some recognition as having been in the news lately. It has, as one of the focal points of the *Wyatt v. Stickney* case.

Wyatt v. Stickney has, of course, become a watershed of patients' rights cases, in which a federal judge (the highly respected Judge Frank Johnson) ordered the State of Alabama to humanize its hospitals, provide adequate staff, and give its patients adequate treatment. There were specifics enough in his decree to fill a volume, ranging from staff-to-patient ratios to the frequency of linen changes.

Which brings us back to our classified ad. To meet Judge Johnson's decree, Bryce Hospital has been attempting for many months to recruit five board-eligible or board-certified psychiatrists (in addition, of course, to a large number of other personnel required by the court decree). It has been unsuccessful.

We think it should be successful and will be. Conversations with officials of the hospital lead us to believe that the hospital is in no way seeking a life-time commitment from the psychiatrists it recruits. A younger psychiatrist willing to face the enormous challenge of operation of a state hospital under court decree to provide adequate care, an older psychiatrist willing to devote a sabbatical to the task, perhaps a senior psychiatrist willing to come out of retirement—all these are possible among the 22,000 psychiatrists in the country today.

More is at stake here than just *any* hospital's recruiting new staff. Bryce is being looked at throughout the country by civil liberties groups, the health care professions, and the judiciary. It presents a challenge not only to the five psychiatrists who will eventually work there, but to the profession in demonstrating that it can undertake and perform well its housekeeping.

Excerpted and reprinted with permission from *Psychiatric News*, March 6, 1974, p. 2.

RIGHT TO PSYCHIATRIC TREATMENT

Jonas B. Robitscher, M.D.

PSYCHIATRY'S RESPONSE TO THE
RIGHT TO TREATMENT

What reception has the concept of the right to treatment received in psychiatric circles? Lawyers were interested in the concept from its inception, but Birnbaum, who is not a psychiatrist, had to wait a number of years to obtain a hearing in the psychiatric journals and at psychiatric meetings. When psychiatry did respond, the reception was mixed. The concept got a strong boost in 1967 from the Director of the National Institute of Mental Health, the most influential figure in psychiatry, who stated that adequacy of treatment was an area in which the courts should be involved, even though the possible danger in judicial definitions of adequate treatment or mental health was apparent:

It is society's responsibility to provide for adequate treatment. It is the psychiatrist's responsibility to treat adequately in the light of present knowledge. It is the court's responsibility, under due process of law, to protect the liberties of persons involuntarily detained, and to rule on practice for the individual case at hand.[1]

However, the concept has not been supported by many psychiatrists, and the APA has opposed it. Following the first *Rouse* decision, the Council of the APA in February 1967 approved a position statement on the question of the adequacy treatment. While acknowledging that staff shortages exist in state hospitals, the position statement declared that the proposal for release of patients when "ideal staff ratios cannot be maintained to provide adequate treatment . . . [is] tantamount to an oversimplified gospel of perfection. Clearly, in the perspective of the over-all mental health manpower shortage in our country, one must settle for something less until personnel shortages can be overcome."[2] The position statement preferred the vague standard of the Model Draft Act: "every patient is entitled to treatment to the extent that facilities and personnel are available."[3] In 1969 the APA dealt the Birnbaum plan a second blow by discontinuing its formulation of minimal patient-staff ratios for private mental hospitals.[4]

THE SPECIAL PROBLEMS OF THE
STATE MENTAL HOSPITAL

Will the right to treatment solve the problem of the state mental hospital? It can focus attention on the problem and give it more publicity than would be available by any other means and thereby hasten change.

Real differences exist between state hospital personnel and the personnel of the private sector of psychiatry. In order to fill quotas of physicians, most states do not require licensure for state mental hospital physicians; the result, therefore, is that the state hospital physician is frequently foreign-born, speaking English as a second language. Furthermore, since state hospital psychiatric practice generally does not include the opportunity for verbal therapy on a one-to-one basis, the state hospitals usually attract and hold physicians who are comfortable dispensing drugs—tranquilizers or anti-depressants—or who enjoy administration more than individual therapy. This is in contrast to the model of private psychiatric practice which continues to be verbal psychological investigation. Moreover, even where hospitals do employ group therapy methods, they often rely on untrained personnel as group leaders.

State hospitals have been further hampered by their geographical inaccessibility, a product of society's desire to push the problems of the mentally ill out of view. The state hospital physician who wants to follow a patient and ease his transition back into the community is not in a position to offer a continuing rela-

---

[1] Yolles, The Right to Treatment, 28 *Psychiat. Dig.* 7, 13 (Oct. 1967).

[2] American Psychiatric Association, Official Actions, 123 *Am. J. Psychiat.* 1460 (1967).

[3] *Id.*

[4] American Psychiatric Association, Standards for Psychiatric Facilities 29 (1969).

Excerpted and reprinted with permission from 18 *Villanova Law Review*, (November 1972).

tionship to the patient after discharge. The main problems of the state hospitals that President Kennedy's Commission found in 1961— their geographical isolation from the community, their emphasis on inpatient rather than outpatient care, their size, and their impersonality—will remain even if patient-personnel ratios are improved.[5]

Modern psychiatry has five main components: private office practice; private inpatient services; services offered without consideration as to ability to pay through community mental health/mental retardation centers; university and teaching-hospital programs stressing research and psychiatric education for residents; and the state hospital system. The first four of these components interact with each other. Private practitioners contribute time to teaching-hospitals and are employed in part-time jobs in community mental health centers affiliated with university departments of psychiatry. Teaching-hospitals and university psychiatry departments provide model care for some inpatients.

Only the state hospitals is isolated. It is isolated geographically because mental hospitals have traditionally tried to insulate society from the hospital population, but it is isolated more thoroughly by the lack of interaction with the private sector, the university sector, and those organizations like the APA and the Group for the Advancement of Psychiatry ("GAP") which represent the more genteel kind of psychiatric practice.

Proposals to Implement the Right to Treatment

The remainder of this Article suggests an eight-point program of social-legal approaches to the problem of offering adequate treatment to patients in state mental hospitals.

Universities and Training-hospitals Must Become Involved in the Problem of the State Hospital's Neglected Patients

University-affiliated and private hospital-affiliated training programs have, until recent years, been interested only in affluent (or insurance rich) patients and in those indigent patients who made good teaching cases. A new development has been their sponsorship of community mental health and mental retardation programs, and through these, they have for the first time provided services across-the-board for all social classes. But this democratization of psychiatry applies only to outpatient

[5] Joint Commission on Mental Illness and Health, Action for Mental Health (1961).

community mental health centers convenient to a university or private hospital; the state hospital system continues to be outside the scope of psychiatry's elite private sector. Further, the system is self-perpetuating. Desirable residents who have their choice of residencies are trained at university hospitals where there is emphasis on research and on training for private practice but where there is no training for public institutional work; less desirable residents, especially the foreign-born who cannot meet state licensure requirements, have no alternatives to the state hospital system. Total institutions—state hospitals, homes for the retarded, juvenile rehabilitation centers— have been of interest to sociologists and even to historians, but they have not been sufficiently used as a placement opportunity for training under university sponsorship for medical students, psychiatric residents, or psychology, sociology, and social work degree candidates.

The advantages of university interest are two-fold: a source of young "bodies"—interns, residents, medical students, and degree candidates who in receiving training also provide services—and a source of senior personnel supervising the training program. The resulting improved intellectual atmosphere makes the institution a desirable place to work, yet these advantages are denied to the state hospital system under its present alienation from the mainstream of psychiatry. The self-perpetuating aspects of present methods of personnel selection ensure an ever-deepening chasm.

University-affiliated programs can provide help in other areas besides therapy. The decision to commit, the decision to hold a subject in a state hospital because he is considered incompetent to stand trial, and the decision to recommend treatment for addiction in lieu of a court sentence, are within the bailiwick of hospital personnel; as a result, they need sociological and legal information about consequences of possible decisions if they are to act intelligently. The intellectual side of psychiatry —its university and private hospital component —must now fulfill these functions for state hospital patients.

The System of Public Hospitals and Private Hospitals will Have to Be Merged into a Single System

As valuable as the interrelationship of university and state hospital through a common teaching program may prove to be, the inequity of a dual system of medical care will dictate merger. Responsible action by the university to improve state hospital services is only the first step toward such a merger.

The system which provided for a disparate kind of care for private, as opposed to ward, patients has disappeared from general hospitals under the onslaught of health insurance, Medicare, and Medicaid. Psychiatry, where these benefits are limited, remains the only branch of medicine that unblushingly maintains the dual approach—$7 a day for care of public patients, $100 a day for care of private patients.

It is submitted that there is no greater justification for economic segregation than for other forms of compulsory segregation and discrimination. Just as separate and unequal facilities based on racial factors have been seen to violate constitutional safeguards, at some point separate and unequal psychiatric facilities based on ability to pay will also be seen to violate the constitutional right to treatment.

There Must Be Federal Participation in Upgrading the State Hospital System

The policy of non-involvement on the part of the federal government was demonstrated in the testimony of Attorney General Robert Kennedy at congressional hearings on the constitutional rights of the mentally ill:

The Department . . . makes no surveys or investigations of State mental institutions to determine general conditions therein. It has no authority with respect to the manner in which patients are admitted or in connection with the quality of care and treatment accorded them. Such matters are within the exclusive jurisdiction of the States.[6]

Since that time, the federal government has shown itself increasingly willing to intervene against discrimination and to regulate in the interests of health, and this kind of concern will have to be extended to state hospital patients.

Patients Themselves Must Be Involved in the Improvement of the State Hospital System

Many mental hospitals now have some kind of patient-participatory self-government, although patients complain that the areas where they are allowed to make decisions are circumscribed and unimportant. Patients with legitimate demands for hospital improvement are often considered troublemakers, their requests are ignored, or they are penalized for their complaints. State hospitals will have to heed patients' requests for their own representatives at hospital staff and trustees meetings. In addition to the involuntary patients' major grievance of loss of freedom, they have unnumerable minor grievances against the hospital as a milieu for dignified living. Much as prisoners complain of the atmosphere of bureaucracy, insensitivity, and cruelty in which their legitimate requests go unanswered, mental patients have complaints about food, living conditions, and administrative policies. The complaints are often disregarded, creating a poor atmosphere for therapy. Thus, there seems to be a clear need to provide an ombudsman in the state hospital system. The ombudsman could receive the recurring complaints of mental patients: a lack of electrical outlets in a dayroom depriving patients of good reading light; a patient who wants to see his doctor about a weekend pass, but is repeatedly put off; a ward's complaint that a pay telephone is not available; continued censorship of mail in spite of an announced new policy against censorship.

The Care of Mental Patients Requires so Much Manpower that a More Efficient Use of Paid Nonprofessional Short-time and Volunteer Help is Needed

To overcome the shortage involves the recruitment of the untrained, but at the same time the interested and the concerned. The use of volunteers and short-timers has serious drawbacks. For example, untrained personnel can be a disruptive influence on mental patients. Using volunteer and short-time manpower can easily backfire because legislatures are then relieved of the pressure to provide more money for trained personnel—the goal of the right to treatment movement. Moreover, volunteers and short-timers who participate in a program for only a limited period of time require training—a drain on existing manpower and much of which goes to waste when the volunteer ceases his activity.

The advantages of securing voluntary help, however, seem to outweigh its disadvantages. Society has increasingly relegated responsibility for the individual in trouble—mental patient, geriatric patient, orphan, delinquent, prisoner—to a professional corps which maintains the individual and keeps him from interacting with society; we prefer to segregate our unfortunates. This abdication of responsibility works only when government funds provide the manpower for this kind of insulated system. Since the funds are not inexhaustible and since the competition for them is increasing, the use of volunteers is needed to maintain even the present unsatisfactory levels of providing care. As a result, to improve the system, a large-

[6] Hearings on Constitutional Rights of the Mentally Ill Before the Subcomm. on Constitutional Rights of the Senate Comm. on the Judiciary, 87th Cong., 1st Sess. 401 (1961) (emphasis added).

scale use of volunteers is needed. Volunteers and short-timers will provide a bridge between the institution and the community.

The State Hospital System Must Make Greater Use of Part-time Professional Personnel

A psychiatrist who would be loath to devote his whole professional life to a state hospital population might be willing to spend one-half or three-fourths of his time in such a post. The wall that divides the state hospital system from the remainder of psychiatry will have to fall at some point, and psychiatrists as well as other highly trained personnel, such as nurses, psychologists, and social workers, will have to be given positions that allow them to alternate with other less taxing, and more financially rewarding, kinds of professional experience.

[P]rivate practitioners who now have no contact with the state hospital system are needed to upgrade that system. By working as part-time personnel, they not only bring their skills, but also, hopefully, are in contact with the training-hospital and university-affiliated personnel who also would be involved.

Proper Use of the Mental Hospital Requires Stricter Attention to the Criteria of Committability

The chief irregularity in our commitment procedures comes not at the time of the initial commitment, when many psychiatric patients are indeed a danger to themselves or to others and in need of involuntary commitment, but at a later stage, when the patient could be given increasing freedom, moved to a halfway facility, or released.

A recent National Institute of Mental Health study of patients at St. Elizabeth's Hospital in the District of Columbia indicated that 68 per cent of the patients had no behavior problems requiring continued hospitalization.[7] They could not be considered dangerous to themselves or to others and could be transferred to their own homes, to foster homes, or to nursing homes, with psychiatric outpatient care available when needed. Hospital officials, generally agreeing with the diagnostic findings of the report, nevertheless said they could not find "nearly enough acceptable alternative facilities"[8] in the Washington area.

Another alternative to total institutionalization is the day hospital, where patients can receive a complete program of psychiatric rehabilitation, but not be separated from their families at nights and on weekends. One research group has reported that the use of the day hospital offers patients an opportunity for a quicker recovery. But even therapists who had seen the greater efficacy of day care treatment preferred to commit patients for inpatient care.[9] Administrative pressure could be employed constructively to counteract that preference. The halfway house provides another alternative to the state mental hospital.

Stricter commitment proceedings, legal counsel for patients at commitment proceedings, constant concern over the patient's committability, and more alternatives to commitment provide methods of decreasing the burden of the state hospital so that better care can be provided for fewer patients.

The Basic Reform that is Needed, However, is the Formulation of Objective Standards of Care so that Adequacy of Treatment Can Be Evaluated

The APA has always been a leader in the formulation of such standards. Recently it has supplemented its standards for adults by publishing its first official standards for psychiatric facilities serving children and adolescents.[10] It has proposed that all health facilities, public and private, attempt, as much as possible, to meet the standards of practice required for accreditation by the Joint Commission on Accreditation of Hospitals ("JCAH").[11] However, APA standards for mental hospitals fail to provide definite guidelines for the measurement of patient care because former numerical ratios of patients to personnel have been eliminated, because many criteria are unduly vague, and because the APA has consistently recognized differing standards of care for public and private mental hospitals.

Some psychiatrists feel that not only is it an imposition to be required to formalize and fully specify treatment standards, but it is also a threat to the autonomy of the therapist. Nevertheless, private mental hospitals are accustomed to conforming their standards to those of the JCAH in order to be eligible for federal funds for their Medicare and Medicaid patients, and medicine generally is accepting the increasing scrutiny of utilization review committees.

---

[7] *Psychiatric News*, Oct. 16, 1971, at 3, col. 4.
[8] *Id.*

[9] Herz, Endicott, Spitzer, and Mesnikoff, Day Versus Inpatient Hospitalization: Controlled Study, 127 *Am. J. Psychiat.* 1371 (1971).
[10] American Psychiatric Association, Standards for Psychiatric Facilities Serving Children and Adolescents (1972).
[11] Joint Commission on Accreditation of Hospitals, Standards for Accreditation of Hospitals (1969).

Objective standards for psychiatric care are overdue; they are needed for the effective use of psychiatric treatment review boards. The promulgation of standards of care and the enforcement of those standards are essential, but, more importantly, there must be an acceptance of responsibility for the plight of the state hospital by others as well as by judges, legislators, and hospital administrators. [The] attack on the problem, no matter how well considered and humane, will not be successful without the support of psychiatry's private practitioners, its university-affiliated and training-hospital-affiliated programs, the young, the volunteers—in short, without help from soicety as a whole.

LEGAL PROBLEMS INVOLVED IN IMPLEMENTING THE RIGHT TO TREATMENT

Grant H. Morris

I. INTRODUCTION

Within the last twelve years, the concept of a legally enforceable "right to treatment" for institutionalized mental patients has been asserted. The "right to treatment" advocates argue that if a mentally ill person has been hospitalized by the state involuntarily because he needs mental treatment, the state has an obligation to furnish that treatment. Even if the individual has been institutionalized as "dangerous to himself or others" instead of "in need of care and treatment," since there has been involuntary confinement without a finding of guilt of a crime, and without rigorous criminal process safeguards, it is a duty of the state to make that confinement as short as possible, by providing adequate treatment. Stated in these simple terms, few lawyers and few psychiatrists are opposed to the principle of a "right to treatment."

It seemed as if members of our two great professions had finally found an issue upon which they could agree and that the iron curtain of icy silence existing between us might melt into meaningful dialogue. However, the difficult problems involved in defining and implementing the right to treatment have quickly returned us to the Cold War. What constitutes adequate treatment? Who should determine adequacy? Are courts competent to enforce a right to treatment? Is release of an inadequately treated, but dangerous patient appropriate? What is adequate treatment for an untreatable patient? These are but a few of the important, and as yet, unresolved issues.

II. GENERAL POLICY ISSUES

The "right to treatment" concept received its major judicial impetus in the landmark case of *Rouse* v. *Cameron.*[1] In that decision, Chief Judge David Bazelon, writing for the majority of the court, declared that since the purpose of involuntary hospitalization is treatment, not punishment, the hospital has a duty to furnish treatment, and the patient has a legal right to receive that treatment. In other words, if a patient is not receiving adequate treatment, he has a right to secure his release from the mental hospital even though he remains mentally ill. Judge Bazelon and others have indicated that grave constitutional problems involving due process and cruel and unusual punishment would arise if involuntarily hospitalized persons could be retained in the institution without affording them adequate treatment.[2]

Thus, within the first six years of the

[1] 373 F.2d 451 (D.C. Cir. 1966).
[2] Bazelon, *Rights of Mental Patients to Treatment and Remuneration for Institutional Work—Prior Court Decisions and Legislation*, PA, BAR ASSN. Q. 534, 544 (June 1968); Note, *Civil Restraint, Mental Illness and the Right to Treatment*, 77 *Yale L.J.* 87, 97–104 (1967).

Excerpted and reprinted with permission from *The Bulletin of the American Academy of Psychiatry and the Law* 1, no. 1, (Autumn 1972): 1–37.

Read at annual AAPL meeting, Ann Arbor, Michigan, October 19, 1972. Material based on a forthcoming book to be published by Charles C Thomas Co.

"Right's" existence, the answers to the two questions were (1) the courts determine adequacy, and (2) the determination of adequacy is made for the individual aggrieved patient who sues for his release from confinement.

However, this resolution of the issues was not without controversy. The American Psychiatric Association questioned the competence of the courts to determine adequacy, and in an official policy statement asserted: "The definition of treatment and the appraisal of its adequacy are matters for medical determination."[3] The psychiatrists were not the only critics. Even the judges sitting in the same court as Judge Bazelon differed in their views as to the appropriate treatment standard required by the right. Judge Bazelon in *Rouse* phrased the test in terms of suitable and adequate treatment for the particular individual in the light of existing medical knowledge. In a subsequent case,[4] Judge Edgerton required only treatment which is selected by a reasonable and permissible decision on the part of the hospital within a broad range of discretion. And in a third case,[5] Judge Burger, wrote a concurring opinion in which he intimated that simply *any* treatment at all satisfies the right to treatment requirements.[6]

Additionally, the method by which a patient raised the issue of adequacy of treatment, i.e., a writ of habeas corpus seeking release from the institution, has been questioned. As one attorney recently wrote, "Habeas corpus appears to be an inadequate vehicle for meaningful reform because even successful litigation will limit relief to one individual."

Judge Bazelon himself, seemed willing to throw the ball into someone else's court, when he admitted:

I, of course, believe the judiciary can play a role, but I will be the first to admit that, in most instances, the legislature can do a better job. A court can only lay down broad policy outlines, but the legislature can create specific procedures and institutions to implement the right to treatment.[7]

However, in most states, the legislatures simply have not done a better job.

When the answer to the question: "Who determines adequacy?" shifted to "the legislature" instead of "the courts," the answer to the other question: "Adequacy for whom?" shifted to "all the patients in the institution—collectively" instead of "the individual aggrieved patient." To the extent that legislatures focused on the problem at all, they focused on the generalized problem of treatment for *all* institutionalized patients.

In my opinion, *both* the legislature and the courts have a role in determining adequacy—the legislature in establishing meaningful standards applicable to all patients, and the courts in determining whether adequate treatment has been accorded in individual cases. My recommendation[8] for a "Right to Treatment Law" is derived from and patterned after a comprehensive bill introduced in, but not enacted by, the Pennsylvania legislature.[9] Within very broad guidelines, the approach I adopted provides for a determination of adequate treatment standards by mental health professionals.

While I feel that the task of delineating treatment standards applicable to all patients is largely within the province of the mental health professional, the task of assisting the individual patient in achieving his full measure of adequate treatment falls within the bailiwick of the lawyer. The difficult and delicate problem is to provide a way in which the patient can effectively enforce his right to treatment, without necessarily impairing the therapeutic relationship existing between the patient and treating personnel.

However, attorneys have not as yet become involved to any great extent with mental patients' problems. Lawyers lack expertise in this neglected area. Statutory duties for the attorney are virtually nonexistent, and lawyers who have worked in the civil commitment area often act only in a ceremonial manner. Additionally, patients' legal problems are often financially unprofitable to an attorney. A lawyer who services many clients may find that the occasional mental patient client, whom he must visit in an institution rather than in his own office, consumes too much of his working time over inconsequential, though complex, matters. However, these reasons do not justify a continuance of the existing situation.

Recent statutory developments in New York suggest a workable solution to the problems involved in enforcing patients' right to treatment and other related rights. In 1965 new laws modifying mental hospitalization procedures went into effect. A special service was created, the Mental Health Information Service, in each of the four Judicial Departments of

[3] Council of the American Psychiatric Association, *Position Statement on the Question of Adequacy of Treatment*, 123 *Am. J. Psychiatry* 1458 (1967).

[4] *Tribby* v. *Cameron*, 379 F.2d 104 (D.C. Cir. 1967).

[5] *Dobson* v. *Cameron*, 383 F.2d 519 (D.C. Cir. 1967).

[6] See P. Marschall, "A Critique of the 'Right to Treatment' Approach," 37 at 49–51 in G. Morris, ed., *The Mentally Ill and the Right to Treatment* (1970) for a discussion of these three cases.

[7] Bazelon, supra note 3, at 544.

[8] My proposal is reprinted as Appendix A.

[9] Senate Bill No. 816, General Assembly of Pennsylvania, 1969 Session.

the state, responsible to the Appellate Division of each department. The Mental Health Information Service is staffed primarily by lawyers. Its function is to review the status of involuntary patients, inform them of their rights under the law, including the right to be represented by legal counsel and to seek independent medical opinion, assemble information for the court whenever a hearing is requested, and advise patients when they seek aid.

Although there are differences between each of the four services, they have generally proved to be an invaluable asset in aiding patients, without unduly hampering administration of the institutions. Contrary to the fears of some hospital personnel, the presence of specially trained mental health lawyers in the institutions themselves has resulted in less conflict and less litigation. Lawyers who work full-time on mental patients' problems and who continually observe the difficulties involved in working in and administering the institutions themselves, develop an expertise in avoiding rather than promoting litigation. Only in the most extreme situations do competent attorneys utilize the formalized relief provided by judicial intervention.

The desire of service workers to reach a negotiated settlement of a dispute—a settlement which satisfies both the psychiatrist and the patient—has been attested to repeatedly.[10]

It should be remembered that the New York Mental Health Information Service deals primarily with legal problems involved in civil commitment. However, such an agency could easily be assigned the role of counseling patients and insuring protection of their legally recognized interests.

I have proposed that a new state-wide agency, called the Mental Patients' Legal Assistance Service, be created as an autonomous agency independent of the mental institutions and of the Department of Health. The service should have the function of protecting the legal rights of mental patients, including the right to treatment. Service personnel should perform this function by fulfilling the following duties:

1. inform and advise patients of their legal rights;
2. study and review all patient records to determine whether patients' rights are being
3. investigate any violations of rights which

appear on patients' records and any and all other violations which are complained of or observed;
4. determine whether a patient's voluntary and informed consent has been obtained for any therapy, procedure, or operation requiring patient consent;
5. act informally to correct any violations of patients' rights;
6. counsel and represent patients in court in all legal disputes in situations where service personnel determine that a right has been violated and the violator refuses to stop the violation, subject to a patient's right to retain independent legal assistance.

The service should be staffed primarily by full-time attorneys who receive such training and such psychiatric and other assistance as is necessary to perform their duties. Service personnel should be stationed in and available to patients at state mental institutions.

III. SPECIFIC TREATMENT PROBLEMS AND SPECIFIC TREATMENT RIGHTS

The above stated proposals attempt to create a framework for establishing minimum treatment standards that can be applied to *all* mental patients in the state mental hospitals, and an agency to enforce an individual patient's rights to receive treatment as required by those standards. However, there are major treatment problems that may involve only some patients and that cannot be dealt with by proclaiming generalized treatment standards.

The Voluntary Patient

In *Rouse* v. *Cameron*, Judge Bazelon reasoned that if the state *involuntarily* deprives a person of his liberty and confines him because he is in need of treatment, it has the obligation to accord him that treatment or to release him. This is logical in a situation where an individual has brought a writ of habeas corpus and is attempting to obtain his release from confinement. But to what extent is the right-to-treatment approach appropriate to the *voluntary* patient, the one who seeks not release from confinement, but rather treatment for his condition?

For example, let me focus on the aged and their need for rehabilitative programs. Should an elderly person have to be involuntarily confined in a mental institution before he can claim that he is not receiving adequate treatment? It seems senseless to so restrict the right to treatment. The voluntary aged mental patient should be accorded the right to complain of inadequate treatment as well. And what of the elderly person in a nursing home?

[10] Zitrin, Herman, and Kumasaka, supra note 25, at 33–34; Rozensweig, "Compulsory Hospitalization of the Mentally Ill," 61 *Am. J. Public Health* 121, 123–34 (Jan. 1971); Gupta, *Mental Health Information Service: An Experiment in Due Process* 5 (unpublished manuscript). observed;

Should he not also be entitled to complain of inadequate programs and services? And finally, what about the elderly person who still maintains his own home, or who lives with his children—does the state not owe him access to rehabilitative programs which he may want to voluntarily attend?

It seems to me that the ultimate goal of a right-to-treatment philosophy is a requirement that the state provide *more* treatment; i.e., adequate treatment to meet the medical needs of its citizens. An approach such as that suggested in *Rouse* v. *Cameron*, that would permit the state to simply release all involuntarily confined mental patients and completely avoid the obligation to provide adequate treatment, is deficient.

Special Treatment Measures for Dangerous Patients

The difficult problem presented by the dangerous or allegedly dangerous patient is worth specific mention at this point. During a psychotic episode when a patient acts in a manner that threatens serious bodily harm to himself, other patients, or staff, he must be restrained temporarily. There is no time to seek a court order authorizing such restraint. While I recognize this, I feel that statutory safeguards are necessary to prevent misuse or overuse of restraint or seclusion. I have proposed a statute to provide:

Patients admitted to mental institutions shall have the right to be free from mechanical or physical restraint or seclusion. Restraint or seclusion shall not be used as punishment, nor shall patients be threatened with restraint or seclusion.

When a patient acts in a manner that threatens serious bodily harm to himself, other patients, or staff of the institution, he may be temporarily restrained by ward personnel only until a physician can be immediately summoned. The physician shall determine and order the minimal restraint that is necessary to prevent the patient from committing the destructive acts. The decision to temporarily restrain a patient and a physician's decision to order restraint or seclusion shall be recorded on the patient's clinical record, together with an explanation justifying the decision. No physician's order for restraint or seclusion shall be for a period of time longer than twenty-four hours. Any subsequent necessity for restraint or seclusion shall be determined by a physician after a personal examination of the patient while under restraint or seclusion. Subsequent orders for restraint or seclusion shall be recorded as above. The patient may contest the physician's decision to order or reorder restraint or seclusion.

The use of tranquilizing drugs has reduced the incidence of and need for physical restraints. However, there is a danger presented by the potential overuse of drugs to achieve the same result as physical restraint. The Mental Treatment Standards Committee may be the appropriate body to examine the use of tranquilizing drugs in the institutions and to establish guidelines as to their appropriate use.

On rare occasion, a patient's dangerous propensity to commit destructive acts cannot be adequately controlled by temporary use of tranquilizers, restraint, or seclusion. In any situation where a patient's alleged "dangerousness" or any other circumstance warrants a substantial restriction on either that patient's rights as a patient or restrictions on "typical" or "normal" treatment opportunities afforded other patients generally, judicial intervention is necessary to scrutinize the propriety of such deprivation.

The Mental Treatment Standards Committee should be empowered to establish guidelines on what constitutes a substantial restriction on treatment opportunities afforded patients generally. For example, mere placement of a patient in a locked ward may not, in and of itself, constitute a substantial restriction on a patient's treatment opportunities. However, transfer to a locked ward for an indefinite length of time with a restriction on movement of the patient to occupational or other therapeutic programs, might constitute such restriction. If such a standard was established, the institution would be called upon to justify in a court hearing a proposed placement of this restriction on any patient.

The Right to Decline Certain Treatments

Currently, a person involuntarily committed to a mental hospital is, by virtue of his status, considered subject to treatment.

While as yet no definite answer can be given or even suggested as to the extent of the patient's right to refuse treatment or his duty to accept treatment, an attempt should be made to formulate some workable principles in this area. The rules relating to the administration of treatment by non-mental hospitals are well settled. Except in emergency cases, before a physician administers treatment or performs an operation, he must obtain the consent of the patient, or if the patient is a minor, he must obtain the consent of the patient's parent or guardian. Absent in adjudication of incompetency of a mental patient, these rules should apply to him as well—at least as to those therapies that involve significant danger to the physical or mental well-being of the patient. I have proposed a statute to provide:

Therapies or procedures involving any significant degree of danger to the physical or mental well-being of the patient and all surgery except those operations performed on an emergency basis to save life, limb, sight or hearing, shall require the written, voluntary, and informed consent of the patient prior to their administration or performance. If the patient is a minor or is mentally incapable of executing a valid consent, the written consent of the guardian of the patient shall be substituted for the consent of the patient. Additionally, therapies, procedures, or operations requiring consent shall be permitted only by order of the patient's physician and only when no less dangerous therapy can achieve the necessary and therapeutically desirable result. The decision to order such therapy, procedure, or operation shall be recorded on the patient's clinical record prior to its performance together with an explanation justifying the decision. Prior to its performance, the patient shall have the right and opportunity to contest the necessity to perform such therapy, procedure, or operation or the necessity to substitute another's judgment for his, or the validity of the written consent obtained from him.

Lobotomy and other psychosurgery, aversive conditioning therapies, and clinical investigations, research, experimentation or testing of any kind seem to be obvious examples of procedures involving a significant degree of danger to the physical or mental well-being of mental patients. Occupational therapy, recreational therapy, group therapy, and other psychotherapies do not seem to involve such risks. Electro-convulsive therapy involves certain dangers, although the risk of injury has been reduced in recent years.[11] The Mental Treatment Standards Committee is the appropriate body to examine these and other therapies and to determine which therapies involve the degree of danger necessary to invoke the requirement of consent.

The Chronic Patient—The Imposition of a Time Limit to Treatment

It is well known that a mental patient receives a more intensive treatment program upon initial admission to a mental hospital than after he has remained for a time and been assigned to a "continued treatment" ward. There are significantly fewer patients per physician in admissions wards than in continued treatment wards. The problem is not one of willful withholding of treatment to patients who have been institutionalized for a time, but, rather, the problem of allocating

[11] Persons temporarily detained pursuant to Mich. Comp. Laws §330.19, Mich. Stat. Ann. §14.809 may receive "medical or psychiatric treatment excluding shock treatment." This appears to be at least some statutory recognition of the danger involved in shock therapy.

inadequate numbers of treating personnel where they will do the most good. But if the goal of treatment remains the same (rehabilitation of the individual to the extent that he is able to function adequately outside the institution), a patient's need for treatment opportunities does not necessarily decrease with a continuing increase in length of stay.

Pursuant to the legislation I have proposed, the Mental Treatment Standards Committee should establish minimum standards to be utilized in admissions or intensive care units. It would be unrealistic for me to propose that continued treatment wards be expected to meet those standards. However, it is undesirable to propose the establishment of "lesser-than-minimum-standards" that would satisfy the treatment requirement for continued treatment wards. I feel that the proper approach is as follows:

1. A patient should be retained in an intensive care ward that meets the minimum treatment standards established by the Mental Treatment Standards Committee until he can be released to the community as sufficiently rehabilitated, or until he has received the maximum benefit from such treatment. A patient should be permitted to allege that he has received the maximum benefit from treatment.

2. Continued confinement of the individual after he has received the maximum benefit from treatment cannot be justified on a "need-for-treatment" basis.

3. If a patient is to be retained thereafter, some other basis to justify the commitment must be utilized. A new hearing with the requisite procedural safeguards should be held at this time. An appropriate placement in a new institutional setup or release should be ordered accordingly.

For example, indefinite commitment of individuals with sociopathic personalities who have not responded to mental hospital treatment can be justified only as preventive detention. If the real basis for the commitment is alleged danger to society and not "need for treatment," and if this justification is legally sufficient and socially desirable, the individual should be accorded a trial, with stringent criminal process safeguards. Accuracy of the prediction of dangerousness should be required. If committed, the individual should be placed in a detention facility, not a hospital. Similarly, if there is justification for retaining chronic schizophrenics because of their inability to care for themselves, a new hearing should be required to establish this, and placement should be in an extended care facility, not a hospital.[12]

[12] I do not at this time express any opinion as to wether these non-treatment confinement arrangements are legal or desirable.

APPENDIX A:

PROPOSED RIGHT TO TREATMENT LAW

Section 2. Establishment of Mental Treatment Standards Committee. . . .

(b) The Mental Treatment Standards Committee shall be composed of seven members as follows:

1. a licensed non-administrator psychiatrist who is a member of the American Psychiatric Association;

2. a licensed physician who is not a psychiatrist and who is a member of the American Medical Association;

3. a psychiatric social worker who is a member of the Committee of Psychiatry of the National Association of Social Workers and who has had at least five years experience in institutional psychiatric social work;

4. a clinical psychologist holding a Ph.D. and who is member of the Clinical Psychologists of the American Psychological Association;

5. a licensed psychiatrist who is a member of the National Association of Medical Superintendents of Mental Hospitals and who has had at least five years of experience as a mental institution administrator;

6. a registered professional nurse who is a member of the Psychiatric and Mental Health Division of the American Nurses Association; and

7. the Director of Mental Health.
Section 3. Preparation and Adoption of Minimum Standards.—

a) The Mental Treatment Standards Committee shall prepare and adopt a "Manual of Minimum Standards for Treatment of Mentally Ill Patients in State Mental Institutions," which shall, in the opinion of the committee, be acceptable to the professional associations named in Section 2 and represented by the members of the committee. "Treatment" is defined as those forms of therapy from which a patient can gain sufficient benefit to substantially aid in his adjustment for his return to society, in the reasonable belief of a psychiatrist. Custodial care shall not constitute treatment within the meaning of the act.

b) These standards shall be prepared and adopted in accordance with the definition of "treatment" and shall specifically include, but not be limited to the following matters:

1) the number of professional and non-professional staff, whose responsibilities are directly related to patient population, including the maximum number of patients for each psychiatrist, physician, clinical psychologist, social worker, industrial therapist, nurse, and attendant or aide;

2) the required minimum qualifications for each professional and non-professional staff position, referred to in clause (1) of subsection (b) of Section 3, including degrees, licensure, certification, apprenticeship, and experience;

3) the minimum number of individual consultations each patient shall have with a psychiatrist and other appropriate professional personnel and the minimum number of hours of such individual consultations each patient shall have in each thirty day period;

4) the frequency and extent of general physical examinations; and,

5) requirements for maintenance of the individualized treatment plans for each patient which shall include but not be limited to: (i) the initial diagnosis, (ii) the manner in which the facilities and programs of the particular institution can improve the patient's condition, (iii) the treatment goals, and (iv) the treatment regimen that is planned to accomplish these goals, subject to the limitation provided in subsection (e) of Section (3).

c) Individualized treatment plans shall be periodically reviewed and updated at no greater interval than every three months.

d) The minimum standards for numbers and qualifications of staff and number of individual consultations shall be no lower than the standards established by the American Psychiatric Association; and they shall also include requirements that all psychiatrists and medical practitioners must have the qualifications that are required to obtain Michigan licensing for private practice.

e) The committee shall not include in its standards any requirements relating to selection and conduct by individual psychiatrists, physicians, or clinical psychologists of their treatment methods or procedures, nor the judgment, skill or care used by these practitioners. The standards promulgated by the committee shall be expressed in objective terms so far as possible in order to minimize the necessity for subjective evaluation of departmental and institutional compliance, in judicial review.

f) The committee shall present to the Governor within six months after its appointment the completed "Manual of Minimum Standards for Treatment of Mentally Ill Patients in State Mental Institutions" and the minimum standards as promulgated by the committee and set forth in such manual shall be the minimum standards of treatment for all patients confined in state mental institutions in Michigan, beginning one year after such presentation, and such manual shall be a public document.

g) The Governor shall immediately upon receipt of said manual from the committee furnish to the Director of Mental Health and the Superintendent of each state mental institution copies of the manual and shall allocate sufficient resources necessary for the state mental institutions to be able to provide at least the minimum staffing standards.

h) The Department of Mental Health shall make studies to determine the additional personnel necessary to meet the requirements of this act. A report shall be prepared and be presented to the Legislature within one year from the effective date of this act, giving cost and other appropriate data.

Section 4. Patients' Legal Right to Minimum Standards of Treatment.

a) Beginning one year after the presentation of the manual to the Governor, every person who is then or at any time thereafter confined, voluntarily or involuntarily, in a state mental institution, shall have the legal right to receive at all times while so confined at least minimum treatment as herein defined.

b) The decisions of the Mental Treatment Standards Committee reflected in the standards adopted in the manual are subject to judicial review in the same manner as are rules of other administrative agencies.

c) The right to minimum standards of treatment provided by this act shall not include the right to have reviewed the judgment, skill, or care used by individual psychiatrists, physicians or clinical psychologists. Any such rights and remedies existing by common law or other statutes shall not be hereby impaired.

EDITORIAL NOTE: The United States Court of Appeals for the Fifth Circuit on April 26, 1974 (*Donaldson* v. *O'Connor*, No. 73–1843, 42 LW 2577) affirmed a verdict of the U.S. District Court for the Northern District of Florida, assessing $28,500 in compensatory damages and $10,000 in punitive damages against the Superintendent of the Florida State Hospital and plaintiff Donaldson's attending physician. Donaldson was committed to the hospital in 1959, instituted the suit, contending that he had a constitutional right to treatment or to be released, in February 1971, and was not released until July 31, 1971. The court found that defendants, in violation of Donaldson's Fourteenth Amendment rights, failed to provide treatment and wrongfully continued to detain him despite his non-dangerousness. Cert. granted 95 S. Ct. 171 C 1974.

B.   Right to Refuse Treatment

THE LIMITS OF THERAPY

Nicholas N. Kittrie

Surely the right to live one's life free from bodily and psychological alteration is basic to our scheme of society. The ability to remain as you are is clearly a right suggested by the general pattern of the Bill of Rights. The First Amendment prohibitions against state invasion of religious freedom and interference with the free transmission of ideas demonstrate that a man's thoughts, mind, conscience, and psychological processes are not to be manipulated or coerced by the state. Furthermore, the Eighth Amendment indicates that there are limits of human dignity beyond which the state cannot go in defending itself against the most heinous of offenders. Thus, even under a narrow construction of the Ninth Amendment, room can be found for the right to personality and bodily integrity.

Perhaps the question should not be what the past use of the Ninth Amendment has been, but whether it has any import for us today. If the framers of the Constitution could have foreseen the therapeutic power, would they not have made some provision to protect individual dignity and integrity? Should we not have the wisdom to react to new dangers using the broadsword they gave us in the Ninth Amendment?

Seeking to define the future limits of therapy, one might outlaw certain surgical, chemical, or psychological techniques altogether, or at least insist that the measure of treatment be proportionate to the severity and social hazard of the deviation. Speaking with regard to classical criminal law, the German philosopher Immanuel Kant stressed that "punishment can never be imposed merely for the purpose of securing some extrinsic good, either for the criminal himself or for civil society; it must in all cases be imposed (and can only be imposed) because the individual upon whom it is inflicted has committed an offense. . . .

The right of retaliation . . . properly understood . . . is the only principle which . . . can definitely guide a public tribunal as to both the quality and quantity of just punishment." One could insist that therapeutic controls should be similarly measured.

One might attempt to delineate personality characteristics that would be immune from alteration. Or one might approach the solution altogether differently. Since the therapeutic state claims for itself a parental role, emphasizing the individual's salvation and well-being over the public's retributive and protective urge, perhaps the propriety of therapy should depend on whether the treatment is constituted for the patient as an end in himself rather than as a means to broader social aims. It is wrong, it has been insisted, to use a person simply as a means to benefit others. What this means is that the aim of treatment should be the patient's own self-fulfillment, not his greater service to or conformity with societal imperatives for the benefit of society. But could we secure a synthesis of the diverse concepts of man's role in the universe, and a consensus among the diverse insights into the sociopsychological makeup of the human nature, which would be necessary for such self-fulfillments? There is a challenge.

Only the future will substantively define the scope of the individual's right not to be altered. Under the criminal process, in an admittedly retributive society, the Eighth Amendment provided a measure for punishment, but little attention has been given in the past to the limits upon the therapeutic process. In tomorrow's manipulative yet assertedly benevolent therapeutic state, the Ninth Amendment should undoubtedly be used in order to furnish a new scale for measuring the type and scope of justified state "treatment."

Excerpted and reprinted with permission from Kittrie, *The Right to Be Different* (Baltimore: The Johns Hopkins Press, 1971), pp. 392–94.

Such limitations on the therapeutic power may indeed hinder the "cure" of many patients. But what kind of a cure is sought by treatments which seek only to preserve the external shell of the treated? Since the therapeutic power seeks justification in the name of therapy and humanity, what reasonable objection could be raised against protections against the very destruction of the essence of humanness? Should we not be willing to accept these limitations to preserve human variation and pluralism in the same way that we have been willing to accept limitations on the exercise of the police power in order to preserve liberty at the expense of more crime, delinquency, and offensive behavior?

TOKEN AND TABOO: BEHAVIOR MODIFICATION, TOKEN ECONOMIES, AND THE LAW

David B. Wexler

I. PSYCHOLOGY AND TOKEN ECONOMIES

A. General Considerations

Many behavior modification practitioners apply clinically the learning theory principles of Skinnerian operant conditioning. Operant theory is bottomed on the principle, amply demonstrated by empirical data, that behavior is strengthened or weakened by its consequences.[1] The frequency of a behavior increases if it is followed by desirable consequences, whereas it will be extinguished if the positive consequences are discontinued or if the consequences are aversive.[2]

The application of operant conditioning to humans has come a long way since 1949, when a severely regressed person was taught to raise his arm by a procedure that rewarded appropriate arm motions by the subsequent squirting of a sugar-milk solution into his mouth. Now, a multitude of therapeutic behavior modification systems are in operation on ward-wide and institution-wide scales. By and large, these programs seek to shape[3] and maintain appropriate behavior patterns—designated as "target behaviors" or "target responses"— by rewarding or "reinforcing" the desired responses. Usually, rewards are dispensed in the form of tokens or points—known as "secondary" or "generalized" reinforcers—which can then be converted, pursuant to a specific economic schedule, to "primary reinforcers" such as snacks, mail-order catalogue items, and the like.

B. Token Economies

Teodoro Ayllon and Nathan Azrin pioneered the token economy concept on a ward of chronically psychotic female patients at the Anna State Hospital in Illinois. Because of their adaptation to long periods of stagnant hospitalization, chronic patients typically suffer from extreme apathy and dependency. This condition, known as institutionalization, impedes the chronic's chances for improvement or release. To overcome this problem, Ayllon and Azrin rewarded target behaviors that would reverse the institutionalization syndrome. Work assignments within the hospital and various self-care behaviors were rewarded with tokens. The self-care category included grooming, bathing, toothbrushing, bed-making, and the like. Work assignments included kitchen chores, serving in the dining room, assisting in the laundry, janitorial work, and related tasks.

For the token economy to succeed, it is necessary to insure that the items or events purchasable with the tokens are effective

---

[1] A good introductory text on operant conditioning is J. R. Millenson, *Principles of Behavioral Analysis* (1967).

[2] For a good introduction to behavior modification and how it contrasts with traditional dynamic concepts, see L. Ullmann and L. Krasner, *Case Studies in Behavior Modification* (1965): 1–65.

[3] "Shape" is a technical term used by operant psychologists to describe the process of gradually building a new behavior by rewarding closer and closer approximations to it.

Excerpted and reprinted with permission from 61 *California Law Review* 81 (January 1973).

reinforcers—in lay terms, that they would in fact be desired by the patients. To solve this problem, the Anna State Hospital psychologists applied "Premack Principle."

It was noted that certain patients often hoarded various items under their mattresses. The activity in this case, in a general sense, consisted of concealing private property in such a manner that it would be inaccessible to other patients and the staff. Since this event seemed to be highly probable, it was formally scheduled as a reinforcer. Keys to a locked cabinet in which they could conceal their private possessions just as they had been doing with the mattresses were made available to patients.

Another activity that was observed to be highly probable was the attempt of patients to conceal themselves in several locations on the ward in an effort to enjoy some degree of privacy. A procedure was therefore instituted whereby a patient could obtain a portable screen to put in front of her bed or access to a bedroom with a door. Another event that had a high probability of occurrence for some patients was a visit with the social worker or psychologist. This was used as a reinforcer by arranging appointments with either of these staff members.

Ground privileges and supervised walks by the staff were also established as reinforcers by application of the Premack Principle, since patients were frequently observed to "stay at the exit to the ward and try to leave." The opportunity to attend religious services was also used as a reinforcer, since several patients attended frequently when they were allowed to freely.

Thus, personal cabinets, room-dividers, visits with the professional staff, ground privileges, supervised walks, and religious services were all made contingently available to the patients: they could be purchased if the patient had performed a sufficient number of target responses to have earned the requisite tokens to purchase the reinforcers. They were otherwise unavailable. Other reinforcers in the Anna State Hospital program included a personal chair, writing materials and stationery, movies, television programs, and various commissary items.

By using these "strong, albeit untapped" sources of motivation, the Ayllon and Azrin economy produced rather impressive results when measured by standards of work performance. They compared the work output of their patients during a specified period of the token economy with a subsequent experimental period during which the various reinforcers were freely available without tokens—a situation which "approximated the usual conduct of a mental hospital ward." Ayllon and Azrin found that patient performance during the experimental period plummeted to less than one-fourth the token economy level. Hence, they concluded that "the performance on a usual ward would be increased fourfold by instituting this motivating environment."

Nonetheless, the Anna State Hospital program did not change the behavior of 8 out of 44 patients involved. Eight patients, who expended fewer than 50 tokens within 20 days, all earned by self-care rather than from job assignments, were relatively unaffected by the reinforcement procedure. Statistical comparison of them with the other patients revealed no difference in diagnosis or age. It appears that their failure to modify behavior appreciably stemmed from the relative absence of any strong behavior patterns that could be used as reinforcers. The only two behaviors that existed in strength were sleeping and eating. The present program did not attempt to control the availability of food.

Many token economy programs have been patterned after the Ayllon and Azrin model. In Atthowe's program for chronic patients at the Palo Alto Veterans Administration Hospital, for example, patients earned points not only for their industrial therapy job assignments but also for participating in group activities, in recreational therapy, and for attending weekend movies. [S]everal programs have taken the step recommended but not taken by Ayllon and Azrin and have made food and beds available only on a contingent basis. Indeed, those programs have exceeded the Ayllon and Azrin recommendation by using beds and meals as reinforcers on a ward-wide basis. . . .

One of the token economies that hinges food and beds on appropriate behavioral responses—a chronic ward at the Patton State Hospital in San Bernardino, California—is "willing to let a patient go for as long as five days without food, or until he has been reduced to 80% of his previous body weight."[4]

At Patton, newly admitted patients are placed in the orientation group, where living conditions are exceedingly drab, and where the subsistence-level existence can be purchased for a small number of tokens. After a patient has adapted well to the orientation group, he is elevated to the middle group, where conditions are better but are considerably more expensive. Patients in the middle group are

---

[4] Schaefer, "Investigations in Operant Conditioning Procedures in a Mental Hospital," in *Reinforcement Theory in Psychological Treatment—A Symposium* 25 (J. Fisher and R. Harris, eds., 1966) (Calif. Ment. Health Res. Monog. No. 8).

given five months to be promoted to the rather luxurious ready-to-leave group, but if after three months in the middle group a patient is not adequately facing the eventual prospect of life on the outside, he will be returned to the orientation group. Margaret Bruce, a psychiatric technician at the Patton State Hospital, described the orientation group in these words:

This group sleeps in a relatively unattractive dormitory which conforms to bare minimums set by the state department of mental hygiene. There are no draperies at the windows or spreads on the beds, and the beds themselves are of the simplest kind. In the dining room the patient sits with many other patients at a long table, crowded in somewhat uncomfortably. The only eating utensil given him is a large spoon. The food is served in unattractive, sectioned plastic dishes. So long as he is in this group, he is not allowed to wear his own clothes and cannot go to activities which other patients are free to attend off the unit. He may not have permission for off-the-ground visits, and the number of visitors who can see him is restricted.

During this time, the patient learns that his meals, his bed, his toilet articles, and his clothes no longer are freely given him. He must pay for these with tokens. These tokens pay for all those things normally furnished and often taken for granted. In the orientation group most of the things the patient wants are cheap; for example, it costs one token to be permitted to go to bed, one token for a meal. Patients find it easy enough to earn the few tokens necessary for bare subsistence.[5]

II. Law and Token Economies

Until very recently, the judicially manufactured "hands-off" doctrine enabled the courts to duck important questions regarding the limits of administrative discretion in the operation of prisons and mental institutions.[6] Accordingly, the correctional and therapeutic establishments were in effect given, by default, the legal nod to manage their institutions—and to conduct their therapy[7]—as they saw fit. But the last few years have witnessed a remarkable turnabout in the willingness of courts to scrutinize living conditions in total

institutions. Already, some bold and far-reaching decisions have been rendered,[8] and there is the further possibility of widespread legislative action.[9] From the sparce legal precedents, one can detect a rather clear trend, and the emerging law bears rather directly on the rights of patients subjected to a token economy.

[I]t will be recalled that the principle target response of most token economies is adequate functioning on an institutional work assignment. Many persons both within and without the legal profession, however, find it objectionable in effect to require patients—especially involuntarily committed patients—to work for mental institutions, particularly without standard compensation. Though the work assignments are often cast in therapeutic terms, such as overcoming apathy and institutionalization, the critics view the jobs as simple labor-saving devices which exploit patients and, indeed, which sometimes make hospital retention of particular patients almost indispensable to the functioning of the institution.

That patient job assignments are in fact often labor-saving is beyond question, as is the fact that work output will increase substantially when work is contingently reinforced by the standard reinforcers employed by token economies. During a patient vacation period [at Anna State Hospital] "the additional work required to keep the ward functioning . . . had to be made up by paid employees whose hours almost doubled."[10]

It seems clear that the law will not tolerate forced patient labor that is devoid of therapeutic purpose and which is required solely as a labor-saving technique. The Second Circuit, invoking a Thirteenth Amendment involuntary servitude rationale, so held in 1966.[11] Since then, recognition that there is not always a sharp line dividing therapeutic and non-therapeutic assignments has led to varying legal theories for dealing with—or for avoiding—the problem.

---

[5] Bruce, "Tokens for Recovery," 66 *Am. J. Nursing* (1966): 1799, 1800–01.

[6] E.g., Note, "Beyond the Ken of Courts: A Critique of the Judicial Refusal to Review the Complaints of Convicts, 72 *Yale L. J.* 506 (1963).

[7] E.g. N. Kittrie, *The Right to Be Different: Deviance and Enforced Therapy* (1971): 307–08. Cf. *O'Donoghue* v. *Riggs*, 73 Wash. 2d 814, 820 n.2, 440 P.2d 823, 828 n.2 (1968): "One who enters a hospital as a mentally ill person either as a voluntary or involuntary patient, impliedly consents to the use of such force as may be reasonably necessary to the proper care of the patient."

[8] *Covington* v. *Harris*, 491 F.2d 617 (D.C. Cir. 1969); *Wyatt* v. *Stickney*, 344 F. Supp. 373 (M.D. Ala. 1972) (Bryce and Searcy Hospitals).

[9] E.g., Cal. Welf. & Inst'ns Code § 5325 (West Supp. 1971).

[10] T. Ayllon and N. Azrin, *The Token Economy: A Motivational System for Therapy and Rehabilitation* (1968), p. 210.

[11] *Jobson* v. *Henne*, 355 F.2d 129, 132 n.3 (2d Cir. 1966). The court also noted that if concededly involuntary labor is non-therapeutic, even compensation for the work will not necessarily satisfy Thirteenth Amendment requirements, for "the mere payment of a compensation, unless the receipt of the compensation induces consent to the performance of the work, cannot serve to justify forced labor." Id.

One rule . . . suggested by . . . a leading mental health lawyer [is] "If a given type of labor *is* therapeutic, we would expect to find patients in private facilities performing that type of labor. Conversely, labor which is not generally performed in private facilities should be presumed . . . to be cost-saving rather than therapeutic."[12]

The "avoidance" approach is exemplified by the elaborate decision in *Wyatt* v. *Stickney*,[13] in which the court barred all involuntary patient labor involving hospital operation and maintenance—whether therapeutic or not— but permitted voluntary institutional work of either a therapeutic or a non-therapeutic nature, so long as the labor is compensated pursuant to the federal minimum wage law.[14] To insure the voluntary nature of any institutional work assignment undertaken, the *Wyatt* court specified further that "privileges or release from the hospital shall not be conditioned upon the performance of labor"[15] involving hospital maintenance.

The approach taken by the landmark *Wyatt* decision, if widely followed, would have an immense impact on traditional token economies. Patients could not be forced in any way to perform institutional labor assignments— and the force could not legitimately be exerted indirectly by making basic reinforcers "contingent" upon appropriate performance. Further, if patients should decide voluntarily to undertake institutional tasks, the minimum wage is the legally required "reinforcer." Under *Wyatt*, therapeutic assignments unrelated to hospital operations can constitute legitimate target responses that can be rewarded without regard to the minimum wage. But, perhaps most significant for token economies, *Wyatt* and related legal developments seem to have a great deal to say regarding the definition of legally acceptable reinforcers. *Wyatt*, together with an occasional piece of proposed or enacted[16] legislation, has begun the process of enumerating the rights guaranteed to hospitalized mental patients. The crux of the problem, from the viewpoint of behavior modification, is that the items and

activities that are emerging as absolute rights are the very same items and activities that the behavioral psychologists would employ as reinforcers—that is, as "contingent rights."

According to the *Wyatt* court, a residence unit with screens or curtains to insure privacy, together with "a comfortable bed, . . . a closet or locker for [the patient's] personal belongings, a chair, and a bedside table are all constitutionally required."[17] Under *Wyatt*, patients are also insured nutritionally adequate meals with a diet that will provide "at a minimum the Recommended Daily Dietary Allowances as developed by the National Academy of Sciences."[18] *Wyatt* further enunciates a general right to have visitors,[19] to attend religious services,[20] to wear one's own clothes[21] (or, for those without adequate clothes, to be provided with a selection of suitable clothing), and to have clothing laundered.[22] With respect to recreation, *Wyatt* speaks of a right to exercise physically several times weekly and to be outdoors regularly and frequently,[23] a right to interact with members of the other sex,[24] and a right to have a television set in the day room.[25] Finally, apparently borrowing from Judge Bazelon's opinion for the District of Columbia Circuit in *Covington* v. *Harris*,[26] Judge Johnson in *Wyatt* recognized that "patients have a right to the least restrictive conditions necessary to achieve the purposes of commitment"[27]—presumably including, if

[17] *Wyatt* v. *Stickney*, 344 F. Supp. 373, 381–82 (M.D. Ala. 1972) (Bryce and Searcy Hospitals).

[18] Id. at 383.

[19] Id. at 379. See also Cal. Welf. & Inst'ns. Code § 5325(c) (West Supp. 1971).

[20] 344 F. Supp. at 381.

[21] Id. at 380. See also Cal. Welf. & Inst'ns. Code § 5325(a) (West Supp. 1971).

[22] 344 F. Supp. at 381.

[23] Id.

[24] Id.

[25] Id. at 382.

[26] 419 F.2d 617 (D.C. Cir. 1969).

[27] *Wyatt* v. *Stickney*, 344 F. Supp. 373, 379 (M.D. Ala. 1972) (Bryce and Searcy Hospitals). The "least restrictive alternative" or "less drastic means" rationale was first applied in the mental health law area in *Lake* v. *Cameron*, 364 F.2d 657 (D.C. Cir. 1966), an opinion authored by Judge Bazelon, which held that commitment itself should be ordered only if no suitable but less drastic alternatives to commitment could be located. For a discussion of the constitutional doctrine of "less drastic means" in the commitment context, see Wexler, Scoville et al., "The Administration of Psychiatric Justice: Theory and Practice in Arizona," 13 *Arizona Law Review* 1 (1971). Hereafter referred to as *Psychiatric Justice Project*. See also Chambers, "Alternatives to Civil Commitment of the Mentally Ill: Practical Guides and Constitutional Imperatives," 70 *Mich. L. Rev.*

[12] Ennis, "Civil Liberties and Mental Illness," 7 *Crim. L. Bull.* (1971): 101, 123 (emphasis in original).

[13] *Wyatt* v. *Stickney*, 344 F. Supp. 373 (M.D. Ala. 1972) (Bryce and Searcy Hospitals).

[14] Id. at 381. The minimum wage law is the Fair Labor Standards Act, 29 U.S.C. § 206 (1971). Judge Johnson in *Wyatt* further ordered that payment to patients for such work shall not be applied to offset hospitalization costs. Id. at 13.

[15] 344 F.Supp. at 381.

[16] E.g., The Lanterman-Petris-Short Act, Cal. Welf. & Inst'ns. Code § 5325 (West Supp. 1971).

clinically acceptable, ground privileges and an open ward.

Thus, the usual target behaviors for token economies would be disallowed and the usual reinforcers will be legally unavailable. Chronic patients at Anna State Hospital who had to work for screens and personal lockers to insure privacy would, under *Wyatt*, have those items provided noncontingently. The "least restrictive conditions" rationale would presumably also invalidate programs, such as the one at Anna State Hospital,[28] in which ground privileges or supervised walks are available only by purchase, and programs in which outright release from the institution is conditioned upon the accumulation of a set number of tokens or points.

III. ANALYSIS AND IMPLICATIONS

The important question of the therapeutic or non-therapeutic nature of institutional labor is unfortunately far more complex than would be indicated by the black or white treatment it has received from both legal and psychological quarters. For instance, [the] initially attractive and easy-to-apply rule of thumb—that types of patient labor performed at public but not at private hospitals should be presumed cost-saving rather than therapeutic—simply cannot withstand close scrutiny. Private hospital patients are typically skilled, of adequate means, and in the hospital for a short stay. Chronic psychotics at state institutions are almost invariably persons who have been hospitalized and unemployed for long periods of time; they are overwhelmingly poor, unskilled, of advanced age, and likely to suffer considerable stigmatization upon release from the hospital.

Given this characterization of chronic mental patients, combined, of course, with apathy, dependency, and institutionalization, ambitious employment opportunities for released chronics are virtually out of the question. Indeed, when viewed from that perspective, together with the fact that work of almost any kind is probably superior to idleness in offsetting apathy, a wide range of institutional work activities have both therapeutic value and realistically approximate future employment goals.

[E]vidence that the motivation behind establishing such target behaviors is indeed

therapeutic rather than simply cost-saving can be gleaned . . . from examples where cost-saving was not in issue. One Veterans Administration program for discharged chronics, for instance, provides patients with token-earning formal classes in shopping, washing, ironing, and mending clothing, and related tasks.[29] Moreover, in one of the few reported instances where released chronics managed to adjust successfully to a form of community life and to remain employed, the nature of the employment was perfectly consistent with training provided by standard institutional tasks.[30]

When the group of patients was about to leave the hospital for the community, for example, it originally planned on opening a restaurant, the bulk of positions to consist of "cook, assistant cook, dishwasher, busboys, waiters and cashier." Eventually, however, the men settled on janitorial work and gardening as their source of income, but even those jobs were performed inadequately[31] until the men received specific training for the work.

From these examples, it should be apparent that many forms of institutional labor, even though concededly cost-saving, prevent apathy and prepare patients for life, however marginal, on the outside. If the performance of therapeutic institutional labor by patients is to be encouraged, however, certain safeguards should perhaps be required to insure that no patient becomes indispensable to his supervisor, a possibility which might result in the patient's continuation on the job becoming more important to the staff than his welfare, his treatment, or even his discharge. Administrative precautions taken in the Anna State Hospital program may prove instructive as legal guidelines: Ayllon and Azrin insisted upon periodic job rotation and, moreover, established a firm rule that "no patient was ever allowed to obtain a position for which she alone was qualified." Instead, "a position was established only when several patients were known to be capable of filling that position."

If, given certain safeguards, voluntary insti-

---

[29] Spiegler, The Use of a School Model and Contingency Management in a Day Treatment Program for Psychiatric Outpatients 4 (paper presented at Rocky Mountain Psychological Association Convention Denver Co., May 1971).

[30] E.g., G. Fairweather, D. Sanders, H. Maynard, D. Cressler, & D. Bleck, *Community Life for the Mentally Ill: An Alternative to Institutional Care*, p. 207 (1969). Indeed, the relapse rate for released chronics is so high and employment prospects are so dim that some commentators have questioned hospital release as an appropriate therapeutic goal.

[31] Id. at 5.

(1972): 1107. In *Covington* v. *Harris*, 419 F.2d 617 (D.C. Cir. 1969), Judge Bazelon simply extended the doctrine to life within the confines of the hospital environment.

[28] *Token Economy*, p. 226.

tutional labor by chronic patients is to be encouraged, what of *Wyatt*'s minimum wage mandate? Such a mandate, besides vitiating any cost-saving benefits of patient performance, might cause serious complications. First, it will inevitably divert scarce legislative appropriations away from other hospital and therapeutic uses. Second, a minimum wage requirement may encourage the hospital—and indeed the encouragement may be compounded by union and community pressure—to fill its institutional positions with permanent outsiders instead of with patients, perhaps leaving the patients to pursue less therapeutic activities. In other words, a minimum wage requirement may possibly result in greater expenditures for less effective therapy.

Thus, although compensating all institutional tasks with the minimum wage appears to be an attractive goal, it is clear that several major problems might be created by that requirement. It is clear, too, that various safeguards short of the minimum wage can be invoked to prevent patient peonage, and that voluntary patient labor can probably be encouraged either by monetary rewards somewhat below the minimum wage or by whatever other reinforcers satisfy the *Wyatt* test.

The major problem faced by the token economy is the current trend toward expansion of the category of protected inmate interests. The law, relying on concepts such as freedom and dignity, would require, for example, that all patients be accorded minimal levels of privacy and comfort. To the behavioral psychologist, who operates from the premise of determinism, philosophical notions of "freedom" and "dignity" are irrelevant.[32] Rather, the psychologist views privacy or comfort as no more than useful tools which he can manipulate to make a psychotic's behavior more appropriate and socially adaptive—a goal which presumably all agree is in the best interest of both the patient and the society. In the psychologist's view it would surely be an ironic tragedy if, in the name of an illusory ideal such as freedom, the law were to deny the therapist the only effective tools he has to restore the chronic psychotic to his health— and his place in the community.

Wyatt thus poses a painful dilemma. The behavior modifier suggests that chronic psychotics respond initially to only the most primitive reinforcers, and, therefore, only their contingent availability can motivate development of socially adaptive behavior. It follows, the behaviorists claim, that if the basics are made freely available as rights rather than as reinforcers, chronic psychotics may be destined to spend their lives functioning poorly in an institutional setting, whereas if those basic rights are converted into contingent reinforcers, there may be a real prospect of clinical improvement and discharge.

If the empirical evidence supported the claim that token economies relying on primitive reinforcers worked very well with chronic patients—that, for example, virtually all patients improved dramatically and were able to earn the reinforcers required for a decent existence or if the evidence demonstrated that no less drastic means could accomplish similar results—a reevaluation of the emerging law might very well be in order. But a review of the pertinent literature suggests that behavior modification proponents may have difficulty sustaining a burden of proof with respect to those matters.

First of all, while most token economy outcome studies report favorable results,[33] the successes are far from overwhelming. Even in a project as dramatic as the Anna State Hospital study, 8 of the 44 subject patients were basically unresponsive to the program, and success for the remaining patients was measured solely by their work output. When judged by release data rather than by measures of work output, decreased apathy, or improved clinical state, results of token economy systems with chronic psychotics have not been encouraging. Even in the Atthowe and Krasner project at the Palo Alto Veterans Administration Hospital, which reported a doubling of the discharge rate, 11 of the 24 released patients returned to the hospital within 9 months,[34] a more rapid relapse than is normally found in studies of chronic patients.

We must also consider whether the results achieved by token economies—whatever they may be—could be matched or surpassed by less drastic means. Information is wanting, perhaps in part because behavior modifiers have not employed reinforcers other than the basics in standard use. It may be, for example, that creative observation of patient behavior preferences would reveal frequent behavior patterns, other than basic behaviors, which could be utilized as reinforcers. Also, although it is an impure technique according to ortho-

[32] See B. F. Skinner, *Beyond Freedom and Dignity* (1971).

[33] See, e.g., Gripp and Magaro, "A Token Economy Program Evaluation with Untreated Control Ward Comparisons," 9 *Behav. Res. & Therapy* (1971): 137 (summarizing results achieved by other researchers).

[34] Atthowe and Krasner, "Preliminary Report on the Application of Contingent Reinforcement Procedures (Token Economy) on a 'Chronic' Psychiatric Ward," 73 *J. Abnormal Psych.* (1968): 37, 40.

dox behaviorism, another practical approach is simply to ask the patients what they would like to possess or to do.

By exploring creatively for reinforcers, it is likely that therapists could construct a list of idiosyncratic objects and activities—mail order catalogue items, soft-boiled rather than standard hard-boiled eggs, and feeding kittens are actual clinical examples—that could be made available contingently in order to strengthen appropriate target responses. Moreover, to the extent that effective reinforcers are in fact idiosyncratic, it follows almost by definition that their contingent availability could not conflict with the legally emerging absolute general rights of patients.

A system of positive behavior modification based heavily on idiosyncratic reinforcers might be clinically as well as legally superior. Psychologists employing such systems have been able to devise individual treatment plans assuring each patient independent diagnostic and therapeutic attention.

But individualized treatment plans, required by *Wyatt* and perhaps part of the emerging right to treatment,[35] are not incompatible with the operation of ward-wide or hospital-wide general treatment systems designed to overcome general patient problems, such as indecisiveness, dependency, or apathy. In fact, the most fruitful combination might be to combine individualized treatment programs with an efficient, easy-to-administer general therapeutic system. If, however, the criteria for a successful system is efficacy with the least drastic deprivations possible, it appears that token economies for chronic psychotics may well finish no better than second best.

[35] E.g., Birnbaum, 'The Right to Treatment," 46 *A.B.A.J.* (1960): 499; *Rouse* v. *Cameron*, 373 F.2d 451 (D.C. Cir. 1966).

KNECHT v. GILLMAN

ROSS, Circuit Judge.

This is an action by Gary Knecht and Ronald Stevenson, both in the custody of the State of Iowa, against officials of that state, under 42 U.S.C. § 1983. Their complaint alleged that they had been subjected to injections of the drug apomorphine at the Iowa Security Medical Facility (ISMF) without their consent and that the use of said drug by the defendants constituted cruel and unusual punishment in violation of the eighth amendment. The trial court dismissed their complaint for injunctive relief. We reverse with directions to enjoin the defendants from further use of the drug except pursuant to specific guidelines hereinafter set forth.

The summary of the evidence showed that apomorphine had been administered at ISMF for some time prior to the hearing as "aversive stimuli" in the treatment of inmates with behavior problems. The drug was administered by intra-muscular injection by a nurse after an inmate had violated the behavior protocol established for him by the staff. Dr. Loeffelholz testified that the drug could be injected for such pieces of behavior as not getting up, for giving cigarettes against orders, for talking, for swearing, or for lying. Other inmates or members of the staff would report on these viola-

tions of the protocol and the injection would be given by the nurse without the nurse or any doctor having personally observed the violation and without specific authorization of the doctor.

When it was determined to administer the drug, the inmate was taken to a room near the nurses' station which contained only a water closet and there given the injection. He was then exercised and within about fifteen minutes he began vomiting. The vomiting lasted from fifteen minutes to an hour. There is also a temporary cardiovascular effect which involves some change in blood pressure and "in the heart." This aversion type "therapy" is based on "Pavlovian conditioning."[1]

The record is not clear as to whether or not

[1] Pavlovian conditioning is based on the theory that when environmental stimuli or the kinetic stimuli produced by the incipient movements of the punished act are made contiguous with punishment, they take on some of the aversive properties of the punishment itself. The next time the organism begins the act, particularly in the same environment, it produces stimuli which through classical conditioning have become aversive. It is these aversive stimuli which then prevent the act from occurring. Singer, Psychological Studies of Punishment, 58 Calif. L.Rev. 405, 423 (1970).

488 F.2d 1136 (1973).

the drug was always used with the initial consent of the inmate. It has apparently been administered in a few instances in the past without obtaining written consent of the inmate and once the consent is given, withdrawal thereof was not permitted. Apparently, at the time of trial apomorphine was not being used unless the inmate signed an initial consent, but there is no indication that the authorities now permit an inmate to withdraw his consent once it is given. Neither is there any indication in the record that the procedure has been changed to require the prior approval of a physician each time the drug is administered. Likewise there is no indication that there has been any change in the procedure which permits the administration of the drug upon reports of fellow inmates despite a recommendation by the magistrate that this practice should be avoided.

The testimony relating to the medical acceptability of this treatment is not conclusive. Dr. Steven Fox of the University of Iowa testified that behavior modification by aversive stimuli is "highly questionable technique" and that only a 20% to 50% success is claimed. He stated that it is not being used elsewhere to his knowledge and that its use is really punishment worse than a controlled beating since the one administering the drug can't control it after it is administered.

On the other hand, Dr. Loeffelholz of the ISMF staff testified that there had been a 50% to 60% effect in modifying behavior by the use of apomorphine at ISMF. There is no evidence that the drug is used at any other inmate medical facility in any other state.

The Iowa Security Medical Facility is established by Section 223.1, Code of Iowa, 1973. It is an institution for persons displaying evidence of mental illness or psychological disorders and requiring diagnostic services and treatment in a security setting. The patients admitted to the facility may originate from the following sources:

1) residents of any institution under the jurisdiction of the department of social services;
2) commitments by the courts as mentally incompetent to stand trial under Chapter 783 of the Iowa Code;
3) referrals by the court for psychological diagnosis and recommendations as part of the pretrial or presentence procedure or determination of mental competency to stand trial;
4) mentally ill prisoners from county and city jails for diagnosis, evaluation, or treatment.

Section 223.4, Code of Iowa, 1973.

Those transferred from institutions where they were committed pursuant to civil statutes or those who were committed by order of the court prior to conviction, suffer a compromise of their procedural rights in the process of the transfer to ISMF. The constitutional justification of this compromise of procedure is that the purpose of commitment is treatment, not punishment. *Cf.* McKeiver v. Pennsylvania, 403 U.S. 528, 522, 91 S.Ct. 1976, 29 L.Ed.2d 647 (White J., concurring) (1971); Sas v. Maryland, 334 F.2d 506, 509 (4th Cir. 1964). Beyond this justification for treatment is the clear command of the statutes that the purpose of confinement at ISMF is not penal in nature, but rather one of examination, diagnosis and treatment. Naturally, examination and diagnosis, by their very definition, do not encompass the administration of drugs. Thus, when that course of conduct is taken with respect to any particular patient, he is the recipient of treatment.

The use of apomorphine, then, can be justified, only if it can be said to be treatment. Based upon the testimony adduced at the hearing and the findings made by the magistrate and adopted by the trial court, it is not possible to say that the use of apomorphine is a recognized and acceptable medical practice in institutions such as ISMF. Neither can we say, however, that its use on inmates who knowingly and intelligently consent to the treatment, should be prohibited on a medical or a legal basis. The authorities who testified at the evidentiary hearing indicate that some form of consent is now obtained prior to this treatment. The only question then is whether, under the eighth amendment, its use should be prohibited absent such consent; and if so what procedure must be followed to prevent abuses in the treatment procedures and to make certain the consent is knowingly and intelligently made.

[1] At the outset we note that the mere characterization of an act as "treatment" does not insulate it from eighth amendment scrutiny. In Trop v. Dulles, 356 U.S. 86, 95, 78 S.Ct. 590, 2 L.Ed. 2d 630 (1958), the Supreme Court stated that the legislative classification of a statute is not conclusive in determining whether there had been a violation of the eighth amendment. Instead, the Court examined the statute by an "inquiry directed to substance," reasoning that "even a clear legislative classification of a statute as 'nonpenal' would not alter the fundamental nature of a plainly penal statute." Trop v. Dulles, *supra*, 356 U.S. at 95, 78 S.Ct. at 595.

Other courts have examined nonpenal statutes in the manner suggested by the Supreme Court in *Trop*. The contention that a state's incarceration of runaway juveniles could not violate the eighth amendment because the statute did not authorize any punishment of juveniles was struck down in Vann v. Scott, 467 F.2d 1235, 1240 (7th Cir. 1972):

Whatever the State does with the child is done in the name of rehabilitation. Since—the argument runs—by definition the treatment is not "punishment," it obviously cannot be "cruel and unusual punishment." But neither the label which a State places on its own conduct, nor even the legitimacy of its motivation, can avoid the applicability of the Federal Constitution. We have no doubt that well intentioned attempts to rehabilitate a child could, in extreme circumstances, constitute cruel and unusual punishment proscribed by the Eighth Amendment.

The absence of criminal incarceration did not prohibit a federal court from entertaining an eighth amendment claim to test the conditions of confinement in a boys' training school:

The fact that juveniles are *in theory* not punished, but merely confined for rehabilitative purposes, does not preclude operation of the Eighth Amendment. The reality of confinement in Annex B is that it is punishment.

Inmates of the Boys' Training School v. Affleck, 346 F.Supp. 1354, 1366 (D.R.I. 1972).

Such findings of cruel and unusual punishment have been sustained with respect to the death penalty,[2] penal incarceration for status,[3] civil commitment for status without treatment,[4] strerooms and solitary confinements,[5] tranquilizing drugs,[6] and corporeal punishment for prisoners.[7] However, any such determination rests on the facts of a particular case.

[2] Here we have a situation in which an inmate may be subjected to a morphine base drug which induces vomiting for an extended period of time. Whether it is called "aversive stimuli" or punishment, the act of forcing someone to vomit for a fifteen minute period for committing some minor breach of the rules can only be regarded as cruel and unusual unless the treatment is being administered to a patient who knowingly and intelligently has consented to it. To hold otherwise would be to ignore what each of us has learned from sad experience—that vomiting (especially in the presence of others) is a painful and debilitating experience. The use of the unproven drug for this purpose on an involuntary basis, is, in our opinion, cruel and unusual punishment prohibited by the eighth amendment.

In this case the trial court should enjoin the use of apomorphine in the treatment of inmates at the ISMF except when the following conditions are complied with:

1. A written consent must be obtained from the inmate specifying the nature of the treatment, a written description of the purpose, risks and effects of treatment, and advising the inmate of his right to terminate the consent at any time. This consent must include a certification by a physician that the patient has read and understands all of the terms of the consent and that the inmate is mentally competent to understand fully all of the provisions thereof and give his consent thereto.

2. The consent may be revoked at any time after it is given and if an inmate orally expresses an intention to revoke it to any member of the staff, a revocation form shall be provided for his signature at once.

3. Each apomorphine injection shall be individually authorized by a doctor and be administered by a doctor, or by a nurse. It shall be authorized in each instance only upon information based on the personal observation of a member of the professional staff. Information from inmates or inmate aides of the observation of behavior in violation of an inmate's protocol shall not be sufficient to warrant such authorization.

[2] Furman v. Georgia, 408 U.S. 238, 92 S.Ct. 2726, 33 L.Ed.2d 346 (1972).

[3] Robinson v. California, 370 U.S. 660, 82 S. Ct. 1417, 8 L.Ed.2d 758 (1962).

[4] Rouse v. Cameron, 373 F.2d 451 (D.C. Cir. 1966); New York State Ass'n. for Retarded Children v. Rockefeller, 357 F.Supp. 752 (E.D.N.Y. 1973); Martarella v. Kelley, 349 F.Supp. 575 (S.D.N.Y. 1972).

[5] LaReau v. MacDougall, 473 F.2d 974 (2d Cir. 1972), cert. denied, — U.S. —, 94 S. Ct. 49, 38 L.Ed.2d 123 (1973); Gates v. Collier, 349 F.Supp. 881 (N.D. Miss. 1972); Landman v. Royster, 333 F.Supp. 621 (E.D. Va. 1971); Inmates of Boys' Training School v. Affleck, 346 F.Supp. 1354 (D.R.I. 1972).

[6] Nelson v. Heyne, 355 F.Supp. 451 (N.D. Ind. 1972).

[7] Jackson v. Bishop, 404 F.2d 571 (8th Cir. 1968); Nelson v. Heyne, 355 F.Supp. 451 (N.D. Ind. 1972); Landman v. Royster, 333 F.Supp. 575 (S.D.N.Y. 1972).

The judgment of the district court is reversed with directions to grant the injunction under the terms hereinbefore set forth.

PROBLEMS IN OBTAINING INFORMED CONSENT FOR ELECTROSHOCK THERAPY

Zigmund M. Lebensohn, M.D.

Defining and obtaining truly informed consent is a difficult problem in medicine. It is even more difficult in psychiatry, where serious questions regarding the mental competence of the patient to give such consent may be legitimately raised.

The competent and conscientious psychiatrist confronted with a desperately suicidal or agitated patient who, in the doctor's opinion, would recover rapidly with electroshock therapy (EST), is faced with an almost insoluble dilemma. If he tells the patient *all* the possible complications that may occur, the patient may become so anxious and frightened that his condition may worsen. By refusing to give permission for EST, he may well close the door to recovery. On the other hand, if the patient does sign the permit, the courts may well question whether he was mentally competent to understand what he had signed. If the doctor does not inform the patient, but proceeds with the treatment on the basis of a permit signed by a relative, the possible legal pitfalls are legion.

In actual practice, as in every day life, some kind of compromise is almost always essential. If every patient given a drug by his doctor were asked to read and sign an informed consent prior to taking the drug, and if this consent form contained within it all the possible dangers, warnings, contraindications, precautions, and adverse reactions listed in the "package insert" supplied by the pharmaceutical manufacturer, it is very doubtful if any patient would ever take any drug, including aspirin. There is a well known dictum in medicine that any drug potent enough to do good is also potent enough to do harm under certain and often unpredictable circumstances. Penicillin has saved countless thousands of lives, yet each year some persons die due to severe sensitivity to this antibiotic. The same may be said for many other drugs or therapeutic procedures, which certainly includes electroshock therapy. Very often the condition for which EST is recommended is a desperate life-threatening condition, with suicide as one of the realistic hazards. In advising a patient and his family regarding the risks of treatment, the risks of *not* treating the patient must also be presented. Under no circumstances, however, is the patient given EST against his will.

There is no doubt that prior to administering any procedure that involves rendering the patient unconscious, the patient should be *informed* and give his *consent*. The problem, then, is: To what extent should he be informed; and how valid is his consent? Patients can literally be harmed by being presented with too many of the gory details. I well remember a depressed school teacher in her forties who had recovered from a previous depression ten years earlier after a course of EST. She entered the hospital for the express purpose of receiving EST and expected to recover rapidly, just as she did ten years ago. She was ready, willing, and able to sign the permit without a word of explanation. I insisted that she read a three-page mimeographed memo explaining the details of EST. Even though she had already had a favorable experience with the treatment in the past, reading the details of what she had gone through created so many doubts and misgivings in her mind that she hesitated and became indecisive and confused. She finally signed the permit (as did her husband), but the results of EST this time were not as rapid or as dramatic as they were ten years earlier. It seemed clear that this overly sensitive and anxious woman would have done better without being asked to read all the details of the treatment.

It is of interest to note that the Helsinki code, which offers ethical guidelines for researchers, emphasizes that consent should be obtained "consistent with patient psychology." This means that the phlegmatic, well-adjusted patient could receive a fuller description of the details of the contemplated procedure, while the anxious, over-sensitive patient could be told much less. The courts tend to insist on rigid standards in regard to informed consent, whereas, they might do better by adopting the

---

This selection was written expressly for this volume and has not been previously published.

more flexible standard followed in the medical clinics.

With specific regard to electroshock therapy, every attempt should be made to explain the procedure and all the possible risks. No patient should ever be given EST against his will and I know of no situation in the United States where this occurs.

On the Psychiatric Unit of Sibley Memorial Hospital the patient and the next of kin are asked to read a brief document describing the treatment, listing the hazards, outlining the post-treatment course, and discussing the results of treatment. Some hospitals require the patient to sign a statement that he has read and understood the information, in addition to the standard consent form. The information that the patient should have should certainly include the material covered under the headings *Technique*, *Risks*, and *Convalescence*, in the preceding section on "The Place of Electroshock Therapy (EST) in Present-Day Psychiatry" (pp. 000).

Competence to Give Informed Consent in Psychiatry

There is a widespread misconception that all patients in psychiatric hospitals are ipso facto incompetent. Nothing could be further from the truth. In fact, most patients who are depressed, even depressed enough to require EST, are still able to read and understand a brief, clearly written description of the treatment method that has been recommended. In any case, an attempt should be made to inform the patient either verbally or in writing. If the patient is so mentally disturbed that he is incapable of giving informed consent, even when the treatment is carefully and patiently explained, then a parent, legal guardian, or other person legally responsible for the patient, may give consent. The consent of an adult's next-of-kin, although not legally binding, is very useful to obtain and often serves to prevent possible law suits. In emergency situations when the patient is desperately ill and unable to give informed consent, the signature of the next-of-kin is often accepted as a practical measure to save a human life.

The Importance of Records

It is of greatest importance that the physician make careful notes and keep full documentation in his office and in the hospital file, proving that he had informed the patient of the hazards of the procedure to which the patient has given his consent. I know of one colleague who went so far as to tape record a long session in his office, during which a son gave permission to treat his 80 year old mother with EST. She had a severe cardiac condition and a recent hip fracture and was obviously a grave risk. However, her mental condition (agitated depression and senility) threatened to aggravate her heart condition and made her so unsteady that another fracture could easily have occurred. Eventually the son gave his consent and the doctor, using the most careful precautions, proceeded with the treatment. Fortunately, she had an excellent result with recovery and was able to return to her son's home, so that the tape recording never had to be used in court.

The growing emphasis in the medical community on obtaining informed consent has caused a number of commercial firms to sell printed forms to doctors, describing a wide variety of procedures ranging from tonsillectomy to pulmonary resection. Although such forms may be better than none, it is usually best for each hospital, clinic, or department to devise its own form, which reflects local practice. Most such forms usually contain a statement at the bottom to be signed by the patient (or the person legally authorized to act for the patient) certifying that the patient has read the contents of the form and understands the risks involved. In addition, the patient must also sign the standard hospital consent form.

It is clear that the number of legal forms are rapidly multiplying in the practice of medicine. Perhaps this is inevitable. Yet, even the most expert form devised by man is no protection against a law suit if complications intervene. Perhaps the best protection of all lies in the quality of the relationship between the doctor, his patient, and the patient's family. If the doctor has established a good, warm, open relationship and has explained the procedure honestly, in all its aspects, to the best of his ability, and has kept good records, then he should have little to fear. In this sense, the informed patient (if properly informed) is the cooperative patient; and the cooperative patient is essential to the practice of good medicine.

_____ Hospital Department of Psychiatry

Details of Electrotherapy*

Electrotherapy is an accepted form of treatment for certain types of psychiatric disorders.

* Also known as electroshock therapy or electroconvulsion therapy.

CONSENT FOR ELECTRO SHOCK TREATMENT

I, ..., a patient in

the .... Hospital, and I ....

...................................., **of** ....
                                              Address

being the ...., and nearest relative
                        Relationship

of ...., do hereby authorize and
                        Patient

direct Dr. .... or his designee, to administer

electroshock treatment, having been fully informed of its nature and purpose, I also agree to hold

the .... Hospital, all its officers and employees, and the attending physician free from

liability for any injury which may result from such treatment.

....
    Witness   Patient's Signature   Date

....
    Witness   Relative's Signature   Date

It has been used successfully in thousands of cases in this country and abroad since its introduction in 1938. It is one of the most effective ways of treating depression and certain other symptoms in patients who might otherwise require prolonged hospitalization.

The psychiatrist himself gives the treatment, using a specially designed electronic instrument. The treatment consists of passing a carefully controlled electric current between two electrodes applied to the patient's temples. In most instances, the patient is given intravenous anesthesia and medication prior to treatment to reduce tension and produce muscular relaxation. The patient experiences no discomfort or pain during the treatment; he does not feel the electric current and has no memory of the treatment. When the treatment is given, the patient becomes immediately unconscious and has generalized muscular contractions of a convulsive nature. These contractions, which are "softened" by the intravenous medication, last from 30 to 60 seconds. Complete relaxation follows. Several minutes later, the patient gradually regains consciousness and shows a transitory confusion, similar to that seen in patients emerging from brief anesthesia. Within an hour or so, this confusion clears and the patient is able to recognize his surroundings. Following this, the patient has breakfast and is permitted to be up and about. Headache and nausea sometimes occur, but these are infrequent and usually respond rapidly to simple treatment.

The number of treatments in any given case will vary with the condition being treated, and the individual response to treatment. The frequency of treatment will also vary with each case. As the treatments progress (usually after the 4th or 5th treatment), a certain amount of haziness of memory and confusion develops. This memory impairment is transitory and usually clears up within several weeks following the last treatments.

Electrotherapy, like any other medical or surgical procedure, involves a certain amount of calculated risk. Fatalities are extremely rare. Complications, although infrequent, may include fractures and/or dislocations of the extremities, or fractures of the vertebrae. These may sometime occur, in spite of all precautions, and must be looked upon as a recognized hazard of the treatment. Should such an injury occur, the patient and his family will be notified and appropriate treatment instituted.

On discharge from the hospital, the patient begins a "convalescent period" of several weeks duration during which he must be under strict supervision of some member of the family or some responsible person selected by the family. This precaution is necessary because of the temporary mental confusion and impairment of memory which is a side effect of the treatment. During this entire period, the patient should not drive an automobile, transact business or carry on his usual employment until the doctor gives permission. Alcoholic beverages are prohibited. He should not be permitted to leave the house unless accompanied by a responsible companion because of the possibility that he may wander off and get lost. Some degree of supervision is most important and must be provided by a responsible person.

Finally, a word about the results of treatment. Although the results in most cases are gratifying, not all cases will respond equally well. As in all forms of medical treatment, some patients will recover promptly; others will recover only to relapse again and require further treatment; still others may fail to respond at all.

When the patient is treated by the ambulatory or outpatient method, the family, or someone designated by the family, has very definite responsibility for the patient's care. The patient must be escorted to the hospital or other place of treatment. The responsible person stays with the patient until he reacts from the treatment and then escorts him back home. During the approximately two-week period of treatment, and for at least two to four weeks following termination of treatment the patient must be under the strict supervision and companionship of the family.

The above information has been prepared to answer some of the most frequently asked questions concerning electrotherapy. The psychiatrist will be glad to answer any further questions that may occur to the patient or his family.

I CERTIFY: I have read or had read to me the contents of this form and I understand the risks involved in this procedure:

Date: _____

Signed: _____
(By patient or person legally authorized to consent for patient)

Witness: _____
(THIS IS *not* A CONSENT FORM. A CONSENT FORM MUST ALSO BE SIGNED BY THE PATIENT.)

Editorial Comment

In Chapter 4, some newer, still controversial and by and large experimental psychiatric modalities that have become the center of controversy in forensic psychiatric circles were presented. Here we take up the thorny issues of selection of patients for these procedures (particularly behavior modification programs and psychosurgical procedures) and, equally important, the protection of the patient's rights by due consideration to informed consent. In the first selection, Dr. Bertram Brown speaks from his position as director of the National Institutes of Mental Health. The second selection is from a symposium conducted by the National Institute of Neurological Disease and Stroke in which many of the leading clinicians, researchers, and scholars in this area participated. The statement represents a consensus of their views. The reader should also refer to the editorial note in Chapter 15 on "behavior modification" in corrections.

TESTIMONY OF BERTRAM BROWN

I know the Subcommittee is quite familiar with the three cardinal principles of DHEW policy guidelines for the protection of human research subjects. They are, briefly: that the rights and welfare of the subjects involved are adequately protected, that the risks to the individual are outweighed by the potential benefit to him or by the importance of the knowledge to be gained, and that informed consent is obtained in an adequate and appropriate manner.

The securing of informed consent poses a difficult problem even when the human subjects are of normal intelligence and are emotionally health and mature. It becomes infinitely more complicated when the subjects are seriously disturbed, below normal intelligence, or children and when the proposed procedures involve serious risks and irreversible consequences. But a clinical investigator may not avoid the solemn responsibility of securing informed consent merely because it is difficult.

DHEW guidelines describe the basic elements of an informed consent as follows:

1. A fair explanation of the procedures to be followed, including an identification of those which are experimental:
2. A description of the attendant discomforts and risks;
3. A description of the benefits to be expected;
4. A disclosure of appropriate alternative procedures that would be advantageous for the subject;
5. An offer to answer any inquiries concerning the procedures; and
6. An instruction that the subject is free to withdraw his consent and to discontinue participation in the project or activity at any time.

All this assumes that the human subject is himself capable of giving an informed consent. While the DHEW guidelines speak of obtaining consent from the subject "or from his authorized representative," they leave to applicable local law such difficult questions as (1) who may consent for the patient when he is incapacitated—next-of-kin? court appointed

Excerpt from *Congressional Record*, March 29, 1973, from speech by Senator Bealle summarizing and quoting testimony of Dr. Bertram Brown, Director of the National Institute of Mental Health.

guardian? (2) under what circumstances can a substitute or agent consent instead of the patient? (3) may parents ever consent to a risky procedure on behalf of a child when the benefit is primarily for science and the benefits for the child are minimal?

Some hospitals and institutions have been drawing up very detailed and comprehensive procedures for solving these questions. They require the presence of the subject's personal physician, personal lawyer, and immediate kin with periods of time being allotted for reflection, questioning, and debate before consent is given. This is an area that will be receiving increased attention as we work with our sister agencies to refine and expand the DHEW requirements for research on human subjects.

The ethical and moral problems posed by current medical, biological, and behavioral techniques are of considerable concern to Government agencies as well as the health professions, the scientific communities, religious groups, the Congress, and the lay public.

Knowledge, or at least the application of knowledge to wield political or social power, has always been a potentially dangerous concomitant of scientific inquiry. Even new knowledge which at first appears to have only beneficial consequences can create new problems. Potter, in a book called Bioethics puts it quite succinctly: ". . . once we have made the choice to open Pandora's Box of Knowledge, we can never put back its contents, and mankind must continue to search forever for the wisdom that is needed to cope with the avalanche of new knowledge that is upon us." We must somehow evolve a system of technology assessment whereby the state of knowledge can be assessed and its readiness for application can be addressed within the context of relevant social, human, and ethical issues. Such a system would assure the timely application of relevant technology and help prevent the premature use of those techniques not thoroughly explored for their human and social implications.

SUMMARY OF CONCLUSIONS ON BRAIN RESEARCH AND VIOLENT BEHAVIOR

GENERAL

The study of the individual exhibiting violent or aggressive behavior is an important undertaking and fully deserving research support and encouragement. Though there are fairly solid areas of understanding and agreement based on the past research, many regions are ambiguous or unknown. To date, the study of violence by the clinical disciplines does not appear to have been a popular area, with the greatest interest having been demonstrated by psychiatry and neurosurgery, with interest shown by neurology or neuropathology.

PATIENT SELECTION

Evaluation of the clinical studies performed to date, and particularly those investigations of treatment outcome, is made very difficult by

the heterogeneity of patient selection. This is probably the core problem in all clinical studies in this area. There are many dimensions of human violence, perhaps both qualitative and certainly quantitative, and this variable is compounded by the individual's degree of psychiatric illness, mental retardation, presence or absence of epilepsy, and genetic constitution— not to mention the cultural and social factors.

The discussants recognized the great difficulty in this area but recommended that future studies be undertaken only with every reasonable effort being made to select patients that can be considered as homogeneous or as common groups.

PRE-TREATMENT EVALUATION

Regardless of the nature of the treatment modality (psychiatric, medical, or surgical),

Excerpted and reprinted with permission from "Report on the Biomedical Research Aspects of Brain and Aggressive Violent Behavior," Oct. 23, 1973, Department of Health, Education, and Welfare, National Institute of Health, National Institute of Neurological Diseases and Strokes.

the outcome can only be evaluated in the light of the assessment of the patient before treatment. Recommendations in this area include:

1. The institutional or clinical record is notoriously inadequate in regard to the documentation of violent or aggressive behavior. Every effort should be made to secure a reliable history by interview with family, associates, social agencies, and from all professional sources.
2. The assessment of the individual prior to treatment should be made while he is not receiving any psychotrophic agent. In view of the relatively long-lasting effects of some of these compounds, the period of observation should be at least one to two months.
3. Every effort should be made to use standardized, reproducible behavioral rating scales in the pre-treatment period. Better scales than are presently available may need to be developed in order to evaluate behavior in real situations.
4. The behavioral ratings should be performed by trained evaluators who have no investment in the outcome of the study and who are not members of the research team.
5. A neuropsychologist should be involved in both the pre- and post-treatment evaluation.
6. Biochemical determinations, such as those now being developed in the study of bipolar illness and in the treatment of schizophrenia should be performed.
7. Advantage should be taken of such devices as the video-tape in the assessment of behavior.

POST-TREATMENT EVALUATION

The same methods of assessment, with the same rigor, must be applied during the post-treatment period as during pre-treatment. Again, the evaluation should be performed by individuals who are not members of the research team. The duration of the follow-up must be of sufficient length as to provide meaningful information. A suggestion was made that a central registry of patients be established to facilitate long-term follow-up in view of the mobility of modern society.

SURGICAL TREATMENT FOR AGGRESSION AND VIOLENCE

The discussants are aware of some of the unique features surrounding the use of this modality. Though seemingly beyond the direct assignment to the participants in this review, the matter of informed consent and possible legal restriction is a current issue. Aside from this consideration, the suggestion can be made that surgical procedures should be undertaken only after an adequate trial of other types of treatment. This would be in keeping with the traditional medical model of the treatment of peptic ulcer by diet and antacids before gastric resection, or the use of every major anticonvulsant in epilepsy before surgery is considered. As developed in the body of this report, there are alternatives to surgery; however, they need to be examined for effectiveness with as much rigor as the surgical treatments themselves.

SURGERY REPORT BOTTLED UP

A report bottled up in the federal bureaucracy since January recommends a temporary halt to most psychosurgery, the brain operation that some opponents call "murder of the mind."

Psychosurgery is defined in the reports as the destruction of brain tissue with the primary intent of altering behavior, thought, or mood.

The January 21 report was from the National Institute of Mental Health to its parent agency, the Department of Health, Education, and Welfare. It was based on consultation with scientific, legal, social, and ethics experts.

HEW spokesmen said the report is being considered, but that no action has been taken and none is likely soon.

"Psychosurgery should be regarded as an experimental therapy at the present time," says the report, signed by Dr. Bertram S. Brown, director of the institute. "As such it should not be considered to be a form of therapy which can be made generally available to the public

The Washington Post, Wednesday, June 5, 1974, p. A9.

because of the peculiar nature of the procedure and of the problems with which it deals."

This and the report's other recommendations would have the effect of ending most psychosurgery until proper guidelines can be drafted, the report said.

The effect of holding up the report is to allow the surgery to continue without any guidelines as to patient selection and alternative treatment.

The report estimated that 100 to 1,000 psychosurgery operations are performed annually, an unspecific estimate that indicates the lack of solid information available about the procedure.

Among the report's other recommendations:

No psychosurgery should be performed on involuntarily confined persons or on persons incapable of giving informed consent.

A registry should be established to monitor the types of patients chosen, outcomes of the treatment, and other aspects of psychosurgery.

LOBOTOMY

Nicholas N. Kittrie

In 1890, Dr. G. Burkhardt, a Swiss psychiatrist, began to remove portions of patients' brains. He believed that mental troubles had their seats in various parts of the brain and that by surgically removing the affected area, sick and dangerous individuals would be transformed into persons harmless to society and themselves. He was reported to be successful in his goal, but was forced to discontinue his operations because of ethical pressures from his colleagues. In 1935 two Portuguese physicians, Moniz and Lima, performed the first pre-frontal lobotomy. They were led to this treatment by evidence that certain mental abnormalities were linked to physical damage and disease of the frontal lobes of the brain. The patient's behavior was changed as a result of the operation, which consisted of removing a small round portion of skull bone near the temple and severing the connection between the frontal lobes of the brain and the midbrain by inserting a knife into the white matter of the brain and twisting it. In 1936 Walter Freeman and James W. Watts introduced the operation into the United States.

Although the operation met with some early criticism and resistance from the medical profession, the successes of Freeman and Watts soon made the treatment acceptable. Freeman and Watts had through lobotomy changed irritable, uncooperative, unclean, and helpless chronic schizophrenics into quite, clean, cooperative, and self-sufficient patients, some of whom could be sent home as employable. These successes generated a search for other uses of prefrontal lobotomy, and for a time the operation was an accepted treatment for the early stages of schizophrenia, manic depression, and even neurosis.

The treatment's frequent side effects, however, prevented its becoming routine. From Dr. Freeman's records of 624 lobotomies, he reported 24 fatalities (3.6%), and 321 (51.5%) patients with undesirable side effects, such as partial paralysis, loss of bladder control, and convulsions. The introduction of new surgical techniques reduced these figures to more tolerable levels. The transorbital lobotomy, in which an icepick-like instrument inserted into the brain through the eye socket is used to cut the frontal lobes, had a fatality rate of only 1.7 percent and an undesirable side effect rate of 5.2 percent. In addition, the number of patients who experienced undesirable behavioral complications (such as indolence, excessive profanity, and sexual irregularities) from the transorbital lobotomy was only one-tenth that of the prefrontal lobotomy. With these developments, lobotomy's acceptance by the medical profession spread. In fact, swift use of the operation on new

---

Excerpted and reprinted with permission from Kittrie, *The Right to Be Different* (Baltimore: The Johns Hopkins Press, 1971), pp. 305–8.

patients was urged because statistics showed that the chance of favorable results was doubled when the mental patient had been in the hospital less than six months.

In the early fifties, however, the old and lingering doubts concerning lobotomies were given substance. Research disclosed that the operation destroyed the capacity to form abstract thoughts and robbed the individual of ambition, conscience, and planning abilities. The lobotomized person could react quickly to

stimuli, but was unable to reflect before reacting on the wisdom or effects of his response. With these developments, psychiatrists began to use lobotomies with much more restraint. It remains a rarely used treatment—a last resort for extremely dangerous and incorrigible patients. Its use to relieve the custodial burdens of the mental hospital staffs is acknowledged, but the introduction of drugs for much the same purpose has further diminished lobotomy's use as a palliative.

ELIMINATING THE UNFIT—IS STERILIZATION THE ANSWER?

Elyce Zenoff Ferster

Recent lower court decisions in California and Ohio have focused public attention on the use of sterilization as an instrument of social policy. The author traces the history of sterilization in the United States and analyzes current legislation and practices. The scientific premise upon which eugenic sterilization is based is now subject to considerable doubt. Nonetheless, sterilization has found questionable new support among those seeking to reduce welfare rolls.

I. EUGENIC STERILIZATION

Although in 1895 the word "eugenics" as it is used today was completely unknown, by 1917 fifteen states had adopted eugenic sterilization laws, and at the end of another twenty year period a total of thirty-one states had enacted such legislation. An examination of all the factors responsible for this rapid growth would encompass many economic and political factors which are beyond the scope of this article, but there is no doubt that three events which occurred at the end of the nineteenth century played a most important part in the adoption of legislation authorizing compulsory

sterilization. They were the launching of the eugenics movement by Sir Francis Galton, the re-discovery of Mendel's laws of heredity, and the development of simple, non-dangerous surgical techniques for the prevention of procreation.

The term "eugenics" is derived from a Greek word meaning "well born." In 1883 Sir Francis Galton coined the word and defined it as "the study of agencies under social control that may improve or impair . . . future generations either physically or mentally." In 1904 he officially launched the eugenics movement which had a two-fold aim: (1) positive eugenics—encouragement of the propagation of the biologically fit and (2) negative eugenics—discouragement of the reproduction of inferior stock. During this same period, the laws of heredity formulated by the Austrian monk, Gregory Mendel, forgotten since their publication forty years earlier, were rediscovered. Although Mendel's work had been confined to the transmission of simple traits in plants, the eugenicists assumed that the Mendelian principles were equally applicable to complex traits in human beings. The proponents of this view decided that mental illness,

The research on which this article is based was supported by United States Public Health Service Grant MH 01947–01; Director, Richard C. Allen, Co-Director, Elyce Zenoff Ferster, The George Washington University. Excerpts reprinted with permission from 27 *Ohio State Law Journal* 591 (1966). Most of the footnotes have been omitted and those retained have been renumbered consecutively.

mental retardation, epilepsy, criminality, pauperism and various other defects were hereditary. Considerable agitation for corrective action was based upon the premise that these various conditions were hereditary. Since attempts at cure were considered futile for hereditary defects, measures which would prevent reproduction by "the unfit" appeared to be the only way to eliminate these conditions.

II. HISTORICAL BACKGROUND

Some of the proponents of eugenic sterilization were so zealous that they began sterilizing people before there was legislative authorization for the procedure. In the middle of the 1890's, F. Hoyt Pilcher, Superintendent of the Winfield Kansas State Home for the Feeble-minded, castrated forty-four boys and fourteen girls. Public sentiment is considered responsible for the ending of this activity. Dr. Martin W. Barr, Superintendent of the Pennsylvania State Training School, claimed that he performed the first sexual sterilization to prevent procreation in 1889. Three years later when he was president of what is now known as The American Association on Mental Deficiency, he reported the operation and asked, "What state will be the first to legalize this procedure?" Another impatient eugenicist was Dr. Harry C. Sharp who devised the surgical operation known as vasectomy. He reportedly sterilized 600 or 700 boys at the Indiana reformatory before the adoption of the Indiana Act. It is also claimed that superintendents of institutions in several states were secretly sterilizing feeble-minded persons.

The legislative history of eugenic sterilization began in 1897 when a bill authorizing such operations was introduced in the Michigan legislature. This bill was defeated and it was Pennsylvania, eight years later, which became the first state to pass a sterilization bill. It was entitled "An Act for the prevention of idiocy" and required that "each and every institution . . . entrusted . . . with the care of idiots . . . appoint a neurologist and a surgeon . . . to examine the mental and physical condition of the inmates." If, in their opinion, procreation was inadvisble, and there was no probability of improvement of the mental condition of the inmate, the surgeon was authorized "to perform such operation for the prevention of procreation as shall be decided safest and most effective." Governor Pennypacker refused to sign the bill and returned it to the senate with this message:

This bill has what may be called with propriety an attractive title. If idiocy could be prevented by an Act of Assembly, we may be quite sure that such an act would have long been passed and approved in this state. . . . What is the nature of the operation is not described, but it is such an operation as they shall decide to be "safest and most effective." It is plain that the safest and most effective method of preventing procreation would be to cut the heads off the inmates, and such authority is given by the bill to this staff of scientific experts. . . . The bill is, furthermore, illogical in its thought. . . . A great objection is that the bill . . . would be the beginning of experimentation upon living human beings, leading logically to results which can readily be forecasted. The chief physician . . . has candidly told us, . . . that "Studies in heredity tend to emphasize the wisdom of those ancient peoples who taught that the healthful development of the individual and the elimination of the weakling was the truest patriotism—springing from an abiding sense of the fulfillment of a duty to the state . . . .

Although many sterilization bills have been introduced in Pennsylvania subsequent to this veto, none has succeeded in becoming law.

It was Indiana which finally enacted the first sterilization law in 1907, two years after Pennsylvania's first attempt. However, the Indiana statute was eventually declared unconstitutional as were all other similar laws which came before the courts prior to 1925.

The statistics concerning sterilization during this early period are quite interesting. As of January 1, 1921, the states reported a total of 3,233 sterilizations performed since 1907, the beginning of legalized operations. If we add the known unauthorized operations in Kansas and Indiana, the sterilization total up to 1921 is approximately 3,900. More than twenty per cent of these operations were executed either without any statutory authority or under laws which were subsequently declared unconstitutional. The balance of the sterilizations took place under laws which had never been constitutionally tested. It is also noteworthy that although many people believed that sterilization is usually recommended for the mentally retarded rather than the mentally ill, more than eighty per cent of the sterilizations reported in 1921 were performed upon mentally ill persons.

III. BUCK V. BELL

The advocates of eugenic sterilization achieved a substantial victory in 1925 when the courts of two states held their sterilization laws valid. The first decision was rendered on June 18, 1925, by the Supreme Court of Michigan in the case of *Smith* v. *Wayne*. A few months later on November 12, 1925, in the case of *Buck* v. *Bell*, the Supreme Court of Appeals of Virginia held a sterilization statute to be a valid enactment under the state and federal constitutions. An appeal was taken from this decision to the United States Supreme Court. In a brief opinion which is probably best remembered for Mr. Justice Holmes' comment: "Three generations of imbeciles are enough," the Court held that the law in question was a reasonable regulation under the police power of that state and did not violate either the due process or the equal protection clause of the fourteenth amendment.

Carrie Buck, the plaintiff in the case, was an eighteen-year-old woman committed to the Virginia State Colony for Epileptics and Feeble-minded. She was the daughter of a feeble-minded mother and the mother of an illegitimate feeble-minded child. The Virginia court found that Carrie Buck was "the probable potential parent of socially inadequate offspring likewise afflicted. . . ."

No objection was made to the procedural provisions of Virginia law. Instead the attack was made upon the substantive law, the contention being that the sterilization order could not be justified upon the existing grounds. Justice Holmes speaking for the Court said:

We have seen more than once that the public welfare may call upon the best citizens for their lives. It would be strange if it could not call upon those who already sap the strength of the state for these lesser sacrifices, often not felt to be such by those concerned, in order to prevent our being swamped with incompetence. It is better for all the world, if instead of waiting to execute degenerate offspring for crime, or to let them starve for their imbecility, society can prevent those who are manifestly unfit from continuing their kind. The principle that sustains compulsory vaccination is broad enough to cover cutting the Fallopian tubes. . . . Three generations of imbeciles are enough. [274 U.S. at 207.]

This decision was followed by an abundance of eugenic sterilization legislation. Twenty statutes were passed in the ensuing ten years, most of them closely patterned after the Virginia law. Only nine cases have been found, involving the validity of sterilization laws applicable to the mentally ill and the mentally retarded, since *Buck* v. *Bell*. Three of these laws were declared unconstitutional, but they were based on procedural deficiencies rather than the substantive issues determined in *Buck* v. *Bell*. In the six cases which upheld the laws, five rely on the decision in *Buck* v. *Bell* and the sixth was concerned with the adequacy of the law's procedural provisions.

The only sterilization law considered by the United States Supreme Court subsequent to *Buck* v. *Bell* was an Oklahoma statute which provided for the sterilization of habitual criminals. The Court held the law unconstitutional on the grounds that its exception of "persons convicted of offenses arising out of violation of the prohibitory laws, revenue acts, embezzlement or political offenses" violated the constitutional prohibition against class legislation. Although this case did not consider the same issues as *Buck* v. *Bell*, some legal scholars have suggested that Justice Jackson's concurring opinion might be interpreted as casting doubts upon the validity of all sterilization laws. Critics of the *Buck* v. *Bell* decision have also speculated on the possibility of a reversal of opinion by the Supreme Court if a question is raised with respect to another eugenic sterilization law. The reasons for this view and criticisms of *Buck* v. *Bell* will be discussed hereafter.

IV. ANALYSIS OF CURRENT STATUTES

At present twenty-six states have eugenic sterilization laws,[1] twenty-three of which are compulsory.[2] Mentally retarded persons are subject to the laws in all of these states, and in all but two states they are also applicable to the mentally ill.[3] Epileptics are still included in fourteen states.[4] In twelve states criminals are subject to sterilization.[5] A few of these laws

[1] Alabama, Arizona, California, Connecticut, Delaware, Georgia, Idaho, Indiana, Iowa, Maine, Michigan, Minnesota, Mississippi, Montana, Nebraska, New Hampshire, North Carolina, Oklahoma, Oregon, South Carolina, South Dakota, Utah, Vermont, Virginia, West Virginia, Wisconsin. A total of thirty-one states have enacted such laws. The laws of New York, New Jersey, and Washington were declared unconstitutional and have not been reenacted. See Smith v. Bd. of Examiners, 85 N.J.L. 46, 88 Atl. 963 (Sup. Ct. 1913); Osborn v. Thomson 103 misc. 23, 169 N.Y. Supp. 638 (Sup. Ct.), *aff'd mem*, 185 App. Div. 902, 171 N.Y. Supp. 1094 (1918); *In re* Hendrickson, 12 Wash. 2d 600, 123 P.2d 322 (1942). Kansas and North Dakota both repealed their statutes.

[2] Connecticut, Minnesota, and Vermont have voluntary sterilization laws. Connecticut changed from an involuntary to a voluntary law in 1965.

[3] Alabama and Nebraska. The Nebraska sterilization law included the mentally ill until 1957. Neb. Acts 1957, ch. 391.

[4] Arizona, Delaware, Idaho, Indiana, Mississippi, Montana, New Hampshire, North Carolina, Oklahoma, Oregon, South Carolina, Utah, Virginia, West Virginia.

[5] Cal. Pen. Code §§ 645, 2670; An Act to Modify the Statute Concerning Operations to Prevent Procreation, Conn. P.A. 536 (1965); Del.

are clearly eugenic, two are clearly punitive,[6] and the purpose of the others is unclear. Seventeen of these laws apply to persons confined in hospitals or other institutions, while nine laws also apply to persons who are not confined.

The involuntary procedure is usually commenced by an application from the superintendent of the institution to a designated administrative agency which has the authority to grant a sterilization order. Although most of the states now require notice, a hearing, and judicial appeal, six states do not require a hearing and three make no provision for judicial appeal. The majority view of the few state supreme courts which have considered the procedural provisions of sterilization laws is that the patient must be given notice and accorded a hearing or else be allowed to appeal the sterilization order to a court. Although a California district court of appeals came to a contrary decision, the California sterilization law was subsequently amended in 1951 and now provides for both notice and judicial appeal. The usual ground for issuing the sterilization order is that "according to the laws of heredity, the person is the probable potential parent of socially inadequate offspring likewise afflicted."

On only twenty-three occasions have cases involving the sterilization of inmates of state institutions come before the courts. According to the Human Betterment Association, one would expect to find the curtailment of rights in an area as important as procreation strongly contested. They conclude that the dearth of cases "speaks well not only of the care and forethought state legislators have given to the consideration of the provisions of the laws but also of the care exercised in their application by administrators."

However, it is possible that the lack of cases is due to other reasons. One of them could be the inability of a mentally ill or mentally retarded person to handle his defense. For that matter it is possible that he does not even understand the nature of the action. In most proceedings affecting personal or property rights, it is taken for granted that the parties are represented by attorneys. Where they cannot afford legal representation, it is usually provided by legal aid, a public defender, or a court-appointed counsel who receives compensation from the state. Very few states provide for court appointed counsel in sterilization proceedings. It is impossible to estimate what effect this policy may have had on the status of sterilization legislation. For example, it has been asserted that the suit in *Buck* v. *Bell* was a friendly one selected by the superintendent of the State Colony for Epileptics and Feebleminded to be used as a test case. Carrie's guardian is alleged to have been appointed by the state, not the county, and to have been paid twenty-five dollars for the entire case, which averaged out to one dollar a month.

V. STERILIZATION PRACTICES

The number of sterilizations per year has decreased steadily during the last twenty years from 1638 in 1943 to 467 in 1963. Currently, five states are not using their eugenic sterilization laws. In fact no operations have been performed in any of these states for approximately ten years. In eight other states, operations have averaged seven or less per year in the period 1959 to 1964. Only six states averaged more than fifteen operations per year during this period, and even these states, with the exception of Delaware, show a steady decrease in the number of sterilizations performed between the years 1943 and 1963.

The decrease is probably due to a rejection of the view that mental illness and mental retardation are hereditary. The decrease was not caused by court decisions. Sterilization orders have not been attacked in the courts during this period. Nor have there been many amendments of the sterilization laws by the state legislatures. California did change its procedures to provide for a hearing in 1951 and there was a sharp drop in the number of operations after this amendment. However, California officials point out that the number of sterilizations began to drop sharply several years prior to the amendment. In 1943 there were 459 sterilizations in the state, but by 1951 the number of operations had dropped to 150. State officials believe that the downward shift in the California sterilization rate reflects a change in the attitude of the people who administer the law about the hereditary aspects of and need for sterilizations, rather than a response to outside pressure.

Code Ann. tit. 16 § 5703 (1953); Ga. Code Ann. § 99–1303 (1955); Idaho Code Ann. § 66–803 (1949); Ia. Code Ann. § 145.2 (Supp. 63); Mich. Stat. Ann. §§ 14.381, 14.382 (Supp. 1965); Okla. Stat. tit. 43A § 341 (1961); Ore. Rev. Stat. 436.010 (1965–1966); Utah Code Ann. § 64–10-7 (Supp. 1961); Wis. Stat. Ann. § 46.12 (1957).

[6] California provides for sterilization as a penalty for the crime of carnal abuse of a female under ten, Cal. Pen. Code § 645. Washington has a similar statute. Wash. Rev. Code Ann. § 9.92.100 (1961). Nevada also had a similar law but it was declared unconstitutional in Mickle v. Henrichs, 262 Fed. 687 (D.D. Nev. 1918), and was repealed by chapter 45 of the 1961 Statutes of Nevada.

The variation in the use of sterilization laws from state to state also appears to be caused by different views about the hereditary nature of mental disability and the desirability of the operation. This topic will be discussed subsequently.

The difference in the rate of sterilizations performed annually in each state has little relationship to the population differences between the states. For example, California with a population of over eighteen million people performed 17 sterilizations in 1963 while North Carolina with a population of not quite five million sterilized 240. Nor is the difference in the number of sterilizations between the states necessarily related to the substantive or procedural provisions of the law. For example, Virginia which reports the second highest number of annual sterilizations limits the application of its law to a eugenic basis and has strict procedural requirements, performed 39 sterilizations while Wisconsin, which has approximately the same population, may sterilize "when procreation is inadvisable" and there are no specific provisions for objections, guardian ad litem, transcripts, or judicial review, reported eight sterilizations.

Virginia sterilization procedures were studied during a seven-state study of "The Mentally Retarded and the Law" conducted by the Institute of Law, Psychiatry and Criminology of the George Washington University. A random sample of sterilization records at two state hospitals for the retarded and observations of four hearings showed that the state meticulously observes the procedural requirements of notice, appointment of a guardian ad litem, patient's presence at hearings, etc.[7] However, the guardian ad litem said little or nothing at the four hearings observed.

It is of interest that in Virginia there appears to be little difficulty in proving that the conditions are hereditary while several other states reported that they are unable to furnish such proof. It is not necessary to furnish such proof in many jurisdictions because the statute authorizes sterilization on such grounds as "for the good of the patient and society."

A large number of states do not have "to prove" anything because they operate their laws only on a voluntary basis. Again, there does not seem to be any relationship between this policy and the rate of sterilizations per year. North Carolina, the state with the highest number of sterilizations operates its program on a voluntary basis but so do several states with much lower annual rates.

[7] Nineteen cases at one hospital and ten cases at another hospital for the year 1965 were selected on a random basis.

The reasons for the policy of performing sterilizations only when consent of the person or a relative has been obtained are not known. The policy may be motivated solely by therapeutic considerations. However, the constitutionality of many of these laws has never been tested. The use of consent may be motivated by a desire to avoid an attack on either the procedures or the substantive basis of the laws.

The belief that mental illness, mental retardation, and criminality are inherited was the basis of the eugenicists' argument for compulsory sterilization and was also the basis of the United States Supreme Court's opinion that the Virginia sterilization law was constitutional. The consistent downward trend of sterilization statistics for a period of two decades may mean that attitudes towards the inheritability of these conditions have changed. However, even if there has been a change of attitude, a prediction that in another two decades the United States will no longer have involuntary sterilization laws is not justified. Mental illness, mental retardation, and criminality still exist in this country and many people now urge that the mentally ill, the mentally retarded, and criminals are unfit parents and should be sterilized for that reason. It is worthy of note that approximately seventy per cent of reported sterilizations in 1963 took place in four states in which sterilization on non-eugenic grounds is authorized.

VI. Current Views on Sterilization Legislation

A. Scientific

The American Neurological Association's Committee for the Investigation of Eugenical Sterilization summarized the main arguments of the proponents of sterilization as follows:

1. Mental illness, mental deficiency, epilepsy, pauperism, and certain forms of criminality are steadily increasing;

2. Persons with these diseases propagate at a greater rate than the normal population;

3. These conditions are hereditary;

4. Environment is of less importance than germ plasm in the creation of these conditions. Implicit and sometimes explicit in this point of view is that euthenics is against natural selection because it keeps alive the unfit and, therefore, is against the racial welfare.

Although it was accepted by the state legislatures and the courts that at least the inheritability of these conditions had been scientifically proven, studies undertaken in the last twenty-five years have thrown substantial doubt upon this conclusion. The most important of these studies was that conducted by the American Neurological Association. They made the following answers to the statements of the advocates of eugenic sterilization laws:

1. There is nothing to indicate that mental disease and mental defect are increasing, and from this standpoint there is no evidence of a biological deterioration of the race.
2. The reputedly high fecundity of the mentally defective groups . . . is a myth based on the assumptions that those who are low in the cultural scale are also mentally and biologically defective.
3. Any law concerning sterilization . . . under the present state of knowledge (of heredity) should be voluntary . . . rather than compulsory.
4. Nothing in the acceptance of heredity as a factor in the genesis of any condition considered by this report excludes the environmental agencies of life as equally potent, and in many instances as even more effective.

Concerning the claim of eugenicists that the efforts of society to help the unfit works against the welfare of the race the Committee said: "It is precisely in those communities where social care is good that we find the evidence of the finest culture and, on the whole, the best biology. It is in those communities where social care is poor that the population presents an appalling spectacle of degradation."

One year later the American Medical Association's Committee to Study Contraceptive Practices and Related Problems reported: "Our present knowledge regarding human heredity is so limited that there appears to be very little scientific basis to justify limitation of conception for eugenic reasons. . . . There is conflicting evidence regarding the transmissibility of epilepsy and mental disorders."

A recent opinion to the same effect is that expressed by the Mental Health Committee of the South Dakota Medical Association in the Explanation of the Proposed South Dakota Mental Health Act:

Medical science has by no means established that heredity is a factor in the development of mental disease with the possible exception of a very few and rare disorders. The Committee holds that the decision to sterilize for whatever reason, should be left up to the free decision reached by patient and family physician mutually and that the State has no good reason to trespass in this area.

The scientific arguments against sterilization were ably summarized in 1960 by Dr. Bernard L. Diamond when he served as a special consultant to the American Psychiatric Association for its report on mental health legislation in British Columbia:

[A]ll laws providing for the sterilization of the mentally ill or defective which have as their basis the concept of the inheritability of mental illness and mental deficiency are open to serious question as to their scientific validity and their social desirability.

Laws of this type followed logically from prevailing psychiatric concepts of the late 19th and early 20th centuries, in which mental illness, be it psychosis, psychoneurosis, or mental deficiency, was regarded as inherited deficiencies or weaknesses. Particularly in relation to mental deficiency, the development of fairly precise tests of intelligence, such as the Stanford-Binet test, promulgated the idea that intelligence was a fixed attribute of the individual and was primarily determined by genetic factors. Legislative bodies were impressed by lurid clinical descriptions of the Jukes and the Kallikaks—families in which antisocial behavior or mental deficiency recurred in generation after generation.

Present day psychiatry, although still vitally interested in the possible genetic factors in mental illness and mental deficiency, avoids the sweeping generalizations so prevalent in the past. Genetics has evolved into a much more precise science and very significant work is being done on the inheritance of mental illness. Nevertheless, this is a field of great conflict; there has been much learned in recent years of the impact of environment on child development; of the essential role of psychodynamic factors in personality development and production of mental illness; and of the susceptibility of the child in utero to unfavorable metabolic and infectious conditions of the mother.

In short, the present state of our scientific knowledge does not justify the widespread use of the sterilization procedures in mentally ill or mentally deficient persons. . . .

It is sometimes proposed that sterilization is demanded, irrespective of the uncertainties of our knowledge of heredity, in that a mentally ill or feebleminded person is incapable of providing the emotional and material environment required to raise a normal child. Perhaps this is so, but it raises issues of a sociological and political nature of a very uncertain character and it may be most dangerous to apply such sociological concepts under the guise of a genetic thesis that is far from proven and highly uncertain in its application.

No attempt has been made to make a complete survey of recent scientific literature and count the number of proponents and opponents of sterilization laws or to evaluate their arguments. These are tasks beyond the author's qualifications. However, the views presented here do show that there is a conflict of opinion about the inheritability of the conditions covered by eugenic sterilization laws. The existence of this conflict is extremely important because to date the legislatures and the courts have assumed that there was undisputed proof of the hereditary nature of these conditions.

B. States Without Sterilization Laws

The most reliable indication of a state's attitude about sterilization laws is, of course, the presence or absence of such legislation. There are twenty-four states which do not have sterilization laws. Nineteen of these states have never had a sterilization law.[8] Opinions of institution personnel, judges, and organizations who work with the mentally disabled are not state policy but their attitudes towards sterilization would undoubtedly be given serious consideration by legislators.

Institution personnel, including superintendents, assistant superintendents, staff physicians, and social workers in six states without sterilization laws[9] were asked about institution policy and their own attitudes towards sterilization by the study on The Mentally Retarded and the Law. In four of these states, operations are not performed at the institution and the institution does not recommend that the operation be done elsewhere. In the fifth state, parents occasionally take the retarded child to the family physician for the operation but this action is neither approved nor disapproved by the hospital.

Parents, in the sixth state, are sometimes told that a child could possibly return to the community if the operation were performed. One institution official in that state reported that he had performed 50 to 60 sterilizations during the last two years always with parental permission.[10] He has a theory that the operation has beneficial effects on a variety of conditions including excessive masturbation, menstrual problems, excessive body hair and acne. Another institution physician in the same state said: "I, on occasion have let my knife slip in

surgery and cut the tubes but with most nurses present I would not do it as they have large mouths." Two opinions of the state attorney general within the last six years have advised the institutions that they do not have statutory authority to perform such operations and that the consent of the parents is not sufficient authorization.

There were other staff members of the institutions within this state who favored a sterilization law besides the two physicians who reported performing sterilization operations. However, a contrary view was expressed by the officials who wrote the state plan to combat mental retardation. They said, "It is questionable whether . . . legislation providing for eugenic sterilization of the mentally retarded is desirable or necessary at this time." They also advised that a re-evaluation of the ground upon which compulsory sterilization is based should be made before any legislation is considered.

Institutional personnel favored a sterilization law in only one additional study jurisdiction. The principal reason advanced was that many girls would be released because they are being kept in institutions for the sole reason that it is feared they might become pregnant.

In the other four jurisdictions, institution officials were opposed to involuntary sterilization laws. One superintendent said that many girls who could be in the community are committed solely because a judge thinks they might become pregnant. He believes that this is an unfortunate situation but is happy that his state does not have a sterilization law. Some officials in these states do not consider pregnancy a problem because "contraceptive devices have made sterilization obsolete." Another official said that pregnancy is not a great problem for the retarded because the rate of pregnancies of normal high school girls who become pregnant is much higher than the rate of retardates.

Intrauterine devices and pills are preferred to sterilization because they are not permanent. One interviewee drew an analogy between life imprisonment and a death sentence, in the sense that if a mistake is made it can be reversed if an intrauterine device has been used. Other interviewees preferred birth control devices because they believe some retarded persons can function as parents after counselling and treatment.

Most of the interviewees who opposed sterilization mentioned at least two of the reasons listed below:

1. The difficulty of determining who should be sterilized because of the imperfections of intelligence tests and the lack of

---

[8] Kansas, New Jersey, New York, North Dakota, and Kansas formerly had sterilization laws.

[9] Florida, Illinois, Maryland, Massachusetts, New Jersey, and Washington.

[10] Note that these sterilizations alone would give the state a sterilization rate of 25 to 30 a year which is higher than the reported rate of 20 states which have sterilization laws.

knowledge concerning the role of cultural deprivation in familial retardation;

2. The doubt that anyone is qualified to make decisions about who should be sterilized;
3. The fear that sterilization laws will be used punitively;
4. The belief that involuntary sterilization is immoral.

All of the state planning reports on mental retardation discuss prevention, but none of them recommend involuntary sterilization legislation to achieve this goal. Two states, Colorado and Kentucky, recommend the adoption of a voluntary sterilization law, but most of the recommendations concern improved prenatal care, greater use of measles vaccine, routine testing of infants for phenylketenuria (PKU), genetic counselling, establishing prenursery schools for children from deprived homes, and intensive research into the biological and behavioral causes of retardation.

The opinion that reduction of public welfare costs justifies the use of sterilization has been expressed by several judges during the last few years. In addition to expressing their views, they have acted on them by ordering sterilizations despite the lack of an applicable sterilization law.

Two of the judges preside over probate courts in Ohio, a state which has never had a sterilization law. They have ordered the sterilization of five mentally retarded females, and one of the judges has said that he intends to continue this practice. The reasons for the decisions and the legal theory on which they are based are given in the opinion, *In re Simpson* [180 N.E.2d 206, Ohio P.Ct., 1962], the first of these cases to attract public attention.

In 1962 Rosie Lee Simpson filed an affidavit in the probate court of Muskingum County alleging that her eighteen-year-old daughter Nora Ann was "feeble-minded." There was undisputed evidence that Nora Ann had an I.Q. of 36, was unable to care for her year-old illegitimate child, and had been promiscuous with a number of men since the birth of her child.

The court took judicial notice of the fact that the county's 1962 quota of commitments to the Columbus State Hospital had been filled for many months and that the waiting list for 1963 was nearing the quota limit.

The court ruled that Nora Ann was "feeble-minded" within the meaning of the sattute and ordered her to submit to an operation which would prevent the birth of additional children "such operation having been found to be necessary for the health and welfare of said Nora Ann Simpson."

The court relied on section 5125.30 of the Ohio Revised Code which provides that the probate judge shall "make such order as he deems necessary . . . to provide for the detention, supervision, care and maintenance of feebleminded persons . . ." when the hospital is unable to receive them as authority for his sterilization order. He also cited section 2101.24 of the code: "The probate court shall have plenary power at law and in equity fully to dispose of any matter properly before the court, unless the power is expressly otherwise limited or denied by statute." The court claimed that the authority granted to it by the statutes is extremely broad.

The fact that the interpretation was extremely broad is not disputed, but the interpretation has been severely criticized. After a full discussion of the court's reasoning, a recent article concluded that "It is difficult if not impossible to avoid the conclusion that this court has simply conjured up a novel power without historical or statutory basis." Another law review article called *In re Simpson* the best example of "perversion of the law."

The judge's reasons for ordering the operation were that it was in the best interest of Nora Ann and society. The advantage to Nora Ann was that she would be condemned "to a lifetime of frustration of drudgery as she continued to bring children into the world for whom she was not capable . . . of providing proper care." Society will benefit by saving on welfare payments:

Application has been made to the Muskingum County Welfare Department for Aid for Dependent Children payments for the child already born. To permit Nora Ann to have further children would result in additional burdens upon the county and state welfare departments which have already been compelled to reduce payments because of shortage of funds and have consistently importuned the General Assembly for additional appropriations.

Although the opinion mentioned no evi- of the hereditary nature of Nora Ann's "feeble-mindedness," the judge prophesied that "there is further probability that such [future] offspring will also be mentally deficient and become a public charge for most of their lives."

Although the judge subsequently issued sterilization orders for a fifteen-year-old girl and a young married woman, again without benefit of sterilization law, he does favor such legislation. He testified in favor of a sterilization bill before the state legislature in 1963 and urged the adoption of such legislation in an address before the Ohio Welfare Conference: "I appeal to you to start a campaign in your own community for compulsory sterilization. This is a positive action which can be taken to help reduce the ever-expanding cost of public welfare."

In 1966, another Ohio probate judge issued sterilization orders for mentally retarded sisters aged nineteen and twenty-two and wrote an opinion which is substantially similar to *In re Simpson*.

In addition to the Ohio cases, there have been three California sterilization cases in the last few years. California law provides for sterilization of the mentally ill, the mentally retarded, and certain sex offenders. However, the code provisions were not applicable to any of these cases and were not relied on by the courts. In each case the sterilization order was a condition of probation.

Miguel Andrada chose probation rather than a jail sentence when he pleaded guilty to a charge of non-support of his minor children. After the operation, he regretted the decision and began litigation which culminated in his asking the United States Supreme Court to review the case and decide if "conditioning probation upon sterilization constituted cruel and unusual punishment and violated procedural due process." However, the Supreme Court denied certiorari.

This was not the first case, and presumably not the last case in which the Pasadena Municipal Court Judge offered probation conditioned on sterilization in non-support cases.

In the second case, *People* v. *Tapia* [No. 73313, Santa Barbara Supra Ct., July 7, 1965] a man and a woman were convicted of a conspiracy to defraud the welfare department. The defendants were offered a reduction of their sentence which would have the effect of fixing their crimes as misdemeanors rather than felonies and also a reduction of the probation period to be spent in jail from one year to six months "upon the filing of a stipulation by counsel or a report from the Santa Barbara County Hospital that the defendants have voluntarily submitted to the operations."

During the hearing on probation and sentencing the judge appeared torn between his belief that the county welfare department wished to make an example of this case to deter others and the fact that the crime specified in the code was a misdemeanor. The basis of the male defendant's conviction appeared to be the jury's finding that he had "knowledge of the existence of this peculiar Welfare and Institutions Code Rule which makes a man

under these circumstances or tries to make him at any rate responsible for the support of children who are not his own and who are also living in the family." Although the probation officer recommended against probation because the defendant still denied his crime and was therefore unrepentant, the judge believed this should not be controlling because Mr. Palafax did not have a previous criminal record, had kept a steady job for many years, and voluntarily supported his own child. However, the judge believed that both defendants had produced enough children. He recessed the hearing so that their attorneys could ask them if they would consent to sterilization if they were granted probation. The defendants did not want to make the decision during the hearing. Therefore, the judge said that he would grant probation for a three-year period, one year of which was to be spent in jail which would be automatically reduced to six months if the operations were performed.

In the most recent California case, a twenty-one-year-old girl was offered a choice between sterilization and probation, or a six months jail sentence, the maximum penalty for her offense. The girl Nancy Hernandez was married at the age of seventeen and received an interlocutory divorce in late 1965. At the time of her arrest she and her two daughters, one two years old, and the other two months old, were living with Joseph Sanchez, the father of the youngest child. The Welfare Department was contributing to the support of Mrs. Hernandez and the infant, and the older child was presumably being supported by her father, Tony Hernandez.

Mrs. Hernandez was arrested at the apartment when police who entered the apartment with a search warrant found marijuana and heroin there. Mrs. Hernandez was charged with and pleaded guilty to being in a room where narcotics are being unlawfully smoked or used with knowledge that the activity was occurring. The probation report said that "she is a likeable person, apparently easily influenced by her associations, that she appears genuinely sorry for having committed the offense, that she has no prior criminal record . . . and that in the opinion of the probation officer she would be amenable to probation. . . ." The report recommended probation for three years under the following conditions: that she commit no further crimes; that she not frequent any place where narcotics are dispensed or sold, or associate with users of narcotics and that she obtain permission from her probation officer or the court before leaving the county. The sterilization provision was added by the judge at the time of the probation hearing. Although no reason was given for the addition of the sterilization provision at the time of the hearing, he subsequently said "this woman is in danger of continuing to lead a dissolute life and to be endangering the health, safety and lives of her minor children."

Although Mrs. Hernandez agreed to the sterilization provision at the time of the hearing, she subsequently changed her mind and refused to sign the probation order. Her attorney's motion to strike the sterilization condition from the probation order was denied but the jail sentence was reduced from six months to three months.

Mrs. Hernandez served only a few hours of her three-month term. Her court-appointed attorney filed a writ of habeas corpus with the superior court. The superior court granted the writ, ordered the sterilization provision stricken from the probation order and released Mrs. Hernandez to the supervision of the probation officer. Although the superior court judge said that there was only one question before him on the merits of the case, "Did the Municipal Court judge have the power to impose sterilization as a condition of probation?," almost half of his opinion was devoted to the problem of public support of illegitimate children and their mothers.

The court held that Mrs. Hernandez was not subject to sterilization under any of the three code provisions authorizing such aertions and that consequently the municipal court judge exceeded his judicial power when he issued a sterilization order in this case. The superior court believed that the sterilization provision was an attempt to punish Mrs. Hernandez for living with the father of her illegetimate child at the taxpayers' expense. Although the court condemned her illicit conduct, it also emphasized that this conduct does not of itself render her and the illegitimate child ineligible for aid. Furthermore, Mrs. Hernandez was neither convicted of nor charged with any violation of the welfare law. The opinion recognized that it is understandable for taxpayers to ask why they should pour their hard-earned tax dollars into supporting such a condition. The answer, however, the court said, is plain. "The answer is because it is the law."

The judge was sharply critical of attempts to change the law by judicial action. "In short, as applied to cases such as the one before this Court, if the aid to needy children provisions of our welfare statutes are not to the liking of a particular judge, he may not ignore them, or substitute a penalty of his own which is not authorized by law. It is for the people of their legislative representatives to make any change in the law that they deem desirable."

The following comments by the judge in the Hernandez case are equally applicable to the other California cases of sterilization by judicial order and also to the Ohio cases:

In our Country we are a people governed under law and not by the whims and caprice of men in power. . . . The courts and judges in the Judicial Branch may not enact laws nor may they set aside a law if it is constitutionally valid. They may affect law by judicial interpretation where its meaning is in doubt but they may not create a law where none exists nor may they alter the plain meaning of a statute to conform to their personal beliefs. . . . Judges may not ignore a law simply because they do not like it or believe in it. . . . Nor may a court act in excess of the power given it under the law. If an officer of the executive branch of government or a judge of the judicial branch should be permitted to act contrary to law or in excess of the power given him by law, this would mark a departure from our fundamental concept of rule by law and it would mean a reverting back to rule by men, that is to say rule in accordance with the whim, caprice and prejudices of men in power. This is wholly repugnant to our concept of government.

C. States with Sterilization Laws

Although twenty-three states have involuntary sterilization laws, this fact is not as strong an indication of support as it might appear at first glance. Only a year ago, the number would have been twenty-six states. In 1965 two states, Kansas and North Dakota, repealed their laws, and Connecticut changed from an involuntary to a voluntary law. Also, only five states, Delaware, Iowa, Michigan, North Carolina, and Virginia, perform twenty-five or more sterilizations annually, and in all but one of these states the number of sterilizations has decreased during the last twenty years.

The majority of the state mental retardation planning reports neither recommend increased use of sterilization nor do they advocate repeal of such legislation. They are similar to the plans of the states without sterilization laws in that they emphasize the importance of prevention but usually do not recommend sterilization as the means to achieve this goal.

The Utah report is an exception. It describes the state's program as a preventive measure not only for hereditary biological defects but also for *prevention of the propagation of cultural impoverishment recently recognized as a primary factor in the largest clinical category of mental retardation.*" (Emphasis added.)

The attitude of the state toward its sterilization law is principally a reflection of the views of the institution superintendent, if the extent to which the law is used is a criteria of "attitude." For example, Delaware sterilizations declined between 1952 and 1962 but in 1963 it had the highest number of reported state sterilizations per 100,000 population. Delaware also appointed a new superintendent of hospitals in July, 1961, who believed it would be possible to release more patients if they had been sterilized so "I began to push the matter and more patients were released. . . ." Georgia's annual sterilization rate dropped from 112 to 1959 to an all-time low of seven operations in 1963. There were no changes in the sterilization law during that period. "The changes have been in the philosophy of the superintendent, not making it necessary for the Eugenics Board to make any decisions."

Although sterilization is not mentioned in Virginia's Plan for Comprehensive Action to Combat Mental Retardation, there is support for the state's sterilization program in both the legislature and in the institutions. In 1960 the Virginia Advisory Legislative Council was told to review the sterliization law "in the light of knowledge most recently available to the medical profession in the fields of hereditary forms of mental illness, mental deficiency, and epilepsy in the treatment thereof."

It reported that "We are advised that there are no medical or other scientific data indicating that a change in the basis set out in the statute for the sterilization of inmates of institutions is either imperative or desirable." The Council's conclusion about scientific evidence is puzzling, to say the least, considering the vast amount of information expressing a contrary view which has been published. Also, it is worthy of note that the Virginia Planning Report on Mental Retardation which was prepared only a few years later says:

The complexity of the problem of mental retardation is further increased by the fact that many specific determinations of MR have not, as yet, been discovered. "Well over a hundred etiologies, diseases and syndromes have been described in which mental retardation represents a more or less important symptom. About 20 per cent of these are encountered with sufficient frequency to have practical importance."

. . .

Not as many cases of retardation are due to genetic factors as was once believed by earlier investigators. In some individuals organic damage to some part of the nervous system can be detected as a causative factor in retardation. Prenatal infections, prematurity, birth trauma, childhood diseases, anoxia, dietary deficiencies, metabolic disorders, blood sensitivities, sociocultural deficiencies are among some of the known causes of this complex problem.

A questionnaire about sterilization administered in 1964 at one of the state institutions for the mentally retarded shows that the staff physicians and the social workers were in favor of sterilization, also favored the sterilization of the parents and/or siblings of the patient; and half of them thought the hospital should perform more sterilizations. The interviews conducted by the "Mentally Retarded and the Law" project in the same and one additional institution also showed support for the state policy. Several interviewees also recommended involuntary sterilization on non-eugenic grounds.

In 1962 the legislature did pass a noneugenic sterilization law but it is a voluntary one. It authorizes the sterilization of any person over the age of twenty-one upon the written request of the person and that of his spouse, if there is one. The law also applies to minors if they are mentally ill, retarded, or epileptic. If the applicant is under twenty-one the statute also requires judicial determination that the operation would be in the best interest of the minor and of society.

Statistics for Connecticut, Minnesota, and Vermont, the three states with voluntary eugenic sterilization laws show the same downward trend in annual sterilizations as the states with involuntary laws. Neither Minnesota nor Vermont reported any sterilizations in 1963, and Connecticut, which was operating under an involuntary law at the time, reported only three.

The sparing use of their eugenic sterilization laws by an overwhelming majority of the twenty-six states which have them indicates their doubts about the effectiveness and/or the constitutionality of these provisions. States that use their laws extensively may share these doubts. For example, North Carolina which reported more than 50 per cent of the total 1963 sterilizations requires the consent of a relative and bases its sterilization program primarily on fitness for parenthood rather than eugenic grounds.

D. The Legal View

There are two legal viewpoints concerning the constitutionality of compulsory sterilization laws. The first theory which became prominent was that the constitutionality of sterilization statutes depends upon their scientific validity. Many proponents of this view believe that the scientific premises upon which the statutes rest are erroneous and that consequently compulsory sterilization is an arbitrary and unreasonable deprivation of liberty.

Proponents of the second theory consider the right of procreation as a fundamental liberty which cannot be interfered with by a government order. They contend that compulsory sterilization would violate substantive due process even if the laws were based on scientific evidence. The analogies used by Justice Holmes to uphold this type of legislation have been severely criticized by some of the proponents of this view Justice Holmes said, "The principle that sustains compulsory vaccination is broad enough to cover cutting the Fallopian tubes." However, when the Massachusetts Supreme Court upheld the vaccination law, it said:

If a person should deem it important that vaccination should not be performed in his case, and the authorities should think otherwise, it is not in their power to vaccinate him by force, and the worst that could happen to him under the statute would be the payment of the penalty of five dollars.

Thus it has been argued that the vaccination and sterilization laws are not analogous because "so far as concerns liberty, there would appear to be a real difference between assessing a fine and compelling submission."

Justice Holmes also believed that if the nation could call upon its best citizens to sacrifice their lives in time of war, it should be able to "call upon those who already sap the strength of the state" to make a lesser sacrifice. This analogy has been contested on the ground that there is a necessity and an urgency that causes us to sacrifice men in self-defense which is wholly lacking in the case of eugenic sterilization.

The fear has also been expressed that the logic in the decision in *Buck* v. *Bell* might be extended beyond its present limited boundaries:

There are other things besides physical or mental disease that may render persons undesirable citizens or might do so in the opinion of a majority of a prevailing legislature. Racial differences, for instance, might afford a basis for such an opinion in communities where the question is unfortunately a permanent and paranoid issue.[11]

In view of suggestions made by some eugenicists, the fear that the scope of eugenic sterilization laws may be expanded is not irrational. A Model Eugenical Sterilization Law proposed that the following persons be subject to sterilization:

(1) Feeble-minded; (2) Insane (including the psychopathic); (3) Criminalistic (including the delinquent and wayward); (4) Epileptic; (5) Inebriate (including drug-habitues); (6) Diseased (including the tuberculous, the syphilitics, the leprous, and others with chronic, infectious, and legally segregable diseases); (7) Blind (including those with seriously impaired vision); (8) Deaf (including those with seriously impaired hearing); (9) Deformed (including the crippled); and (10) Dependent (including orphans, ne'er-do-wells, the homeless, tramps and paupers).[12]

This model law also recommended the sterilization of those persons who, although they did not exhibit any of the above traits, have offspring, one-fourth of whom show such traits or one-half of whom carry genes for such qualities even if the offspring does not function as a socially inadequate person.

Existing sterilization laws are also subject to criticism on the grounds that they violate procedural due process. Since sterilization is a drastic remedy and generally a permanent infringement of bodily integrity, those affected by laws authorizing it are at least entitled to every reasonable precaution. Thus far they have not been adequately protected. The sterilization of persons without legal authorization, before testing the constitutionality of the laws, sterilization under unconstitutional laws, and the lack of representation by counsel, are all clear illustrations of this disregard of rights. In fact, it is likely that if the United States Supreme Court reviewed some of these statutes, it would declare them unconstitutional, because the Court placed great emphasis on the procedural protections of the Virginia statute in *Buck* v. *Bell*.

Many of the criticisms of eugenic sterilization laws are equally applicable to sterilization based on environmental factors. The whole sterilization battle over the efficacy, morality and constitutionality of such legislation may be in the offing, this time with the proponents using social deficiencies rather than hereditary deficiencies as the justification.

VII. The Future of Sterilization Legislation

Involuntary eugenic sterilization was advocated to save civilization from the imminent danger of being overrun by defective stocks who were already eating it away like internal parasites. Mental illness, mental retardation, epilepsy, and criminality were all believed to

[11] Smith v. Bd. of Examiners, 85 N.J.L. 46, 53, 88 Atl. 963, 966 (1913).

[12] Laughlin, Eugenical Sterilization in the United States 446–47 (1922).

be hereditary. Consequently, cure for these conditions was hopeless and prevention was the only answer. For example, it was alleged if sterilization was permitted the total number of retardates would be "greatly reduced in one generation and might in several generations be practically rooted out of the human race."

Sterilization has proved a striking failure as a means of reducing the "unfit." Although the law is often accused of being painfully slow in its acceptance of scientific progress, this was not true in the case of sterilization. Legislators and judges accepted the claims of the eugenicists with such rapidity that today many persons question whether this swift acceptance was wise from either a scientific or a legal point of view.

The legal basis for involuntary eugenic sterilization exists but the number of operations decreases each year. During the last two decades, there has been increasing opposition to sterilization on the grounds that scientific knowledge of hereditary factors in mental disability is not sufficient to warrant its widespread use, certainly not an involuntary basis. There is also opposition to sterilization on theological, moral, and social grounds. However, the objections on scientific grounds seem to have been the major cause of the drop in the number of sterilizations.

We may have an opportunity to measure the extent of moral, social, and theological objections to sterilization as a means of eliminating the unfit. It is possible that within the next few years there will be a new campaign to use sterilization to save society. This time we will be promised salvation from "poor parents" rather than "poor heredity."

Society is still burdened with mental illness, mental retardation, crime, and poverty. In fact, for a variety of reasons they appear to be even larger problems than they were in the 1900's. We are still searching for ways to eliminate them and sterilization is still advocated as at least one of the solutions to the problem.

Three types of sterilization are presently being suggested: voluntary sterilization of the mentally disabled on eugenic grounds; voluntary sterilization without any specific grounds; and involuntary sterilization of the "unfit" on grounds of social inadequacy.

Voluntary sterilization of the mentally disabled already exists in three states. It is used infrequently in these states undoubtedly for the same reasons that the majority of the involuntary laws are inactive. Therefore, it is doubtful that the adoption of such legislation by other states would result in any substantial reduction of mental illness or mental retardation.

Voluntary sterilizations are performed for both therapeutic and non-therapeutic reasons without specific legislation in many states. The number of persons who have had such operations is unknown because the operations on males usually take place in a physician's office and are not reported to any central agency. Although women are operated on in hospitals, statistics are not kept on the number of operations. Many physicians refuse to perform such operations because of uncertainty about the type of situations in which voluntary sterilization is justified under state law. Two states, Virginia and North Carolina, recently adopted legislation which solves this problem. In both states physicians are exempt from civil and criminal liability, except for negligence, for non-therapeutic operations if there is compliance with the provisions of the statute.

There is still considerable controversy about the propriety of allowing people to use sterilization to limit their families for economic reasons or because the family does not want any more children. An analysis of this controversy is outside the scope of the present article. Let us assume for the purposes of this article that such legislation is desirable for the general population. There are still special problems concerning the applicability of a voluntary sterilization law, on eugenic or socio-economic grounds to the mentally disabled and others classified as unfit.

One aspect of the problem although pointed out thirty years ago in the American Neurological Association's report is still valid today:

[T]he word voluntary is frequently a mere subterfuge, in that it is often a condition of discharge from the institution that the patient be sterilized, and consequently the individual involved is in the position of being confined or confinable until he gives his consent for sterilization, which hardly makes the bargain free and equal and nullifies the real meaning of the word voluntary.

The choice of a twenty-one-year-old of sterilization over six months in jail also raises questions about the real meaning of the word voluntary. And how voluntary would be the consent of a mother faced with a choice of a sterilization or discontinuance of welfare assistance?

Another problem about voluntary laws is their application to children. North Carolina and Virginia both sterilize very young children under their eugenic sterilization laws. Virginia sterilizes children as young as six years of age[13] and 30 per cent of North Carolina's

---

[13] One of the Virginia sterilization hearings observed by the Mentally Retarded and the Law concerned a six-year-old boy.

sterilizations between 1962 and 1964 were performed on children between ten and nineteen years old. Neither state's voluntary sterilization law specifies any minimum age.

In fact, the application is not voluntary but is made on petition of a parent or a next friend. A court must determine that the operation would be in the child's best interest. However, one wonders what information the judge is to be given to make this decision. Will a psychiatric opinion on the effects of such an operation for the child's mental health development be required? Is a social worker going to do a study on the child and the family? What are the circumstances which make such an operation "in the best interests of the child"? These and similar questions deserve serious study by legislators considering voluntary sterilization legislation.

Another problem about voluntary sterilization laws is the capacity of a mentally disabled person to consent. Although some mentally ill and mentally retarded persons are capable of understanding the nature and consequences of the operation, others are not. Connecticut has attempted to solve the problem of consent of the incompetent under a voluntary law by providing for consent of the next of kin, or if there is none, with the approval of the board of trustees of the institution. This procedure does enable the operation to be performed but it does not make the operation a voluntary one.

Do these problems mean that the mentally disabled, criminals, and the poor should be denied the benefits of voluntary sterilization? The answer to this question depends on the answers to many other questions including the following:

1. How many persons in these groups who understand the consequences of the operation, and who are in a position to make a free choice, wish to have it performed?
2. What are the attitudes towards the operation of those who have had it?[14]
3. What are the possibilities of adverse consequences to the sterilized person's mental health?

4. Do the people in these groups have adequate information and training about other birth control methods?
5. What are the possibilities that a person who does not understand the nature and consequences of the operation will become pregnant without the use of any birth control method? With the use of a birth control method other than sterilization?
6. Under what conditions is sterilization in the best interests of a minor?
7. Are we willing to compensate the professionals, psychiatrists, social workers, etc., whose services are necessary in these cases?
8. Are we willing to make non-political appointments of reasonably compensated attorneys who will give the necessary legal services to the poor, the incompetent, and minors for whom sterilization is recommended?

The sterilization proposal which would affect the most people is involuntary sterilization on grounds of social inadequacy. Again, this is not a new proposal. Many of the current involuntary sterilization laws provide for sterilization on other than eugenic grounds. However, the constitutionality of sterilization on this basis has not been decided. The arguments advanced in its favor are the same as those used by proponents of eugenic sterilization. Society has the right to protect itself from being swamped by mental illness, mental retardation, crime, poverty, etc., and the high financial costs of these conditions.

The difference between the two proposals is that the eugenicists argued that the prevention of procreation was necessary because children of parents having these conditions would have these same defects, by reason of heredity. Now, the claim is that the children will have the defects because the parents are too socially inadequate to fulfill the responsibilities of parenthood.

It has been suggested that before we decide on the desirability we must attempt to answer the question, "What are we trying to prevent?"

Are we trying to prevent the entrance into our society of offspring who because of the hereditary or environmental effects of their parents' mental disorders probably will be too socially inadequate to be able to stay out of a mental institution; too socially inadequate to be able to stay out of a penal institution; too socially inadequate to be able to earn a minimum livelihood so as not to be a burden upon the state; too socially inadequate to be able to conform to the publicly proclaimed sex mores that are often not followed in private life; or, too so-

---

[14] A follow-up study of 110 sterilized mentally retarded patients who were discharged between 1949 and 1958 showed that: "Almost two-thirds of the discharged patients did not approve of the sterilization operation which they had to undergo. Women, particularly the married, were most likely to object to sterilization, and men, particularly the unmarried, least likely. Sabaugh & Edgerton, "Sterilized Mental Defectives Look at Eugenic Sterilization," Eugenics Q. 9 (1962): 221–22.

cially inadequate to be able to achieve some other goal of our culture?[15]

Some proposals appear to be aimed primarily at cutting welfare costs.

Bills for compulsory sterilization of unwed mothers have been seriously debated in such states as Mississippi, North Carolina and Iowa and advocated in many others (including a number of northern states). Most of the proposals have failed of adoption, but they offer racist politicians and others opportunities for massive fulminations on illegitimacy. AFDC cost, and related subjects, which appear to be aimed at intimidating unwed mothers from applying for public assistance.[16]

The attempt to cut welfare costs also seems to have been the primary reason for the decisions in the Andrada, Palafax, and Hernandez cases.

When welfare costs are not mentioned, the argument is simply that the child, even if of normal intelligence, will be gravely handicapped by the mere fact of being reared by a feebleminded parent. Similar arguments are made about a child whose parents are mentally ill or criminals. However, not all authorities agree. Leo Kanner, an eminent child psychiatrist, said:

In my 20 years of psychiatric work with thousands of children and their parents, I have seen percentually at least as many "intelligent" adults unfit to rear their offspring as I have seen such "feebleminded" adults. I have . . . and many others have . . . come to the conclusion that to a large extent independent of the I.Q., fitness for parenthood is determined by emotional involvements and relationships.[17]

[15] Birnbaum, "Eugenic Sterilization," *A.M.A.J.*, 175 (1961): 951, 956.
[16] Jaffee, "Family Planning, Public Policy and Intervention Strategy," *J. Social Issues* (in press).
[17] Kanner, *A Miniature Textbook of Feeblemindness* (1949), pp. 4–5.

The same arguments used to attack the constitutionality of involuntary eugenic sterilization laws are applicable to involuntary sterilization on an environmental basis. However, there are two additional arguments agains tthe latter type of law. In *Buck* v. *Bell*, the United States Supreme Court proceeded on the assumption that the disabilities covered by the law were hereditary and could not be ameliorated. This is not true of sterilization on an environmental basis. In many instances environment can be changed and we are currently engaged in massive efforts to do this by providing improved pre-natal care, training mothers in child care. Project Head Start, and numerous other programs for children and adults. Also, there were no practical alternatives to sterilization for preventing procreation at the time of *Buck* v. *Bell*, but this is not true today.

Proponents of involuntary sterilization, both in the past and today, seem to imply that those who oppose these laws place the right of procreation above the welfare of society. It is possible that the day will come when this statement is accurate. The hereditary nature of these conditions may be established, or all reasonable attempts at improving the environment and rehabilitation of the disabled may fail, or food and air shortages may become so severe that there might not be enough to bear the burden of any further growth in population; then, there will be a choice between sterilization and the rights of the individual. If the time comes when any of these conditions exists, and if efforts at birth control fail, and if we can decide who should be sterilized and who is qualified to make this decision, then perhaps legislation authorizing involuntary sterilization could be justified.

[Charts of sterilization laws and procedures omitted.]

RELF v. WEINBERGER AND NATIONAL WELFARE RIGHTS ORGANIZATION v. WEINBERGER

GESSELL, Judge

Although Congress has been insistent that all family planning programs function on a purely voluntary basis, there is uncontroverted evidence in the record that minors and other incompetents have been sterilized with federal funds and that an indefinite number of poor people have been improperly coerced into accepting a sterilization operation under the threat that various federally supported welfare benefits would be withdrawn unless they submitted to irreversible sterilization.

When such deplorable incidents began to receive nationwide public attention due to the experience of the Relf sisters in Alabama, the Secretary took steps to restrict the circumstances under which recipients of federal family planning funds could conduct sterilization operations. On August 3, 1973, the Department published in the *Federal Register* a notice of Guidelines for Sterilization Procedures under HEW Supported Programs. 38 Fed. Reg. 20930 (1973). Notices of proposed rule making were duly published in the *Federal Register* on September 21, 1973. 38 Fed. Reg. 26459 (1973). Interested persons were given an opportunity to participate in the rule making by submitting comments on the proposed regulations. The final regulations here under attack were issued on February 6, 1974.

Briefly, they are as follows:

1. Legally competent adults must give their "informed consent" to sterilization. Such consent must be evidenced by a written and signed document.
2. Legally competent persons under the age of 18 must also give such written consent. In these situations, a special Review Committee of independent persons from the community must also have determined that the proposed sterilization is in the best interest of the patient, taking into consideration (a) the expected mental and physical impact of pregnancy and motherhood on the patient, if female, or the expected mental impact of fatherhood, if male, and (b) the expected immediate and long-term mental and physical impact of sterilization on the patient. 42 CFR § 50.206(a); 45 CFR § 205.35 (a)(4)(i). The Review Committee must also (a) review appropriate medical, social and psychological information concerning the patient, including the age of the patient, alternative family planning methods, and the adequacy of consent, and (b) interview the patient, both parents of the patient (if available), and such other persons as in its judgment will contribute pertinent information. 42 CFR § 50.206(b)(1, 2); 45 CFR § 205.35(a)(4)(i)(A,B). However, parental consent is not required. 42 CFR § 50.203(c); 45 CFR § 205,35(a)(t)(ii).
3. Legally incompetent minors must be afforded the above safeguard, and, in addition, a state court of competent jurisdiction must determine that the proposed sterilization is in the best interest of the patient. 42 CFR § 50.203(c); 45 CFR § 205.35(a)(1)(iv)(A,B).
4. The sterilization of mental incompetents of all ages must also be sanctioned by a Review Committee and a court. However, personal consent is not required—it is enough that the patient's "representative" requests sterilization. 42 CFR § 50.203(a); 45 CFR § 205.35(a)(1). Although defendants interpret the term "representative" to mean a person empowered under state law to consent to the sterilization on behalf of the patient, no such definition appears in the regulations themselves.

Plaintiffs do not oppose the voluntary sterilization of poor persons under federally funded programs. However, they contend that these regulations are both illegal and arbitrary because they authorize *involuntary* sterilizations without statutory or constitutional justification. They argue forcefully that sterilization of minors or mental incompetents is necessarily involuntary in the nature of things.

United States District Court for the District of Columbia, Civil Action No. 73–1557 (RELF), and Civil Action No. 74–243 (NWRO), March 15, 1974.

For the reasons developed below, the Court finds that the Secretary has no statutory authority under the family planning sections of the Social Security or Public Health Services Acts to fund the sterilization of any person incompetent under state law to consent to such an operation, whether because of minority or of mental deficiency. In short, federally assisted family planning sterilizations are permissible only with the voluntary, knowing and uncoerced consent of individuals competent to give such consent. This result requires an injunction against substantial portions of the proposed regulations and their revision to insure that all sterilizations funded under the family planning sections are voluntary in the full sense of that term and that sterilization of incompetent minors and adults is prevented.

The dispute with regard to minors and mental incompetents centers around two aspects of the statutory language. On the one hand, Congress included in every section mentioning family planning a requirement that such services be voluntarily requested. 42 U.S.C. §§ 300a–5, 602(a)(15), 708(a), 1396(a)(4). On the other hand, these sections purport to offer family planning services to all poor people and two of them specifically include minors. 42 U.S.C. §§ 602(a)(15), 1396d(a)(4). The Secretary argues that this juxtaposition indicates that Congress intended that minors personally and incompetents through their representatives would be able to consent to sterilization under these sections. That conclusion is unwarranted.

Although the term "voluntary" is nowhere defined in the statutes under consideration, it is frequently encountered in the law. Even its dictionary definition assumes an exercise of free will and clearly precludes the existence of coercion or force. *Webster's Second New International Dictionary* 2858 (2d ed. 1961). See also *United States* v. *Johnson*, 452 F.2d 1363, 1372 (D.C. Cir. 1971); *United States* v. *Thompson*, 356 F.2d 216, 210–21 (2d Cir. 1965), *cert. denied*, 384 U.S. 964 (1966). And its use in the statutory and decisional law, at least when important human rights are at stake, entails a requirement that the individual have at his disposal the information necessary to make his decision and the mental competence to appreciate the significance of that information. See, e.g., *Dusky* v. *United States*, 362 U.S. 402 (1960); *Elder* v. *Crawley Book Machinery Co.*, 441 F.2d 771, 773 (3d Cir. 1971); *Pearson* v. *United States*, 325 F.2d 625, 626–67 (D.C. Cir. 1963).

No person who is mentally incompetent can meet these standards, nor can the consent of a representative, however sufficient under state law, impute voluntariness to the individual actually undergoing irreversible sterilization. Minors would also appear to lack the knowledge, maturity and judgment to satisfy these standards with regard to such an important issue, whatever may be their competence to rely on devices or medication that temporarily frustrates procreation. This is the reasoning that provides the basis for the nearly universal common law and statutory rule that minors and mental incompetents cannot consent to medical operations, see *Restatement of Torts* § 59 (1934), or be held to contractual obligations, see 43 C.J.S. Infants § 71 et seq.; 17 C.J.S. Contracts § 133.

The statutory references to minors and mental incompetents do not contradict this conclusion, for they appear only in the context of family planning services in general. Minors, for example, are not legally incompetent for all purposes, and many girls of child-bearing age are undoubtedly sufficiently aware of the relevant considerations to use temporary contraceptives that intrude far less on fundamental rights. However, the Secretary has not demonstrated and the Court cannot find that Congress deemed such children capable of voluntarily consenting to an irreversible operation involving the basic human right to procreate. Nor can the Court find, in the face of repeated warnings concerning voluntariness, that Congress authorized that such a serious deprivation be imposed upon mental incompetents at the will of an unspecified "representative."

Since these conclusions are based on statutory rather than constitutional grounds, the Court need not reach the question of whether involuntary sterilization *could* be funded by Congress.

C. *Additional Rights of the Mentally Impaired*

THE ERVIN ACT—SECTION 9(a)
PUBLIC LAW 88–597, 88TH CONGRESS

Sec. 9. (a) Any person hospitalized in a public or private hospital pursuant to this Act shall be entitled (1) to communicate by sealed mail or otherwise with any individual or official agency inside or outside the hospital, and (2) to receive uncensored mail from his attorney or personal physician. All other incoming mail or communications may be read before being delivered to the patient, if the chief of service believes such action is necessary for the medical welfare of the patient who is the intended recipient. However, any mail or other communication which is not delivered to the patient for whom it is intended shall be immediately returned to the sender. But nothing in this section shall prevent the administrator from making reasonable rules regarding visitation hours and the use of telephone and telegraph facilities.

(b) Any person hospitalized in a public hospital for a mental illness shall, during his hospitalization, be entitled to medical and psychiatric care and treatment. The administrator of each public hospital shall keep records detailing all such care and treatment received by any such person and such records shall be made available, upon that person's written authorization, to his attorney or personal physician. Such records shall be preserved by the administrator until such person has been discharged from the hospital.

(c) No mechanical restraint shall be applied to any patient hospitalized in any public or private hospital for a mental illness unless the use of restraint is prescribed by a physician and, if so prescribed, such restraint shall be removed whenever the condition justifying its use no longer exists. Any use of a mechanical restraint, together with the reasons therefor, shall be made a part of the medical record of the patient.

(d) No patient hospitalized pursuant to this Act shall, by reason of such hospitalization, be denied the right to dispose of property, execute instruments, make purchases, enter into contractual relationships, vote, and hold a driver's license, unless such patient has been adjudicated incompetent by a court of competent jurisdiction and has not been restored to legal capacity. If the chief of service of the public is hospitalized is of the opinion that such patient is unable to exercise any of the aforementioned rights, the chief of service shall immediately notify the patient and the patient's attorney, legal guardian, spouse, parents, or other nearest known adult relative, and the United States District Court for the District of Columbia, the Commission on Mental Health, and the Board of Commissioners of the District of Columbia of that fact.

(e) Any individual in the District of Columbia who, by reason of a judicial decree ordering his hospitalization entered prior to the date of the enactment of this Act, is considered to be mentally incompetent and is denied the right to dispose of property, execute instruments, make purchases, enter into contractual relationships, vote, or hold a driver's license solely by reason of such decree, shall, upon the expiration of the one-year period immediately following such date of enactment, be deemed to have been restored to legal capacity unless, within such one-year period, affirmative action is commenced to have such individual adjudicated mentally incompetent by a court of competent jurisdiction. . . .

(f) Any patient, and the patient's spouse, parents, or other nearest known adult relative, shall receive, upon admission of the patient to the hospital, a written statement outlining in simple, nontechnical language all release procedures provided by this Act, setting out all rights accorded to patients by this Act, and describing procedures provided by law for adjudication of incompetency and appointment of trustees or committees for the hospitalized individual.

THE THERAPEUTIC BILL OF RIGHTS

Nicholas N. Kittrie

1. *No person shall be compelled to undergo treatment except for the defense of society.* The therapeutic state must be separated into its two major model components: (a) the welfare offerings which are successors to the old poor laws, and (b) the social-defense preventive measures which have replaced the criminal process. The first model should be essentially voluntary and informal. Brought under it will be the neglected child as contrasted with the delinquent child, the docile public drunk as contrasted with the dangerous alcoholic, the senile mental patient as contrasted with the threatening maniac. The second model, continuing in great part to be involuntary and limited to those who have committed crimes or who pose a clear and present danger to themselves or others, must be carefully circumscribed with regard to both criteria and procedures.

2. *Man's innate right to remain free of excessive forms of human modification shall be inviolable.* A new body of laws must be developed within the framework of the Constitution in order to guard against the therapeutic state and its possible zeal in carrying out compulsory societal experiments.

3. *No social sanctions may be invoked unless the person subjected to treatment has demonstrated a clear and present danger through truly harmful behavior which is immediately forthcoming or has already occurred.* Generally, an overt act should be required. For those who are so incompetent, lacking in lucidity, or immature in age that they cannot be left at large, even though not publicly dangerous, greater emphasis must be placed upon voluntary welfare services in a community setting in lieu of total institutionalization.

4. *No person shall be subjected to involuntary incarceration or treatment on the basis of a finding of a general condition or status alone. Nor shall the mere conviction of a crime or a finding of not guilty by reason of insanity suffice to have a person automatically committed or treated.* This is necessary to protect against the dangers of vague and uncertain criteria and the undue expansion of such designations as "mental illness," "psychopathy," "alcoholism," "addiction," and "juvenile delinquency," and to guarantee that all subjected to compulsory controls be accorded equal rights.

5. *No social sanctions, whether designated criminal, civil, or therapeutic, may be invoked in the absence of the previous right to a judicial or other independent hearing, appointed counsel, and an opportunity to confront those testifying about one's past conduct or therapeutic needs.* While it may not be necessary or desirable to follow the mandates of the constitutional Bill of Rights fully, they can be used as guides for deciding what rights must be required. The drafting of acceptable procedures will require a great deal of imagination. The legal profession and the therapists must together work to implement procedures that will serve both the humanistic goals of the *parens patriae* while protecting the individual from the dangers to freedom inherent in the social-defense goals of the therapeutic state. Due to the alleged diminished mental capacity of those coming under the therapeutic controls, the deviant's right to counsel should be absolute; under no circumstances should he be asked or allowed to waive such right.

6. *Dual interference by both the criminal and the therapeutic process is prohibited.* The double-barreled approach presently in effect in the narcotics and psychopathy arenas offends the philosophies of both the criminal law and the therapeutic state. Furthermore, it subjects one to a tribute in terms of time spent under compulsory sanction that is often out of proportion to

Excerpted and reprinted with permission from Kittrie, *The Right to Be Different* (Baltimore: The Johns Hopkins Press, 1971), pp. 402–4.

the offensive behavior. The state should be entitled to either criminal or therapeutic controls in a given case. The insistence upon both reveals an incredible disregard for individual liberty and dignity.

7. *An involuntary patient shall have the right to receive treatment.* If no treatment is available, then any restraint must be justified solely upon the danger the individual represents to society. A separate hearing with full constitutional safeguards should be accorded on the question of dangerousness. Unless it is likely that the individual will beyond a reasonable doubt be harmful, he should be released. Persons retains for their dangerousness alone should be detained in special institutions. Our therapeutic centers must cease being the repositories of highly dangerous, untreatable offenders.

Some further steps must be taken, however, in order to guarantee that the treatment received by an involuntary patient be genuine. Perhaps commitment under therapeutic programs should not be indeterminate, but should be limited to a specific term based on medical estimates of the time required for cure. If this time is considered reasonable by the committing court, it shall establish a treatment review date based on the prognosis. If the term is excessive when judged by the nature of the dangerous act committed and compared with the corresponding penal term for the same act, the committing court may establish its own review date. If the patient is not released by the review date, the therapists shall have the burden of showing cause why the individual should continue treatment. Interim amendments to the treatment plan and revision of the review date may be obtained through the committing court. In addition, boards of visitors, consisting of medical, social, be-

havioral, and legal specialists, should be appointed in every state. These boards would make regular institutional visits to assess the continuing need and efficacy of the treatment of individuals. The boards would also have the obligation to evaluate periodically the treatment facilities and report their findings to the public and responsible public officials. Furthermore, the Department of Public Welfare of each state should keep a full centralized record on all involuntarily committed persons, which should be open for inspection by attorneys and other interested persons.

8. *Any compulsory treatment must be the least required reasonably to protect society.* No person should be subjected to full-time institutionalization or other drastic controls if lesser measures—in the form of voluntary welfare, probation, halfway houses, and so forth—are adequate to protect society while providing the necessary treatment.

9. *All committed persons should have direct access to appointed counsel and the right, without any interference, to petition the courts for relief.* To make this right meaningful, a responsible member of the community, including members of the bar, should be appointed as the next friend for every committed patient. Such a plan would act as a check against institutional abuses, increase community-wide awareness of institutional problems, and provide a liaison between the patient and the legal process.

10. *Those submitting to voluntary treatment should be guaranteed that they will not be subsequently transferred to a compulsory program through administrative action.* All involuntary patients must be accorded the same substantive and procedural safeguards. Such assurance should encourage the seeking of voluntary treatment.

MILLS v. BOARD OF EDUCATION

MEMORANDUM OPINION, JUDGMENT
AND DECREE

WADDY, District Judge.

This is a civil action brought on behalf of seven children of school age in which they seek to enjoin the defendants from excluding them from the District of Columbia Public Schools and/or denying them publicly supported education and to compel the defendants to provide them with immediate and adequate education and educational facilities in the public schools or alternative placement at public expense.

THE PROBLEM

The problem of providing special education for "exceptional" children (mentally retarded, emotionally disturbed, physically handicapped, hyperactive and other children with behavioral problems) is one of major proportions in the District of Columbia. The precise number of such children cannot be stated because the District has continuously failed to comply with Section 31–208 of the District of Columbia Code which requires a census of all children aged 3 to 18 in the District to be taken. Plaintiffs estimate that there are ". . . 22,000 retarded, emotionally disturbed, blind, deaf, and speech or learning disabled children, and perhaps as many as 18,000 of these children are not being furnished with programs of specialized education."

Plaintiffs allege in their complaint and defendants admit as follows:

"Peter Mills is twelve years old, black, and a committed dependent ward of the District of Columbia resident at Junior Village. He was excluded from the Brant Elementary School on March 23, 1971, at which time he was in the fourth grade. Peter allegedly was a 'behavior problem' and was recommended and approved for exclusion by the principal.

"Duane Blacksheare is thirteen years old, black, resident at Saint Elizabeth's Hospital, Washington, D.C., and a dependent committed child. He was excluded from the Giddings Elementary School in October, 1967, at which time he was in the third grade. Duane allegedly

was a "behavior problem." Despite repeated efforts by his mother, Duane remained largely excluded from all publicly-supported education until February, 1971. Education experts at the Child Study Center examined Duane and found him to be capable of returning to regular class if supportive services were provided. Following several articles in the *Washington Post* and *Washington Star*, Duane was placed in a regular seventh grade classroom on a two-hour a day basis without any catch-up assistance and without an evaluation or diagnostic interview of any kind. Duane has remained on a waiting list for a tuition grant and is now excluded from all publicly-supported education.

"George Liddell, Jr., is eight years old, black, resident with his mother, and an AFDC recipient. George has never attended public school because of the denial of his application to the Maury Elementary School on the ground that he required a special class. George allegedly was retarded. George remains excluded from all publicly-supported education, despite a medical opinion that he is capable of profiting from schooling.

"Steven Gaston is eight years old, black, and unable to afford private instruction. He has been excluded from the Taylor Elementary School since September, 1969, at which time he was in the first grade. Steven allegedly was slightly brain-damaged and hyperactive, and was excluded because he wandered around the classroom. Steven has remained excluded from all publicly-supoprted education.

"Michael Williams is sixteen years old, black, resident at Saint Elizabeth's Hospital, Washington, D.C., and unable to afford private instruction. Michael is epileptic and allegedly slightly retarded. He has been excluded from the Sharpe Health School since October, 1969, at which time he was temporarily hospitalized. Thereafter Michael was excluded from school because of health problems and school absences.

"Janice King is thirteen years old, black, and unable to afford private instruction. She has been denied access to public schools since reaching compulsory school attendance age, as a result of the rejection of her application, based on the lack of an appropriate educational program. Janice is brain-damaged and retarded, with right hemiplegia, resulting from a childhood illness.

"Jerome James is twelve years old, black, resident and an AFDC recipient. Jerome is a retarded child and has been totally excluded from public school.

The Defense

These defendants say that it is impossible to afford plaintiffs the relief they request unless:

(a) The Congress of the United States appropriates millions of dollars to improve special education services in the District of Columbia; or

(b) These defendants divert millions of dollars from funds already specifically appropriated for other educational services in order to improve special educational services. These defendants suggest that to do so would violate an Act of Congress and would be inequitable to children outside the alleged plaintiff class.

This Court is not persuaded by that contention. [5-8] The defendants are required by the Constitution of the United States, the District of Columbia Code, and their own regulations to provide a publicly-supported education for these "exceptional" children. Their failure to fulfill this clear duty to include and retain these children in the public school system, or otherwise provide them with publicly-supported education, and their failure to afford them due process hearing and periodical review, cannot be excused by the claim that there are insufficient funds. In Goldberg v. Kelly, 397 U.S. 254, 90 S.Ct. 1011, 25 L.Ed.2d 287 (1969) the Supreme Court, in a case that involved the right of a welfare recipient to a hearing before termination of his benefits, held that Constitutional rights must be afforded citizens despite the greater expense involved. The Court stated at page 266, 90 S.Ct. at page 1019, that "the State's interest that his [welfare recipient] payments not be erroneously terminated, clearly outweighs the State's competing concern to prevent any increase in its fiscal and administrative burdens." Similarly the District of Columbia's interest in educating the excluded children clearly must outweigh its interest in preserving its financial resources. If sufficient funds are not available to finance all of the services and programs that are needed and desirable in the system then the available funds must be expended equitably in such a manner that no child is entirely excluded from a publicly supported education consistent with his needs and ability to benefit therefrom. The inadequacies of the District of Columbia Public School System whether occasioned by insufficient funding

or administrative inefficiency, certainly cannot be permitted to bear more heavily on the "exceptional" or handicapped child than on the normal child.

Judgment and Decree

Plainitffs having filed their verified complaint seeking an injunction and declaration of rights as set forth more fully in the verified complaint and the prayer for relief contained therein; and having moved this Court from summary judgment pursuant to Rule 56 of the Federal Rules of Civil Procedure, and this Court having reviewed the record of this cause including plaintiffs' Motion, pleadings, affidavits, and evidence and arguments judgment is entered in this action as follows:

[10] 1. That no child eligible for a publicly supported education in the District of Columbia public schools shall be excluded from a regular public school assignment by a Rule, policy, or practice of the Board of Education of the District of Columbia or its agents unless such child is provided (a) adequate alternative educational services suited to the child's needs, which may include special education or tuition grants, and (b) a constitutionally adequate prior hearing and periodic review of the child's status, progress, and the adequacy of any educational alternative.

2. The defendants, their officers, agents, servants, employees, and attorneys and all those in active concert or participation with them are hereby enjoined from maintaining, enforcing or otherwise continuing in effect any and all rules, policies and practices which include plaintiffs and the members of the class they represent from a regular public school assignment without providing them at public expense (a) adequate and immediate alternative education or tuition grants, consistent with their needs, and (b) a constitutionally adequate prior hearing and periodic review of their status, progress and the adequacy of any educational alternatives; and it is further ORDERED that:

3. The District of Columbia shall provide to each child of school age a free and suitable publicly-supported education regardless of the degree of the child's mental, physical, or emotional

disability or impairment. Furthermore, defendants shall not exclude any child resident in the District of Columbia from such publicly-supported education on the basis of a claim of insufficient resources.

4. Defendants shall provide each identified member of plaintiff class with a publicly-supported education suited to his needs within thirty (30) days of the entry of this order.

5. Defendants shall cause announcements and notices to be placed in the *Washington Post, Washington Star-Daily News*, and the *Afro-American*, in all issues published for a three week period thereafter at quarterly intervals, and shall cause spot announcements to be made on television and radio stations for twenty (20) consecutive days, and thereafter at quarterly intervals, advising residents of the District of Columbia that all children, regardless of any handicap or other disability, have a right to a publicly-supported education suited to their needs, and informing the parents or guardians of such children of the procedures required to enroll their children in an appropriate educational program. Such announcements should include the listing of a special answering service telephone number to be established by defendants in order to (a) compile the names, addresses, phone numbers of such children who are presently not attending school and (b) provide further information to their parents or guardians as to the procedures required to enroll their children in an appropriate educational program.

6. Within twenty-five (25) days of the entry of this order, defendants shall file with the Clerk of this Court, an up-to-date list showing, for every additional identified child, the name of the child's parent or guardian, the child's name, age, address and telephone number, the date of his suspension, expulsion, exclusion or denial of placement and, without attributing a particular characteristic to any specific child, a breakdown of such list, showing the alleged causal characteristics for such nonattendance (e.g., educable mentally retarded, trainable mentally retarded, emotionally disturbed, specific learning disability, cripples/other health impaired, hearing impaired, visually impaired, multiple handicapped) and the number of children possessing each such alleged characteristic.

7. Notice of this order shall be given by defendants to the parent or guardian of each child resident in the District of Columbia who is now, or was during the 1971–72 school year or the 1970–71 school year, excluded, suspended or expelled from publicly-supported educational programs or otherwise denied a full and suitable publicly-supported education for any period in excess of two days. Such notice shall include a statement that each such child has the right to receive a free educational assessment and to be placed in a publicly-supported educational program suited to his needs. Provision of notification for non-reading parents or guardians will be made.

8. Defendants shall utilize public or private agencies to evaluate the educational needs of all identified "exceptional" children and, within twenty (20) days of the entry of this order, shall file with the Clerk of this Court their proposal for each individual placement in a suitable educational program, including the provision of compensatory educational services where required.

SOUDER v. BRENNAN

ROBINSON, J.

This is an action for declaratory and injunctive relief presently before the Court on Plaintiff's motion for Summary Judgment. Plaintiffs are three resident patient-workers at various state hospitals for the mentally ill or mentally retarded,[1] the American Association on Mental Deficiency, and the National Association for Mental Health. Plaintiffs seek a determination that the minimum wage and overtime compensation provisions of the Act, 29 U.S.C. §§206–207 apply to patient-workers of non-Federal hospitals, homes, and institutions of the mentally retarded and mentally-ill (hereafter collectively referred to as the mentally ill). Plaintiffs further seek to compel the defendant Secretary of Labor and his subordinates to undertake enforcement of the said minimum wage and overtime compensation provisions.

It is undisputed that the Department of Labor has a declared policy of non-enforcement of the minimum wage and overtime provisions with regard to patient-workers at non-Federal institutions for the mentally-ill. It is also clear to the Court that if the Fair Labor Standards Act does apply to such patient-workers then the policy of non-enforcement is a violation of the Secretary's duty to enforce the law. Accordingly, the issue for resolution here is the applicability of the Fair Labor Standards Act to such patient-workers. This is a legal issue properly disposed of here by summary judgment.

The 1966 Amendments to the Fair Labor Standards Act of 1938, extended coverage under the minimum wage and overtime provisions of the Act for the first time to, inter alia, employees of public and private non-Federal hospitals and institutions for the residential care of the mentally ill. It is clear that these amendments were intended to cover the regular professional and non-professional staff of such institutions. Neither the statutory language nor the legislative history of the 1966 amendments, however, makes any direct reference to the status of patient-workers in such institutions. This fact is a matter of concern to the Court for there are significant questions of policy and practicality underlying extension of the Act to patient-workers.[2] Nevertheless, extensive review has convinced the Court that the Act does so apply and that Plaintiffs are entitled to summary judgment.

A basic canon of statutory construction is that when statutory language is clear on its face and fairly susceptible of but one construction, that construction must be given to it. Even where there is legislative history in point, albeit ambiguous or contradictory, it is unnecessary to refer to it and improper to allow such history to override the plain meaning of the statutory language. Most certainly, then, the absence of any legislative history in point should not outweigh the words of the statute.

The words of the statute here in question say simply that "employ" means "to suffer or permit to work," that "employer" specifically includes "a hospital, institution, or school" for the residential care of the mentally ill. The terms of the Fair Labor Standards Act have traditionally been broadly construed and the Congress is not only aware of but has approved

---

[1] Plaintiff Nelson Eugene Souder was, at the date this lawsuit was filed, a resident-worker at Orient State Institute, Orient, Ohio. Mr. Souder was released from Orient State Institute on convalescent leave status on March 24, 1973. Mr. Souder is 47 years old and mentally retarded. He has resided at Orient State Institute since 1940.

Plaintiff Joseph Lagnone is a 32 year mentally-retarded resident-worker at Pennhurst State School and Hospital, Spring City, Pennsylvania, where he has resided since 1955.

Plaintiff Edwin Leedy died during the pendency of this action. He was a 62 year old mentally ill resident-worker at Haverford State Hospital, Haverford, Pennsylvania, where he worked from 1956 until his death in 1973.

[2] The questions of policy and practicality are intertwined, the most obvious being questions as to whether extension of coverage will in the long run be in the best interests of the patient-workers and the public. Significantly increased costs for the operation of institutions may result, but these, on the other hand, may be offset by increased or newly imposed charges on patients for their care. The possibilities and implications of such developments are at least areas in which the Court would have expected some legislative inquiry.

---

367 F. Supp. 808 (D.C. 1973).

of such broad construction. Economic reality is the test of employment and the reality is that many of the patient-workers perform work for which they are in no way handicapped and from which the institution derives full economic benefit. So long as the institution derives any consequential economic benefit the economic reality test would indicate an employment relationship rather than mere therapeutic exercise. To hold otherwise would be to make therapy the sole justification for thousands of positions as dishwashers, kitchen helpers, messengers and the like.[3]

Further support for this approach can be found in the fact that the Act contains specific exemption provisions, yet Congress did not see fit to specifically exclude patient-workers from coverage. The specific exemptions granted are numerous and detailed, indicating clearly that Congress is quite capable of specifically excluding from coverage some of those who might otherwise be covered by the general provisions. Congress did not exclude patient-workers from coverage and, therefore, the Court cannot do so.

Plaintiffs have moved for certification of the case as a class action pursuant to Rule 23, Federal Rules of Civil Procedure. The Court finds that the prerequisites of Rule 23(a) have been met and that Defendants have acted or refused to act on grounds generally applicable to the class, Rule 23(b)(2), and the motion to certify the class will therefore be granted. The class will be defined as follows: All patient-workers in non-Federal institutions for the residential care of the mentally ill and mentally retarded who meet the definition of employee, 29 U.S.C. § 203(d), (e), (g).

The Secretary will be ordered to implement reasonable enforcement efforts applying the minimum wage and overtime compensation provisions of the Fair Labor Standards Act to patient-workers at non-Federal institutions for the residential care of mentally ill.

ORDER

A. NOTIFICATION TO THE CLASS. That the Secretary of Labor, his officers, agents, servants, and all persons acting or claiming to act in his behalf and interest [hereinafter, the "Sec-

retary"], undertake the following notification activities:

1. Within 120 days from the date of this Order, notify the Superintendent of each non-Federal facility for the residential care of the mentally ill and/or mentally retarded, and the chief executive officer or officers of the supervising state agency for mental health and/or mental retardation, that they have the same statutory responsibility to compensate patient-workers as non-patient workers, and that defendants intend to enforce the minimum wage and overtime compensation provisions of the Fair Labor Standards Act on behalf of patient-workers.

2. Within 120 days from the date of this Order, inform the Superintendent of each non-Federal facility for the residential care of the mentally ill and/or mentally retarded; and the chief executive officer or officers of the supervising state agency for mental health and/or mental retardation of their obligation to maintain records of hours worked and other conditions of employment under 29 U.S.C. §211(c) and 29 C.F.R. Part 516 for patient-workers, just as is required for non-patient employees at the same facilities.

3. Within 120 days from the date of this Order, contact the Superintendent of each non-Federal facility for the residential care of the mentally ill and/or mentally retarded and request that he inform patient-workers at his facility of their rights under the Fair Labor Standards Act. Indications that proper attention has been given to informing the patient-workers of their rights will be:

a. That the Superintendent has notified *in writing* every resident and his guardian of his rights under the Fair Labor Standards Act, as declared in this decision;

b. That copies of such written notifications have been posted on every living unit of residential facilities for the mentally ill and/or mentally retarded;

c. That efforts have also been made to notify all residents *orally* of their rights— e.g., by holding group meetings for present residents and by establishing procedures under which each new resident will be notified of his rights within one week of his admission. In order to increase the chances that plaintiffs will fully comprehend such oral presentations, defendants may suggest to the Superintendents and to the chief executive officers of the supervising state agencies that representatives of concerned

---

[3] The fallacy of the argument that the work of patient-worker is therapeutic can be seen in extension to its logical extreme, for the work of most people, inside and out of institutions, is therapeutic in the sense that it provides a sense of accomplishment, something to occupy the time, and a means to earn one's way. Yet that can hardly mean that employers should pay workers less for what they produce for them.

organizations be invited to observe and perhaps to participate at such meetings;

d. That non-patient employees of all non-federal facilities for the residential care of the mentally ill and/or mentally retarded and their collective bargaining representatives or other representatives who deal with the employer on their behalf with respect to wages, hours, or other terms and conditions of employment, have been notified of this decision.

B. REASONABLE ENFORCEMENT ACTIVITIES. Within one year from the date of this order, defendants shall contact every institution to which the Order applies so as to establish and implement the necessary procedures [including any special certifications under 29 U.S.C. §214] whereby every patient-worker in such institutions will be paid the wages due him. After the Department of Labor has made its initial efforts to aid the institutions in establishing their procedures for paying wages, it shall continue in the second year to give attention to investigation and enforcement of employment situations affecting the patient-workers. Thereafter, "reasonable" enforcement shall be defined to include those activities which are necessary to ensure the benefits of 29 U.S.C. §§206 and 207, to which patient-workers are entitled.

C. IMPLEMENTATION REPORTS. That the Secretary shall keep written records of his enforcement activities, wihch shall be available to the public through the Labor Department's Advisory Committee on Sheltered Workshops at six-month intervals. These reports should include a description of the activities taken to comply with the Order; the number of investigations of alleged violations of rights of patient-workers under the Fair Labor Standards Act (including a breakdown by type of establishment and number of workers involved at each such establishment), and the reason for such investigations; the results of each such investigation; and the disposition of each investigation confirming statutory violations, including lawsuits, settlements, and other enforcement activities.

SUGGESTIONS FOR ADDITIONAL READING

Abeson, A. "Right to Education," *MH* 57, no. 2 (Spring 1973): 34.

Allen, R. *Legal Rights of the Disabled and Disadvantaged.* U.S. Gov't. Printing Office, 1969 (HE 17.20:L 52).

Allen, R. A., Ferster, E. Z., and Weihofen, H. *Mental Impairment and Legal Incompetency.* Prentice-Hall, 1968.

Asch, S. *Mental Disability in Civil Practice.* Rochester, N.Y.: Lawyers Co-operative Pub. Co., 1973.

Brakel, S., and Rock, R. *The Mentally Disabled and the Law* (revised ed.). Univ. of Chicago Press, 1968.

Breggin, Peter. "The Second Wave: Psychiatric Surgery Experiences Worldwide Resurgence," *MH* 57, no. 1 (Winter 1973): 10.

Breggin, Phyllis. "Underlying a Method: Is Psychosurgery an Acceptable Treatment for Hyperactivity in Children?" *MH* 58, no. 1 (Winter 1974): 19.

Mental Health Law Project. Basic Rights of the Mentally Handicapped: Right to Treatment, Right to Compensation for Institution-Maintaining Labor, Right to Education. National Association for Mental Health, 1973.

Practising Law Institute, The Mental Health Law Project. *Legal Rights of the Mentally Handicapped* (3 vols.), 1974.

Robitscher, J. "Courts, State Hospitals, and the Right to Treatment," *Amer. J. Psychiat.* 129, 3 (September 1972): 74.

Weihofen, H. *Legal Services and Community Mental Health Centers.* Joint Information Service of American Psychiatric Association and National Association of Mental Health (1969).

11

Guardianship and Incompetency

This chapter deals with a variety of situations in which a person's ability to manage himself and his affairs is in question. Usually, all of these problems are described under the single word "incompetency." The first two selections are the products of extensive empirical studies, one on the laws affecting the retarded and one on determination of civil incompetency. Both studies were supported by the National Institute of Mental Health. The two selections enumerate some of the legal problems of the incompetent and those who deal with them, and also suggest some solutions. The last two selections are cases in which a court must decide whether the alleged incompetent is capable of handling her property. The difference between the two cases is that in the first case the issue is whether Mrs. Stevenson should lose the right to manage her property, while in the second case, the issue is whether Mrs. McConnell should have this right restored.

LEGAL NORMS AND PRACTICES AFFECTING THE MENTALLY DEFICIENT

Richard C. Allen, LL.M.

Since a primary reason for the existence of legal rules and procedures is to facilitate and enhance the rendition of protective services, consistent with safeguarding fundamental human rights, several of the findings of the civil phase of our study will be presented in the context of the question: Whom do protective services fail to protect? Lest our findings seem wholly negative, the reader is asked to bear in mind that these comments, as was true of our research, are intended to identify laws and practices that should be changed. There is, however, a positive side. We also found in our researches dedicated, effective and creative people, exciting and imaginative programs, and laws and practices intelligently conceived and soundly and appropriately administered.

First, protective services do not protect when legal proceedings become routinized and pro forma and when decision-makers lose sight of both the nature of the services available and the needs of the people to be served. It has long been known that institutionalization and legal incompetency are quite different, though related, concepts; thus, a determination that a mentally retarded person is in need of institutional care should not automatically deprive him of all civil rights. Yet, in two of the states in which we conducted studies, although the law expressly declares that institutional commitment does not of itself constitute a finding of legal incompetency, other statutes and hospital regulations prohibit *all* residents of institutions for the mentally retarded from holding a driver's license, making a will, marrying, executing a contract (even one involving a small purchase or a magazine subscription), and from having any right of management of property. And seldom did we find, in either commitment or in guardianship proceedings, a

Excerpted and reprinted with permission from *American Journal of Orthopsychiatry* 38, 4 (1968): 635.

meaningful inquiry into the needs and capabilities of the alleged retardate. Petitions and medical certifications often simply parrot statutory language, and judges and attorneys regard their role as essentially clerical.

Second, protective services do not protect when there is a lack of adequate staff and physical facilities. In every state there is a need for many more community facilities to serve as alternatives to residential care: day care centers, sheltered workshops, recreational programs, family casework, job placement, private boarding facilities, developmental centers and the like. All residential care institutions suffer from severe shortages of funds and trained personnel. At one institution, for example, there is no resident psychologist, and hence inmates are never retested. At another, with a patient population of over 3,500, only four patients have been placed in day work in the community. At still another, with a high proportion of educable patients, there is no educational program at all. And in several states, little or nothing has been done to develop vocational training, and work assignments are based more on institutional needs than on habilitation of patients. We did not find any court with sufficient staff to adequately oversee the discharge of fiduciary responsibility by guardians or institutional personnel.

Third, protective services do not protect when important decision-makers are ignorant of them or of their appropriate use. In the course of our study, we have interviewed many parents of institutionalized and noninstitutionalized retarded children. For the most part they seem not to be aware of alternatives available in planning for their children's future, alternatives such as the *inter-vivos* trust. Few parents of institutionalized children have given any thought to making provision for them on their reaching the age of majority. Guardianship is not seen as an appropriate recourse because of the expense and associated stigma, and often institutionalization has been resorted to as the only available means of ensuring that the child will receive adequate protection when the parents are gone.

The Task Force on Law of the President's Panel on Mental Retardation recommended that there be an "outside" guardian for every retarded person involuntarily admitted to an institution, who could check on his treatment, care, and release possibilities. Yet, we found that guardianships are rarely obtained in any of the states included in our survey; and when they are, the proceedings are most frequently initiated by the state as a means of enforcing cost of care or to meet the eligibility requirements for receipt of aid to the totally and permanently disabled.

Further, we were surprised to find in several of the states studied, that there are hundreds of inmates of state hospitals for the mentally ill with a primary diagnosis of mental retardation. Some were sent there as a matter of administrative convenience; others, out of sheer ignorance. Virtually no education or other special programs are provided for them.

Fourth, protective services do not protect when they impose coercive sanctions unnecessarily, or for longer periods than necessary, or when more appropriate noncoercive measures are available. The first "general principle" declared by the Task Force on Law is to ". . . minimize intervention by the law insofar as possible." Yet in some states certain protective services (e.g., special education or vocational training) cannot be obtained without a formal commitment procedure.

Another illustration of excessive protective intervention may be found in our eugenic sterilization practices. Today 26 of our states have eugenic sterilization laws, 23 of which are compulsory. The number of reported sterilizations per year has decreased steadily, fromr over 1,600 some 25 years ago to less than 500 today, a decrease in large part due to the widespread rejection of the view that mental illness and mental retardation are hereditary.

Our empirical studies have shown, however, that the problems associated with eugenic sterilization are not confined to states with compulsory laws. In states with a "voluntary" statute, "consent" is often more theoretical than real (for example, it may be made a condition of discharge from an institution that the patient "consent" to sterilization), and in one state our field investigators observed a "voluntary" sterilization proceeding for a six-year-old boy. We found further that sterilization operations are conducted outside the institutions in states with no sterilization law. In one state, an institution official told our interviewers that he had performed 50 to 60 such sterilizations during the past two years. If true, his activities alone would give the state a sterilization rate higher than the reported rate of 20 states that have sterilization laws! Another institutional physician in the same state told our field investigators: "I, on occasion, have let my knife 'slip' in surgery and cut the tubes, but with most nurses present I would not do it, as they have large mouths."

The Task Force on Law and several state mental retardation planning committees have equivocated on the matter of involuntary sterilization. We have been unable to find persuasive scientific proof either of the inheritability of the defects for which sterilization is now being imposed or of the fact that a child—even if of normal intelligence—will be seriously handicapped by the fact of being reared by a retarded parent. With the increasing availability of improved supervision and protective services and of birth control devices far less drastic and irrevocable than surgical procedures, it is our finding that there is no sound basis for sanctioning the continuance of involuntary sterilization—under whatever euphemism it may be applied.[1]

Fifth, protective services do not protect when the legal provisions under which they may be rendered are phrased in terms which, because of their ambiguity or inappropriateness, make it difficult to identify the categories of persons eligible to receive them. Our researchers have disclosed that a bewildering array of terms is used in statutes, administrative regulations, and official communications, many of which have no precise or generally understood meaning. We found 14 terms in general use intended to indicate the existence of some degree of impairment in intellectual functioning (including, of course, the ubiquitous epithets: "feeble-minded," "backward," and "inferior"); 32 terms with some etiological connotation; 13 intended to indicate degree of impairment; and nine which refer to level of functioning for some specific purpose (e.g., "slow-learner," "custodial," "marginal dependent," "trainable"). In one state alone (and that a state with a recently enacted and fairly enlightened mental health code) more than half a hundred different terms apparently intended to denominate some or all retarded persons appear in various statutes.

Special problems arise in cross-disciplinary and transjurisdictional communication. For example, the term "mentally deficient" appears in the title of this paper, but in the text the phrase "mentally retarded" has been used. This latter phrase is the generic term for subnormal intellectual development in this country, and in at least one state "mental deficiency" connotes a greater degree of impairment, with special legal implications. But in many other countries "mental deficiency" is the preferred generic term, and "mental retardation" is used to identify persons who are functioning below their presumed capacity.

More significantly, we found that in most of the areas in which we conducted empirical research, descriptive terms tend to become affixed to people as permanent labels. Thus, a child who is denominated "trainable" may be denied exposure to "educational" programs, although he may well be capable of benefitting from them; or, determination of a regardate's need for a particular protective services becomes transmuted into a general declaration of incompetency for all purposes.

Sixth, protective services do not protect when custodial care, because of its ease of application, becomes the treatment of choice over other protective services more appropriate to the needs of the retardate. I have mentioned that institutionalization is often used as a substitute for guardianship, in large part because of inadequacies in our guardianship laws. It is sometimes also used as a kind of disposal system for children with behavioral problems.

Our opinion samples have shown that a substantial majority of psychiatrists, obstetricians, pediatricians, neurologists, and general medical practitioners in the United States believe that during the first few years of life care in the home is greatly to be preferred to institutional care, unless gross physical anomalies or an impossible family situation make institutionalization necessary, both because of the cruciality of these early years in the development of the child and because of the difficulty of arriving at a definitive diagnosis of mental retardation in infancy. Yet we found a number of institutions which routinely accept children under six years of age, and we found medical staff members in key decision-making positions who recommend that all retarded children be institutionalized as soon after birth as possible.

Seventh, protective services do not protect when they are rendered by a multiplicity of agencies with ambiguously defined and often overlapping jurisdiction. In our researches, many instances were found in which effective help was denied, not because of failure to recognize need, or even lack of facilities or appropriate laws and regulations, but because of uncertainty as to which bureaucratic domain had decision-making authority.

Eighth, and finally (for the present writing), protective services do not protect when they do not respect the dignity and worth of the individual. Within the residential care institution, as the Task Force on Law pointed out: "There are, of course, degrees of further confinement and restraint of liberty possible. . . ." It went on to note that "every means should be sought to minimize the need for physical restraint and to scrutinize its use." Most institutions, we found, employ "seclusion" and other restraints as means of protecting patients

---

[1] Fester, E. 1966. Eliminating the unfit—is sterilization the answer? *Ohio State Law J.* 27: 591–633.

or controlling their behavior. And in most institutions such restraints are applied humanely and in the interest of the patient. In some, however, discretion to employ them is given to untrained ward attendants, and that discretion is often exercised less for the patient's well-being than for the comfort of the staff. In one institution, seclusion was regularly applied for much longer periods than permitted by hospital regulations and under conditions which would not be permitted in the most repressive penal institution. In another, ward attendants had obtained prescriptions for tranquilizing drugs at one time or another for many of the patients in their wards; once obtained, these prescriptions were refilled and administered by attendants with no medical control whatever.

Many other illustrations might be cited, but perhaps the greatest abridgment is society's failure to provide adequate laws, facilities, and trained personnel to safeguard that elemental right enunciated by the World Health Organization more than a dozen years ago:[2]

The Task Force on Law report begins with a quotation from a law book published in 1712, which includes the phrase:

> . . . for it is most certain, that our Law hath a very great and tender consideration for Persons naturally Disabled. . . . They are under the Special Aid and Protection of his Equity, who is no less than Keeper of the King's Conscience.

It is as true today as it was 250 years ago, that that cornerstone of our legal system, *equal justice under law*, will remain a half truth unless it embraces as well that concept of equity, *equal justice for the inherently unequal*.

[2] The Mentally Subnormal Child. 1954. World Health Organization, Geneva, Switzerland.

HOSPITALIZATION AND INCOMPETENCY

Elyce Zenoff Ferster

INTRODUCTION

The term "incompetent" is usually[1] used to refer to a person who has been adjudged incapable of managing his own property or handling his own affairs. The adjudication may be the result of a judicial action brought for the specific purpose of determining competency or it may be the by-product of an action brought to determine whether a person requires care in a mental hospital or in a school for the mentally retarded. Incompetency proceedings as such are described elsewhere[2]; in this chapter we will consider incompetency as a concomitant of hospitalization.

[1] See Part II, Chap. 1, "The Semantics of Incompetency" [in Allen, Ferster, Weihofen, *Mental Impairment and Legal Incompetency* (Englewood Cliffs, N.J.: Prentice-Hall, Inc., 1968)].

[2] *Ibid.*, Part III, Chap. 1; ad hoc determinations of incompetency are discussed in Appendix A.

STATUTORY, CASE LAW, AND LITERATURE REVIEW

It was unnecessary for the Mental Competency Study to undertake an extensive review of the statutes and case law in the fifty states, or of the literature dealing with the relationship between hospitalization and incompetency since one of the authors had recently completed this task.[3] The following are some of the most significant findings derived from this prior study:

1. The effect of a hospitalization order on the competency status of a patient varies from state to state. In a few states the hospitalization order is also an adjudication of incompetency;

[3] See Lindman and McIntyre, eds., *The Mentally Disabled and the Law* (1961), Chap. 8. A complete resurvey was made, however, for the states in which empirical research was to be conducted.

Reprinted, with permission, from Allen, Ferster, and Weihofen, *Mental Impairment and Legal Incompetency* (Englewood Cliffs, N.J.: Prentice-Hall, 1968).

in others it results in at least presumptive incompetency; and in still others there is a complete separation of hospitalization and incompetency.

2. In many states the effect of a hospitalization order on competency cannot be determined from the written law.

3. It is also unclear in many states how voluntary or temporary observation hospitalization may affect competency.

4. Some states which purport to have separated hospitalization and incompetency permit the rights of patients who have not been adjudicated incompetent to be markedly restricted by administrative regulations.

5. In some states in which a hospitalization order renders one legally incompetent, discharge from the hospital does not effect a restoration to competency. Thus the status of incompetency persists even after termination of the factual circumstances which produced it.

These findings were taken into account during the planning of this portion of the empirical study. For example, it was sought to select a group of states for empirical study which would present a diversity of approaches to the matter of the relationship between hospitalization and competency. Research was then undertaken in a number of institutions for the mentally ill and the mentally retarded[4] as well as in the courts to seek to determine what restrictions on property management, voting, drivers licensure, marriage, etc. are imposed, and to identify the problems, if any, caused by existing laws and practices.

HOSPITALIZATION AND INCOMPETENCY MERGED

An order of hospitalization for an indeterminate period[5] is also an adjudication of incompetency in Colorado,[6] the District of Columbia[7] and Ohio.[8] However, appointment of a guardian[9] is not automatic.[10] In fact, less than twenty-five per cent of the patients in any of these jurisdictions have guardians.[11] It is probable that there are many patients with substantial assets who do not have a guardian.[12] Neither the court, the hospital nor any other state agency or official conducts a thorough investigation of the extent and nature of the patient's property; appointment of a guardian is sought only when some relative or friend becomes concerned about the patient's estate.

When a guardian is appointed, such appointment is not necessarily contemporaneous with the adjudication of incompetency. A considerable period of time, even a number of years,

---

[4] The practices hereafter described apply to both the mentally ill and the mentally retarded unless otherwise indicated.

[5] Voluntary and temporary hospitalization are not merged with incompetency in these jurisdictions.

[6] Colo. Rev. Stat. §§ 71-1-11(1) & (2), 71-1-26 (1963).

[7] The District of Columbia law was amended recently to separate hospitalization and incompetency for the mentally ill. Ferster, in "The Law in Transition: Civil Incompetency in the District of Columbia" (16 American L. Rev. 236 [1967]), describes incompetency procedures in the District under both the old and the new law. Involuntary hospitalization and incompetency are still merged for the mentally retarded, however.

The statutes provide that no resident of the District Training School may execute any contract, deed, will or other instrument without an order of approval form a judge of the U.S. District Court. D.C. Code §§ 32-628 (Supp. V., 1966). The Superintendent knows of no such orders ever having been granted, and no student at the school has had a guardian appointed for him.

[8] Indeterminate judicial hospitalization "is an adjudication of legal incompetency" (Ohio Rev. Code Ann. § 5122.36 [Page Supp. 1965]).

[9] The term "conservator" is used in Colorado, "committee" in Colorado and "guardian" in Ohio. The term "guardian" will be used throughout this chapter to refer to the person who is appointed by a court to care for the estate and/or person of a patient.

[10] The District of Columbia and Ohio statutes permit appointment of a guardian but do not require it. (Act of March 3, 1901, ch. 854, § 115[b], as added 32 Stat. 524 [1902], as amended; Ohio Rev. Code Ann. § 5122.36 [Page Supp. 1965].) In Colorado the statutes are conflicting. One section makes the appointment mandatory, (Colo. Rev. Stat. § 153-9-2[1] [1963]) and another says that the guardian ad litem is to make a recommendation as to appointment of a guardian (Colo. Rev. Stat. § 71-1-8[3] [1963]). But in practice a guardian is appointed only when deemed "necessary" by the court, with criteria for such appointment varying with the individual judge.

[11] In 1962, 20.8 per cent of the patients at St. Elizabeths Hospital had guardians (letter from Dale Cameron, Superintendent of St. Elizabeths Hospital, to the Mental Competency Study, June 27, 1963). The Superintendent of Longview State Hospital in Ohio estimated that 15 to 20 per cent period had guardians. The Colorado court records of the patients hospitalized for an indeterminate were examined in each of three counties: guardians were appointed for long term patients in 23.3 per cent of the Boulder cases, 22.1 per cent of the Denver cases and 20.9 per cent of the Pueblo cases.

[12] The county judge for the Denver area estimates that 35 to 40 per cent of the adjudicated patients have sufficient assets to warrant appointment of a conservator and the county attorney would put the figure at 50 per cent.

may have elapsed between adjudication and appointment.[13] Since incompetency has been "determined" at the time of hospitalization, it is not considered to be an unresolved issue when an application for the appointment of a guardian is made. In effect, appointment is automatic when an application is made.[14]

The duties of the guardian appointed in this fashion are the same as those of a guardian appointed for a person who is not committed to a mental hospital. His primary function is to manage the patient's estate, even if he is also nominally a guardian of the person.[15] In none of these jurisdictions are the duties of a guardian of the person specifically enumerated nor is there any supervision of his activities in that capacity.

Although hospitalization and incompetency are merged in these jurisdictions, release from lhe hospital is not necessarily an automatic restoration to competency. Whether release and restoration are merged may depend on the type of release. Conditional release[16] does not act as an automatic restoration to competency in any of these jurisdictions.[17] This means that a majority of the patients remain legally incompetent for some time after release,[18] since hospitals prefer to give conditional rather than absolute discharges.[19] An unconditional release "as cured" acts as an automatic restoration to competency in the District of Columbia[20] and Ohio[21] and in some counties in Colorado.[22]

---

[13] For example, the files of 38 of the 230 appointments of guardians made in the District of Columbia during 1962 were examined. Of this number, 18 of the patients had been adjudicated in 1962, 7 in 1961, 9 between 1950 and 1960, 3 in the 1940's, and 1 in 1925.

[14] Though in practice it may not be quite so "automatic." For example, in Ohio, a special guardian of the estate may be appointed for indeterminately hospitalized persons without notice. Ohio Rev. Code Ann. § 5123.42 (Page Supp. 1965). However, the county judges in Hamilton and Greene County do not use this procedure; instead they use the regular incompetency procedure which requires notice and a hearing. Ohio Rev. Code Ann. § 2111.04 (Page Supp. 1965). The District of Columbia also gives notice to all patients before appointing a guardian, though this is not required by statute, and appoints a guardian ad litem if there are no relatives residing in the jurisdiction.

[15] In Colorado, the guardian is only for the estate. Colo. Rev. Stat. § 153–9–2(1) (1963). Since there is no judicially appointed guardian of the person, an informal practice has evolved: if the patient is in a state hospital, the hospital is designated 'custodian'; if he is in a private hospital, a relative or close friend is asked to be "custodian." The county attorney asks the custodian periodically to visit the patient to see that he is "well cared for." If the patient is deteriorating, the "custodian" is to see that he has additional treatment, and when necessary to contact the guardian for additional funds. In Ohio and, previous to 1964, in the District of Columbia, the court may appoint a guardian of the person, of the estate or both. Ohio Rev. Code Ann. § (Page Supp. 1965); D.C.: 2111.06 Act of March 3, 1901, ch. 854, § 115(b), as added 32 Stat. 524 (1902), as amended. In practice the appointment is usually for both the person and the estate and the same person serves in both capacities. In Ohio, even if a guardian has not been requested, the head of the hospital is ex officio guardian of the person for the purpose of retaining the patient in the institution. Ohio Rev. Code Ann. § 5123.03 (Page Supp. 1965).

[16] Conditional release (which may also be called conditional discharge, convalescent leave, parole, etc.) means that the patient is released temporarily but may be returned to the hospital without further judicial proceedings.

[17] E.g., a conditional discharge does not constitute an adjudication of competency. Colo. Rev. Stat. 71–1–28(3) (1963). In fact, conditional release does not act as an automatic restoration of competency in any jurisdiction. Lindman and McIntyre, *The Mentally Disabled and the Law*, 227.

[18] For example, under the D.C. law which was in effect at the time of the study, a patient could not apply for court restoration until he had been on conditional release for six months. Act of Aug. 9, 1939, ch. 620, § 10, 53 Stat. 1298, as amended.

[19] For example, during fiscal year 1962, 1439 patients were placed on conditional release by St. Elizabeths Hospital, and in Colorado the great majority of patients are released conditionally.

[20] Automatic restoration resulted from discharges "as recovered" or "socially recovered" (i.e., although a nucleus of illness remains, the patient has sufficiently recovered to manage his own life and is not dangerous). Restoration was not automatic if the discharge was "as improved" or "unimproved."

[21] Persons who receive a final discharge are automatically restored to competency. Ohio Rev. Code Ann. § 5122.36 (Page Supp. 1965). If a special guardian for the estate has been appointed as part of the hospitalization proceeding he will be dismissed automatically on motion. However, in the counties studied, guardians were appointed only under the regular incompetency procedure; thus the discharged patient would presumably have to go through the regular restoration procedure for non-hospitalized persons.

[22] The Colorado procedure is rather confusing. The statute says:

If, in the opinion of the superintendent or chief medical officer of a hospital, any respondent adjudicated and committed thereto is no longer mentally ill or mentally deficient, the superintendent or chief officer shall file in the court by which the respondent was adjudicated a verified

The hospitals do not routinely inform the patient about his legal status on discharge. Therefore when restoration is not automatic many of the patients do not know that they are still legally incompetent.[23]

SEPARATION OF HOSPITALIZATION AND INCOMPETENCY

The trend in legislation during the last fifteen years has been toward a complete separation of hospitalization and incompetency.[24]

statement setting forth that the respondent is no longer mentally ill or mentally deficient and should be discharged. The court may, on its own motion in such case, enter an order of competency. [Colo. Rev. Stat. § 71–1–27 (1963).]

Some judges believe that the statute is mandatory and that they must enter a restoration when such a statement is filed. Other judges believe, and this appears to be the correct interpretation of the statute, that they may exercise discretion as to whether to enter a restoration order.

Exact figures were not available as to the number of patients for whom a statement is filed in court; it is estimated that slightly more than half of those discharged are so certified by the hospital.

[23] Ferster, "Civil Incompetency in the District of Columbia," 32 *Geo. Wash. U. L. Rev.* 243 (1963).
The patients in one state hospital in Colorado are now well informed about restoration procedures. In 1962 the hospital hired an attorney, one of whose duties was to advise patients about to be discharged as to their legal status.

[24] The idea that hospitalization and incompetency should be determined separately is not a new one as the following comment of Isaac Ray on a proposal to merge hospitalization and competency indicates.

It would be a sufficient objection to this course, that there is no necessary relation between the two things,—placing a person in a hospital for the purpose of procuring his recovery, and subjecting him to interdiction. This is clearly shown by the customs of our people; for of the thousands of persons in our hospitals and asylums, not one in twenty is under guardianship. Had there been anything essentially wrong in this, it would hardly have been left to this day and generation to discover it. No one, with any practical knowledge of the matter,—of the feelings and motives that govern men when brought face to face with the question of confining an insane friend,—can fail to see that this course is quite incompatible with the first two requisites above mentioned. What is implied by interdiction? It implies the taking of property out of the hands of its rightful owner, and giving the control of it to another. It implies the settlement of his affairs, the termination of his business relations, the dissolution of partnership, the resignation of every office of honor or trust,—all in a manner more or less prejudicial to his interests, and solely to meet an exigency that may be of very brief duration. Surely, an attack of

This trend appears to be a reflection of the belief held by an increasing number in both the medical and legal professions that there is no necessary relationship between a person's need to be cared for in a mental hospital and his capacity to handle his own affairs.[25]

insanity is afflictive enough, without any supererogatory misery like this. . . .
There is another and a very important reason why this measure should be avoided if possible. When the patient comes to himself, and learns that his business, successfully established by many years of industry and enterprise, has been wound up, at considerable sacrifice, as he must know, and that he is unable to dispose of a single dollar of his hard earnings, the intelligence will scarcely help to promote his recovery. . . . [Confinement of the Insane, 3 *Am. L. Rev.* 193, 208–9 (Jan. 1869).]

[25] The Group for the Advancement of Psychiatry describes "combining the need for hospitalization with a finding of legal incompetence" as one of the major defects in laws governing hospitalization of the mentally ill. It recommends that these two issues should be separated and that psychiatric patients in public and private hospitals should retain "all civil and political rights guaranteed by law unless specifically revoked by individual incompetency proceedings." Group for the Advancement of Psychiatry, Report No. 61, *Laws Governing Hospitalization of the Mentally Ill* 156–57 (1966). The American Bar Foundation's Study on "The Rights of the Mentally Ill" concluded that "a hospitalized patient may be quite capable of handling certain of his own affairs. . . . Mental disabilities are of such a variety and degree that any automatic connection between incompetency and hospitalization is without justification. Their merger may result in an unnecessary deprivation of personal and property rights." It recommended that: *"The determination of an individual's capacity to handle his own affairs should be disassociated from the question of his need for hospital treatment."* Lindman and McIntyre, *The Mentally Disabled and the Law*, 228.

The Committee on Legislation and Psychiatric Disorder of the Canadian Mental Health Association also recommended that "competency legislation should be other than and quite separate from legislation dealing with hospitalization of the mentally disordered. This principle should hold whether or not the individual is a patient in a psychiatric facility and whether or not he is certified or committed." Canadian Mental Health Association, *The Law and Mental Disorder* 30 (1964). Their recommendation was based on an empirical investigation of the competency of hospitalized persons.

A total of approximately 1000 admissions to three Canadian Mental Hospitals including informal, legal and certificated admissions was examined by the treating physicians specifically regarding competency. About 35 per cent of the certificated or legally admitted patients and about 25 per cent of the informal admissions were considered at the time of admission incapable of handling their business affairs. The reasons for

A total of 182 attorneys, psychiatrists and psychologists were asked their opinion on this issue by the Mental Competency Study. Eighty-eight per cent of the interviewees answered "no" to the question "Should a person committed to a mental hospital be conclusively presumed incompetent as a matter of law?" Approximately half of the interviewees were from states which merge hospitalization and incompetency; and of the interviewees from these states alone, again some eighty-eight per cent disapproved automatic incompetency for involuntarily hospitalized patients. More than half of all the interviewees would give no weight at all to the fact of hospitalization in an independent competency proceeding, and less than one-fifth would assert that involuntary hospitalization should give rise to a presumption of incompetency in such a proceeding.

In five of the eight states studied (California, Massachusetts, New York, North Carolina and Texas) the issue of incompetency is determined separately from indeterminate hospitalization, at least in theory. Texas is the only one of them—in fact, it is the only state in the country—which determines both issues separately, though in the same proceeding. The Texas procedure will not be discussed in some detail.

The Texas law was widely acclaimed at the time of its adoption. The fact that both issues would be considered in the same proceeding, it was felt, would eliminate the problem of no action being taken to protect the patient's assets if he did not have interested friends or relatives in the jurisdiction. Two other important features of the law were automatic appointment of an attorney ad litem and the requirement that two physicians must appear *and testify* at the hearing.

As a prerequisite for filing a petition for indefinite hospitalization and a determination of competency, the allegedly ill person must have been a patient during the year preceding the filing of the petition, for at least sixty days, under a court order for temporary hospitalization.[26] The petition must include the certificate of a physician who has examined the allegedly ill person within 15 days of making the certificate.[27]

When the county judge receives the petition and medical certificate he is required to appoint an attorney ad litem to represent the person,[28] who is to receive reasonable compensation. The attorneys ad litem are selected by the judge from among the younger members of the bar. Involuntary hospitalization cases are heard one day a month and the same attorney is appointed for all of the cases to be heard on a particular day. The number of cases in a month averages about thirty and the attorney ad litem receives ten dollars per case.

The allegedly ill person is personally served with notice at least seven days before the hearing.[29] The notice contains information about the time of the hearing, its purposes, the right to a jury trial,[30] [the right] to be present at the hearing and to consult with the attorney ad litem.

The hearings are conducted in a room at the hospital. Approximately ten per cent of the patients whose cases are being heard are present. The attorney ad litem is there, and two physicians who have examined the person within fifteen days prior to the hearing must appear and testify.[31]

At the conclusion of the testimony, the judge or jury, as the case may be, determines:

(1) whether the proposed person is mentally ill, *and if so,*

(2) whether he requires hospitalization in a mental hospital for his own welfare and protection or the protection of others, *and if so*

(3) whether he is mentally incompetent.[32] [Emphasis added.]

The following is a brief description of one of the hearings observed by a member of the Mental Competency Study staff:

The hearings I attended were conducted in . . . a lecture room at the . . . Hospital. Seated on a small stage at a long table were . . . the attorney ad litem, ———— and ————

inability were not only mental disability but the effects of physical separation or the urgency of business matters that required attention. One psychiatric hospital which treats only certified acutely ill patients and where the superintendent has discretionary powers to advise on competency has recommended no patient incompetent in the last 1500 admissions. [*Ibid.*]

26 Tex. Civ. Stat. Ann. Art. 5547–40 (Vernon, 1958). This determination cannot be made at the hearing for temporary hospitalization, so temporary patients are considered competent. Voluntary patients are also considered competent. Tex. Civ. Stat. Ann. Art. 5547–24 (Vernon, 1958).

27 Tex. Civ. Stat. Ann. Art. 5547–42 (Vernon, 1958).

28 Tex. Civ. Stat. Ann. Art. 5547–43 (Vernon, 1958).

29 Tex. Civ. Stat. Ann. Art. 5547–44 (Vernon, 1958).

30 Jury trials are rare. There were none in 1963. In 1964, there was a jury trial which resulted in the person's release from the hospital. After this case several other patients had jury trials. Four or five of them were released by the jury and in several other cases the hospital withdrew the petition.

31 Tex. Civ. Stat. Ann. Art. 5547–49(d) (Vernon Supp., 1965).

32 Tex. Civ. Stat. Ann. Art. 5547–51(a) (Vernon, 1958).

[the judge and the chief clerk of the court]. While awaiting the various doctors, I asked —————— [the attorney ad litem] if he had contacted any of the proposed patients. He had not. This was the first time he had served as an attorney ad litem. . . . The hearings began at 2:00 PM and ended at 3:05 PM— an hour and five minutes for forty (40) persons; about a minute and a half per patient! All the doctors were sworn . . . prior to testifying. As each case was called, the doctor would give the height, weight, and color of hair and eyes of the patient. These data are for the form sent to the Department of Public Safety concerning driver's licenses. Next, the Judge would read the patient's name and state the dates of the medical examination. Without pausing or looking up he would then read to the doctors, apparently from the Order of Commitment, "Is it your opinion and both of you agree that (he) is a mentally ill person and needs medical care and treatment for his own welfare and protection or the protection of others and is mentally incompetent?" The doctor answered yes and the next case would be called in like fashion. . . . All of the proposed patients were ordered indefinitely committed and all were found to be incompetent.[33]

The invariability of a "finding" of incompetency made at such a hearing is not unusual.[34] A random sample of ten per cent of the petitions filed in the same court during the preceding year was examined, and again all of the persons who were committed were also "found" to be incompetent.[35]

There are, of course, two possible explanations for the fact that all of the persons found to be in need of indeterminate hospitalization were also adjudged incompetent. One is that all of them were in fact incompetent. This appears to be the view of the hospital, but is not substantiated by the available data.[36] The other possibility is that the persons involved in the determination do not understand the con-

cept of competency, the purpose of the separation of hospitalization and incompetency, or their own role in the proceeding. There is ample evidence to support this theory.

County judges in Texas are usually not attorneys, and therefore may not understand the legal issues involved in these proceedings. Two policies followed by the judge seem to indicate a lack of understanding of the law. The first is [his] reading [of] the statutory questions about hospitalization and incompetency as if they were merged when the statute clearly separates them. The other is his instructions to the attorneys. He tells them that their duties are to appear at the hearing, see that the notices are complied with, and sign the jury waiver form. This is not the usual meaning of a statutory direction that an attorney is to be appointed "to represent" the proposed patient.

The attorneys ad litem do not appear to understand the proceedings. For the most part they are young and inexperienced. They do not see the allegedly ill person before the hearing; in fact, they often do not see the patient at all, since only a few patients attend the hearing. They do not examine the hospital records nor interview the hospital personnel. In short, they have no information about the patient's competency nor do they even appear to recognize that it is a separate issue to be determined at the hearing.

The hospital personnel also appear to be unaware of the issues involved in determining competency. The examining physician does not know the extent of the patient's property, and is unaware of what criteria to apply in arriving at an opinion of competency. In fact it is doubtful that a separate determination of competency is made by the physician.

The procedures and objectives of such legislation must be understood by the principal participants in order for it to function effectively. Widespread ignorance of or inattention to the distinction between a person's need for care in a mental hospital and his capacity to handle his own affairs has substantially nullified what was intended as a rational and progressive legislative enactment.

Before 1958, when hospitalization and incompetency were merged under Texas law, discharge did not automatically restore the patient to competency. A restoration proceeding conducted by the county judge who had committed the patient was required.[37] In the-

[33] Observation of Indefinite Commitment Proceedings, Dec. 18, 1963.

[34] Subsequent interviews with attorneys ad litem also confirmed the typicality of the hearing as to number of cases heard, length of time of hearing, etc.

[35] A total of 410 persons were hospitalized for an indeterminate period in the county studied in 1963. The figure is higher than it would be for most counties of a similar population because a state hospital is located there and almost all of the proceedings involved persons who were in the hospital on temporary orders. Ninety-five per cent of the cases involved persons who were residents of another county.

[36] For example, hospital personnel said that a high percentage of the proceedings involved older persons who were having problems in handling their property. However, our survey of cases decided during 1963 showed that about half involved persons under 65.

[37] Vernon's Texas Civ. Stat. Art. 5561b, repealed by Tex. Acts of 1957, Ch. 243, § 103, cited in Texas Research League, Report No. 13, *Legal Structure for the State Hospital System* 23–24, 23 n. 3 (1955). It appears that the superintendent was permitted, but not required, to issue a certificate.

ory, the patient did not have to initiate the proceedings. The judge was to convene the proceeding at the earliest possible time after receiving a certificate from the superintendent of the hospital that the patient was no longer of "unsound mind."[38] However, an overwhelming majority of judges did not institute restoration proceedings when they received such certificates.[39] When the Texas Mental Health Code was passed, there was no provision for judicial restoration. Presumably, there was no need for this type of provision. The legal status of patients not *specifically* found incompetent was to remain unaffected by their hospitalization.[40] Consequently, they had no need for any proceeding; and for those patients who had been found incompetent the statute provided that "The discharge of a patient who has been found to be mentally incompetent terminates the presumption that he is mentally incompetent."[41]

However, a year later a provision was added permitting discharged patients to file an application with the county court "that he is not now mentally ill or incompetent."[42] Understandably, there has been a good deal of confusion about the purpose and meaning of this section. According to the Handbook, *Interpretation of the Mental Health Code*:

This new procedure provides a judicial determination of the fact of the former patient's mental health and competence, it is *in addition to* the administrative finding made by the medical authorities in discharging the patient. Its legal effect is the *same* as that of the administrative determination.[43] [Emphasis added.]

It is difficult to understand how patients could be benefited by the enactment of legislation which "permits" initiation of a proceeding that costs a patient time and money, and burdens the court with additional work, if the legal effect of the determination sought has

already been obtained by virtue of other sections of the Code.

The Attorney General's interpretation of the new provision is different from that of the Handbook. He has ruled:

If the Legislature had intended that . . . discharge was also to act as a restoration of sanity or competency, the enactment of Article 5547–83(c), which provides for adjudicating that one who has been committed to a mental hospital and thereafter released is no longer mentally ill or incompetent, would be unnecessary.[44]

The Attorney General's Opinion quoted above was given in response to questions about patients who had been adjudicated incompetent. However, the statute must also apply to persons committed to a hospital as temporary patients or who, although committed for an indeterminate period of time, are not found incompetent.[45] Under the Attorney General's interpretation it appears that these patients must also be restored by a new judicial proceeding, despite the fact that the preceding subsection of the statute specifically states that one's commitment "does not abridge his rights as a citizen or affect his property rights or legal capacity."

The Handbook suggests the reason the provision was added: "To title examiners, purchasers of the real estate and the like, it [the new procedure] may represent persuasive documentary proof of the mental competency of the former patient at some subsequent time."[46]

Unfortunately, the effect of the amendment appears to be to reunite hospitalization and incompetency. Why should a patient who has not been adjudicated incompetent and whose property rights and legal capacity have not been affected by his hospitalization need a court order "that he is not now mentally ill or incompetent"? Since the amendment of the Mental Health Code it is probable that separation of hospitalization and incompetency was never understood or accepted by the business community or the bar.

It may be that the amendment was passed in an attempt to clarify the competency status of discharged persons who had been adjudicated incompetent at the time the court ordered them hospitalized for an indeterminate period. If so, the attempt has been unsuccessful. If the judicial procedure has the "same legal effect"

---

[38] *Ibid.*, 24.

[39] *Ibid.*, 25, 48.

[40] "The judicial determination that a person is mentally ill or the admission or commitment of a person to a mental hospital, without a finding that he is mentally incompetent, does not constitute a determination or adjudication of the mental competency of the person and does not abridge his rights as a citizen or affect his property rights or legal capacity." Tex. Civ. Stat. Ann. Art. 5547–83(b) (Vernon Supp. 1965).

[41] Tex. Civ. Stat. Ann. Art. 5547–81(b) (Vernon 1958).

[42] Tex. Civ. Stat. Ann. Art. 5547–83(c) (Vernon Supp. 1965).

[43] Ruud, *Interpretation of the Mental Health Code* 10 (Hogg Foundation for Mental Health; rev. ed., 1962).

[44] Tex. Atty. Gen. Op. No. C–4 (Jan. 23, 1963), affirming Op. No. WW–796 (Feb. 24, 1960).

[45] Tex. Civ. Stat. Ann. Art. 5547–83(c) (Vernon Supp. 1965).

[46] Ruud, 10.

as discharge (the interpretation favored by the Handbook), it is superfluous and should be repealed to end the confusion or amended so that its purpose is clear. If the new procedure is necessary to restore the person to competency (the position of the Attorney General), then the provision that "discharge . . . terminates the presumption that he is mentally incompetent"[47] should be repealed or amended and patients told at the time of discharge how to apply for restoration.[48]

The other four jurisdictions (California, Massachusetts, New York and North Carolina) have separate proceedings for determining the need for hospitalization and for determining the patient's capacity to handle his own affairs. However, in all of them the situation is similar to Texas; that is, separate determination of hospitalization and incompetency exists more in theory than in fact. In Massachusetts,[49] and New York,[50] even voluntary

[47] Tex. Civ. Stat. Ann. Art. 5547–83(b) (Vernon Supp. 1965).

[48] They are not given this information now, and, in fact, are told that they do not need formal restoration.

[49] "No patient (includes patients under Section 86 Voluntary) in an institution under the Department of Mental Health or in an institution licensed by the aforesaid Department shall be permitted to make a will, to execute any contract, deed, mortgage or other legal conveyance, or sign any bill, check, bond, draft, promissory note, or other evidence of indebtedness." Mass. Dept. Mental Health Reg. No. 9, item 2a (1955).

Officials of the Department of Mental Health insist that the regulation is not based on a presumption of incompetency, but is instead intended to relieve their personnel from the tasks of assessing competency. . . . The following are the exceptions to the regulation:

[1] Upon the written order of the Department and a Judge of a Court . . . showing that the Judge had knowledge that the person whose signature is sought was an inmate of an institution for care and treatment of the mentally ill, mentally defective or epileptic at the time the order was issued.

[2] A patient in a state institution may endorse checks if the money is to be deposited in the office of the Institution Treasurer to be available for the patient's use.

[3] Applications, checks and documents relating to Old Age Assistance may be signed by the patient if in the opinion of the superintendent he is competent to do so. [*Ibid.*, item 2b.]

If the Department receives a request for permission to execute an instrument, its practice is to require, instead, that a guardian or conservator be appointed for the patient. Not surprisingly, very few requests—perhaps two a year—are received from the hospitals. None of the officials of the Suffolk County Probate Court were aware of the regulation, and neither the Register nor the

patients are prohibited from managing their own affairs by administrative regulation. In North Carolina, the patient's exercise of his civil rights may be restricted by the superin-

Assistant Register could recall ever having received a petition for a court order. A brief check with the Superior Court confirmed the fact that no such petitions are filed.

[50] Service of Legal Processes upon Institutions and Patients, and the Execution of Instruments by Patients. (All Institutions) . . . Except as otherwise provided by this order, no mentally ill, mentally defective or epileptic patient shall be permitted to sign any bill, check, draft or other evidence of indebtedness: to make a will, or to execute any contract, deed, mortgage or other legal conveyance, except upon the order of the commissioner or of a judge of a New York State Court of record or of a federal court, showing that the judge had notice of the fact that the person whose signature is sought to be obtained was at the date of the order a patient in an institution for the care and treatment of the mentally ill, the mentally defective or the epileptic. A patient may endorse checks without reference to this order if the money is to be deposited in the institution's business office to be made available for the patient's use. In his discretion, and without departmental approval, the director or officer in charge may permit patients to draw or endorse checks when the sum involved does not exceed two hundred dollars. The director or one of his assistants designated by him shall be present whenever a patient affixes his signature to any check or legal document.

3.(a) In his discretion and without the order of the Commissioner or of a judge of a New York State court of record or of a federal court, the director or officer in charge may permit a patient, who does not have a committee or guardian, to execute or issue instruments affecting such patient's property, rights or obligations, provided, however, that the facts and circumstances surrounding such transaction, including the document to be executed by the patient shall be carefully scrutinized by the director or officer in charge who shall also interview or cause the patient to be interviewed by a staff physician for the purpose of determining:

[1] That the patient has sufficient mental capacity to understand the transaction and does understand the nature and consequences of his act in executing and issuing the instrument, and

[2] That the patient is willing to sign and execute the instrument.

(b) The director or officer in charge shall enter or cause to be entered in the patient's case record a descriptive note of the transaction and a certification by the interviewing physician that, in his opinion, the patient

[1] Understood the nature and consequences of his act in signing and executing the instrument.

[2] Was willing to sign and execute the instrument.

[N.Y. Dept. Mental Hygiene Gen. Order No. 10 (July 1, 1964).]

tendent of the hospital.[51] New York[52] and North Carolina[53] also have special statutes for appointing guardians for mental patients. Under these statutes proof of hospitalization is sufficient evidence to authorize appointment of a guardian. California does not have this type

of statute, but in practice guardians are appointed on this basis.[54]

Theoretically there is no need for a restoration statute for persons discharged from mental hospitals or institutions for the retarded in jurisdictions that do not merge hospitalization and incompetency. However, both California[55]

[51] Subject to reasonable rules and regulations of the hospital and except to the extent that the chief medical officer of the hospital determines that it is necessary for the medical welfare of the patient to impose restrictions, every patient shall be entitled . . . to exercise all civil rights, including the right to dispose of property, execute instruments, make purchases, enter into contractual relationships, and vote, unless he has been adjudicated incompetent under the provisions of G.S. chapter 35 and has not been restored to legal capacity. [N.C. Gen. Stats. § 122–46(a) (iii) (1964).]

[52] At the time of the empirical study New York had a special proceeding for adjudication of incompetency of persons judicially committed to state institutions. It was initiated by the director of the institution through the Attorney General. The allegation of the director of the institution that the patient was incompetent was sufficient for the appointment of a guardian. N.Y. Mental Hygiene Law § 102 (Supp. 1965). The procedure was simple and cost only $25.

In 1964 the law was amended to include any patient in a mental institution. Also the term "incompetent" was dropped and in its place the criterion "unable adequately to conduct his personal or business affairs" was used.

These changes were introduced through the Department of Mental Hygiene, which submitted the following statements in support of the bill:

Because these procedures are applicable only to court certified patients, there has been a tendency, when it has been imperative that a committee be appointed to manage a patient's estate, that the person be certified solely for the purpose of eligibility for the appointment of a committee under these provisions. The increasing volume of admissions under other than court certification procedures has increased the need for an expeditious and less costly method of appointment of a committee for such persons. It has also been widely recognized that much harm is done to patients both currently and in later years by reason of their adjudication as incompetents. It is recognized that persons may not be able to adequately manage their personal and business affairs solely by reason of their being patients and thus removed from the business world who, in fact, are not incompetent. . . .

There is certainly just and equitable basis for the sovereign state, through its duly constituted judiciary, to take jurisdiction of the property and affairs of one of its wards who is an inmate of a state institution in order to protect the ward and his business interests during such institutionalization without basing it upon the fiction of mental incompetence. . . .

Many agencies, individuals, bar associations, lawyers and jurists have expressed dissatisfaction with these provisions of law and seen the need for a method of conservatorship of the property of an inmate of an institution solely by reason of the fact that he is institutionalized and needs this assistance and also to avoid the stigmas and

other disabilities resulting from a declaration of incompetence. [N.Y. Dept. Mental Hygiene Legis. Memo., Appointment of Committee of Inmate of State Mental Institution (1964).]

Although it is apparent from the foregoing that the proponents of the bill believe that the amendments will somehow make adjudications under this procedure something less than or different from a declaration of incompetency, it is by no means certain that it does. The statutory standard "unable adequately to conduct his personal or business affairs" seems to be, in effect, a definition of legal incompetency. In 1965, the provision was amended again. One of the amendments concerns voluntary patients and will be discussed later. The other provides for discharge of the guardian when the patient is released and the director of the institution issues a certificate that he is able adequately to conduct his personal or business affairs.

[53] In North Carolina a guardian will be appointed for any person confined in a state institution or in a hospital licensed and supervised by the state on the sworn certificate of the superintendent that such patient is "insane." N.C. Gen. Stats. § 35–3 (Supp. 1965).

[54] Although there is no special incompetency procedure for hospitalized persons in California, the judges interviewed all believed that proof of commitment, in the absence of other proof, would be sufficient ground for appointment of a guardian.

[55] When a committed or voluntary patient is released from a state hospital, or a veterans hospital, and, in the judgment of the superintendent, he is "capable of taking care of himself and his property," or was not mentally ill when admitted, he may be issued a "certificate of competency" by the superintendent of the hospital. The certificate has the same effect as a judgment of restoration to competency. This procedure cannot be used by patients with guardians. Cal. Welf. & Inst. Code § 6729 (Deering Supp. 1965). The Certificate of Competency says, "I will certify the above-named person has been released from the hospital and is now competent, as provided in Section 6729 of the Welfare and Institutions Code."

In practice, certificates are not given to all released patients, but only to those absolutely discharged. Hospital policy is to issue the certificate "so long as the patient is not overtly unable to take care of himself and his property."

Committed persons without guardians who are discharged and have not been given a certificate of competency and those who are on parole or leave, may apply to the superintendent for a "certificate of sanity." Cal. Welf. & Inst. Code §

and North Carolina[56] have such statutes, and in New York ex-patients have been restored by court order, though there is no specific statute authorizing the procedure.[57] Massachusetts

does not have a restoration procedure for discharged patients but it does have a procedure under which "any person adjudicated by any court to be a mentally ill person, whether or not in custody, may petition for adjudication of his or her recovery and competence."[58]

Persons who have been patients in mental hospitals have often found that their competency is questioned. For example, in California, a hospital superintendent reported that large numbers of patients were coming back to the hospital to request certificates of competency because they were unable to persuade the State Department of Professional and Vocational Standards to recommend restoration of their licenses or because they have difficulty conveying property. Refusal to deal with former mental patients unless they have a court order or a certificate attesting that they are "competent" is largely based on two misconceptions. The first is that anyone who is sick enough to need care in a mental hospital, especially if he has been "committed," is incapable of exercising his civil rights and taking care of his property. The second is a misunderstanding of the reluctance of psychiatrists to describe a patient as "cured." Many people think the refusal is based on the psychiatrist's belief that the person is still sick, when in fact it may simply be that the term "cured" is deemed inappropriate to describe anyone's mental condition.

Another factor which undoubtedly fosters suspicion of a former patient's competence is that the laws separating hospitalization and incompetency are in many jurisdictions quite recent, and there is often a considerable time lag before people understand and accept any radical change in the law. Also, many of the statutes are ambiguous and may conflict with other statutes and administrative regulations. Last, but certainly not least as a significant cause of confusion, is the provision of restoration procedures for persons who are presumably not legally incompetent. Such provisions can only perpetuate the misidentification of hospitalization with incompetency, and the confusion that still abounds in this area of the law.

HOSPITAL PRACTICES

In each jurisdiction officials were interviewed to find answers to the following questions:[59]

6734 (Deering Supp. 1965). The superintendent may insist on an examination of the patient or such other proof as he deems necessary before issuing such a certificate. It is issued if he finds that the patient "has recovered his reason and is sane, or was not mentally ill when admitted to the hospital." (*Ibid.*) The standard, then, is different from that for issuance of a "certificate of competency." Filing of a "certificate of sanity" with the committing court has, however, the same effect as filing a "certificate of competency." Further, there is provision for judicial review if the superintendent refuses to issue a "certificate of sanity." The superintendent must certify in writing his reasons for refusing the certificate and the patient or "a relative or friend" may petition a superior court for an order that the person is "sane and restored to reason." Cal. Welf. & Inst. Code § 6735 (Deering Supp. 1965).

Patients committed to private hospitals cannot get any kind of certificate from the superintendent of such hospitals. They must file a petition in court and have a hearing.

A "certificate of competency" may be issued to a discharged mentally retarded person, since it is available to "any person released from a state hospital." Cal. Welf. & Inst. Code § 6729 (Deering Supp. 1965). Institutions for the care and treatment of the mentally retarded are called "state hospitals." Cal. Welf. & Inst. Code § 7000.

According to the Chief Social Worker at a hospital for the mentally retarded, very few of the patients are, in fact, discharged with certificates of competency. Such certificates are issued to patients who are judged to have a near-normal I.Q. A certificate is not issued as a matter of course, but only on request, or in case circumstances necessitating such issuance later arise. At most, two such certificates are issued per year.

There is presumably no way for a mentally retarded person to be restored if the hospital refuses to issue a certificate of competency. A "certificate of sanity" or a judicial declaration of sanity would be unavailable since these statutes apply only to persons who have been "adjudged to be mentally ill." Cal. Welf. & Inst. Code § 6734 (Deering Supp. 1965).

[56] N.C. Gen. Stat. Ann. § 35–4.2. (1950) provides a procedure for restoration of persons who have been discharged from state or private mental hospitals but have no guardian. When a petition for restoration is filed, the clerk of the superior court will appoint one or more licensed physicians to examine the applicant. After a hearing before the clerk, or the clerk and a jury, "the clerk shall determine the competency of the person and may if it is deemed proper issue an order restoring any right of which the person may have been deprived by his commitment."

[57] Allen, Ferster, Weihofen, *Mental Impairment*, Part IV, Chap. 1, "Guardianship and Incompetency."

[58] Mass. Ann. Laws Ch. 123, § 94A (1965).

[59] These questions were asked of hospital officials in state hospitals for the mentally ill and the mentally retarded, VA hospitals and private hospitals.

1. If a person is legally incompetent by reason of the fact of his hospitalization is he allowed by the hospital to do any of the following:
   enter a contract (including endorsing a check?) convey property? make a will? sue or defend a legal action? marry? drive an automobile? practice a profession?
2. Does the hospital follow the same or different practices with respect to a person conditionally released?
3. If a person is not legally incompetent by reason of his hospitalization is he prohibited by the hospital from performing any of the functions listed? If so, under what circumstances?

The answers showed that if a patient does not have a guardian his legal status as a "competent" or "incompetent" person is not determinative of whether he may execute a legal instrument, drive an automobile, marry, etc. While he is in the hospital, the policies and procedures of the hospital determine the extent to which he manages his own affairs and exercises his civil rights. Indeed, legal status is not even an important factor in such policies and procedures. Hospital policies vary depending on the act to be performed and therefore are discussed separately for each category of jural activity. When the patient is on conditional release, the hospitals usually have little or no knowledge about the patient's activities in these areas and do not attempt to supervise them.

Execution of Legal Instruments

Contracts, deeds, and wills are executed by legally incompetent patients in Colorado, the District of Columbia, Ohio and Texas. In some instances the act is performed with the hospital's express permission, while in others, the hospital is unaware of the patient's business activities.

None of the large state hospitals believe that they can effectively prevent a patient from executing legal instruments or conducting other business activities. Patients can send checks and other instruments through the mail, and families can bring documents and even a notary with them when they visit the patient. Some hospitals attempt to control the execution of legal instruments by limiting visitors to approved persons and by having nurses and attendants check waiting rooms for unauthorized visitors. However, they doubt that these procedures are fully effective.

In many cases it may be known that a patient wants to make a contract, a deed or a will. One state hospital makes no attempt

either to prevent or to authorize the desired activity because the superintendent does not deem it to be the function of the hospital "to determine the legal effect of any action a patient may take." However, if the situation is regarded as "extreme" the superintendent will file a petition for guardianship. All of the other hospitals surveyed either allow the patient to perform the act or tell him he may not do so. The decision is based on the hospital's evaluation of the person's capacity to perform the specific act[60] and the usual practice is to note the date of the transaction and the hospital's opinion on the patient's records. However, in one hospital a patient may be allowed to execute an instrument even if he is thought to lack capacity to do so if the transaction is thought to be a desirable one. Also, several hospitals permit patients to make small gifts, purchase clothing, and subscribe to magazines, because the legal risk is small and making the transaction is deemed of therapeutic benefit.

Hospitals do not usually prevent a patient from making a will if they believe he is incapable, but they do note their opinion to that effect on his record. One of the hospitals reported that in the last few years there has been a marked decrease in the number of patients who make wills. The superintendent believes that patients no longer regard the hospital as a place in which they will remain until death, and therefore feel less need to make a will during their hospitalization.

Patients who are legally competent (e.g., voluntary and temporary patients) are not prohibited from executing instruments in these states but if the hospital believes that a patient

[60] Only one hospital, a private one, reported that it does not allow any legally incompetent patients to execute contracts or deeds. In fact, it does not allow these patients to handle any financial affairs or even see the bills they receive. The director believes that it is in the patient's best interest "to follow a policy consistent with the law." However, a legally incompetent patient may be allowed to make a will.

If the patient is legally competent but the treating physicians believe that the document should not be executed, the relative or lawyer is told "that paper will never hold up" and "we are prepared to swear to that." For example, a husband came to visit his wife and asked her to sign papers conveying her interest in a business they own. A nurse observed the husband shuffling the papers and insisted he speak to the director before proceeding. The husband reluctantly agreed and was told that the wife was not psychiatrically able to sign. The director also called the husband's lawyer, related the incident and told him the conveyance would be void because of the wife's mental condition. The lawyer agreed to wait until the wife's condition improved.

lacks capacity to perform the act, they will advise him of their opinion and may also inform the family or the patient's attorney.

In New York and Massachusetts, hospitalization and incompetency are separate; however, both states have departmental regulations which in effect make all patients "incompetent" by denying them the power to make a will, execute contracts, deeds or other conveyances or sign any checks, promissory notes, etc. except upon order of the department or of a judge.[61] The practice in both states is similar to that in the states discussed above. Patients are allowed to perform these functions if they are considered "competent." In Massachusetts, the assessment is made by an outside psychiatrist employed by the patient or his representative. The New York regualtion has an exception which permits a patient to execute instruments if the staff physician, after examination, believes that he understands the nature and consequences of the act.[62]

Neither California nor North Carolina has statutes or regulations which prohibit patients from executing legal instruments. However, the policies and practices of the hospitals in these states are similar to the other states studied. Patients who wish to execute a legal instrument are examined by one or more members of the hospital staff. If the finding is that the patient is "incompetent," he is not permitted to execute the contract or deed even though his legal status is that of a competent person.

INSTITUTIONS FOR THE MENTALLY RETARDED

Although the study of institutions for the mentally retarded was less extensive, the results were similar to those of the study of mental hospitals. Some legally incompetent patients in these institutions do make contracts and execute instruments, in some cases without the institutions' knowledge and in others with the institutions' express permission. For example, one institution reported that patients sometimes purchase an item on time payment while on leave. When the bills arrive, the hospital in many cases informs the vendor that in its judgment the patient was not competent to contract and offers to restore the purchased article on refund of money paid. Vendors have invariably accepted this offer and none has litigated the question of mental capacity. Another institution reported that patients are allowed to make contracts and deeds if the other party knows of the patient's status as a resident of the institution and if in the institution's judgment the patient understands the nature and consequences of the act.[63]

MANAGEMENT OF PATIENT'S FUNDS

It is a general practice among hospitals to maintain a "patients' bank" or fund, in which money belonging to patients is kept and against which they are allowed to draw. The money may be used for items of personal need or comfort.[64] In some states, regulations permit depositing in the fund money received from any source, including earnings from work done in the hospital.[65]

Although a ledger account is set up for each patient, the funds are usually mingled for purposes of deposit or investment. In some states interest or increment is not credited to the individual accounts but is put into a benefit fund which may be expended for the education or entertainment of all patients.[66]

Although individual patient accounts are usually less than $500, in two state hospitals studied some of the accounts were over $2,000. In some states, a maximum is fixed by statute or regulation.[67] However, one hospital, with no statutory authority to do so, maintains a bank account in which it deposits the funds of patients and controls their use during the period of hospitalization. One patient came to this hospital with $15,000 in cash on his person,

---

[61] N.Y. Dept. Mental Hygiene Gen. Order No. 10 (July 1, 1964); Mass. Dept. Mental Health Reg. No. 9, Item 2 (1955).

[62] N.Y. Dept. Mental Hygiene Gen. Order No. 10 (July 1, 1964).

[63] A more extensive study of the legal problems of the mentally retarded is currently under way: *The Mentally Retarded and the Law*—a three-year project conducted by The George Washington University Institute of Law, Psychiatry and Criminology and supported by a grant from the National Institute of Mental Health (U.S. Public Health Service. Grant MH–01947).

[64] E.g., "Any of the funds belonging to a patient deposited in the patients' personal deposit fund may be used for the purchase of personal incidentals. . . ." Cal. Welfare & Institutions Code § 6657 (Deering Supp. 1965).

Authorized Purposes for Expenditure: "(a) Personal needs and comforts of the patient [obtained at the institution]. . . . (b) Items that are deemed beneficial to the patient, obtained from local merchants. . . . (c) Dentures, eyeglasses, and like articles necessary for the physical health of the patient. . . ." (Mass. Dept. Mental Health Reg. No. 27, Item A3 [1955].)

[65] Mass. Gen. Laws Ann. Ch. 123, § 39 (Supp. 1965).

[66] E.g., Tex. Rev. Civ. Stat. Art. 3183C (Supp. 1963).

[67] E.g., New York, $2500, N.Y. Mental Hygiene Law § 34(14), (Supp. 1065); Ohio, $50, Ohio Rev. Code Ann. § 5123.42 (Page Supp. 1965).

which was deposited in the account. Few states provide any safeguards, such as an audit by an outside agency, although in many states hospital superintendents are under bond.

The extent to which patients may draw on these funds varies from hospital to hospital. In one VA hospital, patients "on privileges" (i.e., not locked wards) are allowed to withdraw up to $21.00 a week; larger withdrawals, up to $300, may be authorized by the ward physician. One state hospital allows withdrawals of up to $30 a month, but several restrict withdrawals to very small amounts ("cigarette and candy money"). All of the hospitals referred to are located in jurisdictions which do not merge hospitalization and incompetency, and the patients whose funds are thus controlled are legally competent to expend them in any way they like.

The funds are permitted to be used for many purposes. In Massachusetts, patients are permitted to spend it not only for small canteen articles but for other items such as dentures and eyeglasses.[68] The New York law specifically permits using the money to provide "luxuries" as well as comforts and necessities, including support and burial expenses.[69] In many states, if money in the fund exceeds a certain amount it may be used to pay for hospital care. In California, this amount is $500.[70] Discretion is used in determining whether any of the money should be used for hospital care even if the funds exceed this amount. The patient's age and prognosis, the number of his dependents and his financial needs are taken into consideration in making this determination.

Institutions for the retarded also manage funds on behalf of patients. In one institution, most accounts are less than $500. The account can be drawn against for the purchase of radio sets, watches, etc. or making gifts, even though state law declares persons committed to such an institution to be incompetent. The institution policy is defended on the ground that if the state permits the institution to administer funds without a formal proceeding it presumably intends that the authorities exercise their best judgment in the management of the fund. In another state, where hospitalization is not an adjudication of incompetency, patients are "permitted" to spend three dollars a week, sometimes four or five dollars by special request.

[68] Mass. Dept. Mental Health Reg. No. 27, Item 3 (1955).

[69] N.Y. Mental Hygiene Law § 34(14) (Supp. 1965).

[70] Cal. Welfare & Institutions Code § 6657 (Deering Supp. 1965).

Hospital practices concerning management of patients' money seem to be unrelated to the legal status of the individual patients. The hospitals are making decisions for legally competent patients which should be made by the patient if he is legally competent. If the patient is deemed incapable of handling his money, the solution would appear to be to change his legal status and have a guardian appointed to handle his affairs. If the hospital authorities are to have the responsibility of initiating such proceedings this duty should be made explicit. It may be that for therapeutic reasons the action should be initiated by another state agency and the hospital's role limited to informing the agency that such action seems indicated. If a legally incompetent patient can handle small amounts of money for canteen purposes, the maximum amount which can be held for him by the hospital should be specified by statute, as should the action to be taken if the patient has funds exceeding the specified amount.

The suggestion that practices should be changed is not meant as a criticism of the particular decisions which are being made by hospitals, nor is there an implication that the money is not being used for the benefit of the patient. On the contrary hospitals appear to be performing a difficult and time-consuming task conscientiously and humanely, with little guidance.

The question of management of patient funds should be reviewed by state legislatures with attention not only to the problem of the patients' legal status but also the practical problems about his receiving, keeping and using money. Not too many years ago, most patients in state mental hospitals had little money and had little opportunity or inclination to spend any. This situation has been changing rapidly. Patients today may receive money from social security, disability insurance, pension funds, etc. Some of them have remunerative jobs in or outside the hospital. Patients today may go to baseball games and movies, attend dances and go on job interviews. For these activities they need money for clothes, transportation and recreation. They therefore need some place to deposit and withdraw money. Perhaps it should be a trust account; or perhaps a large state hospital can support a small branch bank or a currency exchange. Regardless of the device, the patient's money should be protected by an audit, bond and/or insurance. Also, if the patient is legally competent, keeping his money at the institution should be simply a convenience for him. It should not operate as a restriction on his power to make purchases.

In some cases, the funds of legally incompetent patients (and patients the hospital thinks are incompetent) are allowed to accumulate because the guardianship procedure is cumbersome and expensive. Complaint is also made that when the patient has a guardian it is often both difficult and time-consuming for the hospital to make arrangements for him to obtain canteen money, clothes, etc. The possibility of establishing a system of inexpensive state guardianship, or guardianships administered by non-profit organizations, for incompetent patients with small estates should be explored. The possibility of even patients with guardians being given a small allowance to use for magazine subscriptions, cigarettes, movies, etc. should also be considered.

MARRIAGE

Patients in mental hospitals seem to have little interest in getting married while they are at the hospital. Most of the hospitals report that patients do not ask for permission to marry, and they knew of no instances in which a patient had married during a visit at home. Only two of the hospitals would permit a patient to marry. One, a private hospital, said that it exercises no control to prevent the marriage of a patient "on privileges." The other, a state hospital, reported that some of its patients do marry while they are living at the hospital. A doctor may counsel a patient against marrying for therapeutic reasons, but there is no articulated policy at the hospital forbidding marriage. In fact, a doctor may advise a patient to marry even though legally incompetent, in the case of a woman who is pregnant and wants to legitimize her child.

None of the hospitals interfere with the marriages of patients who are on conditional release. If the hospital is seeing the person on an outpatient basis, it may recommend that the marriage be postponed for therapeutic reasons, but it will not prohibit the marriage or take steps to prevent or annul it.

Patients in institutions for the mentally retarded show a much greater interest in getting married. Some institutions reported that patients have run away to get married and several reported that patients marry while on home leave. One institution will discharge the patient if he marries unless an annulment is initiated by the family or guardian, but the others will allow the patient to remain in the institution and will not attempt to annul the marriage. A few of the institutions reported that they sometimes grant permission for patients to marry. The decision is based on whether the hospital thinks the person is competent to marry, not on his legal status.

SERVICE OF PROCESS

Although the hospitals studied usually allow process to be served on a patient, the manner of service varies considerably. Some hospitals allow service to be made directly on the patient in all cases, others insist that the staff physician determine if service would be harmful, and a few will not allow service to be made directly on the patient. In the latter hospitals, the process server must leave the documents with the superintendent or some other hospital official, who then makes arrangements for their delivery to the patient.[71]

[71] Cf. D.C. Code § 21–1121 (Supp. V 1966) which provides that service on institutionalized mental defectives can be made only by the superintendent or by someone designated in writing by him; N.Y. Dept. Mental Hygiene Gen. Order No. 10, *Service of Legal Processes upon Institutions and Patients, and the Execution of Instruments by Patients* (July 1, 1964):

(ALL INSTITUTIONS)
1. (a) The director or officer in charge of each institution for the care and treatment of the mentally ill, the mentally defective or the epileptic shall not permit the service of any legal process upon any mentally ill, mentally defective or epileptic patient except upon an order of a judge of a New York State court of record or of a federal court, which order shows that the judge had notice of the fact that the person sought to be served was on the date of the order a patient in such institution. The foregoing rule shall not apply to service of the following legal papers, which may be made upon patients without court order:
   (1) citations issued by the Surrogate's Court for probate of wills, letters of administration and for final accounting.
   (2) notice of petition for appointment of a committee and notice of final accounting of committee.
   (b) At the time of the service of any process upon a patient, the director or one of his assistants or the officer in charge shall be present and a descriptive note must be entered in the patient's case record. A copy of the process served, together with a copy of the judge's order, if any, must be filed with the papers relating to the patient. Another copy of the papers, along with an explanatory letter, must be forwarded at once to the committee of the patient, if there be one, or, if there be no committee, then to the nearest known relative or friend. Another copy shall be transmitted to the reimbursement agent for the institution, in the case of state institutions, or to the Department of Mental Hygiene, in the case of licensed private institutions. A final copy is needed in the case of state institutions which must be sent to the Department of Law. The Director or officer in charge is responsible for distribution of the legal papers served upon the institution and/or the patient.
   (c) In order to comply with the foregoing requirements, the process server shall provide

One hospital determines whether the patient is sufficiently "in contact" to understand service but most of the hospitals are concerned about the possible harmful effect of service on the patient. North Carolina has a statute which removes the normal requirement of personal service if the superintendent of the hospital informs the officer charged with the duty of service that service cannot be accomplished without danger or injury to the insane person.[72]

Some hospitals help the patient to obtain legal advise when he is involved in a lawsuit. For example, one hospital employs an attorney who will give the patients advice, but does not handle their cases. Another hospital will suggest that the patient retain an attorney and will recommend one if he has none.

Most of the problems that were described by the interviewees can probably be solved fairly easily by improved communication between the hospital, the legislature, the courts and the bar associations. The major problem concerning service of process seems to be the way in which it is handled. It should be possible for the hospital to be informed in advance of the process server's arrival so that arrangements can be made to prepare the patient, or to accompany the process server and explain the reason for his presence. It should also be possible to make arrangements with the bar association or legal aid for an attorney to explain the case to the patient and to represent him if he does not have his own attorney. Again, this is an area in which the hospitals are doing their best to handle difficult situations with little guidance.

DRIVER'S LICENSURE

Persons hospitalized for mental illness for an indeterminate period are permitted to retain their drivers licenses in only one of the jurisdictions studied, and in that jurisdiction in so doing the hospitals are not complying with state law. Hospital officials do not have authority to decide whether individual patients should keep their licenses in five of these states. In three of them, Colorado,[73] Ohio,[74] and Texas,[75] the clerk of the court has the responsibility of forwarding the license to the motor vehicle department and in Massachusetts[76] and North Carolina,[77] the hospitals are required to inform the motor vehicle department of all such patients who have licenses.

The practice in the District of Columbia and California is substantially the same but it seems to be based on the hospital's voluntary cooperation with the department rather than a legal requirement.

New York hospitals are not required by law to pick up automobile licenses and do not do so. They hold them until the patient's release

---

[73] Revocation is mandatory after a person has been "legally adjudicated insane." Colo. Rev. Stat. § 13–4–22(1) (i) (1963). The clerk of the court in Denver County notifies the Motor Vehicle Bureau of all long-term commitments but this practice is not followed in all counties. The Motor Vehicle Bureau believes that the courts are obliged by statute to notify them but it has no power to compel them to do so.

[74] When any person having an operator's or chauffeur's license is adjuged to be mentally ill, the probate judge shall order the license of such person delivered to the court. The court shall forward such license with notice of such adjudication to the registrar of motor vehicles. The registrar of motor vehicles shall suspend such license until receipt of written notice by the head of the hospital, or other agency which has or had custody of such person, that such person's mental illness is not an impairment to such person's ability to operate a motor vehicle, or upon receipt of notice from the adjudicating probate court that such person has been restored to competency by court decree. [Ohio Rev. Code Ann. § 4507.161 (Page Supp. 1965).]

The probate court does forward licenses to the registrar of motor vehicles when a person is indefinitely hospitalized for mental illness, but not in cases where a guardian is appointed for a non-hospitalized ward.

[75] Cancellation of license: Any finding of any court of competent jurisdiction that any person holding a license "is either insane, feebleminded, an habitual drunkard, an epileptic, an imbecile, an idiot or addicted to the use of narcotics" carries with it a revocation of his license to operate a motor vehicle. It is the duty of the clerk of any court in which such findings are made to certify the same to the Department of Motor Vehicles within ten days. Tex. Civ. Stat. Art. 6687b, § 30 (Vernon 1960). In practice, the hospital usually holds the license of the committed patient because the court clerks frequently do not ask for them. The hospitals hold the license until the patient is released but do not believe they are under any duty to send it to the Department of Public Safety.

[76] Mass. Dept. Mental Health Reg. No. 10 (1955).

[77] N.C. Gen. Stat. § 20–17.1 (1965).

---

five copies when he makes service on a patient in a state institution and four copies when he makes service on a patient in a licensed private institution.

(d) Licensed private institutions shall transmit to the Department of Mental Hygiene a copy of every legal paper relating to a patient which is served on the institution or on the patient.

[72] N.C. Gen. Stat. Ann. § 1–97(3) (1953).

and then return them. However, if they think the patient is in fact "incompetent" to drive at the time of release they will notify the licensing authority.

None of the states studied automatically suspends or revokes the licenses of voluntary patients and only one state requires that the hospital notify the motor vehicle department about voluntary patients. None of the hospitals routinely notify motor vehicle departments about voluntary patients, although it is possible that the hospitals in one state notify the department in some instances.[78]

Patients who have been allowed to retain their driver's licenses do drive automobiles while in patient status in some of the hospitals. In some hospitals, permission to drive must be granted by the patient's treating physician before he is allowed to drive, but in others all patients "on privileges" are permitted to drive.

Some institutions for the mentally retarded report that some patients have driver's licenses and do in fact drive to their jobs by car or motorcycle.

Several hospital officials in jurisdictions in which licenses are suspended or revoked when a patient is committed believe that being without a license causes serious problems both to patients who are on conditional release and to those who are well enough to leave the hospital during the day to look for a job. In some of these jurisdictions the patient cannot be given a new license until he has received an absolute discharge, and in others he has difficulty in obtaining a new license because of his prior hospitalization even after absolute discharge.[79]

OTHER ACTIVITIES

Practical difficulties such as the fact that patients are usually not registered to vote in the precinct in which the hospital is located and lack of personnel to take patients to the polls seems to be more significant in determining whether patients vote while at a given hospital than either legal status or the hospital's appraisal of "capacity." However, there is a wide variation in hospital policy. Patients do vote while in some hospitals, while not in others, and in still others the question has apparently never come up.[80]

Very few hospitals have any patients who are actively practicing a profession or engaging in an occupation which requires a license. However, one hospital reported that two attorneys were trying to carry on their practices while in the hospital. Hospitals in two of the states are required to report names of patients holding licenses to the appropriate state agencies.[81] Compliance with this requirement varies widely from hospitals in these states and none of the hospitals reports such information in states which do not impose it as a requirement.[82]

Patients are sued and may themselves initiate legal action. The hospital officials, of course, cannot stop people from suing patients, though some of them will try to help patients settle claims, such as garnishment actions. Patients are discouraged, but not prohibited, from filing actions which appear to be without merit. However, a patient's capacity to bring suit is controlled by state law.[83]

---

[78] In Colorado the Motor Vehicle Bureau may cancel or deny a license when there is some evidence of mental incompetency but no adjudication. See C.R.S. 13–4–3, 13–4–19 (1961 Supp.). If action is taken on notification of a doctor or family member that the person's condition is such that he should not be driving, the licensee has a right to a hearing. However, in practice, usually the license is revoked without the patient being notified.

In the last few years the number of long-term commitments and consequently the number of revocations based on such commitments have gone down. However, cancellations and denials, based on evidence of mental incompetency have gone up. It is probable that the information about voluntary and temporary patients comes from the hospitals.

Revocations		Cancellations-Denials
291	1960	20
289	1961	95
166	1962	356
35	1963 to July	141

[79] See Allen, Ferster, and Weihofen, *Mental Impairment*, Appendix A, "Ad Hoc Determinations of Incompetency—Operation of a Motor Vehicle," for detailed description of the statutes, administrative regulations, and motor vehicle department practices concerning revocation and restoration of driver's licenses.

[80] For state laws governing this subject see *ibid.*, Appendix A, Section 9.

[81] Massachusetts Department of Health Regulation No. 10–1, 2a (1955); Opinion of Attorney Gen. of California, No. 57–261, 1958, vol. 31, p. 186.

[82] For state laws governing this subject see Allen, Ferster, and Weihofen, *Mental Impairment*, Appendix A, Section 8.

[83] For state laws governing this subject see *ibid.*, Appendix A, Section 3.

SYMPOSIUM ON GUARDIANSHIP OF THE MENTALLY RETARDED: CONCLUSIONS

The term "guardianship"[1] refers to a legally recognized relationship between a specified competent adult and another specified person, the "ward"[2] who, because of his tender age or because of some significant degree of mental disability, judicially verified, is considered to lack legal capacity to exercise fully some or all of the rights pertaining to adults generally in the country of which he is a citizen. The guardian is specifically charged with protecting his ward's interests and, for certain purposes, exercising essential rights on his behalf.

The idea that there must be someone formally responsible for protecting those persons lacking mental capacity to safeguard their own interests was established and expressed many centuries ago. Yet today, there is dissatisfaction in many countries because the principle is not expressed in practice in a manner suited to the needs of the retarded, and because many persons who should enjoy the benefits of guardianship are not receiving them.

Today it is increasingly recognized that even for the seriously retarded adult, life should be characterized by a series of personal decisions, each made in response to current circumstances (including current expectations of the future) and each peculiar to the individual's capacities and preferences. Many of these decisions involve selection of appropriate medical care; training in personal, social, or vocational skills as appropriate; use of leisure time; living arrangements, and the like. Thus an individual life plan is becoming possible for each of the retarded, a plan based on individual needs and preferences, and constructed from the increasing variety of options that are becoming available through public and voluntary initiative. There is, consequently need for a personal coordinator or decision-maker on a continuing basis.

Another serious difficulty arises because the law usually represents incompetence in simple black and white terms, with the result that most guardianships of the person are looked on as plenary guardianships. The effect is well expressed by the word *interdiction* (prohibition), which has until recently been in use in the statutes of many of the Latin countries. The person interdicted (declared incompetent) is deprived of the legal capacity to act in any way on his own behalf. Even though he may have a guardian appointed to exercise some of his rights, the emphasis usually is on the deprivation of rights rather than on implementing rights constructively through informed representation. Moreover, the idea that the person himself can properly retain and exercise some personal and even property rights, selectively, according to his individual capacity, is not adequately expressed in most existing statutes pertaining to guardianship.

Although it is possible in most countries to establish guardianship of property without invoking guardianship of person, this distinction does not really reflect the character of the guardianship most appropriate for the protection of the mentally retarded whose faculties are only partially impaired. The result of this deficiency in the legal system has been twofold: on the one hand there has been a reluctance to invoke guardianship on behalf of a person who needs only moderate protection, since to do so would clearly place him under greater legal incapacity than necessary; on the other hand, where the need for protection is pressing but not complete, it has often been considered necessary to place a seriously retarded person under plenary guardianship when a more limited form would have been sufficient, if it had been available.

Still another complication arises because guardianship, for good reason, is seen as a service which should be applicable to anyone whose faculties have been impaired regardless of cause—mental illness, senility, and the like. The laws pertaining to guardianship are usually

[1] In French: "tutelle"; in Spanish: "tutela."
[2] In French: "pupille"; in Spanish: "pupilo."

Excerpted and reprinted with permission from a symposium held at San Sebastian, Spain, May 29–31, 1969, sponsored by the International League of Societies for the Mentally Handicapped.

structured with the needs of this large group in mind, overlooking the fact that the retarded have a lifelong handicap and, unlike most other candidates, have never experienced a period of normality during which they may have freely exercised their rights to marry, to make a will, to express their wishes about future guardianship, to decide where to establish a residence, etc. Moreover, since they have never experienced normality, they do not know how to protest against denial of the rights which pertain to it.

What procedures should be followed in adjudication of the need for guardianship?

Guardianship proceedings should be as informal as possible, consistent with fairness and the preservation of civil rights.

This goal is simple to state and to accept, but extremely difficult to realize in practice. Jurists who have not looked into these matters in detail and who read the recommendations which follow may be inclined to think that their own countries are exceptions and that the present laws and procedures there are adequate. The participants in the Symposium, members of the legal profession and laymen alike, do not share that view and ask for a genuine reevaluation of the extent to which actual practice falls short of this goal in every country.

If greater use is to be made of guardianship in the future, and if each individual guardianship is to be established with more attention to individual needs as well as rights, it will be necessary to establish the principle that the extension of guardianship to those genuinely in need of it is in the public interest and is not merely a personal or private concern.

It is in the light of this principle that the participants accepted the following guidelines for the procedural aspects of guardianship.

To secure his rights, the individual concerned is entitled to a hearing before an impartial tribunal.

The tribunal or decision-making body should be a court. However, consistent with national law, an administrative body acting judicially might be used. If the latter is used, it should not be part of an agency that renders services to the retarded, and there should be provision for appeal to the courts. The judge or chairman of the decision-making body should be a lawyer, preferably one with a knowledge of the mentally retarded and special competence in dealing with their needs. If the decision-making body is to be a court, consideration should be given to conferring jurisdiction upon a special court, as for example, a family or children's court.

It should be possible for a person on his own application, to secure the appointment of a guardian with specified duties, where it is found to be in the best interests of the applicant and of the community, without a specific declaration that he is incompetent.

Interested persons, to be designated in the various countries, may request the appointment of a guardian for another. However, no person should, on the application of another, be declared in need of guardianship (within the frame of reference here discussed) unless it is found that:

1. He is mentally retarded.
2. By reason of mental retardation he is substantially deprived of capacity to manage his person or his property or both.
3. The appointment of a guardian is found to be in the best interests of the person and the community.

These three conditions must all be satisfied and the decision-making body should have the recommendation of a multiprofessional and interdisciplinary team with respect to them. In particular the decision-making body should be required by statute to avail itself of the expertise of behavioral scientists or, as an alternative, such expertise should be represented in the membership of the decision-making body.

Notice, in simple language and explaining all rights, must be given to the individual concerned and certain other designated persons and/or agencies, when guardianship proceedings are to be initiated.

The tribunal has a duty to ensure that the subject of the proceedings has independent legal representation. In addition the individual concerned has a right to be present at the hearing and to be heard. If he is incapable of being present, the decision-making tribunal has a duty to visit him at the place where he is.

The establishment of the need for guardianship and the appointment of a guardian when necessary is in the public interest. Because it is desirable that there be no significant deterrent to the initiation of appropriate proceedings, it is recommended that the parties themselves not be required to bear the costs of the proceedings, including representation. If, within the framework of a particular jurisdiction, costs must be assessed, they should be minimal, with liberal provisions for waiver. In such cases, the attorney as well as members of the tribunal are to receive salaries or other compensation from other appropriate sources.

The order issued by the tribunal appointing a guardian should be specific in respect of any restriction of the ward's rights as well as in respect to the scope of guardianship. The restrictions and the scope of guardianship should be as limited as possible, taking into account the capabilities of the retarded and the need for his protection.

According to the circumstances of the case, the tribunal at the time of appointing the guardian should stipulate intervals at which the tribunal shall make inquiry into the need for continued guardianship and its scope.

What procedures should be followed in appointing, recalling, and discharging guardians?

The decision-making body, after having decided on the need for guardianship, should select and appoint that guardian who can best serve the special needs of the individual as determined by the body.

There are, in most jurisdictions, guidelines—statutory or otherwise—for the discharge of the duties of guardians of property. However, there seems to be an almost a total absence of any guidelines for the guardian of a person. We see this as a serious defect that should be remedied. Human and social factors should be given the primacy they deserve.

Any party, or the tribunal on its own motion, should be empowered to seek recall and replacement of a guardian. Where appropriate, the recommendations of the multiprofessional interdisciplinary team should be solicited and considered.

Any party to a guardianship proceeding should have a right of appeal from any decision made with respect to the need for guardianship, its extent and character, or the selection of the guardian. The tribunal should have authority to make changes in the guardianship as needed to meet changed conditions.

Any interested person or agency should have the right to initiate proceedings for restoration of an individual's capacity. The procedure and question of costs should be essentially the same as a proceeding to determine the need for guardianship in the first instance, with similar protection of civil rights.

What provisions should be made for supervising guardians and for overview of the system of guardianship?

The participants agreed that there must be in each country adequate machinery for the effective supervision of guardians, individually and collectively, and for reinforcing the system of guardianship through constructive review.

The appointing tribunals or judges have the ultimate responsibility to revise their orders of guardianship, to recall or discharge guardians, and to decide disputes that arise among parties who are affected by guardianship orders. How-

ever, it is unreasonable to expect the courts themselves to engage in the kind of constant monitoring of the system that the participants envision as necessary if the benefits to guardianship as heretofore outlined are to be realized. In no country are the courts currently in a position to discharge properly their responsibilities respecting guardianship as presently defined, to say nothing of responsibilities that the Symposium anticipates they will increasingly assume. Certainly the judges engaged in this difficult work in the future will have to be given opportunities to familiarize themselves with the problem of mental retardation and its relation to guardianship of the person. However, better orientation of judges will not suffice in itself. The courts or tribunals will need the support of a well-staffed agency—public and permanent—which, among other things, has the power and duty to bring before the courts some of the information on which court action should be taken.

The character of this agency will vary from country to country, as will its location within the governmental structure. In some countries, it will find a place in the Ministry of Justice. In any case, it was generally agreed that it should not be located in any government agency that is responsible for direct services for the case, training, or treatment of the retarded.

—Gathering information on the overall system, for the purpose of evaluating its effectiveness and proposing necessary changes.

—Reviewing reports filed by guardians (not to the exclusion of judicial review of the same).

—Investigating individual cases, either in response to complaints or on its own initiative, including direct contact with wards on a random sampling basis.

—Bringing to the attention of the courts pertinent information on which court action is necessary.

—Reviewing the work of professional guardians in relation to the number of wards accepted by each and advising courts relative to limiting the number of wards any one guardian can properly serve.

—Identifying persons needing guardianship who might otherwise not have an application made on their behalf.

—Initiating the necessary legal action where families or other concerned persons do not do so.

—Advising courts on the criteria for the selection of guardians.

—Providing interim services by assigning a person to act as temporary mentor in emergencies, or while a new guardian is being selected.

—Securing competent professional persons to assist the courts as expert witnesses, members of the evaluation teams, etc.

It is possible that in some countries the training and recruitment of guardians might also be considered a function of this agency.

In order to carry out these functions, the public agency must maintain good formal and informal lines of communication with other agencies in the public and voluntary sectors, which are active in promoting the interests of the mentally retarded. The use of an advisory council, which includes representatives from parent associations and professional groups, should be considered.

Parents' associations have a special responsibility to develop within their own organizations better understanding of the principles of law and science underlying guardianship and to strengthen their structures to meet the new opportunities for action that will arise as a result of these recommendations.

AGREEMENTS OF THE MENTALLY DISABLED: A PROBLEM OF NEW JERSEY LAW

Raymond D. Cotton

The involvement of the state in the problems of the mentally ill is twofold: 1) in a negative sense, restrictions are imposed on their rights and privileges in the conduct of their personal and business affairs; 2) on the positive side, the state seeks to institute measures for their proper care and treatment.

This discussion is limited to the legal incidents that arise from agreements[1] to which one of the parties is mentally ill or mentally deficient.[2]

AGREEMENTS OF THE UNADJUDICATED

The legal determination of the effect given an agreement in which one of the parties is mentally disabled often depends upon whether that party has been judicially declared insane or incompetent. This section considers those cases in which, prior to a dispute about the transaction, there was no such adjudication.

New Jersey could have followed one of two roads. The first was taken in *Dexter v. Hall*,[3] in which the United States Supreme Court stated that the "fundamental idea of a contract is that it requires the assent of two minds. But a lunatic, or a person *non compos mentis*, has nothing which the law recognizes as a mind. . . . [thus] he cannot make a contract which may have any efficacy as such." Six states currently adhere to this legal position by statute[4] and three by case law.[5]

New Jersey law, however, follows the authority of the famous English case of *Molton v. Camroux*,[6] which was concerned with

---

[1] This term is used to mean consensual transactions, including *inter alia* contracts, gifts, and conveyances. Green, "The Operative Effect of Mental Incompetency on Agreements and Wills," 21 *Texas L. Rev.* 554 (1943) [hereinafter cited as Green, 21 *Texas L. Rev.*]; *see* 1 S. Williston, *Contracts* § 2 (3d ed. 1959).

[2] *See* A. Allen, E. Ferster & H. Weihofen, *Mental Impairment and Legal Incompetency* 32 (1968); *see also* R. Hurley, *Poverty and Mental Retardation: A Causal Relationship* 13 (1969).

[3] 82 U.S. (15 Wall.) 9 (1872).

[4] Cal. Civ. Code § 38 (West 1954); Idaho Code Ann. §§ 31–106 (1948); Men. Rev. Codes Ann. §§ 64–110 (1970); N.D. Cent. Code § 14–01–Ok (1960); Okla. Stat. tit. 15, § 22 (1961); S.D. Code § 30.0801.

[5] Dougherty v. Powe, 127 Ala. 577, 30 So. 524 (1900) (deed); Elder v. Schumacker, 18 Colo. 433, 33 P. 175 (1893) (deed); Bowman v. Wade, 54 Ore. 347.??? P. 72 (1909) (mortgage).

[6] 154 Eng. Rep. 1107 (Ex. 1849).

Excerpted and reprinted with permission from *Rutgers Camden Law Journal* 3:241, 1971.

an attempt by a deceased "lunatic's" representative to recover premiums paid to his ward for an annuity. The court declared that, "when the state of mind was unknown to the other contracting party, and no advantage was taken on the lunatic, the defence cannot prevail, especially where the contract is not merely executory, but executed in the whole or in part and the parties cannot be restored altogether to their original position."

In the frequently cited case of *Matthiessen & Weichers Refining Co. v. McMahon's Administrator*,[7] the superintendent of McMahon's business delivered certain goods into the possession of Matthiessen under an oral contract between the principals. There was no evidence that McMahon had been adjudicated "insane" or incompetent. The only evidence of incompetence that the deceased exhibited were symptoms of a disordered intellect that began with the delivery of the goods, and continued until his death. The jury found McMahon competent to make the bargain. The effect of such a finding was that if Matthiessen was acting "without the knowledge of such circumstances as would put a reasonably prudent man upon inquiry, [and] made the bargain in good faith, then that would be a good bargain, and neither McMahon nor his representative could set up the insanity against it."

There are, however, two groups of exceptions to the above qualification: 1) "valid" contracts and contracts for necessaries; 2) contracts in which the insane person returns the entire consideration before he rescinds. If he fails to return the consideration, he will be held liable upon contract, but on the grounds that the "lunatic has received and enjoyed an actual benefit from the contract."

Miller v. Barber[8] was a case in which defendant was adjudicated incompetent prior to the commencement of a trial on the merits and subsequent to the time when the transaction was consummated. Defendant executed an assignment of a leasehold and received $3,500 from plaintiff. Soon after the assignment, defendant was declared a "lunatic" by a commission in lunacy issued by the Chancery Court. At the trial on the merits, the jury found that defendant was not capable of understanding the nature and effect of the transaction in which he had engaged on the day the assignment was made.[9]

On appeal the court held that the deed was voidable, and that it could only be avoided by

first returning the consideration, less proper set-offs. Until avoided, though made under questionable circumstances, the deed was to remain good in law.

The notion of a "voidable" agreement is troublesome. A "voidable" agreement may mean any one of the following: 1) that the agreement is valid until disaffirmed; 2) that the agreement is imperfect, but it can be made perfect by ratification; or 3) that as between the parties the contract may be set aside, but an assignee without notice can enforce it.

New Jersey seems to adopt the view that although the agreement is valid, it is subject to being extinguished by the occurrence of certain subsequent events. As was seen in *Miller v. Barber*, when a previously made assignment deed is in question, the deed will be recognized as valid until the conditions of avoidance are met.

Avoidance

Professor Corbin in his *Legal Analysis and Terminology*[10] would probably view avoidance as a power-immunity. It is a power in that the legal relation of *A*, an incompetent, to *B* can be altered by *A*'s voluntary act.[11] And it can be thought of as an immunity because *B* has no legal power to affect the relation of himself to *A*. For example, if *A*, a mental incompetent, owns Blackacre and conveys it to *B*, *A* can assert the power of avoidance by tendering the consideration and still remain safe from *B*'s ability to affect *A*'s relationship to the land. In other words, avoidance renders one able to "terminate such rights and duties as the transaction has created, those of the other party as well as [one's] own."[12]

In order to have this power-immunity attach, a certain degree and kind of mental incapacity must be proved. And to define such a standard it is necessary to determine why the law provides for special incidents to surround the acts of a mentally disabled individual.

Professor Green suggests that the law seeks to foster three types of protection: 1) protection of society from the acts of the mental incompetent; 2) protection of the incompetent

---

[7] 38 N.J.L. 536 (E. & A. 1876).

[8] 73 N.J.L. 38, 62 A. 276 (Sup. Ct. 1905).

[9] Sbarbero v. Miller, 72 N.J. Eq. 248, 252, 65 A. 472, 474 (Ch. 1907).

[10] 29 *Yale L.J.* 163 (1919).

[11] It should be noted that if New Jersey followed the void per se rule, *A*'s voluntary act could not have brought about a formal contract, and thus *A* would have no "power" in this context.

[12] 1 A. Corbin, *Contracts* § 6 n.9 (1963). Viewing "avoidance" from only one side it has been defined as "the ability of one party to 'get out' of the contract in some manner, *if he wishes*." Note, "Mental Illness and the Law of Contrasts," 57 *Mich. L. Rev.* 1021, 1026 n.27 (1959).

from society, because of the unequal position which he occupies in relation to his fellow men; and 3) protection of the family or dependents of the incompetent.[13] Both the second and third forms of protection are probably operable when the agreement turns out to be disadvantageous and t he incompetent seeks avoidance. These forms of protection must be balanced against the very important public policy of safeguarding the security of transactions.

When the contract is purely executory the balance tips decisively for the incompetent. This usually holds true even though the other party entered "into the contract in good faith, without knowledge of such insanity, and before any adjudication of insanity." As the contract is executed, however, the scales begin to approach equilibrium. And if he is not able to restore the consideration or otherwise place the promisee in *status quo*, the balance often tips against the incompetent.

The Status Quo Requirement. When the healthy party cannot be placed in *status quo* the issue becomes the "insane" party's demand for recision. Nevertheless, the rule stands that recision may not be had on an agreement made in good faith until the consideration is restored, except when the one known to be insane is a victim of fraud.

The Test for Avoidance. The test of the degree and kind of mental incapacity that will have the legal effect of creating the power-immunity of avoidance, should be noted. One commentor has stated that the "sufficient capacity to understand in a reasonable manner the nature of the particular transaction in which he was engaged and its consequences and effects upon his rights and interests" will prevent a deed or contract from being set aside on insanity grounds.[14]

The test currently used in New Jersey is probably derived from the dicta in *Lozear v. Shields.* In *Lozear,* Chief Justice Beasley, speaking for a unanimous court, stated: "Where a pure defense of mental incapacity is interposed, I think the true test . . . is whether the party had the ability to comprehend, in a reasonable manner, the nature of the affair in which he participated." The suit in *Lozear* was an attempt to set aside a sale of real property.

Notwithstanding the vagueness and subjectivity of the New Jersey test, courts have more often than not reached just results.

Nevertheless, it cannot be denied that the courts do express interest in the ability of the individual to understand. This is demonstrated by the two components of the judicial test. There must be some sort of abnormality, behaviorally expressed, which impairs the ability of one to "understand" the nature and effect of the questioned transaction.

The term "understand" has not yet been clearly defined by the courts. A . . . serviceable definition is provided by a South Dakota case. That case states that although understanding includes consciousness, it means more: "It suggests the concept of a mind with the faculty of applying its powers of reason to the elements it comprehends, to the end that a judgment or conclusion may be formed."

Who Can Avoid

The Healthy Party. Cases in which this matter has been decided generally state the healthy party may not assert the other's insanity to obtain avoidance. This rule follows from the proposition that the law has created the power-immunity of avoidance for the protection of the mentally ill party, his estate and his heirs. Also, if the healthy party were allowed to avoid the incompetent's option to ratify would be vitiated.

The Incompetent. The incompetent will not be able to wage his own legal battle until he recovers both his well being and his legal status. Some authorities maintain that upon recovery he must elect to either avoid or ratify, and that not choosing to do the former implies the latter. Many cases have qualified this election by requiring that after recovery, the former incompetent must be aware of the bargain previously made. The question becomes easier to decide if the former incompetent exhibits behavior indicating his willingness to be bound. It is, however, not usually required that he must know of his right to avoid.

The right of avoidance may be asserted for the former incompetent by whoever represents him in court. This is not the case with respect to ratification. New Jersey, however, provides by statute that a guardian may be ordered by the superior court to fulfill any agreement to which the incompetent may have consented.

Finally, one should examine the role of those to whom the power-avoidance descends following the incompetent's death, *i.e.* his heirs, executors and administrators. In New Jersey, it is settled that an heir may, without notifying the executor, bring suit to avoid. The focus here seems to be on the heir's property interests. It is said that the heirs

---

[13] Green, 38 *Mich. L. Rev., supra* note 21, at 1213.

[14] 2 H. Black, *Rescission and Cancellation* § 262, at 736 (2d ed. 1929).

should not be barred from protecting their beneficial interests as no one else will do it for them. If a wrong was committed, moreover, and the heirs were injured, it is a basic principle of equity that they have "a right to demand judicial redress in [their] own name against the wrong-doer."

It is a common-law rule that if a party to a contract or conveyance backs mental capacity, his executor or administrator may, after the incompetent's death, either set aside the contract or avoid it on that ground. New Jersey retains this common-law rule.

ADJUDICATIONS

The two most important categories are adjudications of "insanity" and incompetency. The former may be a prelude to the latter, but it usually results in one's commitment as a patient to an institution for the care and treatment of the mentally disabled. A proceeding for incompetency is usually aimed at securing a guardian for the person and his property.

An insanity proceeding is analogous to a proceeding for incompetency.[15] It is, however,

capable of being pursued independently and has as its purpose the care and treatment of the person. Thus the issue of "insanity" is typically determined relative to possible commitment.

On the certificates of two physicians,[16] and a complaint by a relative, caretaker, or specified public official[17] an order of temporary commitment[18] can be obtained from any court of record in the county where the person resides or may be found.[19] When an order of temporary commitment cannot be obtained and the certifying physicians are of the opinion that "immediate restraint and confinement" are necessary because of the patient's condition, the person may be committed for twenty days by the chief executive officer of the institution.[20] Since all persons "detained" under title 30 are entitled to challenge the legality of their confinement through a writ of habeas corpus proceeding,[21] a final hearing[22] will probably be in order at some time.[23] Even at this stage it is provided that "[t]he court[24] shall hear and determine the matter [of mental disability] in a summary way without a jury, or it may, in its discretion, call a jury to determine the question of mental illness."[25]

That these two classes of adjudications are not the same in their legal effects cannot be doubted. In a recent case, the superior court emphasized that New Jersey law views these proceedings as being different in terms of their legal effects.[26] Consequently, a judgment of mental illness ("insanity") by a county court does not compel a finding of incompetency by any other court. Nor is a finding of incompetency binding with respect to the issue of mental illness or mental retardation.

At present an action may be brought under sections 6-35 and 6-36 of title 3A of the *New Jersey Revised Statutes* to have a person

---

[15] In New Jersey the same statute contains provisions for determining mental incompetency and appointing a guardian. The provision concerning mental incompetency states: "The terms 'mental incompetency' and 'mentally incompetent' refer to the state or condition of a 'mental incompetent' as defined in this section." N.J. Rev. Stat. § 3A:1–1(i) (1951); " 'Mental Incompetent' means a person who as a result of idiocy, insanity, lunacy, unsoundness of mind, or habitual drunkenness, is incapable of governing himself and managing his affairs." *Id.* § 3A:1–1(h).

N.J. Rev. Stat. § 3A:6–36 (1951) provides for the appointment of a guardian.

Contrary to common law tradition and former New Jersey law, *e.g., In re* M. McLaughlin, 87 N.J. Eq. 138, 102 A. 439 (Ch. 1917), the present New Jersey Constitution allows the issue of mental incompetency to be tried without a jury. N.J. Const. art. I, § 9. The legislature accepted this and enacted N.J. Rev. Stat. § 3A:6–35 (1951), making the issue triable to the court, "unless a trial by jury is demanded by the alleged mental incompetent or someone on his behalf." *Id.*

Between the time N.J. Rev. Stat. § 3A:6–35 (1951) and its companion N.J. Rev. Stat. § 3A:6–36 (1960) were enacted, the supreme court supported continuing the practice of jury trial except when the incompetent's estate was less than $2,000. "A decades experience . . . indicated, however, that where there is no contest and little doubt as to the condition of the alleged incompetent, neither his nor the public's interest is served by the cumbersome formality of a jury trial." Thus on July 15 of that year, the supreme court amended N.J. Super. Ct. (Civ.) R. 4:102–6, placing the burden

of requesting a jury upon the incompetent or his representative. N.J. State Comm'n. on Mental Health, Toward Better Mental Health in New Jersey, 167–68 (1961).

[16] N.J. Rev. Stat. § 30:4–29 (Supp. 1965).

[17] *Id.* § 30:4–27.

[18] Commitment per se is probably not admissable on the issues of incompetency or unsoundness of mind." *Id.* § 30:4–24.2.

[19] *Id.* § 30:4–37 (Supp. 1953).

[20] *Id.* § 30:4–38.

[21] *Id.* § 30:4–24.2 (Supp. 1965).

[22] *Id.* § 30:4–42.

[23] Even when the hearing does take place the patient might not be allowed to attend. *Id.* § 30:4–41.

[24] *I.e.* the County Court or the Juvenile and Domestic Relations Court. *Id.* § 19:4–23.

[25] *Id.* § 30:4–42.

[26] *In re* Lambert, 33 N.J. Super. 90, 109 A.2d 423 (Ch. 1954).

declared mentally incompetent and have a guardian appointed. The legal effects of such proceedings are discussed in this subsection.

The Nature of the Guardian's Role

The statutes have limited the powers of the guardian,[27] and these limitations are developed by case law. For example, in *Van Horn v. Hann*[28] the court said that at common law a guardian was merely the curator of the "lunatic's" property. He could make no contracts that would bind the "lunatic." To provide for the maintenance of the "lunatic" and his property, a committee was appointed by the Chancellor. Further, the court in *Cooper v. Wallace*,[29] stated that, as with the committee, the guardian of a "lunatic" in New Jersey is a mere curator without any interest in the property of the "lunatic."[30] On the other hand the guardian is required under statute to provide for the care of the incompetent.[31] Following the common law under the writ de lunatico in quirendo,[31] the guardian acts as an agent of the Chancellor. Thus, the court itself must be looked to for payments of the incompetent's debts.[32] It has been stated that, "[a] decree of a court appointing a guardian for a lunatic is conclusive evidence of the ward's incapacity in relation to all subjects on which the guardian can act."[33] On the other hand, some states have declared that a guardianship proceeding is not binding on those not parties to it. Much seems to turn on the wording of the applicable statute.

The Legal Effect upon the Ward

When an individual is declared mentally incompetent and a guardian is appointed the effect upon the individual so declared is severe. The *Restatement* takes the view that the imposition of a guardian of one's property following an adjudication of "mental illness or defect deprives that individual of the capacity to incur contractual duties.[34]

Void Per Se: Pro and Con

The only semblance of a reason presented by the *Restatement*'s Comment to section 18A (void per se rule) is that such a rule prevents the incompetent's property from being "squandered or improvidently used." Subsequently, the American Law Institute's rationale for section 18A falls into mere assertions: "[G]uardianship proceedings *are* treated as giving public notice of the ward's incapacity. . . . [T]he guardian *is* not required to give personal notice to all persons who may deal with the ward.[35] Also, the control and supervision vested by the court in the guardian "*are* not to be impaired or avoided by proof that the ward has regained his reason . . . unless the guardianship is terminated or abandoned."[36]

In addition, the void per se rule finds support in two rationales. The first is that since the proceedings fix the person's status, they are in rem and thus binding on all the world. The second states that to take any lesser position would unduly hamper the discharge of the guardian's duties.

Further, such a position would better serve the public policy of protecting the incompetent himself, his dependents (by preventing a wasting of the estate), and the public (by preventing his becoming a public charge). To allow the question of incompetency to be challenged by, for example, introducing evidence of "lucid intervals," could subject every transaction of the ward to litigation just as it would have in the absence of guardianship.

Other methods of compromising the competing claims have been in use by the states. In Ohio the ward's incapacity is absolute only with respect to those matters that directly conflict with the guardian's authority.[37] Other states have sought to "extend protection by statute to specific groups or individuals who are apt to deal with incompetents at a distance, and who would be unlikely to discover the fact of guardianship."[38]

Judgments of Mental Illness or Deficiency

Prior Adjudication. In *Leick v. Pozniak*,[39] subsequent to a judgment of incompetency, the patient was committed in October 1933 and was not formally discharged until August 1938. On March 25, 1936, while still in the hospital under court order, the patient signed the bonds and mortgages in question. The former adjudication was given presumptive weight with respect to the incompetency.[40]

It would be useful to consider *Coombs v.*

---

[27] N.J. Rev. Stat. §§ 3A:6–36 to –37 (1951); N.J. Rev. Stat. § 30:4–65 (1937).

[28] 39 N.J.L. 207 (Sup. Ct. 1877).

[29] 55 N.J. Eq. 192, 36 A. 575 (Ch. 1896).

[30] *Id.* at 198, 36 A. at 578.

[31] N.J. Rev. Stat. § 3A:6–36 (1951).

[32] N.J. Rev. Stat. § 30:4–65 (1937).

[33] *See* Annot., 7 *A.L.R.* 568, 593 (1920).

[34] RSC § 18A; *accord*, 32 *Colum. L. Rev.* 504, 513 (1932).

[35] RSC § 18A, Comment a.

[36] *Id.* (emphasis added).

[37] Lee v. Stephens, 50 N.E.2d 622 (Ohio App. 1942).

[38] Ross, 57 *Mich. L. Rev.*, *supra* note 156, at 983 & n.90.

[39] 135 N.J. Eq. 67, 69, 37 A.2d 302, 303 (Ch. 1944).

[40] 135 N.J. Eq. at 69, 37 A.2d at 303.

Witte[41] to examine more closely the nature of this presumption. In that case a husband and wife signed an agreement to sell certain property in August 1925. Ten years prior to the sale, however, the husband had been committed to a state institution for treatment as an "insane person." Discussing the effect of the earlier proceeding, the court said that, "such proceedings are not only evidential on the question of the person's mental condition at the time when they were had, but also of the continued existence of that condition; for where a state of insanity is shown to have existed at a certain time, it is presumed to continue until the contrary is shown."[42]

In *Leick* the rebutting evidence was compelling. On March 25, 1926, the patient was examined by a team of six doctors who unanimously found her competent to execute the deeds.[43]

Contemporaneous Adjudication. In *Hill v. Day*[44] the Vice-Chancellor was faced with deciding whether plaintiff's testator should be bound by an assignment he executed in 1878. The issue arose because the testator had been declared a lunatic two years antecedent to the execution of the assignment.[45] The Vice-Chancellor stated that the above finding was prima facie evidence of the testator's incompetency; he went on to state that since the proceeding was purely *ex parte*, it was not conclusive with respect to the defendants.[46]

The Supreme Court of New Jersey faced this issue in *Coombs v. Witte*.[47] *In that case* the individual in question had been committed as an insane person by the Court of Common Pleas of Cape May County. In discussing the legal effect of such an adjudication, the court stated "[A] judgment of this character in a court vested with jurisdiction to inquire into and determine the existence of lunacy is competent, although not conclusive, evidence of the mental condition of the person who is the subject of the investigation *at the time when the judgment was pronounced*."[48]

Subsequent Adjudication. The effect of a subsequent adjudication of insanity was presented to the New Jersey Court of Equity in *Mieczkowski v. Mieczkowski*.[49] In 1930 Anna Mieczkowski opened a savings account at the local bank. On August 7, 1947, a jury found her a mental incompetent. The jury further found that she had been a mental incompetent twenty-eight years prior to August 7, 1947.[50] The court stated the rule of *Den v. Clark*,[51] which is that an inquisition of lunacy is not conclusive against any person not party to it. The party against whom the inquisition is used may offer it to show that the alleged "lunatic" was of sound mind during any period of time covered by the inquisition.[52]

Since the court's rationale is often repeated, paraphrased, and cited, it would do well to take note of it. The court stated:

The disastrous consequences of retroactive operation of an inquisition, if conclusive, strongly recommend the wisdom and policy of withholding from it such influence. In its nature it is *ex parte*.[53]

As matters currently stand, it is arguable that courts are compelled to do that for which they are here criticized because of the vague standards they must apply. Title 3A, for instance, defines a "mental incompetent" as "a person who as a result of idiocy, insanity, lunacy, unsoundness of mind, or habitual drunkeness, is incapable of governing himself and managing his affairs."[54] Those courts that apply such tests as "the ability to understand the nature and effect of the act in which [the individual] is engaged,"[55] do not help to clarify matters.

More precise measures ought to be enunciated by the Legislature. The process of devel-

---

[41] 104 N.J.L. 519, 140 A. 408 (E. & A. 1928).
[42] *Id.* at 523, 140 A. at 410. "Subject to the general rules and regulations of the locality . . . [and medical reasons], every patient shall be entitled (1) to exercise all civil . . . rights . . . . For the purpose of a patient's exercising his civil rights there shall be no presumption of his incompetency or unsoundness of mind merely because of an admission to a mental hospital." N.J. Rev. Stat. § 30:4–24.2 (Supp. 1968).
[43] 135 N.J. Eq. at 68, 37 A.2d at 303.
[44] 34 N.J. Eq. 150 (Ch. 1881).
[45] *Id.* at 151.
[46] *Id.*
[47] 104 N.J.L. 519, 140 A. 408 (E. & A. 1928).
[48] *Id.* at 523, 140 A. at 410 (emphasis added).

[49] 141 N.J. Eq. 367, 57 A.2d 517 (Ch. 1948).
[50] *Id.* at 368, 57 A.2d at 518.
[51] Den v. Clark, 10 N.J.L. 217 (Sup. Ct. 1828).
[52] *Id.* 218.
[53] The question of a person's sanity in a commitment proceeding is heard in a summary way without a jury, or [the court] may, in its discretion, call a jury to determine the question of mental illness." N.J. Rev. Stat. § 30:4–42 (Supp. 1968).
It would be inconsistent with the common and uniform principles of jurisprudence, to suffer an act of such a nature to sweep away with irresistible force all contracts executed under whatever circumstances of solemnity, and even to abrogate the contract of marriage, at the expense of the undefended and truly unfortunate offspring. Such is the diversity of judgment respecting the state of the mind, that on this, more than perhaps any other question, error may be anticipated from uncontroverted proofs and *ex parte* examinations.
[54] N.J. Rev. Stat. § 3A:1–1(h) (1951).
[55] 37 *N.J.L.* at 113.

oping these should probably begin with the establishment of a small expert committee drawing its membership from practicing lawyers, judges, law professors, and specialists in the executive branch of government. Their draft should be discussed openly and fully by the public and its representatives. Hopefully, a practicable statute could be enacted.

It is to be expected that at least the following questions would be considered by the working groups: Who should be protected—the mental incompetent, his heirs, or the holder in due course? How far should this protection extend? Should the parties be returned to their original conditions? If a sliding scale is devised, what should be the relevant variables? What, if any, other state programs will have to be initiated to implement these decisions?

At present the courts are deciding cases in which mental incapacity is an issue on the basis of traditional contract doctrines. Fre-

quently, the court after weighing the equities decides in favor of one side. Can not the system improve upon such a forced choice situation? Two alternatives come readily to mind.

One might be a kind of transaction insurance fund in which all transfer fees would include a small surcharge. This money would be placed in a limited fund only reachable by an innocent and injured party in cases when a contract or deed were held invalid because of the mental incapacity of one of the parties.

Another possible alternative to traditional contract remedies would require employment of a bankruptcy law concept. In effect the rule would require an equal allocation of loss when a transaction was held void because of a party's mental incapacity.

No matter how precise the details, a restructuring is needed to delineate more clearly the rights and responsibilities of the parties. And it is proper for the legal profession to initiate such an understanding.

IN THE MATTER OF THE INCOMPETENCY OF HELEN FISHER McDONNELL

OWEN, Judge.

In May, 1968, at the age of 73, Helen F. McDonnell was adjudged mentally incompetent. Subsequently, in a separate proceeding, the court appointed guardians for both the person and property of Mrs. McDonnell. In May, 1970, Mrs. McDonnell's sister filed a petition seeking restoration of competency pursuant to the provisions of Section 394.22(15), F.S.1969, F.S.A. A hearing was held in May, 1971, and Mrs. McDonnell appeals from the order denying the petition for restoration of competency.

Appellant contends, and we agree, that the trial court misconstrued the legal effect of the evidence. The issue at a hearing of this type is whether the adjudicated incompetent is of sound mind and is capable of managing her own affairs. Section 394.-22(15) (d), F.S.1969, F.S.A. Although the several physicians who had examined or treated Mrs. McDonnell over the past few years preceding the hearing had variously diagnosed her physical ailments as arteriosclerotic vascular disease, congestive heart failure, early cirrhosis, gastritis and excessive use of alcohol, they all

expressed the view that when Mrs. McDonnell was not drinking she was alert, well-oriented as to her circumstances and surroundings and capable of taking care of herself and of managing her own affairs.

Mrs. McDonnell is a lady of considerable wealth, and thus, there is necessarily a greater concern that she might become the victim of designing persons than would be the case if she were a person of meager means. But her testimony amply demonstrated that she was fully aware of the nature and extent of her financial holdings, and she emphatically declared that if she were restored to competency she would rely upon the services of the same investment counselor that she had utilized before being adjudicated incompetent (and whose services are now being utilized by the guardians of her property). True, prior to the adjudication of incompetency she had on her own made a bad investment of $10,000 and had made an uncollectable loan of $6,000, but as she explained, these experiences had taught her to avoid similar investments or loans in the future. Overlooked is the fact that a very appreciable part of her present estate is

---

266 So. 2d 87 (District of Court of Appeal of Florida, 1972).

attributable to a relatively small investment she had made a number of years ago against the advice of her husband and investment counselor. No one, no matter how astute, is immune from bad investments. It is little more than pure speculation to conclude from these isolated examples that she cannot manage her own property or is likely to dissipate it or become the victim of designing persons. In our present day paternalistic society we must take care that in our zeal for protecting those who cannot protect themselves we do not unnecessarily deprive them of some rather precious individual rights.

[1] Mrs. McDonnell's efforts to be restored to competency were resisted by the guardians of her person, the guardians being her two married daughters. The evidence which they caused to be brought before the court at the time of the hearing on the petition for restoration of competency certainly tends to establish that Mrs. McDonnell indulges in alcoholic beverages to an excess with sufficient frequency as to be harmful to her physical health. On a number of occasions she has become intoxicated to the extent that she has required someone to help her physically. The medical testimony established that her continued excessive use of alcohol would be harmful physically and could impair her ability to manage her own property. Well-intentioned though her daughters may have been in seeking to provide her help for what approaches physical incompetency, it is clear to us that at the time of the hearing on the petition for restoration Mrs. McDonnell was not mentally incompetent. To the contrary, she was of sound mind and capable of managing her own affairs. As such, she was entitled to an order as provided in Section 394.22(15) (d), F.S.1969, F.S.A.

[2] The order appealed is reversed and this cause remanded for entry of an appropriate order consistent herewith. We recognize that the very nature of an inquiry into the mental competency of a person necessarily requires a determination of competency at a specific time, and does not preclude an inquiry into competency at a subsequent date upon a showing of a change of condition.

Reversed and remanded.

REED, C. J., and MAGER, J., concur.

IN RE ESTATE OF STEVENSON

UNDERWOOD, Chief Justice.

Pursuant to a jury verdict in the circuit court of Cook County, the defendant, Ellen Borden Stevenson, was adjudicated an incompetent, and a conservator for her estate was appointed. She appeals directly to this court.

The plaintiffs, who are the three sons and the mother of the defendant, instituted this action by filing a petition alleging that the defendant was incapable of managing her estate because of an imperfection of mentality within the meaning of section 112 of the Probate Act (Ill.Rev.Stat.1965, ch. 3, par. 112,) and praying for the appointment of a conservator for her estate. The petition further alleged that defendant suffered from mental and emotional disturbances which caused her to manifest extreme jealousy, suspicion and hostility toward the plaintiffs and others; that as a result of her condition, her estate had diminished by $400,000 over a 14-year period to a point where her assets totaled $100,000, with liabilities in excess of $80,000; that she did not have sufficient funds to pay taxes and other current debts, although plaintiffs had given defendant substantial sums to assist her financially; that she was being harassed by numerous creditors; that she was unable to properly manage her estate; and that due to her condition, her estate was liable to immediate further waste and loss if it remained under her control. In her answer defendant denied substantially all of plaintiffs' material allegations.

Plaintiffs then presented a verified petition for a pretrial mental examination of the defendant pursuant to Illinois Supreme Court Rule 17—1 (now Rule 215, Ill.Rev.Stat.1969, ch. 110A, par. 215). The petition was supported by an affidavit containing a transcript of a telephone conversation between defendant and one of the plaintiffs. Over the objections of defendant, an order was entered directing defendant to submit to a mental examination. She refused to submit to the examination and also failed to comply with the court's order directing her to submit to a discovery deposition relative to her financial affairs. As a consequence of her failure to comply with these orders, an order was entered pursuant to Supreme Court Rule 19—1 (now Rule 219; Ill.Rev.Stat.1969, ch. 110A, par. 219) debarring defendant from maintaining any defense at the trial relative to her mental condition and ability to manage her financial affairs.

At the trial, testimony was introduced by plaintiffs concerning defendant's financial difficulties over a period of years. There was evidence that the defendant was heavily in debt and had insufficient income to meet her current expenses; that an art center operated by her had closed; that her investments in securities with borrowed money had resulted in forced liquidation of the securities; that mechanic's liens and Federal tax liens of substantial amounts had been filed against her and were being foreclosed; that a mortgage on her home had been foreclosed; and that for a period of time plaintiffs had themselves contributed substantial sums toward the payment of defendant's bills, but that defendant had refused further attempts by plaintiffs to assist her.

There was testimony concerning defendant's conversations with her children and grandchildren and evidence of various personal incidents involving defendant and the plaintiffs. One of the plaintiffs testified that he received numerous telephone calls from defendant at various times of the day and night, some of which he recorded in his home with dictating equipment on the advice of counsel. Over defendant's objections, recordings of a portion of some of these conversations were put in evidence and played for the jury. Other witnesses testified that these conversations were similar to ones they had with defendant as a result of calls from her. Certain letters written by defendant were also put in evidence.

Dr. William Offenkrantz, a psychiatrist, testified for the plaintiffs as an expert witness. In response to a hypothetical question based on the evidence, he testified to the effect that defendant suffered from an imperfection and deterioration of mentality.

Defendant first argues that the trial court improperly ordered her to submit to a pretrial mental examination pursuant to Supreme Court Rule 17—1 (now Rule 215) since her mental condition was not "in controversy" within the meaning of that rule, and furthermore, that the requisite "good cause" for the examination had not been shown. She further argues that she has done nothing in this case to affirmatively put her mental condition in issue, and relying on Schlagenhauf v. Holder, 379 U.S. 104, 85 S.Ct. 234, 13 L.Ed.2d 152, she urges that Rule 215 should not permit discovery in a case of this type, but should be limited to those cases where the party whose examination is sought has in some manner affirmatively raised the question of his physical and mental condition. We do not concur with defendant's suggestion that Rule 215 should be so limited in scope nor do we think that the *Schlagenhauf* case suggests such a limitation.

Our Rule 215 provides in pertinent part that "In any action in which the physical or mental condition of a party or of a person in his custody or legal control is in controversy, the court upon notice and for good cause shown on motion made within a reasonable time before the trial, may order the party to submit to a physical or mental examination by a physician. . . ."

Rule 215 is a rule of discovery, the purpose of which is to permit the discovery of facts which will assist the trier of fact to reach a correct determination of the issues before it. This rule does not permit unlimited and indiscriminate mental and physical examinations of persons but by its terms gives a trial court discretion to order such examinations only when certain requirements are met. The person sought to be examined must be a party (or a person in his custody or legal control), the physical or mental condition of that person must be in controversy, and good cause must be shown for the examination. Then, and only then, is discovery of that person's physical or mental condition authorized by this rule.

The need for careful application of the "in controversy" and "good cause" limitations of the rule is particularly evident in a case of this type where the person sought to be examined has not raised the issue of his physical or mental condition (Schlagenhauf v. Holder, 379 U.S. 104, 85 S.Ct. 234, 13 L.Ed.2d 152.) But to limit the scope of Rule 215 as defendant suggests would not be consistent with either the letter or intent of the rule. Discovery of a person's mental or physical condition may be just as appropriate in a case where the party sought to be examined has done nothing to put his condition in issue as in a case where the party sought to be examined has affirmatively raised his condition either in support of or in defense of a claim. Rule 215 contemplates that the trial court in its discretion may order the physical or mental examination under appropriate conditions when all requirements of the rule have been met, irrespective of who has raised the issue of the person's physical or mental condition.

In the case before us, the pleadings show

without question that the mental condition of the defendant is "in controversy" insofar as it affected her ability to manage her estate. Also, we think that plaintiffs' motion for mental examination of the defendant, when considered with the supporting affidavits, furnishes showing of "good cause" for such examination. In our opinion, the trial court did not abuse its discretion in ordering the mental examination of defendant and in imposing the sanctions it did upon her refusal to comply with its order.

Defendant next challenges the constitutionality of section 112 of the Probate Act which provides the definition of an "incompetent" for purposes of that Act. Section 112, insofar as it is here pertinent, states that "An 'incompetent' under this Act includes any person who because of insanity, mental illness, mental retardation, old age, physical incapacity, or imperfection or deterioration of mentality, is incapable of managing his person or estate * * *." (Ill.Rev.Stat.1965, ch. 3, par. 112.) Defendant urges that the statute is vague, indefinite and uncertain; that the words "imperfection of mentality" have no ascertainable meaning; and that to appoint a conservator for a person who is found to be suffering from an "imperfection of mentality" deprives that person of the constitutional guarantees of due process of law under the State and Federal constitutions.

We do not concur with defendant's construction of the statute. This provision of the Probate Act is concerned with the appointment of a conservator for a person who for any of the reasons enumerated in the statute is incapable of managing his person or estate. The justification for the appointment of a conservator is founded primarily on the incapability of managing one's person or estate and not on the cause of that incapability. Thus, in the case before us, it is not the imperfection of mentality *per se* which would justify the appointment of a conservator, but rather the inability to manage one's estate due to such imperfection of mentality. When read in the context of the statute, the phrase "imperfection of mentality" is not vague, indefinite or uncertain. We are of the opinion that section 112 provides sufficiently definite and clear standards for men of ordinary intelligence to determine the competency of a person under the provisions of the Probate Act. The statute does not possess the constitutional infirmities which defendant suggests.

We do not agree with defendant's final contention that there was no evidence to justify the jury's findings of incompetency. Our examination of the record leads us to the conclusion that there was sufficient evidence to support the jury's verdict and to justify the appointment of a conservator for defendant's estate.

The judgment of the circuit court of Cook County is affirmed.

Judgment affirmed.

SUGGESTIONS FOR ADDITIONAL READING

Allen, Ferster, and Weihofen, *Mental Impairment and Legal Incompetency*. Englewood Cliffs, N.J.: Prentice-Hall, 1968.

Asch, S. *Mental Disability in Civil Practice*. Rochester, N.Y.: Lawyers Co-operative Pub. Co., 1973.

Brakel, S., and Rock, R. *The Mentally Disabled and the Law* (revised ed.). Chicago: University of Chicago Press, 1968.

Ferster, "The Law in Transition: Civil Incompetency in the District of Columbia," 16 *American University L. Rev.* 236 (1967).

Hodgson, R. "Guardianship of Mentally Retarded Persons: Three Approaches to a Long Neglected Problem," 37 *Albany Law Rev.* 407 (1973).

Lindman and McIntyre, eds. *The Mentally Disabled and the Law*. Chicago: University of Chicago Press, 1961.

Perr, I. "Statutory Rape of an Insane Person," 13 *J. of Forensic Sci.* 433 (October 1968).

Zenoff (Ferster). "Civil Incompetency in the District of Columbia," 32 *Geo. Wash. L. Rev.* 243 (1963).

Annotation: "Who May Make Election for Incompetent to Take Under or Against Will," 21 *ALR* 3rd 320, 1968.

Annotation: "Cross-Examination of Witness as to his Mental State or Condition, to Impeach Competency or Credibility," 44 *ALR* 3d 1203, 1972.

Annotation: "Validity and Application of Regulation Requiring Suspension or Disbarment of Attorney Because of Mental or Emotional Illness," 50 *ALR* 3d 1259, 1973.

12

Torts—Traumatic Neurosis

In our consideration of the law of torts, we have omitted the question of the liability of the mentally impaired tort-feasor, which is adequately covered in most elementary tort courses and textbooks. Generally, the law holds that as between two "innocent" persons (the "incompetent" and the person he has injured through his negligent or deliberate act) the necessary economic loss entailed in a tortious injury must be borne by the author of that injury; although his mental disability may be taken into account in determining the existence of "specific intent" or the propriety of "exemplary damages" in certain cases. In this chapter and the one to follow we have concentrated on what we believe to be the most difficult and significant areas of concern: the post-traumatic psychiatric syndrome, usually denominated by both lawyers and psychiatrists as "traumatic neurosis"; and "malpractice" in the rendition of psychiatric treatment.

Dr. Yochelson's and Dr. Modlin's articles are excellent descriptions of the phenomenon of "traumatic neurosis" and the difficulties of psychiatrists and lawyers in dealing with it. The Carter case and the two articles that follow it illustrate current trends in the law—with Workmen's Compensation in the vanguard—and the social-legal-psychiatric issues surrounding them.

TRAUMATIC NEUROSIS

Leon Yochelson, M.D.

The diagnosis, "traumatic neurosis," is used increasingly in civil litigation by physicians and lawyers. Paradoxically, this term has not been included in the *Diagnostic and Statistical Manual of Mental Disorders* (American Psychiatric Association, 1968).* This seemingly strange state of affairs is made somewhat more comprehensible by the fact that, for the most part, the diagnostic manual lists the categories of emotional and mental disorder primarily by the predominance and quality of *symptoms* (anxiety, phobia, depression, etc.) rather than with particular reference to *etiology*. In contrast, the term "traumatic neurosis" would imply that trauma of some sort is the causal (etiologic) factor of the neurosis.

To compound the problem there have been a variety of additional diagnostic labels associated with the term "traumatic neurosis," such as "accident neurosis," "compensation neuro-

sis," "compensationitis," and the like. Such terms at times carry pejorative connotations by the diagnostician, be he attorney or physician, with the implication that the plaintiff deliberately complains of disability only as long as he has something to gain, particularly financially. In many years of studying people who have at some point sustained injuries with subsequent anxiety and who consequently have come to psychiatric examination, I have been impressed by the rather infrequent occurrence of malingering which could be diagnosed psychiatrically with assurance. As a gross generalization, nonmedical investigators may have more to offer by way of proving malingering than do the psychiatrists. In instances where the physician suspects malingering but has no clearcut proof of such, a useful way of responding is to state that the complaining person has no psychiatric diagnosis. Indeed, for the most part, I have been impressed by the genuiness of the complainer's attitudes,

* See Chapter 3, supra.

even though in many cases, the casual observer might jump to the conclusion that the plaintiff was consciously motivated only by financial gain and therefore fabricated or exaggerated his pains.

In a number of informal discussions with physicians and lawyers, I have encountered important biases concerning "traumatic neurosis." These include the assumption, if not the conviction, that the claimant is motivated only for financial gain and that claimants are by and large malingerers. Just the opposite of bias is that the injured party is the victim of a gigantic commercial and insurance conspiracy to deprive him of his due; behind this is the implication that "they (the insurance carrier) can afford it anyway." This biased attitude often is based on a genuine compassion for the injured party, who is seen as the underdog, an exploited David struggling against the Goliath insurance company, an attitude intensified particularly when the claimant is under considerable financial strain. It goes without saying that to perform the highest quality examination, the psychiatrist must be ever alert to the possibility of such biases in himself. To neglect this may well result in the psychiatrist eventually being known as "a plaintiff's doctor" or as "a defendant's doctor."

Should a neurotic condition be present, the diagnosis should conform with the *Diagnostic and Statistical Manual of Mental Disorders.* For the most part, these would include the neuroses (anxiety, hysterical, conversion, dissociative, phobic, obsessive, compulsive, depressive, neurosthenic, depersonalization, hypochondriacal), psychophysiological reactions, and occasionally psychoses. That is to say, a traumatic neurosis usually develops in an individual already vulnerable to varying psychological reactions when exposed to additional stress. It is likely that the stronger or healthier the pretraumatic personality, the greater the intensity of the trauma necessary to produce a significant adverse psychological result. Conversely, it is likely that the greater the vulnerability of the personality, the less intense the injury needs to be in order to produce an adverse psycyological reaction. It follows that the more vulnerable the preexisting personality, the greater care must be taken in the evaluation of the large number of possible causal factors that might be present, any of which could produce identical symptoms. Often, I have heard from those in the legal profession that "one has to take the client as he is" (that is to say, should a vulnerable person be exposed ot injury, whatever psychological reaction ensues should be considered a reaction to the trauma). The usual example given is the story of the "last straw which broke the camel's back." In this situation, the camel had a "weak back" (analogous to the psychologically vulnerable quality in a client), so that the owner always took precautions to give him a fairly light load (analogous to the vulnerable person's due care not to expose himself to additional stress). A culprit enters the picture (analogous to the party causing the client some injury) and puts an extra straw on the camel, resulting in a broken back. Officially, greater interest is placed upon the last straw as the proximate cause of the damage the camel sustained, and lesser attention is paid to the preexistent vulnerable factors (i.e., the load of straws already on the camel's back).

The aforementioned example may be the cause of simplistic thinking and inadequate legal decision unless the situation is examined with utmost thoroughness. Continuing with the analogy: because the moment the "last straw" is added, pain followed immediately, it may be inaccurate to assume (a) that the back indeed was broken and (b) that if indeed there was a fracture, the extra straw was the cause. The benevolent owner of our weak-backed camel may not have known, for example, that his camel had some other condition, such as a cyst in a leg bone, which caused the camel to stumble *as though* his back had been broken; the extra strain (straw) in this case was coincidental in time with, but not causal to, the stumbling and to the painful back. More accurate reference would be to the straw that *allegedly* made the camel *feel* as though his back were broken. Thus, in the effort to give expert opinion as to the relationship between trauma and alleged resultant symptoms, it is extremely important that various aspects of the client's life be studied in detail. Even when the extra straw causes a fracture, note should be made that there are many instances on record wherein the complainant, in all sincerity, attributed his symptoms to the straw, not realizing that certain coincidental factors were more relevantly related to the appearance of his symptoms. It is all too human for a person to attribute his anxieties and pains to external causes rather than to his own internal problems.

Modlin,* in the diagnosis of the traumatic neurosis syndrome, concluded that the following symptoms are observed frequently: anxiety, muscular tension, insomnia, repetative frightening dreams, and irritability and withdrawal from any kind of situation that the patient anticipates would increase his anxiety. Modlin sees these as expressions of a person to a frightening or life-threatening external

---

* See: "The Trauma in Traumatic Neurosis," by Herbert Modlin, infra (Ed.).

stress, particularly when the patient has had little or no warning before the injury, effectively depriving him of the opportunity to muster those defense mechanisms which could have alleviated the emotional impact of that stressful situation. As Freud put it, the person is forcefully reminded of his helplessness. Modlin's concept is valuable, but the reader is cautioned, as Modlin himself points out, that any number of stresses might cause the same symptoms, and that the term "traumatic neurosis" specifies and overemphasizes one factor of stress with the resultant understatement of other stresses and of the individual organism's propensity for "breakdown."

A not uncommon presenting statement of the claimant could be paraphrased as, "I was perfectly well and never had a sick day in my life until the accident of such and such date and from that minute on, I have been a complete nervous wreck and have not been able to do anything." Such a gross generalization indeed merits considerable investigation both medically and legally. From the psychiatrist's point of view such a profound degree of incapacity from trauma alone is validated only occasionally. As we will illustrate later, the opposite presentation may also occur. Here the patient, severely psychically injured, presents little by way of complaint because of the severity of the psychic damage already present. In order to evaluate both these presentations, ancillary information should be obtained whenever possible from medical records, attorney, relatives, friends, school, and employers.

Under ordinary, uncomplicated, and healthy circumstances, the effect of a stressful situation or injury is time-limited. Not infrequently, however, an extremely long-lasting effect is present, a phenomenon which demands that we turn our attention to the psychiatric concepts of "primary and secondary gain." *Primary gain* refers to an advantage accruing to a person when his symptoms offer a symbolic solution to a neurotic problem. A "paralyzed" arm thus "solves" the problem of the fear of striking someone, since no direct action can be taken. In contrast, assume, for example, that a person under emotional pressures of one sort or another reacts with elevated blood pressure (hypertension). The elevation of the blood pressure is a *result* of his emotional state and does not solve any emotional conflict in a basic or *primary* way. Therefore, if our patient's conflict has to do with whether or not to permit the release of certain aggressive feelings, the elevated blood pressure in itself offers no direct solution to the conflicts. However, there may accrue to him a kind of benefit known as *secondary gain*, as a consequence of

the medical or surgical attention he may receive as a result of the hypertension. The recognition of being ill, invalided, and the recipient of treatment, diverts his attention away from the basic conflict of his aggressive feelings, effectively removing from his or anyone else's expectations that he will identify his emotional problem, study it, stand up to it, and solve it. We may generalize and say that such a situation may cause symptoms of *any kind* (i.e., not just hypertension), resulting in the patient's insistent complaints that he is unable to work and is now in a state of invalidism. Invalidism is the price he pays for the privilege of not facing the problems that caused the high blood pressure in the first place. Sometimes the client presents a combination of primary and secondary gain. A young matron some months following a very minor back strain found herself subject to most uncomfortable backaches when she was approached by first her husband and then by her lover. A series of interviews brought to light a background of rather strict morality, which was quite in contrast to her exterior blasé, "sophisticated" manner. For a number of reasons she detested the conventional aspects of her life and was unwilling to assume the kind of moral life for which she had been trained. Her "compromise" was to maintain the myth to herself of her sophistication by arranging sexual encounters. She responded to her early moral training, however, by abstaining from the actual intimacy "because of a most painful back." She could tell herself, "I want to (have sex), and would if I could, but I cannot because of my back." In this situation she had achieved a primary gain in that an emotional conflict was "solved." The neurotic quality of the "solution" was evident in that it deprived her of a healthy sexual adjustment. Also, *secondary gain* took the form of solicitude from her husband and lover. In her particular case it was observed that the two gentlemen did not remain fountains of sympathy for very long.

Physicians have observed in cases of approximately equal severity that one human being appears to surrender completely to his incapacity and become an invalid, whereas another will fight and struggle to heroic dimensions ni order to achieve more independent status. Fortunately, the knowledge of medical psychology has progressed to the point where we may go beyond such generalizations as "motivation." (It goes without saying that there are other factors, such as constitutional and genetic ones, which have tremendously important bearings on the fate of people following injury or illness.) Disheartening situations are likely to occur when a patient fails to respond to the best that medicine and surgery have to offer. In some of these situations the patient is said to have "no motivation," meaning that he fails to cooperate or that he does not want to get well. The concept of motivation regrettably has been clouded by lack of definition and consequent misuse. Often the term "motivation" is used to refer to a quality which a person either has or does not have. Actually, motivation exists in every patient in the sense that it is a posiitve force, used either in the effort to get well or in the conscious or unconscious effort to forestall recovery. Humans have within themselves certain urges, energies, or forces, of many of which they are totally unaware, directing or motivating certain people away from adequate function and toward a degree of invalidism. On a conscious level of experience, a person may exaggerate and dramatize his illness for the purpose of some secondary gain, such as sympathy or money. A greater number of individuals, in whom the motivation process is on the unconscious rather than on the conscious level, may find themselves reacting to a minor injury with an attitude of complete invalidism for the purpose of accruing gain (primary) of which they are not aware. The expression "he doesn't want to get well" could be rephrased more accurately "he wants not to get well." A few are aware of this feeling and may clearly state the wish to remain ill or to die. Most, however, consciously wish to regain health and so state (often too protestingly), in contrast to the deeper unconscious wish for invalidism and the advantages accruing therefrom. The therapeutic challenge to both attorney and physician is to channel energies so that what is negative (pro-invalidism) motivation may be shifted to positive (pro-health) motivation.

The physician is often confronted by a patient who, because of certain personality qualities and defense mechanisms, makes the interviewing process an exceedingly arduous one. A common method is for the patient to avoid certain central subject material, insisting it is not relevant, while at the same time persisting in bringing up tangential subject matter. The following dialogue, between a physician and his patient, is totally without subtlety and is not an infrequent state of affairs. The patient had consulted her physician following an accident. Despite extremely competent medical and surgical evaluation, she persisted in her complaints, despite assurance that she was well. On occasion, such chronic complaints serve as the patient's unconscious statement to the environment that something (in the patient's life) is importantly wrong. Her physician changed

his tactics, and instead of continuing a multitude of already oft repeated studies began to study *the way* the patient complained rather than devoting further time to the complaints themselves. In the next visit, the patient was allowed to go through her usual repetitive complaining of terrible back pain, but only briefly, and then was asked what she thought caused her difficulty.

PATIENT: Something is growing there. I can feel it.

DOCTOR: What do you think it is?

PATIENT: I don't know. Maybe you can't see it because it is still too small, but it's causing pressure and pain.

DOCTOR: But the x-rays and all your studies fail to show that there is anything there. What do you think is causing your trouble?

PATIENT: You told me the x-ray doesn't show anything, but isn't it true that x-rays sometimes don't show everything? You keep asking me what I think it is. I'm sure it's a tumor, probably a cancer. You just don't want to tell me.

DOCTOR: No, that is not so. I would tell you if there were anything wrong.

PATIENT: Then you are telling me that there is nothing wrong. Every doctor I have visited says there is nothing wrong, but I tell you I can feel something there. Are you going to tell me there is nothing wrong just like all the other doctors?

DOCTOR: No, I am not telling you there is nothing wrong. Actually, I think there is something wrong, but it is not your back. Something else is bothering you, perhaps some worry.

PATIENT: There is nothing wrong at all except my back. Don't you try to tell me I have any trouble with my husband. I have accepted him very well.

DOCTOR: Your husband? What about him?

PATIENT: He never talks to me, that's all. But I tell you that he has nothing to do with my back. Can't you see that my back hurts so much I can't even bend over? (*starts to demonstrate*)

DOCTOR: Yes, but tell me more about your husband.

PATIENT: Well, I have complained to him that he never talks to me. He said I should not expect him to talk to me because he was a traveling man for a long time, had to eat in hotels, so he is not in the habit of talking during meals, but I tell you, doctor, I have learned to accept him. Don't you understand that it is my back that is the trouble and not my husband?

The physician was able to experience and note the patient's rigidity of complaints. She engaged in extensive protestation that her marriage was just fine, at the same time revealing a good deal of dissatisfaction with her lot. She was persuaded to have a psychiatric consultation through the firm persistence of the orthopedist that there was indeed something wrong, but that endless reexamination of her back alone would not yield the results she desired. With this excellent preparation by the orthopedist, the psychiatrist was able to continue the interview in a similar vein and learned that there had been an insidiously growing difficulty in the patient's marriage. It became evident that the husband had responded to the patient's increasingly domineering tendencies by withdrawal and silence. His tactics had left the patient disarmed, helpless, and without a worthy opponent to battle. Her tensions had taken the form of a fixation on her back, an area frequently symbolic of conflicts over strength and dominance. The patient's rigidity and a belief that cancer was present amounted to a delusional system, as seen in severe hypochondriasis. The prognosis for cure of this condition was regrettably poor, but it was not hopeless as far as improvement was concerned. In this particular instance, treatment of both the patient and her husband resulted in a sufficient mellowing of personality traits in each so as to permit them at least a tolerable accommodation. Correspondingly, there was a reduction in the intensity of her back symptoms. Had the total focus of medical attention remained on the bodily symptoms, and had the assumption been that the accident was totally responsible for those symptoms, the outlook for improvement would have been exceedingly poor.

The following case illustrates a preexistent neurosis aggravated by a life-endangering complication to a severe injury:

Mr. A, a middle-aged married executive was struck a glancing blow by a heavy truck as he was standing near a loading platform in conference with a colleague. He sustained an exceedingly serious compound comminuted fracture of a leg, was hospitalized immediately and appeared to adjust reasonably well to the multiple orthopedic procedures required over a period of some months. After an extended hospital stay, he was driven home, looking forward to getting back to his office soon. As he started up the stairs to his room, he was seized with excruciating pain in the chest and was filled with a terrifying apprehension that he was about to die. He was returned to the hospital immediately and found to have pulmonary emboli (obstruction to the main blood vessels of the lungs). After a lengthy critical period at death's door he survived. Following this latter event, symptoms of anxiety and depression he had known about a decade previously returned. De-

tailed psychological study failed to reveal the presence of any other current factors pertinent to his reaction. Rather, his chronic sense of inadequacy and feelings of depression (which he had overcome in the decade prior to the accident) had increased when the unexpected thought of his own death brought into awareness some of the ancient hostilities (death wishes) toward loved ones.

The next clinical example illustrates the use by a well-meaning but inadequate personality of a nondamaging situation to explain his symptoms:

Mr. B was a 60-year-old salesman, who while putting a small carton in his stationary automobile was mildly jostled when his car was struck a glancing blow by a vehicle in the process of parking. Since then (now lasting for about two years) he has felt unable to work because of pain on the left side of his head "which moves to the left arm and the left leg." He has felt "nervous," by which he meant "shakey inside" and that his "head thumped." He also complained of a difficulty in concentrating following his "accident"; for example, one day he decided to stop work early to return home, only to find that he had unwittingly driven himself to a race track (which he had occasionally visited). His general attitude was that his "life was fine" until the accident. However, detailed scrutiny of his history revealed that he had been a chronically complaining and anxious individual, not marrying until his late 40's after his parents were no longer on the picture (he needed someone to look after him). He also had a poor occupational adjustment, with frequent changes of work and marginal income, despite his statement that he had earned "a very good living." As he identified the many failures in his life, his standard reaction was to attribute each failure to some circumstance in his environment, avoiding a healthier self-scrutiny. Continuing examination revealed his reluctance to face his marital problems squarely. To do so, of course, would have risked his sacrificing his passive dependency upon his wife. A somewhat stronger personality, in exploring that aspect of his life, would have initiated a significant improvement in his symptoms. In summary, his symptoms and life adjustment were absolutely no different following the "accident" than they had been for many years previously.

The case of Mrs. C exemplifies the presence of psychological symptoms following an accident and their successful treatment, but the inaccurate attribution of the return of symptoms to the accident:

Mrs. C had been a passenger in an automobile driven by her son. She was amnesic for the details of the accident and "came to" in a hospital emergency room. General bruising and a fine-line fracture of the skull were discovered. Symptoms included headaches and back pain. With treatment she improved gradually during the following two to three months. About six months following the accident, Mrs. C was hospitalized because of an agitated state which was attributed to the aforementioned accident. Detailed psychiatric examinations revealed that after recovery from the accident she suffered the loss by death of a relative. Her husband's alcoholic tendencies and the chronic illness of one of her children prevented her from obtaining the emotional support she needed during that crisis. In addition, scrutiny of her life history revealed chronic anxieties and exaggerated guilt feelings associated with her mother's excessive domination. To make matters worse, the mother decided to move close to Mrs. C's home "to help out." In this case, Mrs. C had demonstrated improvement of the direct sequelae of her accident. Later on she required extensive psychiatric help, but for personal matters precipitated by factors unrelated to the accident.

The case of Mr. D illustrates the reluctance of the patient to view his life broadly and objectively, as well as the influence of famliy circumstances and attitudes which increased his tendencies toward invalidism.

Mr. D was referred for psychiatric examination at the request of his defendant employer. He was accompanied by a relative who showed marked solicitude by helping him (holding his hand) from the waiting room into the consulting room. He gave no evidence of discomfort in remaining seated for the examination, which lasted two hours. He alleged that while pushing a hand truck up a ramp his leg slipped (unwitnessed), causing him to feel a twinge in the corresponding hip. He continued working the rest of his shift but by the next morning "my wife had to help me out of bed." With aspirin he reported back to work, but by the third day continuing pain resulted in examination by orthopedic specialists, who recommended a lumbo-sacral support. Though not part of his complaints, inquiry revealed he had been depressed and had lost about 20 pounds in the few weeks prior to his psychiatric examination. Mr. D complained that he is aware of "pain all the time" in his lower back and left hip, that despite the use of a bed board he awakens five or six times a night but that he had no recollection of dreams. He believed that his "nerves" were "a little above average" (i.e., he was a little tense), but he exhibited no tremors and gave no history of sensations of anxiety. He had been spending his time reading and watching television, fixing his own breakfast, driving his wife around and picking her up at work. He had been able to do this, he added, by the use of a contour seat and power appliances in his car. Weather permitting, he walked in front of his apartment building and spent time chatting with neighbors, but felt he could not work, even with retraining opportunities.

Psychiatric history revealed a somewhat unstable adolescence and an irregular work history which the patient, despite his intelligence, was unable or unwilling to explain. One sibling had "a bad back" and another had been involved in an auto accident for which a settlement was made

for "whiplash." The patient had lost several relatives by death around the time of his own unwitnessed accident, and he grieved particularly over the loss by accident of a particularly beloved one. This last item was far more traumatic than the alleged accident and a much more relevant cause of his symptoms. His claim of invalidism was a kind of partial dying, a depressive reaction unrelated to "the accident."

There has been an assumption that litigants recovering substantial settlements following negligence trials quickly "get well" and return to effective work. Psychiatric experience does not bear out this assumption. It may be stated as a generalization that when the claimant rigidly misidentifies the etiology of his symptoms and insists that his psychiatric disability is based on physical trauma, the psychological symptoms will continue. So long as he misidentifies the cause(s) of his difficulties, so long will his symptoms continue.

There appears to be general agreement that the slower the process of litigation, the more likely it is for psychological complaints to continue.

Most people subject to injury with no (or only a few seconds) preparation, suffer a high degree of fright, ranging in severity from mild fear up to a panic state. It is undestandable that the dramatic quality of the accident, together with the intensity of the emotional reaction to it, encourages the sufferer to assume that whatever (other) difficulties are present in his life are due to the accident. The following case illustrates a patient's unwitting utilization of a minor accident to explain her difficulty, and of the subsequent great improvement when the valid cause for her psychiatric symptoms was identified.

Mrs. E was referred for psychiatric examination by her attorney when she related to him that following an auto accident she not only sustained a "whiplash" but also had very "shaky nerves." This, she explained, was the result of her car being struck (mildly) from behind while waiting for a signal light to change. Inquiry was made into her activities the day of the accident and it evolved that she had (just prior to the accident) visited another attorney's office where she had been notified that her divorce papers were finalized. Feelings of anxiety and depression were already being experienced in the attorney's office. With a good deal of grief, Mrs. E described her feelings of guilt at having accepted her chronically ill husband's pressure for a divorce so that she might have a fuller and freer life. She had felt a sense of disloyalty to him, although their unique circumstances made it clear to her that his judgment was sound. As she described this situation she spontaneously and emotionally stated that her personal problem had much more to do with her state of "nervousness" than did the accident and that she would instruct her attorney to make claim only for whatever damages there were to her automobile and for the examination and x-rays immediately following the accident. It has been of interest to note that her symptoms subsided quickly and that about three years later Mrs. E remarried, apparently successfully, as her annual Christmas notes to the doctor indicate. Mrs. E's self-honesty was her most valuable therapeutically.

Despite the fairly strong tradition that claims for psychic damages have not been very successful in the absence of physical injury, recently there appears to be a growing incidence of cases in which psychic damages are claimed in the absence of physical injury. Examples of such situations include claims of psychic injury over witnessing injury to someone else, alleged adverse effects upon mental health by housing discrimination, claim of cancerphobia at a physician's mention that cancer can be a complication of skin radiation, and the like.

The case of Mrs. F illustrates the effect upon the emotional life of an individual faced with sudden and spectacular danger or harm, but without actual impact or tissue injury.

Two years prior to her first psychiatric interview, while she was at home with her children one afternoon, a storm caused large tree branches to brush against overhead electric wires nearby. This resulted in a considerable degree of sparking and noises of such magnitude that they were heard by neighbors some blocks away. Despite her great fear, she functioned well during the several hours she and her children were captive in the house and it did not take her long to get over the panic she had experienced during this dramatic episode. Some months later, nothing having been done about the proximity of tree branches and wires, a similar situation occurred a half block from her home. Following this, she began to experience very frequent doubts as to the safety of her children and herself whenever the possibility of a storm arose. She was reassured somewhat by the prospect that she and her husband would be able to move into a new residence. A third episode of "wires buzzing and cracking off and on throughout the night, finally falling into the street" caused her tension to increase to the point that even when a storm was only suspected she would feel panicky. She would try to maintain a calm exterior while arranging to take the children out of their home on some pretext to shop or visit friends. This phobic reaction diffused and she found herself anticipating storms, listening carefully to weather broadcasts, and increasing the time she and the children were away from home even when the weather was clear. Her sleep became interrupted by nightmares of electrical wires falling. She became jumpy when exposed to anything unexpected, particularly noise. Domestic tension occurred as she became increasingly dependent upon her husband. There was some

improvement when her family was finally able to move, but the fear of electrical wires, even in calm weather, persisted, making travel difficult.

Mrs. F's early life was very family-oriented, with a history of only one childhood phobia. In Mrs. F's instance, predisposing personality vulnerability was fairly minor. She had previously made a good occupational adjustment, a fairly solid marital adjustment, accepted the challenge of several dramatic, fearful, life-endangering episodes. She very willingly entered psychiatric treatment.

The genuiness of complaints presented by a claimant is often suspect and is in part explained by our general culture, in which great emphasis is placed upon money, and the consequent suspicion that anyone's motive in entering the courtroom is solely monetary. It should be kept in mind, however, that some people's motivation is only secondarily financial. With some individuals the primary motivation for litigation is to achieve a sense of self-justification, even a feeling of righteousness, that whatever difficulties or invalidism exist are present not because of difficulties in coping with life's problems but rather due to some event, such as an accident, coincidental with those problems. In the following case of Mrs. G, a sense of pride far outweighed financial considerations.

Mrs. G was married, childless, highly regarded assistant to a caterer, who upon finishing an assignment at a client's home waited in the rain to be picked up by her husband. After a lengthy interval, she walked to the corner for a bus. While waiting near the curb, her umbrella-holding hand was brushed by an automobile passing very close to the curb. She slipped, fell, and was immediately taken to a nearby hospital by the concerned driver of the vehicle. Bruising and muscle strain were diagnosed and her convalescence proved uneventful. She was discharged in two days, but then returned to the hospital after another two or three days in a state of such severe emotional depression that extensive psychiatric treatment was necessary. Diagnosis of "traumatic neurosis" was made on the basis that the patient had been well until the moment of the accident. It was assumed that her depression was just as much the result of the accident as were her bruises and muscle strains. More detailed psychiatric interviewing revealed much that she had not shared with her attorney or doctors previously, even during the time she was receiving extensive psychiatric treatment. The following sequence of events elicited during the additional interview proved illuminating: Going back to the aforementioned time when she had finished her catering assignment and waited for her husband, it was learned that she had been quite crestfallen and disappointed at her husband "standing her up" and failing to call for her, particularly in such very rainy weather. It was then learned that once in the emergency room of the hospital following the brush with the automobile, she requested that her husband be notified. This was done by telephone in her presence and he nonetheless failed to come to the hospital immediately, or even to visit her the next day. Thirdly, prior to her discharge she had phoned him asking him to call for her when she was due to leave the hospital. He again failed her and she managed to get home by public transportation. On her return home (which was not unexpected) she encountered an openly amorous situation between her husband and another woman, a good friend of the patient. A severe depression quickly ensued, necessitating her hospitalization and rather urgent psychiatric treatment. Questioned as to why she had not revealed this information to the psychiatrist at the hospital, she acknowledged that pride and a sense of shame at her husband's activities had prevented her. She passively permitted the assumption that her mood was a psychiatric complication induced by the auto accident.

Attention to this situation not only resulted in just compensation for her bruises and strained muscles (not for the depressive mood) but also enabled the plaintiff and her husband to reexamine their relationship with profit to their marriage. Her experience in discussing the situation with the psychiatrist gave her the courage to insist upon a confrontation with her husband, resulting in an improved marital situation. If the plaintiff's depressive reaction had been compensated as caused by the auto accident, the plaintiff and her husband would have continued their domestic maladjustment, presumably to the point of even greater chaos.

Frequently the complainant is vigorous in describing his symptoms and what he believes is wrong with him. On occasion, however, quite the opposite is the case. The following case illustrates a situation in which the complainant (a 27-year-old house painter) was injured quite severely when as a pedestrian, he was struck by a car, approximately a year before the psychiatric examination. His medical records revealed a chronic dizziness and consequent inability to work on a scaffold. Medical and neurological examination revealed no explanation for the persistence of the symptom.

Throughout an extended interview, Mr. H responded to questions with casualness and with a marked tendency to gloss over what ultimately turned out to be major defects in memory. His manner was that of an individual trying to demonstrate that his memory was intact, that he was quite well, and that he had recovered from whatever injuries he had in the accident. (The tendency to conceal memory defects is not an uncommon defense mechanism against the emotional pain and anxiety aroused by diminished mental alertness and intellectual functioning.)

During the interview Mr. H stated that he had been in an auto accident, but only with great effort and slowness did he finally guess its date. He was able to remember that he and a girl friend had had dinner and were crossing the street to hail a taxi. He recalled a car hitting them without warning, his falling down, but then had no memory until he "came to" at a hospital. He minimized the length of time he was unconscious and appeared reluctant to confront the fact that he could not remember a number of details both before and after the accident. With further tedious questioning he recalled that he had several stitches on his head. Since then he felt "dizzy" (by which he meant that when he moved he had the sensation of his surroundings moving about him); he still experienced pain on the left side of his head and face. When asked the global question "How do you feel?" he responded that he was "all right"; a more detailed functional inquiry elicited, for example, that despite his initial statement that he was "sleeping OK," he had difficulty sleeping any length of time because of discomfort in the areas of injury. Similarly, when questioned about dreams he first casually stated that he did not have any, but then acknowledged that he had had very frequent dreams of the accident in which he was running but was unable to avoid being struck by a car.

Despite Mr. H's denials of any other changes, the functional inquiry revealed that since the accident he had been experiencing significantly less sexual desire, that he had weaker erections, and that he "dated" women much less. When asked how he explained these changes, he answered "maybe I am too old." When questioned about his mood, he related that when he was "dizzy" he tended to be sad, whereas prior to the accident he had "melancholy feelings" only as a very temporary response to some bit of bad news. In contrast, his feelings of depression since the accident have been more prolonged, a matter he correlated with the presence of pain in his head. He denied any suicidal preoccupation or activity. Further inquiry revealed that he had been troubled by two varieties of noise, one of machines or sirens making very loud sounds and the other of sudden and unexpected noise which caused a mild to moderate "jumping" (startle reaction).

At some point (his memory was deficient) he made an effort to return to work but became "dizzy," fell, and did not feel well enough to continue. When asked questions designed to determine his vulnerability to irritability he indicated that he found himself quickly angered when he thinks of what happened to him (i.e., the accident), and that he has been able to relax only by shifting his mind away from the subject.

During this examination, Mr. H did not show symptoms of gross anxiety. However, he looked somewhat depressed, some of the time appearing abstracted or bland. (Information from those who knew him prior to the accident described him as a lively, communicative, alert, and socially active individual). Occasionally an appearance of alertness became evident on his face when he was in a situation calling for automatic reactions, such as saying "hello" or "goodbye." There was no abnormal mental content, hallucinations, or delusions. His thinking tended to be concrete. For example, when asked to interpret the proverb of "people in glass houses should not throw stones" he responded with "I don't know whether one should throw stones."

He had suffered a combination of tissue damage to the brain* as well as the psychological consequences of "a traumatic neurosis." Memory was poor even a year following the accident. His level of anxiety had decreased somewhat as evidenced by the cessation of the recurrent traumatic nightmares and the diminishing of the startle reaction. It was not possible to state at the time of this examination whether there would be a continuing improvement of his memory difficulty and his personality change.

SUMMARY AND CONCLUSIONS

The psychiatric approach to traumatized patients is a multifaceted affair, including detailed study of the circumstances of the

* See criteria for diagnosis of organic brain syndrome in the APA *Diagnostic and Statistical Manual*, Chapter 3, supra (Ed.).

trauma, the context in which the trauma occurred, exploration of the pretrauma personality characteristics, previous manner of experiencing stress, the ability to tolerate unexpected apprehension-inducing situations, and the reactions of significant people. Social, medical, and legal biases should be noted in the interest of the utmost objectivity. Particular importance is placed upon the patient's mode of communication, his willingness to stay with central themes, or the rigid adherence to diversionary subject material. Care should be taken to distinguish those traumatic situations that produce psychiatric complications from other situations in which the injured party mistakenly attributes all of his life's problems to some injury. Between the extremes of this polarity are instances wherein previous problems are aggravated. These must be distinguished from those cases wherein after recovery from trauma, the claimant attributes to the injury symptoms which really derive from coincidental or post-accident problems.

THE TRAUMA IN "TRAUMATIC NEUROSIS"

Herbert C. Modlin, M.D.

If present trends continue, an increasing percentage of the psychiatrist's practice will include patients referred with a presumptive diagnosis of a nonorganic illness long designated "traumatic neurosis." The number of such cases seen at the Menninger Clinic in the past five years has shown a steady annual rise.

Several factors contribute to this development: In the first place, the law seems to have acquired, and entrenched, a diagnostic concept of traumatic neurosis and to have accorded it the status of an officially recognized illness, even though medicine does not. The concerted, multipronged campaign of recent years to eliminate the stigma of mental illness has achieved much deserved success; but one fruit of this humane labor is a multiplication of personal injury claims pressed on the grounds that psychiatric sequelae of automobile, home, public carrier, and industrial acci-

dents are as justly compensable as physical injuries.

In addition, American courts are handing down increasingly liberal interpretations that extend the scope of tort law and workmen's compensation laws and are allowing markedly more generous awards in personal injury claims. This makes the personal injury case an attractive field for some lawyers. It has been reliably estimated that (disregarding divorce actions) 75 per cent of cases now pending on the dockets of all courts in the land are personal injury suits—this in spite of the fact that industrial accident claims are now largely handled by workmen's compensation commissioners.

Also, the number of automobile accidents continues to mount. Statistics compiled by the Travelers' Insurance Company indicate that in 1958, 2,825,000 victims of automobile acci-

Reprinted with permission from the *Bulletin of the Menninger Clinic,* 24: 49–56; copyright 1960 by the Menninger Foundation.

dents were treated by physicians. This is roughly a 100 per cent increase in ten years. Many if not all of these accidents were in some degree psychologically disturbing to the victims. It thus becomes incumbent upon psychiatry to study experimental and experiential evidence of the so-called traumatic neurosis and to evaluate the present state of knowledge concerning its manifestations, genesis, and course.

On reviewing the literature one might conclude that we seem to be confused about the clinical and theoretical validity of this term. A neurosis is a neurosis, whatever the particular precipitating stress; and "traumatic neurosis" specifies and overemphasizes one factor of stress with resultant understatement of other stresses and of the individual organism's propensity for breakdown. Psychiatrists' clinical observations attest that a variety of stresses may activate approximately the same constellation of symptoms in a given person. On the official list of mental disorders published by the American Psychiatric Association (and also by the American Medical Association) traumatic neurosis is not authorized as an acceptable diagnosis. However, in the medical and especially in the legal literature "traumatic neurosis" has been used, and is still, to designate a variety of syndromes more or less related to accidents; regardless of whether these syndromes are classifiable more particularly as reactions of anxiety, depression, conversion, or serious disorganization not ordinarily called neurosis.

Contributing to our inconsistent and diverse opinions on traumatic neurosis is the personal bias of some psychiatrists toward these litigious patients and their legal claims. Many physicians—and psychiatrists not excepted—become well known to the attorneys of their communities as "plaintiffs' doctors" or "defendants' doctors," because of the emotionally charged, unscientific attitudes they reveal regarding personal injury suits.

A detailed analysis, including follow-up study, is currently being made of 40 patients referred to our clinic with the preliminary diagnosis of traumatic neurosis. This report from material of that study will be limited to one facet among the many that should be re-examined. It will not explore (1) predisposition to neurosis, (2) the psychosocial setting for the neurosis, (3) the effects of monetary gain upon the illness, (4) the course and treatment of the illness, and (5) the complications of a concomitant head injury. It is confined to a clinical analysis of the psychological stress factor in a single syndrome frequently seen following accidents. In this text the symptom picture will be called the traumatic neurosis syndrome. It includes these symptoms:

1. Anxiety, varying from mild apprehensiveness to panic.
2. Chronic muscular tension manifested by an inability to relax, tremor, restlessness, and insomnia.
3. Repetitive frightening dreams, reproducing directly or symbolically the traumatic incident.
4. Irritability, usually expressed at home, particularly regarding the children and their noise; there may be a startle reaction.
5. Withdrawal, or, to use Fenichel's term, traumatophobia—the avoidance of any experience that might increase excitation —most commonly expressed by loss of sexual interest, poor concentration and memory, avoidance of social contacts, intolerance of discussing symptoms or the traumatic event.

One-third of the patients among the 40 studies presented this syndrome in spite of dissimilarity of traumatic incidents and the variety of personality organizations among the patients. This suggests that the syndrome may be a fundamental, nonspecific, organismic reaction to severe external stress of a frightening or life-threatening kind. This particular coincidence of symptoms, with variations, has been described in the psychiatric literature since World War I. Clinical understanding of it, and related reactions called shell shock, combat exhaustion, and flight fatigue, has always been obscured by the multiple stresses peculiar to war conditions. Accounts of clinical studies, research projects, or even case reports from civilian practice are exceedingly rare in the literature pertaining to this subject. Since the facts of military psychiatry are not easily applicable, without verisimilitude, to the facts of peacetime psychiatric practice, it is unfortunate that most of our knowledge in this area was gleaned from wartime experience. Through study of the traumatic neurosis syndrome in civilian life, uncomplicated by bullets, bombs, foxholes, extreme cold and hunger, exhaustion, troop demoralization, and "Dear John" letters, we may gain clearer understanding of the basic, irreducible stresses and dynamics involved.

Lawyers, patients and their relatives, judges, juries, and doctors generally, seem puzzled by the appearance of incapacitating psychic sequelae to an accident in which the patient sustained little or no physical injury. In my own clinical observations of such patients, I have thus far tentatively identified two sets of circumstances operative in initiating the syndrome, in the first of which (illustrated by Cases A and B which follow) the patient-to-be experiences a brief forewarning of an impending disaster. As a most common example, a rider in an automobile realizes that a crash is imminent and in the few seconds before the impact contemplates his possible annihilation. In the second set of circumstances (Cases C and D), the accident occurs suddenly, unexpectedly, without forewarning. A common example is an industrial accident in which a construction worker is struck by a falling brick or a tool dropped from above him.

Case A—Twenty-nine-year-old Mrs. E. G. was riding one afternoon with her husband who was driving at 50 miles per hour along a highway. Upon reaching an intersection they struck a car which had entered the intersection from their right without observing a stop sign. As they had approached the crossing Mrs. E. G. clearly saw the other car, suddenly realized that it was not slowing to a stop. She was, for an instant, paralyzed with horror, and then began to scream. She was momentarily dazed by the collision, but was able to get out of the car without assistance.

When I saw her six months subsequently she had recovered from her physical injuries. She was chronically tense and regularly exhausted at the end of the day. By remaining quiet and in seclusion at home she avoided distressing feelings of apprehension and panic which had become her chief complaint about two months after the crash. She even severed contact with her neighbors, previously an important part of her day. She had lost her sense of humor and had become hypersensitive. When her husband teased her in his usual fashion, she frequently burst into tears. The insomnia of the first few months had improved, but she still had occasional, brief dreams of a large, black car hurtling toward her. Sexual relations with her husband had been resumed after a three months' moratorium although she had not regained her former enthusiasm.

Case B—A 36-year-old traveling salesman was driving with his wife in a strange town at dusk. His car stalled as he was crossing some railroad tracks and, in attempting to restart it, he flooded the engine. While waiting for the engine to drain, he suddenly noticed a locomotive rolling slowly toward him. He gripped the wheel and stared in terror for perhaps ten seconds before the engine struck the car, dragged it along the tracks, then shoved it to one side. Physically, he suffered only bruised ribs; psychologically he was seriously shaken. His wife was not hurt.

Immediately following the accident he was

so uneasy, weak, and disorganized that his wife persuaded him they should stay in the town four days before starting the 200 mile trip home. Six months afterward he came to us. He was apprehensive, frightened, insecure, and seeking in all directions for help. He complained of difficulty in concentration and memory, was emotionally sensitive and tearful, sexually impotent, and withdrawn from all social contacts. He had tried to resume his job but had been discharged for incompetence.

In the light of current psychodynamic theory, the pathological reaction to stress in Cases A and B seems explicable as follows: Facing definable external danger the organism mobilized for emergency action. On the physiological level, the fight-flight mechanism operates automatically, through the autonomic nervous system and the consciously controlled skeletal musculature, to equip the organism for attack to reduce the source of danger or destroy it; or to retreat to lessen the threat or avoid it entirely. If, however, as in the two instances just cited, action either toward or away from a threatened destruction is blocked, if the protective fight-flight mechanism has time to become mobilized but cannot operate, then the mental apparatus is suffused with an excessive amount of stimulation. On the psychological level, the alarm devices of the ego have kept pace with the physiological alerting. The normal ego has quantities of energy available to bind or discharge excessive amounts of excitation; but if the discharge route is blocked, and homeostatic balance is disrupted, free-floating anxiety and continuing tension result.

Several of our cases seem to have evolved from the differing second set of precipitating circumstances. The end result, the traumatic neurosis syndrome, as the next two cases (C and D) show is the same, but some of the psychic mechanisms involved are not.

Case C—A 45-year-old married man had for 25 years been a truck and construction equipment driver. He was a dependable worker, sought after by local contractors, and had been steadily employed. He was last hired as a driver of an earth mover on the midnight-to-morning shift. After dumping one load of dirt he did not notice that the now empty truck body had not fallen entirely back down to its horizontal position but remained caught, projecting slightly above the top of the truck's cab. He was driving along a temporary road at 35 miles per hour when the edge of the elevated truck body struck a low railroad bridge. In the crash, heard a quarter-mile away, the steel bridge was so buckled that trains had to be rerouted.

His first awareness of an accident came five

minutes later when he regained consciousness to find himself lying on the seat of the cab with his feet out the window. When I examined him two months later, he presented nearly every symptom of a traumatic neurosis syndrome: anxiety, panic attacks, severe tension, insomnia, nightly dreams in which he drove his earth mover into a blank wall, irritability, startle reaction, loss of sexual interest, avoidance of people, difficulty in concentration, and complete refusal to get into a wheeled vehicle.

Case D involves a domestic accident. Mrs. C. L., 40 years of age, lived in one side of a duplex with her husband and son. One night at 3:00 A.M. while the family slept, the gas furnace exploded. The son was blown against a wall; Mr. C. L. was propelled through the front door; both sustained fractured arms. A woman living in the other side of the duplex was killed and her husband badly injured. Mrs. C. L. received a fracture-dislocation of the hip and a triple fracture at the ankle. These injuries ultimately healed but she remained psychologically ill. She became my patient two years after the accident. She was tense, tremulous, apprehensive, restless, sensitive to noises, cried readily, experienced poor concentration, loss of interest and ambition, persistent insomnia, and typical repetitive dreams of an exploding light bulb, and could not stand to be around people.

In this set of circumstances, suggested as operative in initiating the syndrome, the essential feature of the traumatic incident is its completely unexpected suddenness. Each patient in these representative cases (C and D) first became aware that an accident had occurred when he regained consciousness after the fact. Realistic external danger no longer existed to be met and handled. The fight-flight mechanism probably was temporarily mobilized but found no substantial target to act against. Action was not necessarily blocked; it was irrelevant. One immediate task the ego must accomplish in such situations is to regain its suddenly disrupted contact with reality and to grasp and justify what has just happened. The bewildered ego is flooded with alarm and anxiety because it has failed in its self-preservative duty; perception of external reality is a basic organism-protecting function of the ego. It constantly sifts, judges, and disposes of the stream of incoming stimuli; it anticipates sources and quantities of possible excitation and, leaning on past experience and tested adaptive devices, prepares in advance to meet possible influxes of excitation in order to maintain the homeostatic balance of the organism at a tenable level of tension.

An additional component of such situations

as just illustrated is that jeopardy occurs in familiar and presumably safe surroundings. The victim recognizes possible hazard (falling from a height, breakdown of machinery, errors of fellow humans, "acts of God"), but his accustomed experience without serious injury, and his own self-protective dexterity acquired through routine precautionary practices and automatic response to danger signals (whether in walking a scaffold or driving a car in congested traffic), have lulled his natural sense of peril into a private feeling of personal immunity to calamity. Thus reassured, his psychological guard is down and he is maximally vulnerable to psychic assault.

In our medical jargon are many descriptive handles—retirement neurosis, compensation neurosis, Sunday neurosis, fate neurosis, traumatic neurosis—and we rarely consider seriously using these terms as true diagnostic labels. Each of them denotes a partial truth in emphasizing a particular environmental component of the patient's life or a particular reactionary attitude of the patient toward an aspect of his environment. Neurotic symptoms, however, are more a function of the reacting organism than a signification of an external stress; and most neurotic syndromes reveal, in their symbolic symptomatology, specific ego weakness in the sick individual. The traumatic neurosis syndrome may be an exception to this generally held formulation in that it appears nonspecific in terms of psychosexual development. It has been called an "ego neurosis," to differentiate it from the classical "id neurosis." This is not to advocate adding, at present, another term to our diagnostic list, since for classification purposes, anxiety reaction seems an adequate label for the syndrome.

A number of recent developments in the personal injury arena indicate that psychiatrists and lawyers are and will be having increased interprofessional contact. Ninety per cent of our patients with some form of post-accident psychiatric disability were referred to our clinic by lawyers. There is considerable agreement among students and exponents of behavioral science that the law sorely needs the psychiatrists' expert help in arriving at a just disposition of these civil suits. Since the medical expert's evidence largely determines the outcome of personal injury litigation, should we not look for occasion to contribute the insights of dynamic psychiatry to the education of the law and to its possible modification through its having gained a more scientific understanding of human behavior?

Should not a physician view his every contact with a lawyer and his every appearance in court or before a workmen's compensation commissioner as a potential opportunity to instruct as well as to present medical testimony? This is a challenge to our skill in communicating across professional borders. Should not questions on both direct and cross-examination be answered fully, with as detailed explanations as can be appropriately inserted, rather than with just a "Yes" or "No"? Even though lawyers request a "Yes" or "No" answer, the expert witness is not obliged to give it and, in the interest of making his meaning clear and accurate, he sometimes should not give it.

We should try in presenting clearly what we know, to be equally definite and honest about what we do not yet know. Thus we can constructively serve the law and our patients involved with the law, not by becoming amateur lawyers or lawyers' psychiatrists, but by developing professional poise which is the hallmark of conviction born of knowledge and experience, and confidence born of integrity and purpose, and authority that we ourselves have assessed.

Concerning traumatic neurosis—that inexact, jargonish, but hard-to-get-rid-of phrase—we need to reexamine our concepts, gained mostly from military experience, with special reference to the psychological trauma in an accident which triggers the illness. This paper offers for consideration a suggestion, based on observed data and applied theory, that two sets of circumstances are identifiable as commonly precipitative to a traumatic neurosis syndrome. Future studies should explore other important facets of this characteristic human reaction to sudden, external danger.

CARTER v. GENERAL MOTORS CORPORATION

Ordinarily, compensation under our workmen's compensation act is awarded for incapacity to work because of the crushing of a hand or foot, the inhalation of silicotic dust, or other similar injury arising out of and in the course of employment. Benefits are not awarded for the injury as such, but rather for the loss of earning capacity. Hence, even this Michigan Court, years ago, recognized the right of a claimant under the act to compensation for loss of such earning capacity caused by a mental or emotional disability resulting from a physical injury to claimant or even resulting from observing a physical injury to a fellow employee of claimant. In due course we shall examine the authorities so holding, including decisions of this Court made venerable by age and by the compelling logic of their reasoning, for it is upon those past decisions of this Court that our decision in this case is firmly planted. Our decision is that workmen's compensation benefits are payable for incapacity to work because of a claimant's paranoid schizophrenia arising out of and in the course of employment.

Plaintiff had worked as a machine operator for defendant, General Motors Corporation, with intermittent layoffs, since 1953. On October 8, 1956, he was recalled to work after a 5-month layoff and worked for 4 days on a "brace job" and then was transferred on October 12th to a "hub job." This operation required him to take a hub assembly (consisting of a case and cover) from a nearby fellow employee's table to his own workbench, remove burrs with a file and grind out holes in the assembly with a drill, and place the assembly on a conveyor belt. Plaintiff was unable to keep up with the pace of the job unless he took 2 assemblies at a time to his workbench, and he feared another layoff should he prove unable satisfactorily to do the work. He was instructed repeatedly by his foreman not to take 2 assemblies at a time because the assembly parts became mixed up on the conveyor belt when he did so. However, plaintiff continued having trouble "getting on to the job" as it was supposed to be performed. Thus, when he took only 1 hub assembly at a time, he fell behind; when he fell behind, he took 2 assemblies; but, when he took 2 assemblies, he got the assemblies mixed up and was berated by the foreman.

We are told that the dilemma in which plain-

Supreme Court of Michigan, 361 Mich. 577, 106 N.W.2d 105 (1960).

tiff found himself resulted on October 24, 1956, in an emotional collapse variously described as paranoid schizophrenia and schizophrenic reaction, residual type. He was subsequently hospitalized for a period of 1 month, during which time he received shock therapy. In July of 1957, he filed an application for hearing and adjustment of claim for compensation under the workmen's compensation act.

It should be noted that there is not involved in this case a psychosis resulting from a single fortuitous event nor is there involved a psychosis resulting from a direct physical blow to plaintiff's body. Instead, there is involved a psychosis claimed to be the result of emotional pressures encountered by plaintiff daily in the performance of his work.

The referee entered an award of workmen's compensation for a disability described as "traumatic neurosis, traumatic psychosis, functional disability and sequelae thereof." The workmen's compensation appeal board, by a divided vote, affirmed the award for total disability from October 24, 1956, until January 7, 1957, plus reimbursement for medical and hospital care. The appeal board, in addition, allowed to plaintiff continuing compensation from and after January 7, 1957.

Pertinent quotations from the 3 opinions filed by members of the appeal board follow:

1. Chairman McLaughlin:

. . . Plaintiff sustained a personal injury arising out of and in the course of employment and due to causes and conditions characteristic of and peculiar to the business of his employer. . . . As the result of the injury plaintiff has been totally disabled since October 24, 1956, from doing the work he was performing for defendant prior to that date. Plaintiff cannot safely be subjected to pressures or strains. He is not able to perform work which is highly competitive or requires a certain production rate. Plaintiff is and has been since October 24, 1956, disabled from earning full wages at the work in which he was last subjected to the conditions resulting in disability.

2. Member Storie:

. . . The disability is due to an aggravation of a pre-existing condition by more than one nonfortuitous event. I hold that disability is compensable under the provisions of Part II of the Workmen's Compensation Act and concur with Chairman McLaughlin in granting compensation. . . .

3. Member Ryan:

. . . I do not agree that the plaintiff's disability is due to causes and conditions charac-

teristic of and peculiar to the defendant's business. . . .

There is nothing in this case identifiable as an occupational risk.

The job was a simple job and the foreman's instructions were even simpler. Nothing more emanated from the employment.

The disability arose out of the plaintiff's own feelings and misapprehension and from within himself completely.

The order of the appeal board is attacked, among other reasons, because no 2 members of the 3-member board found plaintiff's disability compensable under the same section of the act. Nevertheless, the decision of 2 of the 3 members of the board was that plaintiff suffered a compensable injury. Section 11 of Chapter 1A of the act creating the workmen's compensation appeal board (C.L.S. 1956, § 408.11 [Stat. Ann. 1959 Cum. Supp. § 17.6 (17)]) provides that the "decision of a majority of the board shall be the decision of the board." It is not unusual for members of a body performing a judicial function to arrive at the same conclusion via diverse reasoning. See, for example, *Samels* v. *Goodyear Tire & Rubber Co.* (317 Mich. 149, 26 N.W.2d 742) where 6 justices of this Court voted to affirm an award of compensation, 3 justices grounding their decision on part 2 and 3 justices on part 7. The decision of the board is within the statutory mandate.

However, in order to uphold the board's decision awarding *any* compensation, this Court must be satisfied, first, that there is competent evidence to uphold the finding of causal connection made by a majority of the board, and second, that plaintiff suffered a disability which is compensable under the act.

As to the first point, the only medical testimony offered is that of the treating physician. He testified as follows:

. . . the patient saw himself as in an impossible situation in which he couldn't win. He couldn't please the foreman operating the machine in his job the way he was. If he attempted to do it the foreman's way he would fall behind in his work and the men on the line would complain and the foreman would get after him for this. So he really felt himself caught in an impossible situation which had no solution. . . .

My feeling is that Mr. Carter showed some evidence of instability earlier in his life. Namely, this episode in the service when he went AWOL relatively frequently and was discharged for that reason. That apparently subsequent to this he was able to make a fairly satisfactory adjustment, but that he managed to avoid situations wherein he felt trapped. For instance, he mentioned that on his construction job he was all over, that he worked in many different places. And apparently in his experience with General Motors, too, he was never on a job where he felt he could not meet the demands of the job. Now, I feel that here we had an unhappy combination of circumstances, that after a period of a layoff the man comes into a new job which for somebody, I think with the relative inflexibility of personality that this man had, required some adaptation. So that already he was working in a new position with which he was not familiar and he found himself in a—as I believe I described it before, in what to him was an impossible situation. Namely, that he could not meet the foreman's demands and stay on the work and doing it the way the foreman wanted him to do, and on the other hand, if he did keep up, then his job was threatened in that fashion. So that he actually felt that the job which he had described to his wife as liking very much was threatened in either way. We frequently see a situation of this type where the person feels himself trapped in a situation that has no solution, at least to them, precipitating a schizophrenic breakdown. And I think the indications are that this is what occurred here. . . .

I think that he has had the personality predisposition towards the development of this illness for a number of years. This is what usually happens, but then this is the straw that breaks the camel's back, and they develop the actual psychosis in which they are out of touch with reality. Now, we have no reason to believe that he was before out of touch with reality.

This was competent expert opinion testimony, upon which the board could and did base a finding of causal connection. Such a factual determination is binding upon this Court, there being competent evidence to support it. (*McVicar* v. *Harper Hospital*, 313 Mich. 48, 20 N.W.2d 806; *Redfern* v. *Sparks-Withington Co.*, 353 Mich. 286, 91 N.W.2d 516, and C. L. 1948, § 413.12 [Stat. Ann. 1950 Rev. § 17.186].) It may be noted that the defendant offered no medical testimony to rebut that given in behalf of claimant by Dr. Lawrence P. Tourkow, a specialist in the field of psychiatry and psychiatric consultant to the public schools and the board of health of the city of Highland Park. The record discloses that Dr. Tourkow's professional qualifications as an expert witness were not challenged by defendant.

The second point, whether or not plaintiff suffered a disability compensable under the act, presents a more difficult question. This Court has previously held that emotional disabilities are compensable under the act. (*Klein* v. *Len H. Darling Co.*, 217 Mich. 485, 187 N.W. 400; *Karwacki* v. *General Motors Corp.*, 293 Mich. 355, 292 N.W. 328; *Hayes* v. *Detroit Steel Casting Co.*, 328 Mich. 609, 44

N.W.2d 190; and *Redfern* v. *Sparks-Withington Co.*, *supra*.) Whether the cause of such emotional disability is a direct physical injury (*Redfern* v. *Sparks-Withington Co.*) or a mental shock (*Klein* v. *Len H. Darling Co.*), we have held the disability compensable. What distinguishes the case at bar from our other decisions which recognize the compensability of such disabilities is that this plaintiff's disability was caused by neither a single *physical* injury to plaintiff nor by a single mental shock to him. Instead, his disability was caused by emotional pressures produced by production-line employment not shown by him to be unusual in any respect—that is, not shown by him to be any different from the emotional pressures encountered by his fellow workers in similar employment. As noted above, the finding of causal relationship between plaintiff's disability and the pressures of his employment was supported by the evidence. The question then becomes, must industry, under our laws, bear the economic burden of such disability? Implicit in the question as stated is the further question: Is a worker unable to work because of a mental injury caused by his employment? Our answer may be found in this Court's prior decisions and in the decisions of other courts in other jurisdictions with comparable laws which have considered the problem.

We make no claim that it is universally held that a mental disorder which is precipitated solely by a mental stimulus, as opposed to a physical impact, is considered a compensable personal injury. There are those jurisdictions in which no nervous disorder is compensable. For example, *Star Publishing Co.* v. *Jackson* (115 Ind. App. 221, 58 N.E.2d 202) was a 1944 Indiana case involving a linotype operator who developed a recurring spasm in his left hand. Diagnosed, and proved, as an occupational neurosis caused by the antagonistic relationship between the claimant and his foreman, this disability was held not compensable. See also *McGill Manufacturing Co.* v. *Dodd*, 116 Ind. App. 66, 59 N.E.2d 899, for a similar holding.

In New Jersey, a stenographer was called an "idiot" by a co-worker when she misunderstood what she was supposed to do. This incident upset her, and she was subsequently treated for a nervous disorder. Her petition was dismissed by a referee in a proceeding under the New Jersey workmen's compensation act, for the following reason: "I am satisfied that the petitioner did not meet with an accident arising out of and in the course of her employment; in fact, there was not one iota of testimony to even suggest an *accidental occurrence*." (*Voss* v. *Prudential Insurance Co.*, 187

A. 334, 14 N.J. Misc. 791.) (Emphasis supplied.) The referee's reason for denying compensation is inapplicable in Michigan in the light of our recent holdings in *Sheppard* v. *Michigan National Bank* (348 Mich. 577, 83 N.W.2d 614), and *Coombe* v. *Penegro* (348 Mich. 635, 83 N.W.2d 603).

There is Michigan precedent also, long-established precedent at that. It was in January of 1920 that Otto Klein died. Just a few weeks earlier he had let a piece of machinery slip from his hands. It fell to the floor below, striking a fellow employee. Though the injury to his co-worker was not serious, Otto Klein thought he had caused his death. The mental and nervous shock caused by this accident to his fellow employee, at his hands, resulted in a neurotic condition, causing Mr. Klein's death. His injury and death were held compensable notwithstanding that (as this Court said in *La Veck* v. *Parke, Davis & Co.*, 190 Mich. 604, 605, 157 N.W. 72, L.R.A. 1916D, 1277) no "visible accident occurred and no event causing external violence to applicant's body" occurred. *Klein* v. *Len H. Darling Co., supra.* The philosophy expressed by Justice Weist, concurring, is worth repeating here (217 Mich. 485, 187 N.W. 403):

At first I was inclined to disagree with Mr. Justice Moore, but upon reflection I am convinced he is right. An accident happened in which the deceased was an actor, and the shock to him was so acute and so depressed his vital forces as to kill him. We must not overlook man's nervous system and mental makeup and their intimate relation to his vital forces.

This man died because his vital forces could not meet and withstand the acute depression occasioned by what he had done in the course of his employment. The injury to him was no less real and fatal in its consequences than a mortal wound. "Accidents," within the comprehension of the workmen's compensation law, include all accidents actionable at law and all former nonactionable accidents, except in case of intentional and willful misconduct on the part of the employe.

In 1943, in *Rainko* v. *Webster-Eisenlohr, Inc.* (306 Mich. 328, 10 N.W.2d 903) this Court said that it is not necessary to establish physical injury resulting in outward evidence of violence or trauma to justify an award of compensation. Plaintiff was one of 30 women victims of "mass hysteria" caused by an odor from gasoline vapor of less than toxic concentration in the area where the women worked in a cigar factory. The women collapsed, one after another, and plaintiff was left with dizzy spells, nausea, rash, hyperactive reflexes, an epigastric tenderness, anemia, and loss of

weight. The Court sustained an award of compensation.

This Court's most recent statement respecting compensability of a neurotic condition may be found in *Redfern* v. *Sparks-Withington Co.* (*supra*, 353 Mich. at page 299, 91 N.W.2d at page 518): "In this State, the rule is well established by a line of authority dating from 1922 that where occupationally-incurred injury to the body and/or shock to the nervous system produces a neurosis resulting in disability or death, it is compensable."

In *Redfern*, plaintiff while at work was struck on the back by a steel weight and was thereafter disabled from working by what the medical witnesses described as "conversion hysteria." There was no organic cause for her loss of feeling and strength in her right hand and arm, swelling and pain in the right shoulder and neck area, and general fatigue. Compensation was allowed.

It would be well to note that, in the case at bar, although there was no evidence of psychosis prior to October, 1956, the expert testimony did indicate that plaintiff had a personality disorder all his life and that he had a predisposition to the development of a schizophrenic process.

There was also evidence that the plaintiff had been examined in the emergency room of the Highland Park General Hospital 4 days before the last day he worked, and that his condition at that time was described as "bronchial asthma and anxiety." An exhibit submitted by the defendant was a report from a doctor examining the claimant just prior to October 24, 1956, wherein Mr. Carter was advised to take a leave of absence for 2 or more weeks because of a severe state of anxiety and tension. It would appear, therefore, that the series of events in the instant case served to aggravate a pre-existing latent mental disturbance. That such is not a bar to compensation may best be pointed out by quoting from the Court's opinion in *Karwacki* v. *General Motors Corp.* (*supra*, from pages 356 and 357 of 293 Mich., at page 328 of 292 N.W.): "The testimony . . . supports the finding of the department that the accidental injury aggravated a pre-existing latent mental disturbance, resulting in a disabling condition. The result is comparable to situations wherein an accidental injury has aggravated and precipitated a preexisting latent physical ailment, resulting in disability. Awards of compensation in such cases have been sustained in a multitude of instances."

Appellant contends that there was no single event which precipitated plaintiff's psychotic breakdown and that, therefore, there can be no award of compensation under part 2 of the act. Appellant recognizes that for an award under part 2, no longer is it necessary to find an "accident" or a fortuitous event, citing *Sheppard* v. *Michigan National Bank, supra,* and *Coombe* v. *Penegor, supra,* but appellant further states that it appears from these cases that part 2 applies only to single event injuries. However, it does *not* appear from the Sheppard and Coombe cases that injuries not attributable to a single event are not covered by part 2.

This Court in the past has sustained an award of compensation under part 2 where the physical injury was not occasioned by a single event. In *La Veck* v. *Parke, Davis & Co.* (190 Mich. 604, 157 N.W. 72, L.R.A. 1916D, 1277), the plaintiff's paralysis was attributed to a cerebral hemorrhage caused by prolonged work in a heated kitchen. In affirming an award, the Court said (190 Mich. at page 610, 157 N.W. at page 74): "According to the testimony of some of the physicians that result could be traced to the unusual hours of work and the unusual conditions. It was an unexpected consequence from *the continued work in the excessively warm room.*" (Emphasis supplied.)

Further, to relegate the applicability of part 2 solely to single event injuries, would be to ignore express statutory language referring to multiple event injuries. Section 1 of part 2 provides for a " 'date of injury' . . . in the case of an injury not attributable to a single event," evidencing a legislative intent that such injuries should be compensable.

The case at bar involves a series of mental stimuli or events—(the pressure of his job and the pressure of his foreman)—which caused an injury or disability under the act, causal connection in fact having been found by the board, supported by competent evidence. We find further that Mr. Carter's disabling psychosis resulting from emotional pressures encountered by him daily in his work is compensable under part 2 of the act. Such conclusion renders unnecessary any discussion of the applicability of part 7 to the facts of this case.

Appellant further contests the portion of the appeal board's order awarding continuing compensation based on its finding of a continuing disability. The existence or extent of an injury or disability is a finding of fact and will not be disturbed where supported by competent evidence. (*Finch* v. *Ford Motor Co.,* 321 Mich. 469, 32 N.W.2d 712; *Walding* v. *General Motors Corp.,* 352 Mich. 372, 89 N.W.2d 537.) The testimony of the only medical witness was to the effect that the plaintiff could be employed again, but not on this same type of job, where it is necessary to keep up with a production line.

If there were testimony that claimant's inability to work on a production line was caused by the paranoid schizophrenia condition for which we have held he is entitled to compensation benefits, he would be entitled to continuing payment of such benefits. However, Dr. Tourkow testified that as of September 11, 1957, Mr. Carter no longer showed any symptoms of paranoid schizophrenia or other psychosis. He testified that Mr. Carter should not be employed again in production work, not because of his paranoid schizophrenia, but for the same reason he should not have been employed in such work in the first place: Mr. Carter has a personality configuration that makes him more susceptible than others to psychotic breakdowns when subjected to pressures such as are encountered in production line employment. Under the circumstances, we find no evidence to support the appeal board's award continuing compensation benefits beyond September 11, 1957.

The order of the appeal board should have terminated payment of benefits to Mr. Carter on September 11, 1957, and upon remand to the appeal board it shall be so modified. In all other respects the order is affirmed. No costs.

[Dissenting Opinion]

Justice Souris refers to decisions from Michigan and from other jurisdictions to sustain his opinion. An analysis of these cited cases discloses that while they sustain the compensability of emotional disability, in each instance there was some precipitating factor as disclosed by the following:

Plaintiff's husband's death resulted from shock caused by dropping an object on a fellow employee, knocking said fellow employee unconscious (*Klein* v. *Len H. Darling Co.,* 217 Mich. 485, 187 N.W. 400); plaintiff became emotionally disabled after a piece of hot metal entered his glove (*Karwacki* v. *General Motors Corp.,* 293 Mich. 355, 292 N.W. 328); plaintiff, after suffering the loss of an eye by an occupational injury, developed a post-traumatic neurosis and was unable to work (*Hayes* v. *Detroit Steel Casting Co.,* 328 Mich. 609, 44 N.W.2d 190); plaintiff was injured when a 15-to-20-pound steel weight struck her between her shoulder blades and she subsequently suffered conversion hysteria (*Redfern* v. *Sparks-Withington Co.,* 353 Mich. 286, 91 N.W.2d 516); plaintiff and 30 other employees suffered mass hysteria caused by an odor of gasoline vapor, after which plaintiff was unable to work because of dizziness (*Rainko* v. *Webster-Eisenlohr, Inc.,* 306 Mich. 328, 10 N.W.2d 903); plaintiff's husband died from shock and excitement and overexertion in attempting to pull a fire from a boiler in order to prevent an explosion (*Monk* v. *Charcoal Iron Co.*, 246 Mich. 193, 224 N.W. 354); plaintiff tried to lift a 25-pound tray of cards and suffered an injury when she attempted to yank it free (*Sheppard* v. *Michigan National Bank*, 348 Mich. 577, 83 N.W.2d 614); plaintiff suffered an injury when he exerted great effort to tighten a load binder (*Coombe* v. *Penegor*, 348 Mich. 635, 83 N.W.2d 603).

The final Michigan case cited by Mr. Justice Souris—*La Veck* v. *Parke, Davis & Co.* (190 Mich. 604, 157 N.W. 72, L.R.A. 1916D, 1277), is the only case where there was not an overt act or a direct physical injury leading to neurosis. In this case claimant was awarded compensation for a cerebral hemorrhage induced by heat and overexertion. The court held that since evidence that tends to sustain a determination of the Industrial Accident Board is not subject to review, in appellate proceedings, on writ of certiorari to review the award of compensation for paralysis that resulted from heat and excessive exertion rupturing a small blood vessel of the brain (claimant having suffered from arteriosclerosis for 2 years prior to his injury), the question whether it was caused by an accident arising out of or in the course of claimant's employment was for the lower tribunal and would not be reversed unless a total lack of evidence upon that issue was disclosed.

Justice Souris refers to *Klein* v. *Len H. Darling Co., supra*, as Michigan precedent and quotes the concurring opinion of Justice Wiest. The following sentence in Justice Wiest's opinion (217 Mich. at page 495, 187 N.W. at page 403) clearly distinguishes the Klein case from our present appeal: "An accident happened in which the deceased was an actor, and the shock to him was so acute and so depressed his vital forces as to kill him."

Karwacki v. *General Motors Corp., supra*, is cited to establish that "a pre-existing latent mental disturbance" is not a bar to compensation, but the Karwacki case is not similar to the instant case as is disclosed by the following statement in the opinion: "The testimony . . . supports the finding of the department that the accidental injury aggravated a pre-existing latent mental disturbance, resulting in a disabling condition."

In deciding this appeal we cannot forget the fact that a majority of the commission found there was no accident, and plaintiff, while performing a simple job comparable to others employed, suffered a mental breakdown because he could not adequately perform that simple job.

Sheppard v. *Michigan National Bank* and *Coombe* v. *Penegor, supra*, are majored in Justice Souris' opinion with the statement that

it does not appear "that injuries not attributable to a single event are not covered by part 2." I do not believe either of these cases is of compelling weight, because in both cases there was a single precipitating event, and in neither case did we have a plaintiff that possessed such a mentality as to cause him to lose all control of himself without any accidental or unusual event.

Redfern v. *Sparks-Withington Co., supra*, is referred to as this Court's most recent statement respecting compensability of a neurotic condition. Suffice to say, in a 5 to 3 decision we held that a neurosis developing from an injury is compensable if directly caused thereby and not collateral thereto. There was no injury or comparable facts in this present appeal.

Defendant submits 2 questions in its statement of questions involved: "1. Is the plaintiff's disability the result of a personal injury arising out of and in the course of his employment under either part 2 or part 7 of the Michigan workmen's compensation law?" My answer to question No. 1 is "No." "2. Is there any competent evidence in the record to sustain the finding of the workmen's compensation appeal board that the plaintiff is entitled to continuing compensation?"

The hearing referee (James A. Broderick) found "that said defendant pay compensation at the rate of $36 per week for total disability to said employee from October 24, 1956, to January 7, 1957, inclusive; and, that said defendant shall reimburse said employee $863.27 for medical and hospital care."

Appellee's position on this point is set forth in his brief as follows:

The undisputed medical testimony accepted by the appeal board relative to disability was presented by the treating physician, Dr. Tourkow: Plaintiff should not be employed on a job which is highly competitive. He should not be placed upon a job where he would have to maintain a certain rate of production. He certainly would not be employable in piece work. The type of job that Dr. Tourkow felt that the plaintiff would be able to handle would be a job where he would be able to function at his own level of production without having to push himself. Dr. Tourkow testified that plaintiff was well motivated toward working; that plaintiff actually wanted to work but that he would advise very strongly against anything which would resemble the competitive situation which produced plaintiff's psychotic break. . . .

The plaintiff has been able to do a certain amount of casual farm labor, but that is a far cry from a competitive production-line job. Because of the very nature of plaintiff's disability, the plaintiff himself is incapable of making a reliable judgment as to his own capacity. . . .

The plaintiff's right to compensation for a disability does not depend upon his being totally disabled from doing *any* work but on his being disabled from earning full wages in the work in which he was last subjected to the conditions resulting in his disability. . . .

The appeal board has made a finding of fact, a finding based on uncontradicted testimony. Defendant should not now be permitted to circumvent the appeal board's finding on this or any other factual issue.

The 3 members of the board filed lengthy opinions but only briefly referred to continuing disability.

Chairman McLaughlin found:

Plaintiff contends that he did sustain such an injury and that he is entitled to compensation beyond January 7, 1957, and until further order of the department.

We find as follows: Prior to October, 1956, plaintiff had a personality configuration which made him particularly susceptible to the development of a schizophrenic psychosis. Nevertheless plaintiff had suffered no mental breakdown and had not been out of touch with reality prior to October 24, 1956. There was no psychosis before such date. . . . The date of injury and date of disablement is October 24, 1956. As the result of the injury plaintiff has been totally disabled since October 24, 1956, from doing the work he was performing for defendant prior to that date. . . .

The award of the hearing referee shall be modified to thus provide for continuing compensation from and after January 7, 1957, the date on which the referee stopped compensation.

Commissioner Storie stated:

The record is void of any showing of other "events" which could reasonably be held to have been the precipitating cause of plaintiff's disability. It is evident that this well qualified medical witness is of the opinion that the events created by and encountered during the course of the employment could have been "the straw that breaks the camel's back" in the instant case. We then clearly have a disability and an unexpected result that arose out of and in the course of this employee's employment with defendant company. . . .

From the proofs presented it would be mere speculation for us to hold that plaintiff would have been disabled because of the pre-existing condition even though he had not been employed by defendant company. There are no suggested reasons for plaintiff's mental break-

down other than those which did occur during the course of his employment. . . . Since plaintiff's capacity to earn cannot be measured against his incapacity the continuing award entered by the hearing referee is proper.

As hereinbefore noted, Commissioner Ryan found that plaintiff was not entitled to compensation.

Plaintiff's exhibit 1 was a statement of Dr. Warner to the president of Local 235, under date of January 29, 1957, in which he said:

Mr. James Carter was hospitalized at St. Clair Hospital from 10–27–56 to 11–23–56. During his hospitalization he was treated for a nervous disorder which we have not been able to diagnose. He was given a thorough physical examination and was found to be in excellent condition. . . .

Our last contact with him was on January 21, and he was physically fit to return to his employment.

Dr. Tourkow referred to the St. Clair Hospital diagnosis as follows:

Well, actually, this was the diagnosis they arrived at at St. Clair Hospital, was paranoiac schizophrenia, and it certainly would be in keeping with these progressively developing feelings that the foreman was persecuting him, you see. Right now I don't see any evidence of paranoid schizophrenia per se. I do see some very minimal leftover of a schizophrenic process, but really if you didn't know that the person had had this before, you wouldn't make a diagnosis solely on the symptoms. So this is why I used the term "in remission" in my present diagnosis. In remission means that he's now not psychotic, he's not showing any symptoms right now.

The record discloses that plaintiff had this personality disorder all his life. He proved that he could not adjust to rules or regulations while in the army, but repeatedly went AWOL.

I agree with appellant's statement that: "The testimony does not indicate that plaintiff's disability is due to causes and conditions peculiar to his employment. His disability is due to and arises out of his mental condition." And, I also agree with appellant that the answer to its question No. 2 should be "No," and conclude that the decision of the workmen's compensation appeal board should be reversed.

Reversed. No costs.

WORKMEN'S COMPENSATION FOR PSYCHIATRIC DISORDERS

Norman Q. Brill, M.D., and John F. Glass, M.A.

The concept of workmen's compensation for employees with industrial accidents has been so expanded that it includes many disorders in which the causal relationship between the special hazards of employment and the illness becomes increasingly obscure. In *Carter* v. *General Motors*, a precedent was established of compensating an employee for a psychiatric breakdown not associated with any physical injury, accident, specific event, or unusual stress or incident. To help avoid the perversion of the original intent of workmen's compensation, industry will have to concern itself with emotional as well as physical requirements of its employees, without diminishing the individual's sense of responsibility for his own welfare.

In recent years, there has been an increase in the number of workmen's compensation claims involving psychiatric disorders that have been attributed to emotional stresses on the job unassociated with any accident or physical injury. These cases have caused considerable concern among medical, legal, industrial, and insurance groups, and they raise a number of complex social, moral, and legal questions. A few example cases will illustrate the nature of some of the issues and complications.

1. A structural steel and iron worker was working on a scaffold which collapsed, sending a fellow worker plunging to his death. The claimant was able to jump to safety, suffering only minor bruises. He maintained that the spectacle of his co-worker's death caused an anxiety reaction which made it impossible for him to continue at his job. Compensation (fifty per cent permanent partial disability) was awarded, and the decision was eventually upheld by the Texas Supreme Court (*Bailey* v. *American General Insurance Co.*, 154 Texas 430, 279 SW 2d 315, 1955).

2. In Los Angeles, a workmen's compensation award was granted to a former municipal employee who claimed she "developed an ulcer" while serving as manager of the City Hall information desk. Later vetoing the award, the mayor stated that he found it difficult to understand how the claimant's job could be of "such pressure and intensity" as to bring about an ulcer, and he expressed concern for the establishment of a precedent in the settlement of claims for conditions of this nature if this claim were approved.

The third example involved a civil service employee who claimed that a preexisting condition of migraine was aggravated to a point of full disability by tension and frustrations arising from the duties of his government employment.

3. A 43-year-old white married man became ill in 1942 when he was a permanent officer in the army. He suffered from migraine headaches attributed to tension associated with increased responsibilities. He received a medical disability discharge for migraine headaches in 1944. His headaches persisted. In 1950, after working for several years as an executive secretary to a civil service scientific procurement board, he began to become more tense than usual as a result of schism between the civil service commission and the board on which he served, and he was compelled to take off several days from work because of his severe headaches. In 1952 a perforated peptic ulcer developed and he was operated on. An uneventful recovery and remission of headaches and stomach pains followed. About six months later he again became tense in his job and the headaches and stomach distress returned. His doctor finally advised him to give up his job and the claimant was granted disability retirement in 1954. He applied for compensation for his headaches and ulcer which he claims were severely aggravated by the stress of his job.

The report submitted to the Bureau of Employees' Compensation with regard to the relationship between the claimant's disability and his government employment included this opinion: "His symptoms are psychophysiological. They are the result of continued emotional tension. . . . A simple answer to the causal

Reprinted with permission from *JAMA* 193, no. 5 (August 2, 1965): 345–48.

relationship between job frustrations and the aggravation of his illness is not possible. Emotional adjustment is always a function of predisposition and stress."

What is stressful for one person may not be stressful for another. If one is to avoid reductio ad absurdum in formulating any workable concept of causal relationships as it relates to compensability, it is necessary to consider only that stress which is objective (rather than subjective) and unusual. Exposure to an affectionate display may result in an emotional illness in individuals who have by virtue of unresolved conflicts within themselves an inability to deal with it. Life itself is characterized by a combination of both objective and subjective stresses. If illness caused by subjective stress were considered compensable, then an illness of emotional origin could be compensable, since no job is free of stress and the illness could be attributed to job stress.

The stress to which the claimant was exposed was in part the result of his own actions (sincere as they may have been) and to varying degrees was characteristic of any executive position. It was not of a degree that could be expected to produce illness in any person, and his reaction to it (as to other stresses that were clearly usual ones) was the result of his own severe predisposition. Even his application for federal employees' compensation was admittedly to some extent a manifestation of his neurosis and of his dependent strivings. From this standpoint, there is no causal relationship between the claimant's past or present disability and his government employment.

This case emphasizes two of the thorniest problems associated with psychiatric compensation cases: the claim of aggravation of a pre-existing disorder, and the determination of whether the condition was truly related to the job itself.

Historical Considerations

In most workmen's compensation statutes, only work-connected injuries arising "out of and in the course of employment" which cause disability resulting in temporary or permanent loss of wage earning capacity are compensable. The underlying philosophy of workmen's compensation is social protection, rather than righting a wrong.

Workmen's compensation laws were based on the idea that industrial hazards constitute an insurable risk inherent in production. They were never intended to provide a substitute for pensions and sickness insurance. When work-

men's compensation laws first appeared around the end of the last century, the hazards of industrial life were greater than they are today, and industrial accidents relatively more common. Early workmen's compensation claims dealt almost exclusively with accidental injuries such as loss of fingers or limbs, loss of eyesight, fractures, and other "break or smash" injuries of a relatively obvious nature. Only later was it commonly recognized that illnesses as well as injuries can result from specific industrial hazards, and a variety of occupational diseases began to be covered by workmen't compensation.

The line of demarcation between occupational and nonoccupational disability has become increasingly blurred because of the complex etiology of many industrial disabilities. Ulcer, arthritis, and especially heart diseases are troublesome and raise many of the problems associated with psychiatric disorders. In one notable case, for instance, a 56-year-old employee who suffered a stroke while asleep in bed was awarded compensation, his doctor ascribing the malady to overwork (*Lumberman's Casualty Co.* v. *Industrial Accident Commission*, 29 Cal. 2d 492, 1946).

A similar case noted by Waters involves a claim for benefits under workmen's compensation by the widow of a law school dean who suffered a fatal acute coronary occlusion after speaking before a legal fraternity. The state industrial commission rejected the claim, but was overruled by a district court which accepted testimony that the stress of the dean's law school duties caused the attack.

There have been other cases where an employee received compensation for a heart attack following an argument or harsh words exchanged with an employer or fellow employee. These cases reflect the increasingly liberal interpretation, especially by the courts, of workmen's compensation laws.

Claims for Psychiatric Disorders

Workmen's compensation claims involving psychiatric disorders have a relatively recent history. Since about 1940, disability from a nervous or mental disorder has been considered fully compensable when attributed to or precipitated by a physical injury. According to Larson, many cases involving almost any kind of conceivable neurotic or hysterical symptom have been granted compensation. Denial of compensation in such cases has been based not so much on the theory that traumatic neuroses are not compensable, but on the ground that the evidence failed to establish a causal connection between the injury and the neurosis. The problem of "traumatic neuroses" has been dealt with extensively in the literature.

Our interest is in mental and nervous disorders attributed to emotional or psychic stress where no physical injury or impact is involved. These cases have caused the most controversy recently.

One of the early cases of this type involved a claimant who was frightened by an electric flash near her caused by a short circuit in a motor. She fainted and was caught before she fell by another employee. As a result of the mental association this created she fainted again the next time she saw this co-worker, and it became impossible for her to work because of this neurosis (*Burlington Mills* v. *Hagood*, 177 Va. 204, 13 SE 2d 291, 1941).

A similar case in which compensation was awarded involved a claimant who developed a hysterical paralysis of her left side "as a result of" fright caused by a loud noise and flash of light created when lightning struck the building in which she worked (*Charon's Case*, 321 Mass. 694, 75 NE 2d 511, 1947).

These and other cases were the precedents on which current policies of many jurisdictions are based. Several states, notably New York, Indiana, New Jersey, and Nebraska, still do not allow recovery for mental illness in the absence of some element of accidental physical injury. In Florida, if both the cause and the result are considered "mental," compensation will be denied under its statute which states that nervous or mental injury resulting from fright or excitement does not constitute compensable accidental injury.

In 1960 the Michigan Supreme Court handed down an important and controversial decision:

In *Carter* v. *General Motors* (361 Mich. 577, 106 NW 2d 105, 1960) a divided court (five to three) sustained a compensation award to James Carter, a machine operator, for a psychosis resulting from emotional pressure encountered on his job. Carter was an assembly-line worker whose job required him to take a hub assembly from a nearby fellow employee's table to his own work bench, remove burrs with a file and grind out holes in the assembly with a drill, and place the assembly on a conveyor belt. He was unable to keep up with the pace of the job unless he took two assemblies at a time to his work bench. His foreman instructed him repeatedly not to do this because the assembly parts became mixed up on the conveyor belt when he did so. He continued having trouble handling the job. When he took only one hub assembly at a time, he fell behind, and when he fell behind he would take two assemblies at a time, get them mixed up, and receive criticism from his foreman. On

Oct. 24, 1956, Carter suffered an emotional collapse which was diagnosed as a paranoid schizophrenic reaction. He was hospitalized for a month and received shock therapy during this time. In July, 1957, he filed a claim for compensation which was granted, and he received a permanent total disability rating. An appeal was taken to the Supreme Court of Michigan which affirmed the awarding of compensation for temporary disability, but reversed the award with respect to permanent disability on the attending physician's testimony that as of September, 1957, the claimant no longer showed symptoms of a psychosis.

The majority opinion based its decision of causality on the medical testimony of the attending physician who stated that:

We frequently see a situation of this type where the person feels himself trapped in a situation that has no solution, at least to him, precipitating a schizophrenic breakdown. . . . and I think the indications are that this is what occurred here. . . . I think that he has had the personality predisposition toward the development of this illness for a number of years.

The Carter case was unique in that not only was there no physical injury, but also no accident or specific single incident or definable event that precipitated the breakdown. There was no hazardous condition or unusual stress associated with the job. In most prior workmen's compensation claims, at least one of these conditions had been present. The majority of the supreme court rejected the distinction between physical and mental injuries, and in effect ruled that a schizophrenic breakdown due to ordinary work pressures constitutes a compensable personal injury. Furthermore, the Michigan court reaffirmed rulings in previous cases that held that physical impact is not a requisite, that mental disorders precipitated solely by a "mental" stimulus can be considered a compensable injury.

(The minority opinion in the Carter case criticized the majority opinion for allowing compensation where no accidental injury occurred, no special hazards were involved in the job, and Carter's disability resulted from neither a single physical injury nor a single mental shock, as had been the case in most previous court decisions in psychiatric disorder compensation cases. A dissenting Justice stated: "I do not believe that the injury arose out of employment . . . there is nothing in this case identifiable as an occupational risk. The job was a simple job and the foreman's instructions were even more simple. Nothing more emanated from the employment. The disability arose out of the plaintiff's own feelings and misapprehension and from within himself completely.")

A great deal of controversy was stirred up by this case. The following is representative of the opinion of those who felt the court went too far:

It is indicative of the trend of judicial reasoning to make an employer responsible under workmen's compensation laws for any and all human ills that may arise out of and in the course of employment. While I, personally, deplore this trend, I believe it is inevitable that it will be extended and that other states will follow this decision in making injuries and illnesses compensable where they arise during the course of employment, irrespective of the requirement that they should have been caused by an accident. The very definition of the term "occupational disease" referred to in the court's opinion, excludes diseases of ordinary life. . . . Industry is going to have to live with unfortunate decisions of this type unless aroused public opinion, led by the medical and legal professions, puts a halt to this type of decision.

PREVALENCE OF CASES

It is difficult to determine how often psychiatric and other illnesses are attributed to job stress, since there are no statistical records identifying psychiatric cases as such. There are relatively few reported cases involving overwork or stress associated with usual job duties and most of these involve cardiac and gastric (ulcer) disabilities. The flood of cases feared as a result of the precedent set by the Carter case apparently has not occurred.

A district medical director of the Labor Department, Bureau of Employees Compensation, stated:

I believe that under various disguises, psychiatric disorders play a major role in our compensation work. . . . A very common situation is that of an apparently inadequate or emotionally disturbed employee who suffers an injury, even a trivial injury, and instead of making the expected recovery remains partially or totally disabled thereafter. We see a number of cases of coronary thrombosis attributed to overwork and stress on the job. There are some claims of hypertension and its complications, peptic ulcer, and one I recall of miscarriage of pregnancy, all attributed to stress (R. L. Griffith, in a personal communication to the author, Dec. 16, 1959).

The consensus of opinion as to prevalence seems to be that there are a considerable number of cases where some form of psychiatric

disorder is involved in conjunction with another injury or disease, and a relatively small number similar to the Carter case where no physical injury is involved. The number of these cases, however, is continually increasing as the distinction between occupational and non-occupational disabilities becomes more and more hazy through the ever widening interpretation of workmen's compensation acts by the courts and compensation authorities.

PHILOSOPHICAL CONSIDERATIONS

It has been frequenlty charged that the original intent of workmen's compensation has been perverted, and that it is becoming social sickness insurance, the cost of which is being borne unjustly by industry and the consumer.

The logical outcome of this process, should it continue, would be the extension of the benefits of the compensation system to all sick or injured employees, making no distinction between those hurt within the plant and those hurt in their own automobiles or bathtubs. Such an extension, of course, would make workmen's compensation into something never contemplated and would violate completely the basic principle that the expense of *work* injuries is to be a part of the cost of production. However, if we are to approach that result inevitably as we now seem to be doing, perhaps the time will come when we must answer certain questions frankly—notably, the question whether we actually intend to make industry pay for all disabilities of employees regardless of fault, and if so, under what rules, and subject to what limitations.

There undoubtedly has been and will continue to be misuse of workmen's compensation laws. In a larger sense, the problem is a dilemma of our modern society: how to provide a needed social service, workmen's compensation in this case, without at the same time having the individual lose his sense of responsibility for his own welfare. The recent occurrence of suits being filed against tobacco companies by persons suffering from lung cancer raises a similar problem. A further extension of this problem exists in common law where there is currently great controversy over cases where a third party who witnessed or somehow was involved in an accident without receiving any direct injury sues for damages suffered as a result of the incident. In *Ameya v. Home Ice, Fuel & Supply Co.* (23 Cal. Rptr. 131, 1962) the First District Court of Appeal in California awarded damage to a mother for the emotional stress she suffered in witnessing from a distance her child being run over by a negligently operated truck. The court held that "when one is negligent in the operation of an automobile, he should as a reasonable man, foresee that that class of persons who may suffer harm from his misconduct includes a parent whose emotional distress issues from exposure of the child to injury by reason of negligence." While such considerations are not directly applicable to workmen's compensation, where negligence is not in issue, they have an indirect bearing.

Life is characterized by stress, both interpersonal and intrapsychic. No job is free from stress. It is one thing to provide sickness insurance that will cover the varied manifestations of disordered emotional states, and it is another to attribute these states incorrectly to isolated or specific job stresses. There are two questions that society must answer: Who should be liable for the costs of mental disorders not expressly a result of a work-related injury? To what extent are mental disorders caused by work?

Much has been said and written about the hazards of being an executive. Catch phrases like "slow up or blow up," "most executives die young," and "executive crack-up" emphasize the emotional stress of being an executive. There are studies, however, which have indicated that the emotional health of executives is as good as that of others and perhaps even a little better. One might wonder about the stress of being on an isolated "listening post" for a long time, or operating an over-loaded switchboard.

In a broader sense, the problems of compensating psychiatric disabilities and the misuse of workmen's compensation arise to some extent because workmen's compensation is now operating in an industrial society quite different from that of 75 years ago. Only one out of five of the nation's disabling accidents now arises at work. Automobile accidents claim far more victims than occupational accidents. Absenteeism caused by nonoccupational disability is now estimated to be ten times as great as that resulting from work injuries, according to Sommers. Thus, the legitimate role of workmen's compensation is becoming increasingly limited, especially in light of the great increase in private health-care coverage and the growth of union and industrial health and welfare programs.

How does industry view the problem of compensability of psychiatric disorders? Employers deplore the current trend of expanding coverage of workmen's compensation to cover psychiatric disorders, the diseases of aging, and other illnesses not specifically attributable to work-connected injuries. These disabilities cause far more difficulties for industry than accidents resulting from industrial hazards. There is increasing reluctance of industry to hire older workers on the grounds that the risk is too great and insurance costs too high.

Until recently, employers have been far more concerned with the physical health of their employees than with their mental health. Industry is becoming increasingly involved and interested in mental-health problems. One indication of this is that the number of psychiatrists working full or part time as consultants to industry has more than doubled in the last four years.

How much responsibility industry should take for the mental health of its employees is a question that deserves further study. Unlike accident prevention, safety, and other physical health programs of industry, preventive mental health activities by industry are much more controversial, since questions of individual freedom and privacy arise. Industry has had bad experiences with paternalism. There is a tremendous amount that industry can do, however, to make work less stressful and to meet certain emotional needs related to work.

One could ask, for instance, should James Carter have been placed on an assembly-line job? Should the company have determined his predisposition to mental breakdown? Should he have been hired in the first place? Would his breakdown have occurred had he been placed in a less stressful situation? These are all questions with no simple answers and with great social implications. What would the alternatives have been to his receiving workmen's compensation for his psychotic break? If he had no health insurance and no substantial savings, the chances are that his support and medical care would have been provided by the community and the burden carried by the taxpayer.

THE PSYCHIATRIST AND THE DEFENSE COUNSEL

Alexander H. Hirschfeld, M.D., and Robert C. Behan, M.D.

Losses due to psychiatric disturbances in individual negligence cases today may come to more than $150,000. Counsel who loses such a defense can sometimes feel angry at physicians and judges, not to mention having a sense of overwhelming helplessness. Still, mature thoughtfulness and some sensitive awareness to emotional problems can reduce, sometimes eliminate, these losses. Such mature deliberation first will indicate that the present issue is only a small segment of a much larger problem, the evolution of concepts of legal recovery for damages. A historical perspective of this could well go back to King John facing his barons under the tree at Runnymede, setting up the early rights of, and procedures for, redress. From this moment on, property franchises have been further and further refined until, among lawyers, a great sense of understanding has developed. On the other hand, only recently has the law attempted to deal more effectively with the rights of individuals, with what might be called human rights. For example, wide acceptance of the evil of child labor is less than a century old.

Each such step requires time and seems also to demand the subduing of great passions on both sides. The story is told of a great 19th century English prime minister who rose in Westminster Abbey in the midst of a sermon to scream at the top of his lungs as he left the church, "This fool," referring to the archbishop, "believes that there is morality in international relations." Despite emotion like this, and despite the time required to quell and to argue it, every such step and each such controversy tends to add a little more truth to our knowledge and a bit more form to our law. At this moment, not enough dust has settled in the great controversies over civil and human rights for us yet to see clearly what truths will emerge from this particular fight. . . .

Yet to the trial lawyer who is involved in the fray and who has individual cases to try, such waiting is a luxury. Accordingly, he must try to see as much and as clearly as he can, even though final answers have yet to be found.

Still, even though time is against the current adversaries, the present cases can be clarified somewhat with historical understanding. It is now clear that the public's interest in the plight of the individual has focused more and more on the underprivileged, the hurt, and the disabled. Earlier in the fight the American society's interest in disabled men resulted in an increasing tendency to award victims relief when their bodies were smashed or dismembered. Recognition of this principle resulted in defense attorneys losing more cases while plaintiff's counsel were victorious. With the advent of such devices as the roentgen ray, controversy diminished because the matter of proof became simpler. Both sets of lawyers now knew where they stood.

However, there was another aspect, and that was whether it could be proved that a man had contributed to the negligence which caused an accident. As time went on some areas of the law were further refined and the concept of Workmen's Compensation emerged, where it was agreed the victim's negligence was not germane. Again, there was a settling down and the lawyers knew where they were.

It would be unfair to view this remarkable progression without giving much credit to the legal profession. Through adroit use of the adversary system, certain plaintiff's lawyers fought with great theoretical agility and courage to establish their points. They have ultimately secured legal recognition of more and more truth. This, however, was only done with the limiting theoretical agility and courage of defense counsel who forced better and better definition of the truth as it came to the bar.

The present issue, that which involved psychiatrists, has been a challenge to the concept that disability and injury can only be physical. Much argument has been wasted on the assumption that if it is difficult to measure it must not be real. Whether or not it is a pleas-

Defense Attorneys Seminar, Detroit, Michigan, November 6, 1964; excerpted with permission from *Insurance Counsel Journal* 32 (April 1965): 215–20.

ant morsel to digest, the decisions of the highest courts recognize that a man can be hurt mentally, sometimes even more seriously than he can be hurt physically.[1]

In the establishment of this step, plaintiff's counsel have sought guidance from those who are familiar with the workings of the mind. They have introduced the expert in psychiatry. Some have used him well; a few have been quite unscrupulous; occasionally either lawyer or physician has been frankly dishonest. In general, however, the last group is fortunately small.

Since the psychiatrist came into the court as the instrumentality used to bludgeon the defense, understandably its counsel were at first quite hostile to this group of specialists. Still, some attorneys for the company have overcome this reaction and have used psychiatrists as rebuttal witnesses. Unfortunately, in the early days such clinicians were hired to testify principally that patients were malingering, not a very efficacious move, because in the vast preponderance of litigation it is not wholly true that plaintiffs are malingerers.

A better step has to be taken. This is the first point of this paper and undoubtedly the most important. Plaintiff's counsel who have really advanced the role of the psychiatrist in pleading for damages have not come up with their theories while on their feet in the courtroom. They have not come to decisions about what psychiatric theory to use, *and what to suppress,* simply by responding to expediency of the moment. Rather, they have spent years in the study of this medical discipline and have understood something which was not included in the legal curriculum. Again and again these men are still seen in the audiences of medical meetings when the essays concern disability.[2] *Only when their opponents develop similar understanding and similar grasp will they be equals in argument.*[3] Since the plaintiff's counsel, at this stage of the game, have done their preliminary study and theoretical preparation, the roles of attorneys are now reversed,

at least in Michigan. Today the defense has to probe in order to come up with something new and in order to broaden understanding. This, as has been noted, is the first and most important point of this paper: Defense counsel have to do a great deal of studying and learning about psychiatry if they are effectively to advance their side of the argument about emotional damage.

This is no easy matter. To become a psychiatrist requires not only a medical degree, but 4 to 6 years of postgraduate training. In fact, to be eligible to pass one's boards in psychiatry requires a minimum of 7 years of postgraduate work, and in practice rarely takes less than 10. Even at that, only a limited percentage of those eligible are ever able to pass the examinations when given. While it is unreasonable to suppose that this amount of training is necessary in order to acquaint a lawyer well with the discipline of psychiatry, the facts are mentioned to give substance to a significant conclusion: It is unwise for the attorney to expect mastery of such a body of material in a matter of 3 or 4 hours.

If, then, the first requirement of the improved defense against psychiatric claims is deeper and broader knowledge by the lawyer, what is the second? It is making the same demand of the medical expert. This has two segments. In the first place, the psychiatrist has to supply more information than simply and ineffectually to call the plaintiff a liar. This statement goes to the issue of the term "malingerer." If the interviewer has the opportunity to know the plaintiff at all thoroughly, he can testify as in this hypothetical example:

"Doctor, is this patient aware of the nature of his suit?"

"Yes. He hopes to win $8,000. He told me so."

"Does he have any idea what he will do with this money?"

"Yes. He plans to buy a house on Cape Cod for $6,500 of the total. He has priced the property he is interested in."

"You mean, Doctor, he went to Cape Cod to examine this?"

"Yes. He also figured that he would have $1,500 reserve left over, and that his early reitrement would provide him with $275 a month for life, on which to live."

"Now, Doctor, is a man who has figured a money value for an injury, who has shopped for a house in a distant place, who has figured for a proper reserve to hold onto this land, who has calculated his disability pension, and who has made life plans for living comfortably within these limits—is such a man likely to give up his symptoms?"

---

[1] Carter v. General Motors Corp., 361 Mich. 577 (1960).

[2] D. Loria, "Recognizing and Handling a Traumatic Neurosis Case," *Michigan State Bar Journal* (July, 1956).

[3] The authors have presented these concepts only after a considerable amount of thought. Great care has been taken so that a destructive attitude would be avoided. In fact, the authors have come to respect and appreciate the selective tactics of the opposing attorneys in the adversary process. Only the observation itself is presented here that the plaintiff's attorney has a noticeable advantage because of his more thorough preparation in understanding the emotional nature of these injuries.

"No."

"Is it possible that such symptoms, whcih were originally related to an accident, are now related to an entirely different cause?"

"Yes."

"Do you mean, Doctor, that the same symptoms can have different causes?"

"Yes, counselor. For example, a pain in the abdomen can be caused by appendicitis; the next day it can be the result of surgical manipulation."

"Is this true in emotional diseases?"

"It can be."

"Doctor, what does this mean in the present instance?"

"It means the patient now has made some conscious and consciously acted upon decisions. He has decided whether or not having continued pain will get him certain clear-cut rewards."

With such information in the record, one doesn't have to call the patient names. Rather, a nontechnical description of the victim's thinking is clearly outlined, and juries or referees can understand it easily. Whether or not this is good legal technique is beyond the judgment of a physician; he can only observe that it is the truth and assume there is ample legal skill to get such material into the record in a proper technical manner.

But we are discussing what to expect of the medical expert. The question for him is whether such material can come out as the result of an hour's interview before trial. The answer is a sharp no. Such information derives from sufficient time with the patient, plus enough discussion between the attorney and the clinician. This should be a dialogue in which the attorney explains the points of law and in which the psychiatrist reviews the clinical material and ways in which to present it. This is not done to make the psychiatrist a "good" witness, but to make his testimony specific rather than vague, to make it relevant and to the issues, and to avoid misunderstandings which come from unprobed differences in point of view.

A case in point deserves attention. A prominent and effective plaintiff's attorney has put his thoughts in writing.[4] He says: "Where good medical and surgical specialists maintain that the patient has recovered from an injury but where the patient still complains with definiteness and apparent honesty as to the continuation of symptoms, a psychiatric examination is almost mandatory. In this type of

[4] J. W. Kelman, "Emotional Sequelae of Trauma," NACCA Transcript 17th Annual Convention, 1963. Copyright 1964, The W. H. Anderson Company.

case, a frequent attack on claimant's right to compensation charges is that he has become accustomed to being supported by the insurance company and being dependent upon it and refuses to leave his newly-acquired 'mother.' This attack is meaningless. The real question is whether or not the patient feels the pain or is untruthful. If he really feels the pain, the fact that he has *unconsciously* become dependent upon the insurance company is not material. The material points are (1) is he really disabled and (2) is his disability related to the injury." His observations about the unwise or unprepared psychiatrist, with the latter's vague allusions to the motherhood of the insurance carrier, are gems. But, if the physician has no idea of the material issues, how can he be other than vague? If he does know the business before him, he might well testify that the patient has captured the accident symptoms for an entirely different disability complex; then the doctor may leave speculations about maternity to subsequent theoretical psychiatric meetings. Such testimony can only be meaningful if the doctor is aware of the issues to which he must speak.

The second part of this more demanding use of the psychiatrist is wider employment of medical records. Here one runs into legal entanglements, but again the resourcefulness of defense counsel must be called upon. Medical records are important history; in fact, a great internist used to wag his finger at students and tell them that a history is always more important than a physical examination. In psychiatry this is even more true; it is the essence. Again, a case is illustrative.

A steelworker hurt his back when lifting a heavy plate. He was soon totally disabled, suffering not only from back pain but also from depression, headache, stomach disorder, and dizziness. Careful examination of the patient revealed only that he had previously had the same difficulty and had collected heavily for the injury. He further gave the history that for reasons he could not remember he had been discharged from service during the war. After that, he had been twice retrained in new labor skills and each time the job disappeared, again for reasons he could not remember.

In a careful study of the patient's records the reason for his amnesia became much clearer. When he had wanted to prove his instability in order to get out of the service, his memory had been much less faulty. At that time he recalled that at either 2 or 3 years of age he had fallen and hurt his back. For a full year thereafter, at this tender age, he had backache, headache, dizziness, stomach distress, and depression. He couldn't walk. His record also showed that he had what was called meningitis before the war with the same symptoms. He also found that after the war he couldn't do the jobs because when any pressure developed he had headache, backache, stomach distress, depression, and dizziness.

In a patient of this kind, the physician who has made an adequate study not only of the patient but of his records should be able to make an important contribution to the legal source which engages him. It can be shown beyond any reasonable doubt—medically, at least—that this patient is now acting the same way he always did, *when he didn't like or could not do what was expected of him*. This is not a new disease. In the particular case involved, for example, the disease had been present in almost pure and recorded form for nearly 45 years. It is absurd to bring a medical expert in to testify that an acute injury to this patient's back did not aggravate his prior disease, at least for a time. However, and this is an important point which was brought out in the *Carter* decision,[5] with the passage of time the patient has reverted to a prior, unstable emotional state, and is not suffering from a new disease caused by the accidental injury.

Only after the lawyer has this much medical material can he decide upon his proper defense. If his medical expert has given him a satisfactory review of the present status and of the record, counsel can devise both examination and cross-examination. The importance of the latter is enormous, because, in our experience, it is dealing with the testimony of the hostile psychiatrist which most frequently defeats the lawyer.

Usually the cross-questioning attempts to get the witness to agree with defense psychiatrist, and this fails. The weapons which can be used more hopefully are further information and direct challenges to theoretical concepts. The phrase "theoretical concepts" is carefully chosen.

When a medical expert appears in court, he is usually asked to describe his training and his hospital affiliation. He is further asked to tell if he belongs to a faculty and to give his list of memberships in learned societies. Under these circumstances and barring any interference from opposing lawyers, the qualification of a psychiatrist may sometimes take 20 or 25 minutes. It may be impressive indeed. The other method of dealing with this problem is usually having opposing counsel graciously rise to say he is familiar with the doctor's work.

In contrast to this, when a physician is introduced to a medical meeting and when his peers are the judges of his expertise, the introduction is quite different. Indeed, a moment *is* given his general background, but far more important will be the discussion of the physician's experience in the particular area to be discussed *and how successful he has been in dealing with it*. In the medical milieu, men are seldom regarded as experts unless their theories are tried and found useful.

What about the experience of a psychiatric witness in traumatic cases? Has most of his information come from treating this kind of patient? No, more likely he has had one or two patients in treatment for some such disorder as covert homosexuality which interferes with his marriage. During therapy this man had an accident, and he brought his reactions to the clinician. This patient, who has already come to the therapist for help, has strong motivation to get well, or he has some other compelling circumstance which has driven him into the doctor's office. The chances are great that his educational and cultural patterns, as well as his psychological make-up, are quite different from most accident cases. It can be dangerous to draw analogies between people so dissimilar.

Or has the testifying expert drawn his experience from the war neuroses? Here the danger of analogy is even more apparent and greatly misleading. It is difficult to observe that one can be entrapped into believing that emotional reactions to battlefield destruction and sudden death of close associates are similar to reactions of workers to twisted backs. Yet some psychiatrists believe they are the same. In fact, it is this false comparison which has led to constant use of the term conversion hysteria in our courts. In truth, conversion hysteria was frequently seen on battlefields; critical examination indicates it is much less frequent in civilian life. But how is the court going to know this unless the experience of the psychiatrist is placed on record?

And how much experience does the testifying doctor really have? Last year when Dr. Behan and I published our study of about 300 such cases in the Journal of the American Medical Association,[6] we indicated that we had examined each of these patients from 2 to 20 hours. We were surprised to discover that no other psychiatrist in the United States apparently has recorded this number of patients examined in such depth.

A second matter comes to mind when one

6 A. H. Hirschfeld and Robert C. Behan, "The Accident Process, Part I: Etiological Considerations of Industrial Injuries," *Journal of the American Medical Association*, 186 (Oct. 19, 1963): 193–99.

thinks of qualifying the psychiatrist. What about his biases, and how do they affect his theories? The court is to hear the doctor's opinion, is even to use it to guide the law toward decision. Then surely the court has a right to know what prejudices might be incorporated into the professional knowledge of the witness. Is this a management man? Does he always defend the underdog? A monumental psychiatric treatise has been published on these questions, and should be part of every trial lawyer's library. It is "The Fallacy of the Impartial Expert" by Bernard Diamond.[7]

In addition to knowing the vagaries of the individual doctor, the lawyer may want to learn something of his generic breed. There are some issues on which a person may take a categorical stand, in contrast to a specific position on special situations. The physician should be able to distinguish for the court which point of view is being adopted in his testimony. For example, there are psychiatrists who believe that the mind is the function of the brain. Therefore, nothing will happen to the patient's thinking unless something first occurs in the brain. This means, as a matter of principle, the expert must testify that the patient's brain was hurt if his behavior changed after an accident. He would not be a very good defense witness, no matter what other facts might pertain to the case at the bar. If such a clinician sees a normal electroencephalogram, he only alleges that these tests are not refined enough to determine this type of damage. It is the same with microscopes; they are too gross.

Other psychiatrists have all kinds of generic rules. For example, Freud described certain genital threats to small children, pointing out that these are very significant. Experienced psychoanalysts emphasize this in certain types of cases. However, when some physicians testify, they see almost all insults to the body as reactivation of this early problem. This is important, not as an illustration of truth or untruth, but because the court is entitled to know if the judgment is generic or whether specific facts in a particular case lead to unique conclusions. A similar generic interpretation would be seen in others who feel adult traumata always reactivate inferiority complexes. Many of these men tend to group themselves with others who hold similar beliefs, and so there are various schools.

Qualifying psychiatrists should include some rather elaborate evaluation of such attitudes

as have just been named. Although lawyers are shrewd enough to observe these positions, and discuss them privately, they seldom deeply examine into these attitudes when the doctor is on the stand. Yet, some of these postures make the doctor an advocate, not an expert, and by definition raise questions about ability to deal with the specific facts in any one case.

More complete illustration of this proposition can be made by analogy to orthopedics rather than directly to psychiatry. How many times has the court been puzzled by two well-trained orthopedists who read X-rays differently? One says the roentgen evidence shows a ruptured disc; the other denies it. This can happen with objective evidence, visually presented to and studied by the witnesses. To discern more about such opinions—and this is the point—the examining counsel can try to discover whether the physicians feel specific evidence in the case at bar is being considered, or whether the doctor classifies all such cases this way, since here the individual's uniqueness is most pertinent. Psychiatrically, this is a central determination. The progress of both law and medicine is characterized by increasing evidence of each patient's uniqueness. Whereas the test was once, how do people usually react to such emotional stimulation, our disciplines are now concerned with how and why a certain individual responded to these stimuli. Thus, a generic answer by the medical witness, one describing how other people react, is less meaningful than an answer on the present facts alone.

The end of the questioning deserves attention too. This is the fourth and last point. The problems of prognosis and treatment must be inquired into, because there must be some basis of determining medical costs in the future. Most psychiatrists answer these questions cautiously, because success of psychotherapy depends upon many factors, not the least of which is the attitude of the patient. Usually, however, one of the lawyers coaxes a guess, "Do you think two years of thrice weekly sessions would be a good test, Doctor?"

Here is another spot in which to check up on the expert. "In your own experience, Doctor, how do such patients react?" This is a good question. Most psychiatrists have never treated such an individual for this disorder. And the majority of clinicians will be glad to admit this to the court, given the chance. They dislike pulling numbers out of the air.

For those few doctors who claim to understand the prognosis, special care should be exercised in questioning. They may believe accident victims all have bad outlooks in treatment, and they will support this view with

---

[7] B. L. Diamond, "The Fallacy of the Impartial Expert," *Archives of Criminal Psychodynamics*, 3 (Spring, 1959): 221–36 [also reprinted herein, Chapter 6—Ed. Note].

theoretical deductions. These must be suspect, as was the theory of the doctor who didn't believe in psychometrics. Only if such an expert can offer evidence of having properly tried known methods which failed a significant number of times will he be believed. To our knowledge such psychiatrists are few indeed.

The enormous lack of knowledge is the paradox of the problem between the psychiatrist and the defense counsel. It stands against other areas in which there is a great store of information. The problem, then, is for each group to devote time and study to the other. In a world where specialties are constantly proving too small to encompass their problems, here is an opportunity for interdisciplinary cooperation in which both participants will profit.

SUGGESTIONS FOR ADDITIONAL READING

Curran, *Law and Medicine.* Boston: Little Brown & Co., 1960, 1960, pp. 282–91.

Keiser, L. "The Traumatic Neurosis," *Trial Magazine* (April/May 1970): 59.

Keiser, L. *The Traumatic Neurosis.* Philadelphia: J. B. Lippincott Co., 1969.

"Neurosis and Trauma," Transcript of American Psychiatric Association Round Table Meeting, May 10, 1960.

Robitscher. *Pursuit of Agreement: Psychiatry and the Law.* Philadelphia: J. B. Lippincott & Co., 1966, chapter 12.

Smith. "Problems of Proof in Psychic Injury Cases," 14 *Syracuse L. Rev.* 586 (1962–63).

Stetler and Moritz. *Doctor and Patient and the Law,* 4th ed. St. Louis: C. V. Mosby, 1962, chapter 9.

Tanay, E. "Psychic Trauma and the Law," 15 *Wayne Law Rev.* 1033 (Summer 1969).

Annotation: "Right to Recover Damages in Negligence for Fear of Injury Another, or Shock or Mental Anguish at Witnessing Such Injury," 29 *ALR* 3d 1337, 1970.

For collected case references, see:

"Sufficiency of Proof that Mental or Neurological Condition Complained of Resulted from Accident or Injury in Suit Rather than from Pre-existing Condition," 2 *ALR* 3d 487.

13

Torts–The Doctor as Defendant

There have been relatively few malpractice cases arising out of psychiatric treatment, and most of these have concerned the issue of informed consent, especially incident to electroshock therapy, and the problem of evaluating the appropriateness of the psychiatric regimen in a case in which a depressed patient has injured or killed himself or another. The rules of law are not basically different from those applicable to other areas of medical practice, but the fact that the patient has some degree of mental or emotional impairment complicates the issue of consent, and renders more difficult appraisal of the reasonableness of the treatment. The five cases below, and the article by Dr. Bellamy, raise the issues most likely to be encountered in legal actions in which the doctor is the defendant.

MITCHELL v. ROBINSON

BARRETT, Commissioner:

William Mitchell has been awarded $15,000 damages against the Doctors Robinson and their associates, particularly Dr. Jack DeMott, for malpractice, and the essentially meritorious problem is whether upon the record there is any evidence to support the jury's finding of negligence.

Mitchell and Dr. DeMott were boyhood schoolmates in Independence, Kansas, attended Kansas University at the same time, and were both living in Independence when Dr. DeMott began the practice of medicine there. So when in 1951, at age thirty-five, Mitchell was beset with serious emotional problems he sought out Dr. DeMott who was then a specialist in neurology and psychiatry and was then associated with the Doctors Robinson and the Neurological Hospital in Kansas City, Missouri. Mitchell had "a rather severe emotional illness," process schizophrenia, but he was not mentally incompetent; his illness was characterized by serious depression and rather severe anxiety, complicated by alcoholism. It is not necessary at this

point to detail his case history and symptoms; it was the opinion of the doctors that he should have "combined electro-shock and insulin sub-coma therapy." The general purpose of electroshock treatment is to build up the patient's "defenses and controls and self-confidence" while insulin relieves "basic anxiety" and "disturbance of the mood." The desired physical reaction and intended purpose of electroshock is to induce convulsive seizures of forty to fifty seconds duration. The desired physical reaction of insulin shock is the induction of unconsciousness, a "sub-coma" state, but it is neither intended nor desired, as it is with electroshock, that the patient suffer a convulsion. One of the unpredictable results of insulin shock, however, is an unpreventable convulsion and one of the hazards of convulsions, whether from insulin or electroshock, is fractured vertebrae, fractured legs, and various other injuries.

On October 25, 1951, Mitchell had his first electroshock treatment, the next day another, and, after two days' rest, his first insulin shock October 28 and the next day another, and on

Supreme Court of Missouri, 334 S.W. 2d 11 (1960).

the 30th his third electroshock and on the 31st another insulin treatment. There were convulsions with the electroshock treatments but no untoward results; the insulin treatments came off with normal results and reactions except that on the 31st Mitchell suffered a convulsion and that particular treatment was successfully terminated by an intravenous injection of glucose. Insulin treatment, reduced to 25 units, was resumed November 2, but Mitchell went out for a walk and came in drunk and the treatments were "started over" again on November 4 with 25 units, increased to 40 units November 5, and on November 7, with his seventh insulin treatment of 40 units, he had a "hard generalized convulsion," a grand mal seizure, which resulted in a compression fracture of the fifth, sixth, and seventh dorsal vertebrae. It is to recover damages for these specific injuries that Mitchell instituted this action.

These briefly noted facts are excerpted as background for certain basic distinctions in this and other malpractice cases and eventually to point up the problem precisely involved upon this appeal. The appellant doctors, relying on the general rules (*Williams* v. *Chamberlain*, Mo. 316 S.W. 2d 505), contend that their motions for a directed verdict should have been sustained because "There was no expert testimony to show that the insulin therapy administered to Mitchell failed to conform to the required standards of an ordinarily careful and prudent neurologist or psychiatrist in the community," indeed, the greater part of their brief is devoted to this subject. This phase of appellants' argument has but little if any bearing upon the basic problem involved here; it may be that they could not anticipate just what position the plaintiff would take. But the plaintiff has made it perfectly clear that there is no claim of negligence in any of these general respects; in his brief he repeatedly disclaims any such reliance: "Under point I(a) appellants say there was no expert testimony to show that the insulin therapy administered to Mitchell failed to conform to the required standards. *That is not the complaint.* . . . Plaintiff does not question the technique of administering the insulin, nor does he deny that it should have been administered. . . . There (*Steele* v. *Woods*, Mo. 327 S.W. 2d 187), as here, there was no complaint that the operation was not recommended by good medical practice and was not competently done." Furthermore, there is no question here as to the plaintiff's consent to the treatment (annotation 139 A.L.R. 1370) or claim that the procedure extended beyond that contemplated by the consent. Annotation 56 A.L.R.

2d 695. Again the plaintiff disclaims: "Indeed, he consented to that. . . . Mitchell had already given his oral consent."

On the other hand, despite the repeated disclaimers, the plaintiff immediately argues, inconsistently, that "The issue on the second ground of negligence is whether defendants owed plaintiff a duty to use ordinary care to prevent injury to him during the insulin treatment. On this issue, as well, the defendants provided the necessary expert evidence." At another point the plaintiff says: "But he also proved the defendants were negligent *after* it had been administered in that they failed to use ordinary care to prevent the convulsion by giving him an injection of glucose, when they had ample opportunity to give him the injection. He proved they were negligent in failing to prevent injury from the convulsion after it had begun by guarding him with proper restraints—ankle and wrist cuffs, and a complete body covering as described by Dr. Pool." Upon this phase of the argument the fact was that when the insulin was administered to Mitchell, and all other patients receiving the treatment, he was placed on his back upon a hospital bed with a heavy leather "waist belt" or restraint around the middle of his body. And on this particular occasion, as on other occasions, five attendants were present at the bedside, two colored maids, a male attendant, a nurse, and Mrs. Wuebbold, the experienced (more than twenty years) supervisor of insulin therapy—it was she who administered the insulin. The defendants produced as a witness Dr. Pool, a radiologist connected with a veterans' hospital, Fort Roots Hospital, North Little Rock, Arkansas. While he was neither a neurologist nor a psychiatrist and disclaimed any special qualification in these fields he had made two case studies of the incidence of fractures from shock therapy as they occurred in his hospital. In one study of 46 insulin shock patients he testified that eighteen per cent of them sustained fractures, that in the course of combined electro and insulin shock treatment of 53 patients nineteen per cent sustained fractures, and in another group of 32 patients twenty-five per cent sustained fractures. In his cross-examination Dr. Pool said that in Fort Roots Hospital patients receiving shock treatments were placed in a heavy canvas shroud covering their bodies from head to foot. Another of the defendants' witnesses, Dr. Bills, a neuropsychiatrist, said that wrist and ankle cuffs were sometimes employed. Mrs. Wuebbold, Dr. Bills, and others said that when the first signs of a convulsive seizure appeared a twitching about the eyes and mouth, glucose was administered to restore consciousness, terminate the treatment, and thus prevent a convulsive seizure. These and other circumstances are pointed to, the fact that Mrs. Wuebbold stood at his bedside and saw the face twitching but did not administer glucose, and it is argued that the jury could reasonably draw the inference that the defendants failed to use ordinary care to prevent an injury during treatment in that they could and should have employed all or some of these measures or expedients and thus have prevented the convulsive fractures.

Aside from the disclaimers and the inconsistency of the plaintiff's argument, the insuperable difficulty with this theory of liability is that he did not offer any expert medical testimony upon any of these subjects and the testimony pointed to does not support the inference of negligence in failing to prevent injury during treatment or in failing to employ other restraints or in failing to administer glucose. While the defendants' witnesses testified that wrist and ankle cuffs or other restraints were sometimes employed or glucose used (as it was successfully on Mitchell's sixth insulin treatment), without exception they all testified that the procedures, measures, restraints, and treatment employed on the occasion of his seventh insulin treatment were all in accordance with recognized medical practice in such cases in Kansas City and no other inference is fairly permissible from the testimony. These are not matters of common knowledge or within the experience of laymen and expert testimony is necessary to establish negligence in these respects (*Williams* v. *Chamberlain, supra; Steele* v. *Woods, supra*) and proof that some other measure was possible or that elsewhere some other type of restraint was in use does not support the inference of negligence or here supply the deficiencies in the plaintiff's proof. (*Spain* v. *Burch,* 169 Mo. App. 94, 154 S.W. 172; *Farber* v. *Olkon,* 40 Cal.2d 503, 254 P.2d 520; Regan, *Doctor and Patient and the Law,* Sec. 38, p. 284.) In short and to clarify the meritorious problem involved here, there was no substantial evidence of negligence in these particular respects as the plaintiff partially and conjunctively submitted in instruction one.

One further preliminary matter should be noted; in most of the cases involving fractures from shock therapy the determinate problem has been whether res ipsa loquitur was applicable and almost without exception it has been held that the doctrine was not applicable, and, as the doctors urge, proof alone of an unintended convulsion and fractures does not establish negligence. (*Farber* v. *Olkon, supra; Johnston* v. *Rodis,* 102 U.S. App. D.C. 209,

251 F. 2d 917; *Quinley* v. *Cocke,* 183 Tenn. 428, 192 S.W. 2d 992. But compare "The California Malpractice Controversy," 9 *Stanford L.R.* 731, and *Salgo* v. *Leland Stanford Jr. Univ. Bd. of Trustees,* 154 Cal. App. 2d 560, 317 P. 2d 170; in which res ipsa loquitur was held to be applicable to paralysis resulting from or as a complication of an aortography.) It is not claimed that res ipsa loquitur has any part in this case but contrary to the doctors' contention, even though there is but a plea of "general negligence," the plaintiff is entitled to hypothesize any submissible act of negligence supported by his evidence, particularly any negligent fact issue tacitly tried by the parties as was the case here. (V.A.M.S. § 509.500; *Hales* v. *Raines,* 162 Mo. App. 46, 141 S.W. 917.)

This finally brings us to the really meritorious question of whether in the circumstances of this case, the illness and treatment involved, the doctors were under a duty to inform the plaintiff that one of the hazards of insulin treatment is the fracture of bones not involved in either the illness or the treatment. That the hazard exists is beyond question; Dr. G. Wilse Robinson, Jr., said that fractured bones, serious paralysis of limbs, irreversible coma, and even death were hazards incident to shock therapy and further that there are no completely reliable or successful precautions. In their amended answer the defendants "state that the fracture of bones is a danger and risk that is inherent in insulin shock therapy, and that compression fractures of the spine, and fractures of the limbs can and frequently do occur when said insulin shock therapy is properly administered." The plaintiff's principal claim here is that "there was evidence of a negligent failure to disclose to plaintiff the hazards of insulin treatment," and, of course, evidence that plaintiff would not have consented to the treatment had he known of the dangers. In his argument plaintiff states his position in this language: "He relies on defendants' negligent failure to warn him of the danger of injury from this therapy and on defendants' negligent assurance that there was no danger, and failure to use due care as submitted to the jury." The appellants, on the other hand, do not attempt to demonstrate or elaborate, they simply say that "Failure to inform Mitchell of the risks of the treatment, if there was such a failure, is not negligence." Thus, the serious hazards being admitted, the problem is whether in the circumstances of this record the doctors were under a duty to inform their patient of the hazards of the treatment, leaving to the patient the option of living with his illness or of taking the treatment and accepting its hazards. (*Mohr* v. *Williams*, 95 Minn., 261, 268, 104 N.W. 12, 14, 1 L.R.A., N.S., 439.)

To begin with, it must be said that very little thoughtful consideration has been given this specific problem, particularly with respect to electroshock and insulin therapy. According to Dr. Robinson the shock treatments for emotional disturbance and mental illness came into use in this area about 1940 and with the advent of the so-called tranquilizer type drugs electroshock and insulin therapy are not employed as often as they were a few years ago. Kansas solved the problem, at least as to its public institutions, by passing a statute which provides that "no person" suffering physical or mental injuries from shock treatment "shall . . . have a cause of action for damages against any physician or technician" unless the injury or death resulted from "gross negligence." (G.S. Kan. 1959 Supp. 76-1239 and see 2 Kan. L.R. 393.) Here the doctors rely on but two cases in support of their statement that failure to warn of the hazards is not negligence, *Steele* v. *Woods, supra*, recently decided by this court, and *Hunt* v. *Bradshaw*, 242 N.C. 517, 88 S.E. 2d 762, 763. These cases involved a dangerous operation and a most needful postoperative treatment; neither case was concerned with shock treatment or in fact with failure to warn of the hazards of any dangerous medical procedure. In the North Carolina case it was alleged that the paralysis of the plaintiff's arms and legs resulted from the doctor's negligence in attempting to remove a piece of steel lodged in the vicinity of the plaintiff's brachial plexus. The essentials of the case turned on the general rules and the failure of the plaintiff to adduce expert medical testimony in support of his charges of negligent care in operating and negligence in advising the operation. However, the plaintiff said, "I asked him about the operation, if it was a very serious one, and he said it wasn't nothing to it, it was very simple." The court noted that the plaintiff's evidence was sufficient to support a finding that the operation was of a very serious nature, but in connection with the plaintiff's statement and whether the operation was advisable the court said: "It is understandable that the surgeon wanted to reassure the patient so that he would not go to the operation room unduly apprehensive. *Failure to explain the risks involved, therefore, may be considered a mistake on the part of the surgeon, but under the facts cannot be deemed such want of ordinary care as to import liability.*"

Aside from the fact that the case did not hinge on or involve failure to warn of hazards connected with the operation, the court's italicized statement is inapplicable to this case because the hazards were not withheld from Mitchell because of the doctors' desire to protect him or to reassure him or because they did not want him to enter upon the treatment apprehensive of the results. Dr. DeMott and Dr. Robinson insist that they did warn Mitchell of the dangers and risks of the treatment, including the possibilities of fractures from either intended or unintended convulsive seizures. Upon this precise point the burden of the doctors' argument is that "Mitchell's contrary testimony is not substantial and competent to sustain his verdict in view of Dr. DeMott's testimony that in the mental and emotional state that Mitchell was in at the time of the conferences, he could not possibly have an accurate memory of the conferences after the passage of a number of years." And while on this subject it is just as well to note that Mitchell testified that he did indeed remember the conferences and he said that Drs. Robinson and DeMott recommended the electroshock and insulin therapies, that he personally had no knowledge of the possibilities of fractures from insulin, that they explained the "process" to him "but there was nothing in his conversation to me that indicated any risk or disability as a result of the insulin treatment or any risk of disability at all." He categorically denied that either of the doctors advised him of the possibility of bone injuries or death from the treatments. He said that he asked Dr. DeMott if there was any danger and "his answer was that the treatments had only a temporary effect, a confusion that would last only a matter of an hour or so. He didn't say there would be any lasting effect at all"—in fact the doctor replied, "no danger."

Following a varicose vein operation a paravertebral block is a necessary procedure to prevent impairment of circulation, gangrene and sometimes loss of extremities. In *Steele* v. *Wood, supra*, the other case relied on by the appellants, plaintiff submitted her case upon the theory that the doctor failed to advise her of the necessity of such a procedure. When Mrs. Steele entered the hospital for a second operation, the varicose vein operation, her husband signed a consent form but for some unexplained reason she did not sign a written consent. The doctor did not inform the husband of the necessity for a paravertebral block; he claimed however that he advised Mrs. Steele of the necessity for the procedure but she refused to have the nerve block and thereby contributed to her consequent disabilities. One of the doctor's expert witnesses testified that it was the duty of the doctor to inform the patient or some member of the family of the necessity for the treatment. The court held that as a part of the applicable general rules, it was the duty of the doctor to prescribe the treatment and that whether it was offered and refused was a matter of fact for the jury to resolve. In concluding that the plaintiff made a submissible case the court said: "And we think expert testimony is not required in order to establish whether or not a doctor has complied with his duty to communicate the advice of a treatment, admittedly necessary, under a given state of facts." [327 S.W. 2d 199.] So in this case, the plaintiff explicitly denying and the doctors affirming that they advised the plaintiff of the hazards of shock therapy, a fact issue was presented upon which there was no necessity for expert medical testimony. This case, *Steele* v. *Woods,* does not explicitly hold that it is the duty of a doctor to warn his patient of the hazards of a proposed treatment but there is a lesson in the case and its plain implications are certainly no comfort to the doctors here.

Mitchell did not sign a written consent to the treatment; however, in his brief he repeatedly states that he needed the treatment and "Indeed, he consented to that," but, he says, he would not have consented had he been informed of the hazards. His then wife (they were divorced in 1952 and both have remarried) did sign a consent which contained this sentence: "This is to certify that I have been informed of the possible dangers of shock treatment with curare and electroshock, or metrazol, or with insulin in the case of William Mitchell and that I hereby give permission to the Neurological Hospital and staff to administer this treatment and request that this be done. We assume responsibility for any complications or accident resulting from the administration of these treatments." Mitchell testified that he did not authorize his wife to sign the consent and that he never heard of it until long after he had been discharged from the hospital and therefore had no notice from the consent of the hazards of the treatment. It is not necessary to say whether the consent that Mitchell's wife signed was a valid assumption of the hazards of the treatment, the problem is whether it warned of the dangers and according to him he never heard of it and here, as in the Steele case, the doctors contend that they personally gave him the warning. (See *Rothe* v. *Hull,* 352 Mo. 926, 935, 180 S.W. 2d 7, 12.) The consent signed by the wife and the doctors' claim of a personal warning is some recognition by them of an obligation or duty to warn.

As indicated, these two cases relied on by the appellants were not concerned with shock therapy and they do not plainly consider the basic problem of whether the doctors were under a duty to warn their patients of the hazards of the particular procedure or treatment involved in those cases. And, it may be added, a case fairly meeting and considering the problem in connection with shock therapy or in comparable circumstances has not been found. In the rather bizarre case of *Lester* v. *Aetna Casualty & Surety Co.* (5 Cir., 240 F. 2d 676), the doctors deemed it unwise and unsafe to advise the patient of the hazards of shock treatment and it was held that his wife's written consent did not deprive the husband of the right to contract without due process of law—the only question involved upon the appeal. In the Rodis cases (*Johnston* v. *Rodis,* 102 U.S. App. D.C. 209, 251, F. 2d 917, 918; *Johnston* v. *Rodis,* D.C., 151 F Supp. 345) it was held that res ipsa loquitur was not applicable when the plaintiff sustained five or six fractures of her arm in electroshock treatment. However, the United States Court of Appeals in reversing the judgment said: "The statement attributed to the defendant, that shock treatments are 'perfectly safe,' contains less of prediction and more of present fact. We think this statement, if the defendant made it and did not qualify it in any way, might properly be found to be a warranty." *Salgo* v. *Leland Stanford Jr. Univ. Bd. of Trustees,* 154 Cal. App. 2d 560, 317 P. 2d 170, 181, did not involve shock therapy, the principal question was whether res ipsa loquitur was applicable to paralysis resulting from an aortography. But the plaintiff, his wife, and his son testified that they had not been informed that an aortography was to be performed and of course they had no knowledge of the dangers of this new and very hazardous procedure. The doctors, while admitting that the details of the procedure were not outlined and explained, contradicted the plaintiff's testimony. The trial court gave a rather broad instruction upon the duty of a physician "to disclose to the patient all the facts which mutually affect his rights and interests and of the surgical risk, hazard and danger, if any . . ." The instruction continued: "A physician violates his duty to his patient and subjects himself to liability if he withholds any facts which are necessary to form the basis of an intelligent consent by the patient to the proposed treatment. Likewise the physician may not minimize the known dangers of a procedure or operation in order to induce his patient's consent. . . . One is to explain to the patient every risk attendant upon any surgical procedure or operation, no matter how remote; . . ." The implication of the case is that the doctor is under a duty to warn the patient of the hazards of the procedure, but in considering this instruction in connection with the hypothesis of res ipsa loquitur the court arrived at this rather ambiguous if not inconclusive result: "The instruction given should be modified to inform the jury that the physician has such discretion consistent, of course, with the full disclosure of facts necessary to an informed consent."

While the fairly relevant cases may be indicative but inconclusive the authoritative literature is more specific and helpful to a positive and rather confident conclusion. The subject of the thoughtful article, by a doctor-law teacher, in 41 Minn. L.R. 381, is "A Reappraisal of Liability for Unauthorized Medical Treatment," but in considering *Hunt* v. *Bradshaw, supra,* and the leading cases of *Schloendorff* v. *Society of New York Hospital,* 211 N.Y. 125, 105 N.E. 92, 52 L.R.A., N.S., 505 (Cardozo), and *Mohr* v. *Williams,* 95 Minn. 261, 104 N.W. 12, 1 L.R.A., N.S., 439, all cited by the parties here, the author has this to say (p. 427): "If the sole basis or reason for bringing an action is the former, i.e., disappointment as to the outcome of the operation, there is no real loss in denying recovery. On the other hand, *serious objection may be raised to denying recovery where the reason for bringing the action is failure of communication by the doctor to patient.* The proper solution of this problem, in the opinion of the author, is to recognize that *the doctor owes* a *duty to his patient to make reasonable disclosure of all significant facts,* i.e., the nature of the infirmity (so far as reasonably possible), the nature of the operation, and *some of the more probable consequences and difficulties inherent in the proposed operation. It may be said that a doctor who fails to perform this duty is guilty of malpractice."* [Italics supplied.]

There is no problem here as to so doubtful a matter as the proper diagnosis of Mitchell's illness or as to the prognosis following treatment, matters which may be conclusions or which lie in the field of speculation, as contrasted with matters of fact, which the doctors could not intelligently communicate to their patient—another suggested qualification upon the imposition of liability. (41 Minn. L.R. 381, 429.) The rather high incidence of unintended convulsions and resultant fractures in insulin treatment was a well-known fact, and the final result here was not a matter of supposition as it often is with diagnosis and there was no problem as to the success or failure of the procedure in so far as it related to the primary objective of the treatment. There is no complaint here of the success or result of the treatment; the treatment improved Mitchell's

emotional illness (although he was again under the care of these same doctors in 1957 and 1958 before his case was tried in October, 1958, the suit having been filed in 1952). The incidental hazard here of convulsive fractures was not a danger inseparable from the hazards attendant to many comparatively simple operations or techniques such as the danger of tetanus, infection, or of failure or death under anesthesia. Compare: *Spain* v. *Burch, supra; Kenny* v. *Lockwood* (1931), 1 D.L.R. (Ontario) 507; and *Williams* v. *Chamberlain, supra.* There was no emergency here, it was not even claimed that Mitchell was critically or dangerously ill and that immediate spectacular treatment was imperative. He was "emotionally" ill and the treatment was "recommended," but it was not immediately necessary to save his life or even his sanity. The doctors said he had "a rather severe emotional illness," he was "upset, agitated, anxious, depressed, crying." He had been drinking excessively, he was having marital difficulties, was not sleeping well, could not think things through, had unsuccessfully attempted to work for his father and later unsuccessfully attempted to work for his then father-in-law. As indicated, when Mitchell came to the doctors he was not mentally incompetent or in delirium, he had some understanding of his problems and the need for treatment.

In the particular circumstances of this record, considering the nature of Mitchell's illness and this rather new and radical procedure with its rather high incidence of serious and permanent injuries not connected with the illness, the doctors owed their patient in possession of his faculties the duty to inform him generally of the possible serious collateral hazards; and in the detailed circumstances there was a submissible fact issue of whether the doctors were negligent in failing to inform him of the dangers of shock therapy.

Even though there was a submissible case, solely upon the indicated hypothesis, it is not possible to affirm the judgment plaintiff has obtained. The principal instruction, instruction one, is indeed a very sketchy submission of his basic theory and right of recovery and that theory is submitted conjunctively with extraneous matter and another hypothesis upon which he was not entitled to recover as previously indicated, one that required expert medical testimony. It is not necessary to say, however, that instruction one, standing alone, demands the granting of a new trial. At the behest of the defendants the court gave instruction 7, all of which was probably not justified, which in substance submitted whether the doctors did warn Mitchell and whether his injuries resulted "solely" from a danger inherent in insulin therapy. At the request of the plaintiff the court gave instruction 7a which the plaintiff says is a "proper counter or converse" of instruction 7. Instruction 7a begins by telling the jury that instruction 7 "is known as a sole cause instruction and submits the issue of sole cause of injury without any contributing negligence whatever on the part of defendants as submitted in instruction number one." The instruction, all in one sentence, then proceeds, "and if from the greater weight of all the credible evidence in the case you believe and find that negligence, if any, on the part of defendants toward plaintiff as submitted in said instruction number one caused or directly contributed to plaintiff being so injured, if so, then your finding under said instruction number 7, that is, upon the issue of sole cause submitted therein, must be in favor of plaintiff William Mitchell and against defendants." In the first place, instruction 7, whatever its basic

defects, is not a "sole cause" instruction, was not intended to be, was not made so by the mere use of the word "solely," and in the circumstances of this record and this case it is not believed that the doctrine of sole cause could have the slightest application. In the second place, instruction 7a is not a true "counter or converse" instruction, particularly of instruction 7, and it does, repeatedly and abstractly and therefore confusingly and erroneously inject into the case the false issue of "sole cause." (*Stupp* v. *Fred J. Swaine Mfg. Co.*, Mo. 229 S.W. 2d 681.) From all that appears from this instruction, either factually or by direction, the negligence referred to and to be found in instruction one was the conjunctively submitted hypothesis for which there was no evidentiary support and so the instruction may have been quite misleading as well as confusing. For these indicated reasons the judgment is reversed and the cause remanded.

GEDDES v. DAUGHTERS OF CHARITY OF ST. VINCENT DE PAUL, INC.

Miss Geddes was a life-long resident of Natchez, Mississippi, who was 59 years of age at the time of the trial of this case. Prior to the events which gave rise to the present litigation, Miss Geddes was retired and lived in her family home supported by the income from an inherited trust, which was administered by Francis Geddes, her brother and closest living relative. Miss Geddes had a long history of a number of ailments including alcoholism, drug addiction and a series of abdominal problems. The last mentioned problems resulted from a ruptured appendix which she suffered when she was a teenager. She had no history of previous treatment for a mental disorder.

In 1959, Miss Geddes was taken by her brother to the Natchez Sanitarium at Natchez, Mississippi, for treatment after he had been summoned to her home by her maid when the maid was unable to arouse Miss Geddes. At this institution she was under the care of a Dr. Stowers who had treated Miss Geddes before for other illnesses and who diagnosed her present condition as a probable addiction to a

sedative. After several weeks of treatment at the Natchez Sanitarium, Dr. Stowers concluded that psychiatric care would be required and recommended that Miss Geddes be transferred to the De Paul Hospital in New Orleans. After consultation with Dr. Stowers and with her brother, Miss Geddes agreed to be taken to the De Paul Hospital for treatment.

Miss Geddes was driven to the De Paul Hospital by her brother, accompanied by two nurses. Upon their arrival she was taken directly to the room assigned her while her brother took care of the details of the admission procedure. A psychiatrist, Dr. William Sorum, was given charge of Miss Geddes' case and saw her at regular intervals during her hospitalization at De Paul Hospital which lasted for one year and 22 days.

Miss Geddes testified, in effect, that when she was discussing with her brother and Dr. Sorum the matter of her going to the De Paul Hospital, she was not told that said hospital was a mental institution nor was she told that she had a mental condition and was going to

United States Court of Appeals, Fifth Circuit, 348 F.2d 144 (1965).

receive psychiatric treatment at De Paul's; that at the time she entered De Paul's she did not know it was a mental institution and thought it to be a general medical hospital at which she was to receive medical treatments for the abdominal adhesions which had troubled her for a number of years; that she never requested nor authorized anyone to administer treatment to her for a mental condition; and that she did not realize that the hospital was a mental institution until some two days after her admission when she heard some of the other patients discussing their various ailments and was asked by them the nature of her own mental problems. This testimony was substantiated, at least to some degree, by the hospital record wherein an entry note made by a nurse on the date of Miss Geddes' admission to the hospital shows that Miss Geddes at that time stated to the nurse: "I had adhesions. That's what I'm in here for now."

Following Miss Geddes learning that the De Paul Hospital was a mental institution she requested of Dr. Sorum and the various nurses and nuns on the staff that she be released and allowed to leave the hospital. These requests were viewed by the hospital as the customary and usual complaints almost universal among psychiatric patients and were ignored. On a few occasions Miss Geddes was permitted to leave the hospital to go shopping and/or attend various entertainment attractions in New Orleans. However, on each of said occasions she was accompanied by an employee of the hospital as an attendant and was given by the hospital staff a small amount of money which was sufficient only to cover her expenses for the day.

In August, 1960, Miss Geddes sent a letter to an attorney in Natchez, Mississippi, asking that he assist her in getting out of the hospital. Shortly thereafter there was instituted on behalf of Miss Geddes in a civil district court of the Parish of Orleans a habeas corpus proceeding naming the Daughters of Charity of St. Vincent de Paul, Inc., as the respondent. A hearing in that proceeding resulted in the court ordering and directing the hospital to release Miss Geddes. Subsequent to the conclusion of that proceeding Miss Geddes instituted this action seeking to recover the damages she suffered and expenses incurred as a result of her alleged false imprisonment at De Paul Hospital.

Under Louisiana law there are two essential elements to the tort of false imprisonment, namely, (1) there must be a detention or restraint of the person, and (2) such detention or restraint must be unlawful. (*Crossett* v. *Campbell*, 122 La. 659, 48 So. 141 [1909]; and *Sweeten* v. *Friedman*, 9 La. App. 44, 118 So. 787 [1928].)

As to the first element, the defendants contend that the restraint of Miss Geddes was not sufficient to meet the requirements of a false imprisonment in that there were reasonable means of escape available to Miss Geddes which she failed to exercise. While there is evidence that would support a finding that there were reasonable means of escape available to Miss Geddes which she failed to exercise, there is evidence that would support a finding that no such means of escape were available. The evidence reflects that while Miss Geddes was in the hospital there were at least two locked doors barring her from leaving the institution, and there is ample evidence from which the jury could reasonably infer that the hospital personnel would have prevented Miss Geddes from leaving the hospital had she attempted to do so. As to the trips Miss Geddes occasionally was permitted to take to downtown New Orleans, the evidence shows she was always escorted on said trips by a nurse or other attendant and was given only five to ten dollars in money to cover her expenses of the trip which was not sufficient money to get her back to Natchez, her hometown, and she knew no one in New Orleans to whom she could turn for help had she been able to elude her companion. Such facts as those coupled with her ill health, age, and weakened condition are such that we must conclude that reasonable men in an impartial exercise of their judgment could reach different conclusions as to whether there were reasonable means of escape available to Miss Geddes during all or any part of the time she was confined in the De Paul Hospital.

It is without dispute that Miss Geddes was not confined in the De Paul Hospital as a result of formal commitment proceedings. As to the lawfulness of the detention of Miss Geddes, the defendants maintain that the restraint which was imposed, if sufficient to constitute an imprisonment, was lawful because Miss Geddes voluntarily presented herself for treatment at the hospital and, therefore, consented to such restraint as may have been imposed. Thus, the lawfulness of the detention or restraint was consented to by Miss Geddes. (*Hunter* v. *Laurent*, 158 La. 874, 104 So. 747, 750 [1925]; *Banks* v. *Food Town, Inc.*, La. App., 98 So.2d 719, 722 [1957]; *Coates* v. *Schwegmann Bros. Giant Super Markets, Inc.*, La. App., 152 So.2d 865 [1963].)

While it is true that Miss Geddes agreed to be taken to the De Paul Hospital and entered said hospital without any objection on her part, she contends that she did not *voluntarily* enter the hospital or consent to be treated here because she was not aware of the fact that the hospital was a mental institution at the time she entered and did not learn such fact until about two days after she was admitted. If Miss Geddes, at the time she entered the hospital, did not know it was a mental institution and that she was to receive psychiatric treatments there, it cannot be said that she voluntarily entered the hospital and consented to receive psychiatric treatment. As above demonstrated, there was sufficient evidence to warrant a jury finding that Miss Geddes at the time she entered the De Paul Hospital did not know that it was a mental institution and did not consent to receive psychiatric treatment there.

Furthermore, as above indicated, there is evidence to the effect that commencing approximately two days after her admission to De Paul's, Miss Geddes, on four or five occasions, "begged" Dr. Sorum to release her from the hospital and in addition thereto on several occasions requested both the head nurse and the nun in charge of her ward in the hospital to release her and let her go home. This evidence is of itself sufficient to authorize a jury finding that, at some point subsequent to her entry in the hospital and during her stay therein, Miss Geddes withdrew her consent to detention in the hospital given on her original entry and that further detention at the hospital subsequent to such withdrawal of the consent constituted a false imprisonment, even though the jury might have believed and found that Miss Geddes, upon her original entry in the hospital, consented to be detained therein and to be given psychiatric treatments.

For the reasons above stated, we are convinced that the evidence required that the issues as to the false imprisonment of Miss Geddes and her damages, if any, resulting therefrom be decided by the jury and that it was error for the court to decide them as a matter of law and direct a verdict in favor of the defendants.

The judgment of the trial court is reversed and the case is remanded for further proceedings not inconsistent with this opinion.

BAKER v. UNITED STATES

Plaintiff's ward, Kenneth Baker (hereinafter referred to as the patient) was referred to the Veterans Administration Hospital in Iowa City, Iowa, on August 23, 1960, by his attending physician, Dr. C. E. Schrock, M.D. The patient, then 61 years of age, had been under Dr. Schrock's care for approximately 60 days prior thereto. In a medical certificate accompanying the patient's written application for admission to the V.A. Hospital, Dr. Schrock indicated the following:

Brief History: Progressive symptoms of depression past three months. Suicidal content evident, no real response to medication to date.

Symptoms: Depressed, self accusatory, sleep disturbance and periods of confusion. Suicidal content.

Diagnosis: Involuntary, psychotic reaction.

The patient's wife testified that at the time of patient's application for admission she conferred with Dr. James A. Kennedy, M.D.

(then acting Chief of the Neuropsychiatric Service at the V.A. Hospital) and advised him that there was a suicidal tendency on the part of her husband and told him about finding a gun her husband had hid in one of the buildings on the farm about three weeks before. Dr. Kennedy interviewed the patient for an hour to an hour and a half, visited with the patient's wife and brother, examined the admitting certificate above referred to, and advised the patient's wife that the patient would be admitted provided certain financial data concerning the patient was furnished (the doctor requested this data [sic] for the purpose of confirming that the patient's belief as to his state of poverty was in fact a delusion and completely unfounded). This data [sic] was furnished the next day and Dr. Kennedy then ordered his admission to Ward 10E, an open ward, because as the doctor testified "in my opinion he did not present himself as a suicidal risk." The patient remained on this open ward on the 10th floor for the next three days and

United States District Court, S.D. Iowa, 226 F. Supp. 129 (1964).

had free access to go to the 3rd floor for meals, to the canteen, and to go outside. On August 27, 1960, the patient left the ward on the 10th floor voluntarily and went to the grounds immediately outside the hospital building. At about 7:30 p.m., the patient jumped into a window well 13 feet deep in an obvious suicide attempt. He suffered scalp wounds, fractures of the left clavicle, the 8th, 9th and 10th ribs, and the left transverse processes of the 3rd, 4th and 5th lumbar vertebral bodies. About six hours later the patient suffered an occlusion of the left carotid artery. Thereafter the patient suffered a complete paralysis of his right side. On April 19, 1961, the patient was removed to Restopia, a private nursing home, where he now remains. The patient is completely and permanently disabled both mentally and physically and requires constant nursing attendance.

In considering the various allegations of negligence it should first be observed that there is no evidence indicating that hospital employees failed to carry out the orders of Dr. Kennedy or any other physicians in the care of the patient. Failure on the part of hospital employees to carry out the instructions of a patient's physician may constitute a violation of the standard of care required of hospitals. (*Shover* v. *Iowa Lutheran Hospital*, 252 Iowa 706, 107 N.W.2d 85 [1961].) Neither is there evidence indicating any appreciable change in the patient's condition from the time of his admission to the time of the suicidal attempt which might require action on the part of hospital employees not covered by Dr. Kennedy's instructions. (*Bradshaw* v. *Iowa Methodist Hospital*, 251 Iowa 375, 101 N.W.2d 167 [1960].) It should also now be observed that the window well into which the patient leaped was enclosed by a heavy mesh wire fence which was at least three feet high. This was not a case of the patient falling into the window well but the injury was caused by a deliberate leap of the patient over the fence into the window well.

Although it may have been better practice to cover the window well[1] the Court finds that under the evidence in this case the defendant was not negligent in failing to close the window well with a suitable covering.

The negligence, if any, which was the proximate cause of the patient's injuries arises out of the failure of Dr. Kennedy to properly diagnose the patient as a sufficient suicide risk

so as to require closer supervision than was furnished by the immediate assignment of the patient to an open ward. A closed ward on the 9th floor was available to which patients were assigned when close supervision was deemed advisable. The issues are: What standard of care was required of the hospital and its staff? Was that standard of care violated in assigning the patient to an open ward?

There appear to be no Iowa cases involving the standard of care required of mental hospitals toward their patients. But it appears generally that the care required of a hospital includes giving such care to a patient as the hospital knew or in the exercise of reasonable care should have known was required. This duty is measured by the degree of care, skill and diligence customarily exercised by hospitals generally in the community. A hospital is not an insurer of a patient's safety and is not required to guard against that which a reasonable person under the circumstances would not anticipate. *Shover* v. *Iowa Lutheran Hospital, supra,* 252 Iowa 712, 107 N.W.2d 85; *Bradshaw* v. *Iowa Methodist Hospital, supra,* 251 Iowa 384–385, 101 N.W.2d 167; 41 C.J.S. Hospitals § 8c(3), pp. 349-350.

The standards of care required of mental hospitals in other jurisdictions follow these same general standards. (*Mounds Park Hospital* v. *Von Eye,* 245 F.2d 756, 70 A.L.R.2d 335 [8 Cir. 1957].) It is particularly recognized in the treatment of mental patients that diagnosis is not an exact science. Diagnosis with absolute precision and certainty is impossible. Further the objective is treatment not merely incarceration. Treatment requires the restoration of confidence in the patient. This in turn requires that restrictions be kept at a minimum. Risks must be taken or the case left as hopeless. See *Fahey* v. *United States,* 153 F. Supp. 878, 885 (S.D.N.Y. 1957), reversed on other grounds, 2 Cir., 219 F.2d 445; *Mills* v. *Society of New York Hospital,* 242 App. Div. 245, 274 N.Y.S. 233, 270 N.Y. 594, 1 N.E.2d 346 (1936). The standard of care which stresses close observation, restriction and restraint has fallen in disrepute in modern hospitals and this policy is being reversed with excellent results. See Perr, "Suicide Responsibility of Hospital and Psychiatrist," 9 *Cleveland-Marshall L. Rev.* 427. This trend in the treatment and care of the mentally ill is reflected in regulations promulgated by the Administration of Veterans Affairs pursuant to the authority granted in 38 U.S.C.A. § 621.

Treatment and care of the Mentally Ill. The policy of the V. A. is to allow each psychiatric patient the maximum independence that his condition permits and to administer the hos-

---

[1] The investigating board appointed to investigate the suicide attempt by the patient recommended that a suitable covering be placed over all window wells as an added precaution and this was done.

pital so as to allow as normal a life as possible for the patient. All medically accepted therapeutic facilities will be available to each patient as required and if necessary such facilities will be made available by transfer to appropriate hospital. [Reg. M2–10 change to Par. 102.]

The difficulty lies in the application of the foregoing policy. Each case must rest on its specific facts. The assignment of the patient to an open ward by Dr. Kennedy is the critical issue before this Court. Was the doctor negligent? In *Wilson* v. *Corbin,* 241 Iowa 593, 599, 41 N.W.2d 702, 705 (1950), the Iowa Supreme Court said:

A physician is bound to use that degree of knowledge, skill, care, and attention ordinarily exercised by physicians under like circumstances and in like localities. He does not impliedly guarantee results. Bartholomew v. Butts, supra, 232 Iowa 776, 779, 5 N.W.2d 7, 9, and citations.

Of course malpractice may consist in lack of skill or care in diagnosis as well as in treatment. In re Estate of Johnson, 145 Neb. 333, 16 N.W.2d 504, 511, and citation; Kuechler v. Volgmann, 180 Wis. 238, 192 N.W. 1015, 31 A.L.R. 826, 829, and citation; 41 Am.Jur., Physicians and Surgeons, section 92.

A patient is entitled to a thorough and careful examination such as his condition and attending circumstances will permit, with such diligence and methods of diagnosis as are usually approved and practiced by physicians of ordinary learning, judgment and skill in the community or similar localities. A physician does not insure the correctness of his diagnosis. Ramberg v. Morgan, 209 Iowa 474, 477, 218 N.W. 492. See also In re Estate of Johnson, supra, 145 Neb. 333, 16 N.W.2d 504, 510, and citations; Hill v. Boughton, 146 Fla. 505, 1 So.2d 610, 134 A.L.R. 678, 682; 41 Am.Jur., Physicians and Surgeons, section 92.

Ordinarily, evidence of the requisite skill and care exercised by a physician must come from experts. Bartholomew v. Butts, supra, and citations. But there are exceptions to this rule. Whetstine v. Moravec, 228 Iowa 352, 370 et seq., 291 N.W. 425 and citations, especially Kopecky v. Hasek Bros., 180 Iowa 45, 49, 162 N.W. 828, 830, also cited with approval in Wambold v. Brock, 236 Iowa 758, 762, 19 N.W.2d 582, 584; Peterson v. Hunt, 197 Wash. 255, 84 P.2d 999, 1000, and citations.

See also, *Lagerpusch* v. *Lindley,* 253 Iowa 1033, 115 N.W.2d 207 (1962).

In the case at hand plaintiff offered evidence of practices followed at the State University of Iowa Psychopathic Hospital in the same city and during the same period of time as here involved. In this connection, Dr. Paul

Huston, Director of that hospital since 1956, testified as follows:

A. The first step would have been to establish the diagnosis and to determine if in fact this man was depressed, as the note from the referring physician had indicated. Since the referring physician had indicated that there was suicidal content to this man's thinking, we would have paid particular attention to this in order to determine what kind of precautions would be necessary in handling the case.

Q. And what kind of precautions would be used until it was found definitely he was subject to that suicidal content or was not?

A. Well, this varies some. It depends upon the presence or absence of the suicidal content. If present, this means certain precautions. If they are absent, then precautions aren't generally taken. If one is unsure, one is apt to be conservative and keep the patient under observation for a few days and try to determine whether there are suicidal thoughts in the patient's mind. Now as to the exact nature of precautions, this means generally that the patient is never let out of somebody's sight, out of sight of an employee of the hospital, a nurse or an attendant. It means that he does not have access to materials which he could readily destroy himself with—knives, razors, belts, and so on. If the suicidal intent is prominent, then an attendant even accompanies the patient to the bathroom. He isn't left alone, you see. So that it varies, depending upon the degree or judgment of the degree of the suicidal impulse and whether it's present or not.

Q. Doctor, would a patient such as referred to there in Exhibit 1 have been given free access to go and come from his quarters and freedom of the building and grounds at the Psychopathic Hospital during the month of August, 1960?

A. This would be very difficult to determine. The patient, when he arrived at the hospital, may not have been as depressed as was indicated by the referral note from Doctor Schrock. In Doctor Kennedy's report, he made a very definite attempt to determine the depth of the depression. He brought out that there had been history of it and that there were certain signs present now. But this comes, in the end, to a matter of judgment. It's entirely possible to miss a depression or suicidal thought on the first examination. On the other hand, if the referring physician has referred to this, then one is perhaps inclined to be more conservative and take extra precautions. So that, this is an extraordinarily difficult question to answer, you see.

Q. Well, ordinarily, doctor, what would be the practice in a case such as Mr. Baker where there is suicidal content indicated by the referring doctor?

A. We would have taken this very seriously.

Q. And what procedure would have been followed in regard to his care and treatment there at the Psychopathic Hospital during that time?

A. I think we would have been conservative in our approach to it.

Q. And what do you mean by that?

A. Well, I can't say for sure, I didn't see the patient, you see. But we possibly would have written in the note 'suicidal precautions' at least for a few days until we got a chance to know this patient better, and this would have meant that he would have been under observation and that somebody would have watched him closely all the time.

. . .

Q. To summarize your testimony then, doctor, in this particular case, such as Mr. Baker, you would have been on the conservative side as I understand your testimony. Is that correct?

A. Yes, I think so. If you are going to err, err on the conservative side, I feel. But again let me emphasize, I wasn't there, I didn't examine the patient. It's impossible to say what I would have done had I seen him, you see.

Dr. H. J. Madsen, Director of the 1540 bed Neuropsychiatric Veterans Hospital at Knoxville, Iowa, expressed the opinion that the patient received perfectly acceptable psychiatric care.

In reviewing the conduct of Dr. Kennedy it will be considered that he was aware of Dr. Schrock's note on the medical certificate as to the patient's mental condition prior to admission and the statement made by the patient's wife concerning the finding of a hidden gun, as heretofore related.[2] It will also be considered that the doctor conducted a lengthy interview and examination of the patient and made his own judgment that the circumstances did not require assignment of the patient to a closed ward or that other precautions be taken. Without reviewing all of the facts in detail it is sufficient to state that the Court finds that Dr. Kennedy exercised the proper standard of care required under the circumstances. Calculated risks of necessity must be taken if the modern and enlightened treatment of the mentally ill is to be pursued intelligently and rationally. Neither the hospital nor the doctor are insurers of the patient's health and safety. They can only be required to use that degree of knowledge, skills, care and attention exercised by others in like circumstances. . . .

[2] There was no evidence of an actual attempt by the patient to commit suicide.

MERCHANTS NATIONAL BANK AND TRUST COMPANY OF FARGO v. UNITED STATES

MEMORANDUM OF DECISION

RONALD N. DAVIES, District Judge.

This is an action brought by the Merchants National Bank and Trust Company of Fargo, a corporation, as Administrator and Personal Representative of the Estate of Eloise A. Newgard, deceased, against the United States of America, to recover damages by reason of the alleged negligent conduct of the defendant's agents and employees which resulted in the killing of Eloise A. Newgard by her husband, William Bry Newgard,[1] in Detroit Lakes, Minnesota, July 31, 1965. Jurisdiction is predicated upon Title 28, U.S.C.A. § 1346 et seq., commonly described as the Federal Tort Claims Act. The suit is brought on behalf of

[1] He will be referred to hereafter as Newgard, as not to confuse his name with that of his father, William S. Newgard.

the three minor children of the decedent: Elizabeth, born September 16, 1955, Ann Marie, born April 13, 1958, and Robert William, born December 28, 1960.

Basically, the questions here presented are factual in nature, necessitating a somewhat detailed statement of the evidence developed upon trial.

Early in the morning of January 17, 1965, Dr. Mack V. Traynor, a Fargo physician, was called to the Newgard apartment in Fargo, North Dakota, by Newgard's wife, Eloise. She was frantic-voiced and said she needed help. The doctor, promptly responding to the call, found Newgard glassy-eyed and making senseless talk about horses, cattle "and God most of the time." Dr. Traynor felt Newgard was completely psychotic. Earlier that same morning Eloise had telephoned her pastor, Reverend Richard C. Faust, who knew both Newgard and his wife. He, too, came to the apartment. A daughter, Elizabeth, admitted him. Eloise asked for his help. From elsewhere in the apartment Newgard was shouting "get him out." Reverend Faust says that Newgard finally appeared, yelling that he was "the reincarnation of Jesus Christ." He was clad in boxer shorts and T-shirt. Newgard pulled his shorts down, exposed himself and said he was "going to repopulate the world." Newgard accused his wife of unfaithfulness and threatened to kill her. Reverend Faust also understood Newgard to say that the "God of Fire" would repopulate the world.

Both the Newgards had taught Sunday school in his church, but Reverend Faust had so many complaints about Newgard, he was forced to relieve him of his teaching assignment. Reverend Faust later in the morning of January 17, 1965, was able to get Newgard to St. Luke's Hospital in Fargo by literally marching him there through the streets.

Dr. Albert C. Kohlmeyer, a well qualified psychiatrist, saw Newgard the same day in the Neuropsychiatric Institute section of the hospital. He found him very agitated, "carrying on" about religious ideas and testified that Newgard thought "he was Christ or some representative of Christ." Because of his delusional ideas, the psychiatrist thought Newgard was psychotic and although he saw Newgard only a couple of days, it was his belief that Newgard's illness had been coming on for a long time. Dr. Kohlmeyer felt Newgard was a schizophrenic, chronic, with acute exacerbation, paranoid type.

On January 19, 1965, the Cass County, North Dakota, Mental Health Board after a hearing, ordered Newgard committed to the State Hospital at Jamestown, North Dakota. Later because he was a veteran, an amended

order was issued by the board, making the commitment a dual one so that Newgard could eventually be transferred to the Veterans Administration Hospital at Fort Meade, South Dakota. Effective March 23, 1965, Newgard was transferred to Meade where he was admitted to a ward and placed under the direct supervision of Dr. Leonard S. Linnell, a medical doctor and psychiatrist. This was Dr. Linnell's first position as a psychiatrist since completion of his residency in psychiatry at the University of Minnesota and the Veterans Administration Hospital in Minneapolis.

Dr. Linnell had access to the records of Newgard from the North Dakota State Hospital at Jamestown, which he says he studied, he had access to the mental health records and the commitment papers which he studied and, of course, at all times while Newgard was at Meade he had access to any of Newgard's files and records of whatever kind of nature.

For a number of weeks Newgard was treated with tranquilizers and saw a clinical psychologist, Dr. Jesse H. Craft, weekly, for psychotherapy and examinations. During the course of Newgard's treatment and care he was interviewed by Dr. Linnell about once a week. The psychiatrist also sent Newgard to Dr. Truman M. Cheney, a vocational psychologist, for testing and reporting his job aptitudes. Newgard was given various jobs around the hospital, a procedure followed by Meade in the treatment of hospital patients and which is followed in hospitals of a similar nature. On or about May 25, 1965, Newgard received a letter from his father according to Dr. Linnell, advising Newgard an uncle had died. Newgard got permission from Dr. Linnell to attend the funeral and for that purpose was given a pass for one week's leave of absence "to his parents' home in North Dakota." Dr. Linnell told Newgard to go to the funeral and to his parents' home and to return to the hospital and not to make any other visits. It is quite evident that Dr. Linnell did not know where or when the funeral was to be held or even the city in North Dakota in which Newgard's parents lived. Nor did he consult any other member of the staff at Meade prior to releasing Newgard to attend a funeral conducted at Leeds, North Dakota, which was already over long before Newgard reached Fargo by bus on the day thereof. Dr. Linnell did, however, have Mrs. Lois Powers, a social worker at Meade, telephone Eloise Newgard as the patient's guardian, that Newgard was to be released to attend his uncle's funeral.

Mrs. Newgard, frightened for her life, sought help from people in Fargo who eventually got in touch with County Judge Paul M. Paulsen, Chairman of the Cass County Mental

Health Board, who had Newgard taken into custody at the bus station in Fargo. Here it is noteworthy that Dr. Linnell called Judge Paulsen by long distance telephone on the day Newgard was released, ostensibly to attend the funeral and visit his parents' home. Dr. Linnell told Judge Paulsen, referring to Newgard, "Nobody need to be afraid because this man is cured and he wouldn't hurt anybody." Judge Paulsen thereupon told Dr. Linnell that everyone who knew about Newgard, his condition and his commitment, felt Newgard was far from well mentally and that he was a dangerous man and should not have been released. Dr. Linnell told Judge Paulsen also that "there is nothing to worry about; this man I have told not to stop in Fargo" and "not to try to see his wife." The Cass County Mental Health Board met next day and directed the sheriff of Cass County to return Newgard to Meade. On May 27, 1965, Cass County deputies Dewey Eagle and Archie Vraa did so.

After Newgard's return to Meade the authorities there began thinking about getting Newgard work in the Meade area. Sometime early in July, 1965, Eloise Newgard learned that Dr. Linnell and the Meade authorities were about to discharge Newgard, and very much concerned for her safety, callede Meade and talked to Dr. Curt L. Rosenbaum, Meade's Chief of Staff. Dr. Rosenbaum says she was upset and hung up on him. Dr. Rosenbaum himself never diagnosed Newgard, although he conceded there was no way it could be said Newgard's condition was in complete remission when he arrived at Meade. Dr. Harland T. Hermann, Chief of Psychiatry at Meade, evaluated Newgard's case thereafter. Unfortunately his written report was in some manner lost since it could not be found in the Meade records and files, but Dr. Hermann remembers making it and Dr. Linnell remembers seeing it. Dr. Hermann advised Dr. Linnell not to discharge Newgard.

Sometime before July 18, 1965, Dr. Truman M. Cheney, Counseling Psychologist at Meade, had made arrangements to put Newgard on leave at the ranch owned by Mr. and Mrs. Clarence A. Davis located some ten miles north of Belle Fourche, South Dakota. Dr. Cheney told Mr. Davis that Newgard had had "a mental disturbance, a nervous breakdown" and that Newgard wanted hard work to forget some of his troubles and for rehabliitation purposes. Mr. Davis had never before had a Meade patient working on his ranch.

On July 18, 1865, Newgard was released by Dr. Linnell on work leave to rancher Davis. When asked what instructions he had received from Dr. Cheney with respect to Newgard, Mr. Davis replied:

"None whatsoever that I can recall. I don't believe there was anything said about any way that he would conduct himself, that he thought that he was completely arrested from his troubles and just needed a chance to work and get better rehabilitated again. But there was no reservations made of what I should do with him or for him; or there was no given pattern where I should pay the money or who I should give the money to or whether he was free to come and go. I assumed from the way they talked that I was to pay him and he was to come and go as he pleased."

Dr. Cheney on the other hand testified he had told Mr. Davis that Newgard had an emotional problem, that he might be nervous, that Newgard was upset because his wife was suing him for divorce, and that he had instructed Mr. Davis to call Meade if Newgard gave indication of unusual behavior.

Dr. Cheney conceded, on cross-examination, that he had not told Mr. Davis what constituted "unusual behavior." It is Dr. Cheney's testimony that Dr. Linnell told him that Newgard could work in the immediate Fort Meade area, but that he would have to be kept in South Dakota and "more or less" under hospital surveillance. Dr. Cheney did not tell Mr. Davis that Newgard was under any hospital surveillance, that he could not leave South Dakota, or even that he was a mental patient.

Dr. Linnell testified that he received reports from Dr. Cheney that Newgard was doing well in his work and adjusting on the Davis ranch. This testimony is flatly contradicted by Dr. Cheney himself who testified that his only contact with Mr. Davis after Newgard was first placed on the Davis ranch, was after Newgard had gone to Detroit Lakes and killed his wife.

The second weekend when Newgard left the Davis ranch for the last time, Mr. Davis believed he was "going back to Sturgis" and took Newgard, with another employee, into Sturgis and left them off at the hotel in Belle Fourche. At no time during Newgard's stay at the Davis ranch was Mr. Davis ever contacted by any representative of Meade. So far as Mr. Davis was concerned he had simply hired another farmhand, quite free to come and go as he chose.

Dr. Russell O. Saxvik, a psychiatrist, former North Dakota State Health Officer and former Superintendent of the North Dakota State Hospital at Jamestown, testified he was acquainted with the standards of practice in mental hospitals in this area. He thought Jamestown State Hospital and Meade standards were comparable. He testified further that the Davises should have been given specific instructions with respect to Newgard, which the Court finds were not given. He further testified that a mental hospital would want to know the whereabouts of a patient on leave and that Mr. and Mrs. Davis should have been told to notify Meade immediately, if Newgard left the ranch, and that Meade in turn should have alerted the committing health board, which in the instant case was Cass County, North Dakota. Not one of these things was done in Newgard's case, although clearly the standards of practice in the area required that they be done. Moreover, Dr. Rosenbaum, one of the Government's own expert witnesses, testified that when a man has gone from an area in which he was given leave of absence "the matter should have been pursued, no question about that at all."

It develops that on July 24, 1965, Newgard left the ranch for the weekend. He was to have returned Monday, July 26th, but Newgard went to his parents' home at Mayville, North Dakota. His wife Eloise had no idea he was in Mayville and was there herself only for a brief visit. Newgard wanted his wife to return with him to Fargo but she declined. Newgard then called Mr. Davis, advising him he would return to work on the ranch on Tuesday, which he did. On the night of Friday, July 31, 1965, Mr. Davis again took Newgard into Belle Fourche, having paid him his wages. Newgard got possession of a car and ultimately drove to his mother-in-law's home in Detroit Lakes, Minnesota, where on July 31, 1965, he first attempted to run Eloise Newgard down with the car and failing that, got out of the vehicle, shot and killed her.

The Government sought to make much of Eloise Newgard's meeting her husband in Mayville, Sunday, July 25, 1965, which was entirely circumstantial so far as she was concerned as the record reflects, and to make much of Eloise's alleged failure to telephone Meade as to his whereabouts. It ought not to be forgotten that Eloise A. Newgard was a well trained and responsible registered nurse; that she had worked in a hospital for mental patients; that she knew Newgard was mentally ill and under the supervision of Meade; that she knew he was going back to the ranch and supposedly, at any rate, that Newgard was under the care and supervision of Meade personnel. Her conduct was that of any normally prudent person with any common sense. She wanted him away from her because of his mental illness and her deathly fear of him. She encouraged his going back to South Dakota; and he went back.

Similarly the Government made much of Eloise Newgard visiting her husband at Meade in mid June, 1965, when she journeyed down to South Dakota with her mother, Mrs. Daniel-

son, and the three Newgard children. On that occasion Eloise Newgard talked to Mrs. Lois Powers, the social worker, and to Dr. Linnell. There was a good deal of testimony concerning Eloise's attitude and conduct at Meade, but one inference is clearly drawn from the credible evidence in this action, and that is that Dr. Linnell believed almost everything Newgard told him without investigating or causing to be investigated any of Newgard's statements. Dr. Linnell quite evidently preferred "exaggeration" to "delusional" in describing Newgard's statements and appeared convinced that Eloise Newgard needed psychiatric help herself.

The evidence supports the inference that had Dr. Linnell devoted more of his time and talents to Newgard and less of them attempting to diagnose Newgard's wife, conceivably she would never have met so tragic and untimely a death. This Court thinks it abundantly clear, from the record in this case, that Dr. Linnell knew that Eloise Newgard was afraid of her husband, and it is utterly incredible that she would not have mentioned it to Dr. Linnell or that he would not have questioned her about it at their conference in Meade in June, 1965. Yet that is Dr. Linnell's testimony.

Dr. Linnell ignored and rejected every warning signal that Newgard was delusional at Meade and every warning signal that Eloise A. Newgard had every reason to be in mortal fear of her husband because of his prior conduct and the nature of some of the letters he wrote her while a patient at Meade. Dr. Linnell felt the recommittal order of the Cass County Mental Health Board of May 27, 1965, was "incorrect". Along with its recommittal order the Cass board sent to Meade Newgard's letter to his wife dated May 22, 1965. Dr. Linnell still referred to Newgard's cattle deals as "not a case of delusional thinking, it was exaggeration." Donald E. Frees, a social worker at the Veterans Administration Hospital in Fargo, made a thorough, comprehensive and very revealing report on the family history of the Newgards at the request of Meade. Dr. Linnell saw this instrument and conceded that he had no information that would provide him any basis for disregarding the information in Mr. Frees' report. Yet it is clear from the evidence that Dr. Linnell ignored the report. Had he even heeded the warning implicit in the summary of the social worker, Mr. Frees, which suggested that Newgard had become quite astute at manipulating people, it might have given the doctor pause, but it did not. It is worth noting that Dr. Rosenbaum testified that psychiatrists could not rely upon what a patient tells them in amental hospital and that is why they have social service reports. Dr. Rosenbaum was shown Mr. Frees' report and testified that it was better than average.

One of the Government witnesses testifying was Dr. Jesse H. Craft, a clinical psychologist on the Meade staff, who evaluated Newgard. Dr. Craft gave Newgard certain tests and submitted a written evaluation to Dr. Linnell as a diagnostic aid to the psychiatrist. His testing showed, among other things, clues of organic brain damage. Dr. George B. Kish, the Chief Clinical Psychologist at Meade, testified he did not agree with Dr. Craft that there was evidence of brain damage, even though Dr. Kish had not read all the reports on Newgard. Dr. Craft had been questioned under oath by Mr. Olin M. Stansbury, Jr., a Field Examiner for the Veterans Administration and one of the Government's attorneys in this trial. Among the questions asked of Dr. Craft by Mr. Stansbury on December 10, 1965, under oath, were these:

Q. Have you been informed of the facts on the commitment to the effect that he had choked his wife and had a loaded pistol in the home the day that his wife had asked for his commitment?

A. No, he didn't tell me anything about that.

Q. Did you ever have access to the VA Hospital Correspondence File in which a copy of that transcript is available?

A. No, I didn't.

Q. Had anyone ever told you about that?

A. Not that I recall.

Q. Now, in view of that fact, if in fact it were true, would you have taken his show of jealously (sic) after July 1st more seriously in your recommendations to the Team before they placed him out on leave of absence?

A. *I certainly would if there had been any indication that he had any serious intent toward the wife. I certainly would have recommended against his going.*

Q. Maybe I'm not making myself clear, Doctor, but what I have in mind is if you had all the information that you have had before July 18th with the exception of the fact that you would have been furnished the information from the commitment to the effect that he had tried to choke his wife on or about January 17th, 1965, would that one more piece of information made you hesitant in agreeing with the Team that he should be released on a leave of absence? Just the one fact that one time previously he had tried to choke his wife or had threatened to and apparently had a

loaded gun available in the home to do damage.

A. *I certainly wouldn't have recommended his release had I known that he had any such ideas or had behaved in that way.*

Q. Why?

A. *Because it would have shown more evidence of his homicidal—rather it would have shown evidence of homicidal thinking which I was completely unaware of.*" (Emphasis mine.)

The plaintiff alleges that the Government, acting through its duly authorized agents employed by the Veterans Administration, undertook the custody, care and treatment of Newgard, knowing him to be an insane and incompetent person with homicidal tendencies, and that the Government's inexcusable negligence was the proximate cause of Eloise A. Newgard's death on July 31, 1965, at the hands of her husband.

The plaintiff's burden in this type of case is not an easy one, but it has successfully borne it, in proving, by a preponderance of the relevant, material and credible evidence, that the negligence of the defendant acting by and through its duly authorized agents and employees was indeed the sole and proximate cause of the death of Eloise A. Newgard, and the damages sustained by the plaintiff as a result of her slaying.

The Government contends by way of affirmative defense that the United States is exempt from liability under § 2680(a) of Title 28 U.S.C.A. which provides that § 1346(b) shall not apply to:

"(a) Any claim based upon an act or omission of an employee of the Government, exercising due care, in the execution of a statute or regulation, whether or not such statute or regulation be valid, or based upon the exercise or performance or the failure to exercise or perform a discretionary function or duty on the part of a federal agency or an employee of the Government, whether or not the discretion involved be abused."

It is the Government's position that the granting of the leave of absence to Newgard to work on the Davis ranch near Belle Fourche was the exercise of due care in the execution of a Veterans Administration regulation, and that this falls within the exception set out in § 2680.

Considering the circumstances under which Newgard was placed on leave of absence at the Davis ranch, as disclosed by the credible evidence, the Government's agents and employees not only did not exercise due care;

in the view of this Court they exercised no care at all.

The test of liability under the Federal Tort Claims Act is set out in § 2674, the first paragraph of which reads:

"The United States shall be liable, respecting the provisions of this title relating to tort claims, in the same manner and to the same extent as a private individual under like circumstances, but shall not be liable for interest prior to judgment or for punitive damages."

The Fourth Circuit in White v. United States, 317 F.2d 13, 17 (1963), speaking through Judge J. Spencer Bell, said:

". . . While the policy embodied in the Veterans Administration Regulations that patients should be allowed the maximum of freedom warranted by their condition is a discretionary decision, the application of that policy to an individual case is not within the category of policy decisions exempted by the statute. The application of that policy to the individual case is an administrative decision at the operational level which if negligently done will make the Government liable—whether it involves substandard professional conduct (malpractice) or simple negligence in custodial care. . . ."

This Court is of the opinion that in the case of Newgard the defendant's agents were tortiously negligent both in the matter of substandard professional conduct on the part of Dr. Linnell, and because of gross negligence on the part of Dr. Linnell and Dr. Cheney in the careless custodial care of Newgard. Moreover, Dr. Craft was negligent in not brniging to the attention of the appropriate Meade personnel a letter from Newgard while the latter was on the Davis ranch, in which Newgard made reference to returning to North Dakota and selling some cattle. Newgard's cattle dealings[2] were just as delusional as his horse dealings.

Nor may it be said that Dr. Curt L. Rosenbaum, Meade's Chief of Staff, was not negligent. It was he who received the telephone call from Eloise A. Newgard. Routinely he put a note of the conversation in Newgard's file, but at no time did he direct anyone at Meade to pursue the matter of Eloise Newgard's phone call further to determine what caused her to be upset and allegedly to have hung up the phone on him. Dr. Rosenbaum, as the supervisor of all professional services at Meade, did discuss the matter with Dr. Har-

land T. Hermann, Meade's Chief of Psychiatry, and suggested Newgard should not be released because of his wife's feelings, but he did not, as he should have, follow through on the matter.

Dr. Hermann, a man with impressive credentials as a psychiatrist, conceded that Newgard's leave of absence was not a full discharge and that Newgard was to return to Meade for reevaluation. There is, of course, no question about whether Newgard was a patient under the control of Meade at the time of Eloise A. Newgard's murder. He was.

It is a fair and reasonable inference from the testimony and evidence in this case that the psychiatrists and psychologists at Meade believed Newgard's unsubstantiated and uninvestigated stories about his business ventures and his statements about his wife and that no one placed any credence in the statements of Eloise A. Newgard, Dr. Lancaster, Judge Paulsen, Mr. Rutland, Dr. Kohlmeyer, or Dr. Hubert A. Carbonne. Dr. Carbonne, the record shows, is a psychiatrist certified by the American Board of Psychiatry and Neurology in 1950 and is also a man with impressive qualifications.

It is also a fair and reasonable inference to be drawn from the evidence that Dr. Linnell felt there was something wrong with Eloise A. Newgard; that she was not interested in anything but keeping Newgard away from her; that she did not visit him often enough at Meade; and that her physical fear of Newgard was groundless. Dr. Linnell not only failed to use the facilities available to him to attempt to verify the things Newgard was telling him, and which Dr. Linnell mistakenly described as "exaggeration," but obviously completely ignored the contents of the social service report from Fargo which certainly should have alerted him to the fact that there was something seriously wrong with Newgard.

It is important to note that Dr. Carbonne testified that the purpose of a social worker's report is "to contribute as much information as can possibly be gathered to be presented for the purpose of understanding the patient's problems and *arriving at a diagnosis*." (Emphasis mine.)

Finally, we turn to the amount of damages to be awarded plaintiff. In doing so this Court aligns itself with those courts which hold that the amount of recovery for death by wrongful act should not be diminished by the receipt of social security benefits. The amounts received or to be received by or on behalf of Elizabeth, Ann Marie, and Robert William Newgard are disregarded in reaching the monetary verdict in this case.

---

[2] Sometime during late 1964 or early 1965 Newgard told his pastor, Reverend Faust, he was giving $50,000.00 to the church "through some cattle deal."

Initially it must be borne in mind that the Federal Tort Claims Act limits awards for damages in wrongful death actions to that which is compensatory in nature. 28 U.S.C.A. § 2674. In North Dakota there is no statutory limitation on the amount of recovery. Chapter 32–21–02, North Dakota Century Code. Punitive or exemplary damages are forbidden under the North Dakota statute.

The North Dakota Supreme Court has upon many occasions spoken upon the basis for recovery. In considering damages, pecuniary value of services which the beneficiaries might reasonably have expected may be taken into account. Mortality tables are not binding on the trier of facts. The factors to be considered include the decedent's age, health, condition in life, habits of industry and sobriety, mental and physical capacity, disposition to frugality and customary earnings of the deceased and the use made of them. Damages include the loss of any and all services which children would probably have received from their mother and are not limited to those for loss of money or income. There is evidence in this case that Eloise A. Newgard, had she lived, would have received periodic pay raises. The North Dakota Supreme Court inferentially supports the admissibility of such evidence to show future earning power. Moreover, the expense of educating children was held to be relevant to money or services that could reasonably be expected from the decedent, in the same case.

It is difficult indeed to place a monetary value on the loving care and the advice and guidance of which the Newgard children will be forever deprived through the loss of their mother. It must be included, dispassionately, with the other factors set out herein in reaching the complex and always vexing question of compensatory loss in this type of case, and the declining value of the dollar has been taken into account.

The Court concludes that plaintiff is entitled to recover the sum of Two Hundred Thousand Dollars ($200,000.00) from the defendant, as compensatory damages, arising out of and from the gross negligence of the defendant, acting by and through its agents and employees, which was the sole and proximate cause of the death of Eloise A. Newgard, together with interest after entry of judgment, and costs as provided by law.

ROSENFELD v. COLEMAN

S. Maxwell Flitter, for plaintiff.

PALMER, J., June 8, 1959.—This is a motion to strike off a compulsory nonsuit in a malpractice action wherein plaintiff alleges defendant-psychiatrist negligently caused him to become a narcotic addict.

Nonsuit was entered because the trial judge believed there was no competent evidence of negligence, plaintiff having failed to produce expert testimony as to the professional skill in the locality in which defendant practiced at the time, and there being insufficient evidence that, in treating plaintiff, defendant violated the Anti-Narcotics Act of July 11, 1917, P. L. 758, as amended, 35 PS §851, etc., so as to permit the jury to find him negligent.

Having carefully considered the testimony together with the briefs and argument of counsel, we unanimously agree there is merit in at least a portion of plaintiff's contention and therefore his motion must be granted.

The law governing motions of this type is well settled. We must consider all facts and inferences thereon in the light most favorable to plaintiff, accepting as true all evidence which tends to support his case, giving him the advantage of every fair inference, rejecting antagonistic facts and inferences and resolving all doubts in favor of a jury trial.

Considering the testimony in this light, it appears that from 1945 plaintiff suffered migraine headaches, nervousness and general weakness for which he was treated by various physicians. On October 3, 1955, he consulted defendant, a physician specializing in neuropsychiatry, in the City of Easton, and became his patient.

At the end of October or beginning of

November 1955, he complained of severe pains and defendant gave him a prescription for Demerol, a synthetic narcotic drug, and directed him to have the prescription filled at a drugstore, obtain a syringe and needles and return to defendant's office. Plaintiff did as he was directed and defendant then instructed him in the use of the syringe and needles and told him he should administer the drug himself when he felt he needed it.

About three weeks later, defendant gave plaintiff another prescription for Demerol for self-injection. From October 3 until the time of this prescription, plaintiff visited defendant at his office and was treated psychiatrically; that is, he was asked questions which he answered to the best of his ability, and was counseled by defendant.

Shortly after receiving this second prescription, plaintiff telephoned defendant and told him he had pains and needed help. Upon defendant's instructions, he went to the latter's office where he was handed a Demerol prescription by the doctor, for which he paid $10. From then until May of 1956, plaintiff received no psychiatric treatment from defendant, but did procure from him many prescriptions for Demerol. At no time did defendant or his nurse make any of the injections; they were all made by plaintiff.

In response to an inquiry, defendant on April 25, 1956, addressed a letter to the Division of Narcotic Control of the Pennsylvania Department of Health, referring to plaintiff's addiction to Demerol and stating the prognosis was "not very good." He suggested: "My impression as a Neuro Psychiatrist is that we are dealing with not only a sociopathic behaviour disorder, addict, but his behaviour is that of a hypomanic pattern which at time I feel borders on Manic depressive, Manic, type of affective disturbance."

In the same month defendant told plaintiff he was an addict and there was no help for him unless he went into a hospital. Defendant thereupon committed plaintiff to the Easton Hospital for a period of seven days during which he was withdrawn from the use of the drug. Upon his release, he felt an additional need for Demerol and was again furnished prescriptions by defendant.

Plaintiff testified he was not addicted to the use of the drug in October 1955, when he first visited defendant nor had he ever been so addicted. His testimony in this regard was corroborated by Dr. Joseph M. Brau, who had treated him since 1943. Specifically, Dr. Brau testified that when plaintiff first consulted defendant in October of 1955, which was immediately after plaintiff's last visit to Dr. Brau, he was not an addict.

It is undisputed that plaintiff was addicted to the use of Demerol during the period when he was receiving prescriptions from defendant. He took treatments for withdrawal from its use from Dr. Raymond Wing, during the period October 30, 1956, to January 3, 1957.

Defendant was called as of cross-examination and testified that soon after he began to treat plaintiff in October 1955, the latter confessed he was a Demerol addict and requested prescriptions for the drug.

According to defendant, he felt his patient was suffering from a "psychopathic character disorder" and was "mentally ill." He later became interested in the Demerol addiction which he believed was a result of this mental illness. He prescribed the use of Demerol, which was not dangerous and from which, though habit forming, it was relatively simple to withdraw, to "help the psychotherapy." He tried through psychiatry to make plaintiff understand why he was an habitual user and believed if he were successful in curing the mental disorder, the Demerol addiction would terminate. He admitted the purpose of his treatment was both to cure plaintiff of his mental illness and also to remove him from the drug addiction. By prescribing the use of Demerol at plaintiff's request, he attempted to gain the good will of his patient and so effect a "transference" or "empathy" with him.

In order to get to a jury in Pennsylvania, a plaintiff in a malpractice action must offer expert testimony to establish the measure of professional skill required in the locality at the time of the alleged malpractice. This view is summarized in the majority opinion in Robinson v. Wirts, 387 Pa. 291, 297, as follows: "It is thus abundantly clear that since, in all such malpractice cases involving an appraisal of the propriety and skill of a doctor or surgeon in his professional treatment of a patient, a lay jury would presumably lack the necessary knowledge and experience to render a just and proper decision, they must be guided by the testimony of witnesses having special or expert qualifications. The only exception to this otherwise invariable rule is in cases where the matter under investigation is so simple, and the lack of skill or want of care so obvious, as to be within the range of the ordinary experience and comprehension of even non-professional persons. . . ."

The psychiatric treatment of this plaintiff by this defendant was not "so simple" nor "the lack of skill or want of care so obvious, as to be within the range of the ordinary experience and comprehension of even nonprofessional persons."

Plaintiff's failure to produce such expert testimony, however, is immaterial since there was sufficient evidence of negligence to go to the jury, if the latter believed defendant had violated the provisions of the Anti-Narcotics Act.

Section 1 of that statute, as amended, 35 PS §851, defines "Drugs" as follows:

"Except as limited in section two of this act, the word 'drug', as used in this act, shall be construed to include: . . . any substance or preparation containing any drug found by the United States Secretary of the Treasury, after due notice and opportunity for public hearing, to have an addiction forming or addiction-sustaining liability similar to morphine or cocaine and proclaimed by the president to have been so found by the secretary."

The chemical composition of Demerol nowhere appears in the testimony. However, we know it is the name of a synthetic drug of the Meperidine family. . . .

The case was tried partially on the theory that defendant had violated section 8 of the Anti-Narcotics Act. In his complaint plaintiff alleged the violation of this act and in oral argument prior to granting the nonsuit, his counsel stated, without objection, that Demerol was one of the drugs included in the statute.*

Generally, on appeal, the court will not take judicial notice of matters not appearing in the record. However, where there are undisputed physical facts clearly shown in evidence, our Supreme Court has held that on appeal the court should take judicial notice of the laws of nature or mathematics or quality of matter, or whatever it may be that rules the case, and apply it as the trial court should have done.

In the absence of proof, a trial judge generally is not authorized to take judicial cognizance of the precise meaning of technical terms. On the other hand, the tendency has been to expand the area in which judicial notice will be taken of scientific facts.

We therefore hold that Demerol is a "drug" within the definition of that term in the statute.

Section 8 of the Anti-Narcotics Act provides, in part, as follows, 35 PS §860:

"No physician . . . shall . . . prescribe any of said drugs to any person known to such physician . . . to be an habitual user of any said drugs, unless said drug is prescribed . . . for the cure or treatment of some malady other than the drug habit. . . . In the treatment of drug addiction as such, narcotics must not be

furnished either on dispensing or prescribing in writing by physicians to the addict himself, but must be personally administered by the physician, or be placed in the hands of a nurse, or other reliable person who is not an addict and who is held personally responsible for carrying out the directions of the physician in charge. Written records must be kept of all such administration of narcotics. In every such case the physician shall himself make a physical examination of the patient and shall report, in writing, within seventy-two hours, to the Department of Health, the name and address of such patient, together with his diagnosis of the case and the amount and nature of the drug prescribed or dispensed in the first treatment. When the patient leaves his care, such physician shall report, in writing, within seventy-two hours, to the Department of Health the result of his said treatment."

Defendant testified that plaintiff told him late in October or early November 1955, he was addicted to the use of Demerol. Defendant believed if he was able to affect a cure of plaintiff's mental illness, the Demerol addiction would also be cured, since in his opinion the addiction was the result of the mental illness. He also testified the purpose of his treatment was to cure plaintiff of both his mental illness and his drug addiction.

Plaintiff testified that at the time he first went to the defendant for treatment, he was not addicted to the use of Demerol and he became addicted only while being treated by the doctor and receiving prescriptions from him. He claimed defendant treated him psychiatrically for but a brief period after his initial visit and thereafter he received no psychiatric treatment but rather bought Demerol prescriptions from the doctor. By April 1956, both plaintiff and defendant recognized plaintiff was an habitual user and defendant continued thereafter to prescribe Demerol.

One of the purposes of defendant's treatment was to cure plaintiff's drug addiction. We do not believe the legislature intended to prohibit physicians from prescribing narcotic drugs to known habitual users only where the purpose of such prescriptions is exclusively to cure the addiction. If one of the purposes is to cure the addiction, it would appear to fall within the prohibitory section of the act. Similarly, if one of the purposes of prescribing the drug is to cure a known habitual user from his addiction, the treatment is for drug-addiction "as such," as those words are used in section 8 of the act.

Considering the testimony in the light most favorable to plaintiff, we believe, therefore, there was sufficient evidence to permit the

---

* I.e., that its chemistry and addictive potential clearly fell within the definition of the above paragraph. Demerol is recognized by physicians and by the Bureau of Narcotics and Dangerous Drugs as fully within the category of addictive drugs as defined in paragraph F of the statute.

jury to determine whether defendant prescribed Demerol "for the cure or treatment of some malady *other than* the drug habit" and also whether defendant was treating plaintiff for "drug addiction *as such*" so as to come within the prohibition of section 8 of the statute.

The provisions of this section are mandatory and if the jury found defendant had failed to comply with the duties imposed thereby and as a result plaintiff, without negligence on his part, was injured, the violation of the statute would constitute sufficient evidence of negligence to permit the jury to render a verdict in plaintiff's favor.

The tests for determining whether the violation of a statute constitutes actionable negligence are set forth in §286, A. L. I. Restatement of the Law of Torts, as follows:

"The violation of a legislative enactment by doing a prohibited act, or by failing to do a required act, makes the actor liable for an invasion of an interest of another if:

"(a) the intent of the enactment is exclusively or in part to protect an interest of the other as an individual; and

"(b) the interest invaded is one which the enactment is intended to protect; and

"(c) where the enactment is intended to protect an interest from a particular hazard, the invasion of the interests results from that hazard; and,

"(d) the violation is a legal cause of the invasion, and the other has not so conducted himself as to disable himself from maintaining an action."

As expressed in its title, the purpose of the act is to protect "the public health by regulating the possession, control, dealing in, giving away, delivery, dispensing, administering, prescribing, and use of certain drugs . . ." Clearly one of the intentions of the legislature was to regulate and control the use of narcotics by a known user by preventing him from administering drugs to himself. Plaintiff was a known user and therefore it was the intent of the statute to protect his interest as an individual. This interest was one which the statute was intended to protect. We further believe the act was intended to protect a known user, such as plaintiff, from continued or excessive use of the drug and the jury could find the violation of the statutory duty was the proximate cause of the harm, assuming of course it also would find defendant knew plaintiff was an habitual user at the time he prescribed Demerol for him, and thereafter continued to prescribe the drug.

We believe, therefore, the jury should have been permitted to determine whether defendant violated the provisions of section 8 of the Anti-Narcotics Act. We further believe, if the jury found defendant violated the statute, it would be enough evidence of negligence to support a verdict for plaintiff.

For these reasons, plaintiff's motion to strike off the nonsuit must be granted.

ORDER

And now, June 8, 1959, plaintiff's motion to strike off the compulsory nonsuit hitherto entered against him is granted.

MALPRACTICE IN PSYCHIATRY

William A. Bellamy, M.D.

The purpose of this presentation is to present clinical-legal data and conclusions which may help the physician fulfill his professional and ethical duties, and minimize the risk of committing a negligent tort ("malpractice"). From the findings presented here the psychiatrist may be in a better position to make decisions of importance to his patient as well as to himself, his estate and his family.

Clinical-legal data from five recent appellate court decisions involving psychiatric issues are presented in detail and findings from an earlier

Excerpted with permission from *Diseases of the Nervous System* (February–May, 1965), pp. 25–33. This paper was originally presented as a part of a symposium conducted by the Section of Private Practice of the A.P.A., May, 1963.

published series of 18 cases (nationwide from 1946 to 1961) are reviewed. . . .

Three of the recent and one of the initial 18 pertain to problems of suicide. A study of suicide risks as to referring physician, treating physician and hospital (under locked ward and "open door" circumstances) is presented in detail. In addition are presented: comments on quality of performance of the physician and judge in the court proceedings, a guide to formulating professional liability insurance needs, and other preventive measures. . . .

The 23 cases reviewed fall into four groups:

CHART I

Type of Risk Encountered in Psychiatry

Group	No. Cases	Case Examples
A. Problems of Suicide	4	16, 19, 20, 21
B. Problems of Commit-ment and Hospitali-zation	7	10 to 15 and 22
C. Patient's Assault upon Employee	2	18 and 23
D. Problems of Treatment	10*	1 to 9 and 17

* Seven of these ten cases involved shock therapy.

CLINICAL-LEGAL DATA

A. Problems of Suicide

Case 19. Benjamin v. Havens 373 P. 2d 109 (1962). At the request of the family physician a psychiatrist saw a patient suffering from "agitated depression" and admitted her to an "open ward" facility, even though the husband objected to the open ward. Three months earlier at another hospital the patient had received EST and five more EST's were administered in the second hospital. There was no post shock confusion. On the seventh day the patient asked the nurse to go to the bathroom and permission, as formerly, was granted. The patient then dashed down the main corridor past the nurse on duty at the nurse's station, through an outside door of the Hospital, and leaped or fell through a hedge onto a cement patio. She sustained serious injuries. The patient and her husband brought suit against:

1) Psychiatrist and his wife for failure to select suitable hospital or prescribe necessary restraints.
2) Hospital for failure to constantly watch the patient or restrain her properly.

The husband testified that the day before the psychiatrist was called in, his wife had attempted to break off her toes and to commit suicide by stuffing a nightgown down her throat, and that he had so informed the treating psychiatrist. All three doctors (family physician, treating psychiatrist, and prior psychiatrist) testified that the treaitng psychiatrist had not been told about the attempted suicide.

The psychiatrist admitted that had he known of the attempted suicide he would not have selected Havens since this institution does not accept actively suicidal patients. His orders included, "Watch patient—depressed" and he allowed corridor and bathroom privileges. His letter to the family physician included the phrase "suicidal thoughts." He testified that restraints were contraindicated in this situation in which depressed periods alternated with periods of sociability.

A nurse testified that the patient had begged not to be locked in; that she had used the hospital corridor to go to the bathroom several times unattended; that she gave no signs of her intended dash for freedom or suicide; and that had she given any such indication the nurse would have accompanied the patient to the bathroom.

The jury brought in a verdict of $11,266.00 against the hospital and exonerated the psychiatrist. The trial court judge did not believe that the evidence warranted the award. He set aside the jury's verdict and denied the motion for a new trial as to the psychiatrist. The plaintiffs appealed both rulings.

The appellate court, State of Washington, upheld exoneration of the psychiatrist and granted a retrial against the hospital. The latter opinion was based on the fact that in this hospital the nurses customarily maintained close supervision of the main corridor, but the nurse on duty at the time of the accident was seated at the desk in the nurse's station off the corridor and did not have clear vision up or down the corridor. The possibility of negligence was a proper question for the jury.

The hospital subsequently made a out-of-court settlement for an amount somewhat less than the $11,266.00 jury award.

In a very similar case (Case 16) several years earlier (1948) the attitude of the court was notably more lenient. A man had died by suicide via jumping from his room on the seventh floor of a University Hospital. The relatives sued the psychiatrist for negligence in selecting a hospital unsuited for a suicidal patient and the hospital for not constantly watching the patient. Both the admitting psychiatrist and the hospital were exonerated in trial court, upheld by appellate court. The attitude at that time was that if a hospital accepted mental patients it was not negligent to select that hospital, and that the hospital could not be held negligent unless plaintiff proved that the patient was not properly attended at the critical period of the suicidal act.

Perhaps the pendulum of court decisions is swinging too far toward requiring an ever higher legal duty of care on the part of the psychiatrist and hospital. The "open ward" approach to treatment of the mentally ill is too valuable a tool to be lost through increasing risk. If psychiatry can convince the law that the benefit to the many is more important than an occasional tragic result to a very small number, the law can and will be changed accordingly (by precedent).

Psychiatry did just this in one of the following two cases, although both actions occurred under closed ward circumstances.

Case 20. Stallman v. Robinson, 260 S.W. 2d 743 (1953). On the sixth day in the hospital the patient was given electric shock therapy some time between 8:00 and 10:00 A.M. A nurse testified that when she came on duty at 2:00 P.M. Mrs. Stallman "was in her safety belt, it was locked, and . . . (she was) apparently asleep, so I went on to the next room." At 2:30 P.M. another patient called the nurse to Mrs. Stallman's room. The nurse found that the patient had hung herself from a bathroom fixture in her room by means of strips torn from nightgowns and tied together to form a cord.

The defendants maintained that reasonable care had been provided, and that it was unduly inflammatory to introduce as evidence the strips torn from four nightgowns of various colors and that, furthermore, the torn strips rendered an appearance in court different than the appearance at the time the patient was "cut down."

However, the court considered that the patient had been left unsupervised for several lengthy periods and that the nurse might have reasonably been expected to check more closely the safety belt and condition of the patient, and that to show the torn strips was not inflammatory.

Jury verdict was $9,000.00 against the hospital; sustained by appellate court, Missouri.

The nurse scarcely could have made an actual test of the "locked" safety belt without waking the patient from her sleep. Such constant checks are reacted to, by many patients, as an insult to their integrity, and can increase their lack of inner confidence in themselves. More generally, questionnaires sent by hospitals to their former patient-guests always return the complaint (in high percentage) that they are wakened too often by hospital employees.

Case 21. Gregory v. Robinson, 338 S.W. 2d 88 (1960). While a treating psychiatrist was leaving a locked ward on the third floor of a private hospital and pushing with his back to the door in order to aid the automatic closing device, a patient sitting on his bed 15 feet away ran to the door, pushed his way through, fled down the stairway, leaped through an unbarred window at a stair landing, fell three and a half stories to a cement driveway below and sustained serious injuries which miraculously were not fatal.

The jury found the hospital negligent and awarded $40,000.00 to the plaintiff. The trial judge did not believe that the evidence war-ranted the award and he set aside the jury's verdict. The appellate court, Missouri, upheld absolution of the hospital.

In this case both the trial court and the appellate court judge did appreciate the particular dilemma confronting the psychiatrist and hospital in dealing with the suicidal patient. Consider Judge Eager's deliberations:

The expert testimony developed the following: that the modern concept of treatment in such cases is to allow patients as much freedom as possible, to treat them as individuals, and to try to 'resocialize' them; that therein the physicians knowingly take a calculated risk; that better safeguards could be afforded by strict confinement, but that few patients would be cured; that there is potential for suicide, or of harming others in all acutely depressed mental cases, and that in some patients this may increase when they begin to improve, but certainly not in all; that patients such as plaintiff are being cured regularly by modern treatment; that care in entering or leaving such a ward becomes a sort of automatic reflex and specifically, it was shown here, that it was a constant procedure for the doctors and attendants in this hospital to be careful on entering. . . .

In a minority opinion, Judge Stockman dissented on the basis that it might be possible that the door was hard, or slow, of closing because of defective door-closing mechanism and that this would be a proper question for the jury.

Final action, Supreme Court of Missouri; defendant owners of hospital absolved.

Note: In future claims involving problems of suicide, the above case can be used as logical reference and although it may be an out-of-state decision, nevertheless it may carry weight. In any event, the modern psychiatric concept of treatment with calculated risk is expertly portrayed here. Dr. Robinson and his staff are to be congratulated.

B. Problem of Hospitalization

Case 22. Maben v. Rankin, 55 Cal. 2d 139; 10 Cal. Rptr. 353; 358 P 2d 681 (1961). A husband requested a psychiatrist to hospitalize his wife and administer EST for his mentally ill wife, and signed authorization for both actions. From the patient's symptoms and husband's story, the psychiatrist believed her to be mentally ill, administered sedative and admitted her to a sanitarium of which he was part owner.

The patient-plaintiff alleged that she was not mentally ill but was upset only because of her husband's questionable conduct in marital matters; that she was forcibly rendered unconscious by injection of a sedative; taken to the hospital and given EST without her consent;

and that "the next thing she remembered was that a week later she found herself in the hospital where she remained against her will for 15 days. There was also expert testimony that she had not been mentally ill. . . ."

Other witnesses corroborated the psychiatrist's opinion that the wife was mentally ill, that she was potentially dangerous to her husband and to herself, and that her condition was greatly improved after hospitalization and treatment.

For false imprisonment and assault and battery, trial court awarded $78,000.00 against psychiatrist and hospital. Defendants appealed.

The main issue before the court was: Does admitting a patient outside the laws governing admission necessarily indicate negligence? In California, admission procedures allow for: (1) voluntary admission; (2) emergency 24 to 72 hours hospitalization pending additional psychiatric examination, as required; (3) treatment for 90 days upon certain petitions and examinations; and (4) commitment proceedings.

Had the psychiatrist submitted his reports in proper order or had he called in legal machinery within 24 to 72 hours instead of delaying for two weeks, he would have been on safer grounds.

The appellate judges opined that it was not negligent for the psychiatrist to accept a relative's word in good faith. The fact that the hospital was a charitable facility did not relieve the admitting psychiatrist or hospital of legal duty to comply with laws governing admission of patients. Because the trial judge had erred in giving instructions to the jury, a new trial was granted. The appellate court's opinion included instructions to the new trial court that the fact that the patient had benefited from hospitalization and treatment should be given consideration in the evaluation of damages to the patient, and legal references were cited.

The second trial jury awarded $60,000.00 to the plaintiff.

Evidently, the jury at the second trial did not believe that the ends justified the means, and this patient received cure and a bonus as well. However, in other cases, a husband's intentions could be less honorable. The law zealously guards individual rights, and undoubtedly this is the wisest course in the face of a general world trend toward increased conformity and regulation. In some instances, the individual pays the price of having to be treated more as a prisoner and less as a sick person. . . .

All other problems of hospitalization in this series concerned commitment proceedings (Cases 10 to 15). The main allegations were malicious prosecution, false imprisonment, mistaken diagnosis, libel, or inadequate examination (cursory, or no examination at all).

The law affords protection to the psychiatrist in commitment proceedings so that he may testify without undue fear of reprisal. The privilege is a compromise between competing rights: the right of the public to be protected, and the right of the individual to be protected against false statements, in which the rights of the public are favored. However, the law does not sanction cursory examinations, and false statements are felonies prosecutable under criminal law and subject to exemplary damages: fine, or imprisonment. . . .

In all six commitment cases the defendant was absolved. The district attorney did not prosecute the case in which two physicians (not psychiatrists) allegedly signed an affidavit of mental illness without examining the patient. Nevertheless, it is psychiatry that gets the "black eye" from such allegations and we should endeavor to have psychiatrists appointed as examining physicians in mental cases whenever this is feasible.

C. Assault by Patient

Case 23. Sealy v. Finkelstein 206 N.Y.S. 2d 512 (1961). A practical nurse sued the patient's daughter and the patient's former physician for injuries resulting from assault by a mental patient under the nurse's care.

If a physician or relative does know of assaultive propensities and he does not give warning he may be considered negligent under certain circumstances. However, the fact that a patient is a mental case does not pre-suppose assaultive propensities, nor is it sufficient to maintain that the defendant should have known of assaultive propensities unless the plaintiff can show reason why this should have been known.

Such proof was not shown in this case and the trial judge dismissed the case as without merit. Action was upheld by appellate court, New York; defendants absolved.

In 1957 (Case 18) a cardiac patient suddenly assaulted an attendant. Although the family physician was absolved, the language of the court implied that were the physician a psychiatrist, a higher duty of care might be expected. . . .

D. Problems of Treatment
(Cases 1 through 9, also 17)

The majority (7 of 10 cases) relate to shock therapies.* The courts generally are aware that

---

* The prevalence of malpractice cases involving electroshock is reflected in higher malpractice insurance rates for practitioners who administer ECT than for those who do not.

fractures commonly occur in connection with shock therapies and therefore a fracture itself is not presumed to constitute an inference of negligence. . . .

Shock therapy negligently administered and resulting in damage to the patient carries its risk of course, under negligent tort. . . . In recent years, "unenlightened consent" as a basis of claim for damages from procedures such as shock therapies is being utilized with increasing frequency.

If the physician failed to explain the possible consequence of shock therapy sufficient for the patient (or responsible relative or guardian) to know to what he has consented, this constitutes no consent and the physician has "assaulted" his patient via his "intent to touch."

In order to fulfill his legal duty toward obtaining an informed consent, the physician is not obligated to relate to the patient all the gory details. A note in the record outlining what has been discussed is invaluable to the attorney's defense of the physician. Rodis and Broth have devised a form in which the possible complications of EST are described and the patient and/or guardian is requested to read it and sign to the effect that he has read it and understands what he has read. . . .

COMMENTS ON CLINICAL-LEGAL DATA

1. The quality of performance of physicians on the witness stand was generally very good in these 23 cases. . . .

2. The quality of performance of the judges of trial court and appellate court was also generally good. In my opinion, justice prevailed in most of the 23 cases in this series. . . .

Perhaps we are viewing examples of fine teamwork. The physician relates his observations and his opinions to his attorney; likewise, the plaintiff to his attorney; the attorneys elicit these observations and opinions from the witness under oath; the jury finds as to fact; the trial judge exercises broad powers from his best considered judgment; and finally, by right of appeal, the appellate court reviews the evidence and findings and renders its final legal opinion.

Judges have weeks in which to study a case and their deliberations are made in the relative calm of private chambers. By contrast, the physician-psychiatrist testifies under oath; his advance study and preparation do not always prepare him for certain questions which (if he can formulate an opinion) he is under a legal duty to answer; and he does this under the heat of cross examination. . . .

3. Insurance needs. The largest award in this series was $60,000.00 in a wrongful death action and a like amount in a false imprisonment claim. For every appellate court case there are 100 other clamis, as estimated by Sandor. I do not know how large the awards may have been in cases on the trial court level, nor in those cases which were settled out of court. It seems unlikely that the sum would be as large as $60,000.00. From study of legal trends, awards made against psychiatrists may become larger and larger unless we can reverse certain trends.

The psychiatrist should periodically review his malpractice insurance needs. Insurance is a preventive measure, for the uninsured or inadequately insured physician tends to become alarmed and is more likely to agree to an out-of-court settlement. This encourages nuisance claims, and malpractice problems are thereby increased.

In addition, when a patient in a negative transference reaction may threaten the psychiatrist with a malpractice claim, the psychiatrist may handle the therapeutic problems more calmly to the benefit of himself and his patient, if he does not become unduly alarmed. . . .

From the foregoing thesis, preventive measures logically follow:

1. Every professional practitioner should master his profession.

2. Understand the law. Know your rights as well as your duties under the law.

3. The physician who consults his attorney is practicing "preventive law." The attorney who consults a physician (in a medical case) is practicing "preventive malpractice."

QUESTIONS FOR DISCUSSION

1. What advice would you give a psychiatrist with respect to administration of electroshock or insulin therapy to an emotionally disturbed patient? Would the problem of "informed consent" be different if the patient were: a voluntary patient in a private hospital; an involuntary patient in a public hospital in a state in which commitment is an adjudication of incompetency; an involuntary patient in a state in which incompetency has been "separated" from hospitalization; a patient for whom a guardian has been appointed? (Cf., "Hospitalization and Incompetency," Chapter 8, above.)

2. Would there be a basis for a false imprisonment suit on behalf of: (1) a patient involuntarily admitted on medical certification in accordance with a statute providing f or "emergency" hospitalization, who is not informed of his right to demand a judicial hearing; (2) a patient involuntarily admitted following an *ex parte* commitment hearing, who claims that there was no evidence to support the court's finding that his attendance at the hearing would be detrimental to his health; (3) a "voluntary" patient who alleges that at the time of his admission he was mentally incompetent and incapable of giving his consent; (4) a patient originally admitted by his parents, who alleges that his confinement was continued without court order and against his will after he attained the age of majority?

3. What is the basis for the court's opinion in *Baker* v. *United States*? If it is necessary to strike a balance between effectively safeguarding the pateint's life and providing optimal treatment, do you feel that the court has provided reasonable guidelines in that quest?

4. Dr. Bellamy's paraphrases of and observations about the court decisions described in his article "Malpractice in Psychiatry" are perhaps not legally expert. His article does, however, reflect the attitudes of many psychiatrists relatively sophisticated about the laws applicable to malpractice. What conclusions do you draw from his analyses of the responsiveness of the law to the problems of psychiatric treatment?

SUGGESTIONS FOR ADDITIONAL READING

Asch. *Mental Disability in Civil Practice.* Rochester, N.Y.: Lawyers Co-operative Pub. Co., 1973.

Davidoff, D. The Malpractice of Psychiatrists. Springfield, Ill.: C. C Thomas, 1973.

Davidson. *Forensic Psychiatry*, 2d ed. New York: Ronald Press, 1965, Chapter 16.

Morse. "Psychiatric Responsibility and Tort Liability," *J. of Forensic Sciences* 12 (July 1967): 305.

Perr. "Liability of Hospital and Psychiatrist in Suicide," *Am. J. of Psychiatry* 122 (1965): 631.

Robitscher. *Pursuit of Agreement: Psychiatry and the Law.* Philadelphia: J. B. Lippincott Co., 1966, Chapter 10.

Stetler and Moritz. *Doctor and Patient and the Law*, 4th ed. St. Louis: C. V. Mosby Co., 1962, Chapter 9, and Chapters 19–25.

Ziskin. "Errors in Psychiatric Examinations," *Trial Magazine* (Nov./Dec. 1971): 59.

Annotation: "Liability of Insane Person for His Own Negligence," 49 *ALR* 3d 189, 1973.

Annotation: "Liability of Hospital for Injury Caused through Assault by a Patient," 48 *ALR* 3d 1288, 1973.

Annotation: "Liability of One Releasing Institutionalized Mental Patient for Harm He Causes," 38 *ALR* 3d 699, 1971.

Annotation: "Malpractice—Mental Disease," 99 *ALR* 2d 599 plus later case service.

For collected case references see:

"Malpractice Liability with Respect to Diagnosis and Treatment of Mental Disease," 99 *ALR* 2d 599.

"Liability of Hospital for Injury or Death of Patient as Result of Escape or Attempted Escape," 70 *ALR* 2d 347.

"Legal Risks of Electroshock Therapy," *J.A.M.A.* 196 (May 9, 1966) : 331.

"Therapeutic Restraint," *J.A.M.A.* 197 (July 4, 1966) : 205.

"Responsibility of Psychiatrists for Failure to Control Patients," *J.A.M.A.* 197 (September 26, 1966) : 281.

14

Family Law

Family Law is often thought of as the study of statutes and court decisions that govern disputes between family members. Therefore, to many people Family Law means divorce, alimony, and child custody. However, in many instances the state regulates and intervenes in family affairs when no member of the family has requested its assistance. Therefore, such matters as abortion, neglect, and delinquency are also part of Family Law.

Changes in Family Law during the last few years, especially in the area of the rights of children, have been almost as rapid and extensive as those in the area of patients' rights. Therefore the approach to the two chapters (pointing up the most important issues rather than compiling all the changes) is similar.

The first four selections in this chapter deal with the effect of mental impairment on the right to marry and divorce. The chapter, however, is not limited to discussion of the rights of the mentally impaired. Many of the selections deal with a much broader theme, the way in which law and psychiatry can work together to resolve and prevent family law problems. The next selection, "The Role of the Lawyer in Counseling Divorce Clients" is an excellent illustration of the contribution psychiatry can make in the divorce area. The rest of the chapter also interweaves legal problems and the contributions of psychiatry to the problems of abortion, incest, custody, neglect, and delinquency.

HOMAN v. HOMAN

BOSLAUGH, Justice.

This is an action to annul a marriage between Eugene J. Homan and Lucille Homan, the defendant. Although the action is brought by a guardian and next friend, Eugene J. Homan will be referred to as the plaintiff. The trial court found that the marriage was valid and dismissed the action. The guardian has appealed.

The petition alleged that the ward was mentally incompetent at the time of the marriage. By statute a marriage is void "when either party is insane or an idiot at the time of marriage, and the term idiot shall include all persons who from whatever cause are mentally incompetent to enter into the marriage relation." Section 42–103, R.S.Supp., 1965.

A marriage contract will not be declared void for mental incapacity to enter into it unless there existed at the time of the marriage such a want of understanding as to render the party incapable of assenting thereto. Fischer v. Adams, 151 Neb. 512, 38 N.W.2d 337. Mere weakness or imbecility of mind is not sufficient to void a contract of marriage unless there be such a mental defect as to prevent the party from comprehending the nature of the contract and from giving his free and intelligent consent to it.

Absolute inability to contract, insanity, or idiocy will void a marriage, but mere weakness of mind will not unless it produces a derangement sufficient to avoid all contracts by destroying the power to consent. Aldrich v. Steen, 71 Neb. 33, 98 N.W.2d 445; Adams v.

147 N.W.2d 630 (1967).

Scott, 93 Neb. 537, 141 N.W. 148. A marriage is valid if the party has sufficient capacity to understand the nature of the contract and the obligations and responsibilities it creates. Fischer v. Adams, supra; Kutch v. Kutch, 88 Neb. 114, 129 N.W. 169.

The plaintiff has a history of mental illness and mental deficiency. When he was 5 years old he was ill with scarlet fever and encephalitis which resulted in a permanent impairment of his mental ability. In December 1950, the plaintiff was treated for schizophrenia. Treatment for this condition continued through 1958 but there is no evidence that the plaintiff received any treatment for this condition between 1958 and 1963. The plaintiff attended Immaculate Conception Grade School in Omaha, Nebraska, and completed 3 years of high school. He was then employed as a laborer by Goodwill Industries and later by Armour & Company.

The plaintiff first met the defendant in 1959. They commenced keeping company and approximately 3 months later the plaintiff proposed marriage. The marriage took place about 6 months later on February 27, 1960. The plaintiff was then 29 years of age.

During the courtship the plaintiff made plans to purchase a house and saved a part of his earnings for the downpayment. A property was selected, a mortgage negotiated, and the purchase completed. The parties moved into their first home a week after the ceremony. In March 1962, the parties traded this home for a larger property.

In 1963 the plaintiff was sent home from his employment with instructions to obtain medical treatment. The plaintiff consulted a physician, was referred to a psychiatrist, and was hospitalized.

At the time of the trial the plaintiff was on leave from the hospital. He was living with his parents in Omaha and working part time. The defendant last saw the plaintiff in August 1964. He was placed under guardianship in October 1964. The plaintiff did not attend the trial and, apparently, did not know of the action or the trial.

A marriage is presumed valid, and the bur-

den of proof is upon the party seeking annulment. Adams v. Scott, supra. To succeed in this action it was necessary for the guardian to establish that the plaintiff was mentally incompetent on February 27, 1960.

The plaintiff suffers from a mental impairment that is the result of a childhood illness. This condition is permanent and existed at the time of the marriage. The guardian produced the testimony of the psychiatrist who had treated the plaintiff prior to the marriage. This witness testified that the plaintiff had a mental age of approximately 11 years; an intelligence quotient of between 69 and 75; and that the plaintiff would be classified as a high-grade moron. This witness further testified that, in his opinion, the plaintiff would have an inadequate or superficial understanding of the responsibilities of marriage.

The defendant testified at length concerning her acquaintance and relationship with the plaintiff from the time of their first meeting in 1959 until the hospitalization of the plaintiff in 1963. This evidence contradicts that of the guardian and tends to prove that the plaintiff had a sufficient understanding of the marriage relationship and its obligations and responsibilities. During this time the plaintiff was steadily employed as a maintenance and custodial worker, managed his finances, purchased two properties, and had a reasonably normal life. The evidence supports an inference that the marriage would have continued without difficulty if the plaintiff's mental illness had not recurred in 1963.

Although the plaintiff suffered from schizophrenia prior to the marriage and again in 1963, the evidence shows that this illness was in remission at the time of the marriage and was not a disabling factor at that tmie. Although handicapped mentally, the plaintiff had sufficient ability to transact business and the capacity to enter into the marriage on February 27, 1960.

The marriage in this case may have been unwise or unfortunate, but it was not void. The judgment of the district court is correct and it is affirmed.

Affirmed.

CAHILL v. CAHILL

Action for divorce on the ground of wilful desertion. The trial court found defendant-wife sane, but mentally ill. It ruled that she could not wilfully desert her husband because of her mental illness. Divorce was denied. Custody of the children was awarded to the father. Plaintiff-husband appeals from that portion of the judgment denying a divorce.

The parties were intermarried on March 27, 1943, at Binghamton, New York. Two children were born as a result of this union.

In 1956, the parties moved to Milwaukee, Wisconsin. They purchased a home in Brown Deer, Wisconsin.

The defendant on several occasions left their home in Milwaukee and returned to her father's home in New York. In May of 1957, she remained in New York for over three months, until her husband was able to bring her back to Milwaukee. In 1958, defendant left for New York three times. Two of the trips lasted only for several weeks. One lasted several months.

In late spring of 1957, plaintiff petitioned the Milwaukee county court for a mental examination of his wife. She was admitted to the hospital on October 11, 1957, but she was discharged therefrom on November 18, 1957, as competent.

On April 9, 1959, defendant informed her husband that she was leaving and never coming back. She took the children with her. Plaintiff made various trips to New York in an attempt to convince his wife to return to their home in Milwaukee. In March, 1960, plaintiff succeeded in bringing the older child home. In May, 1960, defendant returned to Milwaukee for a visit, and with the expectation of taking the older child back to New York. The plaintiff secreted the children from his wife and she returned to New York without them.

After commencement of the action, the family court commissioner referred the parties and their children to Dr. James Hurley for a complete psychiatric examination, respecting custody of the children.

On August 2, 1960, Dr. Hurley found defendant sane, but emotionally disturbed. On August 19, 1960, defendant was admitted to a state hospital in New York on account of psychic disorders.

Additional facts will be stated in the opinion.

BEILFUSS, Justice:

Was the trial court's finding that Mrs. Cahill did not wilfully desert her husband against the great weight and clear preponderance of the evidence?

The right to divorce must be predicated upon a violation of the marital relationship as recognized by the divorce statute. One of the grounds enumerated in the statute is wilful desertion.

Sec. 247.07(3), Stats., provides a divorce may be granted, "For the wilful desertion of one party by the other for the term of one year next preceding the commencement of the action."

In *Schopps* v. *Schopps* (1925), 188 Wis. 151, 205 N.W. 829, and *Leach* v. *Leach* (1954), 266 Wis. 223, 63 N.W.2d 73, we recognized four essentials which must be established for a divorce upon ground of wilful desertion. They are (1) a leaving by the other spouse without just cause, (2) such leaving was without intention to return, (3) the separation must be continuous for one year preceding the commencement of the action, and (4) the original leaving, together with the living apart for the statutory period, must be without the consent of the complaining spouse. To these four essentials another should be added, namely, that the leaving and the continued separation for the statutory period was the wilful act of the offending spouse.[1]

If the complaining spouse establishes these five essentials he is entitled to a divorce.

It is without dispute that Mrs. Cahill left the family home in Milwaukee county without just cause; that she did not intend to return; that separation was continuous for more than a year before the commencement of the action;

---

[1] Wilful desertion can be found even though the original leaving was with consent of the other spouse if the complaining spouse offers in good faith to terminate the separation and the other refuses. *Schopps* v. *Schopps, supra.* Also refusal to move to the place of residence selected by the husband can constitute wilful desertion. *Gray* v. *Gray* (1939), 323 Wis. 400, 287 N.W. 708.

Supreme Court of Wisconsin, 26 Wis. 2d 173, 131 N.W.2d 842 (1965).

and that she left and remained separated without the consent of Mr. Cahill.

The trial court found that Mrs. Cahill was not insane but was mentally ill at all times concerned and that the desertion was, therefore, not wilful and denied the divorce.

In addition to the facts set forth above, the only evidence of the mental health of Mrs. Cahill consisted of the testimony of Dr. Hurley and letters from Mrs. Cahill's father, a physician, and physicians who examined and treated Mrs. Cahill at the time of and subsequent to her admission to the hospital in New York on August 19, 1960. These letters have very little probative value because they relate to the situation as it existed after the cause of action occurred in addition to being hearsay. The contents of the letters were also considered by Dr. Hurley in arriving at this conclusion set forth below.

On August 2, 1960, at the request of the family court commissioner, Dr. James Hurley made a complete psychiatric examination of Mrs. Cahill.

Dr. Hurley was called at the trial by the plaintiff-husband and testified at length on examination by counsel for both sides and the court. Dr. Hurley resides in Milwaukee; he does and has for several years conducted an extensive practice in psychiatry. As appears from the opinion of the trial court, Dr. Hurley is an exceptionally well qualified expert in the field of psychiatry.

The testimony of Dr. Hurley stands uncontradicted and unimpeached. He was of the opinion that Mrs. Cahill was emotionally disturbed; that she had a paranoid personality, but had not reached the stage of paranoid schizophrenia and therefore not insane; that she knew the difference between right and wrong and the nature and quality of her acts, and that she did choose her acts even though she had delusions that motivated them.

The trial court's finding that Mrs. Cahill was not insane but mentally ill cannot stand.

Sec. 51.001, Stats., provides:

"*Definitions.* As used in this chapter:

"(1) Mental illness is synonymous with insanity; . . ."

In *State* v. *Esser* (1962), 16 Wis.2d 567, 599, 115 N.W.2d 505, 522, we stated the test of insanity to be:

"The term "insanity" in the law means such an abnormal condition of the mind, from any cause, as to render the defendant incapable of understanding the nature and quality of the alleged wrongful act, or incapable of distinguishing between right and wrong with respect to such act."

The undisputed testimony of Dr. Hurley was that Mrs. Cahill, at the times material, did know the nature and quality of her act in leaving her husband and was able to distinguish between right and wrong with respect to her leaving and intention not to return.

We are not prepared to state that the trier of the fact is absolutely bound by the uncontradicted testimony of an expert. However, we do conclude upon the record of this case that the expert, Dr. Hurley, was competent and well qualified, his testimony was not impeached nor his credibility challenged, and his examination and history of Mrs. Cahill complete so as to afford him ample foundation for his opinion. It is further significant that his examination was conducted and his opinion reached as a result of the request of the family court commissioner. Under these circumstances the trial court was not at liberty to disregard the unimpeached, unequivocal and uncontradicted testimony of Dr. Hurley. This being so, the finding of the trial court that the desertion was not wilful is against the great weight and clear preponderance of the evidence.

In *Caldwell* v. *Caldwell* (1958), 5 Wis.2d 146, 154, 92 N.W.2d 356, 360, a divorce action for cruel and inhuman treatment defended upon the ground of uncontrollable irritability due to ill health, we stated:

Some courts have stated broadly that insanity is a good defense, but the majority view appears to be that if the nature of the mental illness is such that the victim is conscious of what he does and knows that what he does is not right, although in doing the acts he acts under the compulsion of a diseased mind which prevents him from abstaining therefrom, his infirmity is no defense.

To the same effect is 1 Nelson, *Divorce and Annulment* (2d ed.), 355, 356, sec. 9.06:

The fact that conduct complained of was due to hallucinations of the spouse charged with it does not prevent such conduct from constituting ground for divorce, if the hallucinations did not amount to insanity. The same is true as to acts of a paranoiac prior to the time such condition became so advanced as to amount to insanity, or the acts of one suffering from psychoneurosis later developing into insanity.

The term "wilful" has been defined in *Milwaukee Corrugating Co.* v. *Industrial Comm.* (1928), 197 Wis. 414, 420, 222 N.W. 251, 254, thusly:

The words "wilful" and "wilfully" are of somewhat varied signification according to the context in which they are used in particular cases and the nature of the subject under discussion or treatment. They are frequently used in the sense of intentionally, or in other words as implying a purpose or design, or proceeding from a conscious motion of the will as distinguished from accidentally or involuntarily; and they are accordingly used in the sense of or as equivalent to willingly; designedly; purposely; obstinately; stubbornly; inflexibly; perversely; voluntarily; deliberately; with set purpose; being governed by the will, without regard to reason, or without yielding to reason.

We conclude the great weight and clear preponderance of the evidence compel the inferences that Mrs. Cahill was not insane at the time she left her husband and during the statutory period prior to commencement of the action, and that she knowingly and willingly left her husband and their home in Milwaukee with a firm intention not to return.

The finding of the trial court that Mrs. Cahill was mentally ill and did not wilfully desert her husband cannot be sustained.

Mr. Cahill has established his right to a divorce under the statute upon the grounds of wilful desertion. A divorce must be granted to him. Upon remand and granting of a divorce the trial court shall determine Mrs. Cahill's right to a division of property or alimony, or both, as the case may be, and a redetermination of the rights of custody and visitation of the minor children, if advisable, in the sound discretion of the trial court.

Judgment reversed and remanded for further proceedings consistent with the opinion.

HALLOWS, Justice (dissenting):

I respectfully dissent because of my dissatisfaction of this court's definition of "legal insanity." My views are set forth in the dissent in *State* v. *Esser* (1962), 16 Wis.2d 567, 115 N.W.2d 505, and in my concurring opinion in *Kwosek* v. *State* (1960), 8 Wis.2d 640, 100 N.W.2d 339. This court should again take a long, hard look at its definition of legal insanity and the field of mental illness.

WILLIE, Justice (concurring):

I concur in the result reached by the majority. Since, in my view, on this record Mrs. Cahill was not legally insane under the definition of insanity as stated in *State* v. *Esser* by either the majority or by the dissenters, I would conclude that: (1) Mrs. Cahill was not legally insane, and (2) in reaching this conclusion we are not reaffirming the definition of insanity as stated by the majority in *State* v. *Esser*.

I am authorized to state that Mr. Chief Justice CURRIE joins in this opinion.

WIRZ v. WIRZ

NOURSE, Presiding Justice.

Plaintiff sued for divorce charging his wife with "incurable insanity" under the provisions of section 108 of the Civil Code. The trial court denied the decree. The principal question involved on the appeal is the quantum of proof required to establish "incurable insanity."

The code section reads in part: "A divorce may be granted on the grounds of incurable insanity only upon proof that the insane spouse has been confined to an institution * * * for a period of at least three continuous years immediately preceding the filing of the action and upon the testimony of a member of the medical staff of said institution that such spouse is incurably insane." The section requires the court in granting the decree of divorce to make an appropriate order for the support of the spouse, or require a bond therefor.

To prove the issue of "incurable insanity" the plaintiff offered the evidence of Dr. Walter Rapaport, Superintendent and Medical Director of Agnew State Hospital where defendant had been confined since December 15, 1938, under commitment by the superior court. The doctor testified that, in his opinion, the patient would continue to get progressively worse, that "in the realm of reasonable probability, that will be the course." Question: "[I]t is your opinion, is it not, that she is incurably insane and will never be released?" Answer: "That is my opinion." On cross examination Dr. Rapaport testified in answer to a question by the court: "What is your diagnosis, Doctor?" Answer: "The diagnossi is manic depressive; and then they have recurrences. It used to be called circular insanity in the old days, but the condition, if it progresses and remains without improvement over a period of years, indicates a chronic form of manic depressive, from which they do not get well." The trial court did not find that any of this testimony was untrue. It's decision was based upon the ruling that it was necessary for plaintiff to prove that defendant was "absolutely incurably insane; and I don't think any human being can say that about anybody."

The finding of fact on this issue is "That it is not true and that it is not sustained by the evidence submitted that the said defendant Bertha Wirz is incurably insane."

The question presented here is whether the finding that defendant was not incurably insane is contrary to the evidence where the member of the medical staff testified that according to his best opinion defendant was incurably insane, but that he could not go beyond the realm of reasonable probability.

There are no California cases with respect to the proof of incurable insanity and very few outside this state. The authority nearest in point, although there stil is a minor distinction, is Tipton v. Tipton, 1949, 309 Ky. 338, 217 S.W.2d 799. As in our case, the trial judge, who disagreed with the statute permitting divorce on the ground of incurable insanity, KRS 403.020, denied a divorce where the experts testified that according to their opinion defendant would probably not recover and would have to stay permanently in an institution, but refused to say with respect to any patient that he or she was absolutely incurably insane. The Court of Appeals reversed with directions to grant the divorce stating, 217 S.W. 2d at page 801: "Few physicians would testify positively under oath that any mental condition, or any disease for that matter, is incurable. All they can say is that from their experience and in the light of present day medical knowledge, it is their *opinion* that a certain disease is incurable or mental condition is permanent. Many diseases once thought incurable are now curable as medical science advances. If the statute being construed is to have any practical value and accomplish the evident intention of the legislative body, it must be reasonably construed and not given a strained and unnatural construction. We think the expert testimony in this case justifies the court in finding that appellee's condition is permanent and that she will never be able to resume her status as a wife to appellant and

that the lower court erred in dismissing appellant's petition." See also statements to the same effect with respect to propriety of divorce on the ground of incurable insanity. Dodrer v. Dodrer, 1944, 183 Md. 417, 37 A.2d 919 and State v. Brown, 1937, 213 Ind. 118, 11 N.E.2d 679, 682, 13 A.L.R. 1243. The latter case also held that incurable insanity is a recognized mental state which may be established by evidence.

There is another line of cases which has led to judicial discussion of "incurability." A Colorado statute, Rev.St. 1908, § 6068, makes "obtaining of a fee on the representation that a manifestly incurable disease can be permanently cured" a ground for revocation of a medical license. In Graeb v. State Board, 55 Colo. 523, 139 P. 1099, 1101, 47 L.R.A.,N.S., 1063, the Supreme Court of Colorado held 4 to 3 that that provision was invalid for uncertainty because, among other grounds, incurability could be no more than a matter of well-grounded opinion and it could not be said at any point short of death that it is a "manifest" fact. The minority argued that the statute should be interpreted more widely according to its intent to protect hopeless patients from being defrauded by physicians. Both in the Graeb case and in Freeman v. State Board of Medical Examiners, 1915, 54 Okl. 531, 154 P. 56, 58 L.R.A. 1916D, 436, where a statute, Rev. Laws 1910, § 6905, of the same tenor as the one of Colorado did not contain the word "manifest," the principal question was whether the statute applied to promising care to a patient ill in an incurable degree from an illness not necessarily incurable, like tuberculosis. The Oklahoma Court expressly followed the Colorado minority and held that an interpretation according to legislative intent and purpose required the right to revoke the license of a physician who takes a fee for the cure of a patient whose disease has reached a state incurable "according to the [then] general state of knowledge of the medical profession."

We are in accord with the ruling in Tipton v. Tipton, supra, although there is this small distinction that the Kentucky statute expressly states that it is sufficient that at least two psychiatrists declare that "in their opinion" the insanity is permanently incurable. Although our section 108, Civil Code does not specifically mention "opinion" it would seem that our general theory of proof leads to the same effect. Section 1826, Code Civ.Proc. expressly states that absolute certainty is not required "because such proof is rarely possible." Moral certainty or proof which produces conviction in an unprejudiced mind is sufficient even in criminal cases. The moral certainty is not required in civil cases; there "reasonable probability", as testified to by Dr. Rapaport, is normally sufficient and is used as a counterpart to "preponderance of the evidence." Murphy v. Waterhouse, 113 Cal. 467, 473, 45 P. 866, 54 Am.St.Rep. 365. In Liverpool, etc., Ins. Co. v. Southern Pacific Co., 125 Cal. 434, 440, 441, 58 P. 55, 58, it is said: "In civil cases which are decided in favor of the litigant upon a mere preponderance of evidence, the rule of a decision is, after all, but a rule of probability * * *." Compare also Estate of Moramarco, 86 Cal.App.2d 326, 328, 338, 339, 194 P.2d 740. Even where a specially strong degree of proof is required, or where a presumption to the contrary must be overcome, absolute certainty (conclusive proof) is not required. Hobart v. Hobart Estate Co., 26 Cal.2d 412, 446, 159 P.2d 958; In re Estate of Duncan, 9 Cal.2d 207, 217, 70 P.2d 174; In re Estate of Pepper, 158 Cal. 619, 622, 122 P. 62, 31 L.R.A., N.S., 1092; Freese v. Hibernia Sav., etc., Soc., 139 Cal. 392, 395, 73 P. 172. In Simonton v. Los Angeles Trust & Sav. Bank, 205 Cal. 252, 258, 270 P.672, 675, it is pointed out that there is no hard and fast rule for the quantum of proof required under sec. 1826, Code Civ.Proc. in a special case. All the law requires is proof "reasonably certain in view of all the circumstances."

As pointed out in Tipton v. Tipton, and Graeb v. State Board, supra, with respect to incurability of insanity no higher degree of proof than well grounded opinion evidence in the light of present day medical knowledge can be obtained. To require more certainty is unreasonable and would frustrate the intent of the legislature. And it is said: "the objective sought to be achieved by a statute as well as the evil to be prevented is of prime consideration in its interpretation." Rock Creek, etc., Dist. v. County of Calaveras, 29 Cal.2d 7, 9, 172 P.2d 863, 865; 23 Cal.Jur. 764. The objective sought to be achieved was the widening of the possibility of divorce, and the evil to be prevented the permanent union of a sane spouse with an insane one who does not offer hope of recovery. The disapproval by the trial court of that purpose cannot permit him to thwart it nor may we defeat the purpose of the statute by an interpretation which would make it unenforceable.

The question remains whether the court was bound by the expert testimony of Dr. Rapaport. In the Dodrer case, 37 A.2d at page 922, it was held that although the statute requires the affirmative opinion of certain experts, such opinion is not conclusive on the court. This is in accord with the general rule as to opinion evdence in California which is held not to be conclusive. But in Re Estate of McCollum,

59 Cal.App.2d 744, 750, 140 P.2d 176, 179, the only medical expert testified that Mrs. McCollum was incompetent to make a will. The court said: "While this opinion was entitled to be carefully weighed by the trial judge it was not conclusive on the subject, * * * and like the evidence of any other witness could be rebutted by other satisfactory evidence." But in our case there is no rebutting evidence whatever. The rule that uncontradicted testimony of a witness, in no way impeached or discredited, may not be arbitrarily disregarded, applies also to medical expert opinion evidence. In the Mantonya case our Supreme Court said, 33 Cal.2d at page 127, 199 P.2d at page 681: "where there is any real conflict in the evidence the finding of the trier of fact is conclusive. But the trier of fact is not entitled, arbitrarily or upon mere caprice, to disregard uncontradicted, entirely probable testimony of unimpeached witnesses." The rule is pertinent here because the trial judge expressly commended the expert witness for his testimony and stated that he rejected it because he did not "like the policy of the law. I think it is the most unjust law ever enacted, and until it is proved this decree is denied."

On the second ground little need be said. If the trial court was not satisfied with the showing of plaintiff's ability to support the defendant for the remainder of her life expectancy it was authorized by the statute to require a bond therefor "as the circumstances require."

The evidence of plaintiff's ability to support defendant was meager and unsatisfactory as proof. The complaint alleged that the parties owned community property consisting of the home in Redwood City and that plaintiff had the ability to and was willing to support the defendant "for the rest of defendant's life." The ownership of the realty was conceded. Proof was made that plaintiff was employed at wages of $1.88 an hour with reasonable expectancy that the employment would continue. There was no proof of the value of the real property or of the liquitable value of defendant's interest therein. There was no offer to post a bond, and no suggestion of plaintiff's ability to secure payment of the costs of defendant's support. It was shown that for the past ten years she had been under the care of the State and that nothing had been paid by plaintiff for that care. Clearly the purpose of the statute is to permit a bond when the court is not satisfied with the proof that plaintiff's ability to support is absolutely certain. The power of the court under this section is fully considered in Tripoli v. Crivello, 88 Cal.App.2d 760, 99 P.2d 726, where the community property was ordered sold and the wife's share put in trust to cover the cost of her maintenance in the state institution. This provision is designed to make the statute available to those in poor financial circumstances as well as to those who have ample funds to pay for their separation from an insane spouse.

However, since the rule of procedure is settled that a finding of the trial court may not be disturbed on appeal when supported by competent evidence, we must hold that the finding that plaintiff's ability to support the defendant was not proved is a finding on a material question of fact which is just as binding as an affirmative finding that a material issue has been proved.

Judgment affirmed.

GOODELL, J., concurs.

DOOLING, Justice.

I concur. While I appreciate the propriety of the legislature's making any reasonable provision for the future protection of the insane spouse and of the state where a divorce is granted on the ground of incurable insanity, I question the wisdom and justice of making that provision so sweeping that the statute gives rights to the rich while it denies the same rights to the poor. Nevertheless the legislature has seen fit to condition the right to divorce on the ground of incurable insanity on a showing "that there is reasonable ability to support the insane spouse for the remainder of the life expectancy or that such insane spouse has property sufficient" for that purpose. Sec. 108, Civ. Code. The trial court found that these conditions do not exist in this case, the finding has substantial evidentiary support, and under the existing statute this justifies the judgment denying the divorce.

E. v. F.

LOWENGRUB, J. D. C. (temporarily assigned).

An amended complaint was filed in this matter on September 29, 1971 alleging as the ground for divorce from the bond of matrimony defendant's institutionalization in the Camden County Pscychiatric Hospital for Mental Illness (hereinafter called Lakeland), for 24 consecutive months after the date of the marriage and next preceding the filing of that complaint.

The parties were married on September 21, 1963.

On May 24, 1968 defendant was committed to Lakeland on a temporary commitment, and on June 14, 1968 he was transferred to a regular commitment. Defendant's medical diagnosis on admission was paranoid schizophrenia.

Defendant was, as of the date of the trial in this matter, March 1, 1972, an active patient at Lakeland under a program of rehabilitation.

Between June 20 and September 29, 1971 he was permitted to leave the hospital on 15 separate weekend visits with his mother. The

weekend visitations continue to date. There have not been other visitation periods permitted him.

Plaintiff testified that she has not seen defendant since his commitment and, further, that there was no cohabitation between her and defendant since his admission to Lakeland.

Defendant does not deny that he has suffered from mental illness since at least his commitment on May 24, 1968, but he argues that he was not institutionalized for a period of at least 24 consecutive months next preceding the filing of the complaint because he was permitted to leave the hospital on weekends for a period of about three months before the filing date of the amended complaint.

Defendant also argues that the real meaning of the statute is that plaintiff must prove that he was mentally incompetent for the statutory period. He alleges that plaintiff has failed in that burden since no evidence was introduced by her of a determination that he was a mental incompetent.

The hospital records show that defendant was, from the date of his temporary commitment to the trial date, a patient committed to the hospital without benefit of discharge. He was given permission to leave the hospital after application for weekend visits had been made by his mother and approved by the hospital staff member in charge of his case.

Defendant could not leave Lakeland without permission, and although he was away for the weekend, he was subject ot the rules and regulations of the hospital.

Since there is no New Jersey case authority to shed light on the meaning of that portion of N.J.S.A. 2A:34–2(f) requiring institutionalization for "24 or more consecutive months," it would be well to look to the comment to the proposed statute in the final report to the Governor and the Legislature published by the Divorce Law Study Commission, dated May 11, 1970:

The premise is that dead marriages should be terminated at the option of either party. It follows that fault is immaterial. A divorce should not be granted as a reward for virtue or imposed as a punishment for marital sin. The public interest is concerned with the stability of functioning and meaningful marriages. From the standpoint of the non-institutionalized spouse, he or she needs and is entitled to a partner in the household and a surrogate parent for children, if any. It is the absence of the other party from the home, for whatever cause, that constitutes a deprivation.

Moreover, if the family relationship has so far deteriorated that the plaintiff seeks a divorce, there is no social good to be achieved by withholding that remedy. If the marriage remains viable the non-institutionalized spouse will not petition for divorce.

It is apparent, then, that the gravamen of the cause of action is the inability of the institutoinalized spouse to be a working partner in the marriage. A patient who is confined in a mental hospital, and who will not be discharged unless approval is given by the medical staff, is not the spouse in a viable marriage whether he have weekend visitation privileges outside of the hospital or not. In any event, the weekend privileges are not as a matter of right, but are only granted if they are deemed warranted by medical authority.

The continuity of the status of his commitment as a patient in Lakeland was not interrupted by weekend leaves from the hospital. They were and at best are part of a program of rehabilitation with a view to discharge at a subsequent time when the condition of the patient permits.

As to defendant's argument that plaintiff must prove that he was mentally incompetent during the 24-month period, we must first look to the language of the statute for its interpretation. That language is clear and unambiguous. The statute must therefore speak for itself and be construed according to its own terms.

Courts are to interpret the statute as an expression of the legislative will as it is written, and not according to some supposed or unexpressed intention. A court must not presume that the Legislature intended anything more in a statute than that which it actually wrote as to the law.

A person who is declared to be mentally incompetent is one who by age, disease or affliction has become incapable of managing his own affairs.

Illness has been defined as poor health or sickness; loss of health; affliction or disability; an unhealthy condition of the body or mind. Roget's Thesaurus (1969 ed.) 386; Webster's New Collegiate Dictionary (7th ed. 1967) 415.

In another statute our Legislature has defined mental illness as a mental disease of such an extent that a person so afflicted requires care and treatment for his own welfare, or the welfare of others or the community. See N.J.S.A. 30:7B–2(f).

Paranoid schizophrenia clearly comes within the definition of mental illness since mental illness encompasses a general malady of the mind, whereas a mental incompetent is a person who has been declared to be incapable of managing his own affairs. A person may be mentally ill but capable of managing his own affairs. The two conditions are not synonymous.

Plaintiff has established by uncontroverted evidence that defendant was a patient in the Camden County Psychiatric Hospital for a period of at least 24 consecutive months subsequent to the marriage and that the time period next preceded the filing of the complaint. His confinement was a result of his mental illness. A judgment of divorce from bed and board will be granted.

The issue of visitation by defendant of the child of the marriage will be determined at a subsequent hearing.

THE ROLE OF THE LAWYER IN COUNSELING DIVORCE CLIENTS

Caleb Foote, Robert J. Levy, and Frank E. A. Sander

This problem case concerns a hypothetical lawyer who, after twenty years of practice, has been both intrigued and frustrated by the occasional matrimonial cases that have come his way. He likes the challenge of working with such clients and trying to help them resolve their problems but is puzzled by the difficulties he has encountered. In response to a request for a detailed description of a "typical matrimonial case" he has handled, he submitted the problem case which appears below. It is followed by an interview with a psychiatrist who comments upon the lawyer's work and the general problems of lawyers in working with matrimonial clients.

1. PROBLEM CASE

Mr. Arthur is a fifty-six-year-old man who came to see me in regard to his getting a divorce. My law firm has done some legal work for the fairly large manufacturing concern in which Mr. Arthur is employed as vice-president in charge of sales. I have had dealings with Mr. Arthur directly, and these have always gone well, so I suppose that he came to see me about his divorce for that reason. In addition, we have had some social contacts because his youngest son and my oldest are good friends.

Therefore I knew some things about Mr. Arthur before he ever came to discuss the divorce. I knew he has three children: a boy, at present in his second-year residency in internal medicine, married with one child; a girl, married to a yung lawyer in a good firm, also with one child; and a boy who is an engineering student in his senior year at college. I also knew that his wife is a few years younger than he and that it has been rumored that she has been in poor health for a number of years.

In addition I was aware that Mr. Arthur has the reputation of being a hard-driving man with considerable skill but one who somehow was not able to deliver the final 10 per cent of whatever it takes to make him as truly successful as everyone thinks he ought to have been. I knew that his name has just recently been dropped from consideration for promotion to the presidency of the firm in favor of a somewhat younger man, and that this undoubtedly meant that he would not be promoted beyond his present position of vice-president in charge of sales.

When he first came in, Mr. Arthur seemed rather uncomfortable, which I suppose was natural considering what he had in mind. At the outset he said that he had come to see me about getting a divorce, that he had given the matter a lot of thought, and that he didn't want anyone to try to talk him out of it. He said he'd been dissatisfied with his wife and with his life for some time. When I asked him to explain what he meant, he acknowledged that Mrs. Arthur had been sick for some time. But he added that "it really wasn't serious, just some sort of damn allergy" that kept her at home and in bed a good percentage of the time and prevented her "ever going anywhere or having any real fun." He admitted that he was "bored by it all" and "in desperate need for something new and exciting" to keep him from "just plain falling apart."

A little questioning soon revealed that he was thinking of remarriage. As he put it, he was "very interested in" and would "probably marry" the thirty-four-year-old widow of a young man who worked as one of his junior associates until he was killed in an airplane crash fourteen months ago. He said he was in love with this woman and was "sure she's in love with" him. He indicated that he had been seeing her with increasing frequency over the past eight months and found her "exciting, stimulating, interesting, and provocative." He liked playing with her young children (three boys aged ten, five, and three), helping them with their homework, and claimed that they had given him a "new outlook and interest in life."

Excerpted and reprinted from Caleb Foote, Robert J. Levy, and Frank E. A. Sander, *Cases and Materials on Family Law* (Boston: Little, Brown and Company, 1966), pp. 822–35.

I must admit that the whole thing struck me as rather silly. It seemed obvious that he had some sort of crazy idea about being rejuvenated by marrying a younger woman with her young kids. Obviously he would be a good catch for her since it didn't strike me as too likely that anybody except someone like Mr. Arthur would want to marry somebody thirty-four years old with three children. When I asked him if he didn't have his doubts about getting into such a marriage, he said that he did, adding that he often wondered if he'd "be able to satisfy" the younger woman and her children. I told him that I had to agree with these doubts and that if I were in his position, I certainly would have them too.

I asked him if he really was sure of what he was doing. He said that he wasn't absolutely sure but that he really couldn't see any other out. He said he was bored at home and with himself. He said his job didn't really interest or challenge him any more and that he felt as if he were "just playing out the string" at the company. From what I had heard, I suppose he was accurate in that observation.

He told me that he had discussed the "whole idea" any number of times with his wife and that she had agreed to give him a divorce, but that that didn't really satisfy him. He said he'd discussed it "some" with his children and that they'd been no help at all, just saying that they didn't see how he could divorce their mother when she was sick. When he told me that, he slammed his hand down on the desk and exploded that he felt as if he were in a "whipsaw" between "what I want" and "what I feel tied to and obligated to." I asked him how his wife had taken his announcement of wanting a divorce. He said his wife seemed "sort of depressed" since they had the talk in which she agreed to the divorce. He slammed the desk again with his hand and said "the whole damn situation makes me sore as hell" and sometimes "I just feel like telling them all to go to hell and do what I want to do," adding that this "of course" meant to get the divorce and marry the young widow.

Up to this point in our discussion I'd kept fairly quiet, trying only to ask questions to get him to tell me more of the story. It seemed quite clear by this time that Mr. Arthur was trying to ditch his sick wife, on whom he's probably blamed his failure to be promoted at the company, and then marry the younger woman. It even seemed as if he wanted everybody to go along with this: he wanted his wife to give her permission; he wanted his children to support his plan; he probably would want all of iis colleagues to accept the new wife with no questions asked. I guess what I was supposed to be doing was just to pull the legal levers that would make all this come true.

And I certainly wasn't inclined to go along with it. What happened eventually just bore me out, but at this point I was so full of doubts as to the wisdom of what Mr. Arthur was doing that I'd have felt I hadn't done my duty or fulfilled my obligation to my client unless I pointed out how wrong I thought he was. You can't stop a man from making a fool of himself in this free country, but you certainly don't have to stand on the sidelines and cheer him on. My only problem was how to make this clear enough to him so that there could be no doubt where I stood and no doubt about what course I was counseling him to take.

So I asked him if he really thought his wife would stand by and let the divorce go through. He said he was sure she would; after all, they'd talked about it a number of times and she'd finally agreed to let him get the divorce. But I asked him if he didn't think that she'd feel she'd been treated unfairly if he divorced her. He said "No, why should she? After all, I've provided for her very generously and I'll make her a good settlement. What complaints could she have?" I asked him about the children. Wouldn't they be angry with him for leaving their mother high and dry? He said it was none of their business—they were grown up now and leading their own lives the way they wanted to. Why shouldn't he have the same privilege? After all, he said, he was only fifty-six, and with any luck he ought to live another twenty years, and why shouldn't they be happy years? Besides, he wasn't leaving their mother high and dry—he would provide for her very generously, and she could keep the house and the furniture and most of their possessions, so who could say that he was leaving her high and dry?

By this time he was getting pretty worked up about it, and he'd begun to pace up and down in the office. I could really tell I had him on the defensive and on the run, and I didn't want to let him off the hook, so I asked him if he really thought the widow loved him or if she wasn't just looking for a soft touch to help her out of her financial and social dilemma. The question really got him because he began to splutter and stammer, and it took him several minutes to come up with an answer. Even then it wasn't a very satisfactory answer or one that anyone with any intelligence could really believe.

Of course I raised all these doubts in his mind because I really was convinced that he was doing the wrong thnig and that he was just letting himself in for disaster if he stayed on the course he'd set out on. I knew that if I could just get him thinking of the problems he was raising that he'd see the error of his reasoning and come back to his senses.

At this point I thought I'd let him think about it for a while and suggested that we get together to talk about it in a week. He said he thought he'd had enough for one day and thanked me, made another appointment for five days later, and left. I don't know what happened during those five days, but his secretary called me the morning of our appointment to cancel it, and I didn't see Mr. Arthur again. I suppose he talked it over with the widow, and I guess she convinced him to stop raising doubts and to just go to see another lawyer who wouldn't try to counsel him as I was trying to do but would just do what Mr. Arthur wanted him to do.

In any event, that's apparently just what happened. A couple of months later I learned that he had obtained a divorce and married the widow. He went to a lawyer who just pushes these cases through for the fees he gets out of them, no questions asked. Things have gone from bad to worse. Mr. Arthur used to get a lot of pleasure out of his children and grandchildren, but now he hardly sees them any more—the children are very cool. I've also learned through my son that he's doing a lot of drinking. Recently I heard that things aren't going too well for Mr. Arthur in his firm either; they are considering moving him over into some less important position.

2. COMMENT

[A psychiatrist, Dr. Richard G. Lonsdorf of the Law and Medical Schools of the University of Pennsylvania, was interviewed about this case; his comments follow.]

Q. Do you think the lawyer selected this case for discussion because he was satisfied with how he had conducted it?

A. I have the impression from what he said that what he hoped to achieve was to have the client continue on in his marriage. But it is hard for me to see how he really could be satisfied because obviously that didn't happen. I do suspect that he feels he did everything that he could do to bring this about and perhaps that's where his dilemma exists. He must recognize that he left the client with a feeling of dissatisfaction.

Q. In examining what happened, we might start by looking at the interview itself. How do you feel about the way the lawyer handled the interview process?

A. It would help to have an actual transcript, and even more to have a sound film, so we could sense the lawyer's tone of voice and

see what kinds of nonverbal communication were taking place. Still, I think we have a pretty good picture of what went on. We don't seem to have many of the difficulties of interviewing which are so frequently encountered. One thing that is perfectly clear is that to a large extent the lawyer did keep himself out of the first part of the interview. He apparently asked relatively few questions, and one gathers those were only of the sort to move the story along. With a client who is willing to talk, who is in a sense bursting with his problem, one of the best things to do is simply to stand aside and let him spill it out. Not only is this most efficient, but also it gets out many of the ramifications that a question and answer method simply won't elicit. Far too many people have preconceptions of how an interview should run and cannot step aside and allow it to proceed on its own strength and in the way the client wants it to go. Such a structuring of the interview would clearly be a mistake with someone who is as willing to talk as this client seemed to be. With other clients who have more difficulty expressing themselves or in whom the problem is nowhere nearly as well defined or as close to the surface, the question and answer approach may be needed, at least to get things started.

Q. I suppose one test of an interview is whether or not the information necessary for initial planning for the case has been elicited. Would you regard this interview as successful on this score?

A. Obviously I can't answer that from the technical viewpoint of the lawyer. I don't know, since it isn't clearly stated, how long they spent together, but my guess would be that he probably got the basic information from the client in not much more than half or three quarters of an hour. There was an enormous amount of information gleaned in a very short period of time. So I would say that the lawyer really got off to a very fine start.

Q. But you said that something went wrong?

A. Yes, there's a sudden and dramatic shift in the middle of the interview. Somewhere after the client had told the main outlines of his story, our attorney began to get in there with both fists. It seems to me that that is when the trouble began. He obviously was being judgmental and allowing these judgments to interfere with his interview.

Q. But isn't it inevitable that the lawyer would have feelings?

A. Of course, not only lawyers—anyone who interviews.

Q. The case is not a very pretty one, is it?

A. No, and it's not hard to imagine what the lawyer was thinking. A wife who's being ditched after many years of marriage because she's sick and can't have fun with him any more, the alienation of the children— the lawyer's going to come to the view that the client is being what he called "silly."

Q. Silly?

A. I think he really meant bad, morally wrong, sinful, so that an element of condemnation comes into it too. It seems that when this feeling became clear to him, he began to give the client the third degree.

Q. Should he have suppressed these feelings.

A. Just as anyone who listens to a story makes judgments, our lawyer was obviously judging as he went along. It isn't his making judgments that produced the trouble; it is the fact that he let these judgments proceed to dictate the rest of the interview. This is what caused the problem. After he became a district attorney, he never again allowed any of the mixed feelings of the client to come forth. And in taking a strong stand himself, the lawyer forced the client into taking a stronger stand than the client had ever meant to take.

Q. How do we know that? Doesn't the fact that the client went ahead and got his divorce anyway show that he probably felt fairly strongly about it from the outset?

A. Yes, of course he did. But whether or not that would have been the outcome had this interview been handled more skillfully, I'm not at all sure. Of course we can only guess what might have happened if both sides of the client's dilemma had been brought out more skillfully than the lawyer was able to bring them out.

Q. Is it your view that the client was actually very uncertain of himself and that the lawyer in a sense pushed him into his course of action?

A. I certainly had the impression that the client was protesting too much, so to speak, about what he planned to do. His plan of divorcing his wife and marrying the widow seems quite in contrast with what we can infer about the rest of his life. It's as if a man has been a straight arrow for fifty-six years and suddenly decides to throw it all over and change his whole approach to life. This contrast should raise a question in the mind of the lawyer and should start him looking for clues to help explain the shift. Whatever clues were available were lost in this interview as conducted here. If the lawyer simply had given him more time, if there had been fewer judgments expressed or easily inferred in the comments the

lawyer made, if he had allowed the client to expand upon his position and his dilemma a good bit more, the other side of the client's ambivalence would have come out far more strongly. Perhaps a different and more satisfactory ending of their interview might have ensued.

Q. And what prevented this different result?

A. When you attack someone in the way that the lawyer did, you force him to defend his stated position as best he can, and as a result that position simply becomes more entrenched.

Q. Is the lawyer aware of this now?

A. He doesn't seem to be. He blames the client, blames the second lawyer who got the client his easy divorce, and derives a certain amount of self-satisfaction from the fact that his judgment proves to be right in the long run because the client has really gotten into trouble by following the course of conduct of which the lawyer disapproved.

Q. What keeps the lawyer even now in retrospect from being able to see the mistake he has made?

A. Well, he has to be at some sort of peace with himself. I think he is convinced that he did absolutely the right thing, and in some ways he did. He really did look into the situation and see it as something far more complicated and dangerous than a straightforward job of doing what the client said he wanted. The lawyer's intentions were fine; it was his technique that was faulty. He stumbled and fell over his own moral judgments about the client's stated intentions.

Q. How does the lawyer develop an ability to walk this tight rope you've described: having the judgments but not allowing them to interfere with his work?

A. It take a long time to develop these skills. But I don't think the beginning of the development is as difficult as you might think. Obviously the first step is to be aware that we are influenced by and judgmental of the stories our clients and patients tell us. Too often we think we are nonjudgmental in situations where in fact we are judging. To be aware of this fact is the first step toward learning how to deal with it. The second thing is to be aware that the judgments you are making and the conclusions you are drawing aren't necessarily valid for the person with whom you are dealing, no matter how well-intentioned or well-thought-out they may be. It isn't that you submerge the judgments; it's that you are as aware of them as you can possibly be. Any astute or sensitive client is going to be aware of some feelings on your part, and that in itself isn't necessarily bad. The problem comes in learning how to allow the client to develop his own answers to his own problems with nothing more on your part than a kind of general guidance.

Q. Of course, it was guidance that the lawyer was trying to provide.

A. If you want to call hitting the man over the head guidance, okay. As I said before, it isn't in what he was trying to do that he was so wrong; it was in the way that he tried to do it.

Q. So you could say that what the lawyer should have done was to point up to the client the strengths of his situation, where the client now is only oppressed by the negative aspects?

A. You can say this if you want, but it's not going to help much. That's not what I meant. The client is probably already doing this himself. It's like telling him, "You're making $20,000 a year, what are you complaining about?" That's really just another way of whamming him and doesn't help anyone. It is very important for a counselor to accept as real the way in which a client presents his problem even if it seems incredible to an outsider. Suppose you have a very bright guy who's just got his Ph.D. in physics and he comes to you and says in despair, "I don't know anything at all about physics." This is going to seem absurd to you, but you have to recognize that in a certain sense it must be true to the client; for example, he's probably thinking about his relationships with his peers in physics. It isn't going to help the client if you deliver the sermon he's given to himself a thousand times about accentuating the positive. He's got to work the thing through for himself.

Q. In other words, the problems you see in this interview arise as much from the lawyer's feelings as from the client?

A. Exactly. It's very interesting that the lawyer reacted so strongly against the client, whom he characterizes as silly and foolish. Of course we don't know much about the lawyer, either, but if he doesn't normally react with such intensity to the legal problems which come before him, it should have given him a clue to watch out, that perhaps he was emotionally involved in the situation more than any objective examination of the client's problem would have warranted. No lawyer, particularly no married lawyer, is likely to be "neutral" towards a client who brings him a divorce problem. The lawyer's own relationships with his wife and his attitude towards his

marriage and what marriage should be like are going to color his reaction.

Q. So that even if he can't help his own feelings—

A. I re-emphasize that it is not desirable that he block out his feelings, but to the extent possible bring them up to awareness so he can make some allowance for them. Thus if this lawyer had only recognized that he was overreacting emotionally to the client, he could himself have rechecked the validity of what he was proposing to do. With time one can learn to perceive one's own symptoms of excessive reaction and to be skeptical about the conclusions one draws under such circumstances.

Q. And if he had recognized this?

A. The most obvious things he could have done would be simply to have allowed the client to talk a great deal more and to have raised his questions in far more neutral ways. Ask the client if he has any doubts about his course of action, ask him if he has any ideas of how this whole situation developed, and ask such questions in a way that makes it easy for the client to express his own dilemma in as sympathetic a way as he possibly can. It seems clear that he has very mixed feelings about this situation, and sooner or later he's going to give the lawyer the clues to develop the opposite side of his stated feelings. Often he will even supply the right words to use as an opener.

Q. Would you expect this all in the first interview?

A. No, I think not. Probably all that can be expected in the first interview is to let the client develop the story as far as it was developed. At that point the lawyer might simply raise a few questions, say that it isn't at all clear to him exactly how all this came about, that he'd like to think about the situation and would like the client to think some more about it, with a view to returning in two or three days. Most people would be willing to do this, especially when they feel mixed up and when they have already received some help just by finding a sympathetic listener. On a second interview the lawyer will probably get the other side of the coin.

Q. How many interviews would you expect the lawyer to go through with this client?

A. Well, that depends on exactly what his goal is.

Q. What do you think his goal is?

A. I think one of his goals was to prevent the client from making what the lawyer, apparently sincerely, believes would be a mistake for all persons concerned—not just for the client, but for his wife, his children, and perhaps even the widow. But I don't think that's nearly all. The lawyer is quite concerned about imposing his view of what he regards as right conduct and right ethical standards upon the client. I think he's aware of the first goal, but probably unaware of the second. And it is this second goal which severely limits his ability to help the client to try to explore what the client wants to do.

Q. Do you think that a lawyer could really be expected to do the kind of a probing job that you are describing? What are his limits?

A. Anyone who is going to deal with people and their problems ought to have a sufficient amount of training to be able to recognize a situation in which an underlying problem exists behind the superficial one that is presented by the client. All psychiatrists and social workers are familiar with the so-called "calling card" concept, when the client or patient comes in with a stated complaint but in reality he wants to talk about something else that is very much more of a problem to him. The presenting complaint is just the "ticket of admission" to the professional.

Q. But why would this man go to a lawyer?

A. I suppose that in part it has to do with his previous dealings with the lawyer. As the lawyer himself said, these had gone well, and I suppose that in the course of them the client had learned to trust and like him and had some appreciation of his ability to deal with problems. The client came to him really as a problem solver, not as a divorce getter, no matter how directly he states the problem in terms that he knows the lawyer will find acceptable. If he'd come to a doctor, he might have presented a case of headaches or anxiety; if he'd come to a psychiatrist, he might have focused much more directly on what really troubled him. But in any case, he'll frame the problem in such terms as he thinks will fit the expertness of the person whom he has decided to consult.

Q. What sort of help do you think the client was really seeking?

A. I think he was seeking a way out of his entire life dilemma. Clearly this is more than simply getting a divorce. From the lawyer's own observations one can conclude that there are several things that have happened to this man—he was being turned down for promotion in his work; his children had grown up and left home; his wife had been sick; life was no longer as interesting or as challenging as once it had

been. It's not fair to say that he wasn't a successful man, but he had reached the limits of his success. And at this point it must have seemed to him that life was somehow passing him by. Obviously he was looking for a way out, for something new, something to stimulate him, something to produce the interest that he once had in life. It is also clear that he was full of anger about what it was that was happening to him, and as so many people do when they are angry, he just struck out in whatever direction seemed to him to be at all plausible. Whenever you see this combination of events, you have to be very cautious about the underlying depression that exists. That the client was trying to solve a complex problem was clear; that he was solving it in a way that implied large elements of clinical depression is equally clear. What subsequently happened to the client just bears out an increasing amount of depression and an increasing inability to cope with the problems. Anyone who is going to deal with people ought to be able to elicit the clues and hints as to this outcome. This the lawyer did well at the start, but then he tripped over himself and botched it.

Q. Do you see this as a case that a lawyer could carry all the way through to completion?

A. I'm not sure. But I think that after two or three interviews the lawyer could have helped the client to clarify his dilemma to the point that the client might have been interested in developing and resolving it either himself or with some help more expert than it would be realistic to expect the attorney to provide.

Q. Is this the kind of case the lawyer should refer to a marriage counselor?

A. Well, this particular client doesn't really pose so much a problem with marriage as with himself. There are, of course, many cases in which the stresses are truly marital, with difficulties keyed to the interaction of both partners. Here, however, it seems to me that the client himself is the one who is having the difficulty and that everyone else is simply acting and reacting to him. I would think that this case would be better referred to a well-trained social worker, psychiatrist, or clinical psychologist, someone skilled in individual therapy and equipped to deal with what may be severe depression.

Q. Shouldn't the client's wife come into the picture too? Why do you seem to assume that she plays so small a role in the difficulties posed here?

A. I agree that you should get much more information about the wife and that there is a strong possibility that she has something more than a passive role in this marital breakdown. But the husband is the one who is the activist; he is the one who is most interested in doing something about the situation at the present time. So he has to be dealt with first. Until something of a preliminary nature is done with him, it would be a mistake to bring her into it. Later, yes. The more you talk with this client, the more he is going to talk about his wife—he can't avoid it. In due time you will find out more about his complaints about his wife.

Q. Let's go back a moment to your comment that this case is perhaps one you should refer for individual therapy rather than to a marriage counselor. What sort of case should be referred to a marriage counselor?

A. Marriage counselors can best deal with the kinds of cases in which both parties are motivators and actively involved, instead of where one appears to be wholly passive. That kind of therapy starts off on a different premise—a premise that I find quite acceptable—that the marital breakdown is due to the failure of both parties and both are aware of it. Further, typical marriage counseling assumes that neither of the parties is so neurotic as to be unable to work out individual problems which lie outside their mutual failure. Suppose you have a couple who are dissatisfied and angry with one another. Perhaps they fight over money, or the tension may come to a head in a sexual context or about child discipline or over some other aspect of their joint lives. Here a counselor would want to see both parties together first, to get some idea of their interaction, and then he might see each separately for a few sessions before bringing them back together again for a subsequent session or sessions. In the joint sessions the counselor may concentrate sometimes on the husband, sometimes on the wife, and sometimes on how they function as a unit. This is particularly useful where there is a chronic pattern of inability of husband and wife to communicate with one another.

Q. In our present case, isn't it also conceivable that without any expert therapy, either individual or joint, a lawyer might deal adequately with the problem?

A. Certainly. If the lawyer spent two or three or four hours with the client, he might be able to help him through this immediate crisis without any further help. You would know much better whether that was feasible after you'd had two or three inter-

views. It isn't always necessary that there be profound changes or that the dilemma be dealt with in profound terms. Simply to raise the right kinds of questions—different kinds of questions than the client himself has raised—is just as critical and just as important as actually providing the client with specific answers. I can imagine that this might well be the kind of case in which two or three skillful interviews might enable the client to go on and wrestle with the problem himself thereafter and not require a great deal of further treatment other than that which the lawyer had given him through those few interviews.

Q. On the other hand, isn't it even more probable that this client's problem will turn out to be insoluble no matter what kind of help he gets?

A. What do you mean by insoluble?

Q. After all that has happened so far, how can you expect him to go back to his wife and live happily ever after?

A. I don't. I guess it depends on what you mean by "happily." For instance, I can see as a realistic possibility some outcome like this: husband does not divorce his wife or marry the widow. The wife continues sick and perhaps deteriorates slowly and there isn't much basic improvement in the marital relationship, but they continue to live together. Maybe the husband will take up sailing and golf and get his pleasures out of them and out of occasional casual affairs. Is this a "happy" solution? The husband may see it as preferable to divorce and remarriage if he comes to an awareness that by acting out his frustration he will invite a disaster which damages or destroys his relationships with his children, friends, and business associates, and if he realizes that the likelihood of "success" for the second marriage is not too great. But he's not going to end up exuding happiness from every pore. The range of alternative outcomes for this kind of case is rather limited.

Q. So you do think it is within the range of practicality for a skilled lawyer to take this case and achieve an outcome considerably better than what has otccurred?

A. Oh, yes.

Q. Then how does the lawyer develop the necessary skill? How is a social worker or psychiatrist trained?

A. I don't think that is really a germane question. It's not necessary to be a psychiatrist to be able to handle some of these cases. One simple fact that we are going to have to come to terms with is that there are never going to be enough psychiatrists to handle all of the human problems that come along. Any number of people—family doctors, attorneys, ministers, priests, rabbis, what have you—are going to have to have some knowledge of how to cope with these problems if we are ever going to come to any kind of solution.

Q. What, then, does the lawyer need?

A. The first requisites are some intellectualized concepts about how human beings behave—some appreciation of the way people react at different ages, of the kinds of dilemmas and problems that people face at different ages, and of the ways that they have of dealing with these. The lawyer must learn to recognize ways that they have of defending themselves against anxiety and of resolving dilemmas. This particular client is a fifty-six-year-old man. He is faced with the fact that he is now entering his declining years, although he doesn't feel this way yet. Up to this point he has probably been successful in life, but now suddenly he has run into a stone wall and must realize that he can't go any further. His response is one of anger, depression, and disappointment. He probably is angry with himself as well as with a number of people and with his environment for having produced this result, and he doesn't quite know what to do with it all. He wants to escape. He defends himself against having to come face to face with reality by trying to strike out anew with an entirely new family. What he has inadequately realized is the cost of cutting himself off from the family that he has already established. The lawyer needs to recognize that this kind of dilemma will produce depression, anxiety, and behavior that is often ill-designed to serve the purposes of the client who is going to go through with it. And as a lawyer will also see a variety of other clients, he needs knowledge about many different kinds of human behavior.

Q. You are talking about intellectual concepts?

A. Yes. The other side of the coin is simply a matter of practice. There is no way to learn clients, or to learn people, or to learn patients, without seeing clients, people, or patients under different kinds of circumstances. A law student is in a relatively unfortunate position in this respect. One of the most useful aspects of the education of psychiatrists or social workers is the supervision they get in clinical training. They see patients or clients and then discuss their cases with experienced, older practitioners who help them to understand not only what is going on with the client but also the reactions of the therapist himself and how these reactions can interfere with therapy.

This kind of supervision is the heart of almost any training program, but presently legal education rarely provides it for lawyers.

Q. Wait a minute. Do you insist that training under supervision is indispensable?

A. It's hard to get what doctors call clinical judgment without a lot of clinical exposure.

Q. Most lawyers get the exposure; the question is whether there must be a period under supervision. Isn't it quite possible that a law student who likes people, has curiosity about them, feels rapport with them, can be helped a lot without any training under supervision simply by being alerted to the kind of intellectual concepts we have been discussing?

A. Yes, I'd buy that.

Q. Some people just naturally have a lot more interest in and empathy with other people?

A. Of course. Go to any cocktail party and observe the different ways people interact with one another.

Q. At the other extreme, are there people who just can't be taught counseling by any method?

A. I expect so. These are people who like to solve neat analytical problems and who are often not averse to making a lot of money. If they get into medicine, they head for some specialty like surgery, and in law I suppose they would be drawn to some aspect of practice that does not involve them with emotional problems. With such people, hopefully you can help them to recognize and accept this limitation. Perhaps the greatest benefit a person like that can derive from a family law course is to learn to avoid family law practice like the plague and to steer divorce or unwed mother clients to other lawyers.

Q. So at the two extremes we have law students who are so naturally good or bad in their dealings with people that they either don't need or can't profit from training. What about the middle?

A. The main difficulty for most of us comes from the blind spots in ourselves of which we are unaware but to which we could be alerted by a period of counseling under supervision.

Q. You mean a blind spot such as our lawyer's unconscious hostility to his client?

A. Not exactly. Hostilities are much easier to deal with because they're much easier to see. The person who has them feels them; they seem reprehensible to him; he is aware that he needs to get rid of them. Much more difficult are what you might call the loving kind of blind spots. There are people who are so full of the milk of human kindness that they are overwhelmed by a client's problems and are unable to bring reality to them, or they empathize so much with a client's sad situation that they lose perspective themselves as to what can and cannot be done. You might say this is the tender loving mothering type who overwhelms the client, really impeding him in gaining the independence he needs if he is ever to be able to solve problems on his own. These are the kinds of things that supervision can pick up and help a person to recognize in himself.

Q. Wouldn't a lawyer who had these kinds of blind spots need therapy himself?

A. Undoubtedly some do, but often just an understanding of their own personal blind spots will help. I think I might summarize it this way. Many law students can get substantial benefit just from increased intellectual awareness of the concepts on which successful interviewing and counseling are premised. But nothing can really replace the much deeper experience of clinical supervision while dealing with a series of cases.

THE RIGHT TO ABORTION: A PSYCHIATRIC VIEW

INTRODUCTION

During the past two decades there has been an increasing tendency to invoke the psychiatrist as the arbiter at critical points of conflict between existing social policy and individual dissent and disagreement; abortion is one such instance of this tendency. Psychiatrists do have a relevant contribution to make to a resolution of the abortion dilemma, but their contribution is limited. When the psychiatrist serves as the *deus ex machina* of the conflicted social system, he may ease the immediate stress without clarifying or resolving the underlying divisiveness of the community. The unfortunate consequences of this are that society places undue responsibility upon the individual psychiatrist and at the same time shuns its own responsibility to face squarely the serious and sometimes critical issues that have led to such divisiveness. Because of these considerations and because the regulation of access to abortion is, in fact, the product of religious, moral, ethical, socioeconomic, political, and legal considerations, in what follows psychiatric factors are examined in relation to these broader perspectives.

THE OBLIGATIONS OF MOTHERHOOD

Mothering is a task that requires enormous human and emotional resources. It is an obligation that confronts and challenges the

woman's capacity to care night and day. Done in the spirit of love and fulfillment, it is hard but rewarding work. But when the child is unwanted, the task may become onerous and obligations created by such motherhood may become a lifetime sentence, an ordeal emotionally destructive to the mother and disastrous for the child. Despite these serious psychological consequences, motherhood is so universally revered as a natural fulfillment of the life cycle and as a sacred obligation to the potential of a new life that once the woman becomes pregnant, we tend to ignore the element of choice or to condemn those who in a variety of situations would choose abortion. It is out of this social, religious, and psychological climate that laws regulating abortion have been drawn.

THE UNWANTED CHILD

The predicament of the future child, should he be born, also cannot be ignored. More systematic research in this area is badly needed, but one significant study has been carried out in Sweden with 120 children born after an application for a therapeutic abortion had been refused.[1] These children were born dur-

[1] H. Forssman, and I. Thuwe, 'One Hundred and Twenty Children Born After Application for Therapeutic Abortion Refused," *Acta Psychiatrica Scandinavica* 42 (1966): 71–78. In an earlier pa-

Committee on Psychiatry and Law, Group for the Advancement of Psychiatry (G.A.P. Report No. 75, 1969); excerpted and reprinted with permission of G.A.P.

ing the 1939–41 period and followed up until age 21 for assessment in terms of mental health, social adjustment, and educational level. They were compared to a control group composed of the very next same-sexed child born at the same hospital or in the same district to other mothers. The mothers of the control group were not selected on the basis of their maturity, but simply by the criteria of proximity in time, in geography, and in the sex of offspring. The results of this study indicated that "the unwanted children were worse off in every respect. . . . The differences were often significant (statistically) and when they were not, they pointed in the same direction . . . to a worse lot for the unwanted child." This is certainly not unexpected since the adverse consequences of maternal rejection have long been recognized by psychiatrists as one of the major contributing elements of human psychopathology.[2] In fact, some psychiatrists believe that one of the most important goals of preventive psychiatry is the prevention of "unwanted offspring."[3]

Surely, in the face of the population explosion society no longer has a need to compel the birth of such unwanted children. To the contrary, an informed and timely social policy should emphasize that for the sake of the family as well as society such children as are born should be wanted. Stressing this point, Garrett Hardin referred to the positive aspect of abortion:

Critics of abortion generally see it as an exclusively negative thing, a means of nonfulfillment only. What they fail to realize is that abortion, like other means of birth control, can lead to fulfillment in the life of a woman. A woman who aborts this year because she is in poor health, neurotic, economically harassed, unmarried, on the verge of divorce, or immature, may well decide to have some other child five years from now —a wanted child. If her need for abortion is frustrated she may never know the joy of a wanted child.[4]

per Caplan reported that special problems are apt to develop between mother and child when an unsuccessful attempt at abortion has been made. G. Caplan, "The Disturbance of the Mother-Child Relationship by Unsuccessful Attempts at Abortion," *Mental Hygiene* 38 (1954): 67–80.

[2] J. Bowlby, *Maternal Deprivation*, Schocken Books, New York, 1966.

[3] S. Fleck, M.D., in an unpublished paper entitled "Some Psychiatric Aspects of Abortion," presented to the Connecticut Medical Society, May 2, 1968, stated, "Preventive psychiatry's single most effective tool is the prevention of unwanted offspring. . . ."

[4] "Abortion and Human Dignity," Hardin's observation takes on special significance in light of the increasing ability of doctors to diagnose serious genetic defects in the third and fourth months

OTHER CONSIDERATIONS

While many other social, moral, and pragmatic goals may be offered as rationale for retaining the sanctions against abortion, our observation suggests that the historical and scientific developments of the past two decades have attenuated many of these factors. Some examples will illustrate this.

In the past, the threat or fear of pregancy supported our society's taboos about virginity. Whether or not one supports strict sexual sanctions, it is clear that the widespread availability of chemical and mechanical contraceptives has already eroded this traditional fear of pregnancy in many segments of society. Threat of pregnancy as a support of sexual morality and virginity has therefore lost some of its deterrent effect. Furthermore, we would suggest that the psychological cost of unwanted children far outweighs the limited gain in sexual morality that results from the fear of pregnancy.

Abortion at one time constituted a serious surgical procedure; considerable morbidity and some deaths were attendant to it. However, modern surgical techniques together with antibiotics have minimized these risks. The development of the vacuum evacuation procedure has already reduced morbidity and mortality to the status of insignificant factors.[5] Finally, the advent of a new class of risk-free abortifacient drugs can potentially make the interruption of pregnancy a nonsurgical procedure. This would mean that every practicing physician, on a simple prescriptive basis, would be able to terminate pregnancy harmlessly within the early phase of gestation. These developments make it clear that the element of

of pregnancy. For an example of how such a diagnosis led to a therapeutic abortion of a fetus certain to develop into a child requiring life-long institutional care, and allowed the mother to deliver a normal child in a subsequent pregnancy, see the *Boston Globe*, October 16, 1968, p. 3.

[5] For a description of this procedure, see E. Vladov, "The Vacuum Aspiration Method for Interruption of Early Pregnancy," *Obstetrics and Gynecology* 99 (1967): 202. The study offers a favorable comparison between the vacuum aspiration method and the conventional use of curettage. Comparisons were made as to loss of blood, early complications, and late complications. In "Abortion and Human Dignity," Hardin points out that in Hungary, where legal abortion is readily available (and where the vacuum technique has been introduced), the death rate in more than a quarter of a million cases is less than 6 per 100,000. This contrasts with 17 deaths per 100,000 in the United States resulting from the removal of tonsils and adenoids, and with 24 deaths per 100,000 in the United States resulting from childbirth and its complications.

physical risk to the pregnant woman is so small as to be negligible at this point in time and that the risk will, if anything, be still less in the future. These facts make it even more tragic that many American women are forced to seek criminal abortions wherein the risk of morbidity and mortality is relatively high.

An opinion frequently proffered by both medical and nonmedical authorities argues that a woman who aborts undergoes adverse psychological sequelae.[6] One typical view holds that the normal psychophysiological depression that ensues on the interruption of pregnancy combines with a feeling of guilt to produce a focal point for future depressive episodes and that abortion may even in some cases precipitate psychosis or serious neurosis. The published evidence dealing with this supposed deleterious impact of abortion has been summarized by Simon and Senturia[7] and meticulously reviewed by Sloane.[8] Sloane concluded that the earlier findings of serious psychiatric sequelae are (a) often based on a statistically biased self-selection of subjects or are simply case studies without efforts to standardize the sample or balance it against a control group;[9] (b) inadequately differentiated as to pre-existing conditions and abortion sequelae; (c) highly variable (in one study, for example, 43 per cent[10] of aborted women showed moderate to severe guilt, while in another study none of the women could be so designated).[11] Furthermore, the recent more carefully studied cases of Simon,[12] Peck, and Marcus[13] suggest that women who in psychiat-

ric terms are relatively normal respond to abortion with only a mild and self-limited depression without significant symptomatic sequelae. Psychiatrically disturbed women who undergo abortion for the most part remain stabilized or even improve. Simon's excellent retrospective study on women who were therapeutically aborted concludes: "Our study did not produce support for the frequently expressed belief that therapeutic abortion results in involuntary infertility, difficulty in sexual relations, or is a precipitant in involutional depression."[12]

Thus, the dire predictions of dangerous sequelae that had become embedded in medical teaching have not been fulfilled in controlled clinical studies or in our own clinical experience, particularly if the woman was strongly motivated in her desire for an abortion. There are exceptions, of course, but the most notable of these seem to occur when the woman becomes sterile as a consequence of infection at the time of her abortion.[14] The sterility means she can never restitute her loss by attaining motherhood in more gratifying circumstances. Since this occurs most often in nonmedical, illegal abortion, its significance could be markedly reduced if abortion were legalized.

Finally, in the past decade it has been quite difficult for couples who are themselves sterile to adopt children. It has been an era of black market babies, of long waiting and stringent selection of adoptive parents. The past few years have brought a reversal in this trend; in many urban areas it is currently impossible to find adequate foster parents for unwanted infants.[15] The woman who continues the pregnancy of an unwanted child in the hope of finding foster parents for her baby is quite apt to be disappointed. Thus, this justification for requiring the unwilling mother to lend her body to the continued obligation of pregnancy has also diminished.

[6] May Romm, "Psychoanalytic Considerations in Therapeutic Abortion," in *Therapeutic Abortion*.

[7] N. Simon, and A. Senturia, "Psychiatric Sequelae of Abortion: Review of Literature 1935–64," *Archives of General Psychiatry* 15 (1966): 378.

[8] R. B. Sloane, "The Unwanted Pregnancy," *New England Journal of Medicine* 280 (1969): 1206.

[9] F. J. Taussig, *Abortion, Spontaneous and Induced: Medical and Social Aspects*, C. V. Mosby Co., St. Louis, 1936.

[10] K. Malmfors, "Problem of Women Seeking Abortion," in *Abortion in the United States*, M. S. Calderone, ed., Harper & Bros., New York, 1958, pp. 133–36.

[11] B. Brekke, "Other Aspects of Abortion Problems," in Abortion in the United States, pp. 133–36.

[12] N. Simon, A. Senturia, and D. Rothman, "Psychiatric Illness Following Therapeutic Abortion," *American Journal of Psychiatry* 124 (1967): 59.

[13] A. Peck, and H. Marcus, "Psychiatric Sequelae of Therapeutic Interruption of Pregnancy," *Journal of Nervous and Mental Diseases* 143 (1966): 417–25. See also J. Kummer, "Post-abortion Psychiatric Illness—A Myth?" *American Journal of Psychiatry* 119 (1963): 980; M. Ekblad, "Abortion Follow-up Report, *Acta Psychiatrica Scandinavica*, Supp. 99 (1955); and Dr. Fleck's paper cited above in note 3.

[14] Helene Deutsch, *Psychology of Women: (Motherhood)*, vol. II. Research Books Ltd., London, 1947, p. 165.

[15] Of the estimated three million illegitimate children under 18 years of age in the United States in December, 1961, 31 per cent had been adopted. The proportions are strikingly different by race, however; 70 per cent of the white and only 5 per cent of the nonwhite illegitimate children under 18 years of age were adopted. C. Foote, R. J. Levy, and F. E. A. Sander: *Cases and Materials on Family Law*, Little, Brown & Co., Boston, 1966, p. 88.

Editorial Comment

In *Roe* v. *Wade*, 410 U.S. 113 92 S.Ct. 705 (1973) the United States Supreme Court concluded that the right of privacy includes the right to abortion. However, the Court also said that this right is not unqualified and must be balanced against important state interests in regulation. It resolved these competing interests as follows:

a) For the stage prior to approximately the end of the first trimester, the abortion decision and its effectuation must be left to the medical judgment of the pregnant woman's attending physician.

b) For the stage subsequent to approximately the end of the first trimester, the state, in promoting its interest in the health of the mother, may, if it chooses, regulate the abortion procedure in ways that are reasonably related to maternal health.

c) For the stage subsequent to viability the state, in promoting its interest in the potentiality of human life, may, if it chooses, regulate, and even proscribe, abortion except where it is necessary, in appropriate medical judgment, for the preservation of the life or health of the mother. 92 S.Ct. 705, 732 (1973).

However, there are still a number of questions in this area left to be answered.

1. Does the prospective father have a right to prevent an abortion? The United States Supreme Court did not deal with the issue in *Roe* or in the companion case, *Doe* v. *Bolton*, 410 U.S. 179 (1973). In fact, the Court specifically said it did not need to deal with the issue in these cases because no paternal right was asserted in either of them.[1] However, shortly after the Roe decision this question was raised in two cases, both of which involved Florida residents.

In the first case, *Jones* v. *Smith*, 278 So. 2d 339 (1973) an unmarried man argued that he had a right to participate in the decision to terminate a pregnancy, but his attempt to get an injunction preventing the pregnant woman from obtaining an abortion was unsuccessful. The Florida Court of Appeals reasoned that since the woman was in the first trimester of pregnancy, the father's rights during this period, like the interests of the state were subservient to the mother's right of privacy.

A few months later in *Coe* v. *Gerstein*, —— F.Supp. —— (S.D.Fla., 1973), a three judge federal court said that a Florida statute requiring a married woman to have her husband's written consent to obtain an abortion was invalid. The Court was of the opinion that the statute authorized the husband to withhold his consent during the first trimester on the basis of his concern for the potential life of the fetus or the health of his wife. Since Roe forbids the state from interfering with abortion on these grounds, the Court said the state could not delegate such authority to husbands.[2] However, the Court implied that a statute which allowed the husband to object on the basis of his interest in seeing his procreation carried full term might be constitutional.[3]

Therefore, the question of the father's rights to prevent an abortion during the first trimester of pregnancy is still undecided. And the issue of his rights during later stages of pregnancy has not even been litigated.

2. Do parents have a right to prevent or require an abortion? The United States Supreme Court also explicitly postponed consideration of the issue of parental consent for a minor's abortion in Roe. The *Gerstein* court, however, did consider the issue and decided that the Florida statute requiring such consent was unconstitutional. The question has also been raised in Washington and is currently before the Washington Supreme Court.[4]

What if instead of wanting an abortion a pregnant girl refuses a parental order to have an abortion? This issue was presented in In re Smith,[5] and the Maryland Court of Appeals concluded that the decision had to be left to the 16-year-old girl. However, Maryland at that time had a statute giving minors the same rights as adults to receive treatment for pregnancy. What if no such statute exists? Or what if the girl had been 13 instead of 16? There will undoubtedly be further litigation on these questions in the near future.

3. Another important question in the abortion area concerns circumstances under which physicians and hospitals can refuse to perform abortions. For example, some psychiatrists are receiving numerous requests to perform examinations to determine whether an abortion will be "beneficial" or "necessary." Do physicians and hospitals have a right to deny abortions unless a recommendation from a psychiatrist is obtained. There have not been any reported cases on this point as yet, but it seems likely that this policy will be challenged.

[1] *Roe* v. *Wade* at 165 n. 67.

[2] Kay, Sex Based Discrimination in Family Law 413 (1974).

[3] Ibid.

[4] Id. at 416.

[5] 16 Md. APP. 209, 295 A.2d 238 (1972).

EVALUATION OF KENNETH R. ARNOLD

The Jackson Clinic, Psychiatry

January 10, 1960

Honorable Robert T. Morehouse
Judge of the District Court

Dear Judge Morehouse:

In compliance with your order dated December, 1959, I have examined the defendant, Kenneth R. Arnold, his wife, and the complaining witness, Annette Arnold. I have personally seen all these persons in psychiatric interviews on December 5, and December 26, respectively. Furthermore, all these above named persons have been seen by psychiatrists on the staff of the Jackson Psychiatric Clinic for the purposes of history, obtaining of data, and psychiatric examination, and all of them have been given a battery of psychological tests. The examination period lasted from December 5 until December 26. A total of 16 hours of professional contact was spent. On December 29, all the findings were presented in Staff Conference. In the following, I am reporting on my conclusions based on the results of the various examinations that are routine procedures in psychiatric and psychological determinations, and particularly on my own findings and impressions.

SHORT STATEMENT OF THE PROBLEM

Under the given circumstances of the case, a determined attempt was made by all of the evaluators, and particularly by myself, not to judge the existence or non-existence of factual evidence but to concentrate completely on so-called internal evidence as yielded by psychiatric and psychological examinations. On the basis of purely clinical findings, Mr. Arnold presents himself as a passive schizoid and only marginally well-functioning individual, giving some evidence of a disturbed personality development; however, with no indication of an abnormal aggressive or sexually deviant development.

Mrs. Arnold appeared as a hysterical personality with a hysterical character disorder, addictive trends in the sense of alcoholism with somewhat unstable and inadequate impulse control, yet falling in general within the range of so-called normal functioning.

The complaining witness, Annette, an attractive and bright youngster, appeared clinically well composed, completely rational, at ease, and perceptive. She presented the best front of all the persons examined in connection with this case. However, on further examination, she displayed some signs of weakened impulse control, in that respect similar to her mother, unreliability of reported impressions, a tendency to magnify and distort, and considerable ability to fashion her stories according to what she believed the expectations of the examiner to be.

The psychological tests confirmed the clinical impression and fortified the opinions based on the psychiatric interviews.

The father is a severely schizoid, somewhat inadequate personality, with the potential of occasional loss of reliable reality testing. This inappropriateness, inadequacy, and passivity of personality structure is rarely, if ever, associated with the type of person encountered in sexual offenses. Annette's psychological tests show many manifestations of unbridled aggression with uncontroled feeling of rage and anger, given to hostile outbreaks that are then covered over by ingratiating, complaint, naïve and submissive behavior. Considerable sexual confusion and sexual conflicts were evident. They appear mixed with inadequate aggression control and appear merged in generally resentful and revengeful attitudes that are pariculaly directed against the mother.

In view of these findings, it appeared to us, considering our investigations—i.e., on purely internal evidence—as quite unlikely that a personality of the defendant's type should have carried out and maintained sexual relations with his stepdaughter over several years as charged; while it appears compatible with our results that as an outcome of adolescent maladjustment with strong aggressive tensions, the girl might have been able to produce the charges in an attempt to take revenge on an ungratifying and un-understanding evironment in order to permanently escape it and to punish her parents for a real or imagined injustice done to her.

FAMILY, SOCIAL AND PERSONAL HISTORY

The historical information obtained from all three persons coincides in most factual points except, of course, in regard to the alleged offense, over which there is wide discrepancy in description.

The defendant, born in Chicago, is the oldest of four boys. His father died when he was five years old and he has only very scant recollection of him. He was always very close to the mother, who also came to live with him at times and who played an important part in the present case insofar as she accused the victim of having illicit relationships with the defendant's brother. This brother is at present institutionalized in a State Hospital with a diagnosis of paranoid schizophrenia, and had been institutionalized twice before for the same illness. Otherwise, the defendant's family history is non-contributory. The defendant cannot give much pertinent information about his childhood or his development. He describes himself as average in every respect. He recalls considerable financial difficulty after the death of his father. He considered his role always as a helper of the mother who was invariably kind, protective, and wonderful, but he also considers her domineering, headstrong, and pushy. He glosses over this latter observation by insisting that it was all done for the sake of the children. He very quickly assumed a protective role to the other boys that were younger than himself, accepted odd jobs, and somehow neglected his school work so that he never went past the eighth grade, but he earned money from his twelfth year on.

At the age of sixteen, he was once arrested for a minor theft. Outside of that, his record is completely clear up to the present time. He had various occupations as an adolescent and youngster, never really learned a trade although he became interested in cooking and has for most of his life held positions as a chef without having any particular formal training in that occupation. He always stayed very close to home. He had relatively few friends, and his sexual contacts were confined mostly to prostitutes that never meant very much to him. He describes himself as shy and rather afraid of people, fearful that girls would laugh at him because of his awkwardness and his poor looks. Right after the end of the war, he went as Civil Servant to Germany where he served as chef in a hospital. It was there that he met his present wife. At first, he had extreme difficulties being with her because of the then current policy of non-fraternization. She was a German girl, married at that time, somewhat older than himself, who had one daughter, that is, the alleged victim. The courtship lasted

three years, and after overcoming considerable obstacles they got married in Bremerhaven, Germany, eleven years ago. Five more children, three girls and two boys, issued from this marriage. He adopted the stepdaughter and never considered or treated her any different from all the other children, to whom he is very attached.

Returning from Europe, the family went to Mansfield, Ohio, where he worked as a cook for a year and a half, and for another two years drove a taxi-cab. With the money that they saved, they bought a farm in Indiana and stayed there for three years. This is where the first difficulties with Annette started. Up to that time, he had considered her a completely normal, easily manageable girl. Then his wife caught Annette playing with herself and raised a tremendous fuss. She instituted a very strict regime that she had to wear underpants when going to bed in order to prevent her from further masturbation. The defendant was repeatedly asked by his wife to inspect the girl to see whether she had carried out these instructions. From that time on, there were constant conflicts between the mother and the daughter, in which the defendant interfered, frequently on the side of the daughter in order to ward off excessive punishment. The defendant always evaluated Annette as a girl who had occasional bad spells but who was essentially a good child. However, the conflicts did not stop. The girl was also found to make or bring home obscene drawings so the family decided to move to a place where she could go to a Catholic school. He sold the farm and accepted a job as cook in a State Hospital. In 1956, Annette apparently made the first charge that the defendant had tried to touch her, but she never did so directly to him, but to his wife. He was very upset about this allegation and asked the wife to go to the police to clear it up once and for all. The wife refused; the child never retracted her accusation, but did not mention it anymore.

About a year and a half ago, the family came to Disneyland on a vacation. He looked for a job there and found it at Norwalk State Hospital where they could improve their living arrangements and where general conditions were very favorable. He held this job as cook for three months, when he was discharged because he had no Civil Service examination. He then obtained another job at Arcadia where he remained a chef for one and a half years. At this hospital, he also obtained a job for Annette, who for several months worked there to everybody's great satisfaction. He then moved to San Gabriel Hospital in the neighborhood, obtaining a position he still holds.

During all this time there were incessant

quarrels between the girl and her mother, while the mother seemed to be fairly kind and understanding to all the other children. He fears that the wife made a grave mistake by attempting to give the girl a European-type Germanic education; she objected to mascara, lipstick, and her going out with boys. It seemed to him that the girl became more and more mixed up, would tell fantastic stories, fantasying about her real father, that she was a princess and had been kidnapped. She apparently told her teachers that she got nothing to eat at home, and similar stories, but he never paid much attention to it, believing that she was essentially a good kid. He remembers spanking her hard only three times, otherwise he considered himself more as her ally. Whenever she repeated the allegation of his having approached her sexually, which she did again in September, 1957, and now, he wanted to report it to the police and to start an investigation against himself, but his wfie always objected. About a year ago, the defendant's mother and his brother, who is now State hospitalized, came to live with the family, which increased the tension in the home because the wife and his mother did not get along well. He did not have the heart to fight with his mother who was a great help at baby-sitting. The brother developed symptoms of mental illness and it was then that the mother accused Annette of attempting to seduce the brother and of having an affair with him. Hence, the situation at home became turbulent and resulted in a great deal of marital discord between him and his wife who started to drink excessively and accused him of burdening her with his family, of spending money unnecessarily on account of his mother, etc. Finally, the mother left, but the disturbances continued all the more so since Annette started to go out with a twenty-year-old boy who looked like Elvis Presley, and fights between mother and daughter increased. Finally, it came to the point that his wife left him; he went to look for her and found her drunk in a motel. She, at that time, had a nervous breakdown and had suicidal tendencies. He contemplated seriously having her hospitalized in a mental institution. The defendant himself practically "went to pieces" because of the family conflict. He consulted a psychiatrist who advised his transferring the children temporarily to a relative in order to unburden his wife of her responsibilities. He set out to do so, but halfway to Indiana, where he wanted to place the children with a younger brother, his wife begged him to return and he did. The next morning Annette had run away and did not return. He hired private detectives who were able to locate her after several weeks in Chicago where she had gone with money taken from his dresser. The girl was exceedingly defiant, refused to recognize her uncle. The defendant had to go to Chicago himself where he engaged the help of the Juvenile authorities who finally sent her home against her will. At this point, she made the charges of rape. He was arrested and placed in county jail until he bailed himself out. The victim was placed in a foster home in Cornell, California.

He has no specific explanation for the charges except that she is apparently a very upset girl who was always given to making up stories and who was tortured by incessant conflicts with her mother. He pities her more than he resents her, but feels that he is in great danger and that she had done him a great injustice. He emphatically states his sex life was always rather weak but completely normal and that he neither had any desires for Annette nor any other youngsters and certainly never acted in a way that could give support to such a charge because he rather tried to help her and stood up for her against her mother. He points out that he has been alone with her only very infrequently. Hence, the charges appear to him quite absurd.

The mother, who is tense, nervous, and barely controlled, essentially confirms the story of her husband. She admits that she probably treated the girl stricter than was good for her, but she could not help herself. She states that she was constantly irritated by the defiant and teasing atttiude of the girl. She concedes that Annette complained on three or four different occasions about being sexually approached by her husband. She always discussed it with her husband who advised her to go to the police, but she did not want to start something that would ruin them in the neighborhood. She completely disbelieves these charges and thinks that they are the result of the distorted fantasy life of the girl.

Annette states that she has always been extremely unhappy in her home, particularly due to her mother who neglected her and hated her for some reason or other. While she has no complaints against her stepfather prior to four years ago when his sexual advances started, she recalls her mother mistreating. punishing, and slapping her ever since she can remember. She declares herself quite happy and satisfied now that she is with foster parents where she has made excellent adjustment and where she sees for the first time that life can be nice. All her life, she definitely felt treated as a stepchild. Now she is completely through with both her parents, with the stepfather because of his continued sexual attacks and with the mother because she would not stand up for her daughter and would not believe her. She claims not to be vindictive at all but wants to protect potential other victims and feels that her stepfather ought to be in jail.

She describes in great detail the first incident when her stepfather grabbed her, but when she resisted, he let her go. She was "very shook up" and told her mother but the mother would not believe her. This type of incident repeated itself innumerable times and led, in the absence of the mother, to more than a hundred occasions of actual sexual intercourse, "blow jobs," and other sexual activity like touching, mutual masturbation, etc. She is somewhat vague in describing the circumstances, or even the possibilities these very frequent happenings have but states that she was regularly disgusted but gave up defending herself because her stepfather threatened or slapped her around and after complaining several times, she knew that her mother would not believe her and nobody else would help her. She claims she had no sexual contact with any other person except her stepfather.

Annette evaluates her mother very negatively. She considers her as over-strict, inconsistent, and hateful to her. The father has presumably a double personality. He is very nice at work and makes a good impression on everybody, but at home he is like the devil. She despises her home atmosphere because the parents constantly fight. The mother drinks excessively and neglects everything.

Annette insists that running away from home saved her life and her sanity, and when she was forcefully brought back she knew that she had to tell the police because she could not stand it at home any longer. She is now extremely satisfied at her foster-home placement. She feels that both her foster parents are very understanding and real friends. She likes the three other girls that are placed in the same home. She is doing very well at school and is glad that she is out of her own domestic situation, although she misses her two little brothers.

Mental Examination of Defendant

Mr. Arnold is a thirty-seven-year-old, older-looking individual who at present uses a crutch due to a recent fall. He is fully oriented in all spheres, shows no memory defect for recent or more remote events. He appears a rather shy person, easily embarrassed, behaving awkwardly and frequently at a loss to account for the developments around him. His conscious intention is rather to cover up for Annette and for his wife. He attempts to blame everything on his own inadequacy but does not even seem

to be successful in making this inadequacy convincing. He appears as a struggling, barely adequately functioning individual with tenuous object and reality relationships. His predominate mood appears to be one of bewilderment and puzzlement. In his own description, his helplessness emerges as the main complaint. He was buffeted about by the female members of his family, by his mother, particularly by his wife, and now Annette. He appears not to expect anything else, yet he is surprised that it happens over and over again. He is quite responsive, but limited in his responses; shows no discrepancy between intellectual content and emotional reaction, but the latter is within a very limited range; he has little spontaneity, originality or ingenuity visible in his performance; his thought content is exclusively concerned with his present involvement; his plans for the future are unspecific; he visualizes nothing more than a continuation of the present adjustment with Annette being placed away from home. He is fully aware of the seriousness of the charge and the acute danger he is threatened by but has no idea what he could do additionally to defend himself.

The psychological test describes him as an extremely passive, inadequate kind of person who has somewhat less than average intelligence, is very limited in his education and capabilities. He has some difficulty expressing and extreme difficulty in understanding other people, their relationships, and their emotional reactions. He is capable of relating to others only in a highly dependent manner with a strong tendency for withdrawal. His reality testing faculties are usually intact though they are so tenuous that probably there is an occasional loosening and tendency toward discontrol and schizoid regression. There may be also possibilities of occasional aggressive outbursts. However, there are none of the signs customarily found in sex offenders, no loosening of the ordinary controls over sexual or hostile impulses, nor any elaborate fantasies in that direction, nor a severe personality distortion often associated with conditions of that sort. His judgment capacity seemed to be fairly intact. There is no evidence of illusions, hallucinations, or any other signs of major psychotic illness. He has very limited insight into his condition and few adequate plans to remedy it.

Mental Examination of Witness

Annette appears as a well-developed, attractive, and rather intelligent sixteen-year-old girl. She relates quite easily, has very good verbalization, and tells her story, which she admits that she has had to repeat many times in the last few months, in a convincing manner. She is fully oriented in all spheres, and has better than average facility for verbalization. In a manner often seen in adolescence or in other immature people, she uses a black and white technique almost exclusively. She contrasts the impossible circumstances in her home with the ideal ones in the foster home. She idealizes her own motives as being exclusively trying to protect others, serving justice, etc., with those of her parent whom she considers wicked, weak, and treacherous. She contrasts her own disgust and suffering about the sexual assaults with the brutality and glee of her father. She feels there is no other motive to her having left home except to escape a terrible criminal situation to which she saw no other alternative. However, she cannot very well account for a number of factors; for instance, why she did not go to the police earlier, but chose the moment when she was returned home by the Juvenile authorities.

The psychological tests describe her as angry, upset, and somewhat depressed. She attempted to stay aloof from the test and carefully selected the items to which she cared to respond. There was much evidence of anxiety, blocking, and strong reliance on the unconscious mechanism of repression. The test record was characterized by many anxiety indications close to the surface with tendency to and fear of explosive outbursts, which she regularly denies. There is very rich fantasy life concerned with heterosexual material associated with fear and guilt, deep concerns about her body and her body's integrity, and distinct ideas of self-debasement.

Her feelings toward the mother-figure are frankly and intensely hostile, while they are ambivalent in regard to the father, with incestuous fantasies and incestuous fears. She can be described as a hysterical character disorder in an adolescent, maladjustment with depressive features. There is no evidence of a deepgoing personality disorganization, no hallucinations, delusions, or major signs of psychotic illness. Her personality picture is characterized by tensions and anxieties, great discrepancies in thought content and fantasy life that are frequently found in adolescence. Her social awareness is excellent and her reality testing fairly good. She has, however, little or no awareness of any kind of internal problem.

SUMMARY AND RECOMMENDATIONS

On the basis of the findings stated above, it appears that Mr. and Mrs. Arnold are a mar-ginally adjusted couple with innumerable difficulties between each other and in their relationships to the world, which undoubtedly has colored the whole psychological atmosphere of the children. There is indubitable psychological evidence of a long-lasting, ambivalent and then frankly hostile relationship between mother and daughter that is partly admitted, partly covered up by both, and that has, over several years, led to innumerable wild and uncontrolled outbursts on both sides, the mother constantly attempting to impose a strict regime on the daughter, and Annette rebelling against it. In this connection, it may be of significance that Mrs. Arnold used her husband to be her inspector in the so-called educational attempts to prevent the daughter's masturbation. There are, of course, innumerable other conflict areas and complex relationships between father, mother, and daughter, some of which follow rather classically the Oedipal pattern in terms of unconscious fantasies of the parties involved. While the personality of the father that is loosely integrated might permit occasional discontrol, conceivably associated with sexual or aggressive acting out, it appears extremely unlikely that he could consistently have engaged in a prolonged pattern of deviant sexual activity over a period of years. His general inadequacy, helplessness, and passivity speak against this version. Furthermore, he has developed none of the usual signs of sexual psychopathy which, in the case of such prolonged dangerous and guilt-ridden activity, would almost be mandatory. On the other hand, Annette is a girl with excellent social awareness, in constant extreme rebellion against both parents, having a rich fantasy life, and not averse to consciously, and particularly unconsciously, coloring her impressions according to the conceived or picked-up ideas about what would be beneficial to her. The latent aggressive tension existing over a period of years finally was channelized in her running away and in her rebellious resistance toward coming home, where she feels misunderstood and mistreated. Subjectively, she felt so justified in her rebellion that she probably did not and does not see anything wrong in using effective means to bring about her revenge and particularly a permanent separation from the intolerable home environment.

If possible, there should be very strong recommendation for the permanent placement of Annette outside of the home to which she should not be permitted ever to return to live under any circumstances. She is a very endangered yet potentially valuable person. Hence, educational guidance and preferably psychiatric therapy are strongly recommended and appear imperative. It would appear desirable also that the parents' problems should be

brought to the attention of some social agency for some supervision and occasional guidance.

Respectfully submitted,
PETER N. JACKSON, M.D.

GUIDELINES FOR DETERMINING THE PSYCHOLOGICAL BEST INTERESTS OF CHILDREN

Jack C. Westman, M.D., Allen S. Hanson, B.S.

The prevention of mental and behavior disorders includes minimizing faulty personality development and stressful experiences during early life. In particular, the relationship between child neglect and abuse and antisocial behavior in later life has been well demonstrated (6,9). The thesis of this paper is that many of these adverse experiences during the early years of life can be prevented by the application of child development knowledge to legal interventions on behalf of children.

There is a pressing need to bring child development concepts into courts of law in which there is daily exposure to children whose lives are grossly disrupted and who are destined for later antisocial behavior and mental disorder. Attornies and judges routinely are confronted with the responsibility for making judgments and decisions affecting the lives of children. In contrast most child development research has been carried out in the quietude of child study centers remote from the realities of children with disrupted lives (10). Although knowledge is incomplete in many areas, enough is known to permit the infusion of child development thinking into the legal decision-making process. As the physician applying the knowledge of the basic science of child development to clinical situations, the child psychiatrist probably knows as much as anyone and bears the responsibility of at least trying to help beleaguered courts.

Historically, court decisions regarding awarding of custody and placement of children have been determined by an adult-centered point of view. For example, the evaluation of a child's placement with his mother has often been based solely upon psychological studies of the mother and her inferred mothering capacities. The same has been true for fathers, however, mothers also have been favored by a strong

cultural bias toward preserving relationships between children and their biological mothers. From this point of view judgments have been made about maternal fitness on the basis of evaluations of the mother's personality, soundness of mind, and moral attributes. As an example, court decisions have removed children from their mothers because they were regarded as emotionally disturbed, when in fact, their abilities to function as mothers were unimpaired and the children's best interests were not served.

A new wind is blowing in courts focusing attention on the rights of children, specifically in the form of determining the psychological best interests of each child (1,4,8). From this point of view a child's needs are determined and then a specific judgment is made as to whether or not a particular parent can meet those needs. In this situation the question of maternal fitness is replaced by the question of whether or not the psychological needs of a child can be met by his mother. From this perspective a mother who has been successfully treated for her mental illness through the use of chemotherapy, and in that abstract respect judged to be fit as a mother, might not in fact be able to meet her child's psychological needs because of her unresponsiveness to her child. Her symptoms might be in abeyance, but her ability to fill her child's needs is impaired.

Because many children suffer from shifting, temporary resolutions of crises in their lives by courts who are at the mercy of inadequate information, tradition, and biases, practical guidelines are needed for determining the psychological best interests of children (3). Courts often are handicapped by piecemeal information and the adversarial process, which pits expert witnesses against each other, each examining only part of the child's situation:

the psychologist who tested the child, the psychiatrist who evaluated the mother, and the social worker who evaluated the home.

The approach of child psychiatry offers an integrated interdisciplinary assessment based upon knowledge of the child, siblings, parents, school, and community. The evaluation process is based upon as much contact with the child and significant other people as is necessary to gather required information. In a given family each child has unique needs, depending upon his individual characteristics and developmental stage. When his family, school, and community can be viewed from the child's perspective, one can determine his or her needs and how they can be optimally met. The parents, family, and community can be evaluated then in terms of their actual capacities to meet the child's needs, not on abstract conceptions of fitness to be parents.

Since styles of child rearing are strongly influenced by culture, it is necessary to define the psychological goals, environment, and relationships through which a particular child-rearing process takes place. In our society the home with a nuclear family is regarded as the optimal environment and set of relationships for child rearing. Because of the current controversy about the family, leading some to conclude that the "family is dead" and others to advocate alternate child-rearing formats, it is well to face these challenges squarely and examine them in the light of current evidence (2). We know that families in themselves can produce disturbed children, and that pathological families can be the origins of adult maladjustments. It also is true that many children do not live in nuclear families, either because a family did not exist or was broken down. Furthermore, surrogate parents can adequately substitute for biological parents, as found in foster and group homes. At the same time it is clear that institutions in themselves cannot replace small intimate groups. The child who is a state ward is unfortunate unless he manages to find his way into a home with a stable, intact, committed family.

At the most general level, available evidence indicates that the child-rearing process depends upon continuous individual relationships between children and committed adults. Learning takes place through the love of and identification with concerned adults. The relationship between a child and a parent is the vehicle for learning how to manage drives, for modulating emotions, for developing the ability to tolerate frustration, and for acquiring coping skills. Each child needs a committed mentor, preferably two who can support each other, rather than one. From this point of view, the family unit is the most practical and

available means of providing the intimate relationships required for psychological development. It is also to society's advantage to delegate the socialization of children to tax paying adults, rather than construct costly child-rearing environments.

Whether or not legal marriage is an essential ingredient of family living is another hotly debated issue. The fact that family living ordinarily is based upon marriage has led to confusion of husband and wife roles with mother and father roles (7). Marriage itself is not necessary for the satisfaction of husband and wife roles, which are largely related to companionship, sexuality, and recreational activities. Although social pressures to achieve these satisfactions through marriage is strong, it is not compelling, particularly during the present era. It probably is true, however, that marriage is necessary for entering the socially sanctioned child-rearing process. Although not essential for "husband" and "wife" satisfactions, marriage provides for commitment to the continuity of child-adult relationships needed in the child-rearing process. For this reason marriage and family living are socially desirable avenues for satisfying the roles of mother and father.

With these considerations in mind, the evaluation of the psychological best interests of a child in legal matters ordinarily rests upon two assumptions: (1) the child has a fundamental right to self-realization and (2) society places expectations upon the child through the socialization process of child rearing. The growing child, then, faces developmental tasks related both to his own progress toward self-realization and to his socialization. In the final analysis a society's concern is that each individual realize his potential within the context of becoming a contributing or non-burdensome citizen. The following target psychological characteristics are required for competence in our society:

I. *Social Skills*
   A) ability to communicate
   B) ability to learn
   C) ability to relate instrumentally to others
   D) ability to be useful to others
II. *A Value System*
   A) commitment to adopt and adhere to a set social value
   B) commitment to adapting self-interests to social constraints
III. *Basic Knowledge About*
   A) the world
   B) other people
   C) one's self
IV. *Self-control*
   A) ability to delay gratification

B) ability to tolerate frustration
C) ability to work
V. *Self-esteem*
  A) basic self-confidence
  B) basic affection for self
VI. *Self-identity*
  A) unique person
  B) unique gender
  C) unique personality

The formulation of the psychological best interests of a particular child depends upon evaluating the available environmental and relationship options and determining which one offers the greatest potential for fostering the child's achievement of these characteristics needed for social competence. In a clinical child psychiatric setting, the following criteria have been found to be the most helpful in evaluating child-rearing alternatives in terms of their potential for furthering the psychological best interests of children in the legal system:

I. *Evaluation of Child-rearing Environment*
  A) Will the child's epigenetic developmental process* be protected? (Will the dependent years of childhood be free from disruption?)
  B) Will the child be cared for by committed, nurturant adults?
  C) Will the child be exposed to a variety of life experiences?
    1) intimate cross generational small group living (parents, siblings)
    2) neighborhood (peers)
    3) community
    4) school (education and extrafamilial adult relationships)
    5) recreation
II. *The Evaluation of the Quality of Child-rearing Relationships*
  A) Will the child be able to develop bonds with adults?
    1) identification of child with parent figures
      a) developmental stage of child
      b) identification with mothering person
        1) attachment
        2) personality
        3) values
      c) identification with fathering person
        1) attachment
        2) personality
        3) values

  2) identification of parent figures with child
    a) priority of child in parents' life
    b) demonstration of empathy
    c) respect for child's point of view
    d) capacity to communicate with child
    e) acceptance of child's body and its functions
  B) Will the adults be able to manage the the child's behavior?
    1) limit setting
    2) teaching coping techniques
  C) Will the child be able to form bonds with other children?
    1) of varying ages (siblings)
    2) of same age (peers)

When these considerations are applied to the life situations of individual children, it becomes evident that child development knowledge can be applied helpfully in legal adjudications. Expert testimony in these matters should be based upon a coordinated, comprehensive assessment of each child in his family, school, and community with the aim of evaluating child-rearing options in the light of their ability to assure the development of key personality characteristics necessary for the child's competence in his society.

* This term refers to the discrete but overlapping stages of child development from infancy to adolescence, as described in the psychoanalytic literature, especially by Freud and by Eric Erickson.

REFERENCES

1. Adams, Paul, et al. *Children's Rights: Toward the Liberation of the Child.* London: Panther, 1972.
2. Eiduson, B. T., Cohen, J., Alexander, J. "Alternatives in Child Rearing in the 1970's." *American Journal of Orthopsychiatry* 43 (1973): 720–31.
3. Ellsworth, P. C., and Levy, R. J. "Legislative Reform of Child Custody Adjudication." *Law and Society Review* 2 (1969): 167–233.
4. Foster, Henry H., and Freed, Doris J. "A Bill of Rights for Children." *Family Law Quarterly* 7 (1973): 343–75.
5. Hansen, R. W. "The Role and Rights of Children in Divorce Actions." *Journal of Family Law* 6 (1966): 1–14.
6. Robins, Lee N. *Deviant Children Grown Up.* Baltimore: Williams and Wilkins Co., 1966.
7. Veevers, J. E. "The Social Meanings of Parenthood." *Psychiatry* 36 (1973): 291–310.
8. Wadlington, Walter. "The Courts and Children's Rights." *Children* 16 (1969): 138–42.
9. Weininger, Otto. "Effects of Parental Deprivation: An Overview of Literature and Report on Some Current Research." *Psychological Reports* 30 (1972): 591–612.
10. Westman, Jack C. *Individual Differences in Children.* New York: John Wiley & Sons, 1973.

PAINTER v. BANNISTER

Decision of the Supreme Court of Iowa

STUART, Justice:

We are here setting the course for Mark Wendell Painter's future. Our decision on the custody of this seven-year-old boy will have a marked influence on his whole life. The fact that we are called upon many times a year to determine custody matters does not make the exercising of this awesome responsibility any less difficult. Legal training and experience are of little practical help in solving the complex problems of human relations. However, these problems do arise and, under our system of government, the burden of rendering a final decision rests upon us. It is frustrating to know we can only resolve, not solve, these unfortunate situations.

The custody dispute before us in this habeas corpus action is between the father, Harold Painter, and the maternal grandparents, Dwight and Margaret Bannister. Mark's mother and younger sister were killed in an automobile accident on December 6, 1962, near Pullman, Washington. The father, after other arrangements for Mark's care had proved unsatisfactory, asked the Bannisters to take care of Mark. They went to California and brought Mark to their farm home near Ames in July, 1963. Mr. Painter remarried in November, 1964, and about that time indicated he wanted to take Mark back. The Bannisters refused to let him leave and this action was filed in June, 1965. Since July 1965, he has continued to remain in the Bannister home under an order of this court staying execution of the judgment of the trial court awarding custody to the father until the matter could be determined on appeal. For reasons hereinafter stated, we conclude Mark's better interests will be served if he remains with the Bannisters.

Mark's parents came from highly contrasting backgrounds. His mother was born, raised, and educated in rural Iowa. Her parents are college graduates. Her father is agricultural information editor for the Iowa State University Extension Service. The Bannister home is in the Gilbert Community and is well kept, roomy, and comfortable. The Bannisters are highly respected members of the community.

Mr. Bannister has served on the school board and regularly teaches a Sunday school class at the Gilbert Congregational Church. Mark's mother graduated from Grinnell College. She then went to work for a newspaper in Anchorage, Alaska, where she met Harold Painter.

Mark's father was born in California. When he was two and a half years old, his parents were divorced and he was placed in a foster home. Although he has been kept in contact with his natural parents, he considers his foster parents, the McNellys, as his family. He flunked out of a high school and a trade school because of a lack of interest in academic subjects, rather than any lack of ability. He joined the Navy at seventeen. He did not like it. After receiving an honorable discharge, he took examinations and obtained his high school diploma. He lived with the McNellys and went to college for two and a half years under the G.I. bill. He quit college to take a job on a small newspaper in Ephrata, Washington, in November, 1955. In May, 1956, he went to work for the newspaper in Anchorage which employed Jeanne Bannister.

Harold and Jeanne were married in April, 1957. Although there is a conflict in the evidence on the point, we are convinced the marriage, over-all, was a happy one with many ups and downs as could be expected in the uniting of two such opposites.

We are not confronted with a situation where one of the contesting parties is not a fit or proper person. There is no criticism of either the Bannisters or their home. There is no suggestion in the record that Mr. Painter is morally unfit. It is obvious the Bannisters did not approve of their daughter's marriage to Harold Painter and do not want their grandchild raised under his guidance. The philosophies of life are entirely different. As stated by the psychiatrist who examined Mr. Painter at the request of Bannisters' attorneys: "It is evident that there exists a large difference in ways of life and value systems between the Bannisters and Mr. Painter, but in the case, there is no evidence that psychiatric instability is involved. Rather, these divergent life patterns seem to represent alternative normal adaptations."

It is not our prerogative to determine custody upon our choice of one of two ways of life within normal and proper limits and we will not do so. However, the philosophies are important as they relate to Mark and his particular needs.

The Bannister home provides Mark with a stable, dependable, conventional, middle-class, middlewest background and an opportunity for a college education and profession, if he desires it. It provides a solid foundation and secure atmosphere. In the Painter home, Mark thought with an opportunity to develop his would have more freedom of conduct and individual talents. It would be more exciting and challenging in many respects, but romantic, impractical, and unstable.

Little additional recitation of evidence is necessary to support our evaluation of the Bannister home. It might be pointed out, however, that Jeanne's three sisters also received college educations and seem to be happily married to college graduates.

Our conclusion as to the type of home Mr. Painter would offer is based upon his Bohemian approach to finances and life in general. We feel there is much evidence which supports this conclusion. His main ambition is to be a freelance writer and photographer. He has had some articles and picture stories published, but the income from these efforts has been negligible. At the time of the accident, Jeanne was willingly working to support the family so Harold could devote more time to his writing and photography. In the ten years since he left college, he has changed jobs seven times. He was asked to leave two of them; two he quit because he didn't like the work; two because he wanted to devote more time to writing and the rest for better pay. He was contemplating a move to Berkeley at the time of trial. His attitude toward his career is typified by his own comments concerning a job offer:

About the Portland news job, I hope you understand when I say it took guts not to take it; I had to get behind myself and push. It was very, very tempting to accept a good salary and settle down to a steady, easy routine. As I approached Portland, with the intention of taking the job, I began to ask what, in the long run, would be the good of this job: 1) it was not really what I wanted; 2) Portland is just another big farm town, with none of the stimulation it takes to get my mind sparking. Anyway, I decided Mark and myself would be better off if I went ahead with what I've started and the hell with the rest, sink, swim, or starve.

There is general agreement that Mr. Painter needs help with his finances. Both Jeanne and Marilyn, his present wife, handled most of them. Purchases and sales of books, boats, photographic equipment and houses indicate poor financial judgment and an easy come, easy go attitude. He dissipated his wife's estate of about $4,300, most of which was a gift from her parents and which she had hoped would be used for the children's education.

The psychiatrist classifies him as "a romantic and somewhat of a dreamer." An apt example are the plans he related for himself and Mark on February 19, 1963:

"My thought now is to settle Mark and myself in Sausilito, near San Francisco; this is a retreat for wealthy artists, writers, and such aspiring artists and writers as can fork up the rent money. My plan is to do expensive portraits ($150 and up), sell prints ($15 and up) to the tourists who flock in from all over the world."

The house in which Mr. Painter and his present wife life, compared with the well kept Bannister home, exemplifies the contrasting ways of life. In his words "it is a very old and beat up and lovely home." They live in the rear part. The interior is inexpensively but tastefully decorated. The large yard on a hill in the business district of Walnut Creek, California, is full of uncut weeds and wild oats. The house "is not painted on the outside because I do not want it painted. I am very fond of the wood on the outside of the house."

The present Mrs. Painter has her master's degree in cinema design and apparently likes and has had considerable contact with children. She is anxious to have Mark in her home. Everything indicates she would provide a leveling influence on Mr. Painter and could ably care for Mark.

Mr. Painter is either an agnostic or atheist and has no concern for formal religious training. He has read a lot of Zen Buddhism and "has been very much influenced by it." Mrs. Painter is Roman Catholic. They plan to send Mark to a Congregational Church near the Catholic Church, on an irregular schedule.

He is a political liberal and got into difficulty in a job at the University of Washington for his support of the activities of the American Civil Liberties Union in the university news bulletin.

There were "two funerals" for his wife. One in the basement of his home at which he alone was present. He conducted the service and wrote her a long letter. The second at a church in Pullman was for the gratification of her friends. He attended in a sport shirt and sweater.

These matters are not related as a criticism of Mr. Painter's conduct, way of life, or sense of values. An individual is free to choose his own values, within bounds, which are not exceeded here. They do serve, however, to support our conclusion as to the kind of life Mark would be exposed to in the Painter household. We believe it would be unstable, unconventional, Arty, Bohemian, and probably intellectually stimulating.

Were the question simply which household would be the most suitable in which to raise a child, we would have unhesitatingly chosen the Bannister home. We believe security and stability in the home are more important than intellectual stimulation in the proper development of a child. There are, however, several factors which have made us pause.

First, there is the presumption of parental preference, which though weakened in the past several years, exists by statute. Code of Iowa, Section 668.1; *Finken* v. *Porter*, 246 Iowa 1345, 72 N.W. 2d 445; *Kouris* v. *Lunn*, Iowa, 136 N.W. 2d 502; *Vanden Heuvel* v. *Vanden Heuvel*, 254 Iowa 1391, 1399, 121 N.W. 2d 216. We have a great deal of sympathy for a father, who in the difficult period of adjustment following his wife's death, turns to the maternal grandparents for their help and then finds them unwilling to return the child. There is no merit in the Bannister claim that Mr. Painter permanently relinquished custody. It was intended to be a temporary arrangement. A father should be encouraged to look for help with the children, from those who love them, without the risk of thereby losing the custody of the children permanently. This fact must receive consideration in cases of this kind. However, as always, the primary consideration is the best interest of the child and if the return of custody to the father is likely to have a seriously disrupting and disturbing effect upon the child's development, this fact must prevail. *Vanden Heuvel* v. *Vanden Heuvel*, *supra*; *In re Guardianship of Plucar*, 247 Iowa 394, 403, 72 N.W. 2d 455; *Carrere* v. *Prunty*, Iowa, 133 N.W. 2d 692, 696; *Finken* v. *Porter*, *supra*; *Kouris* v. *Lunn*, *supra*, R.C.P. 344(f) 15.

Second, Jeanne's will named her husband guardian of her children and if he failed to qualify or ceased to act, named her mother. The parent's wishes are entitled to consideration. *Finken* v. *Porter*, *supra*.

Third, the Bannisters are sixty years old. By the time Mark graduates from high school they will be over seventy years old. Care of young children is a strain on grandparents and Mrs. Bannister's letters indicate as much.

We have considered all of these factors and have concluded that Mark's best interest demands that his custody remain with the Ban-

nisters. Mark was five when he came to their home. The evidence clearly shows he was not well-adjusted at that time. He did not distinguish fact from fiction and was inclined to tell "tall tales" emphasizing the big "I." He was very aggressive toward smaller children, cruel to animals, not liked by his classmates and did not seem to know what was acceptable conduct. As stated by one witness: "Mark knew where his freedom was and he didn't know where his boundaries were." In two years he made a great deal of improvement. He now appears to be well-disciplined, happy, relatively secure and popular with his classmates, although still subject to more than normal anxiety.

We place a great deal of reliance on the testimony of Dr. Glenn R. Hawkes, a child psychologist. The trial court, in effect, disregarded Dr. Hawkes's opinions, stating: "The court has given full consideration to the good doctor's testimony, but cannot accept it at full face value because of exaggerated statements and the witness's attitude on the stand." We, of course, do not have the advantage of viewing the witness's conduct on the stand, but we have carefully reviewed his testimony and find nothing in the written record to justify such a summary dismissal of the opinions of this eminent child psychologist.

Dr. Hawkes is head of the Department of Child Development at Iowa State University. However, there is nothing in the record which suggests that his relationship with the Bannisters is such that his professional opinion would be influenced thereby. Child development is his specialty and he has written many articles and a textbook on the subject. He is recognized nationally, having served on the staff of the 1960 White House Conference on Children and Youth, and as consultant on a Ford Foundation program concerning youth in India. He is now education consultant on the Project Head Start. He has taught and lectured at many universities and belongs to many professional associations. He works with the Iowa Children's Home Society in placement problems. Further detailing of his qualifications is unnecessary.

Between June 15th and the time of trial, he spent approximately twenty-five hours acquiring information about Mark and the Bannisters, including appropriate testing of and "depth interviews" with Mark. Dr. Hawkes's testimony covers seventy pages of the record and it is difficult to pinpoint any bit of testimony which precisely summarizes his opinion. He places great emphasis on the "father figure" and discounts the importance of the "biological father." "The father figure is a figure that the child sees as an authority figure, as a helper, he is a nutrient figure, and one who typifies maleness and stands as maleness as far as the child is concerned."

His investigation revealed: ". . . the strength of the father figure before Mark came to the Bannisters is very unclear. Mark is confused about the father figure prior to his contact with Mr. Bannister." Now, "Mark used Mr. Bannister as his father figure. This is very evident. It shows up in the depth interview, and it shows up in the description of Mark's lfie given by Mark. He has a very warm feeling for Mr. Bannister."

Dr. Hawkes concluded that it was not for Mark's best interest to be removed from the Bannister home. He is criticized for reaching this conclusion without investigating the Painter home or finding out more about Mr. Painter's character. He answered:

I was most concerned about the welfare of the child, not the welfare of Mr. Painter, not about the welfare of the Bannisters. In as much as Mark has already made an adjustment and sees the Bannisters as his parental figures in his psychological make-up, to me this is the most critical factor. Disruption at this point, I think, would be detrimental to the child even though Mr. Painter might well be a paragon of virtue. I think this would be a kind of thing which would not be in the best interest of the child. I think knowing something about where the child is at the present time is vital. I think something about where he might go, in my way of thinking is essentially untenable to me, and relatively unimportant. It isn't even helpful. The thing I was most concerned about was Mark's view of his own reality in which he presently lives. If this is destroyed I think it will have rather bad effects on Mark. I think then if one were to make a determination whether it would be to the parents' household, or the McNelly household, or X-household, then I think the further study would be appropriate.

Dr. Hawkes stated:

I am appalled at the tremendous task Mr. Painter would have if Mark were to return to him because he has got to build the relationship from scratch. There is essentially nothing on which to build at the present time. Mark is aware Mr. Painter is his father, but he is not very clear about what this means. In his own mind the father figure is Mr. Bannister. I think it would take a very strong person with everything in his favor in order to build a relationship as Mr. Painter would have to build at this point with Mark.

It was Dr. Hawkes's opinion "the chances are very high (Mark) will go wrong if he is returned to his father." This is based on adoption studies which "establish that the majority of adoptions in children who are changed, from ages six to eight, will go bad, if they have had a prior history of instability, some history of prior movement. When I refer to instability I am referring to where there has been no attempt to establish a strong relationship." Although this is not an adoption, the analogy seems appropriate, for Mark, who had a history of instability, would be removed from the only home in which he has a clearly established "father figure" and placed with his natural father about whom his feelings are unclear.

We know more of Mr. Painter's way of life than Dr. Hawkes. We have concluded that it does not offer as great a stability or security as the Bannister home. Throughout his testimony he emphasized Mark's need at this critical time is stability. He has it in the Bannister home.

Other items of Dr. Hawkes's testimony which have a bearing on our decision follow. He did not consider the Bannisters' age anyway disqualifying. He was of the opinion that Mark could adjust to a change more easily later on, if one became necessary, when he would have better control over his environment.

He believes the presence of other children in the home would have a detrimental effect upon Mark's adjustment whether this occurred in the Bannister home or the Painter home.

The trial court does not say which of Dr. Hawkes's statements he felt were exaggerated. We were most surprised at the inconsequential position to which he relegated the "biological father." He concedes "child psychologists are less concerned about natural parents than probably other professional groups are." We are not inclined to so lightly value the role of the natural father, but find much reason for his evaluation of this particular case.

Mark has established a father-son relationship with Mr. Bannister, which he apparently had never had with his natural father. He is happy, well adjusted, and progressing nicely in his development. We do not believe it is for Mark's best interest to take him out of this stable atmosphere in the face of warnings of dire consequences from an eminent child psychologist and send him to an uncertain future in his father's home. Regardless of our appreciation of the father's love for his child and his desire to have him with him, we do not believe we have the moral right to gamble with this child's future. He should be encouraged in every way possible to know his father. We are sure there are many ways in which Mr. Painter can enrich Mark's life.

For the reasons stated, we reverse the trial court and remand the case for judgment in accordance herewith.

Reversed and remanded.

All Justices concur except THORNTON, J., who concurs in result.

Respondent's Brief in Opposition to Petition for a Writ of Certiorari to the U.S. Supreme Court

Glenn R. Hawkes is a child psychologist and, at the time of trial, had been head of the Department of Child Development at Iowa State University for twelve years.

He spent twenty-five hours evaluating Mark and the Bannisters. Following is a synopsis of his testimony:

Mark is now in his latency period of development, which is the very critical stage where he is developing most of his concepts, his attitudes about himself and maleness, and his attitudes about the world.

When he came to Iowa from California, Mark was aggressive, frightened, had difficulty sleeping, and had not internalized many controls. He was anxious and unsettled. He remembers, before coming ot live with the Bannisters, of wondering what was going to happen to him, who was in charge of him, and who he could turn to. He remembers wondering where his father was, and being frightened because he was not there. He remembers being yelled at and someone being angry with him, and thinks it was his father.

A father figure is important in a child's development because he typifies maleness for the child. Before coming to the Bannisters, Mark was confused about the father figure. He was not used to having one because Mr. Painter and Mr. McNelly shared what semblance of a father figure there was. The father image was very tarnished, if it existed at all. He is very confused about what to call Mr. Painter and vacillates between calling him "my father," "Hal," and "that man." He felt he could not depend on Mr. Painter. He remembers very little about his biological mother and sister.

Since coming to Iowa, Mark is making great progress toward emotional adjustment. He does have some anxieties which must be suppressed materially; however, these can be faced in a healthy situation. He has quite a lot of aggression but it is under control.

Mark has spent much time since coming with the Bannisters in determining who he is and where he fits into his environment. This is normal for a child between ages five and seven. He sees his present family as a cooperative unit, and sees a place for each person in it, including himself. He sees his grandfather as his father figure and his grandmother as his mother figure. He has a positive attitude toward families, and it is clear that he structures his family around the Bannisters. He has a very warm feeling for Mr. Bannister; they have the kind of relationship that all fathers would hope they could have with their sons. His relationship with Mrs. Bannister is fine and respectful, and there is a warm bond of affection.

The best way to develop a sense of responsibility in a child is for the parents to be responsible people so as to set a model by which a child builds his life. Mark is very much concerned about good behavior, and is in the process of deciding, through adult models, what is tolerable behavior and what is not.

Mark is very pleased with the progress he has made in school. He is made to feel, by the adults around him, that he is an adequate person. He has adequate contact with children his own age.

I think Mark should be placed with the Bannisters on a permanent basis. The unsettled conditions throughout his life up to the point will cumulatively become more and more detrimental if they are allowed to persist. It is very critical that he have a permanent arrangement. If he were four or five years younger, it would be less important, because there would be time to make up whatever deficiencies might occur because of moving from one place to another. But at this point in Mark's life it is critical that he be established in one place.

While he has been with the Bannisters, he has been through a process of developing a concept of his role in life; it is now well established. By remaining with the Bannisters he can build on the foundation he has. He does not have to go back, pick up the pieces, and start over again. Mark is already in a home where he has a mother and father figure. To move him from this is a rather unthinkable solution to the problem. This is true even if

---

This excerpt is from pages 12–15 of the respondents' brief and is a summary of the testimony of the child psychologist who examined Mark Painter and his grandparents.

you assume the best about Mr. and Mrs. Painter. Leaving Mark with the Bannisters is the only tenable solution.

If the natural parents are suitable persons, a child psychologist would normally recommend that the child be with them only if the child had continuously lived with them in the past. The biological father is necessary only for conception. The psychological father is most important. One has to earn being a father. The persons who become the important figures in a child's life are the mother and father figures, whether there is a biological tie or not. If not, I think our whole system of adoption would be a farce.

If Mark were disrupted at this point, if he is withdrawn from the parental figures established in his own mind and withdrawn from his present environment, he will become unsettled and anxious all over again. There would be a process of rebuilding which would be much more painful, and the chance of success would be much less likely in the second case.

If Mark were moved, there is, in my opinion, a 90 per cent chance that he would either develop a great deal of aggression or would withdraw. Because of the built-up anxiety and potential aggression in Mark at the present time, he would probably become aggressive, which would be acted out in terms of destructive tendencies. A great deal of juvenile delinquents are aggressive people because of inadequacy in their own background. If he withdrew, he would become an inadequate person to the point that he would not be a productive member of society. It is widely recognized in psychological works that adoptions of children from six to eight years old, if there is a prior history of instability, are usually unsatisfactory.

I am appalled at the tremendous task Mr. Painter would have if Mark were to return to him, because he would have to build a relationship from scratch. There is essentially nothing on which to build at the present time. Mark is aware Mr. Painter is his father, but he is not very clear about what this means. In his own mind, the father figure is Mr. Bannister. I think the prognosis would not be good.[1]

[1] We question the propriety of Petitioner [in footnotes appended to his Brief] setting out views of doctors which were not offered in evidence and were not before the Supreme Court of Iowa when it decided this case. The footnotes are intended to bolster Petitioner's assertion . . . that Dr. Hawkes's views "do not represent the opinion of the psychological profession generally or of other experts in the matters of child care." In rebuttal, we set out from the Des Moines Register of February 20, 1966, the following quotation from Richard J. Jenkins, M.D., Professor of Child Psychiatry and Chief of Child Psychiatry Service at the State University of Iowa, Iowa City:

"The decision before the court was whether Mark was to be removed from the home of his grandparents who are presently meeting his needs. . . . It seems clear from the evidence cited that Mark has had a difficult past, and that he showed the effects of it when the Bannisters took him. It is reported that he has made good progress. In a crucial game one does not pull a winning pitcher. The issue in this case is the welfare of the child as against the 'rights' of a father. Children are not possessions. They should never be so regarded."

DOES VIOLENCE BREED VIOLENCE? CONTRIBUTIONS FROM A STUDY OF THE CHILD ABUSE SYNDROME

Larry B. Silver, M.D., Christina C. Dublin, and Reginald S. Lourie, M.D.

A study covering three generations of families of abused children supports the themes that violence breeds violence and that a child who experiences violence as a child has the potential of becoming a violent member of society in the future. The authors believe that the physician has a critical role and responsibilty in interrupting this cycle of violence.

Excerpted and reprinted with permission from *American Journal of Psychiatry* 126, No. 3 (September 1969): 404.

These violent delights have violent ends,
and in their triumph die.

Romeo and Juliet, II, vi, 9.

In 1963 Curtis (2) wrote a brief clinical note entitled "Violence Breeds Violence—Perhaps?" In this report he discussed the battered child syndrome and expressed the concern that ". . . children so treated . . . [may] become tomorrow's murderers and perpetrators of other crimes of violence, if they survive." He further felt that an abused child should have an unusual degree of hostility toward the parents and toward the world in general. The control and channelling of this hostility into nondestructive avenues of release would pose a problem both for the child and for society. In addition, the child would be presented with parental objects for identification who provided an example of the destructive and relatively uncontrolled release of hostile aggression.

As support for this concept, he referred to the studies of Duncan and Easson and Steinhilber (3, 4). Duncan, in a report of a preliminary study of six male adult prisoners convicted of first-degree murder, noted that all were from middle class families of good social standing. He observed that the most striking feature of four of these cases was continuous, remorseless brutality suffered during childhood at the hands of one parent in the face of compliant acquiescence of the other. The remaining two prisoners were overtly psychotic, and no such childhood history was obtained.

Easson and Steinhilber, in a brief clinical account of eight boys who had made murderous assaults—one of them successful—noted that all were from socially acceptable "normal" families. In two of these cases there was a clear history of habitual brutal beating by a parent, and the histories of three others contained remarks that "lead one to wonder if brutality to the child was being concealed."

As members of the Child Abuse Research Group of the Children's Hospital of the District of Columbia as well as participating members of a community-wide interagency committee to plan and coordinate procedures for handling these cases of child abuse, the authors had an opportunity to further investigate the probability that violence breeds violence.

Observations

The study of the 34 cases reflected the frequency of abusive behavior in such families. In more than half of the cases, abuse on the part of one or both parents toward each other or at siblings was found. Of the 19 cases in which siblings were abused, 15 were in families where the child under study had a history of abuse prior to the 1963 episode. The records of the hospital and associated agencies showed that more than one episode of abusive behavior toward the child had occurred in 20 of the 34 cases. Even after referral to community services, abuse or neglect continued or recurred in 12 cases during the four-year period reviewed in the study. This observation of general abusive behavior in these families, rather than selective abuse to a specific child, differs from the "one child in a family" observations of Merrill (6), Zalba (11), and Boardman (1).

Case Reports

In four of the cases there was sufficient evidence to show that the abuser had been abused as a child.

Case 1. W. S., a six-month-old girl, was brought to the emergency room because her mother had knocked her unconscious. The father reported a similar episode previously; however, he had not brought the child in at that time. Information from the Women's Bureau revealed that the mother had been abused by her mother as a child and had been known to the police department since her early teens because of alcoholism and disorderly conduct.

Case 2. E. R. was brought to the emergency room by his father, who complained that the mother had beaten this two-month-old child. In addition to clinical evidence of soft tissue injury, the child showed evidence of neglect (diaper rash, weight loss). The Women's Bureau records noted that the mother had been abused by her father as a child, and she had been known to the police department since her early teens because of alcoholism, assaultive behavior, and disorderly conduct. On the first day following hospitalization of the child, his mother removed him without medical approval. The Women's Bureau went to the home and returned the child to the hospital. On readmission, a fractured skull that had not been present at the time of the original admission was noted.

Case 3. A. T., a six and one-half-year-old child, observed in the emergency room, was found to have multiple hematomas, welts, and contusions. History revealed that the father had beaten the child with a belt. Records showed that the father had been abused as a child, and he was described as violent and abusive to his wife and to the other five siblings. Two months after the event described above, the child was seen in the emergency room after a similar beating; at this time he was noted to have torticollis. Follow-up reports note that four years after the initial event the child was enuretic and had phobias.

Case 4. V. B., a one-year-old child, was seen in the emergency room after a neighbor's complaint led the police to the child's house. He was found alone in a dirty and disorganized house; the refrigerator was broken, and gas fumes were in the room. Clinical evidence of neglect was noted. Women's Bureau records showed that the mother, as a child, had a history of running away from home because of her fear of being beaten by her mother. She had been known to the police department since childhood because of truancy, petty larceny, disorderly conduct, and assaultive behavior. During the four years after the initial episode, reports revealed abusive behavior and neglect toward all five children. One sibling died 14 months after the above incident because of "diarrhea"; another sibling was burned while playing with matches two and one-half years after the initial incident.

At the time of the study, four years after the initial reporting of abusive behavior, seven of the children had already come to the attention of the court because of delinquency. (The first of these children, A. T. [case 3], is discussed above.)

Case 5. D. B., a 13-year-old boy, was initially seen after his mother had hit him with a broom, resulting in multiple contusions. The mother had been abusive to all seven of her children; she had also stabbed her husband five years previously. By age 17 the boy was known to the juvenile court because his behavior was out of control, he was running away from home, and he had broken probation.

Case 6. The father of G. S., an 11-year-old boy, threw battery acid at him, resulting in first and second degree burns on his face. One year prior to this event the child had fractured his leg when he "fell out of bed." Records noted that all six siblings had been known to have been abused. By age 15 he was known to the juvenile court because of his school difficulties, his truancy, and his uncontrollable behavior; he was on probation.

Case 7. S. S., a 15-year-old girl, had been beaten by her father with a heavy cord, resulting in multiple contusions and welts. The father was an alcoholic with at least one previous admission to a mental hospital; he was abusive to all eight children. By age 17 the girl was known to the juvenile court as a delinquent and a truant.

Case 8. B. S., an 11-year-old boy, was beaten by his father with a belt, resulting in soft tissue injury over the face and body. A similar incident had occurred eight years previously; records revealed a long history of abuse and neglect. The father was an alcoholic, and the mother was an alcoholic with a previous admission to a mental hospital. All siblings were known to have been abused at one time or another. By age 15 the boy was known to the juvenile court because of his behavior in school, his delinquency, and his truancy; he was also known to be enuretic.

Case 9. R. W., a nine-year, nine-month-old boy, had been beaten by his father with resulting soft tissue injury. The father had a previous admission to a mental hospital on record. By age 13, R. W. was known to the juvenile court because of assault with a deadly weapon, housebreaking, stealing, and breaking probation.

This theme, violence breeds violence, was painfully intimated recently in newspaper reports about the childhood of Sirhan Bishara Sirhan, the convicted assassin of Robert F. Kennedy. Teachers, pastors, and boyhood acquaintances who had known the subject in Jerusalem reported that he grew up in violence. Salim Awad, the headmaster of the Jerusalem Evangelical Lutheran School, was quoted as saying, "What the [school] records do not show is what went on at home. The father and mother had terrible fights, and the children suffered as a result. Their father beat them . . ." (9).

Pastor Daoud Haddad of the Lutheran Church of the Savior in Jerusalem stated that the father "had frequent violent fits and was given to breaking what little furniture they had, and beating the children. He thrashed them with sticks and with his fists, whenever they disobeyed him" (9).

Salin Atas, a boyhood acquaintance of Sirhan, related an incident when the father heated an iron and pressed it against Sirhan's heel. "I remember Sirhan coming to school with no shoes" (9).

All of these statements have an appalling resemblance to incidents and events in the families studied.

DISCUSSION

A wide range of possible solutions is available to the child who has encountered violence. Special events in the child's life, personal experiences, or interpersonal relationships during the preschool period may lead to reparative intrapsychic defenses such as reaction formation, sublimation, and displacement. The authors would like to call attention to two extreme resolutions available to such children, for there is evidence that these two extremes represent clinically significant outcomes.

The longitudinal study of abused children and discussions with physicians and hospital house staffs suggest that some abused children cope with the emotional stress by choosing "identification with the aggressor" as their major defensive pattern.

Their model for identification and later for imitation shows poor impulse control in general and direct physical expression of aggressive impulses in particular. In addition, early childhood stresses and neglect result frequently in unmet dependency needs that result in oral or primitive patterns of interaction with people and with society.

Although not as easy to document, there are probably many abused children who "identify with the victim." Rather than becoming known to the courts as delinquents or criminals, these individuals become known as the victim: the wife-beater's wife, the person yoked, the person attacked and beaten. At an early age children who are repeatedly battered learn to sense when it is time to go outside, to leave the room, to be quiet. Through painful experience they have learned the consequence of allowing their parents to lose control. But there are other children who, under similar conditions, perform just the act or say just the word that precipitates a beating or abuse. These children seem to have learned that love equals being hurt, and they establish a pattern of inviting the role of harm and of playing the victim.

Milowe and Lourie (8) support this view. They feel that there may be factors in the personality development of some children leading to the child's inviting others to hurt him or to hurting himself, i.e., a "hurt and be hurt" relationship pattern. In another report, Milowe (7) reported the case of a child who was removed from his home because of repeated abuse and who was later abused by a foster parent.

Conclusion

Violence does appear to breed violence. A longitudinal study and review of family backgrounds over three generations shows that some abused children become the abusive parents of tomorrow. The child who experiences violence as a child has the potential of becoming a violent member of society in the future. The physician must be alert to the possibility of the child abuse syndrome; he must be willing to report such cases; he must be willing to join with his community agencies to help these children and their families. No other member of society has such a unique opportunity to interrupt this cycle of violence.

References

1. Boardman, H. E. "A Project to Rescue Children from Inflicted Injuries," *Social Work* 7:43–51, 1962.
2. Curtis, G. C. "Violence Breeds Violence—Perhaps?" *Amer. J. Psychiat.* 120:386–87, 1963.
3. Duncan, G. M., Frazier, S. H., Litin, E. M., Johnson, A. M., and Barron, A. J. "Etiological Factors in First-Degree Murder," *J.A.M.A.* 168:1755–58, 1958.
4. Easson, W. M., and Steinhilber, R. N. "Murderous Aggression by Children and Adolescents," *Arch. Gen. Psychiat.* 4:47–55, 1961.
5. Kempe, C. H., Silverman, F. N., and Steele, B. F. "The Battered-Child Syndrome," *J.A.M.A.* 181:17–24, 1962.
6. Merrill, E. J. "Physical Abuse of Children, An Agency Study in Protecting the Battered Child." Denver, Colo.: Children's Division, American Humane Association, 1962.
7. Milowe, I. D. "Patterns of Parental Behavior Leading to Physical Abuse of Children," presented at the Workshop, Children's Bureau and the University of Colorado, Colorado Springs, Colorado, March 21–22, 1966.
8. Milowe, I. D., and Lourie, R. S. "The Child's Role in the Battered Child Syndrome, *J. Pediat.* 65:1079–81, 1964.
9. *The New York Times*, June 7, 1968, p. 1.
10. Silver, L. B., Barton, W., and Dublin, C. C. "Mandatory Reporting of Physical Abuse of Children in the District of Columbia: Community Procedures and New Legislation," *Med. Ann. D.C.* 36:127–30, 1967.
11. Zalba, S. R. "The Abused Child: I. A Survey of the Problem," *Social Work* 11:3–16, 1966.

CHILD ABUSE
(THE BATTERED CHILD SYNDROME)

C. Henry Kempe, M.D.

Introduction

During the past ten years, all fifty states have enacted child abuse reporting laws which, with very little variation, require physicians and often nurses, teachers, and social workers to report either to the protective service department of the county welfare department, or to the police, incidents of suspected child abuse or serious neglect. Moreover, in some states, such reports can be made by any citizen. The current level of reported cases of suspected child abuse is surprisingly uniform between urban and rural America and stands in 1972 at 380 per million population per year. This means that a total of 60,000 children are reported each year to the authorities as being suspected of being in need of protection by society. In addition, a number of studies have shown that approximately 10% of all trauma seen in emergency rooms in children under the age of 3 is due to inflicted rather than accidental trauma. Other studies suggest that 30% of all fractures seen in children under 2 years of age are inflicted.

Definition

For the past hundred years, the concept of what constitutes "reasonable care and protection" has gradually evolved. Since the beginning of recorded history, and in some parts of the world to this day, children are considered as the true property (chattel) of the parents. This was the case in the United States until approximately 100 years ago. Parents literally had life and death rights over their children and could dispose of them at will. Children were regarded as property by a concept which made sense in a rural society where the number of participating workers in a family greatly enhanced the economic well-being of the group. During the past 100 years, on the other hand,

the rights of children increasingly have come to the fore, and now, in a free and civilized setting, the child is considered to *belong to himself, in care of his parents.*

The most severe form of child abuse is seen in the battered child syndrome. The syndrome lies at one extreme of a spectrum of insufficient care and protection. The term, the battered child syndrome, is used by us to characterize a clinical condition in young children who have received significant physical abuse, generally from a parent or foster parent.

A strictly legal definition of child abuse is "where a child under the age of 16 is suffering from serious physical injury or abuse inflicted upon him by other than accidental means or suffering harm by reason of neglect, malnutrition, or sexual abuse, goes without necessary and basic physical care, including medical and dental care, or is growing up under conditions which threaten the physical and emotional survival of the child."

The above definitions focus on the symptom rather than the underlying pathology. In a study of over 1,000 abusive or seriously neglecting families, we have come to learn that deliberate, premeditated and willful abuse, the old fashioned "cruelty to children," accounts for only 5% of the entire group. These injuries are caused by aggressive sociopaths who are sufficiently pathological to make it unlikely that a change in their personality would be produced through psychiatric intervention. In another 5%, one or the other of the parents is suffering from delusional schizophrenia, and the child is often part of the delusional system to its great peril. The prognosis for ever establishing a reasonable parent/child relationship is again very poor.

The remaining 90% of abusive parents would appear to belong to a great variety of personality types and no one psychiatric definition fits them all. They resemble others in their personality make-up except as it relates to their own childhood experiences. The vast majority

Hearings on the Child Abuse Prevention Act of 1973 before the Subcommittee on Children and Youth, Senate Committee on Labor and Public Welfare, 93rd Congress, 1st Session, at 179 (1973).

of these parents are severely deprived individuals who, in their early infancy, had very little nurturing love from their parents. Abusive parents, as a rule, have, from their earliest childhood, been exploited by their parents, had to conform to rigorous standards of behavior, and almost invariably had to provide a great deal of support and service for their parents. In short, they lacked the usual "ordinary" childhood, which is made up of a great deal of early dependency followed by gradual emancipation. Individuals who have missed such mothering experiences in early childhood become distrustful of their own good qualities, come to feel that they are inferior and "no good" and deserve to be punished, while continuing to hope that at some time a loving relationship will come their way.

They often marry at a young age in the hope of gaining such love and support from their spouses.

Unfortunately, in most cases they tend to marry someone similarly deprived and continue to be two very needy individuals who cling to each other like non-swimmers whose struggling together often results in both of them drowning. For battering to occur, four factors are usually present: (1) *Both parents, regardless of financial or social status, are themselves deprived individuals*; (2) *They see a given child in a very special, unrealistic way.* They tend to see the baby as demanding, unattractive, willful, spoiled, and not living up to their standards. Often, other children in the family are seen quite normally; (3) *A crisis*, such as loss of job, an unwanted pregnancy, prolonged crying, has suddenly developed. Intractable crying is interpreted as being accusatory rather than as a sign that the parents need to attempt to satisfy some need of the child. The parents feel the child is saying, "if you were a good mother or father, I wouldn't be crying like this." Often, these parents desire to be very good parents and to have a very loving relationship with the child. But the supposed rejection on the part of the child results in increased parental anger and frustration when they feel, once more, that someone they love has failed them; (4) There is generally *no lifeline or rescue operation* available to the parents' life. That is, they have no close friends, relatives, or neighbors whom they can readily ask for help in moments of stress. This is true despite the fact that they may live among a variety of people who would be quite willing to help. It is true that truly "unwanted" children are at greater risk, but even with available abortion and the elimination of most unwanted children, the number of abused children would only be decreased by approximately one-half.

THE PROBLEM

In a totalitarian society, where the child's health is a particular concern of the state, universal access to the child from the prenatal period until adult life is insured by compulsory attendance at prenatal and postnatal clinics, nursery schools, and rigid supervision of the child's health care, including nutritional support, developmental evaluation, immunizations, and close and compulsory attention to physical and emotional growth and development. This degree of supervision is also possible in a free, though closed society, such as a kibbutz settlement in Israel, where children, from birth on, are in a community-oriented setting in which the role of the natural parents is deliberately downgraded, with the result that all children are, to a certain extent, considered to belong to all members of the settlement. In our country, on the other hand, the child is essentially a prisoner in his home until he reaches school age. American law demands that parents, at the risk of imprisonment, must present their child to specifically licensed places of education at the age of six years. But we have not yet devised ways in which the child is brought into society before the age of six to insure his basic physical and emotional survival, to say nothing of his optimal development.

It is an interesting paradox that within the American legal system we have a precedent of premarital blood examinations of both partners to detect syphilis so as to prevent the scourge of congenital syphilis; without seeking specific permission, and as a compulsory health measure under the laws of all fifty states, we instill silver nitrate into the eyes of newborn infants to prevent gonorrhea.

THE DIAGNOSIS

Child abuse is diagnosed most often when the child is found to have some suspicious injury. On the other hand, we do not provide basic health screening for possible child abuse and other disturbances in the child under six years of age. (1) The physician may find a child who has one or more fractures, which, on x-ray examination are shown to be in different stages of healing, indicating that the child undoubtedly suffered from more than one episode of trauma, or he may discover a head injury, bite marks, unusual burns, or injuries around the mouth where the bottle was forced or a crying mouth was hit. In many of these instances, the physician is impressed by the truly sincere concern of the parents for their injured child. But there may be a number of crucial points in the history which should make him pause before accepting the parents' explanation for a truly accidental injury: (1) In cases of child abuse and injury, there may be a delay between the time the injury actually occurred and the time that help is sought. (2) The history given is often discrepant, with the physical and x-ray findings simply not fitting the story of the injury. Often the parent gives three or four different stories, or a history of trauma may be denied despite obvious injuries. (3) A history may be elicited of previous accidents, or attendance at more than one physician's office or hospital. (4) The parent's reaction to suggested medical assistance may be inappropriate; they may refuse hospitalization despite the doctor's advice.

Doctors have for years talked about doubtful cases of child abuse (called the "gray area"). This certainly was a serious problem ten years ago when little was known about the total picture, but pediatricians, orthopedists, neurosurgeons, radiologists, and general practitioners who work in accident rooms now are much more sophisticated in interpreting the findings in child abuse cases. If the physician takes into account (1) the extended history, which includes substantive knowledge about the rearing practices used in raising the parents; (2) some appreciation of the way the parents see the child; (3) the presence or absence of a precipitating crisis, such as intractable crying, an unwanted new pregnancy, loss of a job, etc.; and (4) the presence of marked isolation and the absence of a lifeline, the old "gray area" of child abuse has become very small indeed. No more than 2 per cent of all suspected cases of child abuse are now in substantive doubt by the time the juvenile court judge hears the civil case of dependency.

AMERICAN SOCIETY'S RESPONSE TO REPORTS OF CHILD ABUSE

The reporting laws on child abuse do nothing more than provide an official vehicle for bringing the abused and neglected child to the official attention of society. Reporting the case does not, in itself, result in any benefit to the child and society unless proper follow-up procedures are instituted. Ideally, the official report should be evaluated by capable personnel, such as social workers or psychiatrists in a proficient child protective unit of the county welfare department. The nature and degree of evaluation often depends on whether sufficiently adequate intervention, including evaluation of the family, is a policy of the agency and is acceptable

in that community. A protective service department may be intimidated by its employers, the elected or appointed administrators, by a hostile juvenile court judge, or may be made ineffectual by frequent turnover of intake workers or a case load too great to manage competently. If the protective service agency decides that the child is at significant risk and that simple counseling at a relatively superficial level will not suffice, mechanisms exist in all states for further action. Criminal proceedings can be brought by the district attorney for an injury thought to be of sufficient severity to cause serious bodily harm or even death. Not infrequently, the district attorney may be ready to take action but yields to the welfare department, at least for a time, before initiating a second venue of presentation of a dependency petition to the juvenile court, alleging that the child is not receiving "reasonable care and protection." Until recently, these two judicial procedures required identical degrees of proof in order to sustain the charge. In criminal cases, presumption of innocence exists, as does the need for "proof beyond a reasonable doubt"; these are very desirable safeguards. On the other hand, in a civil case before the juvenile court involving the question of dependency, many states have now lowered the required degree of legal proof to "preponderance of evidence" only. In fact, the burden for exact explanation for the child's injuries does no longer lie upon the reporting physician, but rather upon the parents. In some instances, "res ipsa loquitur" (the case speaks for itself), suffices, particularly if the nature of the injury is so evident that the court does not require eye witnesses, a confession, or "proof beyond a reasonable doubt." The court may then find that the child is a dependent in need of supervision. In a dependency hearing, there is no accused person. The court may merely conclude that the child is in need of care and protection, that the home is not safe, or that insufficient care is being exercised by those responsible for caring for the child. Two states, New York and Colorado, require that a guardian ad litem be appointed for such children. It is the duty of the guardian to present to the court information as to the true nature of the family situation, including the psychiatric status of both parents, in order to allow the court to make a wise decision for the disposition of the child. If the dependency petition is sustained, the court makes a decision as to disposition. The judge can either make the child a ward of the state and send it home, applying certain safeguards, or he can place the child in foster care for a time, until there has been a substantive change in the family. He can terminate parental rights if he feels that there is simply no chance of the parent/child relationship ever becoming tolerable. In the truest sense, therefore, the dependency petition with a decision by a judge is the only instance where a final definition of child abuse and neglect is made. Where it is considered that the child belongs to the parents, judges are reluctant to intervene in the sacred parent/child relationship. To the extent that the citizenry feels that the child has very substantive rights to reasonable care and protection of its own, judges will be activists in functioning as parens patriae. Thus, the *challenge* to parental authority occurs when someone in authority decides to bring the child to the court's attention. The *intervention* by society becomes most pertinent when the court hears the case. It can be said that parental rights are challenged with reluctance in most jurisdictions because of the widely held traditional concept of parental supremacy in child raising and the great leeway allowed by the courts in the styles and methods of child raising. More recently, on the other hand, once the child's case is heard by the court, judical intervention occurs more readily because judges increasingly feel that they must concern themselves with the rights of the child and hope to prevent a disaster which would reflect upon the court's more lenient decision should repeated injury or even death occur while the child is a ward of the state.

METHODS OF TREATMENT

There is little evidence that parent therapy is helpful in the 10 per cent of abusive parents who belong to the categories of aggressive sociopaths or delusional schizophrenias and in those who scapegoat a single child, particularly if the child remains in the family, and many disasters have occurred when these kinds of parents have been treated while the child has been left in the home. In these cases, we tend to urge early termination of parental rights and adoption of these children is then possible. The other 90 per cent of abusive parents are readily treatable by reconstituting their sense of trust and by giving them considerable minute-to-minute support over a crucial period of eight to nine months. We use four treatment modalities: (1) lay therapists, (2) Families Anonymous, (3) a crisis nursery, and (4) a therapeutic day care center.

Lay therapists are individuals, both men and women, who have experienced warm and affectionate mothing in their own childhoods and have subsequently been successful parents. Lay therapists are mature persons, generous of spirit, and willing to "mother" a very needy family by providing emotional support, patient listening, a day and night telephone "lifeline" for moments of crisis and stress. They will spend a great deal of time with the abusive family over this period of eight to nine months.

Families Anonymous is the name given a group of abusive parents who meet together once or twice a week and, in a group setting, begin to appreciate the fact that they are not alone in their explosive behavior and that they can derive a great deal of help from each other.

The *crisis nursery* is used at any time, day or night, and with no questions asked, for those moments of crisis or stress when the child can be quickly removed to a place of safety. The child can remain in the crisis nursery for a few hours or a few days until the crisis is over; this method is regarded as a backup to the other treatment modalities.

The *day care center* is a place where abusive parents can see their children vis-à-vis other children and where they can interchange feelings and experiences with other parents who are managing satisfactorily in working out their difficulties. In those cases where the abused child has been in foster care for a period of time, a method which is, incidentally, one we favor, the court then has to answer the question, "is it safe to let the child return home?" As long as the child remains a ward of the state, the child may safely be returned to its home if (1) the parents have gained a better self-image of themselves through the process of having made some friends and having shown that they are reaching out somewhat to society; (2) if they show that they are seeing the child in a positive way, as judged by their comments made during trial visits to the home; (3) when they have learned to use lifelines in comments of crisis other than the lay therapists; and (4) when they have successfully managed a few crises by themselves. In cases where these conditions have been met, no child under our care has been re-injured. The goals of treatment are modest. These parents are so damaged that they are unlikely ever to be generous, wholesome, mature individuals. On the other hand, they still can grow enormously with the kind of treatment described. Specifically contraindicated in treatment is the kind of "insight therapy" which has traditionally been the hallmark of orthodox social case work. Very few of these parents can tolerate much insight, at least early in therapy; if they truly appreciate how deprived their own childhood was they become intensely depressed and often suicidal. Conversely, with a very supportive, loving adult figure in their lives, these parents tend to grow emotionally to a surprising extent and in a reasonable period of time. Within eight months, 80 per cent of our families have their children back in their home permanently, 10 per cent require more time, and in 10 per cent we urge termination of parental rights at an earlier date.

Conclusions

Society has worked out a way to manage failure in marriage; it is called divorce. We should be prepared to accept failures in totally unregulated, random parenthood by permitting, without social stigma, either voluntary or involuntary termination of parental rights for children from those parents who cannot, for one reason or another, give them the minimal physical and emotional support they deserve. Termination of parental rights should become a highly acceptable method of managing parenting failure when adequate diagnostic evaluation suggests that no other method of treatment will succeed.

Recommendations

1) Universal Child Health Supervision

Fundamental to all of our recommendations is the concept that the child belongs to himself and is only in the care of his parents; that he is entitled to the full protection of the Constitution and its amendments; and that the citizenry at large has a substantive involvement with the nurturing of all children.

In order to insure each child's basic rights, society must have *access* to the child from birth until school age, the most critical time of child development. This is best done, in our opinion, through implementation of the concept of universal health supervision in the broadest sense. This is best done through regular well-baby care by the family physician. But 20 per cent of our children fail to receive such care.

We suggest that a health visitor call at intervals during the first months of life upon *each* young family and that she become, as it were, the guardian who sees to it that each infant is receiving his basic health rights.

The system must be equalitarian rather than being directed just toward the poor. It must be recognized as being helpful and supportive to the entire family, and it must broaden the specific role that various helping professions see themselves filling. There is no reason why a social worker, with some additional training in basic health parameters involving physical

and emotional growth and development, cannot be a health supervisor, just as there is no barrier to a public health nurse functioning as an understanding personal advisor in matters not directly concerned with physical health. All helping professions, including physicians, teachers, social workers, nurses, and the new category—health visitors—not yet on the scene must broaden their professional roles so they can serve in this preventive screening capacity. Providing the means for regular health supervision will insure a setting which will permit parents to verbalize their frustration and difficulties, will lead to utilization of additional helping individuals when needed, and will provide a screening tool which will be an additional safeguard in the life of each American child to prevent injury from occurring before society traditionally has had a chance to notice what is happening. It is my view that the concept of the utilization of health visitors would be widely accepted in this country. Health visitors need not have nursing training, and intelligent, successful mothers and fathers could be readily prepared for this task at little cost.

2) Protective Services and Law Guardians

a) Once child abuse has been reported by anyone (including by ordinary citizens), protective service departments must be vigorous in providing an adequate professional evaluation of the family situation. If the parents are not willing to cooperate in this evaluation, the juvenile court should be brought into play at once and a legal guardian appointed at an early date to represent the child who cannot speak for himself.

b) When a child abuse report has been filed, no protective department should be free to ignore the report without taking substantive action. I suggest that a committee of three, representing the protective services department, the juvenile court, and the county medical society, should join in reviewing all such reports, and the request of any one member of the committee should make it incumbent upon the juvenile court to hear the case. Agreement of all three could still permit the extra-legal venue of treatment within the welfare department and, therefore, outside of the jurisdiction of society. It should be stressed that many protective service departments feel that the juvenile court is a place of last resort, and, indeed, many juvenile court judges agree. On the other hand, the child lacks adequate legal protection if its future is determined by a single caseworker, who might be inexperienced, and may wrongly decide that she can manage things without bringing to bear the forces of society on the family pathology Since the child has no part in this decision, the system should require greater safeguards for him. It is proposed that in every case of child abuse a lawyer be nominated by the court to protect the child's interests. It should be pointed out that the Due Process Clause of the 14th Amendment and the rights it represents are not rights for adults alone (In Re Gault, 87 S.Ct. 1428, 1967).

3) National Registry

A national computerized child abuse report registry should be available. The high mobility of abusive parents makes it essential that any physician be able to ascertain whether a given child (as identified by his name, birthdate, and social security number), is listed in a national registry. In this way, it will be possible to discover if a child has experienced repeated injuries, thus increasing the likelihood that a correct diagnosis of child abuse is made.

4) Interim Foster Care

There is a pressing need for the development of a network of adequate foster homes for interim placement of children while parents receive help from lay therapists and Families Anonymous groups. Temporary separation is not meant to be a punitive action and *it is not carried out solely for the child and against the parent; rather, it is for the family*. To produce a significant change in a family, as seems highly possible in 90 per cent of cases, a period of foster care placement should be seen as a temporary measure to help decrease pressure and to minimize crises while parents are learning how to cope with their problems.

5) Innovative Treatment Modalities

It is very clear that, with a few exceptions, the departments of social service in the area states are not able to perform the task of preventing or treating the problems of child abuse and neglect. It is impossible to approach a multidisciplinary problem with a single-discipline service unit. This is true whether the service unit be in social services, medicine. juvenile courts, or law enforcement. We must develop a multidisciplinary service unit which can cut across many of the traditions and unworkable rules and regulations that are built into most protective service departments.

New and broader therapeutic modalities must be available to protective service departments. Traditionally, social case work has been the tool of social workers in welfare departments. Many workers in the field of protective

services soon discover that orthodox case work methods are unsuitable and contraindicated for abusive parents. A great deal of intensive personal commitment of a highly unprofessional kind is far more effective. However, the emotional wear and tear of serving battering parents makes it difficult for most of us to take on the management of more than one or two such families at a time. Social workers should serve as consultants to lay therapists, who will do the day-to-day and night-to-night work on a one-to-one basis. This will in no way diminish the rights and obligations of protective service departments, rather, it will allow them to function more effectively and to greater advantage. Protective service departments are the repository of great talent and great experience, and they have existing tax support. But they are, regrettably, often led by traditionalists in social work who have very little daring in trying innovative approaches in this difficult field. The wide use of lay therapists and of Families Anonymous groups by departments of protective services will go a long way toward making these departments professionally far more effective than they are now. The development of Families Anonymous groups is facilitated by encouragement by professionals, particularly for those abusive families who have very little tolerance for doctors and social workers, but may do quite well with each other in this self-help setting. Each department should have a physician, family doctor, pediatrician or psychiatrist, and someone from the court (probation department) and police as regular members of the child protection team. (The interdisciplinary approach.) None of the above requires much in the way of additional tax funds, but it does require spending existing funds differently. The federal government will need to insist on annual performance reports from the fifty state departments of welfare it now helps to support.

6) Crisis Nurseries and Therapeutic Day Care Centers

A network of crisis nurseries and day care centers in each community should be developed. It is often impossible to find a place outside the home where an infant can quickly obtain emergency care, in spite of the fact that in moments of crisis and stress nothing works as well in protecting children than having them out of the home. There is undoubtedly great fear on the part of welfare departments that if they make it too easy for children to be placed in their care, at any time during the day and night, the department will be overwhelmed by children who might never be reclaimed. This has not been our experience.

We feel that in a civilized society it should be possible to have the child placed where he will be safe when, for one reason or another, the family has decided that it is not competent to manage having him in the home. In the past, the attitude of society toward incompetent parents has been: "you've had your fun, now take care of it." Clearly, the child should not suffer because of the parents' difficulties.

Day care centers that are well planned, uncrowded, and loving can be of value in allowing children to have early social intercourse with others and to minimize the effects of undue isolation. They also tend to bring parents out of isolation to meet other parents and other children and into a setting where questions can be brought out without fear of criticism or derision. Really good day care, which is now generally only open to the well-to-do or to professional women, would also enable some lower socioeconomic mothers to have a respite from child care. It should be an accepted social right that one need not be a perfect mother or father 24 hours a day, seven days a week. In answer to the belief that ready availability of competent day care would weaken the American home, one can point out that "home can be hell."

IN THE MATTER OF N. M. S.

OPINION

J. MURPHY:

The matter before the Court, technically a review of commitment to the Social Rehabilitation Administration concerns the custody of a 9½ year old child, M.[1] who has lived all but the first eight days of her life with one set of foster parents, Mr. and Mrs. J. T. Briefly, the natural mother,[2] Ms. G. P. seeks the return of her daughter. The Social Rehabilitation Administration (SRA), to whom M. was committed for placement in a foster home, has recommended that M. be returned to the natural mother. The foster parents oppose the SRA recommendation. They urge the Court to award custody to them. They are willing to assume all financial obligations for the care of M. should the Court terminate the commitment to SRA and place custody of M. with them. The child personally and through Court appointed counsel strongly rejects the idea of living with her mother and wishes to continue living in the only home she has ever known.

All parties are represented by counsel.

FINDINGS

Over four days, the Court heard from representatives of SRA, the natural mother, the mother's employer, M.'s brother, the brother's basketball coach, a Greek Orthodox Priest (Ms. P. is a Greek Orthodox), a psychologist and psychiatrist, both foster parents, the sisters of the natural mother, and finally from M. In addition, the Court has the benefit of the SRA file on M. as well as the recent psychiatric and psychological evaluations of M. and Ms. P., all made part of the trial record.

Ms. P. is an unwed, 36 year old Greek immigrant who came to this country at the age of 15, with the equivalent of a third grade education. She is now an American citizen. Ms. P. has had four children, all of whom have been conceived and born out of wedlock. Pl., born in 1958, resides with his mother and

---

[1] M. was born N. M. S. In 1971, the natural mother had M.'s family name changed to P., the last name of her oldest son's putative father. This was done over M.'s strong objection as well as a SRA recommendation against the name change. See SRA Report, 8/22/72. M. continues to go by the last name of S.

[2] The Court in its opinion will use the term "natural parent" interchangeably with "biological parent," and "psychological parent" interchangeably with "foster parent." A psychological parent is one to whom the child becomes emotionally attached because of the parent's day-to-day attention to his needs for physical care, nourishment, comfort, affection, and stimulation. J. Goldstein, A. Freud, and A. J. Solnit. *Beyond the Best Interests of the Child* 17 (1973) (hereinafter cited as Goldstein et al.).

Family Division, Superior Court of the District of Columbia, January 17, 1974.

has done so since his birth. A second boy, born in 1959, has been legally adopted. In 1961, a daughter was born. This child is living with a family and Ms. P. regards the child as being informally adopted. M., born on May 11, 1964 at the Georgetown University Hospital, is the last of the four children. On May 14, 1964, the Child Welfare Division was contacted by the Hospital concerning M. On May 19, 1964, M. was placed by the Division on an emergency basis in the T. home where she has since remained. Ms. P. has never attempted to commence a paternity suit or seek support orders in regard to any of the children.

On March 24, 1965, a petition was filed by the Child Welfare Division alleging that M. was homeless and that the natural mother had failed to make a plan for her. The petition requested that M. be committed to the Department of Welfare as a dependent child. At a June 2, 1965, court hearing, at which Ms. P. was present, M. was committed to the Child Welfare Division after the Court found M. to be homeless, without adequate parental care, and within the jurisdiction of the court. This initial commitment has been extended in a number of *ex parte* court hearings.[3] At each of these reviews, the SRA recommended continued commitment of the child because the mother was unable to plan or had not formulated a plan for M.

Over the years, contact has been maintained between M. and the mother. Ms. P visited the T. home when M. was very young, every six weeks to two months. When M. was older, she visited her mother in the mother's apartment or was visited by the mother on an irregular basis. Friction between the parent and child attended these visits. M. did not enjoy visiting her mother. On the day the Ts. were to fetch M. from her mother, M. would constantly ask her mother or brother what time it was. She would refuse to leave the apartment for fear of missing the Ts., and would at times break into tears when she returned to them. The SRA reports also chronicle the difficulties between M. and Ms. P.

Ms. P. discussed from time to time in a vague and general manner with SRA the eventual return of M. to her. However, because of a combination of financial, medi-

cal, and emotional problems, this return was never effected and Ms. P. would always withdraw her requests. Ms. P. suggests she was misled by SRA concerning her rights and that she relied on their advice. She also suggests her lack of sophistication in language and education prevented strong actions on her part. In spite of acquiring a new language and with her limited schooling, she has held a regular reading-type job. She retained a prominent law firm as counsel in Virginia to change her name and that of M.'s to P. The Court finds that her failing to plan for the child was not a result of over-reliance on SBA or because of social limitations. She is an intelligent woman who has an adequate command of the English language. She has been exposed to business for years, has hired legal counsel, and has had social contact with a priest, school officials, and other persons. She has raised a son to his teen-age years and has been active in his school life with no evidence of social limitations. She did not actively seek M. because she lacked the follow-through necessary to bring the child into her life.

The record also reflects that Ms. P. complained to the SRA social workers involved in the case that she was having difficulties with M. in that M. thought of herself as a "T. kid" (although M. used the last name of S.), appeared to be very involved with her foster family, and antagonistic toward and rejecting of her own mother. Yet Ms. P. never asked that M. be removed from the T. home. In fact, she testified she was pleased with the placement. She never requested that SRA arrange psychiatric help for M. and herself. While the mother claims she wants the child, during the pendency of this litigation she has had no contact with M. She has not even requested to visit with M., either in her own apartment or in a neutral territory suggested by SRA.[4] The Court is of the view that Ms. P. regards the child more as an object to be possessed than a child to be loved and cared for. When the child came to visit Ms. P., she never took the child to church, the zoo, a library, a movie, a museum or any social events. There is no evidence of any effort to expose the child to cultural or spiritual values.

Ms. P. is presently employed at a news-clipping service in Washington. She leaves her Arlington apartment early in the morning

---

[3] June 15, 1966; July 13, 1967; February 25, 1969; July 20, 1970; August 23, 1971; October 6, 1972. The practice of *ex parte* reviews year by year has little to be said for it. An interested party has no chance to appear in court. The SRA reports are not subjected to critical analysis in open court. This practice has subjected the SRA and the Court to allegations made by Ms. P. in this case that she was misled over the years by SRA concerning the return of M.

[4] Since mid-summer, the mother has had the benefit of very able counsel, so a claim of inability to cope with the system cannot be suggested. No reason has been advanced why the visits to see the child have been discontinued or why visits pendente lite were not sought. It suggests to the Court that the desire for the child is more impulsive than real.

(around 5:30 or 6:00 A.M.) so that she can arrive home soon after her son Pl. returns from school. She and her son live in a one-bedroom apartment, for which she pays $101 per month rent. Nothing in the mother's present life-style, or in her life-style for the past eight years, suggests any impropriety on the mother's part, although her life prior to the birth of M. was irresponsible. There is no evidence to suggest that Ms. P. could not now care for M. in a material sense, nor has there been such evidence in recent years.

M., the object of this custody struggle, is described by the forensic psychiatry report as "a pretty, engaging, sensitive, articulate youngster . . . who tests in the superior range of intelligence." She does well in school, behaves herself at home, and has no health problems. She has thrived very well in the T. home where the SRA found that she was happy and secure.

Mr. and Mrs. T. presently have five foster children living in their home, including M. Mr. T. is the chief photographer at a local newspaper. Mrs. T. remains at home. They live in a four-bedroom rented house with a yard and trees. The Ts. have, over the years, provided foster care for a total of 15 children committed to the custody of SRA. Nothing suggests that the Ts. have been other than loving, dedicated foster parents, providing a real home for children who otherwise could have been living in institutions. The SRA reports concerning M. state that all the children living with the Ts. seem happy and well adjusted. M. is noted as always being very involved and enthusiastic about family projects. The Court rejects all suggestions by Ms. P. that the Ts. sought to win the child away from her or behave in other than a proper manner. Foster parents have a delicate role to provide a home-like environment without allowing psychological dependency. That dependency developed in this case by the relationship of the foster parents and M. from birth for a continuous 9½ years, and not from any direct effort by the Ts. to win the child away from the mother.

The Social Rehabilitation Administration, has had legal custody of M. since June 2, 1965. At each subsequent court review prior to the sudden change in August 1973, the Administration has recommended that the commitment be continued. The report dated August 22, 1972, noted that Ms. P. continues to reside in the one-bedroom apartment with her son and continues her job as a newsclipper, earning about $75.00 a week. The next report, dated August 7, 1973, contains the recommendation of return to Ms. P. The report states: "After an extensive evaluation of the facts, as they now exist, the agency feels that it would be in M.'s best interest to return her to her natural mother."

Ms. P.'s desire to have the child expressed over the years has not changed. The only difference is that now she has obtained a lawyer.

The incident giving rise to the change in recommendation is clearer than the basis for the recommendation. On June 28, 1973, the Ts. made their annual request that all of the children accompany them on their trip to Kansas to visit relatives. For the first time, Ms. P. objected to the plan. She also requested that M. be immediately discharged to her. The social worker called the Ts. on the phone, told them that their request to take M. to Kansas had been denied, and informed them that M. would be returned to her natural mother in two days. It appears that they did not consult with Ms. P. to determine if she finally had an adequate plan for M. The decision, to abruptly remove this child on two days notice from the only home she has ever known and place her in an environment where she expressly did not want to be, appears to have been made without any consideration of the psychological effect of the decision on the child, and was done with bureaucratic insensitivity.

The SRA did not file, nor has it ever filed, a statement of what it considered in determining that M.'s best interest would be served by living with a person with whom she does not want to live. The SRA representatives who testified in Court relied on an office policy to return children to the natural parent where possible as the prime reason for the return.[5] There is evidence, however, in the testimony from both the SRA representatives and Ms. P., as well as notes in the SRA reports, that Ms. P. threatened to bring a suit against the

---

[5] The agency in theory is to work with child and the natural parent, helping the child prepare for eventual reunion with the natural parent(s). The Court finds that SRA, however, has done little to prepare M. emotionally, mentally, and psychically to return to her mother. Since 1968, when M. was four years old, the reports have noted the difficulties between M. and Ms. P. The agency has made no effort to alleviate the problem between the child and her mother other than by counseling by the social worker over the phone or during sporadic visits. The visits to the foster home were few and far between, in spite of the difficulty between the parent and child. That the social worker's efforts were of no avail is evident by the fact the situation between mother and child did not improve. As noted above, SRA did not seek other professional counseling, and it was a judge of this Court who requested information as to what the import of the child's return would be on the child.

agency for alienation of affection. Although it has been denied, the Court cannot help but find that the threat of a lawsuit was the prime motive for the SRA decision to recommend the child's return to the mother.

FINDING OF NEGLECT

This matter comes before the Court as a review of M.'s commitment as a neglected child. 16 D.C. Code 2301(9) lists the criteria to be considered by the Court in determining whether a child is or continues to be neglected.

(9) The term "neglected child" means a child—

(A) who has been abandoned or abused by his parent, guardian, or other custodian;

(B) who is without proper parental care or control, subsistence, education as required by law, or other care or control necessary for his physical, mental, or emotional health, and the deprivation is not due to the lack of financial means of his parent, guardian or other custodian;

(C) whose parent, guardian, or other custodian is unable to discharge his responsibilities to and for the child because of incarceration, hospitalization, or other physical or mental incapacity; or

(D) who has been placed for care of adoption in violation of law.

M. does not fall within sections (A), (C), or (D).

The Court does find that M. is a "neglected child" within the meaning of subsection (B). Subsection (B) speaks in terms of "care of control." The Court cannot foresee any reason why Ms. P. would not be able to "care or control" M. in a physical and material sense. Ms. P. would be able to adequately clothe and feed M., and attend to her medical needs. But subsection (B) also speaks in terms of mental and emotional health. The Court must consider the emotional and mental needs of the child in reaching a neglect determination. The Court would clearly be disregarding the words of the statute were the Court to base its decision in this case without weighing the emotional and mental impact on M. of the Court's decision.

The Court finds, based on the testimony heard in open court, the SRA reports, and psychiatric-psychological evaluations of M. and her mother, that M.'s mental and emotional health will be adversely affected were she to return to live with her mother. M. has known only one home during her 9½ years.[6] She has thrived extremely well in that home. The SRA reports over the years indicate that M. was and is very happy with, secure in, and well adjusted to the foster home.

The forensic psychiatric report affirms in the Court's mind that the best interests of M. will be served by remaining with the Ts. Although forensic psychiatry does not recommend a specific placement, the report does point out: "From a developmental standpoint, it is a general rule that one seeks to avoid discontinuity as much as possible and would make every effort not to disrupt this youngster's life in the only family in which she has ever lived." According to the report, the mother is "tense, anxious, pressured, and stressed." "She is plagued by guilty feelings about many elements of her life, including her inability to care for M. and wishes to undo M.'s placement."

DISPOSITION

Once the Court finds that a child is neglected within the meaning of 16 D.C. Code 2301(9), the Court must seek an appropriate disposition. 16 D.C. Code 2320 lists the alternatives available: subsection (a) requires that the disposition selected be in the best interests of the child. 16 D.C. Code 2320(a)(3)(C) permits the Court to transfer legal custody to "a relative or other individual who is found qualified to receive and care for the child." The Court is terminating M.'s commitment to SRA and placing legal custody of M. with the Ts., pursuant to this subsection.

The Court has been guided in its decision by the best interests of M. This case is not to be handled as if the child were a chattel or piece of property. The Court is not deciding which party, the natural mother or the foster parents, has the "greater claim" to M. Rather, this is a question of relationships, of ties, affiliations, and attachments. Both the natural mother and the foster parents play a significant role in M.'s life. Two basic relationships exist: one between the child and the foster parents, and one between the child and the natural mother. The Court must decide which of these basic relationships is the most conducive to M.'s physical well-being, mental and emotional development, and supportive of the child as she grows older.

[6] "Psychoanalytic theory . . . establishes, for example, as do developmental studies by students of other orientations, the need of every child for *unbroken* continuity of affectionate and stimulating relationships with an adult." Goldstein et al., *supra* at 5 (emphasis added).

The Court finds that the best interests of this child would not be served by removing her from this warm and happy home she has known all her life, from her foster parents whom she calls "Mommy and Daddy," from her four foster brothers and sisters, to place her in an environment where she feels uncomfortable and anxious, to live in a place she does not want to live and with a woman more an acquaintance than a mother. In reaching its decision, the Court is not finding Ms. P. an unfit mother in a material sense, nor is it finding that the Ts. are more fit than Ms. P. The Court is considering the best interests of M. and M. only.

BEST INTERESTS TEST[6]

The relevant statutes, 16 D.C. Code 2301 and 2320, dictate that only the best interest of the child is to control the court's decision, yet judicial precedent in this jurisdiction recognizes that natural parents do have rights. *Bell* v. *Leonard*, 102 U.S. App.D.C. 179, 251 F.2d 890 (1958). However, the natural rights of a parent must be considered in conjunction with the best interests of the child, and the D.C. Court of Appeals has recognized, as has the U.S. Court of Appeals, that the best interests of the child is the most important consideration.

The controlling principle by which the courts must be guided in cases of this kind is well settled. *The paramount concern is the child's welfare and all other considerations, including the rights of a parent to the child, must yield to its best interests and well-being.* While no precise formulae can be devised to aid the court in its determination as to what is best for the child, certainly the application of this broad principle does not demand that the right of a parent be ignored. *Davis* v. *Jurney*, *supra*, 145 A.2d at 849. (Emphasis added.)

The Court has considered the fitness of Ms. P., as well as her legal rights, in determining what disposition is most appropriate for M. Ms. P. is fit to care for M. in a *material* sense.

---

[6] The Court believes the concept of "least detrimental among available alternatives" is a better test than the heretofore commonly used "best interests of the child" test because of the inherent detriment in any court-ordered placement. A court in a custody case is seeking to salvage as much as possible of a bad situation. "Least detrimental among available alternatives" will reduce the likelihood of the court "becoming enmeshed in the hope and magic associated with 'best,' which often mistakenly leads them into believing that they have greater power for doing 'good' than 'bad.'" Goldstein et al., *supra* at 63.

She has a job, albeit low-paying, and she testifies she can handle the additional expense of M. However, the mother has no real plan for M. now, anymore than she has had in the past, other than to obtain the child.

The Court does find that Ms. P. is unfit to care for M.'s *mental, emotional,* and *psychological* needs. Ms. P. is not in a position to handle M.'s emotional and psychological needs, which would be greatly increased by a forced change of M.'s living and school situation.

THE LEAST DETRIMENTAL AMONG AVAILABLE ALTERNATIVES

The Court has considered various alternative dispositions. One such alternative is to permit the adoption of M. by the Ts. The Court is not willing at this time to follow this alternative. Another alternative would be to continue commitment of M. to the Social Rehabilitation Administration, but the Court was advised during the trial that the Court would have no authority to direct the SRA to continue placement of M. with the Ts. The Court seriously considered placing M. with the natural mother for a period of six months. The Court would monitor the case closely, to see how the return to the natural mother affected M. The Court decided against this alternative because the Court finds it unfair, and potentially very damaging, to experiment with this child in order to satisfy Ms. P.'s desire to have M. with her, which at this time in the Court's view would be clearly adverse to the child's interests.

The Court believes in her own way Ms. P. would try to do what is best for M., but it is a question of too little too late. With the wisdom of hindsight, perhaps if a greater effort had been made years ago to join M. and Ms. P. the reunion now could be done without harm. Time, however, has worked against the reunion because the Ts. are now the child's psychological parents and the child needs continuity of this relationship.[7]

---

[7] "Continuity of relationships, surroundings and environmental influence are essential for a child's normal development." Goldstein et al., *supra* at 31–32. Some current writers believe an absent, inactive adult can never become the psychological parent, regardless of the biological or legal relationship. *Id.* at 19. Further, it appears that multiple placement of a child may put the child beyond the reach of educational influence, and can become the direct cause of behavior which the schools experience as disrupting and the courts label as dissocial, delinquent, or even criminal. *Id.* at 34.

To place the child with the biological mother would require adopting a "per se" rule of biological parent over psychological parent. The Court has considered carefully Ms. P.'s legal position and her desire for her child and believes the child should remain in contact with her mother. The Court believes that with the counseling offered by forensic psychiatry service and the security of knowing she will not ever be removed from her home, the child will develop a mature relationship with Ms. P., so that as she becomes older they might be friends as well as acquaintances.

REMEDY

The Court rules as follows:

(1) For the reasons stated above, M. is to remain with Mr. and Mrs. J. T. Commitment to the Social Rehabilitation Administration is terminated. Legal custody of M. is placed with the Ts.

(2) The Ts. are directed to contact Dr. S. K. K. at the Forensic Psychiatry Office to take advantage of the offer by the staff at Forensic Psychiatry of their professional services. The Ts. are to participate also in the counseling if it is determined necessary or useful by the Forensic Psychiatry Office.

(3) The natural mother may visit the child every six (6) weeks, but only in the T. home. These visits are to be arranged in advance. The mother is also directed to contact Dr. K. so that she may receive the counseling services offered by the Forensic Psychiatry Office.

(4) Forensic Psychiatry is to submit to the Court periodic reports on the nature of the adjustment of the child to the Ts. and to Ms. P. The first such report is to be submitted June 3, 1974.

COMMENT: THE JUVENILE COURT

In a study of 1,214 juvenile courts, Samuel A. Kramer, Ph.D. of the Joint Commission on Correctional Manpower and Training found that about 700 (58 per cent) provide no medical, psychological, or psychiatric examinations or services, and an additional 300 (25 per cent) are able to provide them in less than 10 per cent of their cases.

Even in courts with a psychiatrist or psychologist as a staff member or consultant, his recommendations often are not followed, in large part because of lack of appropriate treatment facilities. The following excerpt illustrates other problems in the interrelationship of judge, juvenile court worker, and consulting psychiatrist.

DISPOSITIONAL DECISION-MAKING IN JUVENILE COURT DELINQUENCY CASES

Richard C. Allen, LL.M.

At a recent conference, the following case was presented: A neglect petition had been filed concerning the children of a Mr. A., a widower. Mr. A. and his two children—a girl of 8 and a boy of 10—live in the home of Mr. and Mrs. B. and their three children, the eldest of whom is 15. Mr. A.'s daughter has had emotional difficulties, and Mr. A., although

The observation above was excerpted for this volume from an unpublished manuscript.

concerned for his children and apparently cooperative with the court worker, is anything but a stable person. Mr. A. and Mrs. B. play the dominant role in the household, with Mr. B. relegated to a status of negligible importance. It was never expressly stated, but apparently generally believed by the workers present, that Mr. A. and Mrs. B. maintain a sexual relationship.

There is no effective control over the children, who have become serious behavior problems at home and at school (the term "bedlam" was rather generally used to describe the household), and the B. children are abusive to the A. children. A hearing was imminent, and the staff was to present a "plan."

The psychiatrist discussed an evaluation of Mr. A. which had been done at a local hospital and which depicted a highly dependent, unstable personality, who had—in the past—engaged in some "acting-out" behavior of a sexual character. He was diagnosed as a sociopathic personality. The consultant then described Mr. A. as a person who needs firm control—which he apparently seeks in establishing relationships with women (in this case Mrs. B.). When he has such a liaison, he is fairly responsible; but here the relationship is not working out, and is hardly one which can be fostered or supported by the court.

The psychiatrist observed that the court does not have access to facilities which can provide the control Mr. A. needs. Psychotherapy would be ineffectual in light of the home relationships. Mr. A.'s daughter had also been evaluated, and—although doing somewhat better in school than she had been at the time of the last hearing—was seen as showing "pseudo-mature" accommodations and apparently seeking to identify with the older B. children.

The consulting psychiatrist concluded: "We must move Mr. A. and his children out of this family situation." He noted that there were two choices: to take the children away from him and make a permanent placement; or to set him up somehow with on-going control. "The latter is not a reasonable possibility; I don't suppose we have a pool of potential wives available." There followed a long pause; then a comment by one of the workers: "I don't see any legal grounds for removal." Then the following colloquy:

DOCTOR: "Would this be a difficult case to convince the court to take the children away?"
WORKER: "Yes, because Mr. A. expresses interest in them. Wouldn't you agree, Miss ——?"
SECOND WORKER: "Yes. We would have to do it over his protest."

DOCTOR: "Well, how do we feel about this family?"
ANOTHER WORKER: "I see those kids being pushed around from foster home to foster home. At least the father is interested in them. I still have the feeling if we work closely with this family it can be worked out."
DOCTOR: "Why didn't you follow your earlier plan to see them intensively? Hasn't this case been before the court for the last two years? Surely a year is plenty long enough to see whether things are going to work out."
WORKER ADDRESSED: "I just had too heavy a case load."
DOCTOR: "Is it realistic to think you could see them once or twice a week?"
WORKER: "No, my work load is just too heavy . . . Well, since we can't work intensively with this family, I guess I would concur in removing the children from the family if a permanent home could be found; but if not, I sure don't like the idea of successive foster homes. An inadequate father is better than no father at all."
GROUP: (Comments of agreement with this point; some indication of positive reaction to Mr. A.: "nice guy," "tries hard," etc.)
DOCTOR: "What about placement with an agency?"
FIRST WORKER: "This is a possibility."

Silence.

DOCTOR: "O.K., any other views on what should be done?"
FIRST WORKER (filling another uncomfortable silence): "How emotionally disturbed is Mr. A.'s daughter? Could we place her for adoption now?"
DOCTOR: "She needs a strong parental figure. It seems to me a good case can be made for permanent removal, but I predict that if the court doesn't move (and there is enough vacillation in our ranks that I am convinced it won't), we will be hearing about this case again from the school and from others."

Silence.

DOCTOR: "I would unequivocally recommend permanent removal and placement for adoption on the ground of long-standing parental neglect, where the father is incapable of changing with any resources available to us. Unless this is done, any change in the sexual character of Mr. A.'s relationship with Mrs. B. may well result in further emotional difficulties for the children. I don't see how you can deal with these people as a family unit. Even an institution would give Mr. A.'s daughter a more stable environment. Her pseudo-mature attitude is alarming—she is building distance defenses against her father, and her efforts to identify with the older girls—at their sexual level—is dangerous for a girl of her age."

FIRST WORKER: "Would you testify at the hearing?"

DOCTOR: "Yes. I think the recommendation should be explicit, so we can say 'I told you so'—not maliciously, but educationally—to educate the court to accept our predictions before the kids get into real trouble."

(The meeting was adjourned, with no apparent agreement as to what recommendation would be made to the judge.)

Here, then, several conflicting points of view appear: The psychiatrist's position that where there is evidence of parental inadequacy, and little hope for strengthening the relationship, the staff should unhesitatingly recommend removal in the interest of the children; and the staff's (largely unexpressed, but clearly apparent) recognition that what they are hearing does not amount to "legal grounds" for removal, and perhaps also their social work predilection for working with the family unit. Again, there is apparent the psychiatrist's wish to utilize staff recommendations to advocate changes in legal criteria—or at least to pinpoint their necessity; and the workers' desire to avoid what they perceive as open conflict with the legal side of the court. Despite the deference accorded to the psychiatrist, it seemed clear that his recommended action (termination of parental rights) would not be followed.

POST-DISPOSITION TREATMENT AND RECIDIVISM IN THE JUVENILE COURT: TOWARDS JUSTICE FOR ALL*

Elyce Zenoff Ferster and Thomas F. Courtless

INTRODUCTION

Dissatisfaction with the juvenile justice system exists throughout the nation and stems from continuously rising rates of juvenile crimes and high levels of recidivism. The basic complaint is that it neither protects the public nor helps the child. There is disagreement, however, about the cause of the system's unsatisfactory performance. Some believe that a separate system of juvenile justice has failed and will continue to fail because not enough is known about the causes of delinquency and effective ways of correcting the delinquent.[1]

Others believe that the system has not failed but rather has never been given an adequate trial because it exists only in form rather than substance. The failure in their view is the community's, not the system's, because it has not provided the personnel, facilities and funds necessary for individualized justice.[2]

The Affluent County study, a portion of which is reported here, was undertaken ot obtain data which would support one or the other of these views. Certainly, the structure of a total juvenile justice system exists in Affluent County. There is a separate division of the police department which deals with juveniles. Detained juveniles are not confined with adults. The court has a separate intake division which screens out some inappropriate cases. In contrast to many jurisdictions, the judges are attorneys and sit only on juvenile cases,

* This study was supported by a grant from the National Institute of Mental Health (No. R 01 M1114500).

[1] President's Commission on Law Enforcement and Administration of Justice, Task Force Report: Juvenile Delinquency and Youth Crime 8 (1967).

[2] *Id* at 7.

Excerpted and reprinted with permission from *The Journal of Family Law* 11, no. 4 (1972): 683–709.

and attorneys for juveniles are frequently present in court. The issue of disposition is considered separately from adjudication. It has probation and after-care services, and the court has access to diagnostic facilities and to some treatment facilities.

In addition, the entire system seems to have a good number of people, from policemen to probation officers to judges, who are sincerely interested in the problems of delinquency. One index of their interest is the wholehearted cooperation they gave to this study, which took considerable portions of their time. Not only did they freely talk about their problems in an open manner but also encouraged the staff to "tell it like it is" in the hopes that this would help them to be of better service. As a *quid pro quo* for this cooperation, we agreed not to identify the persons interviewed, the agencies observed, and to provide only the general characteristics of this jurisdiction.

THE RESEARCH SETTING

Affluent County is a suburb located in a Standard Metropolitan Statistical area in the Middle Atlantic region of the United States. In deciding upon a code name for the county, Affluent was chosen because of the county's position as first in the nation in median family income (over half its residents earn in excess of $10,000 per year).[3]

Several factors influenced the decision to select Affluent County as the locus of research. First, as noted above, the county has, at least in form, all the elements of a complete juvenile justice system as suggested by experts and standard setting organizations. Thus, a study in the county provided a unique opportunity to examine the operation of juvenile justice *in toto*, avoiding the major problem of dealing with a system with one or more missing subsystems.

Secondly, the county was chosen because it has a well-educated middle-class citizenry which is not overwhelmed by the myriad economic, social and health problems besetting most inner-city communities. Selection on the basis of this factor was deliberate. . . .

Still another factor influencing our decision to select Affluent County was the willingness of its juvenile court to participate wholeheartedly in the study. Led by the chief judge, who for some time had been urging a study of the court and related agencies, leading figures in the probation staff and State Department of

Juvenile Services were generally enthusiastic in their response to the research. . . .

This article covers those processes of the juvenile justice system affecting juveniles after the disposition stage has been reached. Thus, we are concerned primarily with the problems of implementing dispositional alternatives, and the resultant impact on Affluent County delinquency.[4] . . .

POST-DISPOSITION TREATMENT AND RECIDIVISM

One of the first problems encountered in attempting to measure the impact of a juvenile justice system is that of defining the term recidivism. . . .

Some jurisdictions, including Affluent County, do not maintain statistics on recidivism and, therefore, have no formal definition of recidivism. For the purposes of this study, a recidivist is defined as a child who is a resident of Affluent County and has had at least two court hearings on a charge of delinquency with the court taking some action other than a dismissal because of lack of jurisdiction or evidence. For example, if the court ordered "probation without verdict" on the first offense and "probation" for a subsequent offense, the child is considered a recidivist.

In 1968, the court records of 126 children who had court hearings were examined. They constituted approximately fifteen percent of the children who had hearings that year. Twenty-seven of these children are not included in this study either because they are not residents of the County or because none of their referrals resulted in any action other than a dismissal. Of the 99 children thus remaining in the sample, 54, or 54.4 percent, were recidivists. Similar recidivism results were obtained for a smaller group of juveniles whose court hearings were observed during the summer of 1969. The recidivism rate for this group of seventy-one children was 50.7 percent.

---

[3] Economic data on Affluent County were taken from City Planning Associates, in, *Population and Social Characteristics* (October, 1968).

[4] Police practices were described in Ferster and Courtless, *The Beginning of Juvenile Justice: Police Practices and the Juvenile Offender*, 22 *Vand. L. Rev.* 567 (1969); detention was covered in Ferster, Snethen, & Courtless, *Juvenile Detention: Protection, Prevention or Punishment?*, 38 *Fordham L. Rev.* 161 (1969); intake was the subject of Fester and Courtless, *The Intake Process in the Affluent County Juvenile Court*, 22 *Hastings L. J.* 1127 (1971); adjudication was discussed in Ferster, Courtless and Snethen, *The Juvenile Justice System: in Search of the Role of Counsel*, 39 *Fordham L. Rev.* 375 (1971).

These data are not very meaningful unless one knows the child's problems and what efforts were made to resolve them. Consequently, each child in the formal sample was analyzed to obtain these data

1. The Non-Recidivists

Eighteen of the forty-five children who did not return to court received some kind of assistance in resolving their problem. Assistance included minimum probation office contacts, individual psychotherapy, family counseling, removal from home to both private and public placements.

Another thirteen children did not need any treatment. They were usually sixteen or seventeen years old with no prior contacts with intake or the police, and their offenses were quite minor. . . .

In another three cases the record is unclear as to whether or not the child received treatment. One child can not be properly called a non-recidivist because he died in a fight with another child soon after his court disposition.

Of the ten remaining cases, there were four recommendations for treatment. It is impossible to determine whether any or all of these ten children needed treatment, nor is it possible to determine if they are truly non-recidivists. No effort was made during the research to determine if these children still reside in the county.

About all that can be said about the non-recidivist is that treatment was successful if it occurred. A more complete picture of the relationship between treatment and recidivism can be obtained from an analysis of the cases of children who were recidivists. . . .

3. Recidivism: Summary and Conclusions

Of the thirty-three recidivists in the three groups, twenty-one were handled unsuccessfully by the court. Four were waived to adult courts. Eleven cases were closed only after the juvenile became eighteen, at which time the court no longer has jurisdiction, or entered the armed forces. These children generally had been known to the court for over three years, and averaged five referrals to court. The six remaining unsuccessful children are either currently under the jurisdiction of a juvenile court, or have physically left the court's jurisdiction. They were known to the Affluent County Juvenile Court for at least three years, and averaged six referrals.

Data from the social and clinical records of these twenty-one children clearly show that family pathology is a significant factor. In sixteen cases (76 percent), there was evidence of either alcoholic or mentally ill parents (11

cases), or parental rejection of the delinquent child (5 cases). In three of the remaining cases, the records reveal that parents actively resisted the court's efforts at rehabilitation by either failing to seek and obtain treatment or services for themselves or their children.

In these twenty-one unsuccessful cases only one child received treatment or services other than routine probation or training school commitment. In this one case, the boy's therapy was to coincide with separate therapy for his parents which was never begun because of parental opposition. It should be emphasized that the court had received recommendations from its staff or professional diagnosticians for treatment or services (other than probation or training school) for ten of these children. In three additional cases, while specific treatment or services recommendations were not made for the children, they were provided for parents and not carried through because of refusals to cooperate.

Significantly, nine of the ten boys whose cases were closed successfully, either received treatment which usually meant removal from an unsatisfactory home (6 cases), or were removed from their homes to those of relatives (3 cases). In other words, the efficacy of treatment or the removal from a damaging home is illustrated dramatically in Affluent County. Children who failed to receive these advantages continued their delinquent activities during the entire period they were of juvenile court age, while those who received help (even though it was often painfully little and painfully delayed) ceased their delinquencies.

The typical adjudicated delinquent[5] in Affluent County has had at least three contacts with the juvenile justice system. He has had at least one contact with the police which did not result in a referral to court and at least two complaints handled judicially. More than a

---

[5] An adjudicated delinquent is one who has been found involved in one or more delinquent acts after a hearing before a juvenile court judge. In Affluent County, a delinquent child is defined by statute as

> . . . any child who violates any law or ordinance of the State or county, or who commits any act which, if committed by an adult would be a crime not punishable by death, or by life imprisonment; who is incorrigible or is beyond the control of his parents, guardian or custodian, or is habitually a truant, or who without just cause or consent, deserts his home or place of abode, who knowingly associates with thieves, vicious or depraved persons, or is growing up in idleness or crime, or knowingly frequents any gambling places, places where beer or intoxicating beverages are sold, or who is guilty of indecent, immoral or lascivious conduct.

third of the delinquents had had an initial contact with the system, a complaint which was handled by the court's intake department and not referred to a judge for a hearing. Therefore, a child in this community is not labeled a delinquent at the first sign of trouble.

It is important to remember that the fact that delinquency adjudications generally do not occur on first offenses does not mean that only children with serious difficulties are adjudicated delinquent. Many children are found delinquent on a first offense as minor as trespassing. On the other hand, some children have several police and intake contacts for quite serious offenses, such as burglary, which do not result in judicial action. The criteria for court referral by the police and the intake department are both vague and inconsistently applied.

The reasons that the police and intake personnel do not refer children to court is that they believe the offense is not dangerous to the child or the community and is atypical of the child's behavior.[6] In many instances, they are correct. When they are wrong, however, the error should not be compounded by equating a new act of delinquency with a willful misuse by the child of an opportunity for assistance. The child is not being given any services by the police or intake when they decide to deal with him informally. The assumption seems to be that no assistance is necessary. Even when the child is placed on informal supervision, this status usually consists only of waiting for a period of time to see if further delinquencies occur.

The strategy of "waiting and seeing" also is used by the judges. Again, the assumption seems to be that the child either has no serious problem or that the problem can be handled without court assistance. As was apparent in the informal cases, the assumption is sometimes correct. More often it is not. Thirty-seven of all the children adjudicated delinquent received a disposition whcih involved no services the first time they appeared in court. In fifteen of these cases, the decision seems to have been correct because the child did not return to court. But by that rationale, twenty-two decisions were erroneous because the children were adjudicated delinquent again at a later time. In fact, fourteen of them had at least three subsequent referrals for delinquency.

There was no way to discern the criteria used by the judges in making these disposi-

tions because there is no social information routinely in the file at the time of disposition other than prior police contacts. One obvious reason why some receive a disposition which involves no services may be that they should never have been referred for hearing. Since the intake criteria are so unclear, some children are adjudicated delinquent who should have been handled informally.

If the court adopts new intake criteria, presumably only those children needing some services will be adjudicated delinquent.

When treatment or service is provided through the court, it is usually probation. Two-thirds of the children who received any service were put on probation. It is difficult to define probation because judges, as well as probation officers, have varying ideas about its purposes and functions. In some probation departments, the officer's role is limited to surveillance. In other words, he is to check up on the probationer to make sure he is fulfilling the conditions of probation. Other departments see the probation officer as a counselor, almost a therapist. His function is to help the probationer solve his problems. Still others consider the proper role of the probation officer to act as a referral source. The officer is to decide what services are appropriate, send the probationer to the proper agency, and report to the court on the progress made by the probationer.[7]

The majority of Affluent County probation officers see themselves as counselors, although a few limit their role to referring the child and his family to other agencies. The judges in Affluent County also view the probation officers as counselors. As one judge said, the probation officer should:

establish relationships with the child and his family; be an effective counsellor with the child which means developing rapport with the child and being a social worker, not simply a person that the child reports to about having kept his hours and conditions of probation.

It was not possible to determine whether or not probation officers' perception of their role is correct because the individual case records often were barren of reports of contacts with the probationers. Unless many of these probation officers did not write up their contacts, which they are supposed to do, many children received little or no contacts. Even if there were counseling sessions, which were not contained in the record, the probation officers'

[6] These views were elicited by personal interviews with the police department's Juvenile Aid Bureau commander, and the court intake department supervisor.

[7] For a discussion of probation officer roles, *see* Diana, *What is Probation*, in Carter & Wilkins, Probation and Parole 39–56 (1970).

estimates of case loads of forty children and time spent in contact with juveniles and families of ten hours a week, indicate that the children could receive a maximum of only fifteen minutes of counseling per week.[8]

It would seem that to be an effective counselor, a probation officer would need to visit a probationer's home periodically. The judges feel strongly that they cannot be adequately informed about a probationer's progress unless home visits are made. The probation officers were noticeably less enthusiastic about making home visits. The great majority considered that home visits inhibit the proper performance of the probation officer's role. They stated that in the home setting the officer is severely limited in efforts at problem analysis, and in communication with the juvenile and his family. In addition, they felt that their exercise of authority was drastically restricted when in the home as opposed to the office setting.[9]

However, the officers also believed that under some circumstances home visits should be made. All of them agreed that a home visit was necessary when the juvenile cannot get to the probation office and the majority of them believed visits shold be made when there are significant family problems or conflicts. . . .

Nevertheless, the officers reported that they had not made a home visit for approximately two-thirds of their active case load.[10]

The extent and type of counseling conducted varies from officer to officer. It ranges from one officer, who refers all cases to an appropriate family agency, to another who does extensive group counseling with juveniles and their families. The case reports of many of the probation officers give the impression that their counseling consists more of meting out discipline for infractions than it does of assisting the child in solving his problems.

In addition to fulfilling the role of counselor, the judges expect the probation officer to know his limitations and, therefore, refer the child and his family to outside community facilities when such action is necessary.[11] The resources available to the probation officer are a family service agency and a mental health clinic. They may also use a court psychiatrist and psychologist for diagnostic services and the county welfare department. The probation officers find the family service agency and the community mental health clinic most helpful. Many of them also said that the court psychiatrist's services had been valuable to them, but no one mentioned either the court psychologist or the welfare department.

Both the judges and the probation officers believe that the mental health clinic is inadequate for their needs, not because the quality of service is poor; rather, the problem is that it cannot provide as much diagnostic and treatment service as is needed. The probation officers also stressed the need for improved relationships between themselves and the schools. Although they did not specify in what ways the situation needed changing, the case records of the children indicate several problem areas.

The schools' almost complete intolerance of aggressively acting-out children is a substantial problem. Even with children as young as first graders, the schools' most usual response to a child's causing a disturbance in the classroom or playground is to remove him from school. Where he is to go and what he is to do seem to be of no concern to the school administration, even when the court, on the recommendation of experts, says that the child should be in school. Similarly, their reaction to truancy usually is to suspend the child for a period of time equal to his truancy. How this procedure solves either the child's inability to do school work or his emotional problems is difficult to comprehend. . . .

At least as important as the school problems are those connected with psychotherapy and outside counseling. As the judges and probation officers recognize, more low-cost community clinics are necessary. However, the resistance to their use by families is perhaps even more serious. The study of recidivists showed that resistance was more responsible for lack of treatment than was a shortage of facilities. This resistance to treatment for themselves or the child on the part of some parents is probably a manifestation of the parental indifference referred to by many probation officers. Many parents tend, according to the officers, to view their children's problems as not including or relating to them. These parents deny responsibility for the difficulties in which their children find themselves. Frequently, these parents view probation or intake officers' attempts to work with them as unwarranted interference.[12]

The judges are of the opinion that they have the power to deal with recalcitrant parents by removing the children from their homes and said that they take such action. However, the case records indicate that this is done infre-

[8] Personal interview with the Chief Judge of the Affluent County Juvenile Court.

[9] Data based on questionnaires administered to all Affluent County probation officers during July, 1969.

[10] *Id.*

[11] Personal interview with the Chief Judge of the Affluent County Juvenile Court.

[12] From questionnaire results.

quently and usually years after the desirability of such action became apparent.

It is possible that this drastic action of removing a child from his home might prove unnecessary in some cases if other measures were taken by the court at an earlier stage. If the parents neglect or refuse to take the child to family services, a psychiatrist, or the probation officer, the court could provide someone to perform this service. In many cases, the parents could be required to reimburse the court as they now do for residential services because they can afford to do so. If the parents undermine the treatment or fail to cooperate by obtaining counseling themselves, the child should be removed for his own protection instead of waiting until he is removed for the protection of the community, which is the usual situation.

Part of the delay in removing children from their homes when such action is necessary is undoubtedly due to a lack of placement facilities.

At the time of the study, there was only one residential group home facility in the communiy and it housed only eight sixteen year old boys. . . .

In addition, there are seven state institutions used by the court including four training schools, the state institution for the retarded, and two state mental hospitals. Although the court regards the training schools as a last resort, they are all too often the only facilities available because of lack of funds for private placements and lack of space elsewhere.

Both the judges and the probation officers believe that a residential treatment center is needed within the county. In fact, the probation staff, in response to a questionnaire, considered such a treatment facility to be the most pressing need in the county. We question this belief on the basis of the data collected throughout the study. Less than ten percent of the children examined at the state diagnostic facility and by community diagnosticians were found to be psychotic or severely disturbed. This finding was confirmed by the project's consulting psychiatrist.[13] Although many additional children in the sample needed counseling or therapy, their treatment needs could be met by a community facility.

The residential facilities most needed by the court are small, long-term group homes which do not require parental participation. Reasons for this need are clear when current disposi-

tional practices are examined. The practice of placing a child on probation for approximately six months or committing him to an institution for less than a year shows that the juvenile system assumes the delinquent is "sick" and will be "cured" by these measures. This medical-model approach often fails. The study of recidivists showed children frequently committing new offenses as soon as the "treatment" was finished and often continued them until they were waived or no longer subject to the court's jurisdiction because of age or residence. The reason for this failure is often that the problem lies not within the child but within his home. In contrast to these failures, many children's delinquencies ceased when a satisfactory living arrangement was found for them. . . .

As was the case with non-residential care, the problem of providing delinquents with appropriate services does not lie wholly with the shortage of available facilities. In some instances, where placement away from home was recommended and a facility was available, parents were antagonistic to the removal and the courts were unwilling to take action over the parental objections. Eventually, the court removed some children despite the parents' wishes but only when the delinquencies had reached the point where the community was endangered. Such delayed action is unsatisfactory for two reasons.

First, the child is sometimes left in an intolerable and damaging situation for years. Secondly, and more importantly from the point of view of the community, the likelihood that the child will develop into a law-abiding citizen is reduced considerably if he remains in a deleterious environment until he is almost an adult.

Another placement need is for adequate foster homes for younger children. The delinquency of some children seems to be related directly to years of poverty, cultural deprivation, and lack of supervision, literally since infancy. Although there were few black children in the study, it seems that the problem of suitable foster homes is particularly acute for them. There seem to be almost no placement opportunities for them.

TOWARD JUSTICE FOR ALL

Since a juvenile justice structure exists in Affluent County in almost perfect form, as does an interested staff, does the high recidivism rate mean that a successful juvenile justice system can not be achieved?

---

[13] The student's consulting psychiatrist was Dr. Donald Hayes Russell. He reviewed the diagnostic reports and dispositional recommendations in the files for children who received predispositional psychiatric and psychological examinations.

On the contrary, we believe that justice for all, the juvenile and the community, can be achieved in Affluent County through a separate juvenile justice system. There is one major handicap, however, which pervades the entire system as it presently functions in the county, and probably in many other jurisdictions throughout the nation. It is the unspoken presumption that taking no action, which is termed "giving the child a chance," is equal to assisting him. The presumption is inexorably tied to the belief that directing a child to "go to school," "mind his parents" or "stop stealing" will have an effect on his behavior. This pattern of response to a juvenile can be observed in all parts of the system. Frequently, the police, intake workers, judges and probation officers all give the child "chances" and not much else.

Their failure to take action stems not from indifference but, to a large extent, from a feeling of powerlessness about changing the child's home life, school situation, or emotional difficulties. Of at least equal significance is the almost total lack of recognition of the rights of children, not only in the juvenile justice system, but in the community as a whole. Of particular relevance are a child's right to be protected from severe familial pathology and his right to receive such treatment and service as deemed necessary by the court.

Historically, the law has always considered children the property of their parents and, although lip service is paid to the concept of acting in the best interests of the child, one need only look at the dispositions in contested adoption, custody, neglect, and delinquency cases to see that children are generally regarded as their parents' property. The exception is when the child's conduct becomes so detrimental to the community that, despite his parents' wishes, he is removed to a training school or prison.

By a combination of changed attitudes and actions, justice for all can become a reality instead of an ideal in Affluent County. First, there must be a recognition that a child who commits a serious offense, or several minor offenses, has a problem and needs not simply another "chance" but active assistance. In the case of children ten and under, a complete mental, physical and home evaluation must be made. It is noteworthy that the overwhelming majority of children in the study who were referred to court in this age group became serious recidivists.

The court needs to adopt specific written criteria for both intake and detention decisions similar to those recommended in our earlier reports.[14] The adoption and implementation of such criteria would have several advantages. First, trauma would be spared some children and their families if those who do not need detention or court services are not forced to receive them. Secondly, personnel costs could be reduced substantially through implementation of more rational procedures. Lastly, and most important, children who need help and often do not receive it under present practices, would receive care promptly.

Additional protection would be afforded juveniles and their families if changes in procedures for notifying and appointing counsel such as those recommended earlier by the project are adopted.[15] However, in order for

[14] The detention criteria are in the project's as yet unpublished final report. They may be summarized as follows:
A. Children shall not be detained if they
   (1) Are under twelve years of age.
   (2) Appear to be so mentally ill as to constitute a danger to themselves or others.
   (3) Have a physical illness or condition which requires medical care (e.g., epilepsy, drug addiction).
B. Children will be detained if they are
   (1) Out-of-state runaways.
   (2) Escapees from institutions for delinquents or criminals.
   (3) Accused of offenses against persons when the victim required medical attention for his injuries.
   (4) Accused of felonies who have more than one prior court referral for running away.
   (5) Accused of selling addictive drugs.
C. Children may be detained if
   (1) They have had three prior delinquency adjudications or five or more adjudications within the last two years.
   (2) They have been referred for running away or being beyond parental care who have previously been in shelter care and while in a shelter facility ran away, assaulted other children or staff or destroyed property.
   (3) They are past the mandatory school attendance age and have dropped out of or have been expelled from school, and are unemployed.

[15] These recommendations are in the project's final report. Briefly they include the following: The court does not comply with all *Gault* requirements when the child is not represented by counsel. In some cases neither the child nor his parents received oral notification of the child's right to be represented by counsel. The court cannot determine whether they know of the right and understand its significance without talking to them.

Moreover, the child's right to counsel in Affluent County seems to be contingent on his parents' willingness to fill out an income state-the right to counsel to be meaningful, those attorneys who practice in the juvenile court must learn that their role is broader than that of functioning solely as an advocate at the adjudicatory stage of the proceedings. In particular, counsel must be sensitized to their duty to represent the child rather than his parents and to inform the court when prescribed treatment is not being carried out.

Too often, whether or not counsel is present, the adjudicatory process seems to serve no useful purpose other than as a device to give a child another chance without really doing anything.

For example, in some cases, though delinquency is clearly established, the case is dismissed either at the hearing or after a month or two. This decision stems from the belief that the offense is not serious enough to warrant a finding of delinquency or that, though the offense is serious, the child has learned his lesson and is unlikely to repeat it. Presumably, the adoption of the recommended intake criteria would eliminate most of these cases of the first type. But where the offense is serious, a social study[16] should be made before dis-

position to see if the child needs services or treatment. Since many of these children have been known to the police or the intake department before, it should not be assumed that the offense is an isolated one whose repetition can be prevented by the family without any assistance from the court.

Dispositions such as essay assignments on "Why I Should Not Steal," or of "probation without verdict" are also of doubtful value. Indicating that an act is wrong is not necessarily related to future deterrence from delinquent activity. The problem with the disposition "probation without verdict" is an entirely different one. The lack of meaningful action in this instance is apt to be on the part of the probation officer rather than the child. Many probation officers believe if the situation is not serious enough to warrant an adjudication of delinquency, it is not serious enough to warrant their time. This is also a peculiar disposition from a legal point of view. Presumably, the child is a probationer involuntarily but there is no legal basis for it without a finding of delinquency.

In Affluent County, as well as most other jurisdictions, the most frequent disposition used by the court once a juvenile has been adjudicated is probation. While probation officers may have somewhat differing views as to what their roles ought to be vis-a-vis a probationer, the Affluent County judges expect the probation officer to provide casework services and to refer probationers to other agencies when appropriate. Thus, the officer is not simply to report on whether or not a juvenile is adhering to the conditions of probation. Examination of case closing memoranda submitted to the judges, however, revealed that frequently the only basis for terminating probation is the absence of further delinquencies during the period of probation. Often these closing memoranda do not support an optimistic view of the juvenile's future behavior. Yet, almost routinely, the judges sign them, closing the cases.

For probation to be more successful, several changes would seem to be in order. More

---

ment. This requirement could exclude a large number of children from representation. First, it excludes children whose parents can retain counsel but refuse to do so. Secondly, it excludes those children whose parents for one reason or another do not fill out a form when their financial status makes their child eligible for court appointed counsel.

Although the majority of children appearing before the court receive oral notice, there are some problems about its content. In some cases the notice statement is incomplete because the child and his family are told only of the right to retain counsel, not of the court's duty to appoint one when they cannot afford it. The child's right to counsel should not be conditioned on his parents' ability to pay or to fill out forms. Nor for that matter should it be subject to the court's assessment of his parents' income.

The principal fact that became clear from the observations is that children without counsel suffer many disadvantages. They cannot effectively cross-examine witnesses or object to testimony. Therefore, it is extremely important that they receive complete, non-prejudicial information about the right to counsel and that counsel by appointed when there is a conflict between the parents' and child's interests or their desire to have counsel.

[16] Prior to making a disposition many juvenile court judges request their probation staff to prepare a pre-dispositional report, usually referred to as a social study. While the content of these studies varies from court to court, there is general agreement as to the elements that ought to be part

of every report. As expressed in *Model Rules for Juvenile Courts,* the social study:

... must . . . be comprehensive and must be analyzed and presented objectively and meaningfully to show the extent and nature of the emotional and behavioral patterns present. the psychological strengths and weaknesses of the individual, and the attitudes and standards of the child and family. Model Rule 29 and comment, *National Council on Crime and Delinquency.* Model Rules for Juvenile Courts 61 (1969).

counseling must be done with the child and his family, either by the probation officer or a suitable family agency. If the child or his family refuse to cooperate, the officer should inform the court promptly rather than waiting to close the case if no further delinquencies are reported. The judge, in turn, should schedule a hearing to review the situation and should issue an order to implement the required services or remove the child from the home. Under present procedures, removal usually takes place eventually, but is frequently too late and for too short a time to be effective.

Often the child's problems do not involve or are not confined to his family. Services may be needed from the school, welfare and mental health administrations. Presently, none of them seem to be providing adequate service to the county's delinquents. To talk of recidivism as the court's failure or the child's failure under these circumstances is unrealistic and unfair. The community must either make sure that these agencies understand that they have a duty to provide services for the court and then give them adequate funding to enable such programs and services to be carried out,

or it must allow the court, properly funded, to establish its own parallel services.

Similarly, when a child requires removal from his home, the court must have some appropriate facility in which to place him. But, in fact, often all the court has is the training school which serves as a holding place while efforts are made to find a more appropriate disposition. Frequently, and not too surprisingly, the effort fails as it has in the past. In fact, the effort begins again when it is time for release and continues unsuccessfully, sometimes throughout the child's minority, because there is either no appropriate facility or no money for placement. . . .

It is possible that our recommendations reflect an overoptimistic view of juvenile criminality and what even a well equipped juvenile justice system can do about it. However, Affluent County, and many other communities, will never know unless serious effort is made toward implementation. The choice is between continuing to give children "chances" instead of services, thereby leaving juvenile crime and recidivism undiminished, or finally implementing individualized justice for juveniles.

SUGGESTIONS FOR ADDITIONAL READING

Avery, J. "The Battered Child," *MH* 57, no. 2 (Spring 1973).

Brakel, S., and Rock, R. *The Mentally Disabled and the Law* (revised ed.). University of Chicago Press, 1971.

Broune, Elizabeth W. *Child Neglect and Dependency: A Digest of Case Law.* National Council of Juvenile Court Judges (1973).

Ferster and Courtless. "The Beginning of Juvenile Justice: Police Practices and the Juvenile Offender," 22 *Vand. L. Rev.* 567 (1969).

Ferster, Snethen, and Courtless. "Juvenile Detention: Protection, Prevention or Punishment?" 38 *Fordham L. Rev.* 161 (1969).

Ferster and Courtless. "The Intake Process in the Affluent County Juvenile Court," 22 *Hastings L.J.* 1127 (1971).

Ferster, Courtless, and Snethen. "The Juvenile Justice System: In Search of the Role of Counsel," 39 *Fordham L. Rev.* 375 (1971).

Ferster and Courtless. "Pre-Dispositional Data, Role of Counsel and Decisions in a Juvenile Court," *Law and Soc. Review* 195 (1972).

Goldstein, J., Freud, A., and Solnit, A. *Beyond the Best Interests of the Child.* New York: The Free Press, 1973.

Polier, Justine, Wise. "Myths and Realities in the Search for Juvenile Justice," 44 *Harv. Educ. Rev.* 112 (1974).

Taschman, H. "In Defense of Children—Advocacy Efforts," *MH* 57, no. 2 (Spring 1973).

Terr and Watson. "'The Battered Child Rebrutalized: Ten Cases of Medico Legal Confusion," 124 *Amer. J. Psychiat.* 1432 (1968).

U.S. Senate, Committee on Labor and Public Welfare, Subcommittee on Children and Youth Hearings on S. 1191—Child Abuse Prevention Act, March 26, 27, 31; and April 24, 1973.

Watson, A. "Psychoanalysis and Divorce," from *The Marriage Relationship*, edited by S. Rosenbaum and I. Alger. New York: Basic Books, 1968.

Wilkerson, Albert E., ed., *The Rights of Children.* Philadelphia: Temple University Press, 1973.

IV

The Psychiatrist and the Criminal Law

15

Mental Impairment and Crime

The chapter begins with excepts from two White Papers prepared for the President's Commission on Law Enforcement and Administration of Justice. Both treat of the relationship of mental impairment to criminal law and corrections, and both grapple with the complexity of social policy determinations in the light of contemporary knowledge—tempered by limitations on that knowledge and by practical realities. Neither paper was substantially drawn upon by that Commission in making its recommendations (which were largely confined to the expressed hope that mentally impaired offenders be diverted early in the criminal process to undefined community treatment programs; see *The Challenge of Crime in a Free Society*, G.P.O., 1967), and they received only limited distribution. However, these treatises, written by leading experts in the field, present a number of challenging and disturbing questions. They deserve more thoughtful consideration than was given to them by the "Crime Commission." The Allen article describes the findings of an empirical study of the mentally retarded offender, who—undiverted—remains in the criminal justice system. Dr. Halleck comments on the role of psychiatry in correction; and Dr. Tanay offers a psychiatric typology of homicide offenders. The chapter concludes with an editorial note on "behavior mod" in correction.

THE MENTALLY DISORDERED OFFENDER

A Consideration of Some Aspects of the Criminal-Judicial-Correctional Process

---

Saleem A. Shah, Ph.D.

INTRODUCTION

This presentation will focus upon a number of issues relating to the labeling, handling, and disposition of persons who have engaged in law-violating behavior and who, in addition, are judged to have various psychiatric and psychosocial problems described as *mental disorders*.

A detailed and exhaustive study of the many issues and problems pertaining to the mentally disordered law-violator would indeed be a major undertaking and one beyond the scope of this paper. The concern here is with some selected areas within two broad aspects: firstly, the many issues of law and legal processes having to do with the mentally ill individual accused or convicted of law violation; secondly, several issues concerning various kinds of programs and facilities for the treatment and handling of such individuals. While many similar problems and considerations also involve the mentally retarded offender, this paper will not deal with this particular group.

A. Scope of the Problem

The mentally disordered offender category is rather broad and covers persons at various stages of the criminal-judicial-correctional

---

process, entails the making of a number of separate and distinct decisions for different purposes, and includes persons suffering from varying degrees of mental disturbance. Any effort, therefore, to deal with this broad group under a single definition, or even a single set of criteria, seems doomed to failure.

We might consider first some of the categories of persons included in various programs for "mentally disordered offenders." These are as follows:

1. Accused persons sent for mental observation and evaluation on a variety of legal issues—mainly for determination of competency to stand trial and criminal responsibility.
2. Persons adjudged incompetent to stand trial.
3. Persons found not guilty by reason of insanity.
4. Criminal sexual psychopaths, or defective delinquents.
5. Psychotic or otherwise seriously disturbed offenders transferred from penal institutions.
6. Transfers from mental hospital, or related institutions, where such persons are considered homicidal, dangerous, or otherwise serious custody problems.
7. Referrals from juvenile courts and institutions, facilities for the mentally retarded, etc., of persons believed to be seriously disturbed, dangerous, or security problems.
8. Offenders adjudged guilty of the charge but sent to mental hospitals, or other special institutions, because of signs of mental disturbance and/or need for special treatment.

Even though such a diverse group of individuals could not be covered by a single set of criteria, they do have in common the feature of having demonstrated a variety of behavioral deviations identified as mental disorders. This latter, then, becomes an area of interest and concern, viz., the particular criteria, or sets of criteria, used to classify certain individuals as suffering from mental disease or disturbance. Obviously, at different stages of the criminal process and for various decisions, the particular criteria applied would differ. Thus, criteria which may be used to determine an accused's competency to stand trial—and these are legal, social, and behavioral criteria—would be quite different from those used to determine whether a particular inmate of a reformatory needs to be transferred to a mental hospital. The criteria, while overlapping, would vary depending upon the particular decision in regard to which

the person is being evaluated and the purpose and objectives involved.

Even though the criteria will therefore differ, there is nonetheless a great need for developing fairly explicit guidelines which may be used in specific situations. Such guidelines, be they "clinical hunches," "rules of thumb," or others, are indeed in use. However, there is general agreement that such implicit and vague criteria need refinement and behavior referents, in order to achieve greater uniformity and reliability.

B. Extent of Mental Disorder among Offenders

It has been estimated that between fifteen to twenty per cent of all criminal offenders have such a significant degree of behavioral deviation that they could be diagnosed psychiatrically and are in need of psychiatric treatment.

There are at least fifty-three facilities which program for mentally disordered offenders in forty-five states and the District of Columbia; of these only seventeen are entirely or almost entirely for mentally disordered offenders. The remaining facilities are mental hospitals with special security units for mentally disordered offenders. Available statistics do *not* provide a breakdown as to the number of persons housed in these special or security units. The fifty-three facilities should not be considered the total number serving this special group of offenders, as other State facilities are also used. Likewise, out-patient, court, legal psychiatric, and community mental health clinics also serve mentally disordered offenders, not to mention the special facilities available within many correctional institutions for such offenders.

In view of the very inadequate and incomplete information available about the extent of serious mental disturbance among offenders, there is an urgent need for a thorough survey of facilities for this population. On the basis of the limited information available, it seems evident that this special group of offenders is of significant size.

C. The Labeling Process and Its Consequences

When studying the criminal labeling and sanctioning process, we can start with the various *social norms* which are designed to regulate social behavior and relationships. Some social norms have considerable force and sanctions to support compliance, while others may have little such force. Among the more universal and permanent social norms are many of those associated with social institutions. Institutional norms tend to be supported by high degrees of consensus and elicit intense reactions when they are violated. Related to this are the central goals or objectives of a culture, i.e., *social values*, which not only are shared widely in the culture, but are regarded as matters of collective welfare and to which are often attached high degrees of emotional belief in their importance. Criminal laws can be seen as norms regulating behavior which are enforced by coercion of the State. Also, such norms involve some basic goals or values held in high regard in the culture. Thus, not only are murder, manslaughter, rape, robbery, and theft violations of legal norms, but the basic values involved include the protection of human life, the protection of sexual and family life, and the protection of property.

While some criminal laws, such as the above, may relate very clearly and obviously to the protection of important social values, others are not so obviously related, but instead may simply reflect the attitudes and expectations of the predominant and influential cultural groups. However, in general, when the violation of certain social norms tends to exceed the tolerance limits of the community, legal norms may be brought into being to sanction and control such violations. Understandably, there are few absolute standards regulating social behavior. Behavior not heretofore labeled "criminal" may come to be so labeled, while other categories of behavior may lose such designation.

Some thought might be given at this point to the labeling process involved in making dispositional decisions about people brought to the attention of law enforcement or other social agencies. Such a labeling process, i.e., whether the individual is to be viewed and handled as a "criminal" or as a "disturbed" person, appears to determine to a large extent the kinds of institutions and agencies which will later deal with him. Likewise, the particular sets of consequences to be experienced—sanctioning, therapeutic, or otherwise—will again depend in large measure on the particular label attached. The practical problems of adapting certain traditional moral, philosophical values, and concepts to the handling of law-violating behavior are nowhere more clear than in determination of criminal responsibility where the defense of insanity has been raised. The labels following this dichotomous classification, i.e., responsible (guilty, blameworthy, "bad") or not responsible (not guilty, not blameworthy, "mad"), lead to differing sets of dispositions, handling, and treatment.

In addition, and this is an even more critical issue, we need to be extremely cognizant of the fact that labeling tends to greatly limit the direction and manner of facilities and services to be utilized. For example, once an offender has been labeled "sick" in regard to some legal decisions or programmatic considerations, focus and concern will tend to be directed more to psychiatric needs than to custody, control, and broad corrective treatment.[1] "Patients" are indeed treated and handled differently from "convicts" and "criminals." However, since such labels are by no means separate and distinct, and since the programs do have similarities, and practical considerations have to be given due weight, we can indeed find "hospitals" with more custody and control features than some "penal" institutions. The overlapping and connecting aspects of various facilities in dealing with our mentally disordered person very quickly become apparent, and increased efforts are needed to provide adequate bridging mechanisms.

Sometimes, however, there seem to be obvious inconsistencies in the labels applied and the nature of the actual resulting consequences. Thus, "sexual psychopaths," identified as requiring "remedial," "curative," and "treatment" services typically end up with indeterminate confinement in special institutions which may be labeled "hospitals." However, such long confinement may not be compared with "incarceration" since the *intent* of the action is "remedial" rather than punitive. Likewise, even though the person may indeed find such experience most punishing, it cannot be described as "punishment" because of the aforementioned "treatment" goals, and because such proceedings are "civil" rather than "criminal." Furthermore, since the proceedings are "civil," in those instances where the individual is later subjected to "criminal" sanctions *after* his presumed recovery through the treatment and curative process, this may not be considered "double jeopardy."

II. THE PRE-TRIAL CONFERENCE[2]

A. Rationale for the Use of Such a Mechanism

If we study the manner in which individuals pass through various stages of the criminal process, a glaring need becomes evident for

[1] Whenever reference is made to "treatment" without any qualifying term such as "psychiatric" or "psychological," the word is used to describe the broad range of educational, vocational, counseling and other programs designed to bring about positive changes in behavior.

[2] This section of the discussion draws heavily on a memorandum prepared for the Crime Commission staff by Professor Abraham Goldstein of the Yale Law School entitled "A Proposal for a Pre-Charge Conference."

mechanisms whereby a variety of dispositional alternatives becomes available at the earliest stages of the process. This possibility of diversion becomes even more important when dealing with various mentally disordered individuals. It is clear that, as one moves forward into the criminal process, the choices decrease, the statutory and other constraints increase, and the relative inflexibility of labeling and dispositional alternatives also increases.

There is some research which indicates that in a large number of cases, whether a law-violator is handled through criminal or mental health agencies seems determined by factors that are largely fortuitous. Likewise many offenses may go undetected; others may come to the attention of health, school, and other social agencies; and still others may be diverted from the criminal process in order to be handled within a therapeutic context. It seems most essential, therefore, to screen out of the criminal process at the very earliest opportunity those deviant persons who, it is felt, should not be subjected to the ponderous machinery of the criminal law, and who may better be handled through various therapeutic-rehabilitative agencies.

With our increasing knowledge regarding deviant and mentally disturbed behavior, it seems appropriate to consider whether certain categories of norm-violations and norm-violating individuals need be subjected to the criminal sanctioning process or whether—keeping in mind both society's and the individual's interests—it might be more appropriate and desirable to deal with the individual through various other social agencies. The thrust of recent court decisions in regard to handling of the chronic alcoholic[3] and the narcotic addict[4] is clearly in the direction of therapeutic measures rather than criminal sanctions in such cases. Similar therapeutic needs and considerations may also involve other forms of deviant conduct which indicate the presence of marked psychological, psychiatric, and related problems. The vagrant, the kleptomanic shoplifter, certain sex offenders, and others with distinct psychological pathology, may be kept entirely outside the criminal process by reason of treatment needs and social policy considerations. Needless to say, treatment of the individual does *not* have to jeopardize the constitutional rights of the person nor the need for protection of the community; appropriate safeguards can be provided.

What is proposed is the setting up of a pre-trial conference which would be used at the "prosecutorial stage," but which also could be used as early as possible in the criminal process, viz., at the pre-charge, pre-arraignment, or pre-indictment stages. An opportunity would be provided to the two attorneys—representing the interests of the community and of the accused—to discuss various dispositional alternatives and to arrive, if possible, at what might be described as a *consensual disposition*. This, it should be clear, is not very different at all from what is already done in terms of "plea bargaining" and related conferences between the two attorneys. Also, since this pre-trial conference would operate within the range of existing "prosecutorial discretion," no legal or organizational changes would be required. The above proposal would seek to make the conference between attorneys a more systematic and formal process leading—through the use of appropriate mental health and related consultation—to more rational and meaningful dispositions. Further, the pre-trial conference would seek to lend greater value to the aforementioned process by providing training for prosecutors in regard to knowledge about and recognition of mental disorders, treatment indications, community resources, and alternative dispositional choices. Some broad guidelines could also be developed and made available to prosecutors to assist in early screening and to provide treatment-oriented criteria for use along with other criteria, in diverting persons from the criminal processes. Some of these guidelines may also be applied at the earlier police stage.

It should be clear that, in order to make the pre-trial conference meaningful, the defendant must be represented by counsel early enough in the legal process so as to participate effectively in such a procedure. The thrust of recent Supreme Court decisions[5] suggests that such early representation has indeed to be provided.

Given certain indications for mental health consultation and information, both the prosecutor and the defense attorney would have available to them consultation in the form initially, perhaps, of a psychiatrist, clinical psychologist, psychiatric social worker, or other mental health professional. The mental health consultant would have access to material regarding the case, including descriptions and details of the offense, accounts of the individual's behavior, previous history of mental disorder and treatment, etc. To facilitate the most rational and careful decision in regard to possible handling and disposition, it would be necessary to have as full "discovery and disclosure" on both sides as possible. However, to

---

[3] Easter v. District of Columbia, 19365 (March 31, 1966).

[4] Robinson v. California, 370 U.S. 660 (1962).

[5] Escobedo v. Illinois, 378 U.S. 478 (1964); Miranda v. Arizona, 384 U.S. 436 (1966).

the extent there may be reasons in certain situations, or in some jurisdictions, for not making full disclosure, the possibility would have to be considered for allowing disclosure with certain safeguards explicitly provided.

In light of evaluation and recommendation by the mental health consultant, the two attorneys may then be able to arrive at some consensual disposition. Or, the consultant may recommend referral to some mental health facility (legal psychiatric or court clinic, or other community mental health agency) for more complete study.

Following fairly complete psychiatric, psychological, and related studies at an outpatient facility (an inpatient facility may be used when specifically indicated), and in light of findings and recommendations, the two attorneys would again consider whether the charge is to be prosecuted or wheather some alternative course may more appropriately be followed.

The decision may be that if the accused cooperates in the recommended treatment program for an agreed upon period of time, the case would—at the satisfactory termination of such period—be dismissed or the indictment dropped. In the event the accused fails to follow through on the agreement the case would then move forward.

It should be emphasized that due process and other constitutional safeguards would have to be provided at each step of the pre-trial conference mechanism. Furthermore, any decision and agreement made by the accused in regard to the consensual disposition and handling would be *voluntary* and be made after the person had the benefit of advice from counsel. Likewise, the accused may, upon advice of counsel or for other reasons, decide *not* to subject himself to the pre-trial disposition but instead to stand trial to contest guilt, or to enter a plea and go through the regular criminal-correctional process. Likewise, the prosecutor would also be free to turn down recommendations of the mental health consultants and take the case to trial.

There will undoubtedly be cases where the prosecutor will deem it necessary to keep some hold on the offender to assure that he continues the course of treatment agreed upon. In fact, in some cases there may be clear indication or explicit recommendation from the mental health agency that the accused requires external constraints to ensure satisfactory cooperation and involvement in the treatment program. Three alternatives might be considered to deal with such situations: (1) a procedure (perhaps termed "administrative probation") which would involve keeping alive the charge of crime for a specified time,

requiring periodic reports, and prosecution if the terms of "probation" are violated. (2) In cases where there is reason to believe that it may not be feasible to try the charge at some distant date, there may be a submission comparable to a "consent decree" to be filed with the court. Such a consent decree would outline the treatment plan and provide that, upon violation of its terms, there would be entered either a plea of guilty of a stipulation of facts, or the depositions of certain witnesses whose testimony might be perpetuated for just such an eventuality. (3) Statutory revisions may be sought which would provide dispositional alternatives similar to "probation before conviction" in Maryland, "case continued without finding" in Massachusetts, or "probation without adjudication" in Florida. Likewise, the Model Sentencing Act makes provisions for sentencing alternatives where, upon fulfillment of the terms of probation, the defendant can be discharged without court adjudication.[6]

There may be cases which are regarded as appropriate for civil commitment. Where the offender wishes to commit himself voluntarily after consulting with his counsel, this should be permitted. However, where he does not wish to do so and where police and prosecutors have power to initiate civil commitment proceedings, there is the risk that such power may be used coercively—either to compel pleas of guilty or to obtain a longer period of confinement than would be possible in the criminal conviction. This could occur because civil commitment brings with it a completely indeterminate confinement, and this often for conditions which are not easily treatable. This risk (which already exists) would probably be aggravated by the pre-trial conference. It would make more apparent, at an early stage, the question whether civil commitment might be appropriate in the particular case. However, with the cloud of indeterminate confinement hanging over the pre-trial conference, it is doubtful that many offenders would participate in it. Two possible solutions might be considered: (1) the prosecutor might be authorized to institute civil commitment proceedings for periods no longer than the maximum sentence which could have been imposed for the offense in issue, thereby reducing the "punitive" potential of civil commitment. If detention beyond that period proves necessary, it might be left to some other official—the superintendent of the hospital or institution to which the person has been committed—to seek it. (2) Police and prosecutors might be elimi-

---

[6] *Model Sentencing Act*, Advisory Council of Judges of the National Council on Crime and Delinquency (NCCD, 1963).

nated from the category of persons authorized to initiate civil commitment, except for emergency situations.

It would be rather essential to bring home to prosecutors and judges that defendants should not be penalized in any way for failing to come to an agreement at the pre-trial conference.

Finally, in the event the case does proceed to trial and the individual is convicted, the findings and recommendations provided by the mental health consultation could be available to the sentencing judge.

III. Special Problem Areas

A. Competency To Stand Trial

In keeping with the common law tenet that an accused may not be tried or sentenced while "insane," the test for mental competence to stand trial follows similar reasoning. The accused is considered eligible for trial if he: ". . . he capable of understanding the nature and object of the proceedings going on against him; if he rightly comprehends his own condition with reference to such proceedings and can conduct his defense in a rational manner, . . . although on some other subject his mind may be deranged or unsound."[7]

The issues of competence to be sentenced and competency for execution of the sentence are also framed in similar terms and involve the same general reasoning.

It has only been in recent years that more attention has been focused on the issue of pre-trial competency in the legal process. While there have been voluminous writings on the subject of criminal responsibility and the insanity defense, the subject of pre-trial competency—which in fact affects more persons and can indeed have a deciding effect much earlier in the legal proceedings—has until recently been somewhat ignored. One consequence of such limited attention to both the legal tests and requirements and also the subsequent handling, treatment, and evaluation of those accused found to be incompetent, has been the long term and almost indeterminate hospitalization of many such persons. Many pre-trial incompetents may have been charged only with misdemeanors, for which even the maximum sentence upon conviction would have been but a few months. Nonetheless, due to lack of adequate staff and facilities in most mental hospitals to undertake adequate treatment and periodic review of these cases, and also because of not infrequent misinterpreta-

tions of the legal requirements pertaining to pre-trial competency, such committed persons often may languish in back wards of State hospitals or similar institutions. These problems are further complicated by the fact that often competency proceedings may be initiated somewhat as an indirect means for obtaining other ends—psychiatric testimony to develop or defeat a defense of insanity, psychiatric intervention to reach some other disposition such as civil commitment or sexual psychopath proceedings, or simply for purposes of delay and discovery.

Some studies have indicated that a large number of the psychiatrists and others conducting pre-trial competency examinations and testifying on this and related issues, do *not* understand the legal questions and considerations involved.[8] Not infrequently the pre-trial competency issue may be confused with the later and separate concern with exculpatory insanity. In addition, frequently there is reference to and use of a variety of medical and psychiatric diagnostic criteria to answer the court's legal questions. Yet, if one thing seems fairly clear, it is that the legal and social criteria involved in the test of pre-trial competency have little if any direct relationship to psychiatric diagnoses. As though the above were not enough, there are the further confounding problems relating to the nature and adequacy of the mental examinations, the bare conclusory form in which reports are often sent to the court, and the tendency of many courts to essentially "rubber-stamp" the psychiatric findings and conclusions instead of exercising audicial judgment.

B. Criminal Responsibility and the Insanity Defense

So much has been written on this topic that one would have to search long and hard to uncover basically novel ideas or thoughts in recent years. In fact, it could well be said that the voluminous literature on the concepts of criminal responsibility and exculpatory insanity as a defense, tends more to becloud and confuse than to clarify the complex issues involved. Indeed, perhaps it would also be both fair and appropriate to say that the question of the insanity defense has been given attention, discussion, and emphasis far in excess of its actual importance in the overall administration of criminal justice. It needs to be borne in mind that in about ninety per cent of criminal cases defendants use the guilty plea, and that

---

[7] State v. Severns, 184 Kan. 313, 336 P.3d 447, 452 (1959).

[8] See, for example, J. A. Hess and T. E. Thomas, "Incompetence to stand trial: Procedures, Results and Problems," *American Journal of Psychiatry*, 119 (1963): 715–20.

in only a relatively small number of cases is the insanity defense raised.[9]

The concept of criminal responsibility is deeply, firmly, and even rigidly rooted in traditional religious, moral, and philosophical beliefs. The doctrine of *mens rea* and criminal responsibility are fundamentally and inextricably tied to the traditional punitive sanctions of the criminal law. The concern is with "blameworthiness" and "punishability" of the individual accused of crime. As a consequence, a considerable amount of time, effort, and expense is involved in the preoccupation with attaching legally appropriate labels on the accused. The courtroom "battle of experts" and the entire trial in such cases revolves around determination of whether the accused is legally to be considered *responsible*—i.e., as blameworthy, "bad," and deserving the punitive sanctions of the law, or whether he is to be considered *not responsible*—i.e., as not blameworthy but rather as "mad," hence deserving treatment rather than punishment. The efforts and energies devoted to the above labeling process seem often so great that the criminal process and societal resources appear too exhausted and inadequate to deal more appropriately with critical decisions relating to the actual disposition of such persons.

The whole issue of exculpatory insanity as a defense aganist criminal responsibility is further complicated and confounded by the confusion of socio-legal criteria with a variety of medical, psychiatric, psychological, or other such criteria. It should certainly be clear that the legal determination at the "fact-finding" or trial stage is basically a social-moral judgment as to how society should handle certain of its deviants. And, while the term "mental disease" or "mental disorder" does appear in various *tests* of criminal responsibility, it is quite clear that the *legal* use of such terms is *not* similar to or synonymous with the mental health usage. However, all too frequently this important and critical distinction is not adequately understood by participants in such legal fact-finding. Failure to fully appreciate the distinctions between criteria used in various *legal* judgments and decisions and those pertaining to treatment and other *mental health* issues, gives rise to many problems.

The above distinction was made very clear in *McDonald* v. *United States*[10] in the District of Columbia. The relevant sections of this opinion state: "What psychiatrists may consider a 'mental disease or defect' for clinical purposes, where their concern is treatment, may or may not be the same as mental disease or defect for the jury's purpose in determining criminal responsibility. . . . We emphasize that, since the question of whether the defendant has a disease or defect is ultimately for the triers of fact, obviously its resolution cannot be controlled by expert opinion" (p. 851).

The point can further be made that when the various insanity tests seek to establish *some relationship* between the mental condition of the defendant and the alleged crime, this again involves an ethical-moral judgment and is not a scientific determination of a causal relationship. Rather, what is at issue is again essentially and primarily a moral judgment: to determine whether the defendant deviates far enough from most people, in terms of his mental functioning and capacity to regulate his behavior, as to require that he not be subjected to criminal sanctions but be treated differently. When these ethical-moral-legal questions are posed to mental ealhealth expert witnesses, certain implicit social values are bound to become involved in their responses—even though these may be couched in technical terminology.

It should be noted that the real difference between the mental health and the legal approach to the issue of criminal responsibility actually has little to do with a philosophy of determinism versus free will. Rather, it has more to do with differing conceptions of the objectives of the criminal process and with questions as to whether the aim of that process is punitive or preventive and therapeutic.

In the past several years there has clearly been a shift away from the punitive emphasis of the criminal law toward rehabilitative and preventive goals. The sharp distinctions between hospitals for mentally disordered offenders and prisons—if ever they were so sharp—seem to be getting increasingly blurred as correctional facilities develop and expand treatment and rehabilitative programs. In fact, one could point to many "correctional" institutions that are more therapeutically oriented and provide better overall treatment and rehabilitation than some "mental hospitals." Likewise, it could not be said that simply by virtue of the labels attached, mental hospitals involved in the handling of law-violators are devoid of sanctions and punitive aspects. For example, Goldstein and Katz have pointed out: ". . . Commitment procedures, however labelled, constitute a sanction, so far as the person confined is concerned, in the form of deprivation of liberty, at least to the extent

[9] E. J. Lindman and D. M. McIntyre, eds. *The Mentally Disabled and the Law* (Chicago: University of Chicago Press, 1961). S. Rubin, *The Law of Criminal Corrections* (St. Paul: West Publishing Co., 1963).

[10] McDonald v. United States, 312 F.2d 847 (1962).

that commitment is without regard to his 'wishes' " (p. 229).[11]

Undoubtedly, there are many complex problems relating to the knotty and vexing issue of criminal responsibility and the insanity defense, and no simple or quick solutions are in view. However, it is imperative that there be a careful and rational analysis of the objectives of the criminal process in light of *present and evolving social needs and problems*. Also, there needs to be an objective and thorough evaluation of the effectiveness of existing legal and other institutions to cope with such societal problems. It seems both inappropriate and archaic to cling rigidly to legal traditions in the implicit if not explicit faith that the age-old moral and ethical values involved in the notions of criminal responsibility have some *absolute* quality which makes them equally relevant to present social needs and situations.

In regard to some practical and specific issues, here too, as in the case of pre-trial mental examinations and the confinement of incompetents, there are serious problems concerning lack of adequate examination, treatment, and periodic review facilities. Likewise, the reports from the hospitals and clinics tend frequently to be brief and conclusory, and significant differences in staff opinions—which may well have a bearing on the legal issues of fact to be determined—often go unreported or may be glossed over. In addition, the criteria for release from the hospital for those acquitted by reason of insanity tend to be too strict and very likely work to keep many persons confined longer than in necessary.

C. Special Statutes

Special statutes are now in existence in roughly half the States and in the District of Columbia aimed at "sexual psychopaths," "sexually dangerous persons," "sex offenders," "mentally abnormal sex offenders," "criminal sexual psychopaths," "psychopathic personalities," "psychopathic offenders," and "defective delinquents."

The first of the so-called sexual psychopath laws was enacted in Michigan in 1935 and was held to be unconstitutional. The Illinois act passed in 1938 and was upheld in the courts; now, half the States have such laws. In 1949 alone six States passed sexual psychopath laws.[12]

It is interesting to note that such laws did not stem either from a sharp increase in sex crimes or certainly from sudden and dramatic advances in psychiatric knowledge in how to deal with sex offenders. It appears that such legislation in many instances arose from public panic when a few serious or particularly heinous sex crimes were committed. Thus, in several instances such statutes were somewhat hurriedly enacted into law. Among many of these earlier sexual psychopath statutes there was no requirement of conviction of a crime. Later statutes, however, followed the usual criminal procedures in requiring a conviction, and some of the other statutes were subsequently revised in this direction.

Of the twenty such laws analyzed by one investigator, ten were found to require conviction of a crime as the basis for jurisdiction, five required a charge of certain particular offenses, and five (District of Columbia, Massachusetts, Minnesota, Nebraska, and New Hampshire) allowed proceedings to be initiated without either conviction or a charge. In Minnesota, for example, sexual psychopath proceedings could be initated merely by the filing of a petition by any person "having knowledge of the facts."[13] Likewise, half of the States do not provide for a jury hearing; in some States the examining physicians need not be psychiatrists; in other States the examining psychiatrists are not subject to cross-examination and the defendant may not introduce his own expert witnesses or even have court-appointed counsel when unable to obtain one himself. In addition, where the commitment is for sexual psychopathy and not for a criminal offense, such commitment is not a bar to a later prosecution for crime. In Illinois, for example, a defendant committed for a crime and found to be a sexual psychopath may be further confined on that basis after serving the original sentence. The constitutionality of such provisions has been upheld by the courts on the grounds that the proceedings are "civil" in nature and hence the customary safeguards of the "criminal" trial need not apply. Thus, since the purpose of such "civil" proceedings has been described as "remedial," "curative," and "regulatory," subsequent "criminal" prosecutions have been held *not* to constitute double jeopardy.

The general administrative experience with such statutes seems to have been that while they have been in effect for a number of years, in most jurisdictions they have been largely inoperative. This might be because of the obvious paucity of treatment facilities for the law

---

[11] J. Goldstein and J. Katz, "Dangerousness and Mental Illness: Some Observations on the Decision to Release Persons Acquitted by Reason of Insanity," *Yale Law Journal* (1960), p. 225.

[12] Lindman and McIntyre, *Mentally Disabled and the Law;* Rubin, *Law of Criminal Corrections.*

[13] Minn. Stats. Ann. #526, 09.

to have any actual meaning. Also, judges and prosecutors, who are endowed by these laws with considerable discretion, may be reluctant to apply them. Since the periods of confinement allowed or even specified by such statutes are usually indeterminate with no minimum or maximum release dates, judges may well be reluctant to commit persons for extended periods—possibly even for life—in the face of inadequate treatment facilities.

The common avoidance of such statutes is probably a sound reaction since they are based on a number of erroneous notions about sex offenders. The assumptions most often attacked are: (1) the sex deviate is more dangerous than other types of criminals; (2) there is a high degree of recidivism of sex deviates—higher than other criminals; (3) such sex deviates can clearly be isolated; and (4) there are in existence both methods of treatment and necessary facilities for treatment that will lead to recovery.

Many studies have been conducted to determine the dangerousness of sex deviates. The findings clearly suggest that not more than about five per cent of convicted sex offenders are of the violent and dangerous type. Also, while there is a popular misconception which holds that sex offenders rather typically progress from minor crimes, like exhibitionism or peeping, to major ones like rape, such a progression is extremely rare. In regard to recidivism rates of sex offenders it has been found that, as a group, such offenders have lower rates. Most sex offenders (except for some minor deviates like exhibitionists, voyeurs, and some homosexuals) seem to run afoul of the law only once.

Even though there has been some feeling that the above statutes were premised upon the ability of "the relatively new science of psychiatry to identify, isolate, and treat such individuals," it is obvious that the vagueness and confusion in psychiatric circles regarding the concept of "psychopathy" has in no significant way been reduced. The label "psychopath" has long tended to be used somewhat as a "wastebasket" category and has been regarded as a dubious concept. The newer label "sociopath," or more accurately but less euphemistically, "antisocial reaction," has in no significant way led to greater uniformity in usage or understanding. Problems of obtaining agreement among clinicians in regard to definition, criteria, prognosis, and treatability remain considerable. Thus, it would not be correct to assume that the impetus for "sexual psychopath" statutes was the sudden and marked increase in diagnostic, predictive, and therapeutic skills in psychiatry. Rather, one is led to conclude that the concept of "sexual psycho-

path" with its "treatment" objectives—in the face of the clear absence of adequate facilities and of effective therapeutic techniques—was invoked to confine for long periods persons whose deviant behavior was found by the community to be highly objectionable and threatening. It seems probable that, in the absence of some "medical" or at least medical-sounding concept and therapeutic intentions, such statutes might well have run afoul of various constitutional protections relating to preventive detention. The irony of the situation is that while these statutes were devised mainly to protect against the more violent and vicious types of sex deviates, the law has more often been applied against the minor sex offender.

A few states, notable among them Maryland, have somewhat similar laws directed at those described as "defective delinquents."[14] The Maryland statute, designed to identify and handle the dangerous and recidivist offender, has attracted much interest and has been in existence for almost twelve years. It provides for a special institution for the indeterminate confinement and treatment of offenders so adjudicated.

This statute may be applied to those criminals convicted and sentenced in the State for: (1) a felony; (2) a misdemeanor punishable by imprisonment in the penitentiary; (3) a crime of violence; (4) a sex crime involving: (a) physical force or violence, (b) disparity of age between an adult and a minor, or (c) a sexual act of an uncontrolled and/or repetitive nature; and (5) two or more convictions for any crimes punishable by imprisonment in a criminal court of Maryland.

In contrast to some of the aforementioned "sexual psychopath" statutes, the Maryland "defective delinquent" statute does explicitly provide for due process and confrontation. For example, the individual must initially be convicted and sentenced in a State court for a crime; the crime must be of a particular type; the person must still be confined; the examination must be made by three persons (a physician, a psychiatrist, and a psychologist) and a majority of the examiners must conclude that the individual is a "defective delinquent"; the person is entitled on request to be examined by a private psychiatrist of his own choice at the expense of the State—unless he himself requested the original examination; he is also entitled to counsel of his choice, or to competent counsel appointed by the Court; the individual also has a choice of a court or jury trial, and may also make application for leave

[14] Annotated Code of the Public General Laws of Maryland, Sec. 5, Art. 31B.

to appeal the order holding him to be a defective delinquent, etc.

Generally, there appear to be rather mixed feelings in regard to the aforementioned statutes providing for indeterminate confinement of certain categories of offenders and law-violators. On the one hand there is recognition of the real need for confining individuals who have demonstrated their threat and danger to the community, and who have been intractable in response to other penal measures. On the other hand, there is serious concern about the loose wording of many such statutes, the invoking of vague and unreliable medical, psychiatric, or related concepts, and the general absence of adequate treatment facilities for so-called civil, remedial, and treatment programs. In addition, use of a particular offense category, viz., sex offenses, can hardly serve as a satisfactory basis for handling under statutes aimed at protecting the community from "dangerous" persons. Offenses other than sexual may be committed by persons equally or far more dangerous.

There is genuine reason for concern in regard to the use and meaning given to the term "dangerous." Very frequently this term is used in various civil and other commitment proceedings and the legal interpretation is rather broad. There is real question whether certain types of property offenders, minor sex offenders such as exhibitionists, voyeurs, and homosexuals engaging in relationships with consenting adults, are indeed to be viewed as so "dangerous" to the community as to justify their incarceration for indeterminate periods. As Szasz[15] points out, what constitutes dangerousness is frequently left unspecified and thus allows for various administrative decisions by lawyers and psychiatrists. Szasz notes further that whether or not the person is dangerous seems not to be the real issue. Rather, it depends upon *who* he is, and *in what way* he is dangerous. Thus, many persons are allowed to be dangerous to others with impunity; many others are allowed to be dangerous in some ways, but not in others; and some forms of dangerous behavior may legally be allowed, e.g., automobile track racing. Drunken drivers are dangerous both to themselves and to others. It could be shown that drunken drivers injure and kill many more people than, for example, persons with paranoid delusions of persecution or the broad range of sex offenders. Nonetheless, persons labeled paranoid and various sex offenders are quite readily committable while drunken drivers are not. Like-

wise, it seems difficult to understand in what ways an exhibitionist, covered by the "sexual psychopath" statutes, is to be considered more "dangerous" than, for example, a bank robber, persons committing assaults with deadly weapons, or persons involved in the manufacture and sale of defective drugs and appliances. What does become clear is that, as in many other areas of legislation and the administration of criminal justice, a variety of social class and related factors operate to determine what categories of offenses or persons are to be subjected to legal control. And, in the absence of financial and other resources, certain segments of the criminally accused population will more likely be subjected to indeterminate confinement than others.

The basic issue here involves some explicit determination as to the nature and degree of social deviancy which should bring the severe consequences of indeterminate confinement, and a careful balancing of the community's rights to be protected from certain individuals versus the rights of the individuals subjected to such consequences.

IV. PROGRAMS AND FACILITIES FOR MENTALLY DISORDERED OFFENDERS

A. General Considerations

1. The Concept of "Mental Disease" and Deviant Behavior. Treatment[16] programs for offenders, and for those among this group also described as "mentally disordered," often make a distinction between persons who are "socially deviant" and those who are "psychologically or psychiatrically deviant." The former, i.e., the "socially deviant," are seen as the "garden variety" offenders requiring the usual correctional handling and treatment; the latter are viewed as "mentally disordered" and in need of some special mental health services. Unquestionably, there is a considerable overlap and no precise distinction or separation is possible. Indeed, as one moves away from the classical psychiatric disorders, viz., the psychoses and neuroses, and deals with the broad range of "personality and sociopathic disorders," manifestations of "social deviance" tend to become definite criteria for application of psychiatric diagnoses. Persons who are psychiatrically deviated frequently manifest their problems in the form of various socially deviant—although not necessarily antisocial—behaviors. However, social deviance does *not*

---

[15] T. S. Szasz, *Law, Liberty and Psychiatry— An Inquiry into the Social Uses of Mental Health Practices* (New York: Macmillan, 1963).

[16] For use of the word "treatment" here, see note 1. "Therapy" is used to indicate psychological or psychiatric treatment methods.

necessarily imply, nor should it automatically suggest, psychiatric disturbance.

Various criticisms of the concept of "mental disease" have stressed the vagueness and circularity of the numerous definitions, and point also to the obvious social, cultural, and value judgment elements involved in the concept. In addition, the term "mental disease" is often used to include such a broad range of psychological and social problems that it becomes imprecise and lacking in clear meaning.

In a discussion relating to this issue Davidson states:

As doctors, we see any major deviation from the norm as unhealthy; and therefore, any such deviation is ill-health or sickness. Thus, in our book we include as mental disorders such deviations as learning difficulties, stress reactions, sexual deviations, mental deficiency, antisocial behavior. By *book*, I mean the volume called *Diagnostic and Statistical Manual of Mental Disorders*, published by this Association (American Psychiatric Association). Now mark this well—it is going to haunt us. This is a list of *mental disorders*. It says so on the cover. Therefore, "transient situational disturbances"—so listed—must be mental disorders; so are alcoholism, habit disturbances, dyssocial reaction, conduct disturbances, mental deficiencies, speech disturbances and so on. . . .

Therefore, these deviations are illnesses. Our categories are so broad that we would squeeze into them such concepts as hostility to an employer, or marital discord over money.[17]

As Davidson warns here, in the absence of precise and strict use of the term, various manifestations of socially deviant and/or undesirable behavior—including law violations—may somewhat automatically come to be seen as indicative of psychiatric disturbance.

2. Psychiatric Diagnoses and Treatment. Despite the lack of uniformity in the use and meaning of various psychiatric diagnostic categories, it is frequently assumed that such labeling provides accurate information about precise treatment needs. The reasoning here would appear analogous to what is sound and established practice in physical medicine: diagnosis precedes and points to treatment. However, in view of the many and marked differences between the concept of disease as used in physical medicine and in the mental health area, psychiatric diagnoses seldom indicate specific treatment procedures.

The landmark research by Hollingshead and Redlich revealed, among many other significant findings, that there was actually little relationship between the psychiatric diagnosis given to patients and the therapy provided. There was, however, a definite relationship between socio-economic (social class) status and type of therapy provided; this finding being true not only in private practice situations but also in clinics and other public supported agencies.[18]

B. Conceptualization of the Problem

To determine the kinds of interventions and programs indicated for various types of mentally disordered offenders, it is desirable first to have some broad conceptual scheme of the tasks, functions, and objectives involved. We could then ascertain the various programs and services needed to achieve these goals. Although concern here is with offenders displaying fairly marked emotional and mental disturbance, many of the therapeutic and rehabilitative programs and recommendations would also apply to and be desirable for the general offender population. As was indicated earlier, no sharp distinctions can be drawn between individuals who are actually distributed along various points of a continuum. Nor can there be such distinctions regarding the services and facilities required to serve these groups of persons.

Treatment and rehabilitation are not the only objectives of the criminal-judicial-correctional process. There are, in addition, concerns about the protection of the community, deterrence of other potential law violators, and future law violations by the offender, and also some adherence to the notion of "just punishment" in relation to the seriousness of the offense committed. However, there does appear to be a definite shift away from the essentially punitive philosophy underlying the criminal process and move toward greater emphasis on treatment and rehabilitation. This latter trend would seem particularly true for the group seen as needing definite mental health services.

Formal labeling in the criminal-judicial-correctional process does relate fairly directly to how an individual is subsequently to be handled. Adjudicated offenders are managed within correctional programs ranging all the way from probation to confinement in maximum security prisons. Persons adjudicated "not guilty by reason of insanity" (NGRI) are handled by programs within mental hospitals or similar facilities. The purpose of the above labeling is to make an ethical-moral-social

[17] H. A. Davidson, "The Semantics of Psychotherapy," *American Journal of Psychiatry*, vol. 115 (November, 1958).

[18] A. B. Hollingshead and F. C. Redlich, *Social Class and Mental Illness* (New York: Wiley, 1958).

value judgment, and the criteria used relate to such legal determination; these criteria do *not* have much relevance to therapeutic and rehabilitative objectives. Yet, in practice, the insanity acquittal often brings about an automatic commitment to a mental hospital. The implication seems to be that the *legal* determination of "not guilty by reason of insanity," involving social-moral considerations, is somehow related to or even synonymous with the *psychiatric* determination regarding hospitalization based upon therapeutic considerations. This point is of particular importance in regard to handling individuals acquitted by reason of insanity, since criteria and considerations used for social value and moral judgments tend to be confused with those directly related to therapeutic needs.

Following adjudication, therefore, specific evaluations are needed to determine programs required for achievement of the therapeutic and rehabilitative objectives. Needless to say, considerations pertaining to protection of the community from violent and dangerous persons are also important and not necessarily contradictory to the above goals. Indeed, it may be essential in handling severe personality disorders, for example, to treat them in highly structured, non-permissive settings which provide rather firm limits.

Thus, such evaluations would ascertain the overall complex of problems—mental health and others—to be dealt with in achieving the goals of the therapeutic and rehabilitative process. These objectives may be described as the bringing about of improved personal and social functioning and cessation of law-violating behavior by the individual.

Correctional programs have the mission of dealing with the broad range of the offender's problems, while also meeting societal demands for protection of the community either through institutionalization or various degrees of supervision in the community. Correctional institutions, for example, have to address themselves to a variety of tasks in addition to those of boarding and housing large populations at very low cost. There are also educational, vocational, industrial, social, medical, mental health, religious, recreational, and other programs to be provided. To a large extent such needs are, and should be, met within correctional settings. For example, because an offender is illiterate he does not have to be shipped out to a special educational facility. While such an individual does have a serious educational problem, the focus of handling is determined in the social system by the fact of the individual's conviction of a crime and the additional decision that he be confined within a correctional institution. The correctional institution, therefore, is expected to furnish remedial educational facilities. However, if the illiterate is also found to be severely retarded and in need of special care and handling, transfer would then be necessary to an appropriate facility.

In this context, assessment of the mental health needs would not seek simply to detect presence of some emotional difficulties in the individual—which could well be a fairly universal finding. Nor would the concern relate to attaching a psychiatric diagnostic label to the problems noted. Rather, the purpose would be to determine the manner in which the specific psychopathology relates to other problems of the individual, and whether the nature and degree of such mental disturbance and handicaps require that it should be made the focus of special therapeutic efforts. In this regard it would, of course, be necessary also to make some evaluations as to whether the detected psychopathology was treatable.

As far as possible a variety of mental health facilities should be available to meet such needs within institutional correctional programs. However, when the nature and/or severity of the psycho-social problems is such as to require special handling, transfer to an appropriate facility would be necessary. Overt psychotics, severe depressives, suicidal risks, and others of this sort would generally require transfer to a mental hospital type facility.

C. Implications for Programs and Services

Insanity Acquittals. As stated before, the "not guilty by reason of insanity" (NGRI) adjudication is an ethical-moral-social value judgment which does not relate to the therapeutic and custodial needs of the individual. The basic objective of programs for persons so adjudicated involves: (1) therapy for the mental disease from which they were suffering at the time of the crime, and (2) proper custodial handling so that the community is protected from individuals who may be dangerous to other persons.

The automatic commitment to mental hospitals in some jurisdictions of persons found NGRI seems to make several implicit if not explicit assumptions—that the individual is still seriously disturbed and requires commitment, that no other treatment and rehabilitative needs are present, and that recovery from the mental disease will invariably or automatically lead to cessation of law violations. These are all very questionable assumptions. The individual may, for example, have recovered from the mental disturbance, or he may have a variety of educational, vocational, and other social problems usually handled within specialized correctional programs. In jurisdictions with broader tests for criminal responsibility, persons with personality disorders may be acquitted by reason of insanity and be sent to mental hospitals for treatment. Since they have been labeled "sick" it is understandable that the mental hospital is seen as the treatment institution. However, many psychiatrists experienced in the care and handling of such persons within typical mental hospital programs state that personality disorders generally may better be treated within good correctional facilities. Furthermore, as was noted earlier, there are correctional facilities which have educational, vocational, and treatment programs surpassing those in some state mental hospitals.

There are conflicting views as to how and in what sorts of settings persons adjudicated NGRI may best be treated. These persons are seen as having two main characteristics: (*a*) they violated a law and thus came within the criminal process, and (*b*) they were judged to be suffering from a "mental disease," which fact removed them from the criminal-correctional process. Such individuals are, therefore, "mentally disordered law-violators." Arguments arise as to whether such persons should be managed in a fashion similar to that for law-violators; or, as mentally disturbed patients. One viewpoint would argue that "a schizophrenic is a schizophrenic and cannot be treated differently because he happened to commit an offense." Another point of view would emphasize the fact that the individual is *not* just a mental patient because, unlike most mental patients, he has committed an offense and furthermore may be dangerous.

There is limited research which would shed light specifically on the above controversy. However, some relevant material is available.

A study of 10,247 male patients released from mental hospitals and followed up for a period of 5.6 years revealed that the annual arrest rate for patients was far lower than that of the general population (122 per 10,000 as compared with 491). Patients who had been in mental hospitals and who had a prior record of arrest had a rate of rearrest which compared favorably with figures available for persons in the general population who had arrest records. Furthermore, arrest rates among patients were *inversely* related to severity of mental symptoms. That is, the more blatant the indications of mental illness during hospitalization, the *lower* was the rate of arrest following release.[19]

There remain many unknown factors in the above study and specific conclusions may therefore be hard to draw in regard to mentally disordered offenders—particularly our NGRI group. However, the study does appear to refute once again the popularly held sterotype about the "dangerous mental patients" released from mental hospitals. Quite obviously, the infrequent acts of violence committed by ex-mental patients seem to draw greater publicity and attention. Mental health professionals experienced in working with both the mental hospital and prison population seem to have little doubt that many more actually dangerous persons are housed in and released from penal institutions than from mental hospitals.

There is another recent study which deals more specifically with mentally disordered law-violators and has rather direct relevance to our NGRI group.

Morrow and Peterson[20] followed up discharged psychiatric offenders, viz., those adjudicated NGRI and "criminal sexual psychopaths" released from Missouri institutions. Among other things, these researchers sought to determine how similar such "psychiatric offenders" were to prison inmates and to other non-criminal psychiatric patients in recidivism patterns and prognostic background variables. The results suggested close similarity between the NGRI group and discharged prison inmates by virtue of their nearly identical criminal recidivism rates, predominance of economic offenses, and prognostic variables common to both these groups. Dissimilarity to non-criminal psychiatric patients was suggested by the lack of prognostic relationship between outcome and either diagnosis or previous psychiatric hospitalization.

In regard then to the sub-group defined as NGRI the above study would seem to refute the argument that a schizophrenic is a schizophrenic regardless of whether he happened to commit an offense. Not only is the diagnostic category broad and unreliable but, in addition, schizophrenics and other patients who commit crimes do indeed become involved in the criminal process and thus have to be viewed and handled somewhat differently from schizophrenics who go directly to mental hospitals for therapy.

However, it is following adjudication that evaluations are necessary to make more rational therapy-revelant decisions concerning the individual, if indeed treatment and rehabili-

[19] New York State Dept. of Mental Health, "Criminal Acts of Ex-Mental Patients." (American Psychiatric Association, Mental Hospital Service, 1962).

[20] W. R. Morrow and D. B. Peterson, "Follow-up of Discharged Psychiatric Offenders," *Journal of Criminal Law, Criminology and Police Science,* vol. 57 (March, 1966).

tation are important objectives in the handling of such persons. The mental health evaluation would have to be broader in scope than it currently seems to be in order that several important matters may be determined: (1) whether the individual is still suffering from mental disturbance, and if so, the nature and severity of the condition; (2) what other therapeutic, custodial, and rehabilitative needs are indicated, e.g., whether the individual requires a variety of educational-vocational rehabilitative services, or whether he may pose a danger to the person of others; (3) in view of the above findings, what particular type of program would be most appropriate for such an individual.

The above evaluation could be conducted in mental hospitals—but with inclusion of professionals able to determine the broader rehabilitative needs of the person—or they may also be conducted within outpatient mental health facilities.

Keeping in mind the aforementioned conceptual scheme for determination of therapeutic and related requirements, it may well be that in a number of NGRI cases the particular need will be for a special facility which could provide a full range of psychiatric services specially geared to such a population, and in addition provide adequate rehabilitative facilities and secure custody for protection of the community. However, such a facility would be more like a hospital than a penal institution.

Other NGRI persons could, depending upon the presence and degree of mental disorder and indications of dangerousness to the person of others, either be discharged outright, or be treated on an outpatient basis in community mental health facilities, or be treated on a day-care or partial hospitalization basis in developing Community Mental Health Centers, or may even be treated in the typical "open" mental hospital. All such recommendations regarding the particular therapeutic needs and related dispositional alternatives would, of course, be made to the court and be subject to judicial review.

Community-Based Correctional Programs. Community-based correctional efforts include work with probationers, parolees, offenders returned to the community through pre-release, halfway house, and other such programs. In the main, such correctional facilities have to obtain mental health services for their clients through already overcrowded community facilities. There are a few locations—mainly large metropolitan areas—where special services are provided through court or legal psychiatric clinics. A few of the larger probation departments have hired their own mental health consultants.

Perhaps a primary need in the above correctional programs relates to the development of sound and reliable criteria to predict probations, parole, and other future adjustment of the mentally disordered offender. While work has been done in development of parole prediction and base expectancy tables, the use of such devices seems rather limited. Such predictive instruments would not, of course, be the only considerations involved in these decisions. It has already been emphasized that such decisions involve issues other than the treatment and rehabilitation of such offenders. However, probation, parole, and other release and program-oriented decisions for mentally disordered offenders should be based upon objective, reliable and scientifically developed instruments which could predict on the basis of complex interactions between particular individuals and the specific environments to which they will be returned. Such probabilistic statements could suggest the kinds of therapeutic and other services indicated to attain particular objectives. Depending upon various social policy and other such considerations, the goals may well vary. They may focus on best chance for rehabilitation, least risk to the community, least overall cost, etc. Validation, verification, and constant efforts to improve such instruments would lead to additions, deletions, and modifications of variables found relevant to the decisions to be made.

This brings us to a discussion of psychiatric and psychological treatment approaches with offenders. Traditional psychotherapeutic concepts, techniques, and methods, used more typically with anxious, motivated, verbal and middle-class patients, seem generally to be neither too relevant nor efficient when applied —or perhaps misapplied—to lower-class persons and offenders. Problems posed by the lack of interest and motivation for behavior change in many of the acting-out personality disorders, for example, are often further compounded by the equally poor motivation of many therapists to work with such persons.

Assumptions are generally made that while some persons may benefit more from psychotherapy than others, certainly no one is likely to be harmed by such treatment. However, many criteria and indications deemed relevant to the use of psychotherapy have not been subjected to evaluative research. It may well be that many of these assumptions and criteria require re-examination.

For example, the PICO (Pilot Intensive Counseling) Project conducted by the California Department of Corrections found that those rated as "non-amenable" to treatment seemed actually to do *worse* when treated with casework counseling than "non-amenables" not so treated.[21] Another study conducted in a naval confinement and retraining installation showed that subjects classified as socially immature *improved* under more-or-less conventional discipline and generally authoritarian supervision, but were actually made *worse* by exposure to intensive psychotherapy.[22]

Much effort has, therefore, to be directed toward development of treatment models and techniques specifically suited to this population, increasing use of behavioral and other approaches showing more promise, and strategies for more effective utilization and development of the rather limited mental health manpower and other resources.

It has long been apparent that many mentally disordered offenders require a program which would provide closer supervision, structure, and treatment than is provided by probation or parole, and yet who do not require institutional confinement. To meet such needs, halfway houses and pre-release guidance centers have been developed. However, typically such programs are for persons being released from penal confinement; they are not available to persons on probation, do not provide longer periods of stay, and do not have special therapeutic facilities for those with serious psychological problems. Persons on probation and parole, including those in halfway houses and pre-release guidance centers, needing particular psychiatric services, could obtain them through existing community mental health agencies. However, many mentally disordered offenders also require educational and vocational rehabilitation, and may need a degree of supervision and control not typically available within mental health programs. Thus, an important need is for the development of small community-based residential facilities combining correctional, mental health, and vocational rehabilitative services.

Such a facility might be referred to as a Community Treatment and Training Center. It would provide essentially residential facilities but could also develop day-care and night-care type services for this particular group of persons. The Center would be designed for persons going through the criminal process who manifest definite mental health problems and vocational and social handicaps; and/or who seem unable to face the demands of independent living in the community due to the above impairment, and who do not appear to require correctional institutionalization. The treatment and training program would be especially designed to equip such persons to function more adequately in the community. There may indeed be some persons who are so handicapped or otherwise impaired that they may remain in such a facility indefinitely. This would apply to some mentally disordered offenders who currently go through correctional institutions on a revolving-door basis. Special provisions would have to be developed to enable such individuals to utilize the facility without having to engage in law violations to become eligible.

The basic concept involved in the development of such centers is to provide services and facilities specially designed to meet the needs of particular target groups. The idea allows considerable flexibility in the design of such programs and could be implemented to serve other groups of persons with various types of psychiatric, social, vocational, and other handicaps, e.g., chronic alcoholics and the mentally retarded.

Depending on the particular target population, program design, local administrative structure, and other such factors, the administration of such facilities may well vary somewhat. However, to the extent that the basic idea proposed here concerns persons who would mainly be adjudicated offenders, such centers could be under Corrections with mental health services provided by State or local agencies. Such an administrative pattern already exists in many States.

For correctional inmates who become psychotic or are otherwise seriously disturbed, mental hospital type facilities are needed. However, in some States the problem seems to be that in view of the increasing trend toward having more "open" mental hospitals, many such institutions are reluctant to accept mentally disordered offenders—some of whom may be dangerous and all of whom would require a degree of secure custody. Several States, therefore, have plans to construct special institutions to house mentally disordered offenders who frequently create serious problems for the general correctional program.

Before States begin to build new and special institutions for the above group, very serious attention should be given to improving mental health staff and facilities *within existing correctional programs* to better handle and treat such persons. It could well be that improved mental health and related facilities within the correctional setting would in many instances

[21] S. Adams, *Interaction between Individual Interview Therapy and Treatment Amenability in Older Youth Authority Wards*, Monograph No. 3, California Board of Corrections (July, 1961).

[22] J. D. Grant and M. Q. Grant, "A Group Dynamic Approach to the Treatment of Non-Conformists in the Navy," *Annals of American Academy of Political and Social Science* (March, 1959), p. 322.

offer a better solution than construction of a new institution.

What seems important, then, in regard to special institutions—both the facilities discussed above and also the smaller residential Community Treatment and Training Centers described earlier—is that Corrections should begin to develop facilities which would combine and integrate therapeutic rehabilitative and custodial features within programs of wider scope. This should certainly be true of any new facilities constructed and also in terms of changes within existing correctional programs. What is, perhaps, even more important and merits special emphasis is that, to the extent a variety of community-based treatment and rehabilitative programs can be developed to provide close supervision and other assistance, there would be less need to resort to long term institutionalization of many offenders. There is evidence from some recent research that intensive community supervision and treatment can be a cheaper and more effective means for handling many law violators.

THE MENTALLY RETARDED OFFENDER

Bertram S. Brown, M.D., and Thomas F. Courtless, Ph.D.

I. INTRODUCTION

The problem of the mentally retarded offender is small in absolute numbers and large in significance. It concerns the overlap of two major aspects of the human condition, behavior and intelligence, an overlap where the unthinking, unfeeling reaction is to castigate the doubly handicapped individuals as both stupid and bad. And yet as a civilization we can be measured by our response to these unfortunates. Less humanistic but as important is that a deeper understanding of the mentally retarded offender may yield important insights into the general problem of anti-social behavior and yield new knowledge in the complex area of retardation.

Viewed historically, professional interest in, and society's responses to, the mentally retarded offender developed within three periods, each manifesting a set of distinct characteristics. Assigning arbitrary levels and dates to these periods, we find a period of Early Enthusiasm: 1890–1920; a period of Denial and Neglect: 1921–1960; and the Contemporary Scene: 1961——. Generalizing rather sweepingly, interest in, and responses to, mentally retarded offenders proceed, during these three periods, from a dramatic emphasis on the offender as almost always feebleminded, through a period of over-reaction entailing the relegation of mental retardation as it relates to criminal behavior to a secondary position so that it is almost totally ignored, to the very recent resurgence of attention given to the relationship between retardation and anti-social behavior.

A. Early Enthusiasm: 1890–1920

During this period two phases may be distinguished. The first of these, historically ranging from the latter part of the nineteenth century until the introduction of intelligence testing in the United States, may be termed a *pre-testing phase* (1890–1914). It is characteristic of much of this phase that mental retardation was linked to crime, with poverty, insanity, and physical and moral degeneracy all in one rather vague category of deviancy. As Martha Clark, a training school worker, stated in 1894: ". . . Crime, imbecility, and insanity are hereditary diseases of the mind. . . . (All) non-organic cases of imbecility show somewhere in the family annals there has been opium-eating, immoral living, drunkenness, insanity, imbecility or actual crime." ("The Relation of Imbecility to Pauperism and Crime," *Arena*, 10 [November, 1894]: 789.)

During this pre-testing phase, mental retardation seemed to be viewed as almost automatically resulting in criminal behavior, and

The paper was reproduced by the President's Commission on Law Enforcement (1967), and no copyright may be placed on material excerpted. Reprinted with the permission of the authors.

Fernald in his now classic article "The Imbecile with Criminal Instincts" (1909) indicated that every feebleminded person was a potential delinquent or criminal "needing only the proper environment and opportunity" to overtly manifest his criminality. This statement is representative of the feeling in the field prior to the introduction of a significant amount of scientific testing.

With the onset of intelligence testing in the United States immediately preceding World War I, an *early testing phase* may be identified within this period. This phase is characterized by a tendency to resist the lumping of such phenomena as mental retardation, crime, insanity, and degeneracy into a broad category of deviancy. During much of this phase the factor of mental defect is made to stand out as a separate and major causal variable in crime and delinquency. Beginning with Goddard's work and lasting until the 1920's, many studies were undertaken employing intelligence tests to determine the proportion of criminal and delinquent populations falling into the retarded range. The reports of these early studies claimed that as many as 100% of such offenders were defective. The enthusiastic and extreme claims of this phase were relatively short-lived.

B. The Period of Denial and Neglect: 1921–1960

Soon after psychometric testing of inmate populations began in the United States an interesting reaction set in. This reaction is manifested by a steady movement away from the position that intelligence is a significant factor in the causation of criminal and delinquent behavior with the accompanying conclusion that most offenders are retarded. The early intelligence testers were, at least partly, responsible for this development. The spotty methodological foundation of much of the ambitious early studies led to an almost ludicrous variety of claims as to the prevalence of mental retardation among criminal populations. . . .

What may be of crucial importance at this stage of the period of "Denial and Neglect" is that within American criminology the reaction away from assigning a causal significance to mental retardation was part of the general ecological school's extension of the theories of the French sociologist Tarde, whose famous Laws of Imitation postulated that behavior is learned in a social process whether it be criminal or non-criminal behavior. More importantly for criminology, it represented a sharp breakaway from the constitutional interpretations pioneered by Lombroso in Italy and the neo-Lombrosians on the European continent.

In many respects the impact of the ecological school in criminology is the decisive factor in current practice and research. The anomie or opportunity structure theoretical frame of reference within which many American criminologists now operate is a logical extension of the concern expressed during the 1920's and 1930's about the deteriorated high-delinquency area. One unfortunate by-product of this development has only recently been offset. It is the almost total neglect of the intelligence factor in explaining criminality and delinquency. The general lack of concern for the retardation factor was verified through a review of twenty criminology texts commonly employed in American colleges and universities in 1960. Most of these make some mention of mental retardation, but only to the extent of indicating that it is not a significant variable, and then summarizing the older studies attempting to establish a relationship between retardation and criminal behavior, highlighting their dubious methodology and possibly erroneous conclusions.

C. The Contemporary Scene: 1961——

Quite recently the issue of the relationship between mental retardation and criminal behavior has received increased attention. Significantly, much of this revived interest has been generated by the legal community and not by criminologists. In 1961, the American Bar Foundation published its landmark volume *The Mentally Disabled and the Law.* (F. T. Lindman and D. M. McIntyre [University of Chicago Press, 1961.]) This extensive study includes one section dealing with the relationship of mental disability and the criminal law. While the major emphasis of this study is directed toward the mentally ill, attention is given to the problems of the retarded or defective accused person. Issues related to the general area of criminal responsibility, a review of defective delinquency and sexual psychopath statutes point to some of the problems involved in dealing with the mentally retarded defendant in a criminal case.

Also in 1961 interest in mentally retarded offenders was greatly stimulated when the late President John F. Kennedy appointed a distinguished panel of physicians, lawyers, scientists, judges, and civic leaders to review the field of mental retardation. In particular, the report of the Presidential Panel's Task Force on Law focused attention on many crucial problem areas involving retarded persons coming into contact with the criminal law. Some of these areas are competency to stand trial, criminal responsibility, admissibility of confessions, and the advisability of incarcerating mentally retarded offenders in penal or correctional institutions. This report has led to new research efforts encompassing retardation and antisocial behavior. An example of such research effort is the three-year empirical study, supported by a grant from Public Health Service, being undertaken by The George Washington University Institute of Law, Psychiatry and Criminology entitled *The Mentally Retarded and the Law*.

II. BRIEF HISTORICAL OVERVIEW OF THE MANAGEMENT AND TREATMENT OF RETARDED OFFENDERS

Generally, one can say that in the United States the treatment or handling of mentally retarded offenders centers historically around attempts to provide separate or special institutional facilities. There is some evidence to indicate that the drive for such management and treatment of the offender conforms to the patterns of interest in the retarded outlined in the first part of this paper. That is, at around the turn of the century there were many proponents of such specialized treatment programs and facilities, but for a substantial period beginning with the 1920's little or nothing seems to have been done to implement the early recommendations beyond a very few pioneer facilities. It can also be stated at this point that much of the strong interest in the provision of separate institutional handling of retarded offenders seems clearly to have been related to the fear that committing retarded offenders to institutions where non-offending retardates were housed had a deleterious effect on the welfare of the non-offenders, and was thus not directed at a more therapeutic setting for the offender.

Attempts to provide specialized facilities for the retarded offender developed a strong sense of urgency after Fernald identified and described the defective delinquent in 1909. Essentially, Fernald's concern for separate institutionalization was based upon the poor influence the defective delinquent had on the non-delinquent defective. In his words: ". . . it is most unfortunate that this criminal type of defective . . . should complicate the care and training of the ordinary defective without criminal habits or propensities. They have had a very bad influence on the ordinary defective who constitutes the legitimate problem of the school for the feebleminded." It should be stressed here that Fernald was not recommending separate facilities because he was concerned for the correctional treatment of the defective delinquent. This is quite clear in his description of this type of offender when he indicated that defective delinquents "cannot be discharged because they are unsafe persons for community life."

Fernald was by no means the first to advocate specialized institutionalization. Clark, in 1894, stated that only by special segregation of the feebleminded offender could society be free from the threat posed by him. In her colorful language, Clark recommended that those children "who in early life portrayed . . . viciousness and . . . [who were] even slightly below par intellectually should be kept from society as we would keep poison from food."

Following Fernald's pioneering statements, Goddard in 1912 made a strong case for special and separate handling of the feebleminded delinquent. Attacking the tendency he saw in society to blame the school and church as well as other institutions for the fact that there are large numbers of mentally retarded offenders (attacking them on the basis that feeblemindedness is caused by heredity or accident rather than by socio-cultural variables), he stressed that penal institutions were inappropriate for their care. He called on the American Prison Association to recommend the removal of these inmates from the prisons to more suitable environments. Based upon his belief that almost all (at least two-thirds) of the feebleminded delinquents come by their defect through heredity, Goddard indicated that the only practicable solution to the problem was a twofold one: sterilization and long-term "colonization and segregation." (H. H. Goddard, "Feeblemindedness and Crime", *Proceedings of the American Prison Association* [1912], pp. 353–57.)

As a result of the contributions of Fernald and others, some early steps were taken to provide separate institutions for the defective delinquent. Davies reported on the establishment of the Massachusetts State Farm (Bridgewater) and the Napanoch (New York) institutions for defective delinquents. (S. P. Davies, *Social Control of the Mentally Deficient* [New York: Crowell, 1939].)

. . .

Recent developments in the handling of defective delinquent offenders include the Patuxent Institution located in Maryland, which by statute is designed to treat the offender who "constitutes a danger to society" and who is either emotionally disturbed or mentally retarded. This special institution, while rather unique on the American scene, by combining emotionally disturbed and/or mentally retarded offenders into the defective delinquency category may be viewed as a return to the much earlier tendency in criminology to categorize a wide variety of deviants into one legally defined administrative entity. Other recent developments in this area include defective delinquency statutes in other jurisdictions as well as sexual psychopathy laws. However, many of these do not provide for the separate handling of such offenders.

Turning, for the moment, to the international scene in the handling and treatment of defective delinquents, it is interesting to note that in contrast to the United States, reports from England and Sweden would seem to indicate that personnel there during the first half of this century were more concerned with providing a therapeutic or treatment orientation in the institutionalization of defective delinquents. Also, they were apparently much less concerned about the effects of combining defective delinquents with non-delinquent defectives.

. . .

It would seem that the English and Swedish ideas of "retraining" and "resocialization," motivating workers in the field in the post-World War II period, have had little in common with the American emphasis on security and custodial care seemingly desired as much for the benefit of non-delinquent defective and the administrator of institutions as for the welfare of the defective delinquent. We know, from the survey of penal and correctional institutions which will be discussed in some detail later, that most institutions in this country are unable or unwilling to provide for the special handling of retarded offenders, either in terms of treatment programs or segregated facilities. In fact, over 90% of all institutions responding to the survey stated that they did not provide special separate facilities for retarded offenders, and over half (56%) were not able to provide any specialized training or therapy services for their retarded inmates.

Certainly, significant attention to the relationship between mental retardation and criminal behavior and the concomitant issue of the treatment and handling of mentally retarded offenders has, until recently, been characterized by a distinct lack of scientific inquiry, and a necessary corollary has been a glaring deficiency in the development of new treatment and handling strategies.

III. THE DEFECTIVE DELINQUENT—
CHANGING DEFINITIONS

The problem of clinical definitions of defective delinquency is necessarily related to the issue of legal control of such offenders. There are, today, statutory definitions of defective delinquents and institutions authorized and designed to deal with such offenders. Before examining a few of these, it is instructive to note what C. S. Chandler and his associates found in a 1958 survey of the arraignment, examination, and confinement of defective delinquents in the United States. (C. S. Chandler et al., "Arraignment, Examination and Confinement of the Mentally Defective Delinquent," American Journal of Mental Deficiency, 63 (January, 1957): 723–29.) They state in the article that "it comes as something of a surprise . . . to learn that there is no agreement as to a definition or description of the defective delinquent. A perusal of the literature indicates that little or no agreement [exists] regarding a definition and interviews with persons in the field confirm this contention. . . . Much of the controversy regarding treatment, place of confinement, etc. has resulted from this confusion." They go on to state that given the absence of a clinical definition, their survey was basically designed to determine whether there exists any "legal basis . . . for defining the defective delinquent, confining him, etc. If such a legal basis did exist, it would be easier to isolate his clinical symptoms and then try to treat him in the light of present-day knowledge."

As a result of the replies to their survey questionnaire, the authors concluded that very few states had made any attempt at the passage of specific statutes dealing with this offender, and that "even among those [states] who do, there is a difference of opinion as to whether the defective delinquent is chronologically a minor or an adult. Questions regarding the upper and lower limits of intellectual attainment have not been adequately resolved. Moreover, the legal responsibilities of the adult defective who has committed criminal acts have not been clearly determined."

Current statutory definitions relating to defective delinquency do not significantly contribute to increased precision in this definitional area. Many of the legally formulated definitions relate primarily to sexual psychopath statutes. For example, in California a sexual psychopath is defined as "any person who is affected, in a disposing way to the commission of sexual offenses, and in a degree constituting him a menace to the health or safety of others, with any of the following conditions: (a) mental disease or disorder, (b) psychopathic personality, (c) marked departures from normal mentality."

In Vermont, the statute defines a "psychopathic personality" to "mean those persons who by a habitual course of misconduct in sexual matters have evidenced an utter lack of power to control their sexual impulse, and who, as a result, are likely to attack or otherwise inflict injury, pain or other evil on the object of their uncontrolled desire." This statute is applied to mentally defective delinquents who are mentally deficient or psychopathic.

There are, however, statutes referring to defective delinquents which do not confine themselves to sexual offenders. For example, Ohio refers to psychopathic offenders, who are defined as persons who exhibit psychopathic personalities. Such an offender is defined by statute as one who manifests "criminal tendencies and who by reason thereof is a menace to the public. Psychopathic personality is evidenced by such traits or characteristics inconsistent with the age of such person, as emotional immaturity and instability, impulsive, irresponsible, reckless, and unruly acts, excessively self-centered activities, deficient power of self-discipline, lack of normal capacity to learn from experience, marked deficiency of moral sense or control." The statute has been applied to mentally deficient offenders since these do exhibit "traits or characteristics inconsistent with the age of such person," and also show a lack of normal capacity to learn from experience. In Oregon, the statute is applied to persons convicted of rape, murder, or manslaughter or other crimes at the discretion of the court, providing the court finds that such person "has mental or emotional disturbance, deficiency or condition predisposing him to the commission of a crime to a degree rendering the person a menace to the safety of others."

The approach taken by Maryland differs significantly from those of other states mentioned in that a specialized institution for the defective delinquent—Patuxent Institution—was established after the enactment of the so-called "defective delinquency statute" in 1951. There is possible under this statute an indeterminate commitment of convicted adult offenders (convicted of a variety of specified offenses) in this institution. A defective delinquent is defined by the statute as ". . . An individual who, by the demonstration of persistent aggravated anti-social or criminal behavior, evidences a propensity toward criminal activity, and who is found to have either such intellectual deficiency or emotional unbalance, or both, as to clearly demonstrate an actual danger to society so as to require such confinement and treatment, when appropriate, as may make it reasonably safe for society to terminate the confinement and treatment." It is interesting to note that this specialized institution, which is unique on the American scene, receives offenders for confinement and treatment who clinically may be subdivided into those who are mentally retarded and those who tend to be sociopathic (anti-social type). The staff of the Institution has published numerous articles describing the operation of the Institution as well as defining the clinical characteristics of the inmates. The definition as derived from most of these articles is clearly one of sociopathic personality disturbance (psychopath under the older nomenclature), and no clear distinction was made in the early articles between inmates who are primarily "emotionally unbalanced" and those who are mentally retarded. From these earlier articles, one might say that one of the most recent innovations in the treatment of the defective delinquent represented a return to the much earlier tendency in the field to categorize a wide variety of deviants into one diagnostic entity. More recently, however, the staff of the Institution has focused its attention both for research and treatment purposes on the mentally retarded offender.

IV. A SURVEY OF THE INSTITUTIONALIZED MENTALLY RETARDED OFFENDER

The review of the literature upon which the comments found in the first two parts of this paper were based revealed that no comprehensive data are currently available regarding the numbers, problems, and treatment of the retarded offender incarcerated in penal and correctional institutions in the United States Consequently, the authors set out to systematically survey a portion of the mentally retarded offender population beginning in December of 1963. For this survey, all penal and correctional institutions in the United States were asked to supply information about the I.Q. distribution of their populations, types of offenses committed by inmates with low reported intelligence, treatment programs available, and management problems and practices related to retarded offenders. The penal and correctional institutions surveyed did not include the approximately 3,000 local jails and workhouses where short-term offenders are confined. The combined populations of the institutions surveyed totaled 217,280 as of December 31, 1963. The great majority of these inmates were serving sentences of one year or longer.

A second phase of the research, dealing with the administration of criminal justice in cases involving retarded offenders and accused persons, was carried out in the summer of 1966 under the auspices of The George Washington University Institute of Law, Psychiatry and Criminology. This phase will be discussed later in this paper.

Completed questionnaires were received from over 80% of the institutions surveyed, representing some 200,000 incarcerated offenders. I.Q. scores were reported on 90,477 of these inmates. While findings relative to the proportion of retardates in the total prison population of the United States must be qualified by the fact that the scores received represented a non-random sampling of the total incarcerated population, an analysis of incomplete questionnaires together with instances in which no replies were obtained revealed no biasing factors such as type of institution for which no I.Q. data were available, geographical location of such institutions, etc.

In generalizing from the data obtained, one must be aware of the problems involved in the determination of operational criteria of mental retardation. The survey results depended upon intelligence testing administered by the responding institutions as the only readily available basis for making decisions regarding retardation on a nation-wide scale. As such, the results, therefore, must be examined in the light of the fact that various correctional and penal institutions throughout the country employ different testing instruments, and dissimilarities in testing situations must be taken into account. Given these limitations, it was decided to operationally define mental retardation for the survey as measured intelligence falling below I.Q. 70. It should be noted that the I.Q. 70 cut-off point is in accord with the criteria established by the American Association on Mental Deficiency ("A Manual on Terminology and Classification in Mental Retardation," *American Journal of Mental Deficiency*, monograph supplement, September, 1959, pp. 58–59). Other elements of the Association's criteria, namely the impairment in adaptive behavior, were, of necessity, impossible to examine given the scope of the survey. From a general perspective, impairment in adaptive behavior is implied by the very fact of institutionalization for anti-social behavior. Adaptive behavior is being more carefully examined for a sampling of incarcerated offenders in the second phase of the study which will be mentioned later in this paper.

A. General Findings of the Major Survey

Summarized below are some of the more significant general findings from the survey:

1. Based on over 90,000 cases of reported I.Q. scores, a mean I.Q. of 93.2 with a standard deviation of 17.1 was computed. Using I.Q. 69 as the upper limit of the mentally retarded range, it was found that about 9.5%

of the reported cases could be classified as mentally retarded. If we were to make some tentative generalizations about all incarcerated adult offenders in the United States, we would estimate that there are currently somewhat over 20,000 inmates in penal and correctional institutions (excluding local jails and workhouses) with I.Q. scores below 70.

Further, it was determined that approximately 1.6% of the surveyed population (1,454 inmates) had I.Q. scores below 55. Making another tentative estimation, this finding would indicate that over 3,300 inmates in our correctional and penal institutions fall below I.Q. 55, and may be moderately to severely retarded (based upon the AAMD classification scheme).

In terms of the percentage of inmates found to fall within the retarded range, the survey did not reveal a return to some of the more outlandish conclusions of the early testing phase discussed at the beginning of this paper. However, in terms of absolute numbers, the problem of the incarceration of mentally retarded offenders may be seen as a significant one with 20,000 possible retardates serving sentences in the United States as criminally responsible adults.

An intensive follow-up of a sample by a psychologist at the Institute of Law, Psychiatry and Criminology indicates that 75% of those selected by the institutional criteria of mental retardation fall below I.Q. 70 on careful retesting. This follow-up is discussed more fully in a later section.

2. The range of reported I.Q. scores for the 90,477 inmates was determined to be from a low of 17 to a high of 145. However, as mentioned earlier, one must reckon with the variety of instruments used to measure intelligence, personnel employed to administer these tests, etc. For example, we found a rather bewildering array of tests used by the institutions to measure intelligence. It must be pointed out, though, that the most frequently employed tests (used by about three-fourths of the institutions reporting) were the Wechsler Intelligence Scale for Children and the Wechsler Adult Intelligence Scale. Although about 75% of the institutions reported that intelligence tests were administered by psychologists, it was found that other institutions used social workers, a few reported the use of classification officers, and five institutions reported using inmates in the administration of testing under the supervision of a psychologist.

3. The proportion of incarcerated offenders falling below I.Q. 70 varies rather sharply

as one controls for geographical region. For instance, the highest percentage of retarded (again using reported I.Q. scores of 69 as the upper limit) among incarcerated adult offenders was found to be 24.3 in the states designated as East South Central (including Kentucky, Tennessee, Alabama, and Mississippi). Following closely behind this region was the West South Central area with a percentage of I.Q.'s below 70 of 20.6 (this region includes Arkansas, Louisiana, Oklahoma, and Texas). The lowest percentage of retarded offenders among incarcerated criminal adults was found to obtain in the Mountain States (Montana, Idaho, Wyoming, Colorado, New Mexico, Arizona, Utah, and Nevada) where only 2.6% had I.Q.'s below 70. The next lowest percentage was found to obtain among the Pacific States (Washington, Oregon, California, Alaska, and Hawaii) with a percentage of 5.4.

These variations, indicating the operation of socio-cultural variables, are consistent with other findings regarding general intelligence throughout the United States. For instance, Throndike and Gallup report similar differences with respect to verbal intelligence, and more recently Ginzberg and Bray, in analyzing rejection rates of registrants for military service during World War II, clearly show that such rejection rates vary by geographical region. This variation conforms quite closely to variation in intelligence testing scores found in the survey of penal and correctional institutions. Particularly, in the Ginzberg and Bray study, the states designated "Far West" had the lowest rejection rates, with states designated as "South East" and "South West" having the highest rates. (For the Thorndike and Gallup findings, see "Verbal Intelligence in the American Adults," *Journal of General Psychology*, 30 [1941]: 75–85. The Ginzberg and Bray study is from *The Uneducated* [New York: Columbia University Press, 1953].)

4. It is perhaps quite significant to note that several institutions reported their inability to determine what the I.Q. distribution was for their populations. These institutions do not routinely test inmates and their records of inmate histories are incomplete at best. However, somewhat over 70% of all reporting institutions did indicate that testing was routine for all admissions.

5. Included in the questionnaire form sent to each institution were questions relating specifically to the offenses committed by those inmates with I.Q. scores below 70. Equiva-

lent information about offenses of the general inmate population was obtained for comparison purposes. Each institution was requested to rank the first, second, and third most frequently committed offense among retarded inmates. After analyzing the replies, it was found that 38% of the institutions ranked the offenses breaking and entering and burglary as most frequently committed by the retarded. About 13% of the institutions reported homicide as the most frequently committed offense. The crime least frequently reported was the combined category of rape and other sexual offenses, this being recorded in only 5% of all institutions responding to this portion of the questionnaire. The findings clearly indicated that, based upon the information supplied by the institutions, the property offenses falling into the general category of larceny breaking-and-entering burglary were by far the most commonly committed offenses by inmates with low reported intelligence. A surprising finding was that homicide was reported as more frequently committed by the institutionalized retarded than among the non-retarded segments of the institutional populations. Later in this paper more data regarding crimes committed by retarded inmates will be reported.

One must bear in mind in interpreting offense data that such crimes reported in this survey relate only to offenses committed by incarcerated retardates and do not justify any superficial generalizations made to the rank ordering of criminal offenses committed by retardates in the total distribution of crimes committed in the United States.

6. Each of the surveyed institutions was asked to supply information about ongoing programs specifically designed for retardates. Seventy-five (or 56%) of those institutions responding to this question reported that no specialized programs of any kind were available. Six responding institutions provided a full range of individual and group psychotherapy, academic and vocational as well as special education programs. Of all institutions reporting some special programs for the retarded, special and/or vocational education was by far the most frequently reported program.

A most significant factor in the general lack of specialized programming for retarded inmates is the general lack of mental health manpower resources available to responding institutions. On the questionnaire form information was requested from each institution concerning the numbers of psychiatrists and psychologists employed by them on full-time or part-time bases. A total of 166 institutions replied to the relevant questions. These institutions housed 153,491 inmates, representing approximately 79% of all inmates incarcerated in state adult correctional and penal institutions. These institutions indicated that they employed a total of 54 psychiatrists full-time, with an additional 165 psychiatrists employed on various part-time and less bases. This makes a grand total of 219 psychiatrists employed by 166 institutions throughout the country. Examining the category "psychologist," it was found that these 166 institutions employed a total of 93 full-time psychologists and 95 on various part-time statuses.

In considering these raw data relative to the employment of psychologists and psychiatrists, one must bear in mind that the 166 responding institutions included specialized facilities for emotionally disturbed and/or mentally retarded offenders, as well as general correctional and penal institutions. When the specialized facilities were considered separately from the others (these constituting 6 of the 166 institutions), it was found that they accounted for 40 of the 54 full-time psychiatrists, and 19 of the part-time psychiatrists. This leaves a total of only 14 full-time psychiatrists being employed by 160 institutions in this country. Examining the category psychologist, 11 of the 93 full-time psychologists were employed by these 6 specialized facilities. This results in a total of 82 full-time psychologists being employed by the 160 general penal and correctional institutions.

Looking of these resources in terms of numbers of inmates, the 6 specialized facilities, housing a total of 6,825 inmates, employ 40 full-time and 19 part-time psychiatrists; 11 full-time and 10 part-time psychologists. We thus have a situation in which a total of 146,662 inmates were confined in non-specialized facilities with access to a total of 14 full-time psychiatrists and 82 full-time psychologists.

An attempt was made through the survey to elicit data from the institutions regarding the numbers of specially trained educational personnel who work exclusively or primarily with retarded inmates. However, the responding institutions included in the tabulation all sorts of educational personnel, including inmates acting as teachers, so that it was impossible to arrive at any meaningful finding regarding this important aspect of institutional programming. It should be noted again, however, that in the questions relating to the types of programs provided by the institutions, over

half of all institutions replying indicated that no special programs (including special education) were being offered.

B. A Follow-up Survey of Inmates with I.Q.'s below 55

After analyzing some of the general data from the institutions it was decided to send follow-up questionnaires to each responding institution with at least one inmate with an I.Q. lower than 55. It was hoped in this way to obtain some supplementary information specifically geared to offenders with high probabilities of being retarded, given the limitations in generalizing on the basis of the I.Q. 69 cut-off point in light of the problems inherent in the use of a variety of instruments and administrative procedures for determining intelligence scores. Through these follow-up questionnaires, data were obtained on a total of 964 adult offenders with I.Q.'s below 55 located in 26 different institutions. Some of the findings from this follow-up questionnaire are of significance for this paper and are summarized as follows;

1. Almost 87% of the 964 offenders with I.Q.'s below 55 fell into the range of I.Q. 40–54 with approximately 8% falling in the range of I.Q. 25–39, and about 5% (52 cases) falling below I.Q. 25.

2. The race and sex distribution of this group of offenders was found to be as follows: approximately 58% were noted as being non-white and 6% were female (for this latter category, the finding is not out of line with the general proportion of the total incarcerated population in this country made up of females).

3. The offense patterns of this grouping of 964 inmates were found to reveal approximately 57% incarcerated for what might be termed crimes against persons, including homicide, assault, and sexual offenses. It is important to note here that statistics compiled by the Federal Bureau of Prisons indicate that for the total population confined to adult institutions in the United States, approximately 27% were committed on the basis of these personal offenses. Significantly, of the group of inmates with I.Q.'s under 55 reported on in our follow-up survey, about 15.4% (90 cases) were committed for criminal homicide offenses. Federal Bureau of Prisons statistics show that commitments generally to institutions in the United States for criminal homicide account for only 5.1% of all commitments (Federal Bureau of Prisons, *National Prisoner*

Statistics, no. 36, United States Department of Justice [December, 1964], p. 3).

It was found that the most frequent single offense category for which this grouping of offenders was committed to institutions was burglary-breaking-and-entering, accounting for about 29% of all cases. This compares closely with the national statistics compiled by the Federal Bureau of Prisons revealing that 28% of all commitments in the United States are for such offenses.

Interpretation of these findings regarding intelligence and criminal offense is difficult. We have no data as to the length of stay for a given offense by a retarded inmate and other variables which may explain the findings. We suspect that retarded offenders sentenced for criminal homicide may have been relatively easier to convict, and tend to remain in the institutions for longer periods of time than those committed for other offenses; and that parole practices and policies may vary. Thus, some of our results in this area may be accounted for by the "loading-up" factor of length of sentence and reduced parole opportunities. What does seem clear, however, is that of the retarded offenders now institutionalized, we found a higher proportion of serious personal offenses than had been previously recognized.

4. As a part of the follow-up survey, institutions were asked to report on any psychiatric or medical diagnoses made as a result of special testing or examination of inmates with I.Q.'s under 55. Most significantly, it was found that in only 11 of the over 900 cases was such additional testing done and reported on in the survey. Penal and corrections institutions do not frequently administer supplemental tests and examinations to inmates with low reported intelligence, and often confine themselves to routine admissions examinations.

5. In addition, each institution was requested to indicate whether a search of their records revealed that the intelligence factor was raised at any time in the trial or post-trial legal histories of these particular offenders. It should be stated here that many institutions were unable to trace this through their records, but in those instances where such searches were made (in 9 institutions), all were unable to determine whether the mental condition of the offender was a significant issue. This facet is being examined in detail by The George Washington University Institute of Law, Psychiatry and Criminology as part of its *Mentally Retarded and the Law* study.

C. Management Problems and Practices

In addition to the statistical data obtained from the survey, special attention was given to the penal administrator's problems and practices in managing retarded inmates, and his recommendations as to the most appropriate handling and treatment strategies he would like to see instituted. Questions related to these matters were open-ended, and a large proportion of the institutions returning questionnaires failed to complete these particular items, or gave incomplete answers. The replies received may be divided into two major parts, management problems and recommendations.

1. Management Problems. The most common complaint for the institutions regarding management problems posed by retarded inmates was that such inmates require constant and individual staff attention. The institutions stated that staffing arrangements are often stretched to the limit and that the needs of retarded inmates are such that they require an undue amount of staff time, thus taking away, in some cases, personnel services essential to the larger non-retarded segments of the institutional populations. The second most frequent problem encountered by the surveyed institutions was that retardates are often victims of exploitation by their more intelligent peers.

Going beyond these two most frequent problems listed by the respondents, one sees in the comments of institutional officials a complex administrative and ethical problem. Each of the responding institutions has a small minority of inmates who may be classed as mentally retarded. In attempting to manage and treat this minority with the manpower and physical resources available, the prison administrator is faced with the possible consequences of inadequately covering the majority of his population. Two prison officials in responding to the questionnaire stated clearly that they could not be placed in the position of showing partiality to the small minority of retarded offenders in setting up programs and management policies.

In discussing disciplinary problems posed by retarded inmates, for example, some institutions reported that they realized the retarded offender may have great difficulty in comprehending what is expected of him in terms of institutional rules and regulations. However, these officials felt it was not possible to apply separate criteria to this group of inmates, and because of this the rule violation rate among the retarded was substantially higher than for other offenders.

In the general area of program management, it is valuable to quote one prison superintendent who rather carefully spelled out the problems he faces:

As we see it, an institution such as ours has a choice of alternative operational policies. The first is the possibility of pitching our program to the needs of the two-thirds majority of normal inmates, in which case the one-third minority of retarded inmates would suffer. A second alternative is to lower our standards and alter our programs as required by the one-third minority, which would deprive the majority group. The third alternative would be to run two separate programs in the same institution, which would require at least a 50% increase in budgeted staff if we are to do justice to both segments of our population.

This particular prison administrator has defined the role of his institution (a state reformatory) as the provision of specialized and individual treatment for youthful offenders. In his words:

Our institution is one designed to deal with the relatively hopeful youthful offender, and our procedure of choice has been to develop a program which presents selective alternatives from which our inmate body are asked to choose on an individualized level. This is deliberately done in the effort to individualize and to humanize the treatment process, as well as to avoid dangers of infantilization and institutionalization. Mentally retarded inmates are in no position to take advantage of such a program by reason of their poor judgment, inadequate concentration, and lack of ease of understanding.

Another institutional administrator likened the situation in his institution and others around the country to the situation obtaining during the development of mass public education in the United States. He stated that the public educational systems of our society tend to be geared toward the average student to the detriment of those falling below as well as significantly above the average. He, as an administrator, is faced with the choice of diluting the general handling and treatment strategies employed by his facility in order to provide more correctional opportunities for retarded offenders, or to neglect the retarded offender in favor of the vast majority of his population.

What seems to result in the forced choice made by prison officials is that the retarded in these institutions are essentially deprived of specialized treatment and handling measures. The consequence of this deprivation as indicated by the officials themselves is that retardates tend to "vegetate." This is particularly true in those institutions classified as maximum security facilities. One administrator, for example, stated that "we are totally unable to do anything except protect these individuals [retarded inmates]. . . . Some no doubt, could make better progress, but when forced to compete in school or work against [those inmates with higher intellectual ability] they became embarrassed and discouraged."

D. A Case Study of an Inmate Sample Analyzed for Socio-Psychological and Legal Variables

Because of the rather large number of incarcerated offenders falling into the low I.Q. levels identified from the survey, it was felt necessary to expand the scope of the research to trace, in effect, the administration of criminal justice in those cases with low reported intelligence. As indicated earlier, approximately 9.5% of all reported I.Q.'s from institutions throughout the country were below 70, and over 1,000 currently incarcerated adult offenders have I.Q. scores reported below 55. The design of this extended study deals specifically with offenders incarcerated in penal and correctional institutions with I.Q.'s reported by these institutions as below 70. It is being conducted under the auspices of The George Washington University Institute of Law, Psychiatry and Criminology as one aspect of a project already being carried out by that staff dealing with the mentally retarded and the law.

The procedure for this study involved the selection of institutions recorded by the original survey as housing inmates with I.Q.'s below 70. A sample of such inmates was selected and was retested by a consulting psychologist using the Wechsler Adult Intelligence Scale, Draw-A-Person, and the Thematic Apperception Test. It was felt that through the use of these instruments it is possible to identify those cases functioning within the retarded range, using criteria based upon psychometric testing independent of the I.Q. scores reported by the institutions.

Five adult penal and correctional institutions in five different states were selected for the study. The field research plan was as follows: one field worker visited each of the five institutions in order to compile a listing of all inmates incarcerated with I.Q. scores falling below 70. From this listing he selected a random sample which was then retested by the clinical psychologist. The institutional field worker was also responsible for collecting detailed socio-psychological, socio-economic, and criminological data on each of the inmates in the sample. A third field worker, an attorney, analyzed the legal data for each case in the sample. This entailed visiting courts to examine transcripts and court records, interviewing responsible personnel in court clinic and probation departments, and conducting other interviews with judges, attorneys (prosecuting and defense), and police personnel. The field study was carried out in the following states: Maryland, Virginia, Florida, Colorado, and Illinois.

The field work phase of the study was completed on September 1, 1966, and only a few tentative findings can be reported from the preliminary analysis of the data.

1. Results of the Testing. In the five states analyzed, the institutions reported a total of 395 inmates with I.Q. scores below 70, based upon their own testing. The mean I.Q. computed for this institutional testing was 62.4. The clinical psychologist, retesting a total of 60 of these inmates using the Wechsler Adult Intelligence Scale, Draw-A-Person, and the Thematic Apperception Test, obtained a mean I.Q. score of 66.0. He determined that 74% of the sample were mentally retarded, with another 8.7% considered to be borderline retarded (with I.Q.'s ranging between 70–74). Generalizing from these findings to the 395 inmates from which the sample was selected, we can tentatively state that 293 are retarded, with another 34 in the borderline retarded range. These results reveal that institutional testing is in general considerably more reliable as an indicator of mental retardation than has been recognized. Slightly over 88% of those found to be mentally retarded on retest were classified as non-white inmates.

At the time of the retesting, the mean age of the sample was 35.4 years, and it is interesting to note that the average lapse in time between the last test given by the institution and the study retest was 25.3 months. In one state, the average lapse of time was found to be 9 years. This finding quite clearly reveals that often in penal and correctional institutional practice the only testing programs undertaken are as one part of the routine admissions process. These facilities do not have the personnel and time required to administer tests to inmates at varying intervals during their confinement.

The mean age of the retardates, at time of criminal conviction, was found to be 28.5 years. The youngest, again at time of conviction, was 14; the oldest was found to be 50.

2. Criminological Findings. The preliminary analysis of the criminological characteristics of that portion of the sample found to be retarded as a result of retesting must be qualified by the fact that most of the sample was taken from penitentiary-type institutions which, in a majority of the states studied, house more serious offenders. Penitentiaries were selected in two states which also have institutions with lesser degrees of security and thus less serious offenders. In two other states, the penitentiaries selected tend to be general purpose institutions for the incarceration of a more heterogeneous offender group. The fifth institution was a reformatory.

With this qualification in mind, it was found that the most frequent crime committed by the incarcerated retardate was first-degree murder, accounting for slightly less than 21% of all the retardates. Other criminal homicides accounted for 17.6% of the sample, and the offense category breaking-and-entering burglary accounted for an equal percentage of the sample. Together, inmates sentenced for all classes of criminal homicide made up nearly two out of five of all offenders included in the sample. When the various crimes committed by the retarded group were combined into the general categories of crimes against persons and crimes against property, the former category accounted for almost 59% of the cases.

One must recognize that the findings above refer only to the offense for which the retardate is currently institutionalized, and do not take into account the characteristics of his criminal career. Attempts were made to examine this career aspect through the study. Some significant findings in this area are: over two-thirds of the retardates committed their crimes alone; they average 2.9 previous convictions for adult crimes (only 20.6% of the retardates had no previous adult convictions); the group, as of the time the data were collected, had spent an average of 7 years in penal and correctional institutions. Examining the past criminal convictions of the retarded group, it was found that in over 60% of the cases, the total criminal career could be classified as property-offense in character.

3. Findings Related to the Administration of Criminal Justice. An attempt was made through the study to ascertain the distribution of certain significant variables in the total process of the administration of justice for those found to be retarded on the basis of the study retesting. Some of the preliminary findings are as follows:

a. Representation by counsel: In only 7.7% of the cases in this sample was there evidence that the retardate was not represented by an attorney. For the cases where representation was found, such representation was court-appointed in slightly over 69% of the cases.

b. *Pleas:* Of the total group of retarded inmates in the sample, almost 59% entered a plea of guilty. Analyzing the court and other records in order to determine the extent of plea bargaining, it was found that in 80% of the cases the original charge on which the retardate was arrested was the same as that for which he was tried and convicted. In no case was there evidence of a lower charge being the basis of arrest when compared to the final charge for which tried.

c. *Confessions:* An analysis of the available records revealed that a confession or incriminating statement was obtained from the retardate in two-thirds of the cases studied.

d. *Pre-Trial and Pre-Sentence Examination of the Accused Retardate:* Analysis of the records indicated that in almost 78% of the cases no pre-trial psychological or psychiatric examination of the accused was made, nor was a social history taken. In those cases where such examinations did occur, 11% were examined as a result of a commitment for observation to a mental hospital; approximately 8% were the subjects of routine probation department examinations in which some mention was made of low intelligence; and in 3% of the cases a routine probation examination was made, but intelligence was not mentioned in the report submitted to the court.

In no case was an examination requested or ordered during the course of the trial. Pre-sentence examinations were made in only 20% of the cases, and these were routine probation department examinations in which no psychometric or psychiatric examinations were administered. In only one such probation department pre-sentence report was mention made of the low intelligence of the convicted person.

e. *Trial:* The issues of competency to stand trial and criminal responsibility were not raised in 92% of the cases under study. In two cases where the retardate was committed for psychiatric observation prior to the trial, a portion of the report submitted to the court indicated that the persons were competent to stand trial, and in a third case (the case of a person who pled not guilty by reason of insanity), a statement appeared indicating that the individual was sane at the time the offense was committed. In only two cases was expert testimony given during the trial (the experts being psychiatrists). In these two cases the experts testified only for the state.

Examining those cases in which pleas of not guilty were entered, it was determined that 40% of the retardates specifically waived jury trials.

f. *Appeal and Post-Conviction Relief Proceedings:* In 88% of the cases of these retardates no appeal was made, and post-conviction relief was not requested in 84% of the cases. In those few cases where appeals or post-conviction relief proceedings were undertaken, the mental condition of the retardate was not given as one of the grounds upon which relief was sought. In the seven cases involving one or both forms of relief, the grounds seemed to be rather evenly divided between inadmissible confessions and the lack of an attorney.

[Section V omitted]

VI. Critical Issues and Recommendations for Action and Research

A. An Overview of the Critical Issues

We see the following as some of the critical issues we face today in the general area of society's response to the mentally retarded offender:

1. There is a serious lack of awareness of the complex legal, sociological, and psychological problems of the mentally retarded offender on the part of both lay and professional persons. To cite only a few of the deficiencies in this area we find that:

   a. The magnitude of the retardate's involvement with the criminal law is almost unknown at the present time. Related to this is:

   b. Epidemiological data on mentally retarded offenders are not now available. . . .

   c. Knowledge of the offense patterns of retarded offenders is at best vague.

2. Currently, there is a striking lack of empirical data clarifying the relationship between intelligence and anti-social behavior. There are virtually no sociologic or psychodynamic formulations to elucidate this relationship.

3. We find that there is a tendency for the rejection of responsibility for retarded offenders on the part of many mental health and correctional professionals. They reject, for different reasons, the retardate as being unsuitable for their respective treatment and handling pro-

grams and facilities. . . . Mental hospitals claim such an offender is not mentally ill, the traditional institutions for the retarded complain that they do not have appropriate facilities for the offender. . . . Correctional institutions would like to remove such persons from their populations on the grounds that the programs available in the correctional setting are totally inadequate and in many cases inappropriate for application to retarded persons.

4. There is a definite lack of adequate socio-psychological definitions for the effective diagnosis and treatment of this offender group. . . . What one institution may call retardation is not so defined in another. . . .

5. Related to the above critical issue is the lack of adequate definitions relative to the legal identification and management of the mentally retarded offender group. Included in this crucial area are problems inherent in the various defective delinquent and sexual psychopathy statutes. In addition, little data are available concerning the effectiveness of these specialized statutes in the handling of mentally retarded persons committing anti-social behavior.

6. There is a very serious shortage of services to this offender group. . . . This deficiency in services is related to several sub-areas:

 a. There is disagreement as to the most appropriate strategies for handling retarded offenders. . . .

 b. There is a lack of mental health and manpower resources in the area of special education, psychiatry, and psychology. . . .

 c. The lack of adequate facilities in the community until recently may be directly related to the placing of mentally retarded offenders in penal and correctional institutions. . . .

7. There seems to be a distinct lack of coordination between and within the agencies having some contact with mentally retarded offenders. . . .

8. There are several crucial legal issues readily identifiable:

 a. Arrest and interrogation. . . . The entire area of the mentally retarded suspect's rights at the time of arrest and during interrogation, and the admissibility of statements and confessions made by such person, needs careful study.

 b. The retention of counsel for mentally retarded accused persons. . . . A factor to be investigated here would be the effect of the Gideon decision with regard to the mentally retarded offender. This decision . . . will result in a significant increase in the involvement of lawyers in criminal law work. . . .

 c. The competency of mentally [retarded] accused persons to stand trial is at best unclarified at this time. Related to this . . . is the issue of the disposition of retardates found to be incompetent to stand trial. . . .

 d. The issue of the determination of criminal responsibility with regard to offenders alleged to be mentally retarded needs further investigation. . . .

B. Recommendations

. . . A general recommendation, which, we feel, must take precedence over the specific recommendations to follow, lies in the urgent requirement for research. . . .

[1.] Agencies processing and/or handling retarded or alleged retarded offenders (e.g., court clinics, probation departments, correctional and penal institutions, etc.) must carry out continuing research regarding

 (1) The intelligence of the cases they handle.

 (2) The relationship between intelligence and types of offenses committed.

 (3) The relationship between intelligence and institutional and other program adjustment.

 (4) The relationship between intelligence and success/failure upon release from various programs.

Such continuing research, the results of which we would recommend being deposited with the central clearing house, would permit us to come substantially to grips with such issues as the magnitude of the involvement of retardates in criminal and delinquent behavior and the efficacy of the variety of treatment and handling strategies currently in vogue.

[2.] Particularly in view of the tendency for the relationship between intelligence and criminal behavior to be de-emphasized in the last thirty or more years, it is extremely important that research into the causal relationship between intelligence and crime be undertaken using the tools now available in the disciplines of sociology, psychology, psychiatry, and criminology.

[3.] It is now recognized that there are no hard and fast rules for determining which kinds of programs will be most effective in dealing with retarded offenders in general. Some of these offenders may respond most effectively to correctional or penal handling; others will require some form of mental hospitalization; still others may be appropriately handled in training schools for the retarded; some can be best dealt with in ongoing community programs now used exclusively for non-offending retardates. What is needed, however, is a greater degree of coordination between and among the various agencies society can muster in responding to the mentally retarded offender.

[4.] We recommend widespread acceptance of the definition of mental retardation adopted by the American Association on Mental Deficiency: "Mental retardation refers to sub-average general intellectual functioning which originates during the developmental period and is associated with impairment in adaptive behavior." We further recommend that more general use be made in the correctional field of the classification of degrees of retardation proposed by the Association.

[5.] In any effort to improve upon the legal identification and management of retarded offenders it is imperative that behavioral science and law professionals actively seek improved communication and cooperation. To this end we specifically recommend:

(1) That legal education be substantially broadened to include course work dealing with basic behavioral science concepts and the accumulation of knowledge through research methods. This can be implemented through three channels, all of which should be actively pursued. The first of these would be in the traditional undergraduate legal education institutions; the second would be through graduate legal education; the third channel includes continuing legal education. The education of behavioral science professionals should be enhanced, most appropriately at the graduate level, through the introduction of courses concerned with the development of basic legal concepts and institutions.

(2) As a means for the development of greater interaction between those in the behavioral science and legal professions as well as providing what might be a more appropriate method of identifying and legally handling retarded offenders, we recommend serious study and, at least on a demonstration basis, implementation of an Exceptional Offender's Court as proposed by Richard C. Allen. Allen's proposal calls for

. . . a specially constituted court, empowered to assume wardship over any adult person shown to be substantially impaired in his intellectual capacity, who has committed an act which, if committed by an adult without such impairment, would constitute a felony or serious misdemeanor. It is suggested further that jurisdiction be transferred to such court at whatever point the existence of severe mental retardation is suspected— whether prior to trial on a criminal charge, or after conviction, sentence, and incarceration for such offense.

Upon referral to such a court, there should first be a determination of the existence of gross intellectual deficit. Such determination should be made by the judge, and should be based on expert evidence presented at a hearing at which the alleged exceptional offender is represented by a guardian ad litem. ("Toward an Exceptional Offenders Court," *Mental Retardation*, 4 (February, 1966): p. 5.)

Flexibility would be the keynote of this court, and procedures involved would be roughly analogous to those of a juvenile court.

(3) Another medium for encouraging greater communication and interaction in this area would be the strengthening of existing clinics attached to criminal courts and the institution of such clinics where they do not now exist. Somewhat later more will be said about access to these clinics by criminal defendants.

[6.] Statutory definitions and related treatment and handling strategies ought to be the subject of serious study to determine the socio-legal adequacy of the definitions, and to identify the problems inherent in and the success of treatment and handling modalities operationally determined by such definitions of defective delinquency established by statute in Maryland, and full advantage taken of the research opportunities inherent in the program of the Patuxent Institution created by the same statute. We might, for instance, be interested in determining if there are any significant differentials in parole outcome of randomly selected offenders who are identifiable as defective delinquents under the statutory requirements who are subjected to ordinary penal incarceration and those committed to Patuxent Institution, or other analogous facilities.

[7.] a. Because of the fact that many penal and correctional institutions have substantial segments of their populations made up of offenders with low measured intelligence (in some cases as high as 25%), it is extremely important that correctional personnel at all levels be at least minimally equipped to handle these inmates. We would recommend that on at least an in-service training basis correctional personnel be given instruction in the handling of retarded inmates.

Beyond the in-service training level, it seems imperative that more intensive education of correctional personnel be undertaken in the form of possible combinations of short-term courses as well as more conventional college programs, which would, among other things, be directed toward assisting correctional workers in their interaction with retarded offenders (as well as those with possible mental illness). We cannot stress too strongly the need for involving the first-line correctional officer in institutions in these programs. This category of correctional personnel has the most frequent, continuous, and intense contact with inmates, and the impact of these contacts will appreciably weaken or strengthen the institutional goal of correction.

b. Extramural correctional services such as probation and parole need strengthening in order to provide adequate ment for the retarded offender. We would recommend here that probation and parole officers be given supplementary education and training designed to assist them in working with retarded offenders; perhaps such training and education could be combined with that recommended for institutional correctional personnel.

In addition, we recommend that retarded probationers and parolees be assigned to special caseloads which would be handled by selected officers trained in the problems of the retarded. These problems would seem to be so different from those of non-retarded offenders that the most effective means for providing adequate supervision would be the assignment of special caseloads where these problems can receive more individual and expert attention.

c. Institutional programs for retarded offenders, especially in the areas of special education and vocational training, require considerable attention. Ways must be found to attract qualified educational personnel in correctional work so that needed programs can be offered. The findings of the survey of the institutions referred to earlier in this paper revealed that over half of all correctional institutions in this country fail to provide any program whatsoever especially directed toward retarded inmates. This is a situation which cannot be permitted to continue.

We recommend that serious study be given to the possibility of establishing regional institutions for mentally retarded offenders. As indicated from the findings of the penal and correctional survey, many institutional administrators feel that they cannot retain specialized personnel and offer unique programs for the small minority of their populations made up of retarded persons. One way of handling this problem would be to create, on a regional basis, specialized institutions for the retarded to which two or more states could commit retardates convicted of criminal offenses.

We further recommend that cooperative efforts be made by the American Association on Mental Deficiency and the American Correctional Association to establish standards for correctional programming for retarded inmates. The AAMD has already become involved in setting standards for residential institutions for the retarded (W. I. Gardner and H. W. Nisonger, "A Manual on Program Development in Mental Retardation," monograph supplement to *American Journal of Mental Deficiency* [January, 1962]), while the American Correctional Association has, for the past several years, produced a manual for correctional standards. Cooperation between the two organizations could provide an excellent basis upon which to build more adequate and appropriate services in penal and correctional facilities. It is doubtful whether such gains can be made without this joint undertaking.

d. Extramural programs for retarded offenders can be dramatically improved through the use of facilities and agencies already operating for non-offending retardates in many cases. The community has, in recent years, experienced an extensive growth in such facilities as day-care centers, sheltered workshops and a variety of educational settings for the non-delinquent retardate. Frequently, such programs are closed to mentally retarded offenders on probation or parole. It may not be practical or wise to expect a community to invest in the development of similar program facilities exclusively for the offending retardate. The possibility of using already existing non-residential facilities for selected offenders should be thoroughly explored. Much in the way of needed programming in this area might be provided if strong citizens' groups such as the National Association for Retarded Children would take a leadership position in this exploration.

[8.] We recommend that states organize comprehensive correctional departments or divisions which would embrace institutional and extramural correctional services. Further, it is recommended that these comprehensive correctional departments be organizationally related to the Departments of Mental Health, and to other administrative divisions within the state having responsibility for training school facilities if this responsibility is not borne by the Department of Mental Health. We recognize that such a recommendation goes beyond the need solely of retarded offenders, but we feel it is only logical that such administrative organization be carried through to the fullest extent possible. Such administrative structuring, we feel, would permit maximum flexibility in designing appropriate programs and management strategies for mentally retarded offenders.

[9.] Those involved in the administration of criminal justice in the United States have been dramatically alerted in recent years to the rights of accused persons through various court decisions regarding criminal responsibility (e.g., Durham), the right of accused persons to have counsel (Gideon), and in the general area of safeguards to be invoked to insure the privilege against self-incrimination through inappropriately obtained confessions and statements. The latter, referring to the Escobedo and Miranda decisions, would significantly affect the use of statements made by accused persons, as well as police interrogation methods. While these decisions, as well as others, have broad impact in the area of the administration of criminal justice, they do have tremendous implications for retarded accused persons and defendants. In the Miranda case, the majority opinion of the Supreme Court refers in several places to the requirement that an accused person must "intelligently" waive his right to remain silent or to have counsel present during police interrogation. We refer here to a most relevant statement by the Task Force on Law of the President's Panel on Mental Retardation, which is as follows:

A retarded person, even when not coerced in the usual sense, may be unable to understand police procedures and their consequences, and therefore may be unable to make a genuine decision in relation to them. He is more likely than the average person to be unaware of his constitutional right to refuse to answer incriminating police questions, and of his right to consult with an attorney; even where the interrogator advises him of these rights, he may be unable to appreciate their significance. . . .

. . .

We do not say that all confessions by mentally retarded defendants should be excluded from evidence. But we do emphasize that courts should fully consider whether the accused's state of mind, in view of his mental retardation, was such that he was unable to give a confession that was genuinely voluntary, reliable, and that may fairly be used against him.

[10.] a. We are greatly impressed with the recommendations incorporated in the Pennsylvania Comprehensive Plan for the establishment, in a model mental health statute of a Mental Health/Mental Retardation Referral and Investigation Service which would be empowered to examine persons taken into custody by police officials. We urge that serious consideration be given to the establishment of such a service unit for the examination of accused persons taken into police custody when there is some indication that mental retardation may be present. The organization of such a referral service might be through the local county departments of mental health, as in the Pennsylvania Model Statute, or could be on a statewide or multi-county regional basis. For many states the regional or statewide basis for organizing the unit would appear to be most appropriate.

b. Going beyond the recommendation indicated above, we suggest that an accused person or someone on his behalf should have the right at any time during the criminal proceedings against him (i.e., prior to the commencement of the trial, during the trial itself, or after trial but prior to sentencing) to request an examination to determine whether he is, and/or to what degree he is, mentally retarded. Such examination would, in the case of indigent defendants, be provided at no cost to the examinee. While this recommendation may appear to be radical to some, we feel that it is a logical and necessary extension of the decision in the Gideon case requiring that a defendant's request for counsel be honored.

The examination called for in this recommendation could be carried out by a referral and investigation service discussed above, or through existing or newly established court clinics. In this latter connection, we recommend for consideration the recently established Georgetown University pre-trial clinic which functions in cooperation with the Legal Aid Services in the District of Columbia.

c. In the matter of incompetency to stand trial and the issue of determinations of criminal responsibility, we are in agreement with the opinion expressed in several state comprehensive plans deploring the practice of automatic commitment, especially in those cases found to be incompetent to stand trial, to a residential facility. Such commitment often results in lifetime segregation from society which is uncalled-for in many cases. We would recommend that when a finding of incompetency to stand trial or a verdict of not guilty by reason of insanity is made that the court clinic or referral and investigation service be empowered to recommend to the court the most appropriate, based upon expert knowledge, disposition. This recommendation would not be binding on the court, although it should be given great weight in the final disposition.

d. Given the state of uncertainty regarding the rules to be applied to determine criminal responsibility (e.g., Durham, M'Naghten, and the American Law Institute formulation), we do not feel it advisable at this time to recommend a specific set of rules.

[11.]   We have come to the inescapable conclusion that it is essential for the strengthening and, perhaps, reform of the administration of criminal justice in those cases involving retarded persons that empirical research into our legal institutions and procedures be undertaken. In general, we are thinking here of empirical legal research such as that being carried out by The George Washington University Institute of Law, Psychiatry and Criminology under a National Institute of Mental Health grant entitled *The Mentally Retarded and the Law*. This research project, dealing with both civil and criminal law, is engaged in compiling statutory and regulatory provisions with regard to the mentally retarded, and examining in the field the operation of these provisions.

. . .

The implications of the findings reported in this paper are as complex and controversial as they are frightening. Society must deal with people who are in ungentle terms seen as both stupid and bad. But our society must be judged by how we deal with the least fortunate amongst us. We cannot hide behind stereotyped, positive prejudice that refuses to face the seriousness and danger of anti-social behavior. We compound the injury by devoting inadequate resources to the pursuit of scientific understanding and possible prevention, and to the practice of humanitarian and enlightened management. The retarded offender is rejected on all sides: by the supporters of mental retardation programs, who feel he is primarily criminal and only secondarily retarded, and by those in the correctional field, who place the retarded offender as low

man on the totem pole of those who might benefit from treatment and rehabilitation programs. The problem of the mentally retarded offender calls for our best efforts as professionals and citizens.

THE RETARDED OFFENDER: UNRECOGNIZED IN COURT AND UNTREATED IN PRISON

Richard C. Allen

The President's Commission on Crime in the District of Columbia reported that "Nearly every agency involved in law enforcement and the administration of justice is impaired by lack of facts."[1] Similarly, the National Crime Commission declared in its report to the President:

Few domestic social problems more seriously threaten our welfare or exact a greater toll on our resources . . . . [Yet] there is probably no subject of comparable concern to which the Nation is devoting so many resources and so much effort with so little knowledge of what it is doing.[2]

And in his Foreword to a recent publication of the Joint Commission on Correctional Manpower and Training, its associate director observed that: ". . . very little research is being done in corrections and . . . there is little agreement on what correctional rehabilitation actually is."[3]

As each of these documents amply illustrates, ignorance of the basic facts of crime causation and lack of research of differential correctional rehabilitative techniques, substantially impairs the effectiveness of crime control. The findings of these Presidential commissions have shed the first rays of light in areas heretofore enshrouded in darkness. But unhappily they have conspicuously failed to illumine the difficult problems presented by the mentally ill and by the mentally retarded offender. Indeed, the National Crime Commission's report virtually ignores them. In only one of its more than 200 recommendations does the commission refer to mentally impaired offenders, and in that Recommendation attempts to write them out of the criminal law-correctional picture.[4]

---

[1] Report of the President's Commission on Crime in the District of Columbia, 1966, p. 355.

[2] The Challenge of Crime in a Free Society: Report of the President's Committee on Law Enforcement and Administration of Justice, 1967, p. 273.

[3] Research in Correctional Rehabilitation, December 1967. Of course some information is scrupulously collected. In the publication cited, the Director of the Research Center of the National Council on Crime and Delinquency at Davis, California, reports that complete records have been

maintained since 1890 of every hanging performed in that State, including information about the age, height, and weight of the prisoner, the length of the drop and the hangman's expert opinion as to how "successfully" the operation was carried out.

[4] Op. cit. supra. Note 2, p. 133: "Procedures are needed to identify and divert from the criminal process, mentally disordered or deficient persons. Not all members of this group are legally insane or incompetent to stand trial under traditional legal definitions."

The Commission recommends:

"Early identification and diversion to other community resources of those offenders in need of treatment, for whom full criminal disposition does not appear required."

Excerpted and reprinted with permission from *Federal Probation* (Sept. 1968): 22.

THE RETARDATE AND CRIME

Although there is a paucity of factual information about mental retardation and crime,[5] there has been no shortage of opinions about it through the years. About a half century ago it was pretty widely believed that every intellectually impaired person was a likely delinquent,[6] and that most criminal offenders were such because of impaired intellect.[7] The polemicists have now come full circle and it is today just as stoutly maintained by some members of the scientific, legal, and correctional communities that mental retardation bears no causal relationship to crime.[8] Indeed this view is so strongly held in some quarters that when staff members of our institute have discussed the preliminary findings of our researches, the most strenuous objection has been voiced by persons ordinarily in the vanguard of liberal reform. As the author once noted:

. . . in our zeal to dispel the chimeras and rubrics that have existed so long, we may have fallen into another kind of error. There seems to be developing a sort of reaction formation in which it has become fashionable to deny that gross intellectual deficit plays any significant role in producing criminal behavior.[9]

Yet would it not be surprising if so major an impairment of one's capacity to compete successfully with his peers, in light of the total inadequacy of institutional and community facilities for the retarded, were not causally related to antisocial behavior? Consider the following composite picture of the mentally retarded young adults who became clients in a rehabilitation project in New York:

The central fact of life of [the retardate] is his history of failure. He is likely to have failed his parents by having been a late walker and late talker and by having soiled himself much longer than did the neighbor's children. He is likely to suffer from physical handicaps.

He fell behind in school. The chances are that he began in regular classes but was transferred to special classes which, while they protected him from hopeless academic competition, probably accentuated for him and his family his difference from other children and his membership in a blemished part of the population.

As he grew older, he lost the few friends he may have had, for his friends absorbed and acted out the cultural values emphasizing the differences between them. As his normal playmates ventured away from the home block, he probably remained behind, restrained by his parents and by his own fears and deficiencies. School chums went on to higher grades while he stayed still. At 17 or before, he left school altogether. As others paired off into heterosexual couples and groups, he was likely to stand out in his loneliness even more obviously. And when others went off to work, he stayed home. He made few if any efforts and felt that it was hopeless to try. In all likelihood, his parents felt the same way.[10]

In a recent publication for the guidance of physicians, the Group for the Advancement of Psychiatry notes the social problems which may follow the failures and frustrations experienced by the retardate, who may "first rebel against the school and later against society itself." The report emphasizes that retardation is neither an inevitable, nor is it ever the sole, cause of antisocial behavior;[11] and it is well to point out that only a very small percentage of the mentally retarded commit criminal acts. But we cannot, if the problem is to be dealt with effectively, choose to remain blind to the fact that a significant number of criminal offenders suffer varying degrees of mental retardation from mild to severe; that they go through the processes of arrest, trial, and conviction without recognition of their condition by key decision makers; and that they are finally consigned to correctional institutions without treatment appropriate to their condition.

[5] ". . . there are currently available little or no systematic data about the prevalence of mental retardation in the anti-social population of the United States." Bertram S. Brown and Thomas F. Courtless, "The Mentally Retarded in Penal and Correctional Institutions," *Amer. J. of Psychiatry*, 124: 9, pp. 1164–1170, l.c. 1164, March 1968.

[6] E.g., see. W. E. Fernald, "The Imbecile with Criminal Instincts," 65 *American Journal of Insanity* 747, 1909.

[7] ". . . the one vital mental constitutional factor in the etiology of crime is defective intelligence." Charles Goring, *The English Convict*. London 1913, quoted in Hartung, *Crime, Law and Society*, Detroit, Michigan, Wayne State University Press, 1965.

[8] Such views are cited and commented upon in Bertram S. Brown and Thomas F. Courtless, "The Mentally Retarded Offender," published by the President's Commission on Law Enforcement and Administration of Justice, 1967, reprinted in Richard C. Allen, Elyce Z. Ferster, and Jesse Rubin, *Readings in Law and Psychiatry*, Baltimore, Maryland, Johns Hopkins Press, 1968.

[9] Richard C. Allen, "Toward an Exceptional Offenders Court," *Mental Retardation*, Volume 4, No. 1, February 1966.

[10] Max Dubrow, Jerome Nitzberg, and Jack Tobias, "Profiles of Failure," *Rehabilitation Record*, March-April 1965.

[11] "Mild Mental Retardation: A Growing Challenge to the Physicians," *Group for the Advancement of Psychiatry Report No. 66*, September 1967.

STUDY OF RETARDATES IN STATE PENAL INSTITUTIONS

In 1963 a questionnaire survey was made of all correctional institutions in the country, with the exception of jails and workhouses where misdemeanants and minor offenders are confined. Responses were received from over 80 percent of the institutions contacted, housing some 200,000 offenders, of which number the reporting institutions have IQ records on about half. The following were among the findings made based on analysis of these records:

1. About 9.5 percent of prison inmates can be classified as mentally retarded, using IQ 70 as the cutoff point [it is estimated that about 3 percent of the general population is mentally retarded].
2. Although more than 70 percent of the reporting institutions routinely test the intelligence of inmates on admission, a number of different tests are used, and testing procedures vary widely; and several reporting institutions make no effort to test the intelligence of their inmates.
3. Nearly 1,500 (1.6 percent) of the inmates had reported IQ scores below 55, ranging down to a low of 17 [well within the "profound" category, for whom full-time nursing care is usually required].
4. There is a general lack of mental health manpower resources within the institutions and consequently virtually no special programs for retarded inmates: 160 institutions, with nearly 150,000 inmates, are served by 14 full-time psychiatrists and 82 full-time psychologists; and more than half of the institutions reporting offer no program of any kind for their retarded inmates—not even a single special education class.[12]

THE MENTALLY RETARDED AND THE LAW STUDY

The Institute of Law, Psychiatry and Criminology has just completed a 3-year empirical study of the operation of civil and criminal laws which affect the mentally retarded and their families—a study made possible through a planning grant from the National Association for Retarded Children and a project grant from the National Institute of Mental Health (MH-01947).[13]

[12] Op. cit. supra, Note 8.
[13] The findings of an earlier study by the Institute of determinations of legal incompetency of the mentally ill and mentally retarded have just been published as Richard C. Allen, E. Z. Ferster, and Henry Weihofen, Mental Impairment and Legal Incompetency, Englewood Cliffs, New Jersey, Prentice-Hall, 1968.

In the criminal law-correctional phase of this study, six adult correctional institutions in six different states, each of which had reported housing inmates with IQ's below 70, were selected, taking into account the character of the institution, the availability of records, and geographic location. The states selected were Colorado, Florida, Illinois, Maryland, Missouri, and Virginia, in each of which, with the exception of Colorado and Missouri, field studies had been conducted in the civil law phase of the project.

To each of the institutions was sent a field worker who compiled from prison records a list of all inmates identified by the institutions as retarded, selected a random sample from this list for retesting, and determined the type and manner of institutional testing and the nature of any educational or other rehabilitative programs provided by the institution for its allegedly retardate population. He also collected detailed sociopsychological, socioeconomic, and criminological data on each of the inmates in the sample.

The sample was then retested by the second member of the team, a clinical psychologist, using the Wechsler Adult Intelligence Scale, Draw-a-Person, and Thematic Apperception tests. The third member of the team, a lawyer, then analyzed the legal data for each case in the sample, including examination of trial transcripts and interviews with judges, prosecuting and defense counsel, probation officers, and police personnel involved in each case. This latter facet of the study sought answers to such questions as: At what point, if at all, was an attorney appointed to represent the accused; was a confession or other statement to the police offered in evidence, and was objection taken to it; was the issue of competency to stand trial raised; was there a referral for an examination or observation; was the defense of lack of criminal responsibility asserted; was there a presentence investigation; and what were the dispositional alternatvies available to the court? The primary focus of inquiry was to determine at what point, if at all, significant decision-makers became aware of the fact of the defendant's mental retardation; and, if this fact was not discovered during the course of the criminal trial, why this was the case, and if it was discovered, what effect, if any, it had.

Correctional institutions use a number of different tests of intelligence. Some are given to large groups of inmates as part of the admissions procedure, sometimes using other inmates to administer and score them. Surprisingly, despite this fact, we found institutional testing to be a fairly reliable indicator of mental retardation. The mean IQ of the sample of 51 inmates whom we retested was 66.0, compared with a mean IQ on institutional testing of 62.4. Further, we found 74 percent of the sample to fall within the retarded range, with an additional 8.7 percent testing in the borderline range (IQ between 70 and 74). Of course, disparities were also discovered. In one state, Missouri, the "Otis Quick Scoring Test" is used. On that test the mean IQ of the supposedly retarded inmates was 61.8; our retesting of a sample of that group showed a mean IQ of 77.8, with only one inmate in the sample scoring below IQ 70.

DIMENSIONS OF THE PROBLEM

Projecting the percentage of retarded inmates identified by the institutions responding to our initial survey to the total prison population, there are in American prisons today nearly 20,000 adult offenders who are substantially intellectually impaired, some 3,300 of whom are classifiable as moderately to profoundly retarded. But the problems which these offenders present transcend their numbers. And, they are rejected at every point where help might be given: by those concerned with treatment for the mentally retarded because they are "criminal," and by corrections because to meet their special needs would exhaust the limited resources of most penal institutions.

The Task Force on Law of the President's Panel on Mental Retardation declared, as though it were axiomatic, that "There is no reason to believe that the small percentage of the mentally retarded who run afoul of the criminal law are prone to commit crimes of violence."[14] Our findings suggest that this rubric, so long accepted in refutation of the once widely held view that all retardates are potential killers, could bear reexamination.

The United States Bureau of Prisons reports that 27 percent of all inmates of adult penal institutions were sent there for having committed assaultive crimes against other people (as opposed to property and other types of offenses), and that 5.1 percent were convicted of some degree of criminal homicide. The largest single offense category is burglary-breaking and entering, which makes up 29 percent of all inmates.[15]

Of the inmates reported by the institutions responding to the Brown-Courtless Questionnaire as having IQ's less than 70, a sample of 964 was selected with measured IQ's below 55. The proportion of this group who had been committed on conviction of burglary-breaking and entering corresponded closely to the figure cited by the Bureau of Prisons for the total prison population (28 percent). However, among this grossly retarded group, 57 percent had been convicted of crimes against the person, and the percentage convicted of homicide was three times as high as that of the total prison population (15.4 percent). And among the prisoners in the six states selected for further empirical research, 72 percent of the sample selected for retesting who were found to be retarded had been incarcerated for crimes against the person and 36 percent for some degree of homicide. Indeed, the most frequent crime committed by inmates identified on retesting as retarded was first degree murder, which accounted for nearly 21 percent of the total.

Perhaps our sample of half a hundred inmates is too small for this apparent predominance of violent crimes to have much significance. Perhaps also the proportion of retarded prisoners who have committed such crimes is inflated by the fact that the retardate is more easily apprehended, more prone to confess, more likely to be convicted, and will probably be incarcerated longer than the nonretarded offender. Also, one might assume that some of the retardates who commit non-assaultive crimes are diverted from the criminal trial process and committed to institutions for the mentally retarded (although we found no evidence that this occurs in any of the courts and other agencies in which our researches were conducted). And finally, it may be more accurate to state that both mental retardation and crime are largely products of certain socioeconomic and cultural factors than to postulate a causal relationship between the two. But however the results of our inquiries may be qualified in light of these factors, one fact rather clearly emerges: The special problem of the mentally retarded offender warrants much greater attention than it has ever been given in the past.

FAILURE OF THE SYSTEM TO IDENTIFY THE RETARDATE

There are several points in the criminal trial process at which the defendant's retardation might be expected to be revealed: in determining his competency to stand trial; in considering the admissibility of his confession; in

---

[14] *Report of the Task Force on Law*, The President's Panel on Mental Retardation, 1963.

[15] United States Bureau of Prisons, *National Prisoner Statistics No. 36*, U.S. Department of Justice, 1963. (The 1963 publication was selected because it most closely corresponded to the dates of the empirical research.)

resolving the issue of his criminal responsibility (insanity); or in the course of a referral for mental examination. In fact, however, it is not discovered, or if it is it plays no significant part in the outcome of the case.

The initial problem, of course, is that none of these legal procedures operates automatically; rather, the issue must be affirmatively raised. And the system works in such a way as virtually to insure that the issue will *not* be raised. Our research suggests that there may be four principal reasons why the fact of a defendant's mental retardation is not disclosed at or prior to trial: failure to recognize it, insensitivity or indifference to it, uncertainty of application of the legal rule, and inappropriateness of the legal result if the fact of mental retardation is established.

The first two reasons cited: failure to recognize the defendant's retardation and indifference to it, are pretty hard to separate. Perhaps the following quotations from our interviews will sufficiently illustrate the point:

. . . we all thought he was dumb, but he was a mean ———, and we were all a little afraid of him (a prosecuting attorney, discussing a subject retested at IQ 57).

. . . I don't recall that any of my clients were retarded (a public defender, several of whose clients were indeed retarded).

. . . He did appear somewhat slow, but most of these migrant farm workers are retarded to a certain extent anyway (said by a judge of a retarded defendant convicted of first degree murder).

A part of the problem is an apparent lack of opportunity to discover the fact of retardation. Most of the prisoners in our sample were poor, most Negro, and most had appointed counsel who spent little time with them. The trial often was little more than a formality: More than 95 percent of the defendants either confessed or pleaded guilty; and the entire proceedings, from arrest to incarceration in prison, often were completed in a matter of weeks. Most of the decision makers lacked even elemental knowledge of what mental retardation is and how it is diagnosed.

Still another reason why the question of a defendant's mental retardation may not be raised, is its questionable relevance to the legal issues to be decided. Space does not permit an adequate review of the laws governing competency, the voluntariness of a confession, or criminal responsibility. However, perhaps the following observations will at least suggest why retardation has but equivocal significance in law.

The Task Force on Law of the President's Panel on Mental Retardation observed that in addition to the capacity to remember and relate facts helpful to counsel in presenting whatever defenses may exist, true competence may require more, indeed more, than a given retardate may possess:

The mentally retarded defendant . . . even though telling the truth, may be incapable of giving the impression of doing so because he is easily confused under the pressure of an effective cross-examination. Thus, he might be discredited in the eyes of judge or jury—or worse, be induced to testify untruthfully.[16]

Yet few courts have taken into account the implications of mental retardation in the criminal trial process.[17]

The cases in our sample were all pre-Miranda.[18] However, it would seem that to whatever extent mental retardation might impair the voluntariness of a confession, it would also cast doubt upon the voluntariness of a waiver of the rights of which the accused is required to be warned under the Miranda decision. And capacity so to act voluntarily may well be impaired by mental retardation.[19] The United States Supreme Court has long held that mental retardation is one factor to be looked at in considering whether a confession was voluntarily given; yet there are few court decisions as enlightened as a recent one by the Supreme Court of Mississippi, which, in overturning the conviction of an 18-year-old boy for molesting a 4-year-old girl, declared that his purported confession should not have been admitted into evidence, despite

---

[16] *Op. cit. supra*, Note 14.

[17] E.g., in *State* v. *Bailey*, 223 La. 40, 96, So. 2d 34, 1957, the trial court's determination that the defendant was competent to stand trial was upheld on appeal despite evidence that the defendant's IQ was 47, and that he had the intelligence level of a 6- to 7-year-old child. However, cf. a case recently decided by the Supreme Court of New Jersey, *State* v. *Caralluzzo*, 228 A. 2d 693, 1967, involving two defendants of about the same degree of impairment as the defendant in *Bailey*.

[18] *Miranda* v. *Arizona*, U.S. Sup. Ct., 384 U.S. 436, 1966, requiring evidence that the accused was warned of his constitutional rights prior to questioning as a condition of the admissibility of a confession.

[19] Several of the inmates in the sample seemed quite closely to fit the descriptive models given by the Task Force on Law (*op. cit. supra.*, Note 14) viz, "Some of the retarded are characterized by a desire to please authority. If a confession will please, it may be gladly given." And " 'Cheating to lose,' allowing others to place blame on him so that they are not angry with him, is a common pattern among the submissive retarded," etc.

statements of the officers who heard it that "He was more than willing to give us a statement for at the time he appeared like he didn't think there was nothing to it."[20] Thus, a confession had been obtained from every retardate in our sample who did not plead guilty except one; virtually all of them were represented by counsel; but in only three cases was admissibility of the confession objected to at trial. Interviews with trial judges, prosecutors, and defense counsel indicate that evidence of retardation is rarely presented on the issue of the admissibility of a confession.

Nor does mental retardation figure prominently in determinations of criminal responsibility. Although the M'Naghten rule is expressed in cognitive terms, and both Durham and A.L.I. carefully distinguish between "mental disease" and "mental defect," most jurisdictions adhere to the rule that mental deficiency alone—however severe—will not warrant a verdict of "not guilty by reason of insanity."[21]

Of course, mental retardation may be one of the constituent elements of the statutory definition of a "defective delinquent" and thus warrant special procedures and places of confinement. Indeed, the "defective delinquency" law[22] and specialized institution for "defective delinquents"[23] of one of the project states, Maryland, are widely known and have been widely commended—and attacked.[24] It is not possible here to discuss the operation of the Maryland law. It will suffice for present purposes merely to observe that even in that State grossly retarded persons were found among the state prison inmates.[25]

Referral for mental examination is provided in the laws of all six of the study states. But prior to conviction, such referral depends upon the raising of one of the issues noted above.[26] After conviction, there is often a presentence investigation report. In our sample of cases, however, in less than half was any presentence investigation report available to the court; and in only a handful of these was any mention made of the offender's mental impairment.

Finally, yet another reason why the issue of mental retardation is not raised is the fact that commitment—either as "incompetent" or "insane"—may well be required to continue "until recovery" or "until sanity is restored."[27] Of course in the case of mental retardation there is little, if any, hope for "recovery" from the underlying condition, as in the case of mental illness. The best that can ordinarily be hoped for is a kind of social recovery in which the retardate is trained to become as self-sufficient as possible. The result then of applying the standard of "recovery" may well in the case of a defendant found competent to stand trial, result in a commitment for years, without any determination having been made either that the defendant did the act complained of, or that he is in need of institutional care. And in the case of a defendant found "not guilty by reason of insanity," may lead to commitment for life, without regard to the nature of the offense committed or the degree of danger, if any, which the retardate may present.

FAILURE TO PROVIDE MEANINGFUL TREATMENT

In 1906 a physician at the Indiana State Prison recommended that "defective" inmates be separated from the others for special treatment. The "special treatment" he had in mind was close custodial care for the longest permis-

[20] *Harvey* v. *State*, 207 So. 2d 108, 1968, the court declaring that ". . . we are not prepared to say that a mentally deficient person of the caliber shown here *can* waive his constitutional rights."

[21] Most of the cases on the point recite the language of *Commonwealth* v. *Stewart*, 225 Mass. 9, 151 N.E. 74, 1926:

"Criminal responsibility does not depend upon the mental age of the defendant, nor upon the question whether the mind of the prisoner is above or below that of the ideal or of the average or of the normal man . . ." (151 N.E. at 74).

[22] Ann. Code Md. Art. 31, 1957.

[23] The Patuxent Institution. For a brief summary of the programs available for retarded inmates, see Boslow and Kandel, "Psychiatric Aspects of Dangerous Behavior: The Retarded Offender," 122 *Am. J. Psychiatry* 646, 1965.

[24] See *Sas, et al.* v. *State of Maryland*, 334 F 2d 506, CA -4, 1964.

[25] See Allen, *op. cit. supra.*, Note 9.

[26] In only one of the cases in our sample was the defense of lack of criminal responsibility raised, and in that one, the plea was changed to "guilty" after the report of the court-ordered psychiatric examination was received, containing the observation:

"In my opinion he could be certified as a mental defective and committed to an appropriate institution. However, in my opinion he is sane and responsible in law for his actions both at the time of the alleged crime and since."

The defendant about whom the psychiatrist was reporting had an IQ score on our retest of 53.

[27] The laws of all six of the study states provide that persons found incompetent to stand trial shall be committed until "recovery" or "restoration." Three of the six provide a similar standard where the defendant is found "not guilty by reason of insanity."

But cf. *Jackson* v. *Indiana*, a 1972 U.S. Supreme Court decision excerpted in Chapter 16 (Ed.).

sible period.[28] In most prisons today, his recommendation is being scrupulously followed.

It is neither ignorance of nor indifference to the special needs of these prisoners on the part of correctional authorities that has produced this situation. Rather, it results from the pathetically limited resources of most prison systems which simply cannot be stretched to provide meaningful programs for both "normal" and retarded inmates.[29]

In the discussion period following presentation of a paper describing some of the findings of the present study at an Annual Meeting of

[28] J. W. Mulligan, "Mental Defectives Among Prisoners," *Proceedings of the American Prison Association*, 1906, p. 198.

[29] As one of our interviewees, a prison superintendent, put it:

"As we see it, an institution such as ours has a choice of alternative operational policies. The first is the possibility of pitching our program to the needs of the two-thirds majority of normal inmates, in which case the one-third minority of retarded inmates would suffer. A second alternative is to lower our standards and alter our programs as required by the one-third minority, which would deprive the majority group. The third alternative would be to run two separate programs in the same institution, which would require at least a 50 percent increase in budgeted staff if we are to do justice to both segments of our population."

the American Psychiatric Association, one of the discussants questioned the extent to which mental retardation should "be permitted as an excuse or defense against criminal action," observing that "there is an implication in this paper that they should somehow receive special consideration."[30]

It is, indeed, special consideration that seems indicated, but not by way of "excuse." Rather, what is here recommended is simply that adequate procedures be designed to enable the fact of mental deficiency to be disclosed at or prior to trial; and that if it be determined that the unlawful act is related to the mental condition of the accused, he receive treatment appropriate to his condition. To follow such a course is both humane and an effectuation of the legal concept of "equal justice." But it is more than that. While the retarded prisoner is perhaps more easily apprehended and convicted, and is certainly confined for longer periods than offenders of normal intellectual capacity, he is eventually released. Thus it is no less than the enlightened self-interest of society that should demand that the mentally retarded prisoner be recognized as such, and that his confinement be rehabilitative rather than merely custodial.

[30] Bertram S. Brown and Thomas F. Courtless, "The Mentally Retarded in Penal and Correctional Institutions," *Amer. J. Psychiat.*, 124: 9, March, 1.c., p. 1170.

Editorial Note: *"Behavior Mod" in Corrections*

Few would dispute that one of the objectives of corrections is modification of the behavior of offenders—that, after all, is what "rehabilitation" means. The term "behavior modification," however, has come to stand for a variety of operant conditioning, psychosurgical, psychopharmacological, and psychotherapeutic techniques, widely believed to constitute a kind of "Clockwork Orange"-like brain washing, involuntarily imposed upon inmates of public institutions and posing the gravest threat to constitutional rights and human dignity.

Dr. Perry London of the University of Southern California wrote recently in the American Psychological Association *Monitor* (April 1974):

"Whether or not behavior scientists really can control much behavior, they have recently convinced the public that they can. Many are sorry now that they have done so. For instead of getting Nobel prizes and gratitude, they have been viewed with increasing suspicion, if not revulsion, and threatened with restriction—of funds, of sponsorship, even of access to subjects for their experiments and objects for their therapeutic benefits."

Focal points of attack have included: the U.S. Bureau of Prison's controversial project START (Special Treatment and Rehabilitative Training) at the Springfield, Missouri prison hospital; alleged use of psychosurgery on inmates of California prisons; techniques used at the Patuxent

Institution in Maryland (see Chapter 18, Part D, post); the planned new Federal Center for Correctional Research at Butner, North Carolina (see Suggestions for Additional Reading at the end of this chapter); and the Center for the Study and Reduction of Violence at U.C.L.A. Constitutional objections have been raised under the First Amendment's protections of freedom of speech, assembly, and religion; the Fourth Amendment's prohibition of unreasonable search and seizures; the proscription under the Fifth Amendment of deprivations of life, liberty, or property without due process of law; the Eighth Amendment's protection against cruel and unusual punishment; the right of privacy subsumed under the Ninth Amendment; and the Fourteenth Amendment's requirement of equal protection of the law. Underlying each of the attacks have been assertions that the programs are punitive rather than therapeutic, and that inmates of prisons and prison hospitals lack capacity to give informed consent to the procedures. As Senator Sam J. Ervin, Jr. declared in a statement before the Senate Health Subcommittee in March 1974:

Prisons exist as a closed society, eluding the public eye behind high walls and restricted contact. Only recently has there been any interest in assuring prisoners the benefits of those constitutional rights which follow them into the prison or jail. Only in the last decade have court decisions sought to insure the rights to counsel, legal materials, correspondence and of freedom from cruel punishment. Testimony before the Health Subcommittee has revealed that in the coercive atmosphere of a prison, inmates are more than willing to submit to drug experiments and other experimental programs in order to secure money or a change of location and conditions or to please the parole board by a record showing cooperation with the prison authority. The use of behavior modification in such a setting poses serious threats to constitutional liberties.

Opponents of "behavior mod" have won impressive first rounds in the cases of Project START and the Violence Center at U.C.L.A. The former program was described by *Psychiatric News* (Feb. 20, 1974), based on reports in the *Washington Post* and responses by the U.S. Bureau of Prisons:

The first level of confinement for START participants is round-the-clock "deadlock." . . . At this level the inmate is allowed out of his cell two hours a week for exercise and twice for showers. The rest of the day he spends in a tile-walled room approximately 6-by-10 feet, behind a steel door with a small window.
If the inmate goes 20 days without a "bad day," . . . he moves to the second level, at which time he is allowed to work three hours a day, eat meals out of his cell, and have one-and-on-half hours of recreation a day.
Gradually, the inmate is allowed more privileges, is allowed to earn money in an adjacent factory six hours daily, and begins to have sentence time off for good behavior restored.
In seven-and-a-half months, he is graduated from the program if he has followed all the rules. The prisoner is then returned to the general population of the penitentiary that referred him to START in the first place.
If the inmate rebels . . . or refuses to follow rules, or becomes verbally abusive to staff members, he is returned to solitary confinement. . . . If he refuses to participate in the program, the prisoner remains in solitary for a year and then is returned to a segregated unit of his home institution.

Psychologist Dr. Albert F. Scheckenbach, consultant to START declared:

"All we're saying [is] 'if you respond like a man, we'll treat you like a man. If you act like a child, we'll treat you like one.'"

But the director of the Institute for Behavior Research, Dr. Harold Cohen, appointed by the U.S. District Court for the Western District of Missouri to chair a panel of experts to study the START program, observed:

"As a behavioral project, it is a failure. It has not produced either the full participation or the expected changes set forth in the original premise. . . . No one should play God, not even an operant psychologist."

Following the report of the panel, the U.S. Bureau of Prisons announced discontinuance of Project START for "economic reasons." The law suit brought by the American Civil Liberties Union on behalf of seven prisoner-participants of START continues.

The Center for the Study and Reduction of Violence at U.C.L.A. received "agreement in principle" in July, 1973 for funding from the California state planning agency which dispenses L.E.A.A. (Law Enforcement Assistance Administration, U.S. Dept. of Justice) block grant funds, to study: abnormal electrical activities within the brains of hyperkinetic children and persons who have committed aggressive or violent sex crimes, possibly with implantation of "depth electrodes"; genetic screening of children to determine correlation of an extra Y chromosome with criminal behavior; treatment of rapists and child molesters with a synthetic female hormone; examination of women to determine the relationship of the menstrual cycle to violence; and development of a "model residential rehabilitation program" for violent sex offenders released from Atascadero State Hospital. Shortly after the U.S. Bureau of Prison's action, closing down Project START, L.E.A.A. announced that it would no longer support any programs involving behavior modification, psychosurgery, chemotherapy, or medical research, on the ground that it lacked "technical and professional skills . . . to screen, evaluate, or monitor such projects." The Violence Center is seeking other sources of funding.

What may be the future course of the behavioral sciences in corrections will depend upon the resolution of a maze of complex scientific, legal, moral, and ethical issues. The following quotes may illustrate the polar extremes of viewpoints bearing upon that resolution: writing in a recent issue of *Psychology Today*, Dr. James V. McConnell, professor of psychology at the University of Michigan, declared that the day has come when ". . . we can combine sensory deprivation with drugs, hypnosis and astute manipulation of reward and punishment to gain almost absolute control over an individual's behavior." Recognizing the existence of difficult legal and moral questions, Professor McConnell observes: "I don't believe the Constitution of the United States gives you the right to commit a crime if you want to; therefore, the Constitution does not guarantee you the right to maintain inviolate the personality forced on you in the first place—if and when the personality manifests strongly antisocial behavior."

And in the March, 1974 issue of *Federal Probation*, William E. Amos, chairman of the Youth Correction Division, U.S. Board of Parole, concludes: "Behavioral sciences at this stage do not know how to rehabilitate criminal offenders. . . . The philosophy of confinement should be deterrence, accountability, and the protection of society—not rehabilitation."

In terms of L.E.A.A. and Bureau of Prison support for behavior mod projects, Senator Ervin's statement of February 19 on the floor of the Senate may define the parameters of the present moratorium: "Until these questions [essentially those referred to above] have been answered, and until strict and comprehensive mechanisms guaranteeing informed consent and the individual privacy, self-determination, and dignity of human subjects of experimentation have replaced the Federal Government's present slipshod methods of funding such projects, such experimentation should be stopped."

PSYCHIATRIC ASPECTS OF HOMICIDE PREVENTION

Emanuel Tanay, M.D.

At this point in history we are using the same tools in relation to homicide that were employed thousands of years ago. We forbid certain forms of homicide and punish transgressions. There has been no significant innovation introduced into homicide control from the days of Hamurabi. There is no body of knowledge dealing with homicidal behavior as such. There is no agency or institution concerned with homicide prevention. We rely exclusively upon the penal-legal system in dealing with homicide.

The social sciences, psychiatry included, neglect the study of homicide. The legal system, on the other hand, is guarding against intrusion and infringement upon its territorial rights in this area. It seems that everyone decries homicide, but no one does anything to prevent it.

The legal system of classification distinguishes, in essence, two types of homicide: (1) approved homicide and (2) disapproved homicide. This type of classification cannot be utilized in devising a scientific approach to prevention.

Excerpted and reprinted with permission from *American Journal of Psychiatry* 128, 7 (January 1972): 815.

CATEGORIZATION

The essence of scientific knowledge is generalization based upon empirical or experimental study of the subject matter. Scientific investigation requires a theoretical frame of reference and the accumulation of empirical data. I approach homicide from the point of view of a psychiatric clinician, deriving data from the evaluation of approximately 100 homicide offenders. My case material led me to classify homicidal behavior into three types. The first category I described as ego-syntonic homicide, the second as ego-dystonic (dissociative) homicide, and the third as psychotic homicide (1).

Ego-syntonic homicide refers to the situation in which the homicidal act was committed without disruption in the functioning of the ego, and was consciously acceptable to the individual committing the act of homicide. The ego-syntonic homicide is a rational, goal-directed act, committed for the purpose of fulfilling a consciously acceptable wish.

The law is explicit about this state of mind when it uses such phrases as "*mens rea*, intent, maliciously, willfully, and knowingly." Inquiry into the state of mind of the perpetrator of homicide at the time of the act has far-reaching implications not only for legal purposes but also for the prevention of homicide.

Ego-dystonic homicide describes a killing that occurs against the conscious wishes of the perpetrator; it is usually carried out in an altered state of consciousness and often occurs without conscious awareness or motivation.

The concept of dissociation is essential to the understanding of ego-dystonic homicidal behavior. This term was introduced by Pierre Janet (1859–1947) to describe a mental state in which a part of the psychic structure is split off from the rest of the personality (2). Dissociation is a defense mechanism involving disruption of the ego. It is analogous to fainting in physiology. In fainting, certain physiological functions are disrupted as an adaptive measure. The essence of the dissociative state is that certain functions of the psychic apparatus escape from the control of the ego and superego. Dissociation is observed in many situations, usually without serious consequences. The term "dissociation" encompasses a variety of altered states of consciousness that result from various causes (psychological, physiological, or pharmacological).

The normal psychic state requires the existence of structures that are coordinated and that maintain a certain hierarchy within the overall organization of the personality. In the normal state, the id can be viewed as subordinated to the ego, the ego as subordinated to the superego. This hierarchy depends upon the integrity of the structural organization of the psychic apparatus. The adequacy of psychic organization is subject to fluctuations in the same individual and varies from person to person. Every human being undergoes a periodic suspension of this hierarchy known as sleep. Breakdown of the psychic organization occurs in a variety of stress situations and is clinically known as dissociative reaction.

Menninger, in his book *The Vital Balance* (3), described this state as ego rupture, which he defined as a major disorganization of the ego that is reversible. He also introduced the term "episodic dyscontrol" (p. 178), which encompasses various situations popularly described as "going to pieces." Other authors have utilized such terms as "situational psychosis," "ten-day schizophrenia," "shell-shock," "combat exhaustion," etc. Menninger pointed out that these conditions are the result of being placed in situations of insoluble conflict. He also described dissociation as a means of controlling agression: ". . . dissociative loss of consciousness is actually a device for the control of aggressions and not merely, as it is sometimes assumed, a self-anesthesizing device in states of fear" (3, p. 242).

Since the terms "situational psychosis," "ten-day schizophrenia," and other similar descriptive labels are not in the current nomenclature, I use the term "dissociative reaction," which is included in the official nomenclature of the American Psychiatric Association.

Dissociative Homicide

The ego-dystonic homicide can best be described as resulting from a process occurring between two individuals whose personalities and life situation determine the deadly outcome. The homicide in these cases represents a resolution of a conflict extending over a long period of time and maintained primarily on an unconscious level. The killing takes place during a disruption of the ego and may be precipitated by a seemingly insignificant provocation. The term "homicidal process" describes the progressive intensification of the sadomasochistic relationship between the perpetrator and the significant person, who usually becomes the victim. I emphasize "usually" since occasionally displacement occurs and a relatively uninvolved person becomes the focus of homicidal discharge.

The perpetrators of this type of homicide do not suffer from superego defects. On the contrary, they show evidence of a strong overcontrolling superego. They lack the capacity to gratify aggressive needs consistently and can do so only in an explosive manner. The history of these individuals frequently reveals violent child-rearing practices that account for the severity of the superego. In the dissociative homicide, the availability of a gun is a crucial factor. Explosive discharges of aggression have occurred in these people before; then they were terminated by verbal or nonlethal physical assaults. The incidence of such episodes, however, is infrequent in this group of perpetrators (1).

Dissociative homicide, then, requires the presence of a number of factors: (1) an over-controlling superego in the perpetrator, (2) a sadomasochistic relationship between victim and perpetrator, (3) the occurrence of an altered state of consciousness, and (4) the presence of a weapon. Dissociative homicide is analogous to nuclear reaction, in which a number of isolated events must occur simultaneously in order to trigger the explosion.

The third category of homicide describes killings that are associated with psychotic states. The incidence of homicide among psychotics is rather rare.

It appears to be almost a banality to stress that there are varieties of homicide. Nevertheless, this emphasis is necessary since we act as if homicide were unitary behavior. There are homicides that represent the ultimate of organization, structure, and preparation. Then, at the other end of the spectrum, are those that are examples of disorganized, unplanned discharge of primitive aggression. A duel may lead to homicide, but it represents an example of organized, ritualized aggression. A lethal confrontation portrayed in a western movie is an organized form of behavior with definite rules or procedures. A gangland killing is an organized form of behavior carried out by those who believe in violence as a means of resolving conflict. These models of ego-syntonic slayings have dominated our handling of homicide.

It is essential for preventive efforts to recognize that ego-syntonic homicide represents only a small part of the incidence of homicide in our culture. The majority of homicides are ego-dystonic.

As long as homicide is viewed primarily as ego-syntonic behavior punitive measures seem an appropriate deterrent device. The recognition of a form of homicide that is nonreflective, ego-dystonic, and representative of a decompensation phenomenon requires a different approach.

PREVENTION OF DISSOCIATIVE HOMICIDE

Prevention involves the systematic application of knowledge designed to eliminate or minimize the factors leading to a morbid condition and its complications. The preventive efforts are designed to reduce the incidence of the condition (primary prevention), shorten the length of associated morbidity (secondary prevention), and diminish the incidence of crippling results (tertiary prevention).

Psychiatry makes significant contributions to the reduction of the incidence of dissociative homicide and complications resulting from it, without being fully aware of it. Systematic preventive efforts should be directed toward a variety of factors that have been isolated as significant in the morbidity and mortality associated with homicidal behavior. A few such factors were named in this paper; many more remain unknown.

Primary prevention involves a reduction of the incidence of the homicidal act itself. Prevention of the psychic disruptions leading to homicide is the most desirable and the least attainable at this time. The theoretical possibilities of primary prevention of the dissociative rage state are not likely to be quickly implemented. The Joint Commission on Mental Illness and Health found no evidence that present-day preventive measures in the field of psychiatry influence the incidence of mental illness: "Primary prevention of mental illness has remained largely an article of scientific faith rather than an applicable scientific truth" (4, p. 76).

The most easily manipulated variable in the homicidal process is the availability of the weapon. Statistical evidence and clinical studies indicate a positive correlation between the incidence of homicide and the availability of weapons. The nature of the weapon immediately available determines the outcome.

The Availability of Guns

The National Commission on the Causes and Prevention of Violence, on the basis of data provided by the Chicago Police Department, concluded that the fatality rate of firearm attacks is about five times higher than the fatality rate of actual attacks with knives (5, p. 41). Since 1900, about 800,000 Americans have been killed with privately owned guns. Each year 17,000 people die by means of firearms.

Nevertheless, the possession of firearms is encouraged and promoted by various private organizations and commercial interests. The explanation given is that guns provide for recreational activities in the form of hunting and target shooting. Furthermore, guns are claimed to be useful for protection. The utility of firearms as protection is a rationalization for the acquisition of an archaic symbol of masculinity. The National Commission on the Causes and Prevention of Violence used statistics from Detroit extensively:

In Detroit, from January 1964 through September 1968, seven residential burglars were shot and killed by their intended victims, an average of just under two a year. . . . When measured against the burglary rate, no more than two in a thousand burglaries in Detroit are foiled by shooting the burglar. . . . While killings by home robbers are a small portion of all homicides (two and three percent in Los Angeles and Detroit), home robbery when it occurs is far more dangerous than home burglary. For example, from January 1964 through September 1968 in Detroit, seventeen victims died as the result of home robberies, compared to three deaths of home burglary victims. Firearms are of limited utility in defending against home robbers because the robber is usually able to surprise and overwhelm his victim. Detroit reported three cases of the victim killing a home robber in five years. In Los Angeles, where about 1,000 home robberies were reported in 1967, eight home robbers were shot and killed from January 1967 to October 1968. . . . During 1967 more lives were lost in home firearm accidents in Detroit—25—than were lost in home robbery and burglary in four and a half years—23 (5, p. 64).

There is at this time no widespread acceptance of the fact that the possession of firearms exposes the owner to the risk of committing involuntary dissociative homicide. Many homicides would be prevented if such awareness existed on the part of physicians, psychiatrists, and law enforcement personnel. Dissemination of this information to the public at large would significantly reduce the number of guns and the incidence of homicide. The triumphs of public health measures, to which we owe the high level of health our society enjoys, were not achieved by education alone. Public health measures require education and effective legislation.

The acceptance of the need for aggressive gratification constitutes, in my opinion, an important preventive measure against homicide and various forms of maladaptive destructiveness. Psychiatry can perform here an important educational role.

Prediction of dangerousness is another important area that psychiatry has avoided for a variety of reasons. Participation in criminal proceedings by psychiatrists is an essential contribution, neglected by American psychiatry. Treatment of various individuals affected by homicidal behavior is another relevant psychiatric activity.

I would like to close with a quotation from Albert Camus: "All I ask is that, in the midst of a murderous world, we agree to reflect on murder and to make a choice" (6, p. 123).

REFERENCES

1. Tanay, E. "Psychiatric study of homicide," *Amer. J. Psychiat.* 125: 1253–1258, 1969.
2. Janet, P. *The Major Symptoms of Hysteria,* 2nd ed. New York: Macmillan Co., 1929.
3. Menninger, K. *The Vital Balance.* New York: Viking Press, 1963.
4. Joint Commission on Mental Illness and Health: Action for Mental Health. New York, Science Editions, 1961.
5. Staff Report to the National Commission on the Causes and Prevention of Violence: Firearms and Violence in American Life. Washington, D.C., U.S. Government Printing Office, 1969.
6. Camus, A., cited in Weinberg, A., Weinberg, L. *Instead of Violence.* Boston: Beacon Press, 1963.

EDITORIAL NOTE: Students who are particularly interested in the raw data from which Dr. Tanay's categories derive are urged to read carefully reference 1, above.

SUGGESTIONS FOR ADDITIONAL READING

Brussel. *Casebook of a Crime Psychiatrist.* New York: Bernard Geis Associates, 1968; Dell Pub. Co., 1970.

Cormier. "Psychiatry in Prison," *MH* 57:4, Special Issue on Prisons (Fall 1973).

Dawson. *Sentencing.* Boston, Mass.: Little, Brown & Co., 1969 ("The Psychiatric Examination," pp. 41–51).

Goldberg. "Patuxent," *MH* 57:4, Special Issue on Prisons (Fall 1973).

Groder. "Butner: A Clear Blueprint," *MH* 57:4, Special Issue on Prisons (Fall 1973).

Guttmacher. *The Mind of the Murderer.* New York: Farrar, Straus & Cudahy, 1960 (Part I: "The Murderer").

Halleck. *Psychiatry and the Dilemmas of Crime.* New York: Harper & Row, 1967.

Katz. *Experimentation with Human Beings.* New York: Russel Sage Foundation, 1972.

MacDonald. *Psychiatry and the Criminal: A Guide to Psychiatric Examinations for the Criminal Courts,* 2d ed. Springfield, Ill.: C. C Thomas, 1969.

MacDonald. *The Murderer and His Victim.* Springfield, Ill.: C. C Thomas, 1961.

Matthews. *Mental Disability and the Criminal Law.* Chicago, Ill.: American Bar Foundation, 1970.

Menninger. *The Crime of Punishment.* New York: Viking Press, 1968 (esp. Chapter 4, "The Cold War between Lawyers and Psychiatrists"; and Chapter 5, "Right and Wrong Uses of Psychiatry").

Morris and Hawkins. *The Honest Politician's Guide to Crime Control.* Chicago: University of Chicago Press, 1970 (esp. Chapter 7, "Crime and the Psychiatrist").

Sadoff. "Mental Illness and the Criminal Process: The Role of the Psychiatrist," 54 *A.B.A.J.* (June 1968): 566.

Scheidemandel and Kanno. *The Mentally Ill Offender: A Survey of Treatment Programs.* Washington, D.C.: American Psychiatric Association, 1969.

Stürup. *Treating the "Untreatable": Chronic Criminals at Herstedvester.* Baltimore, Md.: The Johns Hopkins Press, 1968.

Wellington. "Butner: A Vague Blueprint," *MH* 57:4, Special Issue on Prisons (Fall 1973).

16

Competency to Stand Trial

We continue our inquiry into the role of psychiatry in the criminal law, focusing on an area of decision-making which is of crucial importance, but often overlooked in undergraduate criminal law courses: competency to stand trial. In terms of numbers of persons affected, determinations of incompetency to stand trial are far more significant than verdicts of not guilty by reason of insanity. In a recently published comprehensive survey conducted by the Joint Information Service of the American Psychiatric Association, it was noted that of all admissions to mental hospitals of mentally ill offenders, 52 percent result from determinations of incompetency to stand trial, and only 4 percent from findings of not guilty by reason of insanity. The first article is based on multidisciplinary empirical research and contains a summary of most of the significant problems and recommended solutions. The Ezra Pound case was, of course, a *cause célèbre* in the annals of the criminal law, and is here re-examined by forensic psychiatry's severest critic, Dr. Thomas S. Szasz. The chapter includes the three major U.S. Supreme Court decisions on competency to stand trial: *Dusky*, which raises again some basic problems in construing the legal concepts of "knowledge" and "understanding" (cf. the Allen article in Chapter 3, and the testimony of the psychiatrist in the Andrews case in Chapter 7); *Pate* v. *Robinson* (requiring the court to raise the issue of incompetency *sua sponte* where the evidence suggests doubt as to competency); and *Jackson* v. *Indiana* (the most recent, and perhaps most important, expression by the Court on incompetency determinations). Another empirical research study—this time in the District of Columbia—is represented by the excerpt from the report of a Committee of the Judicial Conference of the District of Columbia Circuit. The *Severns* and *Wilson* cases are concerned with the difficult problems raised by amnesia. And the chapter closes with excerpts from a definitive study by Dr. McGarry and others, supported by the National Institute of Mental Health, and the conclusions and recommendations of the Group for Advancement of Psychiatry.

COMPETENCY TO STAND TRIAL

John H. Hess, M.D., Henry B. Pearsall, S. Ed.,
Donald A. Slichter, S. Ed., and Herbert E. Thomas, M.D.

Mental unsoundness in a person accused of a crime raises two distinct legal questions. One is the question of the individual's responsibility for his behavior, and the other is the question of the individual's competency to enter into the legal procedures of trial or punishment. In recent years considerable attention has been given to matters of responsibility, but relatively little attention has been paid to the problem of incompetency and especially to the consequences of incompetency proceedings. In order to analyze and evaluate the operations

Excerpts from Student Comment, "Criminal Law—Insane Persons—Competency to Stand Trial," 59 *Michigan Law Review* 7 (May 1961): 1078–1100, reprinted by permission of the editors. The authors wish to thank Dr. R. E. Cooper, Medical Superintendent of Ionia State Hospital, and his staff for their co-operation in this study.

of the Michigan law in the area of incompetency to stand trial, two psychiatrists joined two law students to conduct field research at Ionia State Hospital to which all persons found incompetent to stand trial are committed.

This comment reports and analyzes the results of this field research. Attention is given also to the merits of alternative procedures for the commitment and treatment of incompetents.

I. INCOMPETENCY PROCEEDINGS—COMMON LAW

It was the rule at common law that an accused could not be required to plead to an indictment or be tried for a crime when he was so mentally disordered that he could not meet the common law tests of competency; that is, when he could not understand the nature and object of the proceedings against him, comprehend his own condition in reference to such proceedings, and assist in his defense.

The common-law judge had wide discretion in calling and conducting a competency examination. Whether an examination into the defendant's competency would be made at all depended on whether the judge had reason to believe that the defendant was mentally unable to proceed with trial. It was often said that once a competency examination was ordered, the judge was free to use any method for determining the accused's competency which was "discreet and convenient." Also the judge had discretion to summon a jury to make the determination of competency or to make such determination himself. If it was determined that the accused was incompetent, the common-law practice seems to have been to confine him in jail. Indeed, it had been held that in the absence of statutes the judge had power only to order the incompetent confined in jail. He would then be tried at such time as the judge determined his competency restored.

At the common law there was no right of appeal from the incompetency hearing itself, but the issue of the accused's competency could be raised on appeal from the criminal trial. Despite authority that an accused's constitutional rights would be violated if he were tried while incompetent, the judge's decision was generally sustained unless it was clearly arbitrary. Since most states have merely codified the common law in this field, wide discretionary powers continue to be exercised by the trial courts of these states.

II. INCOMPETENCY PROCEEDINGS—MICHIGAN

A. Commitment: Law and Operation

1. *Law.* The Michigan incompetency statute follows the basic pattern of the common law. It requires the court to hold a sanity hearing to determine the accused's competency to proceed with trial when one accused of a felony "shall appear to be insane." The question of the accused's competency can be raised by the accused, the prosecuting attorney, or the court. Whether the defendant "appears to be insane" within the statute may be decided either by the court or by a jury.

If it is determined that the defendant does "appear to be insane," the court fixes a time and place for a hearing of the competency issue at which it "shall call two or more reputable physicians and other credible witnesses to testify at said hearing, and [shall call] the prosecuting attorney to aid in the examination and if it be deemed necessary to call a jury for that purpose, [the court] is fully empowered to compel the attendance of witnesses and jurors."

The statute retains the common-law three-pronged test of incompetency: "[T]he test on the trial of [the defendant's competency] . . . shall be whether such person is [1] capable of understanding the nature and object of the proceedings against him and [2] of comprehending his own condition in reference to such proceedings and [3] of assisting in his defense in a rational or reasonable manner."

It would be expected that if the defendant is found to be incompetent, he would be sent to a rehabilitative institution. This the statute does provide, but it does not use incompetency terminology or refer to the incompetency tests:

If such person is found *insane*, the judge of said court shall order that he be discharged from imprisonment and that he be turned over to the sheriff for safe custody and removal to Ionia state hospital, to which hospital such person shall be committed to remain until restored to sanity.

The use of "insane" and "sanity" can be explained by the fact that it is this same provision which provides for examination and commitment of persons found not responsible for criminal acts. Both these and incompetents are sent to Ionia, and the general word "insane" encompasses the criteria for commitment for both groups. However, with respect to the criterion for commitment of incompetents, reason would indicate that the legislature intended the three-pronged competency test to be used.

2. *Operation.* At the hearing to determine the competency of the accused to stand trial, "two reputable physicians" are required to testify regarding the accused's mental state. The influence which their testimony exerts upon the competency determination is substantial, for they speak as experts in a field shrouded in mystery for both judge and jury. Not understanding the medical complexities associated with mental illness, the legal authorities enunciate legal policy objectives and broad competency tests by way of statute and then rely upon the doctors to apply these tests to the individual defendants.

Our study suggests that the Michigan statute's direction to commit the accused if he cannot meet the competency test is being very loosely applied in many cases. Several records studied at Ionia indicated that the doctors confuse the legal standards for competency with those for responsibility. An example of this confusion of legal concepts was evidenced by a report which read: "This man does not know right from wrong, he is incompetent, he is not able to help his counsel, he should be committed to an institution because he is insane and should be released only when he is found to be sane." Most of the records which did not manifest such confusion were form statements which simply parroted the incompetency test of the statute.

The confusion of legal concepts is caused in part by the imprecise wording of the Michigan statute which codifies the three-pronged common-law test as the criterion for testing the accused's ability to proceed with trial but subsequently uses the word "insane" to indicate the criterion for committing him to Ionia State Hospital. Another probable causal factor is that frequently the "two reputable physicians" who make psychiatric determinations have no psychiatric training. Also, in many cases a report on the defendant's condition is prepared by a social worker or psychologist. After the doctor interviews the patient he adds a covering letter to the psychologist's report suggesting that the accused be committed.

The records also indicate that some of the examining physicians assumed the role of moral experts. In one case the doctor recommended commitment because of the patient's "hostile and aggressive tendencies." However, it may be supposed that those defendants well enough for sentencing to prison exhibit similar tendencies. In another instance the examining physicians said: "We actually feel the patient could cooperate with counsel but that it would be better if he were to be hospitalized in Ionia." This departure from the physician's proper role as expert medical witness seems to be based on two factors. First,

the physician does not understand that the legal objective is the narrow one of determining whether the defendant is competent to proceed with trial, but rather tends to think of his function as a broader one of protecting society, the defendant, or both. Implicit in many of the physician's recommendations is the feeling that the individual defendant is such a pathetic figure and so clearly not responsible for his crime that he should not be consigned to prison. Second, the physicians seem to believe that commitment to Ionia is infinitely preferable to a prison sentence. Misapprehending the purpose of the incompetency proceedings and his role in them, the physician assumes the responsibility for insuring that the defendant is treated in a more humane atmosphere than a prison. Examples of this type of distortion occurred in many of the hospital records studied, but were most prominent in the records of elderly persons or those who were obviously mentally defective.

It is our judgment that as a result of this loose application of the competency tests, persons are being committed to Ionia who are not in fact legally incompetent. This judgment is corroborated by the fact that frequently the Ionia Hospital physicians' diagnosis of the accused varied from the opinion presented to the court by the court-appointed physicians. It was not unusual to find that the hospital staff found a newly-admitted patient was mentally ill but nevertheless able to meet the legal competency standards.

B. Procedures at the Hospital

The Ionia State Hospital is overcrowded and understaffed. The total patient population of 1,484 as of August, 1960, represents a patient excess over maximum capacity of 262 persons or about 21 per cent. Of the total number of patients, approximately 755, or 51 per cent, were committed because incompetent to stand trial. To administer to the needs of these patients there are but four physicians including the superintendent of the hospital. Incompetency as a legal concept is not meaningful to these doctors, for whether a person is "sane enough" for trial is a legal concept incapable of precise medical evaluation and determination. Since the doctors do not understand the law, nor their role in its administration, it is not surprising that clinical results bear scant resemblance to legal policy objectives.

A less obvious but perhaps more important problem concerns the goals of the hospital. Patients' progress notes indicate that the hospital staff frequently does not know what is expected of them. The hospital's objective appears to be to restore the incompetent to "soundness of mind," a goal which could be, and in practice is, very different from the goal of restoring the patient to a condition which would permit him to stand trial. For most categories of patients at Ionia the objective of "restoration to sanity" is sound. It is easy to understand that this objective could be unconsciously applied to the total patient population. Without doubt much of the confusion regarding therapeutic goals for patients who are incompetent to stand trial results from the necessity of establishing different standards of cure for the various classification of patients at the hospital. A lack of clearcut therapeutic goals results in a case such as the following: F. C., a twenty-five-year-old male, has been held as an incompetent patient for four years while hospital personnel work toward achieving "insight into his behavior" and "confession of his crime."

The therapeutic procedures carried out at Ionia State Hospital differ relatively little from those carried on at other state mental institutions. Little in the way of individual attention can be offered. The incoming patient is given a mental and physical examination upon arrival and assigned to a ward. Contact with his staff physician is frequent at first while evaluation is in process, but the longer the patient remains in the hospital, the less frequent are the doctor's interviews. The records studied indicated that only 33 per cent of the patients were seen by a doctor as often as once every three months and 61 per cent were seen by a doctor only every six months. The infrequency of doctor-patient interviews is not solely caused by crowded conditions. Since the interview should further some recognizable goal, if such a goal does not exist, the interview will be unproductive and is therefore less likely to be held.

Other therapeutic efforts consist primarily of relieving the patients of their social and legal responsibilities and exposing them to a healthy hospital environment. Such techniques have definite value, although limited to be sure, and with this minimum treatment alone a large percentage of the individuals committed as incompetent could probably be expected to reach a state of legal competency in a relatively short period of time if the hospital were to concentrate on this goal. Other therapeutic endeavors consist of the extensive use of tranquilizing medication, electroconvulsive shock therapy, and limited group therapy usually conducted by a psychologist, social worker, or "lay therapist."

C. Discharge

In addition to commitment and treatment of incompetents, the Michigan statute provides for their discharge back to the committing court. Since the reason for commitment of the incompetent is his failure to comply with the standards of competency, one would likewise expect that the criterion for discharge back to the committing court would be the accused's ability to "pass" the same competency tests. However, the stated criterion for such discharge is not the three-pronged competency test but that of "restoration to sanity."

When [the accused] . . . shail be *restored to sanity*, and that fact has been determined by the superintendent of said hospital or by any other proceeding authorized by this section, the said superintendent of said hospital shall forthwith certify that fact in writing to said judge and prosecuting attorney. The judge shall thereupon immediately require the sheriff without delay to bring up such person from the said hospital and place him in proper custody until he is remanded to prison, brought to trial or judgment, as the case may be, or is legally discharged.

This use of the "restoration to sanity" standard can again be explained by the fact that the statute covers procedures for commitment and discharge of both incompetents and those found non-responsible. The proposition that the legislature in the case of incompetents intended "restoration to sanity" to refer specifically to the three-part competency test is supported by the Michigan Attorney General's office:

[I]t would seem that the law does differentiate between those individuals who are committed because they are criminally insane, which fact has justified their acquittal on criminal charges, and those individuals who are committed because they cannot stand trial. In the case of a person who is committed after acquittal as criminally insane, the legal and logical test to be applied would seem to be whether he has actually been restored to sanity so that he no longer represents a threat to society.

But, in the case of an individual who is committed before trial, the legal and logical test would seem to be whether he has been restored to sanity to the extent that the reason for his commitment no longer exists, i.e., that he now is capable of understanding the nature and object of the proceedings against him and of comprehending his own condition in reference to such proceedings and of assisting in his defense in a rational and reasonable manner."

It is probable that this vague criterion for discharge—"restoration to sanity"—is partly responsible for the indicated lack of defined therapeutic goals in treatment of incompetents at Ionia. Further, the vague term "sanity" can justify retention of incompetents until it is felt "safe" to return them to society, a criterion for discharge apparently underlying many cases. Moreover, this statutory criterion also justifies the hospital's frequently stated goal of restoring "soundness of mind" to the incompetent before discharging him.

D. Parole

The Michigan incompetency statute was amended in 1947 to provide that any patient may be paroled or given a leave of absence by the hospital superintendent. This amendment, part of the present statute, provides:

The superintendent of the Ionia state hospital may grant a parole or leave of absence to any person committed under the provisions of this section subject to such conditions as may be prescribed by the department of mental health, providing such parole concurred in by the committing court after due notice has been given by mail to the prosecuting attorney of the county from which the patient was committed.

Such paroled person committed under the provisions of this section who has not recovered sanity but whose discharge, in the judgment of the superintendent, will not be detrimental to the public welfare and will not be injurious to the patient, may be discharged, provided such discharge is concurred in by the committing court and due notice has been mailed to the prosecuting attorney of the county in which the patient was committed within 10 days prior to such discharge.

Our study shows that the hospital requires a high degree of mental alertness and exemplary conduct before even considering a patient for parole. Before a patient can be paroled he must come before a staff conference composed of all the doctors plus the ward attendants, psychologists, and social workers. As in the case of doctor visitations, the frequency of a patient's staff conferences varies inversely with the length of his confinement at the hospital. At first he may be "staffed" as often as every three months. But as time passes the meetings are held less and less frequently and it is not unusual for long-time patients to be staff-interviewed less than once every two years. The records indicate that the standards which the doctors set for those seeking parole are "soundness of mind," "social competency," and "emotional maturity." In addition, factors quite apart from the patient's mental state are considered. Whether the patient has a home in Michigan, whether he has a family to look after him, and whether he can find employment are fully as important to his chance for parole as is his mental condition. In one instance, a woman had been in the hospital for over two years and the reports were extremely pessimistic concerning her condition. It appeared that her chances of parole or discharge were exceedingly remote when a letter arrived from a lawyer expressing concern. This was followed by an inquiry from the committing court. Immediately the tone of her progress reports changed and within three months she was paroled.

Once paroled, the patient must meet strict standards of conduct to retain his valued status. He may not drink, drive a car except as necessary in his work, or marry without permission from the hospital. He must report periodically to the parole authorities at a state hospital near his home, and he must be able to hold a job and make a successful adjustment in society. If he is able to maintain these high standards of conduct for a period of three years, he is then eligible for discharge.

Although the statute provides for discharge of paroled persons who have "not recovered sanity," it is clear that anyone meeting the criteria for parole could meet the relatively modest standards required in order to stand trial. The provision for parole makes no sense as part of incompetency to stand trial procedure. If the defendant is well enough for parole, he is well enough for trial. If he is to be tried after discharge from parole, such a procedure denies him his right to a speedy trial guaranteed him by the Michigan constitution and state statute and is vulnerable to a charge of invalidity. If he is not to be tried, but is to be released into society after discharge from parole, the only proper way for the state to hold him as a parolee would appear to be by means of a civil commitment.

III. SOME RESULTS OF THE MICHIGAN SYSTEM

A. Legal Results

We earlier indicated belief that some persons have been sent to Ionia who are not in fact legally incompetent and that there appears to be a conflict between the apparent goals of incompetency law and the hospital goals in treating incompetents. At common law it was for the protection of his rights that an incompetent was not tried, and this same idea appears to be the basis for the Michigan statute. Once the defendant is again competent to stand trial the desire to protect his rights should compel his early return to the committing court for trial. Society also has the "right" to try him at this time. But since the hospital does not concentrate on the goal of making the defendant competent for trial, and in many cases instead concentrates on achieving the more difficult goal of restoring "soundness of mind," many defendants are deprived of a chance to complete their trials.

If our estimate is correct that many incompetents at Ionia could be readied for trial with existing facilities in a short period of time, it is indefensible that for a substantial number of defendants commitment to Ionia is the equivalent of a life sentence. During the period July, 1954, to December, 1960, a total of 470 defendants were committed to Ionia as incompetent to stand trial, a rate of about 84 admissions per year. During this same period approximately 105 were discharged back to the committing court, a rate of little more than 16 per year. Even if there is added to this figure approximately 15 who are paroled in any given year, there are many more admitted to Ionia than are released. How many of the present 755 incompetents will be discharged is impossible to say with complete accuracy, but if the past rates are any guide, the number discharged is likely to fall well short of one-half. The rest can expect to spend the rest of their lives at the hospital. This system accounts for the clear preference of many incompetents for confinement at the state penitentiary at Jackson rather than commitment to Ionia.

Moreover, confinement at Ionia because of incompetence to stand trial is not deemed imprisonment to be computed upon the patient's subsequent conviction and sentence. The sentence begins to run only after conviction. This should be contrasted with the provisions of a Michigan statute which requires an application to the probate court for civil commitment to retain those patients who have been convicted of a crime but who subsequently are sent to Ionia because of mental illness and are still residents at Ionia when their sentences expire. The incompetent who has never faced trial need never be civilly committed under the present procedures.

Instead of protection for the defendant until he is ready for trial, the administration of mental incompetents more closely resembles an alternative to the regular penal system. Through the use of incompetency law, those found dangerous to society by reason of mental affliction can be isolated without the formalities of trial and conviction. Statutory ambiguity and hospital misunderstanding are not solely to blame. Acquiescence by the courts and police in a system producing the above figures on "inflow and outflow" of incompetents suggests satisfaction with the system's operation. The almost total lack of judicial or police inquiry into a patient's progress suggests indifference to whether these persons are ever brought to trial. This is demonstrated by the additional fact that in most cases when the defendant is discharged to the committing court the charges against him are dismissed, and he is released without trial. The authors reviewed the records of 21 incompetent patients discharged back to the committing court for trial. The records showed that 14 of these patients were returned to the Recorder's Court in Detroit. A review of these records at the Recorder's Court by the authors revealed that *not one* of the 14 had been tried after being returned to the court. This fact lends support to the conclusion that the Ionia State Hospital is often used as a place to incarcerate persons without benefit of trial. When this period of incarceration is ended the state apparently considers that adequate punishment has been accomplished. Thus it appears that the emphasis in fact is not on protection of the accused but on protection of society.

Although the Michigan competency statute, providing for examination and commitment of the defendant, is not invalid on its face, commitment for an indefinite period of time and without periodic and thorough review appears to violate the protection afforded the defendant by the due process clause of the federal constitution and the due process and speedy trial clauses of the Michigan constitution.

B. Non-Legal Results

1. *The Doctor at the Incompetency Hearings.* Certainly most doctors would agree that their proper function in hearings to determine competency consists of a scientific evaluation of the patient and an accurate and useful presentation of the scientific conclusions to the court. The abhorrence of the psychiatric discipline for value judgments involving the moral and ethical behavior of its patients is well known; yet in the Michigan commitment proceedings the physician seems to forget this abhorrence when dealing with his legal brethren. All too often in this situation he not only evaluates the defendant's psychological status, but judges his behavior, estimates its social and ethical significance, and decides on a fitting consequence, be it commitment or trial. Such a sacrifice of professional identity and its replacement by a quasi-legal status is not without a price; the physician has enormously complicated if not completely lost his therapeutic advantage. The patient who feels that he has been committed as the result of his confidential utterances to the examining physician loses confidence not in just the "committing doctor" but in *all* physicians.

2. *The Doctor at the Hospital.* The label "hospital" connotes a long tradition of alleviation of pain and suffering dictated by the appropriate and humane application of the science and the art of medicine. Such application is traditionally entrusted to an individual having both in name and in function the title "doctor." The patient admitted to Ionia State Hospital by virtue of the distorted role of the examining physician has already begun to suspect the individual bearing the title "doctor" and to wonder at his intentions.

Many of the patients at Ionia State Hospital do not consider it a hospital, but rather a prison and, in fact, an extremely undesirable prison. For the majority, it is a prison to which one is committed on an arbitrary and incomprehensible basis; it is a prison in which apparent medical functions are carried on in a mechanical fashion without reference to any previous or future framework; it is a prison in which hopes of release gradually are transformed into despair and finally into psychotic delusions. The Ionia atmosphere is predominantly composed of feelings of uncertainty and insecurity. Such feelings have their origin in, and are reinforced by, the uncertainty of the statute, the uncertainty in the mind of the court, and the uncertainty in the minds of the examining physicians. Uncertainty continues at the hospital in the minds of the patient and the doctors.

Is the hospital dealing with an alleged criminal or with a sick human being? Is its role that of a non-judgmental, therapeutically oriented institution, or is it in fact a custodial burying ground for potentially dangerous persons who by social caprice and legal conscience are not sent to prison? Is its goal to restore its patients to health and to social competency or to provide the necessary treatment which would allow the patient to achieve legal competence? It is answers to these questions that Ionia State Hospital lacks, and it is this lack which produces the stultifying mechanical nature of its proceedings and the insidious pessimism of its atmosphere.

Improvement in the hospital's physical facilities or even in the size and quality of its staff could not alone bring about an effective hospital operation. A realizable therapeutic mission is the *sine qua non* of a successful hospital.

3. *Significance for the Patient.* What of the patient? How does he react to the uncertainty and the endless drifting to which he is subjected? The answer is simple: he becomes sicker. The records studied at Ionia are replete with examples of patients who in the initial stages of their hospitalization made significant improvement. However, because such improvement was not measured against any therapeutic framework or applied to any definite goal other than vague concepts of social competency or "restoration to sanity," it passed almost unnoticed. At such a time the patient is struck by the realization that his chances of release are remote. His already sick and flimsy personality structure collapses and the frightening hostility and desolating worthlessness against which the patient has struggled are intensified. Possibilities of mental health become more remote. Questions of parole or discharge become academic. The picture of the gradually decreasing frequency of the doctors' visits and the less frequent staff interviews looms large. Concepts of incurability are considered by both patient and hospital staff. Many human beings are lost, not a dozen or fifty, but literally hundreds, to themselves and to society.

IV. A LOOK AT ALTERNATIVE METHODS

A. Federal Procedure

The examination of the defendant to determine competency under the Michigan statute is generally conducted in the county jail. Examination in a jail atmosphere has been severely criticized on the ground that no thorough physical, mental, or neurological examination is possible under prison conditions and because rarely is a study of a case history of the defendant even attempted.

In an attempt to eliminate these defects, the federal government has enacted a statute which provides that whenever the defendant's mental competency to stand trial becomes an issue in a criminal case, the trial court may order the defendant *to a mental hospital for observation* and examination. If at the end of the examination period the doctors' report indicates a state of present incompetency, the court conducts a competency hearing. If the court is then convinced of the defendant's inability to proceed, it may order his commitment.

However, this system would not solve all of the Michigan problems. Although it is true that an examination at a hospital would be more thorough than one in jail, the confusion which exists in Michigan between non-responsibility and incompetency could still exist. Furthermore, hospital staffs, just like individual doctors, are susceptible to the idea that it is more humane to the defendant to declare him incompetent than it is to require his trial to proceed.

Neither the federal system nor the Michigan system makes provision for the incompetent defendant with a valid defense on the merits to raise initially this defense.

B. *Model Penal Code Approach*

In addition to providing for examination of the accused by a "psychiatrist" rather than by a "reputable physician," the Model Penal Code provides for a determination by the judge at the initial stages of the proceeding of both the defendant's mental competency to stand trial and his responsibility for the criminal act. The latter determination can be made in Michigan only if the accused is competent to stand trial. Under the Model Code, if the medical report by the examining psychiatrist indicates that the defendant suffered from a mental disease which "substantially impaired his capacity to appreciate the criminality of his conduct, or to conform his conduct to the requirements of law, and the court is satisfied that such impairment was sufficient to exclude responsibility, the court shall enter judgment of acquittal on the ground of mental disease or defect excluding responsibility."* This avoids commitment on the grounds of incompetency and removes the threat of a trial. This is important, for the psychiatrists participating in our study strongly believe that the threat of trial and the uncertainty of his status deters the recovery of incompetents at Ionia.

The Model Code's provision for non-responsibility eliminates any reference to "right" or "wrong." A person is non-responsible for criminal conduct if at the time of such conduct as a result of mental disease or defect he lacks substantial capacity either to appreciate the criminality of his conduct or to conform his conduct to the requirements of law. This is a meaningful and significant contribution to the law relating to trial competency. The Model Code recognizes that many commitments for incompetency are the result of dissatisfaction with the harsh tests of responsibility. This dissatisfaction too often leads to prosecution and defense acquiescence in automatic classification of a defendant as incompetent to stand trial and to speedy commitment to a state hospital. The provisions of the Model Code permitting the court to find the defendant non-responsible at the initial sanity hearing will be effective in removing the threat of a trial upon the defendant's hospital release only if there is also liberalization of the traditional M'Naghten rules of criminal responsibility.

C. *Trial on the Merits at the Option of the Defendant*

A defense may exist which does not depend on the competency of the accused for its assertion. For example, counsel for the defendant

* "on motion of the *defendant*" (sec. 4.07) (Ed.).

may be able to show that the prosecution is barred as a matter of law; or that the indictment on its face discloses that the statute of limitations has run; or that he can assert an affirmative defense which does not require the defendant's personal participation. Frequently an affirmative defense is jeopardized by the passage of time. Memories fade, witnesses die or move away, and documentary records may become unavailable. In many cases the defense will be that of non-responsibility; here the longer a trial is postponed, the more difficult it is for the defendant to make such a defense. Indeed, in this situation, it is to the defendant's advantage to be seen by the jury *before* regaining his sanity. The vital question, then, is whether defendant's counsel can proceed with an affirmative defense without, by so doing, foreclosing his client's incompetency plea.

In this country a few states permit a defendant a trial on the incompetency issue along with a trial on the merits. A recently enacted provision of the Texas Criminal Code provides that the jury shall state in the verdict whether the defendant is "sane or insane" at the time of the trial. If the issue of the defendant's competency is tried along with the criminal charge and it is found that the defendant is "insane at the time of the trial," he is then committed to a state mental hospital. When it is determined that he has recovered his "sanity," the proceedings against him continue. Although it is not specifically stated in the statute, the clear implication is that the defendant is entitled to a new trial even if he is found guilty of the crime at the same trial which found him incompetent to stand trial. It also appears that the defendant is entitled to go ahead with the trial on the merits of the criminal charge even though he may in fact be incompetent. In *Ex parte Hodges* the Court of Criminal Appeals of Texas held that the accused was deprived of his rights guaranteed by the sixth amendment of the United States Constitution and by the state constitution to a speedy trial and to effective aid of counsel where the trial court declined to proceed to trial in a murder case and required a preliminary trial to determine the sanity of the defendant.

Two recent English cases have considered the question of a trial on the merits prior to a competency determination. In *Regina* v. *Roberts* the Queen's bench held that the defense counsel could try the general issue of his client's guilt prior to the competency determination without sacrificing the incompetency plea. The nature of the defense which the defendant's counsel wished to raise was not disclosed. The court indicated that in the event the defendant were found responsible for the crime, but at the same time incompetent for trial, he would be sent to a hospital for the criminally insane. The court did not discuss the different and difficult problem of what disposition was to be made of the defendant upon a subsequent restoration to competency. However, in 1957 the Queen's Bench declined to follow the Roberts case, holding that a jury must be sworn to try the fitness of the defendant to plead as a *preliminary* issue. It was said that an insane man cannot be tried.

Professor Foote of the University of Pennsylvania Law School has proposed a plan similar to the procedure followed in *Regina* v. *Roberts* whereby at the defense counsel's option the case would be tried on the merits without foreclosing the defendant's protection of the incompetency plea. His plan includes the following provisions:

(1) In the event that the prosecutor or court moves for pre-trial mental examination to determine competency, if the defendant is unrepresented, counsel should be appointed to represent him on the motion. Only in this way can there be assured full development of an issue which may have an adverse effect on the defendant. If the defendant (perhaps because of illness) refuses counsel, an amicus curiae should be appointed to make an independent presentation of the defendant's interests.

(2) After the court has proceeded to have the defendant mentally examined and has heard evidence on the issue of competency to stand trial, if it finds that the defendant is competent it should so rule and all subsequent proceedings will follow their normal course. If the court is of the opinion that the defendant is incompetent, a ruling to this effect should be deferred if (*a*) counsel moves to dismiss the indictment, or for exclusion of illegally obtained evidence, or raises any other matter which can be determined in a pre-trial hearing, or (*b*) counsel alleges that there is a good faith defense on the merits and chooses to go to trial on the merits notwithstanding defendant's incompetency. In these situations the court shall determine the pre-trial question or proceed to a trial on the merits. If as a result the indictment is dismissed or if there is a finding of not guilty on the merits, that will be the end of the matter, although of course the court or [the prosecuting attorney] . . . can refer the defendant's case to the appropriate local mental health authorities for possible state civil commitment. If there is a verdict of guilty, the court should then rule that the defendant is incompetent, set the verdict aside and commit the defendant . . . until he is sufficiently recovered to be retried or until other appropriate disposition can be made of the case.

(3) The procedures outlined in (2) above should also be made available at defendant's election. Under present law counsel representing a defendant who is both probably incompetent and probably not guilty on the merits is required to make an election prejudicial to his client. If he moves for a pre-trial finding of incompetency, he waives any possibility of seeking a present determination on the merits, whereas if he goes to trial on the merits he waives the incompetency issue.

Professor Foote's plan has considerable merit and should be studied carefully. If the defendant were found not guilty on the merits he would not face the ignomithe of a commitment as a criminally insane person. A civil commitment carries no such stigma, and if the defendant were mentally ill he would be entitled to be treated as a patient, not as a potential criminal. If he were acquitted on grounds of non-responsibility, he would be committed to a hospital, and since he would not have a trial awaiting him upon his discharge his treatment could be geared solely to his mental condition with the threat of trial no longer impeding his cure. If he were found guilty of the crime, he would not be sent to prison, but the verdict would be set aside and he would be committed to a hospital as a person incompetent to stand trial.

The Foote plan does not suggest what should be done with a guilty defendant upon his restoration to competency, other than retrial or "other appropriate disposition." Nor did the Roberts case need to deal with this problem. But the problems attendant to this part of the Foote plan cannot be ignored. Facing a virtual "free trial" at the defendant's option, prosecutors and judges could be expected to raise the issue of the defendant's competency much less frequently. If the defendant were without counsel, it is likely that in many more cases than at present he would be tried and convicted simply because no one raised the competency issue.

V. RECOMMENDATIONS

A. *Statutory Changes*

The present Michigan parole system in conjunction with incompetency law is not only anomalous but may very likely be unconstitutional as well, for if the defendant is well enough for parole he is well enough for trial. Therefore, parole should be eliminated from the Michigan incompetency statute. In addition, the statute should be amended to achieve separation of incompetency from responsibility criteria. The problems of legal incompetency to stand trial and legal responsibility for criminal acts are separate and distinct and to attempt to set up machinery for handling both problems within a single statute only results in confusion. The procedures for examination, commitment, and treatment of incompetents should be described in a separate statute or provision which should make clear that the criteria for finding a person incompetent, commitment, and discharge back to the committing court are the same.

Serious consideration should be given to making the time spent in Ionia as the result of an incompetency commitment a "credit" against any subsequent conviction and sentence. Since the defendants are kept under as rigid supervision and control as they would be in the state prison, and since society is as fully protected by isolating them at Ionia as at Jackson, it would seem fair to allow the time spent at Ionia to be computed against any subsequent sentence. To complement this proposition, consideration should be given to amending the statute to provide for defendant's discharge from Ionia and for civil commitment, if necessary, when the maximum prison sentence would have expired.

An alternative proposal would require amending the statute to provide for a maximum period of time for which the defendant could be committed as incompetent. For example, the statute could provide that at the end of a two-year period he would have to be discharged from Ionia and then either tried or civilly committed. This would set an absolute time limit on the possibility of trial, which should have salutary therapeutic effects, if not during, then certainly after the two-year period, since the uncertainty of a trial appears to be a factor which inhibits recovery from the mental affliction. It would also exert pressure on the hospital staff to ready the defendant for trial. To protect the defendant, the statute should include a provision that no treatment to speed restoration to competency should be given if it would have deleterious effects on final and ultimate recovery. Thus responsibility for the ultimate cure in severe cases of mental illness would be left with civil institutions.

Editorial Note

The confusion between the standards for determining competency to stand trial and criminal responsibility seems difficult to understand, but that it persists, afflicting lawyers and judges as well as psychiatrists, is indisputable (e.g., see *Bruce* v. *Estelle*, 483 F. 2d 1031, CA-5, 1973). It may be well here briefly to note the principal differences between the two determinations:

1. *Nature of the issue*

   a. *the insanity defense (lack of criminal responsibility):*
   An affirmative defense, which in most jurisdictions must be raised by the defendant, and in several jurisdictions the defendant has the burden of proof.

   b. *the competency issue:*
   A procedural issue, based on concepts of a fair trial: as one may not be tried in absentia, so also he may not be tried if, because of mental impairment he cannot meaningfully participate. May be raised by either defense or prosecution, and must be raised by the court if the evidence suggests reasonable doubt of competency (see *Pate* v. *Robinson*, post).

2. *Standard or test*

   a. *the insanity defense:*
   M'Naghten, M'Naghten plus irresistible impulse, *Pike, Durham*, partial responsibility, or a variant of the A.L.I. Model Penal Code test, depending on the jurisdiction.

   b. *competency:*
   A generally accepted two-fold standard: capacity to understand the nature of the charges, plus capacity to assist counsel in presenting whatever defenses may be available.

3. *Point of time-reference*

    a. *the insanity defense:*
    The time of the alleged offense.
    b. *competency:*
    Now—i.e., the time of trial.

4. *Determination*

    a. *the insanity defense:*
    Defendant has right to determination by jury; result may be verdict of not guilty by reason of insanity.

    b. *competency:*
    In most jurisdictions the issue is determined by the court; result of finding of incompetency is deferral of trial.

THE EZRA POUND CASE

Medical Report on Pound—1945

Federal Security Agency
Saint Elizabeths Hospital
Washington 20, D.C.
December 14, 1945

Honorable Bolitha J. Laws
Chief Justice, U.S. District Court
Washington, D.C.

Sir:

The undersigned hereby respectfully report the results of their mental examination of Ezra Pound, now detained in Gallinger Hospital by transfer for observation from the District jail on a charge of treason. Three of us (Drs. Gilbert, King, and Overholser) were appointed by Your Honor to make this examination. At our suggestion, and with your approval, Dr. Wendell Muncie, acting upon the request of counsel for the accused, made an examination with us and associates himself with us in this joint report. Dr. Muncie spent several hours with the defendant, both alone and with us, on December 13, 1945, and the others of us have examined the defendant each on several occasions, separately and together, in the period from his admission to Gallinger Hospital on December 4, 1945, to December 13, 1945. We have had available to us the reports of laboratory, psychological, and special physical examinations of the defendant and considerable material in the line of his writings and biographical data.

The defendant, now sixty years of age and in generally good physical condition, was a precocious student, specializing in literature. He has been a voluntary expatriate for nearly forty years, living in England and France, and for the past twenty-one years, in Italy, making an uncertain living by writing poetry and criticism. His poetry and literary criticism have achieved considerable recognition, but of recent years his preoccupation with monetary theories and economics has apparently obstructed his literary productivity. He has long been recognized as eccentric, querulous, and egocentric.

At the present time he exhibits extremely poor judgment as to his situation, its seriousness, and the manner in which the charges are to be met. He insists that his broadcasts were not treasonable, but that all of his radio activities have stemmed from his self-appointed mission to "save the Constitution." He is abnormally grandiose, is expansive and exuberant in manner, exhibiting pressure of speech, discursiveness, and distractibility.

In our opinion, with advancing years his personality, for many years abnormal, has undergone further distortion to the extent that he is now suffering from a paranoid state which renders him mentally unfit to advise properly with counsel or to participate intelligently and reasonably in his own defense. He is, in other words, insane and mentally unfit for trial, and is in need of care in a mental hospital.

Respectfully submitted,

Joseph L. Gilbert, M.D.
Wendell Muncie, M.D.
Winfred Overholser, M.D.
Marion R. King, M.D.

Politics and Psychiatry: The Case of Mr. Ezra Pound

Thomas S. Szasz

It has been your habit for long to do away with
  good writers,
You either drive them mad, or else you blink
  at their suicides,
Or else you condone their drugs, and talk of
  insanty and genius,
But I will not go mad to please you.
                Ezra Pound (1914)

When psychiatry became a respectable medical specialty—approximately at the beginning of this century—it became fashionable to pin psychiatric diagnoses on well-known personages, both past and present. Frued's (1909) speculations about the psychopathology of Leonardo da Vinci and others are familiar to the contemporary student. It is well known that many nonpsychoanalysts were deeply involved in this game of psychiatric name-calling, or in protests against it. In the little-known work, *The Psychiatric Study of Jesus*, Albert Schweitzer (1913) tried to refute three prominent psychiatrists who claimed that Jesus suffered from paranoia. More will be said about this essay later.

Since its modest beginning early in this century, the enterprise of calling prominent people crazy has proved vastly popular. Not only has this activity received the blessing of the psychiatric profession, but also the endorsement of jurists, politicians, writers, and others. It is hardly surprising, then, that newspapermen, political commentators, and the public at large accept without question explanations that attribute the conduct of some political leaders to common sense, expediency, or meanness, but ascribe the behavior of others to mental illness. The distinction between the mentally healthy and mentally sick leader, man of letters, or scientist is one that the psychiatrist, of course, is expected to make, and which others are expected to accept. Thus, many people seem eager to dispose of the problems posed by men like Fidel Castro, Earl Long, or Adolf Hitler by labeling them "psychotic."

In this chapter, I shall present and analyze the case of Ezra Pound. This case highlights the significance of the Rule of Law for a free society. It illustrates that psychiatric, as against judicial, disposition of alleged lawbreakers permits the exercise of discretionary power in dealing with them. By means of psychiatric incarceration, the modern government is spared from committing "injustices" that may inflame public opinion. Instead of judging the accused guilty and liable to punishment, he is declared mentally ill and not responsible for his conduct. Then, with "kindness" he is committed to a mental institution. So long as more people do not ask where involuntary psychiatric hospitalization and treatment end, and retribution and punishment begin, this form of liberticide is bound to flourish.

THE CASE OF EZRA POUND

When the war in Europe ended in 1945, Ezra Pound was taken into custody by American troops in Italy. He was returned to the United States and indicted for treason. The charge was based on allegedly treasonous broadcasts which Pound made during the war from Rome. It is important to emphasize that Pound insisted that patriotism was his motive. According to a statement by Robert Frost, prepared for a motion for Pound's release in

1958, "He [Pound] never admitted that he went over to the enemy any more than the writers at home who have despaired of the Republic" (Norman, 1960, page 454). Whether Pound's broadcasts were or were not treasonous was, however, never decided. That is, the issue and the evidence on it were never presented to a jury. Hence, no judicial decision on his guilt or innocence was ever rendered. Instead, it was decided—jointly by the government and by Pound's defense—that Pound be declared mentally unfit to stand trial and that he be hospitalized in a psychiatric institution. This was speedily accomplished. It took the jury all of three minutes to decide that Pound was of "unsound mind." He spent the next thirteen years in St. Elizabeths Hospital.

How could this happen? When Pound was indicted for treason, he was fifty-nine years old. He was one of the outstanding and most influential poets of his time. He had married, raised a family, looked after his affairs, helped his colleagues and friends, and never before had any brushes with either policemen or psychiatrists. Eccentric, peculiar, conceited—yes. But was he insane, in the sense that he did not know what he was doing? And, more specifically, was he so out of his mind that he could not assist in his own defense?

Let us remember that the prosecution (the United States Government) and the defense agreed that Pound was mentally unfit to be tried, and so informed the judge. The judge accordingly impaneled a jury, stating: "In the event the jury finds that his mental state is as has been represented to me, then Mr. Pound will not be brought to trial because, under the law, it would not be proper to prosecute him if his mental condition is as has been stated to me" (page 419).

The doctors who had examined Pound in the Gallinger Municipal Hospital (for the prosecution) testified that Pound suffered from a "paranoid state." One of the chief witnesses at Pound's insanity hearing was Dr. Winfred Overholser, Superintendent of St. Elizabeths Hospital, under whose care Pound was to spend the next thirteen years of his life. Here are the reasons Overholser gave to support his opinion that Pound should not be tried:

He is thoroughly convinced that if he had been allowed to send his messages to the Axis, which he wished to send, prior to 1940, there would have been no Axis even. In other words, that if given a free hand by those who were engaged in stultifying him, he could have prevented the war.

He lays a great deal of his difficulties at the door of the British Secret Service, and other groups, which have opposed him.

He assures me, too, that he served a very

useful purpose to the United States by remaining at the Italian prison camp to complete his translation of Confucius, which he regards as the greatest contribution to literature.

He is sure he should not have been brought to this country in the capacity of a prisoner, but in the capacity of someone who was to be of great benefit to the United States in its postwar activities.

I might state that this constitutes a grandiosity of ideas and beliefs that goes far beyond the normal, even in a person who is as distraught in his mind as he is [page 419].

Dr. Overholser was then cross-examined by Mr. Isaiah Matlack, counsel for the Department of Justice.

Q. Now, what part does his background history play in your opinion as to his present sanity?
A. It shows that we are dealing now with the end-product of an individual who throughout his lifetime has been highly antagonistic, highly eccentric, the whole world has revolved around him, he has been a querulous person, he has been less and less able to order his life. This has been a gradual evolution through his life, so that now we are dealing with the end-product, so to speak [page 419].

Notice how general and vague these observations of Overholser's are. No evidence was introduced to prove that, in spite of his peculiarities, Pound could not be treated as a responsible defendant. Instead, unproved allegations were insinuated, such as his being "less and less able to order his life." This psychiatric accusation was simply untrue. Before the American troops landed in Italy, Pound was able to order his life well enough to stay out of the hands of psychiatrists. Whereas, since the end of the European War he had been a prisoner, his life having been "ordered" for him.

To recapture the atmosphere of the jury trial in which Pound's sanity was adjudicated, it is necessary to know the instructions that Judge Bolitha J. Laws, who conducted the proceedings, gave to the jurors. After outlining the case and the problem before the court, Judge Laws addressed the jurors as follows:

It has been testified to before you correctly that we brought him to the point of having him examined by psychiatrists and physicians on mental disease; we brought Dr. Overholser, who is the head of St. Elizabeths Hospital, one of the outstanding institutions of the United States, and run by the United States, and we brought to examine him also Dr. King who, as you have been told on the witness stand, holds a responsible position in the Public Health

Service which attends to the mental as well as the physical condition of persons in the penal institutions throughout the United States. We brought into consultation also Dr. Gilbert, who is the head of the Division of Psychiatry at Gallinger Hospital with which I think you are doubtless familiar. Then there was permitted to examine him at the request of Mr. Cornell, who appeared for Mr. Pound, Dr. Muncie, who is a leading psychiatrist, and I think the head of the department at Johns Hopkins University. You heard his qualifications.

These doctors, after consultation, filed a written certificate with the Court indicating their *unanimous view that Mr. Pound under his then present state of mind was not in a position to stand trial*, to cooperate with his counsel, and go through with a serious charge of this nature.

Government counsel have cooperated very readily in the investigation and were very fair in the entire situation and they, feeling that the code of law which I have explained to you should be compiled with, filed in this court a motion that a jury be impaneled to pass upon this proposition. I agreed with the view of Government counsel that a jury be impaneled to look into it *notwithstanding the unanimous opinion of these psychiatrists*, and that is the reason why you have been impaneled today to hear the whole story, and those physicians have been questioned before you fully with regard to the situation.

It therefore becomes your duty now to advise me whether in your judgment you find that Mr. Pound is in position to cooperate with his counsel, *to stand trial without causing him to crack up or break down;* whether he is able to testify, if he sees fit, at the trial, to stand cross-examination, and in that regard, of course, you have heard the testimony of all these physicians on the subject and there is no testimony to the contrary and, of course, *these are men who have given a large part of their professional careers to the study of matters of this sort*, who have been brought here for your guidance.

Under the state of the law you are not necessarily bound by what they say; you can disregard what they say and bring in a different verdict, *but in a case of this type where the Government and the defense representatives have united in a clear and unequivocal view with regard to the situation, I presume you will have no difficulty in making up your mind.* [Italics added. Norman, 1960, pages 423–24.]

The jury was out three minutes and brought in a verdict of "unsound mind." Pound was remanded to St. Elizabeths Hospital.

Pound remained at St. Elizabeths Hospital from 1945 until 1958, when he was released as "incurably insane, but not dangerous." He was retained all this time despite the fact that barely one year after his commitment, under pressure of Pound's defense attorney, Overholser stated that "in his opinion (1) the defendant has been insane for many years and will never recover his sanity or become mentally fit to stand trial to the indictment, (2) the defendant's mental condition is not benefited by his close confinement at St. Elizabeths Hospital where he is kept in a building with violent patients because of the necessity of keeping him under guard, and it would be desirable from the point of view of the health and welfare of the defendant if he could be removed to a private sanitorium, and (3) the defendant is not violent, etc." (page 424).

Eleven years elapsed after this, until, on April 14, 1958, a motion was filed in the United States District Court for the District of Columbia for dismissal of the original indictment. This motion was supported by statements from Winfred Overholser, Robert Frost, and a number of prominent writers and poets. Frost's eloquent statement was read in court:

I am here to register my admiration for a government that can rouse in conscience to a case like this. Relief seems to be in sight for many of us besides the Ezra Pound in question and his faithful wife. He has countless admirers the world over who will rejoice in the news that he has hopes of freedom. I append a page or so of what they have been saying lately about him and his predicament. I myself speak as much in the general interest as in his. And I feel authorized to speak very specially for my friends, Archibald MacLeish, Ernest Hemingway, and T. S. Eliot. None of us can bear the disgrace of our letting Ezra Pound come to his end where he is. It would leave too woeful a story in American literature. He went very wrongheaded in his egotism, but he insists it was from patriotism—love of America. He has never admitted that he went over to the enemy any more than the writers at home who have despaired of the Republic. I hate such nonsense and can only listen to it as an evidence of mental disorder. But mental disorder is what we are considering. I rest the case on Dr. Overholser's pronouncement that Ezra Pound is not too dangerous to go free in his wife's care, and too insane ever to be tried—a very nice discrimination [page 454].

On April 18, 1958, with the consent of the government, the indictment against Pound was dismissed by Judge Laws.

What happened next? Pound resumed his habitual style of living. He was hyperactive, flamboyant, at times bizarre. He visited with friends, and annoyed some congressmen. Soon, he and his wife sailed for Italy. On arrival, he greeted the reporters and photographers with a Fascist salute and announced that "all America is an insane asylum" (page 458). Since then he has lived with his daughter and son-in-law. At the time of this writing (November,

1961), Pound is still alive. Nor has he required further psychiatric "help." For a seventy-five-year-old man who was pronounced incurably insane sixteen years ago, this is not a bad record.

A CRITICAL ANALYSIS OF THE POUND CASE

What can we learn from the Pound affair? Perhaps the first to criticize the use of psychiatry in this case was Wertham (1949). He thought it virtually self-evident that Pound was sane enough to be tried, and cited evidence to support his view. For example, when taken into custody Pound was quoted as having said: If a man isn't willing to take some risk for his opinions, either his opinions are no good or he is no good" (page 596). Accordingly, Wertham suggested that Pound's insanity was contrived by those in charge of his case, and, more generally, that "His 'insanity' is an example of how we are trying to explain away profound defects in society by placing them outside society, in the sphere of individual pathology" (page 600). Moreover, Wertham observed, if mercy to a great man was the intent of the insanity defense, it could have been "better accomplished democratically by the proper use of clemency than by the dangerous abuse of psychiatry" (page 594).

George Orwell, who demonstrated his knowledge of psychology in his book *Nineteen Eighty-four* (1949), did not regard Pound as a deluded mental patient, but as a Fascist who was nevertheless a fine artist and a respectable human being:

When one thinks of all the people who support or have supported fascism, one stands amazed at their diversity. What a crew! Think of a programme which at any rate for a while could bring Hitler, Pétain, Montague Norman, Pavelitch, William Randolph Hearst, Streicher, Buchman, Ezra Pound, Juan March, Cocteau, Thyssen, Father Coughlin, The Mufti of Jerusalem, Arnold Lunn, Antonescu, Spengler, Beverly Nichols, Lady Houston, and Marinetti all into the same boat. But the clue is really very simple. They are all people with something to lose, or people who long for a hierarchical society and dread the prospect of a world of free and equal human beings [Orwell, 1943, page 150].

Is this not a more meaningful appraisal of the problem which Pound presented to his American captors than calling him a paranoid? And would it not have been more honest to try him? As it is, Pound, self-confessed Fascist, succeeded in provoking his country to treat him with the Fascist methods he so fervently espoused. He was thus imprisoned without benefit of trial. But, someone may object, this is not so. He was not imprisoned at all; he was hospitalized as a mental patient. How was Pound's hospitalization generally perceived? In a review in the *New York Times* (1961), of a biography of Pound by Mullins (1961), Herbert Creekmore wrote: "It is sad that Pound was imprisoned [*sic*], and I think it was unjust, especially in that he was held for twelve years." Creekmore's review elicited several letters to the Editor, but no one commented on, and I assume therefore that no one objected to, Creekmore's referring to Pound's detention as imprisonment. Psychiatric hospitals are, of course, prisons. One of the principal aims of this book is to impress this fact upon the reader, and to show the maneuvers that legislators, attorneys, and physicians use to deceive the public as well as one another of the facts.

The Pound case affords an example of the type of psychiatric participation in the criminal process which substitutes the Rule of Men for the Rule of Law (Hayek, 1957, 1960). Although there are laws that govern the use of psychiatric action in criminal law, one cannot predict whether or not psychiatric participation will be enlisted in any particular case. The severity of the expected punishment seems to be an important variable. If the penalty is heavy—especially if it is death—the likelihood of psychiatric participation is great.

Not only is the use of psychiatric opinion in criminal cases unregulated by strict rules of law, but also the interpretation of the opinion permits so much latitude that the very possibilities of consistency and predictability are negated. The judicial process is thus allowed to drift from the impartial and predictable enforcement of rules toward an unpredictable decision of each case on what is thought to be its own merits.

Lacking the integrity of a scientific definition, the concept of mental health—and its antonym, mental illness—has succumbed to what Bertrand Russell (1953) called the cult of common usage. In contemporary America it has come to mean conformity to the demands of society. According to the commonsense definition, mental health is the ability to play the game of social living, and to play it well. Conversely, mental illness is the refusal to play, or the inability to play well (see Chapter 1 [of Szasz, *Law, Liberty and Psychiatry*]).

Are there differences between social nonconformity or deviation and mental illness? I submit that the difference between saying "He is wrong" and "He is mentally ill" is not factual but psychological. If we take the actor seriously, regard him as having human rights and dignities, and being essentially like us—

we speak of disagreement, deviation, crime, perhaps even treason. Should we feel, however, that we cannot communicate with him, that he is different from us—we then speak of insanity, mental illness, emotional immaturity, racial inferiority, and so forth. Once a person is placed in the second category, *what* he says becomes irrelevant, though *why* he says it may be considered interesting.

Thus, a serious disagreement implies a basically dignified human relationship. At least in the context of the conflict, the participants treat each other as equals. In contrast, a situation in which the position of only one of the participants is taken seriously, while that of his opponent is disregarded, bespeaks a relationship between a superior and an inferior, a master and slave. When initiated by the former, it is a means of degrading his partner. When it is invited by the latter, or is placidly accepted by him, it is self-inflicted degradation.

Occasionally both parties benefit from this shift in attitude. Since kindness, or at least pretended kindness, toward the sick is an integral part of our ethic, the offender who is considered mentally ill may be treated more sympathetically than he might otherwise be. The stronger or superior member of the conflicting pair may also benefit from this arrangement. First, he does not have to take seriously the charges of a critic who is his inferior; second, he avoids the guilt feelings which are invariably associated with meting out punishment. These feelings tend to be particularly distressing when someone who is loved or admired is punished. Prominent artists, Ezra Pound among them, fall into the group of the admired, and hence are not expected to adhere completely to the social rules binding for others. The parental obligation to punish children for infraction of rules gave rise to the saying, "It hurts me more than it hurts you!" This saying is as misleading as it is incomplete. Still, it suggests what parents feel when they discipline their children. Enlarged, this phenomenon is analogous to that of a nation judging and punishing one of its revered members.

Still, it may be asked, what can be the objection to showing kindness to Pound, as was allegedly done by not bringing him to trial? Is this not a fair way to treat the so-called mentally ill criminal? The basic objection is that the social sanctions employed in such cases violate the principles of the open society, by substituting for the Rule of Law the Rule of Men. If this violation of the Rule of Law is due to the humanistic wish to be kind to those who break the laws, it is committed unnecessarily, for trial and, in case of guilt, conviction of offenders need not prevent us from treating them with decency and kindness.

I have previously criticized the practice of giving psychiatric testimony in ordinary criminal trials (see Chapter 10). This practice is particularly undesirable in cases of political offense. When psychiatrists participate in the social disposition of such persons, they renounce the ethics of science for the values uppermost in society at any given time.

Let us recall in this connection that many prominent men have served time in jail for political offenses. Castro, Gandhi, Hitler, Nehru, Russell, Sukarno, to name a few, have all been sentenced to jail for opposing laws. In the past, Galileo, Jesus, and Socrates found themselves in opposition to duly appointed social authority. These men were taken seriously, and were punished in the manner prescribed by law. Surely, the way Pound was treated impugns his stature.

Pound was originally confined in a mental hospital ostensibly because of his alleged mental illness. Was he released because he recovered? Or because there was a change in the political climate? Or because he was punished enough? The psychiatrists in charge of Pound stated that he was still mentally ill, indeed that he would never be sane enough to stand trial. But, they added, he was no longer a danger to himself or to others. Appropriately enough, reporting on these developments, *Time* magazine (April 28, 1958) captioned his picture with the words: "Freedom for the warped." Are we to assume that he was given the precious gift of freedom *because* he was warped? Had he not been warped, but healthy, would he have continued to be deprived of his freedom?

It seems to me, as it did to Wertham (1949), that Pound played the game against the United States, played it well and honorably —but lost! As we have noted, Pound was not alone among artists in his admiration of "strong" men. George Bernard Shaw, for example, also admired the Fascist leaders. The point is, however, that Pound allegedly violated the laws of his country. The Rule of Law demands that the government play the game seriously, according to the rules: that is, that Pound be tried, sentenced if guilty, and later, if it be deemed just, pardoned and released. It may be objected that avoidance of trial on the grounds of insanity is part of the laws of our country. That is true. But as Hayek has shown, a duly constituted law is not the same as the Rule of Law. The latter is characterized by its consistency and inflexibility, in brief, by the fact that it is applied predictably and without exceptions. Since the issue of insanity is raised in some cases but not in others, and when raised is interpreted in an unpredictable manner, it serves as a particularly useful means for individualizing the administration of justice. But we cannot have our cake and eat it too. Exceptions to the Rule of Law on the grounds of mental illness are exceptions nonetheless, and compare with those that favor or penalize a group because of race or religion.

ON THE DISCRETION TO INVOKE
PSYCHIATRIC ACTION: AN EXAMPLE
OF THE RULE OF MEN

As the Rule of Law requires impartial application of rules to all men, so the Rule of Men allows discretion in the choice of rules for each case. The psychiatric disposition of alleged offenders means, first, that the legal and psychiatric authorities are free to seek or avoid psychiatric participation in the criminal process, and second, that they have wide and arbitrary powers to judge a person's sanity.

Until charged with an offense Pound's sanity had never been questioned. In other words, the issue of commitment never arose in his role as private citizen. It is important to keep this in mind, because the subsequent psychiatric picture of him implied that the diagnosis of Pound's paranoia was a purely medical finding, unrelated to his indictment.

What were the grounds for this diagnosis? The main ones were Pound's eccentric and grandiose behavior, and his belief in a "self-appointed mission to 'save the Consittution.'" To be sure, such conduct is sometimes labeled "paranoid," but not always. The labeling also depends on who the person to be diagnosed happens to be. This is where the psychiatric diagnostic and dispositional process can be shown to be crassly arbitrary. In this procedure, men do not apply established rules impartially, but instead follow their own desires.

Men other than Pound have exhibited traits of eccentricity, egocentricity, and grandiosity. Indeed, Jesus was said to have shown these "symptoms," and, accordingly, several psychiatrists diagnosed him as having suffered from paranoia. Schweitzer's study (1913), referred to earlier, was an attempt to refute the works of three psychiatrists, each of whom claimed to have established that Jesus was mentally abnormal.

De Loosten, a German, described Jesus as a "hybrid, tainted from birth by heredity, who even in his early youth as a born degenerate attracted attention by an extremely exaggerated self-consciousness combined with high intelligence and a very slightly developed sense of family and sex. His self-consciousness

slowly unfolded until it rose to a fixed delusional system, the peculiarities of which were determined by the intensive religious tendencies of the time and by his one-sided preoccupation with the writings of the Old Testament" (Schweitzer, 1913, page 37).

Hirsch, an American, diagnosed Jesus as paranoid. Said he: "Everything that we know about him conforms so perfectly to the clinical picture of paranoia that it is hardly conceivable that people can even question the accuracy of the diagnosis" (page 40). To which Schweitzer added: "At the conclusion of this exposition he goes so far as to assert that no textbook on mental disease could provide a more typical description of a gradually but ceaselessly mounting megalomania than afforded by the life of Jesus" (page 41).

Binet-Sanglé, a Frenchman, also considered Jesus paranoid. Wrote Schweitzer: "Binet-Sanglé wishes to establish the secretiveness of the paranoid. He adduces as evidence of this the fact that the Nazarene regarded his Messiahship and certain points in his teaching secrets to be veiled, gave evasive answers to questions and was brought to admit his system of delusions only under the stress of emotion, as, for example, in the proceedings at the trial" (page 44).

Schweitzer rallied to the defense. He argued, quite cogently, that it is difficult to know what the behavior of Jesus was really like, and, in any case, it must be evaluated in the context of the society in which he lived. Concluded Schweitzer: "The only symptoms to be accepted as historical and possibly to be discussed from the psychiatric point of view—the high estimate which Jesus has of himself and perhaps also the hallucination at the baptism—fall far short of proving the existence of mental illness" (page 72).

Of greater interest than the efforts of those hostile to Jesus to incriminate him as paranoid, and of those friendly to him to exonerate him, in Schweitzer's quaint protestation of impartiality. In the Preface of his book, he wrote:

That I command the impartiality necessary for this undertaking I believe I have proved by my former studies in the field of the life of Jesus. Should it really turn out that Jesus' object world must be considered by the doctor as in some degree the world of a sick man, still this conclusion, regardless of the consequences that follow from it and the shock to many that would result from it must not remain unuttered, since reverence for truth must be exalted above everything else. With this conviction I began the work, suppressing the unpleasant feeling of having to subject a great personality to psychiatric examination, and pondering the truth that what is great and profound in the ethical teachings of Jesus would retain its significance even if the conceptions in his world outlook and some of his actions had to be called more or less diseased [page 28].

Thus, instead of acknowledging his proreligious, and especially his pro-Christian, bias, Schweitzer claimed that he was impartial.

It is of particular interest to us, as students of the Pound case, that Overholser (1948), who found Pound to be paranoid, wrote a warmly approving Foreword for the American edition of Schweitzer's book. This is an excellent example of the discretionary attitude toward psychiatric evidence. That Overholser sided with Christ and Schweitzer, rather than with the psychiatrists who called Jesus paranoid, is not surprising. We may well ponder whether, and for how long, the Superintendent of the United States Government's number one mental hospital could retain his position if he publicly announced that Jesus was a paranoid. However, he could claim with impunity—indeed, with public approbation—that a person indicted for treason by the government was paranoid.

And so, as in Orwell's *Nineteen Eighty-four,* history is made by "bringing facts up to date." The great poet, Robert Frost, applauds as a "very nice discrimination" Overholser's pronouncement that Pound is not too dangerous to be released, but too insane ever to be tried. And so, in 1961, before a Hearing of a United States Senate Subcommittee, the following statements were made about Pound:

Mr. Creech [Counsel for the Subcommittee]. I note that you say with regard to Ezra Pound, or similar-type individuals, they should not be confined without a civil commitment proceeding. What is your feeling with regard to the psychopath?

Mr. Krash [Attorney, testifying]. Well, first, as to Ezra Pound, Ezra Pound was suffering from paranoia. He was not a psychopath. *Paranoia is an extremely severe illness, an extreme form of insanity.*

Senator Keating. He was not what we call a sociopath?

Mr. Krash. No, not at all. He was suffering from paranoid psychosis. He was insane. *There is no question whatever about that.* He was also not dangerous, may I say. [Italics added. Krash, 1961b, page 613.]

These divergent attitudes toward diagnosing Pound and Jesus are instructive. There are, of course, endless inconsistencies in applying psychiatric criteria to contemporary cases as well. If Pound was considered insane because of his extremist views, why not also Robert Welch,

leader of the John Birch Society? He claimed that President Eisenhower is a Communist sympathizer, and has asked for the impeachment of Chief Justice Warren. Should Welch be committed as a "dangerous paranoid"? Of course, say some psychiatrists. In response to an article on the "Rampageous Right" in the *New York Times Magazine* (November 26, 1961, Victor Bloom, a Detroit psychiatrist, wrote (December 17, 1961): "If the group in question [that is, the Birchers and other right-wing groups] were instead an individual, and the material presented to a body of psychiatrists intent on formulating a diagnosis, that diagnosis would unquestionably be 'paranoid psychosis.' " I submit, however, that those who advocate restraining Welch on psychiatric grounds would infringe on his right to free speech just as surely as if he were tried and incarcerated on a trumped-up charge.

There are, finally, many cases of grossly peculiar behavior on the parts of defendants for which psychiatric participation in the criminal process is never sought. When the famous psychiatrist Wilhelm Reich (1954) was accused of violating the provisions of the Federal Food, Drug, and Cosmetic Act, he sent a response to the Federal Judge in Portland, Maine, with statements such as these:

According to natural, and in consequence, American Common Law, no one, no matter who he is, has the power or legal right to enjoin. . . . The stir to mate in all living beings, including our maturing adolescents; The emergence of abstractions and final mathematical formulae concerning the natural life force in the universe and the right to their dissemination among one's fellow men [page 541].

Why was the question of insanity never raised in this case? Surely, these brief quotations alone provide ground enough for raising this issue. (I do not say this, of course, because I advocate psychiatric participation in this type of social problem.) Perhaps the fact that Reich was a famous psychiatrist was a deterrent. For if there are no Rules of Law for mental illness, and if the existence of mental illness can be established only by the testimony of psychiatric experts, can the sanity of the expert be questioned?

EDITORIAL NOTE: Ezra Pound spent thirteen years in St. Elizabeths Hospital. Following his release, and the dismissal of charges against him, Pound left the United States to return to his beloved Venice. In 1972, the American press had three occasions to review for their readers the trial and commitment of Ezra Pound: in March, when the University of Maine notified him that he was to receive an honorary degree, and then had to rescind the offer when its board of trustees vetoed the award; in July, when a panel of distinguished writers and critics voted him the Emerson-Thoreau Medal of the American Academy of Arts and Sciences, which action was revoked by the Academy's governing board; and in October, when Pound died at the age of 87.

MILLER v. BLALOCK

. . . This is an appeal from orders of the Western and Eastern Districts of Virginia denying the petitioner's applicaitons for writs of habeas corpus.

The petitions challenge for a second time the validity of the procedures followed in committing Miller to a mental hospital. In a former opinion, Miller v. Blalock, 4 Cir., 356 F. 2d 273, we found that Miller, an accused but unconvicted felon, had "been confined for an indefinite opportunity to be heard before a competent tribunal." We remanded the case to the district court "with instructions to release the prisoner unless the state affords petitioner the hearing to which he is entitled within a reasonable time." Id. at 276.

The Corporation Court of the City of Norfolk then entered an order appointing the director of the mental institution in which Miller was incarcerated and two other physicians on his staff as a commission to "inquire into the facts as to the sanity and mentality of said Sam Miller and report their findings to this court." The court appointed an attorney to represent Miller.

Two weeks later the commission sent its findings to the court. The entire report follows:

In accordance with your Order dated April 5, 1966, the above named (Sam Miller) was examined by the undersigned commission, April 18, 1966. He was examined in the presence of Mr. D. Burke Graybeal, Attorney at Law, who was appointed by the Court to represent him. The commission was appointed to inquire into the sanity and mentality of the said Sam Miller and report their findings to the Court.

This is to report that as a result of our examination we find him to be psychotic (insane), and incompetent at this time and unable to stand trial on the charges pending against him. We are in accord with the official diagnosis, namely Schizophrenic Reaction, Paranoid Type, that has already been made.

Without further hearing, the court ordered Miller confined to the hospital.

Upon oral argument, counsel for the state conceded that the hearing did not comport with the standards of due process. We agree. The report of the commission is entirely conclusory. There are no findings of underlying facts to show whether the petitioner can assist in his defense at his pending criminal trial. There is nothing in the record to show that Miller had an opportunity to introduce any evidence on his behalf or to cross-examine witnesses against him. The procedure for committing an accused but unconvicted felon should contain safeguards at least equivalent to those provided in the procedures for civil commitment.

We recognize Virginia's strong interest in protecting her citizens from mentally ill persons with violent tendencies. And it is Virginia who should set standards of mental competency and who should spell out the procedures for the commitment of the mentally ill. It is only when those standards and procedures fail to protect substantial rights under the Fourteenth Amendment that the federal courts must provide appropriate remedies. . . .

Vacated and remanded.

---

411 F. 2d 548 (CA-4, 1969).

DUSKY v. UNITED STATES

[Reversing 8th Circuit Court of Appeals decision affirming a conviction, and remanding the case for a new hearing to ascertain petitioner's present competency to stand trial, and for a new trial if petitioner is found competent.

HELD: In view of the doubts and ambiguities regarding the legal significance of the psychiatric testimony, the case should be remanded, the court declaring:]

We also agree with the suggestion of the Solicitor General that it is not enough for the district judge to find that "the defendant [is] oriented to time and place and [has] some recollection of events," but that the "test must be whether he has sufficient present ability to consult with his lawyer with a reasonable degree of rational understanding—and whether he has a rational as well as factual understanding of the proceedings against him."

U.S. Supreme Court 362 U.S. 402 (1960).

PATE v. ROBINSON

MR. JUSTICE CLARK delivered the opinion of the Court.

In 1959 respondent Robinson was convicted of the murder of his common-law wife, Flossie May Ward, and was sentenced to imprisonment for life. Being an indigent he was defended by court-appointed counsel. It was conceded at trial that Robinson shot and killed Flossie May, but his counsel claimed that he was insane at the time of the shooting and raised the issue of his incompetence to stand trial. On writ of error to the Supreme Court of Illinois it was asserted that the trial court's rejection of these contentions deprived Robinson of due process of law under the Fourteenth Amendment. His conviction was affirmed, the court finding that no hearing on mental capacity to stand trial had been requested, that the evidence failed to raise sufficient doubt as to his competence to require the trial court to conduct a hearing on its own motion, and further that the evidence did not raise a "reasonable doubt" as to his sanity at the time of the offense. . . .

The State concedes that the conviction of an accused person while he is legally incompetent violates due process, *Bishop* v. *United States*, 350 U.S. 961 (1956), and that state procedures must be adequate to protect this right. It insists, however, that Robinson intelligently waived this issue by his failure to request a hearing on his competence at the trial; and, further, that on the basis of the evidence before the trial judge no duty rested upon him to order a hearing *sua sponte*. A determination of these claims necessitates a detailed discussion of the conduct of the trial and the evidence touching upon the question of Robinson's competence at that time.

The uncontradicted testimony of four witnesses called by the defense revealed that Robinson had a long history of disturbed behavior. His mother testified that when he was between seven and eight years of age a brick dropped from a third floor hit Robinson on the head. "He blacked out and the blood run from his head like a faucet." Thereafter "he acted a little peculiar." The blow knocked

U.S. Supreme Court 383 U.S. 375 (1966).

him "cockeyed" and his mother took him to a specialist "to correct the crossness of his eyes." He also suffered headaches during his childhood, apparently stemming from the same event. His conduct became noticeably erratic about 1946 or 1947 when he was visiting his mother on a furlough from the Army. While Robinson was sitting and talking with a guest, "he jumped up and run to a bar and kicked a hole in the bar and he run up in the front." His mother asked "what on earth was wrong with him and he just stared at [her], and paced the floor with both hands in his pockets." On other occasions he appeared in a daze, with a "glare in his eyes," and would not speak or respond to questions. In 1951, a few years after his discharge from the service, he "lost his mind and was pacing the floor saying something was after him." This incident occurred at the home of his aunt, Helen Calhoun. Disturbed by Robinson's conduct, Mrs. Calhoun called his mother about six o'clock in the morning, and she "went to see about him." Robinson tried to prevent Mrs. Calhoun from opening the door, saying "that someone was going to shoot him or someone was going to come in after him." His mother testified that, after gaining admittance, "I went to him and hugged him to ask him what was wrong and he went to pushing me back, telling me to get back, somebody was going to shoot him, somebody was going to shoot him." Upon being questioned as to Robinson's facial expression at the time, the mother stated that he "had that starey look and seemed to be just a little foamy at the mouth." A policeman was finally called. He put Robinson, his mother, and aunt in a cab which drove them to Hines Hospital. On the way Robinson tried to jump from the cab, and upon arrival at the hospital he was so violent that he had to be strapped in a wheel chair. He then was taken in an ambulance to the County Psychopathic Hospital, from which he was transferred to the Kankakee State Hospital. The medical records there recited:

The reason for admission: The patient was admitted to this hospital on the 5th day of June, 1952, from the Hines Hospital. Patient began presenting symptoms of mental illness about a year ago at which time he came to his mother's house. He requested money and when it was refused, he suddenly kicked a hole in her bar.

Was drinking and went to the Psychopathic Hospital. He imagined he heard voices, voices of men and women and he also saw things. He saw a little bit of everything. He saw animals, snakes and elephants and this lasted for about two days. He went to Hines. They sent him to the Psychopathic Hospital. The voices threatened him. He imagined someone was outside with a pistol aimed at him. He was very, very scared and he tried to call the police, and his aunt then called the police. He thought he was going to be harmed. And he says this all seems very foolish to him now. Patient is friendly and tries to cooperate.

He went through an acute toxic episode from which he has some insight. He had been drinking heavily. I am wondering possibly if he isn't schizophrenic. I think he has recovered from this condition. I have seen the wife and she is in a pathetic state. I have no objection to giving him a try.

After his release from the state hospital Robinson's irrational episodes became more serious. His grandfather testified that while Robinson was working with him as a painter's assistant, "all at once, he would come down [from the ladder] and walk on out and never say where he is going and whatnot and he would be in a daze and when he comes out, he comes back just as fresh. He just says he just says he didn't do anything. I noticed that he wasn't at all himself." The grandfather also related that one night when Robinson was staying at his house, Robinson and his wife had a "ruckus," which caused his wife to flee to the grandfather's bedroom. Robinson first tried to kick down the door. He then grabbed all of his wife's clothes from their room and threw them out in the yard, intending to set them on fire. Robinson got so unruly that the grandfather called the police to lock him up.

In 1953 Robinson, then separated from his wife, brought their eighteen-month-old son to Mrs. Calhoun's home and asked permission to stay there for a couple of days. She observed that he was highly nervous, prancing about and staring wildly. While she was at work the next day Robinson shot and killed his son and attempted suicide by shooting himself in the head. It appeared that after Robinson shot his son, he went to a nearby park and tried to take his life again by jumping into a lagoon. By his mother's description, he "was wandering around" the park, and walked up to a policeman and "asked him for a cigarette." It was stipulated that he went to the South Park Station on March 10, 1953, and said that he wanted to confess to a crime. When he removed his hat the police saw that he had shot himself in the head. They took him to the hospital for treatment of his wound.

Robinson served almost four years in prison for killing his son, being released in September, 1956. A few months thereafter he began to live with Flossie May Ward at her home. In the summer of 1957 or 1958 Robinson "jumped on" his mother's brother-in-law and "beat him up terrible." She went to the police station and swore out a warrant for his arrest.

She described his abnormalities and told the officers that Robinson "seemed to have a disturbed mind." She asked the police "to pick him up so I can have him put away." Later she went back to see why they had not taken him into custody because of "the way he was fighting around in the streets, people were beating him up." She made another complaint a month or so before Robinson killed Flossie May Ward. However, no warrant was ever served on him.

The killing occurred about 10:30 P.M. at a small barbecue house where Flossie May Ward worked. At that time there were ten customers in the restaurant, six of them sitting at the counter. It appears from the record that Robinson entered the restaurant with a gun in his hand. As he approached the counter, Flossie May said, "Don't start nothing tonight." After staring at her for about a minute, he walked to the rear of the room and, with the use of his hand, leaped over the counter. He then rushed back toward the front of the restaurant, past two other employees working behind the counter, and fired once or twice at Miss Ward. She jumped over the counter and ran out the front door with Robinson in pursuit. She was found dead on the sidewalk. Robinson never spoke a word during the three to four minute episode.

Subsequently Robinson went to the apartment of a friend, Mr. Moore, who summoned the police. When three officers, two in uniform, arrived, Robinson was standing in the hall approximately half way between the elevator and the apartment. Unaware of his identity, the officers walked past him and went to the door of the apartment. Mrs. Moore answered the door and told them that Robinson had left a short time earlier. As the officers turned around they saw Robinson still standing where they had first observed him. Robinson made no attempt to avoid being arrested. When asked his address he gave several evasive answers. He also denied knowing anything about the killing.

Four defense witnesses expressed the opinion that Robinson was insane. In rebuttal the State introduced only a stipulation that Dr. William H. Haines, Director of the Behavior Clinic of the Criminal Court of Cook County would, if present, testify that in his opinion Robinson "knew the nature of the charges against him and was able to cooperate with counsel" when he examined him two or three months before trial. However, since the stipulation did not include a finding of sanity the prosecutor advised the court that "we should have Dr. Haines' testimony as to his opinion whether this man is sane or insane. It is possible that the man might be insane and know

the nature of the charge or be able to cooperate with his counsel. I think it should be in evidence, Your Honor, that Dr. Haines' opinion is that this defendant was sane when he was examined." However, the court told the prosecutor, "You have enough in the record now. I don't think you need Dr. Haines." In his summation defense counsel emphasized "our defense is clear. . . . It is as to the sanity of the defendant at the time of the crime and also as to the present time." The court, after closing argument by the defense, found Robinson guilty and sentenced him to prison for his natural life.

The State insists that Robinson deliberately waived the defense of his competence to stand trial by failing to demand a sanity hearing as provided by Illinois law. But it is contradictory to argue that a defendant may be incompetent, and yet knowingly or intelligently "waive" his right to have the court determine his capacity to stand trial. See *Taylor* v. *United States*, 282 F.2d 16, 23 (C.A. 8th Cir. 1960). In any event, the record shows that counsel throughout the proceedings insisted that Robinson's present sanity was very much in issue. He made a point to elicit Mrs. Robinson's opinion of Robinson's "present sanity." And in his argument to the judge, he asserted that Robinson "should be found not guilty and presently insane on the basis of the testimony that we have heard." Moreover, the prosecutor himself suggested at trial that "we should have Dr. Haines' testimony as to his opinion whether this man is sane or insane." With this record we cannot say that Robinson waived the defense of incompetence to stand trial.

We believe that the evidence introduced on Robinson's behalf entitled him to a hearing on this issue. The court's failure to make such inquiry thus deprived Robinson of his constitutional right to a fair trial. See *Thomas* v. *Cunningham*, 313 F.2d 934 (C.A. 4th Cir. 1963). Illinois jealously guards this right. Where the evidence raises a "*bona fide* doubt" as to defendant's competence to stand trial, the judge on his own motion must impanel a jury and conduct a sanity hearing pursuant to Ill. Rev. Stat., c. 38, § 104-2 (1963). *People* v. *Shrake*, 25 Ill. 141, 182 N.E.2d 754 (1962). The Supreme Court of Illinois held that the evidence here was not sufficient to require a hearing in light of the mental alertness and understanding displayed in Robinson's "colloquies" with the trial judge. 22 Ill. 2d, at 168, 174 N.E.2d, at 823. But this reasoning offers no justification for ignoring the uncontradicted testimony of Robinson's history of pronounced irrational behavior. While Robinson's demeanor at trial might be relevant to the ultimate decision as to his sanity, it cannot be relied upon to dispense with a hearing on that very issue. Cf. *Bishop* v. *United States*, 350 U.S. 961 (1956), reversing, 223 F.2d 582, 585 (C.A.D.C. Cir. 1955). Likewise, the stipulation of Dr. Haines' testimony was some evidence of Robinson's ability to assist in his defense. But, as the state prosecutor seemingly admitted, on the facts presented to the trial court it could not properly have been deemed dispositive on the issue of Robinson's competence.

Having determined that Robinson's constitutional rights were abridged by his failure to receive an adequate hearing on his competence to stand trial, we direct that the writ of habeas corpus must issue and Robinson be discharged, unless the State gives him a new trial within a reasonable time. . . . It has been pressed upon us that it would be sufficient for the state court to hold a limited hearing as to Robinson's mental competence at the time he was tried in 1959. If he were found competent, the judgment against him would stand. But we have previously emphasized the difficulty of retrospectively determining an accused's competence to stand trial. *Dusky* v. *United States,* 362 U.S. 402 (1960). The jury would not be able to observe the subject of their inquiry, and expert witnesses would have to testify solely from information contained in the printed record. That Robinson's hearing would be held six years after the fact aggravates these difficulties. . . .

If the State elects to retry Robinson, it will of course be open to him to raise the question of his competence to stand trial at that time and to request a special hearing thereon. In the event a sufficient doubt exists as to his present competence such a hearing must be held. If found competent to stand trial, Robinson would have the usual defenses available to an accused.

The case is remanded to the District Court for action consistent with this opinion.

It is so ordered.

MR. JUSTICE HARLAN, whom MR. JUSTICE BLACK joins, dissenting.

The facts now canvassed by this Court to support its constitutional holding were fully sifted by the Illinois Supreme Court. I cannot agree that the state court's unanimous appraisal was erroneous and still less that it was error of constitutional proportions.

The Court appears to hold that a defendant's present incompetence may become sufficiently manifest during a trial that it denies him due process for the trial court to fail to conduct a hearing on that question on its own initiative: I do not dissent from this very general proposition, and I agree also that such an error is not "waived" by failure to raise it and that it may entitle the defendant to a new trial without further proof. . . . However, I do not believe the facts known to the trial judge in this case suggested Robinson's incompetence at time of trial with anything like the force necessary to make out a violation of due process in the failure to pursue the question.

Before turning to the facts, it is pertinent to consider the quality of the incompetence they are supposed to indicate. In federal courts— and I assume no more is asked of state courts —the test of incompetence that warrants postponing the trial is reasonably well settled. In language this Court adopted on the one occasion it faced the issue, "the 'test must be whether . . . [the defendant] has sufficient present ability to consult with his lawyer with a reasonable degree of rational understanding —and whether he has a rational as well as factual understanding of the proceedings against him.'" *Dusky* v. *United States*, 362 U.S. 402. In short, emphasis is on capacity to consult with counsel and to comprehend the proceedings, and lower courts have recognized that this is by no means the same test as those which determine criminal responsibility at the time of the crime. The question, then, is not whether the facts before the trial judge suggested that Robinson's crime was an insane act, but whether they suggested he was incompetent to stand trial.

The Court's affirmative answer seemingly rests on two kinds of evidence, principally adduced by Robinson to prove an insanity defense after the State rested its main case. First, there was evidence of a number of episodes of severe irrationality in Robinson's past. Among them were the slaying of his infant son, his attempted suicide, his efforts to burn his wife's clothing, his fits of temper and of abstraction, and his seven-week incarceration in a state hospital eight years before the trial. This evidence may be tempered by the State's counterarguments, for example, that Robinson was found guilty of his son's killing and that alcoholism may explain his hospitalization, but it cannot be written off entirely. The difficulty remains that while this testimony may suggest that Flossie May Ward's killing was just one more irrational act, I cannot say as a matter of common knowledge that it evidences incapacity during the trial. Indeed, the pattern revealed may best indicate that Robinson did function adequately during most of his life interrupted by periods of severe derangement that would have been quite apparent had they occurred at trial. The second class of data pertinent to the Court's theory, remarks by witnesses and counsel that

Robinson was "presently insane," deserves little comment. I think it apparent that these statements were addressed to Robinson's responsibility for the killing, that is, his ability to do insane acts, and not to his general competency to stand trial.

Whatever mild doubts this evidence may stir are surely allayed by positive indications of Robinson's competence at the trial. Foremost is his own behavior in the courtroom. The record reveals colloquies between Robinson and the trial judge which undoubtedly permitted a reasonable inference that Robinson was quite cognizant of the proceedings and able to assist counsel in his defense. Turning from lay impressions to those of an expert, it was stipulated at trial that a Dr. Haines, Director of the Behavior Clinic of the Crimi-

nal Court of Cook County, had examined Robinson several months earlier and, if called, would testify that Robinson "knows the nature of the charge and is able to cooperate with his counsel." The conclusive factor is that Robinson's own lawyers, the two men who apparently had the closest contact with the defendant during the proceedings, never suggested he was incompetent to stand trial and never moved to have him examined on incompetency grounds during trial; indeed, counsel's remarks to the jury seem best read as an affirmation of Robinson's present "lucidity," which would be highly peculiar if Robinson had been unable to assist properly in his defense. . . .

In my view, the Court of Appeals should be reversed and the District Court's dismissal of the petition reinstated.

JACKSON v. INDIANA

. . . MR. JUSTICE BLACKMUN delivered the opinion of the Court. . . .

Petitioner, Theon Jackson, is a mentally defective deaf mute with a mental level of a pre-school child. He cannot read, write, or otherwise communicate except through limited sign language. In May 1968, at age 27, he was charged in the Criminal Court of Marion County, Indiana, with separate robberies of two women. The offenses were alleged to have occurred the preceding July. The first involved property (a purse and its contents) of the value of four dollars. The second concerned five dollars in money. The record sheds no lights on these charges since, upon receipt of not guilty pleas from Jackson, the trial court set in motion the Indiana procedures for determining his competency to stand trial. . . .

As the statute requires, the court appointed two psychiatrists to examine Jackson. A competency hearing was subsequently held at which petitioner was represented by counsel. The court received the examining doctors' joint written report and oral testimony from them and from a deaf school interpreter through whom they had attempted to communicate with petitioner. The report concluded that Jackson's almost nonexistent

communication skill, together with his lack of hearing and his mental deficiency, left him unable to understand the nature of the charges against him or to participate in his defense. One doctor testified that it was extremely unlikely that petitioner could ever learn to read or write and questioned whether petitioner even had the ability to develop any proficiency in sign language. He believed that the interpreter had not been able to communicate with petitioner to any great extent and testified that petitioner's "prognosis appears rather dim." The other doctor testified that even if Jackson were not a deaf mute, he would be incompetent to stand trial, and doubted whether petitioner had sufficient intelligence ever to develop the necessary communication skills. The interpreter testified that Indiana had no facilities that could help someone as badly off as Jackson to learn minimal communication skills.

On this evidence, the trial court found that Jackson "lack[ed] comprehension sufficient to make his defense," § 9–1706a, and ordered him committed to the Indiana Department of Mental Health until such time as that Department should certify to the court that "the defendant is sane." . . .

U.S. Supreme Court 406 U.S. 715 (1972).

Counsel argued that Jackson's commitment under these circumstances amounted to a "life sentence" without his ever having been convicted of a crime, and that the commitment therefore deprived Jackson of his Fourteenth Amendment rights to due process and equal protection, and constituted cruel and unusual punishment under the Eighth Amendment made applicable to the States through the Fourteenth. The trial court denied the motion. On appeal the Supreme Court of Indiana affirmed with one judge dissenting, 253 Ind. 487, 255 N.E. 2d 515 (1970). Rehearing was denied with two judges dissenting. We granted certiorari. . . .

In Baxstrom v. Herold, 383 U.S. 107, 86 S. Ct. 760, 15 L. Ed. 2d 620 (1966), the Court held that a state prisoner civilly committed at the end of his prison sentence on the finding of a surrogate was denied equal protection when he was deprived of a jury trial that the State made generally available to all other persons civilly committed. Rejecting the State's argument that Baxstrom's conviction and sentence constituted adequate justification for the difference in procedures, the Court said that "there is no conceivable basis for distinguishing the commitment of a person who is nearing the end of a penal term from all other civil commitments." . . . The Court also held that Baxstrom was denied equal protection by commitment to an institution maintained by the state corrections department for "dangerously mentally ill" persons, without a judicial determination of his "dangerous propensities" afforded all others so committed.

If criminal conviction and imposition of sentence are insufficient to justify less procedural and substantive protection against indefinite commitment than that generally available to all others, the mere filing of criminal charges surely cannot suffice. This was the precise holding of the Massachusetts Court in Commonwealth v. Druken, 356 Mass. 503, 254 N.E. 2d 779, 781 (1969). The *Baxstrom* principle also has been extended to commitment following an insanity acquittal, Bolton v. Harris, 130 U.S. App. D.C. 1, 395 F. 2d 642 (1968); Cameron v. Mullen, 128 U.S. App. D.C. 235, 387 F. 2d 193 (1967); People v. Lally, 19 N.Y. 2d 27, 277 N.Y.S. 2d 654, 224 N.E. 2d 87 (1966), and to commitment in lieu of sentence following conviction as a sex offender. Humphrey v. Cady, 404 U.S.—, 92 S. Ct. 1048, 31 L. Ed. 2d 394 (1972). . . .

Were the State's factual premise that Jackson's commitment is only temporary a valid one, this might well be a different case. But the record does not support that premise. One of the doctors testified that in his view Jackson would be unable to acquire the substantially improved communication skills that would be necessary for him to participate in any defense. The prognosis for petitioner's developing such skills, he testified, appeared "rather dim." In answer to a question whether Jackson would ever be able to comprehend the charges or participate in his defense, even after commitment and treatment, the doctor said, "I doubt it, I don't believe so." The other psychiatrist testified that even if Jackson were able to develop such skills, he would *still* be unable to comprehend the proceedings or aid counsel due to his mental deficiency. The interpreter, a supervising teacher at the state School for the Deaf, said that he would not be able to serve as an interpreter for Jackson or aid him in participating in a trial, and that the State had no facilities that could, "after a length of time," aid Jackson in so participating. The court also heard petitioner's mother testify that Jackson already had undergone rudimentary out-patient training communications skills from the Deaf and Dumb School in Indianapolis over a period of three years without noticeable success. There is nothing in the record that even points to any possibility that Jackson's present condition can be remedied at any future time. . . .

We are unable to say that, on the record before us, Indiana could have civilly committed him as mentally ill under § 22–1209 or committed him as feeble-minded under § 22–1907. The former requires at least (1) a showing of mental illness and (2) a showing that the individual is in need of "care, treatment, training or detention." § 22–1201 (1). Whether Jackson's mental deficiency would meet the first test is unclear; neither examining physician addressed himself to this. Furthermore, it is problematical whether commitment for "treatment" or "training" would be appropriate since the record establishes that none is available for Jackson's condition at any state institution. The record also fails to establish that Jackson is in need of custodial care or "detention." He has been employed at times, and there is no evidence that the care he long received at home has become inadequate. The statute appears to require an independent showing of dangerousness. . . . Insofar as it may require such a showing, the pending criminal charges are insufficient to establish it, and no other supporting evidence was introduced. For the same reasons, we cannot say that this record would support a feeble-mindedness commitment under § 22–1907 on the ground that Jackson is "unable properly to care for [himself]." . . .

More important, an individual committed as feeble-minded is eligible for release when his condition "justifies it," and an individual civilly committed as mentally ill when the "superintendent or administrator shall discharge such person *or* [when] cured of such illness." . . . Thus in either case release is appropriate when the individual no longer requires the custodial care or treatment or detention which occasioned the commitment, or when the department of mental health believes release would be in his best interests. The evidence available concerning Jackson's past employment and home care strongly suggests that under these standards he might be eligible for release at almost any time, even if he did not improve. . . .

As we noted above, we cannot conclude that pending criminal charges provide a greater justification for different treatment than conviction and sentence. Consequently, we hold that by subjecting Jackson to a more lenient commitment standard and to a more stringent standard of release than those generally applicable to all others not charged with offenses, and by thus condemning him in effect to permanent institutionalization without the showing required for commitment or the opportunity for release afforded by § 22–1209 or § 22–1907, Indiana deprived petitioner of equal protection of the laws under the Fourteenth Amendment. . . .

The federal statute, 18 U.S.C. §§ 4244 to 4246, is not dissimilar to the Indiana law. It provides that a defendant found incompetent to stand trial may be committed "until the accused shall be mentally competent to stand trial or until the pending charges against him are disposed of according to law." Section 4247, applicable on its face only to convicted criminals whose federal sentences are about to expire, permits commitment if the prisoner is (1) "insane or mentally incompetent" and (2) "will probably endanger the safety of the officers, the property, or other interests of the United States, and . . . suitable arrangements for the custody and care of the prisoner are not otherwise available," that is in a state facility. See Greenwood v. United States, 350 U.S., at 373–374, 76 S. Ct., at 414–415. . . .

In *Greenwood* the Court upheld the pretrial commitment of a defendant who met all three conditions of § 4247, even though there was little likelihood that he would ever become competent to stand trial. Since Greenwood had not yet stood trial, his commitment was ostensibly under § 4244. By the related release provision, § 4246, he could not have been released until he became competent. But the District Court had in fact applied § 4247, and found specifically that Greenwood would be dangerous if not committed. This Court approved that approach, holding § 4247 applicable before trial as well as to those about to be released from sentence. 350 U.S., at 374,

76 S. Ct., at 414. Accordingly, Greenwood was entitled to release when no longer dangerous, § 4248, even if he did not become competent to stand trial and thus did not meet the requirement of § 4246. Under these circumstances, the Court found the commitment constitutional.

Since *Greenwood*, federal courts without exception have found improper any straightforward application of §§ 4244 and 4246 to a defendant whose chance of attaining competency to stand trial is slim, thus effecting an indefinite commitment on the grounds of incompetency alone. . . .

These decisions have imposed a "rule of reasonableness" upon §§ 4244 and 4246. Without a finding of dangerousness, one committed thereunder can be held only for a "reasonable period of time" necessary to determine whether there is a substantial chance of his attaining the capacity to stand trial in the foreseeable future. If the chances are slight, or if the defendant does not in fact improve, then he must be released or granted a §§ 4247–4248 hearing. . . .

Some States appear to commit indefinitely a defendant found incompetent to stand trial until he recovers competency. Other States require a finding of dangerousness to support such a commitment or provide forms of parole. New York has recently enacted legislation mandating release of incompetent defendants charged with misdemeanors after 90 days of commitment, and release and dismissal of charges against those accused of felonies after they have been committed for two-thirds of the maximum potential prison sentence. . . . Recommendations for changes made by commentators and study committees have included incorporation into pretrial commitment procedures of the equivalent of the federal "rule of reason," a requirement of a finding of dangerousness or of full-scale civil commitment, periodic review by court or mental health administrative personnel of the defendant's condition and progress, and provisions for ultimately dropping charges if the defendant does not improve. One source of this criticism is undoubtedly the empirical data available which tends to show that many defendants committed before trial are never tried, and that those defendants committed pursuant to ordinary civil proceedings are, on the average, released sooner than defendants automatically committed solely on account of their incapacity to stand trial. Related to these statistics are substantial doubts about whether the rationale for pretrial commitment—that care or treatment will aid the accused in attaining competency—is empirically valid given the state of most of our mental institutions.

However, very few courts appear to have addressed the problem directly in the state context. . . .

In a 1970 case virtually indistinguishable from the one before us, the Illinois Supreme Court granted relief to an illiterate deaf mute who had been indicted for murder four years previous but found incompetent to stand trial on account of his inability to communicate, and committed. People ex rel. Myers v. Briggs, 46 Ill. 2d 281, 263 N.E. 2d 109 (1970). . . .

It is clear that Jackson's commitment rests on proceedings that did not purport to bring into play, indeed did not even consider relevant, *any* of the articulated bases for exercise of Indiana's power of indefinite commitment. . . . At the least, due process requires that the nature and duration of commitment bear some reasonable relation to the purpose for which the individual is committed.

We hold, consequently, that a person charged by a State with a criminal offense who is committed solely on account of his incapacity to proceed to trial cannot be held more than the reasonable period of time necessary to determine whether there is a substantial probability that he will attain that capacity in the foreseeable future. If it is determined that this is not the case, then the State must either institute the customary civil commitment proceeding that would be required to commit indefinitely any other citizen, or release the defendant. Furthermore, even if it is determined that the defendant probably soon will be able to stand trial, his continued commitment must be justified by progress toward that goal. In light of differing state facilities and procedures and a lack of evidence in this record, we do not think it appropriate for us to attempt to prescribe arbitrary time limits. We note, however, that petitioner Jackson has now been confined for three and one-half years on a record that sufficiently establishes the lack of a substantial probability that he will ever be able to participate fully in trial. . . .

Both courts and commentators have noted the desirability of permitting some proceedings to go forward despite the defendant's incompetency. For instance, § 4.06(3) of the Model Penal Code would permit an incompetent accused's attorney to contest any issue "susceptible of fair determination prior to trial and without the personal participation of the defendant." An alternative draft of § 4.06(4) of the Model Penal Code would also permit an evidentiary hearing at which certain defenses, not including lack of criminal responsibility, could be raised by defense counsel on the basis of which the court might quash the indictment. Some States have statutory provisions permitting pretrial motions to be made or even allowing the incompetent defendant a trial at which to establish his innocence, without permitting a conviction. We do not read this Court's previous decisions to preclude the States from allowing at a minimum, an incompetent defendant to raise certain defenses such as insufficiency of the indictment, or make certain pretrial motions, through counsel. Of course, if the Indiana courts conclude that Jackson was almost certainly not capable of criminal responsibility when the offenses were committed, dismissal of the charges might be warranted. But even if this is not the case, Jackson may have other good defenses that could sustain dismissal or acquittal and which might now be asserted. We do not know if Indiana would approve procedures such as those mentioned here, but these possibilities will be open on remand.

Reversed and remanded. . . .

REPORT OF THE JUDICIAL CONFERENCE OF THE DISTRICT OF COLUMBIA CIRCUIT

Report of the Committee on Problems Connected with Mental Examination of the Accused in Criminal Cases, before Trial

Institute of Criminal Law & Procedure
Georgetown University Law Center
Washington, D.C.

PROCEDURE IN EXAMINATION

Immediately after admission of the accused to Saint Elizabeths Hospital, a psychiatric resident in training takes a case history and performs a brief physical examination. Routinely the accused is given blood tests, urinalysis and chest x-rays. If special medical tests are indicated, they are scheduled for early administration. Reference is made to a medical staff member for diagnosis and/or treatment if the resident has reason to suspect the existence of a physical ailment.

Within the first thirty days an effort is made to contact all authorities and institutions that might have relevant information about the accused. Included are penal institutions, other hospitals, and the Veterans Administration. Also during the first thirty days a social worker takes a detailed case history of the accused.

It is the practice for psychiatric residents in training to interview the patient on several occasions between his entry into the hospital and the staff conference, the meeting at which the hospital's formal opinion is formulated concerning the competence and, if the hospital has been so directed, the responsibility of the accused. These interviews are summarized and transmitted to the staff psychiatrists for evaluation at the staff conference. The psychiatric resident may see the accused on a greater number of occasions if the accused is extremely agitated. The average number of resident contacts following intake is two or three, each of approximately thirty minutes duration.

Throughout the accused's commitment period, nurses, recreational therapists, and ward attendants are encouraged to make notes of unusual occurrences; if made, these notes are recorded in the accused's file that is sent to the staff conference.

Between the day of admission and the day of the staff conference (which typically was held between the eightieth and eighty-fifth days when the period of commitment was ninety days) the accused generally is seen by a staff psychiatrist only at "rounds," which are usually made twice weekly. At "rounds" if the accused has a special problem he will be able to consult with the staff psychiatrists; otherwise, there is no scheduled contact between the accused and staff psychiatrists.

An extensive battery of psychological tests is performed in the latter part of the accused's stay. This timing is simply the hospital's choice; the tests could be given at any time. The following tests are routinely performed: Wechsler Bellevue Intelligence Scale, Wechsler Memory Scale, Bender-Gestalt, Rorschach, and Projective Drawings. Also employed, but with less frequency, are the Color-Form Sort, Szondi, and Thematic Apperception tests.[1]

The staff conference is, as indicated, the culminating event in the accused's examination. He appears for evaluation before hospital doctors and others who have the benefit of the data accumulated while he has been in the hospital. The staff conference is attended by the following personnel with the indicated frequency: senior staff psychiatrist (always); social worker (often); staff physicians (often); psychologist (always); psychiatric residents in training (often). Recently the administration

[1] This testing exceeds in its scope, by far, that performed in mental hospitals in most other jurisdictions, so the responses to a questionnaire sent to mental hospital superintendents indicated.

of Saint Elizabeths has deliberately reduced the number of psychiatrists attending most staff conferences so as to make fewer of them subject to subpoenas to testify and thus reduce the imposition on their working time caused by courtroom appearances. In some cases the senior staff psychiatrist may decide that the diagnosis is so clear-cut that no staff conference is needed and none is held.

In a substantial number of cases the staff conference may be the first and only time at which a senior staff psychiatrist has spoken with the accused. The staff members review the data that have been developed concerning the patient, including the summary of his commitment period experience prepared by a psychiatric resident in training. At the staff conference the accused is personally interviewed for approximately twenty to thirty minutes, following which another twenty or thirty minutes is devoted to discussion and evaluation of his condition.

Although procedures at the District of Columbia General Hospital are similar to those at Saint Elizabeths Hospital, there are some important differences. First, the intake examination of the accused is performed by a staff psychiatrist, not a resident. Second, the staff psychiatrist sees the accused on a number of occasions during the thirty-day commitment period. At least several hours are spent with the accused by the staff psychiatrist. At the end of the commitment period the staff psychiatrist who has worked with the accused makes his evaluation without resort to the staff conference technique, although on occasions a staff psychiatrist may informally consult with his colleagues.

The psychiatric examination made by Legal Psychiatric Services, usually made at the cell block in the United States Court House, is comparable in duration to the actual psychiatric examination made at Saint Elizabeths Hospital. That is, even though a defendant is in Saint Elizabeths Hospital for sixty days or more, he spends no more time being examined by psychiatrists than the defendant visited at the cell block by psychiatrists from Legal Psychiatric Services. A major difference is that at the present time Legal Psychiatric Services often administers no psychological or medical tests and does not have the benefit of reports made by hospital personnel on patients' ward behavior. Most of the referrals to Legal Psychiatric Services are limited to competence evaluations; further, the committing judge frequently requests a report within twenty-four hours. This may be because the judge has observed aberrational behavior in a defendant in the course of a trial, for example. The staff conference device is used with some frequency.

THE PSYCHIATRIC REPORT TO THE COURT

Following examination and observation of the defendant, the hospital authorities transmit to the court a report concerning his mental condition. The hospital authorities are directed, in the statutory language, to apprise the court whether in their opinion "the accused is of unsound mind or mentally incompetent."

The committee has examined a large number of these reports in the files of the court. Most commonly, the reports merely set out the ultimate conclusion of the hospital. The reports typically have not contained the psychiatric diagnosis of the accused or described the procedures followed in arriving at a diagnosis, and they have rarely delineated any reasons for the conclusion reached.[2] Dissenting views expressed at the staff conference have not been reported by Saint Elizabeths Hospital. It has been suggested that there were two basic reasons for the brief, conclusory nature of these reports. First, some psychiatrists have thought that the court preferred such reports. Second, some psychiatrists have seen no point in a lengthy, detailed report that may serve as the basis for subsequent legal attack. The attitude probably stems in part from psychiatrists' understandable desire to spend more time at the hospital with their patients and less time in court as witnesses. Very recently the Court of Appeals has indicated that only a rather fuller statement than has been typical complies with the statutory words "report" and "certificate," since these must be construed in the context of a statute that requires a judicial determination of competence,[3] and the Chief Judge of the District Court has asked the hospital that in the future its reports comport with the Court of Appeals' view.

A report from the hospital to the court, typical of the period studied by the committee, where the hospital was asked to express an opinion as to competence to stand trial and criminal responsibility, read as follows, following a standard-form introduction:

[The accused's name] case has been studied since the date of his admission to [name of institution] and he has been examined by several

---

[2] The District of Columbia practice as to use of conclusory terms is very typical. See Hess and Thomas, *Incompetency to Stand Trial: Procedures, Results, and Problems* (Am. J. Psychiatry, 119 [1963]: 713, 715–16) relating experience in Michigan. Most respondents to a questionnaire sent to the prosecutors reported that in their jurisdictions conclusory reports were widely used. In many instances, however, these reports also contained a detailed description of the accused's medical condition.

[3] Holloway v. United States, D.C. Cir. No. 18,-017, decided Nov. 5, 1964.

qualified psychiatrists attached to the medical staff of this hospital as to his mental condition. On November 27, 1961, [the accused] was examined and the case reviewed in detail at a medical staff conference. We conclude, as the result of our examinations and observation, that [the accused] is mentally competent to understand the nature of the proceedings against him and to consult properly with counsel in his own defense, although he has not recovered from his mental illness. It is our opinion that he was suffering from mental disease on or about December 13, and December 15, 1960, and that the criminal offenses, if committed by him, were products of this mental disease.

Occasionally, the hospital report has specified the psychiatric diagnosis, e.g., the accused has a "passive aggressive personality" or he suffers from "schizophrenia."[4] In some instances a more detailed report is submitted. One report described the accused's mental condition in these words:

Neurological examinations, including an electroencephalogram, indicate the presence of an epileptic condition. This condition, however, is not the cause of criminal acts involving financial gain or well-constructed secretive behaviour. . . .
Psychiatric examinations reveal him to be sane, competent, and capable of participating in his own defense. It is our opinion he is responsible for his actions.
. . .

RECOMMENDATIONS OF THE COMMITTEE ON PRE-TRIAL MENTAL EXAMINATIONS AS AMENDED AND ACTED UPON BY THE JUDICIAL CONFERENCE

[Conference amendments shown by strike-outs (deletions) and italics (additions)]
. . .

The Requesting Party and the Request

Recommendation 1. The statute should be made to provide that an order for a mental examination shall be granted simply on request of either of the parties or on the court's own motion; and that, upon objection to a request or to a suggestion by the court that it intends to order an examination *sua sponte*, there shall be a hearing and the court shall deny the request or withdraw its proposed *sua sponte* order if it is made clearly to appear to the court that the conduct of a mental examination is unnecessary or would be contrary to the interests of justice or fairness.

The Scope of the Prescribed Examination

Recommendation 2. The statute should be made to provide that a mental examination may be conducted for the purpose of inquiring into an accused's mental condition at the

[4] The medical terminology is not explained.

time of the commission of the offense with which he is charged as well as into his fitness to stand trial, which is the present judicially-approved practice. ~~and further provision should be made that only the kind or kinds of examination that are requested or that the court deems appropriate shall be conducted~~. *In all cases in which an examination is ordered, the order should direct that the accused be examined as to both of these aspects of his mental condition, except that, where neither party has requested inquiry into the accused's mental condition as of the time of the alleged offense and the court does not deem such inquiry necessary, the order should direct that the examination be limited to the accused's fitness to stand trial.*

The Representation of the Accused

Recommendation 3. The ordering or conduct of a statutory mental examination should be made impermissible unless at the time of the order and during the period when the examination is conducted the accused is represented by counsel.

Informal, Extra-Statutory Procedures

Recommendation 4. The prosecuting authorities should be prohibited from having an accused mentally examined except ~~for custodial purposes~~ *as necessary from a medical standpoint to determine the appropriate manner of custody*, without a court order for such an examination.

The Psychiatric Clinic

Recommendation 5. There should be established a psychiatric court clinic, which would initially perform about half of the pre-trial mental examinations of accused felons. ~~It would be staffed by three psychiatrists and one attorney, each working part time, and two psychologists, a social worker, and two secretaries working full time.~~

The Period of Commitment

Recommendation 6. The court's order for a mental examination should designate a maximum period of hospitalization of thirty days (with the possibility of extension contemplated).

Bail

Recommendation 7. The status of the accused who has been enlarged on bail should not be changed because of a pre-trial mental examination being ordered for him, and an accused who is otherwise eligible for bail should not be denied bail because a pre-trial mental examination is ordered for him; if, however, the examining psychiatrists report that the accused's confinement is necessary for an effective examination, the court should be empowered to commit to a mental hospital *for that purpose.*

The Uncooperative Witness, the Psychiatrists' Confidences, and the Privilege Against Self-Incrimination

*Recommendation 8.** An accused who refuses to cooperate in a pre-trial mental examination should not be made punishable as for contempt, nor should such an accused be denied the opportunity to raise the insanity defense; whether other indirect sanctions should be available, such as the presentation of evidence at the accused's trial concerning his refusal to cooperate, should be left to judicial decision; the accused should be informed in advance by the court ~~that he is not under any compulsion to answer questions or otherwise cooperate and that statements he makes in the course of his examination, bearing on the issue of his guilt apart from mental responsibility, may not be admitted as evidence in any criminal proceeding against him; he should also be informed by the court~~ *of his pertinent rights and duties in regard to his mental examination including* any other consequences of his cooperation or failure to cooperate that there may be under then-existing constitutional, statutory and case law.

The Report of the Examination

Recommendation 9. The report of a court-ordered pre-trial mental examinaton should be made in substantial detail, recounting what was done to get at the facts concerning the accused's mental condition and what those facts are, not merely the conclusions the psychiatrists have drawn from those facts.

How the Determination of Competence Should be Made

Recommendation 10. The statute should be made to provide expressly that every determination of competence to stand trial should constitute an exercise of judicial judgment.

Factors in the Determination of Competence

Recommendation 11. The traditional statement of the standard of competence—ability to understand the proceedings against one and to participate in one's defense—should be specified as such in the governing statute and should be considered as subsuming a number of important subsidiary factors.

The Duration of the Commitment

*Recommendation 12.** When, at any time after an accused's commitment as incompe-

* Recommendations 8 and 12 were not formally adopted by the Judicial Conference. Ed. Note.

tent, those treating him certify that it is improbable that he will be restored to competence in the foreseeable future, and when, after an accused has been committed as incompetent for two years, those treating him certify that he probably will not be restored to competence within the next six months, the court should be directed to dismiss the criminal charges against the accused and to order civil commitment proceedings instituted.

Reviewing the Incompetent's Case: Periodic Hospital Review

Recommendation 13. It should be made the obligation of the authorities in charge of the institution in which an accused adjudged incompetent is confined to make a report at least every six months on the accused's status and progress; copies of the report should be sent to the committing judge, the United States Attorney's Office, and counsel for the accused in order that any appropriate judicial action may be taken.

Reviewing the Incompetent's Case: Examination by a Private Psychiatrist

Recommendation 14. An accused who has been adjudged incompetent should be entitled once every twelve months upon request to an examination by a psychiatrist not on the staff of Saint Elizabeths Hospital; the court would designate the psychiatrist.

Raising Legal Defenses During Incompetence

Recommendation 15. It should be made clear that legal objections that do not require the assistance or participation of the accused may be presented to and passed upon by the court after the adjudication of an accused as incompetent; the court's disposition of any motion or other request for relief so presented would be as final as any order of the same kind in any other criminal proceeding except that if, after restoration to competence, the accused demonstrates that the presentation of any such request was prejudiced by his inability to participate, an order adverse to the accused would be reopened by the court.

The Incompetent and the Right to a Speedy Trial

Recommendation 16. The trial court should be empowered to dismiss the charges against an accused and order him discharged where the court is of the view that so much time has elapsed since his commitment that it would be unjust to resume the criminal proceeding.

STATE OF KANSAS v. WALTER RAY SEVERNS

PARKER, C. J.: This is the second appearance in this court of an appeal by Walter Ray Severns in a criminal action, the present appeal being from a conviction of murder in the second degree.

A historical review of the background of this criminal prosecution from the date of its inception is essential to a proper understanding of the events and circumstances giving rise to the instant appeal.

In 1943 the defendant, after having been first examined and found sane by a sanity commission, was tried in the district court of Sedgwick County on an information charging him with murder in the first degree of Inez Viola Burling, a child eight years of age. Such child was a niece of the defendant's wife and was living in the Severns home at the time of her death. At the conclusion of the trial, at which the defendant testified as a witness in his own behalf, the jury found him guilty as charged and determined the punishment to be death. Following the denial of his motion for a new trial the trial court rendered judgment on the verdict. Thereupon defendant appealed to this court, specifying that the court erred in its rulings on the introduction of evidence, in submitting the cause to the jury on the charge of murder in the first degree, and in instructing the jury. On review of the appeal we held his claims of error with respect to rulings on the introduction of evidence and in submitting the cause to the jury on the charge of murder in the first degree were without merit but reversed the judgment solely on the ground of error in other instructions.

It is neither necessary nor required that we here review the sordid facts on which, in the first appeal, we held specifically that under the evidence of record the trial court would have committed error had it failed to give an instruction on murder in the first degree, or detail the reasons given for reversing the case on the basis of error in other instructions. It suffices to say those facts and reasons are already spread at length on the pages of our reports and readily available to readers of this opinion, who may desire further information with respect thereto, upon resort to *State* v. *Severns*, 158 Kan. 453, P.2d 488.

After his first conviction the defendant was incarcerated in the state penitentiary pending his appeal. Sometime thereafter the then Warden of the penitentiary requested the district court for a hearing under the provisions of G.S. 1935, 62–2406, now G.S. 1949, 62–2406, providing for a commission to examine into the sanity of a person awaiting the death penalty. Pursuant to this request the district court caused an investigation to be made and, after a conference with the members of the trial sanity commission, denied the request.

On November 19, 1944, following our reversal of the previous judgment and sentence and prior to the date set for his second trial, a new commission was appointed. It found defendant to be suffering from a prison psychosis, rendering him insane and unable to comprehend his position and to make his defense. Thereupon, as requested (sic) by statute (G.S. 1949, 62–1531), he was admitted to the State Hospital for the dangerous insane at Larned where he remained, undergoing treatment, until May 15, 1957, when, under direction of proper officials of that institution, he was returned to the court from which he was received to again stand trial for the crime of murder in the first degree as charged in the information.

Upon defendant's return to Sedgwick County the district court appointed counsel to represent him. Thereafter, and on May 27, 1957, his counsel, E. Lael Alkire, filed a motion alleging in substance that (1) defendant might be an insane person, hence incapable of comprehending his position and of advising his attorney of such defenses as he might have; and (2) that he had been a sufferer from a mental illness known as schizophrenic reaction, catatonic type, and as a result, by-product, or residual thereof, he was suffering from memory gaps, and unable to remember anything whatsoever concerning the alleged crime and therefore incapable of defending himself. Such motion then asked for the appointment of a commission to determine whether the defendant (1) was presently sane or insane; (2) was suffering from a mental disturbance known as schizophrenic reaction, catatonic type, and

Kansas Supreme Court 184 Kan. 213, 336 P. 2d 447 (1959).

(3) as a result of his mental illness he had suffered a loss of memory, particularly as to the time pertinent to the alleged crime and the occurrences surrounding it.

The court granted the foregoing motion and appointed a commission, consisting of three qualified physicians. This commission conducted a series of examinations and then returned its report. Portions thereof, set forth in the abstract as pertinent to this appeal, read:

1. From a review of reports received from the Larned State Hospital—the social history, the psychological testing, and the psychiatric interview—it would be our impression that this patient is suffering from a condition diagnosed as schizophrenic reaction, paranoid type, in partial remission manifested by massive repression resulting in memory loss, by flatness of affect, by hyper-alertness, and that the manifestations of his illness are now on a characterological level.

2. It is our opinion that at the present time this person would be considered competent, that he knows the nature of the alleged crime and that he knows right from wrong; that his memory loss is not on an organic basis, nor is it a form of malingering but is part of the mental illness which is still present.

3. The question as to whether or not the memory loss makes this patient unable to take part in his own defense must be answered as a legal question and not as a medical one. One may argue that he would be capable of assisting in his own defense because at the present time he is competent, knows right from wrong, and has sufficient judgment, even though he does not remember the events of the crime. Or one might argue that because he does not remember the events of the crime, he could not help prepare his defense.

4. . . . However, it is recognized that the presence of a mental illness does not necessarily mean that a person was incompetent or does not know the nature of his acts, or right from wrong.

5. As to the outlook of this patient, the psychological tests would indicate that this patient would react poorly to stress and that under stress there would be a possibility of a return of more severe symptoms. It would also be expected that this person's control of his impulsive behavior would be poor and, therefore, he would be expected to have a greater tendency to impulsive destructive behavior than the average person; that the possibility of expecting a greater social remission or social recovery from this patient by further treatment would be considered poor to hopeless.

It should be noted that at the time of the return of the report all three members of the commission were personally present; that, for the benefit of court and counsel, each member was sworn as a witness and examined at length; and that their statement was in line with the findings made in such report. It should also be noted that, when the examination of the members of the commission was concluded, defendant's counsel moved for an order continuing the trial of the case indefinitely on grounds the defendant was still technically insane, in that he had suffered a memory loss, could not assist in his defense, and should be returned to the state hospital for further treatment; and that after a full and complete hearing on this motion the trial court made certain written findings which read:

THE COURT FINDS that the defendant, Severns, is not insane, nor an idiot, nor an imbecile; that he is able to comprehend his position at the present time, with reference to the charges pending against him; that he knows right from wrong at the present time; and that at the present time, he knows the nature of his acts.

THE COURT FURTHER FINDS that the defendant, Severns, is suffering from a memory loss which memory loss includes that period of his life immediately prior to and following the alleged offense charged in this case; that said memory loss covers a greater period of time than that herein mentioned, but that the only pertinent memory loss relating to this case is as above outlined; that said memory loss is not of an organic basis and is not a form of malingering.

THE COURT FURTHER FINDS that returning the defendant to the Larned State Hospital would be useless, from a standpoint of expecting additional improvement, the defendant having probably reached his maximum recovery.

THE COURT FURTHER FINDS that this case was heretofore, and in the April term, 1943, tried, and that there is available a transcript of the testimony of said trial, and that apparently the defendant at that time had not been adjudged insane, but that pending an appeal and while he was committed to the Kansas State Penitentiary at Lansing, Kansas, and prior to the time he was remanded for a new trial as ordered by the Supreme Court of the State of Kansas, he became insane.

IT IS THEREFORE THE JUDGMENT OF THIS COURT that the motion of defendant be denied, that the trial proceed as scheduled on June 24, 1957, and that the loss of memory between the first trial and this trial is not sufficient in and of itself to prevent the defendant from proceeding to trial as herein ordered.

Following action as just indicated the defendant was again tried on the information by a jury which found him guilty of murder in the second degree. Later, his motion for a new trial having been overruled, judgment was rendered on the verdict and defendant was sentenced to confinement in the state penitentiary for the commission of such offense. Thereupon he perfected the instant appeal and brings the case to this court under a specification of error, which raises but one question, to which we shall presently refer.

Supplementing what has been heretofore related, it should be stated the record discloses that in the first trial appellant testified as a witness in his own behalf, that the transcript of his testimony and that of all other witnesses testifying in such case was at all times available to him and his counsel prior to and during the second trial, and that, with special reference to his testimony in the first case, the trial court, in a "Memoranda of Findings" on file in such case stated: "Walter Ray Severns took the stand in his own behalf, and while his answers were barely audible, and sometimes inaudible, they were intelligent answers."

The general premise on which appellant founds his right to relief in this case is set forth in that portion of his single specification of error which reads:

The Trial Court erred in requiring the appellant to stand trial when the appellant, under the facts and the Trial Court's findings, had suffered an involuntary loss of memory, which memory loss, as found by the Court, covered specifically the time of the alleged crime, and which memory loss was brought about as a residual or by-product of insanity, and did, in truth and in fact, render the appellant incapable of speaking in his own defense, whatever it might have been, or of having others speak for him. . . .

In connection with the claim thus made it will be helpful to this opinion, from the standpoint of brevity, to state at the outset:

1. That there cannot be and is no dispute between the parties regarding the correctness of the facts, events, conditions, and circumstances set forth in the preceding historical review.

2. That in his brief and on oral argument appellant concedes (a) *the only question raised by his appeal is whether the trial court erred in requiring him to stand trial when, under the existing facts and its findings, he had suffered an involuntary loss of memory covering specifically the time*, and (b) that, if properly placed on trial, all subsequent proceedings were regular and the record with respect thereto discloses no sound ground for reversal of the judgment.

In support of his position on the conceded single question involved, which we have heretofore underlined for purposes of emphasis and future reference, appellant spends much time and space on contentions to the effect that at

common law, and in most jurisdictions by express statutory provision, the universal rule is that a person while insane cannot be tried or convicted for the commission of a crime. We are not disposed to labor arguments advanced, or the numerous decisions cited, by appellant in support of his claim this rule of law is well-established. It suffices to say this court is committed to such rule by statute (G.S. 1949, 62–1531) as well as its decisions. See *In re Wright*, 74 Kan. 406, 407, 86 Pac. 460, where it is said: "It is universally conceded that a defendant cannot be compelled to answer to, or defend against, a criminal charge when by reason of an insane mental condition he is unable to do so in a rational manner . . ." (p. 408).

. . .

The test of insanity of an accused precluding his being *put on trial* for a criminal offense is his capacity to comprehend his position, understand the nature and object of the proceedings against him, and conduct his defense in a rational manner. Stated in different fashion, if the accused is capable of understanding the nature and object of the proceedings going on against him; if he rightly comprehends his own condition with reference to such proceedings, and can conduct his defense in a rational manner, he is, for the purpose of being tried, to be deemed sane, although on some other subject his mind may be deranged or unsound.

Having established the issue presented when the question of sanity at the time of trial is raised it can now be pointed out that, in the face of the present record, we are here concerned with but one of the three tests, to which we have just referred, in our consideration of appellant's sole claim of error. This, we may add, is true for two reasons. First, because both the sanity commission and the trial court, based on facts which were supported by substantial competent evidence and for that reason cannot be disturbed, found that appellant understood the nature and object of the proceedings against him, comprehended his position at the time, and knew the difference between right and wrong. Second, for the reason that, by its very nature and appellant's own admissions, such claim of error is limited to the question whether the sustaining of his memory loss compels a conclusion he was unable to conduct his defense on the trial of this case in a rational manner, under the existing facts and circumstances.

Before giving further consideration to the decisive question raised by appellant it should be also stated that counsel for both parties assert they have been unable to find any reported cases, either in this jurisdiction or elsewhere, that, under the facts and circumstances of record, may be regarded as controlling precedents and, we may add, our extended research of such authorities has failed to disclose any.

True, we find three cases where memory loss is considered and recognized as a sufficient ground for requiring a hearing on the question whether an accused, by reason thereof, is unable to conduct his defense in a rational manner and therefore should not be forced to go to trial. One of such decisions is *Youtsey* v. *United States,* 97 Fed. 937, where a judgment convicting a defendant of embezzlement was reversed because of failure of the trial court to grant a hearing on that question. Another is *United States* v. *Chisolm,* 149 Fed. 284, where a hearing was granted and such question submitted to a jury for its determination under lengthy instruction, at the close of which the jury found the accused was of sufficient sane mind and in such possession of his mental faculties as to make it proper to proceed with his trial. Still another is *State* v. *Swails,* 223 La. 751, 66 So.2d 796, where an accused charged with murder, who had been found insane and committed to a mental hospital, was seeking relief from the hospital and the right to be tried for the crime, while the state was claiming loss of memory as to the events occurring at, before, and after the commission of the crime charged rendered him incapable of making a rational defense and hence required his return to the hospital. The court held against the state's contention and remanded the case for trial. Since the foregoing decisions are clearly distinguishable, from the standpoint of facts and principles involved, and are not to be regarded as controlling precedents, further discussion respecting them would be purely academic. Indeed, our only purpose in here mentioning them is to give readers of this opinion an opportunity to review the few reported appellate court decisions we have been able to find in which memory loss, standing alone, has been relied on as precluding trial of the accused in a criminal action.

Absent controlling precedents, and with full recognition of the rule announced in *In re Wright, supra,* and other decisions of like import, it becomes obvious the all-important question, on which appellant relies to sustain his position the judgment should be reversed, must be determined in the light of the facts before the trial court at the time it reached its conclusion his loss of memory between the first and the second trial was not sufficient in and of itself to prevent him from again proceeding to trial for the crime of murder. We therefore turn to those matters, mindful as we do so, that under the record as presented, the findings and conclusions of the sanity commission respecting the mental status of the appellant must be accepted as controlling and that, except for its conclusion to the effect it was possible for appellant to conduct his defense in a rational manner, the same holds true of all findings and conclusions made by the trial court with respect to the same subject.

What were the facts, matters, and things of record on which the trial court had a right to rely, as we must assume it did, in reaching its decision? Without attempting to recite all of them, it may be stated the more important were:

That a sanity commission, theretofore appointed for the purpose of determining the appellant's mental status, had made its report and found the appellant would be considered competent, that he knew the nature of the alleged crime, and that he knew right from wrong.

That the respective members of such commission had testified as witnesses with respect to their findings and, under oath, had stated in substance that while the appellant was suffering from a memory loss which included that portion of his life immediately prior to and following the alleged offense, he was, except for such memory loss, otherwise normal and from a medical standpoint to be considered as competent.

That the report of such commission contained no finding that the appellant's memory respecting the events, circumstances, and conditions surrounding the commission of the alleged crime could not be refreshed.

That the records of the court disclosed that in the first trial appellant had testified as a witness in his own behalf; that while so testifying his answers to questions propounded to him, although barely audible, were intelligent answers.

That the transcript of the record in the first case had been preserved and was available to appellant and his attorneys, who could read it and thus ascertain the names of all witnesses who testified in the first case; apprise themselves of the defense made in that trial; acquaint themselves with the testimony of such witnesses, including that of appellant while testifying as a witness in his own behalf; refresh appellant's memory with respect to all the facts and circumstances, testified to by him at that time; and become fully cognizant of any and all other matters transpiring during the trial of such action which might affect appellant adversely or otherwise on the trial of the second action.

That, under the peculiar facts and circumstances of the case, having testified as a witness on his own behalf at the first trial and particularly since he had sustained a memory loss as to the events, conditions, and circumstances relating to the commission of the alleged crime, appellant would be entitled, on a proper showing, to have his former testimony received in evidence of the second trial.

That the availability to appellant and his counsel of the full and complete record of the first trial was entitled to weight and consideration in determining whether, standing alone, appellant's memory loss precluded him from making a rational defense.

That appellant, like any other defendant, was entitled to a fair trial but not a perfect one. (See *Lutwak* v. *United States*, 344 U.S. 604, 97 L.Ed. 593, 73 S.Ct. 481; *Steele* v. *United States*, 243 F.2d 712.)

That having had an opportunity to observe the conduct, attitude, and demeanor of the appellant, who was present at all preliminary stages of the proceedings leading up to and including the date of making of its own findings, it (the trial court) had a right to exercise sound judicial discretion in determining whether the appearance, demeanor, and conduct of appellant, throughout such proceedings, were of such character as to warrant a conclusion he was capable, with the assistance of his attorneys, to conduct his defense in a rational manner.

Based on what has been heretofore stated and held we are unwilling to say the confronting facts, conditions, and circumstances of this case required the trial court to hold, as a matter of law, that appellant's loss of memory between the first and second trials was sufficient, in and of itself, to preclude him from conducting his defense in a rational manner or prevent him from proceeding to trial for the crime of murder. Moreover, we are convinced, that in the face of the facts, matters, and things of record, to which we have referred throughout this opinion, that tribunal did not abuse sound judicial discretion in holding that his loss of memory between the first and second trials was not sufficient, in and of itself, to prevent him from proceeding to trial. Therefore, since no irregularities in the subsequent trial or resulting judgment are assigned as error, it necessarily follows that the trial court did not err in overruling appellant's motion for a continuance of the trial, based on the premise he was still technically insane in that he had suffered a memory loss and hence could not assist in his defense; or in rendering judgment in accord with the verdict, finding him guilty of murder in the second degree.

The judgment is affirmed.

WILSON v. UNITED STATES

J. SKELLY WRIGHT, CIRCUIT JUDGE. This appeal presents the unusual situation of the Government conceding a claim which is usually hotly contested—that the appellant suffers from permanent retrograde amnesia as a result of which he has no recollection of any of the events alleged in the indictment. The question raised on appeal is whether it is a denial of due process or of the right to effective assistance of counsel to try a defendant suffering from such a loss of memory.

Appellant was tried and convicted in five counts of assault with a pistol and robbery. The evidence presented at trial was certainly sufficient to sustain the conviction absent the amnesia. The testimony revealed that on October 2, 1964 at about 9:00 P.M., Gerald Fells, who had just parked his car and begun walking down the street, was robbed at gunpoint by two men who took his car keys and stole his car. The robbers held handkerchiefs to their faces and consequently Mr. Fells could not make a positive identification. Nevertheless he testified at trial that appellant "closely resembled" one of his two assailants.

A short time later, at about 9:20 P.M., two men held up a pharmacy on Connecticut Avenue and escaped with over $400 in cash and three bottles of the drug desputal. At trial an employee of the pharmacy positively identified appellant as one of the robbers. Soon after the robbery a police lookout was broadcast for two Negroes driving Mr. Fells' yellow Mustang and believed to have committed the

391 F. 2d 460 (CA–D.C. 1968).

pharmacy holdup. Two officers in a police cruiser spotted the stolen car heading south on Connecticut Avenue and began to pursue it. During the ensuing high-speed chase the suspects' stolen car missed a curve, ran off the road, and crashed into a tree. One of the two men found in a demolished car was dead; the other, the appellant here, was unconscious. Money, a gun, a bottle of desputal, some of Mr. Fells' effects, and a stocking mask and hat resembling those worn by the robbers were found scattered about the wreckage.

In the accident appellant fractured his skull and ruptured several blood vessels in his brain. He remained unconscious for three weeks. He still suffers from a partial paralysis and a slight speech defect. He cannot now, and almost certainly never will, remember anything that happened from the afternoon of the robberies until he regained consciousness three weeks later. Except for this memory loss appellant's mental condition is normal. He suffers from no mental disease or defect, and apparently never has.

On February 23, 1965, appellant was committed to St. Elizabeths Hospital for a mental examination pursuant to 24 D.C.Code § 301 (1967). The hospital reported that, although appellant was now of sound mental health, his amnesia rendered him incompetent to stand trial. On the basis of that report, the District Court judge held a competency hearing, found appellant incompetent to stand trial, and committed him to the hospital, where he remained for 14 months. Then, in August 1966, the hospital reexamined its position and concluded that since appellant was not now suffering from mental disease or defect, and probably was not suffering from such a disorder at the time of the crime, there were no grounds to keep him hospitalized. The court was invited to "make appropriate disposition" of the case. Accordingly Judge McGuire held a second competency hearing in September 1966. The Government's witness, Doctor Economon, testified that appellant had permanent retrograde amnesia and would not be able to aid in his own defense in terms of remembering any of the acts alleged in the indictment. He had "no doubt" that appellant was not feigning. However, the doctor also testified that the appellant did have a rational understanding of the charges against him, that he suffered from no mental disorder, and that, but for the amnesia and slight physical sequelae of the accident, he was in good health. On November 25, 1966, Judge McGuire filed a memorandum opinion finding appellant competent to stand trial. United States v. Wilson, D.D.C., 263 F.Supp. 528.

Judge McGuire abjured a *per se* approach

to the question of incompetency by reason of amnesia, opting instead for a case-by-case determination of competency:

". . . [T]his Court holds that amnesia per se in a case where recollection was present during the time of the alleged offenses and where defendant has the ability to construct a knowledge of what happened from other sources and where he has the present ability to follow the course of the proceedings against him and discuss them rationally with his attorney does not constitute incompetency per se, and that a loss of memory should bar prosecution only when its presence would in fact be crucial to the construction and presentation of a defense and hence essential to the fairness and accuracy of the proceedings. . . .

". . . [T]he rule to be applied in this case is whether insufficient information concerning the events at the time of the commission of the crime and evidence relating thereto is available to the defense so that it can be said that the presence of such an amnesia as we have here precipitates a situation in which defendant's memory is indeed a faculty crucial to the construction and presentation of his defense. . . ." 263 F.Supp. at 533–534.

Judge McGuire left open to defense counsel renewal of his claim of incompetence if formal discovery and other sources of information did not disclose sufficient facts to enable appellant to receive a fair trial. Appellant renewed his claim of incompetency before trial, but Judge McGarraghy, the trial judge, found appellant competent. He was then tried without a jury and convicted.

We agree with Judge McGuire's general approach to assessing the question of competency. However, we remand to the trial judge for more extensive post-trial findings on the question of whether the appellant's loss of memory did in fact deprive him of the fair trial and effective assistance of counsel to which the Fifth and Sixth Amendments entitle him.

The Government relies on our decision in Hansford v. United States, 124 U.S.App.D.C. 387, 365 F.2d 920 (1966), to argue that amnesia, without an accompanying mental disease or defect, can never render the accused incompetent to stand trial. It cites a Yale Law Journal note, *Amnesia: A Case Study in the Limits of Particular Justice*, 71 Yale L.J.109 (1961), for the proposition that "there is no record of any court holding a defendant incompetent to stand trial solely on the basis of amnesia." Id. at 116. But as that same article points out, this doctrinaire approach produces anomalous results. "[F]or while the policy underlying the doctrine of competency focuses on the impairment of the rational ability of the accused to conduct his defense, the rule presently applied by the courts is conditioned upon the fortuitous presence of a narrowly defined mental disorder." Ibid. Instead, as Judge McGuire said, the question must come down to whether, "in the light of the personal intellectual or emotional deficiencies of the accused he can perform the functions essential to the fairness and accuracy of the particular proceedings in which he is presently involved." 263 F.Supp. at 533.

Whether the accused suffers from a mental disorder as defined in the American Psychiatric Association Manual is not decisive. Nor is it enough that the evidence of the defendant's guilt is substantial. He is entitled to a fair trial as well as a trial in which he is proven guilty. To have a fair trial the defendant must be competent to stand trial. The test of competency must be whether he has sufficient "present ability to consult with his lawyer with a reasonable degree of rational understanding —and whether he has a rational as well as factual understanding of the proceedings against him." Dusky v. United States, 362 U.S. 402, 80 S.Ct.788, 4 L.E.d.2d 824 (1960). The accused must be able to perform the functions which "are essential to the fairness and accuracy of a criminal proceeding." Pouncey v. United States, 121 U.S.App.D.C.264, 266, 349 F.2d 699, 701 (1965).

A prediction of the amnesic defendant's ability to perform these functions must, of course, be made before trial at the competency hearing. But where the case is allowed to go to trial, at its conclusion the trial judge should determine whether the defendant has in fact been able to perform these functions. He should, before imposing sentence, make detailed written findings, after taking any additional evidence deemed necessary, concerning the effect of the amnesia on the fairness of the trial. In making these findings the court should consider the following factors:

1. The extent to which the amnesia affected the defendant's ability to consult with and assist his lawyer.
2. The extent to which the amnesia affected the defendant's ability to testify in his own behalf.
3. The extent to which the evidence in suit could be extrinsically reconstructed in view of the defendant's amnesia. Such evidence would include evidence relating to the crime itself as well as any reasonably possible alibi.
4. The extent to which the Government assisted the defendant and his counsel in that reconstruction.
5. The strength of the prosecution's case. Most important here will be whether the Government's case is such as to negate all reasonable hypotheses of innocence. If there is any substantial possibility that the accused could, but for his amnesia, establish an alibi or other defense, it should be presumed that he would have been able to do so.
6. Any other facts and circumstances which would indicate whether or not the defendant had a fair trial.

After finding all the facts relevant to the fairness of the trial, considering the amnesia, the court will then make a judgment whether, under applicable principles of due process, the conviction should stand.

If the court determines that the conviction may not stand because of the unfairness of the trial caused by the defendant's amnesia, the court will vacate the conviction and give the Government an opportunity to retry the case. If on retrial the Government is unable to overcome the unfairness which would have thus voided the first conviction, the indictment will be dismissed.

So ordered. . . .

FAHY, SENIOR CIRCUIT JUDGE (Dissenting):

. . . Appellant by reason of physical brain injury has not simply been completely and permanently deprived of all knowledge of the robbery itself but of all knowledge of anything covering the entire period surrounding it. To try him for crimes which occurred during this period is thus to try him for something about which he is mentally absent altogether, and this for a cause not attributable to his voluntary conduct. The effect is very much as though he were tried in absentia notwithstanding his physical presence at the time of trial. . . .

The remand proceedings required by the court cannot solve the problem presented by this case. Appellant will no more be able to assist his counsel, and his counsel will no more be able effectively to assist him, at the remand hearing than at the trial itself. The terms of the remand in substance require a hearing on the issue of prejudice. To try separately this issue would leave us where we are now, with the added difficulty that at the remand hearing it appears appellant would be required to testify whether or not he wished to do so, raising another Fifth Amendment problem. If the case is to turn on the issue of prejudice we should determine now that prejudice is inherent in the situation. Denial of the effective assistance of counsel, all else aside, establishes prejudice. Chapman v. State of California, 386 U.S.18, 23, 87 S.Ct.824, 17 L.Ed.2d 705. . . .

COMPETENCY TO STAND TRIAL AND MENTAL ILLNESS

A. L. McGarry, M.D.

THE PROBLEM

Historically, competency to stand trial is based on our English common law heritage, holding that a person must have the capacity to adequately defend himself against his accusers in a court of law. The criteria for this capacity include an understanding of the nature of the legal process, a recognition of the consequences that could follow from the accusation, and the ability to assist legal counsel in one's own defense. These criteria are intended to provide due process of law safeguards.

Most frequently the alleged incompetency of criminal defendants is raised on the basis of possible mental illness. It is evident from our own preliminary work and that of others that great confusion has reigned and irrelevant medical criteria have been applied to the determination of competency by the psychiatric profession on whom the burden has fallen to provide expert examination and testimony on the issue. It has become equally apparent that the courts themselves have often confused the criteria for competency with the separate and different legal criteria for criminal responsibility. This confusion about the criteria for competency by psychiatry and the law has been compounded by a lack of relevant communication on the issue between the disciplines of psychiatry and law.

There is certainly nothing new in the observation that the disciplines of psychiatry and the law have had difficulty in communicating with each other. To suggest that the central problem is one of communication, two ways, is to observe the obvious. It is none the less so. Thus, when a court takes the trouble (which it usually doesn't) to articulate the tripartite common law criteria for competency and gets back the answer "Schizophrenia," we are witnessing the interdisciplinary lack of rational communication which has governed the handling of the competency issue in this country with rare exceptions.

The result has been that many people, who have been judged to be incompetent for trial, have been unnecessarily and inaccurately committed to our mental hospitals and denied their right to trial. These commitments have proven to be stigmatizing and antitherapeutic. It is clear, in Massachusetts at least, that these committed incompetents, without trial, have been subjected to society's severest sanctions against both the criminal and the mentally ill and in the past have been provided with the safeguards of neither.

Recent publications have given us a clearer picture of the dimensions of the competency issue nationwide. In the first place, in terms of people whose lives and freedom are affected, competency is a vastly more important issue than criminal responsibility.[1]

Matthews (1966) reported that the use of these procedures has been growing. Given the very crowded and growing calendars of our courts and the general lack of satisfaction with our penal system it is not surprising that there should be increased pressure for seeking alternatives. Generally competency procedures are easily invoked (and constitutionally required when there is any doubt),[2] timesaving

---

[1] Thus in Massachusetts in fiscal year 1970 there were 2,101 mental hospitalizations pretrial and no commitments posttrial as not guilty by reason of insanity. Nationwide it is estimated that of 29,000 mental hospitalizations in 1967, 15,000 were for incompetency and 1,450 were as a result of not guilty by reason of insanity verdicts (Scheidemandel and Kanno 1969). It is our impression that the latter statistic is highly inflated (see table IV in the reference). But there is wide variation from one jurisdiction to the next. Whereas Massachusetts had 2,101 observational admissions in F.Y. 1970 (14.2 percent of all admissions to Massachusetts mental hospitals) MacDonald (1969) reports that in 17 years of his extensive forensic experience in Colorado the issue of competency for trial has been raised only once.

[2] Pate v. Robinson, 383 U.S. 375 (1966).

Final Report—Laboratory of Community Psychiatry, Harvard Medical School; excerpted and reprinted with permission from Dept. of Health, Education, and Welfare Publication No. (HSM) 73–9105 (NIMH Project 7R01–MH–18112–01, June 1972).

as far as the court is concerned. As this project and the work of others has documented, however, this well-meant set of motivations has led to excessive use of these procedures with destructive consequences for the patient-defendants involved and at great and wasteful expense to the public treasury.

In recent years there has been growing pressure from civil liberty advocates to do away with involuntary civil commitment of the mentally ill, or at least to tighten and narrow the standards for involuntary commitment or make the procedures more complex and onerous. The recently passed Lanterman-Petris-Short Act in California is an example of the latter. One practical consequence of these changes is the sharply increased alternative use of the criminal process and pretrial mental hospital commitment for the mentally ill. It is a simple matter to allege "disturbing the peace" and order an admission of a mentally ill person as an alternative to complex and restrictive civil procedures. Thus at Metropolitan State Hospital serving Los Angeles, pretrial competency commitments have increased six-fold since the new act.[3] The effect is to criminalize the treatment of the mentally ill. Other jurisdictions which may be embarking on a similar escalation of the use of pretrial competency procedures will do well to read this record of Massachusett's mistakes, abuses and agonizing reforms in this area. . . .

SIGNIFICANT CONCLUSIONS AND PRODUCTS OF THE PROJECT

The research and documentation which support the conclusions arrived at are contained in the text which follows this subsection of the report. The salient conclusions arrived at in this project are as follows:

1. Brief screening examinations on the issue of competency can prevent many unnecessary admissions to mental hospitals, particularly if such instruments as the Competency Screening Test (CST) and the Competency Assessment Instrument (CAI), developed by the project (see below) are utilized.
2. The legal criteria for competency to stand trial can be accurately translated into psychological and clinical terms and re-translated into relevant legally oriented data.
3. Psychiatrists who are knowledgeable about the criminal justice system and the rele-

[3] Personal communication, Seymour Pollack, M.D., University of Southern California.

vant criteria for competency to stand trial, can effectively serve the courts on the issue.
4. Incompetency to stand trial on the basis of mental illness is rare and is usually quickly responsive to treatment.
5. In Massachusetts, excessive conservatism regarding release and excessive restrictiveness in management have governed the care and treatment of alleged offenders committed as incompetent to stand trial.
6. The mental health system in Massachusetts, although there have been recent improvements, has consistently required higher standards of competency than relevant case law would indicate is required. There appears to be a bias among mental health professionals against returning defendants for trial.
7. Civil commitment of mentally ill alleged offenders led to significantly shorter mental hospitalizations than for comparable incompetent defendants who were committed under criminal sanctions with charges still outstanding. In the latter group, hospitalization tended to be excessively prolonged.
8. Unless criminal charges can be otherwise disposed of, it is in the best interest of the mentally ill defendants to stand trial as expeditiously as possible.
9. The interpersonal skills and sustained involvement of defense counsel are important and overlooked factors in the functioning competency of mentally ill defendants. A skillful, supportive attorney who devotes adequate time to working with mentally ill defendants can maximally facilitate the coping strengths of such defendants. The converse is equally true.
10. A Competency Screening Test (CST) has been developed which provides a summative score of competency to stand trial. . . .
11. A legal psychiatric instrument, the Competency Assessment Instrument (CAI), has been developed which provides quantifiable criteria for competency to stand trial. The instrument is an attempt at an assessment of all possible legal grounds for a finding of incompetency. It is expressed as a series of thirteen ego functions related to what is required of a defendant in criminal proceedings in order that he may adequately cope with and protect himself in such proceedings. . . .
12. Serious abuses of due process in the use of competency procedures in the Massachusetts criminal justice system have been

found by the project and largely corrected.

13. When civil measures for the mental hospital commitment of the mentally ill are procedurally onerous and criminal procedures less so, there is a likelihood that the criminal route for the commitment of the mentally ill will be used excessively. In Massachusetts the decision to hospitalize for a competency workup originates, in large measure, from the judge, and the grounds for such admissions appear to be inadequately reviewed by the judge or challenged by defense counsel.

14. Inappropriate and unnecessary mental hospitalizations on the competency issue appear to rise largely from over-taxed courts seeking alternatives to the penal system.

15. The great majority of defense counsel interviewed in this project were not aware of the common law criteria for competency to stand trial.

16. The common law criteria for competency for trial appear to apply in the statutory and case law of all American legal jurisdictions with minor variations. However, there continues to be confusion in many jurisdictions between the criteria for competency and those for criminal responsibility. Competency criteria are elementary, vague, and of little help to the examining psychiatrist. Attempts by appellate courts to define criteria more precisely, particularly the *degree* of capacity or incapacity which establishes competency or incompetency, have been inconsistent and idiosyncratic.

17. There is great variation and much vagueness among American legal jurisdictions both in terms of the weight of evidence required to make a finding of incompetency, and once the incompetency issue is raised, whether the presumption is one of competency or incompetency. Insofar as it can be discerned, most jurisdictions appear to make the rebuttable presumption that once the issue is raised the defendant is incompetent and his competency must be proved (usually by the prosecution). This is likely to weight in the direction of a finding of incompetency.

18. Although there is an abundance of case law and statutes citing mental illness as a basis for a finding of incompetency for trial, there is a paucity which cite mental retardation. It is our impression that the competency issue is raised too often for the mentally ill and too infrequently for the mentally retarded.

19. Massachusetts' new Mental Health Re-

form Act of 1970 (effective date November 1, 1971), which had significant input from this project (the principal investigator and co-principal investigator were the primary draftsmen of the Act), has had a striking impact, particularly on competency procedures. Based on the statistics of the first 6 months under the new Act and projected for its first year, there will be 1,000 fewer admissions annually to Massachusetts mental hospitals for competency workups. In addition, the number of prolonged commitments arising from these observational admissions will have been halved (from 76 in fiscal year 1971 to about 40 for the first year under the new Act).

This section of the report has been limited to the *salient* conclusions and products of the project. A more detailed account of our conclusions may be obtained by reading the published papers supported by the project. . . .

Although the work of this project had a very minor role in the large scale judicial hearings at Bridgewater in 1967, 1968, and 1969, the outcome of these reviews has had such a substantial impact at Bridgewater, that they are worthy of description here.

The *Baxtrom* v. *Herold*[4] decision of the United States Supreme Court in 1966 was interpreted by the then Massachusetts Attorney General Elliott Richardson as requiring the *retroactive* judicial review of the constitutionality of the commitment of many of Bridgewater's patients. A similar interpretation in New York had led to extraordinary changes at Dannemora and Matteawan in New York (Hunt, Wiley 1967). In essence, the *Baxtrom* decision required that men committed to specialized security mental hospitals such as Bridgewater, who were not actually serving criminal sentences, were entitled to the same due process safeguards as patients committed elsewhere in mental hospitals. In addition, the committing court is required by the *Baxtrom* decision to make a separate finding that "strict security is required" before commitment to a security institution is justified and constitutional. The impact of this decision led to a review of patients who had accumulated at Bridgewater over the years whose criminal sentences had expired. The reviewing justice also interpreted the decision as covering men committed to Bridgewater as incompetent to stand trial who had served enough time there, so that if they had been convicted of their alleged crime they would already have reached parole eligibility (a principle which had been

---

[4] Baxstrom v. Herold, 383 U.S. 107 (1966).

articulated in the early drafts of the Mental Health Reform Act of 1970). . . .

In all, 267 men were reviewed in June and October of 1968. The principal investigator, representing the Department of Mental Health, organized and supervised screening psychiatric examinations of all these men. He also supervised testimony in those cases in which the Department of Mental Health felt there was sufficient danger to others should they be released from Bridgewater. Only 22 out of the 267 men were evaluated as dangerous. Only 9 of the 22 were recommitted to Bridgewater by the Presiding Justice. Most of these men were transferred to Department of Mental Health facilities. In an unpublished followup study by the principal investigator, 43 percent of these men had reached the community by June of 1971.

These significant reductions at Bridgewater change a census which had approached 800 in the early 1960's to 245 in December 1970. These changes were brought about by the significantly fewer men being indefinitely committed in the past few years (particularly the These changes were brought about by the significantly fewer men being indefinitely committed in the past few years (particularly the incompetent for trial group), recent policy changes in the Department of Mental Health which have opened its institutions to Bridgewater transfers, and new activism on the part of the Bridgewater staff in negotiating with courts to resolve criminal charges. Of these Eighty-seven were observational commitments. 245, only 158 were indefinite commitments. These statistics are all the more impressive when one notes that over the decade Bridgewater pretrial observational admissions sharply rose (from 129 to 1960 to 501 in 1971).

More important to note is that Bridgewater has clearly been transformed from a custodial to an actively treatment-oriented facility. Professional staff has been impressively augmented (from 3 physicians in 1963 to 7 in 1970; from 1 nurse in 1963 to 30; from 4 social workers to 7), and links to the community, such as tutors and student volunteers from Bridgewater State Teachers College, have been developed. There is a new spirit of activism at the institution. What is sometimes lacking in sophistication in these programs is made up for in zeal. Ground breaking for a new, cottage type $10,000,000 institution at Bridgewater took place in 1971. Although it does not yet approach a model institution for mentally disordered offenders there is no question that much has been accomplished over the last few years. . . .

NECESSARY AND RECOMMENDED REFORMS

In the light of the work of this project and the documentation of abuses and inequities contained in this report and in the publications of others in the field, consideration of the following procedural and substantive principles in competency proceedings are recommended.

1. *Only when a bona fide doubt is established regarding an accused's competency for trial should competency proceedings be invoked.*
2. *A screening examination by a qualified expert (not necessarily a psychiatrist) should be carried out in the courthouse or place of detention or on an outpatient basis.* The examiner should be provided with the police arrest report and such other data as are available with relation to the facts of the case.
3. *If, after such screening examination, a doubt still exists, more intensive and prolonged examination should take place.* Consideration should be given to accomplishing such examination on an outpatient basis. If necessary, brief, observational inpatient hospitalization may be ordered and such order of admission should be accompanied by the police arrest report and such other data as are available with relation to the facts of the case. The period of observational admission should have no minimum term.
4. *Appropriate notice of and a prompt judicial hearing on the competency issue should be given to the patient-defendant with independent expert examination available to the defense.*
5. *A presumption of competency should exist which is rebuttable only if, by a "preponderance of evidence," the accused is found, after an adequate judicial hearing, to be incompetent to stand trial.*
6. *Procedures should be available whereby an incompetent defendant and/or his counsel may present evidence of a defense on the merits without risk of conviction.* The granting of a judicial hearing to consider such evidence should be up to the discretion of the trial judge following an affidavit requesting such a hearing from the defense counsel or the defendant. The basis for such request should be expressed in such an affidavit. The prosecution should be represented at the hearing. Following the hearing, if the trial judge finds a lack of substantial evidence to support a conviction, he should dismiss the indictment or other charges and order the release of the defendant from criminal

custody, or he should reduce the charges to those for which substantial evidence to support a conviction does exist.

7. *Following a finding of incompetence, full civil safeguards and procedures now must be provided if prolonged mental hospital commitment is sought.* Consideration should be given to outpatient or partial hospitalization of the patient-defendant.

8. *A "statute of limitations" should be running at the time of a finding of incompetency.* Various formulae could be adopted depending on social policy in a given jurisdiction, but no defendant should be kept in criminal custody with charges still outstanding for longer than he could have been sentenced if he was found guilty of the most serious crime with which he is charged. Further hospitalization beyond such term should be on a voluntary or civil basis with charges dismissed.

9. *Flexible management of committed incompetents, including outpatient management, by the administrators of the holding institution should be possible.* Notice to the committing court of proposed decreased controls over the patient-defendant could be given to the prosecutor and the committing court. But only after a judicial hearing, called within a limited period of time, should such a decrease in controls be subject to a countermanding order by the committing court.

10. *Periodic clinical review of committed incompetents should be required every 3 months of such commitment and easily invoked periodic judicial review at the same interval by any of the parties (i.e., defendant, defense counsel, prosecution) should be available.* The judge or hospital administrator should be able to invoke a prompt judicial review of the competency issue at any time. . . .

The courts are obviously seeking something from our hospitals other than competency determinations *per se.* It appears that our desperately overtaxed courts are seeking constructive alternatives to the criminal justice and penal systems as they currently exist. If the competency route has been a false solution and has accomplished more harm than good, we must seek ways in which the courts and their disturbed offenders can be more effectively helped by the behavioral disciplines. Possibly, our emerging community mental health centers, utilizing civil and voluntary procedures for alleged offenders, may yet make a significant contribution.

Our mental health resources must be more creatively and effectively deployed in attempting to meet these great challenges. We must more constructively integrate and advance the social and rehabilitative aims that are common to both the mental health and criminal justice systems.

THE NATURE OF COMPETENCY

To be fit for trial, it is assumed that a person must have minimal affective and cognitive resources available to him to assume the role of a defendant in court. Lacking these resources, the individual would be deprived of his due process right to testify in his own defense, to confront witnesses against him, and to maintain an effective *psychological presence* in court beyond his mere physical presence there. The issue of competency is thus an essentially legal issue, not a psychiatric issue. The criteria for competency to stand trial are concerned with the protection of the individual in the criminal system in order that he may be assured of a fair trial. No other area of the person's physical or emotional health is an issue. Whether or not the person has physical or psychological defects is irrelevant except to the extent that they substantially interfere with fitness for trial.

The common law criteria for competency are defined as (1) an ability to cooperate with one's attorney in one's own defense, (2) an awareness and understanding of the nature and object of the proceedings, (3) an understanding of the consequences of the proceedings. Within the framework of these criteria, a judgment must be made as to whether an accused person should stand trial without undue delay or whether the trial should be deferred until such time as the accused shall meet a minimal standard based on these criteria.

The determination of competency in the broadest sense must be based on some evaluation of these criteria. It must be a prediction because the judgment of the actual performance of the defendant in the role of defendant has not occurred. An assessment of the defendant's ability to perform adequately at his trial must be made by individuals considered most expert to evaluate fitness for trial.

It is important that the assessment or evaluation of the defendant be made with a clear understanding of the requirements of the legal system. Psychological evaluation must be directed toward determining how well the individual will be able to meet the minimum requirements of the three common law criteria for competency. Issues such as legal responsibility for the offense or possibility of rehabilitation are not relevant considerations. Also, mental illness or pathology *per se* are not equivalent to capacity to stand trial, although such matters may be involved in a determination of competency.

The test which follows has been developed for the purpose of quickly screening defendants in order to make recommendations regarding their competency to stand trial. . . .

Brief Definitions

1. *Appraisal of available legal defenses:* This item calls for an assessment of the accused's awareness of his possible legal defenses and how consistent these are with the reality of his particular circumstances.

2. *Unmanageable behavior:* This item calls for an assessment of the appropriateness of the current motor and verbal behavior of the defendant and the degree to which this behavior would disrupt the conduct of a trial. Inappropriate or disruptive behavior must arise from a substantial degree of mental illness or mental retardation.

3. *Quality of relating to attorney:* This item calls for an assessment of the interpersonal capacity of the accused to relate to the average attorney. Involved are the ability to trust and to communicate relevantly.

4. *Planning of legal strategy including guilty pleas to lesser charges where pertinent:* This item calls for an assessment of the degree to which the accused can understand, participate, and cooperate with his counsel in planning a strategy for the defense which is consistent with the reality of his circumstances.

5. *Appraisal of role of:*
   a. Defense counsel
   b. Prosecuting attorney
   c. Judge
   d. Jury
   e. Defendant
   f. Witnesses

This set of items calls for a minimal understanding of the adversary process by the accused. The accused should be able to identify prosecuting attorney and prosecution witnesses as foe, defense counsel as friend, the judge as neutral, and the jury as the determiners of guilt or innocence.

6. *Understanding of court procedure:* This item calls for an assessment of the degree to which the defendand understands the basic sequence of events in a trial and their import for him; e.g., the different purposes of direct and cross examination.

7. *Appreciation of charges:* This item calls for an assessment of the accused's understanding of the charges against him and, to a lesser extent, the seriousness of the charges.

8. *Appreciation of range and nature of possible penalties:* This item calls for an assessment of the accused's concrete understanding and appreciation of the conditions and restrictions which could be imposed on him and their possible duration.

9. *Appraisal of likely outcome:* This item calls for an assessment of how realistically the accused perceives the likely outcome and the degree to which impaired understanding contributes to a less adequate or inadequate participation in his defense. Without adequate information on the part of the examiner regarding the facts and circumstances of the alleged offense, this item would be unratable.

10. *Capacity to disclose to attorney available pertinent facts surrounding the offense including the defendant's movements, timing, mental state, and actions at the time of the offense:* This item calls for an assessment of the accused's capacity to give a basically consistent, rational, and relevant account of the motivational and external facts. Complex factors can enter into this determination. These include intelligence, memory. and honesty. The difficult area of the validity of an amnesia may be involved and may prove unresolvable for the examining clinician. It is important to be aware that there may be a disparity between what an accused is willing to share with a clinician as opposed to what he will share with his attorney, the latter being the more important.

11. *Capacity to realistically challenge prosecution witnesses:* This item calls for an assessment of the accused's capacity to recognize distortions in prosecution testimony. Relevant factors include attentiveness and memory. In addition, there is an element of initiative in that if false testimony is given, the degree of activism with which the defendant will apprise his attorney of inaccuracies, is of importance.

12. *Capacity to testify relevantly:* This item calls for an assessment of the accused's ability to testify with coherence, relevance, and independence of judgment.

13. *Self-defeating v. self-serving motivation (legal sense):* This item calls for an assessment of the accused's motivation to adequately protect himself and appropriately utilize legal safeguards to this end. It is recognized that accused persons may appropriately be moti-

vated to seek expiation and appropriate punishment and the deliberate failure by the accused to avail himself of appropriate legal portections. Passivity or indifference do not justify low scores on this item. Actively self-destructive manipulation of the legal process arising from mental pathology does justify low scores.

MISUSE OF PSYCHIATRY IN THE CRIMINAL COURTS: COMPETENCY TO STAND TRIAL, CONCLUSIONS AND RECOMMENDATIONS

1. Psychiatrists should screen every defendant whose competency is questioned, *before* he is transported to an institution for the criminally insane. Thus, when the issue of competence is initially raised, the psychiatrist can participate in the threshold question. This is particularly desirable when it is the prosecution or the court which raises the question of the defendant's competency. Statistics such as those from the Massachusetts Department of Mental Health for fiscal 1971 reveal that only 74 out of 1,806, or 4.1 percent of pretrial admissions to Massachusetts mental hospitals during this period resulted in findings of incompetency. These statistics more than suggest a need for screening examinations prior to such stigmatizing admissions.

    In part, the decision to admit such a defendant to a psychiatric facility is inescapably a medical decision because the detention period is usually much longer than that required for diagnosis alone. Some treatment may and will be given, and the defendant will be exposed to an institutional environment which may or may not be medically appropriate. Psychiatrists should resist referrals for extensive diagnosis *or treatment*, even when they come from a court, unless they feel that there is a genuine psychiatric need for the treatment and stay involved.

2. Many of the persons found incompetent to stand trial by the court are not dangerous to themselves or to society. It is therefore inexcusable to continue their confinement in maximum-security institutions. Such nondangerous defendants, who would otherwise be eligible for bail, should be hospitalized or treated at the same hospitals and in the same manner as any other mental patient. The treatment should be that best calculated to restore the defendant's mental health as soon as possible. Where medically indicated, treatment should include outpatient care as well as hospitalization. The dangerous incompetent defendant who would not otherwise be bailable should if necessary be confined and treated in a maximum-security institution.

3. It is the belief of this committee that new techniques and drugs currently available can bring most persons initially found to be incompetent to a competent state well within six months of initiation of treatment. At present, this is the maximum length of time normally required to treat most civilly committed patients in hospitals. After six months of treatment, the vast majority of all defendents originally adjudged incompetent will fall into one of two categories: (a) they will be competent to stand trial; or (b) they will be found to be suffering from a type of mental disability such as that due to gross mental retardation, brain damage, or some chronic deteriorated state which makes it possible for the psychiatrist to predict that the defendant will never regain competency. The first group, of course, should stand trial. Criminal charges against the second group should be dropped, and they should, instead, be subject to commitment proceedings where their danger to society is reassessed and the type of institutionalization required, if any, is determined. Those persons who will never return to competency, and who pose no threat to themselves or the community, should be released.

Committee on Psychiatry and the Law, Group for the Advancement of Psychiatry (G.A.P. Report No. 89, February 1974): excerpted with permission of G.A.P.

4. There will be a small number of incompetency cases which do not fit into either of these categories. For these few, the judge should hold a hearing and, if indicated, grant a six-month extension of the initial treatment period. At the end of the extension period, comprising a total of twelve months' treatment, the defendant should be returned for trial or civilly committed to that institution best equipped to treat him.

Given the adversary background of the criminal law, these new procedures, the primary aim of which is to prevent abuse and allow for adequate treatment of the defendant, will themselves be tested and exploited. Criminal defendants charged with grave offenses may well attempt to malinger for 12 months on the expectation of escaping trial. Experience suggests that this may occur. However, simply to avoid such a possibility, it is unnecessary to retain our current system, which discourages malingering by permanently confining all defendants found incompetent in hospitals where living conditions are often worse than prison conditions.

As an alternative, this committee suggests the following: If the alleged crime is a serious felony, and the question of competency has not been resolved after one year, the court should have the discretion of retaining the criminal charges and its jurisdiction over the defendant, with the power to proceed to trial at some future time when and if the question of competency is resolved. The maximum length of the delay should bear a reasonable relationship to the jail term applicable as the criminal penalty for the crime alleged.

Many of the reforms proposed by this committee could be implemented or initiated by psychiatrists even without passage of new statutes.

Psychiatrists who become involved in evaluating problems of defendant competency should take the following steps:

1. They should, whenever possible, attempt to participate in the initial screening process when the issue of competency is first raised.
2. Psychiatrists who occupy positions in hospitals for the criminally insane should take note of the fact that in many jurisdictions patients referred to them by the courts come with a provision allowing "no more than x number of days" of hospitalization. They can therefore within legal bounds examine the defendant-patient on the day of arrival and if a decision of competency can be reached at that point, he should be returned immediately to the court.
3. If the court finds the defendant incompetent, the psychiatrist should work against a deadline of six months of hospitalization. Recognizing that competency is a much lower standard than care, the psychiatrist should aim at returning all such defendants to the court within a month or two. Certainly this task should take no longer than six months.
4. As soon as the psychiatrist decides it unlikely that the defendant will ever regain competency, he should so inform the court and the defendant's lawyer, at this time emphasizing that further confinement in that particular institution may be detrimental to the defendant's mental health.
5. As soon as the psychiatrist decides that an incompetent defendant is not dangerous, he should so inform the judge and attorneys. He should, if indicated, recommend outpatient treatment, placing the burden of opposing such medically appropriate treatment on the legal system.

By such legally responsible procedures psychiatrists can and should refuse to participate in practices which are detrimental to patients under their care. In the opinion of this committee, passive collaboration in legally ambiguous but abusive practices has been perhaps the most common failing of twentieth century psychiatry. To the extent that such passive collaboration is based on ignorance, it is our hope that this report will be helpful. We are convinced, however, that progressive reform requires more than information—it requires the willingness, the courage, and the activism of individual psychiatrists, supported by their profession, to challenge established practices whenever they are detrimental to patients entrusted to their care.

Problem Assignment

Consider the following (fabricated) evaluation. What problems, inadequacies do you see in it? What questions would you have for the psychiatrist as prosecutor or defense counsel?

U. X. Oricide, charged with the murder of his wife and infant daughter, was referred by the court, on motion of defense counsel, to a state hospital for observation and an evaluation of his competency to stand trial. Under applicable state statutes the court will make the final determination of competency, based on the report of the hospital and any other evidence presented by the parties. The report received by the court following the 90-day period of observation is as follows:

U. X. Oricide was referred to this hospital on _____ by the _____ court under Section _____ of the Penal Code. He was retained under observation for 90 days, as required by law, and was seen by me on three occasions. On the basis of that observation and clinical interviewing totaling approximately 2½ hours, the following report is respectfully submitted.

Mr. Oricide is a rather stocky, 36-year-old white male of average intelligence. He is oriented as to time and place, and, although understandably under considerable emotional stress, is in good contact with reality. He spoke freely with me about the crimes with which he is charged, his earlier life, and the impending trial. It is my diagnosis that Mr. Oricide is a paranoid personality, but is not insane. He has always been intensely jealous of his wife, and his suspicions of her infidelity—apparently totally without foundation—bordered on the delusional. It was this pathological suspicion that was the impelling factor in the murders.

There is no question but that he knows the difference between right and wrong. In fact, he is now bitterly remorseful and says he hopes the law will execute him for having killed his wife (he accepts the fact that he killed the child as well, although he has no memory of the event).

Mr. Oricide is quite capable of standing trial. The following medication should be continued during transit as well as while he is in the custody of the court: Aventyl 50 mg. three times a day; Stelazine 5 mg. in the morning; Mellaril 50 mg. at bedtime.

(Signed)
O. M. NIPOTENT, M.D.

SUGGESTIONS FOR ADDITIONAL READING

A.L.I. Model Penal Code, Art. 4, Proposed Official Draft, 1962, and Comments in Tentative Draft No. 4.

"Amnesia as Affecting Capacity to Commit Crime or Stand Trial," 46 *ALR* 544 (1972).

Annotation: "Incompetency at Time of Offense or Trial as Ground for Vacating or Setting Aside Sentence under 28 USC Sec. 2255, 7 *ALR* Fed 565 (1971).

Brakel and Rock, eds. *The Mentally Disabled and the Law* (revised ed.). Chicago: Univ. of Chicago Press, 1971, pp. 408-21.

Bendt, Balcanoff, and Tragellis. "Incompetency to Stand Trial: Is Psychiatry Necessary?" *American Journal of Psychiatry* 130, 1, (Nov. 1973).

Bukatman, Foy, and Degrazia. "What is Competency to Stand Trial?" *American Journal of Psychiatry* 127 (March 1971): 1225-29.

Buschman and Reed. "Tranquilizers and Competency to Stand Trial," 54 *ABAJ* 284 (March 1968).

Comment: "Amnesia: A Case Study in the Limits of Particular Justice," 71 *Yale L.J.* 109 (1961).

Committee on Psychiatry and Law. *Misuse of Psychiatry in the Criminal Courts: Competency to Stand Trial*. New York: Group for the Advancement of Psychiatry, 1974.

Cooke, Johnston, and Pogany. "Factors Affecting Referral to Determine Competency to Stand Trial," *American Journal of Psychiatry* 130 (August 1973): 870–75.

Haddox and Pollack. "Psychopharmaceutical Restoration to Present Sanity (Competency to Stand Trial)," 17 *J. of Forensic Sciences* 568 (October 1972).

Koson and Robey. "Amnesia and Competency to Stand Trial," *American Journal of Psychiatry* 130 (May 1973): 588–92.

Lewin. "Incompetency to Stand Trial: Legal and Ethical Aspects of an Absurd Doctrine," *Arizona State Law Journal* 19, 1 (1969).

Lipsitt, Lelos, and McGarry. "Competency for Trial: A Screening Instrument," *American Journal of Psychiatry* 128 (July 1971): 105–9.

Matthews. *Mental Disability and the Criminal Law.* American Bar Foundation, 1970, Chapter III.

McGarry. "The Fate of Psychiatric Offenders Returned for Trial," *American Journal of Psychiatry* 127 (March 1971): 713–20.

Robey. "Criteria for Competency to Stand Trial: A Checklist for Psychiatrists," *American Journal of Psychiatry* 122 (December 1965).

Scheidemandel and Kanno. *The Mentally Ill Offender.* American Psychiatric Association, 1969.

Steadman. "Some Evidence on the Inadequacy of the Concept and Determination of Dangerousness in Law and Psychiatry," *Journal of Law and Psychiatry*, 1, no. 4 (Winter 1973): 409–26.

Szasz. *Psychiatric Justice.* N.Y.: MacMillan, 1965 (and see review by Weihofen, 19 *J. Legal Ed.* 117 [1966]).

For the special problems presented by the "sedated" or amnesic defendant, see: "Propriety of Criminal Trial of One under Influence of Drugs or Intoxicants at Time of Trial," 83 *ALR* 2d (161).

17

Criminal Responsibility—The Insanity Defense

We begin the chapter with excerpts from articles on homicide and the insanity defense by two distinguished forensic psychiatrists—separated in time by nearly a century and a half; the first, by Isaac Ray, was written some five years before the House of Lords formulated the M'Naghten Rules, but might almost have been written as a dissent to the *Andrews* decision by the Supreme Court of Kansas (see Chapter 7, supra). M'Naghten (or M'Naghten plus irresistible impulse) remains the law of most American jurisdictions, but the federal courts (with the exception of the First Circuit, which has not as yet ruled on the matter) have all adopted the A.L.I. Model Penal Code rule, or some variation of it (e.g., that of the *Currens* case). The Gray article describes the historical development and current state of the various rules. The tortuous course of the District of Columbia is represented by the *Durham*, *Washington*, and *Brawner* decisions; by the Report of the Commission on Crime in the District of Columbia, and by the Allen article reviewing *Brawner* and the unresolved issue of abolition of the insanity defense. The issue of the committability of one criminally convicted or found not guilty by reason of insanity is considered in the U.S. Supreme Court's decision in *Baxstrom* v. *Herold*, and in the D.C. case of *Bolton* v. *Harris*, the effect of which was largely nullified by the District of Columbia Court Reform and Criminal Procedure Act of 1970. Abolition of the insanity defense was the purported objective of S1400—the Nixon administration proposal for revision of Title 18, U.S. Code; its actual effect is speculated upon in the N.Y.U. Colloquium. The *Adams* and *Hawkins* cases involve problem issues in administering an insanity defense; and *Lee* v. *County Court* and the 1974 Amendments to the Federal Rules of Criminal Procedure deal with the question whether a defendant who pleads insanity can be compelled to submit to a psychiatric examination, and what sanctions can be imposed by the court if he refuses. The chapter closes with two psychiatric evaluations.

A TREATISE ON THE MEDICAL JURISPRUDENCE OF INSANITY

(Excerpts)

Isaac Ray

. . . The circumstances under which the homicidal act is perpetrated furnish strong ground for believing that they depend on mental alienation in some form or other; so different are these circumstances from those which attend the commission of crime. In homicidal insanity, murder is committed without any motive whatever strictly deserving the name; or at most, with one totally inadequate to produce the act in a sane mind. On the contrary, murder is never criminally committed without some motive adequate to the purpose in the

Published in London in 1838 by G. Henderson.

mind that is actuated by it and with an obvious reference to the ill-fated victim. Thus, the motive may be theft, or the advancement of any personal interest, in which case it will be found that the victim had or was supposed to have property, or was an obstacle to the designs or expectations of another. Or it may be revenge, and then the injury real or imaginary will be found to have been received by the murderer from the object of his wrath. In short, with the criminal, murder is always a means for accomplishing some selfish object, and is frequently accompanied by some other crime; whereas, with the homicidal monomaniac, murder is the only object in view, and is never accompanied by any other improper act.

The homicidal monomaniac, after gratifying his bloody desires, testifies neither remorse, nor repentance, nor satisfaction, and if judicially condemned, perhaps acknowledges the justice of the sentence. The criminal either denies or confesses his guilt; if the latter, he either humbly sues for mercy, or glories in his crimes, and leaves the world cursing his judges and with his last breath exclaiming against the injustice of his fate.

The criminal never sheds more blood than is necessary for the attainment of his object; the homicidal monomaniac often sacrifices all within his reach to the cravings of his murderous propensity.

The criminal lays plans for the execution of his designs; time, place and weapons are all suited to his purpose; and when successful, he either flies from the scene of his enormities, or makes every effort to avoid discovery. The homicidal monomaniac, on the contrary, for the most part consults none of the usual conveniences of crime; he falls upon the object of his fury, oftentimes without the most proper means for accomplishing his purpose; and perhaps in the presence of a multitude, as if expressly to court observation; and then voluntarily surrenders himself to the constituted authorities. When, as is sometimes the case, he does prepare the means, and calmly and deliberately executes his project, his subsequent conduct is still the same as in the former instance.

The criminal often has accomplices and always vicious associates; the homicidal monomaniac has neither.

The acts of homicidal insanity are generally, perhaps always, preceded by some striking peculiarities in the conduct or character of the individual, strongly contrasting with his natural manifestations; while those of the criminal are in correspondence with the tenor of his past history or character.

In homicidal insanity, a man murders his wife, children or others to whom he is tenderly attached; this the criminal never does, unless to gratify some evil passion, or gain some other selfish end, too obvious to be overlooked in the slightest investigation.

A stronger contrast than is presented, in every respect, between the homicidal act of the real criminal and that of the monomaniac, can hardly be imagined; and yet we are obliged to acknowledge that men of learning and intelligence have often refused to acknowledge it. . . .

FORENSIC PSYCHIATRY IN THE LEGAL DEFENSE OF MURDER

Emanuel Tanay, M.D.

The crime of murder exists in some form in all known societies. In the disposition of those who are found guilty, the law places little reliance upon behavioral sciences. Homicide occurs for diverse reasons. The law recognizes this fact by providing several legal categories of homicide, one of which is "not guilty by virtue of insanity." The concept of insanity in determining responsibility for the crime is defined according to legal criteria. The litera-

Excerpts from authorized reprint, *Journal of Forensic Sciences* 17, no. 1. Copyright 1972. American Society for Testing and Materials, 1916 Race Street, Philadelphia, Pa. 19103.

ture on the issue of criminal responsibility is extensive, but that issue will not be the subject of this paper.

The act of homicide is not only a physical but also a psychological event. The state of mind of the perpetrator during the execution of the crime is of crucial legal consequence; therefore, the psychiatrist is an important resource to the legal process in determining his condition. For historical reasons, the law has made an attempt to place the primary focus of attention on the act itself. The dominance of the act was an important political achievement assuring equality before the law. The act of murder was to be adjudged and punished the same whether committed by a prince or a pauper—at least this was the hope. The political organization of society has changed, as well as the psychological sophistication of the public at large. Society is ready to shift the emphasis from the act to the actor. The need for psychiatric participation in this process will increase in the future.

Psychiatric contributions to the litigation process in general, and the handling of homicide in particular, are based upon clinical skill, experience, and some degree of legal sophistication. Without clinical expertise in the subject matter, the psychiatrist is a mere figurehead, utilized in the courtroom for ritualistic purposes. Scientific knowledge of the subject, however, is not enough for the purpose of meaningful participation in the legal process. It is essential that a psychiatrist be familiar with the legal setting in which he renders his services. It goes without saying that the legal profession also needs psychiatric sophistication in order to be receptive to psychiatric contributions.

Within the psychiatric and legal professions, there has been opposition to such cross-education. In both professions, one encounters those who champion the slogan "A little knowledge is a dangerous thing." They refuse to recognize that nothing is more dangerous than ignorance and that the so-called little knowledge can be valuable for the acquisition of further in-depth knowledge. Information about psychiatry will not transform the lawyer into a psychiatrist, but it might help him to become a better lawyer. Information about the law will not make the psychiatrist an attorney, but it will help him to become a better practitioner within the scope of his own profession.

VARIETIES OF HOMICIDE *

It is almost banal to stress that there are varieties of homicide; nevertheless, it is neces-

* For a more expanded discussion see Tanay's article supra, p. 611.

sary, since society treats homicide as if it were unitary behavior. There are homicides which represent the ultimate of organization, structure, preparation, and execution; at the other end of the spectrum, there are those which are nothing more than a disorganized, unplanned discharge of primitive aggression. A duel may lead to homicide, but it represents an example of organized, ritualized aggression. A lethal confrontation portrayed in a Western is an organized form of behavior with definite rules of procedure. A gangland killing is an organized form of behavior carried out by those who believe in violence as a means for resolution of conflict. Such models of egosyntonic modes of homicidal behavior have dominated our handling of homicide. It is essential to recognize that they represent a small fraction of the homicides in our culture.

As long as homicide is viewed primarily as reflective, egosyntonic behavior, punitive measures seem appropriate. The recognition of a form of homicide which is nonreflective, egodystonic, and represents a decompensation phenomenon requires a different approach. The egodystonic homicide can be best described as the conclusion to a process occurring between two individuals whose personalities and life situation determine the homicidal outcome. The homicide in these cases represents a resolution of conflict extending over a long period of time and maintained primarily on an unconscious level. The homicide takes place during a disruption of the ego and may be precipitated by a seemingly insignificant provocation. The term "homicidal process" is used here to describe the progressive intensification of the sadomasochistic relationship between the perpetrator and the significant person who usually becomes the victim. "Usually" is emphasized, as occasionally displacement occurs and an uninvolved person becomes the focus of the homicidal discharge.

The perpetrators of this type of homicide do not suffer from superego defects; on the contrary, they show evidence of a strong overcontrolling superego. These are people who do not have the capacity to gratify their aggressive needs consistently and do it in an explosive manner. The history of these individuals usually reveals violent childrearing practices, which account for the severity of the superego. In the dissociative homicide, the availability of a gun appears to be a crucial variable. Explosive discharges of aggression may have occurred in these perpetrators before and were terminated by verbal or nonlethal physical assaults. The incidence of such episodes, however, is generally rare in this group. Dissociative homicide usually requires the presence of a number of factors: an overcontrolling superego in the perpetrator, a sadomasochistic relationship between victim and perpetrator, the occurrence of an altered state of consciousness, and the presence of a weapon. Dissociative homicide is analogous to a nuclear reaction, in which a number of isolated events must occur simultaneously in order to trigger the explosion.

INSANITY AS A DEFENSE

The never-ending controversy and outpouring of literature on the subject of insanity as a defense is usually conducted without consideration of those facts essential to the whole interaction. On one side, the proponents of insanity as a defense visualize the execution of mentally ill citizens for crimes which they have committed in a state of mental derangement. The opponents of insanity as a defense, on the other hand, see murderers who go scot free because skilful attorneys, with the help of unscrupulous psychiatrists, mislead innocent juries into acquittal. This discrepancy might offer stimulating mental exercise to those who engage in this polemic, but it seems to have little basis and relationship to the transactions which occur in the criminal courts of the nation. A few oversimplified generalizations may be made:

1. Insanity as a defense is raised almost exclusively in cases of involuntary homicide and only when the perpetrator of the involuntary homicide is charged with first-degree murder.

2. The perpetrators of homicide who plead insanity as a defense are neither mentally ill nor criminals.

3. The concept of insanity is a legal fiction without much relationship to the realities of the functioning and malfunctioning of the human mind.

4. The determination of insanity in criminal law is to a minimal degree influenced by psychiatric thinking or psychiatric participation.

5. Insanity is raised as a defense in a small proportion of the cases of homicide. A great many perpetrators of homicide who are legally and factually entitled to this defense do not make use of it.

Defense by reason of insanity exists in law due to the simple fact that there *are* some crimes which are committed as a result of insanity, that is, some crimes are symptoms of a mental disorder. The defense by insanity has a variety of useful functions, which appear to have been lost in the hue and cry against alleged coddling of criminals. Such a defense is essential for the internal coherence of the legal structure. If criminal sanctions are based on criminal responsibility, then involuntary behavior has to be excluded from the criminal process. Furthermore, the defense by insanity fulfills an important social function by protecting sick people from punishment and, perhaps, further aggravation of their condition.

The existence of the defense by insanity proclaims that the law recognizes the fact that certain forbidden conduct is more appropriately handled by treatment than by punishment. This issue is particularly critical in view of the fact that penal institutions in our society do not regularly provide treatment for mentally ill prisoners. The controversy about the defense by insanity would be much less intense if such treatment were generally available in penal institutions. Punishment of those who have transgressed provisions of the criminal law while lacking the ability to control their behavior is offensive to the sense of justice and, therefore, undermines respect for the law. Such punishment has no justification regardless of the basic objectives of criminal law, whether they be those of retribution, deterrence, or rehabilitation. Furthermore, the defense by insanity has some fiscal significance, as it reduces the burden on the penal system of having to care for people who do not require the complex and expensive services of penal institutions.

The defense by insanity also provides for the inclusion of psychiatry into the courtroom, which is certainly beneficial to the law and possibly useful to psychiatry. Psychiatry has a humanizing influence upon criminal law. The best example of this is the handling of suicide. Through the medium of the defense by insanity, the handling of suicide has been transformed from a felonious offense to a medical entity, exciting little interest in the criminal law. Society does not appear to have suffered as a result of this evolution, and certainly the individual citizens afflicted by suicidal impulses are better served by psychiatry, inadequate as it is, than by the criminal process. I believe that defense by insanity, which now is rarely utilized, poorly presented, and frequently unsuccessful, will, nevertheless, succeed in transforming the present irrational handling of homicidal offenders into a realistic and useful system of disposition.

THE MODEL FOR HOMICIDE

In handling homicide, the law utilizes the model of the criminal man who wilfully and maliciously kills another human being for some utilitarian purpose. This model fits certain homicidal offenders. There is, however, no doubt that the majority of the perpetrators of homicide do not fit this particular model. They can be accommodated within it only by doing violence to basic legal principles, to the sense of justice, and, last but not least, to the findings of behavioral sciences. The law as a rational system cannot survive if it continues to disregard scientific reality in principle or in practice.

In addition to the model of the criminal man, the law has utilized the model of the sick man who is excluded from criminal sanction. This model has led a shadowy existence and has been treated as a stepchild of psychiatry and the law. Defense by insanity is prominent in the law library but disreputable in the courtroom. The indiscriminate charge of first-degree murder utilized in most homicides by the prosecution raises no legal eyebrows. The assertion of defense by insanity, however, renders the legal or psychiatric practitioner suspect of intellectual dishonesty.

There is a common myth to the effect that crafty defense attorneys, with the cooperation of unscrupulous psychiatrists, bring about acquittals of murderers. In reality, the opposite is true. The majority of attorneys handling homicide cases are unskilled in the preparation and presentation of insanity as a defense, and only a small number of attorneys have prepared and used such a defense repeatedly. There may be a number of unscrupulous psychiatrists, but very few psychiatrists of any kind are willing or able to participate in the legal process. It is, therefore, not surprising that insanity is used as a defense infrequently and rarely with success. Between 60 and 80 percent of all homicides involve impulsive violence towards someone with whom the perpetrator has had an intense relationship. Most of these would qualify for raising insanity as a defense. Only 2 percent of cases charged with homicide lead to acquittal by reason of insanity.

In involuntary, dissociative homicide the defendant usually has no other defense than that of insanity. He asserts it not because of the prospect of avoiding punishment but due to the fact that he has no other option. In this type of homicide the perpetrator usually reports the crime himself. He frequently has made a confession and reinforced it by many self-incriminating statements. The act frequently is committed in the presence of witnesses. The initial comments by the perpetrator, as well as his behavior, are often designed to assure him of a charge of first-degree murder.

In the cases of egodystonic and psychotic homicide, success in apprehension and prosecution is aided by forces rooted in the psychology of the perpetrators of these acts. In the 80 to 90 homicides which I have examined, in only a few were even half-hearted attempts made to elude apprehension. In many instances, the perpetrator calls the police or reports the crime at the police station. It hardly requires the skills of Sherlock Holmes or the resources of Scotland Yard to deal with this particular category of homicidal offenders. Furthermore, it does not require brilliant advocacy to persuade a jury that the accused did know what he was doing and, therefore, that it is the duty of the jury to find him guilty of first-degree murder. For reasons which seem beyond comprehension, prosecutors in this country consider it their duty to obtain a first-degree conviction as often as possible. For example, a man who killed his mother suddenly, without any intense interaction with her, and then proceeded to have sexual relations with her dead body, was charged with first-degree murder!

Plea of Insanity

Insanity as a defense is asserted in only a small proportion of all cases where it could be legally applied. There are a variety of reasons for the striking underutilization of this defense. The law limits the raising of the defense by providing a legal restrictive formula for its presentation. Another limiting factor is the lack of familiarity on the part of attorneys with this defense. There is also the reality of lack of sufficient witnesses competent in psychiatry. The public attitudes which are exemplified by the attitudes of juries are another consideration. The practical utility of insanity as a defense at the present time is, therefore, insignificant in the handling of homicide. It is a defense scarce in the courtroom although plentiful in literature. . . .

There are various forces which work against the involvement of practicing psychiatrists in the legal process. Some of these are (1) psychiatric theory and dogma proclaim treatment to be the exclusive concern of the psychiatrist; (2) lack of understanding of the law due in part to the lack of teaching of forensic psychiatry during the training of psychiatrists; (3) the hostility of the law towards intrusion by psychiatrists into the legal domain; and (4) individual abuses by attorneys of physicians in general and psychiatrists in particular in matters of scheduling of testimony and payment for services rendered. These various factors condition the average psychiatrist to avoid courtroom involvement with a phobic intensity.

CONCLUSIONS

It is, at times, amusing to hear lawyers and judges expound about the virtues and vices of psychiatry, without having had the opportunity to work with a practicing psychiatrist in their entire professional careers. Similarly, psychiatrists give pronouncements on the involvement of psychiatry with the law without having had the opportunity and challenge of being significantly exposed to legal processes. Psychiatry has a legitimate interest in attempting to contribute to the development and practice of law. Law constitutes a significant aspect of social reality. Prevention of psychiatric morbidity is intimately involved with the administration of justice. Law, on the other hand, needs the resources of psychiatry for theoretical and practical reasons. The legal precepts which govern human behavior require the data of the social sciences, including psychiatry. The practical administration of justice in the individual case calls for the collection and interpretation of relevant information of psychosocial nature. This is best performed by various behavioral scientists, including psychiatrists. This collaboration between the law and the behavioral sciences is desirable in all areas of the law; however, it appears to be most crucial in the handling of homicide.

The ideals of law and psychiatry can be best achieved through cooperative efforts in theoretical formulation and practical application. It is, therefore, in the best interest of law, psychiatry, and society to further the development and growth of the psychiatric subspecialty of forensic psychiatry.

DANIEL M'NAGHTEN'S CASE

The prisoner had been indicted for [the murder of Edward Drummond, private secretary to Sir Edward Peel]. . . . The prisoner pleaded Not Guilty.

Evidence having been given of the fact of the shooting of Mr. Drummond, and of his death in consequence thereof, witnesses were called on the part of the prisoner, to prove that he was not, at the time of committing the act, in a sound state of mind. . . .

LORD CHIEF JUSTICE TINDAL (in his charge): —The question to be determined is, whether at the time the act in question was committed, the prisoner had or had not the use of his understanding, so as to know that he was doing a wrong or wicked act. If the jurors should be of opinion that the prisoner was not sensible, at the time he committed it, that he was violating the laws both of God and man, then he would be entitled to a verdict in his favour: but if, on the contrary, they were of opinion that when he committed the act he was in a sound state of mind, then their verdict must be against him.

Verdict, Not Guilty, on the ground of insanity.

This verdict, and the question of the nature and extent of the unsoundness of mind which would excuse the commission of a felony of this sort, having been made the subject of debate in the House of Lords, it was determined to take the opinion of the Judges on the law governing such cases. . . .

LORD CHIEF JUSTICE TINDAL: . . . The first question proposed by your Lordships is this: "What is the law respecting alleged crimes committed by persons afflicted with insane delusion in respect of one or more particular subjects or persons: as, for instance, where at the time of the commission of the alleged crime the accused knew he was acting contrary to law, but did the act complained of with a view, under the influence of insane delusion, of redressing or revenging some supposed grievance or injury, or of producing some supposed public benefit?"

In answer to which question, assuming that

House of Lords, 1843, 10 Cl. & F. 200, 8 Eng. Reprint 718.

your Lordships' inquiries are confined to those persons who labour under such partial delusions only, and are not in other respects insane, we are of opinion that, notwithstanding the party accused did the act complained of with a view, under the influence of insane delusion, of redressing or revenging some supposed grievance or injury, or of producing some public benefit, he is nevertheless punishable according to the nature of the crime committed, if he knew at the time of committing such crime that he was acting contrary to law; by which expression we understand your Lordships to mean the law of the land.

Your Lordships are pleased to inquire of us, secondly, "What are the proper questions to be submitted to the jury, where a person alleged to be afflicted with insane delusion respecting one or more particular subjects or persons, is charged with the commission of a crime (murder, for example), and insanity is set up as a defence?" And, thirdly, "In what terms ought the question to be left to the jury as to the prisoner's state of mind at the time when the act was committed?" And as these two questions appear to us to be more conveniently answered together, we have to submit our opinion to be, that the jurors ought to be told in all cases that every man is to be presumed to be sane, and to possess a sufficient degree of reason to be responsible for his crimes, until the contrary be proved to their satisfaction; and that to establish a defence on the ground of insanity, it must be clearly proved that, at the time of the committing of the act, the party accused was labouring under such a defect of reason, from disease of the mind, as not to know the nature and quality of the act he was doing; or, if he did know it, that he did not know he was doing what was wrong. The mode of putting the latter part of the question to the jury on these occasions has generally been, whether the accused at the time of doing the act knew the difference between right and wrong: which mode, though rarely, if ever, leading to any mistake with the jury, is not, as we conceive, so accurate when put generally and in the abstract, as when put with reference to the party's knowledge of right and wrong in respect to the very act with which he is charged. If the question were to be put as to the knowledge of the accused solely and exclusively with reference to the law of the land, it might tend to confound the jury, by inducing them to believe that an actual knowledge of the law of the land was essential in order to lead to a conviction; whereas the law is administered upon the principle that every one must be taken conclusively to know it, without proof that he does know it. If the accused was conscious that the act was one which he ought not to do, and if that act was at the same time contrary to the law of the land, he is punishable; and the usual course therefore has been to leave the question to the jury, whether the party accused had a sufficient degree of reason to know that he was doing an act that was wrong; and this course we think is correct, accompanied with such observations and explanations as the circumstances of each particular case may require.

The fourth question which your Lordships have proposed to us is this:—"If a person under an insane delusion as to existing facts, commits an offence in consequence thereof, is he thereby excused?" To which question the answer must of course depend on the nature of the delusion: but, making the same assumption as we did before, namely, that he labours under such partial delusion only, and is not in other respects insane, we think he must be considered in the same situation as to responsibility as if the facts with respect to which the delusion exists were real. For example, if under the influence of his delusion he supposes another man to be in the act of attempting to take away his life, and he kills that man, as he supposes, in self-defence, he would be exempt from punishment. If his delusion was that the deceased had inflicted a serious injury to his character and fortune, and he killed him in revenge for such supposed injury, he would be liable to punishment. . . .

DURHAM v. UNITED STATES

Before EDGERTON, BAZELON, and WASHINGTON, Circuit Judges.

BAZELON, Circuit Judge. Monte Durham was convicted of housebreaking by the District Court sitting with a jury. The only defense asserted at the trial was that Durham was of unsound mind at the time of the offense. We are now urged to reverse the conviction (1) because the trial court did not correctly apply existing rules governing the burden of proof on the defense of insanity, and (2) because existing tests of criminal responsibility are obsolete and should be superseded.

I

Durham has a long history of imprisonment and hospitalization. In 1945, at the age of 17, he was discharged from the Navy after a psychiatric examination had shown that he suffered "from a profound personality disorder which renders him unfit for Naval service." In 1947 he pleaded guilty to violating the National Motor Theft Act and was placed on probation for one to three years. He attempted suicide, was taken to Gallinger Hospital for observation, and was transferred to St. Elizabeths Hospital, from which he was discharged after two months. In January of 1948, as a result of a conviction in the District of Columbia Municipal Court for passing bad checks, the District Court revoked his probation and he commenced service of his Motor Theft sentence. His conduct within the first few days in jail led to a lunacy inquiry in the Municipal Court where a jury found him to be of unsound mind. Upon commitment to St. Elizabeths, he was diagnosed as suffering from "psychosis with psychopathic personality." After 15 months of treatment, he was discharged in July 1949 as "recovered" and was returned to jail to serve the balance of his sentence. In June, 1950, he was conditionally released. He violated the conditions by leaving the District. When he learned of a warrant for his arrest as a parole violator, he fled to the "South and Midwest obtaining money by passing a number of bad checks." After he was found and returned to the District, the Parole Board referred him to the District Court for a lunacy inquisition, wherein a jury again found him to be of unsound mind. He was readmitted to St. Elizabeths in February, 1951. This time the diagnosis was "without mental disorder, psychopathic personality." He was discharged for the third time in May, 1951. The housebreaking which is the subject of the present appeal took place two months later, on July 13, 1951.

According to his mother and the psychiatrist who examined him in September, 1951, he suffered from hallucinations immediately after his May, 1951, discharge from St. Elizabeths. . . .

[Durham's] conviction followed the trial court's rejection of the defense of insanity in these words:

I don't think it has been established that the defendant was of unsound mind as of July 13, 1951, in the sense that he didn't know the difference between right and wrong or that even if he did, he was subject to an irresistible impulse by reason of the derangement of mind.

While, of course, the burden of proof on the issue of mental capacity to commit a crime is upon the Government, just as it is on every other issue, nevertheless, the Court finds that there is not sufficient to contradict the usual presumption of [sic] the usual inference of sanity.

There is no testimony concerning the mental state of the defendant as of July 13, 1951, and therefore the usual presumption of sanity governs.

While if there was some testimony as to his mental state as of that date to the effect that he was incompetent on that date, the burden of proof would be on the Government to overcome it. There has been no such testimony, and the usual presumption of sanity prevails. . . .

Mr. Ahern, I think you have done very well by your client and defended him very ably, but I think under the circumstances there is nothing that anybody could have done. [Emphasis supplied.]

We think this reflects error requiring reversal.

In *Tatum* v. *United States* we said, "When lack of mental capacity is raised as a defense to a charge of crime, the law accepts the gen-

United States Court of Appeals, District of Columbia Circuit, 214 F.2d 862 (1954). The footnotes of the court have been renumbered, and some have been omitted.

eral experience of mankind and presumes that all people, including those accused of crime, are sane." So long as this presumption prevails, the prosecution is not required to prove the defendant's sanity. But "as soon as 'some evidence of mental disorder is introduced, . . . sanity, like any other fact, must be proved as part of the prosecution's case beyond a reasonable doubt.' " Here it appears that the trial judge recognized this rule but failed to find "some evidence." We hold that the court erred and that the requirement of "some evidence" was satisfied.[1]

In Tatum we held that requirement satisfied by considerably less than is present here. Tatum claimed lack of memory concerning the critical events and three lay witnesses testified that he appeared to be in "more or less of a trance," or "abnormal," but two psychiatrists testified that he was of "sound mind" both at the time of the examination and at the time of the crime. Here, the psychiatric testimony was unequivocal that Durham was of unsound mind at the time of the crime. Dr. Gilbert, the only expert witness heard, so stated at least four times. . . . Intensive questioning by the court failed to produce any retraction of Dr. Gilbert's testimony that the "period of insanity would have embraced the date July 13, 1951." And though the prosecution sought unsuccessfully in its cross- and recross-examination of Dr. Gilbert to establish that Durham was a malingerer who feigned insanity whenever he was trapped for his misdeeds, it failed to present any expert testimony to support this theory. In addition to Dr. Gilbert's testimony, there was testimony by Durham's mother to the effect that in the interval between his discharge from Saint Elizabeths in May, 1951, and the crime "he seemed afraid of people" and had urged her to put steel bars on his bedroom windows. . . .

. . . [O]nce the issue of insanity is raised by the introduction of "some evidence," so that the presumption of sanity is no longer absolute, it is incumbent upon the trier of fact to weigh and consider "the whole evidence, including that supplied by the presumption of sanity . . ." on the issue of "the capacity in law of the accused to commit" the crime. Here, manifestly, the court as the trier of fact

did not and could not weigh "the whole evidence," for it found there was "no testimony concerning the mental state" of Durham.

For the foregoing reasons, the judgment is reversed and the case is remanded for a new trial.

II

It has been ably argued by counsel for Durham that the existing tests in the District of Columbia for determining criminal responsibility, i.e., the so-called right-wrong test supplemented by the irresistible impulse test, are not satisfactory criteria for determining criminal responsibility. We are urged to adopt a different test to be applied on the retrial of this case. This contention has behind it nearly a century of agitation for reform.

A. The right-wrong test, approved in this jurisdiction in 1882, was the exclusive test of criminal responsibility in the District of Columbia until 1929 when we approved the irresistible impulse test as a supplementary test in *Smith* v. *United States*. The right-wrong test has its roots in England. There, by the first quarter of the eighteenth century, an accused escaped punishment if he could not distinguish "good and evil," i.e., if he "doth not know what he is doing, no more than . . . a wild beast." Later in the same century, the "wild beast" test was abandoned and "right and wrong" was substituted for "good and evil." And toward the middle of the nineteenth century, the House of Lords in the famous M'Naghten case restated what had become the accepted "right-wrong" test in a form which has since been followed, not only in England but in most American jurisdictions,[2] as an exclusive test of criminal responsibility. . . .

---

[1] In its brief, the prosecution confounds the "some evidence" test with the "evidence sufficient to create a reasonable doubt" test, despite our explanation in Tatum that the " 'evidence sufficient to create a reasonable doubt' test" applies only after the issue has been raised by "some evidence" and that the burden is already upon the Government to prove the defendant's sanity beyond a reasonable doubt. 88 U.S. App. D.C. at page 390, 190 F.2d at page 616.

[2] Weihofen, "The M'Naghten Rule in Its Present-Day Setting," *Federal Probation* 8 (September, 1953); Weihofen, *Insanity as a Defense in Criminal Law* (1933), pp. 15, 64–68, 109–47; *Leland* v. *State of Oregon*, 1952, 343 U.S. 790, 800, 72 S. Ct. 1002, 96 L. Ed. 1302.

"In five States the M'Naghten Rules have been in substance re-enacted by statute." Royal Commission Report 409; see, e.g., "Sec. 1120 of the [New York State] Penal Law [McK. Consol. Laws, c. 40] [which] provides that a person is not excused from liability on the grounds of insanity, idiocy, or imbecility, except upon proof that at the time of the commission of the criminal act he was laboring under such a defect of reason as (1) not to know the nature and quality of the act he was doing or (2) not to know that the act was wrong." Ploscowe, "Suggested Changes in the New York Laws and Procedures Relating to the Criminally Insane and Mentally Defective Offenders," 43 *J. Crim. L., Criminology and Police Sci.* 312, 314 (1952).

As early as 1838, Isaac Ray, one of the founders of the American Psychiatric Association, in his now classic *Medical Jurisprudence of Insanity,* called knowledge of right and wrong a "fallacious" test of criminal responsibility. This view has long since been substantiated by enormous developments in knowledge of mental life. In 1928 Mr. Justice Cardozo said to the New York Academy of Medicine: "Everyone concedes that the present [legal] definition of insanity has little relation to the truths of mental life."

Medico-legal writers in large number,[3] The Report of the Royal Commission on Capital Punishment 1949–1953, and The Preliminary Report by the Committee on Forensic Psychiatry of the Group for the Advancement of Psychiatry present convincing evidence that the right-and-wrong test is "based on an entirely obsolete and misleading conception of the nature of insanity." The science of psychiatry now recognizes that a man is an integrated personality and that reason, which is only one element in that personality, is not the sole determinant of his conduct. The right-wrong test, which considers knowledge or reason alone, is therefore an inadequate guide to mental responsibility for criminal behavior. As Professor Sheldon Glueck of the Harvard Law School points out in discussing the right-wrong tests, which he calls the knowledge tests:

[3] For a detailed bibliography on Insanity as a Defense to Crime, see 7 The Record of the Association of the Bar of the City of New York 158–62 (1952). And see, e.g., Alexander, *The Criminal, the Judge and the Public* 70 et seq. (19–31); Cardozo, *What Medicine Can Do For the Law* 28 et. seq. (1930); Cleckley, *The Mask of Sanity* 491 et. seq. (2d ed., 1950); Deutsch, *The Mentally Ill in America* 389–417 (2d ed., 1949); Glueck, *Mental Disorder and the Criminal Law* (1925), *Crime and Justice* 96 et seq. (1936); Guttmacher & Weihofen, *Psychiatry and the Law* 218, 403–23 (1952); Hall, *Principles of Criminal Law* 477–538 (1947); Menninger, *The Human Mind* 450 (1937); Hall & Menninger, "Psychiatry and the Law"—a Dual Review, 38 *Iowa L. Rev.* 687 (1953); Overholser, *The Psychiatrist and the Law* 41–43 (1953); Overholser & Richmond, *Handbook of Psychiatry* 208–15 (1947); Ploscowe, "Suggested Changes in the New York Laws and Procedures Relating to the Criminally Insane and Mentally Defective Offenders," 43 *J. Crim. L., Criminology and Police Sci.* 312, 314 (1952); Ray, *Medical Jurisprudence of Insanity* (1st ed., 1838; 4th ed., 1860); Reik, "The Doe-Ray Correspondence: A Pioneer Collaboration in the Jurisprudence of Mental Disease," 63 *Yale L. J.* 183 (1953); Weihofen, *Insanity as a Defense in Criminal Law* (1933), "The M'Naghten Rule in Its Present-Day Setting," *Federal Probation* 8 (September, 1953); Zilboorg, Mind, Medicine, and Man 246–97 (1943), Legal Aspects of Psychiatry, American *Psychiatry 1844–1944,* 507 (1944).

It is evident that the knowledge tests unscientifically abstract out of the mental make-up but one phase or element of mental life, the cognitive, which, in this era of dynamic psychology, is beginning to be regarded as not the most important factor in conduct and its disorders. In brief, these tests proceed upon the following questionable assumptions of an outworn era in psychiatry: (1) that lack of knowledge of the 'nature or quality' of an act (assuming the meaning of such terms to be clear), or incapacity to know right from wrong, is the sole or even the most important symptom of mental disorder; (2) that such knowledge is the sole instigator and guide of conduct, or at least the most important element therein, and consequently should be the sole criterion of responsibility when insanity is involved; and (3) that the capacity of knowing right from wrong can be completely intact and functioning perfectly even though a defendant is otherwise demonstrably of disordered mind.[4]

Nine years ago we said:

The modern science of psychology . . . does not conceive that there is a separate little man in the top of one's head called reason whose function it is to guide another unruly little can called instinct, emotion, or impulse in the way he should go.[5]

[4] Glueck, "Psychiatry and the Criminal Law," 12 *Mental Hygiene* 575, 580 (1928), as quoted in Deutsch, *The Mentally Ill in America* 396 (2d ed., 1949); and see, e.g., Menninger, *The Human Mind* 450 (1937); Guttmacher & Weihofen, *Psychiatry and the Law* 403–8 (1952).

[5] Holloway v. United States, 1945, 80 U.S. App. D.C. 3, 5, 148 F.2d 665, 667, certiorari denied, 1948, 334 U.S. 852, 68 S. Ct. 1507, 92 L. Ed. 1774.

More recently, the Royal Commission, after an exhaustive survey of legal, medical, and lay opinion in many Western countries, including England and the United States, made a similar finding. It reported: "The gravamen of the charge against the M'Naghten Rules is that they are not in harmony with modern medical science, which, as we have seen, is reluctant to divide the mind into separate compartments—the intellect, the emotions, and the will—but looks at it as a whole and considers that insanity distorts and impairs the action of the mind as a whole." (Royal Commission Report 113.) The Commission lends vivid support to this conclusion by pointing out that "It would be impossible to apply modern methods of care and treatment in mental hospitals, and at the same time to maintain order and discipline, if the great majority of the patients, even among the grossly insane, did not know what is forbidden by the rules and that, if they break them, they are liable to forfeit some privilege. Examination of a number of individual cases in which a verdict of guilty but insane [the nearest English equivalent of our acquittal by reason of insanity] was returned, and

By its misleading emphasis on the cognitive, the right-wrong test requires court and jury to rely upon what is, scientifically speaking, inadequate, and most often, invalid and irrelevant testimony in determining criminal responsibility.

The fundamental objection to the right-wrong test, however, is not that criminal irresponsibility is made to rest upon an inadequate, invalid or indeterminable symptom or manifestation, but that it is made to rest upon *any* particular symptom. In attempting to define particular faculties are destroyed or gravely have assumed an impossible role, not merely one for which they have no special competence. As the Royal Commission emphasizes, it is dangerous "to abstract particular mental faculties, and to lay it down that unless these particular faculties are destroyed or gravely impaired, an accused person, whatever the nature of his mental disease, must be held to be criminally responsible. . . ." In this field of law as in others, the fact finder should be free to consider all information advanced by relevant scientific disciplines.

Despite demands in the name of scientific advances, this court refused to alter the right-wrong test at the turn of the century. But in 1929, we reconsidered in response to "the cry of scientific experts" and added the irresistible impulse test as a supplementary test for determining criminal responsibility. Without "hesitation" we declared, in *Smith* v. *United States,* "it to be the law of this District that, in cases where insanity is interposed as a defense, and the facts are sufficient to call for the application of the rule of irresistible impulse, the jury should be so charged." We said:

. . . The modern doctrine is that the degree of insanity which will relieve the accused of the consequences of a criminal act must be such as to create in his mind an uncontrollable impulse to commit the offense charged. This impulse must be such as to override the reason and judgment and obliterate the sense of right and wrong to the extent that the accused is deprived of the power to choose between right and wrong. The mere ability to distinguish right from wrong is no longer the correct test either in civil or criminal cases, where the defense of insanity is interposed. The accepted rule in this day and age, with the great advancement in medical science as an enlightening influence on this subject, is that the accused must be capable, not only of distinguishing between right and wrong, but that he was not impelled to do the act by an irresistible impulse, which means before it will justify a verdict of acquittal that his reasoning powers were so far dethroned by his diseased mental condition as to deprive him of the will power to resist the insane impulse to perpetrate the deed, though knowing it to be wrong.[6]

As we have already indicated, this has since been the test in the District.

Although the Smith case did not abandon the right-wrong test, it did liberate the fact finder from exclusive reliance upon that discredited criterion by allowing the jury to inquire also whether the accused suffered from an undefined "diseased mental condition [which] deprive[d] him of the will power to resist the insane impulse. . . ." The term "irresistible impulse," however, carries the misleading implication that "diseased mental condition[s]" produce only sudden, momentary, or spontaneous inclinations to commit unlawful acts.[7]

As the Royal Commission found:

. . . In many cases . . . this is not true at all. The sufferer from [melancholia, for example] experiences a change of mood which alters the whole of his existence. He may believe, for instance, that a future of such degradation and misery awaits both him and his family that death for all is a less dreadful alternative. Even the thought that the acts he contemplates are murder and suicide pales into insignificance in contrast with what he otherwise expects. The criminal act, in such circumstances, may be the reverse of impulsive. It may be coolly and carefully prepared; yet it is still the act of a madman. This is merely an illustration; similar states of mind are likely to lie behind the criminal act when murders are committed by persons suffering from schizophrenia or paranoid psychoses due to disease of the brain.

We find that as an exclusive criterion the right-wrong test is inadequate in that (*a*) it does not take sufficient account of psychic realities and scientific knowledge, and (*b*) it is based upon one symptom and so cannot validly be applied in all circumstances. We find that the "irresistible impulse" test is also inadequate

rightly returned, has convinced us that there are few indeed where the accused can truly be said not to have known that his act was wrong." (*Ibid.,* at 103.)

[6] 59 App. D.C. at page 145, 36 F.2d at page 549.

[7] Impulse, as defined by Webster's New International Dictionary (2d ed., 1950), is: "1. Act of impelling, or driving onward with *sudden* force; impulsion, esp., force so communicated as to produce motion *suddenly* or *immediately.* . . . 2. An incitement of the mind or spirit, esp. in the form of an *abrupt* and vivid suggestion, prompting some *unpremeditated* action or leading to unforeseen knowledge or insight; a *spontaneous* inclination. . . . 3. . . . motion produced by a *sudden* or *momentary force.* . . ." (Emphasis supplied.),

in that it gives no recognition to mental illness characterized by brooding and reflection and so relegates acts caused by such illness to the application of the inadequate right-wrong test. We conclude that a broader test should be adopted.[8]

B. In the District of Columbia, the formulation of tests of criminal responsibility is entrusted to the courts[9] and, in adopting a new test, we invoke our inherent power to make the change prospectively.

The rule we now hold must be applied on the retrial of this case and in future cases is not unlike that followed by the New Hampshire court since 1870.[10] It is simply that an accused is not criminally responsible if his unlawful act was the product of mental disease or mental defect.[11]

We use "disease" in the sense of a condition which is considered capable of either improving or deteriorating. We use "defect" in the sense of a condition which is not considered capable of either improving or deteriorating and which may be either congenital, or the result of injury, or the residual effect of a physical or mental disease.

Whenever there is "some evidence" that the accused suffered from a diseased or defective mental condition at the time the unlawful act was committed, the trial court must provide the jury with guides for determining whether the accused can be held criminally responsible. We do not, and indeed could not, formulate an instruction which would be either appropriate or binding in all cases. But under the rule now announced, any instruction should in some way convey to the jury the sense and substance of the following: If you the jury believe beyond a reasonable doubt that the accused was not suffering from a diseased or defective mental condition at the time he committed the criminal act charged, you may find him guilty. If you believe he was suffering from a diseased or defective mental condition when he committed the act, but believe beyond a reasonable doubt that the act was not the product of such mental abnormality, you may find him guilty. Unless you believe beyond a reasonable doubt either that he was not suffering from a diseased or defective mental condition, or that the act was not the product of such abnormality, you must find the accused not guilty by reason of insanity. Thus your task would not be completed upon finding, if you did find, that the accused suffered from a mental disease or defect. He would still be responsible for his unlawful act if there was no causal connection between such mental abnormality and the act.[12] These questions must be determined by you from the facts which you find to be fairly deducible from the testimony and the evidence in the case.

The questions of fact under the test we now lay down are as capable of determination by the jury, as, for example, the questions juries must determine upon a claim of total disability under a policy of insurance where the state of medical knowledge concerning the disease involved, and its effects, is obscure or in conflict. In such cases, the jury is not required to depend on arbitrarily selected "symptoms, phases or manifestations" of the disease as criteria for determining the ultimate questions of fact upon which the claim depends. Similarly, upon a claim of criminal irresponsibility, the jury will not be required to rely on such symptoms as criteria for determining the ultimate question of fact upon which such claim depends. Testimony as to

---

[8] As we recently said, ". . . former common law should not be followed where changes in conditions have made it obsolete. We have never hesitated to exercise the usual judicial function of revising and enlarging the common law." Linkins v. Protestant Episcopal Cathedral Foundation, 1950, 87 U.S. App. D.C. 351, 355, 187 F.2d 357, 361, 28 A.L.R. 2d 521. Cf. Funk v. United States, 1933, 290 U.S. 371, 381–382, 54 S. Ct. 212, 78 L. Ed. 369.

[9] Congress, like most State legislatures, has never undertaken to define insanity in this connection, although it recognizes the fact that an accused may be acquitted by reason of insanity. See D.C. Code § 24–301 (1951). And as this court made clear in Hill v. United States, Congress has left no doubt that "common-law procedure, in all matters relating to crime . . . still continues in force here in all cases except where special provision is made by statute to the exclusion of the common-law procedure." 22 App. D.C. 395, 401 (1903).

[10] State v. Pike, 1870, 49 N.H. 399.

[11] Cf. State v. Jones, 1871, 50 N.H. 369, 398.

[12] "There is no *a priori* reason why every person suffering from any form of mental abnormality or disease, or from any particular kind of mental disease, should be treated by the law as not answerable for any criminal offense which he may commit, and be exempted from conviction and punishment. Mental abnormalities vary infinitely in their nature and intensity and in their effects on the character and conduct of those who suffer from them. Where a person suffering from a mental abnormality commits a crime, there must always be some likelihood that the abnormality has played some part in the causation of the crime; and, generally speaking, the graver the abnormality . . . the more probable it must be that there is a causal connection between them. But the closeness of this connection will be shown by the fact brought in evidence in individual cases and cannot be decided on the basis of any general medical principle." (Royal Commission Report 99.)

such "symptoms, phases, or manifestations," along with other relevant evidence, will go to the jury upon the ultimate questions of fact which it alone can finally determine. Whatever the state of psychiatry, the psychiatrist will be permitted to carry out his principal court function which, as we noted in *Holloway* v. *U.S.*, "is to inform the jury of the character of [the accused's] mental disease [or defect)]." The jury's range of inquiry will not be limited to, but may include, for example, whether an accused, who suffered from a mental disease or defect, did not know the difference between right and wrong, acted under the compulsion of an irresistible impulse, or had "been deprived of or lost the power of his will. . . ."

Finally, in leaving the determination of the ultimate question of fact to the jury, we permit it to perform its traditional function, which, as we said in Holloway, is to apply "our inherited ideas of moral responsibility to individuals prosecuted for crime. . . ." Juries will continue to make moral judgments, still operating under the fundamental precept that "our collective conscience does not allow punishment where it cannot impose blame." But in making such judgments, they will be guided by wider horizons of knowledge concerning mental life. The question will be sim-

ply whether the accused acted because of a mental disorder, and not whether he displayed particular symptoms which medical science has long recognized do not necessarily, or even typically, accompany even the most serious mental disorder.

The legal and moral traditions of the western world require that those who, of their own free will and with evil intent (sometimes called *mens rea*), commit acts which violate the law, shall be criminally responsible for those acts. Our traditions also require that where such acts stem from and are the product of a mental disease or defect as those terms are used herein, moral blame shall not attach, and hence there will not be criminal responsibility.[13] The rule we state in this opinion is designed to meet these requirements.

Reversed and remanded for a new trial.

---

[13] An accused person who is acquitted by reason of insanity is presumed to be insane (Orencia v. Overholser, 1947, 82 U.S. App. D.C. 285, 163 F.2d 763; Barry v. White, 1933, 62 App. D.C. 69, 64 F.2d 707), and may be committed for an indefinite period to a "hospital for the insane." D.C. Code § 24–301 (1951). [Cf. Bolton v. Harris and D.C. Court Reform and Criminal Procedure Act of 1970, post.]

REPORT OF THE PRESIDENT'S COMMISSION ON CRIME IN THE DISTRICT OF COLUMBIA

(Excerpts)

THE MENTALLY ILL OFFENDER[1]

The District of Columbia followed the *M'Naghten* and irresistible impulse rules until 1954 when the Court of Appeals in *Durham* v. *United States* announced a new test of criminal responsibility. Under this standard "an accused is not criminally responsible if his unlawful act was the product of mental disease or mental defect." The Court of Appeals found that the "right-wrong" test did not "take suffi-

cient account of psychic realities and scientific knowledge." It also concluded that the irresistible impulse test gave "no recognition to mental illness characterized by brooding and reflection and so relegates acts caused by such illness to the application of the inadequate right-wrong test." The *Durham* rule was designed to reconcile the legal test of criminal responsibility with advances in psychiatric knowledge. Specifically, it was framed to permit psychiatrists to testify in their own terms concerning the accused's mental condition, thereby facilitating the kind of communication between psychi-

[1] Footnotes omitted.

Washington, D.C., 1966.

atric experts and the courts which was felt to be impeded by the existing tests.

Various objections were leveled against the *Durham* test. It was argued that there was ambiguity in the requirement that the criminal act be shown to be the "product" of the mental disease. Other critics expressed concern that undue weight was being accorded to the opinions of psychiatrists. These problems were considered by a unanimous *en banc* decision of the Court of Appeals in 1962 in *McDonald v. United States.* In addition to defining more rigorously the amount of evidence required for a defendant to raise the issue of insanity, the court emphasized in *McDonald* that the issue should be left in the hands of the jury; whether a psychiatrist deemed a particular defendant to be mentally diseased was not dispositive. The court also defined a "mental disease or defect" to include "any abnormal condition of the mind which substantially affects mental or emotional processes and substantially impairs behavior controls." The *Durham* test, as amplified by *McDonald,* is similar to the "substantial capacity" standard of the American Law Institute.

A defendant is presumed to be sane. An accused who claims he is not criminally responsible has the initial duty of introducing "some evidence" showing that he suffered from a mental disease or defect at the time of the alleged offense. If some evidence of lack of mental responsibility is received, then in the trial courts of the District, as in all Federal courts, the prosecution bears the burden of proof on the sanity issue. In such a case the prosecution must prove beyond a reasonable doubt either that the accused was not mentally diseased, or that the crime was not the product of mental disease. If the prosecution does not carry its burden, the jury, after finding that the defendant committed the act, may then find him not guilty by reason of insanity. . . .

The Commission does not purport to judge whether persons committed to Saint Elizabeths Hospital as not guilty by reason of insanity are confined for too long or too short a time. That is a medical question which is properly entrusted to the specialists at the hospital. These comparisons [charts comparing median periods of confinement of convicted persons and persons committed to Saint Elizabeths on finding of not guilty by reason of insanity] have been made by the Commission primarily in response to criticisms that persons found not guilty under the *Durham* rule are avoiding confinement or escaping punishment for their acts. The majority of the Commission believes that the facts do not support such a conclusion. . . .

For nearly a decade following announce-ment of the *Durham* rule in 1954, there was widespread debate in the District concerning the desirability of the new test. Over a hundred appellate decisions involving the insanity issue were decided by the United States Court of Appeals; judges, juries, lawyers, and psychiatrists struggled with the application of the new standard for criminal responsibility. Much of the debate, however, was stilled by the 1962 decision of the Court of Appeals in *McDonald v. United States.* Appellate cases involving the *Durham* rule have decreased since then and insanity acquittals have stabilized at two to three per cent of all defendants in the United States District Court.

Although we are unable to judge whether too many or two few persons are being found not guilty by reason of insanity, the number of defendants whose criminal behavior is excused under the *Durham* standard is relatively small. The *Durham* rule does not appear to offer a readily available opportunity for criminal offenders to escape the consequences of their acts, particularly in view of the statute requiring commitment of those found not guilty by reason of insanity. Experience at Saint Elizabeths Hospital demonstrates that most persons found not guilty by reason of insanity under the *Durham* rule are indeed suffering from mental disease or defect and that they are sufficiently ill to remain in the hospital for substantial periods of time.

The majority of the Commission therefore concludes that there is no pressing need for change in the law. As an original proposition, several members of the Commission might favor replacement of the *Durham* rule with the American Law Institute standard of criminal responsibility or the very similar formulation passed by Congress in the recently vetoed Omnibus Crime Bill. The majority does not believe, however, that the advantages of such a substitution clearly outweigh the possible disadvantages. Even a comparatively minor change in the wording of the legal test might spawn another decade of litigation, without any assurance that it would produce a significant change in the number of persons found not guilty by reason of insanity or would improve the accuracy of those determinations.

The Commission is concerned, however, about the nature of the psychiatric testimony elicited under the *Durham* rule. *Durham* was intended to enable psychiatrists to testify freely and completely without the evidentiary limitations of a right-wrong or irresistible impulse test. Based on such expert testimony, the jury was supposedly equipped to reach a just decision concerning the defendant's mental condition. Due to failures by both lawyers and psychiatrists, this essential testimony has often evolved into a series of complex, unexplained psychiatric conclusions of little value to the jury. In order to remedy this deficiency, lawyers must make every effort to ask questions which promote lucid testimony and psychiatrists must in turn attempt to translate their professional terminology into lay language and explain reasons for their conclusions. . . .

This Commission has considered the problem of the adult mentally ill offender whose condition becomes an issue in criminal proceedings. Other aspects of the relationship between mental illness and criminal activity are equally important, however, and must in the future command greater attention.

Notwithstanding the *Durham* rule, many people with "mental problems" are convicted and sent to correctional institutions rather than Saint Elizabeths Hospital. The study by the Stanford Research Institute reveals that 1.7 per cent of adult felons convicted in the District of Columbia in fiscal 1965 had been in mental institutions, 2.7 per cent had had psychiatric treatment, 1.4 per cent had "serious mental illness," and 12.5 per cent had "other mental problems." These persons either did not raise the insanity defense or the defense was rejected by the judge or jury. A substantial number of children adjudicated as juvenile delinquents also show signs of emotional disturbance.

Whether the offender is confined in prison, juvenile training school, or mental hospital, one aim of the community must be to help him become a useful, law-abiding person. Yet there is not a single psychiatrist on the staff of the Receiving Home, the facility in the District in which juvenile offenders are detained following arrest, and only one of the staff at the Children's Center, which serves about 2,000 retarded, delinquent, or dependent persons. There is no psychiatrist on the staff of the Youth Correction Center at Lorton. Diagnosed psychotics are often kept in our prisons for months before transfer to Saint Elizabeths Hospital; pre-psychotics are given no hospitalization. These shortages rate a high priority among the community's concerns.

The Commission recognizes that the *Durham* rule or other formulations of criminal responsibility are not the only mechanisms for handling the mentally ill offender; other alternatives must be constantly explored. For example, in Maryland procedures have been devised for committing mentally ill offenders and incorrigibles to a special treatment-oriented institution until "it is reasonably safe for society to terminate the confinement and treatment." It has also been proposed that the criminal process be separated into two steps, the first limited to ascertaining whether the defendant committed the alleged crime without consideration of his mental condition, and the second involving selection by experts of the appropriate course of treatment. Underlying these and other alternatives is the growing recognition that the dichotomies which now characterize the law's handling of this problem—sane or insane, guilty or not guilty, prison or hospital—must be replaced by emphasis on gradations of mental condition and the need for a wide range of specialized correctional and treatment facilities. . . .

MINORITY REPORT[2]

. . . In applying the *Durham* rule and its concomitants, the District Court and the Court of Appeals have been plagued with difficult problems of interpretation. Since 1954 there have been a hundred or more cases on this subject in the Court of Appeals, many with dissenting and concurring opinions. For examples of the problems, there may be mentioned the following: What types of afflictions can constitute a "mental illness or mental defect"? What does the word "product" mean? What is "some evidence" under *Durham*? Of the last example, I refer to *Logan* v. *United States*, 109 U.S. App. D.C. 104 (1960), where there was testimony that actions of defendant when drinking were "different from what other people would do" in the same condition, and to *Clark* v. *United States*, 104 U.S. App. D.C. 27 (1958), where there was testimony of the defendant that he "must have been insane." This evidence was considered sufficient to satisfy the requirement of the "some evidence" rule and thereby place the burden on the prosecution to establish, *beyond a reasonable doubt*, a negative, i.e., that defendant was *not* suffering from a mental disease, etc.

Also, it should be pointed out that underlying these problems are the varied use of medical terms by psychiatrists and the question of the weight to be given expert testimony as opposed to lay testimony. "In considering *Durham* it was noted that a reputable school of psychiatrists considers most antisocial acts to be symptomatic of mental disease or defect and that since under *Durham* mental disease or defect excuses from criminal responsibility, in most cases at least a sound ground exists for a juror's reasonable doubt as to almost *any* defendant's legal sanity." (Italics supplied.) Since common sense dictates that a psychiatric interview and testimony based thereon should be given substantial, if not determinative, weight, in many cases the expert may usurp

[2] Footnotes omitted.

the jury's function—allowing little or no credence to a layman's views on sanity. Indeed, in *Douglas* v. *United States*, 99 U.S. App. D.C. 232 (1956), the Court of Appeals, by implication at least, held that lay testimony alone of sanity was insufficient to overcome psychiatric testimony of insanity and prevent a directed judgment of acquittal by reason of insanity.

However, the case of *McDonald* v. *United States*, 114 U.S. App. D.C. 120 decided October 8, 1962, answered to a degree some of the above mentioned perplexities that the *Durham* decision had created. As to the amount of evidence needed to overcome the initial presumption of sanity, and to place the burden of proof on the Government, the court, at 122, stated that:

The subject matter being what it is, there can be no sharp quantitative or qualitative definition of "some evidence." Certainly it means more than a scintilla, yet, of course, the amount need not be so substantial as to require, if uncontroverted, a directed verdict of acquittal [by reason of insanity].

Relating to the variety of psychiatric labels and the weight to be given to expert psychiatric testimony, the court said this:

[T]he jury, in considering an insanity plea, must weigh all the evidence, including the presumption of sanity. . . . Whether uncontradicted expert testimony overcomes the presumption depends upon its weight and credibility, and weight and credibility ordinarily are for the jury. . . . Our purpose now is to make it very clear that neither the court nor the jury is bound by *ad hoc* definitions or conclusions as to what experts state is a disease or defect. What psychiatrists may consider a "mental disease or defect" for clinical purposes, where their concern is treatment, may or may not be the same as mental disease or defect for the jury's purpose in determining criminal responsibility.

Finally, and perhaps most importantly, the court set forth an additional definition of "mental disease or defect," namely, "a mental disease or defect includes any abnormal condition of the mind which substantially affects mental or emotional processes and substantially impairs behavior controls."

Thus, in *McDonald*, the trial courts were given some guidelines as to how much evidence is needed to raise the insanity defense and shift the burden of proof to the prosecution, and, once the defense is raised and the burden shifted, the weight the jury or court should give to expert and lay testimony in determining the criminal responsibility of the

accused. *McDonald*, as did *Durham*, left the ultimate burden of proving the defendant's sanity beyond a reasonable doubt upon the prosecution.

While *McDonald*, as stated, relieved some of the difficulties inherent in the *Durham* rule, like the redoubtable Hydra, problems survived the decision and more have arisen. What follows is a discussion of some of these existing problems with specific recommendations for remedies where they would seem to be appropriate.

Several cases have illustrated that there has also arisen a dispute in the Court of Appeals about the meaning of *McDonald*, especially with regard to what constitutes "some evidence" and the weight that should be accorded to expert testimony. I feel that this is unfortunate, but see no alternative to leaving the matter to judicial interpretation. An *en banc* decision further delineating and defining "some evidence" would be helpful, in providing uniformity and certainty in the law. . . .

As hereinbefore mentioned, there are psychiatrists who believe antisocial acts are symptomatic of a mental disease or defect. Stated more bluntly, these psychiatrists have the opinion, and will so testify, that any person who commits a crime is suffering from a mental disease and that the crime is the product of the disease. When a psychiatrist of this school testifies as to the criminal responsibility of one who commits a crime, an antisocial act, "a sound ground exists for a juror's reasonable doubt as to . . . defendant's legal sanity," and this is all that is required for a verdict of "not guilty by reason of insanity." In such cases, the prosecution is thus placed in the position of being required, by reason of the burden of proof, to remove any and all reasonable doubt that the accused was *not* mentally ill in order to avoid a verdict of "not guilty by reason of insanity." This burden, which in many cases is insuperable, results in a defendant, with such psychiatric testimony at his disposal, being found not guilty by reason of insanity and placed in a mental institution eligible for an early release from custody under circumstances hereinafter set forth. In this manner the public safety is endangered, disrespect for the law is generated, and fear of punishment is decreased. This latter encourages infractions by others because of a belief that if they violate the law and are apprehended, they can "bug out," to use their picturesque but expressive vernacular.

In the District of Columbia the problem has become more acute for still another reason, which I shall now discuss. In addition to whatever opinions a defendant is able to obtain from private psychiatrists who adhere to the view above expressed that antisocial conduct can be equated with mental disease, the official staff position of Saint Elizabeths Hospital, to which the Government looks for psychiatric testimony, since 1959 has been that "people suffering from sociopathic personality disturbance should be 'labeled' as diseased, as mentally ill." Some staff psychiatrists of the hospital have wavered in, and some have disagreed with this view, but the staff position has remained unchanged since then. On the other hand, there is substantial psychiatric support for the previously held opinion of Saint Elizabeths Hospital that antisocial acts are not necessarily indicative of a mental disease or defect. For example, the Commission on Mental Health of the District Court adheres to this earlier opinion of long standing; and in the American Law Institute Model Code, in order to prevent miscarriages of justice flowing from this relatively recent concept, it is provided that antisocial conduct be expressly excluded from the terms "mental disease or defect."

I do not subscribe to the view that an abnormality manifested only by antisocial acts should be completely excluded from the term "mental disease or defect," as provided in the A.L.I. Model Code, because I feel that the criminal responsibility of a sociopath or psychopath depends upon the degree of the "illness," and that an antisocial act in some cases may be symptomatic of a "mental disease or defect." I only say that the present requirement of the law which places the burden on the Government to prove beyond a reasonable doubt that the defendant was *not* suffering from a mental illness at the time of the offense in cases involving sociopathic behavior is an unjustifiable burden and on occasions results in otherwise guilty defendants going unwhipped of justice. Placing the burden, as I have suggested, would avoid this onerous requirement of the law, and tend to remove this avenue of escaping punishment. It would at the same time still provide defendants with the full spectrum of psychiatric defenses and testimony.

In this connection, it is interesting to mention how this changed position of Saint Elizabeths Hospital came about in 1959. In *Blocker* v. *United States,* 107 U.S. App. D.C. 63, defendant, who had been indicted for murder in the first degree, defended on the ground of insanity. This defense was rejected by the jury, and he was found guilty, sentenced to death, and appealed. Three psychiatrists testified at his trial, two called by the defense, one by the prosecution. All three were on the staff of Saint Elizabeths Hospital. The psychiatrist called by the Government testified that he found nothing wrong with defendant. The other two concluded that he suffered from a sociopathic personality disturbance with chronic alcoholism, but that this was not considered to be a mental disease or defect, thus removing the evidential basis for the insanity defense under the *Durham* rule. Less than a month after this verdict was returned, the Assistant Superintendent of Saint Elizabeths Hospital testified in another case that the Superintendent and he were then agreed "that people suffering from sociopathic personality disturbance should be 'labeled' as diseased, as mentally ill, mentally sick, suffering from mental disease." Counsel for defendant Blocker, on learning of this testimony, moved for a new trial on the basis of "new medical evidence." This motion was denied, but the Court of Appeals thought it should have been granted and the case was reversed and remanded for a new trial.

This later position of Saint Elizabeths Hospital, which as we have stated has since become its official position, was an abrupt about-face from the position previously taken. Defendant Blocker was accordingly retried, but in the retrial the court placed the burden of proof on the defendant and he was convicted a second time and sentenced to death. Again the case was appealed and again was reversed, this time because of the Court's instruction placing the burden on the defendant to establish the defense of insanity. He was later tried for the third time and convicted of second degree murder. On appeal from this last conviction, the sentence was affirmed on the lesser included offense of second degree murder.

Another reason for my recommendation, which pertains to all mental illnesses, including those of the sociopathic variety, is that by placing the burden of proof by a preponderance of the evidence on defendant, a harmful hiatus would be removed from the law. This hiatus or inconsistency in the law, and evils flowing therefrom, arise from the difference in the quantum of proof required to acquit a defendant by reason of insanity (that is, a failure by the prosecution to prove beyond a reasonable doubt that defendant was *not* suffering from a mental disease, or if he was that the crime was *not* the product of the disease) and the quantum of proof required to enable a defendant found not guilty by reason of insanity to gain his release after commitment to Saint Elizabeths Hospital, hereinafter set forth. At present, as stated, any reasonable doubt of an accused's sanity requires a jury to acquit him by reason of insanity. Such an acquittal, however, is not adjudication of insanity or mental incapacity, *Green* v. *United States,* 122 U.S. App. D.C. 33, 35 (1965), but is merely a finding by the jury that the government failed to carry its burden as above stated. However, once acquitted, and committed to a mental hospital, pursuant to D.C. Code 24–301 (d) 1961, a preponderance of the evidence that he "has recovered [*sic*] his sanity and will not in the reasonable future be dangerous to himself or others" is sufficient for defendant to obtain his unconditional release by habeas corpus under D.C. Code 24-301 (e). It thus takes less proof for a defendant to obtain a verdict of not guilty by reason of insanity than it does to obtain a release after such a verdict; and it might be argued at first blush that this is desirable from the standpoint of protection of society. But it does not work out that way. For example, an accused whose mental condition at the trial stage meets the unconditional release test above stated, may nevertheless be found not guilty by reason of insanity if he can muster up "some" evidence of insanity (e.g., evidence that criminal conduct connotes insanity) requiring a verdict of not guilty by reason of insanity under the onerous burden now placed on the Government to establish sanity beyond a reasonable doubt. In such circumstances, the accused would be committed to a mental hospital and shortly thereafter would be unconditionally released and commingling with the public, freed from punishment for his criminal acts. This is a fact and not a theory.

In this connection, and in further support for a shift in the burden of proof from the Government to the defendant, it is appropriate to lay bare some of the bizarre results growing out of the acceptance by the staff of Saint Elizabeths Hospital that a sociopathic personality disorder, *per se*, constitutes a mental disease. Almost one-fourth of all admissions to Saint Elizabeths Hospital after verdicts of not guilty by reason of insanity are classified as persons suffering from a personality disorder. These are defendants some of whom would otherwise be found guilty and held accountable to society for their crimes. Instead, they escape punishment. not for the reason that they have been found to be mentally ill because, as above stated, a verdict of not guilty by reason of insanity is not such a finding, but because the prosecution has been confronted with the almost impossible burden of proving beyond a reasonable doubt that they were not suffering from a mental disease at the time of the offense, in the face of psychiatric testimony from Saint Elizabeths Hospital that they were. . . .

BAXSTROM v. HEROLD

MR. CHIEF JUSTICE WARREN delivered the opinion of the Court.

We granted certiorari in this case to consider the constitutional validity of the statutory procedure under which petitioner was committed to a mental institution at the expiration of his criminal sentence in a state prison.

Petitioner, Johnnie K. Baxstrom, was convicted of second degree assault in April 1959 and was sentenced to a term of two and one-half to three years in a New York prison. On June 1, 1961, he was certified as insane by a prison physician. He was then transferred from prison to Dannemora State Hospital, an institution under the jurisdiction and control of the New York Department of Correction and used for the purpose of confining and caring for male prisoners declared mentally ill while serving a criminal sentence. In November 1961, the director of Dannemora filed a petition in the Surrogate's Court of Clinton County stating that Baxstrom's penal sentence was about to terminate and requesting that he be civilly committed pursuant to § 384 of New York Correction Law.

On December 6, 1961, a proceeding was held in the Surrogate's chambers. Medical certificates were submitted by the State which stated that, in the opinion of two of its examining physicians, Baxstrom was still mentally ill and in need of hospital and institutional care. Respondent, then assistant director at Dannemora, testified that in his opinion Baxstrom was still mentally ill. Baxstrom, appear-

U.S. Supreme Court, 383 U.S. 107 (1966).

ing alone, was accorded a brief opportunity to ask questions. Respondent and the Surrogate both stated that they had no objection to his being transferred from Dannemora to a civil hospital under the jurisdiction of the Department of Mental Hygiene. But the Surrogate pointed out that he had no jurisdiction to determine that question—that under § 384 the decision was entirely up to the Department of Mental Hygiene. The Surrogate then signed a certificate which indicated he was satisfied that Baxstrom "may require mental care and treatment" in an institution for the mentally ill. The Department of Mental Hygiene had already determined *ex parte* that Baxstrom was not suitable for care in a civil hospital. Thus, on December 18, 1961, the date upon which Baxstrom's penal sentence expired, custody over him shifted from the Department of Correction to the Department of Mental Hygiene, but he was retained at Dannemora and has remained there to this date.

Thereafter, Baxstrom sought a writ of habeas corpus in a state court. An examination by an independent psychiatrist was ordered and a hearing was held at which the examining psychiatrist testified that, in his opinion, Baxstrom was still mentally ill. The writ was dismissed. In 1963, Baxstrom applied again for a writ of habeas corpus, alleging that his constitutional rights had been violated and that he was then sane, or if insane, he should be transferred to a civil mental hospital. Due to his indigence and his incarceration in Dannemora, Baxstrom could not produce psychiatric testimony to disprove the testimony adduced at the prior hearing. The writ was therefore dismissed. Baxstrom's alternative request for transfer to a civil mental hospital was again denied as being beyond the power of the court despite a statement by the State's attorney that he wished that Baxstrom would be transferred to a civil mental hospital. . . .

We hold that petitioner was denied equal protection of the laws by the statutory procedure under which a person may be civilly committed at the expiration of his penal sentence without the jury review available to all other persons civilly committed in New York. Petitioner was further denied equal protection of the laws by his civil commitment to an institution maintained by the Department of Correction beyond the expiration of his prison term without a judicial determination that he is dangerously mentally ill such as that afforded to all so committed except those, like Baxstrom, nearing the expiration of a penal sentence.

Section 384 of New York Correction Law prescribes the procedure for civil commitment upon the expiration of the prison term of a

mentally ill person confined in Dannemora.[1] Similar procedures are prescribed for civil commitment of all other allegedly mentally ill persons. All persons civilly committed, however, other than those committed at the expiration of a penal term, are expressly granted the right to *de novo* review by jury trial of the question of their sanity . . . Under this procedure any person dissatisfied with an order certifying him as mentally ill may demand full review by a jury of the prior determination as to his competency. If the jury returns a verdict that the person is sane, he must be immediately discharged. It follows that the State, having made this substantial review proceeding generally available on this issue, may not, consistent with the Equal Protection Clause of the Fourteenth Amendment, arbitrarily withhold it from some.

The Director contends that the State has created a reasonable classification differentiating the civilly insane from the "criminally insane," which he defines as those with dangerous or criminal propensities. Equal protection does not require that all persons be dealt with identically, but it does require that a distinction made have some relevance to the purpose for which the classification is made. Classification of mentally ill persons as either insane or dangerously insane of course may be a reasonable distinction for purposes of determining the type of custodial or medical care to be given, but it has no relevance whatever in the context of the opportunity to show whether a person is mentally ill *at all*. For purposes of granting judicial review before a jury of the question whether a person is mentally ill and in need of institutionalization, there is no conceivable basis for distinguishing the commitment of a person who is nearing

[1] As it appeared when applied to petitioner in 1961, N.Y. Correction Law § 384 provided in part:

"1.Within thirty days prior to the expiration of the term of a prisoner confined in the Dannemora State Hospital, when in the opinion of the director such prisoner continues insane, the director shall apply to a judge of a court of record for the certification of such person as provided in the mental hygiene law for the certification of a person not in confinement on a criminal charge. The court in which such proceedings are instituted shall, if satisfied that such person may require care and treatment in an institution for the mentally ill, issue an order directing that such person be committed to the custody of the commissioner of mental hygiene to be placed in an appropriate state institution of the department of mental hygiene or of the department of correction as may be designated for the custody of such person by agreement between the heads of the two departments."

the end of a penal term from all other civil commitments.

The statutory procedure provided in § 384 of New York Correction Law denied Baxstrom the equal protection of the laws in another respect as well. Under § 384 the judge need only satisfy himself that the person "may require care and treatment in an institution for the mentally ill." Having made such a finding, the decision whether to commit that person to a hospital maintained by the Department of Correction or to a civil hospital is completely in the hands of administrative officials. Except for persons committed to Dannemora upon expiration of sentence under § 384, all others civilly committed to hospitals maintained by the Department of Correction are committed only after judicial proceedings have been held in which it is determined that the person is so dangerously mentally ill that his presence in a civil hospital is dangerous to the safety of other patients or employees, or to the community.[2]

This statutory classification cannot be justified by the contention that Dannemora is substantially similar to other mental hospitals in the State and that commitment to one hospital or another is simply an administrative matter affecting no fundamental rights. The parties have described various characteristics of Dannemora to show its similarities and dissimilarities to civil hospitals in New York. As striking as the dissimilarites are, we need not make any factual determination as to the nature of Dannemora; the New York State Legislature has already made that determination. By statute, the hospital is under the jurisdiction of the Department of Correction and is used for the purpose of confining and caring for insane prisoners and persons, like Baxstrom, committed at the expiration of a penal term. Civil mental hospitals in New York, on the other hand, are under the jurisdiction and control of the Department of Mental Hygiene. Certain privileges of patients at Dannemora are restricted by statute. Moreover, as has been noted, specialized statutory procedures are prescribed for commitment to hospitals under the jurisdiction of the Department of Correction. While we may assume that transfer among like mental hospitals is a purely administrative function, where, as here, the State has created functionally distinct institutions, classification of patients for involuntary commitment to one of these institutions may not be wholly arbitrary.

The Director argues that it is reasonable to classify persons in Baxstrom's class together with those found to be dangerously insane since such persons are not only insane but have proven criminal tendencies as shown by their past criminal record. . . .

We find this contention untenable. Where the State has provided for a judicial proceeding to determine the dangerous propensities of all others civilly committed to an institution of the Department of Correction, it may not deny this right to a person in Baxstrom's position solely on the ground that he was nearing the expiration of a prison term.[3] It may or may not be that Baxstrom is presently mentally ill and such a danger to others that the strict security of a Department of Correction hospital is warranted. All others receive a judicial hearing on this issue. Equal protection demands that Baxstrom receive the same.

The capriciousness of the classification employed by the State is thrown sharply into focus by the fact that the full benefit of a judicial hearing to determine dangerous tendencies is withheld only in the case of civil commitment of one awaiting expiration of penal sentence. A person with a past criminal record is presently entitled to a hearing on the question whether he is dangerously mentally ill so long as he is not in prison at the time civil commitment proceedings are instituted. Given this distinction, all semblance of rationality of the classification, purportedly based upon criminal propensities, disappears.

In order to accord to petitioner the equal protection of the laws, he was and is entitled

---

[2] . . . Former § 412 of Correction Law, permitting commitment to Matteawan State Hospital of any patient who had previously been sentenced to a term of imprisonment, without the benefit of the proceeding accorded others under § 85 of Mental Hygiene Law, was held unconstitutional as a denial of equal protection in *United States ex rel. Carroll v. McNeill*, 294 F. 2d 117 (C.A. 2d Cir. 1961), probable jurisdiction noted, 368 U.S. 951, vacated and dismissed as moot, 369 U.S. 149, and was repealed by N.Y. Laws 1965, c. 524. Even that provision required a showing that the person still manifested criminal tendencies.

[3] In oral argument, counsel for respondent suggested that the determination by the Department of Mental Hygiene to detain a person in Dannemora must be based not only on his past criminal record, but also on evidence that he is currently dangerous. Far from supporting the validity of the procedure, this only serves to further accent the arbitrary nature of the classification. Under this procedure, all civil commitments to an institution under the control of the Department of Correction require a determination that the person is presently dangerous; all persons so committed are entitled to a judicial proceeding to determine this fact except those awaiting expiration of sentence. Their fate is decided by unreviewable determinations of the Department of Mental Hygiene.

to a review of the determination as to his sanity in conformity with proceedings granted all others civilly committed . . . He is also entitled to a hearing under the procedure granted all others . . . to determine whether he is so dangerously mentally ill that he must remain in a hospital maintained by the Department of Correction. . . .

It is so ordered.

Editorial Note

Following the U.S. Supreme Court's decision in *Baxstrom*, the *New York Times* reported (Feb. 24, 1966) that 460 inmates of Dannemora would have to be released unless civilly committed, noting that "State officials say many of them are potentially dangerous." However, in fact, most of these patients were found to be free of dangerous mental illness and were freed from confinement (see 17 Buffalo L. Rev. 651, 1968).

BOLTON v. HARRIS

BAZELON, Chief Judge

In this appeal from denial of habeas corpus, appellant attacks the mandatory commitment provisions of D.C.Code §24–301(d) [hereinafter Subsection (d)] and the release provisions of D.C.Code §24–301(e). These provisions apply after a successful voluntary plea of not guilty by reason of insanity. The primary contention is that these provisions violate equal protection because they do not afford safeguards available for those civilly committed under the Hospitalization of the Mentally Ill Act of 1964. . . .

Subsection (d) provides for automatic commitment without any hearing, even though acquittal by reason of insanity reflects only a reasonable doubt that the defendant was sane at the time of the offense. . . . A patient confined under Subsection (d) may be released only upon order of the court. The order must be based upon either the certificate of the Superintendent of Saint Elizabeths Hospital or the patient's petition for habeas corpus. The Superintendent may certify either that the patient has recovered his sanity, that he will not be dangerous to himself or others in the foreseeable future, and that he is entitled to unconditional release; or that, while not fully recovered, he is eligible for conditional release. In either case, the court may release the patient on the certificate or it may hold an evidentiary hearing concerning his recovery. It has been held that for release on habeas, the patient must prove beyond a reasonable doubt that he is free "from such abnormal mental condition as would make the individual dangerous to himself or others in the foreseeable future." and, according to some cases, that the Superintendent's refusal to issue a certificate is arbitrary and capricious.

So construed, this statutory scheme would conceivably allow a patient committed under Subsection (d) to remain in the hospital for the rest of his life without a judicial determination that he is mentally ill or that he is still likely to commit dangerous acts. In sharp contrast the 1964 Hospitalization of the Mentally Ill Act, enacted subsequent to the decisions referred to above, requires a judicial determination and places the burden of proving insan-

396 F.2d 642 (1968) (CA–DC).

ity on the Government. It also requires the hospital to examine a civilly committed patient at least every six months and to release him without a court order if the chief of the patient's service then deems him recovered. . . .

Commitment without a hearing is permissible for the period required to determine present mental condition. The jury's finding of a reasonable doubt as to defendant's sanity at the time of the offense provides sufficient warrant for further examination.

The length of time required for such examination will vary, of course, with the individual case. It will be the responsibility of the court to establish this period, just as it now orders the hospital to make a determination and report its findings when the question of an accused's competency to stand trial is raised. The courts in this jurisdiction have sufficient experience with the problems involved to make individual judgments.

Once the examination period is over, however, there is no rational basis for denying a hearing. It is true that persons acquitted by reason of insanity have committed criminal acts and that this fact may tend to show they meet the requirements for commitment, namely illness and dangerousness. But it does not remove these requirements. Nor does it justify total abandonment of the procedures used in civil commitment proceedings to determine whether these same requirements have been satisfied. Hence persons found not guilty by reason of insanity must be given a judicial hearing with procedures substantially similar to those in civil commitment proceedings. . . . After acquittal by reason of insanity there is also need for a new finding of fact. The trial determined only that there was a reasonable doubt as to the defendant's sanity in the past, present commitment is predicated on a finding of present insanity. . . .

The question then arises how a person thus committed can obtain release. We uphold the release provisions of §24–301(e) even though they differ from civil commitment procedures by authorizing court review of the hospital's decision to release a patient. We do not think equal protection is offended by allowing the Government or the court the opportunity to insure that the standards for the release of civilly committed patients are faithfully applied to Subsection (d) patients.

We note, however, that under civil commitment procedures, a patient is entitled to periodic examinations by the hospital staff and has the right to be examined by an outside psychiatrist. If just one of the examining physicians believes he should no longer be hospitalized, he is entitled to a court hearing. Subsection (e) provides none of these safeguards. Because we find no rational justification for withholding these safeguards from a Subsection (d) patient, we construe Subsection (e) to require them.

Subsection (d) patients may also establish their eligibility for release by a writ of habeas corpus. This court has often debated what the burden of proof should be in such habeas proceedings. But it follows from our view of the requirements of equal protection that the burden for Subsection (d) patients must be the same as that for civilly committed patients. While the criminal acts committed by a Subsection (d) patient may be evidence indicating whether or not the burden has been met, they do not justify a different burden.

Unfortunately, the cases in this jurisdiction do not make clear what the burden of proof is in habeas proceedings challenging civil commitment. It could be argued that the Government should have the burden of proving that the patient is still committable, since this is where the burden lies in the initial commitment proceedings. But the traditional rule in habeas corpus proceedings is that the petitioner must prove, by the preponderance of the evidence, that his detention is illegal. We conclude that the traditional rule should apply, particularly since we have previously held that the hospital must assist the court in acquiring all the relevant information on the patient's condition, treatment, etc. Thus, the court must find, by the preponderance of the evidence, that the patient's commitment is no longer valid—i.e., that he is no longer "likely to injure himself or other persons" due to "mental illness. . . .

Accordingly, we reverse the judgment and remand with directions to issue the writ unless the Subsection (d) commitment procedures required by this opinion are instituted within thirty days.

District of Columbia Court Reform and Criminal Procedure Act of 1970, 91st Congress, 2d Session, 1970

"If any person tried upon an indictment or information for an offense raises the defense of insanity and is acquitted solely on the ground that he was insane at the time of its commission, he shall be committed to a hospital for the mentally ill until such time as he is eligible for release pursuant to this subsection. . . .

"A person confined pursuant to paragraph (1) shall have a hearing, unless waived, within 50 days of his confinement to determine whether he is entitled to release from custody. . . . (T)he court shall provide such person with representation by counsel. . . . The person confined shall have the burden of proof. If the court finds by a preponderance of the evidence that the person confined is entitled to his release from custody, either conditional or unconditional, the court shall enter such order as may appear appropriate. . . ."

"No person accused of an offense shall be acquitted on the ground that he was insane at the time of its commission unless his insanity, regardless of who raises the issue, is affirmatively established by a preponderance of the evidence."

WASHINGTON v. UNITED STATES

A strong minority of this court has consistently advocated that psychiatrists be prohibited from testifying whether the alleged offense was the "product" of mental illness, since this is part of the ultimate issue to be decided by the jury. We now adopt that view. The term "product" has no clinical significance to the psychiatrist. Thus there is no justification for permitting psychiatrists to testify on the ultimate issue. Psychiatrists should explain how defendant's disease or defect relates to his alleged offense, that is, how the development, adaptation and functioning of defendant's behavioral processes may have influenced his conduct. But psychiatrists should not speak directly in terms of "product," or even "results" or "causes."

It can be argued that psychiatrists should also be prohibited from testifying whether the defendant suffered from a "mental disease or defect," since this too is part of the ultimate issue. But unlike the term "product" the term "mental disease or defect" may have some clinical significance to the psychiatrist. Moreover, prohibition of testimony about "mental disease or defect" would not be a panacea. Other words and other concepts may similarly be transformed into labels. For example, in *McDonald* we spoke about "abnormal" conditions of the mind, about impairment of mental and emotional processes, and about control mechanisms.

At least for now, rather than prohibit testimony on "mental disease or defect" we shall try to help the psychiatrists understand their role in court, and thus eliminate a fundamental cause of unsatisfactory expert testimony. A copy of the explanatory instructions to psychiatrists which we have set out in the appendix should accompany all orders requiring mental examinations so that the psychiatrists will be advised of the kind of information they are expected to provide. To insure that counsel and the jury are also so advised, the trial judge should give the explanatory instruction in open court to the first psychiatric witness immediately after he has qualified as an expert. It need not be repeated to later witnesses.

390 F.2d 444 (1967) (CA–DC).

[APPENDIX]

Court's Instruction to Expert Witness in Case Involving the "Insanity Defense"

Dr. ―――, this instruction is being given to you in advance of your testimony as an expert witness, in order to avoid confusion or misunderstanding. The instruction is not only for your guidance, but also for the guidance of counsel and the jury.

Because you have qualified as an expert witness your testimony is governed by special rules. Under ordinary rules, witnesses are allowed to testify about what they have seen and heard, but are not always allowed to express opinions and conclusions based on these observations. Due to your training and experience, you are allowed to draw conclusions and give opinions in the area of your special qualifications. However, you may not state conclusions or opinions as an expert unless you also tell the jury what investigations, observations, reasoning, and medical theory led to your opinion.

As an expert witness you may, if you wish and if you feel you can, give your opinion about whether the defendant suffered from a mental disease or defect. You may then explain how defendant's disease or defect relates to his alleged offense, that is, how the development, adaptation and functioning of defendant's behavioral processes may have influenced his conduct. This explanation should be so complete that the jury will have a basis for an informed judgment on whether the alleged crime was a "product" of his mental disease or defect. But it will not be necessary for you to express an opinion on whether the alleged crime was a "product" of a mental disease or defect and you will not be asked to do so.

It must be emphasized that you are to give your expert diagnosis of the defendant's mental condition. This word of caution is especially important if you give an opinion as to whether or not the defendant suffered from a "mental disease or defect" because the clinical diagnostic meaning of this term may be different from its legal meaning. You should not be concerned with its legal meaning. Neither should you consider whether you think this defendant should be found guilty or responsible for the alleged crime. These are questions for the court and jury. Further, there are considerations which may be relevant in other proceedings or in other contexts which are not relevant here; for example, how the defendant's condition might change, or whether there are adequate hospital facilities, or whether commitment in the courtroom is the kind of opinion you would give to a family which brought one of its members to your clinic and asked for your diagnosis of his mental condition and a description of how his condition would be likely to influence his conduct. Insofar as counsel's questions permit, you should testify in this manner.

When you are asked questions which fall within the scope of your special training and experience, you may answer them if you feel competent to do so; otherwise you should not answer them. If the answer depends upon knowledge and experience generally possessed by ordinary citizens, for example questions of morality as distinguished from medical knowledge, you should not answer. You should try to separate expert medical judgments from what we may call "lay judgments." If you cannot make a separation and if you do answer the question nonetheless, you should state clearly that your answer is not based solely upon your special knowledge. It would be misleading for the jury to think that your testimony is based on your special knowledge concerning the nature and diagnosis of mental conditions if in fact it is not.

In order that the jury may understand exactly what you mean, you should try to explain things in simple language. Avoid technical terms whenever possible. Where medical terms are useful or unavoidable, make sure you explain these terms clearly. If possible, the explanation should not be merely general or abstract but should be related to this defendant, his behavior, and his condition. Where words or phrases used by counsel are unclear, or may have more than one meaning, you should ask for clarification before answering. You should then explain your answer so that your understanding of the question is clear. You need not give "yes or no" answers. In this way any confusion may be cleared up before the questioning goes on.

Some final words of caution. Because we have an adversary system, counsel may deem it is his duty to attack your testimony. You should not construe this as an attack upon your integrity. More specifically, counsel may try to undermine your opinions as lacking certainty or adequate basis. We recognize that an opinion may be merely a balance of probabilities and that we cannot demand absolute certainty. Thus you may testify to opinions that are within the zone of reasonable medical certainty. The crucial point is that the jury should know how your opinion may be affected by limitations of time or facilities in the examination of this defendant or by limitations in present psychiatric knowledge. The underlying facts you have obtained may be so scanty or the state of professional knowledge so unsure that you cannot fairly venture any opinion. If so, you should not hesitate to say so. And again, if you do give an opinion, you should explain what these facts are, how they led to the opinion, and what, if any, are the uncertainties in the opinion.

ADAMS v. UNITED STATES

BAZELON, Chief Judge:

The appellant contends that the trial court erred as a matter of law in rejecting his insanity defense. The case arises from the holdup of a National Capital Housing Authority office on June 21, 1967. Four employees witnessed the robbery and getaway, at least one of whom saw the license plate of the rented car in which the hold-up man drove away. The appellant was arrested several hours later when he attempted to pay the rental fee for the car.

After a trial without a jury, Adams was convicted for robbery of property belonging to the United States, assault with a dangerous weapon and carrying a dangerous weapon under 18 U.S.C. §2112 (1964) and 22 D.C. Code §§502, 2901 (1967). The evidence of guilt was strong, and the defense relied principally upon the claim that the offense was the product of mental illness. . . .

After a series of petty offenses as a juvenile for which he was placed under probation, the appellant was sent to the National Training School in 1938 for housebreaking. He has spent 28 of the 31 years since then in a succession of reformatories and prisons. Most of his numerous convictions are for housebreaking. On the nine occasions he has been free in the past 30 years, he has never succeeded in staying out of jail for as long as a year; in the last 20 of these years his longest period of freedom has been five months. . . .

The experts testifying at trial presented conflicting explanations for the appellant's repeated offenses. Dr. William Schwartz, the staff psychiatrist at Saint Elizabeths Hospital who had examined Adams during his Section 301(a) commitment, diagnosed the appellant as suffering from an antisocial-reaction personality disorder. He acknowledged, however, "[T]he label . . . is simply picked out of a book. It really doesn't completely describe Mr. Adams."

. . . Dr. Schwartz stated that his evaluation was based upon his personal interviews with Adams and the results of psychological tests conducted at the hospital, he also attached substantial importance to the appellant's criminal record. . . . He refused, however, to follow the prosecutor's invitation to say that recidivism alone would indicate a mental disturbance. . . .

Dr. Elliott Blum ,a psychologist at Saint Elizabeths Hospital who also testified for the defense, agreed with Dr. Schwartz that the appellant suffered from a psychiatric problem but differed as to its dynamics. On the basis of a psychological test he administered before the 1967 trial, and to a lesser extent on the basis of certain 1960 tests performed at Saint Elizabeths during an earlier Section 301(a) commitment, Dr. Blum "felt Mr. Adams was somewhat more tormented inside than an antisocial reaction is and he has more anxiety than the antisocial reaction". . . . Dr. Blum was inclined to believe that Adams' criminal offenses represented a species of defense mechanism rather than a primary manifestation of his character. The high anxiety levels shown by the appellant in the psychological test results, together with certain test responses indicative of a schizophrenic thought process, suggested to Dr. Blum that Adams "is a very immature, a very insecure, very inferior feeling person who instead of being overwhelmed with his symptomatology in terms of just, as we say, go off the deepend, he is able to utilize certain types of defenses, certain types of adaptive behavior which keeps his self-esteem up to a level where he will not fall apart."

Accordingly, Dr. Blum preferred to describe the appellant as a pseudo-neurotic schizophrenic. . . .

Dr. Morris Platkin, the psychiatrist in charge of the maximum security facility at Saint Elizabeths Hospital, testified for the Government in rebuttal that the appellant was without mental disorder. Although Dr. Platkin had never examined Adams, he had scrutinized the hospital records and presided over the steaff conference in 1967 at the time of the appellant's pretrial commitment. Adams' behavior patterns did not, for Dr. Platkin, indicate a sociopathic personality of the antisocial reaction type: "[M]y interpretation of what is meant by sociopathic personality is—an antisocial reaction is the type of individual who to begin with his criminal activities are generally of the manipulating kind. They do not involve aggressiveness whether against an individual or property in the sense of breaking into. They would involve, for example, check writing or various types of confidence activities. . . . [I] don't believe I have ever met a sociopath who has committed housebreakings. This isn't the kind of things that they do." . . .

Dr. Platkin concluded—as undoubtedly would much of the community—that a perfectly rational economic man with "limited schooling . . . and the lack of technical knowledge" might turn to robbery and housebreaking as the easiest, indeed perhaps the only way to satisfy his expensive tastes. . . .

And Dr. Blum, criticizing the view that Adams has simply devoted a life to earning a good living in a businesslike if criminal manner, stated, "I think a professional criminal would be a well—the best professional criminal is a well integrated individual. Mr. Adams is not. A professional criminal has friends and can stick to a job, how be it but he can stick to it. A professional criminal can meet stresses and can meet every day living and has loyalties towards different groups and things of this sort. . . ."

Dr. Schwartz gave probably the best explanation of their disagreement: "It is simply that the time the hospital has for examining these patients, we can not learn to know what the basic motivation is of the patient. . . ."

This case presents neither the powerful showing of mental illness nor the sort of bizarre crime suggestive on its face of mental illness which have characterized the cases in which this court has found an insanity acquittal required as a matter of law. The expert testimony was in conflict. It is true that Dr. Platkins's opportunity to evaluate the appellant's mental condition was limited at best. But we have affirmed convictions, however uneasily, in other cases where rebuttal testimony left much to be desired.

Guided by the prior decisions of this court, to which we adhere, and the evidence in this case, we affirm the conviction. In doing so, we cannot but note that society has proven even less able to cope with this man than he with it. . . . Dr. Schwartz testified, "The treatment that we can offer him is very inadequate and the chances of his personality improving . . . are very slim." If this is true, perhaps society must continue simply to lock up the appellant each time he offends. By doing so we may protect our homes. But the present criminal process allows us to pursue this legitimate goal only by the fiction that he is an evil man. The fact that the insanity defense as presently conceptualized and administered plays handmaiden to this social hypocrisy further reveals our inadequacy to respond selectively or constructively to offenders.

Affirmed.

EXCERPTS FROM THE AMERICAN LAW INSTITUTE MODEL PENAL CODE, 1962, PROPOSED OFFICIAL DRAFT

Section 4.01. Mental Disease or Defect Excluding Responsibility.

(1) A person is not responsible for criminal conduct if at the time of such conduct as a result of mental disease or defect he lacks substantial capacity either to appreciate the criminality [wrongfulness] of his conduct or to conform his conduct to the requirements of law.

(2) As used in this Article, the terms "mental disease or defect" do not include an abnormality manifested only by repeated criminal or otherwise anti-social conduct.

Section 4.02. Evidence of Mental Disease or Defect Admissible When Relevant to Element of the Offense; [Mental Disease or Defect Impairing Capacity as Ground for Mitigation of Punishment in Capital Cases].

(1) Evidence that the defendant suffered from a mental disease or defect is admissible whenever it is relevant to prove that the defendant did or did not have a state of mind which is an element of the offense.

[(2) Whenever the jury or the Court is

Reprinted with permission, American Law Institute.

authorized to determine or to recommend whether or not the defendant shall be sentenced to death or imprisonment upon conviction, evidence that the capacity of the defendant to appreciate the criminality [wrongfulness] of his conduct or to conform his conduct to the requirements of law was impaired as a result of mental disease or defect is admissible in favor of sentence of imprisonment.]

Section 4.03. Mental Disease or Defect Excluding Responsibility Is Affirmative Defense; Requirement of Notice; Form of Verdict and Judgment When Finding of Irresponsibility Is Made.

(1) Mental disease or defect excluding responsibility is an affirmative defense.

(2) Evidence of mental disease or defect excluding responsibility is not admissible unless the defendant, at the time of entering his plea of not guilty or within ten days thereafter or at such later time as the Court may for good cause permit, files a written notice of his purpose to rely on such defense.

(3) When the defendant is acquitted on the ground of mental disease or defect excluding responsibility, the verdict and the judgment shall so state.

Section 4.05. Psychiatric Examination of Defendant with Respect to Mental Disease or Defect.

(1) Whenever the defendant has filed a notice of intention to rely on the defense of mental disease or defect excluding responsibility, or there is reason to doubt his fitness to proceed, or reason to believe that mental disease or defect of the defendant will otherwise become an issue in the cause, the Court shall appoint at least one qualified psychiatrist or shall request the Superintendent of the Hospital to designate at least one qualified psychiatrist, which designation may be or include himself, to examine and report upon the mental condition of the defendant. The Court may order the defendant to be committed to a hospital or other suitable facility for the purpose of the examination for a period of not exceeding sixty days or such longer period as the Court determines to be necessary for the purpose and may direct that a qualified psychiatrist retained by the defendant be permitted to witness and participate in the examination.

(2) In such examination any method may be employed which is accepted by the medical profession for the examination of those alleged to be suffering from mental disease or defect.

(3) The report of the examination shall include the following: (a) a description of the nature of the examination; (b) a diagnosis of the mental condition of the defendant; (c) if the defendant suffers from a mental disease or defect, an opinion as to his capacity to understand the proceedings against him and to assist in his own defense; (d) when a notice of intention to rely on the defense of irresponsibility has been filed, an opinion as to the extent, if any, to which the capacity of the defendant to appreciate the criminality [wrongfulness] of his conduct or to conform his conduct to the requirements of law was impaired at the time of the criminal conduct charged; and (e) when directed by the Court, an opinion as to the capacity of the defendant to have a particular state of mind which is an element of the offense charged.

If the examination can not be conducted by reason of the unwillingness of the defendant to participate therein, the report shall so state and shall include, if possible, an opinion as to whether such unwillingness of the defendant was the result of mental disease or defect.

The report of the examination shall be filed [in triplicate] with the clerk of the Court, who shall cause copies to be delivered to the district attorney and to counsel for the defendant.

Section 4.08. Legal Effect of Acquittal on the Ground of Mental Disease or Defect Excluding Responsibility; Commitment; Release or Discharge.

(1) When a defendant is acquitted on the ground of mental disease or defect excluding responsibility, the Court shall order him to be committed to the custody of the Commissioner of Mental Hygiene [Public Health] to be placed in an appropriate institution for custody, care and treatment.

(2) If the Commissioner of Mental Hygiene [Public Health] is of the view that a person committed to his custody, pursuant to paragraph (1) of this Section, may be discharged or released on condition without danger to himself or to others, he shall make application for the discharge or release of such person in a report to the Court by which such person was committed and shall transmit a copy of such application and report to the prosecuting attorney of the county [parish] from which the defendant was committed. The Court shall thereupon appoint at least two qualified psychiatrists to examine such person and to report within sixty days, or such longer period as the Court determines to be necessary for the purpose, their opinion as to his mental condition. To facilitate such examination and the pro-

ceedings thereon, the Court may cause such person to be confined in any institution located near the place where the Court sits, which may hereafter be designated by the Commissioner of Mental Hygiene [Public Health] as suitable for the temporary detention of irresponsible persons.

(3) If the Court is satisfied by the report filed pursuant to paragraph (2) of this Section and such testimony of the reporting psychiatrists as the Court deems necessary that the committed person may be discharged or released on condition without danger to himself or others, the Court shall order his discharge or his release on such conditions as the Court determines to be necessary. If the Court is not so satisfied, it shall promptly order a hearing to determine whether such person may safely be discharged or released. Any such hearing shall be deemed a civil proceeding and the burden shall be upon the committed person to prove that he may safely be discharged or released. According to the determination of the Court upon the hearing, the committed person shall thereupon be discharged or released on such conditions as the Court determines to be necessary, or shall be recommitted to the custody of the Commissioner of Mental Hygiene [Public Health], subject to discharge or release only in accordance with the procedure prescribed above for a first hearing.

(4) If, within [five] years after the conditional release of a committed person, the Court shall determine, after hearing evidence, that the conditions of release have not been fulfilled and that for the safety of such person or for the safety of others his conditional release should be revoked, the Court shall forthwith order him to be recommitted to the Commissioner of Mental Hygiene [Public Health], subject to discharge or release only in accordance with the procedure prescribed above for a first hearing.

(5) A committed person may make application for his discharge or release to the Court by which he was committed, and the procedure to be followed upon such application shall be the same as that prescribed above in the case of an application by the Commissioner of Mental Hygiene [Public Health]. However, no such application by a committed person need be considered until he has been confined for a period of not less than [six months] from the date of the order of commitment, and if the determination of the Court be adverse to the application, such person shall not be permitted to file a further application until [one year] has elapsed from the date of any preceding hearing on an application for his release or discharge.

Section 4.09. Statements for Purposes of Examination or Treatment Inadmissible Except on Issue of Mental Condition.

A statement made by a person subjected to psychiatric examination or treatment pursuant to Sections 4.05, 4.06 or 4.08 for the purposes of such examination or treatment shall not be admissible in evidence against him in any criminal proceeding on any issue other than that of his mental condition but it shall be admissible upon that issue, whether or not it would otherwise be deemed a privileged communication [, unless such statement constitutes an admission of guilt of the crime charged].

UNITED STATES v. CURRENS

BIGGS, Chief Judge.

Currens, the appellant, was convicted by a jury of a violation of Section 2312, Title 18 U.S.C., the National Motor Vehicle Theft Act, the so-called "Dyer" Act, and was committed as a young adult offender to the custody of the Attorney General for treatment and supervision pursuant to Section 5010 (b) of the Youth Corrections Act, 18 U.S.C. §5010 (b), until discharged by the Federal Youth Correction Division pursuant to law. . . .

We come now to another question which must be decided before we can reach the issue of what rule of criminal responsibility should be imposed in respect to Currens: whether that of M'Naghten or Durham or some other. We are aware that some jurists and legal scholars are of the view that, as a matter of law, a psychopath is not "insane." This view seems to be based on a fear that a rule recognizing that a psychopath may not be capable of possessing a "guilty mind" would open the door to the acquittal of persons accused of crime solely on the basis of a history of recurrent antisocial conduct. It is readily apparent that this objection to the inclusion of psychopaths among those entitled to raise the defense of insanity assumes a particular definition of psychopathy; viz., that the term psychopathy comprehends a person who is a habitual criminal but whose mind is functioning normally. Perhaps some laymen, and, indeed, some psychiatrists, do define the term that broadly; and insofar as the term psychopathy does merely indicate a pattern of recurrent criminal behavior we would certainly agree that it does not describe a disorder which can be considered insanity for purposes of a defense to a criminal action. But, we are aware of the fact that psychopathy, or sociopathy, is a term which means different things to experts in the fields of psychiatry and psychology. Indeed, a confusing welter of literature has grown up about the term, causing some authorities to give up its use in dismay, labelling it a "waste basket category." (See, e.g., C. E. Partridge, "Current Conceptions of Psychopathic Personality," *American Journal of Psychiatry*, 10 (1930): 53–59.)

We have examined much of this literature and have certainly found it no less dismaying than those authorities to which we have just referred. Our study has, however, revealed two very persuasive reasons why this court should not hold that evidence of psychopathy is insufficient, as a matter of law, to put sanity or mental illness in issue. First, it is clear that as the majority of experts use the term, a psychopath is very distinguishable from one who merely demonstrates recurrent criminal behavior. For example, Dr. Winfred Overholser, Superintendent of Saint Elizabeths Hospital in the District of Columbia, has stated that the Hospital takes the unequivocal position that sociopathy is a mental disease. Dr. Overholser, in stating that this is the position of the Hospital, uses the words "the Hospital" in the same sense that a judge uses the term "the court" in expressing the judgment of his tribunal. Moreover, the American Psychiatric Association in 1952 when it published its *Diagnostic and Statistical Manual: Mental Disorders* (Mental Hospital Service), altered its nomenclature (p. 38), removing sociopathic personality disturbance and psychopathic personality disturbance from a non-disease category and placing them in the category of "Mental Disorders." See also note 11, cited to the text, p. 16, in the concurring opinion of Judge Burger in

Blocker v. *United States*, D.C. Cir. 1961, 288 F.2d 853.

One of the most respected, perhaps the leading, modern works on psychopathy is *The Mask of Sanity* by Hervey Cleckley, M.D. (Mosby, 1941). Dr. Cleckley's findings are best summarized in Professor Robert W. White's *The Abnormal Personality* (Ronald Press, 1948) at p. 401 as follows: "He (Cleckley) rules out those cases in which social standards are rejected only in respect to some one particular kind of behavior: for example, alcoholism or deviant sexual behavior in a person otherwise adapted to social demands. He also rules out those cases in which delinquency and crime have been adopted as a positive way of life—in which the person is an enemy of society but is capable of being a loyal and stable member of a delinquent gang. There remains a group characterized by a diffuse and chronic incapacity for persistent, ordered living of any kind. These are, in Cleckley's view, the true psychopathic personalities. They need not be diagnosed negatively, by exclusion of other possibilities. They constitute a true clinical entity with a characteristic pattern of symptoms." After some discussion, Professor White concludes (p. 404): "It is clear that we are dealing with a fairly serious disorder. There are grave disturbances in the patient's affective life as well as in foresight and the control and organization of behavior. Cleckley considers the condition serious enough to be classed as a psychosis. Although the patient outwardly presents a 'convincing mask of sanity' and a 'mimicry of human life,' he has lost contact with the deeper emotional accompaniments of experience and with its purposiveness. To this extent he may be said to have an incomplete contact with reality, and it is certainly very hard to approach him and influence him therapeutically."

Thus, it can be seen in many cases the adjective "psychopathic" will be applied by experts to persons who are very ill indeed. It would not be proper for this court in this case to deprive a large heterogeneous group of offenders of the defense of insanity by holding blindly and indiscriminately that a person described as psychopathic is always criminally responsible.

Our second reason for not holding that psychopaths are "sane" as a matter of law is based on the vagaries of the term itself. In each individual case all the pertinent symptoms of the accused should be put before the court and jury and the accused's criminal responsibility should be developed from the totality of his symptoms. A court of law is not an appropriate forum for a debate as to the meaning of abstract psychiatric classifications. The criminal law is not concerned with such classifications but with the fundamental issue of criminal responsibility. Testimony and argument should relate primarily to the subject of the criminal responsibility of the accused, and specialized terminology should be used only where it is helpful in determining whether a particular defendant should be held to the standards of the criminal law.

It is for such reasons that we feel sure that the Court of Appeals for the District of Columbia Circuit has applied the Durham formula to all types of mental illness including psychopathy or sociopathy. Whether a psychopath or a psychotic suffers from illness of such a nature that he should not be held to criminal responsibility is a jury question in the District of Columbia. *Taylor* v. *United States,* 1955, 95 U.S. App. D.C. 373, 222 F.2d 398, 404; *Stewart* v. *United States,* 1954, 94 U.S. App. D.C. 293, 214 F.2d 879, 881. Indeed, in the case last cited a charge to the jury that a psychopath "is not insane within the meaning of the law" has been held by the Court of Appeals for the District of Columbia Circuit to be reversible error. We think that that Court, in permitting an insanity defense to be employed in the case of a sociopath, is pursuing the correct course, for the mental condition of the accused is one of ultimate fact to be found by the jury, which must always determine the defendant's *mens rea* or lack of it.

For purposes of the present case it is sufficient to point out that the evidence introduced on the issue of Currens' criminal responsibility consists of substantially more than his history of recurrent criminal behavior. A reasonable jury could infer that Currens is mentally incapable of ordered social living; that he is subject to hysterical episodes; that under stress he has many symptoms of the incapacitating disease of schizophrenia; and that he is generally subject to depression, fright, and losses of contact with reality. On the basis of such evidence we believe that a jury reasonably could find that he did not possess the necessary guilty mind when he committed the crime of which he is accused.

The court below, relying on the decision of the Supreme Court of the United States in *Davis* v. *United States, supra,* its first Davis decision in 1895, on the second Davis decision, *Davis* v. *United States,* 1897 (165 U.S. 373, 378, 17 S. Ct. 360, 41 L. Ed. 750), and apparently on *Matheson* v. *United States,* 1913 (227 U.S. 540, 33 S. Ct. 355, 57 L. Ed. 631), charged the jury as to Currens' criminal responsibility in terms of the M'Naghten Rules but added glosses of temporary insanity and irresistible impulse. The backbone of the charge given by the court below was the

knowledge of right and wrong by the accused, the so-called "right-and-wrong" test of M'Naghten.

We think that there are cogent reasons why the M'Naghten Rules should not be followed or applied today in the courts of the United States. The M'Naghten Rules are to be found, as we have said, in 8 English Reports, Reprint, at p. 722 *et seq.* (1843), and were engendered by the excitement and fear which grew out of the acquittal of Daniel M'Naghten who had attempted to assassinate Sir Robert Peel, Prime Minister of England, but who instead shot Peel's private secretary, Drummond, because M'Naghten had mistaken Drummond for Peel. The offense against Drummond followed a series of attempted assassinations of members of the English Royal House, including Queen Victoria herself, and attacks on the Queen's ministers. Some of these were considered to have grown out of Anti-Corn-Law League plots. When M'Naghten was acquitted at his trial (*The Queen* v. *M'Naghten,* 4 State Trials, N. S. 923 [1843]), public indignation, led by the Queen, ran so high that the Judges of England were called before the House of Lords to explain their conduct. A series of questions were propounded to them. Their answers, really an advisory opinion which was delivered by Lord Chief Justice Tindal for all fifteen Judges, save Mr. Justice Maule, constitute what are now known as the M'Naghten Rules. These Rules have fastened themselves on the law of England and on the law of almost all of the States and on all of the federal courts save one.* The earlier rule of English law, first established in Hadfield's case (27 State Trials 1281) in 1800, was in substance the product rule of *Durham* v. *United States,* 1954 (94 U.S. App. D.C. 228, 214 F.2d 862), and of *State* v. *Pike* (49 N.H. 399), which has been in effect in New Hampshire for over ninety years. The M'Naghten Rules, which applied primarily the test of knowing the difference between right and wrong, are set out in the ancient book, written by William Lambard of Lincolns Inn, *Eirenarcha,* reprinted at least seven times between 1582 and 1610. At "Cap. 21.218" of this work, Lambard stated: "If a mad man or a naturall foole, or a lunatike in the time of his lunacie, or a childe y apparently hath no knowledge of good nor euil do kill a mã, this is no felonious acte, nor any thing forfeited by it . . . for they cãnot be said to haue any understanding wil. But if upo examination it fal out, y they knew what they did, & y it was ill, thē seemth it to be otherwise." It will be observed that Lambard laid

---

* No longer true. See headnote to this chapter (Editor).

down as his test of criminal responsibility "knowledge of good or evil." The phraseology quoted is as antique and creaking as the doctrine of criminal responsibility it announces. For the words "knowledge of good or evil," the phrase "knowledge of right and wrong" was substituted. This essential principle, embodied in the M'Naghten Rules, is not 118 years old. The substance of the M'Naghten Rules was set out in the *Eirenarcha* over 375 years ago, published in a year in which belief in witchcraft and demonology, even among well-educated men, was widespread. The *Eirenarcha* itself contains a statute imposing severe penalties for injuries or death caused by witchcraft. The principles of law embodied in the volume are, of course, typical of the thinking of the times.

The M'Naghten Rules are unworkable for a number of reasons. We will try to state some of them. The Supreme Court in its decision in *Hotema* v. *United States*, 1902 (186 U.S. 413, 420, 22 S. Ct. 895, 46 L. Ed. 1225), makes it plain that knowingly violating a criminal law will impose criminal responsibility upon a defendant even if he believes his act to be morally right. See also in this connection *Saure* v. *United States* (9 Cir., 241 F.2d 640, 649). As an example of the unrealistic effect of the M'Naghten Rules in such a situation we cite Hadfield's Case, 27 State Trials (1800). Hadfield, an old soldier who had served at Freymar and had there sustained terrible head wounds, attempted to kill George III because he viewed himself as the saviour of mankind and felt he had to become a sacrifice as had Jesus Christ, and consequently he had to be executed in accordance with law in order to attain this end. He concluded that killing the King was the best way to attain quick martyrdom. He failed in the attempt but wounded an equerry. Hadfield was acquitted. The jury, under an instruction from the Chief Justice, found that Hadfield was under the "influence of insanity at the time the act was committed" and was not under the "guidance of reason." In substance the test applied was the product test of Durham or the proximate cause test set out in the dissenting opinion in United States ex. rel. *Smith* v. *Baldi* (3 Cir., 1951, 192 F.2d 540, 568). It was good law in England for some 12 years. Hadfield in fact was insane, mentally ill or mentally diseased, yet he would have had to have been declared "sane" under the M'Naghten Rules had that test been applied to him.

Our institutions contain many patients who are insane or mentally ill or mentally diseased and who know the difference between right and wrong. A visit of a few hours at any one of our larger State institutions within this Circuit will convince even the lay visitor of the correctness of this statement. The test, therefore, of knowledge of right and wrong is almost meaningless.

Further, the M'Naghten Rules are a sham, as Mr. Justice Frankfurter made plain in his testimony before the Royal Commission on Capital Punishment. He stated in part: ". . . The M'Naghten Rules were rules which the Judges, in response to questions by the House of Lords, formulated in the light of the then existing psychological knowledge. . . . I do not see why the rules of law should be arrested at the state of psychological knowledge of the time when they were formulated. . . . If you find rules that are, broadly speaking, discredited by those who have to administer them, which is, I think, the real situation, certainly with us—they are honoured in the breach and not in the observance—then I think the law serves its best interests by trying to be more honest about it. . . . I think that to have rules which cannot rationally be justified except by a process of interpretation which distorts and often practically nullifies them, and to say the corrective process comes by having the Governor of a State charged with the responsibility of deciding when the consequences of the rule should not be enforced, is not a desirable system. . . . I am a great believer in being as candid as possible about my institutions. They are in large measure abandoned in practice, and therefore I think the M'Naghten Rules are in large measure shams. That is a strong word, but I think the M'Naghten Rules are very difficult for conscientious people and not difficult enough for people who say, 'We'll just juggle them' . . . I dare to believe that we ought not to rest content with the difficulty of finding an improvement in the M'Naghten Rules. . . ."

Mr. Justice Douglas also has indicated his disapproval of the M'Naghten Rules in his article "The Durham Rule: A Meeting Ground for Lawyers and Psychiatrists" (41 *Iowa L. Rev.* 485 [1956]).

Mr. Justice Cardozo, in an address before the New York Academy of Medicine in 1928, after referring to the M'Naghten Rules, asked that a definition of insanity be framed, ". . . that will combine efficiency with truth." He said further: "If sanity is not to be a defense, let us say so frankly and even brutally, but let us not mock ourselves with a definition that palters with reality. Such a method is neither good morals nor good science nor good law." "What Medicine Can Do for Law," from *Law and Literature and Other Essays and Addresses* by Benjamin N. Cardozo ([New York: Harcourt, Brace, 1931], at p. 108).

The Royal Commission on Capital Punishment expressed an unfavorable conclusion respecting the M'Naghten Rules with only one of the twelve commissioners dissenting. The Commission said that ". . . the test of responsibility laid down in England by the M'Naghten Rules is so defective that the law on the subject ought to be changed." (*Report*, Royal Commission on Capital Punishment, 1953, p. 275.)

The Committee on Psychiatry and the Law of the Group for the Advancement of Psychiatry has recommended the abolition of the M'Naghten Rules. The Report of the Committee states: "The law, however, does not allow the psychiatrist to communicate his unique understanding of psychic realities to the Court and Jury. More often, the mutual quest for the 'whole truth' cannot get past a barrier of communication which leaves the psychiatrist talking about 'mental illness' and the lawyer talking about 'right and wrong.' "

We state again, as was said in the dissenting opinion in United States ex rel. *Smith* v. *Baldi, supra* (192 F.2d at p. 567), that the M'Naghten Rules assume: ". . . the existence of a '. . . logic-tight compartment, in which the delusion holds sway leaving the balance of the mind intact . . .'; the criminal retains enough logic . . . so that from this sanctuary of reason he may inform himself as to what the other part of his mind, the insane part, has compelled or permitted his body to do. If the sane portion of the accused's mind knows that what the insane part compels or permits his body to do is wrong, the body must suffer (by punishment). . . . The human mind, however, is an entity. It cannot be broken into parts, one part sane, the other part, insane."

The vast absurdity of the application of the M'Naghten Rules in order to determine the sanity or insanity, the mental health or lack of it, of the defendant, by securing the answer to a single question: Did the defendant know the difference between right and wrong, appears clearly when one surveys the array of symptomatology which the skilled psychiatrist employs in determining the mental condition of an individual. This is not the place to set this out in detail, but the extent of its substance is suggested by psychiatric textbooks. For example, Henderson and Gillespie in *Textbook of Psychiatry* give 11 pages of "Symptomatology"; Strecker, Ebaugh, and Ewalt in their *Practical Clinical Psychiatry* devote 43 pages to "Methods of Psychiatric Examination"; and Noyes, *Modern Clinical Psychiatry,* employs 25 pages to describe "Symptoms of Mental Disease." These symptomatologies are general in their nature. Many more pages of these works are devoted to descriptions of specific mental diseases. How, conceivably, can the criminal responsibility of a mentally ill defendant be determined by the answer to a single question placed on a moral basis? To state the question seems to us to answer it. All in all, the M'Naghten Rules do indeed, as has been asserted so often, put the testifying psychiatrist in a strait-jacket.

Moreover, the question as to the defendant's knowledge of right and wrong puts the psychiatrist, if he can answer the question and does answer it, in a position in which he must state a moral judgment, and in doing so he cannot avoid usurping to some extent the function of the jury.

In concluding this phase of this opinion we point out that many highly civilized European nations have adopted rules of law relating to the criminal responsibility of offenders suffering from mental disorders or mental weaknesses which bear no relation to the M'Naghten Rules. These nations include Sweden, Denmark, Norway, France, Belgium, Germany, Luxembourg, and Finland. Scotland does not follow the M'Naghten Rules. No harm seems to have inured to the administration of criminal justice in their courts by not asking the testifying psychiatrist whether the accused knows the difference between right and wrong.

Finally, we must point out that the M'Naghten Rules are not only unfair to the individual defendant but are dangerous to society. As was stated in "The Guilty Mind," "[T]he mental competency of recidivists should be questioned by realistic means at the earliest possible stage. So long as the courts judge criminal responsibility by the test of knowledge of right and wrong, psychotics who have served prison terms or are granted probation are released to commit increasingly serious crimes, repeating crime and incarceration and release until murder is committed. Instead of being treated as are ordinary criminals, they should be confined to institutions for the insane at the first offense and not be released until or unless cured." The throwing of the mentally ill individual from the jail back into the community, untreated and uncured, presents a great and immediate danger.

. . . We are of the opinion that the following formula most nearly fulfills the objectives just discussed: The jury must be satisfied that at the time of committing the prohibited act the defendant, as a result of mental disease or defect, lacked substantial capacity to conform his conduct to the requirements of the law which he is alleged to have violated. . . .[1]

---

[1] [Footnote by the Court] The test approved is drawn from part (1) of the test proposed, after long and careful consideration, by the American

We are of the opinion that the following would be an acceptable charge: "If you the jury believe beyond a reasonable doubt that the defendant, Currens, was not suffering from a disease of the mind at the time he committed the criminal act charged, you may find him guilty. If you believe that he was suffering from a disease of the mind, but believe beyond a reasonable doubt that at the time he committed the criminal conduct with which he is charged he possessed substantial capacity to conform his conduct to the requirements of the law which he is alleged to have violated, you may find him guilty. Unless you believe beyond a reasonable doubt that Currens was not suffering from a disease of the mind or that despite that disease he possessed substantial capacity to conform his conduct to the requirements of the law which he is alleged to have violated you must find him not guilty by

reason of insanity. Thus, your task would not be completed upon finding, if you did find, that the accused suffered from a disease of the mind. He would still be responsible for his unlawful act if you found beyond a reasonable doubt that at the time he committed that act, the disease had not so weakened his capacity to conform his conduct to the requirements of the law which he is alleged to have violated that he lacked substantial capacity to conform his conduct to the requirements of that law. These questions must be determined by you from the facts which you find to be fairly deducible from the evidence in this case. . . ."

The judgment of conviction will be reversed and a new trial ordered, with directions to proceed in accordance with this opinion.

Law Institute in its Model Penal Code, which is as follows: "Mental Disease or Defect Excluding Responsibility."

(1) "A person is not responsible for criminal conduct if at the time of such conduct as a result of mental disease or defect he lacks substantial capacity either to appreciate the criminality of his conduct or to conform his conduct to the requirements of law."

(2) "The terms 'mental disease or defect' do not include abnormality manifested only by repeated criminal or otherwise anti-social conduct."

We are unable to accept the phrase "to appreciate the criminality of his conduct." This phrase would overemphasize the cognitive element in criminal responsibility and thus distract the jury from the crucial issues while being little more than surplusage. The cognitive element would rarely be significant, and indeed would be absent, in the case of an individual in an extreme state of stuporous catatonic schizophrenia, a condition of living death, and in the case of the raving maniac or the imbecile. While persons in the two latter categories may commit acts which are essentially criminal in their nature, they are nonetheless

rarely brought to trial but rather are committed forthwith to mental institutions.

As we have indicated earlier in this opinion, we agree fully with part (2) of the American Law Institute proposal set out above.

The test approved by us, while based primarily on the American Law Institute proposal, is similar to that approved in part (c) of that suggested by the Royal Commission on Capital Punishment, which in turn borrowed it from the British Medical Association. The full text recommended by the Commission is as follows: "The jury must be satisfied that, at the time of committing the act, the accused, as a result of disease of the mind (or mental deficiency) (a) did not know the nature and quality of the act, or (b) did not know that it was wrong, or (c) was incapable of preventing himself from committing it."

[A footnote after the words "as a result of disease of the mind (or mental deficiency)"] is cited to subheading B of the Commission's Report, "Mental Deficiency"; and the reason why the phrase "or mental deficiency" was placed in parentheses need not be given here. See Royal Commission on Capital Punishment, pp. 110, 111, and pp. 117, 118.

Parts (a) and (b) of the test suggested by the Royal Commission lead straight back to the M'Naghten Rules and in our judgment, for reasons already stated, should be eschewed.

THE INSANITY DEFENSE: HISTORICAL DEVELOPMENT AND CONTEMPORARY RELEVANCE

Sheila Hafter Gray

The use of insanity to excuse criminal conduct seems to have first appeared at the end of the reign of Henry III in the form of king's pardons granted to those he judged insane. These pardons became so frequent that they were ultimately granted as a matter of course if the situation so dictated. The courts later adopted insanity as a valid defense, and by the 16th century it was well-established in the criminal law.

Although it was held, even as late as 1724, that an accused must be totally deprived of reason for the insanity defense to apply, there were efforts to introduce partial insanity as a defense. At the end of the 17th century, Sir Mathew Hale, in his attempt to categorize the recognized defenses to criminal charges, developed in some detail the concept that partial insanity was sufficient to prove the absence of criminal intent. He proposed a rule whereby a person would not be held responsible if, at the time of the offense, his mental capacity was less than that of a child of 14 years. His test did not gain wide use, however, possibly because an understanding of the relationship between mental age and mental capacity had not yet developed in scientific circles. Furthermore, society at that time was not willing to accept the possibility of large scale exoneration of criminals on the ground of insanity, possibly because no alternative to imprisonment could be envisioned. The requirement of total insanity embodied in the traditional "wilde beeste" test therefore continued to prevail.

In 1800, *Hadfield's Case* (27 How. St. Tr. 1281 (K.B. 1800) added insane delusions to the "wilde beeste" test as a basis for a finding of insanity. Hadfield, a soldier who had suffered severe head injuries in battle, attempted to assassinate the king in order to attain the martyr's death he believed to be his destiny. His delusion was held to be sufficient ground for acquittal. This defense, although not widely successful, led to acquittal in some cases. In 1840, for example, Edward Oxford, acting under a similar delusion, attempted to assassinate Queen Victoria and Prince Albert. He too was acquitted on the ground of insanity.

Three years later, the case of Daniel M'Naghten led to a substantial change in the legal rule used to determine insanity. M'Naghten had been found not guilty by reason of insanity of the murder of Sir Robert Peel's secretary, Edward Drummond. Lord Chief Justice Tindal had instructed the jury to decide whether, at the time of the crime, the defendant "had or had not the use of his understanding, so as to know that he was doing a wrong or wicked act." If he did not know that he was violating the law, he was to be acquitted; but if he was "in a sound state of mind," he was to be found guilty. When the verdict was rendered, however, the public and the Queen were so disturbed over the obvious ambiguities of the charge that the House of Lords was asked to define what constituted a sound mind and under what circumstances the insanity defense would apply in the future. Lord Tindal set out a double test, requiring that the defendant either not know what he was doing (total insanity) or not know that it was wrong.

DEVELOPMENT AND MODIFICATION OF *M'Naghten*

We cannot understand the subsequent development of the insanity defense, however, without taking into account the position of psychiatry, both as a body of knowledge and as a group of practitioners, in relation to the courts. The first systematic application of medical science to jurisprudence was proposed by Hale, as part of his aforementioned categorization of criminal defenses. Although he defined his terms according to contemporary medical understanding of the conditions he described, these definitions were not legal rules

Excerpts reprinted with permission from 10 *Am. Crim. L. Rev.* 559 (Spring 1972).

but rather examples to help judges instruct juries who tried the cases in which the insanity defense was raised. Hale made it clear that mental incapacity was to be a question of fact to be determined by the jury. The evidence presented by medical experts was, however, given no greater weight than that of lay witnesses.

It was not until *M'Naghten's Case* that the testimony of psychiatrists, as experts in the field of mental disease and deficiency, was accorded special status. For the first time they could offer an opinion concerning an event which they had not actually witnessed, but about which they might reconstruct information using their newly developed techniques. While physicians still could not determine the fact of insanity, they were permitted to testify whether the accused had been suffering from a disabling disease at the time of the alleged offense and to state whether the criminal act was a product of that disease. Pandora's Box was opened just enough for the courts to view its contents; but it took 85 years for another court to muster the courage to lift the lid once again.

The *M'Naghten* rule, later modified beyond recognition by experts and jurists alike, became the basic rule in the English and American courts for almost 100 years. The promulgation of the [New Hampshire] rule, heavily influenced by the American psychiatrist, Isaac Ray, marked the first instance in which the courts responded to the budding science of psychiatry. Its carefully drafted language made psychiatric testimony useful because it permitted the expert to formulate the relationship between criminal intent and mental state in a particular case. Furthermore, the rule allowed wide leeway in the definition of "disease of the mind" and yet prevented acquittals based solely on the presence of mental illness at the time of the crime. But *M'Naghten* soon became a rigid codification of early examples of its application, as the New Hampshire Supreme Court had envisioned when it rejected the test in 1869.

The narrow interpretation of *M'Naghten* led to two major erroneous consequences. First, the words of the test came to be interpreted as requiring a cognitive understanding of the difference between right and wrong. Secondly, the concept of "disease of the mind" came to be held by some psychiatrists to encompass only psychosis itself. The latter is illustrated by Frederic Wertham in a case involving a pedophiliac whom he believed should be held responsible under *M'Naghten* because "the law of legal insanity is not intended to exculpate such a person who does not suffer from a psychosis, *i.e.,* a major dis-

ease, and who is not committable." Psychiatric experts seemed to forget that the *M'Naghten* rule refers to the "true capacity of the individual." Instead, these experts sought to modify the law by attempting to codify each new psychiatric theory and to substitute their findings for those of the jury as they became more confident of their ability to postdict human behavior.

The recent experience in the District of Columbia illustrates the futility of the constant recodifications of medical theories. *M'Naghten*, adopted as the rule in the District of Columbia in 1882,[1] was broadened to include the "irresistible impulse" test in 1929[2] in response to the requests of a number of psychiatrists who argued that unlawful acts often arise from an impulse, a force from within, that could become strong enough to overcome the defendant's cognitive knowledge of the legal or moral wrongfulness of an act. Even this rule was not satisfactory, however, and in 1954 the *M'Naghten* rule was broadened almost to the point of nonexistence when the United States Court of Appeals for the District of Columbia Circuit held in *Durham v. United States*[3] that "an accused is not criminally responsible if his unlawful act was the product of a mental disease or defect."

The *Durham* rule was a reformulation of the New Hampshire test announced in *State v. Pike*,[4] with one major and critical difference: the New Hampshire rule was an evidentiary one while *Durham* was a substantive rule of law.[5] This was a victory for the postdicters;

[1] United States v. Guiteau, 12 D.C. (1 Mackey) 498 (1882).

[2] Smith v. United States, 36 F.2d 548 (D.C. Cir. 1929).

[3] 214 F.2d 862 (D.C. Cir. 1954).

[4] 49 N.H. 399 (1869). Judge Doe, in his concurring opinion, stated the rule as follows:

The whole difficulty is, that courts have undertaken to declare that to be law which is a matter of fact. The principles of the law were maintained at the trial of the present case, when, experts having testified as usual that neither knowledge nor delusion is the test, the court instructed the jury that all tests of mental disease are purely matters of fact, and that if the homicide was the offspring or product of mental disease in the defendant, he was not guilty by reason of insanity.

Id. at 442.

[5] The change from an evidentiary to a substantive rule made all the difference in the long run, for making legal standards of medical theories which by their very nature must grow and change is the danger about which the court in *Pike* warned. More recently, Dr. Thomas Szasz has pointed out the folly of *Durham:*

To believe that one's own theories are facts is considered by many contemporary psychiatrists

but it was a pyhrric victory for they found they could not postdict with the degree of certainty required in criminal cases. But within a few years, the *Durham* rule itself rigidified. Meeting the test became a game of semantics, requiring definition and redefinition of "product" and "mental disease or defect."[6] Perforce,

---

as a "symptom" of schizophrenia. Yet this is what the language of the *Durham* decision does. It specifies some of the shakiest and most controversial aspects of contemporary psychiatry (i.e., those pertaining to what is "mental disease" and the classification of such alleged diseases) and by legal fiat seeks to transform inadequate theory into "judicial fact."

Szasz, "Psychiatry, Ethics, and the Criminal Law," 58 *Colum. L. Rev.* 183, 190 (1958), *quoted in* Reid, "Understanding the New Hampshire Doctrine of Criminal Insanity" 69 *Yale L.J.* 367, 389–91 (1960).

[6] In Carter v. United States, 252 F.2d 608, 617 (D.C. Cir. 1957) "product" was defined to mean that, but for the mental disease, the accused would not have committed the act. In McDonald v. United States, 312 F.2d 847 (D.C. Cir. 1962), "mental disease or defect" was defined as "any abnormal condition of the mind which substantially affects mental or emotional processes and substantially impairs behavior controls." Chief Judge Bazelon described the nature of the semantic game in Washington v. United States, 390 F.2d 444 (1967):

[T]he jury was often subjected to a confusing mass of abstract philosophical discussion and fruitless disputation between lawyer and witness about legal and psychiatric labels and jargon. Dr. Hamman's entire testimony on direct examination was that Washington did not have a "passive-aggressive personality," . . . did not have "an irresistible impulse," was "not mentally ill," and was not "abnormal from the standpoint of psychiatric illness".

Id. at 447–48.

Since the *M'Naghten* decision, medical terms have frequently been heard in court. The following are but a few: "defect of reason," "disease of the mind," "nature and quality of the act," "behavior controls,' "mental disease or defect," "capacity . . . to appreciate the criminality of his conduct," and "capacity to conform his conduct to the requirements of law." *See* Washington v. United States, *supra* at 452 n.23. Chief Judge Bazelon concluded after considering the history of the use of medical terminology in the courts that such terminology is vague and gives a false impression of scientific exactness. Professor Alan M. Dershowitz is quoted in the Bazelon opinion as going so far as to recommend that no legal rule should ever be phrased in medical terms. The trend appears to be away from the *Durham-Carter-McDonald* line of cases, which were attempts at defining and refining the meaning of medical terms, and into an area which leaves much to the common sense judgment of the jury.

the rule left little room for the introduction of yet newer medical discoveries.[7]

Recognizing the inadequacies of *Durham*, the United States Court of Appeals for the Third Circuit in *United States* v. *Currens*[8] adopted a test to determine criminal responsibility based on the American Law Institute's Model Penal Code formulations for the insanity defense.[9] The Third Circuit rejected *Durham* for its failure to provide the jury with a standard to relate a defendant's mental disease to mens rea requirements.[10] Focusing on the guilty mind of the accused,[11] it adopted the following formulation:

The jury must be satisfied that at the time of the committing of the prohibited act the defendant, as a result of mental disease or defect, lacked substantial capacity to conform

[7] *Durham* has been accepted in only two other jurisdictions, Maine and the Virgin Islands. A. Goldstein, *The Insanity Defense* 83 (1967). However, the impact of *Durham* has been enormous, forcing a complete reevaluation of the tests for criminal responsibility. *See* Goldstein & Katz, "Abolish the 'Insanity Defense'—Why Not?," 72 *Yale L.J.* 853, 855 n.5 (1963) (*Durham* cited in 140 cases between 1957 and 1963).

[8] 290 F.2d 751 (3d Cir. 1961).

[9] The court referred to the ALI Model Penal Code § 4.01(1) (Tent. Draft No. 4, 1955) which provides that:

(1) A person is not responsible for criminal conduct if at the time of such conduct as a result of mental disease or defect he lacks substantial capacity either to appreciate the criminality of his conduct or to conform his conduct to the rerequirements of the law.

(2) The terms "mental disease or defect" do not include an abnormality manifested only by repeated criminal or otherwise antisocial conduct.

290 F.2d at 774.

[10] The court concluded:

[*Durham*] omits the most important step in deciding the issue of criminal responsibility, namely that of determining the total mental condition of the defendant at the time he committed the act, and providing the jury with a standard by means of which an ultimate social and moral judgment can be rendered.

Id.

[11] The court stated:

Our . . . objective is, therefore, to verbalize the relationship between mental disease and the concept of 'guilty mind' in a way that will be both meaningful to a jury charged with the duty of determining the issue of criminal responsibility and consistent with the basic aims, purposes and assumptions of the criminal law.

Id. at 773.

his conduct to the requirements of the law which he is alleged to have violated.[12]

Although the District of Columbia Circuit has not as yet adopted the *Currens* formulation, there are at least indications that it is currently being considered to replace the *Durham* rule.[13] Thus, the game of redefinition of terms to limit application of the test may begin anew.

Modern Psychological Theory and Its Application to Criminal Responsibility

As we have pointed out, many psychiatrists shared with the legal profession profound misconceptions about the significance of the *M'Naghten* rule. While the psychiatrists and legal scholars attempted to alter the rules, there developed, ironically, a substantial body of psychological, and particularly psychoanalytic, knowledge which suggested that most, if not all defendants who now qualify under *Currens* could have qualified under *M'Naghten* or even the ancient formula of Sir Mathew Hale.

An examination of the meaning of the right-wrong test will serve to illustrate the interchangeability of the various formulations. Narrow interpretations of the *M'Naghten* rule suggested that verbalization of a moral principle implied understanding. But Jean Piaget's studies have shown that while a young child has some vague notion about the "rules of the game" of justice and morality, these mental faculties do not develop into their fully mature forms until the age of 15 years.[14] Interestingly enough, however, the younger child may be able to verbalize these rules which he cannot follow, thereby giving an interviewer the impression that he actually "knows" right from wrong. But his behavior indicates he can neither comprehend nor conform his conduct to the rules he has previously articulated.[15]

Thus, in normal children, there seems to be an intrinsic connection between morality and the ability to think logically which is not established until early adolescence. Cross-cultural studies indicate that these basic mental faculties develop similarly in all cultures provided there is sufficient development of civilization.[16] However, in social groups, where there is a deficiency in educational opportunity or other stimulating social interaction, children who show normal intelligence on *performance tests* tend to be severely retarded in tests of *intellectual function*.[17] They do not achieve the level of abstract thinking which normally develops between the ages of 12 and 15 years.[18] Based on Piaget's studies, one could argue that they never develop the functions necessary for a valid moral sense as defined by law.[19]

The implications of these recent psychological studies assume further importance in the light of the growing and increasingly disturbing body of knowledge which points to the conclusion that children in the ghettos of America often do not achieve an adult level of abstract thinking. Roger Hurley has assembled a massive amount of data which clearly supports the idea that "poverty in America is one of the most significant causes of mental retardation—far beyond the more publicized damage believed to be done by heredity or uncontrollable accidents suffered by prominent, prosperous families."[20] He further shows how the difficult social and family situation of the poor makes it impossible for the child to develop his innate psychological capabilities, explaining:

A very intimate relationship exists between the stultification of the child's intellectual development and his psychological maturation and well-being [i.e., development of his character]. Because the impoverished child does

---

[12] *Id.* at 774.

[13] The court in *Brawner v. United States* specifically requested that the amici curiae discuss the feasibility of replacing *Durham* with the A.L.I. test from which the *Currens* test was adopted. Brief for William Dempsey as Amicus Curiae at Appendix A, Brawner v. United States, Crim. No. 22,714 (D.C. Cir., filed Feb. 6, 1969).

[14] *See generally* Flavel, *The Developmental Psychology of Jean Piaget* (1963).

[15] "It is clear that the mechanism which Piaget holds responsible for the development of a rational morality is exactly the same as that which he thinks engenders rationality in general. . . . [L]ogic is the morality of thought just as morality is the logic of action." *Id.* at 296.

[16] J. Piaget, *Psychology and Epistomology* 50 (1971).

[17] *Id.* at 49.

[18] *Id.* at 62.

[19] These important studies on the development of intellectual function are strikingly similar to the formulations of Sir Mathew Hale for the age of 14 as the cut-off point in evaluating partial insanity. Hale's standards for the insanity test are as valid and applicable today, based on Piaget's studies, as they were in the 17th century. Indeed, our juvenile court system is a reflection of the premise that before a certain age a youth will not be held responsible as would an adult for comparable conduct. *See* Louisell & Diamond, "Law and Psychiatry: Détente, Entente, or Concomitance," 50 *Cornell L.Q.* 217, 232 n.72 (1965).

[20] R. Hurley, *Poverty and Mental Retardation: A Causal Relationship* 45 (1969).

not prosper and does not develop the intellec‐ tual equipment needed to function effectively in our society, because he remains embedded in a whole subculture of misfortune, his psychological orientation becomes gnarled and unhealthy.[21]

Gustav Bychowski has also documented the stultifying effect of the impoverished environment of the child, emphasizing the deleterious effect upon his psychic drives and paying special attention to the fate of inborn aggression.[22] While these internal forces are normally neutralized and diverted to socially productive goals, the threatening environment of the impoverished child intensifies them. This not only leads to a heightened capacity for violent behavior in the adult, but it also deprives the ego of a major source of energy for the task of intellectual and moral development.[23] It should also be noted that it is the general instability of deprived families rather than the absence of money that does the damage.[24]

[21] *Id.* at 86.

[22] Bychowski, "Psychoanalytic Reflections on the Psychiatry of the Poor," 51 *Int. J. Psychoanalysis* 503 (1970).

[23] *Id.* at 509; *see* Hartmann, "Notes on the Theory of Sublimation," 10 *Psychoanalytic Study of the Child* 9–29 (1955), for a comprehensive review of the theory of socialization of psychic drives.

[24] Pavenstedt notes that many well organized families living at or below welfare standards manage to raise their children to be reasonable, socially productive, law-abiding citizens. *The Drifters: Children of Lower Class Families passim* (E. Pavenstedt ed. 1967). *See generally* Hurley, *supra* note 70; Bychowski, *supra* note 72. Recent social trends which lead to the breakdown of family structure are more causative than impecuniousness. The social welfare system in this country has been a prime culprit in this regard. *Cf. Hurley, supra* at 165.

We see similar psychological deviation in children of affluent parents whose gratifying permissive attitudes have inhibited the child from developing moral standards. The author has on several occasions examined and/or treated affluent defendants. One young lady had been engaging in petty thievery at least since she had entered grade school. Whenever she was caught, the father compensated the victim handsomely with cash far in excess of the value of the articles stolen; and she was always permitted to keep the pilfered goods. At the age of 19 she was finally apprehended by the police, but the father's political influence enabled her to be transferred immediately to an

Taken together, the results of this psychological research reveal that to grasp effectively, rather than merely to verbalize, the difference between right and wrong described in the *M'Naghten* test, an individual must have reached a specified level of psychological development. This finding becomes of the utmost importance when we realize that a substantial proportion of the criminally accused have never reached this stage of mental development. Thus, under the allegedly conservative *M'Naghten* rule, a large number of those criminally accused could plead not guilty by reason of insanity if knowledge of right and wrong were defined in light of recent psychological discoveries.

This is not to suggest that a new rule should supplant *Currens,* but rather to show that any broad rule can be used if it is reinterpreted in each case in light of its facts and contemporary scientific understanding. The combination of increased knowledge and open-minded interpretation could have made *M'Naghten* an effective insanity test and could now do the same for *Currens.* We need no new rules, but rather careful application of those we have.

---

expensive private mental hospital. On examination she proved indeed to be suffering from latent schizophrenia (which soon became acute) as are many of our poor offenders.

Other studies further cement the relationship between family disorganization and improper psychological development. Charles A. Malone and his research team found persons in the Boston slum who are so disorganized that they cannot even belong to a poverty culture. *See The Drifters, supra, passim.* In a population that contains many white people as well as Blacks it was found that

[t]he primary social-psychological characteristic that appeared during the course of our study is the enormous confusion in each family about the differences between adults and children. . . . All our adults showed persisting failure to exercise self-restraint or self-discipline at crucial points when their own anxieties are aroused. . . . My first impression . . . was that we were watching 'families of children' in action. You could hardly distinguish the adults from the children except for the fact that the former were larger.

Id. at 312–13.

It is no surprise that these people have a high degree of delinquency. *See* Bychowski *supra* note 72 (wherein he makes a convincing argument for viewing "hippies" and lower class social misfits as environmentally-produced schizophrenics; a view which conforms with the author's experience).

UNITED STATES v. BRAWNER

LEVENTHAL, Circuit Judge:

The ALI's primary provision is stated thus in its Model Penal Code, see § 4.01(1).

Section 4.01 Mental Disease or Defect Excluding Responsibility

(1) A person is not responsible for criminal conduct if at the time of such conduct as a result of mental disease or defect he lacks substantial capacity either to appreciate the criminality [wrongfulness] of his conduct or to conform his conduct to the requirements of the law.

We have decided to adopt the ALI rule as the doctrine excluding responsibility for mental disease or defect, for application prospectively to trials begun after this date.

History looms large in obtaining a sound perspective for a subject like this one. But the cases are numerous. And since our current mission is to illuminate the present, rather than to linger over the past, it suffices for our purposes to review a handful of our opinions on the insanity defense.

1. The landmark opinion was written by Judge Bazelon in *Durham* v. *United States,* 94 U.S.App.D.C. 228, 214 F.2d 862 (1954). *Durham* adopted the "product rule," pioneered in *State* v. *Pike*, 49 N.H. 399, 402 (1869–70), and exculpated from criminal responsibility those whose forbidden acts were the product of a mental disease or defect.

Few cases have evoked as much comment as *Durham*. It has sparked widespread interest in the legal-judicial community and focused attention on the profound problems involved in defining legal responsibility in case of mental illness. It has been hailed as a guide to the difficult and problem-laden intersection of law and psychiatry, ethics and science. It has been scored as an unwarranted loophole through which the cunning criminal might escape from the penalty of the law. We view it more modestly, as the court's effort, designed in the immemorial manner of the case method that has built the common law, to alleviate two serious problems with the previous rule.

The first of these was a problem of language which raised an important symbolic issue of the law. We felt that the language of the old right-wrong/irresistible impulse rule for insanity was antiquated, no longer reflecting the community's judgment as to who ought to be held criminally liable for socially destructive acts. We considered the rule as restated to have more fruitful, accurate and considered reflection of the sensibilities of the community as revised and expanded in the light of continued study of abnormal human behavior.

The second vexing problem that *Durham* was designed to reach related to the concern of the psychiatrists called as expert witnesses for their special knowledge of the problem of insanity, who often and typically felt that they were obliged to reach outside of their professional expertise when they were asked, under the traditional insanity rule established in 1843 by *M'Naghten's* Case, whether the defendant knew right from wrong. They further felt that the narrowness of the traditional test, which framed the issue of responsibility solely in terms of cognitive impairment, made it impossible to convey to the judge and jury the full range of information material to an assessment of defendant's responsibility.

2. Discerning scholarship now available asserts that the experts' fears and concerns reflected a misapprehension as to the impact of the traditional standard in terms of excluding relevant evidence.

Wigmore states the rule to be that when insanity is in issue, "any and all conduct of the person is admissible in evidence." And the cases support Wigmore's view. The almost unvarying policy of the courts has been to admit *any* evidence of abberational behavior so long as it is probative of the defendant's mental condition, without regard to the supposed restrictions of the test used to define insanity for the jury.[1]

Moreover if the term "know" in the traditional test of "know right from wrong" is taken as denoting affective knowledge, rather than merely cognitive knowledge, it yields a rule of greater flexibility than was widely supposed to exist. Livermore and Meehl, "The

---

[1] A. Goldstein, *The Insanity Defense* 54 (New Haven: Yale University Press, 1967), citing 1 Wigmore Evidence §228 (1940) and numerous cases.

Virtues of M'Naghten," 51 *Minn.L.Rev.* 789, 800–08 (1967).*

We need not occupy ourselves here and now with the question whether, and to what extent, the *M'Naghten* rule, ameliorated by the irresistible impulse doctrine, is susceptible of application to include medical insights and information as justice requires. In any event, the experts felt hemmed in by the traditional test; they felt that they could not give the jury and judge the necessary information in response to the questions which the traditional test posed.

3. A difficulty arose under the *Durham* rule in application. The rule was devised to facilitate the giving of testimony by medical experts in the context of a legal rule, with the jury called upon to reach a composite conclusion that had medical, legal and moral components. However the pristine statement of the *Durham* rule opened the door to "trial by label." *Durham* did distinguish between "disease" as used "in the sense of a condition which is considered capable of either improving or deteriorating," and "defect," as referring to a condition not capable of such change "and which may be either congenital or the result of injury, or the residual effect of a physical or mental disease." 94 U.S.App.D.C. at 241, 214 F.2d at 875. But the court failed to explicate what abnormality of mind was an essential ingredient of these concepts. In the absence of a definition of "mental disease or defect," medical experts attached to them the meanings which would naturally occur to them—medical meanings—and gave testimony accordingly. The problem was dramatically highlighted by the weekend flip flop case, In re Rosenfield, 157 F.Supp. 18 (D.D.C.1957). The petitioner was described as a sociopath. A St. Elizabeths psychiatrist testified that a person with a sociopathic personality was not suffering from a mental disease. That was Friday afternoon. On Monday morning, through a policy change at St. Elizabeths Hospital, it was determined as an administrative matter that the state of a psychopathic or sociopathic personality did constitute a mental disease.

The concern that medical terminology not control legal outcomes culminated in *McDonald* v. *United States,* 114 U.S.App.D.C. 120, 312 F.2d 847, 851 (en banc, 1962), where this court recognized that the term, mental disease or defect, has various meanings, depending upon how and why it is used, and by whom. Mental disease means one thing to a physician bent on treatment, but something different, if somewhat overlapping, to a court of law. We provided a legal definition of men-

tal disease or defect, and held that it included "any abnormal condition of the mind which substantially affects mental or emotional processes and substantially impairs behavior controls." (312 F2d at 851). "Thus the jury would consider testimony concerning the development, adaptation and functioning of these processes and controls."

While the *McDonald* standard of mental disease was not without an attribute of circularity, it was useful in the administration of justice because it made plain that clinical and legal definitions of mental disease were distinct, and it helped the jury to sort out its complex task and to focus on the matters given it to decide.

4. The *Durham* rule also required explication along other lines, notably the resolution of the ambiguity inherent in the formulation concerning actions that were the "product" of mental illness. It was supplemented in *Carter* v. *United States,* 102 U.S.App.D.C. 227 at 234, 235, 252 F.2d 608 at 615–616 (1957):

The simple fact that a person has a mental disease or defect is not enough to relieve him of responsibility for a crime. There must be a relationship between the disease and the criminal act; and the relationship must be such as to justify a reasonable inference that the act would not have been committed if the person had not been suffering from the disease.

Thus *Carter* clarified that the mental illness must not merely have entered into the production of the act, but must have played a necessary role. *Carter* identified the "product" element of the rule with the "but for" variety of causation.

The pivotal "product" term continued to present problems, principally that it put expert testimony on a faulty footing. Assuming that a mental disease, in the legal sense, had been established, the fate of the defendant came to be determined by what came to be referred to by the legal jargon of "productivity." On the other hand, it was obviously sensible if not imperative that the experts having pertinent knowledge should speak to the crucial question whether the mental abnormality involved is one associated with aberrant behavior. But since "productivity" was so decisive a factor in the decisional equation, a ruling permitting experts to testify expressly in language of "product" raised in a different context the concern lest the ultimate issue be in fact turned over to the experts rather than retained for the jurors representing the community.

The problem was identified by then Circuit Judge Burger in his concurring opinion in *Blocker*:[2]

---

* See testimony in *State* v. *Andrews,* ch. 7, *supra* (Ed.).

[2] *Blocker* v. *United States* 110 U.S. App. D.C. 41, 51, 228 F.2d 853, 863 (en banc 1961).

The hazards in allowing experts to testify in precisely or even substantially the terms of the ultimate issue are apparent. This is a course which, once allowed, risks the danger that lay jurors, baffled by the intricacies of expert discourse and unintelligible technical jargon may be tempted to abdicate independent analysis of the facts on which the opinion rests. . . .

It was in this context that the court came to the decision in *Washington* v. *United States*, 129 U.S.App.D.C. 29,390 F2d 444 (1967), which forbade experts from testifying as to productivity altogether. Chief Judge Bazelon's opinion illuminates the bases of the ruling, as one intended "to help the psychiatrists understand their role in court; and thus eliminate a fundamental cause of unsatisfactory expert testimony," namely, the tendency of the expert to use "concepts [which] can become slogans, hiding facts and representing nothing more than the witness's own conclusion about the defendant's criminal responsibility."

The core rule of the ALI has been adopted, with variations, by all save one of the Federal circuit courts of appeals, and by all that have come to reconsider the doctrine providing exculpation for mental illness. Their opinions have been exceptionally thoughtful and thorough in their expositions of the interests and values protected. *United States* v. *Freeman*, 357 F2d 606 (2d Cir. 1966); *United States* v. *Currens*, 290 F.2d 751 (3d Cir. 1961); *United States* v. *Chandler*, 393 F.2d 920 (4th Cir. 1968); *Blake* v. *United States*, 407 F.2d 908 (5th Cir. 1969); *United States* v. *Smith*, 404 F.2d 720 (6th Cir. 1968); *United States* v. *Shapiro* 383 F.2d 680 (7th Cir. 1967); *Pope* v. *United States*, 372 F.2d 710 (8th Cir. 1967); *Wade* v. *United States*, 426 F.2d 64 (9th Cir. 1970); *Wion* v. *United States*, 325 F.2d 420 (10th Cir. 1963).

These opinions show that the ALI rule has proved peculiarly subject to successful adaptation, permitting variations but within a framework of uniformity.

A principal reason for our decision to depart from the *Durham* rule is the undesirable characteristic, surviving even the *McDonald* modification, of undue dominance by the experts giving testimony.

Our ruling today includes our decision that in the ALI rule as adopted by this court the term "mental disease or defect" includes the definition of that term provided in our 1962 en banc *McDonald* opinion, as follows:

[A] mental disease or defect includes any abnormal condition of the mind which substantially affects mental or emotional processes and substantially impairs behavior controls.

McDonald v. *United States*, 114 U.S.App.D.C. at 124, 312 F.2d at 851.

A number of proposals in the journals recommend that the insanity defense be abolished altogether. This is advocated in the amicus brief of the National District Attorneys Association as both desirable and lawful. The amicus brief of American Psychiatric Association concludes it would be desirable, with appropriate safeguards, but would require a constitutional amendment. That a constitutional amendment would be required is also the conclusion of others, generally in opposition to the proposal.

This proposal has been put forward by responsible judges for consideration, with the objective of reserving psychiatric overview for the phase of the criminal process concerned with disposition of the person determined to have been the actor. However, we are convinced that the proposal cannot properly be imposed by judicial fiat.

To obviate any misunderstanding from our rejection of the recommendation of those projudicial abolition of the insanity defense, we expressly commend their emphasis on the need for improvement of dispositional resources and programs. The defense focuses on the kind of impairment that warrants exculpation, and necessarily assigns to the prison walls many men who have serious mental impairments and difficulties.

We have also pondered the suggestion that the jury be instructed that the defendant lacks criminal responsibility if the jury finds that the defendant's mental disease impairs his capacity or controls to such an extent that he cannot "justly be held responsible."

However, there is a substantial concern that an instruction overtly cast in terms of "justice" cannot feasibly be restricted to the ambit of what may properly be taken into account but will splash with unconfinable and malign consequences. The Government cautions that "explicit appeals to 'justice' will result in litigation of extraneous issues and will encourage improper arguments to the jury phrased solely in terms of 'sympathy' and 'prejudice.' "

There is wisdom in the view that a jury generally understands well enough that an instruction composed in flexible terms gives it sufficient latitude so that, without disregarding the instruction, it can provide that application of the instruction which harmonizes with its sense of justice. The ALI rule generally communicates that meaning.

Statistical data concerning the use of insanity in criminal trials in this jurisdiction were presented in the December 15, 1966, Report of the President's Commission on Crime in the District of Columbia. These data have been up-dated in Mr. Dempsey's brief, with the aid of data helpfully supplied by the United States Attorney's office. At least since *Durham* was modified by *McDonald,* insanity acquittals have run at about 2% of all cases terminated. In the seven years subsequent to *McDonald* jury verdicts of not guilty by reason of insanity averaged only 3 per anum. In trials by the court, there has been an annual average of about 38 verdicts of not guilty by reason of insanity; these typically are cases where the Government psychiatrists agreed that the crime was the product of mental illness. We perceive no basis in these data for any conclusion that the number or percentage of insanity acquittals has been either excessive or inadequate.

In adopting the ALI formulation, this court does not follow the *Currens* opinion of the Third Circuit, which puts it that the sole issue in every case is defendant's capacity to control his behavior, and that as a matter of analysis a person who lacks substantial capacity to appreciate the wrongfulness [criminality] of his conduct necessarily lacks substantial capacity to control his behavior. Like the other circuits, we resist the *Currens* lure of logic in order to make certain that the jury will give heed to the substantiality of a defense of lack of substantial capacity to appreciate wrongfulness, a point that may elude a jury instructed solely in terms of control capacity.

Section 4.01 of the Model Penal Code as promulgated by ALI contains in subsection (2) what has come to be known as the "caveat paragraph":

(2) The terms "mental disease or defect" do not include an abnormality manifested only by repeated criminal or otherwise anti-social conduct.

The purpose of this provision was to exclude a defense for the so-called "psychopathic personality."

Our own approach is influenced by the fact that our rule already includes a definition of mental disease (from *McDonald*). Under that definition, as we have pointed out, the mere existence of "a long criminal record does not excuse crime." *Williams* v. *United States,* 114 U.S.App.D.C. 135, 137, 312 F.2d 862, 864 (1962). We do not require the caveat paragraph as an insurance against exculpation of the deliberate and persistent offender. Our *McDonald* rule guards against the danger of misunderstanding and injustice that might arise, say, from an expert's classification that reflects only a conception defining all criminality as reflective of mental illness. There must be testimony to show both that the defendant was suffering from an abnormal condition of the mind and that it substantially affected mental or emotional processes and substantially impaired behavioral controls.

In this context, our pragmatic approach is to adopt the caveat paragraph as a rule for application by the judge, to avoid miscarriage of justice, but not for inclusion in instructions to the jury.

Finally, we have not accepted suggestions to adopt a rule that disentangles the insanity defense from a medical model, and announces a standard exculpating anyone whose capacity for control is insubstantial, for whatever cause or reason. There may be logic in these submissions, but we are not sufficiently certain of the nature, range and implications of the conduct involved to attempt an all-embracing unified field theory.

Our decision accompanies the redefinition of when a mental condition exonerates a defendant from criminal responsibility with the doctrine that expert testimony as to a defendant's abnormal mental condition may be received and considered, as tending to show, in a responsible way, that defendant did not have the specific mental state required for a particular crime or degree of crime—even though he was aware that his act was wrongful and was able to control it, and hence was not entitled to complete exoneration.

Some of the cases following this doctrine use the term "diminished responsibility," but we prefer the example of the cases that avoid this term.

Neither logic nor justice can tolerate a jurisprudence that defines the elements of an offense as requiring a mental state such that one defendant can properly argue that his voluntary drunkenness removed his capacity to form the specific intent but another defendant is inhibited from a submission of his contention that an abnormal mental condition, for which he was in no way responsible, negated his capacity to form a particular specific intent, even though the condition did not exonerate him from all criminal responsibility.

Our rule permits the introduction of expert testimony as to abnormal condition if it is relevant to negative, or establish, the specific mental condition that is an element of the crime.[3]

The Appendix to *Washington* still stands in

---

[3] Since the defense relates to a specific mental element of a crime, it is not applicable to "malice" established on an objective standard in a case of second degree murder. Whether it may be applicable in a case where malice is established on a subjective standard, so as to reduce the offense to manslaughter, is a matter that requires further analysis and reflection.

effect, although we do not retain *Washington* insofar as it reflects the product rule, and we permit testimony by an expert, and cross-examination, on the causal relationship between the mental disease and the existence of substantial capacity for control (and knowledge) at the time of the act. The jury will consider this testimony under the instruction on need to acquit if as a result of mental disease or defect there is a lack of substantial capacity to control the behavior in question (or appreciate its wrongfulness). We think this sufficiently communicates to the jury the kind of hard question it is called upon to decide, and the instructions will make clear that the jury is not foreclosed by opinions of experts.

The case is remanded for further consideration by the District Court in accordance with this opinion.

BAZELON, Chief Judge, concurring in part and dissenting in part:

In place of the *Durham* jury instruction, juries will now be instructed in terms of the American Law Institute test that a person is not responsible for a criminal act if as a result of mental disease or defect he lacks substantial capacity either to appreciate the wrongfulness of his conduct or to conform his conduct to the requirements of law. But the adoption of this new test is largely an anticlimax, for even though *Durham's* language survived until today's decision, the significant differences between our approach and the approach of the ALI test vanished many years ago.

Neither *Durham* nor *Brawner* lets slip our well-guarded secret that the great majority of responsibility cases concern indigents, not affluent defendants with easy access to legal and psychiatric assistance. In a long line of cases we have been asked to confront difficult questions concerning the right to an adequate psychiatric examination, the right to psychiatric assistance in the preparation of the defense, the right to counsel at various stages of the process, the role and responsibility of a government expert who testifies on behalf of an indigent defendant, the burden of proof, the right to treatment during postacquittal hospitalization, and many more. If the promise of *Durham* has not been fulfilled, the primary explanation lies in our answers, or lack of answers, to those questions. I fear that it can fairly be said of *Brawner,* just as it should be said of *Durham,* that while the generals are designing an inspiring new insignia for the standard, the battle is being lost in the trenches.

ABOLITION OF THE INSANITY DEFENSE

Richard C. Allen

Durham-McDonald is not significantly different in substantive content from the A.L.I. test. . . . As we have already pointed out, we did not adopt the new rule in the contemplation that it would affect a significant number of verdicts.

From Judge Leventhal's majority opinion in
United States v. Brawner
471 F. 2d 469 (D.C. cir. 1972)

[O]n the whole I fear that the change made by the Court today is primarily one of form rather than of substance. . . . What should by now be clear is that the problems of the responsibility defense cannot be resolved by adopting for the standard or for the jury instruction any new formulation of words.

From Judge Bazelon's concurring opinion in
United States v. Brawner
471 F. 2d 469 (D.C. cir. 1972)

Over a hundred years ago, a distinguished lawyer declared that the legislatures should "amend the law so as to require the question of insanity to be determined by a competent tribunal after a conviction of the fact of guilt." He urged that the instruction to the jury should not be " 'was the defendant capable of judging between right and wrong,' a proposition which

---

Excerpted from "The Brawner Rule—New Lyrics for an Old Tune," *Washington University Law Quarterly* (Winter 1973): 79–86.

no jury can determine, but 'did he . . . commit the specific act charged,' for whether he committed it sane or insane, the result is . . . that the safety of society requires that he should be placed in seclusion for such a period as will promote the joint ends of personal reformation and the preservation of the well being of the community at large."[1]

How modern and enlightened the words sound, even today! How eminently sensible to bring to an end the labeling process that has occupied nearly all the attention of specialists in both law and the behavioral sciences, and get to the potentially far more fruitful business of protection of society and reformation of the offender, which is, of course, the *raison d'être* of the criminal law. The idea sounds new even today, because, except for three abortive efforts several decades ago,[2] it has never been tried. The author recalls that when Dr. Cameron—then Superintendent of St. Elizabeths Hospital—propounded it in testimony before Senator Ervin's Subcommittee on Constitutional Rights of the Senate Judiciary Committee in the early 1960's, it was headline news in the *Washington Post,* which described it as "daringly innovative."

In the last few years, the proposal has gained powerful adherents: Karl Menninger,[3] Sheldon Glueck,[4] Seymour Halleck,[5] and Norval Morris,[6] to name a few.[7] The author's colleague at the National Law Center, Professor David Robinson, in his *Consultant's Report to the National Commission on Reform of Federal Criminal Laws,* offered several cogent

arguments for abolition, which may be summarized as follows:[8]

1. Trained mental health personnel—especially psychiatrists—are in critically short supply. Devoting their services to assistance in disposition and in treatment of people who need treatment, "seems far more sensible than encouraging their presence in courthouses so that they will be available to engage in retrospective reconstructions of criminal responsibility."

2. All of the prevailing insanity tests are vague, and perhaps meaningless, inviting "semantic jousting, metaphysical speculations, [and] intuitive moral judgments in the guise of factual determinations."

3. None of them offers much in the way of a guide to determining either "blameworthiness" or the infinitely more important question whether an offender ought to be institutionalized, and if so where and with what rehabilitative program.

4. The criteria for release of persons committed after a verdict of not guilty by reason of insanity are imprecise, and their application is erratic and often oppressive.

5. It makes good therapeutic sense to treat deviants as responsible for their conduct rather than as helpless victims of their "sickness."

6. The insanity defense fails to recognize the influences of social factors in restricting behavioral choices (*e.g.,* the offender suffering from delusions is exculpated, but the offender suffering from a ghetto environment and a delinquent sub-culture is not).

7. The defense overlaps with the mens rea requirement, and neither can be used effectively to determine dangerousness or need for treatment.

His recommendation was rejected by the Commission—as the idea has nearly always been rejected—with reluctance. And although it was rejected again in *Brawner,* the Court of Appeals has indicated that it is still under consideration. In *Washington* the court observed:

[I]t may be that psychiatry and the other social and behavioral sciences cannot provide sufficient data relevant to a determination of criminal responsibility no matter what our rules of evidence are. If so, we may be forced to elimi-

[1] F. Wharton and M. Stille, *Medical Jurisprudence* § 277, at 290 (2d ed. 1860).

[2] Washington, Louisiana and Mississippi. In all three, the highest court of the state declared abolition of the insanity defense unconstitutional. State v. Lange, 168 La. 958, 123 So. 639 (1929); Sinclair v. State, 161 Miss. 142, 132 So. 581 (1931); State v. Strasburg, 60 Wash. 106, 110 P. 1020 (1910). This prompted both the American Psychiatric Association and Dempsey to declare in their briefs amici that a constitutional amendment would be required; the Court in *Brawner* observed that in any event abolition could not be accomplished by "judicial fiat."

[3] K. Menninger, *The Crime of Punishment* (1969).

[4] S. Glueck, *Law and Psychiatry: Cold War or Entente Cordiale?* (1962).

[5] S. Halleck, *Psychiatry and the Dilemmas of Crime* (1967).

[6] Morris, "Psychiatry and the Dangerous Criminal," 41 *S. Cal. L. Rev.* 514 (1968).

[7] *See also* Goldstein and Katz, "Abolish the Insanity Defense—Why Not?," 72 *Yale L.J.* 873 (1963).

[8] 1 Working Papers of the National Commission on Reform of Federal Criminal Laws 229 *et seq.* (1970).

nate the insanity defense altogether, or re-fashion it in a way which is not tied so tightly to the medical model.[9]

And in *Murdock*:

Under each of the prevailing tests of criminal responsibility, the operation of the defense has been haphazard, perfunctory, and virtually inexplicable. If we cannot overcome the irrational operation of the defense, we may have no honest choice but to abandon it and hold all persons criminally responsible for their action.[10]

The defense of insanity is perhaps the most overwritten area in the law. It is really difficult to say anything new about it. As has been indicated, the proposal for abolition—novel as it may sound—has been around for a hundred years, and the arguments for and against have been so often stated that one has a feeling of *déjà vu* in discussing contemporary writings on the subject. But let us review the principal arguments *against* abolition:

1. The behavioral sciences have not advanced far enough to provide answers to such questions as moral culpability, dangerousness and treatability.[11] But if we are awaiting a scientific breakthrough on questions of moral blameworthiness, we will doubtless still be waiting on Judgment Day (when, presumably, the only authoritative decision on that score will be issued). And surely the treatment and release decision can more appropriately be made—despite the primitive state of our knowledge—after expert study and diagnosis of the offender, rather than by a legislature's prospective judgment, based on a description of a piece of behavior ("anybody who does this . . . gets that"), or through our present system of sentencing, prison and parole (which, as indicated by the statistics on recidivism, often works against both protection and rehabilitation).

2. The deterrent impact of the criminal law would be weakened.[12] But the reverse is true. It is the present haphazard and discriminatory insanity defense, postponing punishment for some, and avoiding it for others (who "couldn't help" what they did), which weakens the deterrent value of law.

3. It would obscure the "real issues." In a recent article a psychiatrist observes:

Prosecutors often distort the real issues involved in the determination of criminal responsibility. In each case in which the author has testified, for example, she has been asked on cross-examination by the prosecution (or directly by the court) some question about "treatability," that is, what disposition could be made of the allegedly insane defendant.[13]

But is not prognosis a "real issue"? Have we become so wrapped up in a game of labeling defendants "sane" or "insane" that we have lost sight of its purposes? Or perhaps it is indeed a game: "Do not pass go, do not collect $200."

4. "[E]liminating the insanity defense would remove from the criminal law and the public conscience the vitally important distinction between illness and evil. . . ."[14] To which the author can only comment: "Right on!" The dichotomy which the law has tried to maintain between the "mad" and the "bad" is a patent absurdity, whose loss will be little missed, save by professional testifiers and psychiatrist-baiting cross-examiners.

Perhaps the most telling objection to continuation of the quest for separation of the "sane" from the "insane" is that humanity just is not divisible into such discrete categories. If the elusive group we are seeking to define with our reformulations of rules are those without "free will"—without the capacity to choose to obey the rules of society—then where are they to be found? And how? The "sickest" of us, in the most remote back ward of a primitive state hospital, have some capacity to respond to rules, some consciousness of moral accountability (indeed, for some it is inability to deal with an overwhelming sense of guilt and unworthiness which has resulted in their need for hospitalization). And the "wellest" of us have areas of ego weakness, in which our range of behavioral choices is narrowed by our hereditary equipment and our experiences. If those we are trying to identify are the "treatables"—those who can benefit from mental health care—then we are simply not asking the right questions. How in any event can a lay jury be expected, on the basis of a few days or weeks of trial, to make a diagnosis and prescription of treatment—especially when the information on which it must act is filtered through the mechanisms of adversary inquiry, often focused on moral blameworthiness?

[9] Washington v. United States, 390 F.2d 444, 457 n.33 (D.C. Cir. 1967).

[10] United States v. Alexander & Murdock, 471 F.2d 923 (D.C. Cir. 1972).

[11] *See, e.g.,* Judge Haynesworth's opinion in United States v. Chandler, 393 F.2d 920 (4th Cir. 1968).

[12] *See* Erickson, "Psychiatry and the Law: An Attempt at Synthesis," 1961 *Duke L.J.* 30.

[13] Gray, "The Insanity Defense: Historical Development and Contemporary Relevance," 10 *Am. Crim. L.Q.* 559 (1972).

[14] A. Goldstein, *The Insanity Defense* 223 (1967).

Once the label is applied—"sick" or "well," "responsible" or "insane"—who is benefited? A dear friend of the author, Dr. Seymour Pollack, appeared last year as a guest speaker in the author's Criminal Law and Procedure class, and told us about his experience in the Sirhan Sirhan case. Pollack appeared as a witness for the prosecution, and Dr. Bernard Diamond, also an eminent California forensic psychiatrist, appeared for the defense. Both made heroic investments of time—literally hundreds of hours of clinical interviewing, examination of reports and documents, conference with counsel, and testifying in court. To what end? Was society one whit better protected by it all? Was Sirhan Sirhan's condition—whatever it may be—improved in the slightest degree? We enjoyed the discussion of the case, and I think the students learned something from our analysis of the direct and cross-examination of these extraordinarily well-qualified experts. But I for one could not help but think how much more productive would have been the devotion of their considerable talents to something like providing consultation services to probation officers, setting up group therapy programs in correctional institutions, or establishing halfway houses for the vast majority of offenders, who cannot profit from—and indeed will be harmed by—incarceration in a prison. The author's first collaborator in teaching law and psychiatry at the Menninger School of Psychiatry, Dr. Joseph Satten, put it this way:

[T]he psychiatrist can make his greatest contribution in legal situations if he enters after the question of guilt and innocence has been resolved and when the only question is what to do with the individual in his own and society's best interest. In other words, the psychiatrist can do the most good when he remains in his clinical, treatment-oriented role.[15]

Finally, the defense of insanity works directly against both the goals of protection of society and reformation of the offender. As to the former, since the defense is just that—an affirmative defense—it may be raised or not raised at the option of the defendant. Should not treatment, when treatment is needed to effect behavioral change, be a part of the armamentarium of society, along with incarceration, vocational training, probation, and the other correctional tools? As to the latter, the whole process leading to an adjudication of non-responsibility may be counter-

therapeutic. Is not the whole objective of therapy to help the patient accept the fact that he is responsible for what he does, and that he must take control of his life and make choices of behavior on reality-oriented grounds and not on fantasies? For the psychopath-sociopath-antisocial personality, an acquittal "by reason of insanity" provides the one, irrefutable defense against any efforts at behavioral change: "I can't help myself; I'm sick!" Shades of "Dear Officer Krupke!"

This section of the article has been, perhaps, more polemical than specific. There are problems in effecting abolition of the insanity defense which demand fuller exposition. There is the problem of constitutionality if the change is made by the courts or the legislatures[16] (which the author is happy to leave to other scholars). And there is the problem of mens rea. Many of the substantive offenses are statutorily defined in terms of mental state (like malice aforethought, deliberately and premeditatedly, willfully, maliciously, with intent to . . . , etc.), and each may well involve the kind of intra-psychic foray now conducted under the rubric of the insanity rule (as California has discovered under its bifurcated trial system). And there is also the problem of the stigma and deprivation of civil and jural rights which now follows a criminal conviction. Perhaps the only way effectively to abolish the insanity defense is to abolish as well the moral condemnation of the criminal law, substituting for it a simple process of adjudicating the operative facts of guilt.

But, most important of all, if the defense of insanity is removed, something must be put in its place. And it is on this point that the brief of the National District Attorneys Association[17] is deficient. The essential *quid pro quo*, in the author's opinion, is establishment of a real system of corrections, with differential treatment modalities geared to individual needs and capabilities, and not to reified labels. A system primarily community-based is needed, instead of the fortress-like prisons and "hospitals" (often differing from prisons only in that the guards wear white coats) of the present criminal justice system.

There is, of course, a danger in all this—that of developing a *Clockwork Orange*-like therapeutic state. The author recognizes the

---

[15] Satten, "The Concept of Responsibility in Psychiatry and Its Relationship to the Legal Problems of 'Criminal Responsibility,'" 4 *U. Kan. L. Rev.* 361, 363 (1956).

[16] *See* note 2 *supra.*

[17] Brief amicus in *U.S.* v. *Brawner*, 471 F.2d 969 (D.C. Cir. 1972), recommending abolition of the defense except as mental impairment may negate capacity to entertain specific intent. Cf. § 502, S. 1400, 93rd Congress, 1st Session, March 27, 1973 (Administration Bill to revise Title 18, U.S. Code).

problem—it is real, but not insoluble. If the present system of determining "insanity" is to be abandoned for one in which triers of fact decide only the factual questions of who did what to whom, and whether the thing done is proscribed by law, and whether the whole process of proof conforms to due process safeguards, and in which the disposition decision is made after trial, by a more expert tribunal, after more intensive study than can be provided via the trial process, then that decision too must accord that elemental fairness subsumed in the phrase "due process of law." There must be provision for notice, representation, a right to independent evaluation, hearing, confrontation, and judicial review. And perhaps there should also be membership on the dispositional panel of judges and lawyers as well as behavioral scientists, for their decisions involve social and legal, as well as medical and psychological, considerations.

A society must decide where it will spend its limited chips. If the optimal treatment for a given offender is one-to-one psychotherapy three times a week for a period of years, society has, it would seem, the right to say that it would prefer to devote its resources to other things (say, school mental health programs), and to take its chances with more traditional handling of the offender. Again, if "dangerousness," or the likelihood of repetition of the offense were the only criteria for release, most first degree murderers would be back on the streets within a few months, and most exhibitionists would be incarcerated (in hospital or prison) for life. But there is a social interest at stake, and perhaps the deterrence objective of the criminal law makes necessary some period of punitive custody for an offense as serious as murder; and perhaps society must accept the risk that the exhibitionist will repeat his offense under some future stress, if the only alternative is life imprisonment.

POSTLUDE

This article was subtitled: "New Lyrics for an Old Tune." The words of the *Brawner* rule are somewhat less ambiguous than those of *Durham-McDonald*—somewhat more in accord with what we know about human personality, but the tune is still the same and it is discordant, out of harmony with the objectives of the criminal law. Psychiatrists used to be called "alienists," and those whom they treated were regarded as "alien"—to be identified, separated from the "sane" and shuttled off to some remote, secure place. Whatever ultimately happens to the insanity rule—whether it is refined, substituted for, or scrapped—what happens to the mentally impaired offender is of infinitely greater importance. The Roman poet Terence said it simply and well: "I am a human being . . . and nothing that is human is alien to me."

ADMINISTRATION BILL S. 1400, 93D CONGRESS, 1ST SESSION

Introduced March 27, 1973 by Senators Hruska and McClellan (the Administration Bill for Revision of Title 18, U.S. Code)

Sec. 502 *Insanity*

"It is a defense to a prosecution under any federal statute that the defendant, as a result of mental disease or defect, lacked the state of mind required as an element of the offense charged. Mental disease or defect does not otherwise constitute a defense."

Note: other provisions contain procedures:

1. for pre-trial psychiatric examination for persons filing notice of intention to introduce evidence of insanity at time of offense;

2. for hearing to determine dangerousness of persons found not guilty by reason of insanity, and commitment of persons so found;

3. for hearing on the present mental condition of persons found guilty of the offense charged, at the instance of the defendant or the court, and for commitment of persons found in need of custody, care or treatment in a mental institution; and

4. for commitment following expiration of sentence of persons suffering from a mental disease or defect as a result of which his release would create substantial danger to himself or to the person or property of others.

PRESIDENT NIXON'S PROPOSAL ON THE INSANITY DEFENSE

N.Y.U. COLLOQUIUM

The topic under discussion was "President Nixon's Proposal On The Insanity Defense." The proposed statute supported by the President reads:

§502. Insanity
It is a defense to a prosecution under any federal statute that the defendant, as a result of mental disease or defect, lacked the state of mind required as an element of the offense charged. Mental disease or defect does not otherwise constitute a defense.

The panelists were:

Moderator: Professor Henry H. Foster, Jr.; Professor of Law, New York University School of Law.
Morris Herman, M.D.: Professor and Acting Chairman, Department of Psychiatry, School of Medicine New York University.
Arthur Zitrin, M.D.: Professor of Psychiatry, School of Medicine New York University. Formerly Director of Psychiatry of Bellevue Hospital.
Professor Gerhard O. W. Mueller: Professor of Law, New York University School of Law and Director of New York University Law School Criminal Law Education and Research Center.
Professor H. H. A. Cooper: Deputy Director, Center of Forensic Psychiatry and Deputy Director, New York University Law School Criminal Law Education and Research Center.

FOSTER: It has been said that the measure of a civilization is the way in which it treats the most despised among us. That is, criminals and the insane. The two avowed functions of the criminal process I would assert are first to find the truth and second, and equally important, to do so by a fair and civilized process.

The matters we discuss tonight arise against the background of extensive discretion in the criminal processes. And in one sense we are talking about the quality of mercy, in another sense we are talking about the theory and purpose of punishment. And still in another sense we hope to be talking about what is functional and what will work. Although it's not necessarily true that to understand is to forgive, we must understand human behavior if the law is to be an effective means of social control. To have the beginning of understanding perforce we must consult other disciplines such as psychiatry, sociology, criminology and others. In addition to the larger moral and philosophical issues we hope to consider the practical aspects of the insanity defense. In the first place it should be noted that the defense is rarely used and succeeds in only a negligible fraction of cases. Under the so-called *Durham* rule in the District of Columbia, at most 2 to 3 percent of all criminal cases were terminated by an acquittal by reason of insanity. And of those acquittals 70 percent were by the judge without a jury. Throughout the rest of the country perhaps 1 percent or less of such pleas succeed and ordinarily are asserted in only the most serious cases. In New York during the 1960's there were only 11 successful "not guilty by reason of insanity" pleas in the whole state, averaging a little over one per year. Either the cases where the plea might have been advanced were disposed of by a guilty plea or were resolved on the issue of competency to stand trial. Or perhaps there are cases where counsel for the defense preferred Sing Sing to Matteawan.

With regard to the specific proposal we are to consider, it may be understood that substantially the same proposal was considered and rejected by the National Commission on Reform of the Federal Criminal Law under the chairmanship of former Governor Pat Brown, by the full court of the Circuit Court of Appeals for the District of Columbia in the *Brawner* case, and was rejected even by Senator McClellan when he drafted a revision to the Federal Criminal Code. The proposal of President Nixon we will consider tonight is attributed to Assistant Attorney General Henry Petersen.

Excerpts reprinted with permission from *Journal of Psychiatry and Law* 297 (Fall 1973).

MUELLER: Anglo-American law has never been interested in mental illness, insanity, in the medical sense as such. We have always, supposedly, been interested in the effects which mental illness may have on any of the justiciable issues that may be before the court.

The *M'Naghten* rules very simply, in 1843, meant to focus on the two halves of the crime concept that are relevant. The judges in *M'Naghten* did not want a defense simply in terms of broad questions of rationality, simply in terms of broad mental illness. They did not want to distinguish between the mentally ill and the mentally nonill. Rather, they asked, "Was there mental illness and did that mental illness have the effect of depriving the defendant of a capacity to form the action to engage in the relevant action involved?" In other words, they said, "Did the defendant know the nature and the quality of his act?" Or, in the alternative, "Did the defendant lack the capacity by reason of such mental illness to form the requisite criminal intention, evil intention?" . . . That was the intent of 1843. Unhappily the test of 1843 fell into the hands of a lot of lawyers. They looked up the modern meaning of these words, and ultimately we wound up with a test which simply asked whether or not the defendant knew the difference between right and wrong. Well even if he is a tottering idiot or a human vegetable he might have some apperception of right and wrong, and under those circumstances almost anybody could be sent to the gallows. . . .

Now, the latest experimentation with insanity tests is the test which is proposed by President Nixon in Senate Bill 1400. . . .

Here is likely what is going to happen. . . . If for example, the intention to kill a human being is an element, or an ingredient within the criminal definition of murder or of involuntary (sic) manslaughter, and if the defendant was so mentally ill that he could not form this requisite intent, then the defendant is to be exculpated. While this is true of previous tests this one goes further, because if the defendant by bringing in a psychiatrist only throws some reasonable doubt about his capacity to formulate the requisite criminal intent, then he's entitled to an acquittal.

Now in the past, the defendants in criminal cases could bring in their psychiatrists only when they had made an insanity defense. . . . Now the defendant can bring in a psychiatric expert with respect to every individual and discrete psychological element of the crime. . . . Every time the issue comes up as to whether or not an individual psychological or axiological element was constituted by the defendant, a psychiatrist is now competent to say, "Maybe not." In other words, he may testify that since the defendant is suffering from such and such a disease and in general such and such diseases have such and such an effect, the defendant may not have entertained the necessary mental state for the commission of the offense. Now it probably will depend on how this test is interpreted in the court. . . . But I think the opportunity for a much broader psychiatric intervention is given. . . .

One word in conclusion—there's another point in the Nixon draft which refers to psychiatric testimony . . . and that is in section 2003 with respect to the presentence report and commitment. And there's a further reference with respect to the . . . potential imposition of capital punishment. . . . These are relatively orthodox provisions that simply say that when it comes to sentencing, the defendant's character, background, mental, emotional, and physical health are obviously issues and, of course, relevant testimony may be introduced. So my conclusion is right now that if Nixon wanted to get a tough conservative bill—he did not succeed. I think what we will experience in this country is a considerable broadening of the power and influence of psychiatrists during the trial of criminal cases in the United States.

COOPER: There are many ways in which, if you like, criminal intent can be perverted, diverted, changed. . . . If, for example, we take the position of strict liability, we simply forbid a particular line of conduct, then it is of no importance, whatsoever, to consider the state of mind with which the individual acted because the law has postulated this is not an element of the offense. The question of the quality of mind and what it means in psychiatric terms is a relatively late development, . . . and it is a sophisticated development but it is one which has not come even, to full fruition in the latter half of this century. . . .

It's easy to set standards, legislatively. What most standards turn out to be in terms of criminal policy in the administration of criminal justice depends very much on the judges, and what the judges make of those words under our Anglo-American system. And whether or not this latest proposal will be interpreted in liberal or conservative fashion is what will determine the extent of responsibility, criminal responsibility, in this case. It is not difficult to guess at what lies behind this proposal. It is not difficult to see the objectives of those who drafted it. It is not difficult to predict . . . that their objectives will not be realized if in fact the judges take a contrary view. In the civil law system the matter is very complicated, indeed, because they have refinement which is unknown to Anglo-American jurisprudence. They do not talk, for example, simply about capacity or responsibility or even imputability. Those of you who are familiar with some of the civil law works in this area might know, for example, the work of a great Spanish jurist Jimenez de Asúa where three huge volumes deal with what we would term "*mens rea*." They deal exhaustively with every aspect of criminal responsibility. They deal with this with a refinement which is unknown to the common law. They do this because they try to give every possible solution to every conceivable future case so as to tie the hands of the judges.

In the Anglo-American system what the issue of responsibility means and what is in fact the insanity defense at any particular point in time depends very much on the adventuressness or timorousness of the particular judges on the court at any one time.

FOSTER: It is true that every word in the *M'Naghten* formula has received differing definitions and constructions; often in the same jurisdiction. It is true that we are in a semantical bog, so to speak, when we start talking about any test of responsibility. Yet, it seems to me, that to opt for this proposal may involve the implication that the law is willing to forsake the moral, ethical responsibility that it has assumed for centuries. To my mind it would be the equivalent of removing the reasonable man from the whole structure of negligence law.

I have no doubt about the sponsorship of this particular proposal and the backing it has received. I have no doubt about public sympathy for law and order and I suppose that the public may well support any measure that it construes as designed to make it tough on criminal defenses. Yet, even though we have a movement for no-fault insurance, no-fault divorce, it seems to me that this is peculiarly an area for maintaining the notion of blameworthiness which is what I think the *M'Naghten* rules and all of the other tests proposed so far have been all about. Just as proximate cause is a shorthand expression in the law of torts as to whether or not liability should be imposed on the basis of blameworthiness or the allocation of the loss, so too in the criminal area this matter of responsibility is a similar judgment on culpability or blameworthiness, and I would hesitate long before I would excise or eradicate from the criminal law this difficult, perplexing job.

HERMAN: Basically the psychiatrist is a specialist in behavior and a person who evaluates a human being behaviorally in a specific fashion that can be recorded, documented and transmitted. Now he necessarily feels that he wants a forum to transmit this. . . . And this was one of the very important arguments in relation to the *M'Naghten* rules, that these rules constricted the doctor in being able to transmit this information in full form and that the questions that were put to him were such that it did not enable him to give full documentation. . . . Any rule that will enable the psychiatrist to give testimony on a full basis we can live with, . . . but we have another . . . concern . . . in what happens to the individual. . . . We also are interested in the question of the violation of liberties involved. . . .

Now any experienced psychiatrist in the forensic field knows that the rules are very important to lawyers. They live by rules and words and definitions and . . . sometimes it appears to us that they're more important than the human beings involved. I'm sure we're wrong but this is the attitude we get—to such a degree that there are a significant number of psychiatrists who won't partake in the operation whatsoever. They're really overwhelmed by the aspect of advocacy that's involved, and the apparent inhumanity aspects that pertain to this procedure, and they see no merit in it. As a matter of fact psychiatrists such as Cameron advocate, and others like him have advocated, a kind of avoidance of the whole problem, saying that what you should concern yourself with in court and in law is (putting it in a general, nonlegal fashion): Did he do it or didn't he do it? Is he accountable for the act (never mind responsible, but accountable in some other general way)? And if he did the act then let's decide and then bring in the psychiatrist to help to determine what are you going to do with the offender after you've made this decision.

Many psychiatrists advocate that psychiatrists get out of the courtrooms because their major function ought to be after trial in relation to disposition and care. Now the American Psychiatric Association recently also came out with an amicus curiae statement asking for abolition—abolition of the responsibility aspect in court and removing psychiatrists from any kind of participation in this determination. Now many problems persist, as long as this is not yet current. Psychiatrists do try to fit into the framework of law, but use whatever means are available to influence changes within the law, while recognizing that society in the long run is the organization that decides what exists in its midst. We cannot autocratically make these changes. Therefore, we must also act with another cloak and that is, we have to ask you to influence society to adopt changes and to modify the patterns they already have.

FOSTER: Dr. Zitrin, could you tell us a little bit about the competency to stand trial issue and how it's checked out in places such as Bellevue Hospital? I direct your attention specifically to this because this is the practical phase of these cases. If the person is screened out and held incompetent to stand trial the chances are that he will be sent to an institution, either a civil hospital or to Matteawan. (I'm talking now about state rather than federal cases.) And he will be kept until he is competent to stand trial and returned for that purpose at which time the district attorney will have some discretion as to whether to press charges or not.

ZITRIN: We at Bellevue often have the responsibility of deciding whether defendants who have committed a crime are competent to stand trial, whether they, because of mental disease or illness, lack the capacity to be able to understand the nature of the charges against them or assist in their defense. One of the reasons why there are so very few cases . . . where the insanity defense is offered is because many of these people are screened out beforehand because they are found not competent to stand trial. . . . This screening procedure precludes the insanity defense in a great many cases and perhaps we'll have the opportunity to return to this in some of the discussion.

I want to spend just a few minutes sharpening the issue a little bit. We're talking about President Nixon's—not President Nixon's insanity defense which is what my inclination is to say—President Nixon's proposal.

Now first, what was the express purpose of this legislation to start with? It is designed, they say, to curb unconscionable abuse of the insanity defense by criminals. Now, precisely what kind of abuse of the insanity defense by criminals has there been? The facts I think are really quite different. First of all, when the insanity defense is used, and used successfully, no one walks away from the courtroom free. All these patients are incarcerated. They're hospitalized and in many instances for a longer period of time than they would have been jailed had they been found guilty of the crime with which they were charged. Also there are very few federal defendants who raise the insanity defense and even fewer prevail when they do raise that defense. One administration official estimated that there were fewer than 100 defendants a year out of more than 50 thousand federal criminal cases brought annually to raise that defense and the number has been decreasing each year.

In addition the proposal would not be applicable to most crimes committed in the District of Columbia where the largest number of insanity defenses are ordinarily raised. And I'm inclined to agree with Dershowitz when he said recently (as quoted in the *New York Times*) that the most likely result of the Nixon proposal is that nothing very much would change. Here I disagree with you Gerhard, I think there would be very little difference under this law, very little difference from what we see today. As Dershowitz said "the battlefield may shift from the issue of right versus wrong to the equally troublesome one of intent." But it's his feeling and I'm inclined to agree that the jurors will hear the same kind of testimony or at least testimony not very substantially different from what they hear today. There will be the same kinds of unseemly battles of psychiatric experts that neither enlighten a jury, in my view, nor advance the cause of justice. My feeling is that we need not more but fewer psychological concepts in our criminal law. Most of these I think, are vague or indefinable—intent, insanity, and mental illness. They're imprecise and I think that instead of introducing more such concepts into the law we should remove as many as possible. This has been done in the civil law for the most part and many crimes are, I understand, defined without any reference whatsoever to intent. I believe that this is a model that we can use in the criminal law as well. My point of view is, very simply, perhaps simplistically, that the jury should restrict itself to deciding whether the accused committed the act or not. . . .

Let's keep the psychiatrist out of the court when this issue is being determined. Let's bring him in to talk about the things that he knows best, let's bring him in at the stage of the proceeding where I think he can make a more important and less controversial contribution to the cause of justice in determining what disposition is most suitable for a particular defendant.

Now exactly how that should be done, whether by a panel of psychiatrists or other professionals or in a separate court proceeding, a trial with a jury hearing testimony, is something about which there are differences of opinion. However, I'd be inclined to take the psychiatrist out of the court when the issue of guilt or innocence is being decided.

FOSTER: Well, quite recently there was a study by the University of Virginia Law School's research team—research group— which concluded that a constitutional amendment would be essential and necessary to do what you suggest. The two cases in point, one from Washington and one from Mississippi, both held it would be unconstitutional to do what you suggest; namely to have the jury determine guilt alone and then have a panel determine the disposition of the offender in terms of his mental state.

COOPER: I have read some portions of the *Hadfield* case referred to by Professor Cooper. It was in 1800, 40 years before *M'Naghten*. A very enlightened discussion. . . . Guilty intent —*mens rea*—product of mental disease; all of that is in there. . . . These are part and parcel of the entire experience of having to pass on the guilt or innocence of the individual. If the psychiatrists don't do it, somebody else will do it. . . .

MUELLER: I simply wanted to disagree with Arthur Zitrin because I think along with Andy Watson and various other of my criminal law colleagues, that there is quite clearly a potential for greater defense strategy in federal criminal cases in the Nixon proposal. Now it may not have been intended but it is definitely there. I think the potential for greater psychiatric intervention is there as well. And I think there is another important potential as well— a potential for legal education to develop theories concerning the psychological element of crimes, theories not yet satisfactorily worked out. But these elements of the crime, the psychological and axiological elements, call them the *mens rea* elements will be very important under this test, and that I think is a very positive thing.

But now there's one very large issue; the trouble with Dr. Cameron's position, with which I think both of our psychiatrists are in sympathy, is that it avoids not only the insanity plea, but also the question of responsibility. That to me is quite unfortunate. Government does not have the right to deal with deviance as such. There is no such right. Let everybody deviate as much as he cares. Government has a right to deal only with such persons who have committed a crime. But whether or not a deviant has committed a crime depends precisely on whether or not he fulfilled all the the elements of the crime and that means the psychological elements as well, his *mens rea*, his intent to kill, or to steal. If that intent is not present, then the crime is not consittuted and government has no right to deal with this human being. Consequently, I'm afraid we do need psychiatrists and they cannot avoid the issue. They have to come in and tell us whether or not a given mental illness had the effect of depriving the defendant of this capacity.

Now there lurks an even bigger issue in the background. Of course once somebody is acquitted because, on the basis of mental illness he could not form the requisite mental element, there still is a temptation on the part

of society to put him away. Well that second putting away, in other words the confinement, of deviants who have not committed a crime, is a very, very tough and dangerous issue. It's the issue that crops up in the Soviet Union all the time, and it has cropped up in this country with Ezra Pound and various other people. When do you have the right to put a deviant away, who's dangerous and how do you measure this dangerousness? I'm satisfied for the time being that our legal concepts here are OK. Dangerousness is to be measured both in terms of dangerousness to oneself and to the lives and safety of others. Perhaps we can live with this concept. But I much prefer putting that question into the criminal trial to begin with, and in a manner more easily answerable with the aid of psychiatry: Was a crime involving certain elements, some of them psychological, committed by the defendant?

COOPER: I find myself in the very difficult position of having to say that what we are really debating here tonight is not a medical problem nor a legal problem—it is essentially a moral problem.

Somehow or other we must look at this on two levels. If it becomes a question, if you like, in lawyers' terminology, of responsibility and the reproachability, which is really blameworthiness, . . . but this is considered usually . . . in a highly charged political atmosphere and very often in connection with the death penalty.

FOSTER: . . . What I'm suggesting is that in a country, including federal jurisdictions, where typically the judge is a former prosecutor and has that background and as often as not—more often than not—he starts with a bias in criminal cases. Once we start getting rid of the responsibility element and focus solely upon the *mens rea* and the *actus reus* we're going to find that the requisite criminal intent is narrowed down consistently. That I would predict would be the consequence of the adoption of this rule. And if that were true, we would be, in effect, routinely convicting people who in psychiatric judgment had no free choice regarding what they did. . . . Frequently at trial the district attorney asks the psychiatric witness, "Did this man know that he was in a house? Did he recognize, did the patient recognize this was a human being across from him? Did he know that this was a knife he had in his hand and that he stabbed him?" What I'm afraid of here . . . is that this is the satisfaction of the element of criminal intent which will suffice under a tough law and order approach to these problems. If there is what the psychiatrist calls sensorium or cognition, that will be isolated and removed from the total dynamics of the individual. This I think is the great peril that we face in any such approach as here suggested, assuming that it may be constitutional, which certainly is not free from doubt.

ZITRIN: There's been a good deal of concern expressed about the guilt and the stigma attached to a finding of guilt, particularly if the guilty person lacked the guilty mind we call *mens rea*. Let me summarize Wooten's recommendation on the defense of insanity. She would recommend a legal system in which there would be a "conviction" without blame, without stigma as we know it today. Whenever a person is found to have committed an act proscribed by law, *mens rea* would be discarded from the definition of legal accountability, the state of the offender's mind being relevant only to his postconviction disposition. Based on predictions of future recurrence of socially dangerous conduct, as well as other criteria that would be used, the choice of disposition would be wide in each case ranging from immediate release to various forms of individualized treatment. The connotations of

that kind of conviction would be very different from those which adhere today to a finding of guilty and the state of the individual's mind would be important in determining what happens after the determination of guilt or innocence is made. . . .

WEINSTEIN: I believe that we are approaching the point in psychiatry where there is some evidence that we can explain in some depth why an individual does a particular act. To leave to the jury only the question of whether a defendant has done the act or has not may be a retreat from dynamic psychiatry. I think it's a position which can only set back our system of law which has advanced in its sophistication, its compassion and its civilized qualities by looking to why an individual has done a particular act. I think, furthermore, that it's inappropriate to deprive the jury of this privilege of trying to determine why an indviidual did a particular act and thereby perhaps exculpating him from "guilt," in the sense that we talk about ordinarily.

In the last comment that Dr. Zitrin made about an ideal society where the jury's finding would only be something other than guilt— well I'll wait until that society and that legal system exists before I would eliminate the insanity defense as we know it today.

UNITED STATES v. HAWKINS

. . . The principal issue presented on this appeal, and which we think to be dispositive of it, is whether the prosecutor's improper closing and rebuttal arguments were so highly prejudicial as to require reversal.

Interspersed throughout the Government's closing and rebuttal arguments were the following:

CLOSING ARGUMENT

"You can read the paper in the big cases and it always is there, isn't it, Sirhan Sirhan, Jack Ruby, Ammidown, Timm and Caldwell, when they were caught red-handed in front of an

audience or bevies of people, they turn to insanity because that is their only hope."

"Now, oh, he is dangerous, he is a murderer. But he is not mentally ill. Sirhan Sirhan and Jack Ruby and Ammidown, they didn't fool anybody, nor does he, has he?"

". . . He is not crazy, ladies and gentlemen, or insane, you know somebody passed me in the hall a moment ago and said you'll never get first degree murder—

THE COURT: Wait a minute let's don't talk about things like that.
MR. ROBINSON: I[t] was going to be an analogy [*sic*], Your Honor.

---

480 F.2d 1151 (1973) (CA–DC)

THE COURT: No, you cannot make that analogy and the jury will disregard it.

MR. ROBINSON: Mr. Robinson [you] might think you can't get first degree murder in the case like this, because it's what somebody might say is 'a Saturday night special.' I mean, you don't have a $50,000 suburban house that you live in like Mrs. Ammidown, you don't have a deputy chief of the city like Heidi Ann Fletcher, a police officer got shot.

But you see, ladies and gentlemen, this is the worst kind of murder, I mean its the worst. 15 years old, he never even knew Watusi Jones. Mrs. Ammidown at least knew Mr. Ammidown, there was friction. He never even knew the man that murdered him."

At the conclusion of the Government's closing argument both defense counsel moved for a mistrial based on the Government's comparison with the *Ammidown* case. This motion was denied.

REBUTTAL

"How many policemen die a year in this country in the line of duty? How many in Washington, D.C. alone? How many officer Sigmons get shot down in a bank robbery by a Mr. Timm? Do we just cover them all, these deaths, with a blanket of insanity?

"And let them all go to a nice hospital under some kind of a charade of a defense? Or do we stand up tall and we defend those men who lost their lives in the line of duty? . . .

". . . He was intelligent and Napoleon was a genius and he tried to wreck all of Europe. He bolled [*sic*] over anybody that got in his way. Hitler was a genius in his own way. But he's not a Hitler or a Napoleon, but he ran in gangs, gangs from which all the gangsters have gone to jail, and what I am saying, ladies and gentlemen, it is time for the final gangster to go to jail and not to a hospital.". . .

Here, as in United States v. Clinton L. Phillips,* the same Government attorney resorted to arguments clearly designed to arouse the passion and prejudice of the jury. When a defendant's sole defense is insanity, a prosecutor cannot be permitted to compare that defense to other infamous crimes where that defense has been raised and rejected.

Once again, as in United States v. Clinton L. Phillips, *supra*, we quote from Brown v. United States, 125 U.S. App. D.C. 220, 224, 370 F.2d 242, 246 (1966):

"While such an argument is always to be condemned as 'an appeal wholly irrelevant to any facts or issues in the case,' Viereck v. United States, 318 U.S. 236, 247, 63 S.Ct. 561, 566, 87 L. Ed. 734 (1943), and as a dereliction of the prosecutor's high duty to prosecute fairly, see Berger v. United States, 295 U.S. 78, 88, 55 S.Ct. 629, 79 L. Ed. 1314 (1935), in the context of current events, raising the spectre of [heinous crimes] . . . was an especially flagrant and reprehensible appeal to passion and prejudice.

Although the prosecutor 'may strike hard blows, he is not at liberty to strike foul ones. It is as much his duty to refrain from improper methods calculated to produce a wrongful conviction as it is to use every legitimate means to bring about a just one.' Berger v. United States, *supra*, 295 U.S. at 88, 55 S.Ct. at 633; Viereck v. United States, *supra*, 318 U.S. at 248, 63 S.Ct. at 567."

Reversed.

* 155 U.S. App. D.C.—, 476 F.2d 538 (decided May 16, 1973) (Per Curiam).

LEE v. COUNTY COURT

SCILEPPI, Judge. We have been called upon to decide questions relating to the effect of a plea of not guilty by reason of insanity on a defendant's constitutional rights. . . .

In 1964, Rufus Lee, petitioner herein, was indicted for the murder of two women which occurred on November 5, 1964, two days after his release from a mental institution. . . . Lee . . . pleaded not guilty by reason of insanity and in preparation for the new trial, the District Attorney's motion for a mental examination was granted by the County Court in February, 1969. Defendant, asserting his privilege against self incrimination, refused to submit to the examination and was found in contempt of court. The Appellate Division reversed the contempt order [32 A.D.2d 885, 302 N.Y.S.2d 171] and the County Court once again granted the District Attorney's application for an examination to be held on September 19, 1969. This order provided that defense counsel and an assistant district attorney could be present at such examination and further directed that:

"Defendant, or defendant's attorney, shall note his objections for the record and such objection shall be passed upon by the Trial Court prior to the trial of this indictment; and it is, further

"Ordered, that in the event that this defendant shall refuse to answer questions deemed pertinent by the designated psychiatrists, then this court will entertain a motion by the People of the State of New York to strike defendant's defense of insanity and deny the defendant the right to call psychiatric witnesses in his behalf."

On the advice of counsel, petitioner refused to answer questions concerning his behavior on the day of the crime and those relating to this conduct in October, August, and July of 1964. Absent defendant's answers to their questions, the psychiatrists were unable to proffer an opinion as to Lee's capacity to commit the crime* and on motion of the District

Attorney, the County Court ordered that Lee's plea of not guilty by reason of insanity be stricken; that he be precluded from offering psychiatric evidence on his behalf; and that the matter proceed to trial. Lee, thereupon commenced in the Appellate Division, the instant article 78 proceeding in the nature of prohibition seeking an order preventing the trial court from striking his insanity defense and from directing that he proceed to trial without being able to present evidence of his insanity. The Appellate Division vacated the order striking the defense, but directed that Lee submit to another mental examination without the presence of nonmedical personnel and the matter is here on cross appeals from the Appellate Division order. . . .

Petitioner Lee argues that the privilege against self incrimination allows a defendant, who pleads not guilty by reason of insanity, to refuse to answer questions put to him by court-appointed psychiatrists during a pretrial mental examination and that the court improperly struck the plea when defendant relied upon his privilege. Thus, we are called upon to determine whether the privilege obtains at an examination pursuant to section 658 of the Code of Criminal Procedure and if so, whether it is waived when a defendant interposes the defense of insanity.

These are not questions which lend themselves to facile solutions. The People have a right to expect that criminal transgressors will be brought to justice. However, it is our concern with injustice which mandates that constitutional rights be safeguarded and that procedures evolve which protect the interests of both society and defendants alike. . . .

Traditionally, the privilege against self-incrimination has been deemed to protect against so-called testimonial disclosures (8 Wigmore, Evidence, §§2263–2265). . . . Following this rationale, the Supreme Court wrote in Schmerber v. California, 384 U.S. 757, 763–764, that: ". . . [B]oth federal and state courts have usually held that it offers no protection against compulsion to submit to fingerprinting, photographing, or measurements, to write or speak for identification, to appear in court to stand, to assume a stance, to walk, or

---

* It appears that in the years since the commission of the crime, Lee's mental condition has improved and that no one suggests that he is now incompetent to stand trial (per curium).

267 N.E. 2d 452, 318 N.Y.S. 2d 449 (1971).

to make a particular gesture. The distinction which has emerged, often expressed in different ways, is that the privilege is a bar against compelling 'communications' or 'testimony,' but that compulsion which makes a suspect or accused the source of 'real or physical evidence' does not violate it."

Thus, if statements made by a defendant during pretrial psychiatric examinations are nothing more than the exhibition of a part of the body, i.e., the mind, the privilege would not obtain (see Danforth, Pretrial Mental Examination, 19 *Rutgers L. Rev.* 489, 493). It is our view, however, that these examinations do not readily fit into the Schmerber dichotomy. In formulating an opinion on a defendant's mental capacity, the physicians must draw from both physical and verbal responses. Inasmuch as these responses are relevant on a material element of the crime, *mens rea*, we are unable to analogize them to the mere exhibition of one's body. While strong argument can be advanced that the privilege against self-incrimination should not be extended beyond what is generally considered its present scope (see Friendly, The Fifth Amendment Tomorrow: The Case For Constitutional Change, 37 *U. of Cincinnati L. Rev.* 671), recent decisions of the Supreme Court of the United States have extended the application of the privilege. . . . Accordingly, it is our view that the privilege does obtain during pretrial psychiatric examinations. . . . This is not to say that a defendant who proffers an insanity defense may hide behind that defense because of his privilege and thereby make the People's burden of proving sanity insurmountable. In People v. Di Piazza ([24 N.Y.2d] at p. 352, 300 N.Y.S.2d at p. 553, 248 N.E.2d at p. 418) we said that where a defendant defends by reason of insanity and requests a mental examination, "he may not complain that his privilege against self-incrimination or his right to counsel was violated." Though it is true that in the instant case it was the District Attorney who requested the examination, it is our view that it is not who requests the examination which controls, but rather the plea of not guilty by reason of insanity, which is the basis of the psychiatrist's competency to testify at the trial. Nor does the mere fact that the examination is requested by the District Attorney necessarily mean that the physician will be a witness for the People. In point of fact, the record herein indicates that the court-appointed psychiatrists testified for the defendant. . . .

Accordingly, we hold that the privilege is waived when a defendant interposes his insanity defense. In so doing, we note that several jurisdictions have considered the problem, reaching substantially the same result (see, e.g., In re Spencer, 63 Cal. 2d 400, 46 Cal. Rptr. 753, 406 P.2d 33; State v. Whitlow, 45 N.J.3, 210 A.2d 763; . . . United States v. Baird, 2 Cir., 414 F.2d 700; . . .; contra, Hunt v. State, 248 Ala. 217, 27 So. 2d 186; . . .; French v. District Ct., 153 Colo. 10, 384 P.2d 268; People v. English, 31 Ill. 2d 301, 201 N.E.2d 455; . . .). Lest there be any doubt, we are not saying that because of this waiver, the psychiatrist is a competent witness on all matters concerning the commission of the crime. A defendant's waiver of privilege because of his plea of insanity only permits the physician to testify as to the facts which formulate the basis of his medical opinion on the question of sanity. To prevent the psychiatrist from giving the basis of his opinion would vastly limit the value of psychiatric examinations. . . . This is not to say, however, that any admission as to the crime in question can be considered by the jury in their determination of whether the defendant committed the acts which constitute the crime charged. Nor shall the District Attorney be permitted to use the psychiatric examination as a source of evidence which would be relevant on the issue of guilt.

From the foregoing analysis concluding that the privilege was waived by the plea. Lee had no constitutional right to refuse to participate in the examination ordered below.

We now turn to the question whether the County Court properly struck the plea. The court's action was predicated on its view that Lee could not raise an insanity defense and at the same time refuse to submit to an examination. While we agree with that view, we are of the opinion that, inasmuch as a defendant's capacity to commit a crime is not placed in issue by his availability for examination, but by his plea, striking the plea is not a proper sanction for a refusal to co-operate. Since these examinations are the most effective aid to a determination of the merits of the defense, we hold that where a defendant chooses to deprive the triers of fact of this essential evidentiary source, by refusing to submit to pretrial mental examination, he cannot at the trial, offer psychiatric evidence on his capacity to commit the crime. If the defendant wishes to call psychiatrists on his behalf, he must first demonstrate to the court in the absence of the jury, that he has, prior to the trial, fully co-operated and submitted to a mental examination, where one has been sought by the People. If this obligation is not met by the defendant, the court shall deem the offer of psychiatric testimony inadmissible; and unless the defendant has other proof relevant to his defense, the People's burden of proof shall be satisfied by the presumption of sanity which remains in the case. Since in such a case, no issue of fact as to insanity would be presented for the jury, the court shall be permitted to charge that as a matter of law the defendant is sane. Where, however, the defendant has other proof of his defense of insanity, and the court finds that the defendant did not co-operate at pretrial psychiatric examinations sought by the People, this other nonpsychiatric proof, if otherwise competent, shall be admissible. In such a case the court shall instruct the jury as to the presumption of sanity and that they must consider whether defendant's nonpsychiatric proof has rebutted the presumption. Additionally, the court shall be permitted to instruct the jury that the defendant has failed to co-operate (see Burgunder v. State, 55 Ariz. 411, 103 P.2d 256) and the failure to co-operate should be considered by them in determining the merits of the defense (see Note, Pretrial Mental Examination and Commitment, 51 *Geo. L.J.* 143, 152–153). . . .

It is argued, however, that the Appellate Division erroneously ordered that the examination be conducted without the presence of nonmedical personnel. With this we agree. . . .

In United States v. Wade, 388 U.S. 218, the Supreme Court held that the Sixth Amendment to the Federal Constitution mandates the presence of counsel at critical stages of the prosecution to preserve the right to a fair trial. A "critical state" was defined as "any stage of the prosecution, formal or informal, in court or out, where" "the presence of his counsel is necessary to preserve the defendant's basic right to a fair trial as affected by his right meaningfully to cross-examine the witnesses against him and to have effective assistance of counsel at the trial itself" (Wade, supra, at pp. 226–227). Since pretrial psychiatric examinations are a critical stage in the prosecution of one accused of a crime under the Wade rationale, the defendant is entitled to have counsel present to make more effective his basic right to cross-examination (see Note, Right to Counsel at the Pretrial Mental Examination, 118 U. Pa. L. Rev. 448; State v. Whitlow, supra, 45 N.J.3, at pp. 26–28, 210 A.2d 763). Inasmuch as defense counsel is given the right to be present, it is only fair to allow the District Attorney the same right.

We see no merit to the argument that defense counsel should be permitted to take an active role at the examination, or that he should be allowed to advise his client not to answer questions put to him by an examining psychiatrist or make objections. As in Wade situations, the function of counsel is limited to that of an observer. Both the defense attorney and the prosecutor may take notes and save their comments or objections for the trial and cross-examination of the examining psychiatrist. Additionally, a copy of the medical report must be furnished to both sides, and although no stenographic transcript of the examination is required, if one is made, it shall be made available to both sides prior to trial.

Accordingly, the order appealed from should be modified by allowing the presence of defense counsel and the District Attorney at the psychiatric examination to be held, but merely as observers.

FULD, Chief Judge (dissenting in part). . . . . . . I strongly disagree . . . with the court's further determination that defense counsel must be barred from taking an active role during the interrogation of his client at a psychiatric examination. . . . A defendant's Sixth Amendment right to assistance of a lawyer exists separate and apart from his Fifth Amendment privilege against self-incrimination and, quite obviously, the fact that one accused of crime may have waived his privilege cannot—as is suggested (opn., p. 714)— destroy or impair his constitutional right to an attorney. I think it self-evident that to restrict a defendant's right to a lawyer upon his pretrial mental examination—at least when he is being questioned for the purpose of determining his mental condition at the time of the crime—will frequently have the effect of substantially abridging, if not eliminating, every right he may have to the effective assistance of counsel in the preparation of his defense. . . . Without the benefit of counsel to advise him, it is quite likely that the . . . accused will unknowingly provide the prosecution with sufficient evidence to secure his conviction by defeating his defense of insanity before the trial has even begun. In such a situation the harm done to the defendant's case is irreparable. *When the sole issue is the defendant's sanity at the time of the crime, the right to the assistance of counsel is thus as important at the time of the defendant's mental examination as it is at the time of the trial itself*." (Emphasis supplied.) . . .

Amendments to the Federal Rules of Criminal Procedure
Effective August 1, 1974

NEW RULE 12.2
NOTICE OF DEFENSE BASED UPON
MENTAL CONDITION

(a) *Defense of insanity.* If a defendant intends to rely upon the defense of insanity at the time of the alleged crime, he shall, within the time provided for the filing of pretrial motions or at such later time as the court may direct, notify the attorney for the government in writing of such intention and file a copy of such notice with the clerk. If there is a failure to comply with the requirements of this subdivision, insanity may not be raised as a defense. The court may for cause shown allow late filing of the notice or grant additional time to the parties to prepare for trial or make such other order as may be appropriate.

(b) *Mental disease or defect inconsistent with the mental element required for the offense charged.* If a defendant intends to introduce expert testimony relating to a mental disease, defect, or other condition bearing upon the issue of whether he had the mental state required for the offense charged, he shall, within the time provided for the filing of pretrial motions or at such later time as the court may direct, notify the attorney for the government in writing of such intention and file a copy of such notice with the clerk. The court may for cause shown allow late filing of the notice or grant additional time to the parties to prepare for trial or make such other order as may be appropriate.

(c) *Psychiatric examination.* In an appropriate case the court may, upon motion of the attorney for the government, order the defendant to submit to a psychiatric examination by a psychiatrist designated for this purpose in the order of the court.

(d) *Failure to comply.* If there is a failure to give notice when required by subdivision (b) of this rule or to submit to an examination when ordered under subdivision (c) of this rule, the court may exclude the testimony of any expert witness offered by the defendant on the issue of his mental state.

TWO PSYCHIATRIC EVALUATIONS

Kermit S. Birnham

January 31, 1959

Honorable L. J. Wentworth
Judge of the District Court

Dear Judge Wentworth:

In accordance with your instructions, I examined the defendant on January 10, 1959, and on January 28, 1959; I have also read the transcript of the Grand Jury hearing and the material in the District Attorney's files on this case. I wish to report the following to the Court:

Short Statement of the Problem

This 33-year-old individual gloatingly brags about the commission of at least 11 murders. He shows absolutely no regret or guilt about these deeds; on the contrary, he indulges in an exhibitionistic display of triumphant satisfaction over his accomplishments. Although he is fully oriented and appears rational and coherent, his thinking is delusionally distorted —probably as the result of an underlying paranoid, megalomanic, schizophrenic psychosis. However, according to present legal tests of insanity, he must be considered legally sane at the time of commission of the crimes and legally sane at the present time.

Family, Social and Personal History

The defendant speaks of his childhood and early years with great bitterness and hate—directed at his Catholic foster-parents ("hypocrites right down the line"); his parochial-school education; Christian morality in general; and society as a whole. All of these, he holds responsible for depriving him physically and breaking him spiritually from the earliest time he can remember.

He was, he says, "born a charity case and will probably die one." Although he does not remember anything before the age of five, he believes he was placed in some kind of foundling home in New York (he was born in Manhattan or the Bronx) before he was given to his foster-parents, who did not tell him that he was not their own child. Not until 1947 (when he needed a birth certificate before he could apply for the Merchant Marines) did he find out that his name was not the same as that of these "parents"; then he was told that his own parents had died shortly after his birth, but he suspects that he was merely the product of an "irresponsible good time."

His devoutly Catholic foster-parents sent him to the Sacred Heart parochial school in New York, from which he graduated. In this strict "inhibiting" environment, he says, he lived a "narrow, shallow life—merely existing from day to day," learning no trade, acquiring no abilities or ambitions, losing "freedom of thought and action," and developing a thorough-going hatred for "Christian charity," which "always had a price tag attached to it." When he finally ran away from home (after one year in a public high school), he was "completely confused and a mess."

First, he joined the C.C.C., where he remained for over a year and adjusted fairly well there. Then, immediately after Pearl Harbor, he enlisted in the army and served for a year and a half, before he was discharged on the grounds of homosexuality, to which he confessed. Regarding his sexual adjustment in general, he says that his "Christian upbringing" instilled sexual inhibitions and shame in him and left him totally ignorant of sexual matters. When he subsequently made some attempts at heterosexual adjustment, he claims that the girls he "went after" would have nothing to do with him and that he therefore turned to homosexuality.

After his discharge from the army, he spent the next few years in an apparently aimless manner—drifting from one odd job to another and finally engaging in a series of armed robberies for about two years (which he looks upon as a happy period of his life). Eventually he was apprehended and convicted of grand theft and sentenced to San Quentin, where he says he was classified as psychoneurotic. He is particularly resentful of the fact that he was forced to serve his entire sentence (of five or six years), whereas other first offenders who had committed the same kind of crime were usually paroled after a year or so.

He looks upon this period of confinement in San Quentin as the supreme illustration of the persecution and suffering he had always endured at the hands of society. During this period, he made his plans for revenge. He would kill and destroy as often as he could, in order to compensate himself for the "thousand times he had died as a child" and particularly in order to eliminate certain "types" (specifically, sailors, children, and women). At first, he thought of derailing a train, in order to "see the monkeys drown"; but he later abandoned this plan as too impersonal, since he preferred to "know his customers."

He was released from San Quentin in 1957, at which time he tried to enlist in the Merchant Marine; however, he was turned down —for which he blames "administrative pressure" and the government in general, which he declares he hates. He then returned to his former life as a transient, working at odd jobs and carrying out his plans to revenge himself on society. In pursuit of these plans, he deliberately began committing a series of murders, leaving only the choice of his victim to chance. He frequently changed residences so as to minimize the danger of discovery, and seems to have killed people in a number of different places—although the total number of his victims is not yet completely clarified, he himself boasts of 11 "to his credit" and mentions Oakland, San Francisco, Los Angeles, and various other places as the location of his different murders. His sole aim was to take as many lives as he possibly could, in order to make his revenge on society most complete.

The defendant's accounts of the specific crimes for which he is now being tried are similar to those recorded in the Grand Jury transcript and in the District Attorney's files; and he takes pleasure in describing these deeds in great detail. However, he completely refuses to give any information about six crimes, of which presumably the authorities have not yet been informed.

Mental Examination

(The psychiatric examination took place in the hospital of the County Jail, where the defendant was seen twice for periods of approximately 1 and ½ hours each. During the second examination, the presence of a deputy sheriff nearby was noted and exploited by the defendant, who gleefully included this additional "audience" in his exhibitionistic display.)

The defendant is fully oriented in all spheres and shows no disturbance in any area of memory; in fact, he appears to be hypermnesic, remembering even minute details of past events—particularly of his various criminal deeds. His productions are extremely colorful and vivid, and are often punctuated by lurid and frequently gory descriptions. Only after repeated questioning and on closer examination does it become obvious that these seemingly very fantastic and florid outpourings are also repetitive, almost stereotyped, and characterized by a certain emotional emptiness that is only superficially covered up by extreme bravado.

His verbalization is excellent, and the sequence of his thoughts appear coherent and rational; however, his conclusions are so absurd and the actual content of his ideas so bizarre that his over-all production seems to indicate an underlying, well-developed system of delusions. Frequently he pursues a thought to such an extent and in such detail that his outpourings can be classified as "ranting and raving." This is particularly noticeable when he indulges in grandiose fantasies about the final glory of his own execution and the events he envisions as preceding it. For instance, he is firmly convinced that he can extract large amounts of money from either the press or the police or the district attorney's office for information about the "six carcasses that are still my own possession." He takes great pleasure in "protecting" the six crimes which are still his alone, since the five to which he has already confessed "don't belong to me any more." However, he is even more pleased about the money he will make from these six murders; and since he has had no response to his first offer (i.e., to sell his information for $500 per crime), he plans to keep raising the price until finally, on the day of his execution, it will be $50,000 or maybe $5,000,000 or possibly fifty million dollars. He will force the mayor of the city of Los Angeles to present the money to him in a big televised ceremony and then will use the money to secure for himself a "Christian burial," in order to mock Christianity which has inflicted such harm on him. He returns over and over again to the idea of

purchasing a Catholic funeral so that he can laugh about the hypocrisy of the priest, who will say nice things about him because he has been paid to do so. In these fantasies, he loses even the superficial aspects of rationality.

On other occasions, however, he is able to present a façade of reasonableness—although even then his train of thought generally leads him to totally absurd conclusions, which he does not recognize as such. Over and over again, he rants about (1) the frustrations of his childhood; (2) his miserable upbringing; (3) the hypocrisy of Christian morality, and the contrast between professions of Christian charity and the actuality of Christian brutality. He states, probably delusionally, that he was incessantly beaten by Catholic nuns and priests—which resulted in three things: fear, shame, and cowardice.

It is an interesting feature of his thinking that he divides everything into three parts. For instance, he attributes his "downfall" to three factors: (1) lack of formal education; (2) his police records; (3) the bad army discharge and his unjust imprisonment in San Quentin. He also primarily hates three types of people, whom he prefers to kill: (1) sailors; (2) "kids"; (3) women. He despises sailors because he believes that they have more sexual freedom than anybody; because they have "more to live for sexually," it is all the more pleasurable for him "to make them die." "Kids," who come second in preference as victims, also have "more of everything," and by killing them, one can hurt more than one person. Girls "never would give me anything" and are "only after money"; therefore, they too deserve to be killed. He volunteers a description of what he considers the usual relationship between male and female: "The girl is always after money; the man is always after sex." Therefore, he approves of rape, though he himself prefers to kill. In a rambling and irrelevant fashion, he adds that he would gladly kill a police sergeant or all the reporters in the world because they want to exploit him commercially.

Throughout the interviews, he was obviously preoccupied with essentially the same subjects (which, in his typical fashion, he separated into three parts): (1) Christian morality and its hypocrisy—and, connected with this, the fantasies of his revenge, culminating in his execution and funeral; (2) The accumulation of money in payment for information on his crimes, since he has never been able to make money by honest work; (3) The murders which he has "rightfully" committed in order to revenge himself upon the society that crippled him during his childhood and continued to plague him throughout his life.

He has an overwhelming need to explain his actions in a "scientific" manner—without noticing, however, that his so-called conclusions are not only illogical, weird, and peculiar, but grotesque distortions of a wildly roaming pathological imagination. For example, he states in great detail that he suffers from Christian inhibitions against sexuality and violence; that he is a man who believes in reason rather than force; that he is in many respects more Christ-like than Jesus himself, who resorted to violence in chasing the money-changers out of the temple (this story, he repeated on several different occasions during the interviews).

On the other hand, he describes his various killings with obvious relish and seems to get tremendous satisfaction from enumerating his various victims (referring to two separate "lists"—one of them, consisting of the five "public" crimes; the other, including the six victims who "still belong to him"). He speaks, for instance, of victim "Number 2"—an engineer in San Francisco with whom the defendant had had an affair—and is particularly triumphant about having killed this man because he was so successful and wealthy; therefore, in killing him, the defendant was able to destroy all of his property and future expectations, in addition to his life. He applies the same kind of reasoning when he refers to the "Rice kid," who also had future expectations, as well as a father who loved him; here again, the defendant considers himself particularly fortunate, since he succeeded in destroying "the future" of the boy and in hurting his father as well.

He uses vivid gestures to describe how he slashed the bellies of his victims and then cut their throats, and savors with sadistic pleasure the recalling of their suffering. He also glories in the power that was his when he had a knife in his hand, for then he was a "big man," "the lord of the universe," no longer the "victim of persecution by Christians" but able to "make things go the way [he] wanted them to." He sees no contrast between these accounts and his former professions of nonviolence.

In "scientifically" accounting for and justifying his deeds, he again enumerates *three* instances of deprivation and persecution: (1) that he was circumcised before he was 4½ years old and society had no right to "bother with his body"; (2) that his foster-parents destroyed his faith in reasoning; and (3) that he was forced into a Catholic school and was not given the "democratic privilege" of attending a public school. However, in spite of all his former handicaps, he feels that he has now finally succeeded in triumphing over society because "they can kill him only once," while he has 11 bodies to his credit; thus, even if he considers his own life four times as valuable as his victims' lives, he is "still ahead three to one." This supreme triumph has given him, for the first time in his life, a feeling of perfect calm, relaxation, and happiness; he has an excellent appetite and sleeps well—whereas, before, he was always tense, anxious, and full of fears. Now he has found complete peace and just hopes that he can maintain it to the end, "when gas time comes." He says he is fine at the moment but that he might "need some help" a couple of days before the execution, when a possibly unconscious desire to live may disturb his tranquility. Right now, he is not only reconciled to his death but sees his execution as his final triumph over society.

He then proceeds to develop a very elaborate fantasy about "shaking down" the jurors at his trial and then sharing the money he receives with the public defender. He imagines that it will be up to him to disqualify any juror who does not want to pay him a certain sum. He also looks forward to prolonging his trial, which he plans to adorn with unheard-of sex tales. He plans to shock the jury and the public by revealing disgusting and revolting details during the trial, and he hopes to succeed in destroying the Christian reputation of the victims whose bodies he has taken. Then he somewhat irrelevantly alludes to the case of Whittaker Chambers, who "sold the country down the river" and made money from it; but again he returns to speak with satisfaction of his intention to "shake down" the jury for more than $450—which is the total amount he ever made by honest work. In the next sentence, however, he mentions the sum of $50,000, which he expects to get. He says he is more important and powerful than the State Department, which only tells other people whom to kill in wars, while he decides for himself whom to kill and then carries out his plans.

He is mortally afraid only of being sent to a hospital, where he may receive shock treatment and thereupon surrender his information without being aware of it. He insists somewhat over-anxiously that he is completely sane, and says he knows that society considers all of his actions as wrong—although he himself feels perfectly justified in having acted as he did. In fact, he stresses that if he were released, he would continue to kill until they caught him again. He breaks into prolonged laughter at the thought that according to Christian doctrine, God will have to forgive him, although he has no redeeming features at all; and he takes considerable pride in the fact that he has become "Number 1 on the hate list of the public."

There is a great deal more material in the same vein. What is particularly striking, however, is his repetition of the same thoughts and his elaboration of them in the same pseudo-systematic and pseudo-rational manner.

Throughout the examinations, the defendant was perfectly at ease, showed no signs of anxiety or depression, or even any kind of emotional participation—except that he enjoyed himself vastly and appeared to look upon the interviews as opportunities for a major performance and particularly for describing details which he expected would shock his "audience." He appeared quite cordial and relaxed, and consequently showed a totally inappropriate emotional reaction in regard to the heinous details contained in his stories. He displayed neither contrition nor regret, but gloated throughout and expounded his distorted pseudo-philosophical views with apparently complete conviction.

At the present time, no definite hallucinations can be elicited. There is, however, little doubt that his whole thinking is based on delusional ideas, which are not in the least modified by any new experiences or reality-testing on his part. For instance, at the time of the first interview, he had expected a large pay-off from the police within the next few days; but he showed no disappointment, at the second interview, that he had not yet received any money—on the contrary, this made him feel even better, because he thereby could raise the price. This episode illustrates the delusional features of his thought, in that his beliefs are not subject to correction in the face of further facts or experiences.

As indicated, his affect is totally inappropriate and distorted; he has no fear, no concern about himself or anybody else, no realization of the true significance of his actions, while his thought content is obsessively preoccupied with grandiose and megalomanic ideas. His judgment in personal and impersonal matters is completely deranged, and there is absolutely no insight.

Mental Condition at the Time of Commission of Crime

An evaluation of this 33-year-old individual of above-average intelligence—who proudly brags of the commission of 11 murders—presents a most unusual problem. Not only the number of his crimes, but also the bizarre, senselessly cruel and sadistic manner which characterizes these callous murders, makes this case an extraordinary psychological phe-nomenon. The vicious terror of this man's actions is underscored by his provocative, gloating boastfulness about his accomplishments and the almost incomprehensible total absence of shame, guilt, or concern for his victims, for society, or even for his own survival.

A psychiatric evaluation cannot overlook the fact that the nature and quality of this man's deeds—and his attitude of boastful braggadocio toward them, without any signs of remorse—by necessity creates most intense feelings of revulsion and repugnance in any observer. This reaction is further enhanced by the equally inevitable realization that this intensely sadistic, psychopathic individual—who is undoubtedly an acute and most dangerous menace to society—has always led a totally worthless life.

The moral condemnation of an individual, seemingly without any redeeming features, who commands neither pity nor sympathy and makes human understanding most difficult, is reinforced by the recognition that even with the help of the best available social and medical resources, he has to be considered at present as incurable, with an utterly hopeless prognosis. Therefore, even the raising of the issue of insanity—which could result in preserving this man's life and permitting him to continue his explosively menacing existence in a hospital—must necessarily provoke strong emotions about the social and human desirability of protecting an individual who appears, according to all civilized human standards, a virtually inhuman, fiendish monster.

However, this examiner, appointed by the Court to give his expert opinion as a neuro-psychiatrist, cannot permit his clinical insight to be obscured by these considerations—regardless of the legal and social consequences of his findings. From a psychiatric point of view, it appears undeniable that this man's thinking processes are based on a complicated interlocking set of delusions which ingeniously support each other so as to give a superficial semblance of reasoning—although they are in fact a mere caricature of rationality.

The psychopathic component in this individual's personality make-up is quite overt and obvious. He displays extreme emotional immaturity; his anxiety threshold is very low; he is unable to mobilize adequate defenses against any frustrations; and therefore he very characteristically succumbs to every temptation and translates every sexual or aggressive impulse into immediate action. His sex life is completely disordered; he is dominated by intense sadistic, hostile, and sexualized destructive impulses, which manifest themselves in a curious mixture of homosexual violence and murder. All of those tendencies, as well as his readiness to resort to glib rationalizations and projection—so that he sees only the flaw and faults of others, particularly of "society," and does not recognize his own responsibility for his deeds—would tend to confirm the diagnosis of a psychopathic or sociopathic personality, characterized by a total absence of effective defenses and inhibitions as well as by sexual psychopathy.

But this is by no means the complete picture. This man, who is a voracious reader (his favorite books, interestingly enough, being Hitler's *Mein Kampf* and Tolstoy's *War and Peace*) and who makes a pretense of being an intellectual, believes firmly that he is basically non-violent and that he was perfectly justified in leading a one-man war against "Christian morality." He sees himself as an exalted Christ-like figure, who has suffered from unjust and cruel persecutions and who therefore has been driven to righteous retaliation. Even aside from the formal characteristics of his thinking processes (his curious organization of ideas into patterns of three), his ideation makes it possible for him (without any external or internal contradictions) to justify mass-murder and even to boast about it with undisguised glee. His murderous accomplishments have totally relaxed all of his anxieties and produced a state of remorseless calm and triumphant self-satisfaction—which certainly has to stand as the epitome of an inappropriate emotional response.

The ugly, undisguised cruelty of his actions is perceived by him as contributing to his own glory and to the accomplishment of a revenge which he justifies at great length with his special brand of reasoning, which leads to utterly fantastic conclusions. His fantasies concerning the extraction of money from law-enforcement officers lack any basis in reality. Furthermore, his entire ideology of revenge against Christianity (his gleeful anticipation of his own funeral as a supreme mockery of the hypocrisy and mercenariness inherent in Christianity); the strange calculations he uses to prove his triumph over society (in that society can take only one life from him, while he has taken eleven from it); and his frequent pseudo-religious allusions (such as his identification with Christ, Cain, and the Christian saints) are almost textbook examples of delusional, paranoiac, and megalomanic thinking. Under the conditions of a restricted, purely clinical psychiatric examination, no diagnostic conclusions can be arrived at with complete certainty; but the rampant delusional thinking-disturbance—combined with his totally inappropriate affective response—strongly suggests the presence of a schizophrenic psychosis, with paranoid, megalomanic delusions of grandeur.

Nevertheless, since the defendant is fully aware of the fact that his actions are considered "wrong" by society, although he himself does not look upon them as such—and since he was aware of the consequences of these actions, and in fact gleefully looks forward to his own execution as his final triumph—he must be considered, according to present legal definitions of insanity, as legally sane at the time of commission of his crimes.

Mental Condition at the Time of Examination

The above considerations apply to the defendant's present status. For the reasons stated above' he must be declared legally sane at the present time.

Respectfully submitted,
Kenneth N. Pierpont, M.D.

MARTIN S. CLAYTON

Psychiatric Consultation

(Requested by Jones, Jones, and Smith, Attorneys-at-Law, Elgin, Illinois.)

Dates of examination: *Place:*
1. March 12, 1964   Elgin Police Station, Elgin, Illinois
2. March 22, 1964   Kane County Jail, Geneva, Illinois
3. March 25, 1964   Kane County Jail, Geneva, Illinois

The Incident

On Wednesday, March 11, 1964, Martin S. Clayton shot and seriously wounded his estranged wife and their fifteen-year-old daughter as they sat in their car in front of their home in Elgin, Illinois.

Past History

The patient was born on October 24, 1916, and reared in Dundee, Illinois. He is the oldest in a sibship of nine. His father was a farmer. The latter, at the age of thirty-eight, was admitted to Elgin State Hospital on December 28, 1927, and discharged on April 9, 1930. At that time Martin was eleven years old. The father had been heavily addicted to alcohol, which necessitated his commitment. According to the record available, he was considered by hospital authorities to be psychotic. Martin's grandfather was likewise a patient at Elgin State Hospital. He was admitted the first time on January 29, 1915, discharged on June 21, 1915, and admitted a second time on December 14, 1926, and discharged on February 26, 1927. Like his son, Martin's father, the grandfather had also been addicted to alcohol and had developed ideas of persecution which resulted in a psychosis, as evident from the hospital record. Martin vividly remembers the hospitalizations of his father and grandfather and remembers the disruptions they caused in the household.

Martin Clayton has a grammar school education. The relationship between his father and mother was not too friendly but he is not aware of any violence between the two. He himself received corporal punishment on several occasions. After leaving grammar school, Martin worked for a short time for his father. At the age of eighteen, he became an automobile mechanic and worked for a Chevrolet Agency in Dundee for six years. He then found employment at the Elgin Foundry. At the age of twenty-six, in 1942, he enlisted in the Army and saw combat in the Philippines. He received several decorations and an honorable discharge in 1946. He had reached the rank of Corporal 5th grade and was never subjected to disciplinary action. After his discharge he returned to this area and immediately began to work for a potato chip factory. He did *not* draw any unemployment compensation after his return, as was customary among many recent veterans. Soon after he found employment with the Acme Transfer Company in Elgin, as a truck driver, and he has held this position uninterruptedly ever since, up to the occurrence of the incident. He now holds an eighteen-year seniority with this company. He has frequently worked overtime and he states that his work is satisfactory. He has always enjoyed good physical health with the exception of rather frequent headaches when under tension. For the past ten years he has become intoxicated on several occasions.

Marital History

He met his future wife through a mutual friend of theirs, and after a short courtship, married her in 1942, while in the military service. His wife is four years his junior and was divorced at the time the two met. This did not disturb the patient. He found her beautiful and compatible and "loved her then and loves her now." The patient soon after left for Fort Knox, Kentucky, but frequently visited his wife, who remained in Elgin. There had also been frequent correspondence, and the patient remembers one minor incident when a letter meant for a former lady acquaintance was erroneously mailed to his wife by him.

A son was born to the couple a few months after the marriage had taken place. He had been preconceived, but Martin felt at no time, nor does he feel now, that he was forced into marriage on the strength of his wife's premarital pregnancy. The couple had a daughter in 1948. All in-laws connected with this union had fully accepted the respective spouses and had approved of the marriage.

While overseas the patient did not seek the company of other women and was satisfied that his wife was true to him. After his return from the Army, he moved in with his wife's family, the wife having stayed with her parents during his tour of duty. This, retrospectively, was a grave mistake, since difficulties soon started with the mother-in-law. The wife's father had died shortly before Martin's return; an elderly sister of the mother-in-law resided then and continues to reside in the household.

The patient was subjected to the opinions, approvals and disapprovals of altogether four women: wife, daughter, mother-in-law, and her sister. Among many other discrepancies, the mother would constantly throw up to the young couple was the fact that they were not paying sufficient rent. During unavoidable family arguments she would, without exception, side with the daughter. Yet she was, and continues to be, very fond of the grandchildren, of whom there is now only the granddaughter left. The wife worked before the marriage and worked later, intermittently; at the time of the incident she was employed by at a ladies' clothing store.

As early as 1951 the young couple made plans with regard to acquiring their own home. To this the mother-in-law reacted with severe threats, such as "disowning" the daughter. Finally, when the couple's daughter was experiencing difficulties in school, the couple was advised to establish a home of their own, which they did. The advice had been given by a school counselor. Yet, to this day the wife resents this move and frequently expresses her disapproval of it by "blaming" the patient for it. After the couple moved into their own home, the wife continued to see her mother every day, without fail. It was also during the early fifties that the patient began to drink.

The patient at this time remains particularly sensitive about the fact that the mother-in-law would constantly try to influence his son, who was later killed in an accident, against him. She used to tell the boy that his father was "no good" and "had no interest in him." The boy, however, never reacted with disrespect toward his father, in spite of his grandmother's insinuations. As a matter of fact, he, the boy, grew up to be "the apple of the father's eye." He graduated from high school at the age of eighteen, worked for a dry-goods firm in Elgin, and found his death in a car accident while riding with three others during October of 1962. After this, the patient felt he had lost his best friend and that "the bottom had dropped out from under him." The four women in his life continued to aggravate him by frequently stating that the boy had not meant much to him. Instead of bringing the parents closer together, the boy's death drove them more apart. "I died with him." The mother-in-law now began to influence the patient's daughter against him. The latter had been witnessing frequent arguments between her parents and would now side in strongly with her mother and grandmother. "You have a bad father," she would be told by both. It was not till 1963 that the couple finally moved out with the daughter. The down payment for the house was available from mutual savings and the payments are being met jointly by husband and wife.

Soon after the couple moved into their own home, the patient began to apply himself by remodeling and repairing the premises, an effort which was not the least appreciated by wife and daughter. This disappointed him and his drinking increased. During February of this year the fifteen-year-old daughter became an object of marital dispute. She had been seen with girl friends of whom the parents had not approved. The same night she did not return home till 11:00 P.M., which was unusual. During an argument with the daughter, the patient hit her in the face, which the wife strongly resented. As far as the patient remembers, he left home then, returned intoxicated later, had arguments with his wife, punched his fist through a bedroom door, but did not lay a hand on any member of his family. Nevertheless, the wife called the police, but did not press any charges. The same night, wife and daughter left the home for her mother's.

Now follows a period during which the patient became very despondent, hoping his family would return. During the two weeks which ensued he repaired the damage he had done to the property and pleaded with wife and daughter to come home and live with him. There were frequent telephone calls made by him, but his family remained adamant and refused to join him. In a mood of extreme despondency the patient conceived ideas of suicide. On the night of the incident described initially, he had once more been drinking and had armed himself with a loaded gun left behind by his deceased son, who was an avid hunter. Under the influence of alcohol his suicidal ideas became stronger, a phenomenon well known to occur in depressed individuals. The two weeks of living in isolation, of feeling rejected by his family by their repeated refusals to join him, his preoccupation with his deceased son, whom he now missed more than ever, [and] finding himself completely without an ally, had deepened his depression to a degree that suicide seemed to be the only way out of his dilemma.

That night he drove around aimlessly, but finally cornered his wife and daughter who were sitting in a car. His wife had failed to call him on that day, contrary to her promises. He remembers having asked his wife if she was avoiding him. He further remembers that the tone and content of the conversation which followed was not friendly. In his own words, all of a sudden "everything seemed to go goofy," and he feels that it was at that moment that he tried to do away with himself, but that "the gun did not work." He then returned home and tried to reload the gun. (It had originally been loaded by the son.) The patient stated that he himself had had no experience in handling small firearms. Characteristically, he now returned to the scene of the incident. He wanted to be sure that the victims had been properly taken care of. He then, under a degree of stress never before experienced in his life, went to see his aged mother, whom he felt he had "hurt" by his recent behavior, after which he drove to the hospital to turn himself over to the authorities.

Psychiatric Findings

When seen at the Elgin Police Station shortly after committing the deed, the patient was overtly depressed. His main concern was with the conditions of his wife and daughter, which at that time remained fair. He knew that he had done wrong and was full of remorse. His suicidal ideas had vanished since now he felt that he was needed, his wife and daughter having been seriously injured. Soon he began to talk about his son, whom he now missed more than ever. He functioned with a blood pressure of 160/110, which denotes an elevation. In general, he repeated what has already been recorded under Past History and Marital History, although much more time was spent on these during subsequent visits to the County Jail. He stressed that since the boy's death his relationship with his wife had become more strained. He added that during the past two weeks he had been praying a great deal. Basically, he stated, he is not inclined toward violence and that he merely wanted to "scare" his wife and daughter.

He mentioned that his wife had suggested some time ago that he should undergo psychiatric treatment. He had been suffering from poor sleep for the past two weeks. He had also been crying, which was a new experience for him. Regarding the incident, he stated that he felt he was "going blank," but said that primarily he intended to kill *himself*.

During the two subsequent visits at the County Jail the patient was more composed but still remained depressed. It was this depression which at times made it difficult for him to concentrate and develop his thoughts logically. He remained remorseful and guilt-laden and feared that his wife would divorce him. This would mean a great blow to him, since he still loves her. He would also miss his daughter, should the divorce materialize. He is convinced that never again will he resort to violence or even do as much as lay hand on his wife or daughter. Ever since having been in custody his mind has constantly dwelled on wife and daughter. He hopes he will eventually be accepted by them again. He was very emphatic in stating that, although the marriage had been unhappy, and although he had had no sexual relations with his wife for the past three years, he had never sought the company of other women.

At times the patient was somewhat slow in grasp, at other times he was rather circumstantial. At all times one had the impression that this was a man very much in need of guidance and very insecure, who had taken much abuse during his entire lifetime and had "bottled up" this abuse for many years. The patient gave an over-all impression of inadequacy and of having had difficulties all his life in making decisions. This, however, should not be confused with not being dependable. As a matter of fact, once the patient had found his proper place, be that in the army or even in the disrupted home, one could depend on him. His blood pressure during the visits in jail had decreased to 150/100.

Formulation, Summary, and Conclusion

The psychiatric literature generally agrees that in cases such as this the motive for suicide is primary and that any other incidents connected with the planning of this act are secondary ramifications. Thus it is clear that Mr. Clayton on the day of the deed was extremely depressed. The factors leading to this depression were manifold.

The patient comes from a family where there was mental illness of the paternal grandfather and the father. Both had been hospitalized at Elgin State Hospital and had been found mentally ill. The two hospitalizations took place about one year apart, when Clayton was only eleven years old. At that age such an incident leaves a lasting impression on a youngster. This is the period in his development when he needs a *strong* father on whom he can lean and to whom he can go for advice and guidance. The mentally ill grandfather and father made for a poor fabric in Mr. Clayton, rendering him initially weak for the turbulent life to come.

The marriage from the beginning was unhappy. The environment in which the couple lived and reared their children was extremely unhealthy. Obviously the mother-in-law ruled the roost, keeping the patient frustrated and disappointed perennially. The wife sided in with her mother, which made matters worse. As a result of this unhealthy climate, the daughter became maladjusted, which was noticed by the teachers. Apparently the only person on whom the patient could lean was the son. He lost him in 1962 and for practical purposes is still mourning him. The insulting remarks the mother-in-law expressed, when she said he had been a poor father to the boy, were apt to increase the patient's feelings of worthlessness. It was now a situation of four women against one man. This is an unusual situation which demands extraordinary strength on the part of the man. This strength Mr. Clayton did not have. His moderate drinking was an expression of his futile attempt to "forget" the entire situation. It did not work, and as time went by he became more depressed. Finally, he was abandoned by his wife and daughter, and his living alone, not knowing if they would ever return, deepened his depression. This, together with his state of mourning, finally led to the decision to commit suicide. Persons suffering from depressions as deep in quality as Mr. Clayton's are liable to do most anything, since their judgment has become extremely impaired and since they can no longer make sound plans. They act on impulse, a behavior which they can no longer control. Every individual has his own private capacity of human endurance. In Mr. Clayton's case, considering the poor fabric of which he was made and the severe disappointments he had suffered, one can say that he was driven beyond human endurance and acted without control. Technically, such states are called Dissociative Reactions. They are short lived and the person recovers from it, as is the case in this patient.

On the other hand, much can be said about Mr. Clayton's positive personality traits. He has an excellent work record with his employer and has held the same position ever since 1946. He was subjected to no disciplinary measures while in the Armed Services and remained true to his wife while away from her. He tried to be a good husband and father but was severely frustrated in this attempt. This was due to no fault of his own.

Mr. Clayton is not basically inclined toward violence. A study of his over-all personality indicates this. In spite of all the emotional injuries he suffered, he continues to love his wife and daughter. He is full of remorse at this time and fears future isolation, should his wife divorce him. Mr. Clayton needs a healthy home life and understanding. Ideally, the couple, possibly also the rest of the family, should receive psychiatric guidance so that they may live more harmoniously together. Punishment would create additional resentment in the patient and may drive him into another state of depression, possibly even deeper than the one he recently experienced.

QUESTIONS FOR DISCUSSION

1. In each of the tests of criminal responsibility, who is the law seeking—and who should it seek—to identify? The mentally ill? The undeterrable? The psychiatrically treatable? The psychotic? The dangerous? Those without "understanding"? Those without "free will"? The "unblameworthy"? Other?

2. For what purpose are they to be so identified? Because it is inhumane to punish the "sick"? Because they will receive more appropriate treatment in a mental hospital than in a correctional facility? Because punishing such persons cannot deter others? Because they can be detained longer than if convicted of the offense? Because they will not "appreciate" what is being done to them? Other?

3. Which of the formulations places greater emphasis on the *cognitive* faculty of the defendant, and which on his *volitional* capacity?

4. Which of the rules seem to require the psychiatrist to testify in "absolute" terms? Which permit him to speak in terms of gradations of impairment?

5. What ethical problems are posed to the lawyer when he believes his client to be seriously mentally ill but his client refuses to agree to raise the defenes of insanity?

6. What ethical problems are presented to the lawyer when his mentally ill client is

charged with an offense, conviction of which will probably carry a minimal sentence, whereas commitment to the state hospital may well result in detention for many years?

7. May a lawyer ethically advise his client not to raise the defense of insanity because he knows that the state hospital facilities are inadequate and his client would probably not receive appropriate treatment there?

8. Should the issue of criminal responsibility remain as an affirmative defense? Or should the prosecution be permitted to introduce evidence to support a finding of not guilty by reason of insanity—even over the objections of the defendant? Cf. *Lynch* v. *Overholser*, U.S. Supreme Court, 369 U.S. 705, 1962.

9. If commitment following a verdict of not guilty by reason of insanity is not automatic, might juries be deterred from rendering such verdicts in cases involving extreme violence? See Judge Bazelon's analysis of the problem in *Bolton*, and the Congressional response. Cf. the recent decision by the Supreme Court of Arizona in *State* v. *Clemans*, 515 P. 2d 324, 1974.

10. Compare the *caveat* paragraph of the A.L.I. test with the definition of Antisocial Personality in the *Diagnostic and Sta-*

tistical Manual of Mental Disorders (Chapter 3), and consider Judge Biggs' comments in *Currens*. Are psychopaths-sociopaths-antisocial personalities excluded by the *caveat* paragraph? Should they be?

11. If the Nixon administration proposal on insanity (S 1400) is adopted:

    a) Might it have the effect of enlarging the rule of partial responsibility, where it exists, by extending the rule to non-specific intent crimes, and by imposing it upon jurisdictions which do not now recognize it?

    b) Could a court retain its present insanity rule by the expedient of defining "state of mind required as an element of the offense charged" to include, in every case, for example, "substantial capacity to appreciate the wrongfulness of the act and to conform one's conduct to the requirements of the law?"

12. Should voluntary drug or alcohol intoxication producing a temporary psychosis come within the insanity defense? What if the defendant is drug addicted or an alcoholic? See the recent decision of the California Supreme Court in *People* v. *Kelly*, 516 P. 2d 875, 1974.

13. What do you think of the arguments for and against abolition of the insanity defense?

14. The Birnham and Clayton evaluations should be studied not only in the context of an impending decision about criminal responsibility but also in light of the guidelines for psychiatric reports described in Chapter 5.

In appraising these evaluations, consider the following:

    a) The Birnham evaluation seems concerned exclusively with the issue of criminal responsibility. Do you see anything in the letter to Judge Wentworth that might have relevancy on the issue of competency to stand trial?

    b) What do you think about the propriety of a psychiatrist's stating as his "expert" opinion that: ". . . according to present legal tests of insanity, he [the examinee] must be considered legally sane at the time of commission of the crime and legally sane at the present time"?

    c) The psychiatrist in the Birnham case notes with candor his emotional reactions to the defendant; then observes that: ". . . this examiner, appointed by the court to give his expert opinion as a neuropsychiatrist, cannot permit his clinical insight to be obscured by these considerations." Do you think he has been successful in avoiding this?

    d) After reading the Clayton evaluation, do you feel you understand the dynamics of the shooting incident? Has the psychiatrist sufficiently supported his findings and recommendations?

    e) For what purposes might this evaluation be used by Clayton's defense counsel, for whom it was prepared?

    f) How well do these two evaluations (Birnham and Clayton) measure up in terms of the guidelines suggested in Chapter 5 of this book? What, if any, additional information would you have wanted to have in each case?

SUGGESTIONS FOR ADDITIONAL READING

Annotations:

"Instructions in Criminal Case in which Defendant Pleads Insanity as to his Hospital Confinement in the Event of Acquittal," 11 *ALR* 3d 737, 1967.

"Modern Status of Rules as to Burden and Sufficiency of Proof of Mental Irresponsibility in Criminal Case," 17 *ALR* 3d 146, 1968.

"Mental or Emotional Condition as Diminishing Responsibility for Crime," 22 *ALR* 3d 1228, 1968.

"XYY Syndrome as Affecting Criminal Responsibility," 42 *ALR* 3d 1414, 1972.

"Admissibility on Issue of Sanity of Expert Opinion Based Partly on Medical, Psychological, or Hospital Records," 55 *ALR* 3d 551, 1974.

Brakel and Rock. The Mentally Disabled and the Law (revised ed.). Chicago: Univ. of Chicago Press, 1971, chap. 11.

Goldstein. *The Insanity Defense.* New Haven: Yale Univ. Press, 1967.

Lewinstein. "The Historical Development of Insanity as a Defense in Criminal Actions," 14 *J. Forensic Sciences* 275 (Part I); 14 *J. Forensic Sciences* 469 (Part II), 1969.

Matthews. *Mental Disability and the Criminal Law.* American Bar Foundation, 1970.

Scheidemandel and Kanno. *The Mentally Ill Offender.* American Psychiatric Assoc., 1969.

Simon. *The Jury and the Defense of Insanity.* Boston, Mass.: Little, Brown & Co., 1967.

Symposium on Law and Psychiatry, 10 *American Criminal Law Review*, Spring 1972.

Symposium on United States v. Brawner, *Washington Univ. Law Quarterly*, Winter 1973.

Szasz. *Law, Liberty and Psychiatry.* New York: MacMillan, 1963.

Weihofen. *The Urge to Punish.* New York: Farrar, Straus & Cudahy, 1956.

18

Special Categories of Offenders

In this concluding chapter, we present materials introducing four "special categories" of offenders: the drug addict, the alcoholic, the sex offender and "sexual psychopath," and the "defective delinquent." The first category is represented by the landmark case *Robinson* v. *California*, and the recently issued Second Report of the National Commission on Marihuana and Drug Abuse. The *Easter* decision by the U.S. Court of Appeals for the D.C. Circuit seemed almost mandated by the decision by the U.S. Supreme Court in *Robinson*; but the promise of *Robinson* was soon dashed by the decision in *Powell* v. *Texas*. The section on alcoholism concludes with Section 2.08 of the Model Penal Code.

Sexual offenses and the problems incident to their occurrence—and enforcement of the laws prohibiting them—are discussed in the Robitscher article and the editorial by Dr. Lanham. The *Stone* v. *Wainwright* decisions concern the proscription of consensual sodomy—the "abominable and detestable crime against nature" first denounced in the reign of Henry VIII; and Section 213 of the Model Penal Code represents a major departure from traditional handling of "morals" offenses (and see the recent change in the classification of homosexuality by the American Psychiatric Association noted in chapter 3). Sexual psychopathy proceedings are denominated "civil," but in their application bear a frighteningly close resemblance to imprisonment, as *Dittrich* and *Barnett* illustrate. These cases were deliberately selected as "horrible examples" of the operation of sex psychopathy statutes: the former case is almost a blueprint of how to get rid of an unwanted spouse without divorce and have him imprisoned without conviction in the bargain—with all due legal solemnity; the latter case may well reach a desirable result, assuming that treatment can be provided (an unsafe assumption in most states—see the Koocher article which precedes the cases), but it is a veritable grab-bag of medical misinformation. You may wish to read again the discussion of sexual psychopath laws in the Shah article in Chapter 15, and consider what, if any, remedial legislation is needed. Finally, we offer some arguments pro and con on Maryland's "defective delinquency" statute, plus a couple of recent cases dealing with it. A number of states have enacted similar "civil commitment" statutes, under various nosological rubrics and definitions. The similarity of the treatment regimen under such statutes to what was earlier described as "behavior mod" is more than superficial, and has engendered the same kind of civil libertarian opposition.

In his essay on *Morals and Conduct*, John Dewey observed that "Judgment in which the emphasis falls upon blame and approbation has more heat than light. It is more emotional than intellectual. It is guided by custom, personal convenience and resentment rather than by insight into causes and consequences." That such an emphasis persists may be reflected in the arrest statistics annually reported by the F.B.I. in its Uniform Crime Reports, based upon reporting by state and local law enforcement agencies around the country. In 1972, for example, arrests for narcotic drug law offenses (more than half of which involved marihuana!) exceeded those for all violent offenses combined; and "crimes without victims" (prostitution, consensual sex offenses, drug possession, gambling, curfew, drunkenness, vagrancy, etc.) led to more than twice as many arrests as the total of all violent and property offenses. Perhaps neither the sanction nor the treatment model is fully adequate to meet the complex issues involved in these "special categories"; and each adds its own increment of difficulty and potential for oppression. The former may offer "cures" worse than the perceived disease; and the latter often involves indeterminate commitments for "treatment" when in fact no treatment is provided. It is hoped that the materials included, along with the Suggestions for Additional Reading, will provide the reader with a basis for further exploration of these issues and preferred solutions.

A. THE DRUG ADDICT

ROBINSON v. CALIFORNIA

Mr. Justice STEWART delivered the opinion of the Court.

A California statute makes it a criminal offense for a person to "be addicted to the use of narcotics." This appeal draws into question the constitutionality of that provision of the state law, as construed by the California courts in the present case.

The appellant was convicted after a jury trial in the Municipal Court of Los Angeles. The evidence against him was given by two Los Angeles police officers. Officer Brown testified that he had had occasion to examine the appellant's arms one evening on a street in Los Angeles some four months before the trial. The officer testified that at that time he had observed "scar tissue and discoloration on the inside" of the appellant's right arm, and "what appeared to be numerous needle marks and a scab which was approximately three inches below the crook of the elbow" on the appellant's left arm. The officer also testified that the appellant under questioning had admitted to the occasional use of narcotics.

Officer Lindquist testified that he had examined the appellant the following morning in the Central Jail in Los Angeles. The officer stated that at that time he had observed discolorations and scabs on the appellant's arms, and he identified photographs which had been taken of the appellant's arms shortly after his arrest the night before. Based upon more than ten years of experience as a member of the Narcotics Division of the Los Angeles Police Department, the witness gave his opinion that "these marks and the discoloration were the result of the injection of hypodermic needles into the tissue into the vein that was not sterile." He stated that the scabs were several days old at the time of his examination, and that the appellant was neither under the influence of narcotics nor suffering withdrawal symptoms at the time he saw him. This witness also testified that the appellant had admitted using narcotics in the past.

The appellant testified in his own behalf, denying the alleged conversations with the police officers and denying that he had ever used narcotics or been addicted to their use. He explained the marks on his arms as resulting from an allergic condition contracted during his military service. His testimony was corroborated by two witnesses.

The trial judge instructed the jury that the statute made it a misdemeanor for a person "either to use narcotics, or to be addicted to the use of narcotics. . . . That portion of the statute referring to the 'use' of narcotics is based upon the 'act' of using. That portion of the statute referring to 'addicted to the use' of narcotics is said to be a status or condition and not an act. It is a continuing offense and differs from most other offenses in the fact that [it] is chronic rather than acute; that it continues after it is complete and subjects the offender to arrest at any time before he reforms. The existence of such a chronic condition may be ascertained from a single examination, if the characteristic reactions of that condition be found present."

The judge further instructed the jury that the appellant could be convicted under a general verdict if the jury agreed *either* that he was of the "status" *or* had committed the "act" denounced by the statute. "All that the People must show is either that the defendant did use a narcotic in Los Angeles County, or that while in the City of Los Angeles he was addicted to the use of narcotics. . . ."

Under these instructions the jury returned a verdict finding the appellant "guilty of the offense charged." An appeal was taken to the Appellate Department of the Los Angeles County Superior Court, the "highest court of a State in which a decision could be had," in this case, 28 U.S.S. §1257. See *Smith* v. *California,* 361 U.S. 147, 149; *Edwards* v. *California,* 314 U.S. 160, 171. Although expressing some doubt as to the constitutionality of the "crime of being a narcotic addict," the

U.S. Supreme Court, 370 U.S. 660 (1962). Footnotes have been omitted.

reviewing court in an unreported opinion affirmed the judgment of conviction, citing two of its own previous unreported decisions which had upheld the constitutionality of the statute. We noted probable jurisdiction of this appeal, 368 U.S. 918, because it squarely presents the issue whether the statute as construed by the California courts in this case is repugnant to the Fourteenth Amendment of the Constitution.

The broad power of a State to regulate the narcotic drugs traffic within its borders is not here in issue. More than forty years ago, in *Whipple* v. *Martinson*, 256 U.S. 41, this Court explicitly recognized the validity of that power: "There can be no question of the authority of the State in the exercise of its police power to regulate the administration, sale, prescription and use of dangerous and habit-forming drugs. . . . The right to exercise this power is so manifest in the interest of the public health and welfare, that it is unnecessary to enter upon a discussion of it beyond saying that it is too firmly established to be successfully called in question." 256 U.S., at 45.

Such regulation, it can be assumed, could take a variety of valid forms. A State might impose criminal sanctions, for example against the unauthorized manufacture, prescription, sale, purchase, or possession of narcotics within its borders. In the interest of discouraging the violation of such laws, or in the interest of the general health or welfare of its inhabitants, a State might establish a program of compulsory treatment for those addicted to narcotics. Such a program of treatment might require periods of involuntary confinement. And penal sanctions might be imposed for failure to comply with established compulsory treatment procedures. Cf. *Jacobson* v. *Massachusetts*, 197 U.S. 11. Or a State might choose to attack the evils of narcotics traffic on broader fronts also—through public health education, for example, or by efforts to ameliorate the economic and social conditions under which those evils might be thought to flourish. In short, the range of valid choice which a State might make in this area is undoubtedly a wide one, and the wisdom of any particular choice within the allowable spectrum is not for us to decide. Upon that premise we turn to the California law in issue here.

It would be possible to construe the statute under which the appellant was convicted as one which is operative only upon proof of the actual use of narcotics within the State's jurisdiction. But the California courts have not so construed this law. Although there was evidence in the present case that the appellant had used narcotics in Los Angeles, the jury were instructed that they could convict him if they disbelieved that evidence. The appellant could be convicted, they were told, if they found simply that the appellant's "status" or "chronic condition" was that of being "addicted to the use of narcotics." And it is impossible to know from the jury's verdict that the defendant was not convicted upon precisely such a finding.

The instructions of the trial court, implicitly approved on appeal, amounted to "a ruling on a question of state law that is as binding on us as though the precise words had been written" into the statute. *Terminiello* v. *Chicago*, 337 U.S. 1, 4. "We can only take the statute as the state courts read it." *Ibid.*, at 6. Indeed, in their brief in this Court, counsel for the State have emphasized that it is "the proof of addiction by circumstantial evidence . . . by the tell-tale track of needle marks and scabs over the veins of his arms, that remains the gist of the section."

This statute, therefore, is not one which punishes a person for the use of narcotics, for their purchase, sale, or possession, or for antisocial or disorderly behavior resulting from their administration. It is not a law which even purports to provide or require medical treatment. Rather, we deal with a statute which makes the "status" of narcotic addiction a criminal offense, for which the offender may be prosecuted "at any time before he reforms." California has said that a person can be continuously guilty of this offense, whether or not he has ever used or possessed any narcotics within the State, and whether or not he has been guilty of any antisocial behavior there.

It is unlikely that any State at this moment in history would attempt to make it a criminal offense for a person to be mentally ill, or a leper, or to be afflicted with a venereal disease. A State might determine that the general health and welfare require that the victims of these and other human afflictions be dealt with by compulsory treatment, involving quarantine, confinement, or sequestration. But, in the light of contemporary human knowledge, a law which made a criminal offense of such a disease would doubtless be universally thought to be an infliction of cruel and unusual punishment in violation of the Eighth and Fourteenth Amendments. See *Francis* v. *Resweber*, 329 U.S. 459.

We cannot but consider the statute before us as of the same category. In this Court, counsel for the State recognized that narcotic addiction is an illness. Indeed, it is apparently an illness which may be contracted innocently or involuntarily. We hold that a state law which imprisons a person thus afflicted as a criminal, even though he has never touched any narcotic drug within the State or been guilty of any irregular behavior there, inflicts a cruel and unusual punishment in violation of the Fourteenth Amendment. To be sure, imprisonment for ninety days is not, in the abstract, a punishment which is either cruel or unusual. But the question cannot be considered in the abstract. Even one day in prison would be a cruel and unusual punishment for the "crime" of having a common cold.

We are not unmindful that the vicious evils of the narcotics traffic have occasioned the grave concern of government. There are, as we have said, countless fronts on which those evils may be legitimately attacked. We deal in this case only with an individual provision of a particularized local law as it has so far been interpreted by the California courts.

Reversed.

Mr. Justice DOUGLAS, concurring. . . .

Today we have our differences over the legal definition of insanity. But however insanity is defined, it is in end effect treated as a disease. While afflicted people may be confined whether for treatment or for the protection of society, they are not branded as criminals. . . .

We should show the same discernment respecting drug addiction. The addict is a sick person. He may, of course, be confined for treatment or for the protection of society. Cruel and unusual punishment results not from confinement, but from convicting the addict of a crime. The purpose of §11721 is not to cure, but to penalize. Were the purpose to cure, there would be no need for a mandatory jail term of not less than ninety days. . . . A prosecution for addiction, with its resulting stigma and irreparable damage to the good name of the accused, cannot be justified as a means of protecting society, where a civil commitment would do as well. Indeed, in §5350 of the Welfare and Institutions Code, California has expressly provided for civil proceedings for the commitment of habitual addicts. Section 11721 is, in reality, a direct attempt to punish those the State cannot commit civilly. This prosecution has no relationship to the curing of an illness. Indeed, it cannot, for the prosecution is aimed at penalizing an illness, rather than at providing medical care for it. We would forget the teachings of the Eighth Amendment if we allowed sickness to be made a crime and permitted sick people to be punished for being sick. This age of enlightenment cannot tolerate such barbarous action.

Mr. Justice WHITE, dissenting. . . .

The Court clearly does not rest its decision upon the narrow ground that the jury was not expressly instructed not to convict if it believed appellant's use of narcotics was beyond his control. The Court recognizes no degrees of addiction. The Fourteenth Amendment is today held to bar any prosecution for addiction regardless of the degree or frequency of use, and the Court's opinion bristles with indications of further consequences. If it is "cruel and unusual punishment" to convict appellant for addiction, it is difficult to understand why it would be any less offensive to the Fourteenth Amendment to convict him for use on the same evidence of use which proved he was an addict. It is significant that in purporting to reaffirm the power of the States to deal with the narcotics traffic, the Court does not include among the obvious powers of the State the power to punish for the use of narcotics. I cannot think that the omission was inadvertent.

The Court has not merely tidied up California's law by removing some irritating vestige of an outmoded approach to the control of narcotics. At the very least, it has effectively removed California's power to deal effectively with the recurring case under the statute where there is ample evidence of use but no evidence of the precise location of use. Beyond this it has cast serious doubt upon the power of any State to forbid the use of narcotics under threat of criminal punishment. I cannot believe that the Court would forbid the application of the criminal laws to the use of narcotics under any circumstances. But the States, as well as the Federal Government, are now on notice. They will have to await a final answer in another case. . . .

DRUG USE IN AMERICA: PROBLEM IN PERSPECTIVE

The Assumptions and Premises of Present Policy

Elimination of Non-Medical Drug Use. American drug policy has been predicated on one fundamental notion: that the societal objective is to eliminate "non-medical" drug use. Inquiry has rarely been addressed to whether this goal is desirable or possible. Failure to address such questions is abetted by the exclusion of certain drugs and certain types of drug taking from the realm of social distress. For example, the non-medical use of alcohol and tobacco would be inconsistent with the declared goal; thus, statutory vocabulary and social folklore have established the fiction that they are not drugs at all. Although use of these substances may arouse concern, they are not viewed in the wider context of drug use.

Another area excluded from public discussion is drug use sanctioned by medical judgment. While most medically-approved consumption of psychoactive drugs is substantially different from the situation where the individual chooses to use the drug himself, this is not always true. The absence of the intervening judgment of a third party does not mean that the individual's motivation is "non-medical," or hedonistic. Nor does the intervention of medical judgment assure that the drug will be used for medically-intended purposes.[1]

Drug policy makers cannot truthfully assert that this society aims to eliminate non-medical drug use. No semantic fiction will alter the fundamental composition of alcohol and tobacco. Further, even if the objective is amended to exclude these drugs, human history discounts the notion that drug-using behavior can be so tightly confined as a medical system implies. The substantial increase in self-medication in recent years illustrates

[1] The third party judgment may intervene directly, as is the case with prescription drugs, or indirectly, as is the case with over-the-counter preparations previously approved for this purpose by the Food and Drug Administration.

this truth. The backyard pharmacy, where neighbors diagnose their friends' ailments and share their prescription drugs with them, the proliferation of over-the-counter preparations, the advertising of mood-altering drugs, and the popularity of minor tranquilizers are all manifestations of an important contemporary trend.

The medical/non-medical distinction has become increasingly blurred as emotional ailments increase. Many individuals tend today to assess their own needs and define the purposes for which they use a drug. For this reason, generalized societal proclamations regarding the need to eliminate non-medical drug use raise an important question that must be honestly answered: how does the daily use of a prescribed barbiturate to bring a person "down" from the day differ from the similar use of a self-prescribed minor tranquilizer or, for that matter, a martini?

Deferring for the moment our own view as to what society's objective in this area ought to be, we do know that it is not as clear cut as official pronouncements imply. In determining the appropriate objective, a task that we will undertake in Chapter Four, policy makers must recognize the scope and complexity of drug-using behavior and develop rational distinctions between that which should be disapproved and that which should be tolerated, or even approved. Within the area of disapproval, policy makers should not consider all disapproved drug use to be of equal importance; priorities must be assigned on the basis of actual and potential social consequence, and not just on the basis of numbers of users.

Risk-Taking and Health. Often cited in support of societal disapproval of non-medical drug use is the proposition that individuals should not risk their health by using drugs. Without regard to the philosophical propriety of this premise as a guide for social policy, this view appears to be somewhat at odds with the facts about drug use and with prevailing social attitudes toward risk-taking in other areas.

Excerpts from Second Report of the National Commission on Marihuana and Drug Abuse, 1973.

Much emphasis has been placed on whether or not a drug is a dangerous drug; and analogies have been drawn between "street" drugs and such substances as cyclamates. These examples illustrate how closely public discussion of drug abuse has become tied to matters of individual health. In supporting present social policy, spokesmen often list those drug effects which are potentially harmful to individual health rather than focusing on the social consequences of drug-using behavior.

The Commission believes that persons who take this approach have misconstrued the nature of the drug issue. The assumption that all psychoactive drug use is a high-risk behavior presumes a progression from irregular use of low doses to continuous use of high doses, thereby ignoring pharmacological variations among drugs and the importance of frequency of use, method of administration, dose, and non-drug factors as determinants of risk. In fact, injury to health is associated primarily with chronic heavy use and at times with the acute effects of high doses.

Further, there is no correlation whatsoever between the capacity of psychoactive drugs to induce behavioral disorders and their capacity to induce organic or somatic toxicity or pathology. Of the drugs which are most commonly associated with dependence or drug-induced behavior, alcohol produces the most clearly established and reproducible brain pathology. Cocaine, amphetamines and other stimulants, heroin and morphine-like drugs, and cannabis do not appear to have this effect. On the other hand, very heavy use of phenacitin, which has no significant behavioral impact at all, may produce renal damage, and heavy tobacco smoking is associated with greatly increased risk of lung cancer. If the standard for social policy were potential injury to individual health, barbiturates, alcohol, and tobacco would present the clearest cases for prohibition. Yet, the latter two are available for self-defined purposes, and the former is widely used in the practice of medicine.

Nonetheless, the approach often applied to "drugs of abuse" is the same as that applied to non-psychoactive substances: risks to individual health will be tolerated only if the medical needs for the substance justify the risks. But individuals would not choose to use psychoactive drugs if they did not perceive some advantage to themselves. So the fundamental question arises: Who is to weigh the perceived advantages of drug use against the risk, the individual or the society?

To deal with this question, we must examine the pattern of social response to risk-taking behavior in general. For example, we urge our youth to be curious and to explore. Until recent years, Americans tended to place a premium on high-powered automobiles. We tolerate the private ownership of firearms. We tend to applaud the courageous mountain climber or other adventurer who ignores the risks in the effort to establish human dominion over nature. In short, risk-taking behavior is permitted and often encouraged by many of our social institutions, which defer to individual judgment the weighing of often intangible benefits against the quite tangible risks.

Society has long been aware of the individual and social risks of alcohol use. Even with the effort now being made to inform the public of the risks of tobacco use, society still permits this drug to be widely available. In both cases, society clearly subordinates the risks inherent in such behavior, deferring instead to individual judgment.

The Commission is not suggesting that health risks are irrelevant to the formulation of drug policy. However, whatever appropriate weight is given to health considerations, it is a peripheral, rather than focal, concern. Drug policy must be based on the social consequences of drug use, and on the social impact of drug-induced behavior.

Motivation for Mood Alteration. Subsumed within the societal goal of eliminating non-medical drug use is the value judgment that use of drugs for the explicit purpose of mood alteration is *per se* undesirable. To harmonize this judgment with approved conduct, we avoid analyzing the motivations of similar behaviors.

As noted earlier, we do not verbalize the motivation for alcohol use in terms of pleasure but rather in terms of the drug's function as a relaxant, as a social lubricant, and as a beverage. We do not think about the alcohol experience as an altered state of consciousness but rather as a means to some other end, such as promoting conviviality or stimulating conversation.

Within the medical setting, the individual is increasingly making the decision to use medically approved drugs and selecting them according to their capacity to alter his mood. The National Survey shows that 15% of the adult population reported that they "take a pill to calm down or cheer up" when they feel "out of sorts . . . not really sick, but nervous, or depressed or under stress." Eighteen percent of the public reported that they used alcohol for similar purposes. The use of a variety of new mood altering drugs to cope with stress is undoubtedly a significant social development, particularly among women. This option to employ drugs for what is essentially an individual diagnosis of felt needs has, to a large extent, changed public perception concerning the role of the drugs as mood alterants in our society.

Whatever the biological and psychological foundations for the common human desire to alter consciousness, policy makers must recognize that drugs have always been used for this purpose. Most societies have institutionalized at least one form of drug-induced mood alteration; only the drugs differ, not the essential purpose. Instead of assuming that mood alteration through some drugs is inherently objectionable, while similar use of others is not, the public and its leaders must focus directly on the appropriate role of drug-induced mood alteration. It is no longer satisfactory to defend social disapproval of use of a particular drug on the ground that it is a "mind-altering drug" or a "means of escape." For so are they all.

Drugs and Individual Responsibility. Implicit in present policy is the concern that many individuals cannot be trusted to make prudent or responsible decisions regarding drug-taking. Certain drugs are thought to possess even greater powers than they have, including the capacity to overbear individual will. Most people are not accustomed to thinking about drug effects in terms of probabilities and uncertainties, of dose-response curves, of multiple effects (some desirable and some undesirable), of reactions which vary from individual to individual and from time to time in the same individual.

A deep-seated popular belief that some drugs diminish or destroy the individual's capacity to control his behavior is reflected in hypotheses such as "drugs cause crime" or "drugs cause dropping out" or "drugs cause mental illness." Any perceived correlation between use of the drug and the unwanted consequence is attributed to the drug, removing the individual from any and all responsibility. Similarly, while it is true that certain drugs offer more intense psychological rewards than others, seduction characteristics are attributed to all psychoactive drugs, suggesting a chain of progression from light to heavy use, from weak to stronger drugs, all without the intervention of individual choice.

A drug has no effect until it interacts with an organism. The effects of any drug, psychoactive drugs included, are mainly dose related. At low or moderate doses they are determined mainly by non-drug factors, such as the psychological characteristics of the individual, the reasons why he uses the drug, what he expects the effects will be, the physical and social setting in which he uses it, and how he perceives its use or non-use in relation to self-defined goals. Further, how his friends, subculture, and his society define and respond to his drug use are equally important factors. These psychological and social criteria not only influence the reaction to a specific drug but they are key factors in determining use or non-use, selection of substance, and the pattern and circumstances of use.

An Overview of the Present Response

Because of this confusion about objectives, the formal institutional response to the drug problem has been more reflexive than rational, more situation-oriented than strategic. The *ad hoc* responses to use of specific psychoactive drugs have interfered with examination of the fundamental questions relating to behavior patterns and the appropriate means of social control.

Research has provided us with an almost endless stream of psychoactive substances. The tendency is to identify a new substance, determine its potential hazards as a chemical and then to insert it into the existing system. This procedure tends to perpetuate the public focus on the drugs rather than on the prevention of behavior about which society is concerned. When the drug appears in the streets, as it inevitably does, social institutions respond as if the behavior was unanticipated, and because they are ill-prepared to deal with the situation, an atmosphere of crisis is generated.

Because the focus has always been on the elimination of prohibited substances altogether and on the elimination of the street use of therapeutically useful drugs, social institutions have directed primary attention to the problem of *use* of *specific drugs*. Patterns of drug-using behavior have been ignored except as an afterthought of intervention. When increases in prohibited drug use continue to escalate, policy makers respond, not by reassessing the problem from different perspectives, but rather by pressing for ever-more costly mechanisms of control; costly both in terms of resources and important social values. Drug policy can be thus summed up: increased use of disapproved drugs precipitates more spending, more programs, more arrests and more penalties, all with little positive effect in reducing use of these drugs.

Details of the present institutional response share the confusion of purpose which characterizes the entire social response. We will sketch a few of the key features here although these matters will be considered in some depth in Chapter Four.

Risk-Education. An important operating assumption of the present response is that if people are educated about the risks of drug taking, they will not use drugs. It is presumed that presentation of information regarding dangers and risks can quiet curiosity and the desire for anticipated pleasant psychological sensations, the factors which account for most individual drug experiences.

Society's experience in attempting to discourage use of substances not labeled as drugs is instructive. Campaigns have been mounted in the past, both through the mass media and the schools, about the dangers of alcohol use and cigarette smoking. Facts have been marshaled, scientific opinion has been mobilized, and the adverse consequences of use of these drugs have been amply demonstrated by the number of alcoholics within the United States and the number of persons dying yearly from heart disease, lung cancer and other respiratory ailments. Still the consumption of alcohol continues and the number of persons smoking cigarettes increases.

This same kind of educational effort has been directed at the illicit drugs with no apparent impact on behavior. Little insight has been gained as to why this approach has not worked with alcohol and cigarettes, or as to whether risk-oriented curricula may actually arouse interest rather than dampen it. Further, assuming that such programs might be useful, little thought has been given to how to transmit the information, the assumption again being that the facts speak for themselves. This vast expenditure of time, money and effort has apparently paid few measurable social dividends, and those that have claimed success have done so not on the basis of scientific proof, but on the basis of impressions and anecdote.

Coercion. If information about risks and moral suasion is insufficient to convince many people not to use drugs, it is assumed that the threat of a criminal sanction will do so. While a criminal proscription does function as a deterrent to some degree for all behavior, the strength of this factor varies according to the nature of the offense, the characteristics of the actor, the probability of detection and the certainty of punishment. With regard to drug consumption, all of these factors diminish the utility of the criminal sanction. Drug consumption is an expressive conduct which normally occurs in private among groups which are least influenced by legal condemnation. In addition, the consumption-related offenses[2] are no

longer supported by the strong social consensus which once existed, and the emerging ambivalence is reflected in the dispositional decisions of police, prosecutors and courts.

We note that drug consumption offenses have not been remarkably successful in curtailing use in general. However, it is important here, as elsewhere, to distinguish between different patterns of drug-taking behavior. On the one hand, the law may deter indiscrete use and continued use of a prohibited drug. On the other hand, e xperimental behavior, particularly by youth, is unlikely to be deterred by the law alone. For those who are dependent upon prohibited drugs, such as the heroin-dependent person, the deterrence concept is functionally inapplicable.

Sickness. Anyone choosing to use drugs, despite the enumerated risks, moral suasion and threat of criminalization, is often considered abnormal, emotionally ill and weak of character. The last decade has seen the pendulum of legislative opinion swing toward the belief that drug dependence and even drug *use* is a "medical" problem, that it can be "treated," and that the user can be "rehabilitated." Like many ideas which aim to correct those previously in vogue, the medical approach has itself become a runaway concept. Policy makers have adopted policy guidewords such as "treatment," "rehabilitation," "contagion," and "epidemic," without regard to their utility in the present context.

The "sickness" label has been attached to all users of prohibited drugs without regard to their patterns of drug-taking behavior. While very few question that persons compulsively using drugs are in need of some form of therapeutic assistance, the same is rarely true for the experimental and recreational user. To label drug users in general as mentally ill is to place a large segment of American society in need of formal medical assistance.

With regard to drug dependence in particular, the public has been led to believe that this condition is as definable and treatable as ordinary illnesses of the body. In reality, there is not, at the present time, any generally applicable cure for drug-dependent persons let alone non-dependent users of drugs. "Success" in treatment programs has been difficult to define, reflecting the complex relationship between drug use, social functioning and mental health. Even when measured against their

---

[2] Throughout this Report, consumption-related offenses will refer to offenses such as use, possession for personal use, presence in a place where

prohibited drugs are being used. Unless stated otherwise, "possession" means possession for personal use.

own criteria for evaluation, most treatment programs can demonstrate only limited "success."

Public policy is committed to the treatment and rehabilitation of all drug-dependent persons. While thousands of persons have been aided by treatment efforts in recent years, social objectives continue to outstrip professional understanding of the condition and official capacity to deliver the necessary services.

Perpetuating the Problem. Because of the intensity of the public concern and the emotionalism surrounding the topic of drugs, all levels of government have been pressured into action with little time for planning. The political pressures involved in this governmental effort have resulted in a concentration of public energy on the most immediate aspects of drug use and a reaction along the paths of least political resistance. The recent result has been the creation of ever larger bureaucracies, ever increasing expenditures of monies, and an outpouring of publicity so that the public will know that "something" is being done.

Perhaps the major consequence of this *ad hoc* policy planning has been the creation, at the federal, state and community levels, of a vested interest in the perpetuation of the problem among those dispensing and receiving funds. Infrastructures are created, job descriptions are standardized, "experts" are created and ways of doing business routinized and established along bureaucratic channels. During the last several years, drug programming has become a multi-billion dollar industry, one administering to its own needs as well as to those of its drug-using clientele. In the course of well-meaning efforts to do something about drug use, this society may have inadvertently institutionalized it as a never-ending project.

All of these responses stem from one fundamental flaw in present drug policy: the problem is defined incorrectly. The uneasiness which the Commission has encountered among thoughtful observers and officials arises largely from their own perceptions that the present response, although massive, has so far been relatively ineffective. Yet, any challenge to the basic premises of policy may be viewed by some as a disavowal of the entire social response. The Commission does not believe the present policy should be abandoned out of hand. Instead, we hope that policy can be made more coherent and more flexible. In order to do so, we must put aside preconceived notions, setting out afresh to redefine the problem.

DEFINING THE PROBLEM

The Meaning of Drug Use

Throughout history man has used available psychoactive substances to seek relief from cold, hunger, deprivation, anxiety, pain and boredom. He also has used such substances to receive pleasure or to achieve new experiences. Various cultures have sought out and used naturally-occurring plants for their psychoactive ingredients, discovering their effects by trial and error. Modern man has consciously created new chemical substances and institutionalized their availability for similar uses.

Drugs have effects other than those which are sought; and all drug-effects vary with amount and frequency of use, the characteristics of the user, and the set and setting in which they are used. Consequently, different cultures have applied different values to the presumed consequences of drug use, whether beneficial or deleterious. Each society has decided which needs are legitimate, which effects are valuable and which risks are tolerable. These judgments are based on prevailing values concerning specific drugs, their effects, the reasons for which they are used, and the people who use them.

Man does not ordinarily continue to do something that does not fulfill some real or imagined need. To persist, behavior must be reinforced. To the extent that it does fulfill a need, it will recur, often at some risk unless it interferes with some more important need. The need for a drug may be closely related to its real or imagined effects or it may be grounded in social rather than chemical elements. Use of specific substances may determine group membership, or status within a group, or among groups. It may function as either a symbol or symptom of rebellion, alienation, independence or sophistication.

To better understand current self-defined drug use and to determine the scope of social concern, one must go beyond the cataloguing of substances (pharmacologically defined where possible), the listing of effects, and the counting of users and non-users of drugs. The inquiry must shift from drugs to people, from pharmacological effects to the meaning and function of drug use.

The Incidence of Drug Use. The nature and scope of society's drug problem at any given time are generally perceived in terms of the incidence of non-medical use of legal and illegal substances. Tables 1 and 2 present data of this kind obtained in the Commission-sponsored National Survey. . . .

Table 1. Incidence of Use of Illegal Drugs[1] 1972

	Ever used (Percent)		Present use[2] (Percent)	
	Youth	Adult	Youth	Adult
Marihuana	14	16	7	8
LSD or hallu-cinogens	4.8	4.6	3.1	1.5
Cocaine	1.5	3.2	1.1	1.6
Heroin	.6	1.3	.2	.1

[1] The Commission emphasizes that the National Survey was a household survey and therefore the sample did not include the transient "street" population among whom use of heroin and cocaine is presumably high.

[2] For LSD, cocaine, and heroin, "most recent use" of 6 months or less was regarded as "present use."

Table 2. Incidence of Nonmedical Use of Legal Drugs 1972

	Youth (Percent)	Adults (Percent)
Over-the-counter prepara-tions (ever use)	6	7
Prescription (ever use):		
Stimulants[1]	4	5
Sedatives[2]	3	4
"Minor tranquilizers"[3]	3	6
Alcohol:		
(present use)[4]	24	53
Beer	17	38
Wine	9	18
Liquor	6	26

[1] Includes amphetamine and amphetaminelike substances.

[2] Includes barbiturates and several nonbarbiturate substances, such as glutethimide.

[3] Includes substances, such as meprobamate, diazepam, and chlordiazepoxide.

[4] Present use of alcohol includes use within past 7 days.

Criminogenic Effects

Summary. In conclusion, the research findings concerning the associations between drug use and crime have been complicated by the interplay between the pharmacologic properties of the drugs and the psychosocial characteristics of the individuals who use them. Inferences which might have been drawn from laboratory research have suffered primarily from the difficulties attending replication of non-pharmacological variables; and while naturalistic studies are appropriate to this area of investigation, they have been plagued for the most part by deficiencies in research design and sampling procedures. Nonetheless, the following tentative conclusions appear justifiable from the data available:

- Alcohol, the most commonly used drug, is strongly associated with violent crime and with reckless and negligent operation of motor vehicles.

- Research findings linking barbiturate and amphetamine users with criminal behavior, especially assaultive offenses, are increasing, but no definitive association has yet been established in this country; however, a strong association has been demonstrated between amphetamine use and violence in Sweden and Japan.

- Research data are generally lacking regarding the actual relationship between cocaine use and criminal behavior; however, the pharmacologic effects of the drug would seem to suggest a potential for drug-induced violent behavior similar to that shown for amphetamine and barbiturate users.

- Marihuana use, in and of itself, is neither causative of, nor directly associated with crime, either violent or non-violent. In fact, marihuana tends to be underrepresented among assaultive offenders, especially when compared with users of alcohol, amphetamines and barbiturates.

- Use of opiates, especially heroin, is associated with acquisitive crimes such as burglary and shoplifting, ordinarily committed for the purpose of securing money to support dependence. Assaultive offenses are significantly less likely to be committed by these opiate users, especially in comparison with users of alcohol, amphetamines and barbiturates.

- Except in relatively rare instances generally related to drug-induced panic and toxic reactions, users of hallucinogens, non-barbiturate sedative-hypnotics, glue and similar volatile inhalants are not inclined toward assaultive criminal behavior. It should be noted, however, that some of the non-barbiturate sedatives, notably methaqualone, and the hydrocarbon solvents have a potential for inducing violent behavior although the incidence of such behavior is currently low.

Involuntary "Civil" Commitment: The Problems of a Therapeutic Response

As we have noted, drug-dependent persons have been covered by the general mental illness commitment statutes of most states for many years, although these procedures have rarely been invoked. Beginning with the California, New York and federal (NARA) civil commitment programs, many states enacted separate statutes specifically dealing with drug-dependent persons. At the present time, 34 states have involuntary commitment laws which apply expressly to drug-dependent persons. In 24 of these states a person may be committed upon a showing of "addiction" or "drug dependence;" the remaining 10 states require a showing of "dangerousness" as well. The consequences of commitment under these therapeutic programs vary widely. In 17 states, confinement is indefinite. In the others the possible periods of commitment range from 30 days in Washington and Montana to 10 years in California.

By and large, persons against whom civil commitment petitions are filed are entitled to very few procedural safeguards, and the details of commitment procedure differ enormously from state to state. Almost every state permits the subject to be detained pending a hearing without any kind of preliminary adjudication,[3] although some states limit the time of pre-hearing detention. In most states commitment proceedings are conducted without a jury. Eight states do not provide for representation by counsel, and Indiana and Illinois appoint the District Attorney to represent indigent patients. Several states do not even give the patient notice that a proceeding is being initiated against him. As is true in most procedures shaped by the therapeutic premise, a patient's silence is generally regarded as proof of his illness rather than as the exercise of a constitutional right.

Only Nebraska and Wisconsin require the state to demonstrate the grounds for commitment beyond a reasonable doubt. In most states, the petitioner need only establish "addiction" or dependence on the basis of a preponderance of the evidence. Only nine states accord the patient an immediate appeal of a commitment order, and in the other states review is limited to habeas corpus or permitted only after completion of a specified period in treatment.

Very few of the state legislatures have applied fundamental controls to the treatment process itself. It is now generally accepted that a person committed for purposes of treatment has a right to receive treatment, though the contours of this right remain ill-defined. This area requires the most careful legislative attention, yet, very few states have spoken to the issue in even an oblique way.

[3] Pennsylvania and Hawaii actually permit the person to be confined without a hearing until he himself protests.

Nine states require the facilities to provide "adequate and appropriate" or "humane" treatment; and Massachusetts requires the preparation of individual treatment plans. To date very few states actually have special facilities for drug-dependent persons; the common outcome for the drug-dependent person is commitment to the state mental hospital. Moreover, patients may be held in jails while awaiting space in a treatment institution.

At the present time, involuntary commitment laws are clearly superfluous and rarely invoked. The criminal justice system still functions as the method by which most drug-dependent persons enter treatment. Involuntary civil commitment may have a useful role after the criminal justice framework has been disengaged from the area of drug consumption, but, even then, it should be limited to individuals who have refused to enter treatment voluntarily, who present a clear and immediate danger to the safety of themselves or others, and for whom treatment is available. In the meantime, existing laws require a fundamental restructuring in terms of procedure, substantive criteria for commitment, length of commitment, and nature of treatment services.

Therapy and the Criminal Process

Despite the increased substitution of treatment for criminal punishment, the criminal justice system remains the primary means of detecting drug users and asserting control, either punitive or therapeutic, over them. Many awkward and undesirable features of the present response reflect the fact that the therapeutic approach to drug use and dependence is still a stepchild of the criminal process. To correct this situation, it is necessary to develop a formal process, with appropriate internal and external restraints, for asserting therapeutic control, for choosing the least restrictive method of treatment adequate to the case, and for assuring that the treatment is satisfactorily administered.

Concluding that possession of prohibited substances except marihuana for personal use should remain a criminal offense, we believe the criminal justice system must continue to serve as the mechanism for detecting those in need of assistance and channelling their entry into a treatment system. The Supreme Court's decision in *Robinson v. California* made it clear that traditional criminal justice concepts are constitutionally suspect when applied to drug-dependent persons. In this case, the Court held only that a person may not be punished for being drug-dependent, reasoning that this status was not a matter of free moral choice. Many commentators, however, think that the rationale in *Robinson* precludes making drug-dependent persons criminally responsible for much of their status-related behavior as well (Silverman, 1973). Although the Supreme Court has not yet exempted drug-dependent persons from traditional criminal prosecution for the *acts* which are symptomatic of the illness, such as possession of the drug upon which he is dependent or being under the influence of the drug, its decision in *Robinson* indicates a change in the operation of the criminal justice system when it deals with the dependent offender.

In the Commission's view, the criminal justice system may properly function in such cases as a detection mechanism. However, since the premises of free choice and punishment are not always applicable to the behavior of drug-dependent persons, the process after detection must shift to determining whether the relationship between the person's status and his anti-social behavior permits application of the punitive premise. For certain conduct (possession for personal use, being under influence and other consumption-related behavior), the Commission believes that criminal responsibility may not be affixed.[4] For other conduct, involving violence or the threat of violence against the person, the possible relationship with drug dependence is more tenuous, and the public interest in preserving order and safety is so great that criminal liability must be assessed. For other behavior, the Commission believes that the participants in the criminal process (the district attorney and the judge) must have the discretion to determine whether or not the drug-dependent person should be held accountable.

When punitive intervention is inappropriate, the Commission does not conclude that society must forego control altogether. Instead, in such cases it may be constitutionally permissible to rest formal control on the therapeutic premise and on the state's *parens patriae* power, if treatment is indeed available and the nature of control is no more restrictive than necessary to provide effective treatment. As we have noted, the constitutional bounds of therapeutic intervention seem to be narrowing. Nonetheless, the Commission believes that imposition of therapy is a legitimate exercise

of state power, as long as control is asserted only when the individual's drug dependence has had a substantially detrimental impact on his capacity for normal functioning, unnecessary restraint is avoided, adequate treatment is provided, and the entire process is subject to strict procedural limitations.

It is important to emphasize that the distinction between punishment and therapy is not a matter of procedural labels. As experiences with the juvenile court and commitment procedures for mental illness indicate, "civil" procedures do not guarantee a therapeutic result. The Commission is convinced that the criminal justice system may be utilized to assert control for therapeutic purposes provided that the indicia and implications of criminality which would render the process constitutionally impermissible are avoided.

In this regard the Commission recommends that all states attempt to rationalize the operation of the criminal justice system as a process for identifying drug-dependent persons and for securing their entry into a treatment system. The states should establish, as part of the comprehensive prevention and treatment program, a separate treatment process which runs parallel to the criminal process, and which may be formally or informally substituted for the criminal process.

In the long run, however, the Commission believes that coercive intervention should not rest simply on the need for therapy alone. Primarily, entry into treatment should become voluntary, and society should aim to maximize the number of drug-dependent persons who seek assistance on their own. The legal status of dependence on opiates, barbiturates

Table 3. Federal Expenditures for Drug Law Enforcement

(In millions of dollars)

Agency	Fiscal year				
	1969	1970	1971	1972	1973
Justice:					
LEAA	0	0.6	2.2	16.6	30.3
BNDD	16.8	25.8	41.3	59.7	71.2
Other	0.3	1.3	3.5	0.3	4.8
Treasury:					
IRS	0	0	0	7.6	18.9
Customs	3.1	12.4	30.2	46.8	54.3
State	0.3	1.3	1	1.0	1.6
Aid	0	0	4.4	20.7	42.7
Agriculture	0	0	0	2.1	1.8
DOT	0		0	0.5	0.5
Law enforcement, total	20.5	41.4	81.6	155.3	226.1

[1] Less than $100,000.

---

[4] That drug-dependent persons may not be held criminally responsible for consumption-related conduct does not mean that the criminal justice system has no rule in the treatment process. See the Commission's recommendation regarding the possession penalty on pages 273–74 and regarding treatment and rehabilitation on pages 338–42.

or any other drug restricted to medical channels should compare to that of alcohol dependence: coercive intervention should be limited to those persons posing an immediate and substantial danger to their own safety or the safety of others. This leads us to consideration of the third justification for control: prevention. . . .

CONCLUSION: THE POSSESSION OFFENSE AND ITS ENFORCEMENT

Having discussed deterrence, therapy and prevention as justifications for assertion of control over persons who have chosen to consume prohibited substances, we can now draw some conclusions concerning the appropriate scope and method of intervention.

The Commission recommends that the unauthorized possession of any controlled substance except marihuana for personal use remain a prohibited act. The Commission further recommends that as a matter of statutory or enforcement policy, assertion of control over the consumer should not be tied to concepts of criminal accountability but rather to concepts of assistance appropriate in the individual case. The primary purpose of enforcement of the possession laws should be the detection and selection of those persons who would benefit by treatment or prevention services.

Treatment and prevention programs will be detailed in later sections; the role of the legal system will be outlined here.

For those drug-dependent persons who are apprehended for consumption-related offenses, including possession, one of the following dispositions is in our view constitutionally required and should be mandatory:

(a) diversion to a treatment program in lieu of prosecution; or
(b) diversion to a treatment program after conviction but before entry of judgment by the court.

Failure by an individual to comply with the conditions of treatment would result in his return to the court for prosecution or sentencing. In that event, he should be subject to punishment by up to one year imprisonment, a fine of up to $500 or both.

For those non-drug-dependent persons who are apprehended for consumption-related offenses, including possession, one of the following dispositions should be mandatory:

(a) diversion to a prevention services program in lieu of prosecution;
(b) diversion to a prevention services program after conviction but before entry of judgment by the court:
(c) a fine of up to $500; or
(d) probation with appropriate conditions.

Failure by the individual to comply with the conditions of prevention services under alternatives (a) or (b) would result in his return to the court for prosecution or sentencing. In that event, he should be subject to punishment by up to one year's imprisonment, a fine of up to $500 or both.

The Commission supports the conditional discharge provisions of the Comprehensive Drug Abuse Prevention and Control Act of 1970, which includes expungement of criminal records. Experience with this provision and a similar one in the Uniform Controlled Substances Act,[5] indicates that they are useful in providing flexibility in the criminal justice process.

These recommendations should be implemented by the state legislatures and the Congress by amendments of their possession laws, or as part of a comprehensive drug dependence treatment and rehabilitation act, such as that now before the National Conference of Commissioners on Uniform State Laws. . . .

CONCLUSIONS AND RECOMMENDATIONS ON TREATMENT OF DEPENDENCE

Earlier, we raised the question whether drug dependence can meaningfully be regarded as an illness and whether the concept of treatment can be applied meaningfully. We can answer these questions with a qualified "yes." The successes of recently developed methods of therapy indicate that the social functioning of opiate-dependent persons can be improved through a wide range of services, although neither social reintegration nor abstinence can be guaranteed.

Several qualifications are necessary, though. First, treatment of drug dependence must be approached pragmatically. If treatment "success" means no less than a quick and complete cessation of drug-taking, treatment programs will often fail to achieve either that utopian goal or more limited results which are within reach. Flexibility in both method and objective are critical to any effective treatment response to drug dependence. Jerome H. Jaffe, Director of the Special Action Office for Drug Abuse Prevention in the White House, has noted in this connection:

[5] The Uniform Controlled Substances Act does not provide for expungement of the criminal record.

Ideally, a treatment program should attempt to help all compulsive narcotic users become emotionally mature, law abiding, productive members of society who require no drugs or additional medical or social support to maintain this ideal status. But, this is an ideal set of goals, a set that society does not expect any other group with medical or psychiatric disabilities to meet. For example, we do not expect middle-aged people with mild congestive heart failure to become marathon runners; we do not even insist that, after some arbitrary period of treatment, they abstain from digitalis, diuretics, and visits to the doctor. Compulsive drug use should also be thought of as a chronic disorder, and many cases require continual or intermittent treatment over a period of years. It follows, then, that, while all treatment programs should attempt to help every individual reach all the components of the ideal set of goals, any evaluation of the overall effectiveness of any specific treatment must take into consideration the fact that different programs tend to place their emphasis on different goals. (Jaffe, 1973)

The second caveat is that treatment is neither available nor appropriate for all kinds of drug use or drug dependence. The experimental, recreational or circumstantial user of drugs is generally no more "sick" than the social drinker; it becomes an absurdity to talk of treating such a person. Nonetheless, there have been serious proposals to commit any person detected using marihuana, for example, to long periods of drug treatment. The Commission finds such proposals overreactive and misguided. Misusing drug treatment programs in such a way would not only waste their resources but would also turn drug treatment into another form of incarceration.

Even among chronic users, whose drug use has escalated to intensified patterns and who might legitimately be classified as drug-dependent, treatment is not always appropriate. Chronic drug use is not necessarily symptomatic of psychiatric disorders, and legal standards for therapeutic control must reflect a meaningful and accurate definition of the "illness" of drug dependence.

Finally, recognizing the complex etiology of drug dependence, rehabilitation policy must not focus so closely on the dependent individual that it loses sight of preventive approaches. Medicine has discovered that some of the best remedies for physical diseases are social remedies; improving nutrition, shelter, and living conditions in general. If this is true for illnesses like malaria and tuberculosis, how much more true for "social diseases" like drug dependence.

In accord with the observations in this section and the earlier ones on consumption-intervention and the governmental response, the Commission makes the following recommendations concerning treatment and rehabilitation policy:

Federal Funding and Services

Through block and formula grants to the states, the federal government should have major responsibility for funding treatment and rehabilitation services administered by the states. However, the federal government should retain discretionary funds for direct funding of demonstration and special projects in the field of treatment and rehabilitation. Such funds should be used for innovative and experimental programs, as well as for providing services to communities not receiving sufficient funding from the state.

Except for offenders within federally-operated correctional institutions, the federal government should not have direct operating responsibility for providing treatment and rehabilitation services. Services provided to persons entering treatment on a voluntary basis or through involuntary civil commitment proceedings should be provided only at the state level. Services provided to persons charged with or convicted of federal criminal offenses who are not in a federal correctional facility should be provided through state-operated programs and facilities on a reimbursable basis. The public health hospital operated by the federal government in Lexington, Kentucky should continue to be utilized for clinical research purposes only and the fifty-bed clinical research unit of the facility should be maintained for human research.

Federal Evaluation

The federal government should sponsor a program to evaluate existing drug treatment and rehabilitation programs to see whether they (1) are cost effective; (2) are designed to deal effectively with their client populations; and (3) have established suitable criteria and objectives.

After such an evaluation the federal government should establish performance criteria for state drug treatment and rehabilitation programs.

All drug treatment and rehabilitation programs receiving federal funds should demonstrate effective effort consistent with the performance criteria established, and undergo an annual evaluation by independent evaluators having no vested interest in either the funding agency or the service delivery agency.

State Treatment Programs

Each state should establish a comprehensive statewide drug dependence treatment and rehabilitation program including integrated health, education, information, welfare and treatment services, which should be administered as part of the state's broader health care delivery and human resources development systems. The program should:

(a) Provide a full range of treatment and rehabilitation services throughout the state, including emergency, residential, and outpatient services for drug-dependent persons, persons incapacitated by controlled substances or persons under the influence of controlled substances.

(b) Include medical, psychiatric, psychological and social service care; vocational and rehabilitation services; job training and career counselling; corrective and preventive guidance; and any other rehabilitative services, including maintenance, designed to aid the person to gain control over or eliminate his dependence on controlled substances and to make him less susceptible to dependence on controlled substances in the future.

(c) Emphasize the development of community-based emergency, outpatient and follow-up support services.

(d) Utilize and coordinate all appropriate public and private resources, wherever possible utilizing the facilities of and coordinating services with community mental health services and general hospitals.

(e) Allocate services within the state according to an overall plan based on the estimated size and location of the current potential populations of drug-dependent persons in various communities.

The state administrator of such a comprehensive drug dependence treatment program should have statutory responsibility for:

(a) Establish standards and guidelines for effective drug dependence treatment services provided by public or private agencies participating in the program.

(b) Evaluate, on a continuing basis, all public and private treatment services included in the program, in order to assure that such services are adequate and effective according to defined objectives and standards.

(c) Prepare, publish and distribute annually a list of all public facilities and those private facilities to which public agencies are authorized to refer individuals for treatment services.

(d) Assure that the courts of each jurisdiction within the state are periodically notified of facilities through which services are available within the jurisdiction and of the types of treatment offered at each facility, thereby assuring that formal control is not asserted over a person for purposes of treatment when appropriate facilities are not available.

(e) Assure that the services offered within each community include drug-free programs as well as maintenance programs, thereby assuring that persons seeking or referred for treatment have the option of participating in a drug-free program.

The Role of the Legal System in State Programs

Each state should review its current statutory mechanisms regarding the process by which drug-dependent persons are permitted or compelled to enter treatment. Those states which have not already done so should modify existing legislation to encourage drug-dependent persons to seek treatment voluntarily. In order to maximize the attractiveness of voluntary programs, formal legal processes should be avoided entirely and absolute confidentiality of the treatment records should be assured.

Whenever a state chooses to exert formal control over a drug-dependent person for purposes of treatment, either through criminal process or an involuntary civil process, treatment services should be administered in accordance with the following standards:

(a) Each person has a right to receive such individual treatment as will give him a realistic opportunity to overcome his dependence on controlled substances.

(b) An individual treatment plan, guided by sound medical and clinical judgment and maximizing freedom of choice of the patient, shall be prepared and maintained on a current basis for each person.

(c) No person should be required to receive chemical treatment or maintenance services without his consent, and in the case of a person under 18 years of age, without additional consent of his parents or legal guardian.

(d) Each individualized treatment plan should employ methods which restrict the drug-dependent person's liberty only when less restrictive alternatives would be inconsistent with necessary and effective treatment.

(e) No person should be required to be a subject for experimental research without his expressed and informed consent.

(f) All persons should be required, as a condition of participation in a treatment program, to comply with reasonable conditions, including surveillance techniques such as urinalysis.

The state, through legislation or administra-tive action, should assure that private and public hospitals do not discriminate in either admission or treatment policy against any person on the grounds of use of or dependence on controlled substances.

Uniformity of State Law

In connection with these above recommen-dations, the Commission supports the adop-tion of the Uniform Drug Dependence Treatment and Rehabilitation Act presently being considered by the National Confer-ence of Commissioners on Uniform State Laws. . . .

B. THE ALCOHOLIC

EASTER v. DISTRICT OF COLUMBIA

JUDGE FAHY:

In the Court of General Sessions of the District of Columbia, at a trial by a judge without a jury, appellant DeWitt Easter was found guilty of having been "drunk and intoxicated" on a stated date in a street in Washington, in violation of our Code provision reading: "No person shall . . . be drunk or intoxicated in any street, alley, park, or parking . . ." D.C. Code § 25–128(a). He was given a suspended sentence of ninety days imprisonment. That he was drunk or intoxicated at the time and place stated was proved and was uncontested. His defense was that he was a chronic alcoholic.

The judge did not rule that the evidence fell short of establishing that appellant was a chronic alcoholic. The judge ruled that the evidence to that effect was not pertinent; that is, that chronic alcoholism was not a defense to a charge of intoxication in a public place.

The District of Columbia Court of Appeals affirmed the conviction. *Easter* v. *District of Columbia*, D.C. App., 209 A.2d 625. We allowed an appeal to this court. Sitting *en banc* we heard and now decide the case.

I

Our decision is that chronic alcoholism is a defense to a charge of public intoxication and, therefore, is not a crime in violation of Section 25-128(a) of our Code. We think this follows, in the first place, from the Act of Congress of August 4, 1947, entitled "Rehabilitation of Alcoholics," 61 Stat. 744, c.472, now embodied in our Code as Sections 24-501 *et seq.*

In aid of its purposes, one of which is "to establish a program for the rehabilitation of alcoholics, promote temperance, and provide for the medical, psychiatric, and other scientific treatment of chronic alcoholics" the Act provides,

the courts of the District of Columbia are hereby authorized to take judicial notice of the fact that a chronic alcoholic is a sick person and in need of proper medical, institutional, advisory, and rehabilitative treatment, and the court is authorized to direct that he receive appropriate medical, psychiatric, or other treatment as provided under the terms of this chapter.

D.C. Code § 24-501 (1961 ed.).

361 F.2d 50 (1966) (CA–DC). Footnotes omitted.

A "chronic alcoholic" is defined in the Act: The term "chronic alcoholic" means any person who chronically and habitually uses alcoholic beverages to the extent that he has lost the power of self-control with respect to the use of such beverages, or while under the influence of alcohol endangers the public morals, health, safety, or welfare.

D.C. Code § 24-502 (1961 ed.).

We are concerned in this case only with that part of the above definition which refers to loss of the power of self-control with respect to the use of alcoholic beverages.

The above statutory provisions, considered in the full context of the Act of which they are a part, preclude attaching criminality in this jurisdiction to intoxication in public of a chronic alcoholic. An essential element of criminal responsibility is the ability to avoid the conduct specified in the definition of the crime. Action within the definition is not enough. To be guilty of the crime a person must engage responsibly in the action. Thus, an insane person who does the act is not guilty of the crime. The law, in such a case, based on morals, absolves him of criminal responsibility. So, too, in case of an infant. In case of a chronic alcoholic Congress has dealt with his condition so that in this jurisdiction he too cannot be held to be guilty of the crime of being intoxicated because, as the Act recognizes, he has lost the power of self-control in the use of intoxicating beverages. In his case an essential element of criminality, where personal conduct is involved, is lacking. This element is referred to in the law as the criminal mind. See *Carter* v. *United States,* 102 U.S. App. D.C. 227, 235, 252 F.2d 608, 616, where the subject is well discussed. It is there stated in terms of the common-law axiom, "Actus non facit reum, nisi mens sit rea." Coke, Third Institute *6 *107.

The Act of 1947 does not state that a chronic alcoholic is suffering from a mental disease which causes the loss of control; the defense is not in terms of insanity. The condition is defined as a 'sickness," and Congress did not find it necessary to specify whether it is mental, physical or a combination of both. Whatever its etiotogical intricacies it is deemed a sickness which is accompanied with loss of power to control the use of alcoholic beverages. The congressional judgment is supported not only by the evidence in this case adduced in the Court of General Sessions but by the record of the hearings on the Act of 1947, the entire legislative history of the Act, and by an additional abundance of authorities, some of which are enumerated in Appendix B to this opinion. As Congressman Miller of Nebraska

stated on the floor of the House during the debate on the Act: "Jail is not the answer to their trouble. We think they are sick people and need scientific and technical attention of psychiatrists and medical personnel." 93 Cong. Rec. 3357 (1947).

It is suggested that the public nature of the intoxication adds a factor which precludes the defense—that if suffering from the sickness is not a crime, manifesting it in a public place is. But nothing whatever indicates that Congress intended to limit the scope of the Act to persons sick in privacy. It is clear the Act was primarily concerned with persons found in public places. The provisions which contemplated their institutional care, instead of the jail, show indubitably that the non-criminal approach of Congress applies to the chronic alcoholic floundering in a public place. The lack of power of self-control referred to cannot be limited to absolution of criminality for drinking or being drunk in a nonpublic place. No statute in the District of Columbia makes such an act or circumstance criminal. The very nature of the sickness goes where its victim goes.

It should be clear from the above that chronic alcoholism resulting in public intoxication cannot be held to be criminal on the theory that before the sickness became chronic there was at some earlier period a voluntary act or series of acts which led to the chronic condition. A sick person is a sick person though he exposed himself to contagion, and a person who at one time may have been voluntarily intoxicated but has become a chronic alcoholic and therefore is unable to control his use of alcoholic beverages is not to be considered voluntarily intoxicated. We desire to make clear, however, that we are not absolving the voluntarily intoxicated person of criminal responsibility for crime in general under applicable law. See *Harris* v. *United States,* 8 App. D.C. 20, 36 L.R.A. 465.

We find no basis for judicial repudiation of the Act of 1947. The fact that in the intervening years the facilities contemplated by the Act have not been made available does not detract from the legal effect of those provisions of the Act which define the nature of the sickness. One who has committed no crime cannot be validly sentenced as a criminal because of a lack of rehabilitative and caretaking facilities.

In event of a determination of chronic alcoholism under the procedures of D.C. Code §24-504, commitment for treatment is not mandatory. In the judge's discretion the accused may be released. But he may not be punished.

II

Our decision would be the same were we without the guidance furnished by the Act of 1947. One who is a chronic alcoholic cannot have the *mens rea* necessary to be held responsible criminally for being drunk in public. This is so for the same reason which led Congress to that enactment, namely, that a chronic alcoholic is in fact a sick person who has lost control over his use of alcoholic beverages. This is demonstrated by the hearings on the Act of 1947, by the evidence taken in the present case, and by the wealth of material available and appropriate to be considered by the court. See Appendices A and B.

The same basic problem now before us was recently before the Court of Appeals for the Fourth Circuit in *Driver* v. *Hinnant,* 356 F.2d 761. This was a habeas corpus proceeding attacking in the federal courts a conviction of Driver of public intoxication by the courts of North Carolina. Under a State statute it was a misdemeanor to be found "drunk or intoxicated on the public highway, or at any public place or meeting." Even without benefit of such a statute as our Act of 1947, the court sustained the defense of chronic alcoholism. The court said in part:

As defined by the National Council on Alcoholism, he [a chronic alcoholic] is a "person who is powerless to stop drinking and whose drink seriously alters his normal living pattern." The American Medical Association defines "alcoholics" as "those excessive drinkers whose dependence on alcohol has attained such a degree that it shows a noticeable disturbance or interference with their bodily or mental health, their interpersonal relations, and their satisfactory social and economic functioning." The World Health Organization recognizes alcoholism as "a chronic illness that manifests itself as a *disorder of behavior*." (Emphasis added.) It is known that alcohol can be addicting, and it is the addict—the involuntary drinker—on whom our decision is now made. Hence we exclude the merely excessive— steady or spree—voluntary drinker.

This addiction—chronic alcoholism—is now almost universally accepted medically as a disease. The symptoms, as already noted, may appear as "disorder of behavior." Obviously, this includes appearances in public, as here, unwilled and ungovernable by the victim. When that is the conduct for which he is criminally accused, there can be no judgment or criminal conviction passed upon him. To do so would affront the Eighth Amendment, as cruel and unusual punishment in branding him a criminal, irrespective of consequent detention or fine.

Although his misdoing objectively comprises the physical elements of a crime, nevertheless,

no crime has been perpetrated because the conduct was nither actuated by an evil intent nor accompanied with a consciousness of wrongdoing, indispensable ingredients of a crime. Morissette v. United States, 342 U.S. 246, 250-252, 72 S.Ct. 240, 96 L.Ed. 288 (1952). Nor can his misbehavior be penalized as a transgression of a police regulation— malum prohibitum—necessitating no intent to do what it punishes. The alcoholic's presence in public is not his act, for he did not will it. It may be likened to the movements of an imbecile or a person in a delirium of a fever. None of them by attendance in the forbidden place defy the forbiddance.

. . .

Of course, the alcohol-diseased may by law be kept out of public sight. Equally true, the North Carolina statute does not punish them solely for drunkenness but rather for its public demonstration. But many of the diseased have no homes or friends, family or means to keep them indoors. Driver examples this pitiable predicament, for he is apparently without money or restraining care.

Footnote 3 of Judge Bryan's opinion [in the Driver case] calls attention to reliance by the District Court in the Driver case upon the definition of a chronic alcoholic contained in the Act of 1947.

Judge Bryan also stated for the court that *Robinson* v. *State of California*, 370 U.S. 660, 82 S.Ct. 1417, 8 L.Ed.2d 758, "sustains, if not commands, the view we take." In *Robinson* the Supreme Court held invalid as cruel and unusual punishment prohibited by the Eighth and Fourteenth Amendments a California statute which made drug addiction a crime. The Court said such addiction was a status involuntarily assumed, and therefore to punish it as a crime violated the constitutional provision. Since, as we have seen, public intoxication of a chronic alcoholic is not a crime, to convict one of it as though it were would also be cruel and unusual punishment. The fact that in our case the sentence of 90 days was suspended, whereas in *Robinson* there was imprisonment, is immaterial on the question of cruel and unusual punishment; it is the fact of criminal conviction that is critical:

. . . in the light of contemporary human knowledge, a law which made a criminal offense of such a disease [mental illness, leprosy, or venereal disease] would doubtless be universally thought to be an infliction of cruel and unusual punishment in violation of the Eighth and Fourteenth Amendments.

370 U.S. at 666, 82 S.Ct. at 1420.

In *Driver* Judge Bryan stated it is "cruel and unusual punishment in branding him a criminal, irrespective of consequent detention or fine."

We hold, therefore, by reason of the Act of 1947, for the independent reasons which underlay the theory of that Act, and on the precedential authority of *Driver* . . . that the public intoxication of a chronic alcoholic lacks the essential element of criminality; and to convict such a person of that crime would also offend the Eighth Amendment.

We close this discussion with the observation that confinement, e.g., for inquiry or treatment, lies within the means available for dealing, constitutionally, with a menace to society. This appears from passages in *Robinson* v. *State of California, supra,* 370 U.S. at 664-665, 82 S.Ct. 1417; *Driver* v. *Hinnant, supra.* We are not called upon to speculate as to the range and nature of permissible detention which could be authorized by Congress beyond that contemplated in the Act of 1947.

III

It follows that the evidence of chronic alcoholism adduced in this case was pertinent. It established the defense.

Expert medical and psychiatric evidence, not sought to be rebutted, proved that appellant was a chronic alcoholic who had lost self-control over his use of alcoholic beverages. His condition, with its unusual physical manifestations, was arrayed fully before the trial judge and need not be repeated here in detail. Since 1937 appellant has been arrested for intoxication or associated conduct 70 times, 12 times in 1963 alone. On innumerable occasions he has been intoxicated but not arrested. The condition had progressed for many years, definitely since the 1930's, resulting in a broken home life, recurrent hospitalization, and loss of steady employment.

Reversed, with direction to remand to the Court of General Sessions for dismissal of the information.

APPENDIX A

Excerpts of Testimony from Hearings on H.R. 496 before Subcommittee on Health, Education, Recreation of the House Committee on the District of Columbia, 80th Cong., 1st Session (1947).

Chronic alcoholism is a disease. It is one which requires treatment and attention just as the narcotic habit demands treatment.
—Congressman Miller, of Nebraska

This is not a measure to approach the moral aspects of drinking, nor is this an opinion as to the drinking of alcoholic beverages, but we are approaching the problem from the standpoint of a man suffering from a disease such as cancer, tuberculosis, or like diseases which also have an economic influence on the lives of our people.
—Congressman Hébert, of Louisiana

On a certain day last week, in which we had in our institution [the D.C. penal institution] 559 inmates, that is, people committed for intoxication, 5 per cent had been committed 100 times or over before; 64 per cent of these people in our institution had served time 10 times or more; only 1 of the 559 had been there only once, and so on. . . . In other words, the drink problem in terms of those who get arrested and convicted is primarily a problem of recidivism.
—Donald Clemmer, Director, Department of Corrections, District of Columbia

Our hearts and minds particularly go out to those individuals. We know they are derelicts, many of them, practically hopelessly involved in this alcoholic confusion.

• • •

We are hopeful a bill of this character will no doubt in the case of many men do a great deal of good. I would say if we got 5 per cent out of these alcoholic cases restored to normal health and good citizenship, it will have been well worth the effort put forth in this Congress, I am sure. It is perfectly obvious that it will reduce our work, be for the interest of the individual, it being for his protection. . . .
—Inspector Walter H. Thomas, Acting Major and Superintendent, Metropolitan Police, District of Columbia

Through my experience I have been educated as it were to the point that your committee has arrived at, that alcoholism is a disease and that it is not criminal behavior, and that progress in meeting the situation cannot be made, in my mind, unless we break down in its entirety the concept that the alcoholic is a criminal.
—Judge Fay Bentley, Juvenile Court District of Columbia

And see the testimony before the Subcommittee of Dr. Robert H. Felix, Chief, Mental Hygiene Division, U.S. Public Health Service; Captain Rhoda Milliken, Head of Women's Division, Metropolitan Police Force, D.C.; and others.

APPENDIX B

Report of the Board of Trustees of the AMA, *Journal of the American Medical Association,* 162 (1956): 749.

Among the numerous personality disorders encountered in the general population, it has long been recognized that a vast number of such disorders are characterized by the outstanding sign of excessive use of alcohol. All excessive users of alcohol are not diagnosed as alcoholics, but all alcoholics are excessive users. When, in addition to this excessive use, there are certain signs and symptoms of behavioral, personality, and physical disorder or of their development, the syndrome of alcoholism is achieved. The intoxication and some of the other possible complications manifested in this syndrome often make treatment difficult. However, alcoholism must be regarded as within the purview of medical practice.

Trotter, *An Essay, Medical, Philosophical, and Chemical, on Drunkenness* (2d ed., 1804).

The habit of drunkenness is a disease of the mind. [p. 179]
But others think that is physical and must be slowly dropped since it has become a "part of our nature." [p. 181]

Committee on Prisons, Probations and Parole in the District of Columbia, Report (1957).

Alcoholism is a serious problem in the District of Columbia. [p. 83]
Repeaters accounted for 9,288, or 68 per cent, of the total number of arrests. Police records, reveal, moreover, that the average person arrested for intoxication during the test period had *a record of 12 prior arrests for the same offense.* [p. 93]
More than 90 per cent of the 16,267 persons committed to the District Jail for intoxication during fiscal 1956 had served prior prison terms for the same offense. Many who were discharged from the Workhouse on Monday, reappeared for another term before the week was up. The Committee believes that anything more futile than this process of getting drunk, being arrested, receiving 10, 15, or 30-day sentences, going to the Jail and to the Workhouse, serving time, going out and getting drunk again, can scarcely be imagined. The rate of recidivism, moreover, is the best evidence that existing procedures are failing to rehabilitate the alcoholic. [p. 102]
The Committee cannot emphasize too strongly that not all persons committed for intoxication are chronic alcoholics. Many are relatively youthful offenders who were simply intoxicated at the time of arrest; a somewhat larger group are "problem drinkers," bordering on chronic alcoholism—but who have families, job prospects, and a desire to "get back home and back to work"; finally, the great majority of the approximately 14,000 intoxicants committed each year to the Workhouse are chronic skid-row alcoholics.
Most of the intoxicants in the first two groups should be handled, in any future program, in such a manner as to avoid incarceration. . . .
However, the vast majority of offenders are chronic skid-row alcoholics who are primarily

"custody cases." A great number are sick, infirm, and mental cases. [p. 103].

Haggard and Jellinek, *Alcohol Explored* (1942).

It is necessary to recognize that the confirmed inebriate is a person requiring medical attention, and society must face the issue of treating him as an irresponsible individual until he can be rehabilitated. . . . It is clear that courts require the aid of medical agencies in diagnosing and classifying the types of inebriates who come to their attention, thus enabling them to dispose of each case in the appropriate manner. [p. 273]

MacCormick, "Correctional Views on Alcohol, Alcoholism and Crime," Alcoholism and Crime *Conference* 61 (Chatham, Mass., 1962).

My professional and personal interest in the alcoholic and in alcoholism began during the six years, 1934 to 1940, when I was Commissioner of Corrections in New York City. . . . [p. 61]
I am not sure whether I was more impressed by the inhumanity of our methods of dealing with the alcoholic or by the futility of the process. [p. 61]
In spite of the significant increase in the understanding of alcoholism which has taken place in the past 25 years, however, alcoholics for the most part are still dealt with in the legal and penal setting rather than by methods which are appropriate for persons presenting a socio-medical problem. [p. 63] . . . it would be a step in advance if laws and local ordinances throughout the country were changed so that they could be committed under health or welfare laws rather than under penal statutes. [p. 64]

Murtagh, "The Derelicts of Skid Row," *Atlantic Monthly*, 209, no. 3 (1962): 77. (Chief Magistrate to the City of New York, 1950–60.)

Incarceration never cured a derelict, never did and never will. The problem of the skid-row derelict is basically social, medical, and spiritual in nature. Whether the derelict is a true alcoholic or merely a problem drinker, he usually has a much more deep-seated pathology, an emotional disturbance, if you will, that is an enigma to all of the disciplines. The penal approach to his problem is at best but a feeble attempt. . . . [p. 80]

National Institute of Mental Health, United States Department of Health, Education and Welfare, Alcoholism, Public Health Service Pub. No. 730 (rev., 1963).

Only within the last two decades has alcoholism come to be accepted as a medical problem. [p. 9] The term "alcoholism" is not easy to define. It is generally used to cover a whole range of individual and social problems connected with the use of alcoholic beverages. People whose drinking causes them to become enmeshed in these problems are called "alcoholics."

The World Health Organization describes alcoholism as ". . . a chronic illness that manifests itself as a disorder of behavior. It is characterized by the repeated use of alcoholic beverages to an extent that exceeds customary dietary use or compliance with social customs of the community and that interferes with the drinker's health or his economic or social functioning."

The National Council on Alcoholism defines an alcoholic as a "person who is powerless to stop drinking and whose drinking seriously alters his normal living pattern."

It has been shown that alcohol can be physically addicting. The drinker may develop a tolerance to alcohol so that the same amount produces progressively less effect, and he craves larger and larger amounts. Eventually he must keep on drinking in order to avoid the severe and painful symptoms that result from abrupt withdrawal of alcohol. These symptoms include weakness, severe tremors, fever, and in some cases, convulsions and delirium tremens.

. . . Alcoholism occurs when people continue to drink heavily in spite of the painful and injurious consequences they suffer. [pp. 2–3]

Goff, "Correction and the Alcoholic," *The Court and the Chronic Inebriate: Conference Proceedings* 21 (U.S. Department of Health, Education and Welfare, 1965).

The dilemma of handling cases of alcoholism involving chronic public intoxication appears to be deeply routed [*sic*] in an underlying philosophy of justice which looks at chronic public intoxication as controllable by traditional correctional means. It is fed by the implied and sometimes expressed belief that the disease can be "punished away." Until there is greater recognition both intellectually and emotionally of alcoholism as a disease, the "exercise in futility" of punitive measures to cope with the chronic police court offender will continue.

What we propose would use repeated offenses of public intoxication as an indication, not of the need of the individual for increased penalties, but of the need of the individual for nonpunitive state handling. Legislative procedure should permit the commitment of selected alcoholics on a civil, not criminal basis, to specialized facilities and programs under the jurisdiction of medical and welfare authorities, for an intermediate period not exceeding one year. [p. 24]

Hall, "Drunkenness as a Criminal Offense," *Quarterly Journal of Studies on Alcohol* 1 (1941): 751.

The trend of legislation is to treat habitual drunkenness as a disease of mind and body, analogous to insanity, and to put in motion the power of the state, as the guardian of all its citizens, to save the habitual drunkard, his family, and society from the consequences of his habit. It is not a penal but a paternal statute. This statute is limited to persons who have lost the power or will to control their appetite for intoxicating liquors, and have a fixed habit of drunkenness, who are in need of care and treatment, and to those it would be dangerous to leave at large. [p. 758]

. . . excepting where serious personal injury is involved, there is no obstacle to elimination of punitive methods where others are reasonably indicated. [p. 763]

Alexander, *Jail Administration* (1957), pp. 237-40.

The alcoholic is the most common type of prisoner found in American jails. Usually he is committed for drunkenness, drunken driving, vagrancy, or as a public nuisance.

But the jail is not the answer to the problem of the alcoholic, despite the fact that it has had to deal with drunks from time immemorial and will continue to deal with them for some foreseeable years ahead. The unending series of fines which must be lain out in jail, and short jail sentences repeated endlessly month in and month out, year in and year out, bear not the slightest semblance of an intelligent approach to the treatment and solution of the alcoholic's problem. [p. 237]

Roche Laboratories, *Aspects of Alcoholism* (1963).

[Alcoholism is] a condition which belongs in the realm of public health, but excludes the occasional excessive drinker whose disorderly conduct or automobile accident make him more the concern of the civic authorities than of health personnel. [p. 9]

Pittman and Gordon, *Revolving Door, A Study of the Chronic Police Case Inebriate* (1958).

The newer concept of alcoholism as a social, mental, and physical illness is in gross conflict with punishment and confinement for the habitual public inebriate. [p. 141]

The results of our investigation negate completely the assumption that incarceration acts as a deterrent to the chronic public inebriate. [p. 139]

Note, "Legislation for the Treatment of Alcoholics," 2 *Stan. L. Rev.* 515 (1950).

What is alcoholism? Authorities stress the fact that it is a health problem and not a penal one. It is a resultant of two factors: the individual's original psychological maladjustment, and the depressant effect of alcohol which creates of itself new maladjustments. The alcoholic feels he cannot successfully adjust to his environment without alcohol, but actually he cannot adjust successfully so long as he uses alcohol. The problem, then, is not solely alcohol but the *individual* and the manner in which he uses it. When an alcoholic shows pronounced mental and physical degeneration, he is termed "chronic." [pp. 515–16; footnotes omitted]

Hall, "Intoxication and Criminal Responsibility," 57 *Harv. L. Rev.* 1045 (1944).

The disparity between judicial and available knowledge is indicated by the need to point out that one of the commonest of expert agreements is that "alcoholic addiction" (dipsomania) is a disease. [p. 1073]

The Correctional Association of New York and the International Association of Chiefs of Police, *Alcohol and Alcoholism, A Police Handbook.*

Alcoholism is a disease. The definition of a disease is: "a disturbance in function or structure of any organ or part of the body, possessing certain recognizable symptoms." Alcoholism fits this perfectly. The victim drinks repeatedly to drunkenness—despite the fact that it injuries him physically or mentally, or endangers his earning capacity, or adversely affects his (or her) social and family life.

. . .

The cause of the disease are [*sic*] not yet known, but it seems to be a combination of many physical and mental factors. [p. 14]

Celebreze, Opening Remarks, HEW National Conference on Alcoholism (1963).

. . . alcoholism ranks as our fourth major health problem, following closely after cancer, heart disease, and mental illness. [p. iii]

MCGOWAN, Circuit Judge:

I concur in the result reached by Judge Fahy, and in Parts I and III of his opinion. My reasons for doing so are stated hereinafter.

It was not argued to us on this appeal that we invalidate the D.C. Code provision against public intoxication on its face or as applied to any and all people found drunk in public places. What we were urged to do was to say that henceforth in this jurisdiction one charged with public drunkenness may assert chronic alcoholism as a defense and introduce evidence in support of that defense. This is what I consider we are doing in this case; and I agree that a remand is unnecessary only because the evidence of chronic alcoholism as to the appellant is clear.

We may, in my view, summon this defense into being because we have both the authority and the duty to shape the criminal jurisprudence of the District of Columbia in accordance with civilized notions of justice. We are not like the ten other federal courts of appeals, whose authority over state criminal law derives only from the commands of the Constitution. In particular, we are not in the position of the Fourth Circuit when, in *Driver* v. *Hinnant,* 356 F.2d 761 (1966), it decided that the Eighth Amendment barred the conviction and imprisonment of a chronic alcoholic under a North Carolina statute directed at public drunkenness.

Our authority in this regard exists in any event, absent only an affirmative and valid legislative proscription of what we propose to do. Far from there being in effect such a veto by Congress in this instance, our duty to do as we do here is, if not compelled, at least strongly indicated and emphasized by the Act of August 4, 1947. In that statute Congress exhibited an extraordinarily sensitive awareness of the problems of acute alcoholism and enacted a singularly enlightened—and noncriminal—approach to be followed in this jurisdiction. Had Congress acted to implement this statute with the necessary appropriations and facilities, this appeal would presumably never have reached us. The substantive statute remains on the books. Only the implementation is missing.

The urgent need of that implementation is accentuated by what we do today. The community will not tolerate uncontrolled drunkenness in public places, and will insist that the police act to remove it as before. The power of the police in this respect is, in my view, unaffected by today's ruling. But it does underscore the necessity of coming to grips with the ultimate disposition of the chronic alcoholics among those so removed. Congress has already done so in the 1947 Act. All it needs to do now is to put some flesh on those bones.

DANAHER, Circuit Judge, with whom BURGER and TAMM, Circuit Judges, join, concurring in the result:

I join Judge McGowan in concluding that "a remand is unnecessary only because the evidence of chronic alcoholism as to this appellant is clear." I share his view that we have here been asked to say that henceforth "one charged with public drunkenness may assert chronic alcoholism as a defense and introduce evidence in support of that defense."

My real problem stems from the alternative clause in D.C. Code § 24-502 (1961). Its definition of a "Chronic alcoholic" as one "who chronically and habitually uses alcoholic beverages to the extent that he has lost the power of self-control with respect to the use of such beverages," is clear enough. As here applied, so far, so good.

But the statute goes on to extend that category to include one who "while under the influence of alcohol *endangers* the *public* morals, health, *safety, or welfare."* (Emphasis added.)

I am confident that Congress in its obvious purpose of seeking means for accomplishing the possible rehabilitation of the unfortunate victims of alcoholism had no thought whatever of addressing itself to some revised standards for determining criminal responsibility as to yet other crimes than public drunkenness. I wish to note my complete understanding that we are not now doing so. All too often this court has been confronted with circumstances of crime where intoxication has been urged as a ground of exculpation. See, e.g., *Bishop* v. *United States*, 71 App.D.C. 132, 135-136, 107 F.2d 297, 301-302 (1939); *Heideman* v. *United States*, 104 U.S. App.D.C. 138, 259 F.2d 9439 (1958), cert. denied, 359 U.S. 959, 79 S.Ct. 800, 3 L.Ed.2d 767 (1959).

Obviously the application of any rule of law will depend upon the circumstances of a particular case. In the instant situation this appellant meets the definition of a chronic alcoholic because, by reason of his habitual use of alcoholic beverages, he "has lost the power of self-control with respect to the use of such beverages."

POWELL v. STATE OF TEXAS

Mr. Justice Marshall delivered the opinion of the Court.

In late December 1966, appellant was arrested and charged with being found in a state of intoxication in a public place, in violation of Vernon's Ann, Texas Penal Code, Art. 477 (1952), which reads as follows: "Whoever shall get drunk or be found in a state of intoxication in any public place, or at any private house except his own, shall be fined not exceeding one hundred dollars."

Appellant was tried in the Corporation Court of Austin, Texas, found guilty, and fined $20. He appealed to the County Court at Law No. 1 of Travis County, Texas, where a trial *de novo* was held. His counsel urged that appellant was afflicted with the disease of chronic alcoholism," "that his appearance in public [while drunk was] . . . not of his own volition," and therefore that to punish him criminally for that conduct would be cruel and unusual in violation of the Eighth and Fourteenth Amendments to the United States Constitution. . . .

The principal testimony was that of Dr. Davis Wade, a Fellow of the American Medical Association, duly certificated in psychiatry. . . . Dr. Wade sketched the outlines of the "disease" concept of alcoholism; noted that there is no generally accepted definition of "alcoholism"; alluded to the ongoing debate within the medical profession over whether alcohol is actually physically "addicting" or merely psychologically "habituating"; and concluded that in either case a "chronic alcoholic" is an "involuntary drinker," who is "powerless not to drink," and who "loses his self-control over his drinking." He testified that he had examined appellant, and that appellant is a "chronic alcoholic," who "by the time he has reached [the state of intoxication] . . . is not able to control his behavior, and [who] . . . has reached this point because he has an uncontrollable compulsion to drink." Dr. Wade also responded in the negative to the question whether appellant has "the willpower to resist the constant excessive consumption of alcohol." He added that in his opinion jailing appellant without medical attention would operate neither to rehabilitate him nor to lessen his desire for alcohol.

On cross-examination, Dr. Wade admitted that when appellant was sober he knew the difference between right and wrong, and he responded affirmatively to the question whether appellant's act in taking the first drink

U.S. Supreme Court, 88 S. Ct. 2145 (1968).

in any given instance when he was sober was a "voluntary exercise of his will." Qualifying his answer, Dr. Wade stated that "these individuals have a compulsion, and this compulsion, while not completely overpowering, is a very strong influence, an exceedingly strong influence, and this compulsion, coupled with the firm belief in their mind that they are going to be able to handle it from now on causes their judgment to be somewhat clouded. . . ."

We know very little about the circumstances surrounding the drinking bout which resulted in this conviction or about Leroy Powell's drinking problem, or indeed about alcoholism itself. The trial hardly reflects the sharp legal and evidentiary clash between fully prepared adversary litigants which is traditionally expected in major constitutional cases. The State put on only one witness, the arresting officer. The defense put on three—a policeman who testified to appellant's long history of arrests for public drunkenness, the psychiatrist, and appellant himself.

Furthermore, the inescapable fact is that there is no agreement among members of the medical profession about what it means to say that "alcoholism" is a "disease. . . ." In other words, there is wide-spread agreement today that "alcoholism" is a "disease," for the simple reason that the medical profession has concluded that it should attempt to treat those who have drinking problems. There the agreement stops. Debate rages within the medical profession as to whether "alcoholism" is a separate "disease" in any meaningful biochemical, physiological or psychological sense, or whether it represents one peculiar manifestation in some individuals of underlying psychiatric disorders. . . .

The trial court's "finding" that Powell "is afflicted with the disease of chronic alcoholism," which "destroys the afflicted person's will power to resist the constant, excessive consumption of alcohol" covers a multitude of sins. Dr. Wade's testimony that appellant suffered from a compulsion which was an "exceedingly strong influence," but which was "not completely overpowering" is at least more carefully stated, if no less mystifying. Jellinek insists that conceptual clarity can only be achieved by distinguishing carefully between "loss of control" once an individual has commenced to drink and "inability to abstain" from drinking in the first place. Presumably a person would have to display both characteristics in order to make out a constitutional defense, should one be recognized. Yet the "findings" of the trial court utterly fail to make this crucial distinction, and there is serious question whether the record can be read to support a finding of either loss of control or inability to abstain.

Dr. Wade did testify that once appellant began drinking he appeared to have no control over the amount of alcohol he finally ingested. Appellant's own testimony concerning his drinking on the day of the trial would certainly appear, however, to cast doubt upon the conclusion that he was without control over his consumption of alcohol when he had sufficiently important reasons to exercise such control. However that may be, there are more serious factual and conceptual difficulties with reading this record to show that appellant was unable to abstain from drinking. Dr. Wade testified that when appellant was sober, the act of taking the first drink was a "voluntary exercise of his will," but that this exercise of will was undertaken under the "exceedingly strong influence" of a "compulsion" which was "not completely overpowering." Such concepts, when juxtaposed in this fashion, have little meaning. . . .

It is one thing to say that if a man is deprived of alcohol his hands will begin to shake, he will suffer agonizing pains and ultimately he will have hallucinations; it is quite another to say that a man has a "compulsion" to take a drink, but that he also retains a certain amount of "free will" with which to resist. . . .

There is as yet no known generally effective method for treating the vast number of alcoholics in our society. Some individual alcoholics have responded to particular forms of therapy with remissions of their symptomatic dependence upon the drug. But just as there is no agreement among doctors and social workers with respect to the causes of alcoholism, there is no consensus as to why particular treatments have been effective in particular cases and there is no generally agreed-upon approach to the problem of treatment on a large scale. Most psychiatrists are apparently of the opinion that alcoholism is far more difficult to treat than other forms of behavioral disorders, and some believe it is impossible to cure by means of psychotherapy; indeed, the medical profession as a whole, and psychiatrists in particular, have been severely criticised for the prevailing reluctance to undertake the treatment of drinking problems. Thus it is entirely possible that, even were the manpower and facilities available for a full-scale attack upon chronic alcoholism, we would find ourselves unable to help the vast bulk of our "visible"—let alone our "invisible"—alcoholic population.

However, facilities for the attempted treatment of indigent alcoholics are woefully lacking throughout the country. It would be tragic to return large numbers of helpless, sometimes dangerous and frequently unsanitary inebriates to the streets of our cities without even the opportunity to sober up adequately which a brief jail term provides. Presumably no State or city will tolerate such a state of affairs. Yet the medical profession cannot, and does not, tell us with any assurance that, even if the buildings, equipment and trained personnel were made available, it could provide anything more than slightly higher-class jails for our indigent habitual inebriates. Thus we run the grave risk that nothing will be accomplished beyond the hanging of a new sign—reading "hospital"—over one wing of the jailhouse.

One virtue of the criminal process is, at least, that the duration of penal incarceration typically has some outside statutory limit; this is universally true in the case of petty offenses, such as public drunkenness, where jail terms are quite short on the whole. "Therapeutic civil commitment" lacks this feature; one is typically committed until one is "cured." Thus, to do otherwise than affirm might subject indigent alcoholics to the risk that they may be locked up for an indefinite period of time under the same conditions as before, with no more hope than before of receiving effective treatment and no prospect of periodic "freedom."

Faced with this unpleasant reality, we are unable to assert that the use of the criminal process as a means of dealing with the public aspects of problem drinking can never be defended as rational. The picture of the penniless drunk propelled aimlessly and endlessly through the law's "revolving door" of arrest, incarceration, release and re-arrest is not a pretty one. But before we condemn the present practice across-the-board, perhaps we ought to be able to point to some clear promise of a better world for these unfortunate people. Unfortunately, no such promise has yet been forthcoming. . . .

Ignorance likewise impedes our assessment of the deterrent effect of criminal sanctions for public drunkenness. . . .

Obviously, chronic alcoholics have not been deterred from drinking to excess by the existence of criminal sanctions against public drunkenness. But all those who violate penal laws of any kind are by definition undeterred. The longstanding and still raging debate over the validity of the deterrence justification for penal sanctions has not reached any sufficiently clear conclusions to permit it to be said that such sanctions are ineffective in any particular context or for any particular group of people who are able to appreciate the consequences of their acts. . . .

Appellant, however, seeks to come within the application of the Cruel and Unusual Punishment Clause announced in Robinson v. State of California, 370 U.S. 660, 82 S. Ct. 1417, 8 L. Ed. 2d 758 (1962), which involved a state statute making it a crime to "be addicted to the use of narcotics." This Court held there that "a state law which imprisons a person thus afflicted [with narcotic addiction] as a criminal, even though he has never touched any narcotic drug within the State or been guilty of any irregular behavior there, inflicts a cruel and unusual punishment . . ." Id., at 667, 82 S. Ct., at 1420–1421.

On its face the present case does not fall within that holding, since appellant was convicted, not for being a chronic alcoholic, but for being in public while drunk on a particular occasion. The State of Texas thus has not sought to punish a mere status, as California did in Robinson; nor has it attempted to regulate appellant's behavior in the privacy of his own home. Rather, it has imposed upon appellant a criminal sanction for public behavior which may create substantial health and safety hazards, both for appellant and for members of the general public, and which offends the moral and esthetic sensibilities of a large segment of the community. . . .

It is suggested in dissent that Robinson stands for the "simple" but "subtle" principle that "[c]riminal penalties may not be inflicted upon a person for being in a condition he is powerless to change." Post, at 2171. In that view, appellant's "condition" of public intoxication was "occasioned by a compulsion symptomatic of the disease" of chronic alcoholism, and thus, apparently, his behavior lacked the critical element of mens rea. Whatever may be the merits of such a doctrine of criminal responsibility, it surely cannot be said to follow from Robinson. The entire thrust of Robinson's interpretation of the Cruel and Unusual Punishment Clause is that criminal penalties may be inflicted only if the accused has committed some act, has engaged in some behavior, which society has an interest in preventing. . . .

If Leroy Powell cannot be convicted of public intoxication, it is difficult to see how a State can convict an individual for murder, if that individual, while exhibiting normal behavior in all other respects, suffers from a "compulsion" to kill, which is an "exceedingly strong influence," but "not completely overpowering. . . ."

It is not difficult to imagine a case involving psychiatric testimony to the effect that an individual suffers from some aggressive neurosis which he is able to control when sober; that very little alcohol suffices to remove the inhibitions which normally contain these aggressions, with the result that the individual engages in assaultive behavior without becoming actually intoxicated; and that the individual suffers from a very strong desire to drink, which is an "exceedingly strong influence" but "not completely overpowering." Without being untrue to the rationale of this case, should the principles advanced in dissent be accepted here, the Court could not avoid holding such an individual constitutionally unaccountable for his assaultive behavior. . . .

We cannot cast aside the centuries-long evolution of the collection of interlocking and overlapping concepts which the common law has utilized to assess the moral accountability of an individual for his antisocial deeds. The doctrines of *actus reus, mens rea,* insanity, mistake, justification, and duress have historically provided the tools for a constantly shifting adjustment of the tension between the evolving aims of the criminal law and changing religious, moral, philosophical, and medical views of the nature of man. This process of adjustment has always been thought to be the province of the States.

Nothing could be less fruitful than for this Court to be impelled into defining some sort of insanity test in constitutional terms. Yet, that task would seem to follow inexorably from an extension of *Robinson* in this case. If a person in the "condition" of being a chronic alcoholic cannot be criminally punished as a constitutional matter for being drunk in public, it would seem to follow that a person who contends that, in terms of one test, "his unlawful act was the product of mental disease or mental defect," Durham v. United States, 94 U.S. App. D.C. 228, 214 F. 2d 862, 875, 45 A.L.R. 2d 1430 (1954), would state an issue of constitutional dimension with regard to his criminal responsibility had he been tried under some different and perhaps lesser standard, e.g., the right-wrong test of *M'Naghten's Case.* The experimentation of one jurisdiction in that field alone indicates the magnitude of the problem [citing D.C. cases]. Formulating a constitutional rule would reduce, if not eliminate, that fruitful experimentation, and freeze the developing productive dialogue between law and psychiatry into a rigid constitutional mold. It is simply not yet the time to write the Constitutional formulas cast in terms whose meaning, let alone relevance, are not yet clear either to doctors or to lawyers.

Affirmed.

Mr. Justice BLACK, whom Mr. Justice HARLAN joins, concurring. . . .

Those who favor holding that public drunkenness cannot be made a crime rely to a large extent on their own notions of the wisdom of such a change in the law. A great deal of medical and sociological data is cited to us in support of this change. Stress is put upon the fact that medical authorities consider alcoholism a disease and have urged a variety of medical approaches to treating it. It is pointed out that a high percentage of all arrests in America are for the crime of public drunkenness and that the enforcement of these laws constitutes a tremendous burden on the police. Then it is argued that there is no basis whatever for claiming that to jail chronic alcoholics can be a deterrent or a means of treatment; on the contrary, jail has, in the expert judgment of these scientists, a destructive effect. All in all these arguments read more like a highly technical medical critique than an argument for deciding a question of constitutional law one way or another.

Of course, the desirability of this Texas statute should be irrelevant in a court charged with the duty of interpretation rather than legislation, and that should be the end of the matter. But since proponents of this grave constitutional change insist on offering their pronouncements on these questions of medical diagnosis and social policy, I am compelled to add that, should we follow their arguments, the Court would be venturing far beyond the realm of problems for which we are in a position to know what we are talking about. . . .

Jailing of chronic alcoholics is definitely defended as therapeutic, and the claims of therapeutic value are not insubstantial. As appellees note, the alcoholics are removed from the streets, where in their intoxicated state they may be in physical danger, and are given food, clothing, and shelter until they "sober up" and thus at least regain their ability to keep from being run over by automobiles in the street. Of course, this treatment may not be "therapeutic" in the sense of curing the underlying causes of their behavior, but it seems probable that the effect of jail on any criminal is seldom "therapeutic" in this sense, and in any case the medical authorities relied on so heavily by appellants themselves stress that no generally effective method of curing alcoholics has yet been discovered.

Apart from the value of jail as a form of treatment, jail serves other traditional functions of the criminal law. For one thing, it gets the alcoholics off the street, where they may cause harm in a number of ways to a number of people. . . . In addition, punishment of chronic alcoholics can serve several deterrent functions. . . . Civil commitment facilities may not be any better than the jails they would replace. In addition, compulsory commitment can hardly be considered a less severe penalty from the alcoholic's point of view. . . .

I agree with Mr. Justice MARSHALL that the findings of fact in this case are inadequate to justify the sweeping constitutional rule urged upon us. . . .

The argument is made that appellant comes within the terms of our holding in *Robinson* because being drunk in public is a mere status or "condition." Despite this many-faceted use of the concept of "condition," this argument would require converting *Robinson* into a case protecting actual behavior, a step we explicitly refused to take in that decision. . . .

The test urged would make it necessary to determine not only what constitutes a "disease," but what is the "pattern" of the disease, what "conditions" are "part" of the pattern, what parts of this pattern result from a "compulsion," and finally which of these compulsions are "symptomatic" of the disease. The resulting confusion and uncertainty could easily surpass that experienced by the District of Columbia Circuit in attempting to give content to its similar, though somewhat less complicated test of insanity. . . .

Mr. Justice WHITE, concurring in the result.

If it cannot be a crime to have an irresistible compulsion to use narcotics, Robinson v. State of California, 370 U.S. 660, 82 S. Ct. 1417, 8 L. Ed. 2d 758, rehearing denied, 371 U.S. 905, 83 S. Ct. 202, 9 L. Ed. 2d 166 (1962), I do not see how it can constitutionally be a crime to yield to such a compulsion. . . .

Unless *Robinson* is to be abandoned, the use of narcotics by an addict must be beyond the reach of the criminal law. Similarly, the chronic alcoholic with an irresistible urge to consume alcohol should not be punishable for drinking or for being drunk.

Powell's conviction was for the different crime of being drunk in a public place. Thus even if Powell was compelled to drink, and so could not constitutionally be convicted for drinking, his conviction in this case can be invalidated only if there is a constitutional basis for saying that he may not be punished for being in public while drunk. The statute involved here, which aims at keeping drunks off the street for their own welfare and that of others, is not challenged on the ground that it interferes unconstitutionally with the right to frequent public places. . . .

The trial court said that Powell was a chronic alcoholic with a compulsion not only to drink to excess but also to frequent public places when intoxicated. Nothing in the record before the trial court supports the latter conclusion, which is contrary to common sense and to common knowledge. . . .

Mr. Justice FORTAS, with whom Mr. Justice

DOUGLAS, Mr. Justice BRENNAN, and Mr. Justice STEWART join, dissenting.

The defense established that appellant had been convicted of public intoxication approximately 100 times since 1949, primarily in Travis County, Texas. The circumstances were always the same: the "subject smelled strongly of alcoholic beverages, staggered when walking, speech incoherent." At the end of the proceedings, he would be fined: "down in Bastrop County, it's $25.00 down there and it's $20.00 up here [in Travis County]." Appellant was usually unable to pay the fines imposed for these offenses, and therefore usually has been obliged to work the fines off in jail. The statutory rate for working off such fines in Texas is one day in jail for each $5 of fine unpaid. Texas Code Crim. Proc. Art. 43.09.

Appellant took the stand. He testified that he works at a tavern shining shoes. He makes about $12 a week which he uses to buy wine. He has a family, but he does not contribute to its support. He drinks wine every day. He gets drunk about once a week. When he gets drunk, he usually goes to sleep, "mostly" in public places such as the sidewalk. He does not disturb the peace or interfere with others. . . .

Dr. Wade testified that he had observed and interviewed the appellant. He said that appellant has a history of excessive drinking dating back to his early years; that appellant drinks only wine and beer; that "he rarely passes a week without going on an alcoholic binge"; that "his consumption of alcohol is limited only by his finances, and when he is broke he makes an effort to secure alcohol by getting his friends to buy alcohol for him"; that he buys a "fifty cent bottle" of wine, always with the thought that this is all he will drink; but that he ends by drinking all he can buy until he "is passed out in some joint or on the sidewalk." According to Dr. Wade, appellant "has never engaged in any activity that is destructive to society or to anyone except himself." He has never received medical or psychiatric treatment for his drinking problem. He has never been referred to Alcoholics Anonymous, a voluntary association for helping alcoholics, nor has he ever been sent to the State Hospital.

Dr. Wade's conclusion was that "Leroy Powell is an alcoholic and that his alcoholism is in a chronic stage." Although the doctor responded affirmatively to a question as to whether the appellant's taking the first drink on any given occasion is "a voluntary exercise of will," his testimony was that "we must take into account" the fact that chronic alcoholics have a "compulsion" to drink which "while not completely overpowering, is a very strong influence, an exceedingly strong influence," and that this compulsion is coupled with the "firm belief in their mind that they are going to be able to handle it from now on." It was also Dr. Wade's opinion that appellant "has an uncontrollable compulsion to drink" and that he "does not have the will power [to resist the constant excessive consumption of alcohol or to avoid appearing in public when intoxicated] nor has he been given medical treatment to enable him to develop this will power. . . ."

The issue posed in this case is a narrow one. There is no challenge here to the validity of public intoxication statutes in general or to the Texas public intoxication statute in particular. This does not concern the infliction of punishment upon the "social" drinker—or upon anyone other than a "chronic alcoholic" who as the trier of fact here found cannot "resist the constant, excessive consumption of alcohol." Nor does it relate to any offense other than the crime of public intoxication.

The sole question presented is whether a criminal penalty may be imposed upon a person suffering the disease of "chronic alcoholism" for a condition—being "in a state of intoxication" in public—which is a characteristic part of the pattern of his disease and which, the trial court found, was not the consequence of appellant's volition but of "a compulsion symptomatic of the disease of chronic alcoholism. . . ."

It is true, of course, that there is a great deal that remains to be discovered about chronic alcoholism. Although many aspects of the disease remain obscure, there are some hard facts—medical and, especially, legal facts—that are accessible to us and that provide a context in which the instant case may be analyzed. We are similarly woefully deficient in our medical, diagnostic, and therapeutic knowledge of mental disease and the problem of insanity; but few would urge that, because of this, we should totally reject the legal significance of what we do know about these phenomena. . . .

This Court reversed Robinson's conviction on the ground that punishment under the law in question was cruel and unusual, in violation of the Eighth Amendment of the Constitution as applied to the States through the Fourteenth Amendment. The Court noted that narcotic addiction is considered to be an illness and that California had recognized it as such. It held that the State could not make it a crime for a person to be ill. Although Robinson had been sentenced to only 90 days in prison for his offense, it was beyond the power of the State to prescribe such punishment. . . .

Robinson stands upon a principle which, despite its sublety (sic), must be simply stated and respectfully applied because it is the foundation of individual liberty and the cornerstone of the relations between a civilized state and its citizens: Criminal penalties may not be inflicted upon a person for being in a condition he is powerless to change. In all probability, Robinson at some time before his conviction elected to take narcotics. But the crime as defined did not punish this conduct. The statute imposed a penalty for the offense of "addiction"—a condition which Robinson could not control. Once Robinson had become an addict, he was utterly powerless to avoid criminal guilt. He was powerless to choose not to violate the law.

In the present case, appellant is charged with a crime comprised of two elements—being intoxicated and being found in a public place while in that condition. The crime, so defined, differs from that in *Robinson*. The statute covers more than a mere status. But the essential constitutional defect here is the same as in *Robinson*, for in both cases the particular defendant was accused of being in a condition which he had no capacity to change or avoid. . . .

The findings in this case, read against the background of the medical and sociological data to which I have referred, compel the conclusion that the infliction upon appellant of a criminal penalty for being intoxicated in a public place would be "cruel and inhuman punishment" within the prohibition of the Eighth Amendment. This conclusion follows because appellant is a "chronic alcoholic" who, according to the trier of fact, cannot resist the "constant excessive consumption of alcohol" and does not appear in public by his own volition but under a "compulsion" which is part of his condition.

I would reverse the judgment below.

EXCERPTS FROM THE AMERICAN LAW INSTITUTE MODEL PENAL CODE, 1962 PROPOSED OFFICIAL DRAFT

SECTION 2.08 INTOXICATION

(1) Except as provided in Subsection (4) of this Section, intoxication of the actor is not a defense unless it negatives an element of the offense.

(2) When recklessness establishes an element of the offense, if the actor, due to self-induced intoxication, is unaware of a risk of which he would have been aware had he been sober, such unawareness is immaterial.

(3) Intoxication does not, in itself, constitute mental disease within the meaning of Section 4.01.

(4) Intoxication which (a) is not self-induced or (b) is pathological is an affirmative defense if by reason of such intoxication the actor at the time of his conduct lacks substantial capacity either to appreciate its crimi-

Reprinted with permission, American Law Institute.

nality [wrongfulness] or to conform his conduct to the requirements of law.

(5) Definitions. In this Section unless a different meaning plainly is required:

(a) "intoxication" means a disturbance of mental or physical capacities resulting from the introduction of substances into the body;

(b) "self-induced intoxication" means intoxication caused by substances which the actor knowingly introduces into his body, the tendency of which to cause intoxication he knows or ought to know, unless he introduces them pursuant to medical advice or under such circumstances as would afford a defense to a charge of crime;

(c) "pathological intoxication" means intoxication grossly excessive in degree, given the amount of the intoxicant, to which the actor does not know he is susceptible. . . .

C. THE SEX OFFENDER AND THE "SEXUAL PSYCHOPATH"

A PROPOSED "DANGEROUS SEX OFFENDER" LAW

Nathan T. Sidley, M.D., and Francis J. Stolarz, J.D.

Sex offender laws and other forms of preventive detention designed to protect the public from dangerous individuals have been criticized because of their subjectivity. The authors propose legislation that would ensure against abuse of the laws by the following means: strict definitional criteria of the dangerous sex offender in terms of predictability, requirement of proof of dangerousness, and

time-limited commitments. They feel that implementation of this kind of law will restrict those incarcerated to the truly dangerous offenders and will help avoid overinclusive commitments.

Despite their unimportance compared to other criminals, people who commit sex crimes seem to attract more attention from legisla-

Revised version of a paper read at the 125th annual meeting of the American Psychiatric Association, Dallas, Tex., May 1–5, 1972. Reprinted with permission from *American Journal of Psychiatry* 130:7 (July 1973).

tures than do most offenders. This is not surprising, of course, for sex itself is more interesting than most other areas of activity. Yet the excess of attention and interest has not always led to the most effective laws.

One facet of sex legislation pertains to what one might call "dangerous sex offenders." Thirty states and the District of Columbia have such laws. The general idea behind them is that there are individuals who are uncontrollably sexually dangerous, who present threats to the community, and who should be locked up and/or treated until they are "cured." In practice the effect of these special laws is that people who are considered to be sexually dangerous tend to be treated differently and more punitively than people who are equally or more dangerous in some other area of behavior.

It is particularly important to note that although their ostensible purpose is to protect the public, dangerous sex offender laws are not designed as public health laws. There is no clinical entity of "sex crime," nor is there an epidemiology of "sex crime." Legislatures have not called in public health specialists as consultants when drafting such laws. Furthermore, there are no known public health measures that are effective in lowering the general incidence of sex crimes.

These laws thus function so as to deal with *specific* cases. They tend to be enacted after the occurrence of specific crimes, such as the Raymond Ohlsen case in Massachusetts, in which a man with an aggressive pedophiliac history murdered two boys shortly after his release from prison. (This is, of course, another factor leading to ineffective legislation. Public fear runs high at such times, and a legislature is under pressure. In such circumstances even the little knowledge about sex crimes that is available is not always attended to. It is of interest that strong public reactions more often follow violent sex crimes against children than those against adults. Although this may be due to psychological reasons, nevertheless offenders who act violently against children tend to be the most dangerous sex offenders.) The law asks the question of the specific case, "Is this individual another Raymond Ohlsen?" If the answer is yes, the individual is committed.

The function of the statutes is thus to enable a decision to be made about cases at hand. If a violent sex crime is committed by a man of the street, there is no way that legal process can prevent it. If a violent sex crime is committed by a person previously involved in the legal process, the process must ask itself, "Could that crime have been prevented by holding the individual in custody (or treating him, etc.)?" Legal process ought not to miss the opportunity for crime prevention and protection of the community when the opportunity is at hand. Therefore, although legal process is not a public health facility, and although the amount of sex crime trauma prevented in this manner is a negligible fraction of the total amount, the small opportunity for prevention should be grasped.

In this situation legal process sets for itself an excessively high level of aspiration. The fundamental issue faced by legal decision makers and psychiatrists, who are invariably associated with these proceedings, is that of prediction, i.e., prediction of recidivism. Prediction of events involving human behavior is difficult in general, but it is especially difficult when those events are rare. Most difficult is the prediction of behavior under unspecifiable circumstances, particularly when only meager information concerning prior conditions is available.

Yet these are precisely the circumstances in which accurate predictions are demanded of psychiatrists and judges. For all but a few cases it is an impossible situation. It is bad enough that the public should set impossible standards for decision makers, but it is serious when, as sometimes happens, the decision makers, themselves believe that they can perform the impossible. It is worse when they criticize themselves for not attaining the impossible, as in a situation in which someone previously examined and declared not to be dangerous subsequently commits a seriously injuring offense.

There is a way, however, in which a situation that is impossible to predict can be converted into a feasible one in which the predictor cannot be "wrong." That is, of course, to predict that an individual will commit a dangerous act, then to lock him up and prevent him from doing so ("preventive detention"), a good example of a self-fulfilling prophecy. And this is what is done. Decision makers become conservative and incarcerate individuals about whom they have doubt. Thus many individuals who would never commit a subsequent sex offense, let alone an injurious one, are erroneously locked up because of decision-making conservatism. This is an intolerable situation!

SOME FACTS

Detailed actuarial information necessary to make intelligent predictions about sex offenders' recidivism is presently unavailable, and the kind of information required to make accurate specific predictions about many individual cases will probably not be available in our lifetime. There is some trend information that is worth considering, though, for it helps a bit in dealing with cases.[1] The basic problem, however, is classification, and all classifications of sexual offenders suffer severely from lack of homogeneity within classes and from occasional multiple class membership for some individuals.

Considering primarily the age and sex of the victim and the presence or absence of force or threats is nevertheless useful, for it presents a framework that is of some help in prediction (1). We thus consider: 1) heterosexual *offenders* (who *have not* used force or threats) against children under age 12, minors under 16, and adults; 2) heterosexual aggressors (who *have* used force or threats) against children under 12, minors under 16, and adults; 3) homosexual *offenders* (homosexual aggressors are very rare); and 4) exhibitionists and peepers (who do not have any physical contact with the sexual object and can be grouped together).

The primary consideration for our purpose is this: With some exceptions, the major group that is of concern with respect to recidivism leading to sexual crimes of violence is that of heterosexual aggressors against children under 12. Sometimes other aggressors repeat, but usually they don't, while some peepers are not consummatory peepers but are instrumental peepers reconnoitering for a more serious crime, during which they injure a victim. Although individuals in the other classes may have criminal careers lasting for years, they seldom use any violence. It is well known that once ordinary pedophiles (heterosexual offenders against children under 12), homosexuals, and exhibitionists are detected, they rarely progress to more serious sex crimes. Indeed, ordinary pedophiles (no use of force or threats) tend mainly to be older offenders who approach little girls known to them and who often live in the same household; these offenders tend to be a moralistic, almost prudish group. The incidence of ordinary pedophilia is great, running to perhaps half a million offenses annually in the United States (2).

Note, however, that heterosexual aggressors against children are the most criminally recidivistic of any group, i.e., not merely sex offenders but all offenders. Most come from broken homes, many are of below-average intelli-

gence, and most are heavy drinkers and are intoxicated when committing their offense. Their victims tend to be strangers, and they have little concern for the feelings or welfare of their victims.

The likelihood of recidivism for a first-time sexual offender is only about one in ten, for a second-time or subsequent sex offender it is about one in three, while one out of two second-time or subsequent sex offenders with other crimes on their record tend to be repeaters. Aggressors are more recidivistic than nonaggressors, while the likelihood of recidivism is negatively related to the age of the victim.

The greater the number of sex offenses on a person's record, the greater the variety, i.e., an offender does not necessarily stick to one type of offense.

The role of alcohol in sex offenses is truly impressive. In many, probably over half, of the sex crimes involving aggression the offender is an alcoholic or a heavy drinker, and he commits his offense while intoxicated. A high proportion of nonaggressive sex offenses, particularly pedophilia, also involve alcohol.

Perhaps the fundamental problem, though, despite knowledge of facts like these, is that sex offenders are not uniform and what is true for one member of a class is not true for others. Thus if it is known that 50 percent of a certain class of offenders are recidivists, that is not much help in trying to decide whether the person before us will recidivate or not. The sad situation is that we do not know much about prediction for those offenders. Even more disappointing is that prediction will probably always be quite limited in this area because of the fortuitous association of circumstances that lead to sex crimes, e.g., alcohol, the presence of a potential victim, the absence of others, etc.

PROPOSED LEGISLATION

There is no law that can improve the ability of psychiatrists to predict future sexual violence. However, the law can do something to ensure that only those most likely to commit dangerous sexual crimes will be subject to incarceration. We wish as much as possible to prevent the occurrence of injurious sex crimes on the part of those who are exposed to the control of legal process, and we also wish to strenuously protect the rights of those subject to preventive detention as dangerous sex offenders so as to avoid locking up the wrong people. No completely satisfactory balance point exists, but we believe that the legislation proposed herein provides a more useful balance point than most.

---

[1] The facts subsequently presented have been abstracted and rounded out to very simple figures, because there is variation among different sources and because there seems to be no practical legal benefit in being more precise.

The most important aspect is the definition of, or the criteria to be fulfilled before a person can be regarded as a dangerous sex offender. First, in his past history he must have committed a sexual offense in which his victim was physically injured. Second, the person making predictions about the offender's future behavior must be able to demonstrate convincingly (i.e., beyond a reasonable doubt) that the offender will, within a period of one year, unless he is incarcerated or treated, commit a sexual offense that will result in physical injury to his victim. These criteria are strict, but there are offenders who meet them.

Other provisions of the proposed law are as follows.

Only those individuals who are *convicted* of one of various sexual felonies, such as rape [Model Penal Code 213, 1 (a) (d)], gross sexual imposition [Model Penal Code 213, 1 (2) (a) (b)], deviate sexual intercourse by force or imposition [Model Code 213.2 (1) (a) (d), 213.2 (a)], corruption of minors and seduction [Model Penal Code 213.3 (1) (a)], or sexual assault [Model Penal Code 213.3 4 (1) (4)], or of the attempt to commit any of the foregoing crimes would be eligible for processing as dangerous sex offenders.

A commitment as a dangerous sex offender would require a hearing in which the defendant would be entitled to a jury, legal counsel, subpoena power for witnesses, independent psychiatric examinations, and any other rights held by those who are defendants in a criminal trial. Such a hearing would only be held if a majority of the examining psychiatrists clearly felt that the individual was a dangerous sex offender. If an examination or hearing indicated that the individual was not a dangerous sex offender, then ordinary criminal disposition of his case would be undertaken.

A treatment center would be established and maintained by the state agency responsible for mental health rather than by the agency responsible for prisons. The superintendent would be responsible for security but would be encouraged to use outpatient rather than inpatient facilities when feasible. He would recommend appropriately to the court when he felt that an individual was no longer a dangerous sex offender.

A person would be committed as a dangerous sex offender for an indefinite length of time not to exceed the maximum period of penalty for the offense of which he was convicted. If the individual were still regarded as acutely dangerous at the end of that time, he would be processed under the laws of the state governing commitment of the dangerously mentally ill. The individual would be entitled to reexamination yearly. No psychotherapist treating the individual would participate in the examination process without the individual's permission.

Any individual might volunteer for treatment in the treatment center.

Finally, the agency in charge of administration of these statutes would be authorized to budget for research up to ten percent of the total amount allocated for their implementation.

With the exception of the criterion and budget sections, the other provisions of this proposal are found in the laws of one jurisdiction or another. Few jurisdictions provide the safeguards of a criminal proceeding, however. The first provision is the most critical one, for it places strict definitional criteria on the meaning of dangerous sex offender. These criteria are highly circumscribing, but there are offenders who meet them. An example would be a heterosexual aggressor who commits multiple crimes against children, who does so while intoxicated, who is a chronic alcoholic, who has a long criminal career, who has no insight, etc.

It is hoped that the effect of this legislation would be to protect more effectively the rights of those facing the possibility of long-term commitment as dangerous sexual offenders by regarding the proceedings as analogous to criminal proceedings rather than civil proceedings as they are now. Further, it is expected that the number of those inappropriately committed to treatment centers for dangerous sex offenders would be decreased without significantly exposing the public to a greater danger from injurious sex crimes than now exists. If these goals are accomplished, society will have a more just and more effective mechanism for dealing with these troublesome cases. We believe that this legislation will be a step toward this end.

DISCUSSION

The suggestions herein represent one manner of dealing with the problem of overcommitment of those alleged to be dangerous sex offenders. Other possible approaches include outright repeal of such laws, commitment of these offenders to mental hospitals, or the expansion of treatment facilities in prisons.

Repeal has appeal. Because of the almost unavoidable potential for abuse of any preventive detention law, such laws are to be feared. However, repeal is not always possible; neither, for that matter, is reform. This proposal represents an attempt to minimize abuse by providing strict criteria and full rights for those under consideration as dangerous sex offenders, yet to provide for some measure of protection of the public and to provide psychiatric treatment rather than criminal punishment for these offenders. As noted earlier, the proposal represents a balance point, a point that we hope can be attained in the real world, maintained with some vigilance, and defended as a reasonable effort to cope with one small aspect of the problem of destructive violence.

Perhaps our most questionable proposal is the notion of a separate institution for dangerous sex offenders. Merely providing separate facilities encourages institutional conservatism, empire building, and abuse. A point perhaps in favor of placing dangerous sex offenders in mental hospitals is that they are likely to be released sooner than if they were in special institutions, if for no other reason than they are not welcome patients at psychiatric hospitals because they are different from most ordinary mental hospital patients. Yet their very difference makes whatever treatment can be given to them more difficult in a state hospital. For those few truly dangerous people who are susceptible to change by treatment,

confinement in a separate unit in a state hospital may be feasible. Chronic, untreatable, psychotic or organically disturbed dangerous sex offenders are suitable candidates for a mental hospital ward for chronic patients.

Finally, the same thing must be said about handling the dangerous in general as for handling the sexually dangerous in jurisdictions where there are no special laws for dangerous sex offenders. Such special laws should be strongly discouraged. Like most efforts to attain desirable goals with inadequate methods, in the long run they tend to do more harm than good.

REFERENCES

1. Gebhard, P. H., Gagnon, J. H., Pomeroy, W. V., et al. *Sex Offenders, An Analysis of Types.* New York: Harper & Row, 1965.
2. Gagnon, J. H., Simon, W. Sexual Encounters Between Adults and Children, SIECUS Study Guide No. 11. New York, Sex Information and Education Council of the US, 1970.
3. American Law Institute: Model Penal Code. Philadelphia: American Law Institute, 1962.

THE DANGEROUS SEX OFFENDER

David A. Lanham, M.D.

I am motivated to write this article by the recent public shock surrounding several sadistic sexual attacks and related murders in this metropolitan area. I believe that there is a great deal of ignorance of the facts concerning potentially dangerous sex offenders in the area. It may well be that many people do not really want to know how complex the issue is. However, it seems appropriate that those of us who deal with these individuals on a continuing basis should share information, and responsibility, with others in the community.

It is extremely difficult to get an accurate census of how many and what types of sex offenders are in the Washington, D.C. Area, which of course encompasses adjoining areas

of Maryland and Virginia. As one index of the extent of the problem, the annual report of the Washington, D.C. Police Dept. for Fiscal Year 1972 lists 670 rape offenses and 318 sex offenses exclusive of prostitution. These figures do not include the suburbs, and it is generally accepted that many rapes and other sex offenses go unreported because of the legal hassles, embarrassment, and shame involved for the victim. If we include under the heading of sex offenders exhibitionists, voyeurs, pedophiles (both homosexual and heterosexual child molesters), sexual sadists, and rapists, we are talking about a very large population indeed. I have not even included incest cases occurring within families with

Reprinted with permission from *Medical Annals of the District of Columbia* 43, no. 2 (February 1974).

both natural and step-children. Exhibitionists and voyeurs must be included in the group because while they usually do not pose a physical threat to their victims, it is not really possible to say that they are not dangerous until they are properly evaluated. For example, a few exhbiitionists do attack, and some voyeurs are only "casing the joint" before breaking and entering.

Hundreds of such offenders are processed through the judicial systems of the District of Columbia and adjoining jurisdictions each year. The public should not be under any illusion that such offenders are found only in the District of Columbia. This means that the number of known sex offenders both from the recent past and in the present who are known in the Courts, probation offices, parole offices, psychiatric hospitals (both public and private), as well as private physicians, psychiatrists and psychologists number in the thousands. To this number we must add the numbers in correctional institutions serving sentences, awaiting trial, out on bail and bond, etc.

It seems to me that in many ways this population actually could well be thought of as a Public Health problem of considerable magnitude. It is an understandable exercise in futility for the media and the public to cry out in pain and alarm each time there is a horrible, vicious case and to attempt to fix blame for the individual case. This is a very large problem, it will not go away, it could be ameliorated but the community must be willing to pay the price.

There are many frustrating paradoxes involved in the problem of the management, of sex offenders. For example, many call for all potentially dangerous sex offenders to be "locked up," and/or summarily executed or castrated. However, at the same time, commissions and groups are advocating virtual abolition of penal institutions and mental hospitals, and the whole thrust is toward rehabilitating offenders in the community. Also, civil liberties groups, often quite properly, are bent on the protection of the rights of the accused and the committed. It is also a fact that many of those in the community who want dangerous offenders locked up or better controlled, are by no means ready to pay increased taxes for decent institutions in which to maintain and attempt to rehabilitate them or for more probation officers, parole officers, and behavioral scientists to work with such offenders.

In my opinion there are also racial and social attitudes involved in some of the reactions to violent sex crimes. The outcry and publicity is great when such offenses occur in places and against persons where they are not expected or somehow not supposed to occur. However, inner city black people are victimized by sex offenders with considerable frequency and I have been impressed by how remarkably little notice has been taken of some of these events which have come to my attention. The tragedy is every bit as real and great, no matter who the victim.

We are dealing with an extremely large and difficult group of individuals with a very fallible and often inadequate human system. Every day Judges and others working within that system must give opinions and make very difficult decisions, in attempting to manage these offenders with what the community is willing to allot for that purpose. All potentially dangerous sex offenders can never be "locked up." The safety of the community must be continually balanced against the civil rights of individuals. For instance, many attorneys have raised serious questions about the constitutionality of indeterminate sentences for so-called sexual psychopaths or "defective delinquents," and the right to bail or bond must always be respected.

Even if many dangerous sex offenders are incarcerated it would not eliminate the first offender, the offender who has not yet been apprehended or identified, or who comes in from other areas. Similarly, every day dangerous sex offenders walk out of prison by expiration of sentence. Very little seems to be made of this, perhaps because it is believed that they have "paid their debt to society," when in actuality there has been little or no real effort at rehabilitation and/or treatment of the underlying psychological disturbance. In that vein, it also should be clearly stated that many sex offenders are very disturbed individuals, ranging all the way from clearly psychotic persons through the whole diagnostic manual of mental diseases (including organic conditions). This is by no means a problem which can be approached from a moralistic point of view.

Our society does not seem to like to face problems for which there are no straight-forward or simple solutions. The problems involved in aberrations of sex and aggression in human beings are more complex than the technical and engineering problems of getting to the Moon. I believe that it is extremely important that physicians and other responsible persons as well as the general public have a better understanding of the scope of this problem and some of the issues involved. There have been sex offenders in all societies. We can work to minimize the problem by early identification, more knowledge and better management. We need more money; however, no matter how much money is spent there will be failures of rehabilitation and treatment and there will continue to be violent sex offenses committed in our community. To a considerable degree I believe the responsibility must be shared by all of us for improving that community and making a more human environment. This is the only hope for true progress with this very difficult problem.

STONE v. WAINWRIGHT

This is an appeal by the State of Florida from the granting of federal habeas relief to two men who had been convicted of violating Florida's "felony sodomy statute," Fla.Stat.Ann. §800.01. Subsequent to the trials at which petitioners were convicted, the Supreme Court of Florida held Section 800.01 to be "void on its face as unconstitutional for vagueness and uncertainty in its language.

The statute under which petitioners were convicted reads as follows:

"800.01 Crime against nature; punishment

"Whoever commits the abominable and detestable crime against nature, either with mankind or with beast, shall be punished by imprisonment in the state prison not exceeding twenty years."

Statutes prohibiting consensual sodomy have increasingly come under constitutional attack in recent years. The challenges that have been brought fall into a wide variety of imaginative theories that can be categorized in two general groups. The first grouping is premised on the theory that the state is without power to regulate consensual sodomy and other sexual activities between or among consenting adults. Specific arguments that have been advanced include allegations that such statutes unconstitutionally (1) invade a prenumbral right to privacy, (2) establish a religion by promoting nonsecular religious morals, (3) impose cruel and unusual punishment by penalizing a condition (homosexuality), (4) impinge Frist Amendment expressional freedoms, and (5) violate due process standards by criminalizing conduct absent either a "rational basis" or a "compelling state interest."

The second general category of attacks against sodomy statutes consists of arguments that admit that the state may permissibly regulate some instances of consensual sodomy but argue that the particular statute involved is constitutionally defective. Perhaps the most common example of this argument is the theory that marital privacy is protected by the Constitution and that therefore any statute that could be or is used to prosecute married persons is unconstitutionally overbroad. Another example is the attack based on the vagueness with which the acts sought to be proscribed are often defined. The term "sodomy" originated in the Bible and appears in the common law, but the various states have, perhaps for euphemistic reasons, selected terms even more arcane than "sodomy," such as "buggery" or "the crime against nature." Thus, when the common citizen is faced with prosecution under a statute employing such indefinite phraseology, he may argue that due process is violated inasmuch as the statute is so vague and lacking in ascertainable standards of guilty conduct as to be incapable of giving a person of ordinary intelligence fair notice that his contemplated conduct is forbidden.

Almost fifty years have passed since the Supreme Court of the United States penned the classic statement regarding the level of linguistical vagueness that a criminal statute must exceed if it is to satisfy due process standards:

"[That the words of a criminal statute] must be sufficiently explicit to inform those who are subject to it what conduct on their part will render them liable to its penalties, is a well-recognized requirement, consonant alike with ordinary notions of fair play and the settled rules of law. And a statute which either forbids or requires the doing of an act in terms so vague that men of common intelligence must necessarily guess at its meaning and differ as to its application violates the first essential of due process of law."

478 F.2d 390 (1973) (CA–5).

Connally v. General Construction Co., 1926, 269 U.S. 385, 391, 46 S.Ct. 126, 127, 70 L.Ed. 322, 328.

As did the District Court, we agree with the Florida Supreme Court that the words "abominable and detestable crime against nature" are fatally vague. Convictions obtained under this statute, rendered void by its vagueness, are repugnant to the Constitution and cannot stand.

Affirmed.

WAINWRIGHT v. STONE

Per curium.

We perceive no violation of the "underlying principle . . . that no man shall be held criminally responsible for conduct which he could not reasonable understand to be proscribed." Stone was convicted for copulation per os and per anum, Huffman for copulation per anum. These very acts had long been held to constitute "the abominable and detestable crime against nature" under §800.01 and predecessor statutes.

Judgment reversed.

U.S. Supreme Court, 94 S.Ct. 190 (1973).

Excerpts from Model Penal Code, American Law Institute Article 213, Sexual Offenses

SECTION 213.0. DEFINITIONS.

In this Article, the definitions given in Section 210.0 apply unless a different meaning plainly is required.

SECTION 213.1. RAPE AND RELATED OFFENSES.

(1) *Rape.* A male who has sexual intercourse with a female not his wife is guilty of rape if:

(a) he compels her to submit by force or by threat of imminent death, serious bodily injury, extreme pain or kidnapping, to be inflicted on anyone; or
(b) he has substantially impaired her power to appraise or control her conduct by administering or employing without her knowledge drugs, intoxicants or other means for the purpose of preventing resistance; or
(c) if the female is unconscious; or
(d) if the female is less than 10 years old.

Rape is a felony of the second degree unless (i) in the course thereof the actor inflicts serious bodily injury upon anyone, or (ii) the victim was not a voluntary social companion of the actor upon the occasion of the crime and had not previously permitted him sexual liberties, in which cases the offense is a felony of the first degree. Sexual intercourse includes intercourse per os or per anum, with some penetration however slight; emission is not required.

(2) *Gross Sexual Imposition.* A male who has sexual intercourse with a female not his wife commits a felony of the third degree if:

    (a) he compels her to submit by any threat that would prevent resistance by a woman of ordinary resolution; or

    (b) he knows that she suffers from a mental disease or defect which renders her incapable of appraising the nature of her conduct; or

    (c) he knows that she is unaware that a sexual act is being committed upon her or that she submits because she falsely supposes that he is her husband.

SECTION 213.2. DEVIATE SEXUAL INTERCOURSE BY FORCE OR IMPOSITION.

(1) *By Force or Its Equivalent.* A person who engages in deviate sexual intercourse with another person, or who causes another to engage in deviate sexual intercourse, commits a felony of the second degree if:

    (a) he compels the other person to participate by force or by threat of imminent death, serious bodily injury, extreme pain or kidnapping, to be inflicted on anyone; or

    (b) he has substantially impaired the other person's power to appraise or control his conduct, by administering or employing without the knowledge of the other person drugs, intoxicants or other means for the purpose of preventing resistance; or

    (c) the other person is unconscious; or

    (d) the other person is less than 10 years old.

Deviate sexual intercourse means sexual intercourse per os or per anum between human beings who are not husband and wife, and any form of sexual intercourse with an animal.

(2) *By Other Imposition.* A person who engages in deviate sexual intercourse with another person, or who causes another to engage in deviate sexual intercourse, commits a felony of the third degree if:

    (a) he compels the other person to participate by any threat that would prevent resistance by a person of ordinary resolution; or

    (b) he knows that the other person suffers from a mental disease or defect which renders him incapable of appraising the nature of his conduct; or

    (c) he knows that the other person submits because he is unaware that a sexual act is being committed upon him.

SECTION 213.3. CORRUPTION OF MINORS AND SEDUCTION.

(1) *Offense Defined.* A male who has sexual intercourse with a female not his wife, or any person who engages in deviate sexual intercourse or causes another to engage in deviate sexual intercourse, is guilty of an offense if:

    (a) the other person is less than 16 years old and the actor is at least 4 years older than the other person; or

    (b) the other person is less than 21 years old and the actor is his guardian or otherwise responsible for general supervision of his welfare; or

    (c) the other person is in custody of law or detained in a hospital or other institution and the actor has supervisory or disciplinary authority over him, or

    (d) the other person is a female who is induced to participate by a promise of marriage which the actor does not mean to perform.

(2) *Grading.* An offense under paragraph (a) of Subsection (1) is a felony of the third degree. Otherwise an offense under this section is a misdemeanor.

SECTION 213.4. SEXUAL ASSAULT.

A person who subjects another not his spouse to any sexual contact is guilty of sexual assault, a misdemeanor, if:

    (1) he knows that the contact is offensive to the other person; or

    (2) he knows that the other person suffers from a mental disease or defect which renders him or her incapable of appraising the nature of his or her conduct; or

    (3) he knows that the other person is unaware that a sexual act is being committed; or

    (4) the other person is less than 10 years old; or

    (5) he has substantially impaired the other person's power to appraise or control his or her conduct, by administering or employing without the other's knowledge drugs, intoxicants, or other means for the purpose of preventing resistance; or

    (6) the other person is less than 16 years old and the actor is at least 4 years older than the other person; or

    (7) the other person is less than 21 years old and the actor is his guardian or otherwise

responsible for general supervision of his welfare; or

(8) the other person is in custody of law or detained in a hospital or other institution and the actor has supervisory or disciplinary authority over him.

Sexual contact is any touching of the sexual or other intimate parts of the person of another for the purpose of arousing or gratifying sexual desire of either party.

SECTION 213.5. INDECENT EXPOSURE.

A person commits a misdemeanor if, for the purpose of arousing or gratifying sexual desire of himself or of any person other than his spouse, he exposes his genitals under circumstances in which he knows his conduct is likely to cause affront or alarm.

SECTION 213.6. PROVISION GENERALLY APPLICABLE TO ARTICLE 213.

(1) *Mistake as to Age.* Whenever in this Article the criminality of conduct depends on a child's being below the age of 10, it is no defense that the actor did not know the child's age, or reasonably believed the child to be older than 10. When criminality depends on the child's being below a critical age other than 10, it is a defense for the actor to prove that he reasonably believed the child to be above the critical age.

(2) *Spouse Relationships.* Whenever in this Article the definition of an offense excludes conduct with a spouse, the exclusion shall be deemed to extend to persons living as man and wife, regardless of the legal status of their relationship. The exclusion shall be inoperative as respects spouses living apart under a decree of judicial separation. Where the definition of

an offense excludes conduct with a spouse or conduct by a woman, this shall not preclude conviction of a spouse or woman as accomplice in a sexual act which he or she causes another person, not within the exclusion, to perform.

(4) *Sexually Promiscuous Complainants.* It is a defense to prosecution under Section 213.3 and paragraphs (6), (7), and (8) of Section 213.4 for the actor to prove by a preponderance of the evidence that the alleged victim had, prior to the time of the offense charged, engaged promiscuously in sexual relations with others.

(5) *Prompt Complaint.* No prosecution may be instituted or maintained under this Article unless the alleged offense was brought to the notice of public authority within 3 months of its occurrence or, where the alleged victim was less than 16 years old or otherwise incompetent to make complaint, within 3 months after a parent, guardian or other competent person specially interested in the victim learns of the offense.

(6) *Testimony of Complainants.* No person shall be convicted of any felony under this Article upon the uncorroborated testimony of the alleged victim. Corroboration may be circumstantial. In any prosecution before a jury for an offense under this Article, the jury shall be instructed to evaluate the testimony of a victim or complaining witness with special care in view of the emotional involvement of the witness and the difficulty of determining the truth with respect to alleged sexual activities carried out in private.

Note: Crimes of "Public Indency" (chiefly prostitution and obscenity) are contained in Article 251; bigamy, incest, and illegal abortion under Article 230, "Offenses Against the Family."

SPECHT v. PATTERSON

Mr. Justice DOUGLAS delivered the opinion of the Court.

We held in Williams v. People of State of New York, 337 U.S. 241, 69 S.Ct. 1079, 93 L.Ed. 1337, that the Due Process Clause of the Fourteenth Amendment did not require a

judge to have hearings and to give a convicted person an opportunity to participate in those hearings when he came to determine the sentence to be imposed. . . .

The question is whether the rule of the *Williams* case applies to this Colorado case

U.S. Supreme Court, 386 U.S. 605 (1967).

where petitioner, having been convicted for indecent liberties under one Colorado statute that carries a maximum sentence of 10 years (Colo.Rev.Stat.Ann. § 40–2–232 (1963)) but not sentenced under it, may be sentenced under the Sex Offenders Act, Colo.Rev.Stat. Ann. §§ 39–19–1 to 10 (1963), for an indeterminate term of from one day to life without notice and full hearing. The Colorado Supreme Court approved the procedure, when it was challenged by habeas corpus (153 Colo. 235, 385 P.2d 423) and on motion to set aside the judgment. 156 Colo. 12, 396 P.2d 838. This federal habeas corpus proceeding resulted, the Court of Appeals affirming dismissal of the writ, 10 Cir., 357 F.2d 325. The case is here on a petition for certiorari, 385 U.S. 968, 87 S.Ct. 516, 17 L.Ed.2d 433.

The Sex Offenders Act may be brought into play if the trial court "is of the opinion that a * * * person [convicted of specified sex offenses], if at large, constitutes a threat of bodily harm to members of the public, or is an habitual offender and mentally ill." § 1. He then becomes punishable for an indeterminate term of from one day to life on the following conditions as specified in § 2:

"(2) A complete psychiatric examination shall have been made of him by the psychiatrists of the Colorado psychopathic hospital or by psychiatrists designated by the district court; and
"(3) A complete written report thereof submitted to the district court. Such report shall contain all facts and findings, together with recommendations as to whether or not the person is treatable under the provisions of this article; whether or not the person should be committed to the Colorado state hospital or to the state home and training schools as mentally ill or mentally deficient. Such report shall also contain the psychiatrist's opinion as to whether or not the person could be adequately supervised on probation."

This procedure was followed in petitioner's case; he was examined as required and a psychiatric report prepared and given to the trial judge prior to the sentencing. But there was no hearing in the normal sense, no right of confrontation and so on.

Petitioner insists that this procedure does not satisfy due process because it allows the critical finding to be made under § 1 of the Sex Offenders Act (1) without a hearing at which the person so convicted may confront and cross-examine adverse witnesses and present evidence of his own by use of compulsory process, if necessary; and (2) on the basis of hearsay evidence to which the person involved is not allowed access.

We adhere to Williams v. People of State of New York, supra; but we decline the invitation to extend it to this radically different situation. These commitment proceedings whether denominated civil or criminal are subject both to the Equal Protection Clause of the Fourteenth Amendment as we held in Baxstrom v. Herold, 383 U.S. 107, 86 S.Ct. 760, 15 L.Ed.2d 620, and to the Due Process Clause. We hold that the requirements of due process were not satisfied here.

The Sex Offenders Act does not make the commission of a specified crime the basis for sentencing. It makes one conviction the basis for commencing another proceeding under another Act to determine whether a person constitutes a threat of bodily harm to the public, or is an habitual offender and mentally ill. That is a new finding of fact (Vanderhoof v. People of State of Colorado, 152 Colo. 147, 149, 380 P.2d 903, 904) that was not an ingredient of the offense charged. The punishment under the second Act is criminal punishment even though it is designed not so much as retribution as it is to keep individuals from inflicting future harm.[1] United States v. Brown, 381 U.S. 437, 458, 85 S.Ct. 1707, 1720, 14 L.Ed.2d 484.

The Court of Appeals for the Third Circuit in speaking of a comparable Pennsylvania statute[2] said:

"It is a separate criminal proceeding which may be invoked after conviction of one of the

[1] Provisions for probation are provided (Colo. Rev.Stat.Ann. § 39–19–5–(3) (1963)); and the Board of Parole has broad powers over the person sentenced. (Colo.Rev.Stat.Ann. §§ 39–19–6 to 10 (1963)).

[2] The Pennsylvania statute (Pa.Stat., Tit. 19, §§ 1166–1174 (1964)) provides that if a court is of the opinion that a person convicted before it of certain sex offenses "if at large, constitutes a threat of bodily harm to members of the public, or is an habitual offender and mentally ill," it may, "in lieu of the sentence now provided by law," sentence the person to a state institution for an indeterminate period from one day to life. Pa. Stat., Tit. 19, § 1166 (1964). The sentence is imposed only after the defendant has undergone a psychiatric examination and the court has received a report containing all the facts necessary to determine whether it shall impose the sentence under the act. Pa.Stat., Tit. 19, § 1167 (1964). If the court, after receiving the report, "shall be of the opinion that it would be to the best interests of justice to sentence such person under the provisions of [the] act, he shall cause such person to be arraigned before him and sentenced to" a state institution designated by the Department of Welfare. Pa.Stat., Tit. 19, § 1170 (1964). After a person is sentenced under the act, the state Board of Parole has exclusive control over him. Pa.Stat., Tit. 19, § 1173 (1964).

specified crimes. Petitioner therefore was entitled to a full judicial hearing before the magnified sentence was imposed. At such a hearing the requirements of due process cannot be satisfied by partial or niggardly procedural protections. A defendant in such a proceeding is entitled to the full panoply of the relevant protections which due process guarantees in state criminal proceedings. He must be afforded all those safeguards which are fundamental rights and essential to a fair trial, including the right to confront and cross-examine the witnesses against him." United States ex rel. Gerchman v. Maroney, 3 Cir., 355 F.2d 302, 312.

We agree with that view. Under Colorado's criminal procedure, here challenged, the invocation of the Sex Offenders Act means the making of a new charge leading to criminal punishment. The case is not unlike those under recidivist statutes where an habitual criminal issue is "a distinct issue" (Graham v. State of West Virginia, 224 U.S. 616, 625, 32 S.Ct. 583, 56 L.Ed. 917) on which a defendant "must receive reasonable notice and an opportunity to be heard." Oyler v. Boles, 368 U.S. 448, 452, 82 S.Ct. 501, 504, 7 L.Ed.2d 446; Chandler v. Fretag, 348 U.S. 3, 8, 75 S.Ct. 1, 99 L.Ed. 4. Due process, in other words, requires that he be present with counsel, have an opportunity to be heard, be confronted with witnesses against him, have the right to cross-examine, and to offer evidence of his own. And there must be findings adequate to make

meaningful any appeal that is allowed. The case is therefore quite unlike the Minnesota statute[3] we considered in State of Minnesota ex rel. Pearson v. Probate Court of Ramsey County, Minn., 309 U.S. 270, 60 S.Ct. 523, 84 L.Ed. 744, where in a proceeding to have a person adjudged a "psychopathic personality" there was a hearing where he was represented by counsel and could compel the production of witnesses on his behalf. Id., at 275, 60 S.Ct. at 526. None of these procedural safeguards we have mentioned is present under Colorado's Sex Offenders Act. We therefore hold that it is deficient in due process as measured by the requirements of the Fourteenth Amendment. Pointer v. State of Texas, 380 U.S. 400, 85 S.Ct. 1065, 13 L.Ed.2d 923.

Reversed.

[3] The Minnesota statute (Chapter 369 of the Laws of Minnesota of 1939) provided that the laws relating to persons found to be insane were to apply to "persons having a psychopathic personality." It defined the term "psychopathic personality" as meaning the existence in a person of certain characteristics which rendered him "irresponsible for his conduct with respect to sexual matters and thereby dangerous to other persons." The statute was not criminal in nature, and was not triggered by a criminal conviction. A person found to have a "psychopathic personality" would be committed, just as a person found to be insane. See Mason's Minn. Stat. c. 74, § 8992–176 (1938 Supp.).

AMERICAN "SEX PSYCHOPATH" LAWS: INJUSTICE IN PRACTICE

Gerald P. Koocher, Ph.D.

In the past 20 years many jurisdictions have acquired statutes for dealing specifically with habitual sex-offenders. These presuppose that treatment facilities and adequate detention facilities exist. Unfortunately, these laws are too frequently applied to the detriment of the offender. What was originally intended as a protective rehabilitative legal tool may result

in highly unjust practices, that would not have remained unnoticed for so long were it not for the bias against sexual offenders.

Generally speaking, "sex psychopath statutes"

(1) Usually create a legal status of psychopathy, which medical and legal authorities have to determine jointly. In the State of Mis-

Reprinted with permission from *Int. J. of Offender Therapy and Comparative Criminology* 17, no. 2 (1973): 148–51.

souri the diagnosis given to such offenders is "criminal sexual psychopath" (CSP).[1]

(2) By definition, persons considered legally insane, psychotic or feeble-minded do not fall under the above term.

(3) Most such statutes require that there be a history of past sexual crimes, as well as the assumption of criminal propensities to commit such offenses again.

(4) All imply that offenders so classified are a danger to others.

(5) All assignments to a "treatment facility" imply an indeterminate commitment.

My paper is mainly concerned with prosecutors who use such laws as tools to keep undesirable individuals away from the general population without sincere regard for the offender's true status and legal rights.

I will focus primarily on the first three points listed above showing how easily these crucial points are disregarded. The fourth and fifth points have been dealt with by Paul Tappan[2,3] in two articles. He notes that there has been a general failure to establish the "treatment facilities" postulated in legislation, and assumes that the ostensibly clinical orientation of these laws is chiefly camouflage.

The following case studies illustrate these points:

James is a 68 year old married white male. His right leg has been amputated ten years ago. His criminal record goes back to 1921 and concerns mainly minor offenses against property. In 1929 he spent some time in a state mental hospital where he was diagnosed as "psychotic." A county court judge classified him as a CSP at the request of the county prosecutor without asking for expert psychiatric testimony. His sex-crime history consists of "child molestation," and dates back to shortly before his arrest. He persuaded a number of neighborhood children (according to their testimony) aged 12 to 14 to climb into bed to perform fellatio on him, for which he rewarded them with candy, money, and cigarettes. He steadfastly claims that this is a "frame up" by neighborhood delinquents. All the children had records of truancy, and some juvenile court records as well. He was "turned in" to the police by one of these children when a truant officer investigated his excessive absences from school.

Several points are clearly in contradiction with the intent of the CSP law. First, this man has a history of psychosis and virtually none of sex-offenses. Second, the children involved were cooperative, active and willing participants, perhaps even responsible for initiating contact. Finally, the subject's physical condition, and the circumstances of the crime appear to rule out any predatory sex-crimes endangering the public.

Eugene is a 48 year old single Negro male, who has been hospitalized as a CSP since 1960. He has a long history of fighting, excessive drinking, and exhibitionism dating back to the age of 18. His Full Scale WAI I. Q. is 55, placing him in the lowest percentage of mental deficiency. His score on the same test in 1960 was 53. He obviously has always been severely retarded, and at present there are in addition indications of organic brain damage. He is clearly not a CSP by definition of the law, yet strangely remains one by definition of the courts.

It is a moot point as to whether he is better cared for on the "inside" rather than on the outside and whether he is in need of custodial care. What is relevant, however, is firstly that he is being detained unjustly, and secondly that any suggestion that suitable therapeutic treatment is available for this type of sex-offender is utterly ridiculous.

Paul is a 44 year old unmarried white male, who is a deaf mute, with a long record of minor offences such as vagrancy, prowling, and exhibitionism. It is possible to communicate minimally with him via written notes. Although standard psychological tests cannot be applied, there is some evidence of feeble-mindedness and of a thought disorder of psychotic proportions. He was classified as a CSP because once he approached two small girls at a public school, picked them up, kissed them on the cheek, and walked away.

Clearly, the CSP laws gave the prosecuting attorney the opportunity to put a problem case out of circulation for a long time, but can this be justified as a case of sex-psychopathy? Legal convenience has taken precedence over the offender's rights.

David probably comes closest to the general image of the sex psychopath, but his case had been handled so ineptly that probably no one will ever be certain. He is a 51 year old married white male, who has a record of exhibiting himself to children in a city park. When first arrested, David who is quite intelligent and well educated, began psychotherapy and was making some progress. Unfortunately, he continued to get arrested for the same offense and was therefore eventually confined to a state hospital. The prosecuting attorney initiated court procedures to have him committed indefinitely as a CSP. David claimed that he had not exhibited himself any more and actually he had never been caught in the act, but had merely been "positively identified" from police photographs and from a "line-up" in which he was the only suspect shown. Recently he was again "positively identified" when charged with three more acts of exhibitionism. Unfortunately for the overzealous prosecutor, David was in maximum security confinement 100 miles away when the offences were supposed to have taken place.

This case shows how minor sex-offenses may be magnified out of all proportion to the detriment of the offender. If David was classified as a CSP, he would be kept confined in a state mental hospital without any chance of individual psychotherapy, taking him away from his home community where he had been receiving such therapy and benefiting from it.

The fact that my examples are drawn specifically from the Missouri State Hospital for the Criminally Insane should not be viewed as a limited indictment, but rather as a generalizable example of situations that exist in many other places. In the two years that I was affiliated with the Hospital I had contact with a large number of sex-offenders appropriately classified as CSP under Missouri law. The public interest and the personal well-being of the vast majority of such patients are well served under the existing statutes, but the inequities of the large numbers of individuals who are unjustly detained should be recognized. In these cases and many others like them, much greater care should be exercised before classifying offenders as "sex psychopaths." These special laws were made for the purpose of achieving therapeutic rehabilitation and we should live up to their intention by carefully discriminating and evaluating rather than using them for an "easy conviction." Many psychopaths react excellently to current psychotherapies, but they must be intelligently selected. Three of the cases quoted above and other sex offenders so classified are totally unsuited for any such treatment even if it were available. Classification procedures allowing wide judicial latitude to unqualified officers of the court, who have the power to decide arbitrarily and possibly unfairly the defendant's whole future, are dangerous for the concept of democratic justice.

REFERENCES

1. Missouri Statutes, Chapter 202.7, approved August 1, 1949.
   Offenders," *Federal Probation*, 1955, 19, 7–12.
2. Tappan, Paul, W. "Some Myths about Sex
3. ——— *Crime, Justice and Correction*, New York: McGraw-Hill, 1960.

EDITORIAL NOTE: "Legislation defining sex psychopaths and establishing administrative procedures for their custody, treatment and release, was passed by some 13 states between 1937 and 1950, and has been extended to other states since that time. The procedures leading up to legislation were similar in many different jurisdictions. In a review of the development of sex psychopath laws, the late criminologist, Edwin Sutherland, in an article entitled 'The Diffusion of Sexual Psychopath Laws', noted a sequence characterised by (a) an upspring of fear within the community as a result of a few serious sex crimes, (b) community response in the form of fear and anxiety, leading to (c) the gathering of information from an appointed committee and recommendations that generally were uncritically accepted by state legislatures. Usually, committees proceed to make recommendations based largely on the absence of facts. Sutherland noted that the laws embodied a set of implicit assumptions that were explicit in much of the popular literature on sex offenses. Such assumptions were largely based on the notion that all sex offenders were potentially dangerous, that they were recidivists, that they can be accurately diagnosed and efficiently treated by psychiatrists. These laws were passed in the name of science, although the scientific method was completely ignored.*"

* From: Eldefonso, Edward, *Law Enforcement and the Youthful Offender*, 2nd Edition. U.S.A., John Wiley, 1973, pp. 428–29.

DITTRICH v. BROWN COUNTY ET AL.

Proceeding by the County of Brown and others for commitment of Benno Dittrich to a state hospital as a psychopathic personality. After findings affirming a probate court's judgment adjudicating respondent to be a psychopathic personality and committing him to a state hospital for treatment and care, he appealed from an order denying his motion for a new trial.
Affirmed.

Supreme Court of Minnesota, 215 Minn. 234, 9 N.W.2d 510 (1943).

A psychopathic personality is defined by §526.09 to mean "the existence in any person of such conditions of emotional instability, or impulsiveness of behavior, or lack of customary standards of good judgment, or failure to appreciate the consequences of his acts, or a combination of any such conditions, as to render such person irresponsible for his conduct with respect to sexual matters and thereby dangerous to other persons."

At the time of trial in the district court, appellant was forty-two years old, married, and the father of six children. His business was that of farming. He was mentally bright, capable, and a good worker. His troubles related to sexual matters. We shall state only such facts relating to those matters as are necessary to an understanding of the case.

Appellant was emotionally unstable with respect to sexual matters and had an uncontrollable craving for sexual intercourse and self-abuse by masturbation. It is undisputed that his behavior otherwise was good and that he had never attacked or made advances to other women. As a result of his sexual excesses committed upon his wife, her health was impaired. Apparently she continued to live with him until the probate court adjudged him a psychopathic personality and committed him to the hospital. He was later released on bond. His wife was not living with him at the time of the hearing of the appeal in the district court.

The only expert testimony relative to appellant's psychopahtic condition was that of two physicians called by the state. Their testimony was conflicting as to whether or not appellant's condition rendered him dangerous to other persons. One of the medical experts called by the state testified that, because of the fact that appellant was separated from his wife and denied normal marital relations, his sexual desire, if not satisfied, "would be like steam under pressure" and that there was "reasonable danger" of his molesitng other women. The other expert testified that, in his opinion, it was unlikely appellant would attack other women. . . .

Here, appellant makes two points, viz.: (1) the evidence was insufficient to establish that he was a psychopathic personality within the meaning of the statute, for lack of any showing that he was dangerous to others; and (2) the court erred in requiring him to offer his evidence before that of the state.

1. The statute requires that, before a per-son may be adjudged a psychopathic personality, two facts must be established, viz.: (1) that such person is irresponsible with respect to sexual matters; and (2) that, because of such fact, he is dangerous to others. It is not seriously disputed here that the evidence sustains a finding that appellant is irresponsible with respect to sexual matters. He claims that the evidence is entirely insufficient to establish that, because of such fact, he is dangerous to others, for the reasons that the evidence is undisputed that he had made no advance or attack upon any other woman and that the medical testimony is equally divided on the point, one expert being of the opinion that he was dangerous in that respect and the other that he was not. The medical expert who gave an opinion that appellant was, because of irresponsibility with respect to sexual matters, dangerous to others, took into consideration the fact that he had not made any advance or attack upon other women. His opinion was that appellant's uncontrollable craving for sexual intercourse, rendering him irresponsible with respect to sexual matters, an irresponsibility manifested by his prior conduct, while he was enjoying marital relations with his wife, would be increased and accentuated by cessation of such relations to a point where there was reason to believe that there was "reasonable" danger that he would attack other women. While the other medical expert was of the opinion that appellant would not attack other women, he was equivocal about the matter. When interrogated as to the likelihood of such attacks, he testified: "I wouldn't say either, the propensities may be present and it may come sometime in the future and it may not. That is all I can say."

The trier of fact is the sole judge of the credibility of witnesses testifying in relation to an issuable fact, not only where there is a conflict in the testimony of witnesses called by different parties, but also where it exists between the witnesses of a party or even in the versions given by a single witness . . .

Although both medical experts testified for the state, the trial court was warranted in adopting the views of the expert who stated that appellant was dangerous to others and in rejecting those of the other expert to the contrary. The finding in accordance with these views is supported by the evidence and is sustained. . . .

Affirmed.

PEOPLE v. BARNETT

Earl Barnett was convicted on 12 counts of an indictment, each charging a separate offense under Penal Code, §288a. From the judgment of conviction, an order denying a new trial, and an order refusing to adjourn the proceedings or suspend sentence to determine whether defendant was a sexual psychopath, he appeals.

Judgment of conviction reversed in part, order denying a new trial affirmed, appeal from order refusing to adjourn the proceedings dismissed, and cause remanded with directions.

SCHAUER, Justice.

Defendant was convicted by the court, without a jury, on twelve counts of an indictment, each of which charged him with a separate offense under section 288a of the Penal Code. Before, during, and following the trial defendant moved the court pursuant to the terms of section 5501 of the Welfare and Institutions Code to grant him a hearing to determine whether he is a sexual psychopath as defined by section 5500 of the same code. On each occasion the motion, based upon affidavits of a brother of defendant to which were appended written statements of three physicians that they considered defendant to be a sexual psychopath, was denied. Thereupon judgment was pronounced and defendant was sentenced to the state prison. He appeals from the judgment of conviction and from an order denying a new trial, and attempts to appeal "from the Court's order refusing to adjourn the proceedings and/or to suspend sentence for the purpose of hearing and determining whether or not the defendant . . . was and is a sexual psychopath." The latter order is, under the circumstances of this record, not appealable, but is reviewed on the appeal from the judgment.

Defendant's chief contention is that the court erred in denying his motion for a hearing to determine whether he is a sexual psychopath. Defendant argues also the sufficiency of the evidence to support his conviction on count three of the indictment. We have determined that upon the showing made defendant is entitled to the hearing he seeks, but that the conviction on count three is supported by the evidence.

The pertinent provisions of the Welfare and Institutions Code which relate to sexual psychopaths presently read as follows:

Section 5500. As used in this chapter, 'sexual psychopath' means any person who is affected, in a form predisposing to the commission of sexual offenses [against children], and in a degree constituting him a menace to the health or safety of others, with any of the following conditions:

(a) Mental disease or disorder.
(b) Psychopathic personality.
(c) Marked departures from normal mentality.

(The words "against children" which appear in brackets in the above section were in effect at the time of the trial of this case but were deleted by amendment in 1945.)

Section 5501. If, when any person is charged with a crime, either before or after adjudication of the charge, it appears by affidavit to the satisfaction of the court that such person is a sexual psychopath within the meaning of this chapter, the court may adjourn the proceeding or suspend the sentence, as the case may be, and thereupon proceed as provided by this chapter. . . .

Section 5502. If upon the hearing on the allegation of sexual psychopathy, the person before the court upon trial or under conviction is found not to be a sexual psychopath, the court may proceed with the trial or impose sentence, as the case may be. If upon the hearing on the allegation of sexual psychopathy, the person is found to be a sexual psychopath, the court may suspend the proceedings and commitment to the Department of Institutions for placement in a State hospital shall proceed, according to the provisions of this chapter. . . .

In support of his contention that the court erred is not granting a hearing to determine whether defendant is a sexual psychopath, defendant relies upon the proposition laid down in *People v. Haley* (1924), 46 Cal. App.2d 618, 622, 116 P.2d 498, to the effect that the provisions of the first paragraph of section 5501, quoted hereinabove, confer

Supreme Court of California, 27 Cal. 2d 649, 166 P. 2d 4 (1946).

upon the court and, as a corollary, require the exercise of, a sound discretion to determine from the affidavit therein described whether defendant is a sexual psychopath and so entitled to a further hearing on the matter, and urges that in view of the uncontroverted allegations of the original affidavit of defendant's brother and of a supplement thereto and of the attached reports of physicians, the court abused its discretion in denying to defendant the requested hearing.

The original affidavit states, among other things, that defendant is forty-five years of age, unmarried, and by occupation an architect; that affiant (who does not claim to be a medical expert) as a result of reading the transcript of the testimony taken before the grand jury upon which the indictment against defendant was returned and of reading the medical statements attached to the affidavit believes that defendant "is affected with a predisposition and uncontrollable desire and impulse to commit sexual offenses against children upon any and all occasions when by chance or otherwise he comes in contact with such children and the opportunity for the commission of said acts is present; is affected in a form predisposing to sexual offenses against children, to wit: That he shows marked departures from normal physical development, normal physiological development which in turn has produced marked departures from normal mentality. That the departures from normal mentality include but are not limited to disorder of his ideation, reasoning and judgment and comprehension concerning all things sexual; disorder in the emotional sphere in relation to sex; and disorder in the very instinctive basis of sex and the desires and impulses that lead therefrom.

That an innate organic inability to profit by experience to fit into social patterns of behavior, or to respond to self-discipline, together with the whole mental picture, indicate the presence of a psychopathic personality; that a review of the testimony taken before the Grand Jury, as aforesaid, indicates that the said Earl Barnett . . . for the past 30 or more years has been homosexual in the gratification of his sexual desires; that he has for more than five or six years last past persistently engaged in sexual offenses with and upon young boys ranging in age from 13 to 18 years old, such offenses including [various described lewd and unnatural practices] . . . but that the central core of his sexual aberration and variation consists of the fixation of attraction, ideation in both consciousness and in his dreams, of boys of 14 or of immature years.

One of the medical statements, in which two physicians joined, reads as follows:

[W]e are of the opinion that he [defendant] is a Sexual Psychopath within the meaning and intent of Section 5500 of the Welfare and Institutions Code. . . . [T]his individual . . . can be classified under well known and generally accepted medical rules with reference to his sex reactions and behavior. He suffers from a congenital condition technically known as inversion. He is an Invert, a type of individual in whom not only is there defective microscopic brain structure, but in addition to this brain defect a congenital variation in the structure of endocrine glands which [has] a determining effect upon character. Such persons all have psychopathic personalities and when their sex life is considered, are Sexual Psychopaths.

. . . [T]his condition is congenital. It is inborn and exists in the microscopic structure of his body. He is in sexual matters an Invert; i.e., one whose interest sexually has been turned congenitally by a power outside of him and apart from any consideration of free will from normal interest and satisfaction in the opposite sex to a condition where he is interested in, attracted by, and obtains sexual satisfaction from his own sex. When this results in obvious and often unlawful, as well as shocking and indecent, anomalies in sexual behavior such acts should be considered not as vicious manifestations of a perverted free will, but rather as the unfortunate and destructive results of a congenitally bad brain and glandular makeup under the influence of the bad habits of a corrupt environment.

. . . [W]hile this inborn basis for inverted and anti-social sex conduct may possibly serve to extenuate the purely moral dereliction involved in his conduct, it renders the individual so afflicted an even greater menace to society, in general, and to the age group of children which he prefers, in particular, than are individuals who may indulge in similar practices for reasons other than an inborn urge, for congenitally afflicted individuals such as the defendant will not abstain, when opportunity affords, from the aberrant sex practices characteristic of their inverted nature, because they cannot.

The other medical statement recites as the opinion of the physician making it that the defendant presents:

1. Certain elements of mental disorder. 2. A psychopathic personality. 3. A marked departure from normal mentality. There are readily apparent anatomic and physiological abnormalities which lie at the basis of the above. . . . [Such abnormalities are then enumerated.] These anatomical and physiological abnormalities are congenital and they have determined in toto the evolution of his sex psychology. He is as he is, for exactly the same reason that a normal man is as he is . . . in the matter of sex. . . .

Just as nature has broadened his pelvis . . . so has nature made him associate words one with the other in a feminine rather than masculine way. Given him the visual imagery of a woman, caused him to seek and retain knowledge that is feminine, caused him to respond to anger provocations more as a woman than a man. Given him likes and dislikes of a great number of sorts, which are common to the female rather than the male. Forced him to choose material for art work, writing, studying, travelling, in a female manner in the ratio of 10 to 2. Nature has so built him that authoritative scientific tests of the total masculinity or femininity in his nature given him a score 85 points away from the average masculine score. (Male average 52: female average 70: Barnett's score—feminine 33) Such a long list of abnormalities, variations, or perversions of mind indicate "certain elements of mental disorder". . . .

On the basis of these abnormalities . . . this subject has found himself in opposition to established modes, customs, and conventions of the society in which he lives. But, unable to change . . . he has not responded to self-discipline; has been unable to profit by experience of mental discomfort and anxiety; and has been unable to fit into social patterns. This status of mind establishes him as a "psychopathic personality."

Such things . . . mark the defendant as one with definite departures from normal mentality. The extent to which the abnormal mentality has expressed itself in untoward behavior moves us to state that the departures from normal mentality are marked.

The analysis of his personality up to this point when coupled with perverted sexual behavior indicate that this man is a homosexual. . . .

The supplemental affidavit, also made by defendant's brother, added no material facts but merely incorporated a copy of the transcript of the grand jury testimony, referred to in the original affidavit.

It is not contended that the trial judge was an expert is such matter. Nevertheless, he determined, contrary to the positive and undisputed statements of the three physicians, that defendant was not affected, in a form predisposing to the commission of sexual offenses and in a degree constituting him a menace to the health or safety of others, with either (*a*) mental disease or disorder, (*b*) psychopathic personality, or (*c*) marked departures from normal mentality. (Welf. & Inst. Code, §5500.)

The People rely upon the declaration in *People* v. *Haley* (1941), *supra,* 46 Cal.App.2d 618, 622, 116 P.2d 498, 501, that it is "not mandatory that the court shall adjourn the criminal proceeding when the affidavit is filed. The word 'may,' as it is used in that section [5501] should not be construed as a mandatory direction to the court regardless of the sufficiency of the showing. It

is merely discretionary. Unless there is an abuse of that discretion the ruling of the court in that regard may not be disturbed on appeal." However, we are of the opinion that where, as here, an unequivocal and uncontradicted showing is made by the affidavit that the accused falls within the meaning of section 5500, the denial by the court (both before, during, and after the trial) of the fuller hearing upon the issue, which is provided for by subsequent sections of the Welfare and Institutions Code, constitutes an abuse of discretion. (We do not imply that postponement of such a hearing until after the trial and adjudication of guilt would be otherwise than proper.) . . .

As stated hereinabove, the court, without a jury, found defendant guilty of the commission of twelve separate sexual offenses, and it cannot be seriously disputed that such offenses constituted him a menace to the health and safety of the boys against whom they were committed. The three physicians, experts in such matters, concurred in the opinion that defendant was congenitally affected with a condition resulting in a psychopathic personality and was therefore powerless to refrain from such offenses. One of the physicians was of the further opinion that defendant was also affected with mental disease or disorder and with marked departures from normal mentality. The conclusion that the trial court, in view of the strong showing made by the defendant, abused its discretion in denying to him a full trial on the issue of sexual psychopathy appears inescapable. . . . We are of the view that substantial justice, in a liberal interpretation and application of this remedial statute and in the light of the facts shown, requires that defendant be granted the hearing he requested. . . .

The judgment of conviction is reversed only insofar as it commits defendant directly to imprisonment in a state prison and otherwise is affirmed as to all twelve counts. The order denying defendant's motion for a new trial is affirmed. The cause is remanded to the trial court with directions "to suspend sentence for the purpose of hearing and determining whether or not the defendant . . . is a sexual psychopath," to grant defendant the requested hearing, and after such hearing commit the defendant to the Department of Institutions or to a state prison as may be determined according to law, and to make such other orders in the premises as may be meet. The purported appeal "from the Court's order refusing to adjourn, the proceedings . . ." is dismissed.

GIBSON, C. J., and SHENK, EDMONDS, CARTER, TRAYNOR, and SPENCE, J. J., concurred.

D.   THE "DEFECTIVE DELINQUENT"*

MARYLAND'S DEFECTIVE DELINQUENT STATUTE: A PROGRESS REPORT

State of Maryland, Department of Public Safety and Correctional Services.

I. OVERVIEW—MARYLAND'S DEFECTIVE DELINQUENT STATUTE

In an opinion in 1931, Judge Joseph N. Ulman stated, "Proper institutions must be provided and the law must be so amended that defective delinquents will be sent to them and kept in them for treatment until cured, if curable, or for life, if not curable."

In 1947, by Joint Resolution, the State Legislature of Maryland directed the appointment of a commission to study the problem. After several years of study, they proposed a new statute that was enacted into law in 1951. The statute was Maryland's approach to dealing with that segment of the criminal population who were defective emotionally and/or intellectually and who were repeated offenders whose anti-social or criminal behavior was deemed physically dangerous to society.

The legislative research report was quite clear in its intent. "The *primary* purpose of such legislation is to protect society from this segment of the criminal population who probably will again commit crimes if released on the expiration of a fixed sentence; and thus they should be detained and specially treated unless and until cured."

To implement the intent, the statute provided for an indeterminate sentence. ". . . An indeterminate sentence, as herein used, is one without maximum or minimum limits in order to confine defective delinquents until, as a result of the special treatment which they need, it is safe to return them to the community. If they cannot be cured, such indeterminate sentence accomplishes their confinement for life, which the protection of society demands. . . . The treatment may, and in many cases would, involve incarceration for life . . . not because of guilt, but to protect the defective himself and society." To implement the Defective Delinquent Statute, the legislature created a special institution known as Patuxent Institution.

The establishment of the Patuxent Institution was hailed at the time both nationally and internationally, on the one hand, as the most logical development resulting from a century of progress in corrections, and as a noble experiment on the other. The idea was coming to prevail that punishment meted out in proportion to the seriousness of the offense is not the only answer to the problem of crime, but that treatment of the offender and protection of society are also important and suggest an indeterminate sentence. If an attempt is made to "cure" the offender of his criminal propensities, it is impossible to predict beforehand when the treatment will take effect. Hence the length of the sentence cannot be foretold in advance. If one is concerned about the safety of society and future potential victims, one likewise cannot foretell beforehand when the threat will disappear, and the judgment regarding the release must be made in due time on the basis of experience, expertise and the best available knowledge. This is why the Patuxent Institution and even the plans for it received such wide attention in the international Congresses on the Prevention of Crime and the Treatment of Offenders in The Hague and Geneva in 1950 and 1955.

During the first ten years of operation (1955–1964), 794 patients were recommended for commitment by the professional staff of the Patuxent Institution. At their formal court hearing, the courts concurred (committed) in 638 cases and disagreed (did not commit) in 156 cases. That is, the courts concurred with the staff recommendation in approximately 80 per cent of the cases. Fol-

---

* See also Brown, Courtless article, Chapter 15. supra, especially pp. 589 et seq.

Patuxent Institution, January 9, 1973.

lowing the course of those patients who have subsequently been completely released, we found that these individuals fall into four categories in regard to treatment. The first group (untreated) are those whom the courts did not commit, contrary to professional staff recommendation. The second group are those who were subsequently released by the courts, contrary to staff recommendation, and who had only received in-house treatment at the time of their release. The third group comprised of individuals who were also released by the courts at subsequent redetermination hearings, contrary to staff recommendation, but who had experienced conditional release status (leaves, work release, parole), prior to their court release. The fourth group are those who had in-house treatment, had served three

Table 1. Recidivism Rates—Comparing Four Groups of Patuxent Patients and the National Recidivism Rate*

	Number	Recidivism rate
National Rate Most Frequently Quoted for Adult Offenders		65%
1. Patients recommended for commitment but not committed by the Courts (not treated, subjected to regular correctional system programs)	156	81%
2. Patients released at rehearing against staff advice, in-house treatment only	186	46%
3. Patients released at rehearing against staff advice, in-house treatment plus conditional release experience	100	39%
4. Patients released at recommendation of staff and Institutional Board of Review, in-house and continued treatment for three years on parole	135	7%

* 217 of the 638 committed patients were not included in Table 1. 166 were still under the jurisdiction of the Institution (in-house and on parole). The remaining 51 were released on legal technicalities and/or were too recently released to meet the criterion for inclusion (opportunity to be in society for three years).

years on parole and whose court release had been initiated by the Institutional Board of Review at the request of the professional staff.

To evaluate the Patuxent experience, the four aforementioned groups were compared for recidivism with each other and with the most frequently quoted national recidivism rates. Recidivism here was defined as conviction for a new offense and data was obtained from F.B.I. follow-up reports. This data may be found in Table I.

The Patuxent results indicate a distinct reduction in recidivism rates, well below national average, for all treated groups. Among all published data available to us, the finding of a 7 per cent recidivism rate in patients released by the Institutional Board of Review stands out dramatically as the lowest rate by far of any ever reported, and reflects the ability of a professional staff working in conjunction with an outside board of professionals from various disciplines to treat dangerous offenders and identify those who have been fully rehabilitated, returning them to society as productive citizens, as the statute envisioned.

The 135 patients comprising Group 4, have been in society for an average of 7.4 years. Some might question the 7 per cent recidivism rate since the first three years in society were accomplished under supervision and continued treatment. This, of course, is as the law intended. However, even if one considers only those patients from this group who were completely beyond any formal control or supervision, 58 patients would fall into this group (at least six years in the community) and their recidivism rate is 12 per cent. It should be further noted that only four of these recidivists spent any time in a correctional institution as a result of their new offense. The longest sentence was three years for shoplifting.

It should be noted that the treatment program of the Patuxent Institution has in a timely fashion responded to the recent emphasis on so-called community-based treatment. The Patuxent Institution has always emphasized the gradual termination of its care of its patients, continuing to work with them after their release from the confines of the institution itself. In recent years a great deal of emphasis has been given to the parole program, the halfway house, leaves, and work releases. The approach of the Patuxent parole is unique assuring the offender, who is back in the community, of supervision and help by the same team of treatment personnel who have been working with him within the institution. The Patuxent parole is kept flexible in the sense that returns to the institution, if needed, can be effected with relatively little formality and just as necessary steps in a continuing treatment program. Thus the Patuxent treatment program is located both within and without the institution.

Of the 638 patients committed between 1955–1964, only 3 per cent (22) have been continuously confined.

The seven per cent rate of recidivism has been accomplished within the limits of fiscal responsibility. During the period 1963–1972, the Maryland State Budget has increased by 301 per cent (mean annual growth rate 17%), the budget of the Division of Correction has increased by 334 per cent (mean annual growth rate 18%), the budget of Patuxent Institution has increased 153 per cent (mean annual growth rate 11%).

"DEFECTIVE DELINQUENT" STILL AN ELUSIVE CONCEPT IN MARYLAND

Margaret C. McDonald

Defective delinquency as a disease entity was given dubious birth in Maryland's State Legislature in 1951 and was followed in 1955 with the creation of an institution devoted solely to treating this disease—Patuxent Institution in Jessup, Maryland. Although many of the defective delinquency statute's early advocates still regard the law favorably, a large number of psychiatrists, lawyers, and sociologists have come to see it as a Frankenstein's monster, which has since grown into something almost impossible to deal with effectively.

The law defines a defective delinquent as "an individual who, by the demonstration of persistent aggravated antisocial or criminal behavior, evidences a propensity toward criminal activity, and who is found to have either such intellectual deficiency or emotional unbalance, or both, as to clearly demonstrate an actual danger to society so as to require confinement and treatment, when appropriate, as may make it reasonably safe for society to terminate the confinement and treatment."

The person so diagnosed is confined at Patuxent for an indeterminate sentence, until the institution's board of review finds him sufficiently rehabilitated to return to society.

PROCEDURE

After being convicted and sentenced in the usual way, any convicted criminal can be referred to Patuxent for examination to determine whether or not he is a defective delinquent. If he fits the legal definition, his original sentence may be revoked and he may be committed indeterminately to Patuxent instead. "The designation of some offenders as mentally ill is extremely arbitrary, as is the identification of those who fall within the statutory definitions of 'defective delinquent' or 'sexual psychopath,' " says E. Barrett Prettyman, president of the District of Columbia Bar Association, in the *American Criminal Law Review*. "As one commentator has implied in regard to the Maryland definition of a 'defective delinquent,' it could include virtually every offender except an unhelmeted motorcyclist."

Psychiatrist Brian Crowley, while testifying in a court debate over Patuxent's constitutionality, asked the presiding judge "whether a man who had been convicted of trespassing eight times on the Capitol steps, was emotionally disturbed, and might trespass again, would be a defective delinquent." The judge replied, "I certainly think so"; at which juncture, according to Dr. Crowley, the state's attorney "almost died of apoplexy."

The characteristics of the defective delinquent, as defined by law, seem to differ little from those of psychiatry's "sociopath" or the law's "recidivist." Indeed, the argument might be made that the new term seems to confuse those who have always dealt with the "defective delinquent" under another name.

Maryland's law is unique in that it is the first to charge the psychiatrist, rather than the

Excerpted and reprinted with permission from *Psychiatric News*, March 21, 1973.

penologist, with the responsibility of "treating and rehabilitating a large group of persons who would otherwise continue lives of tragic consequence to themselves and others." Patuxent looks like a prison, with the same fences and guard towers and the same armed, uniformed guards, yet it is headed, by law, by a psychiatrist, Dr. Harold Boslow, and is defined as "an institution that is neither a prison nor a mental hospital, yet one that retains some important features of both." Patuxent employs seven correctional personnel for every psychologist, psychiatrist, or social worker that it employs.

About this half-and-half approach, Dr. Crowley says, "I think it is very destructive, because you are sent to a place where you are going to get treatment and you get punishment. I think that is worse than simply being sent to a place where you are told that you are going to get punishment. . . . It's a bastardized mixture of punishment and treatment that I think is unfortunate in the extreme."

Another problem that was born with the new disease and the new treatment was a new emphasis. Though group therapy for all patient/inmates, with the purpose of rehabilitation and return to society, is cited as the significant difference between Patuxent and conventional prisons, the emphasis at Patuxent is still on "the protection of society," state Patuxent's annual reports, with rehabilitation taking a distant second place.

Perhaps the major fault most critics of Patuxent find is the indeterminate sentence. Every patient/inmate has to be scrupulously careful of everything he says and does, because at Patuxent, as in *1984,* Big Brother is indeed watching, and any small act he commits or thought he verbalizes can affect the pivotal uncertainty of his life—his release date.

And the only sure way to get out of Patuxent is to participate in therapy. "Participation in any program is voluntary," says the Patuxent Patient Handbook, followed in the same paragraph by ". . . you hold the key to your own future by participation in the institutional program." In other words, you don't have to participate, but you won't get out if you don't.

The patient/inmate soon appears to learn from other inmates to tell his therapist what the therapist wants to hear, in hopes of convincing him of rehabilitation. "Not only must an inmate attend therapy (group sessions are from one to two hours a week)," says Mr. Prettyman, "but he must, once there, comply with certain well-prescribed modes of behavior. He must talk about himself, his relation to his parents, his past sins. He must recognize that he has been sick and gain insight into what his 'problem' has been. Then the offender must begin to recognize that he has been wrong and that it is not in his own interest to cling to his past behavioral pattern.

"Finally, upon ascertaining the nature of his problem, he must evidence a strong intent to overcome it, compensate for it, fight it, or do whatever else is necessary to become a peaceful, useful citizen. The result? Shamming."

A patient/inmate told Mr. Prettyman, "Look, man, most of us are good at shamming. We grew up in the streets surrounded by confidence games. Literature is available to everyone now—hell, we talk as much about the Oedipus complex as about baseball. We know what these cats want to hear. Not the real gory stuff—what you're really thinking—because that scares 'em and makes 'em think you're still dangerous. But you spill your guts in a nice kind of way and act as if you're gaining all these insights. Now that you know yourself and that you killed that girl because you were really killing your mother, you don't have to kill anyone. It doesn't seem to occur to 'em that I might want to kill my mother several times over. Hell, everything I've told 'em is a lie. One big sham."

Dr. Thomas Courtless, a George Washington University sociologist and a caseworker and counselor at Patuxent between 1957 and 1962, favors the indeterminate sentence, calling it "the wedge to drive the sociopath off center. It helps to generate anxiety," he says, "and the rest of the program should channel this anxiety toward change." Forrest Calhoun, one of Patuxent's three associate directors, puts the indeterminate sentence on an even higher pedestal, calling it the "heart and soul" of the defective delinquency statute. He also remarked in a seminar at George Washington University Law School that "a man who fakes change is better than a man who refuses to be in the program at all."

But Mr. Prettyman sees the indeterminate sentence as a definite deterrent to rehabilitation: "The indeterminate sentence is self-defeating as a rehabilitative device. Only by use of [a sentence with a fixed maximum] can any treatment stand a chance of success, for until an inmate knows for certain that he will be released at the very latest on a particular, known date, he will remain outside the purview of meaningful rehabilitation. He may play the game to the point where the authorities are willing to take a chance on his freedom, but from the psychiatric standpoint he will be neither cured nor rehabilitated. The sooner society faces this fact the more quickly it can move on to solving the real problem of why these men had to be institutionalized in the first place."

Convicted criminals, almost to a man, would rather go to a conventional prison than to Patuxent, said several Patuxent patient/inmates. "Inmates weren't glad to come there even then [1957]," Dr. Courtless noted. "They said, 'You're kidding man; I'm not sick.'" Once there, men try to get out by all methods: refusing to be tested, making court appeals, and when all else fails, shamming through the program.

Defective delinquency, a disease with dubious symptoms, is also a disease with dubious cure.

McNEIL v. DIRECTOR, PATUXENT INSTITUTION

MR. JUSTICE MARSHALL delivered the opinion of the Court.

. . . The Maryland Defective Delinquency Law provides that a person convicted of any felony, or certain misdemeanors, may be committed to the Patuxent Institution for an indeterminate period, if it is judicially determined that he is a "defective delinquent." A defective delinquent is defined as:

"an individual who, by the demonstration of persistent aggravated antisocial or criminal behavior, evidences a propensity toward criminal activity, and who is found to have either such intellectual deficiency or emotional unbalance, or both, as to clearly demonstrate an actual danger to society so as to require such confinement and treatment, when appropriate, as may make it reasonably safe for society to terminate the confinement and treatment." Md. Code Ann., Art. 31 B, § 5.

Defective delinquency proceedings are ordinarily instituted immediately after conviction and sentencing; they may also be instituted after the defendant has served part of his prison term. §§ 6 (b), 6(c).[1] In either event, the process begins with a court order committing the prisoner to Patuxent for a psychiatric examination. §§ 6(b), 6(d). The institution is required to submit its report to the court within a fixed period of time. § 7(a).[2] If the report recommends commitment, then a hearing must be promptly held, with a jury trial if requested by the prisoner, to determine whether he should be committed as a defective delinquent. § 8. If he is so committed, then the commitment operates to suspend the prison sentences previously imposed. § 9(b).

In Murel v. Baltimore City Criminal Court, 405 U.S. ——, 92 S.Ct. 2091, 31 L.Ed.2d ——, several prisoners who had been committed as defective delinquents sought to challenge various aspects of the criteria and procedures that resulted in their commitment; we granted certiorari in that case together with this one, in order to consider together these challenges to the Maryland statutory scheme. For various reasons we now decline to reach those questions, see Murel, supra. But Edward McNeil presents a much more stark and simple claim. He has never been committed as a defective delinquent, and thus he has no cause to challenge the criteria and procedures that control a defective delinquency hearing. His

[1] But not after he has served all of it. The statute has always provided that no examination may be ordered or held if the person has been released from custody; since 1971 it has always prohibited the examination if the person is within six months of the expiration of sentence. § 6(c), as amended 1971. The State asserts that about 98% of the referrals to Patuxent are made immediately after conviction. Transcript of Argument, at 27; see Respondent's Brief, at 82 n. 33.

[2] The statute originally required the report to be submitted within six months, or before expiration of sentence, whichever later occurs. Since 1971, it has required a report within six months, or three months before expiration of sentence, whichever *first* occurs. § 7(a), as amended 1971. The state courts have construed the statute to permit extension of the allowable time, however, in the case of a noncooperative defendant who resists examination. State v. Musgrove, 241 Md. 521, 217 A.2d 247 (1966); Mullen v. Director, 6 Md.App. 120, 250 A.2d 281 (1969).

confinement rests wholly on the order committing him for examination, in preparation for such a commitment hearing. That order was made, not on the basis of an adversary hearing, but on the basis of an *ex parte* judicial determination that there was "reasonable cause to believe that the defendant may be a defective delinquent."[3]. . . .

The State of Maryland asserts the power to confine petitioner indefinitely, without ever obtaining a judicial determination that such confinement is warranted. It advances several distinct arguments in support of that claim.

First, the State contends that petitioner has been committed merely for observation, and that a commitment for observation need not be surrounded by the procedural safeguards (such as an adversary hearing) that are appropriate for a final determination of defective delinquency. Were the commitment for observation limited in duration to a brief period, the argument might have some force. But petitioner has been committed "for observation" for six years, and on the State's theory of his confinement there is no reason to believe it likely that he will ever be released. A confinement which is in fact indeterminate cannot rest on procedures designed to authorize a brief period of observation.

We recently rejected a similar argument in Jackson v. Indiana, when the State sought to confine indefinitely a defendant who was mentally incompetent to stand trial on his criminal charges. The State sought to characterize the commitment as temporary, and on that basis to justify reduced substantive and procedural safeguards. We held that because the commitment was permanent in its practical effect, it required safeguards commensurate with a long-term commitment. . . .

A second argument advanced by the State relies on the claim that petitioner himself prevented the State from holding a hearing on his condition. The State contends that, by refusing to talk to the psychiatrists, petitioner has prevented them from evaluating him, and made it impossible for the State to go forward with evidence at a hearing. Thus, it is argued, his continued confinement is analogous to civil contempt; he can terminate the confinement and bring about a hearing at any time by talking to the examining psychiatrists, and the State has the power to induce his cooperation by confining him.

Petitioner claims that he has a right under the Fifth Amendment to withhold cooperation, a claim we need not considered here. But putting that claim to one side, there is nevertheless a fatal flaw in the State's argument. For if confinement is to rest on a theory of civil contempt, then due process requires a hearing to determine whether petitioner has in fact behaved in a manner that amounts to contempt. At such a hearing it could be ascertained whether petitioner's conduct is willful, or whether it is a manifestation of mental illness, for which he cannot fairly be held responsible. Robinson v. California, 370 U.S. 660, 82 S.Ct. 1417, 8 L.Ed.2d 758 (1962). . . .

Finally, the State suggests that petitioner is probably a defective delinquent, because most noncooperators are. Hence, it is argued, his confinement rests not only on the purposes of observation, and of penalizing contempt, but also on the underlying purposes of the Defective Delinquency Law. But that argument proves too much. For if the Patuxent staff was prepared to conclude, on the basis of petitioner's silence and their observations of him over the years, that petitioner is a defective delinquent, then it is not true that he has prevented them from evaluating him. On that theory, they have long been ready to make their report to the Court, and the hearing on defective delinquency could have gone forward.

Petitioner is presently confined in Patuxent without any lawful authority to support that confinement. His sentence having expired, he is no longer within the class of persons eligible for commitment to the Institution as a defective delinquent. Accordingly, he is entitled to be released. The judgment below is reversed, and the mandate shall issue forthwith.

Reversed.

---

[3] Petitioner's Brief, at 6 n. 5; see Art. 31B, § 6(b): request for examination is made to Court "on any knowledge or suspicion of the presence of defective delinquency in such person." It appears that in this case the trial court issued the order *sua sponte*; prior to sentencing he had ordered a psychiatric evaluation by the court's medical officer, who in turn recommended referral to Patuxent for further evaluation and treatment.

MUREL v. BALTIMORE CITY CRIMINAL COURT

SYLLABUS BY THE COURT

Habeas corpus proceedings by inmates committed as defective delinquents. After remand 334 F.2d 506, the United States District Court for the District of Maryland, 295 F.Supp. 389, dismissed petitions, and petitioners appeal. The Court of Appeals, 436 F.2d 1153, affirmed, and certiorari was granted. The Supreme Court held that where statutes governing civil commitment in Maryland were undergoing substantial revision, designed to provide greater substantive and procedural safeguards to committed persons, it was inopportune time for Supreme Court to consider comprehensive challenge to Defective Delinquency Law.

Writ of certiorari dismissed as improvidently granted.

U.S. Su. Ct., 92 S. Ct. 2091 (1972).

SUGGESTIONS FOR ADDITIONAL READING

Alcoholism and Drug Addiction

"Dependence on Cannabis (Marihuana)," Council on Mental Health and Committee on Alcoholism and Drug Dependence. *Journal of the American Medical Assoc.* 201 (August 7, 1967): 108.

"Drug Addiction: Crime or Disease?" Interim and Final Reports of the Joint Committee of the American Bar Association and the American Medical Association on Narcotic Drugs (1961).

Lindesmith. *The Addict and the Law.* Bloomington, Ind.: Indiana Univ. Press, 1965.

"Narcotics and Addiction," special section, *American Journal of Psychiatry* 128 (1972): 7.

Marihuana: A Signal of Misunderstanding. First Report of the National Commission on Marihuana and Drug Abuse. U.S. Government Printing Office, March 1972.

Drug Use in America: Problem in Perspective. Second Report of the National Commission on Marihuana and Drug Abuse. U.S. Government Printing Office, March 1973.

Wittenborn (ed.). *Drugs and Youth.* Springfield, Ill., C. C Thomas & Co., 1969.

Wittenborn (ed.). *Communication and Drug Abuse.* Springfield, Ill.: C. C Thomas & Co., 1970.

Manual on Alcoholism. Committee on Alcoholism of the Council on Mental Health, American Medical Association, 1962.

Social Welfare and Alcoholism. Conference Proceedings. U.S. Dept. of Health, Education and Welfare, 1967.

Alcohol and Alcoholism. National Center for Prevention and Control of Alcoholism, National Institute of Mental Health, 1968.

Selzer. "Alcoholism and the Law: The Need for Detection and Treatment," *Michigan Law Review* 56, no. 2 (December 1957).

Selzer and Payne. "Automobile Accidents, Suicide and Unconscious Motivation," *American Journal of Psychiatry* 119, no. 3 (September 1962).

Alcohol, Alcoholism and Law Enforcement. Law Enforcement Study Center. St. Louis, Missouri: Washington University, 1969.

Allen. *Legal Rights of the Disabled and Disadvantaged.* U.S. Government Printing Office, 1969, pp. 38–48.

Task Force Report: Narcotics and Drug Abuse. President's Comm. on Law Enforcement and Administration of Justice, 1967.

Task Force Report: Drunkenness. President's Comm. on Law Enf. and Admn. of Justice, 1967.

Slovenko. *Psychiatry and Law.* Boston, Mass.: Little, Brown & Co., 1973 (Chaps. 9 and 10).

Slovenko. *Psychiatry and Law.* Boston, Mass.: Little, Brown & Co., 1973, Chapter 12.

McGarry and Cotton. "A Study in Civil Commitment: The Massachusetts Sexually Dangerous Persons Act," 6 *Harv. J. Leg.* (1969): 263.

Annotation: "Applicability, in Proceedings under Statutes Relating to Sexual Psychopaths, of Constitutional Provisions for the Protection of a Person Accused of Crime," 34 *ALR* 3d (1970): 652.

Annotation: "Requiring Complaining Witness in Prosecution for Sex Crime to Submit to Psychiatric Examination," 18 *ALR* 3d (1968): 1433.

Sex Offenders and the "Sexual Psychopath"

Gebbhard, Gagnon, et al. *Sex Offenders.* New York: Harper & Row, 1965.

Karpman. *The Sexual Offender and His Offenses.* New York: Julkan Press, 1954.

Mueller. *Legal Regulation of Sexual Conduct.* New York: Oceana Pub., 1961.

Slovenko. *Sexual Behavior and the Law.* Springfield, Ill.: C. C Thomas & Co., 1965.

Brakel and Rock (eds.). *The Mentally Disabled and the Law,* rev. ed. Chicago: Univ. of Chicago Press, 1971 (Chapter 10).

Robitscher. *Pursuit of Agreement: Psychiatry and the Law.* Phila., Penn.: J. B. Lippincott & Co., 1966 (pp. 154–68).

Halleck. *Psychiatry and the Dilemmas of Crime.* New York: Harper & Row, 1967, p. 252 et seq.

Packer. *The Limits of the Criminal Sanction.* California: Stanford Univ. Press, 1968, p. 301 et seq.

"Defective Delinquency"

Boslow, Rosenthal, et al. "Methods and Experiences in Group Treatment of Defective Delinquents in Maryland," *J. Soc. Therapy* 7 (1961): 65.

Boslow and Kandel. "Psychiatric Aspects of Dangerous Behavior: The Retarded Offender," *Amer. J. of Psychiat.* 122 (1965): 646.

Goldfarb and Singer. "Maryland's Defective Delinquency Law and the Patuxent Institution," *Bulletin of the Menninger Clinic* 34 (1970): 4.

Scheidemandel and Kanno. *The Mentally Ill Offender: A Survey of Treatment Programs,* Joint Inf. Serv., Amer. Psychiat. Assoc. and Nat. Assoc. for Mental Health, 1969, p. 63 et seq.

Carney. "The Indeterminate Sentence at Patuxent," *Crime and Delinquency* 20 (April 1974): 2.

A Psychiatric Glossary

abreaction: Emotional release or discharge resulting from recalling to awareness a painful experience that has been forgotten (repressed) because it was consciously intolerable. The therapeutic effect sometimes occurs through discharge of the painful emotions, desensitization to them, and often, increased insight.

abstinence: Voluntarily denying oneself some kind of gratification; in the area of *drug dependence*, the state of being without the drug on which the subject is dependent. The "abstinence syndrome" is equivalent to *withdrawal symptoms*, and its appearance suggests the presence of physiological dependence or *addiction*.

accident prone: In psychiatry, special susceptibility to accidents due to psychological causes.

acrophobia: See *phobia*.

acting out: Expression of unconscious emotional conflicts or feelings of hostility or love in actions that the individual does not consciously know are related to such conflicts or feelings. May be harmful or, in controlled situations, therapeutic (e.g., in children's play therapy).

acute situational or stress reactions: See *gross stress reaction*.

adaptation: Fitting or conforming to the environment, typically by means of a combination of autoplastic maneuvers (which involve a change in the self) and alloplastic maneuvers (which involve alteration of the external environment). The end result of successful adaptation is termed *adjustment*; "mal-adjustment" refers to unsuccessful attempts at adaptation.

addiction: Dependence on a chemical substance to the extent that physiologic dependence is established. The latter manifests itself as withdrawal symptoms (the abstinence syndrome) when the drug is withdrawn. See also *drug dependence*.

adjustment: The relation between the person, his inner self, and his environment. See also *adaptation*.

adrenergic: Activated or transmitted by adrenalin (e.g., *sympathetic nerve fibers*). See also *sympathetic nervous system*.

aerophagia: Excessive or morbid air swallowing.

affect: A person's emotional feeling tone. "Affect" and "emotion" are commonly used interchangeably.

affective disorder: Any *mental disorder* in which a disturbance of *affect* is predominant. This is a broad concept that includes *depressive neurosis* (see under *neurosis*), the *major affective disorders*, and *psychotic depressive reaction*.

affective personality: See *cyclothymic personality disorders*.

aftercare: Continuing treatment and rehabilitation provided in the community to help the patient maintain and continue to improve his adjustment following a period of hospitalization.

aggression: In psychiatry, a forceful, physical, verbal, or symbolic attack. May be appropriate and self-protective, including healthful self-assertiveness, or inappropriate. Also may be directed outward toward the environment, as in *explosive personality*, or inward toward the self, as in *depression*.

agitated depression: A psychotic depression accompanied by constant restlessness. Sometimes seen in *involutional melancholia* (q.v.). See also *depression*.

agitation: Severe restlessness; a major psychomotor expression of emotional tension.

agnosia: The inability to recognize and interpret the significance of sensory impressions; usually due to an organic brain disorder.

agoraphobia: See *phobia*.

agraphia: See *speech disturbance*.

ailurophobia: See *phobia*.

akathisia: Originally, a difficulty in sitting down. More recently broadened to include restlessness and uncontrolled muscular movements; sometimes seen as side effects in the use of certain *psychotropic* drugs, such as the *phenothiazines*.

alcoholic paranoid state: An *alcoholic psychosis* that develops in chronic alcoholics, usually male, and is characterized by excessive jealousy and delusions of infidelity by the spouse.

Reprinted with permission of the American Psychiatric Association. Third edition by the Committee on Public Information, American Psychiatric Association, 1969.

alcoholic psychoses: A group of major mental disorders associated with organic brain damage and caused by poisoning from alcohol. Includes *delirium tremens, Korsakov's psychosis, alcohol paranoid state* (q.v.), and often *hallucinosis.*

alcoholism: Addiction to or psychological dependence on the use of alcohol to the point that it is damaging to one's physical or emotional health, interpersonal relations, or economic functioning. The inability of a person to do without drinking or to limit his drinking once he starts is presumptive evidence of alcohol addiction.

alexia (dyslexia): See *speech disturbance.*

algophobia: See *phobia.*

alexia (dyslexia): See *speech disturbance.*

algophobia: See *phobia.*

alienation: In psychiatry, the term is used variously. For example: In *depersonalization* phenomena, feelings of unreality or strangeness produce a sense of *alienation* from one's self or environment. In obsessional states (see *obsessions*) where there is fear of one's emotions, avoidance of situations that arouse emotions, and continuing effort to keep feelings out of awareness, there is *alienation* of affect. More broadly, the term is used to denote the state of estrangement the individual feels in cultural settings that he views as foreign, unpredictable, or unacceptable.

alienist: Obsolete legal term for a psychiatrist who testifies in court about a person's sanity or mental competence.

Alzheimer's disease: A pre-senile degenerative organic brain disease. The symptoms are similar to *Pick's disease* (q.v.).

ambivalence: The coexistence of two opposing drives, desires, feelings, or emotions toward the same person, object, or goal. These may be conscious or partly conscious; or one side of the feelings may be unconscious. Example: love and hate toward the same person.

ambulatory schizophrenia: An unofficial term for a person with schizophrenia who functions sufficiently well that he generally does not require hospitalization. If in a hospital, he is kept on open wards or he may be allowed the complete freedom of the community.

amentia: An old term meaning absence of intellect as in severe congenital *mental retardation* (q.v.). The basis of amentia is usually organic and due to a developmental lack of adequate brain tissue. To be distinguished from *dementia* (q.v.).

animia: See *speech disturbance.*

amines: Organic compounds containing the amino group ($-NH_2$). Of special importance in biochemistry and neurochemistry. See also *biogenic amines* and *catecholamines.*

amnesia: Pathological loss of memory; forgetting; a phenomenon in which an area of experience is forgotten and becomes inaccessible to conscious recall. It may be of organic, emotional, or mixed origin, and limited to a sharply circumscribed period of time.

retrograde amnesia: Amnesia for events that occurred *before* a significant point in time.

anterograde amnesia: Amnesia for events that occurred *after* a significant point in time.

amok: A term denoting a relatively rare syndrome seen primarily in Malayan men, in which the individual suddenly becomes frenzied, violent, and even homicidal. The "running amok" episode appears to be an acute dissociative state precipitated by some intense frustration.

amphetamines: A group of chemicals that stimulate the cerebral cortex of the brain. Often misused by adults and adolescents to control normal fatigue and to induce euphoria. Used clinically to treat *hyperkinesis* (q.v.) in some children and to control minor depressions and overeating in adults. Highly addicting.

anaclitic: Literally, leaning on. In psychoanalytic terminology, denotes dependence of the infant on the mother or mother substitute for his sense of well being (e.g., gratification through nursing). Normal in childhood; pathologic in later years if excessive.

anaclitic depression: An acute and striking impairment of an infant's physical, social, and intellectual development that sometimes occurs following a sudden separation from the mothering person. See also *depression.*

anal character: A personality type that manifests excessive orderliness, miserliness, and obstinacy. In psychoanalysis, a pattern of behavior in an adult that is believed to originate in the *anal stage* of infancy. See *psychosexual development.*

anal erotism: The pleasurable part of the experience of anal function. Anal erotism appears in disguised and sublimated forms in later life. See also *psychosexual development* and *anal character.*

anal phase: See *psychosexual development.*

analgesia: A state in which the sense of pain is lulled or stopped.

analysand: A patient in psychoanalytic treatment.

analysis: a common synonym for *psychoanalysis* (q.v.).

analytic psychology: The name given by the Swiss psychoanalyst, Carl Gustav Jung (1875–1961), to his theoretical system, which minimizes the influence of sexual factors in emotional disorders and stresses mystical religious influences. See also *Jung*.

anamnesis: The developmental history of an individual and of his illness, especially a patient's recollections.

anankastic personality: A synonym for *obsessive compulsive personality*. (See under *personality disorders*).

anesthesia: Absence of sensation; may result from nerve damage, anesthetic drugs, or psychological processes such as in *hysterical neurosis, conversion type* (see under *neurosis*) or *hypnosis*.

anhedonia: Chronic inability to experience pleasure. See also *hedonism*.

anima: In Jungian psychology, the inner being of an individual as opposed to the outer character or *persona* that he presents to the world. Further, the anima may be the more feminine "soul" or inner self of a man; the *animus* the more masculine soul of a woman.

anorexia nervosa: A syndrome marked by severe and prolonged inability to eat, with marked weight loss, amenorrhea (or impotence), and other symptoms resulting from emotional conflict. Most frequently encountered in young females.

Antabuse: Disulfiram, a drug used in *aversive treatment* (q.v.) of alcoholism. It blocks the normal metabolism of alcohol and produces increased blood concentrations of acetaldehydes, which cause very unpleasant reactions, including pounding of the heart, shortness of breath, nausea, and vomiting.

antidepressant: Drugs used in treating depressions.

antisocial personality: See under *personality disorder*.

anxiety: Apprehension, tension, or uneasiness that stems from the anticipation of danger, the source of which is largely unknown or unrecognized. Primarily of intrapsychic origin, in distinction to fear, which is the emotional response to a consciously recognized and usually external threat or danger. Anxiety and fear are accompanied by similar physiologic changes. May be regarded as pathologic when present to such extent as to interfere with effectiveness in living achievement of desired goals or satisfactions, or reasonable emotional comfort. See also *panic*.

anxiety hysteria: An early psychoanalytic term for what is now called *phobic neurosis*. See under *neurosis*.

anxiety neurosis: See under *neurosis*.

aphasia: See *speech disturbance*.

aphonia: Inability to produce normal speech sounds. May be due to either organic or psychic causes.

apoplexy: See *stroke*.

apperception: Perception as modified and enhanced by the individual's own emotions, memories, and biases.

apraxia: See *speech disturbance*.

aptitude tests: Tests to measure an individual's various special skills and talents. Used in vocational counseling, such tests provide information regarding mechanical, clerical, musical, artistic, and other special aptitudes. By administering a range of multiple tests, it is also possible to measure such special skills as verbal reasoning, abstract reasoning, numerical ability, space relations, clerical speed and accuracy, mechanical reasoning, spelling, and grammar.

association: Relationship between ideas or emotions by contiguity, continuity, or by similarity. See also *free association*.

asthenic personality: See under *personality disorder*.

ataraxy: Absence of anxiety or confusion; calmness. Thus, *tranquilizers* are frequently called "ataractic" drugs.

atypical child: Nonspecific term for a child with distorted personality development. Applied most often to *autistic children* with perceptual handicaps and brain damage.

aura: In epilepsy, a premonitory, subjective sensation (e.g., a flash of light) that often warns the patient of an impending convulsion.

autism (autistic thinking): A form of thinking marked by extreme self-absorption and egocentricity, in which objective facts are obscured, distorted, or excluded in varying degrees.

> **autistic child:** In child psychiatry, a child who responds chiefly to inner thoughts, who does not relate to his environment; his overall functioning is immature and he often appears retarded. It may be an extension of *early infantile autism*, a manifestation of brain damage, or a sign of *childhood schizophrenia*. See under *schizophrenia*.
>
> **early infantile autism (Kanner's syndrome):** A syndrome beginning in infancy and characterized by self-absorption, inaccessibility, and inability to relate.

autoeroticism: Sensual self-gratification. Characteristic of, but not limited to, an early stage of emotional development. Includes satisfactions derived from genital play, masturbation, fantasy, and from oral, anal, and visual sources.

automatism: Automatic and apparently undirected behavior that is not consciously controlled.

autonomic nervous system: The part of the nervous system that innervates the cardiovascular, digestive, reproductive, and respiratory organs. It operates outside of consciousness and controls basic life-sustaining functions such as the heart rate, digestion, and breathing. It includes the *sympathetic nervous system* and the *parasympathetic nervous system.*

aversive therapy (conditioning): A treatment that suppresses undesirable behavior by associating a painful or unpleasant reaction with the behavior. Some examples are: the use of emetics or *Antabuse* (q.v.) with alcoholics, or the administration of an electric shock following the occurrence of some undesired behavior or symptom. Aversive therapy or conditioning is thought by some (but disputed by others) to be effective in the treatment of such disorders as *enuresis,* writer's cramp, *homosexuality, fetishism, transvestitism,* and *alcoholism.*

battered child syndrome: Physical injury to a child resulting from excessive beating, usually by a parent or parents and usually performed repeatedly over an extended period of time. The presence of mental illness in the parents may be presumed.

behavior disorders of childhood: a group of disorders occuring in childhood and adolescence that are less severe than psychoses but more resistant to treatment than *transient situational disturbances* (q.v.) because they are more stabilized and internalized. They are characterized by overactivity, inattentiveness, shyness, feelings of rejection, over-aggressiveness, timidity, and delinquency. The child who runs away from home or who persistently lies, steals, and teases other children in a hostile fashion falls into this category.

behavior therapy: Any treatment approach designed to modify the patient's behavior directly rather than inquiring into the dynamic causation. Typically, the psychopathology is conceptualized as maladaptive behavior. The treatment techniques are adapted from laboratory investigations of learning and may use principles of classical, instrumental and traumatic avoidance *conditioning, reciprocal inhibition and desensitization,* simple extinction, etc.

behavioral science(s): While strictly speaking physiology, neurology, endocrinology, and other biologically-based sciences may be called behavioral sciences, the term is generally reserved for those sciences focussed on the study of man's interpersonal relationships, values, experiences, activities, and institutions, such as psychiatry, psychology, cultural anthropology, sociology, and political science.

behaviorism: A body of psychologic theory developed by *John B. Watson* (1878–1958), concerned chiefly with objectively observable, tangible, and measurable data, rather than with subjective phenomena such as ideas and emotions.

Bender-Gestalt test: A psychological test in which the subject is presented, once at a time, with nine distinctly different geometric designs and told to copy them on a sheet of paper. He may then be asked to redraw them from memory. As a test for visual-motor coordination and for immediate visual memory, it can be of great help in detecting brain damage.

bestiality: See *sexual deviation.*

biogenic amines: A group of *amines* (q.v.) formed in the living organism, some of which exert an important influence on nervous system activity. Includes *catecholamines* (q.v.) and *indoles* (q.v.).

birth trauma: Term used by Otto Rank (1884–1939) to relate his theories of anxiety and neurosis to the inevitable psychic shock of being born.

bisexuality: Presence of the qualities of both sexes in the same individual. In psychoanalytic theory considered to be a universal trait, so that each individual has both masculine and feminine traits and homosexual and heterosexual tendencies, latent if not overt.

blocking: A sudden obstruction and interruption in the train of thought or speech, typically in the midst of a sentence, due to unconscious factors. Although normal persons may occasionally experience blocking, it is commonly seen in a variety of mental disorders and most often in *schizophrenia.*

body image: The conscious and unconscious picture a person has of his own body at any moment. The conscious and unconscious images may differ from each other.

borderline state (borderline psychosis): An unofficial diagnostic term for a condition in which a person's symptoms are difficult to classify as either psychotic or nonpsychotic. The symptoms may shift quickly from one pattern to another, and often include *acting out* and behavior suggesting *schizophrenia.*

brain syndrome: See *organic brain syndrome.*

brain waves: See *EEG.*

bulimia: Morbidly increased hunger. Same as *polyphagia.*

CA: Abbreviation for chronologic (actual) age. See also *IQ.*

carbon dioxide therapy: See *shock therapy.*

carnal abuse: An unlawful mishandling of the genitalia of another human being. In some jurisdictions, anything from kissing to forcible rape is considered "carnal abuse."

castration: In psychiatry, usually the fantasied loss of the penis. Also used figuratively to denote state of impotence, powerlessness, helplessness, or defeat. See also *castration complex* under *complex.*

castration anxiety: Anxiety due to fantasied danger or injuries to the genitals. May be precipitated by everyday events which have symbolic significance and appear to be threatening such as loss of job, loss of a tooth, or an experience of ridicule or humiliation. See also *castration complex* under *complex.*

castration complex: See under *complex.*

catalepsy: A generalized condition of diminished responsiveness usually characterized by trance-like states. May occur in organic or psychological disorders or under hypnosis.

cataplexy: Momentary loss of skeletal muscular tone with resulting weakness.

catatonic state (catatonia): A state characterized by immobility with muscular rigidity or inflexibility and at times by excitability. Often a symptom of *schizophrenia.*

catchment area: In psychiatry, a term borrowed from the English to delineate geographic area for which a mental health facility has responsibility. See also *community psychiatry.*

catecholamines: A group of *biogenic amines* derived from phenylalanine and containing the catechol nucleus. Certain of these amines, such as *epinephrine* and *norepinephrine,* exert an important influence on nervous system activity.

catharsis: (1) The healthful (therapeutic) release of ideas through a "talking out" of conscious material accompanied by the appropriate emotional reaction. (2) The release into awareness of repressed (i.e., "forgotten") material from the unconscious.

cathexis: Attachment, conscious or unconscious, of emotional feeling and significance to an idea or object, most commonly a person.

causalgia: A sensation of burning pain of either organic or psychic origin.

central nervous system (CNS): The brain and spinal cord.

central (syntactial) aphasia: See *speech disturbance.*

cephalalgia: Headache or head pain.

cerea flexibilitas: The "waxy flexibility" often present in catatonic schizophrenia in which the patient's arm or leg remains passively in the position in which it is placed.

cerebral arteriosclerosis: Hardening of the arteries of the brain resulting in an *organic brain syndrome* that may be either primarily neurologic in nature (e.g., convulsions, *aphasia,* chorea, athetosis, *parkinsonism,* etc.), or primarily mental (e.g., intellectual dulling, memory defects, emotional *liability,* paranoid delusions, confusion, and finally profound dementia), or a combination of both. Cerebral arteriosclerosis typically manifests itself in people over 50 years of age and at the present time accounts for approximately one-fifth of all first admissions to mental hospitals.

character: In psychiatry, the sum of the relatively fixed personality traits and habitual modes of response of an individual.

character analysis: Psychoanalytic treatment aimed at the *character defenses.*

character defense: In psychiatry, any character or personality trait which serves an unconscious defensive purpose. See also *defense mechanism.*

character disorder: A personality disorder manifested by a chronic and habitual pattern of reaction that is maladaptive in that it is relatively inflexible, limits the optimal use of potentialities, and often provokes the very counterreactions from the environment that the subject seeks to avoid. In contrast to symptoms of neurosis, character traits are typically *egosyntonic.* See also *personality.*

character neurosis: Similar to *character disorder* except that the neurotic conflicts are expressed in exaggerated but socially acceptable patterns of behavior and may not be easily recognizable as symptoms.

child analysis: Application of modified psychoanalytic methods and goals to problems of children to remove impediments to normal personality development.

childhood schizophrenia: See under *schizophrenia.*

cholinergic: Activated or transmitted by acetylcholine (e.g., *parasympathetic nerve fibers*). See also *parasympathetic nervous system.*

chromosomes: Microscopic intracellular structures that carry the *genes* for that cell. The normal human cell contains 46 chromosomes.

claustrophobia: See *phobia*.

climacteric: Menopausal period in women. Also used sometimes to refer to the corresponding age period in men.

clinical psychologist: See *psychologist, clinical*.

cognitive: refers to the mental process of comprehension, judgment, memory, and reasoning, as opposed to emotional and volitional processes.

collective unconscious: In Jungian theory, a portion of the unconscious common to all mankind; also called "racial unconscious." See *unconscious*.

combat fatigue: Term for disabling physical and emotional reaction incident to military combat. Paradoxically, the reaction may not necessarily include fatigue.

commitment: In psychiatry, a legal process for admitting a mentally ill person to a mental hospital, usually without his consent. The legal definition and procedure vary from state to state. Typically requires a court or judicial procedure, although not in all states, and sometimes the commitment may be entirely voluntary. A "voluntary" commitment, however is to be distinguished from a "voluntary admission" in that in the former case the hospital has the right to detain the patient for a legally defined period of time after he has given notice that he wishes to leave. See also *habeas corpus*.

communication, privileged: See under *privilege*.

community mental health center: In general, a community or neighborhood-based facility, or a network of component facilities for the prevention and treatment of mental illness, ideally with emphasis on a comprehensive range of services and with convenient accessibility to the population it serves. Since 1964, regulations governing federal support for community centers have required that a center offer at least five services, namely, inpatient, outpatient, partial hospitalization, emergency services, and consultation and education for community agencies. It is also considered desirable that a center should provide diagnostic, rehabilitative, precare and aftercare services, training, research, and public education.

community psychiatry: That branch of psychiatry concerned with the provision and delivery of a coordinated program of mental health care to a specified population (usually all residents of a designated geographical area termed the *catchment area*). Implicit in the concept of community psychiatry is acceptance of continuing responsibility for all the mental health needs of the community — diagnosis, treatment. rehabilitation (tertiary *prevention*) and aftercare, and, equally important, early case-finding (secondary *prevention*), and promoting mental health and preventing psychosocial disorder (primary *prevention*). The organizational nucleus for such services is typically the *community mental health center*. The body of knowledge and theory on which the methods and techniques of community psychiatry are based is often called *social psychiatry* (q.v.). See also *preventive psychiatry*.

compensation: (1) *A defense mechanism*, operating unconsciously, by which the individual attempts to make up for (i.e., to compensate for) real or fancied deficiencies. (2) A conscious process in which the individual strives to make up for real or imagined defects of physique, performance, skills, or psychological attributes. The two types frequently merge.

compensation neurosis: An unofficial term for certain unconscious neurotic reactions in which features of *secondary gain* (q.v.), such as a situational or financial advantage, are prominent. To be distinguished from *malingering* (q.v.) where there is conscious concealment or an ulterior motive to defraud. See also *hysterical neurosis, conversion type*, under *neurosis*.

complex: A group of associated ideas that have a common strong emotional tone. These are largely unconscious and significantly influence attitudes and associations. Three examples are:

> **castration complex:** A group of emotionally charged ideas that are unconscious and which refer to the fear of losing the genital organs, usually as punishment for forbidden sexual desires; includes the childhood fantasy that female genitals result from loss of a penis.

> **inferiority complex:** (Adler) Feelings of inferiority stemming from real or imagined physical or social inadequacies that may cause anxiety or other adverse reactions. The individual may overcompensate by excessive ambition or by the development of special skills, often in the very field in which he was originally handicapped. See also *overcompensation*.

> **Oedipus complex:** (Freud) Attachment of the child for the parent of the opposite sex, accompanied by envious and aggressive feeling toward the parent of the same sex. These feelings are largely repressed (i.e., made unconscious) because of the fear of displeasure or punishment by the parent of the same sex. In its original use, the term applied only to the male.

compression: In psychiatry and neurology, the squeezing of the brain, spinal cord, or nerve fibers by such conditions as fractures, blood clots, tumors, and abscesses.

compulsion: An insistent, repetitive, intrusive, and unwanted urge to perform an act that is contrary to the persons ordinary wishes or standards. Since it serves as a defensive substitute for still more unacceptable unconscious ideas and wishes, failure to perform the compulsive act leads to overt anxiety. Compulsions are *obsessions* (q.v.) that are still felt as *impulses* (q.v.).

compulsive personality: A personality characterized by excessive adherence to rigid standards. Typically, the individual is inflexible, overconscientious, overinhibited, unable to relax, and exhibits repetitive patterns of behavior. See *obsessive compulsive personality* under *personality disorder*.

conative: Pertains to the basic strivings of an individual, as expressed in his behavior and actions; volitional as opposed to *cognitive*.

concussion: The impairment of brain function due to injury caused by a blow on the head. The speed and degree of recovery depend on severity of the brain injury. Symptoms include unconsciousness, disorientation, and paralysis.

condensation: A psychologic process often present in dreams in which two or more concepts are fused so that a single symbol represents the multiple components.

conditioning: Any process by which an individual learns—either consciously or unconsciously—to modify his behavior in the presence of a particular stimulus. Conditioning is employed clinically in *behavior therapy*.

> **classical (Pavlovian) conditioning:** A conditioning process by which an individual learns to make a response mediated primarily by the *autonomic nervous system* (e.g., salivation or pupillary constriction) in the presence of a stimulus that normally does not elicit that response (i.e., a "neutral conditioned stimulus"). This is done by repeatedly exposing the individual to the neutral conditioned stimulus (e.g., the sound of a bell) at the same time or soon before he is exposed to the "unconditioned stimulus" (e.g., food or a bright light) that normally elicits that response in an untrained individual. When it occurs regularly in the presence of the neutral conditioned stimulus, the response is called a "conditioned reflex."

> **instrumental (operant) conditioning:** A *conditioning* process by which an individual learns to make (or to avoid making) specific responses in the presence of a once-neutral stimulus. Conditioning is achieved by repeatedly presenting the individual with a rewarding (or punishing) stimulus after he has performed (or avoided performing) the particular response. The once-neutral stimulus is called a "conditioned stimulus"; and the rewarding (or punishing) stimulus is called a "reinforcing" or "unconditioned" stimulus.

> **traumatic avoidance:** A form of instrumental conditioning in which, after a signal, a particular response must be completed in order to avoid a highly aversive stimulus. Once learned, this type of response is extremely resistant to extinction, particularly when it is difficult for the individual to find out that the traumatic consequences no longer obtain.

confabulation: The more or less unconscious, defensive "filling in" of actual memory gaps by imaginary experiences, often complex, that are recounted in a detailed and plausible way. Seen principally in organic psychotic disorders, such as *Korsakov's psychosis*.

confidentiality: In medicine, the ethical principle that a physician may not reveal the confidences entrusted or any information gained by him in the course of medical attendance unless he is required to do so by law or unless it becomes necessary in order to protect the welfare of the individual or of the community. See also *privilege, privileged communication*.

conflict: In psychiatry, a mental struggle that arises from the simultaneous operation of opposing impulses, drives, or external (environmental) or internal demands; termed *intrapsychic* when the conflict is between forces within the personality, *extrapsychic* when it is between the self and the environment.

confusion: In psychiatry, refers to disturbed orientation in respect to time, place, or person.

congenital: Literally, present at birth. Not synonymous with hereditary or genetic, for it may include conditions that arise during fetal development or the birth process. It does not refer to conditions that appear after birth.

conscience: The morally self-critical part of the self-encompassing standards of behavior, performance, and value judgments. Commonly equated with the conscious *superego*.

constitution: A persons intrinsic physical and psychological endowment; sometimes used more narrowly to indicate the physical inheritance or potential from birth.

constitutional types: Constellations of morphologic, physiologic, and psychologic traits as earlier proposed by various scholars. Galen, Kretschmer, and Sheldon proposed the following major types: *Galen*: sanguine, melancholic, choleric, and phlegmatic types; *Kretschmer*: pyknic (stocky), asthenic (slender), athletic, and dysplastic (disproportioned) types; *Sheldon*: ectomorphic (thin), mesomorphic (muscular), and endormorphic (fat) types, based on the relative preponderance of outer, middle, or inner layers of embryonic cellular tissue.

contusion: A superficial injury produced by a nonlacerating impact; a bruise.

conversion: A *defense mechanism*, operating unconsciously, by which intrapsychic conflicts that would otherwise give rise to anxiety are, instead, given symbolic external expression. The repressed ideas or impulses, plus the psychologic defenses against them, are converted into a variety of somatic symptoms. Example: psychogenic paralysis of a limb that prevents its use for aggressive purposes.

conversion neurosis (reaction): See *hysterical neurosis, conversion type,* under *neurosis.*

convulsive disorders: Primarily the centrencephalic seizures, grand mal and petit mal, and the focal seizures of Jacksonian and psychomotor *epilepsy* (q.v.). These brain disorders, with their fairly characteristic electroencephalographic patterns, are to be differentiated from a variety of other pathophysiological conditions in which a convulsive seizure may occur. For example, seizures may follow withdrawal from alcohol, barbiturates, and a wide variety of other drugs; they may also occur in cerebral vascular disease, brain tumor, brain abscess, hypoglycemia, hyponatremia, high fevers, eclampsia, uremia, and many other metabolic and intracranial disorders. Finally, hysterical seizures and seizures simulated by *malingerers* may, at times, pose difficult diagnostic problems.

coping mechanisms: Ways of adjusting to environmental stress without altering one's goals or purposes; includes both conscious and unconscious mechanisms.

coprophagia: Eating of filth or feces.

coprophilia: Excessive or morbid interest in filth or feces or symbolic representations thereof.

counterphobia: The desire or seeking out of experiences that are consciously or unconsciously feared.

countertransference: The psychiatrist's conscious or unconscious emotional reaction to his patient. See also *transference.*

cretinism: A type of mental retardation and body malformation caused by severe uncorrected thyroid deficiency in infancy and early childhood.

criminally insane: A legal term for psychotic patients who have been found not guilty of a serious crime, such as murder, rape, or arson, "by reason of insanity." See also *Currens Formula, Durham, McNaghten Rule.*

crisis intervention: A type of brief treatment in which a therapist or team of therapists assist a patient and his family with an immediate problem by giving medication, altering environmental circumstances, suggesting changes in patterns of behavior, and making referrals to community agencies.

cross-cultural psychiatry The comparative study of mental illness and mental health among different societies, nations, and cultures. The latter term is often used synonymously with *transcultural psychiatry,* the "trans" prefix denoting that the vista of the scientific observer extends beyond the scope of a single cultural unit.

cultural anthropology The study of man and his works, or of the learned behavior of man: his technology, languages, religions, values, customs, mores, beliefs, social relationships, and family life and structure. Originally restricting its studies to primitive or pre-literate societies and to nonoccidental civilized societies, cultural anthropology in recent years has enlarged its scope of interest to include studies of contemporary Western cultures. Of particular interest to psychiatry is the finding that what is considered as psychopathological is a matter of consensus within a given society. Similar to *social anthropology* and *ethnology.*

cultural psychiatry: A branch of *social psychiatry* (q.v.) that concerns itself with the mentally ill in relation to their cultural environment. Symptoms of behavior regarded as quite evident psychopathology in one society may well be regarded as acceptable and normal in another society.

cunnilingus: Sexual activity in which the mouth and tongue are used to stimulate the female genitals.

Currens Formula: A ruling that a person is not responsible for a crime if, as a consequence of a mental disorder, he did not have "adequate capacity to conform his conduct to the requirements of the law." This formula is applied only in the federal (not the state) courts of Pennsylvania, Delaware and New Jersey, the Third U.S. Circuit. See also *McNaghten Rule* and *Durham.*

cybernetics: Term introduced by Norbert Wiener (1894–1964) to designate the science of control mechanisms. It covers the entire field of communication and control in machines and puts forth the hypothesis that there is some similarity between the human nervous system and electronic control devices.

cyclothymic personality: See under *personality disorder*.

day hospital: See under *partial hospitalization*.

death instinct (Thanatos): In Freudian theory, the unconscious drive toward dissolution and death. Co-exists with and is in opposition to the life instinct (Eros).

defense mechanism: Unconscious intrapsychic processes that are employed to seek relief from emotional conflict and freedom from anxiety. Conscious efforts are frequently made for the same reasons, but true defense mechanisms are out of awareness (unconscious). Some of the common defense mechanisms defined in this glossary are: *compensation, conversion, denial, displacement, dissociation, idealization, identification, incorporation, introjection, projection, rationalization, reaction formation, regression, repression, sublimation, substitution, symbolization, undoing.* See also *mental mechanism*.

déjà vu: The sensation that what one is seeing has been seen before.

delirium: A mental state characterized by confusion and altered, possibly fluctuating, consciousness. Delusions, illusions, hallucinations, and lability of emotions, particularly anxiety and fear are often present.

delirium tremens: An acute and sometimes fatal disorder involving impairment of brain tissue; usually caused by withdrawal from excessive and unusually prolonged alcohol intake and manifested by tremors, frightening *illusions, hallucinations*, and sometimes convulsions. See also *organic brain syndrome*.

delusion: A false belief out of keeping with the individual's level of knowledge and his cultural group. The belief results from unconscious needs and is maintained against logical argument and despite objective contradictory evidence. Common delusions include:

> **delusions of grandeur:** Exaggerated ideas of one's importance or identity.

> **delusions of persecution:** Ideas that one has been singled out for persecution. See also *paranoia*.

> **delusions of reference:** Incorrect assumption that certain casual or unrelated events or the behavior of others apply to oneself. See also *paranoia*.

dementia: An old term denoting madness or insanity; now used to denote organic loss of intellectual function.

dementia praecox: Obsolescent descriptive term for *schizophrenia*. Introduced by Morel (1860) and later popularized by *Kraepelin*.

dementia, senile: See *senile dementia*.

demography: The description of populations in terms of relevant variables such as size, density, growth trends, sex, and age distribution. Such data are frequently related to the incidence and prevalence of disease in the companion science, *epidemiology*.

denial: A defense mechanism, operating unconsciously, used to resolve emotional conflict and allay anxiety by disavowing thoughts, feelings, wishes, needs, or external reality factors that are consciously intolerable.

dependency needs: Vital needs for mothering, love, affection, shelter, protection, security, food, and warmth. May be a manifestation of regression when they reappear openly in adults.

depersonalization: Feelings of unreality or strangeness concerning either the environment or the self or both. See also *neurosis*.

depersonalization neurosis: See under *neurosis*.

depression: Psychiatrically, a morbid sadness, dejection, or melancholy. To be differentiated from grief, which is realistic and proportionate to what has been lost. A depression may be a symptom of any psychiatric disorder or may constitute its principal manifestation. Neurotic depressions are differentiated from psychotic depressions in that they do not involve loss of capacity for reality testing. The major psychotic depressions include *psychotic depressive reaction* and the various *major affective disorders*. (q.v.).

depressive neurosis: See under *neurosis*.

depressive psychosis: See *psychotic depressive reaction*.

deprivation, emotional: A lack of adequate and appropriate interpersonal and/or environmental experience, usually in the early developmental years.

deprivation, sensory: See *sensory deprivation*.

depth psychology: The psychology of unconscious mental processes. Also a system of psychology in which the study of such processes plays a major role, as in *psychoanalysis*.

dereistic: Describes mental activity that is not in accordance with reality, logic, or experience. Similar to autistic. Sée *autism*.

descriptive psychiatry: A system of psychiatry based upon observation and study of readily observable external factors; to be differentiated from *dynamic psychiatry*. Often used to refer to the systematized descriptions of mental illnesses formulated by *Kraepelin*.

desoxyribonucleic acids: See *DNA*.

deterioration: Worsening of a clinical condition, usually expressed as progressive impairment of function; in organic brain syndromes, for example, deterioration refers to a progressive loss of intellectual faculties without implying permanency of change. *Dementia*, in contrast, usually refers to an irreversible decline of mental functions with intellectual disintegration of such a degree as to render fragmentary or to falsify entirely the patient's relationship to his environment. *Regression*, on the other hand, implies that the decline in functioning is reversible, and is more often applied to impairment in the emotional sphere than to intellectual impairment.

determinism: In psychiatry, the postulate that nothing in the individual's emotional or mental life results from chance alone but rather from specific causes or forces known or unknown.

dipsomania: See *–mania*.

disorientation: Loss of awareness of the position of the self in relation to space, time, or other persons; confusion.

displacement: A *defense mechanism*, operating unconsciously, in which an emotion is transferred or "displaced" from its original object to a more acceptable substitute.

dissociation: A *defense mechanism*, operating unconsciously, through which emotional significance and affect are separated and detached from an idea, situation, or object. Dissociation may defer or postpone experiencing some emotional impact as, for example, in selective *amnesia*.

dissociative reaction: Same as *hysterical neurosis, dissociative type* (q.v., under *neurosis*).

distributive analysis and synthesis: The therapy used by the psychobiologic school of psychiatry developed by *Adolf Meyer*. Entails extensive guided and directed investigation and analysis of the patient's entire past experience, stressing his assets and liabilities to make possible a constructive synthesis. See *psychobiology*.

DNA (desoxyribonucleic acid): One of the key chemicals governing life functions. Found in the cell nucleus. Essential constituent of the *genes*. Governs the manufacture of *RNA*.

dominance: 1) In psychiatry, an individual's disposition to play a prominent or controlling role in his interaction with others. 2) In neurology, the (normal) tendency of one half of the brain to be more important than the other in controling behavior (cerebral dominance). 3) In genetics, the ability of one *gene* (dominant

gene) to express itself in the *phenotype* of an individual, even though that gene is paired with another (recessive gene) that would have expressed itself in a different way.

double bind: A type of interaction, noted frequently in families with schizophrenic members, in which one person (often the mother) demands a response to a message containing mutually contradictory signals while the other (the schizophrenic son, for example) is unable either to comment on the incongruity or to escape from the situation. Example: a mother tells her son to act like a man and express his opinion and when he does, berates him as unloving and disloyal.

double-blind study: A research procedure for testing the therapeutic effectiveness of a drug. Neither the research investigator nor the patients know whether the drug being given is the one under investigation, another drug, or a *placebo* until the completion of the study.

double personality: See *personality, multiple*.

Down's syndrome (disease): Preferred term for a common form of mental retardation caused by a chromosomal abnormality; formerly called *mongolism*, a name increasingly regarded as inappropriate and inaccurate.

drawing test: A psychological test in which the subject is asked to draw (but not copy) a person, and then another person of the opposite sex, a tree, a house, an animal, or any other object. Attitudes and traits that are important to the subject may be revealed by the type of body posture he depicts, movements, size of person, omission or distortion of body parts, sex differentiation, etc. Although not as informative as the *Thematic Apperception Test (TAT)* and the *Roschach Test*, the drawing tests offer rather quick and helpful information about problems that may not be very deep-seated but that are troublesome to the subject.

drive: Basic urge, instinct, motivation; in psychiatry, a term currently preferred to avoid confusion with the more purely biological concept of *instinct*.

drug abuse: See under *drug dependence*.

drug dependence: Habituation to, abuse of, and/or addiction to a chemical substance. Largely because of psychologic craving, the life of the drug-dependent person revolves about his need for the specific effect of one or more chemical agents on his mood or state of consciousness. The term thus includes not only *addiction*, (which emphasizes physiologic dependence), but also drug abuse, (where the pathologic craving for drugs seems unrelated to physical dependence). *Alcoholism* is a special type of drug dependence. Other examples are dependence on opiates; synthetic analgesics with morphine-like effects; barbiturates; other hypnotics, sedatives, and tranquilizers; cocaine; marihuana; other psychostimulants; and halucinogens.

DSM-II: Abbreviation for *Diagnostic and Statistical Manual of Mental Disorders*, Second Edition (q.v.).

dummy: British term for *placebo*.

Durham Decision: A ruling which states that a person is not responsible for a crime if his act was the product of mental disease or defect. Currently, this formula applies only in the District of Columbia and the State of Maine. See also *McNaghten Rule* and *Currens Formula*.

dyadic: The relationship between a pair. In psychiatry, refers to the therapeutic relationship between doctor and patient as in "dyadic therapy."

dynamic psychiatry: As distinguished from *descriptive psychiatry* (q.v.), refers to the study of emotional processes, their origins, and the mental mechanisms. Implies the study of the active, energy-laden, and changing factors in human behavior and its motivation. Dynamic principles convey the concepts of change, of evolution, and of progression or regression.

dynamics: See *psychodynamics*.

dysarthria: Impaired, difficult speech, usually due to organic disorders of the nervous system or speech organs.

dyslexia: See *speech disturbance*.

dyspareunia: Pelvic pain, usually emotional in origin, experienced by the female in sexual intercourse.

dysphagia: Difficult or painful swallowing.

dyssocial behavior: In psychiatry, a diagnostic term for individuals who are not classifiable as *anti-social personalities*, but who are predatory and follow more or less criminal pursuits such as racketeers, dishonest gamblers, prostitutes, and dope peddlers. Formerly called "sociopathic personalities."

early infantile autism: See under *autism*.

echolalia: The pathologic repetition by imitation of the speech of another. Sometimes seen in *schizophrenia, catatonic type*.

echopraxia: The pathologic repetition, by imitation, of the movements of another. Sometimes seen in *schizophrenia, catatonic type*.

ecology: Study of relations between individuals and their environments. In psychiatry, especially the study of relations between human beings and human institutions.

ECT (electroconvulsive therapy): See *shock therapy*.

EEG: See *electroencephalogram*.

ego: In psychoanalytic theory, one of the three major divisions in the model of the psychic apparatus, the others being the *id* and *superego*. The ego represents the sum of certain *mental mechanisms*, such as perception and memory, and specific *defense mechanisms*. The ego serves to mediate between the demands of primitive instinctual drives (the *id*), of internalized parental and social prohibitions (the *superego*), and of reality. The compromises between these forces achieved by the ego tend to resolve intrapsychic conflict and serve an adaptive and executive function. Psychiatric usage of the term should not be confused with common usage, which connotes "self-love" or "selfishness."

ego analysis: Intensive psychoanalytic study and analysis of the ways in which the ego resolves or attempts to deal with intrapsychic conflicts, especially in relation to the development of *mental mechanisms* and the maturation of capacity for rational thought and act. Modern psychoanalysis gives more emphasis to considerations of the defensive operations of the ego than did earlier techniques, which emphasized instinctual forces to a greater degree.

ego-dystonic: Aspects of the individual's behavior, thoughts, and attitudes that he views as repugnant or inconsistent with his total personality. See also *ego-syntonic*.

ego ideal: That part of the personality that comprises the aims and goals of the self; usually refers to the conscious or unconscious emulation of significant figures with whom the person has identified. The ego ideal emphasizes what one should be or do in contrast to what one should not be or do.

egomania: See under *mania*.

ego-syntonic: Aspects of the individual's behavior, thoughts, and attitudes that he views as acceptable and consistent with his total personality. See also *ego-dystonic*.

eidetic image: Unusually vivid and apparently exact mental image; may be a memory, fantasy, or dream.

elaboration: In psychiatry, an unconscious psychologic process of expansion and embellishment of detail, especially with reference to a symbol or representation in a dream.

Electra complex: Obsolescent term. Analogous in the female to *Oedipus complex* (q.v. under *complex*).

electroconvulsive treatment: See *shock therapy.*

electroencephalogram (EEG): A graphic recording of minute electrical impulses arising from activity of cells in the brain. Used in neurologic and psychiatric diagnosis and research.

electroshock therapy (EST): See *electroconvulsive treatment* under *shock therapy.*

electrostimulation: See *electroconvulsive treatment* under *shock therapy.*

elope (elopement): In hospital psychiatry, a term sometimes used for a patient's unauthorized departure from a mental hospital.

emotion: A feeling such as fear, anger, grief, joy, or love. As used in psychiatry, emotions may not always be conscious. Synonymous with *affect.*

emotionally disturbed: Often used to describe a person with a *mental disorder.*

emotional health: Often used synonymously with *mental health.*

emotional illness: Often used synonymously with *mental disorder.*

empathy: An objective and insightful awareness of the feelings, emotions, and behavior of another person, their meaning and significance; to be distinguished from sympathy, which is usually nonobjective and noncritical.

encephalitis: A general term used to designate a diffuse inflammation of the brain. The condition may be acute or chronic and may be caused by a variety of agents such as viruses, bacteria, spirochetes, fungi, protozoa, and chemicals (such as lead). In addition to a number of neurological signs and symptoms, a variety of mental and behavioral changes occur during the illness and may persist beyond the acute phase of the illness. See *encephalopathy, organic brain syndromes.*

encephalopathy: A broad term designating any of the diffuse degenerative diseases of the brain. See *Alzheimer's disease, Pick's disease, encephalitis, Parkinsonism, Huntington's chorea, organic brain syndromes.*

encopresis: Inability to retain feces; incontinence. Cf. *enuresis.*

endocrine disorders: Dysfunction of any of the endocrine glands. Of special concern in psychiatry are those *psychophysiologic disorders* in which dysfunction of the endocrine glands may be caused or aggravated by emotional factors, or which, regardless of etiology, may produce varying degrees of mental and behavioral disturbances.

engram: A memory trace. Theoretically, a change in neural tissue that accounts for persistence of memory.

entropy: In psychiatry, diminished capacity for spontaneous change such as occurs in aging.

enuresis: Bed wetting.

epidemiology: In psychiatry, the study of the incidence, distribution, prevalence, and control of mental disorders in a given population. Common terms used in epidemiology are:

> **incidence:** The number of new cases of a mental disorder that occur in a given population over a set period of time, a year, for example.
>
> **epidemic:** Describes a disorder or the outbreak of a disorder that affects significant numbers of persons in a given population at any time.
>
> **endemic:** Describes a disorder that is native to or restricted to a particular area.
>
> **pandemic:** Describes a disorder that occurs over a very wide area or in many countries, or even universally.
>
> **prevalence:** The number of cases of a disorder that currently exists in a given population. **Point prevalence:** The number of cases that exists at a specific point in time. **Period prevalence:** The number of cases that exists in a defined period of time. **Lifetime prevalence:** The number of persons who have had a disorder in their lifetimes.

epilepsy: A disorder characterized by periodic motor or sensory seizures or their equivalents, and sometimes accompanied by a loss of consciousness or by certain equivalent manifestations. May be idiopathic (no known organic cause) or symptomatic (due to organic lesions). Usually accompanied by abnormal electrical discharge as shown by EEG. See also *convulsive disorders.*

> **epileptic equivalent:** Episodic, sensory, or motor phenomena which an individual with epilepsy may experience instead of convulsive seizures.
>
> **Jacksonian epilepsy:** Recurrent episodes of convulsive seizures or spasms localized in a part or region of the body without loss of consciousness. Named after Hughlings Jackson (1835–1911).
>
> **major epilepsy (grand mal):** Characterized by gross convulsive seizures with loss of consciousness.
>
> **minor epilepsy (petit mal):** Minor, nonconvulsive epileptic seizures or equivalents; may be limited to only momentary lapses of consciousness.

psychomotor epilepsy: Recurrent periodic disturbances, usually of behavior, during which the patient carries out movements often repetitive, highly organized but semi-automatic in character.

epileptoid personality disorder: See *explosive personality* under *personality disorders.*

epinephrine: One of the *catecholamines* secreted by the adrenal gland and by fibers of the *sympathetic nervous system.* It is responsible for many of the physical manifestations of fear and anxiety. Also known as adrenalin.

erogenous zone: See *erotogenic zone.*

erotic: Consciously or unconsciously invested with sexual feeling; sensually related.

erotogenic zone: An area of the body particularly susceptible to erotic arousal when stimulated, and especially the oral, anal, and genital areas. Sometimes called *erogenous zone.*

erotomania: See *−mania.*

erythrophobia: See under *phobia.*

ESP: See *extra-sensory perception.*

EST (also ECT): See *electroconvulsive treatment.*

ethology: The scientific study of the behavior of animals in their natural habitats. Also the empirical study of human behavior.

etiology: Causation, particularly with reference to disease.

euphoria: An exaggerated feeling of physical and emotional well-being not consonant with apparent stimuli or events; usually of psychologic origin, but also seen in organic brain diseases, toxic, and drug induced states.

executant ego function: A psychoanalytic term for the ego's management of the *mental mechanisms* in order to meet the needs of the organism. See also *ego.*

exhibitionism: See under *sexual deviation.*

existential psychiatry (existentialism): A school of psychiatry that has evolved out of orthodox psychoanalytic thought and incorporates the ideas of such existentialists as Kierkegaard, Heidigger, Sartre, and others. It focuses on the individual's subjective awareness of his style of existence, his intimate interaction with himself, his values, and his environment. Stress is placed on the way in which man experiences the phenomenological world about him and takes responsibility for his existence. Philosophically, the point of view is *holistic* and self-deterministic in contrast to biologically or culturally deterministic points of view. See also *phenomenology.*

explosive personality: See under *personality disorder.*

extrapsychic: That which takes place between the *psyche* (mind) and the environment.

extrapsychic conflict: See under *conflict.*

extrapyramidal syndrome: A variety of signs and symptoms, including muscular rigidity, tremors, drooling, restlessness, peculiar involuntary movements and postures, shuffling gait, protrusion of the tongue, chewing movements, blurred vision, and many other neurological disturbances. Results from dysfunction of the *extrapyramidal system.* May occur as a reversible side effect of certain psychotropic drugs, particularly *phenothiazines. Parkinson's disease* is an irreversible, organically caused manifestation of this syndrome.

extrapyramidal system: The portion of the *central nervous system* responsible for coordinating and integrating various aspects of motor behavior or bodily movements.

extrasensory perception (ESP): Perception without recourse to the conventional use of any of the five physical senses. See also *telepathy.*

extraversion: A state in which attention and energies are largely directed outward from the self, as opposed to inward toward the self, as in *introversion.*

family therapy: Treatment of more than one member of the family simultaneously in the same session. The treatment may be supportive, directive, or interpretive. The assumption is that a mental disorder in one member of a family may be a manifestation of disorder in other members and in their interrelationships and functioning as a total group.

fantasy: An imagined sequence of events or mental images, e.g., day dreams. Serves to express unconscious conflicts, to gratify unconscious wishes, or to prepare for anticipated future events.

fear: Emotional response to recognized sources of danger, to be distinguished from *anxiety.* See *phobia.*

feeblemindedness: Obsolete. See *mental retardation.*

fellatio: Sexual stimulation of the penis by oral contact.

fetish: An inanimate object, such as an article of apparel, symbolically endowed with special meaning. Often necessary for completion of the sexual act.

fetishism: See *sexual deviation.*

fixation: The arrest of psychosexual maturation. Depending on degree it may be either normal or pathological. See *psychosexual development.*

flagellantism: A masochistic or sadistic act in which one or both participants derive stimulation, usually erotic, from whipping or being whipped.

flexibilitas cerea: See *cerea flexibilitas.*

flight of ideas: Verbal skipping from one idea to another. The ideas appear to be continuous but are fragmentary and determined by chance associations. Sometimes seen in manic-depressive illness.

folie à deux: A condition in which two closely related persons, usually in the same family, share the same delusions.

forensic psychiatry: That branch of psychiatry dealing with the legal aspects of mental disorders.

forepleasure: Sexual play preceding intercourse.

formication: In psychiatry, the tactile hallucination or illusion that insects are crawling on the body.

free association: In psychoanalytic therapy, spontaneous, uncensored verbalization by the patient of whatever comes to mind.

free floating anxiety: Severe, generalized, persisting *anxiety.* Often a precursor of *panic.*

frigidity: Psychogenically inhibited female sexual response manifested by a variety of difficulties ranging from complete lack of sexual response to incomplete orgastic climax.

fugue: A major state of personality dissociation characterized by amnesia; may involve actual physical flight from the customary environment.

functional: In medicine, changes in the way an organ system operates that are not attributed to known structural alterations. While it is true that psychogenic disorders are functional in that their symptoms are not based on any detectable alterations in the structure of the brain or *psyche*, it is not true that all functional disorders of the psyche are of emotional origin any more than functional heart murmurs are based on emotional conflict. A drug-induced, temporary disturbance in central synaptic transmission, for example, may produce psychologic or behavioral abnormalities, but such changes in function are not correctly considered to be psychogenic in origin.

galvanic skin response (GSR): The resistance of the skin to the passage of a weak electric current: an easily measured variable widely used in experimental studies as a measure of an individual's response to emotion-arousing stimuli.

Ganser's syndrome: Sometimes called "non-sense syndrome" or "syndrome of approximate answers" (e.g., "two times two equals about ten"). Commonly used to characterize behavior of prisoners who seek—either consciously or unconsciously—to mislead others regarding their mental state in order to gain an advantage or escape responsibility.

gender identity: Denotes those aspects of appearance and behavior which society attributes to "masculinity' or "femininity." Gender identity is culturally determined and is to be distinguished from sexual identity, which is biologically determined. Such factors as body physique, external genitalia, cultural and parental attitudes and expectations combine to establish gender identity. Arbitrary cultural or group values may cause conflicts about gender identity by labelling certain non-sexual interests and behavior as being "masculine" or "feminine." See also *gender role.*

gender role: The learned roles and images that individuals present to their environment that declare them to be boy or man, or girl or woman. In a sense, *gender identity* is what society expects, while *gender role* is what the individual delivers. Usually the two will be congruent; however, they can be in opposition.

general paresis: See *general paralysis.*

general paralysis (general paresis): A chronic organic brain syndrome resulting from a chronic syphilitic infection. Occasionally associated with other neurological signs of syphilitic involvement of the nervous system. Detectable with laboratory tests of the blood or spinal fluid.

general systems theory: A theoretical framework that views events from the standpoint of the "systems" involved in the event. Systems are groups of organized interacting components. The behavior of each system is determined by its own structure, by the aggregate characteristics of its component systems ("subsystems"), and by the larger systems ("suprasystems") of which it is a component. Consequently, all systems may be viewed as part of an interrelated hierarchy (e.g., from subatomic particles to whole societies). The value of this theory in psychiatry lies in its emphasis on the *holistic* nature of personality (as compared to mechanistic, stimulus-response, and cybernetic theories, for example) and in its potential for advancing interdisciplinary understanding by integrating concepts about all of the systems, subsystems, and suprasystems that affect human behavior.

genes: The fundamental units of heredity. Composed of *DNA* and arranged in a characteristic linear order on *chromosomes* within cells, they determine the *genotype* of the individual.

genetic: (1) In biology, pertaining to *genes* or to inherited characteristics. (2) In psychiatry, pertaining to the historical development of an individual's psychological attributes or disorders.

genital phase: See under *psychosexual development*.

genotype: The total set of *genes* received by an individual at the time of conception; genetic constitution. The obverse of *phenotype*.

geriatrics: A branch of medicine dealing with the processes and diseases of the aging. Growing interest in the psychological aspects of the aging process has stimulated the growth of "geriatric psychiatry."

Gestalt psychology: A German school of psychology that emphasizes a total perceptual configuration and the interrelations of its component parts.

globus hystericus: An hysterical symptom in which there is a disturbing sensation of a lump in the throat. See also *hysterical neurosis, conversion type* under *neurosis*.

glossolalia: Gibberish speech.

grand mal: See *epilepsy*.

grandiose: In psychiatry, exaggerated belief or claims of one's importance or identity; often manifested by delusions of great wealth, power, or fame.

grief: Normal, appropriate emotional response to an external and consciously recognized loss; it is usually self-limited and gradually subsides within a reasonable time. To be distinguished from *depression*.

gross stress reaction: A term employed for an acute emotional reaction incident to severe environmental stress, as, for example, in military operations, industrial, domestic, or civilian disasters, and other life situations.

group process: A general term for the way a group goes about solving a common problem.

group psychotherapy: Application of psychotherapeutic techniques to a group, including utilization of interactions of members of the group.

group work: Recreational, social, educational, and cultural activities in the community to further the satisfactions and growth of participating group members by providing positive experiences through the group activity programs, interaction with other group members, and interaction of the group with the community. The trained group worker is skilled and knowledgable in individual and group behavior and community relations. Also called "social group work." Not to be confused with *group psychotherapy*.

habeas corpus: A legal document that brings into court a person held in custody (e.g., in a mental hospital) to determine whether the custody is legal.

halfway house: In psychiatry, a specialized residence for mental patients who do not require full hospitalization but who need an intermediate degree of protection and support before returning to fully independent community living.

hallucination: A false sensory perception in the absence of an actual external stimulus. May be induced by emotional and other factors such as drugs, alcohol, and stress. May occur in any of the senses.

hallucinogen: A chemical agent that produces hallucinations.

hallucinosis: A condition in which the patient hallucinates in a state of clear consciousness.

hebephrenia: See *schizophrenia*.

hedonism: In psychiatry, constant seeking of pleasure and avoidance of pain. See also *anhedonia*.

hermaphrodite: An individual who possesses both male and female sexual organs to some degree. Almost invariably one sex is predominant.

histrionic personality disorder: See *hysterical personality* under *personality disorders*.

holistic: In psychiatry, an approach to the study of the individual as a unique entity, rather than as an aggregate of physiological, psychological, and social characteristics.

hemostasis: The maintenance of self-regulating metabolic or psychologic processes which are optimal for comfort and survival.

homosexual panic: An acute and severe attack of anxiety based upon unconscious conflicts involving homosexuality.

homosexuality: See *sexual deviation*.

Huntington's chorea: An uncommon hereditary and progressively degenerative disease of the *central nervous system*. Onset is in adult life. Characterized by random movements (lurching, jerking) of the entire body and progressive mental deterioration.

hyperkinesis: Increased or excessive muscular activity seen in some neurological conditions, but more frequently in psychiatric disorders, especially in children.

hyperkinetic: Describes a disorder of childhood or adolescence characterized by overactivity, restlessness, distractibility, and short attention span.

hyperventilation: Overbreathing associated with anxiety and marked by reduction of blood carbon dioxide, subjective complaints of light-headedness, faintness, tingling of the extremities, palpitation, and feelings of inability to get enough air.

hypesthesia: A state of diminished sensitivity to tactile stimuli.

hypnagogic: Related to the semiconscious state immediately preceding sleep; sometimes also loosely used as equivalent to "hypnotic" or "sleep-inducing."

hypnagogic hallucinations: *Hallucinations* occurring during the hypnagogic state. Usually of no pathologic significance.

hypnosis: A state of increased receptivity to suggestion and direction, initially induced by the influence of another person. Often characterized by an altered state of consciousness similar to that observed in spontaneous dissociative conditions. The degree may vary from mild hypersuggestibility to a trance state with complete anesthesia.

hypnotic: Strictly speaking, any agent that induces sleep. While *sedatives* and *narcotics* in sufficient dosage may produce sleep as an incidental effect, the term "hypnotic" is appropriately reserved for drugs employed primarily to produce sleep. See also *addiction, drug dependency, tranquilizer, psychopharmacology.*

hypochondriacal neurosis: See under *neurosis.*

hypomania: A mild form of manic activity. See also *manic depressive illness.*

hysterical neurosis, dissociative type: See under *neurosis.*

hysterical personality: See under *personality disorder.*

hysterical psychosis: An unofficial term for an acute situational reaction in an histrionic type of person, usually manifested by the sudden onset of hallucinations, delusions, bizarre behavior, and volatile affect. As so defined, the term includes such exotic disorders as *amok, koro,* and *latah.*

hysterics: Lay term for uncontrollable emotional outbursts.

iatrogenic illness: An illness unwittingly precipitated, aggravated, or induced by the physician's attitude, examination, comments, or treatment.

ICD (ICD-8, ICDA): See *International Classification of Diseases.*

ICT (insulin coma therapy): See *shock treatment.*

id: In Freudian theory, that part of the personality structure which harbors the unconscious instinctive desires and strivings of the individual. See also *ego, superego.*

idealization: A *mental mechanism,* operating consciously or unconsciously, in which the individual overestimates an admired aspect or attribute of another person.

ideas of reference: Incorrect interpretation of casual incidents and external events as having direct reference to one's self. May reach sufficient intensity to constitute *delusions.*

idée fixe: Fixed idea. Loosely used to describe a compulsive drive, an obsessive idea, or a delusion.

identification: A *defense mechanism,* operating unconsciously by which an individual endeavors to pattern himself after another. Identification plays a major role in the development of one's personality and specifically of one's *superego.* To be differentiated from imitation, which is a conscious process.

identity crisis: A loss of the sense of the sameness and historical continuity of one's self, and inability to accept or adopt the role the subject perceives as being expected of him by society; often expressed by isolation, withdrawal, extremism, rebellion, and negativity, and typically triggered by a combination of sudden increase in the strength of instinctual drives in a milieu of rapid social evolution and technological change.

idiopathic: Of unknown cause.

idiot: Obsolescent term. See *mental retardation.*

idiot-savant: An individual with gross mental retardation who nonetheless is capable of performing certain remarkable "intellectual" feats such as calendar calculation and puzzle solving.

illusion: The misinterpretation of a real experience.

imago: In Jungian psychology, an unconscious mental image, usually idealized, of an important person in the early history of the individual.

imbecile: Obsolescent term. See *mental retardation.*

impotence: Usually refers to inability of the male to perform the sexual act, generally for psychologic reasons; more broadly used to indicate powerlessness or lack of sexual vigor.

imprinting: A relatively recent term used in *ethology* to refer to a process similar to rapid learning or behavioral patterning that occurs at critical points in very early stages of development in animals. The extent to which imprinting occurs in human development has not been established.

impulse: A psychic striving; usually refers to an instinctive urge.

impulse disorders: An unofficial term for a varied group of nonpsychotic disorders in which impulse control is weak. The impulsive behavior is usually pleasurable, irresistible, and *ego-syntonic*.

inadequate personality: See under *personality disorder*.

incompetent: A legal term for a person who, because of mental defect, cannot be held responsible in certain legal procedures such as making a will, entering into a contract, or standing trial.

incorporation: A primitive *defense mechanism*, operating unconsciously, in which the psychic representation of a person, or parts of him, are figuratively ingested. Example: infantile fantasy that the mother's breast has been ingested and is part of one's self.

individual psychology: The system of psychiatric theory, research, and therapy developed by *Alfred Adler* which stresses *compensation* and *overcompensation* for inferiority feelings.

Indoklon therapy: See *shock therapy*.

indoles: A group of *biogenic amines* derived from tryptophan. Certain of these amines, such as tryptamine and serotonin, exert an important influence on the activity of the *central nervous system*.

industrial psychiatry: See *occupational psychiatry*.

inferiority complex: See *complex*.

information theory: A philosophical system that deals with the mathematical characteristics of communicated messages and the systems that transmit, propagate, distort, or receive them.

inhibition: In psychiatry, an unconscious defense against forbidden instinctual drives; it may interfere with or restrict specific activities or general patterns of behavior.

insanity: A vague, legal term for psychosis, now obsolete in psychiatric usage. Generally connotes: (a) a mental incompetence, (b) inability to distinguish "right from wrong," and/or (c) a condition that interferes with the individual's ability to care for himself or that constitutes a danger to himself or to others. See *Currens Formula, Durham Decision, McNaghten Rule*.

insight: Self-understanding. The extent of the individual's understanding of the origin, na-ture, and mechanisms of his attitudes and behavior. More superficially, recognition by a patient that he is mentally ill.

instinct: An inborn *drive*. The primary human instincts include self-preservation and sexuality and—for some proponents—*aggression*, the *ego instincts*, and "herd" or "social" instincts. Freud also postulated a *death instinct*.

instrumental conditioning: See under *conditioning*.

insulin coma therapy: See *shock therapy*.

integration: The useful organization and incorporation of both new and old data, experience, emotional capacities into the personality. Also refers to the organization and amalgamation of functions at various levels of *psychosexual development*.

intellectualization: The *defense mechanism* that utilizes reasoning as a defense against conscious confrontation with unconscious conflicts and their stressful emotions.

intelligence: Capacity to learn and to utilize appropriately what one has learned. May be affected by emotions.

intelligence quotient (IQ): A numerical rating determined through psychological testing that indicates the approximate relationship of a person's mental age (MA) to his chronological age (CA). Expressed mathematically as $IQ = \dfrac{MA}{CA} \times 100$. Thus, if MA=6 and CA=12, then IQ=6/12 × 100 or 50 (retarded). If MA=12 and CA=12, then IQ = 100 (average). If MA=18 and CA=12, then IQ=150 (very superior). (Note: Since intellectual capacity is assumed to be fully developed about age 15, adult IQ's are computed by using a fixed arbitrary value of 15 for CA.)

International Classification of Diseases (ICD): The official list of disease categories issued by the World Health Organization. Subscribed to by all WHO member nations, who may assign their own terms to each ICD category. *ICDA* (*International Classification of Diseases, Adapted for Use in the United States*), prepared by the U.S. Public Health Service, represents the official list of diagnostic terms to be used for each ICD category in this country. *DSM-II* is based upon the eighth revision of the International Classification of Diseases (*ICD-8*) prepared in 1966.

interpretation: The process by which the therapist communicates to the patient understanding of a particular aspect of his problems or behavior.

intrapsychic: That which takes place within the *psyche* or mind.

intrapsychic conflict: See under *conflict*.

introjection: A *defense mechanism*, operating unconsciously, whereby loved or hated external objects are taken within oneself symbolically. The converse of *projection*. May serve as a defense against conscious recognition of intolerable hostile impulses. For example, in severe depression, the individual may unconsciously direct unacceptable hatred or aggression toward himself, i.e. toward the introjected object within himself. Related to the more primitive mechanism of *incorporation*.

introversion: Preoccupation with oneself and accompanying reduction of interest in the outside world. Roughly, the reverse of *extraversion*.

involutional melancholia (involutional psychosis): A *major affective disorder* occurring in late middle life and characterized by worry, anxiety, agitation, and severe insomnia. Feelings of guilt and somatic preoccupations are common and may be of delusional proportions.

involutional paranoid state (involutional paraphrenia): See under *paranoid states*.

inward aggression: See under *aggression*.

IQ: See *intelligence quotient*.

irresistible impulse test: A formula that states that a person is not responsible for a crime if his act was compelled by an irresistible impulse. This is usually construed to mean a psychotic or an obsessive-compulsive (neurotic) impulse and not a simple reaction of rage. Currently, the irresistible impulse test is accepted in 14 states, rejected in the remaining 36.

isolation: A *defense mechanism*, operating unconsciously, in which an unacceptable impulse, idea, or act is separated from its original memory source, thereby removing the emotional charge associated with the original memory.

Jacksonian epilepsy: See *epilepsy*.

kleptomania: See *–mania*.

koro: A culture-bound syndrome, this psychogenic disorder is found primarily among the peoples of Indonesia and South China. Koro is an acute anxiety reaction in which the patient feels that his penis is shrinking and will retract into his abdomen causing him to die. Occasionally, comparable anxiety is expressed by females, who complain of shrinking of their breasts and external genitalia.

Korsakov's psychosis: A mental disorder with brain damage characterized by amnesia, compensatory *confabulation*, disturbance of attention, and peripheral neuritis. Usually associated with *alcoholism* and dietary deficiencies.

la belle indifférence: Literally, "beautiful indifference." Seen in certain patients with hysterical neurosis, conversion type (q.v., under *neurosis*), who show an inappropriate lack of concern about their disabilities.

labile: In psychiatry, pertaining to rapidly shifting emotions; unstable.

lapsus linguae: A slip of the tongue due to unconcious factors.

latah: A culture-bound syndrome seen mostly among Malay-speaking peoples but also observed in the Philippines, Siberia, Lapland, North America, and Africa. Latah is a state of extreme suggestibility and mimicking in response to a sudden stimulus. The subject feels helplessly compelled to imitate any action he sees or repeat any word or sound he hears, regardless of its inappropriateness and unacceptability to him. This psychogenic disorder, with its compulsive *echolalia* and *echopraxia*, is usually relatively brief but may become chronic.

latency period: See under *psychosexual development*.

latent content: The hidden (unconscious) meaning of thoughts or actions, especially in dreams or fantasies. In dreams it is expressed in distorted, disguised, condensed, and symbolic form, which is known as the *manifest content*.

latent homosexuality: See under *sexual deviation*.

laterality: See under *speech disturbance*.

learning disturbance: See under *speech disturbance*.

lesbian: Homosexual woman.

libido: The psychic drive or energy associated with the sexual instinct. (Sexual is used here in the broad sense to include pleasure and love-object seeking.)

lithium therapy: The use of certain lithium salts in the treatment of *manic* and *hypomanic* states of excitement. See also *manic-depressive illness*.

lobotomy: See *psychosurgery*.

logorrhea: Uncontrollable, excessive talking.

LSD (lysergic acid diethylamide): An extremely potent drug that produces symptoms and behavior resembling certain psychoses. These symptoms may include *hallucinations, delusions,* and time-space distortions.

lunacy: Obsolete legal term for a major mental illness.

lunatic: Obsolete legal term for a psychotic person.

magical thinking: A person's conviction that thinking equates with doing. Occurs in dreams, in children and primitive peoples, and in patients under a variety of conditions. Characterized by lack of realistic relationship between cause and effect.

major affective disorders: A group of psychoses characterized by severe disorders of mood— either extreme depression or elation or both— that do not seem to be attributable entirely to precipitating life experiences. Includes *involutional melancholia* and the varieties of *manic-depressive illness.*

major epilepsy (grand mal): See under *epilepsy.*

maladjustment: See *adaptation.*

malingering: Deliberate simulation or exaggeration of an illness or disability that, in fact, is nonexistent or minor, in order to avoid an unpleasant situation or to obtain some type of personal gain. See also *compensation neurosis* and *secondary gain.*

–mania: Formerly used as a nonspecific term for any kind of "madness." Currently used as a suffix with any number of Greek roots to indicate a morbid preoccupation with some kind of idea or activity, and/or a compulsive need to behave in some deviant way. *Phobia* as a suffix is used in a similar way. For example, hellenomania, the tendency to use cumbersome Greek or Latin terms instead of readily understandable English words, characterizes the pseudo-erudite jargon of many fields as evidenced by the various terms (often unpreferred) listed below and elsewhere under *phobia.*

    dipsomania: Compulsion to drink alcoholic beverages.

    egomania: Pathological preoccupation with self.

    erotomania: Pathological preoccupation with erotic fantasies or activities.

    kleptomania: Compulsion to steal.

    megalomania: Pathological preoccupation with delusions of power or wealth.

    monomania: Pathological preoccupation with one subject.

    necromania: Pathological preoccupation with dead bodies.

    nymphomania: Abnormal and excessive need or desire in the female for sexual intercourse. Most nymphomaniacs, if not all, fail to achieve orgasm in the sexual act. See also *erotomania, satyriasis.*

    pyromania: Morbid compulsion to set fires.

    trichotillomania: Compulsion to pull out one's hair.

mania: A mood disorder characterized by excessive elation, hyperactivity, agitation, and accelerated thinking and speaking, sometimes manifested as *flight of ideas.* Mania is seen most frequently as one of the two major forms of *manic-depressive illness.*

maniac: Imprecise, sensational, and misleading lay term for an emotionally disturbed person. Usually implies violent behavior. Is not specifically referable to any psychiatric diagnostic category.

manic-depressive illness: A *major affective disorder* characterized by severe mood swings and a tendency to remission and recurrence. It is divided into the following three subgroups:

    depressed type: A kind of manic-depressive illness consisting exclusively of depressive episodes characterized by severely depressed mood and by mental and motor retardation that may progress to stupor. Uneasiness, apprehension, perplexity, and agitation may also be present.

    circular type: A manic-depressive illness distinguished by at least one depressive episode *and* a manic episode.

    manic type: A kind of manic-depressive illness consisting exclusively of manic episodes characterized by excessive elation, irritability, talkativeness, *flight of ideas*, and accelerated speech and motor activity.

manifest content: The remembered content of a dream or fantasy, as opposed to *latent content*, which it conceals and distorts.

MAO inhibitor (MAOI): *Monoamine oxidase inhibitor* (q.v.).

masculine protest: Term coined by *Alfred Adler* to describe a striving to escape identification with the feminine role. Applies primarily to women but may also be noted in the male.

masochism: See *sexual deviation.*

maximum security unit: A building or ward in a mental hospital or other institutional setting especially designed to prevent the escape of mental patients who have committed crimes or whose symptoms are a physical threat to the safety of others. See also *criminally insane.*

McNaghten Rule (Also M'Naghten, McNaughten, and McNaughton): The formula that holds a person not responsible for a crime if the accused "was laboring under such a defect of reason from disease of the mind as not to know the nature and quality of the act; or, if he did know it, that he did not know that he was doing what was wrong." This is the criminal responsibility formula in most states of the U.S.A. Also see *Currens Formula, Durham Decision*, and *irresistible impulse*.

megalomania: See *–mania*.

melancholia: See *involutional melancholia*.

menarche: The beginning of menstrual functioning.

mens rea: A guilty intent; that is, an intent to do harm. In a criminal case involving a defendant's mental state an important question may be whether he had *mens rea*, the ability to form an intention to do harm.

mental age: The age level of mental ability determined by standard intelligence tests; distinguished from chronologic age. See *intelligence quotient*.

mental deficiency: See *mental retardation*.

mental disease: See *mental disorder*.

mental disorder: Any psychiatric illness or disease included in the World Health Organization's *International Classification of Diseases*, or in the American Psychiatric Association's *Diagnostic and Statistical Manual of Mental Disorders*, Second Edition (1968). Many of these disorders are defined in this glossary.

mental health: A state of being, relative rather than absolute, in which a person has effected a reasonably satisfactory integration of his instinctual drives. His integration is acceptable to himself and to his social milieu as reflected in his interpersonal relationships, his level of satisfaction in living, his actual achievement, his flexibility, and the level of maturity he has attained.

mental hygiene: Measures employed to reduce the incidence of mental disorders through prevention and early treatment and to promote mental health.

mental illness: Same as *mental disorder*.

mental mechanism: A generic term for a variety of psychic processes that are functions of the *ego* and largely unconscious. Includes *perception*, memory, thinking, and *defense mechanisms*.

mental retardation: Subnormal general intellectual functioning, which may be evident at birth or develop during childhood. Learning, social adjustment, and maturation are impaired. Emotional disturbance is often present. The degree of retardation is commonly measured in terms of IQ: borderline (68–83), mild (52–67), moderate (36–51), severe (20–35), and profound (under 20).

mescaline: An alkaloid originally derived from the peyote cactus, resembling amphetamine and adrenalin chemically; used experimentally to induce hallucinations. Used by Indians of the Southwest in religious rites.

mesmerism: Early term for *hypnosis*. Named after *Anton Mesmer* (1733–1815).

metapsychology: The branch of theoretical or speculative psychology that deals with the significance of mental processes; the nature of the mind-body interrelationship; the origin, purpose, and structure of the mind; and similar hypotheses that are beyond the realm of empirical verification.

Methadone: A synthetic narcotic used to treat patients severely addicted to heroin. In effect, it replaces one addiction with another less socially disabling addiction. See also *narcotic blockade*.

Metrazol shock therapy: See *shock treatment*.

migraine: A syndrome characterized by recurrent, severe, and usually one-sided headaches, often associated with nausea, vomiting, and visual disturbances. May be related to unconscious emotional conflicts.

milieu therapy: Literally, treatment by environment in a hospital setting. Physical surroundings, equipment, and staff attitudes are structured in such a way as to enhance the effectiveness of other therapies and foster the patient's rehabilitation. See also *total push therapy, therapeutic community*.

minor epilepsy (petit mal): See under *epilepsy*.

MMPI (Minnesota Multiphasic Personality Inventory): A questionnaire type of psychological test designed for persons sixteen years of age and over. It may be administered individually or in groups. Although the MMPI has certain limitations, as a self-reporting test it is one of the most carefully validated and reliable instruments of its kind.

mongolism: Archaic term for *Down's syndrome*.

monoamine oxidase inhibitor (MAOI): A group of antidepressant drugs that appear to ameliorate the emotional state by inhibiting certain brain enzymes and raising the level of *serotonin*.

monomania: See *–mania*.

moral treatment: A philosophy and technique of treating mental hospital patients that prevailed in the first half of the nineteenth century. It emphasized removal of restraints, humane and kindly care, attention to religion, and performance of useful tasks in the hospital. Historically, the antecedent of the modern *therapeutic community* and *milieu therapy*.

moron: Obsolescent term for an individual with borderline or mild *mental retardation.*

multiple personality: A term used by *Morton Prince* for a rare type of dissociative reaction in which the individual adopts two or more different personalities. These are separate and compartmentalized, with total amnesia for the one, or ones, not in awareness.

mutation: In biology, a change in hereditary constitution that causes genetically transmissable permanent differences between the characteristics of an individual and those of his parents; may occur spontaneously or may be induced by such agents as high-energy radiation. See also *genes*.

mutism: In psychiatry, refusal to speak for conscious or unconscious reasons. Often seen in *psychosis*.

mysophobia: See under *phobia*.

narcissism (narcism): From Narcissus, figure in Greek mythology who fell in love with his own reflected image. Self-love, as opposed to object-love (love of another person). In psychoanalytic theory, cathexis (investment) of the psychic representation of the self with libido (sexual interest and energy). Some degree of narcissism is considered healthy and normal, but an excess interferes with relations with others. To be distinguished from egotism, which carries the connotation of self-centeredness, selfishness, and conceit. Egotism is but one expression of narcissism. See also *cathexis*, and *libido*.

narcoanalysis: See *narcosynthesis*.

narcolepsy: Brief, uncontrollable episodes of sleeping.

narcosis: *Stupor*, of varying depth, induced by certain drugs.

narcosynthesis: Psychotherapeutic treatment under partial anesthesia, e.g. as induced by sodium amytal or pentothal. Originally used to treat acute mental disorders caused by military combat.

narcotic: Any drug, natural or synthetic, that produces sleep or even *stupor* and relieves pain. See *addiction*, *drug dependency*, *hypnotic*, *sedative*.

narcotic blockade: Total or partial inhibition of the euphoria produced by narcotic drugs through the use of other drugs, such as *Methadone*, which can then be used as maintenance

treatment without producing the peaks of elation, *withdrawal symptoms*, and demand for increasing dosage that characterize addiction to opiates.

necromania: See *mania*.

negative feelings: In psychiatry, unfriendly, hostile feelings.

negativism: Perverse opposition and resistance to suggestions or advice. Often observed in people who subjectively feel "pushed around." Seen normally in late infancy. A common symptom in *catatonic schizophrenia* (q.v., under *schizophrenia*).

neologism: A new word or condensed combination of several words coined by a person to express a highly complex idea often related to his conflicts; not readily understood by others; common in *schizophrenia*.

neoplasm: A new growth or tumor. Neoplasms that affect behavior are primarily, but not exclusively, found within the cranial cavity. Such neoplasms may cause mental and behavioral disturbances in addition to neurological signs and symptoms. See *organic brain syndromes*.

nervous breakdown: A nonmedical, nonspecific term; a euphemism for a mental disorder.

neurasthenic neurosis (neurasthenia): See under *neurosis*.

neurologist: A physician with postgraduate training and experience in the field of organic diseases of the nervous system and whose professional work focuses primarily in this area.

neurology: The branch of medical science devoted to the study, diagnosis, and treatment of organic diseases of the nervous system.

neuropsychiatry: Combination of the specialties of neurology and psychiatry.

neuroleptic: A synonym for major tranquilizers. (q.v., under *tranquilizer*).

neurosis (psychoneurosis): An emotional maladaption characterized chiefly by anxiety arising from some unresolved unconscious conflicts. This anxiety is either felt directly or controlled by various psychological mechanisms to produce other, subjectively distressing symptoms. The neuroses are usually considered less severe than the psychoses (although not always less disabling) because they manifest neither gross personality disorganization nor gross distortion or misinterpretation of external reality. The neuroses are classified according to the predominating symptoms. The common neuroses are:

  anxiety neurosis: A neurosis characterized by anxious over-concern occasionally progressing to panic; frequently associated with somatic symptoms.

depersonalization neurosis: A neurosis characterized by feelings of unreality and of estrangement from the self, body, or surroundings. Different from the process of *depersonalization*, which may be a manifestation of normal anxiety or of another mental disorder.

depressive neurosis: A neurosis manifested by an excessive reaction of depression due to an internal conflict or to an identifiable event, such as a loss of a loved person or a cherished possession.

hypochondriacal neurosis: A neurosis characterized by preoccupation with the body and with fear of presumed diseases of various organs. Although the fears are not delusional in quality, they persist despite reassurance.

hysterical neurosis: A neurosis characterized by a sudden psychogenic loss or disorder of function in response to an emotional stress. This disorder is divided into two subtypes:

> **conversion type:** An hysterical neurosis manifested by disorders of the special senses or the voluntary nervous system, such as blindness, deafness, *anesthesia*, *paresthesia*, paralysis, and impaired muscular coordination. A patient with this disorder may show *la belle indifférence* about his symptoms, which may actually provide *secondary gains* by winning him sympathy or relieving him of unpleasant responsibilities. See also *conversion*.

> **dissociative type:** An hysterical neurosis manifested by alterations in the patient's state of consciousness or in his identity, producing such symptoms as *amnesia*, *somnambulism*, *fugue*, or *multiple personality*. See also *dissociation*.

neurasthenic neurosis (neurasthenia): A neurosis characterized by complaints of chronic weakness, easy fatigability, and exhaustion.

obsessive compulsive neurosis: A neurosis characterized by the persistent intrusion of unwanted thoughts, urges, or actions that the individual is unable to stop. The thoughts may consist of single words or ideas, ruminations, or trains of thought that the individual often views as nonsensical. The actions may vary from simple movements to complex rituals, such as repeated handwashing. See also *compulsion*.

phobic neurosis: A neurosis characterized by intense fear of an object or situation that the individual consciously recognizes as

harmless. His apprehension may be experienced as faintness, fatigue, palpations, perspiration, nausea, tremor, and even panic. See also *phobia*.

night hospital: See under *partial hospitalization*.

nihilism: In psychiatry, the delusion of nonexistence of the self or part of the self.

norepinephrine: The neurohormone of the peripheral sympathetic nervous system. A *catecholamine* related to *epinephrine*. Also known as noradrenalin.

nosology: Medical science of classification of diseases.

NREM sleep: See *REM Sleep*.

nymphomania: See *–mania*.

object relations: The emotional bonds that exist between an individual and another person, as contrasted with his interest in, and love for, himself; usually described in terms of his capacity for loving and reacting appropriately to others.

obsession: A persistent, unwanted idea or impulse that cannot be eliminated by logic or reasoning.

obsessive compulsive neurosis: See under *neurosis*.

obsessive compulsive personality: See under *personality disorder*.

occupational psychiatry: A field of psychiatry concerned with the diagnosis and prevention of mental illness in industry and with psychiatric aspects of absenteeism, accident proneness, personnel policies, operational fatigue, vocational adjustment, retirement, and related phenomena.

occupational therapy: An adjunctive therapy that utilizes purposeful activities as a means of altering the course of illness. The patient's relationship to staff personnel and to other patients in the occupational therapy setting is often more therapeutic than the activity itself.

Oedipus complex: See under *complex*.

oligophrenia: A term for *mental retardation*.

onanism: Incomplete sexual relations with withdrawal just prior to emission. Coitus interruptus. Incorrectly used as a synonym for masturbation.

ontogenetic: Pertaining to the biological development of the individual. Distinguished from *phylogenetic*.

open hospital: Literally, a mental hospital, or section thereof, that has no locked doors or other forms of physical restraint.

operant conditioning: See *conditioning.*

oral phase: See *psychosexual development.*

organic brain syndrome (OBS): A disorder caused by or associated with impairment of brain tissue function. It may be manifested by disorientation, loss of memory, and impairment of the ability to learn, comprehend, calculate, and exercise judgment. May be psychotic or nonpsychotic, mild, moderate, or severe. Simple drunkenness is an example of nonpsychotic OBS, and *senile dementia* of the psychotic type.

organic disease: A disease characterized by significant demonstrable structural or biochemical abnormality in an organ or tissue. Sometimes imprecisely used as an antonym for *functional* illness.

organic psychosis: A severe psychiatric disorder resulting from a demonstrable physical disturbance of brain function such as a tumor, infection, or injury. Characterized by impaired memory, orientation, intelligence, judgment, and mood. See also *psychosis,* and *organic brain syndrome.*

orientation: Awareness of oneself in relation to time, place, and person.

orienting reflex (OR): Pavlovian term used to describe response to a novel stimulus which is not sufficiently strong to elicit a specific inborn *unconditioned reflex* and to which an individual has not learned to produce a conditioned reflex. Turning of the head, focusing of the eyes or ears to a nonspecific noise, light, or touch are examples. See *conditioning.*

orthopsychiatry: An approach to the study and treatment of human behavior that involves the collaborative effort of psychiatry, psychology, psychiatric social work, and other behavioral, medical, and social sciences in the study and treatment of human behavior in the clinical setting. Emphasis is placed on preventive techniques to promote healthy emotional growth and development, particularly of children.

overcompensation: A conscious or unconscious process in which a real or fancied physical or psychologic deficit inspires exaggerated correction.

overdetermination: In psychiatry, a term indicating the multiple causality of a single emotional reaction or symptom. Thus, a single symptom expresses the confluence and condensation of unconscious drives and needs as well as the defenses against them.

overt homosexuality: See under *sexual deviation.*

panic: In psychiatry, an attack of acute, intense, and overwhelming anxiety, accompanied by a considerable degree of personality disorganization. See *anxiety.*

panphobia: See under *phobia.*

paranoia: See under *paranoid states.*

paranoid: An adjective applied to individuals who are oversuspicious, some of whom may also harbor grandiose or persecutory *delusions,* or *ideas of reference.*

paranoid personality: See under *personality disorder.*

paranoid states: Psychotic disorders in which a delusion, generally persecutory or grandiose, is the essential abnormality and accounts for disturbances in mood, behavior, and thinking (including *hallucinations*) that may be present. Its two major subdivisions are:

> **involutional paranoid state (involutional paraphrenia):** A paranoid psychosis characterized by delusion formation that begins in the involutional period. Distinguished from *schizophrenia, paranoid type,* by the absence of a schizophrenic thought disorder.

> **paranoia:** An extremely rare condition characterized by the gradual development of an intricate, complex, and elaborate paranoid system based on (and often proceeding logically from) misinterpretation of an actual event. Frequently the individual considers himself endowed with unique and superior ability. In spite of a chronic course, this condition does not seem to interfere with the rest of the individual's thinking and personality. To be distinquished from *schizophrenia, paranoid type,* and involutional *paranoid state.*

paraphasia: See *speech disturbance.*

paraphrenia: A *paranoid state* consisting of a persecutory or grandiose delusional system without the primary disturbances of thinking and affect that characterize *schizophrenia, paranoid type.* See also *involutional paranoid state* under *paranoid states.*

parapraxis: A faulty act, blunder or lapse of memory such as a slip of the tongue or misplacement of an article. According to Freud, these acts are caused by unconscious motives.

parapsychology: The study of metapsychic (psi) phenomena, i.e., events caused or perceived without the ordinary use of physical actions or senses. Example: predicting outcome of throw of dice. See also *psychokinesis* and *extrasensory perception (ESP).*

parasympathetic nervous system: That part of the *autonomic nervous system* that controls the life-sustaining organs of the body under normal, danger-free conditions. See also *sympathetic nervous system.*

parataxic distortion: Sullivan's term for certain distortions in judgment and perception, particularly in interpersonal relations, based upon the observer's need to perceive subjects and relationships in accordance with a pattern set by earlier experience. Parataxic distortions develop as a defense against anxiety.

paresis: Weakness of organic origin; incomplete paralysis; term often used instead of *general paresis.*

paresthesia: Abnormal tactile sensation. Often described as burning, prickling, tickling, tingling, or creeping. May be hallucinatory in certain psychoses or a manifestation of neurological disease.

Parkinson's disease: See *extrapyramidal syndrome.*

parole: In psychiatry, technical term for the conditional release of a patient from a mental hospital prior to formal discharge so that the patient may be returned to the hospital if necessary without legal action. Obsolescent because of its association with parole from prison. Similar in meaning to "trial visit," "on leave," and "home leave."

partial hospitalization: A psychiatric treatment program for patients who require hospitalization but not on a full-time basis. For example:

> **day hospital:** A special facility or an arrangement within a hospital setting that enables the patient to come to the hospital for treatment during the day and return home at night.

> **night hospital:** A hospital or hospital service for patients who are able to work or otherwise function in the community during the day but who require specialized treatment and supervision in a hospital setting after working hours.

> **weekend hospital:** A hospital setting providing a treatment program over weekends. The patient resumes his usual work and activities outside the hospital during the week.

passive-aggressive personality: See under *personality disorder.*

passive-dependent personality: A disorder manifested by marked indecisiveness, emotional dependency, and lack of self-confidence. For diagnostic purposes, once considered to be a subtype of *passive-aggressive personality*. See under *personality disorders.*

pastoral counseling: The use of psychological principles by clergymen in interviews with parishioners who seek help with emotional problems.

pathognomic: A medical term applied to a symptom or group of symptoms that are specifically diagnostic or typical of a disease entity.

pavor nocturnus: Nightmare.

pederasty: See *sexual deviation.*

pedophilia: See *sexual deviation.*

pellagra: A specific vitamin deficiency disease that manifests major mental symptoms, such as *delusions* and impaired thinking. It is correctable by treatment with vitamin B_3 (nicotinamide).

penis envy: Literally, envy by the female of the penis of the male. More generally, the female wish for male attributes, position, or advantages. Believed by many to be a significant factor in female character development.

perception: The *mental mechanism* by which the nature and meaning of sensory stimuli are recognized and interpreted by comparing them with stimuli associated with past experiences.

perseveration: Involuntary and pathological persistence of a single response or idea in reply to various questions. Seen most often in organic brain disease.

persona: A Jungian term for the personality "mask" or facade that each person presents to the outside world. Distinguished from the person's inner being or *anima* (q.v.).

personality: The characteristic way in which a person behaves; the deeply ingrained pattern of behavior that each person evolves, both consciously and unconsciously, as his style of life or way of being in adapting to his environment. See *adaptation, character disorder, personality disorder.*

personality disorders: A group of mental disorders characterized by deeply ingrained maladaptive patterns of behavior, generally life-long in duration and consequently often recognizable by the time of adolescence or earlier. Affecting primarily the personality of the individual, they are different in quality from *neurosis* and *psychosis.*

> **antisocial personality:** A personality disorder characterized by a basic lack of socialization and by behavior patterns that bring the individual repeatedly into conflict with society. People with this disorder are incapable of significant loyalty to individuals, groups, or social values and are grossly selfish, callous, irresponsible, impulsive, and unable to feel guilt or to learn from experience and punishment. Frustration tolerance is low. Such individuals tend to blame others or offer plausible rationalizations for their behavior.

asthenic personality: A personality disorder characterized by easy fatigability, low energy level, lack of enthusiasm, marked incapacity for enjoyment, and over-sensitivity to physical and emotional stress.

cyclothymic personality (affective personality): A personality disorder characterized by recurring and alternating periods of depression and elation not readily attributable to external circumstances.

explosive personality: A personality disorder characterized by gross outbursts of rage or of verbal or physical aggressiveness. Outbursts are strikingly different from the individual's usual behavior, and he may be regretful and repentant for them. See also *aggression.*

hysterical personality (histrionic personality disorder): A personality disorder characterized by excitability, emotional instability, over-reactivity, and self-dramatization that is attention-seeking and often seductive, whether or not the individual is aware of its purpose. Often individuals with this disorder are immature, self-centered, vain, and unusually dependent on others.

inadequate personality: A personality disorder characterized by ineffectual responses to emotional, social, intellectual, and physical demands. While the individual seems neither physically not mentally deficient, he does manifest inadaptibility, ineptness, poor judgment, social instability, and lack of physical and emotional stamina.

obsessive compulsive personality (anankastic personality): A personality disorder characterized by excessive concern with conformity and adherence to standards of conscience. Individuals with this disorder may be rigid, over-inhibited, over-conscientious, over-dutiful, indecisive, perfectionistic, and unable to relax easily.

paranoid personality: A personality disorder characterized by hypersensitivity, rigidity, unwarranted suspicion, jealousy, envy, excessive self-importance, and a tendency to blame others and ascribe evil motives to them.

passive-aggressive personality: A personality disorder characterized by aggressive behavior manifested in passive ways, such as obstructionism, pouting, procrastination, intentional inefficiency, or stubbornness. The aggression often arises from resentment at failing to find gratification in a relationship with an individual or institution upon which the individual is over-dependent.

schizoid personality: A personality disorder manifested by shyness, over-sensitivity, seclusiveness, frequent daydreaming, avoidance of close or competitive relationships, and often eccentricity. Individuals with this condition often react to disturbing experiences and conflicts with apparent detachment and are often unable to express hostility and ordinary aggressive feelings.

persuasion: In psychiatry, a therapeutic approach based on direct suggestion and guidance intended to influence favorably patients' attitudes, behavior, and goals.

perversion: Any *sexual deviation.*

petit mal: See *epilepsy.*

phallic phase: See under *psychosexual development.*

phantom limb: A phenomenon frequently experienced by amputees, in which sensations, often painful, appear to originate in the amputated extremity.

phenomenology: The study of occurrences or happenings in their own right, rather than from the point of view of inferred causes; specifically, the theory that behavior is determined, not by external reality as it can be described objectively in physical terms, but rather by the way in which the subject perceives that reality at any moment. See *existentialism.*

phenothiazine derivatives: A group of *psychotropic* drugs that, chemically, have in common the phenothiazine nucleus but that differ from one another through variations in chemical structure. As a group of drugs, the phenothiazines are also known as *major tranquilizers* possessing marked antianxiety and antipsychotic properties. See *psychopharmacology* and the other terms listed there.

phenotype: The observable attributes of an individual; the physical manifestations of his *genotype* (q.v.).

phenylketonuria: See *PKU.*

phenylpyruvic oligophrenia: See *PKU.*

phobia: An obsessive, persistent, unrealistic intense fear of an object or situation. The fear is believed to arise through a process of displacing an internal (unconscious) conflict to an external object symbolically related to the conflict. (See also *displacement.*) Some of the common phobias are:

acrophobia: Fear of heights.

agoraphobia: Fear of open places.

ailurophobia: Fear of cats.

algophobia: Fear of pain.

claustrophobia: Fear of closed spaces.

erythrophobia: Fear of blushing; sometimes used to refer to the blushing itself.

mysophobia: Fear of dirt and germs.

panphobia: Fear of everything.

xenophobia: Fear of strangers.

phobic neurosis: See under *neurosis*.

phrenology: Abandoned theory of relationship between bony structure of the skull and mental traits.

phylogenetic: Pertaining to the evolutionary or racial history of the species. See also *ontogenetic*.

pica: A craving for unnatural food; a perverted appetite. Example: children eating plaster or dirt. Seen in hysteria, pregnancy, and emotional disturbances in children.

Pick's disease: A presenile degenerative disease of the brain affecting the cerebral cortex, particularly the frontal lobes. Symptoms include intellectual deterioration, emotional instability, and loss of social adjustment. See also *Alzheimer's disease*.

PKU (phenylketonuria): A congenital metabolic disturbance characterized by an inability to convert phenylalanine to tyrosine. Results in the abnormal accumulation of chemicals that interfere with brain development. Transmitted genetically. Treatable by diet when detected in infancy. Detectable by testing the urine for the presence of phenylpyruvic acid. If untreated, mental retardation results. Also known as *phenylpyruvic oligophrenia*.

placebo: Originally, an inactive substance such as a "bread pill" given to "placate" a patient who demands medication that is not necessary. Useful in research and practice because of its potential psychological effect, which may be neutral, therapeutic, or noxious depending on suggestion by the therapist or experimenter and the patient's own expectations, faith, fear, apprehension, or hostility. In British usage a placebo is sometimes called a "dummy."

play therapy: A treatment technique utilizing the child's play as a medium for expression and communication between patient and therapist.

pleasure principle: The psychoanalytic concept that man instinctually seeks to avoid pain and discomfort and strives for gratification and pleasure. In personality development theory the pleasure principle antedates and subsequently comes in conflict with the *reality principle* (q.v.).

polyphagia: Pathological overeating.

porphyria: A metabolic disorder characterized by the excretion of porphyrins in the urine and accompanied by attacks of abdominal pain, peripheral neuropathy, and a variety of mental symptoms.

positive feeling: In psychiatry, warm, friendly feelings, as opposed to negative, hostile feelings.

portpartum psychosis: A psychotic episode, usually schizophrenic in nature, following childbirth. Organic or toxic factors may be responsible.

potency: In psychiatry, the male's ability to carry out sexual relations. Often used to refer specifically to the capacity to have and maintain adequate erection of the penis during sexual intercourse.

preconscious: Referring to thoughts that are not in immediate awareness but that can be recalled by conscious effort.

prefrontal lobotomy: A type of *psychosurgery*.

pregenital: In psychoanalysis, refers to the period of early childhood before the genitals have begun to exert the predominant influence in the organization or patterning of sexual behavior. Oral and anal influences predominate during this period. See also *anal erotism* and *oral phase* under *psychosexual development*.

prevention (preventive psychiatry): In traditional medical usage, the prevention or prophylaxis of a disorder. The modern trend, particularly in *community psychiatry*, is to broaden the meaning of prevention to encompass also the amelioration, control, and limitation of disease. Prevention is often categorized as follows:

> **primary prevention:** Measures to prevent a mental disorder, (e.g., preventing *general paralysis* with adequate doses of penicillin in treating syphilis).

> **secondary prevention:** Measures to limit a disease process, (e.g., through early case finding and treatment).

> **tertiary prevention:** Measures to reduce impairment or disability following a disorder, (e.g., through rehabilitation programs).

primal scene: In psychoanalytic theory, the real or fancied observation by the infant of parental or other heterosexual intercourse.

primary gain: The relief from emotional conflict and the freedom from anxiety achieved by a *defense mechanism*. The concept is that mental states, both normal and pathological, develop defensively in largely unconscious attempts to cope with or to resolve unconscious conflicts. All *mental mechanisms* operate in the service of the primary gain, and the need for such gain may be thought of as responsible for the initiation of an emotional illness. To be distinguished from *secondary gain*.

primary process: In psychoanalytic theory, the generally unorganized mental activity characteristic of unconscious mental life. Seen in less disguised form in infancy and in dreams. It is marked by the free discharge of energy and excitation without regard to the demands of environment, reality, or logic. See also *secondary process.*

prison psychosis: Term for emotional reactions of psychotic depth precipitated by actual or anticipated incarceration.

privilege: The legal right of a patient, always established by statute, to prevent his physician from testifying about information gleaned in the course of his treatment by the physician. Thus, a legal affirmation of the ethical principle of *confidentiality.* Many states have privileged communication laws.

> **privileged communication:** A legal term for information that a patient discloses to his physician while the latter attends him in a professional capacity. The information is termed "privileged" because in some states by law, and universally according to medical ethics, the physician is not allowed to divulge such information without the patient's consent. Also, the medical record of a patient is regarded as a privileged communication in jurisdictions where privilege is established by law, and in any case, as a *confidential* communication where it is not.

process schizophrenia: See under *schizophrenia.*

projection: A *defense mechanism,* operating unconsciously, whereby that which is emotionally unacceptable in the self is unconsciously rejected and attributed (projected) to others.

projective tests: Psychological tests used as a diagnostic tool in which the test material is so unstructured that any response will reflect a projection of some aspect of the subject's underlying personality and psychopathology. Among the most common projective tests are the *Rorschach* (inkblot) and the *Thematic Apperception Test (TAT).*

psychasthenia: Largely obsolete term introduced by *Janet* to include obsessions, compulsions, doubts, feelings of inadequacy, and phobias. See also *neurasthenia.*

psyche: The mind.

psychedelic: A term applied to any of several drugs that may induce hallucinations and psychotic states, including the production of bizarre distortion of time, sound, color, etc. Among the more commonly used psychedelics are *LSD, marijuana, mescaline,* morning-glory seeds, psilocybin.

psychiatric illness: See *mental disorders.*

psychiatrist: A doctor of medicine who specializes in *psychiatry.*

psychiatry: The medical science that deals with the origin, diagnosis, prevention, and treatment of mental disorders.

psychic determinism: See *determinism.*

psychic energizer: A popular term for drugs that stimulate or elevate the mood of a depressed patient.

psychoanalysis: A psychologic theory of human development and behavior, a method of research, and a system of psychotherapy, originally developed by Sigmund Freud. Through analysis of free associations and interpretation of dreams, emotions and behavior are traced to the influence of repressed instinctual drives and defenses against them in the unconscious. Psychoanalytic treatment seeks to eliminate or diminish the undesirable effects of unconscious conflicts by making the patient aware of their existence, origin, and inappropriate expression in current emotions and behavior.

psychoanalyst: A psychiatrist who has had additional training in psychoanalysis and who employs the techniques of psychoanalytic therapy.

psychobiology: The science of the human being as an integrated unit. Specifically, it views the individual not as having a psychological and a biological set of functions, but rather as functioning as an integrated unit. Generally associated with *Adolf Meyer,* who introduced the term in the United States in 1915.

psychodrama: A technique of group psychotherapy in which individuals dramatize their emotional problems.

psychodynamics: The systematized knowledge and theory of human behavior and its motivation, the study of which depends largely upon the functional significance of emotion. Psychodynamics recognizes the role of unconscious motivation in human behavior. It is a predictive science, based on the assumption that a person's total make-up and probable reactions at any given moment are the product of past interactions between his specific genetic endowment and the environment in which he has lived from conception onward.

psychogenesis: Production or causation of a symptom or illness by mental or psychic factors as opposed to organic ones.

psychokinesis: The belief that directed thought processes can influence an event such as a throw of dice. See also *parapsychology* and *extrasensory perception (ESP).*

psycholinguistics: The study of factors affecting activities involved in communicating and comprehending verbal information.

psychologist: One who specializes in psychology. Generally holds a Ph.D. or M.A. degree.

psychologist, clinical: A psychologist with a graduate degree, usually a Ph.D., and with additional supervised training and experience in a clinical setting, who specializes in the evaluation and psychological treatment of mental disorders. Frequently clinical psychologists work in medical settings in collaboration with psychiatrists and other physicians.

psychology: An academic discipline, a profession, and a science dealing with the study of mental processes and behavior in man and animals. See also *psychiatry.*

psychology, analytic: See *analytic psychology* and *Jung.*

psychology, individual: See *individual psychology.*

psychometry: The science of testing and measuring mental and psychologic ability, efficiency, potentials, and functioning, including psychopathologic components. An example is the Stanford-Binet test for intelligence.

psychomotor epilepsy: See under *epilepsy.*

psychomotor excitement: Generalized physical and emotional overactivity in response to internal and/or external stimuli as in hypomania.

psychomotor retardation: A generalized retardation of physical and emotional reactions. The opposite of *psychomotor excitement.*

psychoneurosis: See *neurosis.*

psychoneurotic disorders: See *neurosis.*

psychopathic personality: An informal term for *anti-social personality.* Afflicted individuals are referred to casually as "psychopaths."

psychopathology: The study of the significant causes and processes in the development of mental illness. Also the manifestations of mental illness.

psychopharmacology: The study of the mental and behavioral effects of certain drugs. Some of the many facets of psychopharmacology are described in this glossary under the following terms: *antidepressant, ataractic, neuroleptic, psychedelic, psychic energizer, psychotomimetic, psychotropic, tranquilizer.*

psychophysiologic disorders: A group of disorders characterized by physical symptoms that are caused by emotional factors and that involve a single organ system, usually under *autonomic nervous system* control. Symptoms are caused by physiological changes that normally accompany certain emotional states, but in these disorders the changes are more intense and sustained. Frequently called "psychosomatic disorders." These disorders are usually named and classified according to the organ system involved (e.g., musculo-skeletal, respiratory).

psychosexual development: In psychoanalysis, a term encompassing the various stages of libidinal maturation from infancy to adulthood. The way in which a child experiences these stages significantly influences his basic personality characteristics in later life. The stages are:

> **oral phase:** The earliest of the stages of infantile psychosexual development, lasting from birth to 12 months or longer. Usually subdivided into two stages: the **oral erotic,** relating to the pleasurable experience of sucking; and the **oral sadistic,** associated with aggressive biting. Both oral erotism and sadism continue into adult life in disguised and sublimated forms.

> **anal phase:** The period of pregenital psychosexual development, usually from one to three years, in which the child has particular interest and concern with the process of defecation and the sensations connected with the anus. The pleasurable part of the experience is termed *anal erotism.* See also *anal character.*

> **phallic phase:** The period from about two and a half to six years during which sexual interest, curiosity, and pleasurable experience center about the penis, and in girls, to a lesser extent, the clitoris.

> **latency period:** The period from about five to seven years to adolescence when there is an apparent cessation of psychosexual development.

> **genital phase:** The culminating stage of development in which a person achieves a genuinely affectionate, mature relationship with a sex partner.

psychosis: A major mental disorder of organic or emotional origin in which the individual's ability to think, respond emotionally, remember, communicate, interpret reality, and behave appropriately is sufficiently impaired so as to interfere grossly with his capacity to meet the ordinary demands of life. Often characterized by regressive behavior, inappropriate mood, diminished impulse control, and such abnormal mental content as delusions and hallucinations. The term is applicable to conditions having a wide range of severity and duration. See also *schizophrenia, manic-depressive illness, reactive depression, involutional melancholia,* and *organic brain syndrome.*

psychosomatic: Adjective to denote the constant and inseparable interaction of the *psyche* (mind) and the *soma* (body). Most commonly used to refer to illnesses in which the manifestations are primarily physical with at least a partial emotional etiology. See also *psychophysiologic disorders*.

psychosurgery: Treatment of chronic, severe, and intractable psychiatric disorders by surgical removal or interruption of certain areas or pathways in the brain, especially in the prefrontal lobes.

psychotherapy: The generic term for any type of treatment that is based primarily upon verbal or nonverbal communication with the patient as distinguished from the use of drugs, surgery, or physical measure such as electroconvulsive treatment. The basic treatment method used by psychiatrists either alone or in conjunction with other forms of treatment. See also *psychoanalysis, group therapy*.

psychotic depressive reaction: A psychosis distinguished by a depressive mood attributed to some experience. It is *not* considered one of the *major affective disorders* (q.v.).

psychotomimetic: Literally, mimicking a psychosis. Used to refer to certain drugs such as *LSD* (lysergic acid diethlyamide) or *mescaline*, which produce psychotic states.

psychotropic: A term used to describe drugs that have a special action upon the *psyche*. See *psychopharmacology* and the other terms listed there.

puerperal psychosis: See *postpartum psychosis*.

pyromania: See *–mania*.

q-sort: A personality assessment technique in which the subject (or someone who observes him) indicates the degree to which a standardized set of descriptive statements actually describe the subject. The term reflects the "sorting" procedures occasionally used with this technique.

rapport: In psychiatry, the conscious feeling of harmonious accord, mutual responsiveness, and sympathy that contributes to the patient's confidence in the therapist and willingness to work cooperatively with him. To be distinguished from *transference*, which is unconscious.

rationalization: A *defense mechanism*, operating unconsciously, in which the individual attempts to justify or make consciously tolerable, by plausible means, feelings, behavior and motives that would otherwise be intolerable. Not to be confused with conscious evasion or dissimulation. See also *projection*.

reaction formation: A *defense mechanism*, operating unconsciously, wherein attitudes and behavior are adopted that are the opposites of impulses the individual harbors either consciously or unconsciously (e.g., excessive moral zeal may be a reaction to strong but repressed asocial impulses).

reactive depression: An informal term for *depressive neurosis*.

reactive schizophrenia: See under *schizophrenia*.

reality principle: In psychoanalytic theory, the concept that the *pleasure principle*, which represent the claims of instinctual wishes, is normally modified by the inescapable demands and requirements of the external world. In fact, the reality principle may still work in behalf of the pleasure principle; but it reflects compromises in the nature of the gratification and allows for the postponement of gratification to a more appropriate time. The reality principle usually becomes more prominent in the course of development but may be weak in certain psychiatric illnesses and undergo strengthening during treatment.

recall: The process of bringing a memory into consciousness. In psychiatry, recall is often used to refer to the recollection of facts or events in the immediate past.

reciprocal inhibition and desensitization: A term for a widely used form of behavior therapy. The patient is made comfortable in relaxed, pleasant, supportive surroundings and is then exposed, usually by imagery, to gradually increasing amounts of anxiety-provoking stimuli. The feeling of comfort associated with the situation allows the patient to tolerate increasing amounts of these stimuli and may eventually entirely remove their ability to arouse anxiety.

reference, delusion of (idea of): See *ideas of reference*.

regression: The partial or symbolic return to more infantile patterns of reacting. Manifested in a wide variety of circumstances such as normal sleep, play, severe physical illness, and in many psychiatric disorders.

rehabilitation: The methods and techniques used in a program that seeks to achieve maximal functional and optimal adjustment for the identified patient, and to prevent relapses or recurrences of his condition (because of the latter, sometimes termed *tertiary prevention*). The focus in rehabilitation is on the patient's assets and recoverable functions, rather than on the liabilities engendered by his pathology or the complications of disuse and social deterioration which formerly were often mistakenly considered to be part of the underlying disease process. Includes individual and group psychotherapy, directed socialization, vocational retraining, education. See *community psychiatry*.

REM sleep: One of two kinds of sleep. The term designates the "deep sleep" periods during which the sleeper makes coordinated rapid eye movements (REM's) resembling purposeful fixation shifts, as might be seen in the waking state. REM sleep is also called "dreaming sleep" since there appears to be an intimate relationship with dreaming activity, as if the dreamer were watching the visual imagery of his dream. *NREM* sleep is the term given to the longer period of sleep that begins as the subject passes from wakefulness into a light sleep with *no rapid eye movements* (NREM's).

REM sleep interrupts NREM sleep about once in every ninety minutes and lasts for about twenty minutes. REM sleep is believed to account for one-fifth to one-fourth of the total sleep time. Between the two forms of sleep, there are distinct differences in the *EEG* patterns and in the occulomotor, cardiovascular, respiratory, muscular, and other bodily activities.

remission: Abatement of an illness.

remotivation: A group treatment technique administered by nursing service personnel in a mental hospital; of particular value to long-term, withdrawn patients by way of stimulating their communication skills and interest in their environment.

repetition compulsion: In psychoanalytic theory the impulse to reenact earlier emotional experiences. Considered by Freud more fundamental than the *pleasure principle*. According to Ernest Jones: "The blind impulse to repeat earlier experiences and situations quite irrespective of any advantage that doing so might bring from a pleasure-pain point of view."

repression: A *defense mechanism*, operating unconsciously, that banishes unacceptable ideas, affects, or impulses, from consciousness or that keeps out of consciousness what has never been conscious. Although not subject to voluntary recall, the repressed material may emerge in disguised form. Sometimes used as a generic term for all *defense mechanisms*. Often confused with the conscious mechanism of *suppression*.

resident: An M.D. who has completed his internship and who is in graduate training to qualify as a specialist in a particular field of medicine, such as psychiatry. The *American Board of Psychiatry and Neurology* requires three years of psychiatric residency training in an approved hospital or clinic, together with two years of practice in the specialty of psychiatry, to qualify for examinations.

resistance: In psychiatry, the individual's conscious or unconscious psychological defense against bringing repressed (unconscious) thoughts to light. See also *mental mechanism*.

retardation: Slowing down of mental and physical activity. Most frequently seen in severe depressions, which are sometimes spoken of as retarded depressions. Also a synonym for *mental retardation*.

retrograde amnesia: See *amnesia*.

retrospective falsification: Unconscious distortion of past experiences to conform to present emotional needs.

rigidity: In psychiatry, refers to an individual's excessive resistance to change.

ritual: In psychiatry, any psychomotor activity sustained by an individual to relieve anxiety. Most commonly seen in *obsessive compulsive neurosis* (q.v., under *neurosis*).

RNA: Abbreviation for *ribonucleic acid*. A vital nucleic acid manufactured by *DNA*. Essential for the building of body proteins from amino acids. Appears to play a key role in memory.

Rorschach test: A *projective test* developed by the Swiss psychiatrist, Hermann Rorschach (1844–1922), which seeks to disclose conscious and unconscious personality traits and emotional conflicts through eliciting the patient's associations to a standard set of ink-blots.

sadism: See *sexual deviation*.

satyriasis: Pathologic or exaggerated sexual drive or excitement in the male. May be of psychic or organic etiology. Analogous to *nymphomania* in the female.

schizoid personality: See under *personality disorders*.

schizophrenia: A large group of disorders, usually of psychotic proportion, manifested by characteristic disturbances of thought, mood, and behavior. Thought disturbances are marked by alterations of concept formation that may lead to misinterpretation of reality and sometimes to *delusions* and *hallucinations*. Mood changes include ambivalence, constriction, inappropriateness, and loss of empathy with others. Behavior may be withdrawn, regressive, and bizarre. Currently recognized types of schizophrenia are:

acute schizophrenic episode: A condition characterized by the acute onset of schizophrenic symptoms, often associated with confusion, perplexity, *ideas of reference*, emotional turmoil, excitement, depression, fear, or dream-like dissociation. This term is *not* applicable to acute episodes of the other types of schizophrenia described here.

catatonic type: A schizophrenic disorder manifested in either or both of two ways: (1) by excessive and sometimes violent motor activity and excitement ("excited subtype") or (2) by generalized inhibition manifested as *stupor*, *mutism*, *negativism*, or *waxy flexibility* ("withdrawn subtype").

childhood schizophrenia: Schizophrenia appearing before puberty. It is frequently manifested by *autism* and withdrawn behavior; failure to develop an identity separate from the mother's; and general unevenness, gross immaturity, and inadequacy in development.

chronic undifferentiated type: A condition manifested by definite signs of schizophrenic thought, affect, and behavior that are of a sufficiently mixed or indefinite type that they defy classification into one of the other types of schizophrenia.

hebephrenic type: A schizophrenic disorder characterized by disorganized thinking, shallow and inappropriate affect, inappropriate giggling, silly and regressive behavior and mannerisms, and frequent hypochondriacal complaints. Delusions and hallucinations are usually bizarre and not well organized.

latent type: A condition manifested by clear symptoms of schizophrenia but no history of psychotic schizophrenic episodes. Sometimes designated as incipient, pre-psychotic, psuedo-neurotic, pseudo-psychopathic, or borderline schizophrenia.

paranoid type: A schizophrenic disorder characterized primarily by the presence of persecutory or grandiose delusions, often associated with hallucinations.

process schizophrenia: Unofficial term for schizophrenia attributed more to organic factors than to environmental ones; typically begins gradually, continues chronically, and progresses (either rapidly or slowly) to an irreversible psychosis. See also *reactive schizophrenia*, to which this condition is contrasted.

reactive schizophrenia: Unofficial term for schizophrenia attributed primarily to strong predisposing and/or precipitating environmental factors; usually of rapid onset and brief duration, with the affected individual appearing well both before and after the schizophrenic episode. Differentiating this condition from *process schizophrenia* is generally considered more important in Europe than in this country.

residual type: A condition manifested by individuals with signs of schizophrenia who, following a psychotic schizophrenic episode, are no longer psychotic.

school phobia: A term used when a child, usually a pupil in the early elementary grades, unexpectedly and without apparent reason, strenuously refuses to attend school because of some irrational fear. The underlying psychopathology is believed to be an intense *separation anxiety* rooted in unresolved dependency ties.

scotoma: In psychiatry, a figurative blind spot in an individual's psychologic awareness.

screen memory: A consciously tolerable memory that serves as a cover or "screen" for another associated memory that would be disturbing and emotionally painful if recalled.

secondary gain: The external gain that is derived from any illness such as personal attention and service, monetary gains, disability benefits, and release from unpleasant responsibility. See also *primary gain*.

secondary process: In psychoanalytic theory, mental activity and thinking characteristic of the *ego* and influenced by the demands of the environment. Characterized by organization, systematization, intellectualization, and similar processes leading to logical thought and action in adult life. See also *primary process*.

sedative: A broad term applied to any agent that quiets or calms or allays excitement. While *narcotics*, *hypnotics* and other classes of drugs have calming properties, the term is generally restricted to drugs that are not primarily used to achieve analgesia or sleep. See also *psychopharmacology*.

senile dementia: A chronic *organic brain syndrome* associated with generalized atrophy of the brain due to aging. In addition to the organic symptoms present, self-centeredness, difficulty assimilating new experiences, and childish emotionality are usually prominent. Deterioration may range from minimal to severe.

sensorium: Roughly synonymous with consciousness. Includes the special sensory perceptive powers and their central correlation and integration in the brain. A clear sensorium conveys the presence of a reasonably accurate memory together with a correct orientation for time, place, and person.

sensory aphasia: See *speech disturbance*.

sensory deprivation: Term for experience of being cut off from usual external stimuli and the opportunity for perception. May occur experimentally or accidentally in various ways such as through loss of hearing or eyesight, by becoming marooned, by solitary confinement, by assignment to a remote service post, or by traveling in space. May lead to disorganized thinking, *depression, panic, delusions,* and *hallucinations.*

separation anxiety: The fear and apprehension noted in infants when removed from their mothers (or surrogates) or when approached by strangers. Most marked from sixth to tenth month. In later life, similar reaction may be caused by separation from significant persons or familiar surroundings.

serotonin: A *biogenic amine* derived from tryptophan. Present in the intestine and the brain. A smooth muscle constrictor or stimulator. May influence nervous system activity. See also *indoles.*

sexual deviation: The direction of sexual interest toward objects other than persons of the opposite sex, toward sexual acts not associated with coitus, or toward coitus performed under bizzare circumstances. Examples are:

bestiality: Sexual relations between human and animal.

exhibitionism: Psychiatrically, body exposure, usually of the male genitals to females.

fetishism: A sexual deviation characterized by attachment of special meaning to an inanimate object (or *fetish*) which serves, usually unconsciously, as a substitute for the original object or person. The fetish is essential for completion of orgasm. Rare in females.

homosexuality: Sexual attraction or relationship between members of the same sex.

Overt homosexuality: Homosexuality that is consciously recognized or practiced. **Latent homosexuality:** A condition characterized by unconscious homosexual desires. See also *lesbian.*

masochism: Pleasure derived from physical or psychological pain inflicted either by oneself or by others. When it is consciously sought as a part of the sexual act or as a prerequisite to sexual gratification, it is classifiable as a sexual deviation. It is the converse of *sadism,* and the two tend to coexist in the same individual.

pederasty: Homosexual intercourse between man and boy by anus.

pedophilia: In psychiatry, a sexual deviation involving the use of children for sexual purposes.

sadism: Pleasure derived from inflicting physical or psychological pain or abuse on others. The sexual significance of sadistic wishes or behavior may be conscious or unconscious. When necessary for sexual gratification, classifiable as a sexual deviation.

sodomy: Anal intercourse. Legally, the term may include other types of perversion such as *bestiality.*

transvestitism (transvestism): Sexual pleasure derived from dressing or masquerading in the clothing of the opposite sex. The sexual origins of transvestitism may be unconscious. There is a strong wish to appear as and to be accepted as a member of the opposite sex.

voyeurism: Sexually-motivated and often compulsive interest in watching or looking at others, particularly at genitals. Roughly synonymous with "peeping Tom." Found predominantly in males.

shell-shock: Obsolete term used in World War I to designate a wide variety of psychotic and neurotic disorders presumably due to combat experience. See *conversion, combat fatigue, hysterical neurosis.*

shock treatment: A form of psychiatric treatment in which electric current, insulin, carbon dioxide, or Indoklon®, is administered to the patient and results in a loss of consciousness or a convulsive or comatose reaction to alter favorably the course of the illness. Some common types of shock therapy are:

carbon dioxide therapy: A form of inhalation treatment in which carbon dioxide gas is administered to the point of unconsciousness in order to cause emotional *abreactions* and alleviation of anxiety.

electroconvulsive treatment (ECT): Use of electric current to induce unconsciousness and/or convulsive seizures. Most effective in the treatment of depression. Introduced by Cerletti and Bini in 1938. Modifications are electronarcosis, producing sleep-like states, and electrostimulation, which avoids convulsions.

Indoklon therapy: A form of shock treatment in which a convulsive seizure is produced by intravenous injection or inhalation of the drug, Indoklon.

insulin coma therapy (ICT): A treatment primarily for schizophrenia in which insulin is injected in large enough doses to produce profound hypoglycemia (low blood sugar) resulting in coma. First used by Manfred

Sakel in 1933. Its use in the United States has decreased since the introduction of *tranquilizers.*

Metrazol shock therapy: A form of shock treatment, now rarely used, in which a convulsive seizure is produced by intravenous injection of Metrazol (known as Cardiazol in Europe). Introduced by L. von Meduna in 1935.

subcoma insulin treatment: A treatment in which insulin is administered to induce drowsiness or somnolence short of coma. Used to alleviate anxiety, stimulate appetite, and induce a feeling of well being.

sibling: Term for a full brother or sister.

sibling rivalry: The competition between *siblings* for the love of a parent or for other recognition or gain.

situational depression: See *depressive neurosis* under *neurosis.*

social control: The way in which society or any of its subgroups, various institutions, organizations, and agencies exert influence upon the individual, or groups of individuals, to conform to the expectations and requirements of that society or subgroup. Control may be coercive (as by means of the law) or persuasive (through such devices as suggestion, blame, praise, reward, and recognition). See also *sociology.*

social psychiatry: The field of psychiatry concerned with the cultural, ecologic, and sociologic factors that engender, precipitate, intensify, prolong, or otherwise complicate maladaptive patterns of behavior and their treatment; sometimes used synonymously with *community psychiatry,* although some limit the latter term to practical or clinical applications of social psychiatry. Important in social psychiatry is the ecological approach to maladaptive behavior, which is viewed not only as a deviation of an individual but also as a reflection of deviation in the social systems in which he lives.

social work: The use of community resources and of the conscious adaptive capacities of individuals and groups to better the adjustment of an individual to his environment and to improve the quality and functioning of an individual's external environment.

social worker, psychiatric: A social worker with specialized psychiatric training leading to a graduate degree (M.S.W. or D.S.W.) in social work. Such a worker may utilize all social work techniques such as case work, group work, and community organization in a psychiatric or mental health setting.

socialization: The process by which society integrates the individual and the way in which the individual learns to become a functioning member of that society. See *sociology.*

sociology: The study of the development and governing principles of social organization and the group behavior of men, in contrast to the individual behavior of man. Overlaps to some extent with *cultural anthropology.* Related concepts are defined elsewhere under the following terms: *alienation, social control, socialization.*

sociopath: An unofficial term for *antisocial personality* (q.v., under *personality disorders*).

sodomy: See *sexual deviation.*

soma: The body.

somatic conversion: See under *neurosis, hysterical.*

somatization reactions: See *psychophysiologic disorders.*

somnambulism: Sleepwalking. A dissociated or a fugue-like state in which the person can move about but otherwise is asleep.

speech disturbance: Any disorder of verbal or nonverbal communication that is not due to faulty innervation of the speech muscles or organs of articulation. There is no single cause for any of the speech disturbances, but minimal cortical or subcortical dysfunction, including dysharmony in the physiologic predominance of one cerebral hemisphere over the other, may be an important factor in many patients. Any grouping is highly arbitrary, but the term includes many language and *learning disturbances,* such as those listed below:

aphasia: Inability to utter a sound, word, or phrase, or to find the right name for an object. **Sensory aphasia:** Inability to perceive or understand certain sounds, syllables, or phrases, as in word-blindness. **Central** or **syntactical aphasia:** Speech is fluent but disordered by verbal and grammatical confusions (paraphasia).

alexia (dyslexia): Inability or difficulty in reading, including word-blindness and strephosymbolia (tendency to reverse letters and words in reading and writing).

agraphia (dysgraphia): Inability or disability in writing.

amimia: Inability to gesticulate or to understand the significance of gestures.

apraxia: Loss of previously acquired skilled acts (including speech and writing) or failure to develop normal skills.

Stanford-Binet intelligence scale: An individually administered intelligence test emphasizing verbal facility. Used with individuals from age two through adulthood. The test yields a *mental age* and an *IQ*.

status epilepticus: More or less continuous epileptic seizures. See *epilepsy*.

stereotypy: Persistent mechanical repetition of speech or motor activity. Observed, for example, in *schizophrenia*.

strephosymbolia: See *speech disturbance*.

stress reaction: See *gross stress reaction*.

stroke: Apoplexy; cerebrovascular accident (CVA); gross cerebral hemorrhage or softening of the brain following hemorrhage, thrombosis, or embolism of the cerebral arteries. Symptoms may include coma, paralysis (particularly on one side of the body), convulsions, aphasia, and other neurologic symptoms determined by the location of the lesion.

stupor: In psychiatry, a state in which the individual does not react to his surroundings and appears to be unaware of them. In catatonic stupor, the unawareness is more apparent than real. See *catatonic state*.

stuttering and stammering: Spasmodic speaking with involuntary halts and repetitions, usually considered of psychogenic origin.

subcoma insulin treatment: See under *shock treatment*.

subconscious: Obsolescent term in psychiatry. Formerly used to include the *preconscious* (what can be recalled with effort) and the *unconscious*.

subcoma insulin treatment: See *shock therapy*.

sublimation: A *defense mechanism*, operating unconsciously, by which instinctual drives, consciously unacceptable, are diverted into personally and socially acceptable channels.

substitution: A *defense mechanism*, operating unconsciously, by which an unattainable or unacceptable goal, emotion, or object is replaced by one that is more attainable or acceptable. Comparable to *displacement*.

succinylcholine: A potent chemical used intravenously in anesthesia as a skeletal muscle relaxant. Also used prior to electroconvulsive therapy to minimize the possibility of fractures.

suggestion: In psychiatry, the process of influencing an individual to accept uncritically an idea, belief, or attitude induced by the therapist.

superego: In psychoanalytic theory, that part of the personality associated with ethics, standards, and self-criticism. It is formed by the infant's identification with important and esteemed persons in his early life, particularly parents. The supposed or actual wishes of these significant persons are taken over as part of the child's own personal standards to help form the "conscience." In late life they may become anachronistic and self-punitive, especially in neurotic persons. See also *ego*, *id*.

supportive psychotherapy: A technique of psychotherapy that aims to reinforce a patient's defense and to help him suppress disturbing psychological material. Supportive psychotherapy utilizes such measures as inspiration, reassurance, suggestion, persuasion, counselling, and re-education. It avoids probing the patient's emotional conflicts in depth.

suppression: The conscious effort to control and conceal unacceptable impulses, thoughts, feelings, or acts.

surrogate: One who takes the place of another; a substitute person. In psychiatry, usually refers to an authority figure who replaces a parent in the emotional feelings of the patient (e.g., father-surrogate, mother-surrogate).

symbiosis: In psychiatry, denotes a mutually-reinforcing relationship between two disturbed persons who are dependent on each other.

symbolization: An unconscious mental process operating by *association* and based on similarity and abstract representation whereby one object or idea comes to stand for another through some part, quality, or aspect which the two have in common. The symbol carries in more or less disguised form the emotional feelings vested in the initial object or idea.

sympathetic nervous system: That part of the *autonomic nervous system* that responds to dangerous or threatening situations by preparing the individual physiologically for "fight or flight." See also *parasympathetic nervous system*.

sympathy: Compassion for another's grief or loss. To be differentiated from *empathy*.

symptom: A specific manifestation of a patient's condition indicative of an abnormal physical or mental state. Psychiatric symptoms are often the result of unconscious conflict and may represent in symbolic form an instinctual wish, the defense against such a wish, or a compromise between the two.

syndrome: A configuration of symptoms that occur together and that constitute a recognizable condition. Example: *Ganser's syndrome*.

syntactical (central) aphasia: See *speech disturbance*.

syphilis: A venereal disease, which, if untreated, may lead to *central nervous system* deterioration with psychotic manifestations in its later stages. See *general paralysis*.

t-groups (sensitivity training groups): A group of people who meet to learn about themselves, about interpersonal relationships, about *group process*, and about larger social systems. An important element in the learning is that the group members meet in an unstructured situation and have the task of constructing their own group.

Talion law or principle: A primitive, unrealistic belief, usually unconscious, conforming to the Biblical injunction of an "eye for an eye" and a "tooth for a tooth." In psychoanalysis the concept and fear that all injury, actual or intended, will be punished in kind—i.e., retaliated.

telepathy: The communication of thought from one person to another without the intervention of physical means. Not generally accepted as scientifically valid. See also *extrasensory perception*.

thematic apperception test (TAT): A *projective test* consisting of a series of drawings suggesting life situations, which may be variously interpreted depending on the mood and personality of the subject.

therapeutic community: A term of British origin, now widely used, for a specially structured mental hospital milieu that encourages patients to function within the range of social norms. Special educational techniques are used to overcome the patients' dependency needs, to encourage them to assume personal responsibility, and to speed their social rehabilitation.

tic: An intermittent, involuntary, spasmodic movement such as a muscular twitch, often without a demonstrable external stimulus. A tic may be a disguised expression of a hidden emotional conflict or the result of neurologic disease.

toilet training: The methods used by a child's parents, usually the mother, in teaching and encouraging control of bladder and bowel functions. Occurs at an important period in the formation of the child's personality. Marks the parents' first major effort to control the child and the child's first good chance to resist the parents. Adult attitudes about cleanliness, control, authority, and anger arise in part from this period of toilet training and the method by which it is carried out.

topectomy: A type of *psychosurgery*.

total push therapy: In a hospital setting, the energetic simultaneous application of all available psychiatric therapies to the treatment of a patient, first described by Abraham Myerson (1881–1948). Myerson emphasized physical activity, recreation, praise, blame, reward,

punishment, and involvement in care of clothing and personal hygiene.

toxic psychosis: A *psychosis* resulting from the toxic effect of chemicals and drugs, including those produced in the body.

trance: A state of diminished activity and consciousness resembling sleep. Seen in hypnosis, hysteria, and ecstatic religious states.

tranquilizer: A drug that deceases anxiety and agitation, usually without causing drowsiness. Divided into two groups:

> **major tranquilizers:** Drugs such as *phenothiazines* which produce relief from symptoms of psychosis.

> **minor tranquilizers:** Drugs that are used predominantly to diminish neurotic anxiety.

transactional analysis: A psychodynamic approach that attempts to understand the interplay between therapist and patient—and ultimately between the patient and external reality—in terms of role theory, beginning with an exposure of current, well-defined, explicit roles, and ultimately evoking a recognition of implicit emotional roles and a repetition of earlier interactions that trace the genesis of current behavior.

transcultural psychiatry: See *cultural psychiatry*.

transference: The unconscious "transfer" to others of feelings and attitudes that were originally associated with important figures (parents, siblings, etc.) in one's early life. The transference relationship follows roughly the pattern of its prototype. The psychiatrist utilizes this phenomenon as a therapeutic tool to help the patient understand his emotional problems and their origin. In the patient-physician relationship the transference may be negative (hostile) or positive (affectionate). See also *countertransference*.

transient situational disturbance: A more or less transient disorder of any severity (including psychosis) that represents an acute reaction to overwhelming stress, such as the severe crying spells, loss of appetite, and social withdrawal of a child separated from its mother; or, in an adult, a reaction to an unwanted pregnancy manifested by suicidal gestures and hostile complaints. The symptoms generally recede as the stress diminishes.

transorbital lobotomy: A type of *psychosurgery*.

transsexualism: A term used to describe the wish to change one's sex. Often associated with *transvestitism* and *homosexuality*, it may be manifested by seeking plastic surgery to replace the male's external genitalia with an artificial vagina, electrolysis to remove facial hair, estrogens to stimulate breast enlargement, etc. Also known as "sex-role inversion," transsexualism is believed to have its pathological origins in early childhood, when the future transsexual develops a primary and continuing identification with the parent of the opposite sex and adopts the *gender role* of that parent. See also *gender identity*.

transvestitism (transvestism): See *sexual deviation*.

trauma: In psychiatry, an extremely upsetting emotional experience that may aggravate or contribute to a mental disorder. In medicine, any injury or wound.

traumatic neurosis: The term encompasses combat, occupational, and compensation neuroses. These are neurotic reactions that have been attributed to or follow a situational traumatic event, or series of events. Usually the event has some specific and symbolic emotional significance for the patient. The neurosis may be reinforced by *secondary gain*.

triage. The sorting out and classification of casualties. An essential function for carrying out efficient treatment in war, civil disasters, and other situations where limited resources must be organized to provide service for large numbers of people.

trisomy: The presence of three *chromosomes* instead of the two that normally represent each potential set of chromosomes. Humans have 23 sets of chromosomes. The most significant trisomy in psychiatry is that associated with *Down's syndrome*.

unconditioned reflex (UCR): An inborn physiologic reflex response to a stimulus; e.g., salivation at the sight of food.

unconscious: In Freudian theory, that part of the mind or mental functioning of which the content is only rarely subject to awareness. It is a repository for data that have never been conscious (primary repression), or that may have become conscious briefly and later repressed (secondary repression).

underachiever: Term used in psychiatry for a person who manifestly does not function up to his capacity.

undoing: A primitive *defense mechanism*, operating unconsciously, in which something un-

acceptable and already done is symbolically acted out in reverse, usually repetitiously, in the hope of "undoing" it and thus relieving anxiety.

vaginismes: Painful vaginal spasm, usually occurring in connection with sexual intercourse.

vegetative nervous system: Obsolescent term for the *autonomic nervous system*.

verbigeration: Stereotyped and seemingly meaningless repetition of words or sentences.

vertigo: A type of dizziness or "spinning around," in which the subject feels that he or his environment is spinning. Often associated with faintness.

vitamin therapy: See *pellagra*.

voluntary admission: See under *commitment*.

voyeurism: See *sexual deviation*.

WAIS (Wechsler Adult Intelligence Scale): A verbal and performance test especially designed to measure intelligence in adults.

waxy flexibility: See *cerea flexibilitas*.

weekend hospital: See under *partial hospitalization*.

withdrawal: In psychiatry, a pathological retreat from people or the world of reality, often seen in *schizophrenia*.

withdrawal symptoms: Term used to describe physical and mental effects of withdrawing drugs from patients who have become habituated or addicted to them. The physical symptoms may include nausea, vomiting, tremors, abdominal pain, and convulsions.

word-blindness: See *speech disturbance*.

word salad: A mixture of words and phrases that lack comprehensive meaning or logical coherence, commonly seen in schizophrenic states.

working through: Active exploration of a problem by patient and therapist until a satisfactory solution has been found or until a symptom has been traced to its unconscious sources.

xenophobia: See under *phobia*.

INDEX OF MAJOR CASES

INDEX